# MAMMALS OF THE

# EASTERN UNITED STATES

### Third Edition

# MAMMALS

## OF THE

# EASTERN UNITED STATES

THIRD EDITION

*John O. Whitaker, Jr.*

INDIANA STATE UNIVERSITY

AND

*William J. Hamilton, Jr.*

CORNELL UNIVERSITY

*Comstock Publishing Associates*

A DIVISION OF

Cornell University Press

ITHACA & LONDON

*Library of Congress Cataloging-in-Publication Data*

Whitaker, John O.
    Mammals of the Eastern United States / John O. Whitaker, Jr., and
William J. Hamilton, Jr.—3rd ed.
        p.   cm.
    Includes bibliographical references (p.  ) and index.
    ISBN 0-8014-3475-0 (cloth)
        1. Mammals—East (U.S.)   I. Hamilton, William John, 1902– .
    II. Title.
    QL719.E23W49   1998
    599′.0974—dc21                                           98-11962

*To the memory of*
BILL HAMILTON,
*for his countless contributions to*
*mammalogy and conservation,*
*and for the steadfast help and encouragement*
*he gave me and all his students*

# CONTENTS

# PREFACE

WE DESCRIBE IN THIS volume the land mammals, native or established in the wild, common or rare, inhabiting the states east of the Mississippi River, along with accounts of their habits and distribution. Like its first two editions, the book is designed for students of mammalogy, for professional conservationists, and for the increasing numbers of laymen taking a serious interest in wildlife. There are many good books on the mammals of particular states, but animals are no respecters of political boundaries, and we hope this book helps fill the need for a comprehensive work on *all* eastern mammals. It includes illustrations and distribution maps for essentially all the species, generous lists of references, and identifying keys to all genera, subfamilies, families, and orders. We hope it will suggest to the amateur naturalist or the laboratory professional the joys of capturing and observing mammals and the value of further field study. It should also be useful to those interested in preserving natural areas and in ensuring the survival of endangered or threatened species.

It has been our good fortune to have been able to collect and observe mammals in twenty-six of the twenty-seven states east of the Mississippi River (to date, we have somehow failed to find ourselves in the bottomlands of Mississippi). We have hiked the high reaches of Mount Katahdin in northern Maine, where water shrews and moose keep company, and the cypress swamps of lower Florida, where the spoor of the mountain lion, or Florida panther, may still be seen. We have spent much time studying bats in the caves and mines of southern Illinois, and rodents and insectivores in the mountains of Pennsylvania and North Carolina. We have watched the western harvest mouse move across Illinois into the prairie lobe of Indiana, where the least weasel and pocket gopher live. In Florida, we have trapped the elusive Florida mouse. In the mountains of Kentucky, we have captured wood rats and pine mice, and in the unglaciated foothills of southern Indiana, our pitfall traps have taken smoky and pygmy shrews, species that have flourished in Indiana since glacial times but had gone undetected until 1981. On seemingly countless nights, we have deployed our traps to capture the little brown bats and northern bats that venture out of their caves in winter, and we have mist-netted Indiana bats, evening bats, and other bats over Indiana streams. (If I seem to have been rather too attentive to bats, or to the mammals of Indiana, I plead guilty; they are what I know best.)

To William J. Hamilton, Jr., my mentor and friend of many years, I owe much gratitude, not only for allowing me to join him in writing both this book and its predecessor, the second edition (published in 1979), but also for his help and support in so many other undertakings. When Bill wrote the first edition of *Mammals of the Eastern United States* (published in 1943), it was ahead of its time, and is today generally considered a classic. To me and to many others, it was a bible of mammalogy, but in due course it gave way to the second edition. It is my fond hope that this third edition will be seen to have been greatly improved over the second. Bill read an entire earlier draft of this edition, but not the later drafts, for death came to him on July 27, 1990. I hope he would have been proud of the results. Bill was of course one of the great mammalogists of this century, and he is sorely missed.

This edition has been almost entirely rewritten. All the species accounts have been considerably expanded and updated—the material on parasites and disease, and on subspecies, is altogether new—and a thoroughgoing topical structure has been imposed on their content, both to ensure rigor in our literature search and text preparation and to afford the reader greater ease of reference. Various sections of material from the earlier editions of this work remain, however, where no change was needed or warranted, and the authorship of those paragraphs—some are by Bill Hamilton, some are by me, some are by both of us—has made attribution in running text somewhat imprecise. To spare the reader, I have chosen to use the editorial "we" on most occasions, but any "I" you see is indeed I.

The Appendix, also new to this edition, lists all of the species and subspecies that are currently designated Endangered or Threatened on federal or state lists, as well as those that until recently were under consideration for listing, state by state. We are indebted to the various state agencies, and to those within these agencies, for much help in our preparation of these listings.

The taxonomic arrangement for orders and families in this book, as well as the species names adopted, are those of Jones et al. (1992) in the main, but sometimes follow Wilson and Reeder (1993).

In times past, most subspecies of mammals had been described on the basis of a rather loose morphological-subspecies concept. Because of the great number of subspecies that have been described over the years on this basis, many of them obviously invalid, some have suggested that subspecies be dispensed with altogether. I have always felt, however, that the subspecies taxon should be retained, so long as it is restricted to populations undergoing speciation, i.e., that the concept should be revised as a biological entity paralleling the species concept. Here we have applied a biological-subspecies concept, which requires, first, that a primary isolating mechanism be in place and, second, that the results of evolution through differentiation can be demonstrated in the isolated population(s).

Because information on chromosome numbers has mushroomed in recent decades, and has proved valuable both in taxonomy and in population genetics, we have added diploid numbers to the species accounts, where these are known. Another new feature is the provision of tooth formulas for all species. The Glossary, which defines virtually all of the technical terms used in the text, is also new. Most of the line drawings in this edition appeared in earlier editions of the work; nearly all of the photographs, and all of the color photos, are new to this edition. All of the maps are new.

The Guide to Further Reading lists state and regional mammal books. We think these references are exceedingly valuable to people visiting various of the eastern states.

Many people have helped produce this work. We have benefited greatly from the discussions, ideas, and assistance given by our graduate students over many years. I especially wish to thank Cheryl Bauer, Ronald S. Caldwell, Dennis E. Clark, K. W. Corthum, Jr., Mary Beth Eberwein, Stephen D. Ford, Thomas W. French, Rebecca Goff, Gwilym S. Jones, William Kern, David Pascal, Leslie Rissler, David Rubin, Larry Schmeltz, George R. Sly, Martha Smith, Dale Sparks, Edwin Spicka, Beth Vincent, Janice Webster, and Earl G. Zimmerman. Others who have helped in various ways are Rollin H. Baker, Troy L. Best, Wayne H. Davis, M. Brock Fenton, James S. Findley, Edwin Gould, Katie Gremillion-Smith, Sherry L. Gummer, Donald F. Hoffmeister, Scott Johnson, Ralph D. Kirkpatrick, Thomas H. Kunz, Allen Kurta, William Z. Lidicker, Donald W. Linzey, Joseph E. Merritt, Scott and Lori Pruitt, James Shaw, Harmon P. Weeks, Jr., and Don E. Wilson.

James B. Cope has read and greatly improved

the entire book. I have learned much of pertinence from Russell E. Mumford while working with him all over Indiana. Hobart M. Smith encouraged me to develop the subspecies concept, incorporated it in his own thinking and teaching, and urged me to publish it. James N. Layne and Gordon Kirkland helped the authors come to what we hope is a workable and worthwhile way of approaching the subspecies issue. Layne read the penultimate draft of the entire manuscript; to his careful eye and diverse knowledge we owe many last-minute corrections and improvements. Gwilym S. Jones has examined the range maps and has given much helpful advice, especially on the ranges of mammals in New England, and has helped us with the literature sections. James D. Lazell, Jr., supplied much information on bats and deer, and Roger A. Powell has supplied much on carnivores. Tom French, David Gordon, and William Kern have given helpful advice on insectivores, on the ranges of some New York mammals, and on bats, respectively. Stephen Scheffield has provided much information on the introduction program of the red wolf and also on *Mustela nivalis*. Philip A. Frank provided information on the bats new or verified in Florida, *Molossus molossus* and *Artibeus jamaicensis*. Earl G. Zimmerman furnished information on many of the diploid numbers. A number of people have helped me with ectoparasites; a few of these are Alex Fain, M. Lee Goff, E. W. Jameson, Jerry Krantz, Robert E. Lewis, Richard Loomis, Fritz Lukoschus, Barry O'Connor, Frank Radovsky, Robert L. Smiley, Nixon A. Wilson, and William Wrenn. Michael Pelton supplied information for the *Ursus americanus* map.

Others have read and greatly improved particular sections: Gordon L. Kirkland, Jr. (Shippensburg University, Shippensburg, Pa.), the insectivores; Merlin Tuttle (Bat Conservation International, Austin, Tex.), the bats; Peter D. Weigl (Wake Forest University, Winston-Salem, N.C.), the squirrels; Robert M. Timm (University of Kansas, Lawrence, Kans.), the pocket gophers; John P. Hayes (Hatfield Marine Science Center, Oregon State University, Newport, Ore.), the woodrats; Uldis Roze (The City University of New York, Flushing, N.Y.), the porcupine; Thomas W. French (Massachusetts Department of Natural Resources) and James N. Layne (Archbold Biological Station, Lake Placid, Fla.), the remainder of the rodents; Roger A. Powell (North Carolina State University, Raleigh, N.C.), the carnivores; David S. Maehr (Wilkinson & Associates, Naples, Fla.), the mountain lion; Cathy Beck (The Sirenia Project, Gainesville, Fla.), the manatee; Ronald R. Keiper (Pennsylvania State University at Mont Alto), the Assateague ponies; George A. Feldhamer (Southern Illinois University, Carbondale, Ill.), many of the ungulates; and Alan C. Hicks (New York State Department of Environmental Conservation), the moose.

Thanks are given to all of the photographers, and artists, 38 of them, who contributed their work to this volume, but especially to the late Roger Barbour, for taking so many of the photographs, and to his wife, for allowing us to use them. That about one-third of the photographs in this book are Roger's demonstrates his devotion to his work as well as his consummate ability as a photographer.

We also acknowledge the superb work of our typist, Laura Bakken, and we are grateful for her constant attention to detail, consistency, accuracy, and sense. Our thanks go also to Barbara Green, Debbie Church, and Hilary Philpot for making the range maps.

Without the manifold contributions of Robb Reavill, Peter Prescott, Helene Maddux, Kay Scheuer, Lisa Turner, and others at Cornell University Press, this book could not have been completed. A large measure of thanks must also go to William Carver, who in the end gave the entire volume an extraordinary job of professional editing.

Finally, I wish to thank my late parents and my family for all their help and support over the years.

JOHN O. WHITAKER, JR.
*Terre Haute, Indiana*

# MAMMALS OF THE

# EASTERN UNITED STATES

THIRD EDITION

# INTRODUCTION

To DEFINE A MAMMAL, one need only state that it is an animal more or less covered with hair at some time in its life, and that its young are fed milk produced by the mammary glands of the female. Our warm-bloodedness, another salient aspect of our nature, we share with only the birds. Terrestrial mammals of one kind or another occur everywhere in the eastern United States, from the peaks of the highest mountains to the intertidal zone of the seacoasts, from pristine wilderness to farmland and abandoned urban warehouses.

But over the past two centuries we humans, to serve the needs of an ever-increasing population and in the name of development, have cut the forests, drained the wetlands, paved over the riverbanks, and plowed the grasslands. And we have been doing this so relentlessly that the wildlands that remain today—at least what remains this side of the great deserts and polar regions— are but a minute fraction of the natural habitats that once completely covered the land. The process continues, of course, and in doing so little to reverse it, we court ecological disaster. The problem is that humans, alone among the world's animal species, have ignored the laws of nature that in an earlier day kept us in balance with the environment. We have used our brains to find new ways to produce food, house people, and produce energy to support ourselves—which is well and good, except that the world is finite, the human population is doubling every 35 to 40 years, and somewhere, perhaps close at hand, there lies a population limit beyond which we cannot avoid radical, long-term damage to our environment.

Evidence that we may already have surpassed that limit is the widespread environmental wreckage we leave in our wake at every turn: pollution of air, water, and land; loss of habitat and (concomitantly) loss of unknown numbers of plant and animal species; acid rain, clearcutting, forest fires; holes in the ozone layer and radioactive materials in the seas; and global warming, potentially the most calamitous of all. These all need urgently to be corrected, or reversed, but they are all symptoms of the greater and more urgent problem, that of human overpopulation. If we were to solve that problem, then solutions to all the other problems would begin to fall into place. If we do *not* solve that problem, nature will solve it for us—through starvation, pestilence, and war, thus in ways that a reasoning species should find wholly unacceptable.

## DECLINING HABITATS, RECEDING DISTRIBUTIONS

During our settlement of the North American continent and our exploitation of the land, nearly all of the native mammal species of what is now the eastern United States have suffered radical declines in numbers, and several are threatened, endangered, or already extirpated. This has come about—mostly unintentionally—in a number of ways, but chiefly by the destruction of natural habitats. Species, like individual organisms, cannot survive if they lack adequate habitat.

Some notable exceptions to the all but universal declines are the species that have adapted to the new environments we have created: the common mole, which does well in lawns; the big brown bat, which colonizes and hibernates in buildings; the prairie deer mouse, which can persist in cultivated fields even when vegetation is removed during plowing; the Norway rat and the house mouse, which do well in buildings, trash dumps, and farmlands; the coyote, which has taken advantage of brushlands and has managed, at least partially, to fill the vast niche vacated by the wolf; and the raccoon, gray squirrel, and opossum, which have adapted well to suburban and even urban living. A few species that human institutions have managed, such as the white-tailed deer and the beaver, have done well. Both of these species were near extirpation in many parts of their range, in this century; the white-tailed deer has increased in numbers through management and the extirpation of the larger predators, the beaver mostly through reintroductions and renewed freedom from trapping. The river otter is being successfully reintroduced, and some woodland species such as the pine marten have done well in recent years in limited areas when suitable habitat is available.

But most species have declined, many of them precipitously. Some—the bison (or buffalo), the caribou, the wolverine, the red wolf, and the wapiti (or elk)—are already extirpated throughout the east (though the wapiti and red wolf are now being reintroduced). Others—most prominently the mountain lion, the timber wolf, and the Canada lynx—have been extirpated over vast areas, and some are barely surviving in the east. Many more, including several bats and carnivores, a few rodents, and others, are in trouble, as indicated by their status as threatened or endangered species, at the federal or state levels. The Appendix is a summary of information on the endangered and threatened species and subspecies of each of the eastern states. This summary, compiled as of 1996 with the help and cooperation of the appropriate agencies in each of the states, is in effect a yardstick that can be used in the future to determine how well we are handling the business of saving species.

## WHY STUDY MAMMALS?

There are many reasons for attempting to save and help our mammals, thus to *manage* them (management means establishing and maintaining adequate habitat and sometimes controlling the numbers of animals in particular populations), and there are many reasons for studying them. First, they are part of our natural heritage. Do we have the right to continue to destroy them? To deny them to our descendants? We do not. It is our duty, our obligation, to protect those that remain, to manage them in such a way that they will survive, and perhaps even increase. But if we are to manage species, we need to know as much as we can about them. We need to know the factors that determine adequate habitat, how the animals survive the winters and otherwise accord with their environment, what they eat, and how they interact with other species. The more we know about them, the more we can help them.

What are the effects when some disappear? Often, we do not know. For example, clearcutting to harvest timber removes habitat essential to many of the small mammals and may completely disrupt the normal forest-recovery sequence. Part of the forest-regeneration cycle includes the small mammals that feed on seeds and hypogeous fungi. The fungi and their associated bacteria are crucial to reforestation, but tend to be destroyed by clearcutting, demonstrating once again that radically altering the environment can lead to results we had not anticipated. These relationships, as they are played out in the western United States, have recently been elucidated by Maser (1994).

Farmers have long thought mice to be detrimental to their fields. Mice do feed heavily on waste grain after the harvest, but they also feed on cutworms and other injurious insects and their larvae, and much of the grain they glean from the soil is incidental to the harvest. We suspect that the net effects of mice in most cultivated fields are actually more beneficial than harmful. To be sure, many of our eastern species, such as the meadow vole, the pine mouse, the cotton rat, and at times the cottontail rabbit, are important pests of agriculture, but the worst pests are generally the introduced species, especially the Norway rat and the black rat. These species do millions of dollars of damage to food and many other items, including buildings, and frequently transmit disease organisms. A relatively new invader, currently attaining pest status, is the nutria, which has become exceedingly abundant and is now competing with native muskrats. In order to initiate controls for the harmful mammals, protect those mammals in need of protection, and prevent the spread of disease, we must learn as much as we can about these animals and their parasites. If we can discover the weaker links in the life histories of the harmful species, we may be able to reduce their numbers through the exploitation of these channels.

Aside from management and economic considerations, the study of our native mammals is of absorbing interest in its own right, and holds a fascination quite different from that of bird study. To come upon a red fox hunting mice in the bare March meadows, or to uncover a nest of lustrous-eyed flying squirrels—even to happen upon the serpentine, single-file march of a skunk family on a still June evening—provokes a thrill of a sort occasioned by no other group of animals. For we ourselves are mammals, and our closest kin have much in common with us.

## MAMMALS AND THE LAY OF THE LAND

Though their numbers have almost everywhere declined, mammals abound throughout the world, from the highest mountains to the shores of the seas. There are of course legions of terrestrial, arboreal, and fossorial mammals, everywhere but in Antarctica, but there are also many aquatic mammals, both freshwater and marine, the manatees and their relatives being the most highly adapted to freshwater environments, the whales and the pinnipeds the most thoroughly adapted to the sea (Wozencraft, 1989). There are even flying mammals (bats) and gliding mammals (flying squirrels). In all, there are about 4,629 living species of mam-

mals in the world, in 1,135 genera, 136 families, and 26 orders. They are represented in the eastern United States by 121 species in 68 genera, 26 families, and 11 orders.

There are of course numerous habitats and microhabitats in the eastern United States. There are fields and forest, highlands and bottomlands, lakes, ponds, swamps, marshes, bogs and fens, rocky cliffs and sandy shores, wet prairies and dry prairies. But there are no deserts in the east, and the mountains are of only modest height: the highest, Mt. Mitchell, in North Carolina, is just 2037 meters (6684 feet), and Mt. Washington, in New Hampshire, is 1917 meters (6288 feet) above sea level. Thus there is greater habitat variation (and considerably more land) in the western United States than in the east, yet there is enough habitat variation in the east to support a relatively large biodiversity. And there are some exceedingly interesting habitats in the east—much of Florida and the Keys, the Appalachian Mountains, the Adirondacks, the Pine Barrens of New Jersey, the bayous of Louisiana, the Great Lakes and their associated freshwater dunes, the Dismal Swamp, and the great rivers of the east, such as the Mississippi, the Ohio, the Wabash, the Hudson, the Susquehanna, and the Delaware.

Many mammals present here in late prehistoric times are long since extinct. Some of these are the horse, dire wolf, beautiful armadillo, jaguar, sabertooth tiger, several peccaries, ground sloth, giant beaver, mastodon, mammoth, and some tapirs, stag-moose, and musk-ox. The opossum family evolved much earlier in North America but became extinct here; the modern opossum invaded North America from South America, just 3 million years ago.

## MAMMAL SPECIES NEW TO THIS EDITION

A total of 104 species of mammals, all of them still with us, was included in the second edition; 121 are included in the present edition. The following species have been added to this volume: *Sorex fontinalis*, Maryland shrew, *Artibeus jamaicensis*, Jamaican fruit-eating bat, *Molossus molossus*, little mastiff bat, *Macaca mulatta*, rhesus monkey, *Sylvilagus obscurus*, Allegheny cottontail, *Sciurus aureogaster*, red-bellied squirrel, *Neotoma magister*, Allegheny wood-rat, *Canis familiaris*, feral dog, *Canis rufus*, red wolf, *Felis catus*, feral cat, *Trichechus manatus*, West Indian manatee, *Equus caballus*, feral horse, *Sus scrofa*, feral pig, *Cervus dama*, fallow deer, *Cervus elaphus*, wapiti, or elk, *Cervus nippon*, sika deer, and *Cervus unicolor*, sambar deer.

Of these species, three had previously been considered conspecific with other species, but now appear to be valid species, although there are serious questions about the first two. The Maryland shrew, *Sorex fontinalis*, had been considered conspecific with *Sorex cinereus*; the Allegheny cottontail, *Sylvilagus obscurus*, with *S. transitionalis*; and the Allegheny woodrat, *Neotoma magister*, with *N. floridana*. The red wolf, *Canis rufus*, had apparently been extirpated in the wild, but breeding stock was preserved and small numbers have been reintroduced in North Carolina. Two species of bats, the Jamaican fruit-eating bat, *Artibeus jamaicensis*, and the little mastiff bat, *Molossus molossus*, were not previously known to occur in the eastern United States, but both are now known to be resident in Florida. The feral dog, *Canis familiaris*, the feral cat, *Felis catus*, the feral horse, *Equus caballus*, and the feral pig, *Sus scrofa*, are domestic animals that have either become thoroughly established in the wild or at least have major impacts on native populations. The manatee, *Trichechus manatus*, which occurs primarily in inland waters, is now included. The wapiti, or elk, has been successfully reintroduced. The remaining species (rhesus monkey, red-bellied squirrel, and sika, sambar, and fallow deer) are all exotics that have been introduced intentionally or accidentally, but in any case appear to have become established, although there have been recent efforts to remove the rhesus monkey.

To our knowledge, no species has been extirpated in the eastern United States since the second edition of this book appeared in 1979, but the following are in trouble to one extent or another: *Canis lupus*, gray wolf, *Canis rufus*, red wolf, *Felis concolor*, mountain lion, *Lynx lynx*, lynx, *Eumops glaucinus*, Wagner's mastiff bat, *Oryzomys argentatus*, Key rice rat, and *Myotis leibii*, eastern small-footed myotis.

## What We Have Tried to Do

The objectives of this volume are mainly six. First, we have assembled much of what is known of the natural history of the 121 known species of extant mammals native to or currently established in the eastern United States—that part of the nation east of the Mississippi. We have presented that information in systematic fashion, species by species and topic by topic. Second, we have prepared maps showing, as accurately as could be determined, the current eastern U.S. distribution of all the species and subspecies treated. Third, we have tried to indicate some fruitful areas for further research, for every species. Fourth, by citing and listing a number of pertinent articles and books, we hope we have opened a window into further study of mammalogy. Fifth, to address a long-felt need for a drastic revision of the traditional treatment of subspecies, we have attempted to apply a biological-subspecies concept to the populations of mammals under consideration. Finally, to address another long-felt need, we have included, for every species, a brief listing and discussion of some of its known parasites and diseases—information that, although important both to the animals and to human epidemiology, is seldom addressed by professional mammalogists. In pursuing all of these objectives, we have surely erred, or fallen short, on many occasions, and we welcome corrective correspondence—toward the day when someone undertakes to prepare a further revision of this work.

## Methods Employed in the Species Accounts

Each species account begins with the common and scientific names of that species. Common names vary from place to place. In central Indiana, for example, chipmunks are often called "ground squirrels," and ground squirrels are often called "gophers." In the Deep South, a turtle, the gopher tortoise, is called a "gopher," while pocket gophers there are often called "salamanders" and salamanders are called "lizards." And of course our French-speaking neighbors to the north, in Quebec, and our Spanish-speaking neighbors to the south, in Mexico, employ altogether different sets of common names. It is easy to see how confusion and imprecision can arise from the use of common names. Still, common names have their place, and we have tried to honor those that are in more or less widespread use in the eastern United States.

Scientific names, by contrast, are governed by a set of rules—the International Code of Zoological Nomenclature—such that each animal species has one (and only one) valid name, known and used by biologists throughout the world. The form of the species name is a binomial and is in Latin (occasionally Greek), or at least latinized: that for man, *Homo sapiens*, for example, consists of a generic name (*Homo*) and a trivial name (*sapiens*), the two jointly forming the species or specific name. The name of the original describer is given after the name of the species, thus *Mus musculus* Linnaeus for the house mouse. It was Carl von Linné, the great eighteenth-century Swedish systematist, who first named and described *Mus musculus*.

An author's name in parentheses indicates that the species is currently in a genus other than that in which it was originally described. The site where the type material (the specimen or specimens constituting the basis for the description) was originally collected is called the *type locality*. Later specimens from the type locality are called *topotypes*; the material selected for the topotypes should be the closest to the original that is available. Topotypes, often collected a century or two after a species was originally described, should provide a measure of the evolution occurring in the species since its original description.

In several cases, an entity's status as a species has been, or continues to be, in question among specialists. Some may argue that the entity is properly a subspecies of another species, or that, conversely, it should be split into two or more species. Where dispute of this sort persists, we discuss its ramifications at the outset of the species account.

DESCRIPTION. Most of the species accounts begin with basic descriptive material: shape, coloration, seasonal color changes, variation within the species, contrasts with related species, and special features (a prehensile tail, greatly en-

larged forefeet, a flattened skull, or whatever). The Glossary, at the back of the book, defines many of the terms used here and elsewhere.

Mammals often vary substantially in color even within litters. Notwithstanding this commonplace observation, the original descriptions of many subspecies were based on coat color alone, or coat color and size. A striking instance of the variability of color within a single species can be found in southern U.S. fox squirrels. Here, several very different color phases occur, yet the specimens drawn upon for the original descriptions were collected within a few miles of one another. We discuss these color differences, but often do not recognize the subspecies that others have erected on the basis of color.

Most mammals are colored rather drably, an adaptation allowing them to blend into their background. A number of eastern species, however, including some squirrels, the jumping mice, the golden mouse, and the red-backed vole, are quite colorful. The solitary bats are all quite colorful, and the red bat is exceptional in showing a marked color difference between the sexes: the male is much redder than the female. In many species the young and the adults are colored differently; for example, young mice of the genus *Peromyscus* are steel gray, whereas the adults of most species in the genus are some shade of brown. There are also well-developed seasonal differences; the most dramatic are found in some of the weasels and lagomorphs, which turn white in winter, but more subtle seasonal changes abound. Skunks and, to a lesser degree, porcupines have striking coat patterns, helping them to survive by giving an early warning to would-be predators—tangle with me and you will regret it!

For accurate color descriptions, a color standard should be used, such as Ridgeway's (1912) *Color Standards and a Color Nomenclature*, or the *Munsell Soil Color Charts* (1971). Another approach is to use modern instruments to measure quantitatively the reflectivity of various wavelengths of light, as Bowen (1968) did in his study of *Peromyscus polionotus*.

MEASUREMENTS. On almost any mammal, there are certain measurements to be taken: the *total length* (tip of snout to the tip of the last tail vertebra, not to the end of the hairs), the *tail length* (base of tail to the tip of the last vertebra, the location of the base established by bending the tail up at right angles to the body), and the *hind-foot length* (ankle bend to end of longest claw or hoof). These three measurements, given in this order for a mammal—in text, notes, or on a label—are understood by long-standing agreement among mammalogists to be the *standard* measurements, and they, along with information on weight, are given for each species treated in this volume. Ear length (from the notch at the base of the ear to the tip of the ear) is often a fourth standard measurement, though it is not given routinely because of variation in the way it is measured (which notch to use; and whether from fresh or dry skins). Three other measurements often given for bats are for the wingspread, the forearm (total length), and the tragus (principal ear lobe, notch to tip). Many other measurements on mammal specimens, particularly of the skull, can also be taken. See Hall and Kelson (1959) and Hall (1981) for excellent accounts of procedure and type of skull measurements.

The *diploid number* of an organism, also given under MEASUREMENTS, is the number of chromosomes found in its body cells, as opposed to the haploid number (half the diploid number), which is the number found in its sex cells, the eggs and sperm. (Earlier, it was assumed that animals with different chromosome numbers were by definition different species; some species, however, vary even in this basic characteristic.)

The tooth formula, or dental formula, is another basic characteristic given for each species. For many dogs of the genus *Canis*, for example, it is:

$$\frac{3}{3} \quad \frac{1}{1} \quad \frac{4}{4} \quad \frac{3}{3} \quad = \quad 44$$

This formulation indicates that on each side of the skull there are three incisors, one canine, four premolars, and three molars above and the same numbers below, thus 22 teeth total. That number is then doubled (here, 44) to account for the upper and lower jaws on *both* sides of the skull. The upper incisors are situated in the *premaxillary* bone; the rest of the upper teeth, the canines, premolars, and molars, are in the maxillary bone, the canines foremost. The lower

teeth are in the *mandible*. Premolars and molars differ in that premolars are preceded by milk (baby) teeth, molars are not; because this determination cannot be made simply by examining the teeth, mammalogists often consider premolars and molars jointly as *molariform teeth*, or *cheek teeth*. Using that logic, the formula for *Canis* could be written as:

$$\frac{3}{3} \quad \frac{1}{1} \quad \frac{7}{7} \quad = \quad 44$$

Tooth formulas vary considerably, however, from family to family and from order to order. The formula for the fulvous harvest mouse, for example, is

$$\frac{1}{1} \quad \frac{0}{0} \quad \frac{0}{0} \quad \frac{3}{3} \quad = \quad 16$$

Moreover, the numbers for the upper and lower jaws do not always coincide. The formula for the silver-haired bat, for example, is

$$\frac{2}{3} \quad \frac{1}{1} \quad \frac{2}{3} \quad \frac{3}{3} \quad = \quad 36$$

Because the teeth of shrews are quite difficult to identify, we do not give tooth formulas for them. In shrews, the first incisor is enlarged and has a large, curved front portion and a small cusp at the rear. The next few teeth—the rest of the incisors, the canines, and most of the premolars—are all small and single-cusped. These are called, collectively, *unicuspids*, and their details and positions are very helpful in identifying shrew species. The shrew's unicuspids are followed by the larger molariform teeth.

DISTRIBUTION. Anyone who has tried to prepare range maps recognizes the difficulty of drawing proper boundary lines, since, often, too few data are available, maps vary greatly from source to source, and avid collectors are forever extending the known range of a species. Perfect maps would probably present an array of dots depicting actual collection sites. Even then, the maps would not have remained perfect for long, for the animals themselves refuse to stay at home, and whole populations occasionally succumb to habitat loss or other debilitating factors.

For the range maps in this book, we have tried to show the current range of the eastern U.S. species and their subspecies, relying primarily on the range data in state mammal guides, in

Hall (1981), and in the Mammalian Species accounts currently being published by the American Society of Mammalogists. Occasionally, a state line or international boundary happens to form the limit of a known range, but this seeming coincidence is usually explained by the presence of an impassable river barrier constituting that segment of the state's boundary. Wild animals are of course no respecters of political boundaries; they follow natural ecological associations and constraints of which we are often unaware and which we cannot fully understand.

Range maps, of course, are silent on the matter of abundance. Some species, like the white-footed mouse, are very common throughout much of the range; others, like the hoary bat or the two bog lemmings, are, or appear to be, rare throughout much of their range.

Some of the maps herein may be misleading even within a few years, since some species (for example, the western harvest mouse and the nutria) are rapidly extending their ranges, and others (such as the river otter) are being reintroduced. At the same time, the ranges of, for example, the evening bat, the Allegheny woodrat, Franklin's ground squirrel, and even the eastern fox squirrel are apparently contracting.

The reader will note that many basically northern species follow the Appalachian Mountains through Virginia and West Virginia, finally finding the southernmost extremity of their range in the mountains of Tennessee, North Carolina, and northern Alabama. There are likewise species that shun the higher levels, preferring, for example, the coastal marshes or sandy beaches of the Atlantic Coast or the Gulf of Mexico, or the bottomlands of the Midwest. Islands automatically present primary isolating mechanisms for most mammals, and there may well be insular races yet to be described, some of these probably as separate subspecies.

A few introduced species—in particular the feral house cat, the feral dog, the house mouse, and the Norway rat—tend to concentrate heavily in or near human habitation or development, as opposed to wildlands. Because they occur in such circumstances throughout the eastern United States, we have not given them range maps.

Many of the bats are somewhat migratory, moving between summer and winter quarters.

Three species, however—the hoary bat, the red bat, and the silver-haired bat (the solitary bats)—are highly migratory, undergoing annual movements on a scale more like that of birds, and a fourth species, the gray bat, appears to winter regularly in a handful of eastern caves. Books on birds usually show separate summer and winter ranges for the migratory species, and it is odd that no one has done this for the migratory bats. The explanation lies probably in the sparsity of information on the movements of the bats. For the four mentioned above, we have shown the approximate extent of their migratory movements on their maps, on the basis of the information at hand. We welcome additional information.

HABITAT. In this section of the species treatments we have tried to indicate the general habitat types in which one would be likely to find a particular species, in terms of general landscape aspect (open field, woods, marsh, etc.), and vegetation type. We have also included information on local and regional variation in habitat and, where applicable, positive or negative influences arising from the efforts or negligence of people.

HABITS. Here, we discuss general lifeways (active, solitary, arboreal, etc.), daily and seasonal cycles, hibernation, movements, dens and nests, overt behavior, special abilities (echolocation, swimming, climbing, running, etc.), scent marking, and other typical behaviors of the species.

FOOD AND FEEDING. For each species, we have tried to indicate the general category of foods eaten—thus whether the species are herbivorous, carnivorous, or omnivorous—and the important specific foods taken by that species, when information at that level is available. Some species (artiodactyls, lagomorphs, and the Arvicolinae) feed essentially on 100% plant material, whether herbaceous or woody or mast (nuts and large seeds). These plant foods are ground very finely, and accordingly are difficult to identify in digestive tracts. They usually have to be identified on the basis of epidermal cell shape, trichomes, and other fine anatomical details under high-powered microscopes. Many other herbivores and omnivores feed on seeds, fruits, fungal spores, *Endogone* and related fungi, and/or insects and other invertebrates, such as spiders, centipedes, and earthworms. Such items are usually encountered in larger pieces and can be identified from stomach contents using the dissecting microscope. Some authors have attempted to use fecal analysis for determination of foods eaten, but other than for insectivorous bats, we do not recommend this approach. Fecal analysis can provide some information on diet, but it is usually exceedingly biased by the differential effects of digestion, soft foods being digested much faster and more thoroughly than hard foods. Its advantage is that it is not harmful to the animals.

Insectivorous bats, however, feed almost entirely on adult flying insects, and all of these contain much chitin. Chitin is exceedingly difficult to digest, and such foods go through the digestive tract very rapidly—in as little as 20 minutes in some bats. Therefore, although there remains some question about mayflies and perhaps a few other large, relatively soft-bodied insects, we usually feel fairly comfortable about our results when analyzing guano from bats. See Mumford and Whitaker (1982) and Whitaker (1988) for further information on food-habits analysis.

We have tried also to include information on seasonal shifts in foods, on food-gathering techniques and behavior, and on food storage. The foods of species may also vary greatly between seasons, habitats, and regions. In general, the foods eaten are influenced by the feeding adaptations of the species, the availability of potential food items, and the degree of selectivity of the species. Thus, although the foods eaten at any one time will be within the limits of adaptation of the species, individual animals will necessarily select from among the foods available, and the smaller the amounts and kinds of foods available, the closer the diet will conform to the foods available. Some species are rather specialized: the long-eared bats, for example, are primarily moth feeders; but Mexican free-tailed bats and mice of the genus *Peromyscus* tend to be generalists. Bears and the introduced rats will eat almost anything organic.

REPRODUCTION AND DEVELOPMENT. Here, we have tried to indicate seasonal cycles, prenuptial and mating behavior, gestation and birth, litter sizes, age at first mating, nursing patterns, the growth and development of the young, and the age at which the young are essentially or completely on their own.

POPULATION CHARACTERISTICS. Here, we discuss relative abundance, seasonal cycles, population density, dispersal patterns, annual turnover, home-range size, territory size, and such sex differences as occur in these regards. An animal's home range is the area it covers in its day-to-day travels. Home ranges of individuals may overlap, but territories, which by definition are defended areas within home ranges, do not overlap. Many birds, with their ability to cross large areas rapidly, tend to have large territories, which effectively spreads them out through the available habitat. Mammals, by contrast, often have large home ranges that include small territories. Our treatment of this material closes with the species' typical and longest recorded life spans, when these are known.

ENEMIES. In this section we list primarily those animals—other mammals, raptors, reptiles, and even fish—that are known to prey on the species, but also other mortality factors, including hunting, trapping, auto collisions, habitat destruction, and natural accidents, such as falling from trees or cave walls.

PARASITES AND DISEASE. Most books of this sort offer little or nothing on parasites; diseases, though not often discussed at length, are more apt to be covered. But it has not been our intention to present all available information on this subject in this book; rather, we have attempted to indicate at least the general kinds of parasites that afflict the animals, and to offer more detail where it seemed of particular interest. We hope this treatment will encourage others to be attentive to this important phase of the biology of our mammals.

Trematodes of the lungs of deer are well known, as are the heartworms of canids, but internal parasites are most abundant in digestive tracts, particularly the intestines, of mammals. One can easily find various helminth worms—nematodes (roundworms), trematodes (flukes: unsegmented flatworms with ventral suckers), and cestodes (tapeworms: many-segmented worms with a distinct head). Uncommonly, one can find acanthocephalans (spiny-headed worms with well-developed heads); these often exhibit pseudosegmentation, which may lead one to confuse them with cestodes.

Among the ectoparasites, fleas, biting lice, sucking lice, ticks, mites (including chiggers), and a few flies, beetles, and true bugs may be found. Fleas are laterally flattened, jumping insects often with genal, pronotal, or abdominal combs and highly modified piercing/sucking mouthparts. They are relatively non-host-specific (that is, they are not confined to a single host species), and many different species of them can be found on our mammals. Sucking lice (Anoplura), which have sucking mouthparts, are confined to mammals, and can be found on a number of our species, particularly rodents. Biting or chewing lice (Mallophaga, often called bird lice) have chewing mouthparts and an interesting distribution on mammals: they are found primarily on carnivores, deer, and pocket gophers. Because both kinds of lice are exceedingly host-specific, their presence can be used as taxonomic characters, in the same fashion as morphological or genetic characters. Most abundant on most mammals are ticks and mites (including chiggers). Ticks, which have a piercing/sucking proboscis with backward-projecting spines, are considered to be enlarged mites. All stages—larvae, nymphs, and adults—are found on the host. Ticks lie in wait for a host, take a blood meal, then drop off. Most of those found on mammals are "hard" ticks, of the family Ixodidae, which take one blood meal each as larvae, nymphs, and adults. Ticks found on the big brown bat, "soft" or "bird" ticks of the Argasidae, take numerous blood meals.

Chiggers are larvae (three pairs of legs, rather than the four of the adults) of one mite family, the Trombiculidae. They too have piercing/sucking mouthparts with retrorsely (backward) projecting spines. They are not host-specific, even though they are often found on the same hosts. They are termed *habitat-specific*: they position themselves where they are likely to encounter specific hosts, such as near a woodchuck burrow, which *Euschoengastia marmotae* does. But if another host happens by, it is equally likely to become infected.

Numerous species of mites have been recorded from mammals, some (such as many of the myobiids and listrophorids) being exceedingly host-specific, whereas others, such as *Androlaelaps fahrenholzi*, are at most weakly host-specific, that species having been recorded from well over 100 different host species in North America. Various specialized fly parasites occur on bats, and some large, reddish-brown fly larvae (of *Cuterebra*, a botfly) are often found protruding from the flesh of certain species, notably the white-footed mouse, *Peromyscus leucopus*. Bat bugs (Hemiptera: *Cimex*) are sometimes found on bats, and beetles are found on shrews; the beaver "flea," actually a beetle (*Platypsyllus*; *Platypsyllidae*), is common on beavers.

It is important to note that, in general, mammalian parasites do *not* much affect their hosts or humans. They have become adapted to an existence on their hosts, which for them *are their habitats*; it would be self-defeating for them to harm their hosts in significant ways.

Extensive information on the parasites of mammals is lacking for most states other than for Florida (Forrester, 1992) and Indiana (Whitaker, 1982; Mumford and Whitaker, 1982) in the east, and Utah (Allred and Beck, 1966) in the west (mites only). A guide to the literature of ectoparasitic mites of mammals was presented by Whitaker and Wilson (1974). A similar compilation for more recent mite records is nearly complete.

Many diseases occur in mammals, many can be transmitted to humans, and a number of them are mentioned in the various species accounts. Rabies has long been a problem in carnivores, and more recently it has been known in North American insectivorous bats, as well. Rabies and bat rabies may actually be two different diseases, though they share many similarities. Unlike carnivores, rabid bats do not go mad and attack anything that moves. Rather, they lie still, thus are not dangerous unless handled. Rabies in most carnivores has been kept in check, since most dogs now receive rabies shots, but rabies in raccoons has become a major problem. Tularemia can be a problem in rabbits, and many cottontails are discarded needlessly because people know that white spots on the liver are characteristic of tularemia. In tularemia, there are many small white spots scattered over much of the liver. Many rabbits are discarded, however, because of a few larger white bodies in the liver, these being the harmless immature stages of tapeworms. Black plague or black death, carried by rat fleas, has generally been associated with rats of the genus *Rattus*, and in earlier times the plague killed millions of people. Some diseases we have recently become aware of in mammals are Lyme disease, hantavirus, and the raccoon nematode, *Baylisascaris*. Lyme disease is carried by ticks of deer (the larval ticks are mainly on *Peromyscus*); hantavirus is found mostly in *Peromyscus* and other small mammals; the raccoon nematode, found in raccoon feces, becomes more virulent with time.

RELATION TO HUMANS. Here, we indicate the various ways in which mammal species interact with us: humans acting as predators (hunting and trapping) or as inadvertent enemies (killing them with our automobiles), the mammals acting as pests (carrying diseases and spoiling food, feeding on crops, killing livestock or wildlife), or offering us aesthetic pleasure, or, in the case of the beaver, actually altering the landscape.

SUBSPECIES. Our thinking on subspecies differs greatly from that of most authors. Like many of them, we feel that an excessive number of subspecies have been described for North American mammals, but it is in determining a sound basis for reducing that number where opinions differ. Subspecies and species were traditionally described on the basis of morphological differences alone—differences mostly in external and skeletal form and appearance. We now know, however, that species are composed of series or arrays of populations, each population evolving genetic differences over time, depending on the extent and pace of the environment's variation and the species' adaptation to its environment. Thus the morphological variation so often found between different populations in intergrading series is no more than is to be expected. Such variation will occur gradually or abruptly over a species' range. These levels and patterns of variation should be recorded, but in our opinion are not a sufficient basis for describing subspecies.

Lidicker (1962), in discussing the problem of subspecies, concluded that "statistically significant differences can be found between the vast majority of the population pairs" and that "the ability to prove that two populations are statistically different in one or several characters is only a measure of the persistence and patience of the systematist. To base formal subspecific descriptions on this kind of evidence seems to us to be almost meaningless, as well as a contribution to the degradation of the subspecies category, to the extent of losing it as a legitimate member of the taxonomic hierarchy." Wilson and Brown (1953) proposed dispensing with subspecies designations entirely. We believe the subspecies category should be retained, but that it should be used, as its name suggests, only for units somehow set apart from the others—typically by geographic disjuncture—and evolving toward the species level, not simply for cataloging variation among intergrading series of populations at points along continua of imperceptible character shifts.

Over the last few decades, the biological-*species* concept, which is based on reproductive isolation—related species may occasionally hybridize but cannot and do not reproduce regularly—has replaced the morphological-species concept. Some years ago I proposed (Whitaker, 1970) that a biological-*subspecies* concept likewise be established, to replace the morphological-subspecies concept. I believe that subspecies should be restricted to situations wherein populations or groups of populations appear to be on their way toward becoming new species. Seen in this light, the first step in speciation is the introduction of a *primary isolating mechanism*, the stopping of gene flow between particular populations or groups of populations. Primary isolating mechanisms are often or usually geographic: for whatever reason, groups of populations of a species become separated in space, with uninhabitable areas (mountains, deserts, water, or whatever) between them. Any factor, however, that disrupts gene flow between populations, spatial or otherwise, can be considered a primary isolating mechanism.

When such a mechanism is in place, the development of *secondary* isolating mechanisms can begin; these are mechanisms, driven by the needs of environmental adaptation, that in the course of time prohibit interbreeding even where the primary isolating mechanisms have broken down, that is, when members from the two groups, for whatever reason, are again in contact. If at that point the secondary isolating mechanisms have developed to the extent that the two forms once again in contact *remain distinct* (cannot or do not interbreed), speciation has occurred. In very rare cases, a sudden genetic change—a shift to polyploidy, for example—can create an immediately viable new form; we view this as a situation in which primary and secondary isolating mechanisms are one and the same.

From this concept emerge two criteria for the recognition of subspecies: (1) a primary isolating mechanism is in place but secondary isolating mechanisms are not, and (2) the results of evolution can be observed as morphological (or other) variation between the mutually isolated populations. Most of the mammal subspecies described for the eastern United States were originally erected on the basis that they differed morphologically from the individuals in the population that had prompted the original *species* description, or from other, already described, subspecies, thus usually fulfilling only the second criterion. Authors describing subspecies usually made little or no attempt to determine whether primary isolating mechanisms (or such mechanisms by any other name) were in place.

Accordingly, when we began to assess the subspecies we encountered in the literature, we examined the available information, pro and con, to determine whether there was evidence that two (or more) described subspecies of a species are in fact separated by these mechanisms, or if, on the contrary, there continues to be significant gene flow between them. Where adequate evidence of a primary isolating mechanism was found—either by a documented break in the range of a species or by other evidence indicating a lack of gene flow—and if differentiation had indeed occurred, we accepted that subspecies. Where we saw no evidence of a primary isolating mechanism, we did not accept the validity of the subspecies in question. Those we *have* accepted as valid are given full subspecies accounts in the text, and their boundaries are indicated by solid lines and boldface type on the range maps.

Again, where we find no primary isolating mechanisms, we question the subspecies that have been described, no matter how striking any clinal variation might be. Moreover, we do not accept subspecies in situations in which a former primary isolating mechanism has broken down and an intergrading series once again links the populations involved. The subspecies we question are *not* given separate subspecies accounts; rather, they are simply listed as "other currently recognized eastern subspecies" under the account of the subspecies or species with which we think they should be included. On the maps, their boundaries are indicated by dotted lines. Most of those we reject appear to be portions of series of intergrading populations, rather than evolutionary units on their way to becoming species.

We have not, of course, formally or intensively studied the 260-odd currently recognized subspecies of eastern U.S. mammals, and we have likely overlooked some primary isolating mechanisms, thus some valid subspecies, in some cases. It would thus be taxonomically inappropriate for us to relegate formally to synonymy those subspecies we question or believe to be invalid. Nor have we proposed or described new subspecies of our own. More concentrated work is necessary before sound decisions can be reached on whether particular questionable subspecies are valid, that is, whether both of our subspecies criteria are fulfilled. Our choices should therefore be considered as recommendations to be verified or refuted by more exhaustive investigation. We suggest that the questionable subspecies undergo further study, then be formally synonymized if they are found not to be separated by primary isolating mechanisms—geographic, genetic, or otherwise.

Currently, 224 subspecies of mammals are recognized in the eastern United States, most of them listed in Hall (1981). We have found evidence of our subspecies criteria in 63 of these, leaving 161 that we have questioned. Detailed study may show, of course, that our criteria are fulfilled in some of the 161, and not fulfilled in some of the 63. We welcome such work, for we will feel that our efforts have stimulated new thinking and a viable solution to the subspecies problem.

LITERATURE. Since 1969, the American Society of Mammalogists has been publishing the Mammalian Species series, each number in the series treating a different species. These accounts are by different authors, but each attempts to bring together the pertinent literature and to present it in concise, organized format. The result is an excellent, in-depth series of leaflet-type publications on individual species. New accounts are being steadily added, and over 500 are available as of this writing. This total includes accounts for most of the species covered by this book.

These accounts, which have been drawn upon heavily for this revision, provide a much more extensive literature review for each species than could be furnished here. In this volume, following the text for each species, we present a listing of pertinent literature, which includes all works cited in the species text as well as other, more comprehensive or more detailed papers or books on that species, and works that are not included in the Mammalian Species account. If no Mammalian Species account yet exists for a species, then a more extensive literature listing is included here for that species.

Mammalian Species accounts can be obtained by writing to the secretary-treasurer of the American Society of Mammalogists, as indicated in any current issue of the *Journal of Mammalogy* (currently H. Duane Smith, Monte L. Bean Life Science Museum, Brigham Young University, Provo, Utah 84602). Contact the secretary-treasurer also for information on other publications of the Society (*Journal of Mammalogy*, Special Publications) or for membership in the Society.

Potential authors volunteer to write the accounts by getting approval from the primary editor of Mammalian Species, currently Barbara Blake (Dept. of Biology, Bennett College, 900 East Washington St., Greensboro, North Carolina 27401-3239). The objective in these accounts is to summarize information from all the literature on the species, not to present unpublished data.

## IDENTIFICATION KEYS

Keys are a simple and time-saving means of identifying the taxa of organisms. Without keys, it would be necessary to read the descriptions of numerous taxa before a determination could be made.

The keys in this book, like those in most other works in the natural sciences, are dichotomous, that is, there are two choices at each couplet (two at number 1, two at number 2, and so forth), each choice leading to another couplet, until a taxonomic determination is made. For example, to key an armadillo, read the key to the Orders; from couplet 1 go to couplet 2, then to the second half of couplet 2, in both cases because of the armor.

Once the key has been traversed, the next step is to read the description of the taxon, to verify the taxonomic determination. If it is incorrect, try the key again from the beginning or go back to the couplets you were unsure of, and try the other way. Keys will not work for every specimen, because of variation between species.

## COLLECTING AND TRACKING MAMMALS

Before collecting any mammals, anywhere, one must first determine their legal status, whether permits are needed, and, if so, from what jurisdiction. State laws govern most mammal species, but federal law is preemptive for all species listed as endangered or threatened by the U.S. Fish and Wildlife Service. The best way to determine what permits, if any, are required to collect a given species in a given locality is to consult the appropriate state agency, such as the Indiana Department of Natural Resources, the Florida Department of Fish and Game, or the New York Department of Environmental Conservation. Ask about both federal and state laws and permits.

Federal permits are required to collect species federally designated as threatened or endangered, even if you simply want to catch and release them. State permits cover all the others, and eligibility for permits and the details of pertinent laws differ from state to state. Most states consider certain species to be game species, and as such they may be covered by hunting or trapping licenses. Nongame species are usually covered by scientific collecting permits.

Knowing about the locale in which you wish to collect is also important. You should always obtain permission to make observations or collect on private land. In some areas, as for example state parks in Indiana, all wildlife is protected; in these parks, one must obtain a special permit, over and above a state scientific collecting permit, to capture mammals. Some states may issue salvage permits, which allow you to pick up animals killed on the highway.

In addition, the American Society of Mammalogists and some state and federal agencies have developed standards and guidelines pertaining to the collecting and handling of wild mammals in the field and in captivity. Persons interested in studying mammals should ask the Society and the appropriate state agencies about these also.

Another consideration with regard to collecting mammals is their ultimate resting spot. It is desirable that specimens that have been preserved ultimately be deposited in a museum or collection where they will be properly curated and made available for study by future generations of scientists.

Finally, people working with mammals should be aware of possible diseases or parasites associated with wild species, and take precautions if necessary. Some of the diseases to be aware of are Lyme disease, rabies, hantavirus, tularemia, histoplasmosis, and the nematode parasite of raccoons, *Baylisascaris procyonis*.

Small mammals are generally shy and retiring. Many are nocturnal and dwell beneath the matted grass or the thick humus cover of the forest. There are some, such as the woodchuck and the various ground and tree squirrels, that are readily observed, but in many other cases, we must capture specimens in kill traps or live traps. For some purposes, we need dead animals, for example to study food habits or parasites, to examine the reproductive system, or to do morphological or taxonomic studies, or if a biological survey of the mammal fauna of an area or region must be made and reference specimens retained. But for other types of studies, such as of behavior, population dynamics, or physiology, the animals are needed alive, either to keep in the laboratory for some period of time or to mark and release. Many studies require a balance between field and laboratory work. Environmental conditions can be controlled in the laboratory, so as to simplify and regularize the testing of behavioral stimuli, or to determine cause and effect with respect to various envi-

ronmental factors. One confronts the problem, of course, that confinement affects results, but often we can study certain details or test hypotheses in the laboratory, then see if they are borne out in the field. The laboratory biologist establishes the conditions the way he or she wants them, but then must determine how laboratory conditions affect the results. The field biologist often looks to the field for the situation or conditions he or she wishes to study, but conditions there cannot be precisely controlled. Careful planning, in the laboratory *or* in the field, is crucial to the obtaining of meaningful results.

Small mammals may be kept in aquaria; or one may build larger cages or purchase any of the many commercial cages currently on the market. There are also many sizes and shapes of plastic containers that can serve as animal cages; and a suitable screen cover will keep the occupant inside. Too often, captive mammals are kept under conditions that are too dry for them; damp sphagnum, leaf mold, or sod should be placed in a portion of the container, as well as a suitable nest chamber where the captive can retire to sleep or, if fortune favors, to bear her young.

Capturing animals alive, marking them in various ways, and releasing them will permit recognition of the individual when it is later recaptured, for studies of populations, home ranges, dispersal, and the like. Marking can be by ear or ankle tagging, ear punching, banding, or toe clipping. Gillian K. Godfrey (1954) used a leg bracelet modified to hold radioactive cobalt so that the movements of marked voles could be traced with a Geiger-Muller counter. W. G. Sheldon (1949) put expanding collars on young foxes and secured much information on their movements. Where collars are not practical, a braided polyethylene rope harness with coded color patches has proved effective. The large-eared ungulates have been marked with a washer tag holding a colored plastic disc, permitting the researcher to identify and observe the animal at a distance. The use of commercial fur dyes, also useful in marking animals, is described by Evans and Holdenreid (1943), but such marks persist only until molting occurs. Freeze-marking mammals with a pressurized refrigerant destroys the pigment cells in the hair follicles, and in a few weeks a new growth of unpigmented hairs becomes evident at the brand site (Lazarus and Rowe, 1975).

Techniques for determining movements, home ranges, growth, aging behavior, and other phases of the life history of mammals have been greatly refined in the past 35 years. When the first edition of this book was written, ear tagging and toe clipping were standard procedures for identifying recaptured animals. Now, rapid advances in electronics and radioisotopes have provided new approaches to the field study of wild mammals that have aided greatly in our understanding of their habits and behavior. Packets of cyalume lightstick, as used by fishermen, can be glued to bats and other mammals to permit observation of their movements. Transponders (PIT tags) can be implanted in mammals to mark them individually, just as prices are marked on items in the grocery store. A major advantage this procedure offers is that the life of the transponder is unlimited; as passive devices, they carry no battery or other dischargeable element. A disadvantage is that they cannot be read from a distance. Another approach to tracking is to mark an animal with fluorescein dye, liberate the animal, and then scan for its trail using fluorescent light. Radiotelemetry is discussed by Amlaner and MacDonald (1980) and Mech (1983), and in *Research and Management Techniques for Wildlife and Habitats* (Bookhout, ed., 1996). The latter discusses many techniques for field study and is a mine of information. The cost of tracking equipment is high, but its merits have been amply demonstrated.

Tranquilizers (nicotine salicylate, succinylcholine, and others) shot into the animal with a dart gun have been effective with larger mammals. Once the animal has been immobilized, it can be tagged, radioed, weighed, and otherwise studied before it is released.

It is lamentable that biologists so often take many specimens, then use them only for their own study. We believe one should gather as much information as possible from all animals collected, but also make efforts to see that other workers are afforded an opportunity to gain information from the animals thus sacrificed. Furthermore, workers often expend much time

and effort attempting to study the hard-to-find while ignoring the common mammals, even though the latter may be more in need of study. Often we can obtain a much greater quantity of information right in our own backyard, and larger data sets afford a much better chance of leading to useful generalizations than do chance data concerning rare animals—though of course we need information on the rare animals as well.

Small rodents and shrews are readily trapped with the familiar snap-back mouse trap, although these traps often crush skulls. This problem can be partly remedied by using museum special traps, although they are expensive (the museum special is larger, thus more often misses the skull). These and several other types of traps can now be purchased from B. E. Atlas, 4300 North Kilpatrick, Chicago, Illinois 60641. The large snap-back rat trap is useful for capturing squirrels, wood rats, and even weasels. Steel traps that instantly kill the animal, such as the Conibear trap, are usually used for larger animals. The Tomahawk Live Trap Company of Tomahawk, Wisconsin 54487, carries a large assortment of cage or "live" traps, and Hava-hart or Sherman traps are also much used. Many of the collecting and tracking devices are advertised in the back pages of the *Journal of Mammalogy*.

Various baits have proved useful, but these are often as attractive to ants, crickets, and slugs as to the mammal for which the trap was intended. Consequently, the biologist may find many unsnapped traps from which all bait has been removed. Peanut butter and oatmeal, thoroughly mixed, form a standard bait used by many, although others use peanut butter alone, and some use bacon or other items. We often bait initially with peanut butter or a peanut butter/oatmeal mixture, then rebait as needed with oatmeal by dropping it on the treadles. Suet is attractive to many mammals, particularly during winter, and raisins, wild birdseed, bits of meat, kippered herring, and even table scraps can be used.

Unbaited traps placed directly across the runway of a small rodent or shrew, so that the treadle is tripped as the animal moves by, will serve to catch many small mammals. Traps can also be sunk crosswise in the subterranean burrows of shrews or pine mice, so that the treadle is at the ground level of the burrow. For added effectiveness, the hole can be covered with bark or other material, but be sure the cover is high enough that the treadle will clear it, and be sure you will be able to find the trap when you return! We usually place traps in lines with basically equidistant spacing (often a meter), the ends of the line marked with tape. If traps are to be placed farther apart, we usually mark each trap.

Post holes or sunken cans (pitfall traps) are effective for shrews, and they will often take arvicoline rodents as well. We usually use 1,000-ml plastic beakers and sink them as far under logs or other objects as we can get them. Where small mammals are numerous, they can be caught by hand, but a heavy glove should be worn to guard against the bite of their sharp teeth. We have collected many meadow voles and jumping mice in this fashion, and also chipmunks and ground squirrels.

Shooting was once used extensively to collect bats, but the bats shot must be felled over water or bare ground, since even a small amount of obscuring vegetation in the fading light of a summer evening will usually lead to frustration. In any event, we almost never shoot bats anymore, because of the difficulty of determining their identity in flight, and thus of ensuring that we are not shooting an endangered or threatened species. In caves, bats can often be secured simply by picking them from the walls or ceiling. A pair of long, slender forceps will often prove useful in extracting a bat hidden away in some otherwise inaccessible fissure. A bat trap that has been developed and proved effective in recent years consists of two vertical ranks of piano wire, the two ranks about 8 cm (3 inches) apart, and, within the ranks, wires about 2.5 cm (an inch) apart. The trap is thoroughly described by Tuttle (1974), but we have made much simplified models, often using fishing leader in place of wire. The trap is usually placed over an opening to a cave, mine, or building. The bats attempt to fly through the two ranks of wires but end up between them and are unable to escape. They then slide down the wires into a canvas bag and can easily be secured.

Japanese mist nets are also effective in capturing bats. Mist nets can be obtained from Avinet, P.O. Box 1103, Dryden, New York 13053-1103. Nets must be used with care in caves or other areas where many bats will be caught in a short time, for it often takes some time to remove a single bat from the net. A good place for netting operations is over woodland streams or old roads, but nets must be placed beneath a canopy, such that the branches above the net restrict the area of flight. Otherwise, most of the bats will simply fly up and over the net. After capture, bats may be placed temporarily in a hardware-cloth cylinder or like container. Food-habits information can be obtained by placing the bats in a cup, from which feces can be collected, for a few minutes before the bats are released.

Bat banding has greatly increased our knowledge of chiropteran biology. Suitable bands can be obtained from Lambournes Limited, Shallowford Court, *off* High Street, Henley-on-Arden, Solihull, West Midlands B95 5BY, England; or from A. C. Hughes, 2 High St., Hampton Hill, Middlesex TW12 1NA, England. Small bands placed on the forearm have been carried by some bats for more than 30 years. For Lambourne's bands, use Alloy 2.9 mm for *Myotis* and *Pipistrellus* and Alloy 4.2 mm for *Eptesicus*, *Lasionycteris*, and *Lasiurus*. For Hughes' bands, use 5.30 XB for all North American bats. Lambourne's bands can be purchased with letters and numbers (extra, one-time charge) and Hughes bands come in solid colors (with or without embossed numbers) or as two color stripes (without numbers). Bat detectors, which pick up the supersonic notes of bats, can be used to find bat roosts and feeding areas, and to determine times of activity and other facets of bat behavior. We use them to test the efficiency of our mist nets. National Band and Tag Company (721 York St., Newport, Kentucky 41072) carries an assortment of bands for other species.

Another useful recent technique is to glue tiny radio transmitters on bats and then track them back to their roosts. We snip off a small patch of hair and glue the trap onto the bare skin with colostomy glue. A variety of radio transmitters can be used on other animals, whether placed as implants or mounted on collars. Advanced Telemetry Systems, Inc. (Isonti, Minnesota

55040) and Holohil Systems (RR #2, Wood-lawn, Ontario KOA 3140) carry receivers and transmitters. Mini-mitters are small "beepers" that can be placed in or on mammals, both to track them and to gather data on body temperatures (Mini-mitter Co., Inc., P.O. Box 3386, Sunriver, Oregon 97707).

Bats sent to rabies laboratories can often be obtained in return for identifying the bats. We have obtained extensive information on bat biology from specimens from the Indiana rabies laboratory. Road-killed animals of all kinds are other excellent sources of study material, and would otherwise go to waste. We have gathered many valuable specimens and much useful information from D.O.R.'s (dead on the road).

Fur dealers and trappers, visited in the late fall and winter, can provide valuable specimens. From them, the collector can procure fine skull series and useful measurements of the larger mammals, which are otherwise difficult to secure, and valuable information on primeness, reproduction, the habits of hibernation of the two sexes, food habits, internal and external parasites, and other subjects.

The preparation of mammal skins, skulls, and skeletons for museum purposes is well outlined in Hall (1981) and in *Wildlife Management Techniques Manual*, published by The Wildlife Society (Schemnitz, ed., 1980). Works of this sort will help, but if young collectors first observe an experienced collector preparing a skin, they will save much time and disappointment in their own efforts.

Some object to the sacrifice of any animals. Information is needed on the biology of the various species in order that we might better provide for them later, and often it is necessary to sacrifice a few in order to gain such information. Animals should be sacrificed humanely, but the sacrifice of some may be highly beneficial to the species in the long run.

## RECORDING OBSERVATIONS

We cannot impress upon the reader too strongly the desirability, indeed the utmost urgency, of recording in minute detail everything connected with the collecting of a specimen. It is amazing how much can be written on a museum label measuring but one-half by two inches. One skin and skull with full notes and a well-recorded label are much more valuable than a whole group of specimens with limited data. The following should be recorded on such a small tag: locality; date; collector; sex of specimen (with probable age, as "immature" or "adult"); the conventional measurements (total length, tail length, hind foot length, and, whenever possible, weight, as well as, for bats, tragus, forearm length, and wingspan); condition of the reproductive organs (if a female is pregnant, the number of embryos, their size, and whether the female is or is not nursing; if a male, the size and descent of the testes); stomach and cheek-pouch contents; the presence and identity of internal and external parasites; details of habitat; and anything else felt to be of significance. The name of the species is not necessary: if known, record it on the label; if not, it can be determined (by you or a colleague) at a later date. One can use a fine pen with India ink, though much more suitable pens with permanent black ink, such as the Uniball deluxe (micro, 0.2 mm), are now available. If parasites, stomach materials, or other items are to be stored in alcohol, we recommend that one let the ink on the label dry and then rinse the label in running water before placing it in a vial with the preserved material.

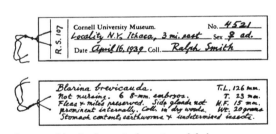

*Front and back of a typical specimen label, prepared in the field*

The mammalogist should keep a catalogue—a consecutively numbered list of all mammals personally processed. It should include one line for each animal collected, with, minimally, its number (in your own series), species, date, and collection locality (state, county, and specific locality, with reference to some recognizable location on a state map). The specimen number designated in the catalogue should be included with all materials preserved from any mammal processed.

It is also imperative that investigators keep full and detailed notes in a field notebook or journal. The field notebook is arranged by species, with one or more pages per species and not more than one species on a page. Field notes should include details on a species' habitat and habits as observed in the field, the conditions under which the specimen was secured, sketches of any soft parts the character of which may be lost in drying (i.e. the position of the teats), the plantar tubercles (on the soles of the feet), the molting pattern, and information on food, reproduction, and parasites. No collector should be concerned lest he keep too many notes, for memory is ephemeral. Notes can always be ignored, but they cannot be accurately retrieved from memory later. More than a century has passed since the renowned American naturalist Elliot Coues (1877) stated the following:

Now you know these things, but very likely no one else does and you know them at the time, but you will not recollect a tithe of them in a few weeks or months, to say nothing of years. Don't trust your memory, it will trip you up, what is clear now will grow obscure; what is found will be lost. Write down everything while it is fresh in your mind; write it out in full; time so spent now will be time saved in the end, when you offer your researches to the discriminating public. Don't be satisfied with a dry-as-dust item: clothe a skeleton of fact and breathe life into it with thoughts that glow; let the paper smell of the woods. There's a pulse in a new fact; catch the rhythm before it dies. Keep off the quicksand of mere memorandum—that means something "to be remembered," which is just what you cannot do. Shun abbreviations; such keys rust with disuse, and may fail in after times to unlock the secret that should have been laid bare in the beginning. Use no signs intelligible only to yourself; your notebook may come to be overhauled by others whom you would not wish to disappoint. Be sparing of sentiment, a delicate thing, easily degraded to drivel: crude enthusiasm always hacks instead of hewing. Beware of literary infelicities: the written word remains after you have passed away: put down nothing for your friend's blush or your enemy's sneer, write as if a stranger were looking over your shoulder.

## HOW AND WHAT TO STUDY

Every species described in this volume would amply repay additional close study, and at the close of each species account we have offered some particulars on that score, with no expectation or intention of having exhausted the more promising prospects. Of the 121 species treated, the young of many have yet to be described; the gestation period of a number of species is unknown; detailed data on food habits have as yet been recorded for relatively few. Home life, seasonal differences in food habits, activity cycle, and behavior are unknown in any detail for many. We need to know more about the winter behavior of many of the species, such as the hibernation and migration of bats. (Where do red and evening bats spend the winter?) We also need a proper evaluation of the soft parts and other structural modifications of many mammals, in relation to the biology of the species. In the field, direct observations of animals feeding can often be made. Burrows can be excavated and the nests and their invertebrate fauna investigated and described. The active periods of both diurnal and nocturnal species can be recorded. These are areas in which mammalogists—professional or amateur, but thoughtful and earnest—can make contributions to the science of mammalogy, often without recourse to museums or natural history laboratories.

We have included in this edition some information on the major ectoparasites of each species. This is an area that has attracted few mammalogists, one in which countless contributions can yet be made. We do want to emphasize the endlessly fascinating possibilities for the mammalogist with an interest in these matters. In lieu of the cumbersome phrase "ectoparasites and other associates," a less specific, shorter, but more descriptive name would seem to be useful, and the term "ectodyte" (as well as the term "endodyte," for internal forms) has been suggested by Whitaker et al. (1993).

Whitaker and Wilson (1974) summarized information on the mites (other than chiggers) of North American mammals. Such a summary is much needed, as well, for the fleas, the ticks, the chiggers, and the endoparasites. Most work to date has been directed simply toward determining the species and abundance of ectoparasites on or in given hosts, and perhaps their location on the bodies of their hosts. Future workers can determine more intimate details of the host-parasite interrelationships, although we use this term loosely, since many of the associates abiding in the fur of mammals apparently cause the host no harm, thus by definition are not parasites.

There is, then, an invertebrate *community* within the fur of the host, just as there is such a community in an old field or woodlot. That in the fur is a much simpler community, in which the lice, fleas, batbugs, batflies, and many of the mites are truly parasitic, though the extent of harm caused is exceedingly variable. Unlike most other communities, this one includes few predators (cheyletid mites, common on rabbits, are thought to be predaceous, but cheyletids are not often common on other mammals). A number of forms are phoretic: they do not feed, but use the host simply as a means of transportation or dispersal. Some mites are parasitic or phoretic on other parasites, as for example on fleas. Nymphal mites of the genera *Cyrtolaelaps* and *Euryparasitus* (Cyrtolaelapidae) are phoretic on their hosts. Female mites of the genus *Pygmephorus* (Pygmephoridae), their first pair of legs enlarged for grasping, are highly modified for a phoretic existence on mammals. The closely related *Bakerdania* is also commonly phoretic on mammals, but is not thus modified. The reason for the difference is unknown, but we would expect it to relate to the various behavior patterns of the mites. Moreover, the males of the pygmephorids have not been found on mammal hosts, a circumstance that raises additional questions. Certain glycyphagid mites, which have evolved claspers for clasping individual hairs, are also highly modified for phoretic life, as deutonymphs. Many are highly host-specific, riding about on the host for extended periods, presumably dropping off in the nest of the host, where they metamorphose to adults and begin breeding. Most hypopi (immature transport stages of certain mites) apparently do not feed, nor do they even have mouthparts (some reside

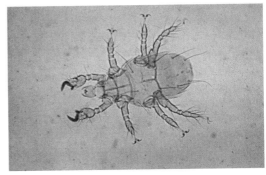

Pygmephorus *female, a phoretic (nonparasitic) mite*

in hair follicles, and some nutrients in this case may pass to the mite through their skins).

Aside from the study of parasites for its own sake, parasite relationships can sometimes provide insight into the evolutionary relationships of their mammalian hosts. This approach is productive only with highly host-specific forms, those that remain on hosts of the same species, or of a related group of species, through time. Close taxonomic relationship between parasites of different hosts often indicates close relationship between those hosts. This observation has been used for studies of the taxonomy of the mammal hosts, and has been especially useful with mallophagan lice in efforts to determine the relationships of pocket gophers (Emerson and Price, 1985). See, also, the exceedingly interesting story of the beaver mites, recounted in the beaver account.

The fleas, lice, ticks, and larger mites infesting many of the species are fairly well known, but only a few hosts have been adequately studied for small ectoparasites. Indeed, new species of mites are still being described from eastern mammals, and will be for decades to come. To find smaller parasites, we use a dissecting microscope and manipulate the hair and skin with dissecting needles. External parasites can be preserved directly in 70% alcohol.

Likewise, internal parasites have been little sought in many of the less-common species, and much remains to be done. The best way to look for larger internal parasites is to carefully cut open the stomach and the length of the intestine. We usually do this using a black background with a dissecting microscope. Most of the worm parasites are white, but some are colored. Nematodes can often be found in the stomach and the intestine, whereas trematodes, cestodes, and acanthocephalans can be found in the intestines, trematodes and cestodes commonly, acanthocephalans rarely. It has always surprised us that numerous trematodes of a number of species are found in bats. The surprise arises from the fact that *all* of the trematodes have a complex life cycle requiring a snail as an intermediate host. It is difficult to see how so many species of trematodes could have undergone the complex evolutionary development necessary to be so often associated with bats. Nematodes can be killed in hot 70% ethyl alcohol, then preserved in a mixture of four parts 70% ethanol and one part glycerine. Other worm parasites can be killed and stored in AFA, a mixture of 20 parts 95% alcohol, six parts commercial formalin, one part glacial acetic acid, and 40 parts distilled water.

The approximate age of many mammals may be determined by tooth wear. This method has been carefully worked out by Severinghaus (1949) for white-tailed deer. Similar procedures have been established for many carnivores, ungulates, and rodents. Tooth wear in *Sorex fumeus* and some other shrews is distinctive, and reliably establishes age classes (Hamilton, 1940). The annulations on the root of the upper canine in the black bear appear to be correlated with age. H. T. Gier (1957) has provided a reconstruction of tooth wear in coyotes from one through eight years. This method may undoubtedly be applied to other carnivores. Epiphyseal cartilage is prominent in many of the long bones of immature animals, but disappears as maturity is reached. The baculum (the bone in the penis of some mammalian groups) has been widely used in an attempt to establish age classes, though this method should be used with caution, for there is wide variation in the rate of development of this structure. The eye lens grows continually throughout life, and thus may act as an indicator of age. This basis has been used with some success; for example, R. D. Lord (1959) used the dried weight of the lens in age studies of cottontail rabbits. The lens-growth curve permits the determination of month of birth of younger rabbits and the year of birth of rabbits older than one year.

Population size, population trends, and the characteristics of population cycles have been studied by many investigators. Their techniques are varied and often complicated. The purpose of population studies is to develop as close an approximation of population sizes and densities as resources permit, and also to indicate the statistical accuracy of such estimates. The various methods employed in such studies were well summarized by Lancia et al. (1996).

The food and feeding habits of some mammals have been much studied, largely because of economic considerations, but the food habits of many or most mammals are deserving of further study. Mammals must select their food from among the available items, their choices affected by their adaptations and their preferences. Their food may vary from day to day, sometimes even within the day. We have found a case of bats, *Tadarida brasiliensis*, eating very different foods during their postdusk and predawn feedings (Whitaker et al., 1996). Foods, of course, often vary markedly with the seasons, as well. The relationship between available food and food actually eaten can indicate both the adaptations and the preferences of the species, but good availability estimates are hard to make. The usual procedure in food-habits research is to examine stomach contents and fecal matter.

For food-habits analysis, the investigator must begin with a thorough knowledge of the potential foods of the species under study. It is essential that a good reference collection of vertebrates, invertebrates, and plant material be available for comparison, but even more valuable is a collection of potential food items made at the time and place of collection of the mammals. It is never possible to identify all the items encountered, but with experience and from use of reference material much or most of the material can be determined, at least to a reasonable taxonomic level, if the worker has sufficient patience. We usually attempt to identify the materials to the lowest possible taxonomic level, within reasonable amounts of time and study.

In recent years the genetics of our wild mammals have been much studied. This information is particularly useful to the student of mammalian evolution and taxonomy. Basic to such study is the determination of the diploid

(2*N*) number of chromosomes (the number in the somatic cells) (Baker and Patton, 1967). This number, when available, has been added to the species treatments in this edition, under MEASUREMENTS.

A rapidly developing area of research is mammalian physiology. (What are the nutritional requirements of the various species? How are they satisfied?) We need to know the energy budgets of most species. We need also to know much more about thermoregulation, metabolic rates, and water balance and about the physiology of sleep, torpor, and true hibernation. Endocrinology is another burgeoning area in mammalogy; see the examples in Gittleman, ed. (1989, 1996).

The references within the text and at the back of the book, and the sections on AREAS FOR FURTHER WORK in the species accounts, suggest countless additional research ideas and approaches. Many opportunities for research on native mammals remain virtually unexplored, and there is little need to travel to distant or exotic areas; opportunities abound at home. Our most common species continue to offer unlimited scope for scholarly studies.

Most of our shrews and bats, many of our smaller rodents, and certainly the fur-bearing predators would repay further work. Many reports, some of them monographic in scope, have been written on our eastern mammals, yet we have barely scratched the surface. During the century and a half that have passed since Audubon and Bachman were amassing observations for their monumental *Viviparous Quadrupeds of North America* (1846–1854), we have added surprisingly little to our knowledge of many southern mammals, and not much more to our knowledge of some northern species.

There are many other sources of information on eastern mammals, some of the most important of which are the various state mammal books listed at the back of the book; the *Journal of Mammalogy*, published by the American Society of Mammalogists; and *The American Midland Naturalist*, published by Notre Dame University. Joseph A. Chapman and George A. Feldhamer's *The Wild Mammals of North America* (1982) is another source of excellent and exhaustive references, especially on the larger species. Further information is provided

by King (1968) and Kirkland and Layne (1989) on *Peromyscus*; by Tamarin, ed. (1985) on *Microtus*; and by Barbour and Davis (1969), Fenton (1983), Hill and Smith (1984), Kunz, ed. (1982), and Tuttle (1988) on bats. The Mammalian Species series currently being published by the American Society of Mammalogists is an excellent source of detailed information on mammals.

For those engaged in bat research, *Bat Research News* will prove invaluable. Address requests for subscriptions to the current publisher and managing editor, G. Roy Horst (Department of Biology, State University College at Potsdam, Potsdam, New York 13676). Allen Kurta (Department of Biology, Eastern Michigan University, Ypsilanti, Michigan 48197) is the current editor for feature articles.

We hope that this volume will help the interested field zoologist, particularly the aspiring mammalogist and the enthusiastic amateur, to gain greater understanding and appreciation of our wild mammals, and that it will indicate or suggest fruitful areas for further study. We hope also that the treatment of subspecies we have used will stimulate further discussion and hasten the transition from a morphological- to a biological-subspecies concept.

## LITERATURE CITED

Allred, D. M., and D. E. Beck. 1966. Mites of Utah mammals. Brigham Young Univ. Sci. Bull. Biol. Ser. 8: 1–123.

Amlaner, C. J., Jr., and D. W. MacDonald. 1980. *A Handbook on Biotelemetry and Radio Tracking.* Oxford, U.K.: Pergamon. 826 pp.

Audubon, J. J., and J. Bachman. 1846–1854. The viviparous quadrupeds of North America. 3 vols. New York: Privately printed.

Baker, R. J., and J. L. Patton. 1967. Karyotypes and karyotypic variation of North American vespertilionid bats. *J. Mammal.* 48: 270–286.

Barbour, R. W., and W. H. Davis. 1969. *Bats of America.* Lexington: Univ. Kentucky Press. 286 pp.

Bookhout, T. A., ed. 1996. *Research and Management Techniques for Wildlife and Habitats.* Bethesda, Md.: The Wildlife Society. 740 pp.

Bowen, W. W. 1968. Variation and evolution of Gulf Coast populations of beach mice, *Peromyscus polionotus. Bull. Fla. State Mus. Biol. Sci.* 12: 1–91.

Chapman, J. A., and G. A. Feldhamer, eds. 1982. *Wild*

*Mammals of North America: Biology, Management, and Economics.* Baltimore: Johns Hopkins Univ. Press. 1147 pp.

Coues, E. 1877. Fur bearing animals: A monograph of the North American Mustelidae. Department of the Interior, U.S. Geological Survey of the Territories, Misc. Publ. No. 8. 348 pp.

Emerson, K. C., and R. D. Price. 1985. Evolution of Mallophaga on mammals. In: K. C. Kim, ed., *Coevolution of Parasitic Arthropods and Mammals*, pp. 233–235. New York: John Wiley and Sons. 800 pp.

Evans, F. C., and R. Holdenreid. 1943. A population study of the Beechey ground squirrel in central California. *J. Mammal.* 24: 231–260.

Fenton, M. B. 1983. *Just Bats.* Toronto: Univ. Toronto Press. 165 pp.

Forrester, D. J. 1992. *Parasites and Diseases of Wild Mammals in Florida.* Gainesville: Univ. Press of Florida. 459 pp.

Gier, H. T. 1957. Coyotes in Kansas. Kansas Agric. Exp. Sta. Bull. 393. 97 pp.

Gittleman, J. L., ed. 1989. *Carnivore Behavior, Ecology, and Evolution*, Vol. 1. Ithaca, N.Y.: Cornell Univ. Press. 620 pp.

———. 1996. *Carnivore Behavior, Ecology, and Evolution*, Vol. 2. Ithaca, N.Y.: Cornell Univ. Press. 644 pp.

Godfrey, G. K. 1954. Tracing field voles, *Microtus agrestis*, with a Geiger-Müller counter. *Ecology* 35: 5–11.

Hall, E. R. 1981. *The Mammals of North America.* 2 vols. New York: Ronald Press. 1181 pp.

Hall, E. R., and K. R. Kelson. 1959. *The Mammals of North America.* New York: Ronald Press. 1083 pp.

Hamilton, W. J., Jr. 1940. The biology of the smoky shrew, *Sorex fumeus. Zoologica* 25: 473–491.

Hill, J. E., and J. D. Smith. 1984. *Bats: A Natural History.* Austin: Univ. Texas Press. 243 pp.

King, J. A., ed. 1968. Biology of *Peromyscus* (Rodentia). Amer. Soc. Mamm. Spec. Publ. 2. 593 pp.

Kirkland, G. L., Jr., and J. N. Layne. 1989. *Advances in the Study of Peromyscus (Rodentia).* Lubbock: Texas Tech Univ. Press. 366 pp.

Kunz, T. H., ed. 1982. *Ecology of Bats.* New York: Plenum Press. 425 pp.

Lancia, R. A., J. D. Nichols, and K. H. Pollock. 1996. Estimating the number of animals in wildlife populations. In: Bookhout, T. A., ed., *Research and Management Techniques for Wildlife and Habitats*, pp. 215–253. Bethesda, Md.: The Wildlife Society.

Lazarus, A. B., and F. P. Rowe. 1975. Freeze marking rodents with a pressurized refrigerant. *Mammal Revue* 5: 31.

Lidicker, W. Z., Jr. 1962. The nature of subspecies boundaries in a desert rodent and its implications for subspecies taxonomy. *Syst. Zool.* 11: 160–171.

Lord, R. D. 1959. The lens as an indicator of age in the cottontail rabbit. *J. Wildl. Mgmt.* 23: 358–360.

Maser, C. 1994. *Sustainable Forestry: Philosophy, Science and Economics.* Delray Beach, Fla.: St. Lucie Press. 373 pp.

Mech, L. D. 1983. *Handbook of Animal Radiotracking.* Minneapolis: Univ. Minnesota Press. 128 pp.

Mumford, R. E., and J. O. Whitaker, Jr. 1982. *Mammals of Indiana.* Bloomington: Indiana Univ. Press. 537 pp.

Munsell Soil Color Charts. 1971. Baltimore: Munsell Color Division, Kollmorgan Corporation.

Ridgeway, R. 1912. Color standards and a color nomenclature. Privately printed.

Schemnitz, S. D., ed. 1980. *Wildlife Management Techniques Manual.* Washington: The Wildlife Society. 686 pp.

Severinghaus, C. W. 1949. Tooth development and wear as criteria of age in the white-tailed deer. *J. Wildl. Mgmt.* 13: 195–216.

Sheldon, W. G. 1949. Reproductive behavior of foxes in New York State. *J. Mammal.* 30: 236–246.

Tamarin, R. H., ed. 1985. *Biology of New World Microtus.* Amer. Soc. Mammal. Spec. Publ. 8. 893 pp.

Tuttle, M. D. 1974. An improved trap for bats. *J. Mammal.* 55: 475–477.

———. 1988. *America's Neighborhood Bats.* Austin: Univ. Texas Press. 96 pp.

Whitaker, J. O., Jr. 1970. The biological subspecies: An adjunct of the biological species. *The Biologist* 52: 12–15.

———. 1982. Ectoparasites of mammals of Indiana. Indiana Acad. Sci. Monogr. No. 4. 240 pp.

———. 1988. Food habits analysis of insectivorous bats. In: T. H. Kunz, ed., *Ecological and Behavioral Methods for the Study of Bats*, pp. 171–189. Washington: Smithsonian Institution Press. 533 pp.

Whitaker, J. O., Jr., C. Neefus, and T. W. Kunz. 1996. Dietary variation in the Mexican free-tailed bat (*Tadarida brasiliensis mexicanus*). *J. Mammal.* 77: 716–724.

Whitaker, J. O., Jr., and N. Wilson. 1974. Host and distribution lists of mites (Acari), parasitic and phoretic, in the hair of wild mammals of North America north of Mexico. *Amer. Midland Nat.* 91: 1–67.

Whitaker, J. O., Jr., W. L. Wrenn, and R. E. Lewis. 1993. Parasites. In: H. H. Genoways and J. H. Brown, eds., *Biology of the Heteromyidae*, pp. 386–478. Amer. Soc. Mammal., Spec. Publ. 10.

Wilson, E. O., and W. L. Brown, Jr. 1953. The subspecies concept and its taxonomic application. *Syst. Zool.* 2: 97–111.

Wozencraft, W. C. 1989. Appendix: Classification of the Recent Carnivora. In: J. L. Gittleman, ed., *Carnivore Behavior, Ecology, and Evolution*, pp. 569–593. Ithaca, N.Y.: Cornell Univ. Press.

## Key to the Orders of Eastern U.S. Mammals

1. Animal having *either* wings *or* a well-developed armor of bony plates over much of the body .............................2
1. Animal having *neither* wings *nor* armor.........3
2. Forelimbs modified to serve as wings; body not armored (bats) ......... Chiroptera (p. 73)
2. Forelimbs not thus modified; much of body covered by well-developed armor of bony plates (armadillo) ......... Xenarthra (p. 160)
3. Animal highly evolved for an aquatic existence: forelimbs paddle-like, hind limbs lacking, tail horizontally flattened (manatee)................... Sirenia (p. 498)
3. Animal not thus evolved ...................4
4. Feet bearing hooves.......................5
4. Feet bearing claws or nails..................6
5. Axis of each limb passing between third and fourth toes, these two toes each bearing an asymmetrical hoof that touches the ground (pigs, deer, moose, etc.) ... Artiodactyla (p. 512)
5. Axis of each limb passing through middle of third toe, this toe bearing a single, enlarged, laterally symmetrical hoof (horses) ............. Perissodactyla (p. 504)
6. Female having an external pouch in which the young are carried for some time after birth; tail prehensile; teeth 50, including five upper incisors on each side; innermost toe of hind foot clawless and thumblike (opossums).......... Didelphimorphia (p. 23)
6. Female having no such external pouch; tail in no case prehensile; teeth less than 50, including less than five upper incisors on

each side; innermost toe of hind foot in no case clawless, and thumblike only in rhesus monkey .................................7
7. Incisor teeth chisel-shaped, separated from grinding teeth by a wide space (gnawing animals)................................8
7. Incisor teeth not chisel-shaped, not separated (or at least not widely separated) from grinding teeth, the tooth row thus essentially continuous..............................9
8. Ears and hind feet much enlarged; tail short; upper incisors four, the frontal pair large and grooved, the second pair rudimentary and placed directly behind the first pair (rabbits and hares) ....... Lagomorpha (p. 165)
8. Ear, hind feet, and tail not as above; upper incisors just two (rats, mice, squirrels, etc.).............. Rodentia (p. 198)
9. Eyes small, often concealed in fur; snout greatly elongated beyond jaw; animal small, its total length usually less than 200 mm (8 inches) (shrews and moles)... Insectivora (p. 29)
9. Eyes obvious; snout not greatly elongated; animal large, its total length usually more than 250 mm (10 inches)..................10
10. Upper incisors two on a side; braincase large, the face flattened and the nose not forming a snout; eyes placed forward (monkeys); claws flattened, forming nails (apes, monkeys, etc.) ........ Primates (p. 156)
10. Upper incisors three on a side; braincase smaller, the face usually forming an elongate snout; eyes placed on sides; claws not thus modified (wolves, weasels, cats, etc.) ............... Carnivora (p. 393)

# 1. ORDER DIDELPHIMORPHIA

## *Opossums*

WE USUALLY THINK of "marsupials," or "pouched mammals," as being primarily Australian, and their center of abundance and diversity is certainly in Australia. Still, three of the 19 families of extant marsupials, the Caenolestidae, Microbiotheriidae, and Didelphidae, are found exclusively in the New World. The Caenolestidae number seven species in three genera, all quite rare and all found in western South America; often called rat opossums, they are somewhat shrewlike in appearance. The Microbiotheriidae (earlier placed in the Didelphidae) was raised to family status on the basis of a single species, the monito del monte, found in Chile and Argentina. Members of the Didelphidae, including the Virginia opossum, have reached Central and North America.

Originally, the opossums were established as one of ten families constituting a single order, the Marsupialia, though even at the time it was recognized that marsupials are a highly diverse group. The pouched mammals have now been divided into no fewer than seven orders: three of them, each with one family, in the New World, the other four, embracing 16 families, in the Australian region. See Marshall et al. (1990) for a discussion of the interrelationships.

The marsupials are characterized by a primitive brain, the presence of epipubic bones, and young born in an undeveloped state. In many species, the female possesses a prominent marsupium, or pouch, for the care of her young; the epipubic bones help support the pouch on the pelvis. The American marsupials all have numerous teeth, 50 being the number in *Didelphis*.

LITERATURE CITED

Marshall, L. G., J. A. Case, and M. O. Woodburne. 1990. Phylogenetic relationships of the families of marsupials. In H. H. Genoways, ed., *Current Mammalogy*, pp. 433–505. New York: Plenum Press.

## OPOSSUMS, Family Didelphidae

The family Didelphidae, the American opossums, is a diverse group comprising about 63 species in 12 genera, all in the New World and most in South America. Of the 63 species, about 11, in seven genera, reach into Central America, and one, the Virginia opossum, *Didelphis virginiana*, is distributed widely in North America. Didelphids vary greatly in size, habits, and habitat, but many have long, prehensile tails. Some of the species in the family have secondarily lost the marsupium, the mother in these cases presumably caring for her young in the traditional way—in a nest.

The Virginia opossum is often referred to as a "living fossil" because of its very primitive characteristics. Indeed, there were didelphids in North America during Mesozoic times, but they became extinct, and *D. virginiana* entered North America from South America much later, during Pleistocene times. The name "opossum" derives from a term for "white animal" in an Algonquian language of Virginia.

### Virginia Opossum
### *Didelphis virginiana* Kerr

DESCRIPTION. The opossum is about the size of a house cat, but has shorter legs, large, naked ears, a long, pointed muzzle, and a long, prehensile tail. Long white hairs overlie the black-tipped underfur, giving the animal a grizzled appearance. The first (innermost) toe of the hind foot lacks a claw and is opposable. The head, throat, and cheeks are whitish, although the cheeks, throat, and chest are often stained

*Virginia opossum,* Didelphis virginiana
*(J. Hill Hamon)*

yellowish-orange. The black, leathery ears are tipped with white, and the tail, except at its blackish base, is generally creamish white. The overall color may vary from blackish to pale gray, and albinos occasionally occur. The female's pouch, in which the young are carried, is studded with 13 teats, 12 in a circle or "U" and one in the center. In the area from Charleston, South Carolina, to southern Florida and west through the Gulf region to Louisiana, the opossum is smaller and darker than it is to the north, the tail is longer and slimmer, and the ears and toes tend to be entirely black.

MEASUREMENTS. Average measurements of 28 individuals from Pennsylvania (Blumenthal and Kirkland, 1976) were: total length 762 (666–883), tail 290 (216–356), hind foot 66 (60–75) mm. From Louisiana (Lowery, 1974), measurements of 44 individuals were: total length 777 (613–940), tail 306 (223–380), hind foot 61 (38–85) mm. Ten males and 18 females from Pennsylvania averaged: 3.4 (2.2–4.0) and 2.4 (1.8–3.0) kg, respectively, whereas 105 males and 74 females from Louisiana (Edmunds et al., 1978) weighed 2.0 (0.9–3.0) and 1.8 (0.3–1.6) kg, respectively. Males are larger than females. There are records of opossums weighing over 7 kg (15.4 lbs).
  Diploid number = 22.

TOOTH FORMULA

$$\frac{5}{4} \quad \frac{1}{1} \quad \frac{3}{3} \quad \frac{4}{4} \ = \ 50$$

DISTRIBUTION. The Virginia opossum occurs commonly over much of the United States, in the east from the Gulf Coast and Florida north to Lake Ontario, central Michigan, and most of Wisconsin. Within the past century, it has extended its range northeastward, and it now occurs sporadically throughout most of New York and southern New England into extreme southern Maine. We cannot be sure of its earlier U.S. range, but Audubon and Bachman (1846–1854) indicated that it occurred east to the Hudson River, which would place it north at least to southern New York in the mid-eighteenth century. Outside of the eastern United States, the Virginia opossum occurs north into southeastern Ontario, west to southeastern South Dakota, eastern Wyoming and Colorado, and southeastern Arizona, and south through most of Central America. There are also substantial introduced populations on the West Coast.

HABITAT. The opossum's adaptability to a great variety of habitats, ranging from forest to purely agricultural lands, explains its success in the eastern United States. It is often quite common even in urban and suburban areas, and many are found dead on the highways.

HABITS. The opossum, shy and secretive, becomes active mainly at night; in winter, it is sometimes out during the day. It climbs well and can even swim. When climbing, it can hang from limbs by its prehensile tail. But although it is well adapted for arboreal life, much of its time is spent on the ground. The opossum is a solitary wanderer, remaining in no one place for long, and may be found far from trees. Its daytime den is in a fallen log, a hollow tree, a cleft in a cliff, a brushpile, a tree nest of a bird or squirrel, a woodchuck or skunk burrow, or a recess under a building, or in any of many other protected situations. Opossums do not dig their own dens, and thus are dependent on other animals, primarily the woodchuck and skunk, for ground burrows. Of 85 dens located by Allen et al. (1985) in Georgia, 76 were associated with pines and nine with upland hardwoods, a proportion roughly comparable to the availability of those habitats in the area. One den was in an old field. Of the 85, 47 were underground, mostly in stump holes; 31 were at ground level (mostly in blackberry thickets or windrows); and seven were arboreal (4–6 meters, or 13–20 feet, above ground, in snags or leaf nests probably used or constructed in years past by squirrels). During the severest winter weather, the opossum may pass a week or more in such a well-protected retreat, but occasionally it is abroad even when near-freezing temperatures prevail; at such times the naked ears and tail may become severely frostbitten.

Nest-building is particularly interesting in this species. Nest materials are grasped in the mouth, then passed under the body to the tail, which is turned forward between the hind legs. The materials are then transported in the grasp of the coiled tail. This behavior has been noted in captives as young as 88 to 92 days old.

Defensive or aggressive behavior in opossums is well-developed; they click, hiss, growl, screech, and bare their teeth, and sometimes extrude a greenish substance from glands near the vent.

Gardner (1982) believes the clicking sounds are made by clashing the canines together. The clicks, aside from their role in aggressive encounters, are used by males during mating behavior, and by females communicating with their young. In male-to-male encounters, open-mouthed threat behaviors accompanied by growling and screeching are common. The males face off, mouths open, ears back, each weaving from side to side, the confrontation ending in a fight or when one or the other retreats.

Scent marking, most pronounced at the height of breeding, may help attract females. The animal licks the sides of its head, then rubs its head against a tree trunk or other object. Holmes (1992) found that females investigated plastic disks marked with the odors of male opossums significantly more than they did those marked with female odors when the disks were presented in male/female pairs.

The opossum may gain some measure of pro-

*Distribution of the*
*Virginia opossum,*
Didelphis virginiana,
*in the eastern United States*

tection from its well-known habit of feigning death when escape is impossible. The maneuver may be quite realistic, for the animal will roll over on its side, shut its eyes, loll the tongue from its open jaws, and drool. Such a disposition may be maintained for some time or, presumably, until the predator has left the scene. Further threat stimulation may cause a return to the death-feigning. This behavior appears to be caused by a temporary paralysis brought on by shock, a condition somewhat similar to fainting. James B. Cope relates that in April 1989 his dog found an opossum, grabbed it by the neck, and shook it for about half a minute, at which point the opossum went limp and "played possum." The dog then lost interest, dropped the opossum, and walked away. The dog stayed in the area for about five minutes, glancing occasionally at the opossum, then left. After ten minutes the opossum got up, remained immobile for about four more minutes, then walked away. This behavior, which Jim has seen on four different occasions, appeared to have saved the life of the opossum.

FOOD AND FEEDING. The opossum is omnivorous, and often forages along small permanent or intermittent streams. Insects, small mammals, green vegetation, fruits and berries, earthworms, and amphibians constituted the bulk of the food contained in 461 New York opossum stomachs examined. Snakes and birds are also eaten. Persimmons, blackberries, apples, and corn "in the milk" are especially favored foods. Hamilton once found a newly hatched box turtle in the stomach of an opossum, and opossums have been known to eat bats. The opossum is killed in great numbers on the highway, probably because of its habit of feeding on road-killed animals; a goodly portion of the diet is in fact carrion, and there is little the opossum will pass up.

REPRODUCTION AND DEVELOPMENT. Remarkable also are the reproductive habits of this curious animal. Males click continually while in pursuit of a female, who is receptive for only a short time. When she accepts him, the male places his front feet on her shoulders, grasps her by the neck with his teeth, shifts his whole weight upon her, and clasps her hind legs with his hind feet. They then roll onto their right sides and

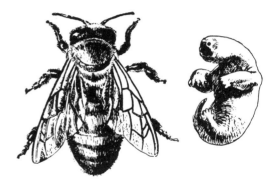

*Honeybee and newborn opossum, to same scale*

mating begins, sustained typically for about 20 minutes. After a gestation of just 12 to 13 days, the tiny young are born. Eighteen or more may be born, though the average is about six to nine.

These "living embryos," weighing only about 0.1 to 0.2 gram and having a crown-rump length of just 14 mm, have a large head and well-developed front legs. After birth they crawl hand over hand to the marsupium, where they immediately grasp one of the 13 teats. There is no actual fusion of tissue during suckling, but the teat expands inside the mouth of the young, forming a relatively permanent attachment that is maintained for 50 to 65 days but does permit some freedom of movement, the nipple serving as a tether. In larger litters, obviously, any young reaching the pouch after the teats are all occupied is doomed to perish, and usually not more than seven or eight are found in the pouch a month after birth. At this time they are about the size of grown house mice. The female supplies milk and a place to live, but otherwise she has little to do with the young except for occasionally cleaning the pouch. More than two months are spent in the pouch, and the eyes of the young open between 58 and 72 days after birth. The young first clamber outside the pouch at about two months; for two to four weeks they cling to the mother's long fur and ride around on her back. Some solid food is taken prior to weaning, which is at about 80 to 105 days. Normally, two litters per year are produced, a third litter only if an earlier one was lost. At about the time the prior litter is weaned, mating occurs again. Pouch young have been found from February through October.

Data obtained by tracking 12 radio-collared

female opossums in southeastern New York are given by Hossler et al. (1994). These females entered the reproductive season in poor condition, but increased their body weight by 11% during lactation. The 12 females used 76 different dens, 73 of them burrows, mostly of woodchucks. All of them used burrows for weaning dens, all of the dens were in highly vegetated areas, and den fidelity was greatest during weaning time. Birth dates varied from 29 February to 3 June; mean birth date for ten first litters was 25 March, and for three second litters it was 1 June. Litter size was positively correlated with fat reserves. The females that had been the earliest to give birth were those that gave birth to second litters: one female produced litters of 9 and 14 young on 29 February and 1 June, and her first litter was just 93 days old when she produced the second.

POPULATION CHARACTERISTICS. Opossums are not territorial, and because they are essentially solitary wanderers, their home ranges are hard to define. Estimates have ranged from 5 to 120 ha (12 to 264 acres), the larger home ranges occurring in more cultivated areas. (Radio-tracking yields much more data, and therefore correspondingly larger home-range estimates, than do trapping mark/release/recapture techniques.) An opossum tends to operate from a succession of dens, each den for a different period of time, and each successive home range is the area occupied temporarily around that den, until in due course the animal moves on. The individual's total home range is therefore the sum total of the several temporary home ranges occupied in a year, some of them overlapping. Many of the den shifts occur at one-day intervals, the opossum staying longer if conditions are favorable.

Published density estimates range from one opossum per 0.4 ha (0.9 acre) to one per 43 ha (106 acres). The lowest counts of opossums occur from January through April. Once independent, young males disperse farther than females do. In captivity, one individual lived to four years, five months, but few individuals, presumably, live much beyond two years in the field, even though they sometimes appear, by toothwear and injuries, to be very old.

ENEMIES. The opossum has many enemies, one of the most deadly, of course, being the automobile. Dogs and great horned owls may be the most serious natural enemies, but many other predators, especially coyotes, foxes, raccoons, bobcats, raptors, and snakes, kill opossums.

PARASITES AND DISEASE. Opossums harbor a great variety of ectoparasites: in Georgia, 27 species were found on 349 opossums; in Indiana, 26 on 66 opossums. The cat flea and other fleas are found on them, along with chiggers and several other species of mites. Four species of mites are host-specific and abundant on opossums: a hypopial glycyphagid mite, *Marsupialichus brasiliensis*, which uses the opossum as a means of transportation, and three truly parasitic forms, *Archemyobia inexpectatus* (Myobiidae), *Ornithonyssus wernecki* (Macronyssidae), and *Didelphilichus serrifer* (Atopomelidae). None of these species would occur in the United States were it not for the South American roots of their host. Among endoparasites, numerous nematodes and trematodes and seven species each of cestodes and acanthocephalans have been reported from opossums. The digestive tract of an opossum may contain hundreds of nematodes.

An organism resembling *Trypanosoma cruzi* (which causes sleeping sickness) was isolated from opossums from Georgia and Florida. Other organisms found in opossums are the fungus *Histoplasma capsulatum*, the causal factor in histoplasmosis; *Pasteurella tularensis*, the causative agent of tularemia; and murine (endemic) typhus. Rabies occasionally infects opossums in the eastern United States, but most or all of the cases examined have been of "dumb" rabies, a condition in which the host is passive. None of these diseases, in the levels at which they seem to occur, appears to pose any significant threat to opossums or to humans.

RELATION TO HUMANS. Contrary to popular opinion, opossums have little impact on either domestic poultry or wildlife. When such items are taken as food, they are most often in the form of animals already dead. Even though the skin of an opossum brought the trapper much less than did most of the other furs, the numbers taken even in such northern states as Pennsylvania and Indiana once made it important in the fur trade. Over one million opossums were harvested from North America as recently as the 1976–77 season, ranking them as the third most frequently taken skin in eight eastern states that year, even though the price averaged only $2.50 per skin, the second lowest for any species (the coarse fur was used chiefly for trimmings). Moreover, the opossum is relished by many people, and thousands are killed each year simply for food, but the market for opossum pelts has all but vanished.

AREAS FOR FURTHER WORK. As is true of all of our wildlife, opossums pose many unanswered questions. Discovering the physiological cause of death-feigning, the food of the recently weaned as compared to that of older animals, and the nature of the nest fauna of this species should all be fascinating. Adults of the hypopial mite *Marsupialichus brasiliensis* have not been described; one could collect them from dead opossums and attempt to allow them to transform to adults. What is the greenish substance produced from the glands near the vent, and what is its function? Rabies strains should be identified in cases of "dumb rabies," in opossums or other animals, to determine if any or most are bat strains. We suspect that dumb rabies occurs when the ultimate infection is a bat strain and that furious rabies results from a "street" rabies strain.

## SUBSPECIES

A southeastern subspecies has been described, but because it intergrades broadly with the nominate form, *Didelphis virginiana virginiana*, we do not recognize it.

*Didelphis virginiana virginiana* Kerr
  As described above.
  Type locality: Virginia.
  Other currently recognized eastern subspecies:
    *D. virginiana pigra* Bangs

LITERATURE

Allen, C. H., R. L. Marchinton, and W. M. Lentz. 1985. Movement, habitat use and denning of opossums in the Georgia Piedmont. *Amer. Midland Nat.* 113: 408–412.

Audubon, J. J., and J. Bachman. 1846–1854. *The Viviparous Quadrupeds of North America.* 3 vols. New York: privately published.

Blumenthal, E. M., and G. L. Kirkland, Jr. 1976. The biology of the opossum, *Didelphis virginiana*, in south central Pennsylvania. *Proc. Pa. Acad. Sci.* 50: 81–85.

Edmunds, R. M., J. W. Goertz, and G. Linscombe. 1978. Age ratios, weights and reproduction of the Virginia opossum in north Louisiana. *J. Mammal.* 59: 884–885.

Fitch, H. S., and L. L. Sandridge. 1953. Ecology of the opossum on a natural area in northeastern Kansas. *Univ. Kansas Publ. Mus. Nat. Hist.* 7: 305–338.

Gardner, A. L. 1982. Virginia opossum *Didelphis virginiana*. In: J. A. Chapman and G. A. Feldhamer, eds., *Wild Mammals of North America*, pp. 3–36. Baltimore: Johns Hopkins Univ. Press.

Hamilton, W. J., Jr. 1958. Life history and economic relations of the opossum (*Didelphis virginiana*) in New York State. Mem. Cornell Univ. Agric. Exp. Sta. 354. 48 pp.

Hartman, C. G. 1923. Breeding habits, development and birth of the opossum. *Smithsonian Report for 1921*, pp. 347–363.

———. 1952. *Possums.* Austin: University of Texas Press. 174 pp.

Holmes, D. J. 1992. Sternal odors as clues for social discrimination by female Virginia opossums, *Didelphis virginiana*. *J. Mammal.* 73: 286–291.

Hossler, R. J., J. B. McAninch, and J. D. Harder. 1994. Maternal denning behavior and survival of juveniles in opossums in southeastern New York. *J. Mammal.* 75: 60–70.

Hunsaker, D., II. 1977. Ecology of New World marsupials. In: D. Hunsaker II, ed., *The Biology of Marsupials*, pp. 95–156. New York: Academic Press.

Lowery, G. H., Jr. 1974. *The Mammals of Louisiana and Its Adjacent Waters.* Baton Rouge: Louisiana State Univ. Press. 565 pp.

McManus, J. J. 1974. *Didelphis virginiana.* **Mammalian Species No. 40.** Amer. Soc. Mammal. 6 pp.

Seidensticker, J., M. A. O'Connell, and A. J. T. Johnsingh. 1987. Virginia opossum. In: M. Novak, J. A. Baker, M. E. Obbard, and B. Mallock, eds., *Wild Furbearer Management and Conservation in North America*, pp. 246–261. Toronto: Ontario Ministry Nat. Resources.

# 2. ORDER INSECTIVORA

## Shrews and Moles

THE ORDER INSECTIVORA, which includes the moles and shrews and their relatives, is represented in all parts of the world except Australia and the southern nine-tenths of South America. Worldwide, there are about 428 species of insectivores in 66 genera and seven families. The two largest and best-known families, and the only two represented in the United States, are the shrews (Soricidae) and the moles (Talpidae). Nearly all have five clawed toes on each foot, a long, pointed snout extending considerably beyond the jaw, and a wedge-shaped skull. The zygomatic arch (an arch of bone forming the outside of each orbit, or eye socket) is lacking in shrews and much reduced in moles. The teeth are sharp and pointed, the canines little differentiated from the incisors or premolars. In the species of the eastern United States the eyes are minute and probably of little use. Prominent scent glands are found in most species.

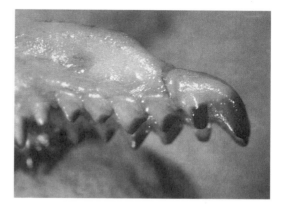

Upper partial tooth rows of two eastern shrews, Sorex cinereus (top; note the four large unicuspids and one minute one behind the large anterior tooth) and Sorex hoyi (bottom; note the three large unicuspids, the third and fifth reduced and positioned in the spaces after the second and fourth), greatly enlarged

### KEY TO THE FAMILIES OF INSECTIVORES

1. Forefeet broad and enlarged, more than twice as large as the hind feet, and adapted for digging; body stout and cylindrical, seemingly lacking a neck; teeth white. . TALPIDAE (moles, p. 64)
1. Forefeet not enlarged, not notably adapted for digging; body relatively thin; teeth tipped with chestnut . . . . . . . . . . . . . SORICIDAE (shrews)

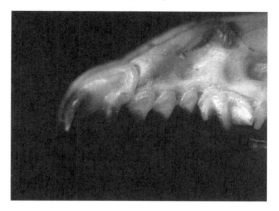

### SHREWS, Family Soricidae

Shrews include about 312 species of small fossorial mammals with soft fur that will lie either forward or backward. The first upper incisors, which protrude forward, are efficient organs with which to gather the tiny prey on which shrews feed. They are both enlarged and pincer- or sickle-like, but have a posterior cusp as well. Behind these enlarged teeth are a series of four or five small teeth called the *unicuspids*. The

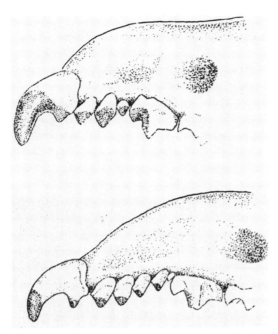

*Upper partial tooth rows of two other eastern shrews,* Cryptotis parva *(top) and* Sorex fumeus *(bottom), further illustrating the varied disposition of the unicuspid teeth in this genus (Thomas W. French)*

number and size of the unicuspids have been much used in shrew identification and classification, but we have not included standard tooth formulas for shrews, since it is not clear, in this case, how "unicuspid" might relate to the incisors, canines, and premolars of the standard formula. In North American shrews, all of which belong to the subfamily Soricinae, the "red-toothed shrews," the teeth have chestnut-colored tips.

Shrews are seldom seen, but are exceedingly active, constantly running about, squeaking, wriggling their noses, and sniffing this way and that. They also have exceedingly high metabolic rates. The heart rate may reach 1200 beats per minute, and respiration rates run from 168 breaths per minute when at rest to 750 per minute when undergoing "average" activity. Few individuals, evidently, live much more than a year; most probably die much sooner. Shrews are among the smallest of mammals, and our pygmy shrew is the smallest of the shrews.

Shrews are often numerous in the forests,

marshes, and meadows, where they consume prodigious quantities of worms, insects, other invertebrates, and some vegetation, and themselves provide food for predatory animals. These tiny animals, particularly those of the genus *Blarina*, often feed on the minute subterranean fungus *Endogone* and fungi of related genera. Shrews have a number of glands, such as lateral, or side, glands and abdominal glands. These often impart an odor to the shrew, and many of them probably function to bring the sexes together. One might think these glands would deter predators, but predators often eat shrews. At least some shrews are known to use echolocation for navigational purposes.

An excellent way to collect shrews is to sink containers such as coffee cans or 1000-ml plastic beakers in the ground with their lips at ground level. Add to these about 25 mm of water. These are called "pitfall traps." For best results they should be checked once a day or at least three times a week, but they can be left in place for longer periods in remote areas. For collecting live shrews, replace the water with dry leaf litter or cotton, and add some food (worms, cat food). Check these live pitfall traps every two hours throughout the night, for shrews in traps die quickly. The pitfalls can be placed along or partially under logs or rocks in woods, or one can erect a fence of hardware cloth or other wire material in open areas, and sink the cans along the fence. Shrews run along or under logs or rocks, or, coming upon an obstacle in the field, will dart along the obstacle seemingly without regard for where it might be taking them. Such pitfall traps will often enable one to capture large numbers of shrews. (We have caught many pine voles and bog lemmings, as well as shrews, in this fashion.) Another way to gain information on shrews is to check discarded bottles. These make excellent shrew traps. Narrow-necked bottles pointing somewhat uphill are the best bets.

KEY TO THE GENERA OF THE FAMILY SORICIDAE

1. Tail long, over 30 mm; unicuspids five, though the third and fifth may be minute, and the braincase rounded . . . . . . . . . . . . . . . . . . . . . *Sorex*

1. Tail short, less than 30 mm; unicuspids four, or, if five, then the lateral edge of the braincase produced into a sharp angle. . . . . . . . . . . . . . . . . . 2
2. Length less than 90 mm; unicuspids only four, but three quite visible from the side; braincase rounded behind . . . . . . . . . . . . . . *Cryptotis* (p. 60)
2. Length more than 90 mm; unicuspids five, four of them visible from the side, the fifth small and hidden behind the fourth; lateral edge of braincase produced into a sharp angle. . . . . . . . . . . . . . . . . . . . . . . *Blarina* (p. 53)

## Shrews of the Genus *Sorex*

The genus *Sorex* includes the smallest of the North American shrews, and many of the shrews in the genus are very difficult to identify. To help in their identification, one can pull back the lip to view the unicuspids (use a hand lens or, better yet, a dissecting microscope).

KEY TO THE LONG-TAILED SHREWS
OF THE GENUS *SOREX*

In using this key, note that *Sorex fontinalis* and *S. longirostris* are very similar to and often confused with *S. cinereus* (see the account for *S. fontinalis*). *Sorex cinereus* is generally larger and has a relatively longer tail (35–46% of total length) and a longer, narrower rostrum. In *S. cinereus* the greatest width across the outside of the first large molariform teeth is usually more than half the distance from the posterior end of the palate to the anterior end of the first incisors; in *S. longirostris* and *S. fontinalis* this width is usually less than half that distance. Moreover, in *S. cinereus* the inner ridge of the upper unicuspids is pigmented; in *S. longirostris* and in *S. fontinalis* these ridges lack pigment.

1. Only three large unicuspid teeth visible in profile, the third and fifth tiny. . . . . . . . . . . . *S. hoyi*
1. Four or five unicuspids visible when viewed in profile . . . . . . . . . . . . . . . . . . . . . . . . . . . . . . . 2
2. Total length usually less than 90 mm, the tail usually less than 36 mm long. . . . . . . . . . . . . . . . 3
2. Total length usually greater than 90 mm, the tail usually more than 36 mm long . . . . . . . . . . . 4
3. Occurs only in southeastern Pennsylvania, northeastern Maryland, and northern Delaware; third and fourth unicuspids subequal in size . . . . . . . . . . . . . . . . . . . . . . . *S. fontinalis*
3. Occurs over a large range in southeastern United States, north to southern Illinois and Indiana and northeast to southern West Virginia and southern Maryland; fourth unicuspid often, but not always, larger than the third. . . . . . . . . . . . . . . . . . . . . . . *S. longirostris*

4. Color generally grayish (*S. fumeus* in summer may be brownish) . . . . . . . . . . . . . . . . . . . . . . . . 5
4. Color generally brown. . . . . . . . . . . . . . . . . . . . . . 7
5. Total length greater than 140 mm; a fringe of stiff hairs on edge of feet. . . . . . . . . . . . . *S. palustris*
5. Total length less than 140 mm; no such fringe on edge of feet . . . . . . . . . . . . . . . . . . . . . . . . . . 6
6. Posterior border of infraorbital foramen behind the space between the first and second upper molariform teeth; tail more than 50 mm long . . . . . . . . . . . . . . . . . . . . . . . *S. dispar*
6. Posterior border of infraorbital foramen ahead of that space; tail less than 50 mm long . . *S. fumeus*
7. Adults distinctly tricolored, the back dark, the sides lighter, and the belly still lighter. *S. arcticus*
7. Adults not tricolored, brown above and lighter below . . . . . . . . . . . . . . . . . . . . . . . . . . *S. cinereus*

## Arctic Shrew *Sorex arcticus* Kerr

DESCRIPTION. In Arctic shrews, there are two separate color patterns, a distinctive tricolor pattern in the adults and older juveniles, and a dull or all-brown phase in the younger juveniles. Animals in the tricolor or "saddle-backed" pattern are easily distinguished from all other eastern shrews. The back is a rich dark brown, distinctly darker than the sides, which in turn are darker than the belly, which is light gray or pale brown. In the other color pattern, the "overall dull," the back is brown grading through lighter brown on the sides to the belly, which is lightest brown of all. Juveniles in July are all dull, and juveniles between July and November may have either pattern, but all juveniles have obtained the tricolor pattern during the fall molt or by November of the year of their birth. Thus arctic shrews taken from November through June show the tricolor pattern, whereas those taken in July are either adults in the tricolor pattern or juveniles in the dull pattern. By August, juveniles have replaced many of the adults, and increasing numbers will take on the tricolor pattern as the season progresses.

*Sorex arcticus* is the only member of the subgenus *Sorex* in its range. This subgenus is characterized by well-developed postmandibular canals and a lack of pigmented ridges on the unicuspids. Moreover, the third unicuspid is larger than the fourth, and there is no accessory cusp on the anterior facet of the first upper incisor.

MEASUREMENTS. Average measurements are: total length 101–124, tail 30–45, hind foot 12–15 mm; and weight 6.0–13.5 grams.

Diploid number = 28 in females, 29 in males. This species (and other members of the *Sorex araneus/arcticus* group) has trivalent sex chromosomes, i.e. three sex chromosomes in males (X, $Y_1$, $Y_2$) (Volobouer and Dutrillaux, 1991).

DISTRIBUTION. In the eastern United States, arctic shrews occur in northern Wisconsin and the Upper Peninsula of Michigan; beyond, their range extends through much of southern and southwestern Canada and Alaska.

HABITAT. Shrews of this species occur most often along the edges of swamps and marshes. Clough (1963) took 28 from a grass/sedge marsh at Madison, Wisconsin. Wrigley et al. (1979) took 167 of them, 78 in grass/sedge marshes, 37 in willow/alder fens, and 23 in mesic shrub areas in Manitoba. Of these, 80% were in hydric, 19% in mesic, and 1% in xeric (dry) sites. Bailey (1929) collected arctic shrews from the marshes surrounding rice lakes and from among old stumps in tamarack swamps in Minnesota. The marsh in which Clough worked, in spring, was covered with water up to 15 cm (6 inches) deep, except for the emergent tussocks, and snow covered the surface in winter. Other common small-mammal inhabitants of the marsh were meadow voles and masked shrews. Whitaker and Pascal (1971) took 18 arctic shrews in an old field in Minnesota.

HABITS. Arctic shrews may be active at any time during the day or night, but are least busy between 600 and 1000 hours. Activity is mostly in

*Distribution of the Arctic shrew,* Sorex arcticus, *in the eastern United States*

short bursts totaling under two hours during the 24-hour period. Shrews, including arctic shrews, dart about quickly when active, always on the run. Captives kept by Clough, however, spent frequent periods inactive, lying on their sides or bellies. On a few occasions they would lie on their backs licking their anal region, perhaps in coprophagy. They dug in loose dirt with the head and forefeet, and sometimes uttered a "low rapid chatter" as they ran about the cage.

FOOD AND FEEDING. Little food-habits information is available, but shrews of this species probably eat small insects and their larvae, small spiders, small centipedes, and similar invertebrate fare. Arctic shrews have been observed taking grasshoppers (*Melanoplus femurrubrum*) from the plant stems where they rest early in the morning. A shrew would climb slowly up an adjacent stem perhaps 25 cm (9 inches) away, then suddenly leap at the grasshopper, grasping it with the forefeet and jaws. This behavior, pursued in the cool early-morning temperatures (6°C, or 43°F), was observed 37 times in a 15-minute period (Buckner, 1964). The legs and wings were not consumed. The behavior then ceased as the air temperatures rose and the grasshoppers became active.

REPRODUCTION AND DEVELOPMENT. In Wisconsin, the breeding season for these shrews is from February through August. All males taken from February through June appeared fertile, but Clough (1963) took no females during this period. It appears that few females become pregnant their first year, although one young taken 15 August contained embryos. Arctic shrews produce young from late April through September, up to three litters per female per year. Twelve embryo counts taken range from four to nine and average 6.8. Of 20 females in a mark-recapture study (Buckner, 1966), nine had one litter, four had two litters, seven had three litters, and three bred in two consecutive years. Buckner estimated nestling mortality at about 50%.

POPULATION CHARACTERISTICS. Clough (1963) found two age groupings, i.e. two generations,

in this species via examinations of tooth wear. The young shrews, which first appeared in traps in July, formed the new generation. Adult animals were taken from January through July, and July was the only month in which both generations were taken. Thus it appeared that the new generation completely replaced the adults by midsummer. In another study, *Sorex cinereus* and *S. arcticus* populations were found to be inversely related to one another in size (Buckner, 1966). Population-density estimates run from 10.1 to 20.6 per ha (4.1 to 8.6 per acre).

ENEMIES. The enemies of this species are presumably the typical predators of small mammals, such as cats, foxes, weasels, hawks, owls, and snakes.

PARASITES AND DISEASE. Several species of mites and ticks are parasites of this host. When Whitaker and Pascal (1971) reported myobiid mites, *Protomyobia brevisetosa*, on this shrew, an interesting situation arose. Letters soon arrived from both E. W. Jameson, Jr., and F. Dusbabek asking if the mites were not *P. onoi*, which they had just described from *Sorex araneus* and *S. unguiculatus* from Eurasia, and which they had predicted, on geographical and ecological grounds, might be on *S. arcticus*. They were correct. This episode is of interest here primarily for indicating the mostly untapped role that host-parasite relations can sometimes play in mammalian taxonomy and zoogeography.

RELATION TO HUMANS. This species benefits us by feeding on various insects and their larvae, but otherwise has little direct relation to our concerns.

AREAS FOR FURTHER WORK. Relatively little is known of the population biology or food habits of this species, and a full ecological study is in order.

## SUBSPECIES

Our eastern populations are currently listed as *Sorex arcticus laricorum*, but we see no reason to distinguish them from the nominate subspecies.

*Sorex arcticus arcticus* Kerr

As described above.

Type locality: Fort Severn, mouth of the Severn River, Hudson Bay, Ontario.

Other currently recognized eastern subspecies:

*S. arcticus laricorum* (Jackson)

## LITERATURE

Bailey, B. 1929. Mammals of Sherburne County, Minnesota. *J. Mammal.* 10: 153–164.

Buckner, C. H. 1964. Metabolism, food capacity, and feeding behavior in four species of shrews. *Canadian J. Zool.* 42: 259–279.

———. 1966. Populations and ecological relationships of shrews in tamarack bogs in southeastern Minnesota. *J. Mammal.* 47: 181–194.

Clough, G. C. 1963. Biology of the arctic shrew, *Sorex arcticus. Amer. Midland Nat.* 69: 69–81.

Kirkland, G. L., Jr., and D. F. Schmidt. 1996. *Sorex arcticus.* **Mammalian Species No. 524.** Amer. Soc. Mammal. 5 pp.

van Zyll de Jong, C. G. 1983. A morphometric analysis of North American shrews of the *Sorex arcticus* group with special consideration of the taxonomic status of *S. a. maritimensis. Naturaliste Can.* 110: 373–378.

Volobouer, V., and B. Dutrillaux. 1991. Chromosomal evolution and phyletic relationships of the *Sorex araneus-arcticus* species group. *Mém. Soc. vandoise des sciences naturelles* 19: 131–139.

Whitaker, J. O., Jr., and D. D. Pascal, Jr. 1971. External parasites of arctic shrews taken in Pine County, Minnesota. *J. Mammal.* 52: 202.

Wrigley, R. E., J. E. Dubois, and H. W. R. Copland. 1979. Habitat, abundance, and distribution of six species of shrews in Manitoba. *J. Mammal.* 60: 520–525.

## Masked Shrew
### *Sorex cinereus* Kerr       Color plate 1

DESCRIPTION. *Sorex cinereus* is one of the smallest shrews. How it got its common name is unclear, since it certainly does not have any obvious mask. Its summer pelage is grayish brown above, light below. The tail is bicolored, fuscous above and buffy below. Winter pelage is darker, a grayish fuscous to dark brown above, much paler below. This shrew is immediately distinguished from adult smoky shrews, *S. fumeus*, by its smaller size and browner color. In summer, however, young smoky shrews are brown and can be difficult to separate from masked shrews. (The head and tail proportions of *S. cinereus* and *S. longirostris* are contrasted on p. 48.)

MEASUREMENTS. Average measurements are: total length 88 (71–111), tail 33 (25–50), hind foot 11 (9–14) mm; and weight 3.6 (2.4–7.8) grams.

Diploid number = 66.

DISTRIBUTION. *Sorex cinereus* has a very wide range, including most of Canada, Alaska, and the northern United States. In the area treated by this volume, it occurs from Maine to Wisconsin, south through New Jersey and northern Illinois, barely into northern Kentucky, and through the Appalachians to northern Alabama.

HABITAT. These little mammals occur from the salt marshes to the high slopes of mountains above timberline. They seem as much at home in the moist, grassy fields and marshes where the meadow voles live as in the dark, moss-carpeted spruce forests. Masked shrews occur in all manner of habitats between, as well, such as hardwood forests, swamps, and bogs, and are often particularly abundant in habitats carpeted with moss. They may also be abundant along the coast; during high water, when their burrows are flooded, large numbers have sometimes been seen on floating driftwood. Masked shrews invade the trapper's cabin in the coniferous forests, and at times fairly swarm in the northern meadows and the dense boreal woods. Few other North American mammals have such a wide range and choice of habitat. Their major requirement is that the area be moist.

HABITS. Masked shrews are active at all hours, but appear to be most active at night. They run rapidly about in and under the leaves, under logs, and in tiny runways through the moss, and they often run along the runs of other species, such as *Microtus pennsylvanicus*. They constantly dart about, poking their noses here and there in search of food and making tiny chipping notes, probably part of their echolocation repertoire.

Shrews do not hibernate. Indeed, their minute tracks may be seen on the snow during bitterly cold weather. It seems incredible that these tiny, hyperactive mammals can produce sufficient heat to maintain a constant body temperature under such conditions.

An interesting assemblage of shrews was seen on a mountain slope at the Coweeta Hydrological Laboratory in North Carolina in late April 1986 (Vispo, 1988). Near sunset on a hot, clear day of an exceedingly dry spring, we heard rustling in the leaves along a 20-meter roadside, and determined that a large number of shrews, probably at least 15, but more likely 30 to 40, were producing the rustling. Many of the shrews proved to be *Sorex cinereus*, but some smoky shrews may have been involved as well. We suspected that they had come together along this road to take advantage of an abundant food source, but moisture may have played a role as well.

FOOD AND FEEDING. The food of the masked shrew is not unlike that of the other, smaller shrews of the genus. Tiny mollusks, insects, small annelids, and the dead bodies of much larger animals are eaten. Their major foods in Indiana are caterpillars, beetle grubs, slugs, snails, and spiders. Ants formed half of the prey items of 31 masked shrews studied in Michigan (Ryan, 1986). Even during midwinter, shrews find sufficient dormant insects to supply their needs. Plant food is eaten sparingly, in greater proportions when the animal is in dire need.

REPRODUCTION AND DEVELOPMENT. A dainty nest of leaves or grasses, 4–6 cm in outer diameter and 2–3 cm in inner diameter, is placed beneath a log or stump or in a shallow burrow. Here the incredibly small young are born, from spring until early fall. About three litters appears to be the rule. Broods number from four to ten newborns each, a large family for such a tiny beast. Forsyth (1976) studied the development of 60 nestlings in nine litters that he found under discarded wooden rabbit traps (69 by 23 by 19 cm) that had been in position for two to three years, in Ohio. The newborns, 12–14 mm crown-rump measurement and weighing about

*Masked shrew,* Sorex cinereus

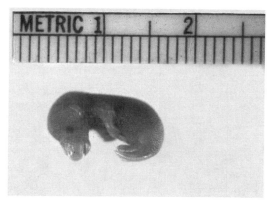

*Newborn masked shrew*

0.3 gram, made feeble clicking noises. Tail and hind foot were 19.1 and 9.3 mm at 11 days and 32.6 and 11 mm at weaning (20 days). Body weights were 3.0 grams at 11 days and 3.5 at weaning. Incisors erupted at 13–14 days. The ears opened at 14–17 days, the eyes at 17–18 days.

POPULATION CHARACTERISTICS. The masked shrew varies greatly in abundance from place to place and from year to year. Quite often, for reasons not known, one's traps may take few of these in the first two or three nights of trapping, but then increase their catch after a few days. One often finds these shrews dead in the woods, particularly in the fall; these are probably old animals, which are thought to die at the close of their first breeding year. Masked shrews apparently do not breed during the summer of their birth, suggesting that their maximum life span is about 15 months. In old animals, the teeth may be worn so badly that the red pigment is entirely gone.

ENEMIES. Every small and abundant mammal is beset by a host of predators, and this species is no exception. Owls, hawks, shrikes, herons, and various predatory mammals take a considerable toll. Notwithstanding the odoriferous lateral scent glands these shrews possess, foxes and weasels kill and eat large numbers. Hamilton once found the sole stomach contents of a 9-kg (20-lb) bobcat to be one shrew of this species. Fish are known to capture them, and a specimen was removed from a merganser.

PARASITES AND DISEASE. Most insectivores and most burrowing animals are highly parasitized, but truly tiny mammals have few external parasites. Small size seems to have won the day in this case, for the masked shrew has few parasites or other associates of the fur, no regularly occurring lice, fleas, or ticks, although a few ticks and fleas do occur. Its principal associate is a tiny mite that is not a parasite at all; it does not even feed, nor does it have usable mouthparts. It is the hypopial stage of the mite *Orycteroxenus soricis*, and it uses the shrew simply as a means of transportation. A nematode, *Capillaria maseri*, is often seen in the urinary bladder of this host.

RELATION TO HUMANS. The benefits of this shrew, like those of other insectivores, cannot be easily measured. Its aggregate destruction of insects must be considerable, and for this we are in its debt.

*Distribution of the masked shrew,* Sorex cinereus, *in the eastern United States*

AREAS FOR FURTHER WORK. Additional study of the development of feeding behavior in the young would be interesting, and the relationship of this species to *Sorex fontinalis* needs to be reassessed.

## SUBSPECIES

Four subspecies, including the nominate, have been described from the eastern United States, but we think all should be reassessed.

*Sorex cinereus cinereus* Kerr

As described above.

Type locality: Fort Severn, Ontario.

Other currently recognized eastern subspecies:
   *S. cinereus lesueurii* (Duvernoy)
   *S. cinereus nigriculus* Green
   *S. cinereus ohionensis* Bole & Moulthrop

### LITERATURE

Blossom, P. M. 1932. A pair of long-tailed shrews (*Sorex cinereus cinereus*) in captivity. *J. Mammal.* 13: 136–143.

Forsyth, D. J. 1976. A field study of growth and development of nestling masked shrews (*Sorex cinereus*). *J. Mammal.* 57: 708–721.

Junge, J. A., and R. S. Hoffmann. 1981. An annotated key to the long-tailed shrews (genus *Sorex*) of the United States and Canada, with notes on Middle American *Sorex*. Occ. Pap. Mus. Nat. Hist. Univ. Kansas No. 94. 48 pp.

Moore, J. C. 1949. Notes on the shrew, *Sorex cinereus*, in the southern Appalachians. *Ecology* 30: 234–237.

Pruitt, W. O. 1954. Aging in the masked shrew, *Sorex cinereus cinereus* Kerr. *J. Mammal.* 35: 35–39.

Ryan, J. M. 1986. Dietary overlap in sympatric populations of pygmy shrews, *Sorex hoyi*, and masked shrews, *Sorex cinereus*, in Michigan. *Canadian Field-Nat.* 100: 225–228.

Vispo, C. R. 1988. An observation of a wild group of masked shrews, *Sorex cinereus*. *Canadian Field-Nat.* 102: 731–733.

Whitaker, J. O., Jr., and L. L. Schmeltz. 1973. Food and external parasites of *Sorex palustris* and food of *Sorex cinereus* from St. Louis Co., Minnesota. *J. Mammal.* 54: 283–285.

## Long-Tailed Shrew *Sorex dispar* Batchelder

DESCRIPTION. The long-tailed shrew is similar in appearance to the smoky shrew, *Sorex fumeus*, but may be distinguished by its longer tail,

*Long-tailed shrew,* Sorex dispar *(Roger W. Barbour)*

slimmer body, and nearly uniform darker coloration. The belly is almost the same color as the back. This species has been likened to a swift, lightweight cruiser, the smoky shrew to a slower, heavier battleship. The two are most difficult to distinguish in winter, when both are slate-colored. At that time the belly of the smoky shrew is slightly lighter than the back.

*Sorex dispar* is apparently very closely related to *S. gaspensis*, which occurs in Canada, in the Gaspé Peninsula and Nova Scotia. The two differ from all other North American *Sorex* in having the posterior border of the infraorbital foramen posterior to the interface of the second and third large molariform teeth ($M_1$ and $M_2$) behind the unicuspids.

MEASUREMENTS. Body measurements (Kirkland and Van Deusen, 1979) of over 150 long-tailed shrews from the northern part of their range were: total length 118.1 (103–137), tail 55.7 (46–65), hind foot 13.8 (12.0–15.5) mm. For 65 individuals from the southern Appalachians, corresponding measurements were: 123 (108–135), 57.8 (49–67), and 14.8 (13.5–18) mm. The weight ranges from 3.1 to 3.8 grams.

Diploid number unknown.

DISTRIBUTION. The long-tailed shrew occurs from western Maine south through the mountainous areas to North Carolina and Tennessee.

HABITAT. This shrew is restricted to upland areas, where it occurs primarily in two types of habitat: under and among rocks or boulders, especially in talus slopes, and along mountain streams. Some have been secured in the recesses of large masses of boulders, where the shade permits the ice to linger into July; and indeed, the best way to trap them is to set mousetraps deep in the dark recesses of rock or talus slopes. Some have been trapped in recent clearcuts in Pennsylvania and West Virginia.

Common boreal associates in *Sorex dispar* habitats are *S. cinereus*, *S. fumeus*, *Peromyscus maniculatus*, and *Clethrionomys gapperi*. We found this species and *S. fumeus* together on Whiteface Mountain, in the Adirondacks of New York; and Earl Poole found *S. cinereus*, *S. fumeus*, and *S. dispar* all in the same locality. Poole accordingly suggested the possibility of a greater difference in habits than is presently known.

HABITS. Little is known of the habits of the long-tailed shrew, but it would seem likely that the habitat of this species, in talus slopes and in the recesses beneath boulders, suggests some specializations.

FOOD AND FEEDING. Paul C. Connor (1960) found the major foods of nine individuals from Schoharie County, New York, to be adult flies, cave crickets, spiders, centipedes, and beetles. Centipedes were the main food component in the stomachs of three individuals from Pennsylvania.

REPRODUCTION AND DEVELOPMENT. Breeding appears to extend from late April to August in this species. Embryo counts have been made in only four individuals: two females from New

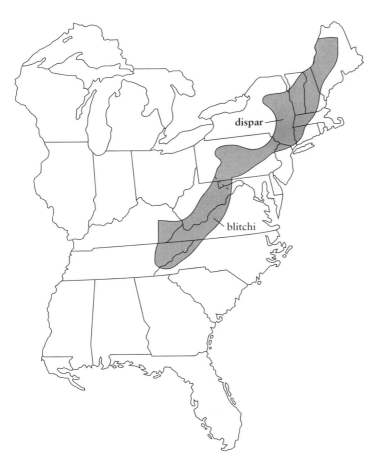

*Distribution of the long-tailed shrew,* Sorex dispar, *in the eastern United States*

York each carried two embryos, and two from Pennsylvania each had five.

POPULATION CHARACTERISTICS. Essentially nothing is known of the population characteristics of this species.

RELATION TO HUMANS. These shrews feed on insects and their larvae, but because of their isolated habitat, they are likely to have little direct relation to humans.

AREAS FOR FURTHER WORK. The habits of the long-tailed shrew are little known, and a study of its entire life history would be valuable if adequate populations could be located. A laboratory behavioral study of echolocation in this species might be particularly valuable, given the deep talus this species often inhabits.

## SUBSPECIES

*Sorex dispar dispar* (Batchelder)
As described above.
Type locality: Beedes River Gorge, Essex Co., New York.
Other currently recognized eastern subspecies:
   *S. dispar blitchi* Schwartz

### LITERATURE

Caldwell, R. S., and H. Bryan. 1982. Notes on distribution and habitats of *Sorex* and *Microsorex* (Insectivora: Soricidae) in Kentucky. *Brimleyana* 8: 91–100.

Connor, P. C. 1960. The small mammals of Otsego and Schoharie counties, New York. New York State Museum and Science Service Bull. No. 382. 84 pp.

Kirkland, G. L., Jr. 1981. *Sorex dispar* and *Sorex gaspensis*. **Mammalian Species No. 155.** Amer. Soc. Mammal. 4 pp.

Kirkland, G. L., Jr., and H. M. Van Deusen. 1979. The shrews of the *Sorex dispar* group: *Sorex dispar* Batchelder and *Sorex gaspensis* Anthony and Goodwin. *Amer. Mus. Novitates* 2675: 1–21.

## Maryland Shrew *Sorex fontinalis* Hollister

The Maryland shrew was originally described as a distinct species, but subsequently, and for many years, it was relegated to subspecific status under *Sorex cinereus*, the masked shrew.

Kirkland (1977), however, found that *S. c. fontinalis* and *S. c. cinereus* overlap geographically in southeastern Pennsylvania, apparently without interbreeding. Junge and Hoffmann (1981) later resurrected *S. fontinalis* as a full species, and Kirkland and Levengood (1987) treated it as a full species and reported its first record in West Virginia. Two years later, van Zyll de Jong and Kirkland (1989) stated that morphometric analysis does not support retaining *S. fontinalis* as a separate species, but acknowledged that a final determination would require more data. Gordon Kirkland (pers. comm.) later informed us that he is still treating *S. fontinalis* as distinct, and we have retained that status here, pending further investigation.

DESCRIPTION. The Maryland shrew is essentially identical to *Sorex cinereus* in color, but is smaller than that species and has a shorter tail, shorter skull, shorter, broader rostrum, and shorter unicuspid tooth row. In all these characters, *S. fontinalis* is similar to *S. longirostris*, the southeastern shrew, and we think *S. fontinalis* should be compared to that species. In *fontinalis*, the third and fourth unicuspids are similar in size; in *longirostris*, the fourth is often larger than the third. Kirkland, too, wonders about the relationship of *fontinalis* and *longirostris*. Could *fontinalis* constitute an intergrade between *longirostris* and *cinereus*? It is obvious that more work is needed to clarify the taxonomy of these shrews.

MEASUREMENTS. Average measurements of 29 individuals are: total length 88.6 (78–97), tail 35.0 (27–39), hind foot 11.2 (10–13) mm. The upper molariform tooth row averages 3.68 (3.5–3.8) mm. This measurement averaged 3.71 and 3.78 in 18 individuals of *Sorex cinereus* from Pennsylvania and West Virginia. The weight is 2.3 to 4.5 grams.
Diploid number unknown.

DISTRIBUTION. This species occurs in northern Maryland, northern Delaware, southeastern Pennsylvania, and northeasternmost West Virginia. Bray (1939) reported it from Virginia on the basis of several specimens, but Handley (1982) reidentified the single specimen he was able to locate as *Sorex longirostris*. The occurrence of the Maryland shrew south of the Potomac in West Virginia, however, does raise the possibility of its occurrence in Virginia.

HABITAT. Most earlier specimens of *Sorex fontinalis* were taken in moist meadows, some in *Microtus* runways. Gordon Kirkland (pers. comm.) recently collected 296 individuals on South Mountain, near Shippensburg, Pennsylvania. He found the species to be about equally common in mature lowland forest, midslope oak forest, ridge forest (oak and black gum), and oak clearcuts 3–4 and 9–10 years old. These data suggest a rather broad ecological distribution, especially since he also took it in meadows, hedgerows, and forests in the Cumberland Valley.

HABITS. Little is known of the habits of this shrew, but they are presumably similar to those of *Sorex cinereus* and/or *S. longirostris*.

AREAS FOR FURTHER WORK. A detailed study of the genetic, ecological, and taxonomic interrelationships of these three species is in order, as well as studies of their life history and ecology.

## SUBSPECIES

None described.
Type locality: Cold Spring Swamp, Prince Georges Co., Maryland.

## LITERATURE

Bray, R. S. 1939. *Sorex fontinalis* in Virginia. *J. Mammal.* 20: 102.

*Distribution of the Maryland shrew,*
Sorex fontinalis, *in the eastern United States*

Handley, C. O., Jr. 1982. Deletion of *Sorex cinereus fontinalis* from taxa known to occur in Virginia. *J. Mammal.* 63: 319.

Hollister, N. 1911. Remarks on the long-tailed shrews of the eastern United States, with description of a new subspecies. *Proc. U.S. Natl. Mus.* 40: 377–381.

Junge, J. A., and R. S. Hoffmann. 1981. An annotated key to the long-tailed shrews (genus *Sorex*) of the United States and Canada, with notes on Middle American *Sorex*. Occ. Pap. Mus. Nat. Hist. Univ. Kansas No. 94. 48 pp.

Kirkland, G. L., Jr. 1977. A reexamination of the subspecific status of the Maryland shrew, *Sorex cinereus fontinalis* Hollister. *Proc. Pa. Acad. Sci.* 51: 43–46.

Kirkland, G. L., Jr., and J. M. Levengood. 1987. First record of the Maryland shrew (*Sorex fontinalis*) from West Virginia. *Proc. Pa. Acad. Sci.* 61: 35–37.

van Zyll de Jong, C. G., and G. L. Kirkland, Jr. 1989. A morphometric analysis of the *Sorex cinereus* group in central and eastern North America. *J. Mammal.* 70: 110–122.

## Smoky Shrew *Sorex fumeus* (Miller)

DESCRIPTION. Aside from *S. palustris*, *Sorex fumeus* is the largest of the eastern long-tailed

*Smoky shrew,* Sorex fumeus, *with earthworm (Roger W. Barbour)*

shrews in total mass. Winter and summer colors are markedly different. Winter pelage is dark mouse-gray above and rather lighter below. In summer the fur is much browner, approaching olive-brown, and paler below, occasionally silvery on the belly. The tail is bicolored, fuscous above and paler below. The ears are relatively prominent. There are two molts annually, the summer pelage being replaced about October

and the winter pelage about April or May, depending on latitude and altitude, though there is much individual variation. The young may be distinguished from the adults by their smaller size, seldom exceeding 6.5 grams, and by the pencil of long hairs on the tail tip, which in the adult disappear, leaving the naked tail tip rounded and smooth. In spring the tails of these shrews become swollen, apparently as a repository of energy.

MEASUREMENTS. Average measurements of 25 adults of both sexes from Ithaca, New York, were: total length 116.8 (110–125), tail 42.6 (37–47), hind foot 12.8 (12.3–14) mm; and weight 7.7 (6.1–11) grams.
Diploid number = 66.

DISTRIBUTION. In the eastern United States the smoky shrew occurs from New England and New York south through the Appalachians to northern Georgia. One individual has been taken from Wisconsin. Vernon Bailey collected a small series in Mammoth Cave, Kentucky, and Ronald S. Caldwell and Hal Bryan (1982) found additional populations in western Kentucky. Caldwell et al. (1982) found the species in the unglaciated hill country of south-central Indiana, where it is quite abundant but had gone undetected. It appears to have arrived there from the south in postglacial times, probably becoming isolated in southern Indiana by the glacial meanderings of the Ohio River. This species also occurs in southeastern Canada, from north of Lake Superior to Nova Scotia.

HABITAT. Shady, damp woods, of either hardwoods or conifers, are the habitat of choice of these shrews, particularly where there are extensive clumps of yew and moss-covered logs and boulders in maple, birch, and hemlock woods. The species has been taken in a variety of habitats, however, such as bogs, swamps, talus slopes, stream banks, and even, sometimes, in grassy areas, but it is seldom found in dry woods and never found in the marshes along the coast. The smoky shrew is not so generally distributed throughout its habitat as are deer mice and short-tailed shrews. Its favorite haunts appear to be the well-traveled highways deep in the leaf mold that cover the roots of the venerable hemlocks and birches to a depth of several centimeters.

Traps set at the entrances to tiny burrows leading into stream banks along shaded brooks in New York, and along mountain roads in North Carolina, have often yielded smoky shrews. Numbers of them have also been taken by pitfall traps placed under the edges of logs or rocks in the ravines of the maple/hickory forests of southern Indiana. Thirteen were taken in one trap under a shale outcrop in one week.

The smoky shrew has an interesting distribution in southern Indiana. It and the pygmy shrew, *Sorex hoyi*, occur only in the uplands and slopes of the unglaciated hill country of the south-central portion of the state, whereas, in the bottoms of the valleys and ravines in this same area, both are replaced by *S. longirostris*. *Sorex cinereus* occurs throughout the state *except* in this unglaciated area, and to the east of this area only *S. cinereus* occurs, whereas, to the west, *S. longirostris* occurs in the uplands, *S. cinereus* in the bottomlands. We believe much of this distribution, both ecological and geographic, to be greatly influenced by competitive interspecific relationships. Kirkland and van Deusen (1979) suggested that *S. fumeus* and *S. dispar* are competitors, and Jameson (1949) suggested interspecific intolerance between *S. fumeus* and *S. cinereus*. (See page 45 for further details concerning these relationships.)

HABITS. In the damp, dark northern woods that support dense growths of ferns and other ground cover, shaded by a canopy of second-growth timber, the smoky shrew lives alongside deer mice, red-backed mice, pine voles, wood-

*Distribution of the smoky shrew,* Sorex fumeus, *in the eastern United States.*

land jumping mice, short-tailed shrews, and hairy-tailed moles. It travels the burrows of other forest mammals, or threads through the leaf mold of the forest floor. In some seasons it is common; at other times it is scarce.

Like other shrews, the smoky shrew does not hibernate. This fact was well emphasized one winter when Whitaker set about two hundred mousetraps in a forest at Oneonta, in central New York, during a very cold period. For five days in a row, the morning temperatures were minus 29°C (minus 20° Fahrenheit) or below, and noon temperatures were minus 20°C or below. On one morning, the temperature at 0800 hours was minus 35°C (minus 31°F); nevertheless, three smoky shrews were taken that morning.

When disturbed, the smoky shrew makes a grating, high-pitched note, similar to that of bats, and if highly agitated the shrew may throw itself on its back and wave its legs, while uttering this note. Smoky shrews continually utter a faint twitter while foraging, undoubtedly a part of their echolocation repertoire. This species has odor-producing lateral glands that may serve to bring the sexes together.

Whitaker once took two shrews of this species together in the same snap trap in an Ithaca, New York, swamp. One was a pregnant female; the other was a male. The ground around the trap, of soft dirt covered with moss, was torn up in a circle about 25 cm (10 inches) in diameter. The male was firmly grasping the fur of the flank of the female and had penetrated the skin slightly. It appeared that the two shrews had been in pitched battle when killed by the trap.

FOOD AND FEEDING. The principal food of the smoky shrew consists of the small invertebrates of the leaf litter. Earthworms, centipedes, insects and their larvae, small salamanders, plant matter, sowbugs, and other small invertebrates make up the greater share. Smoky shrews kept by Hamilton in captivity would bite off pieces of food while holding down an item with the forefeet. Salamanders were killed by severing their spinal cords, but often only the viscera, feet, and heads were eaten. Contrary to popular belief, these shrews never consumed more than about half their own weight in food per day.

(There is some evidence, however, that *Blarina* does consume more than its own weight per day.)

REPRODUCTION AND DEVELOPMENT. These shrews place a nest of shredded leaves and/or grasses in the honeycombed recesses of some half-rotted log or moss-covered stump, or directly beneath a slab of rock. The first litter is born in late April. The young may number from two to eight, averaging about 5.5, and are born blind and naked. Month-old individuals weigh about 4 grams, about half the weight of adults, but by that time a second litter is already on its way. Hamilton collected gravid females in early July and, rarely, in August. Thus two litters are customary and, less often, a third litter is produced in the fall. Lactating individuals may be found as late as October. Smoky shrews do not breed in the year of their birth, but overwinter as immatures, breeding the following spring.

POPULATION CHARACTERISTICS. Because one so seldom collects an adult smoky shrew in the late fall or winter, it seems likely that the adults die off in their second year, following the breeding season. The lifespan of the species is probably about 14 to 17 months. Population-density estimates range up to 143 per ha (57 per acre), but populations of 12 to 35 per ha (5 to 14 per acre) are more likely. At times, smoky shrews may constitute a rather large proportion of the mammal community.

ENEMIES. We may number among the enemies of the smoky shrew all the owls and some of the hawks, foxes, weasels, and other mammalian predators; and short-tailed shrews sometimes prey upon smaller shrews.

PARASITES AND DISEASE. Many ectoparasites and other associates, mostly mites, have been taken from this host. We have taken at least 31 different species from it in Indiana alone (Whitaker and Cudmore, 1987). The most abundant are a myobiid mite, *Amorphacarus hengererorum*, two chiggers, *Euschoengastia whitakeri* and *E. jamesoni*, and two hypopial mites, *Orycteroxenus soricis* and *Xenoryctes nudus*.

RELATION TO HUMANS. These tiny mammals and their confreres are important checks on the populations of many insects. Their effectiveness in destroying the larvae and pupae of forest insect pests can hardly be denied.

AREAS FOR FURTHER WORK. Ecological relationships between this species and the other shrews that occur with it, especially where they concern habitat and food as related to size, are of interest and may vary with habitat and shrew community. Radio-tracking of this species might be difficult, but if successful would pay ample rewards. Besides amassing behavioral data, one should be able to find nests this way, which could lead to studies of the nest fauna.

## SUBSPECIES

*Sorex fumeus fumeus* (Miller)

As described above.

Type locality: Peterboro, Madison Co., New York.

Other currently recognized eastern subspecies:

S. *fumeus umbrosus* Jackson

### LITERATURE

Caldwell, R. S., and H. Bryan. 1982. Notes on distribution and habitats of *Sorex* and *Microsorex* (Insectivora: Soricidae) in Kentucky. *Brimleyana* 8: 91–100.

Caldwell, R. S., C. K. Smith, and J. O. Whitaker, Jr. 1982. First records of the smoky shrew, *Sorex fumeus*, and pygmy shrew, *Microsorex hoyi*, from Indiana. *Proc. Ind. Acad. Sci.* 91: 606–608.

Hamilton, W. J., Jr. 1940. The biology of the smoky shrew *Sorex fumeus fumeus* (Miller). *Zoologica* 25: 473–491.

Jameson, E. W., Jr. 1949. Some factors influencing the local distribution and abundance of woodland small mammals in central New York. *J. Mammal.* 30: 221–235.

Kirkland, G. L., Jr., and H. M. Van Deusen. 1979. The shrews of the *Sorex dispar* group: *Sorex dispar* Batchelder and *Sorex gaspensis* Anthony and Goodwin. *Amer. Mus. Novitates* 2675: 1–21.

Owen, J. G. 1984. *Sorex fumeus.* **Mammalian Species No. 215.** Amer. Soc. Mammal. 8 pp.

Whitaker, J. O., Jr., and W. W. Cudmore. 1987. Food and ectoparasites of shrews of south central Indiana with emphasis on *Sorex fumeus* and *Sorex hoyi*. *Proc. Ind. Acad. Sci.* 96: 543–552.

## Pygmy Shrew *Sorex hoyi* (Baird)

Pygmy shrews were long placed in the genus *Microsorex*, but Diersing (1980) placed them in *Sorex*, where consensus retains them today.

DESCRIPTION. In general appearance, pygmy shrews closely resemble *Sorex cinereus*, the

*Pygmy shrew,* Sorex hoyi *(Robert C. Simpson)*

masked shrew. They differ somewhat from the larger shrews of the genus by their slighter build and shorter tail, but one should examine the unicuspids to verify the identification. The third unicuspid in the upper jaw, wedged in between the second and fourth, is very small (see photo p. 29); it is so small that it cannot be seen without magnification, and even then it cannot be observed from the outside. Moreover, because the fifth unicuspid is also tiny, usually only three unicuspids can be seen from the outside of the tooth row, whereas in *S. cinereus* and most other species of *Sorex*, five may be seen, though the fifth is small. The color of *S. hoyi* is very similar to that of *S. cinereus*, sepia-brown above, smoke-gray below, tinged with light buff. The tail is indistinctly bicolored, dark brown above, lighter below, and darker at the tip.

MEASUREMENTS. Average measurements of 13 individuals from Maine were: total length 85, tail 29.5, hind foot 9.4 mm; and weight 2.5–3 grams. Using pitfall trapping, we have recently taken a number of individuals of this species in south-central Indiana. Data from 71 were as follows: total length mean 73.5 (71–82), tail 24.6 (21–28), hind foot 8.2 (6–9) mm; and weight 2.0 (1.3–2.9) grams. The pygmy shrews of south-central Indiana are the smallest known shrews, averaging 2.0 grams (a dime weighs about 2.6 grams). The barely smaller bumble-bee bat, *Craseonycteris thonglongyai*, of Thailand, which weighs 1.7 to 2.0 grams, is generally considered to be the world's smallest mammal. Diploid number = 62.

DISTRIBUTION. The pygmy shrew occurs in the northeastern United States south to northern Illinois, southern Michigan, southeastern Ohio, and northeastern Kentucky, with a disjunct population in the southern Appalachians extending northward into central Kentucky and south-central Indiana. The range of this species extends westward to the Dakotas and northward to cover much of Canada and part of Alaska.

HABITAT. These shrews make tiny burrows beneath stumps, fallen logs, and the leaf carpet of the forest. We have taken pygmy shrews in open fields, along with *Sorex cinereus*, at Ithaca, New York, and along a woods edge at Oneonta, New York. Paul Connor has taken several in woods. We have also taken over a hundred in Indiana, mostly on the wooded slopes of ravines. One that Schmidt (1931) observed in Wisconsin was eating the contents of a dung-beetle burrow, and was able to enter the burrow without enlarging it to any notable extent. Another that P. B. Saunders captured at Clinton, New York, made holes in the dirt floor of its cage that could easily have been mistaken for those of a large earthworm.

In the woodlands of the south-central Indiana hill country occur one large shrew, *Blarina brevicauda*; one medium-sized shrew, *Sorex fumeus*; one small shrew, *S. longirostris*; and one very small shrew, *S. hoyi* (Cudmore and Whitaker, 1984). One finds *Blarina* throughout the

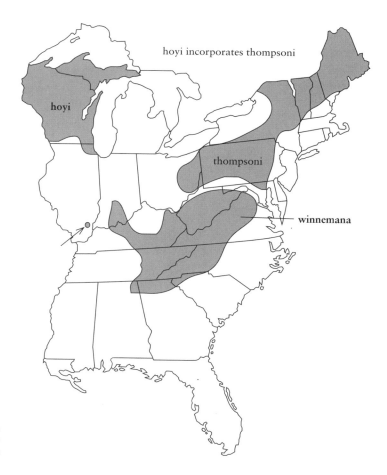

*Distribution of the pygmy shrew,*
Sorex hoyi, *in the eastern*
*United States*

area, *S. hoyi* and *S. fumeus* in the uplands, and *S. longirostris* in the bottomlands. In southeastern Indiana, *S. fumeus* and *S. hoyi* do not occur; there, *S. longirostris* tends to occur in the uplands, *S. cinereus* in the bottoms. In Land Between the Lakes, in western Kentucky and Tennessee, *S. hoyi* likewise occurs more often in the uplands, *S. longirostris* in the bottoms; and *S. fumeus* was not found there at all. In both Indiana and Kentucky, the four species tended to be distributed generally by size, thus fitting the species-assembly rule of Fox and Kirkland (1992), which posits that North American shrew communities will generally include shrews of different sizes, the different species making use of different groups of resources. This process appears to be fueled by interspecific competition.

HABITS. Up until the last few years, most mammalogists would have agreed that pygmy shrews are quite rare, for they were seldom collected, and they can easily be overlooked. (Be sure to check the unicuspids of any small brown *Sorex* you collect, to be sure you do not overlook this species.) The advent of pitfall trapping (in sunken cans) has rapidly changed our views on distribution and abundance, and increased the number of pygmy shrews in collections. They are sometimes quite common, but are simply too small for snap-traps. For example, Elmer Birney has taken numerous individuals in pitfalls in Minnesota, and we have taken over 100 from the slopes and ravines of the oak and maple woods in the unglaciated portion of south-central Indiana.

Long (Mammalian Species, 1974) indicates that pygmy shrews are active the entire year, night or day. They can swim and climb and would hang from the top of a cage by the hind limbs only; and they can jump to a height of 110 mm (3½ feet). When disturbed, they would quiver violently and run to cover; and when foraging, they would run about constantly, sniffing here and there. Apparently, the scent glands, common to all shrews, are better developed in these animals than in some others. Several investigators have remarked on the well-developed side glands of pygmy shrews and the pronounced effluvium often attending them.

FOOD AND FEEDING. The most important foods of 63 pygmy shrews from Indiana, as shown by stomach analysis, were insect larvae, spiders, and beetles. Ryan (1986) found 45.5% of the prey items of 29 pygmy shrews from Michigan to be ants. Caterpillars, beetle larvae, adult flies, and many other invertebrates have also been found in stomachs.

REPRODUCTION AND DEVELOPMENT. The few earlier breeding records suggest that these tiny creatures bear litters during the summer, the usual number of young being five to eight. Long suggests that in Wisconsin, at least, the female may bear only one litter per year. Feldhamer et al. (1993) indicated that the predominant times of births in Land Between the Lakes, in Kentucky and Tennessee, were January through early March and, to a lesser degree, August through December. The young entered the population at adult size about ten weeks after birth.

POPULATION CHARACTERISTICS. We know little of the population characteristics of this species, but they are presumably similar to those of *Sorex cinereus*.

ENEMIES. The enemies of *Sorex hoyi* are poorly known, but are probably similar to those of *S. cinereus*.

PARASITES AND DISEASE. The only regularly occurring associate in the fur of this species in Indiana was the hypopial mite *Orycteroxenus soricis*. As its name suggests, this species is common on many species of shrews.

RELATION TO HUMANS. As do other shrews, the pygmy shrew helps maintain the balance of nature by feeding on numerous insects and their larvae. Until the advent of pitfall traps, the species was thought to be quite rare.

AREAS FOR FURTHER WORK. More information is needed on growth and development, general life history, and relationships with other species.

## SUBSPECIES

Charles A. Long (1974) proposed designating *Sorex hoyi thompsoni* and *S. h. winnemana* as separate species, on morphological grounds, but we do not see sufficient basis for that determination and thus have retained eastern *S. hoyi* as a single species. Diersing (1980) likewise recognized only a single species, though he did retain five subspecies, three of these (*hoyi*, *thompsoni*, and *winnemana*) occurring in the eastern United States.

Because *Sorex hoyi hoyi* and *S. h. thompsoni* appear to intergrade broadly in Canada, we do not recognize subspecies distinction for *S. h. thompsoni*. Moreover, until recently it was thought that there was a hiatus of about 480 km (300 miles) between the northeastern pygmy shrews and those farther south (*S. h. winnemana*), but Kirkland et al. (1987) have reduced the hiatus to about 80 km (50 miles) by turning up four individuals in Pennsylvania. Generally, if there is an intergrading series of populations between two described forms, we would not treat the two as subspecies, but we have provisionally retained *S. h. winnemana* and *S. h. hoyi* as separate subspecies, on the basis of two factors: first *S. h. winnemana* shows little internal variation, which would indicate that little gene flow is invading from populations to the north; and, second, pygmy shrews appear to be extremely rare in Pennsylvania, the area between the two subspecies, which would also tend to limit gene flow between the two. Further work, of course, may well show these forms to intergrade more broadly.

*Sorex hoyi hoyi* Baird

As described above.
Type locality: Racine, Racine Co., Wisconsin.
Other currently recognized eastern subspecies:
    *S. hoyi thompsoni* Baird

*Sorex hoyi winnemana* Preble

This subspecies includes the tiniest of the tiny. The type measures: total length 78, tail 28, hind foot 9 mm. A specimen from the Pisgah Forest of North Carolina measured: total length 80, tail 28, hind foot 10 mm; it weighed only 2.3 grams, or somewhat less than a dime. Average measurements of 71 individuals from the Pisgah Forest were: total length 73.5, tail 24.6, hind foot 8.2 mm; and the average weight of 65 individuals was 2.0 (1.3–2.9 grams).

Type locality: Bank of the Potomac River near Stubblefield Falls, 4 miles [7 km] below the Great Falls of the Potomac, Fairfax Co., Virginia.

## LITERATURE

Caldwell, R. S., and H. Bryan. 1982. Notes on distribution and habitats of *Sorex* and *Microsorex* (Insectivora: Soricidae) in Kentucky. *Brimleyana* 8: 91–100.

Cudmore, W. W., and J. O. Whitaker, Jr. 1984. The distribution of the smoky shrew, *Sorex fumeus*, and the pygmy shrew, *Microsorex hoyi*, from Indiana. *Proc. Ind. Acad. Sci.* 93: 469–474.

Diersing, V. E. 1980. Systematics and evolution of the pygmy shrews (subgenus *Microsorex*) of North America. *J. Mammal.* 61: 76–101.

Feldhamer, G. A., R. S. Klann, A. S. Gerard, and A. C. Driskell. 1993. Habitat partitioning, body size and timing of parturition in pygmy shrews and associated soricids. *J. Mammal.* 74: 403–411.

Fox, B. J., and G. L. Kirkland, Jr. 1992. An assembly rule for functional groups applied to North American soricid communities. *J. Mammal.* 73: 491–503.

Kirkland, G. L., Jr., A. M. Wilkinson, J. V. Plenz, and J. E. Maldonado. 1987. *Sorex (Microsorex) hoyi* in Pennsylvania. *J. Mammal.* 68: 384–387.

Long, C. A. 1974. *Microsorex hoyi* and *Microsorex thompsoni*. **Mammalian Species No. 33.** Amer. Soc. Mammal. 4 pp.

Ryan, J. M. 1986. Dietary overlap in sympatric populations of pygmy shrews, *Sorex hoyi*, and masked shrews, *Sorex cinereus*, in Michigan. *Canadian Field-Nat.* 100: 225–228.

Schmidt, F. J. W. 1931. Mammals of western Clark County, Wisconsin. *J. Mammal.* 12: 99–117.

Whitaker, J. O., Jr., and W. W. Cudmore. 1987. Food and ectoparasites of shrews of south central Indiana with emphasis on *Sorex fumeus* and *Sorex hoyi*. *Proc. Ind. Acad. Sci.* 96: 543–552.

## Southeastern Shrew *Sorex longirostris* Bachman

DESCRIPTION. *Sorex longirostris* is similar to *S. cinereus*, the masked shrew, but is smaller and more reddish in color, and the tail is shorter and more sparsely haired. The head and tail

*Southeastern shrew,* Sorex longirostris
*(Thomas W. French)*

*Masked shrew,* Sorex cinereus *(left), and southeastern shrew,* S. longirostris *(right), showing the greater tail length and greater amount of hair on the tail of* S. cinereus, *and its longer, thinner snout (Thomas W. French)*

proportions of the two are illustrated at right; as indicated, the skull of *S. longirostris* is much shorter and less acutely pointed than is that of *S. cinereus*. This relationship can be shown by measuring the greatest width across the outside of the first large molariform teeth, behind the unicuspids. In *S. longirostris*, this distance is usually less than twice the distance from the posterior end of the palate to the anterior end of the first incisors; in *S. cinereus*, it is more than twice this width. Moreover, the inner ridges of the upper unicuspids lack pigment, whereas these are pigmented in *S. cinereus*. *Sorex longirostris* has a shorter and more crowded unicuspid row, and the third upper unicuspid is usually smaller than the fourth.

MEASUREMENTS. The basal length of the skull is 14–14.2 mm. Measurements of 270 individuals from Georgia and Alabama were: total length 81.9 (68–94), tail 30.1 (24–37), hind foot 10.9 (9.0–12.0) mm. Measurements of 33 from Indiana were: total length 72–90, tail 26–33, hind foot 9–11 mm; and weight 3–4 grams.
 Diploid number unknown.

DISTRIBUTION. *Sorex longirostris* occurs in the southeastern United States from northern Maryland and eastern Virginia south to south-central Florida, west through Alabama and Mississippi, and north through Tennessee and Kentucky to south-central West Virginia and southern In-

diana and Illinois. Elsewhere, this species occurs only in northern Arkansas.

HABITAT. Like most other species of *Sorex*, these shrews are most often taken in moist situations, such as swamps, marshes, and stream and river bottoms, although in Florida it has also been taken in xeric upland habitats (sand pine scrub and sandhill vegetation types). It may also occur in open or wooded areas. One was caught by hand in a patch of virgin forest in southern Indiana, where it had been darting rapidly in and out of the leaves.

 In west-central Indiana, where both species are taken, *Sorex cinereus* generally occurs in the bottomlands, *S. longirostris* in the uplands, though occasionally they are taken together. In the hill country of south-central Indiana, where *S. cinereus* is absent, *S. longirostris* occurs in the bottomlands, *S. fumeus* and *S. hoyi* in the uplands.

HABITS. Relatively little is known about the habits of this shrew, although it is not extremely rare, as once thought. Its habits seem quite similar to those of *Sorex cinereus*.

FOOD AND FEEDING. The most important foods of 90 individuals from Indiana (French, 1984) were spiders (39.3% by volume), lepidopterous larvae (15.7%), Gryllidae (11.3%), adult beetles (7.1%), harvestmen (5.8%), beetle larvae (4.1%), and centipedes (3.9%).

REPRODUCTION AND DEVELOPMENT. Southeastern shrews breed throughout the summer. Pregnant females have been found from 31 March to 6 October, and some females breed during their first season. As do the young of other shrews, southeastern shrews remain in the nest until nearly full grown. Nestlings have been found measuring 71 and 72 mm total length. William L. Engels (1941) found four young in a nest in North Carolina. The nest, placed beneath a well-decayed log in an oak/pine forest, was a shallow depression lined with fragments of leaf litter. Other nests, usually leaf-lined, have been found in or under decaying logs.

POPULATION CHARACTERISTICS. French (1980) estimated population densities at 30 and 45 per ha (12 and 18 per acre) on two Alabama study plots. Southeastern shrews may live up to 18 or 19 months, but most individuals probably live less than a year.

ENEMIES. Few cases of predation have been reported, but of those, most involved owls, particularly barn and barred owls, and domestic cats.

*Distribution of the southeastern shrew,* Sorex longirostris, *in the eastern United States*

The stomach of an opossum from Virginia contained one southeastern shrew; South Carolina specimens were recovered from a barn owl and from the throat of a hooded merganser shot in a rice marsh. The first specimen from Alabama had been collected by a barred owl.

PARASITES AND DISEASE. Several kinds of ectoparasites have been reported from this host, but two of the major ones are a host-specific myobiid mite, *Protomyobia indianensis*, and the same phoretic mite found on *Sorex cinereus*, *Orycteroxenus soricis* (phoretic species use a mammal simply as a means of transportation).

RELATION TO HUMANS. These shrews feed on insects and their larvae, but as with most shrews it is difficult to determine their impact on human concerns.

AREAS FOR FURTHER WORK. Detailed taxonomic, genetic, and ecological studies comparing this species with *Sorex cinereus* and *S. fontinalis* should be very instructive.

## SUBSPECIES

See Jones et al. (1991), but we think the two described subspecies should be reexamined for primary isolating mechanisms. We recognize only the nominate subspecies.

*Sorex longirostris longirostris* Bachman
As described above.
Type locality: Hume plantation [ = Cat Island, in the mouth of the Santee River], South Carolina.
Other currently recognized eastern subspecies:
*S. longirostris fisheri* Merriam
*S. longirostris eionis* Davis

### LITERATURE

Engels, W. L. 1941. Distribution and habitat of *Sorex longirostris* in North Carolina. *J. Mammal.* 22: 447.
French, T. W. 1980a. *Sorex longirostris*. **Mammalian Species No. 143**. Amer. Soc. Mammal. 3 pp.
———. 1980b. Natural history of the southeastern shrew, *Sorex longirostris* Bachman. *Amer. Midland Nat.* 104: 13–31.
———. 1984. Dietary overlap of *Sorex longirostris* and *S. cinereus* in hardwood floodplain habitats in Vigo County, Indiana. *Amer. Midland Nat.* 111: 41–46.
Jones, C. A., S. R. Humphrey, T. M. Padgett, R. K. Rose, and J. F. Pagels. 1991. Geographic variation and taxonomy of the southeastern shrew (*Sorex longirostris*). *J. Mammal.* 72: 263–272.

## Water Shrew *Sorex palustris* Richardson    Color plate 1

DESCRIPTION. The water shrew is a large, soft-furred, dark-colored shrew partially adapted

*Water shrew,* Sorex palustris *(Roger W. Barbour)*

for an aquatic life. The large, broad hind feet are conspicuously fringed with stiff hairs, and the toes are slightly webbed at their base. In winter pelage, the upper parts are very dark, almost black; in the summer, they are slightly paler and more brownish. The underparts are grayish white, the ventral color extending onto the upper lips and part of the flanks. The tail is bicolored, blackish brown above, much paler below. The fourth unicuspid of the water shrew is larger than the third.

MEASUREMENTS. The skull averages 20.1 (19.1–21.7) mm in length. Ranges of measurements are: total length 138–164, tail 63–72, hind foot 19–21 mm; and weight 12–18 grams. Diploid number = 44.

DISTRIBUTION. Water shrews are found in the northeastern United States from Maine to Connecticut, westward to northeastern and southeastern (Westchester County) New York and northeastern and central Pennsylvania. They are also found in Wisconsin, Michigan's Upper Peninsula and the northern part of the Lower Peninsula; and, disjunctively, in the southern Appalachians. The only individual known from New Jersey was taken in 1994 in Sussex County, about 1 km (half a mile or so) north of Warren County and 2 km (a mile or so) east of the Delaware River. *Sorex palustris* is also found over most of southern Canada to southeastern Alaska and in much of the westernmost third of the United States.

HABITAT. As their name implies, water shrews are usually near water. They often occupy the shoreline of rushing mountain streams, the sphagnum swamps bordering beaver meadows, grass/sedge marshes, or willow/grass or willow/sedge associations. They have also been taken in dry creek beds and near small springs. We have collected several on the mud flats of sluggish backwaters, and on the moss-covered boulders

of yellow birch and striped maple thickets on the slopes of Mount Katahdin, Maine.

HABITS. These little mammals swim and dive with great celerity, and can actually run on the surface of the water. Jackson (1961) observed a water shrew near Rhinelander, Wisconsin, run over 1.5 meters (almost 5 feet) across a small pool, the surface of which was glassy smooth. The head and body of the animal were entirely out of the water, the surface tension alone supporting the shrew. At each step a little globule of air appeared to be held by the fibrillae on that foot, and the globule was even discernible in the shadow at the bottom of the pool. These shrews can reduce their own metabolic demands, so as to be able to dive in cold mountain streams even in winter, and they will swim under the ice.

When swimming, water shrews use all four feet

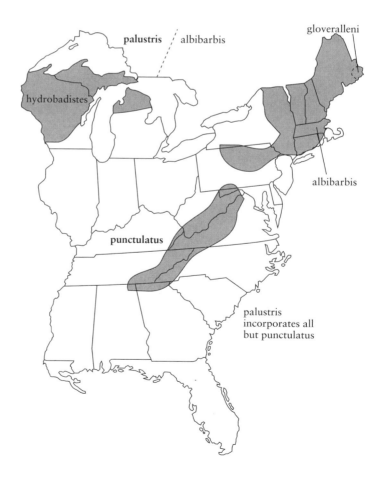

*Distribution of the water shrew,* Sorex palustris, *in the eastern United States*

in a walking motion. They have difficulty remaining underwater, however, because of air entrapped in their hair, which lends much buoyancy. On reaching the bottom, water shrews constantly probe here and there with their snouts, the feet kicking rapidly in order to maintain the nose-down position. To come to the surface they merely stop kicking and immediately rise, like a cork. They usually remain submerged from a few seconds up to a quarter of a minute, but if forced can stay under for up to three-fourths of a minute. On coming to the surface, the animal needs but a few shakes of the body and some combing with the hind feet to dry the coat.

Nests of captive water shrews, which were in tunnels or in or under hollow logs, averaged about 8 cm in diameter, but one was 33 cm across. One nest of sticks and leaves was found just above water level in a beaver lodge. Water shrews use the burrows of other animals or construct short (up to 12 cm) tunnels of their own.

FOOD AND FEEDING. Water shrews eat aquatic and nonaquatic insects and other invertebrates. Among the aquatic insects taken are stonefly, mayfly, and caddisfly nymphs and cranefly larvae. Slugs, snails, and earthworms are important. Fish, fish eggs, and salamanders have been recorded as food, as well as some plant material and the spores of the subterranean fungus *Endogone*.

The vibrissae and the sensitive nose apparently aid in the detection of prey, especially under water. Minnows are apt to be overlooked when still, but are more easily detected when they move. A friend was once troubled by finding that some small predator was continually pilfering the trout eggs from trays he had sunk in flowing water. Baiting a weighted mouse trap with these eggs, he was rewarded by catching several water shrews.

REPRODUCTION AND DEVELOPMENT. Most water shrews apparently do not produce young in the year of their birth. In Montana, first pregnancies occurred in late February. Two or three litters are produced per year, but the gestation period is unknown. It is likely around three weeks, the normal time for most shrews. The number of embryos ranges from three to ten, six being the most common.

POPULATION CHARACTERISTICS. Although the species is not often collected and densities apparently are often low, the water shrew is far more abundant than museum collections would indicate.

ENEMIES. Water snakes, garter snakes, weasels, mink, hawks and owls, and even large frogs may feed on this species. One was removed from the stomach of a trout that was caught 32 km (20 miles) north of New York City, and others have been found in fish.

PARASITES AND DISEASE. The more abundant ectoparasites of this species, at least in New Brunswick (Whitaker and French, 1982), are the hypopial mite *Glycyphagus hypudaei*, the myobiid mite *Protomyobia claparedei*, and the chigger *Miyatrombicula esoensis*. A number of other parasite species have also been identified.

RELATION TO HUMANS. This species is too small and too seldom seen to have much impact on human concerns. They do serve to help maintain the balance of nature, as do all small predators that feed heavily on insects.

AREAS FOR FURTHER WORK. One fortunate enough to live in a region where the species is common could make an interesting and worthwhile contribution to mammalogy by a close study of this handsome big shrew. A study of its feeding behavior would be especially interesting.

## SUBSPECIES

In the eastern United States, four subspecies of *Sorex palustris* are currently recognized (Hall, 1981), *S. p. punctulatus*, *S. p. hydrobadistes*, *S. p. albibarbis*, and *S. p. gloveralleni*. One of these, *S. p. punctulatus*, is found in the southern Appalachians, apparently separated geographically from the northern populations, but we have no evidence of a primary isolating mechanism among the other three, *S. p. hydrobadistes* of Wisconsin and the Upper Peninsula of Michigan, *S. p. albibarbis* of northeastern United

States and southeastern Canada, and *S. p. gloveralleni* of extreme eastern Maine, since they intergrade in Canada through *S. p. palustris*. We therefore suggest that *S. hydrobadistes* and *S. p. albibarbis* be synonymized with *S. p. palustris*, and that two subspecies be retained in the eastern United States, a northern *S. p. palustris* and a southern *S. p. punctulatus*.

### *Sorex palustris palustris* Richardson

This subspecies occurs in the northern reaches of our area. Measurements of six adults from New York and Maine averaged: total length 140, tail 66, hind foot 19 mm; and weight 12–17 grams. Otherwise, as described above.

Type locality: "Marshy places, from Hudson Bay to the Rocky Mountains."

Other currently recognized eastern subspecies:

*S. palustris gloveralleni* Jackson.
*S. palustris hydrobadistes* Jackson
*S. palustris albibarbis* (Cope)

### *Sorex palustris punctulatus* Hooper

This subspecies occurs in the southern Appalachians, where individuals are larger and have grizzled upper parts, pale-gray underparts in winter pelage, and a narrow interorbital space. Measurements of three individuals, as given in the original description, averaged: total length 152–155, tail 64–71, and hind foot 19–20 mm.

Type locality: 6 miles [10 km] northwest of Durbin, Shavers Fork of Cheat River, 3600 ft, Randolph Co., West Virginia.

### LITERATURE

Beneski, J. T., Jr., and D. W. Stinson. 1987. *Sorex palustris*. **Mammalian Species No. 296.** Amer. Soc. Mammal. 6 pp.

Conaway, C. H. 1952. Life history of the water shrew (*Sorex palustris navigator*). *Amer. Midland Nat.* 48: 219–248.

Hall, E. R. 1981. *The Mammals of North America.* New York: John Wiley & Sons. 2 vols., 1181 pp.

Jackson, H. H. T. 1961. *Mammals of Wisconsin.* Madison: Univ. Wisconsin Press. 504 pp.

Whitaker, J. O., Jr., and T. W. French. 1982. Ectoparasites and other associates of some insectivores and rodents from New Brunswick. *Canadian J. Zool.* 60: 2787–2797.

## Shrews of the Genus *Blarina*

These shrews are very large, dark-colored, and short-tailed. They are collectively, one of the very few kinds of mammals that possess poison, and one of the few insectivores that practice food storage. Short-tailed shrews are often mistaken for moles or voles.

KEY TO THE SHORT-TAILED SHREWS
OF THE GENUS *BLARINA*

1. Hind foot (including claw) 13 mm long or longer; condylobasal length of skull 20 mm or greater . . . . . . . . . . . . . . . . . . . . . *B. brevicauda*
1. Hind foot less than 13 mm long; condylobasal length of skull less than 20 mm . . . . . *B. carolinensis*

## Northern Short-Tailed Shrew
### *Blarina brevicauda* (Say)　　　Color plate 1

DESCRIPTION. *Blarina brevicauda* is a large, short-tailed, slate-colored shrew. The short legs,

*Northern short-tailed shrew,* Blarina brevicauda *(Roger W. Barbour)*

minute eyes, and concealed ears are good field characteristics. The sharp-pointed muzzle, which becomes relatively blunt in older individuals, is not nearly so pointed as those of the long-tailed shrews. All New World shrews have deep reddish-brown- or chestnut-tipped teeth, the color becoming less noticeable as the tooth wears down with advancing age. Adults are slaty above and paler beneath; new fur is glossy; and the tail and the feet are dark gray above and paler below. Young short-tails are much darker than the adults, and sometimes appear almost black. Individuals from the Dismal

Swamp of Virginia are more plumbeous and have relatively longer hind feet and a narrower skull.

MEASUREMENTS. Measurements of 60 males (weights for 53) from Indiana averaged: total length 115 (100–126), tail 23 (19–28), hind foot 14.3 (9–16) mm; and weight 17.5 (11.0–26.3) grams. Of 69 females (weights for 67), they averaged: 111.5 (95–125), 22.3 (17–26), 14.2 (9–20) mm; and weight 16.3 (11.4–24.8) grams. Average measurements of 60 adults of both sexes from central New York were: total length 124, tail 24.8, hind foot 15 mm; and the weights of 50 adults of both sexes averaged 19.3 grams. Large individuals may weigh 27 grams, whereas juveniles weigh but 12–15 grams.
  Diploid number = 48 to 50.

DISTRIBUTION. *Blarina brevicauda* is found in the eastern United States from Maine and Wisconsin south to Kentucky and northern Tennessee, and in the mountains to Georgia and Alabama. The species is replaced to the south by a smaller form, *B. carolinensis*. A large *Blarina* was described from Lee County, Florida, as *B. brevicauda shermani*, but we have followed George et al. (Mammalian Species, 1986), who recognize it as a subspecies of *B. carolinensis*. George et al. stated that it "may [yet] prove to be an isolated subspecies of *B. brevicauda* or still another species of *Blarina*." To the west, *blarina brevicauda* occurs to central Nebraska and most of North Dakota; to the north, it ranges across southern Canada to southwestern Saskatchewan.

HABITAT. The ubiquitous *Blarina* is found in a wide variety of habitats, from the salt marshes of the coastal areas to stunted timber growth on the mountains. Because *Blarina* loses much water via evaporation through the skin, it thus requires free water and cannot tolerate unduly hot or dry conditions. In the more northern parts of its range, for example in New York and Michigan, it is found in a variety of habitats, so long as there is enough moisture in the soil to maintain 100% saturation in the air in its burrows. In southern Indiana, Kentucky, and Tennessee, however, it tends to be more restricted to moist woods.

HABITS. The powerful little paws and stout, cartilaginous nose of *Blarina* are real assets as it plows through leaf mold and forest litter, or burrows in the loose, damp soil. It is often very common in such situations, and often finds other animals in traps, leaving nothing but a neatly turned-back skin and a few bones.
  The burrows of this species are usually in the top 10 cm of soil, but may be as deep as 50 cm. They are flattened at top and bottom, and thus can be distinguished from other small-mammal burrows, which are usually more circular in cross section. *Blarina* will burrow under and along rocks and other objects, and will often use the burrows of microtines and moles. Short-tailed shrews dig with their front feet, and kick excess soil from the burrow with the hind feet. If necessary, they will turn around in the burrow and push dirt out with their noses, in bulldozer fashion.
  Shrews are often thought of as solitary, ferocious little beasts, and indeed, when Whitaker put his finger in an aquarium containing a Blarina, the shrew immediately came running over, took one sniff of the finger, and bit it. He suffered no pain or after-effects from toxin. Sometimes, when short-tailed shrews have been kept together in captivity, they have cowered when mice were put in with them. But at other times, the mice were immediately attacked and killed. Jack L. Gottschang, however, kept a house mouse and a short-tailed shrew together in a small cage for many months.
  Shrews' eyes are degenerate, and sight is probably limited to the detection of light, but *Blarina* has a well-developed repertoire of squeaks and clicks, including ultrasonic sounds, for navigation and predation. Gould et al. (1964) first demonstrated that shrews were using echolocation in exploring their environment; and Tomasi (1979) found that echolocation could be used by *Blarina* to locate burrow entrances, determine whether they were open or plugged, and distinguish between the different sorts of material plugging them. They can even use this ability to distinguish openings around corners. The clicks recorded in these echolocation studies ranged from 30 to 55 kHz in frequency.

FOOD AND FEEDING. Most shrews, including *Blarina brevicauda*, feed principally upon the teeming invertebrate fauna that they find in the soil. Earthworms are by far the single most important food of this species, followed by slugs and snails, lepidopterous larvae, and other insects. Spiders, centipedes, and to a lesser extent small salamanders, mice, and an occasional bird are also eaten. A captive 14.8-gram *Blarina* consumed an average of 25.6 grams of food (crayfish and minnows) per day over a ten-day period, and an average of 9.1 cc of water per day over five days (Edgren, 1948). The feces, about 2.5 cm long, dark green, and twisted, are deposited in piles, often along the sides of the burrows. Short-tailed shrews practice at least limited food storage.

*Blarina* and the European water shrew, *Neomys fodiens*, are apparently the only mammals that produce a toxic secretion in the salivary glands. Pearson (1942) studied the toxin in *Blarina* in detail. This poison is secreted from a duct at the base of the incisors and apparently flows along the groove between the two pincerlike incisors. The toxin, introduced into a wound made by the teeth of the shrew, has been found to be powerful enough to kill small mammals, through respiratory failure, when injected by the investigator. A dose of 5.7 mg is lethal for a 20-gram mouse. Some authors have described painful effects upon being bitten (Krosch, 1973). Apparently, the toxin functions primarily in immobilizing smaller prey, particularly snails, so that they can be stored for later use (Tomasi, 1978; Martin, 1981). One often finds piles of stored snails, or the remains of them, in and around *Blarina* burrows. Martin (1984) found that storage occurred mostly in fall and winter, or in times when an overabundance of food was available. *Blarina* is often said to feed frequently on small rodents, but although stomach-contents analysis has not to date supported this claim, it will feed on small mammals, especially the young, under conditions of high small-

angusta
pallida
hooperi
talpoides
aloga
compacta
brevicauda
kirtlandi
telmalestes
churchi
brevicauda
incorporates all
but aloga
and compacta

*Distribution of the northern short-tailed shrew,* Blarina brevicauda, *in the eastern United States*

mammal population. The function of the toxin in the European water shrew, which feeds on sizable fish and frogs, is thought to be to weaken the prey (Churchfield, 1985).

Plant food, including roots, beechnuts, and berries, is also eaten. Martinson (1969) maintained *Blarina* on cracked corn, and Whitaker once found several caches of corn in winter in the burrow labyrinth of *Blarina* under an old sheet of plywood. *Blarina* limits its activity in winter, thus conserving energy, and the food caches help limit energy spent foraging. The subterranean fungus *Endogone* and its relatives are often eaten by *Blarina* and many other small mammals. The spores are found probably by smell, in the litter or upper layers of the soil. The spores appear as grains of dirt at 10 times magnification of the dissecting microscope, but at higher powers one can see that the spores form grapelike bunches with single stems.

REPRODUCTION AND DEVELOPMENT. The northern short-tailed shrew constructs a bulky nest of partly shredded leaves and grasses, beneath some fallen log or stump. Here the young are born, from early spring until late September. The young usually number four to six per litter, but as many as nine have been recorded. Three and perhaps four litters are produced each year, but there are two peaks of breeding, one in spring and one in late summer or early fall.

The testes remain always inside the body cavity, not in a scrotal sac, and the testis varies in length from about 3 mm in winter to three times that in the breeding season. Copulation may last up to 25 minutes, with the male and female locked together, the male all the while inactive and dragged around by the female. At least 20 matings were observed in one pair in one day; the multiple matings are apparently necessary to induce ovulation, which does not occur in the absence of copulation. Gestation is about 21 or 22 days, and weaning (females have three pairs of inguinal mammae) is at about 25 days. Hamilton (1929) described the development, from birth, of a litter of the naked "honeybee"-sized newborn, their eyes and ears still closed. At two days, standard measurements were total length 31, tail 4, and hind foot 4.5 mm; and weight averaged 1.34 grams. At eight days, they were 61, 9.5, and 9 mm, respectively; and 6.2 grams. Hair had appeared, but the teeth had not erupted; at this stage, the young produced a sucking sound and could crawl. At 13 days they measured 73, 12, and 16 mm, respectively, and their weight averaged 9.9 grams. Young shrews thus grow amazingly fast and are half-grown when they are just a month old, which accounts for the fact that nearly all shrews seem to be full grown when trapped. But in spite of their reproductive capability, it is probable that shrews, unlike many mice, do not breed during the season in which they are born.

POPULATION CHARACTERISTICS. In some years the woods fairly swarm with these shrews, but at other times they are quite scarce. Population-density estimates range from 1.6 to 121 per ha (1 to 50 per acre). Home-range size has been estimated at about 2.5 ha (6 acres), although this seems to us much too high; our observation of central New York tunnels indicated that the range of individuals was less than 0.25 ha (0.6 acre). The life of these shrews is short: 6% of the individuals marked by Oliver Pearson one year were recaptured the next; and L. J. Blus (1971) found that 11.1% lived more than one year.

ENEMIES. Owing to their great numbers and small size, short-tailed shrews have many enemies, but many predators discard them because of their odor. The odor arises from a pair of glands located on the sides near the flanks, and is particularly strong-smelling during the reproductive season. It appears to function in indicating the presence of a male *Blarina* in a tunnel, signaling other males not to enter. Often, one is aware, even before a trap is seen, that the trap has taken a shrew, since even the poorly equipped human nose can detect this odor. House cats may be their most important enemy, but hawks, owls, weasels, skunks, snakes, fish, and others kill great numbers.

PARASITES AND DISEASE. Both ecto- and endoparasites are abundant on or in this host. In Indiana, 181 individuals of *Blarina brevicauda* examined yielded averages of 0.46, 1.59, and 4.40 intestinal roundworms, flukes, and tapeworms, respectively, per shrew; and a subcutaneous nematode, *Porrocaecum encapsulatum*, is common. At least 32 species of ectoparasites and other associates were found in the fur of 92 individuals, the most abundant being the mites *Asiochirus blarina*, *Orycteroxenus soricis*, *Androlaelaps fahrenholzi*, *Myonyssus jamesoni*, and *Haemogamasus liponyssoides*, several mites of the genus *Pygmephorus*, and the fleas *Ctenophthalmus pseudagyrtes* and *Doratopsylla blarinae*.

RELATION TO HUMANS. These shrews are beneficial little creatures. They do no damage to our crops, but are of service in helping to control insect populations (see Anderson and Folk, 1993). It is said that in New Brunswick they once destroyed 60% of the larch sawfly population.

AREAS FOR FURTHER WORK. Shrews of this species are known to echolocate, but little is known of the natural conditions under which this occurs. Short-tailed shrews harbor many parasites, and the relation between their parasites and the fauna occurring in their nests would be of interest. Adult mites of the genus *Orycteroxenus* and males of the genus *Pygmephorus*, not yet known to science, could be sought. More information is needed on how much food this and other shrews eat per day.

## SUBSPECIES

Because most of the described subspecies of this species apparently intergrade with one another, we have accepted just four of them.

*Blarina brevicauda brevicauda* (Say)

As described above.

Type locality: West bank of Missouri River, near Blair (formerly Engineer Cantonment), Washington Co., Nebraska.

Other currently recognized eastern subspecies:

B. *brevicauda angusta* (Anderson)
B. *brevicauda churchi* Bole & Moulthrop
B. *brevicauda hooperi* Bole & Moulthrop
B. *brevicauda kirtlandi* Bole & Moulthrop
B. *brevicauda pallida* Smith
B. *brevicauda talpoides* (Gapper)

*Blarina brevicauda aloga* Bangs

Known only from Martha's Vineyard, Dukes Co., Massachusetts, this form is smaller than the mainland form and has a "dark brownish back and very pale—almost whitish—underparts; and . . . a short skull, the rostral portion of which is much broader and stronger, and the nasal aperture larger" than in the mainland form. The border between the dark dorsum and light underparts, including where it passes along the tail, is sharply demarcated. The feet are lighter than those of northeastern mainland individuals. Measurements of ten individuals averaged: total length 119.4 (113–128), tail 25.3 (23–29), hind foot 14.3 (14–15) mm.

Type locality: West Tisbury, Martha's Vineyard, Dukes Co., Mass.

*Blarina brevicauda compacta* Bangs

Known only from Nantucket Island, Massachusetts, this subspecies resembles B. *b. aloga* in size and skull form, but differs greatly in color. It is darker below and more plumbeous above, thus is more like the mainland individuals. Measurements of seven individuals were: total length 117.4 (110–129), tail 23.3 (22–25.5), hind foot 14.4 (13.5–15.0) mm.

Type locality: Nantucket Island, Nantucket Co., Massachusetts.

*Blarina brevicauda telmalestes* Merriam

Known from Dismal Swamp, Virginia, and North Carolina, this subspecies is surrounded by populations of the smaller *Blarina carolinensis*, and is apparently not contiguous with other populations of its own species. Thus this form is separated by a primary isolating mechanism of geographical nature. The measurements of 13 individuals from Lake Drummond, Dismal Swamp, averaged: total length 119.5 (118–128), tail 26.4 (26.4–28), hind foot 16–17 mm.

Type locality: Lake Drummond, Dismal Swamp, Norfolk Co., Virginia.

### LITERATURE

Anderson, D. C., and M. L. Folk. 1993. *Blarina brevicauda* and *Peromyscus leucopus* reduce overwinter survivorship of acorn weevils in an Indiana hardwood forest. *J. Mammal.* 74: 656–664.

Blus, L. J. 1971. Reproduction and survival of short-tailed shrews (*Blarina brevicauda*) in captivity. *Lab. Anim. Sci.* 21: 884–891.

Churchfield, S. 1985. The feeding ecology of the European water shrew. *Mammal Revue* 15: 13–21.

Edgren, R. A. 1948. Notes on a northern short-tailed shrew. Nat. Hist. Misc. Chicago Acad. Sci. No. 25. 2 pp.

George, S. B., J. R. Choate, and H. H. Genoways. 1986. *Blarina brevicauda*. **Mammalian Species No. 261.** Amer. Soc. Mammal. 9 pp.

George, S. B., H. H. Genoways, J. R. Choate, and R. J. Baker. 1982. Karyotypic relationships within the short-tailed shrews, genus *Blarina*. *J. Mammal.* 63: 639–645.

Gould, E., N. C. Negus, and A. Novick. 1964. Evidence for echolocation in shrews. *J. Exp. Zool.* 156: 19–38.

Hamilton, W. J., Jr. 1929. Breeding habits of the short-tailed shrew, *Blarina brevicauda*. *J. Mammal.* 10: 125–134.

Krosch, H. F. 1973. Some effects of the bite of the short-tailed shrew, *Blarina brevicauda*. *J. Minn. Acad. Sci.* 39: 21.

Martin, I. G. 1981. Venom of the short-tailed shrew (*Blarina brevicauda*) as an insect immobilizing agent. *J. Mammal.* 62: 189–192.

———. 1984. Factors affecting food hoarding in the short-tailed shrew, *Blarina brevicauda*. *Mammalia* 46: 65–71.

Martinsen, D. L. 1969. Energetics and activity patterns of short-tailed shrews (*Blarina*) on restricted diets. *Ecology* 50: 505–510.

Merritt, J. F. 1986. Winter survival adaptations of the short-tailed shrew (*Blarina brevicauda*) in an Appalachian montane forest. *J. Mammal.* 67: 450–464.

Pearson, O. P. 1942. On the cause and nature of a poisonous action produced by the bite of a shrew *Blarina brevicauda*. *J. Mammal.* 23: 159–166.

Tomasi, T. E. 1978. Function of venom in the short-tailed shrew, *Blarina brevicauda*. *J. Mammal.* 59: 852–854.

———. 1979. Echolocation by the short-tailed shrew *Blarina brevicauda*. *J. Mammal.* 60: 751–759.

## Southern Short-Tailed Shrew
## *Blarina carolinensis* (Bachman)

DESCRIPTION. This species is the small southern counterpart of *Blarina brevicauda*, the total length of large individuals running not much over 100 mm. The skull is less massive than that of *B. brevicauda*, and the fifth unicuspid, visible in *B. brevicauda*, is usually not visible from the outside in the southern species.

*Southern short-tailed shrew,* Blarina carolinensis *(Roger W. Barbour)*

MEASUREMENTS. Measurements of 17 individuals from northern Florida (weights for 11) were: total length 92.2 (89–102), tail 21 (18–26), hind foot 12.5 (11.5–14) mm; and weight 8.0 (5.5–10.3) grams. Thirty-nine individuals from Virginia and North Carolina measured: total length 95.6 (84–107), tail 19.3 (15–23), hind foot 12.3 (11–15) mm.

There is much karyotypic variation in this species. Excluding *B. c. peninsulae*, *Blarina carolinensis* has a fundamental number of 44 or 45 and diploid numbers of 37, 38, 39, and 46. *Blarina carolinensis peninsulae* has a fundamental number of 52 and diploid numbers of 50 and 52.

DISTRIBUTION. This shrew occurs in the austro-riparian fauna from Virginia, Tennessee, and southern Illinois southward. It is unknown in the southern Alleghenies. The range of this species extends west to eastern Texas and southern Nebraska.

HABITAT. Shrews of this species occur primarily in damp woods.

HABITS. Though the habits of this species have not been well studied, they are presumably similar to those of *Blarina brevicauda*, and much that is said about *Blarina brevicauda* presumably applies here also.

PARASITES AND DISEASE. David Pascal (unpubl.) compared the ectoparasites of this species with those from *Blarina brevicauda*, and found that although the two ectoparasite communities contained the same major species, there were significant differences in relative abundances.

RELATION TO HUMANS. Southern short-tailed shrews, like their northern counterparts, are beneficial in helping to control insects.

AREAS FOR FURTHER WORK. Relatively little information is available on this species. Its life history could be compared in detail to that of *B. brevicauda*. Moreover, what are the status and taxonomic position of *Blarina carolinensis* (or *brevicauda*) *shermani*, if indeed it still exists?

## SUBSPECIES

In southern Illinois (Ellis et al., 1978) and in south-central Virginia (Tate et al., 1980), *Blarina carolinensis* and *B. brevicauda* occur together, thus providing us two eastern U.S. field tests of whether these are both good species.

The conclusion is that they are, since they live side by side but remain distinct, at least in these two areas. The taxonomic status of the southern short-tailed shrew of peninsular Florida, *B. c. peninsulae*, which may represent a separate species, needs further work (see below).

*Blarina carolinensis carolinensis* (Bachman)

As described above.

Type locality: Eastern South Carolina.

Other currently recognized eastern subspecies:
  *B. carolinensis minima* Lowery

*Blarina carolinensis peninsulae* Merriam

*Blarina* from peninsular Florida differs from more northern *B. carolinensis* in being uniformly slate-black above and duller below, and in lacking the sepia-brown tint of its more northern relatives. In addition, it has a larger hind foot and a more massive skull and teeth. The diploid number is 50 or 52; the fundamen-

*Distribution of the southern short-tailed shrew,* Blarina carolinensis, *in the eastern United States*

tal number is 52. *Blarina c. peninsulae* is thus sufficiently different to be considered a separate species (see George et al., 1982), but we do not know the relationship between *B. c. carolinensis* and *B. c. peninsulae* where they meet geographically. George et al. add that the "karyotype and polymorphism [of *peninsulae*] are most similar to those of *B. brevicauda*, suggesting a close affinity to that species." Much more work is needed, but these differences, especially the karyotypic ones but also the morphological ones, would indicate that very little if any gene flow is occurring between *peninsulae* and *carolinensis*. Thus we have accepted *B. c. peninsulae* as a valid biological subspecies, a form occurring only in peninsular Florida. Measurements of 17 individuals of this taxon were: total length 97 (82–110), tail 21.3 (18–25), hind foot 12 (10–14) mm; and weight 9.9 (8.1–11) grams.

Type locality: Miami River, Dade Co., Florida.

*Blarina carolinensis shermani* Hamilton

Short-tailed shrews from Fort Myers, Florida (now likely extirpated), are similar to the large northern *Blarina brevicauda*, but geographically separated. The Fort Myers population is surrounded by populations of *B. c. peninsulae* (which itself is likely wrongly classed), from which it differs in being larger and darker. George et al. (1986) recognize this as a subspecies of *B. carolinensis*, but state that it could be an isolated population of *B. brevicauda* or a new species. Known only from the type locality. Measurements of 27 individuals of this subspecies were: total length 109 (100–116), tail 23.5 (22–25), hind foot 14.1 (13.5–15) mm; and weight 13.8 (11.1–17.0) grams.

Type locality: 2 mi [3 km] north of Fort Myers, Lee Co., Florida.

## Literature

Ellis, L. S., V. E. Diersing, and D. F. Hoffmeister. 1978. Taxonomic status of short-tailed shrews (*Blarina*) in Illinois. *J. Mammal.* 59: 305–311.

Genoways, H. H., J. C. Patton III, and J. R. Choate. 1977. Karyotypes of shrews of the genera *Cryptotis* and *Blarina* (Mammalia: Soricidae). *Experientia* 33: 1294–1295.

George, S. B., H. H. Genoways, J. R. Choate, and R. J. Baker. 1982. Karyotypic relationships within the short-tailed shrews, genus *Blarina*. *J. Mammal.* 63: 639–645.

Pascal, D. D., Jr. 1984. A taxonomic study of midwestern short-tailed shrews (genus *Blarina*) with emphasis upon their ectoparasites. Unpubl. Ph.D. diss., Indiana State University. 185 pp.

Tate, C. M., J. F. Pagels, and C. O. Handley, Jr. 1980. Distribution and systematic relationship of two kinds of short-tailed shrews (Soricidae: *Blarina*) in south central Virginia. *Proc. Biol. Soc. Wash.* 93: 50–60.

## Least Shrew
### *Cryptotis parva* (Say)      Color plate 1

DESCRIPTION. The least shrew seemingly is a small, brownish *Blarina*, only slightly smaller

*Least shrew,* Cryptotis parva, *with earthworm (Roger W. Barbour)*

than *B. carolinensis*, but it may be immediately distinguished from *Blarina* by examining the dentition: in *Cryptotis parva* there are four unicuspids on each side, in contrast to the five of *Blarina*. Summer pelage is brown or sepia, the winter pelage brownish gray to slate, silver-gray below; the slender tail is similarly colored. Individuals from Florida and southeast Georgia are somewhat darker and have somewhat longer tails.

MEASUREMENTS. Measurements of ten New York and Virginia adults averaged: total length 83, tail 17.5, hind foot 11 mm. Twenty-five specimens from Raleigh, North Carolina, averaged: total length 75, tail 16.4, hind foot 10.6 mm; and weight 4.5–5 grams. Measurements of five adults from southeastern Georgia and Florida averaged: total length 79.5, tail 21, hind foot 11 mm; and weight 4–5 grams.

Diploid number = 52.

DISTRIBUTION. *Cryptotis parva* is found from southern Wisconsin, southern Michigan, and central New York south throughout the eastern United States. Across the Mississippi, it occurs to southern South Dakota, northeastern Nebraska, eastern Texas, and south through much of central America.

HABITAT. This diminutive shrew has been trapped in the marshes about New York City, and in New Jersey and Virginia, but in the northern part of its range the species generally inhabits grassy, weedy, and brushy fields. In Indiana we have taken over 200 individuals, all of them in these more customary habitats, none in woods, and none in marshy areas. In the southern part of its range the species occurs in a greater variety of habitats, including woods. In Florida it lives along lake shores in the dense hammocks of the prostrate saw palmetto (*Sere-*

*noa repens*), in marshy areas, or in the pine-woods, or travels the twisting runways of the cotton rats in old fields grown to weeds and sedges. We have caught several in traps that we had placed in *Sigmodon* runways.

HABITS. The life history of the least shrew is not well known, because the species is seldom seen. It must be much more common than is supposed, for owl pellets often contain a surprisingly large number in the very regions where the mammalogist has failed to take it.

The runways of least shrews in the grass are almost the size of a lead pencil. Their burrows are about 13 mm high and 18 mm wide. Davis and Joeris (1945) observed two least shrews building a tunnel together. The nest is a ball of shredded leaves and grasses under a rock slab, stump, or log, or in a shallow tunnel. Hamilton found two nests containing five and three occu-

*Distribution of the least shrew,* Cryptotis parva, *in the eastern United States*

pants, all adults. Davis and Joeris (1945) found 12 individuals in a nest in Texas. H. H. T. Jackson (1961) found 25 individuals in one nest in Virginia, and McCarley (1959) found at least 31 individuals in a nest 100 by 150 mm, also in Texas. These data indicate that least shrews tolerate one another, or possibly even welcome each other, a disposition not generally accredited to shrews. A nest in Florida, of leaves of panic grass under a saw palmetto, was about 13 cm in diameter. Several tunnels led from the nest, which was occupied by just two shrews.

Stewart Springer records four of these shrews huddled together under brush at Englewood, Florida, and two of them lived amicably together for several days. They uttered a noise that Springer likened to the call of a flicker heard at a considerable distance, though it was audible for only about 50 cm (20 inches). Edwin Gould (1969) described twitters, "puts," and clicks from this species, some of them from a nine-day-old young.

FOOD AND FEEDING. The least shrew eats various small insects, mollusks, spiders, and earthworms. Major foods in 109 Indiana specimens, in decreasing order of use, were lepidopterous larvae, beetle larvae, slugs and snails, spiders, and crickets (Whitaker and Mumford, 1972). Digestion is rapid; the consistency of fecal material changed within two hours of a change in diet (Davis and Joeris, 1945). One of the shrews kept by Stewart Springer lived more than a month and ate tree frogs, small-mouth toads, lizards, and a 23-cm (9-inch) crown snake (*Tantilla*), in addition to crickets. The shrew subdued crickets and grasshoppers by biting them in the head. Small insects were entirely eaten, but only the internal organs of the larger ones were eaten, and excess insects were stored in the burrows. The shrew frequently drank water. Its initial weight was 4.97 grams, and it consumed an average of 5.5 grams of food per 24-hour period, the daily totals ranging from 3.5 to 8.1 grams. Thus, like some other species, it averaged more than its own weight in food per day.

This species has been called the "bee shrew" because it has been known to build its nest in beehives, feeding upon the bees and their lar-

vae. In 1985, however, we checked with beekeepers throughout Indiana, and found none that knew of this behavior, although mice (*Peromyscus*) frequently nest in the hives over winter.

REPRODUCTION AND DEVELOPMENT. Breeding is from March to November in the north, but may occur throughout the year in the south. Several litters, numbering from two to seven young each (mean of 4.9), may be produced per year, with gestation about 21–23 days. A female and her nearly grown litter of six young were taken from a nest in eastern Kentucky during mid-April by W. Welter and D. Sollberger. The combined weight of the litter was 17.5 grams, and the mother weighed but 5.4 grams. Before they were fully weaned, the young nursed from a parent weighing one-third as much as the combined youngsters. These authors observed that the mother killed the insects that the young then fed upon. Hamilton captured a female from a salt marsh at Chincoteague, Virginia, that gave birth to six tiny, naked young, the combined weight of these not exceeding 2 grams. Measurements of a newborn weighing 0.32 gram were: total length 22, tail 3, and hind foot 2.5 mm. Vibrissae were already present, but no trace of teeth was seen. Hair developed by the 20th day, and the eyes opened by day 14. Weight at 6 days was 1.0–1.8 grams, at 15 days it was 2.7 grams, at 25 days 3.7–4.6 grams, and it reached the adult level at about one month (Conaway, 1958). The young are not weaned until nearly three weeks old.

POPULATION CHARACTERISTICS. Howell (1954) estimated the home range for *Cryptotis* at 0.23 ha (0.57 acre) for one female and 0.17 ha (0.41 acre) for one male. He estimated population density at at least 1.7 per ha (0.7 per acre), although he thought that this was low, and that the actual value might have been about 5 per ha (2 per acre). One individual kept by Pfeiffer and Gass (1963) from the time it was a nestling died at 21 months, of old age, they thought.

ENEMIES. Owls are probably the chief enemies of this shrew. W. B. Davis (1938) reported the remains of 171 *Cryptotis* in the pellets of barn owls in Texas. These constituted 41% of the total number of mammals taken, and there are many other such reports, from later years. These records indicate not only the abundance of these shrews at times, but the importance of the owl as a predator. Hawks, snakes, and predatory mammals, including dogs and cats, also capture these shrews, as the opportunity affords. In 1949, James B. Cope (1949) found 27 of these shrews (and one *Blarina*) in the digestive system of a rough-legged hawk taken in midwinter in Indiana.

PARASITES AND DISEASE. Few endoparasites were found in the 139 *Cryptotis* digestive tracts examined from Indiana, but the hypopial mite *Orycteroxenus soricis*, found on most species of shrew, was abundant on this host. The flea *Corrodopsylla hamiltoni* was the second most abundant, followed by three other mites, *Androlaelaps fahrenholzi*, *Protomyobia americana*, and *Echinonyssus talpae*.

RELATION TO HUMANS. Like other shrews, this species feeds heavily on insects, but otherwise has relatively little direct relation to human concerns.

AREAS FOR FURTHER WORK. This species is found in much drier situations and is much more social than are other shrews, suggesting that a comparative study of its physiology and behavior would be of interest. Do the young follow one another in train fashion, each one grasping the tail of the one ahead with its mouth, and the first grasping the tail of the mother, as do some Eurasian shrews? Ronald Richards observed caravaning of this sort in unidentified shrews in Bloomington, Indiana, in the fall of 1966. One larger and three smaller shrews emerged from an armful of damp weeds, each linked to the tail of the shrew ahead of it. Richards wondered if these might be *C. parva*.

## SUBSPECIES

*Cryptotis parva parva* (Say)
  As described above.
  Type locality: West bank of the Missouri River near Blair, formerly Engineer Cantonment, Washington Co., Nebraska.

Other currently recognized eastern subspecies:
  *C. parva elasson* Bole & Moulthrop
  *C. parva floridana* (Merriam)
  *C. parva harlani* (Duvernoy)

## LITERATURE

Conaway, C. H. 1958. Maintenance, reproduction, and growth of the least shrew in captivity. *J. Mammal.* 39: 507–512.
Davis, W. B. 1938. A heavy concentration of *Cryptotis*. *J. Mammal.* 19: 499–500.
Davis, W. B., and L. Joeris. 1945. Notes on the life history of the little short-tailed shrew. *J. Mammal.* 26: 136–138.
Gould, E. 1969. Communication in three genera of shrews (Soricidae): *Suncus*, *Blarina* and *Cryptotis*. *Comm. Behav. Biol.*, part A, 3: 11–31.
Howell, J. C. 1954. Populations and home ranges of small mammals on an overgrown field. *J. Mammal.* 35: 177–186.
Jackson, H. H. T. 1961. *Mammals of Wisconsin*. Madison: Univ. Wisconsin Press. 504 pp.
McCarley, W. H. 1959. An unusually large nest of *Cryptotis parva*. *J. Mammal.* 40: 243.
Pfeiffer, C. J., and G. H. Gass. 1963. Note on the longevity and habits of captive *Cryptotis parva*. *J. Mammal.* 44: 427–428.
Whitaker, J. O., Jr. 1974. *Cryptotis parva*. **Mammalian Species No. 43.** Amer. Soc. Mammal. 8 pp.
Whitaker, J. O., Jr., and R. E. Mumford. 1972. Food and ectoparasites of Indiana shrews. *J. Mammal.* 53: 329–335.

## MOLES, Family Talpidae

Moles are relatively large, burrowing insectivores highly modified for a fossorial existence. Their eyes are reduced and barely functional. Their forelimbs—enlarged, turned outward, and tipped with very large claws—are potent digging tools. Moles are almost completely fossorial and their soft and velvety fur can lie in either direction, a modification that permits movement either backward or forward in their burrows. Their teeth are sharp, like those of shrews, but unlike those of New World shrews, they are white. The zygomatic arch is complete. In moles, the testes and the rest of the male reproductive tract become extremely large during the breeding season, forming as much as 14% of total body weight. There is but one litter per year in moles, but this rate of procreation is sufficient to maintain population size, because predation on animals that remain below ground most of the time is low. Growth is rapid in moles, and the young are nearly full grown when they leave the nest to fend for themselves. Moles are good swimmers.

Worldwide, there are 17 genera and 42 species of moles. They occur in North America, from southern Canada to northern Mexico, and in central Eurasia. Three species occur in the eastern United States.

### Key to the Genera and Species of the Family Talpidae

1. Tail long, to 60 mm or more; snout with a fleshy rosette of tentacles; third incisor resembling a canine . . . . . *Condylura cristata* (p. 70)
1. Tail short, less than 40 mm; snout plain; third incisor not resembling a canine . . . . . . . . . . . . . . 2
2. Tail naked; first upper incisor simple . . . . . . . . . . . . . . *Scalopus aquaticus* (p. 66)
2. Tail densely furred; first upper incisor bearing an accessory cusp . . . . . . . . . . *Parascalops breweri*

### Hairy-Tailed Mole *Parascalops breweri* (Bachman)    Color plate 2

DESCRIPTION. The hairy-tailed mole is our only eastern mole with a short, hairy tail. The color

*Hairy-tailed mole,* Parascalops breweri
*(Roger W. Barbour)*

is dark slate to black, slightly paler below. The small eyes are well hidden in the fur, and the soft, thick fur is slightly coarser than that of *Scalopus.*

MEASUREMENTS. Average measurements of 20 adults from New Hampshire, New York, and Pennsylvania were: total length 158 (150–170), tail 27.5 (24–30), hind foot 19 (17–21) mm. Males are slightly larger than females, and weights vary from 40 to 64 grams.

Diploid number = 34.

TOOTH FORMULA

$$\frac{3}{3} \quad \frac{1}{1} \quad \frac{4}{4} \quad \frac{3}{3} \ = \ 44$$

DISTRIBUTION. The hairy-tailed mole ranges through much of the northeastern United States and adjacent Canada, excluding the coast, occurring from southern New Brunswick and Quebec south to the mountains of Virginia, West Virginia, Kentucky, Tennessee, and North Carolina, and west through much of Ohio.

HABITAT. These moles occur from near sea level in the northern part of their range to altitudes of 3000 feet or more in the Appalachians. Their usual habitats range from pasture lands supporting shrubs to well-wooded forests of birch, hemlock, and pines. *Parascalops* prefers a well-drained, light soil, and is seldom taken in wet areas or clay soils. It is most abundant in sandy loams containing sufficient moisture.

HABITS. Hairy-tailed moles are active day or night, probably more so in the daytime, and during the night they often wander from their tunnels to feed on the forest floor. This habit is reflected in the numbers that are caught by cats and other nocturnal predators. Moles of this species have several glands that produce a yellowish liquid and a characteristic odor, especially in females. The irregular and abundant subsurface runways they construct may form a complete network of highways, but the deeper, permanent tunnels are fewer. As winter approaches, these deeper tunnels are repaired or new ones are made, and with the advent of freezing temperatures the mole deserts the upper strata of tunnels and occupies these deeper burrows. The surface ridges produced by tunneling are much less prominent in *Parascalops* than in *Scalopus* or *Condylura*, although excess dirt is often pushed to the surface as molehills, especially in wet weather. Philip L. Wright (1945) wrote of a burrow that was in use up to eight years. Nests about 15 cm (6 inches) in diameter, constructed of dead leaves, are placed 25 to 50 cm (10 to 20 inches) below the surface.

FOOD AND FEEDING. These moles feed chiefly upon earthworms, insects and their larvae, centipedes and millipedes, ants, and other arthropods. A captive mole that weighed 50 grams devoured 66 grams of earthworms and insect larvae in 24 hours. Moles may store earthworms after they have induced paralysis by biting them. Scats, deposited outside the burrows, are cylindrical, tapered at both ends, and about 2.5 by 10 mm long.

REPRODUCTION AND DEVELOPMENT. Mating occurs in late March or early April. The single litter, comprising four or five young (one report was of eight), is produced in late April or May after a gestation period of probably a month to six weeks. The young are blind and helpless at birth, but, like other moles, grow rapidly and are probably weaned and able to shift for themselves when about four weeks old. At this point they are about 13–18 grams shy of the adult weights, and they are sexually mature the following spring. As in other moles, there is a great increase in testis size from nonbreeding to breeding season, from about 2 by 3 mm to 7 by 12 mm. A copulatory plug is formed after mating.

POPULATION CHARACTERISTICS. The hairy-tailed mole is undoubtedly more abundant than trapping records indicate. During the breeding season, W. Robert Eadie (1939) took 11 specimens from an acre in New Hampshire, but this high yield probably represents an influx into an unusually suitable habitat. Normally, this species occurs at rates of about three per ha (1.2 per

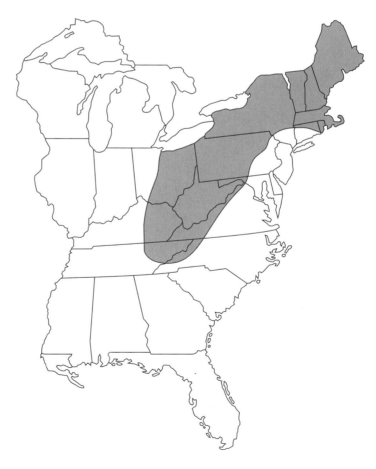

*Distribution of the hairy-tailed mole,* Parascalops breweri, *in the eastern United States*

acre), but sometimes up to 25 to 30 per ha (10 to 12 per acre).

ENEMIES. Cats, dogs, foxes, opossums, owls, copperheads, and a bullfrog all have been known to eat moles of this species.

PARASITES AND DISEASE. Eadie (1949) frequently found acanthocephalans, *Moniliformis* sp., in the intestines, and roundworms were in 15% of the stomachs examined, 36 in one stomach, 27 in another. Most eastern burrowing mammals support large numbers of ectoparasites, and this species is an excellent example. Whitaker and French (1988) examined seven individuals of this species from New York and New England and found a total of 33 species of ectoparasites and other associates, and an average of 82 individuals per host. Included were five species of fleas, at least 27 of mites, and a very infrequently taken mole louse, *Haematopinoides squamosus* (three individuals). The most numerous species were the hypopial glycyphagid mite *Labidophorus nearcticus*, a host-specific species recently described from this host (Fain and Whitaker, 1985); 138 individuals of at least two species of *Bakerdania*; and the widespread insectivore flea *Ctenophthalmus pseudagyrtes*. Mites of the genera *Pygmephorus* and *Bakerdania* (Pygmephoridae) are particularly interesting, since their relationship to the host is unknown, and the whereabouts of the males of these mites is almost completely unknown. These species are decidedly not host-specific; they are perhaps fungivores rather than parasites. The females of *Pygmephorus* are in fact phoretic and have enlarged, crablike front legs for grasping; those of *Bakerdania* lack this modification.

RELATION TO HUMANS. In mountain resorts, this species sometimes does extensive damage to golf greens, but on the whole it seldom interferes with our concerns.

AREAS FOR FURTHER WORK. Much new information could be obtained by a study of the nest and burrow fauna of this species. Of particular interest would be a search for males of *Pygmephorus*.

SUBSPECIES

None described.

Type locality: Eastern North America, the type supposed by Bachman to have been taken on the island of Martha's Vineyard, Massachusetts, a locality where the animal probably does not occur.

LITERATURE

Eadie, W. R. 1939. A contribution to the biology of *Parascalops breweri*. *J. Mammal.* 20: 150–173.

Fain, A., and J. O. Whitaker, Jr. 1985. *Labidophorus nearcticus* n.sp. (Astigmata: Labidophorinae), a new glycyphagid mite from *Parascalops breweri* in the United States. *J. Parasitol.* 71: 327–330.

Hallett, J. G. 1978. *Parascalops breweri*. **Mammalian Species No. 98.** Amer. Soc. Mammal. 4 pp.

Whitaker, J. O., Jr., and T. W. French. 1988. Ectoparasites and other arthropod associates of the hairy-tailed mole, *Parascalops breweri*. *Great Lakes Entomol.* 21: 39–41.

Wright, P. L. 1945. *Parascalops* tunnel in use after eight years. *J. Mammal.* 26: 438–439.

## Eastern Mole *Scalopus aquaticus* (Linnaeus)

The specimen upon which Linnaeus based the original species description of the eastern mole had been found dead in water, a fact that was noted on the original collection label. This happenstance led to his naming the species *aquaticus*, an obvious misnomer, for it is the *least* aquatic of our moles.

DESCRIPTION. Moles of the genus *Scalopus*—there is but one species—are characterized by a short, nearly naked tail and heavy, broad palms. The soft, velvety dorsal fur is silvery or fuscous to blackish brown; the underparts are grayish. The eyes are small, with no external opening, and there are no external ears. The front feet, very large, are naked below and bear little hair above. The palms are wider than long, and the toes, both front and back, are webbed.

MEASUREMENTS. Measurements of a series of males from different parts of the species' range gave the following extremes: total length 152–184, tail 22–30, hind foot 18–21 mm. Females

*Eastern mole,* Scalopus aquaticus *(Roger W. Barbour)*

tail 24.5, hind foot 17.8 mm. In Hillsborough and Pasco Counties, Florida, *Scalopus* is still smaller, and in the region north of Tampa Bay, total length usually does not exceed 140 mm, nor does the hind foot often exceed 17 mm. The smallest, darkest individuals are those from the Miami area. Weights of this species in Pennsylvania range from 40 to 64 grams.

Diploid number = 34.

TOOTH FORMULA

$$\frac{3}{2} \quad \frac{1}{0} \quad \frac{3}{3} \quad \frac{3}{3} \ = \ 36$$

gave extremes of: total length 144–165, tail 15–28, hind foot 18–21 mm; and weight 40–50 grams. Males are thus larger than females, and males from the northern Midwest are the largest. Measurements of twelve adults from northeastern Florida averaged: total length 142,

DISTRIBUTION. *Scalopus* is found from southern Massachusetts and southern Wisconsin south to Florida and Louisiana, but is absent in the Appalachian Mountains region. This species has the largest range of any North American mole,

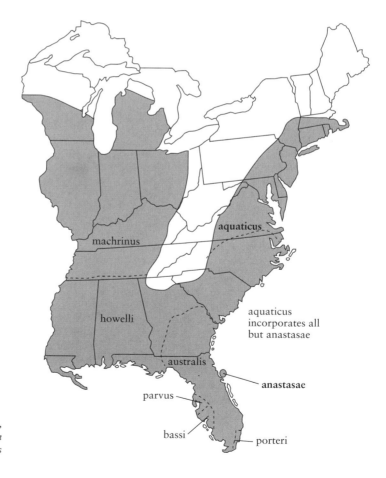

aquaticus

machrinus

howelli

aquaticus incorporates all but anastasae

australis

anastasae

parvus

bassi

porteri

*Distribution of the eastern mole,* Scalopus aquaticus, *in the eastern United States* extending westward beyond our limits to Nebraska, Kansas, and central Texas.

HABITAT. The eastern mole prefers a well-drained, loose, sandy or loamy soil. It avoids heavy clay, gravelly or stony soils, and very dry or very wet soils. It usually frequents open fields and pastures, but occurs also in thin woods and meadows.

HABITS. The eastern mole is much more abundant in our southern states than in the north. After a soaking rain, cultivated fields there will often be riddled with their burrows. Moles are active at all hours, with peaks near dawn and dusk, and they are active throughout the winter. Periods between activity bouts average about 3 hours, but may last up to 6.5 hours.

Eastern moles dig two kinds of burrows: deeper permanent ones and shallow temporary ones just under the surface, used for foraging. The regular, permanent highway of the eastern mole is often constructed 25 cm (10 inches) or

*Burrow of eastern mole*

more below the surface, and the mole retreats here during long periods of dry weather or when frost is in the ground. When making fresh burrows, the mole will push excess soil up through vertical shafts, thus producing "molehills." New burrows just below the surface of the ground, often marked by ridges and new molehills, appear to facilitate the capture of worms and other soil life following a rain. During burrowing, and probably at any other time, moles use the nose as a tactile organ, constantly poking it here and there. In friable soil, these moles

can burrow at a rate of up to nearly 6 meters (18 feet) per hour.

The nest, constructed of leaves and grasses, is placed from several inches to a foot or more below the surface. It is usually beneath a boulder, stump, or bush, and has several approaches, one of which usually enters from below. One nest is used in winter, several in summer. Brown (1972) indicates that in Florida this species does not construct nests.

FOOD AND FEEDING. The principal food of the eastern mole is usually earthworms when available, but many other foods, such as larval and adult insects, slugs, snails, centipedes, and ants are also eaten. Scarab beetle grubs are often eaten, and moles often enter anthills and feed on all life stages of ants. Under normal conditions moles will also eat vegetable matter, in considerable quantities at times. We have seen Indiana specimens whose stomachs were completely filled with grass seeds (Whitaker and Schmeltz, 1974).

REPRODUCTION AND DEVELOPMENT. A single litter of two to five young is produced, usually between mid-April and June, after a gestation of about 45 days. A nest containing four young was found in mid-April on Long Island, but in the South Atlantic states the young are born earlier, perhaps in March. They are blind and naked at birth, but are exceptionally large relative to the size of the mother. When ten days old, they have a fine, velvetlike covering of light-gray fur, which they retain for several weeks. Growth is rapid, and the young are able to leave the nest and shift for themselves when about four weeks old.

POPULATION CHARACTERISTICS. In one study, the home range of males averaged 1.1 ha (2.7 acre), that of females only 0.3 ha (0.7 acre) (Harvey, 1976). Because the male home ranges are so much larger, there is usually a preponderance of males in samples of moles. The fossorial habit of a species generally tends to limit its dispersal and thus gene flow, and the character of soils often limits populations. Moles are good swimmers and probably not much limited by rivers, although the heavy clay soils associated with some rivers may limit dispersal. Hartman (1992) estimated longevity at at least six years, using mark-recapture methods in South Carolina, whereas Davis and Choate (1993) estimated it at greater than 3.5 years in Kansas.

ENEMIES. Dogs, cats, foxes, and coyotes are some of the predators on moles of this species.

PARASITES AND DISEASE. As with most burrowers, and particularly moles, this species harbors many parasites. On 104 moles from Indiana were found four species of fleas, one species of sucking louse, one species of beetle, and at least 20 species of mites, including several new species, one of them, *Scalopacarus*, constituting a new genus.

RELATION TO HUMANS. Moles are considered to be harmful where they disfigure lawns and furnish subsurface highways in gardens for field and pine voles, but their destruction of insects should place them in a more favorable light. A friend once said that these moles had almost eliminated the larvae of Japanese beetles on his grounds. The tunneling activities of moles also aid in the aeration of the soil.

AREAS FOR FURTHER WORK. A radio-tracking study of this or other moles should be instructive. One could, for example, compare summer and winter behavioral activities. How do moles maintain themselves during dry periods when they presumably retreat to their deeper burrows? A study of the nest fauna would also be of interest. What is the effect of this species on populations of prey items?

## SUBSPECIES

*Scalopus aquaticus aquaticus* (Linnaeus)

As described above. This is the subspecies we recognize as occurring through most of the range of the species.

Type locality: Philadelphia, Pennsylvania.

Other currently recognized eastern subspecies:

  *S. aquaticus australis* (Chapman)
  *S. aquaticus bassi* Howell
  *S. aquaticus howelli* Jackson
  *S. aquaticus machrinus* (Rafinesque)

  *S. aquaticus parvus* (Rhoads)
  *S. aquaticus porteri* Schwartz

*Scalopus aquaticus anastasae* (Bangs)

This subspecies is known only from Anastasia Island, St. John Co., Florida. Although its status is questionable, we have provisionally listed it as a separate subspecies. Since it is an island form, a primary isolating mechanism is in place, but the question whether differentiation has indeed occurred on the island needs to be resolved. Two series of four moles each have been collected, but the two series are quite different (Jackson, 1915). Moles of the type series, collected at Point Romo by Outram Bangs, have small, short, heavy skulls; and the face, chin, and wrists are bright orange, paler in winter. The orange color arises apparently from glandular secretion (Eadie, 1954). The moles of the second series, however, collected by Thaddeus Surber at "Espanita" toward the southern end of the island, were essentially identical with the mainland form.

Type locality: Point Romo, Anastasia Island, St. John Co., Florida.

## LITERATURE

Brown, L. N. 1972. Unique features of tunnel systems of the eastern mole in Florida. *J. Mammal.* 53: 394–395.

Conaway, C. H. 1959. The reproductive cycle of the eastern mole. *J. Mammal.* 40: 180–194.

Davis, F. W., and J. R. Choate. 1993. Morphologic variation and age structure in a population of the eastern mole, *Scalopus aquaticus. J. Mammal.* 74: 1014–1025.

Eadie, W. R. 1954. Skin gland activity and pelage descriptions in moles. *J. Mammal.* 35: 186–196.

Hartman, G. D. 1992. Demographic and population genetic structure in the eastern mole, *Scalopus aquaticus howelli* (Insectivora: Talpidae). Unpubl. Ph.D. diss. University of New Mexico, Albuquerque. 171 pp.

Harvey, M. J. 1976. Home range, movements, and diel activity of the eastern mole, *Scalopus aquaticus. Amer. Midland Nat.* 95: 436–445.

Jackson, H. H. T. 1915. A review of the American moles. *North Amer. Fauna* 38: 1–100.

Whitaker, J. O., Jr., and L. L. Schmeltz. 1974. Food and external parasites of the eastern mole, *Scalopus aquaticus*, from Indiana. *Proc. Ind. Acad. Sci.* 83: 478–481.

Yates, T. L., and D. J. Schmidley. 1978. *Scalopus aquaticus*. **Mammalian Species No. 105.** Amer. Soc. Mammal. 4 pp.

## Star-Nosed Mole *Condylura cristata* (Linnaeus)                    Color plate

DESCRIPTION. The star-nose is a black, long-tailed mole. It is characterized most prominently by the 22 fleshy pink projections that fringe the

*Star-nosed mole,* Condylura cristata *(Dwight Kuhn)*

tip of the snout. This singular structure immediately distinguishes *Condylura* from all other moles, and, for that matter, from any other mammal in the world. The forefeet are relatively weaker than those of other eastern moles, but are nevertheless broad and scaly, well adapted for a subterranean life. The ears are larger than in most other species, probably indicating better hearing than inheritance accords most moles. The fur is nearly black on the back, becoming paler on the sides and belly. The tail is long, scaly, scantily haired, and constricted at the base, and often becomes enormously swollen in both sexes during winter and early spring. Immature animals are even darker than adults. The first incisors project forward, the second are tiny, and the third are caniniform.

MEASUREMENTS. Average measurements of 52 adult males and females from central New York were: total length 188, tail 66.5, hind foot 26 mm. The weights of 50 adults of both sexes from New York averaged 52 grams. Individuals from the southern Appalachians and from southern coastal areas are much smaller; nine from this area averaged: total length 165 (158–170), tail 60 (57–63), hind foot 25 (24–26) mm. Diploid number = 34.

TOOTH FORMULA

$$\frac{3}{3} \ \frac{1}{1} \ \frac{4}{4} \ \frac{3}{3} \ = \ 44$$

DISTRIBUTION. The star-nosed mole is found primarily in the Northeast, from New England to eastern South Carolina, extending in the Appalachians to northern Alabama, and west through northern Ohio to Michigan and northern Wisconsin. Specimens have been secured in the Okefenokee Swamp of extreme southeastern Georgia. Moles of this species also occur in southeastern Canada and west to eastern North Dakota and southeastern Manitoba.

HABITAT. The star-nosed mole is usually found in wet situations, be they meadows, fields, woods, or swamps, or along slow-flowing streams with muddy bottoms. It is often found in mucky situations, and mole burrows in muck are almost undoubtedly made by this species. It is less often taken in the damp leaf litter of dense woods, or in relatively dry fields that support a few damp spots, from which its tunnels radiate.

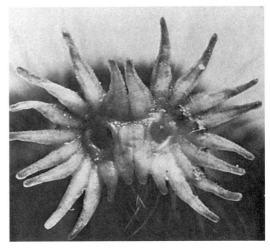

*Tentacles of star-nosed mole (Tony Brentlinger)*

HABITS. Unlike its relatives, *Condylura* is as much at home in the water as it is on land. It is an adept swimmer, using its broad palms as efficient oars, and the tail as an effective scull. It often enters the water in winter, and has even been seen swimming under the ice. We have caught several in a minnow trap in 45 cm (18 inches) of water (Eadie and Hamilton, 1956), and in

Indiana two have been taken in muskrat traps 30 cm (a foot) under water. Frequently, their burrows lead directly into a stream or pool. These moles are active by day or night, and throughout the year, even pushing their tunnels through the snow and occasionally scrambling along on its surface. They may be somewhat gregarious or colonial.

The tunnels of the star-nose are less regular than are those of other moles, forming undulating subterranean highways that are frequented by meadow voles, shrews, and other small mammals. Digging is by lateral thrusts of the forefeet, and the forefeet and shoulders are used to move the loose soil. Excess soil is pushed to the surface, forming molehills. In mucky soil, the mounds are similar to those made by crayfish, but have no opening. The nest of the star-nose is usually composed of grasses, dead leaves, or such other material as is available, and is constructed in some eminence that provides a mea-

sure of immunity from the periodic high water that often floods its chosen habitat. A compost heap is sometimes chosen.

The "star," or assemblage of 22 tentacles, of the star-nosed mole is, of course, its outstanding characteristic. This unique appendage has long been thought to be sensory, usually tactile (Hamilton, 1931; Van Vleck, 1965). Gould et al. (1993) presented behavioral and experimental evidence to support the hypothesis that the star-nosed mole uses an electrical sense to detect prey. The rays, which contain numerous nerves and blood vessels, are in constant motion when the mole is active, and the motion increases with the level of excitation, the rays moving back and forth. Before entering the water, the mole usually dips the paired elongate ventral rays into the water, and, before diving, it often pauses and holds its star below the surface for a few seconds. When under water, it scans with the tentacles. Gould et al. measured

*Distribution of the star-nosed mole,*
Condylura cristata, *in the eastern*
*United States*

the electrical output of the moles, then simulated it. They also simulated the electrical field of earthworms, which star-nosed moles feed on heavily, and five of six moles studied selected the simulated "worm." The moles direct their bites toward areas with strong electrical output, especially the clitellum and reproductive pores, when attacking submerged earthworms.

FOOD AND FEEDING. As is true of most moles, the most important food of the star-nose is often earthworms. Much of its food, however, is secured by rooting in the mud of the stream bottom, where a variety of aquatic annelids and insects, crustaceans, and an occasional small fish are captured. In 107 stomachs of this species from New York (Hamilton, 1931), 49% of the food was annelids, 33% insects, 6.5% crustaceans, 2% mollusks, 2% vertebrates, and the remainder miscellaneous materials. Nine of 18 individuals from Indiana contained 100% earthworms, and three of the remainder contained 90, 66, and 10% earthworms. Other items found were insects, slugs, vegetation, and aquatic items (immature insects and annelids).

REPRODUCTION AND DEVELOPMENT. The testes reach breeding condition by about mid-February, and breeding likely takes place in February and March of the mole's first year. Glands associated with the male reproductive system are particularly active in the breeding season, presumably helping to bring the sexes together. A copulatory plug is formed after mating. The earliest known embryos, observed by Eadie and Hamilton (1956), were seen on 16 March. A single litter of three to seven young, averaging about five, is produced sometime between mid-April and early June, after a gestation of about 45 days. The young are blind and naked at birth, but the nasal rays are already visible. When three weeks old, the young, already well furred, leave the nest to seek their own food and shelter.

POPULATION CHARACTERISTICS. Apparently almost nothing is known of the population characteristics of this species.

ENEMIES. Hawks, owls, skunks, weasels, and cats are the chief enemies of star-nosed moles, and fish are known to take them occasionally.

PARASITES AND DISEASE. Several ectoparasites of star-nosed moles have been reported, among which the more noteworthy are the tiny host-specific hypopus *Orycteroxenus canadensis* (averaging over 250 per mole in 14 of 21 examined from Indiana), the laelapid mites *Haemogamasus ambulans* and *Androlaelaps fahrenholzi*, the host-specific myobiid *Eadiea condylurae*, and the flea *Ctenophthalmus pseudagyrtes*, which is common on shrews, moles, and several burrowing rodents.

RELATION TO HUMANS. Because of its nature and habitat, *Condylura* seldom comes to the notice of the agriculturist, and only rarely does it tunnel in lawns or on the golf green.

AREAS FOR FURTHER WORK. More behavioral work could be done, using earthworms and other prey items, to further test the use of the tentacles as an electrical receptor, and also to test the mole's response to other stimuli—both tactile and olfactory. The use of the various receptors in water could be compared with their use in soil. Very little is known about the home range, tunnels, and population characteristics of the species. And is energy storage the function of the tail enlargement in spring?

## SUBSPECIES

*Condylura cristata cristata* (Linnaeus)
   As described above.
   Type locality: Pennsylvania.
   Other currently recognized eastern subspecies:
      *Condylura cristata parva* Paradiso

### LITERATURE

Eadie, W. R., and W. J. Hamilton, Jr. 1956. Notes on reproduction in the star-nosed mole. *J. Mammal.* 37: 223–231.

Gould, E., W. McShea, and T. Grand. 1993. Function of the star in the star-nosed mole. *J. Mammal.* 74: 108–116.

Hamilton, W. J., Jr. 1931. Habits of the star-nosed mole, *Condylura cristata*. *J. Mammal.* 12: 345–355.

Peterson, K. E., and T. L. Yates. 1980. *Condylura cristata*. **Mammalian Species No. 129.** Amer. Soc. Mammal. 4 pp.

Van Vleck, D. B. 1965. The anatomy of the nasal rays of *Condylura cristata*. *J. Mammal.* 46: 248–253.

# 3. ORDER CHIROPTERA

## *Bats*

CONTRARY TO FOLKLORE and popular belief, most bats not only are harmless but in fact are highly beneficial to humans. Other than for presence of rabies (rare in bats), they should never be killed. Widely held fears of bats derive from long-held myths and misunderstandings. Bats do not become entangled in people's hair; they are not aggressive; and they do not carry parasites harmful to people.

Bats differ from all other mammals by virtue of their specialized forelimbs, which are adapted for flight. Not the gliding of the flying squirrels, but swift, extended, precisely controlled flight. The wings of bats, strong and powerful, consist of an extra-long ulna (forearm), four elongated phalanges (fingers), and soft, pliable, and mostly naked skin joining the phalanges together. The forearm, the longest large bone of the wing, is measured from the elbow to the wrist, or end to end. The thumb, which has become a claw on the front edge of the wing, is used when crawling over surfaces. The interfemoral membrane, a sheet of soft skin like the wings, joins the hind legs and tail. The hind legs are directed outward, the knees bent backwards, owing to a rotation of the hind limb. The hind feet, each bearing five toes, are the hooks that the bats hang from while inactive. The calcar, a cartilaginous process arising from the ankle joint, provides partial support to the interfemoral membrane. Immature bats of all species can readily be distinguished from the adults by holding the wing membrane to the light; the phalanges of young specimens gradually widen at their junction with one another, allowing light to pass through at the joint. If the phalanges meet as solid knobs, the animal is fully adult.

A bat's ear is large, and within its opening is a prominent, upright membranous process, analogous to the lobe at the center of our own ear, called a tragus. Though its function is not well understood, the tragus is probably important in echolocation. Many bats have small eyes, but no bats are blind, and some have excellent vision. Some—primarily the fruit bats, in which echolocation is less effectively developed—have large eyes. Visual cues are apparently used for orientation and for determination of nightly departure time.

The remarkable agility that many bats exhibit in avoiding obstacles and capturing food in flight is made possible by echolocation. A bat emits high-frequency sound pulses (clicks) through its mouth or nose; from the sound waves reflected back to it from contact with nearby objects, it gains information on the location, distance, size, texture, shape, and movement of those objects. Because a pulse returns to the bat's ear in just 0.006 second, the click must be extraordinarily brief, so as not to obscure the returning echo. Bats can discriminate delays in echoes of as little as 70 millionths of a second (Suga, 1990), and objects as small as 0.06 mm (0.002 inch) in thickness.

High-frequency sounds are ideal for echolocation, since they have short wavelengths, and short wavelengths can provide more detailed information about a target. Objects about one wavelength in size reflect sound particularly well. A wavelength—the distance from peak to peak in a sound wave—is about 11 mm at 30 kHz (30,000 Hz), or about the length of a small insect. There is a down side, however: because high-frequency sounds are quickly absorbed by the environment, bats are restricted to a short range of operation. Bats use these sounds at high intensity; they would be very loud to our ears at lower frequencies. Echolocation calls vary in loudness, duration, etc., in the various phases of the bat's approach to an object or prey: the search, approach, and terminal phases. Bats distinguish moving objects from stationary objects (and approaching objects from departing objects) by the Doppler effect, the lowering in pitch we perceive when a swiftly moving car or train goes by us, the pitch dropping because the sound waves are no longer "pushed together," but are in fact "stretched out," or made longer.

Some bats are termed "whispering bats." They produce their echolocation calls at lower intensity, which are useful at much shorter distances. Bats such as *Myotis septentrionalis* and *M. keenii*, which glean items like spiders from leaves, are examples of whispering bats.

The echolocation calls of some bats can be identified (Fenton and Bell, 1981; MacDonald et al., 1994), but only after one has had quite a bit of experience observing known bats under field conditions, in much the same way birders in time come to know bird species by their calls alone. Calls vary with differing field conditions, and the identification of bats by their calls is further complicated by their "honks," specialized calls that help to avoid impending collisions between bats. Honks are especially prevalent around roosts and in other situations where conditions are crowded.

Most bats of the north-temperate region exhibit delayed fertilization: though much of the mating takes place in the fall, actual fertilization—from sperm stored in the uterus—occurs in the spring, when the females ovulate. Matings can also occur in winter and spring. The function of delayed fertilization may be to extend the mating period, thus helping to ensure that all bats are mated, or it may serve to allow embryo development to begin very soon after the females emerge from hibernation.

Most young bats, as they are born, are extruded into a pocket formed by the mother's interfemoral membranes. For several hours after birth, they remain attached by the umbilical cord and crawl about in this membrane, and are freed when the placenta is pulled clear and eaten by the parent. Bats as a group have low numbers of offspring. North American bats have one litter per year, and many have just one young per litter, though most of the rest have two. (The red

bat usually has three or four.) The number of young characteristic of various species is presumably a reflection of mortality rates, those with higher mortality having the greater numbers of young. Hermanson and Wilkins (1986) studied preweaning mortality in *Tadarida brasiliensis* and *Myotis austroriparius* roosting in the same building in Florida. *Tadarida brasiliensis* is a precocial bat with a single young, whereas *M. austroriparius* is an altricial bat producing two young. One might thus expect much greater mortality in the young in *M. austroriparius* than in *T. brasiliensis*, and this is what was found.

As the primary controllers of night-flying insects, including a wide variety of crop pests, bats form a vital element in the maintenance of healthy environments, worldwide. The 20 million Mexican free-tailed bats (*Tadarida brasiliensis*) living in Bracken Cave, Texas, eat roughly a quarter of a million pounds (125 *tons*, or more than 100 thousand kg) of insects nightly. Nevertheless, most North American bat species are declining in numbers, their loss leaving us increasingly reliant on dangerous chemical insecticides of short-lived efficacy.

It has often been suggested that bats eat many mosquitos. Indeed, a small myotis bat is capable of catching 600 or more mosquitos in an hour under laboratory conditions (Griffin et al., 1960). Under field conditions, however, bats seldom eat mosquitos, not because of any aversion to them, but because mosquitos do not usually fly in numbers in the levels of air where the bats are feeding. Rather, mosquitos remain in the vegetation until disturbed. They are also small, thus provide relatively little energy in proportion to the energy used in the pursuit. There are, in fact, relatively few actual records of North American bats feeding on mosquitos under natural conditions. Just six were found among 340 prey individuals in one little brown bat (Buchler, 1976). Whitaker has examined hundreds of scats and stomachs and found mosquitos as follows: 2% of the volume in 15 silver-haired bats, 3.2% of the volume in 31 California myotis, 0.4% of the volume in 67 little brown myotis, and 0.7% of the volume in 23 eastern pipistrelles. Zinn and Humphrey (1981), from an examination of 4, 65, and 24 scats of *Myotis austroriparius* from Florida, reported volumes of mosquitos as 10.0%, 27.6%, and 46.2%.

Mosquitos formed about 3% of the contents of 100 scats of *Myotis lucifugus* from Alaska, where mosquitos abound (Whitaker and Lawhead, 1992). In one hoary bat stomach, Earl Poole found a single mosquito. Among the prey of Indiana bats in a swamp in southern Michigan we recently examined, there were a number of mosquitos. (The bats were captured, and released, by Al Kurta.) The big brown bats and little brown bats most commonly flying around your yard are not feeding heavily on mosquitos.

The failure of bats to focus on mosquitos does not lessen their value to us. The numbers of crop-harming and disease-carrying insects of other kinds eaten are phenomenal, and bats deserve all the protection and help we can give them. An example of a pest species heavily eaten by big brown bats is the spotted cucumber beetle, *Diabrotica undecimpunctata*; its larva is the southern corn rootworm, a major pest of corn crops. Scarab beetles, green stinkbugs, and leafhoppers are other pest species heavily eaten by big brown bats, and other bats eat great quantities of moths, such as cutworm moths, the larvae of which are important garden pests; cutworms cut off cabbage plants at ground level.

Bats tend to differ considerably in their habits, but for many species more data are needed. Still, because many bats are becoming increasingly uncommon, care should be taken not to sacrifice individuals simply for, say, food-habits analysis. But since most bats are insectivorous, and since insects contain highly indigestible chitin, we have an alternative: we can capture live bats, place them in holding containers until they defecate, then examine their guano to compile food-habits information. Information may, of course, be got from bats killed in other ways, or from natural guano deposits, provided the species of bat can be determined.

There has been continuing debate over whether bats feed opportunistically (eat whatever is there) or selectively. We have no doubt that bats select from among the available foods (Whitaker, 1995). In early spring, in cold situations, or where food is otherwise limited, bats will indeed feed more opportunistically, but given ample choice they will show greater selectivity. Barclay and Brigham (1994) showed that, in the laboratory, bats can make detailed discriminations, but they suggested that field evidence does not support the proposition that they make such discrimination under natural conditions. We have much evidence of bats, while flying at the same time and place, feeding differentially, and we believe that observation constitutes strong evidence of selectivity.

Bats may feed at high altitude. At least seven species were detected by Fenton and Griffen (1997) echolocating and producing feeding buzzes at altitudes of 600 meters (2000 ft) above ground in Zimbabwe.

The patterns of predation of bats in flight tend to reflect the patterns of airworthiness inherent in their structure. Two characteristics in particular, *aspect ratio* and *wing loading*, are of significance here. The first of these is the relation between the length and the width of the wing. Those bats with long, narrow wings (high aspect ratio), such as *Tadarida*, fly fast and long but do not maneuver as well as those with wider, shorter wings (low aspect ratio), such as *Lasionycteris noctivagans*. *Lasionycteris* is a slow flyer, but it maneuvers well even in limited space. Wing loading is the relation between body weight and wing surface area. Bats with low body weight in relation to wing surface (low wing loading) have much greater lift, thus greater potential for slow flight and greater maneuverability.

All bats of the eastern United States are capable of hibernation in winter, and they will also reduce metabolism and enter torpor during cool days, as an energy-saving mechanism. Earlier, it was thought that bats and other hibernating animals simply go to sleep in the fall and awake in spring. That is not the case. Hibernating animals wake periodically through the winter. Adult little brown bats, for example, weigh about 6 grams, then put on another 2 grams of fat prior to hibernation, some of it as "brown fat" between the muscle and skin layers between the shoulder blades. Brown fat provides quick energy for use when waking, and the bats wake about once every two weeks. About 75% of the stored fat is used during the combined wakeup periods alone, which total perhaps two and a half days, and the other half gram must serve to maintain the bats' life functions through the entire winter of hibernation.

Nature sometimes seems to move in peculiar ways. Here, an elaborate hibernation process has evolved, one that allows bats to save energy, but then 75% of the energy saved appears to be wasted during their numerous wakeups. The cause of waking during hibernation is not known. It was once thought that it was to empty the bladder, but this does not seem to be the case. Nor is it for feeding, at least in big brown, little brown, or northern bats, although these bats do sometimes fly outside during these moments of wakefulness. We have seen some evidence that big brown bats, at least those hibernating in dry buildings, will drink during flights outside in winter. One of our current speculations, however, is that the exercise may help prevent muscle atrophy, for bats often fly inside the hibernaculum when awake, and it may be no more detrimental for them to fly outside, especially on nights when the temperature approaches or exceeds that inside. The flight speeds of bats vary greatly. Some bats can hover, and many fly at slow speeds. Slower-flying bats often are very maneuverable. Mexican free-tailed bats, when leaving their roost caves, can fly at speeds up to 65 kph (40 mph) or perhaps even 100 kph (60 mph).

We usually think of contracting rabies from dogs or skunks or other carnivores, not from insectivores, but it has long been known that many species of bats, even insectivorous bats, do contract rabies and can transmit rabies by bite. The number of bats contracting rabies, however, is very low (far less than 1%), and even these few bats rarely bite, except in self-defense when handled. Only about 25 people in the United States have ever died of bat rabies. This is a *very* low-risk situation indeed. Bats do not, as was once believed, serve as symptomless carriers, or cause epidemics in other wildlife, and their droppings are no more dangerous than are those of birds (Tuttle and Kern, 1981). We have long considered bat rabies and street or typical rabies to be different diseases. Bat rabies usually results in dumb rather than ferocious behavior—the animal just lies there, rather than attacking. Bat rabies has an exceedingly long incubation period—up to several months, in contrast to the 21 to 28 days or so in street rabies—and negri bodies in the brain typical of street rabies cannot be seen in bats without fluorescent microscopy. Recently, a number of strains of bat rabies have been distinguished, as

well as separate rabies strains in raccoons and skunks (Smith et al., 1995). Krebs et al. (1995) present a general discussion of rabies in wild mammals. Bat parasites—mites, worms, and others—are mostly host-specific and are not of public-health consequence.

For those people who simply leave bats alone, then, the odds of being harmed by them are so remote as to be almost mathematically incalculable, yet the benefits of sharing our neighborhoods with bats are truly staggering.

Where are bats when they are not flying? This depends on the species, time of day, and time of year. Most bats leave their daytime roost and forage at least during the first hours after dusk and the early hours before dawn, and perhaps off and on during the night as well. When not flying at night, they may return to the daytime roost, or they may use a "night roost" near the foraging area. Some bats forage near their daytime roosts, perhaps within 1 to 3 km (0.65 to 2 miles), although some species, such as gray bats and free-tailed bats, may fly much farther. Bats are often thought to live in caves, and many of our eastern species do live (hibernate) in caves in winter, but very few bats, females at least, live in caves in summer. Gray bats and Townsend's big-eared bats are true cave bats, both hibernating there and establishing their maternity colonies there (though not necessarily in the same caves), and southeastern myotis and free-tailed bats often form maternity colonies in caves, but may, alternatively, form them in human structures. Big brown bats and little brown bats probably originally formed maternity colonies in hollow trees, but now they usually form them in buildings; pipistrelles, northern myotis, and evening bats normally use trees, but sometimes form maternity colonies in buildings; and silver-haired bats apparently use hollows in trees for the most part. Indiana myotis usually form maternity colonies under loose bark, and northern myotis may also do this on occasion. *Lasiurus intermedius*, apparently, forms colonies sometimes. Most bats of the genus *Lasiurus*, however, are solitary and migratory, hanging individually among foliage, and *L. borealis* and *L. cinereus* migrate south (often considerable distances), where they spend the winter (in hibernation or feeding, depending on latitude).

In most species, males are not found in the maternity colonies, but rather, are often solitary. In big brown bat colonies the males often live elsewhere in the same buildings; in some bats—*Myotis grisescens*, *M. sodalis*, and *M. lucifugus*—they often form bachelor colonies in caves.

Bats spend considerable time grooming. Feet, tongue, and teeth are used in combing and licking the fur. Grooming keeps the fur neat and clean and may help control parasites.

The primary causes of bat decline, in order of probable importance, are general loss of habitat, including traditional roosting places in old buildings and hollow trees; human disturbance of caves; and thoughtless or careless use of pesticides. In the first instance, humans have simply used up too much of the world's natural environment; for the benefit of all the world's species, including ourselves, we should not allow more land to be "developed." In the second instance, cave explorers can aid greatly in saving our remaining cave-dwellers simply by planning their trips to coincide with seasons when bats are not using the caves in question. Finally, when increasing numbers of bats living in a building become a nuisance, we should not conclude that killing them is our best option; they are best dealt with simply by installing exclusionary barriers, after their nightly or seasonal departure. The most serious health hazards we face from the presence of bats are probably those that arise when we use poisons to kill them in our homes and other structures. Again, the only reasonable way to eliminate bats from buildings is to prevent their access, using hardware cloth or other construction materials, and exclusion should be undertaken only when the bats are absent. One can usually observe the bats emerging from outside the building at dusk, and thus see where their entrances are, and there is often a dark, telltale smudging of dirt around the entrances. An ancillary approach that has had limited success is to erect bat houses nearby before exclusion is effected, in order to give the returning bats an alternate roost. Bat houses should be placed in the sun, at least 2.5 meters (8 feet) high.

Bats, Chiroptera, constitute the second largest order of mammals, numbering about 925 species in 177 genera and 17 families. In numbers of individuals, too, they are exceeded only by the rodents. Bats are worldwide in distribution, occurring in all the tropical and temperate parts of both hemispheres and to the limits of the trees. Many species, however, are becoming increasingly uncommon and, one by one, are being placed on the endangered and threatened lists of various nations, states, and provinces.

Twenty species of bats in 11 genera and three families are known from the eastern United States: one American leaf-nosed bat, Phyllostomidae; three free-tailed bats, Molossidae; and 16 mouse-eared bats, Vespertilionidae.

## LITERATURE CITED

Barclay, R. M. R., and R. M. Brigham. 1994. Constraints on optimal foraging: A field test of prey discrimination by echolocating insectivorous bats. *Anim. Behav.* 48: 1013–1021.

Buchler, E. R. 1976. Prey selection by *Myotis lucifugus* (Chiroptera: Vespertilionidae). *Amer. Naturalist* 110: 619–628.

Griffin, D. G., R. A. Webster, and C. R. Michael. 1960. The echolocation of flying insects by bats. *Animal Behav.* 8: 141–154.

Fenton, M. B., and G. P. Bell. 1981. Recognition of species of insectivorous bats by their echolocation calls. *J. Mammal.* 62: 233–243.

Fenton, M. B., and D. R. Griffen. 1997. High altitude pursuit of insects by echolocating bats. *J. Mammal.* 78: 247–250.

Hermanson, J. W., and K. T. Wilkins. 1986. Preweaning mortality in a Florida maternity roost of *Myotis austroriparius* and *Tadarida brasiliensis*. *J. Mammal.* 67: 751–754.

Krebs, J. W., M. L. Wilson, and J. E. Childs. 1995. Rabies—epidemiology, prevention, and future research. *J. Mammal.* 76: 681–694.

MacDonald, K., E. Matsui, R. Stevens, and M. B. Fenton. 1994. Echolocation calls and field identification of the eastern pipistrelle (*Pipistrellus subflavus*: Chiroptera: Vespertilionidae), using ultrasonic bat detectors. *J. Mammal.* 75: 462–465.

Smith, J. S., L. A. Orciari, and P. A. Yager. 1995. Molecular epidemiology of rabies in the United States. *Seminars in Virology* 6: 387–400.

Tuttle, M. D., and S. J. Kern. 1981. Bats and public health. Milwaukee Publ. Mus. Contr. Biol. Geol. 48. 11 pp.

Whitaker, J. O., Jr. 1995. Food availability and opportunistic versus selective feeding in insectivorous bats. *Bat Research News* Winter 1994: 75–77.

Whitaker, J. O., Jr., and B. Lawhead. 1992. Foods of *Myotis lucifugus* in a maternity colony in central Alaska. *J. Mammal.* 73: 646–648.

Zinn, T. L., and S. H. Humphrey. 1981. Seasonal food resources and prey selection of the southeastern brown bat (*Myotis austroriparius*) in Florida. *Fla. Scientist* 44: 81–90.

## KEY TO THE FAMILIES OF BATS

1. Tail either lacking or extending well beyond interfemoral membrane . . . . . . . . . . . . . . . . . . . . . 2
1. Tail present but not extending beyond inter-femoral membrane . . . . . VESPERTILIONIDAE (p. 80)
2. Tail lacking; leaf on nose (found in Florida Keys) . . . . PHYLLOSTOMIDAE (*Artibeus jamaicensis*)
2. Tail present and extending well beyond inter-femoral membrane; no leaf on nose . . . . . . . . . . . . . . . . . . MOLOSSIDAE (p. 147)

## American Leaf-Nosed Bats, Family Phyllostomidae

There are about 140 species of bats in this family, most of them found in the tropical regions of the New World, where many feed on fruit, often figs. Six species occur in the United States, but only the Jamaican fruit-eating bat, *Artibeus jamaicensis*, occurs in the eastern part of the country (the other five are found in the Southwest). As their common name suggests, phyllostomid bats generally have a leaflike structure projecting upward from the nose. In many, the tail is reduced or lacking. On the whole, these bats have relatively large eyes and poorly developed echolocation.

## Jamaican Fruit-Eating Bat
### *Artibeus jamaicensis* Leach          Color plate

DESCRIPTION. *Artibeus jamaicensis*, a large brown bat, is the only bat in the eastern United States with a *nose leaf and no tail*. It is the only fruit bat in the eastern United States, and is found there only in the Florida Keys. The upper parts are various shades of brown; the underparts are often grayish and usually somewhat paler than the dorsum. There may or may not be facial markings.

MEASUREMENTS. Total length averages about 80, hind foot about 17, forearm 58 (54–60), ear 22 mm; and the weight averages about 42 grams.
Diploid number = 30 or 31.

TOOTH FORMULA

$$\frac{2}{2} \ \frac{1}{1} \ \frac{2}{2} \ \frac{2}{3} \ = \ 30$$

DISTRIBUTION. In the United States, *Artibeus jamaicensis* has been reported from Cudjoe and Ramrod Keys and Key West, Florida. It may occur on other southern Keys, as well, and is apparently resident in the lower Keys.

The species was first reported in the Keys in 1872 (Maynard, 1872), but that record was later discounted (Allen, 1939). On 3 February 1983, L. Page Brown photographed one of several bats that had been flushed from East Martelo Tower, Key West, and the bat in the photograph was identified by James D. Lazell and Karl Koopman (Lazell and Koopman, 1985) as *Artibeus*. Because the bat was not collected, however, this record, too, was discounted (Humphrey and Brown, 1986). In 1984, a small colony of fruit bats (about six) moved into a house on Ramrod Key, but unfortunately were evicted before they could be examined. "Big, tailless, leaf-nosed bats [were] regularly brought into the Monroe County Extension offices on Stock Island" (Lazell, 1989), but none of the specimens had ever been saved. On 28 January 1986, one settled for an instant on a screen on a house on Cudjoe Key. It immediately departed, but had been there long enough to be identified by Lazell (Lazell, 1989). There was a large fig tree, *Ficus citrifolia*, near the house, and a fruit bat was seen to fly into the tree; figs were falling at the time. Finally, on 6 June 1995, Philip Frank collected an adult *Artibeus* from a fence in Key West, thus definitively documenting this species in Florida. On 23 March, 1996, he collected another (Frank, 1997).

*Artibeus jamaicensis* is widespread and often common in Cuba and on other oceanic islands in the Caribbean. Thus its occurrence is not improbable in the southern Keys, especially since it feeds primarily on fig trees, and fig trees are present and fruit year-round there.

HABITAT. In the tropics this bat lives in a wide range of forest types. It roosts in buildings, caves, or hollow trees, or in tents of large, folded leaves that it creates by biting the leaf midribs.

HABITS. These bats may forage in small groups, but are much less active on bright moonlit nights. Individuals caught may produce stress calls, inducing "mobbing" behavior by other members of the group. Besides harems, these bats also form groups of bachelor males and of nonreproductive females. The harems are often in tree hollows; the bachelor males and nonreproductive females are often solitary or in small groups among tree foliage.

FOOD AND FEEDING. Bats of this species, chiefly frugivorous, feed primarily on fig trees, *Ficus* spp., but also feed on pollen, nectar, flower parts, and perhaps insects. Other fruits known to be eaten are mangos, avocados, and bananas. Food passes through the digestive tract in 15–20 minutes, and fecal material often has the odor of the fruit consumed.

REPRODUCTION AND DEVELOPMENT. The reproductive period of this species is tied closely to maximum abundance of the fig. In Panama, birthing peaks in March and April, and a post-partum estrus is followed by a second birthing peak in July and August. This peak, too, is followed by estrus and implantation, but the implanted blastocysts remain dormant from September to November. Development then proceeds normally until births occur in March and April. A single young is produced at each birth, although a few cases of twinning are known. Females form a daytime roost and leave their young in creches near the feeding tree during their nightly feeding forays.

POPULATION CHARACTERISTICS. These bats are polygynous; it has been suggested that males accumulate harems of up to 25 females. Two individuals have been known to live seven and ten years, respectively.

RELATION TO HUMANS. These bats may create a nuisance by forming colonies in houses.

AREAS FOR FURTHER WORK. Information is needed on all phases of the biology of this species, as it is manifested in the Keys.

*Jamaican fruit-eating bat,* Artibeus jamaicensis *(Bruce Hayward)*

## SUBSPECIES

Seven subspecies of *Artibeus jamaicensis* have been described from Central America and the Caribbean area. *Artibeus j. parvipes* Rehn, of Cuba, is the closest one to Florida.

Type locality for the species: Jamaica.

## LITERATURE

Allen, G. M. 1939. *Bats.* Cambridge, Mass.: Harvard Univ. Press. 368 pp.

Frank, P. A. 1997. First record of *Artibeus jamaicensis* Leach (1821) from the United States. *Fla. Scientist* 60: 37–39.

Humphrey, S. R., and L. N. Brown. 1986. Report of a new bat (Chiroptera: *Artibeus jamaicensis*) in the United States is erroneous. *Fla. Scientist* 49: 262–263.

Kunz, T. H., P. V. August, and C. D. Burnett. 1983. Harem social organization in cave roosting *Artibeus jamaicensis* (Chiroptera: Phyllostomidae). *Biotropica* 15(21): 133–138.

Lazell, J. D., Jr. 1989. *Wildlife of the Florida Keys: A Natural History.* Washington, D.C.: Island Press. 250 pp.

Lazell, J. D., Jr., and K. F. Koopman. 1985. Notes on bats of Florida's Lower Keys. *Fla. Scientist* 48: 37–41.

Maynard, C. 1872. Catalogue of the mammals of Florida. *Bull. Essex Inst.* 4: 135–140.

Morrison, D. W. 1978. Foraging ecology and energetics of the frugivorous bat *Artibeus jamaicensis.* *Ecology* 59: 716–723.

———. 1979. Apparent male defense of tree hollows in the fruit bat *Artibeus jamaicensis. J. Mammal.* 60: 11–15.

## Vespertilionid, or Mouse-Eared, Bats, Family Vespertilionidae

The vespertilionid or "evening" bats constitute the largest family of bats. "Evening bats" is a poor name for the family, however, since most bats fly in the evening, and one species, *Nycticeius humeralis,* is formally known as the evening bat. The family includes about 35 genera and 318 species occurring essentially in temperate and tropical areas throughout the world. Only on small, remote islands are there no vespertilionid bats. The biggest genus, with about 84 species, is *Myotis,* the mouse-eared or myotis bats, many species of which are quite difficult to distinguish. There are 14 species of vespertilionid bats in the eastern United States, in seven genera; six of the species are in the genus *Myotis.*

Most North American bats and all but four species of eastern U.S. bats belong to this family. All are insectivorous, and eastern vespertilionids have a well-developed sense of echolocation. They have plain noses, the earlobe forms a tragus, and the tail extends slightly beyond the hind edge of the interfemoral membrane. The front of the skull is flattened, and there is a space between the two front incisors. A few species make very long migrations to their wintering grounds, and most make at least short migrations. Many exhibit delayed fertilization, mating usually in the fall but sometimes in the spring or even in winter. Delayed fertilization may serve as an energy-saving mechanism, and/ or perhaps as a mechanism for ensuring that all females are bred. Young vespertilionids at birth drop into the interfemoral membrane for a time. Many of the species hibernate, and they may readily enter torpor on cool days even during the nonhibernating season, as a means of conserving energy.

There are six main events in the life history of many of our northern insectivorous bats: winter hibernation, a spring staging period, spring migration, the summer birthing period, fall migration, and the fall swarming period prior to hibernation. In the spring staging period, bats gradually begin emerging from hibernation, and there is much activity or "swarming" at the cave entrance. During this period they begin their spring feeding forays, and some copulations may occur during the nightly swarming. The staging period, during which the bats reenter hibernation each day, is relatively short, and, for the females, is followed by the spring migration to the summer or maternity roosts, where birthing takes place. The males are often solitary or aggregated into small groups, sometimes near the maternity roosts, sometimes elsewhere. Fall migration back to the hibernacula proceeds gradually, beginning in late summer, the males tending to precede the females. In the fall, there is a great deal of swarming activity at cave entrances, and most copulations apparently occur at this time. In northern areas, feeding ceases toward the end of this period, and hibernation begins.

KEY TO THE GENERA OF THE FAMILY VESPERTILIONIDAE

1. Ears large, 27–35 mm long . . *Corynorhinus* (p. 141)
1. Ears small, less than 20 mm long . . . . . . . . . . . . . 2
2. Fur strikingly colored, whether yellowish, reddish, or blackish, with silver-tipped hairs . . . . . 3
2. Fur generally brown, or the bat very small with tricolored fur . . . . . . . . . . . . . . . . . . . . . . . . . 4
3. Fur yellowish or reddish; interfemoral membrane usually well furred; upper incisors one on each side . . . . . . . . . . . . . . . . *Lasiurus* (p. 120)
3. Fur blackish or chocolate, with silver-tipped hairs; interfemoral membrane furred for half its length; upper incisors two on each side . . . . . . . . . . . . . . . . . . . *Lasionycteris* (p. 107)
4. Dorsum distinctly tricolored . . . *Pipistrellus* (p. 112)
4. Dorsum not tricolored . . . . . . . . . . . . . . . . . . . . . 5
5. Animal large, the forearm at least 44 mm long . . . . . . . . . . . . . . . . . . . . . . *Eptesicus* (p. 117)
5. Animal smaller, the forearm less than 44 mm long . . . . . . . . . . . . . . . . . . . . . . . . . . . . . . . . . . . 6
6. Tragus elongate and slender; first two premolars tiny, forming a space behind canine; upper incisors two on each side. . . . . . . . . . *Myotis*
6. Tragus small and rounded; first tooth behind canine enlarged; upper incisors one on each side. . . . . . . . . . . . . . . . . . . . . *Nycticeius* (p. 137)

## Bats of the Genus *Myotis*

The bats of this genus are both common and widespread. They form maternity colonies under varying conditions, depending on the species. Most hibernate in caves or mines. Bats of the genus *Myotis* are generally various shades of brown and are often difficult to identify. Two reduced teeth behind the canines form an apparent space.

Bats of the genus *Myotis* are most properly referred to as "myotis," e.g. "southeastern myotis," "gray myotis," but the common names "myotis" and "bat," e.g. "southeastern bat," "gray bat," are often used interchangeably.

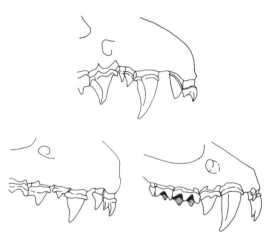

*Partial tooth rows of bats, showing space behind canine holding two small teeth in* Myotis *(top), space with one small tooth in* Pipistrellus *(lower left), and no space, simply a large tooth behind canine, in* Eptesicus *(lower right) (Thomas W. French)*

### KEY TO THE BATS OF THE GENUS *MYOTIS*

1. Hair on dorsum one color from base to tip . . . . . . . . . . . . . . . . . . . . . . . *M. grisescens*
1. Hair on dorsum not all of one color . . . . . . . . . . 2
2. Ear length greater than distance from base of ear to end of nose, extending 2 mm beyond nose; tragus long and pointed . . . *M. septentrionalis*
2. Ear length nearly equal to distance from base of ear to end of nose; tragus shorter and more rounded . . . . . . . . . . . . . . . . . . . . . . . . . . . . . . . 3
3. Bat small, the forearm 30–35 mm long; hind foot small, less than 8 mm long; lips black and a black mask . . . . . . . . . . . . . . . . *M. leibii*
3. Bat larger, the forearm usually at least 36 mm long; hind foot usually at least 8 mm long; lips and face not black . . . . . . . . . . . . . . . . . . . . . 4

4. Metatarsal hairs extending beyond claw nails; keel on calcar lacking or very small; pelage variable . . . . . . . . . . . . . . . . . . . . . . . . . . . . . . . . 5
4. Metatarsal hairs not extending beyond claw nails; calcar with keel; pelage with pinkish cast . . . . . . . . . . . . . . . . . . . . . . . . . . . *M. sodalis*
5. Sagittal crest lacking; hair on dorsum silky, light brown to dark brown . . . . . . . . . *M. lucifugus*
5. Sagittal crest present; hair on dorsum dense and woolly, gray to gray-brown . . *M. austroriparius*

## Southeastern Myotis, Southeastern Bat
### *Myotis austroriparius* (Rhoads)

DESCRIPTION. The southeastern myotis is similar in appearance to the little brown myotis, *Myotis lucifugus*, but the thick, woolly, and somewhat shorter fur and the absence of conspicuously burnished hair tips help distinguish it from that bat. The ventral fur becomes white upon molting in June, and, at least in Indiana, remains white in winter. The color above is dull yellowish or a drab brown.

*A pair of southeastern myotis,* Myotis austroriparius *(Bruce Hayward)*

The skull of this species is slenderer, with a narrower interorbital constriction, than that of *M. lucifugus*, and generally has a low sagittal crest that can be felt through the skin. This bat may be distinguished from other *Myotis* species of the eastern United States by its large hind foot (10–12 mm long) and the lack of a keel on the calcar.

MEASUREMENTS. Average measurements of 20 adults of both sexes from Gainesville, Florida, were: total length 91.5 (84.4–96), tail 41.3 (36.5–44), hind foot 10.7 (10.2–12.5), ear

14–16, forearm 39.8 (35.5–41.7) mm. The wingspread is about 238–270 mm (9.5–11 inches). Males are slightly smaller than the females. Adult males weigh 5–12 grams; nursing females are heavier.

Diploid number = 44.

TOOTH FORMULA

$$\frac{2}{3} \quad \frac{1}{1} \quad \frac{3}{3} \quad \frac{3}{3} \quad = \quad 38$$

DISTRIBUTION. This species has a disjunct distribution. Originally, there were large populations in the Deep South, especially in Florida. The southeastern bat still occurs in Illinois and Kentucky, but it is apparently extirpated in Indiana, where at one time the species regularly hibernated. No maternity colonies were ever discovered in Indiana. This is—or was—the most abundant bat in parts of northern Florida, but the southeastern bats in peninsular Florida are now disjunct from those in the panhandle. This species ranges west of the Mississippi to northeastern Texas and southeastern Oklahoma.

HABITAT. Southeastern bats cluster in caves or buildings or other protected sites, such as hollow trees. They are often seen in the company of free-tailed bats, *Tadarida brasiliensis*, in buildings, or with gray bats, *Myotis grisescens*, in caves. There are nursery caves in Florida that once contained thousands of individuals (see below, under Population Characteristics), but in other parts of the South, where caves are lacking, buildings are the typical nursery sites. There are few males in the nursery colonies, but

Artibeus jamaicensis

*Distribution of the Jamaican fruit-eating bat,* Artibeus jamaicensis, *and the southeastern myotis,* Myotis austroriparius, *in the eastern United States*

most males roost elsewhere, alone or in small bachelor colonies.

HABITS. Most individuals leave the maternity sites about October and congregate to winter in various protected places, usually over water. Typical wintering sites are under bridges and in boathouses, drainpipes, culverts, buildings, hollow trees, and crevices in mangroves. Departure from the winter sites is gradual, extending through late February and March in northern Florida. Movements between summer and winter quarters are usually local, minimally qualifying as migrations. In peninsular Florida, southeastern bats put on little or no fat in the fall and do not hibernate, but move into winter quarters similar to their summer roost sites. Farther north, southeastern bats do hibernate, often in caves.

FOOD AND FEEDING. This bat feeds by flying low over the water. Zinn and Humphrey (1981) found 7.2% Coleoptera, zero Lepidoptera, and 92.8% Diptera in four scats collected on a cold night in early spring; 15.3, 20.8, and 63.9% of the same foods in 24 scats on a warm spring night; and 26.3, 30.5, and 43.1% in 65 scats produced in summer by this species. Many of the dipterans were identified as mosquitos and crane flies.

REPRODUCTION AND DEVELOPMENT. Gene Gardner recently discovered a small maternity colony of southeastern bats in a hollow tupelo tree in a hardwood swamp in southern Illinois, and Virgil Brack (using mist-netting) discovered the general area of an apparent maternity site in Breckenridge County, Kentucky, although he was unable to locate the actual roost. Otherwise, nothing is known of the breeding of the northern populations (those in Illinois and Indiana). In Florida, mating is apparently from mid-February to mid-April, and the nursery colonies that begin forming in mid-March would in earlier years build to 2,000 or even 90,000 individuals in some Florida caves. The caves they occupy generally contain water. There is no delayed fertilization in Florida.

During late April to mid-May, the young are born, about 90% of the females producing two young. This is the only species of *Myotis* in North America that regularly produces more than one young. The greater numbers of young appear to relate to the higher mortality of young in maternity caves containing water; when the young drop, they are seldom retrieved. At birth the young are naked, except for a few facial whiskers and a few hairs on the toes and about the knees. Notwithstanding the transparency of their skin, which gives them a pinkish hue, they are black. Their ears and eyes are closed. But when just three weeks old, they are capable of maintaining themselves.

POPULATION CHARACTERISTICS. Like many other species, this bat is in trouble. It shows great roost fidelity, and Rice (1957) indicated that it requires areas over water for its maternity colonies. He suggested that southeastern bats would abandon caves when water levels dropped, exposing dry cave floor beneath, and that flooding, too, could cause abandonment.

The stronghold of the southeastern myotis had always been in Florida, where an estimated 380,000 individuals were earlier known to live in 15 nursery colonies in caves. In 1991–92, however, visits to all the traditional caves (Gore and Hovis, 1994) disclosed that only five of the caves were still active, and that the total number of bats had been reduced to about 319,000. (That the investigation discovered four colonies not previously known, and that populations increased in two of the caves, is but modest encouragement, since many of the bats seem to be in less desirable situations, i.e. not over water.) Three of the ten abandoned caves had been vacated because their entrances were closed, and in three others the surrounding forest had been cut. Since the original report, Gore (pers. comm.) indicates that the entire population in Sneads Cave, 85,000 bats, was destroyed by flooding in 1994, leaving the total at only 234,000 bats. Several caves, occupied or unoccupied by southeastern myotis, showed signs of excessive human use, and several showed signs of flooding. The stability of the bats' maternity colonies is extremely delicate, and human use, even if minimal, may have led to the bats' exodus. To make matters worse, very few maternity colonies of this bat are known north of Florida. Much more work, obviously, is needed on the status of this species, but it is clear that it needs immediate protection. Perhaps it is time that we protect *all* bats, just as we do migratory birds! The life span of this species is unknown, but we know of no particular reason why it should not live for at least 15 years if it does not meet a violent end. ENEMIES. Predation by rat snakes and corn snakes appears to be common in the caves in Florida, and small carnivores and owls apparently take some individuals. Cockroaches in the bat caves eat the very small young that fall to the floor, rather than in the water.

PARASITES AND DISEASE. Conspicuous parasites on these bats in Florida are the streblid fly *Trichobius major* and the nycteribiid fly *Basilia boardmani*. Chiggers, *Euschoengastia pipistrelli*, are also found. A new mite, *Olabidocarpus whitakeri*, was found on this species in southern Indiana.

RELATION TO HUMANS. As are all eastern bats, those of this species are highly beneficial, because they feed on a variety of nocturnal insects. Like some other bats, they sometimes come into conflict with us by occupying our buildings, but the species appears to be declining in numbers and should be protected.

AREAS FOR FURTHER WORK. Much more information is needed on the distribution, abundance, and food habits of this species, throughout its range. Apparently, it feeds in winter. How does the food taken then compare to that eaten at other seasons? More taxonomic work on this species (see below) is also needed, and a genetic comparison of different populations should prove instructive.

## SUBSPECIES

*Myotis austroriparius* presents a difficult taxonomic problem, one that warrants further work. The species occurs in three main regions of the southeastern United States. The populations there were originally described as three separate subspecies, primarily on the basis of color, as follows: *M. a. austroriparius* (Florida and Georgia and one locality in south-central Alabama); *M. a. gatesi* (southern Mississippi, Louisiana, Arkansas, extreme southeastern Oklahoma, and northeastern Texas); and *M. a. mumfordi* (southern Illinois and Indiana, western Kentucky, western Tennessee, and northern Mississippi). Thus, primary isolating mechanisms are fairly well established, but LaVal (1970) was unable to find characters that would allow us to distinguish the individuals from the three major geographic areas, and he found individuals of all of the colors in all three areas. He therefore did not recognize subspecies. (The color variations appear to be seasonal rather than geographic, but this cannot be gleaned from LaVal's paper.) We follow LaVal and recognize no subspecies.

*Myotis austroriparius* Rhoads
  None recognized.
  Type locality: Tarpon Springs, Pinellas Co., Florida.

## LITERATURE

Bain, J. R. 1981. Roosting ecology of three Florida bats: *Nycticeius humeralis*, *Myotis austroriparius*, and *Tadarida brasiliensis*. Unpubl. M.S. thesis. University of Florida, Gainesville. 130 pp.

Foster, G. W., S. R. Humphrey, and P. P. Humphrey. 1978. Survival rate of young southeastern brown bats, *Myotis austroriparius*, in Florida. *J. Mammal.* 59: 299–304.

Gore, J. A., and J. A. Hovis. 1994. Southeastern myotis maternity cave survey. Final performance report January 1, 1991 to July 31, 1992. Nongame Wildlife Program. Florida Game and Freshwater Fish Commission. 33 pp.

———. 1997. Status and conservation of southeastern myotis maternity colonies in Florida caves. Unpubl. Report, Fla. Game and Freshwater Fish Comm. 23 pp.

LaVal, R. K. 1970. Infraspecific relationships of bats of the species *Myotis austroriparius*. *J. Mammal.* 51: 542–552.

Rice, D. W. 1957. Life history and ecology of *Myotis austroriparius* in Florida. *J. Mammal.* 38: 15–32.

Sherman, H. B. 1930. Birth of the young of *Myotis austroriparius*. *J. Mammal.* 11: 495–503.

Zinn, T. L., and S. R. Humphrey. 1981. Seasonal food resources and prey selection of the southeastern brown bat (*Myotis austroriparius*) in Florida. *Fla. Scientist* 44: 81–90.

## Gray Myotis, Gray Bat
## *Myotis grisescens* A. H. Howell

DESCRIPTION. The gray bat may be at once distinguished from all other members of the genus

*Gray myotis*, Myotis grisescens *(Tony Brentlinger)*

*Myotis* by the pattern of the dorsal fur, which is uniformly colored throughout, rather than being conspicuously darker at the base of the hairs. The insertion of the wing membrane is at the tarsus rather than at the side of the foot, but this character is not evident in study skins. This myotis is similar in general appearance to the southeastern bat, *M. austroriparius*, but slightly larger. The skull is larger than that of *M. lucifugus* and shows evident sagittal and lamboidal crests.

MEASUREMENTS. Average measurements of adults from various parts of the range are: total length 88.6 (80.2–96), tail 38 (32.8–44.2), hind foot 9.9 (8.4–11.2), forearm 43.1 (40.6–

45.8), ear 16, wingspread 275–300 mm. Mohr (1933) found these bats to weigh 7.6 to 9.1 grams during June, 5 to 10 grams in January. Diploid number = 44.

TOOTH FORMULA

$$\frac{2}{3} \quad \frac{1}{1} \quad \frac{3}{3} \quad \frac{3}{3} \ = \ 38$$

DISTRIBUTION. This species is found throughout the limestone region of the southern middle-western and southeastern states, i.e. from southern Illinois and Indiana south to northwestern Florida and west through Missouri and northern Arkansas to southwestern Nebraska and northeastern Oklahoma.

HABITAT. Both this bat and Townsend's big-eared bat may be considered true cave bats, for both of them not only hibernate in caves but bear their young in them.

HABITS. To Merlin Tuttle we owe much of our knowledge of gray bats. Tuttle (1975, 1976a, b) banded over 40,000 of them at 50 caves during his extensive studies of the ecology of the species. Most of the banding (94%) was done in summer at maternity caves, but the banded bats were later sought out in both the maternity and wintering caves. Tuttle found that bats of this species showed strong ties to particular cave systems, both summer and winter, although in late summer they often roost in other caves. They are also highly migratory, moving up to 525 km (325 miles) between different summer and winter caves, thus ensuring optimum conditions for hibernating and raising their young. They spend the summer in fairly large colonies in several states, but especially in Missouri, Tennessee, Kentucky, and Alabama and into the eastern part of the panhandle of Florida. A maternity colony was found in a quarry in Indiana in 1982 (Brack et al., 1984), the only one known in the state. It numbered about 400 bats when found and remained at roughly that number through 1990, when about 480 emerged from the openings in the quarry on 17 September. On similar dates in 1991, 1994, and 1997, the counts were 752, 1101, and 1949, giving some indication of the rate at which a colony of gray bats may expand.

Maternity colonies usually form in warm caves, and are usually not more than a kilometer from rivers, lakes, or reservoirs. Most foraging is within 11 km (7 miles) of the maternity cave, but is sometimes pursued at much greater distances. Smaller juveniles often forage at greater distances. Laval et al. (1977) found, by the use of luminescent markers glued to individuals, that gray bats foraged among trees at least part of the time.

In winter, gray bats congregate to hibernate in huge numbers in a few "cold" caves—cold because they are below sinkholes. Small openings to the surface above the sinkhole allow cold air to enter and become trapped. Five such caves are known in the east and five are known in the western part of the range, four in northern Arkansas and one in Missouri. Tuttle postulated

that probably 90% of the gray bats of the eastern United States earlier used just three main wintering caves: one in northeastern Alabama, one in central Tennessee, and one in eastern Tennessee close to the Virginia border. All three wintering caves were used by at least some bats from each of the summer colonies studied, but most bats from any one summer colony used just one hibernaculum, any one individual repeatedly using a particular wintering cave. The bats in most Tennessee colonies wintered in the winter cave nearest to them, elsewhere in Tennessee, but the greatest number of individuals from one large maternity colony in eastern Tennessee (Tuttle, 1976b) hibernated in the most distant cave (in northeastern Tennessee, about 200 km, or 130 miles, away), and the smallest number went to the nearby east Tennessee wintering cave (perhaps 60 km, or 33 miles, away). Tuttle noted that to go to one of the Tennessee caves the bats

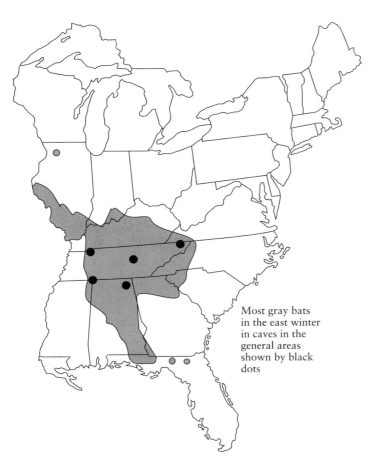

Most gray bats in the east winter in caves in the general areas shown by black dots

*Distribution of the gray myotis,* Myotis grisescens, *in the eastern United States*

were forced to go over or around the Cumberland Mountains. Even the bats from Florida maternity colonies migrated to the north to winter in these same three caves.

Gray bats are essentially restricted to their maternity-cave areas during the reproductive season, and to the three hibernating caves during winter, but they use many other caves as stopovers during migration (late March through late May, and late August through late November). The Florida bats make a broad western curve during their northward migration, which keeps them near the stopover caves. Adults generally migrate before the juveniles, but juveniles were never found alone, and it appeared that at least some adult males remained behind and migrated with them. The bats, often migrating in large groups, reach the hibernating caves between August and October, the females again arriving first. Swarming and mating begin soon after the bats start arriving. Females enter hibernation first (September and early October), right after copulation; males remain active longer, entering hibernation by early November.

Females emerged first from the hibernacula, beginning in late March or early April, followed by subadults, and the adult males last. Gray bats began arriving at the summer caves during the latter part of April. Adult females occupied maternity caves, whereas the males and yearlings usually occupied nearby, but separate, caves. Females move between caves in their home range, and by late July and early August, adults and juveniles from the maternity caves are moving back and forth between maternity and other nearby caves.

Some information on rates of travel is available from Tuttle's work. For example, one adult female traveled 207 km (135 miles) in four nights, for an average of 52 km (34 miles) per night. Of 515 banded individuals in one cluster, 133 were found in a single cluster the following day in a cave 15.8 km (10.2 miles) away. A yearling male traveled 145 km (94 miles) in eight nights, for an average of 18.1 km (11.8 miles) per night.

FOOD AND FEEDING. Rabinowitz and Tuttle (1982) observed gray bats feeding on mayflies over a reservoir in Tennessee, but were unable to find mayfly remains in feces during feeding experiments. They concluded that guano analysis did not work well for determination of mayflies (and perhaps other soft-bodied items). Lacki et al. (1995) found that beetles, especially those of the Carabidae, Chrysomelidae, and Scarabaeidae, were the prominent items eaten by gray bats in Kentucky. Trichoptera, Diptera, and Lepidoptera were other important orders represented. Presumably, this species also feeds heavily on aquatic foods, especially mayflies (Ephemerida) and true flies (Diptera), but although mayflies were present, none were found in guano during these studies.

REPRODUCTION AND DEVELOPMENT. Even though the gray bat frequents caves throughout the year, there is a remarkable segregation of the sexes during the reproductive season. Gray bats swarm to mate at the hibernation sites in September or early October, though some copulations may occur in spring. Fertilization is delayed and ovulation normally follows the spring mating. Pregnant females maintain normal body temperatures, through spring and early summer, even at low air temperatures, by clustering to help facilitate heat retention. The single young is usually born in early June, occasionally in late May, depending on latitude. At birth, the young's weight is about one-third that of the parent. The mother leaves the naked, helpless young hanging from the cave wall or ceiling while she forages, but when three weeks old the young are able to provide for themselves. Colonies begin to decline in late July and August, after the young are weaned, but many gray bats are still in the colonies through much of September.

POPULATION CHARACTERISTICS. Though this species still occurs in large numbers, it has declined dramatically. Partly because of its habit of congregating in large numbers in few caves, especially in winter, it was placed on the federal endangered species list, as of 28 April 1976. Many of the caves used in winter by this species, often no more than vertical pits, are difficult to enter. But for just that reason, these caves have become particularly challenging to spelunkers, and increasingly in recent years they have been entered, provoking the loss of some previously large gray bat colonies. In short, the disturbance of a relatively few caves could wipe out vast portions of the population of this species. Many of the other winter and summer caves used by gray bats have been commercialized, destroyed, or overused. Banding studies by John Hall and Nixon Wilson (1966) indicated that all or most of the bats from summer colonies in Tennessee, Kentucky, and Illinois hibernated in huge colonies in one large cave complex, Coach-James Cave in Kentucky. Estimates from Kentucky—previous totals of over 500,000 gray bats in summer colonies reduced to 61,000 (Rabinowitz and Tuttle, 1980)—indicate the precipitous declines in population that have apparently befallen this species. Twenty-two summer colonies in Alabama and Tennessee declined 76%, from 1,199,000 prior to 1968 to 293,600 in 1976, with one of the largest declining by 95%. More recently, there have been some increases. For example, the summer colony in Jesse James Cave, Kentucky, increased from 230,000 in 1983 to 300,000 in 1997. These bats are also increasing in Arkansas. Some of the changes in winter populations seem to indicate bat movements. Gray bats have been known to live at least 18 years.

ENEMIES. No information is available on predation on this species. It is assumed to be light, as is the case for most other bats, except for the occasional predator that happens to learn how to enter a hibernaculum. Significant mortality of juveniles—the causes unknown—occurs during migration, especially at greater distances (Tuttle, 1977).

PARASITES AND DISEASE. The parasites of this species are not well known, but fleas (*Myodopsylla insignis*) and mites (*Macronyssus jonesi*, three species of *Spinturnix*, and *Olabidocarpus* sp.) are some of the main external parasites in our area. A small sample from Illinois contained intestinal cestodes, trematodes, and nematodes.

RELATION TO HUMANS. The summer colonies of this species are easily disturbed, the entire colony suddenly flying rapidly about the cave. Biologists and cavers should be exceedingly cautious about disturbing either summer or winter colonies, and we should avoid entering their caves at all during the time they are in use by the bats. When the bats are disturbed by people, many young drop from the walls, or lose their grip on flying mothers, thence falling to the cave floor, where they perish. Scores of dead young may be seen beneath bat roosts after a disturbance in early summer.

Clark, LaVal, and Swineford (1978) examined the brains of dead juvenile gray bats taken from beneath maternity roosts in two Missouri caves, and found them to contain lethal concentrations of dieldrin. In another colony, which appeared to be abnormally small, they found more dead bats, a year after the juvenile bats had been collected. This is the first report linking the field mortality of bats directly to insecticide residues acquired through the food chain.

AREAS FOR FURTHER WORK. Much more information is needed on the status of this bat, summer and winter, in major caves in the various states. More information is also needed on the food and feeding of this species. Rabinowitz and Tuttle (1982) observed gray bats feeding on mayflies, but they and Lacki et al. (1995) found few mayfly remains in guano. Rabinowitz and Tuttle concluded that mayflies are usually not identifiable in guano. However, Belwood and Fenton (1976) found that mayflies were identifiable in feces. We think more feeding experiments are in order, using mayflies followed by guano analysis, to determine those characters most useful in identifying mayflies and just how difficult the determination is.

Little is known about navigation in bats. Do they follow natural landmarks, or stars, or what? Can they migrate on cloudy nights or only on clear nights? What about dark vs. moonlit nights?

## SUBSPECIES

None described.
Type locality: Nickajack Cave, near Shellmound, Marion Co., Tennessee.

## LITERATURE

Belwood, J. J., and M. B. Fenton. 1976. Variation in the diet of *Myotis lucifugus* (Chiroptora: Vespertilionidae). *Canadian J. Zool.* 54: 1674–1678.

Brack, V., Jr., R. E. Mumford, and V. R. Holmes. 1984. The gray bat (*Myotis grisescens*) in Indiana. *Amer. Midland Nat.* 111: 205.

Clark, D. R., Jr., R. K. Laval, and D. M. Swineford. 1978. Dieldrin induced mortality in an endangered species, the gray bat (*Myotis grisescens*). *Science* 199: 1357–1359.

Guthrie, M. J. 1933. Notes on the seasonal movements and habits of some cave bats. *J. Mammal.* 14: 1–19.

Hall, J. S., and N. Wilson. 1966. Seasonal populations and movements of the gray bat in the Kentucky area. *Amer. Midland Nat.* 75: 317–324.

Lacki, M. J., L. S. Burford, and J. O. Whitaker, Jr. 1995. Food habits of gray bats in Kentucky. *J. Mammal.* 76: 1256–1259.

Laval, R. K., R. L. Clausen, M. L. Laval, and W. Caire. 1977. Foraging behavior and nocturnal activity patterns of Missouri bats, with emphasis on the endangered species *Myotis grisescens* and *Myotis sodalis. J. Mammal.* 58: 592–599.

Mohr, C. E. 1933. Observations on the young of cave dwelling bats. *J. Mammal.* 14: 49–53.

Rabinowitz, A., and M. D. Tuttle. 1980. Status of summer colonies of the endangered gray bat in Kentucky. *J. Wildl. Mgmt.* 44: 955–960.

Rabinowitz, A., and M. D. Tuttle. 1982. A test of the validity of two currently used methods of determining bat prey preferences. *Acta Theriologica* 21: 283–293.

Tuttle, M. D. 1975. Population ecology of the gray bat (*Myotis grisescens*): Factors influencing early growth and development. Occ. Pap. Mus. Nat. Hist. Univ. Kansas No. 36. 24 pp.

———. 1976a. Population ecology of the gray bat (*Myotis grisescens*): Factors influencing growth and survival of newly volant young. *Ecology* 57: 587–595.

———. 1976b. Population ecology of the gray bat (*Myotis grisescens*): Philopatry, timing and patterns of movement, weight loss during migration, and seasonal adaptive strategies. Occ. Pap. Mus. Nat. Hist. Univ. Kansas No. 54. 38 pp.

———. 1979. Status, causes of decline and management of endangered gray bats. *J. Wildl. Mgmt.* 43: 1–17.

Tuttle, M. D., and D. E. Stevenson. 1977. An analysis of migration as a mortality factor in the gray bat based on public recoveries of banded bats. *Amer. Midland Nat.* 97: 235–240.

## Eastern Small-Footed Myotis, Leib's Myotis
### *Myotis leibii*
**(Audubon and Bachman)**      Color plate 2

The small-footed myotis was long known as *Myotis subulatus*, with an eastern subspecies *M. s. leibii*, but Glass and Baker (1968) showed

that *M. subulatus* was probably an earlier name for the wholly distinct *M. yumanensis*, a western species, leaving *M. leibii* as the earliest available name for this species. Further, van Zyll de Jong (1984) considered the western form of *M. leibii* to be a separate species, *M. ciliolabrum* (Merriam). This interpretation was accepted by Jones et al. (1992) but not by Wilson and Reeder (1993). Obviously, more information is needed before taxonomic consensus can be reached. For present purposes, we accept the determination of Jones but draw upon the literature of *M. ciliolabrum* to support what is known of *M. leibii*.

DESCRIPTION. The small-footed myotis is similar in appearance to the little brown myotis,

*Eastern small-footed myotis,* Myotis leibii
*(Roger W. Barbour)*

*Myotis lucifugus*, but can be distinguished by its smaller size, smaller foot (less than 8 mm long), shorter ears (less than 15 mm long), contrasting black ears and facial mask, dark brown or golden-tinted fur, keeled calcar, and shorter forearm (less than 35 mm long). The face, including the nose, lips, ears, and tragus, is black, giving a masked appearance. The wings and interfemoral membranes are blackish brown. The skull is nearly as long as that of *M. lucifugus*, but more flattened.

MEASUREMENTS. Average measurements of six specimens from New York, Vermont, and Maryland were: total length 77.5 (73–82), tail 32.6 (29.8–35.2), hind foot 6.8 (6.6–7), ear 14–15, forearm 31.8 (30.8–34), wingspread 212–234 mm; and weight 4–6 grams.
Diploid number = 44.

TOOTH FORMULA

$$\frac{2}{3} \quad \frac{1}{1} \quad \frac{3}{3} \quad \frac{3}{3} \quad = \quad 38$$

DISTRIBUTION. The small-footed myotis occurs from northern New England through New York to North Carolina, Tennessee, and northern Georgia, Alabama, and Mississippi west into Arkansas and southeastern Oklahoma. The related *Myotis ciliolabrum* occurs throughout most of the western half of the United States and also into southwestern Canada and northern Mexico.

HABITAT. These bats usually occur in mountainous regions, although in Ontario they do not. They hibernate in caves in winter, but little information is available on their summer habitat. A summer roost was found behind the sliding door of a barn in Ontario. Tuttle and Heaney

(1974) located 12 active roosts of *M. ciliolabrum* in the South Dakota Badlands, two in horizontal cracks in rocks on hillsides, six in crevices in the walls of vertical banks, and four in holes in sloping banks. All of these roosts were small, dry, and shallow, and presented high ambient temperatures (26–33°C, or 80–92°F). Openings into the roosts ranged from 1.5 to 9.0 cm in width.

HABITS. This species is solitary in winter, hibernating in caves or mines, often near the entrance. It has been found in very cold caves and can tolerate lower temperatures than can the little brown bat. Up to 142 individuals have been found hibernating in one cave in Renfrow County, Ontario. Wayne H. Davis has found several small-footed myotis on the ground under rocks in caves. He reports that in one West Virginia cave, they hibernate in crevices in the

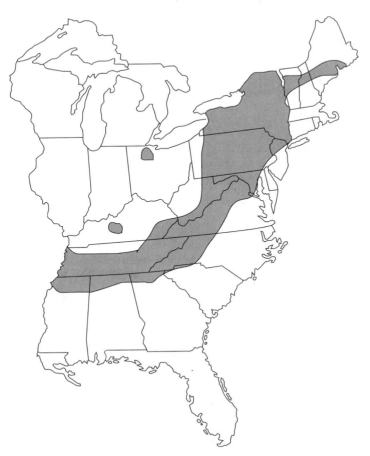

*Distribution of the eastern small-footed myotis,* Myotis leibii, *in the eastern United States*

cracked clay floor. Merlin Tuttle reported two from under a rock in Tennessee. Mohr (1936) collected and marked a large series of this species, all in caves in a limited area in wild, mountainous country rising to 650-meter (2000-foot) altitudes in central Pennsylvania during winter. Mohr stated that this bat is active in late winter and leaves the caves long before the other hibernating bats. "The attitude of the bat as it hangs on the walls or ceilings of the caves is so characteristic that it offers a very definite means of identification at a distance. The arms, instead of hanging practically parallel, are extended about 30° from the vertical, and almost every least [small-footed] bat was found in this position, other bats seldom. The last least bat was taken this year [1933] on April 2. No caves were visited the following week, but visits to Dulany Cave on April 15, Cornwall Cave on April 16, and Aitkin, Little Aitkin, and Stover Caves on April 17 failed to show a single bat of this species, although other hibernating bats were still inactive."

Mohr believed that *Myotis leibii* hibernates in caves of the Appalachians from Vermont to West Virginia, migrating southward during February and March or perhaps earlier, and stopping over for short periods in remote caves in heavily forested sections of the mountains. Other banding information, however, indicates that some may hibernate near their summer quarters. Individuals have been taken near large caves in Kentucky during August, they have been found hibernating in Tennessee caves, and a male and female were found on 19 January in manmade tunnels in North Carolina. Al Hicks has recently found this bat in goodly numbers in winter, and as late as early May, in mines in the Adirondack Mountains of New York. In Arkansas and Oklahoma, Leib's bats may hibernate in "rock glaciers or rock rivers" or in talus caves associated with them.

Bats of this species are among the latest to enter hibernacula in the fall (mid-November) and earliest to leave in the spring (March or early April). They are often active during the milder parts of winter, and marked and released individuals have homed to hibernating caves. One individual was found in a crevice in the floor in Schoolhouse Cave, West Virginia, on 26 January, and an accumulation of feces there suggested that the bat had been active.

FOOD AND FEEDING. There are no data on the food of *Myotis leibii*, but limited information indicates that *M. ciliolabrum* feeds on flies, beetles, leafhoppers, true bugs, and flying ants.

REPRODUCTION AND DEVELOPMENT. Little is known of the breeding of *Myotis leibii* in the east, although one summer colony was found behind the sliding door of a shed in Ontario. Apparently, females normally produce one young per year. The 12 roosts of *M. ciliolabrum* found in South Dakota by Tuttle and Heaney (1974), all in the third week of July, collectively contained 27 small-footed myotis, including seven lactating females, two postlactating females, one nonreproductive female, one adult male, four juvenile males, and seven juvenile females (five bats escaped before they could be sexed and aged). The juveniles varied greatly in age, ranging in weight from 1.6 to 3.9 grams and forearm length from 14.5 to 31 mm. The smallest juvenile had no body fur; the largest was marginally volant. Only two roosts contained more than a single adult or an adult and its young: one consisted of four lactating females and five juveniles, including apparently one set of twins (only *M. austroriparius* among eastern U.S. *Myotis* regularly produces twins); the other consisted of an adult and her young, plus a postlactating female. The single adult male was solitary. The roost housing the nine bats was in a hole in the ground that had an entrance 2.5 by 3.5 cm and inside dimensions of 2.0–3.5 by 15 by 31 cm. Other records consisted of individuals or pairs in a building, among boards resting against a building, under a loose strip of pine bark, under rocks or stones in erosion crevices, and in pockets of eroded sandstone.

Given the underground roosting habits of *Myotis ciliolabrum* in the West, and the records of *M. leibii* found under rocks in caves in the East, it will not be surprising if eastern maternity colonies, too, are found to be under rocks, in underground burrows, or in crevices.

PARASITES AND DISEASE. *Macronyssus crosbyi* and *Spinturnix americanus*, parasitic mites found on various other species of *Myotis*, have been reported from this host as well, along with two species of chigger mites normally found on bats.

RELATION TO HUMANS. This species is uncommon and poorly known, thus has little relation to humans other than that, like other insectivorous bats, it helps maintain the balance of nature by feeding on insects.

AREAS FOR FURTHER WORK. Obviously, little is known of the habits of this interesting but very uncommon species. Where are its maternity colonies? When does it enter and leave them? What does it eat? Does it feed in winter? What is its summer habitat? Does it carry any host-specific parasites?

### SUBSPECIES

None described.
Type locality: Erie Co., Ohio.

### LITERATURE

Best, T. L., and J. B. Jennings. 1997. *Myotis leibii.* **Mammalian Species No. 547.** Amer. Soc. Mammal. 6 pp.

Glass, B. P., and R. J. Baker. 1968. The status of the name *Myotis subulatus* Say. *Proc. Biol. Soc. Wash.* 81: 257–260.

Hitchcock, H. B., R. Keen, and A. Kurta. 1984. Survival rates of *Myotis leibii* and *Eptesicus fuscus* in southeastern Ontario. *J. Mammal.* 65: 126–130.

Jones, J. K., Jr., J. S. Hoffmann, D. W. Rice, C. Jones, R. J. Baker, and M. D. Engstrom. 1992. Revised checklist of North American mammals north of Mexico, 1991. Occ. Pap. Mus. Texas Tech Univ. No. 146. 23 pp.

Mohr, C. E. 1936. Notes on the least bat, *Myotis subulatus leibii*. *Proc. Pa. Acad. Sci.* 10: 62–65.

Tuttle, M. D., and L. R. Heaney. 1974. Maternity habits of *Myotis leibii* in South Dakota. *Bull. S. Cal. Acad. Sci.* 73: 80–83.

van Zyll de Jong, C. 1984. Taxonomic relationships of nearctic small footed bats of the *Myotis leibii* group (Chiroptera: Vespertilionidae). *Canadian J. Zool.* 62: 2519–2526.

Wilson, D. E., and D. M. Reeder. 1993. *Mammal Species of the World: A Taxonomic and Geographic Reference.* Washington: Smithsonian Institution Press, in assoc. with American Society of Mammalogists. 1206 pp.

## Little Brown Myotis, Little Brown Bat
### *Myotis lucifugus* (Le Conte)

DESCRIPTION. The little brown bat is similar to the other species of myotis in the east. It can

*Little brown myotis,* Myotis lucifugus
*(Bruce Hayward)*

be separated from the northern myotis by its shorter ears and shorter, rounded tragus; from the gray bat by its bicolored fur and attachment of the patagium to the ankle; from the Indiana bat by its bigger feet, more heavily furred toes, and lack or near lack of a keel on the calcar; from the small-footed myotis by its longer forearm and lack of a mask; and from the southeastern myotis by its less woolly fur and lack of a sagittal crest. The little brown bat has a furry face, only the nostrils and lips remaining naked. Its ears are moderately long, but when laid forward do not extend beyond the nostrils. The wing membrane between the humerus and knee is sparsely furred, the interfemoral membrane furred not at all. The calcar is unkeeled or only slightly keeled. The color above is a rich brown, at times almost bronze, but the hairs at their base are dark plumbeous or blackish. Ventrally, the distal third of the fur is tipped with buff. Young animals are much darker.

MEASUREMENTS. Average measurements of 18 specimens of both sexes from Center County, Pennsylvania, were: total length 89.2 (79–93), tail 34.6 (31–40), hind foot 9.4 (8.5–10), ear 14–16, forearm 38.1 (35–40), wingspread 222–272 mm. The average weight, during the spring and early summer, is 4–5 grams; just before hibernation, it is 7.5–8.5 grams.

Diploid number = 44. This is the number for all North American *Myotis*.

TOOTH FORMULA

$$\frac{2}{3} \quad \frac{1}{1} \quad \frac{3}{3} \quad \frac{3}{3} \; = \; 38$$

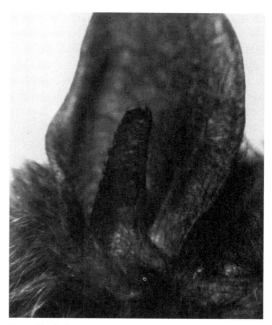

*Ear of little brown myotis, showing tragus*

DISTRIBUTION. The little brown bat occurs from Labrador to Alaska and, in the east, as far south as northern Alabama and Georgia. In the northern part of its range it is often the most abundant of all bats, although, like many other bats, it appears to be declining. Farther south, for example in Illinois, Indiana, and Ohio, red or big brown bats are often the more abundant bat species. This species also occurs throughout much of the west, from Alaska to northern Mexico.

HABITAT. This bat may be looked for almost everywhere. It is most commonly found about farms and towns and villages, and occurs from sea level to the forested mountaintops. In summer, female and young little brown bats can be found in clusters in maternity roosts, most often in buildings or other structures. We suspect, however, that they also roost sometimes in hollow trees, likely their ancestral habitat. Males are generally solitary, but can be looked for elsewhere in the maternity roost or in nearby buildings or trees. In the summer, males are sometimes seen in caves. Little brown bats hibernate in caves in winter, although we once found one in hibernation in an Indiana building in midwinter. Kurta and Teramino (1994) found at least 15,000 bats hibernating in a hydroelectric dam in Michigan. Most were *Myotis lucifugus* and *M. septentrionalis*, but one individual each of *M. sodalis* and *Pipistrellus subflavus* were also found.

HABITS. Shortly before dusk the little brown bat sallies forth from its daylight retreat—in a barn or in the attic of a church or house, or perhaps from behind a sheltering slab of loose bark or from the dark recesses of a cave (mostly males)— to flit over a nearby pond, river, or stream. After sweeping low over the water for a drink, it continues its flight, catching small moths and flies with its wing membranes or tail and then deftly removing them with its teeth, or it may fly to a nearby tree, where it can manage larger prey with greater facility. Often the bat locates a swarm of insects, such as midges, with echolocation, then flies back and forth through the swarm to capture its meal.

Practically from birth, little brown bats produce vocalizations, including the high-frequency sounds used in echolocation. The echoes of the high-frequency calls are used to locate both obstacles and food, and it is also clear that these bats find new roosts by cueing in on the calls of others. The calls last from about 1 to 5 milliseconds and range from about 40 to 80 kHz, most of their energy produced at 45 kHz (Fenton & Bell, 1979). A bat in free flight may produce about 20 pulses per second; and while approaching an obstacle or chasing prey it may produce a "feeding buzz" of over 50 pulses per second. The introduction of bat detectors (devices that pick up high-frequency calls) has helped in locating bats and learning about their behavior. Quite a bit of experience is required, but with a bat detector, differences in the echolocation calls can often be used to distinguish a *Myotis* bat from bats of other genera in the field. It is much more difficult, however, to distinguish a myotis of one species from a myotis of another species. A non-echolocation call used by little brown bats while feeding is a "honk" used to avoid collisions with one another (Barclay et al., 1979).

Three types of roosts are used by little brown bats: day roosts, night roosts, and hibernacula. Day roosts consist of the nursery areas, where the females and young form colonies, and the individual sites occupied by the males. Higher than ambient temperatures are important in choice of nursery roosts, both as an energy-conservation measure and for successful growth of the young. Nursery colonies are often in buildings, but may be in crevices. The day roosts of males and nonbreeding females are usually somewhere apart from the nursery colonies and may be in many types of sites. The bats here hang alone or in small groups, often in buildings, but they may be under tarpaper or loose bark, or in caves or mines. Again, temperature is important in site choice, but these sites range much cooler than the nursery sites, though they often have southwest exposure, which provides heat useful for arousal (Fenton, 1970). Sometimes one finds urine stalactites below where the bats have roosted. The liquid part of the urine has dried, leaving a structure much like a stalactite.

*Distribution of the little brown myotis,* Myotis lucifugus, *in the eastern United States*

*Urine stalactites on ceiling below little brown myotis*

After the initial evening feeding period, the bats usually pack themselves into confined spaces that serve as night roosts. Numbers of bats cramped into confined spaces apparently increase the ambient temperature, helping them to conserve energy and better digest food. Because the night roosts are often in the same building as the day roosts, proximity to feeding site may not be a factor in their being separated from one another. Females enter night roosts while pregnant, but return to the nursery roost when young are present. Night roosts are usually not occupied when temperatures exceed 15°C (60°F). Upon the dispersal of the nursing colonies, these bats, especially the young of the year, appear in numerous day roosts that had been uninhabited during the reproductive period.

By late August and early September the bats have already put on a great amount of fat, amounting to about one-fourth of their body weight. At this time, bats of several species may "swarm" or fly about the entrances of caves or mines. A mist net or Harp trap carefully placed over the entrance will often catch many in a night. The significance of the swarming behavior is not altogether known, but it appears to be an important component of mate-finding. The bats seldom venture far into the opening while swarming; they simply circle about and into and out of the entrance. They probably find the entrances by sensing air currents, and may in that fashion gain information about the potential virtue of caves as hibernacula. Another possibility is that swarming serves as a gathering locus prior to migration, though this seems unlikely, since the bats that swarm do not appear to form migratory flocks. Little brown bats usually hibernate in relatively small clusters and relatively small numbers in nearby caves and mines, although they may have to fly 160–320 km (100–200 miles) to find a suitable hibernaculum. Two little brown bats have been found in hibernation in buildings, one in southern Indiana and one in Cooperstown, New York. See Fenton (1969) for further discussion of these topics.

By late October, little brown bats are migrating to their hibernacula, though dates vary with latitude. Migration may be short or up to several hundred kilometers distant. The hibernacula are usually caves or mines unoccupied by the species during the summer, though males or nonparous females occasionally use them as day roosts. In the hibernacula they hang by their feet, so closely packed at times that a dozen can be picked up in one's hands. At such times the bats feel cold to the touch and exhibit all the characteristics of true hibernation; but unlike a dormant ground squirrel, which takes two to three hours to fully wake, they awake and fly about if handled, all within five to ten minutes. Energy for arousal from hibernation is quickly released by brown fat, and arousal normally occurs about once every two weeks during hibernation. The bats have accumulated about 2 grams of fat to maintain themselves during hibernation, but about 80% of this fat is consumed just for the arousals (Thomas et al., 1990). Little brown bats may even fly outside in winter, but they do not feed at that time (Whitaker and Rissler, 1992, 1993). It is important that arousal not occur too often, for it creates an energy drain that can lead to mortality.

The heart rate in this species generally ranges from 20 to 210 beats per minute, when the bat is at rest. The highest rate was recorded at 1368 beats per minute (Fenton and Barclay, Mammalian Species, 1980), the lowest (at −5°C, or 23°F) at 8 beats per minute.

Little brown bats are common over most of their range. Most species of bats may have radically decreased in numbers in recent years, owing to insecticide poisoning, control measures in buildings, and disturbance to wintering colonies. But although it may be declining at present, we suspect that this species and the big brown bat may be more abundant today than in presettlement days, owing to their ability to adapt to manmade structures.

FOOD AND FEEDING. The little brown bat is wholly insectivorous. The stomachs of those we have examined from Indiana contained the finely ground remains of tiny flies, true bugs (primarily Cicadellidae and Delphacidae), moths, caddisflies, beetles, and many other insects; midges (Diptera, Chironomidae) are a staple. Specimens examined about 20 minutes after they had taken flight already had well-filled stomachs, indicating how rapidly and effectively they feed. In turn, food passes through their digestive tracts very rapidly, within half an hour or so (Buchler, 1975), which permits steady ingestion for more extended periods. Little is known about taste discrimination, but little brown bats will reject some foods (Coutts et al., 1973). Dunning (1968) found that this species (and *Eptesicus*) would not take live *Cycnia tenera* (Lepidoptera: Arctiidae), which give ultrasonic "warning" sounds. And when dead specimens were taken into the mouth, they were immediately ejected, presumably found to be ill-tasting.

Echolocation is often used to capture individual insects. It appears clear, from watching the flight patterns of these bats over streams, and from the great numbers of individual species of tiny flies (often midges) sometimes found in individual stomachs, that this species often feeds by passing back and forth through swarms, rather than by focusing on individual insects. Fenton and Bell (1979) found that there were no social interactions between flying bats, other than "honking" at each other when on collision courses. Little brown bats appear to be "short-range feeders," a strategy compatible with feeding on clumps (or swarms) of insects. (Bats of this species often make several passes through small volumes of air, executing turns within a meter of target.) Those observed by Fenton and Bell hunted in a variety of situations, but when over water they usually flew low. Using a typical feeding "buzz" (the high pulse rates associated with small targets), they would swoop and catch insects. They would also take insects (or even items thrown there by Fenton and Bell) from the surface of the water, apparently in the mouth.

It appears that lactating individuals concentrate more on larger prey, although midges remain a staple. Coutts et al. (1973) found that three males of *M. lucifugus* consumed about 1.22 grams of food per day, six females 0.93 gram per day.

REPRODUCTION AND DEVELOPMENT. In summer, female little brown bats congregate in colonies, while the males remain solitary or form loose clusters. When females are found roosting with males, examination usually proves them to be nonparous or immature animals. The little brown bat mates in the fall and winter at swarming or hibernation sites, the inactive sperm being stored in the uterus during the period of dormancy. When ovulation then occurs in spring, fertilization soon follows. Delayed fertilization apparently allows ovulation to ensue soon after the female's arousal from hibernation, but may also help to get all females mated, by ensuring a long receptive period. Male little brown bats emit a special and specific "copulatory call" that apparently helps calm the female and indicates reproductive rather than aggressive behavior (Barclay and Thomas, 1979). Gestation is about 50–60 days. Active males sometimes attempt to mate in the hibernaculum, even with torpid females. Mating may also occur in the spring, before the bats have left their winter quarters. Breeding colonies generally begin to form in April, often in attics of buildings.

A single young is produced, sometime between mid-June and mid-July. The female hangs with its head up during partus and the young drops into the interfemoral membrane. The newborn bat is flesh-colored, with little fur. Its lacteal dentition is almost fully erupted at birth, and the eyes and ears open within a few hours of birth. While the parent forages during the evening, the young remains hidden in some dark retreat. There is no evidence that the parent ever carries the young on her hunting trips, although it can move the young if disturbed. We saw four females moving young when a barn was being torn down, and caught one such pair. The female weighed 7.33 grams, the pup 2.88 grams. Some mortality may occur when the young drop from the roost.

At about three weeks the young bat begins to fly on its own, at least in the area of the roost. It also starts feeding on insects, and weaning begins about this time, although Buchler (1980) found that the first attempts to catch insects consisted of sitting on a perch and waiting for the insects to come by. Soon, however, the young begins to fly nightly with the adults. By that time it has attained some of the adult proportions, such as in length of forearm, but through their first summer, the young remain lighter in weight than the adults.

POPULATION CHARACTERISTICS. The little brown bat has become heavily dependent on human structures in summer, but not in winter. Maternity colonies are most often in buildings or other structures, such as bridges, particularly in the expansion joints. Buildings most often used are houses, churches, and barns, the maternity colonies numbering from about 30 up to several thousand individuals. The largest colony we have known, in an unused barn at Brazil, Clay County, Indiana, numbered at its height (summer of 1989) about 6,700 individuals. We were pursuing long-term banding studies (we had banded about 1,800 individuals), and the church that owned the barn had allowed it to stand and was cooperating fully with our efforts. But the barn was sold to a second church—Methodists—and, good Christians that they are, they immediately tore the barn down, during the bats' birthing time. We attempted to move some of the bats to a nearby bathouse, but without success. When we introduced a female with a young into the bathouse, the female im-

mediately escaped, but we placed the baby in the bathouse nonetheless. The female returned within 30 seconds and lit on the cage in which the two had been transported, before finally disappearing.

Little brown bats have been known to live to at least 34 years of age. Al Hicks recently found a banded bat in an iron mine at Paradox, New York, that had been banded at the same location on 11 February 1961, 33 years earlier (Davis and Hitchcock, 1995). This is the longest known bat longevity on record.

ENEMIES. Bats have few predators, although an occasional cat, skunk, raccoon, or snake may learn how to enter a cave and capture them. We have seen many wings inside the entrance to Wyandotte Cave in Indiana from bats that had fallen prey to a cat. Adverse climatic conditions probably exact their toll: successive nights of rain or high wind are sometimes sufficient to cause mortality, for bats cannot long endure a fast. Insecticides may accumulate in fat deposits, and bats are sometimes killed upon release of the insecticides by the metabolism of the fat (Geluso et al., 1976). Kunz et al. (1977) documented the mortality of little brown bats at a nursery colony in southern New Hampshire from pesticides (DDT, chlordane). Several people have found bats of this species caught on barbed wire fences and burdocks.

PARASITES AND DISEASE. Intestinal roundworms, flukes, and tapeworms are all found in this host, but none is particularly abundant. Neither are external parasites overly abundant. The most prominent are chiggers, *Euschoengastia pipistrelli*, a macronyssid mite, *Macronyssus crosbyi*, and a flea, *Myodopsylla insignis*. Chiggers are often found in the ears, *Macronyssus* in the fur or often (especially the nymphs) on the membranes of the wings or tail, and the fleas run about in the fur.

RELATION TO HUMANS. These little bats are harmless, and inasmuch as they destroy vast quantities of insect pests, such as cutworm moths and cornborer moths, they should gain our gratitude. Unfortunately, they often seek out our dwellings, where their noise or accumulated droppings may become a nuisance. Bats may best be excluded from buildings by constructing barriers across the places where they enter (see p. 77). Exclusion, however, should certainly not be attempted from May through August, when the young are present. Better yet, one should undertake exclusion, if necessary, only when the bats are absent, i.e. between November and March.

AREAS FOR FURTHER WORK. Much more work on swarming is needed. Studies of the nutrient content of the food of this species, compared with the nutrient content of the guano in this or any other species of bat, would provide information on the nutrients the bats derive from various foods. Whitaker and Rissler (1992) found no bats feeding in the winter, but the slow digestion of remnant items in the digestive tracts apparently continues then. Further work is needed to determine the significance of this process. (Might the bats possess chitinase?) Do little brown bats feed in winter in the southern part of their range? What is the function of winter flight during which the bats do not attempt to feed? Do they drink water at this time? How much energy is expended during flight outside in winter at various temperatures?

## SUBSPECIES

*Myotis lucifugus lucifugus* (LeConte)

As described above. The only subspecies in the eastern United States. Several others, questionable to us, have been described from the western United States.

Type locality: Georgia, probably LeConte Plantation, near Riceboro, Liberty Co.

## LITERATURE

Anthony, E. L. P., and T. H. Kunz. 1977. Feeding strategies of the little brown bat, *Myotis lucifugus*, in southern New Hampshire. *Ecology* 58: 775–786.

Barclay, R. M. R., M. B. Fenton, and D. W. Thomas. 1979. Social behavior of the little brown bat, *Myotis lucifugus*: 2. Vocal communication. *Behav. Ecol. Sociobiol.* 6: 137–146.

Barclay, R. M. R., and D. W. Thomas. 1979. Copulation call of *Myotis lucifugus*: Discrete situation-specific communication signal. *J. Mammal.* 60: 632–634.

Belwood, J. J., and M. B. Fenton. 1976. Variation in the diet of *Myotis lucifugus* (Chiroptera: Vespertilionidae). *Canadian J. Zool.* 54: 1674–1678.

Brenner, F. J. 1974. A five-year study of a hibernating colony of *Myotis lucifugus*. *Ohio J. Sci.* 74: 239–244.

Buchler, E. R. 1975. Food transit time in *Myotis lucifugus* (Chiroptera: Vespertilionidae). *J. Mammal.* 56: 252–255.

———. 1980. The development of flight, foraging and echolocation in the little brown bat (*Myotis lucifugus*). *Behav. Ecol. Sociobiol.* 6: 211–218.

Coutts, R. A., M. B. Fenton, and E. Glen. 1973. Food intake by captive *Myotis lucifugus* and *Eptesicus fuscus* (Chiroptera: Vespertilionidae). *J. Mammal.* 54: 985–990.

Davis, W. B., and H. B. Hitchcock. 1995. A new longevity record for the bat *Myotis lucifugus*. *Bat Research News* 36: 6.

Dunning, D. C. 1968. Warning sounds of moths. *Z. Tierpsychol.* 25: 129–138.

Fenton, M. B. 1969. Summer activity of *Myotis lucifugus* (Chiroptera: Vespertilionidae) at hibernacula in Ontario and Quebec. *Canadian J. Zool.* 47: 597–602.

———. 1970. Population studies of *Myotis lucifugus* (Chiroptera: Vespertilionidae) in Ontario. Life Sci. Contr. Royal Ontario Mus. 77. 34 pp.

Fenton, M. B., and R. M. R. Barclay. 1980. *Myotis lucifugus*. **Mammalian Species No. 142.** Amer. Soc. Mammal. 8 pp.

Fenton, M. B., and G. P. Bell. 1979. Echolocation and feeding behavior in four species of *Myotis* (Chiroptera). *Canadian J. Zool.* 57: 1271–1277.

———. 1981. Recognition of species of insectivorous bats by their echolocation calls. *J. Mammal.* 62: 233–243.

Geluso, K. N., J. S. Altenbach, and D. E. Wilson. 1976. Bat mortality: Pesticide poisoning and migratory stress. *Science* 194: 184–186.

Humphrey, S. R., and J. B. Cope. 1976. Population ecology of the little brown bat, *Myotis lucifugus*, in Indiana and north central Kentucky. Spec. Publ. No. 4, Amer. Soc. Mammal. 81 pp.

Kunz, T. H., E. L. P. Anthony, and W. T. Rumage III. 1977. Mortality of little brown bats following multiple pesticide application. *J. Wildl. Mgmt.* 41: 476–483.

Kurta, A., and J. A. Teramino. 1994. A novel hibernaculum and noteworthy records of the Indiana bat and eastern pipistrelle (Chiroptera: Vespertilionidae). *Amer. Midland Nat.* 132: 410–413.

Thomas, D. W., M. Dorais, and J. Bergeron. 1990. Winter energy budgets and cost of arousals for hibernating little brown bats, *Myotis lucifugus*. *J. Mammal.* 71: 475–479.

*Northern myotis,*
Myotis septentrionalis

Whitaker, J. O., Jr., and L. J. Rissler. 1992. Winter activity of bats at a mine entrance in Vermillion County, Indiana. *Amer. Midland Nat.* 127: 52–59.
———. 1993. Do bats feed in winter? *Amer. Midland Nat.* 129: 200–203.

## Northern Myotis
## *Myotis septentrionalis*
### (Trouessart)                    Color plate 3

The eastern long-eared bat was long known as Keen's bat, *Myotis keenii septentrionalis*, but van Zyll de Jong (1979) decided, on morphological grounds, that the eastern form represents a separate species, which then became *Myotis septentrionalis*. We have followed Jones et al. (1992) in accepting this disposition, but Wilson and Reeder (1992) did not. More work is needed before consensus can be reached on whether these two taxa are members of the same or different species.

DESCRIPTION. The northern myotis is similar in appearance to the little brown bat, *Myotis lucifugus*, but is distinguished by its long ears (about 14 to 18 mm from the notch), which when laid forward extend about 4 mm beyond the nostrils on live individuals. The tragus is also long (about 8 to 10 mm from the notch), narrow, somewhat curved, and much more pointed than that of *M. lucifugus*. In color, too, this species is similar to *M. lucifugus*, but the brown hair tips of the dorsum are neither so long nor so glossy. The ears and the face are usually less blackish than in

*M. lucifugus*. The venter is usually yellowish, but the two species should be laid side by side for such color differences to become apparent. The skull is narrower in proportion to its length than is that of *M. lucifugus*.

MEASUREMENTS. Average measurements of 20 adults from various parts of the range are: total length 84.1 (79.2–87.8), tail 41.7 (36.4–43), hind foot 8.4 (7.2–9.4), ear 17–19, forearm 36.7 (34.6–38.8), wingspread 228–258 mm; and weight 5 to 10 grams.

Diploid number = 44.

TOOTH FORMULA

$$\frac{2}{3} \ \frac{1}{1} \ \frac{3}{3} \ \frac{3}{3} \ = \ 38$$

DISTRIBUTION. In eastern United States this species occurs from Maine to Wisconsin, south to Alabama, Georgia, and the panhandle of Florida. It also occurs in southeastern Canada and west to northern Arkansas, eastern Kansas, the Dakotas, and southern Saskatchewan.

HABITAT. Northern myotis are usually solitary or gathered in small groups, but in spring the females cluster in maternity colonies. Few such colonies have been found, but they are usually small (up to several dozen bats). We think most are in hollows in tree limbs or perhaps under loose bark. We have found several maternity colonies in artificial bat houses in shade. They have also been found behind shutters and in buildings. We found one nursery colony of about 100 individuals in a large, seldom-used warehouse. Among over 400 maternity colonies of bats that we found in buildings in Indiana, this was the only one of this species (although Jim Cope did find one earlier in an Indiana barn). In this building, the bats tended to be in clusters when the pups were young, then tended to spread out over the building later.

Hamilton found several bats of this species behind the shutters of a small cottage on the shore of a lonely lake in eastern New York. They usually left late in the evening, and seldom returned until dawn, probably repairing to a night roost from time to time when they tired of hunting. Hamilton once broke a dead yellow birch stump in a Maine bog and found a northern myotis

tucked away for the day, and three males were found hanging inside a small decorative bell on the front porch of a house in Indiana. During mid-August in a New York cave a single northern myotis was found hanging in the midst of 20 little brown bats.

HABITS. *Myotis septentrionalis* enters hibernation in October and November, and emerges in March or April. It does not make extended migrations, usually choosing to hibernate in nearby caves or mines. It usually hibernates in the same caves or mines in concurrent use by bats of other species, primarily *Eptesicus fuscus, Pipistrellus subflavus, M. lucifugus,* and *M. sodalis,* but generally at different locations within these places, the other myotis often in large colonies, *M. septentrionalis* usually single or in groups of two or three. At least 15,000 bats were found hiber-

*Distribution of the northern myotis,* Myotis septentrionalis, *in the eastern United States*

nating in a hydroelectric dam in Michigan by Kurta and Teramino (1994). Most were *M. lucifugus* and *M. septentrionalis*. The little brown myotis were clustered; the northern myotis were mostly solitary. The northern myotis and other species usually begin to arrive at the hibernating caves in August or September. The northern bats sometimes hang from the ceiling, or can be seen in a crevice, but our limited data suggest that the great majority are completely hidden in tiny cracks and crevices. We are aware of at least two caves and one mine where this appears to be the case. About 100 pipistrelles and 300 little brown bats hibernate at Copperhead Cave, a mine in Vermillion County, Indiana, and are easily seen, but virtually no northern bats can be found there in winter. Nonetheless, from the numbers of them emerging in spring we estimate that perhaps 800 to 1200 northern bats hibernate there (Whitaker and Rissler, 1992). Like the little brown bat, these bats often emerge from caves in winter, in Indiana, and fly about briefly, but the function of this behavior is not known. They do not feed at this time, even when insects are available (Whitaker and Rissler, 1993). An average weight loss of 41% and 43% in hibernating females and males has been reported.

As is true of most eastern species, echolocation is well developed. Stones and Branick (1969) found that some bats with impaired vision were able to return home a distance of 58 km (38 miles), but that none with impaired hearing could.

FOOD AND FEEDING. Little about the food of this species has been published, but reduviids, cicadellids, ichneumons, lepidopterans, and dipterans were found in the stomachs of three individuals from Indiana. Droppings from below a colony in Maine examined by Hamilton revealed finely ground remains of caddisflies, mayflies, and Diptera. Virgil Brack and the author (Whitaker) have examined guano from about 250 individuals of this species, mostly from Indiana but a few from Missouri as well. The data, not yet published, indicate the species to be a moth strategist, but beetles, various flies, caddisflies, and spiders are also important. We suspected this bat to be a moth strategist, since large

ears often seem to be associated with moth feeding. Spiders, often eaten by this species, are presumably gleaned from leaves.

REPRODUCTION AND DEVELOPMENT. There is relatively little information on reproduction in this species, but like many other eastern colonial bats, it does exhibit delayed fertilization. Mating presumably occurs in August and September, when this species can often be found swarming at the entrances to caves, along with such other species as *Myotis lucifugus*, *M. sodalis*, and *Pipistrellus subflavus*. At dusk on an August night, R. E. Mumford and Whitaker set up a mist net just inside the entrance to Ray's Cave in southern Indiana. Within 15 minutes, it was so full of northern bats that we had to remove it.

The largest maternity colony we are aware of was the one referred to above, discovered on 8 July in a large warehouse. It consisted of about 100 individuals in two clusters and included some nonvolants. We have taken females with large embryos in New York State on 21 June, 29 June, and 9 July, but Easterla (1968) reported a young produced on 5 June in Missouri. Kunz (1971) reported pregnant females from 20 May to 23 June, and lactating females from 23 June to 28 July, in central Iowa. The young were first volant by 23 July. It appears that there is much variation in the birth dates of this species, but the single young is often born in July, or later than in most other eastern U.S. bats.

POPULATION CHARACTERISTICS. Maternity colonies number up to perhaps 100 individuals. Large numbers may occur in winter in caves, but they are usually solitary and crawl into tiny cracks and crevices, for the most part out of sight. Some individuals have been known to live as long as 18½ years (Hall et al., 1957).

ENEMIES. Like other North American bats, the northern myotis suffers little predation, though any of the typical predators will kill and eat a bat when the opportunity arises.

PARASITES AND DISEASE. The main ectoparasites of this species are the mites *Macronyssus crosbyi, Acanthophthirius gracilis, Olabidocarpus whitakeri*, and *Spinturnix americanus* and the chigger *Euschoengastia pipistrelli*.

RELATION TO HUMANS. Like other bats, this one eats its share of nocturnal flying insects. Otherwise, it is of little direct consequence to us, since it seldom enters our buildings.

AREAS FOR FURTHER WORK. Relatively little information is available on the biology of this species, and an extensive study of its life history would be in order. Much more work is needed on its maternity colonies and its winter behavior.

## SUBSPECIES

None described; but see the discussion at the head of this species account.

Type locality: Halifax, Nova Scotia.

## LITERATURE

Easterla, D. A. 1968. Parturition of Keen's myotis in southwestern Missouri. *J. Mammal.* 49: 770.

Fitch, J. H., and K. A. Shump, Jr. 1979. *Myotis keenii.* **Mammalian Species No. 121.** Amer. Soc. Mammal. 3 pp. [Much of the material included is on the eastern species, *M. septentrionalis.*]

Hall, J. S., R. J. Cloutier, and D. R. Griffin. 1957. Longevity records and notes on tooth wear of bats. *J. Mammal.* 38: 407–409.

Jones, J. K., Jr., J. S. Hoffmann, D. W. Rice, C. Jones, R. J. Baker, and M. D. Engstrom. 1992. Revised checklist of North American mammals north of Mexico, 1991. Occ. Pap. Mus. Texas Tech Univ. No. 146. 23 pp.

Kunz, T. H. 1971. Reproduction of some vespertilionid bats in central Iowa. *Amer. Midland Nat.* 86: 477–486.

Kurta, A., and J. A. Teramino. 1994. A novel hibernaculum and noteworthy records of the Indiana bat and eastern pipistrelle (Chiroptera: Vespertilionidae). *Amer. Midland Nat.* 132: 410–413.

Stones, R. C., and L. P. Branick. 1969. Use of hearing in homing by two species of *Myotis* bats. *J. Mammal.* 50: 157–160.

van Zyll de Jong, C. G. 1979. Distribution and systematic relationships of long-eared *Myotis* in western North America. *Canadian J. Zool.* 57: 987–994.

Whitaker, J. O., Jr., and L. J. Rissler. 1992. Winter activity of bats at a mine entrance in Vermillion County, Indiana. *Amer. Midland Nat.* 127: 52–59.

———. 1993. Do bats feed in winter? *Amer. Midland Nat.* 129: 200–203.

Wilson, D. E., and D. M. Reeder. 1993. *Mammal Species of the World: A Taxonomic and Geographic Reference.* Washington: Smithsonian Institution Press, in assoc. with American Society of Mammalogists. 1206 pp.

## Indiana Myotis *Myotis sodalis* Miller and Allen          Color plate 3

DESCRIPTION. Because this myotis bears such a strong resemblance to *Myotis lucifugus*, it was

*Indiana myotis,* Myotis sodalis

not described as a distinct species until 1928 (Miller and Allen, 1928). It is best distinguished from that species by its short, inconspicuous toe hairs, by its smaller foot (usually 9 instead of 10 mm long), by its keeled calcar, and by its more uniform and distinctively pinkish-brown fur. The color of *M. lucifugus* is much more variable, but its hair tips are burnished bronze. The toe hairs in *M. lucifugus* are usually quite conspicuous and extend past the knuckle joints; those of *M. sodalis* are inconspicuous and do not extend past the knuckle joints. The well-developed keel on the calcar is an excellent character, but one, unfortunately, that does not

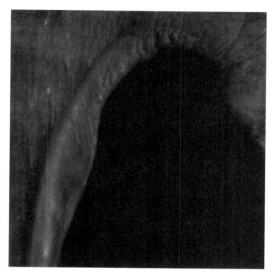

*Keeled calcar of Indiana myotis*

often show on study skins, although moistening the area may allow one to determine this character.

The fur is of an extremely fine and fluffy texture; the hairs have a tendency, owing perhaps to a slight crinkling, to stand out from each other a little, as they do in *Pipistrellus subflavus.* Below, the fur is slaty basally, with grayish-white tips, washed more or less heavily with cinnamon-brown, particularly at the flanks, rather than with the slightly yellowish wash of *M. lucifugus.* The skull usually has a slight sagittal ridge, but the teeth are indistinguishable from those of *M. lucifugus.* The tragus is short and relatively rounded, as it is in *M. lucifugus.* Biologists should give careful attention to all small brown bats, for these two and other species of *Myotis* can easily be confused.

MEASUREMENTS. Average measurements of 36 specimens from various parts of the species' range are: total length 81.7 (70.8–90.6), tail 36.4 (27–43.8), hind foot 7.9 (7.2–8.6), forearm 38.8 (36–40.4), wingspread 240–267 mm; and weight 5–11 grams.
Diploid number = 44.

TOOTH FORMULA

$$\frac{2}{3} \ \frac{1}{1} \ \frac{3}{3} \ \frac{3}{3} \ = \ 38$$

DISTRIBUTION. The Indiana bat occurs throughout much of eastern United States, from the central Mississippi Valley, eastern Alabama, and the panhandle of Florida to New England, but not along the Atlantic Coast. It occurs west through much of Missouri and Arkansas and into northeastern Oklahoma.

HABITAT. The Indiana myotis gathers in summer in small colonies, usually under the loose bark of trees in semi-wooded areas, in upland or bottomland forests, or even completely in the open (Kurta et al., 1993a, b). Gardner et al. (1991), using radio-tracking, found 48 different roost trees in eight Illinois counties. One of the colonies included 95 bats in June 1988, and 50 in September the next year. In two of the 48 roosts there were 18 bats; in six, 8–15 bats; in nine, 2–6 bats; and in 56, lone bats in each when found. Trees used as roosts, in order of preference (the numbers are small), were slippery elm, northern red oak, shagbark hickory, silver maple, cottonwood, bitternut hickory, sassafras, sugar maple, white and shingle oak, and American elm. Most roost sites were under the exfoliating bark of dead trees, but four were under the bark of living trees and three (one bat each) were in cavities; 37 were in uplands and 11 were in floodplains; 32 of the roost trees were in areas with closed canopy, 12 in areas with canopies 30–80% closed. Since most of the roosts are in dead trees, the bats suffer a constant attrition of suitable roost sites, about one-third per year.

Kurta et al. (1993b) found a colony in southern Michigan occupying eight different roost trees, all of them green ash and all in full sun, in an area that was inundated by water for most of the year. The number using any one roost tree varied greatly throughout the summer, and there was much movement between trees, only two trees being used for extended periods. Bats in this colony were present until 15 September. Kurta et al. also discovered a maternity colony of 95 bats in a hollow sycamore tree in total sun in a pasture in Illinois.

Callahan et al. (1997) studied four maternity

colonies and found that Indiana bats used two types of roosts: primary roosts, which they defined as roosts that housed more than 30 bats on more than one occasion, and alternate roosts, which were used by smaller numbers of bats. All primary roosts were in standing dead trees exposed to sunlight, and there were one to three primary roosts per colony. For the four colonies, a total of 54 roost trees, 10 to 20 trees per colony, was located. Two of the colonies had one primary roost tree, one had two, and one had three. Use of alternate roost trees increased in times of higher temperatures and during rainy periods.

In winter, Indiana bats come together from a considerable area to form large clusters in a very few caves for hibernation. Probably over 95% of the bats winter in 15 caves, six of them in Missouri, nine in the eastern United States. That they settle in so few caves is why this species is on the federal endangered list, even though still rather abundant. Fourteen winter hibernacula have therefore been listed as critical habitat for protection by the Environmental Protection Agency. Considering all of the major populations (Priority 1 caves), there has been an estimated decrease of the total population of this species of up to 58% since 1960 and as much as 36% just since 1983 (Clawson, 1991). In great part, these declines have probably resulted from human disturbance, and protection efforts have focused on limiting winter access to these hibernacula, coupled with a censusing of them only every other year. *Myotis sodalis* favors hibernating caves in which temperatures are cooler and more stable than those required by most other *Myotis* species. Summer roosting and feeding habitat has also declined.

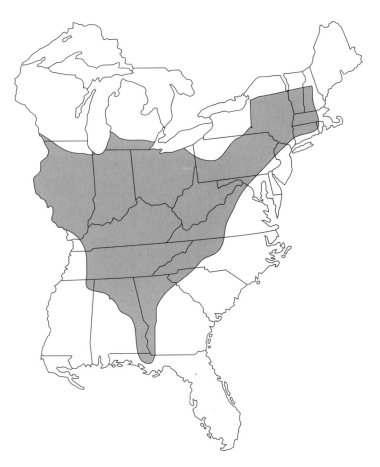

*Distribution of the Indiana myotis,* Myotis sodalis, *in the eastern United States*

HABITS. There are six main annual events in the life of many bats: hibernation, a short spring "swarming" or "staging" period upon emergence from hibernation, spring migration, the summer birthing period, fall migration, and fall swarming prior to hibernation. Indiana bats, like other bats, do not all migrate at once, either in spring or fall. Body fat increases by about 50% prior to hibernation.

In hibernation, *Myotis sodalis* clusters in large, tightly packed, rather characteristic masses, on the walls and ceilings, often all lined up one deep so that only the faces, ears, and wrists show. The cooler sites favored by large colonies

*Hibernating cluster of Indiana myotis in cave in southern Indiana*

offer metabolic advantages, but also a greater chance that bats will need to move occasionally during the winter. Smaller colonies occur in warmer sites, which are less advantageous metabolically but present less chance of disturbance (Clawson et al., 1980). Bats hibernate in portions of the cave where temperatures are 2–5°C (33–42°F), relative humidity is 66 to 95% (average 87%), and there is some movement of air. Because individuals wake from hibernation at perhaps two- to three-week intervals, there are usually a few individuals awake at any one time, at least in a large colony. The heart rate of bats hibernating at 5°C was found to be 36 to 62 beats per minute, which is higher than that of *Myotis lucifugus* (24–32) and *Lasiurus borealis* (10–16) (Davis and Reite, 1967), whereas the rate is around 600 beats per minute in an active bat. Indiana myotis leave the hibernacula in late April to late May or early June, the females leaving first. Often, some males remain

near the hibernacula throughout the summer.

In April and May, Indiana bats gradually emerge from hibernation and enter the staging period, when they begin their feeding forays. Some copulation may also occur at the wintering sites, prior to spring migration. Because most females have emerged by the end of April and presumably have migrated, later spring swarming includes mostly males. Usually, spring migration is generally northward, and the bats move up to several hundred kilometers.

That this species spreads out over a considerable area from its winter hibernating quarters is evidenced by the number of individuals taken in summer in areas where there are no caves. Females congregate at the maternity roost trees at this time and have their young. Cope et al. (1973), using bat detectors, observed Indiana bats making direct flights from the maternity colonies, along hedgerows, toward the feeding area, the nearby river. Patterson and Hardin (1969) recorded flight speeds of 12.8 to 20 kph (8–12.4 mph). In Illinois, mean foraging areas were reported as 51.8 ha (128 acres) for pregnant females and 94 ha (232 acres) for lactating females (Garner and Gardner, 1992). Males and nonbreeding females form separate small colonies, apart from the parous females.

After birthing, and after the young bats have become independent, migration back to the hibernacula begins, the males tending to precede the females. The first bats begin to arrive at the swarming caves in late July, the others then building through late summer and fall, peaking in September and October. Earlier bats are mostly males, but in September the sexes are about equally represented. Bats fly in and out of the entrance throughout the night, but there are few bats inside the caves during the day, especially early in this period. Later, increasing numbers of bats enter hibernation, and swarming behavior decreases. Swarming continues through about the first week in November, and late-arriving females are thus bred, but it is not known if females mate during their first year.

Homing is well developed in this species, vision and echolocation both playing important roles.

FOOD AND FEEDING. These bats forage in upland and bottomland forest, up to about 5 km

(3 miles) from the maternity colony. They feed on a variety of insects, with small Lepidoptera, Diptera, Trichoptera, Hymenoptera, Coleoptera, Plecoptera, Homoptera, and Neuroptera all being recorded. Nonetheless, Indiana bats usually feed on particular prey groups, regardless of habitat, moths most often (Belwood, 1979; Brack and LaVal, 1985), followed by Coleoptera or Diptera. In southern Michigan, however, we found them feeding on caddisflies, dipterans (including many mosquitos), and moths.

REPRODUCTION AND DEVELOPMENT. Until James B. Cope and associates (Humphrey et al., 1977) found and studied three maternity colonies near Richmond, Indiana, little was known of the breeding habits of this species, and only three pregnant individuals had been taken. Copulation occurs primarily during fall swarming, or after bats arrive at the hibernacula in October. The females enter hibernation, but the males remain active for a time and copulate with additional incoming females. Hundreds have been seen copulating at night at Bat Cave Kentucky, in early October. They spread in pairs and copulate on the ceiling of the cave, the sperm remaining in the uteri of the females until spring. Limited copulation may occur in winter or early spring as well. Ovulation, fertilization, and implantation all probably occur after the bats emerge from hibernation.

The colonies studied by Cope were located by using bat detectors to pinpoint the movements and concentrations of bats. They were under loose bark on a dead bitternut hickory, a living shagbark hickory, and a dead cottonwood. Since the development of radio-tracking, many other maternity roosts have been found, in a variety of trees. The maternity colonies of Indiana bats are relatively small, but females and young sometimes exceed 100 individuals. The maximum we know of was about 130 individuals. The single young is born in late June or early July, and lactating females are seen from about 10 June through July. Weaning occurs at 25 to 37 days, and the first young may be volant by mid-July. In two of the three colonies found by Humphrey et al. (1977), 25 females reared 23 young to flying age, and 28 weaned 23 young. The third colony was found at Knightstown, Indiana, on the Big Blue River. The entire colony of 109 bats, captured on 29 July 1978, consisted of 51 adult females and 58 immatures (26 females and 32 males). On 8 September 1984, a farmer at Freelandville, Knox County, Indiana, cut down a dead shagbark hickory in a woodlot a few hundred meters from a farm pond. Out flew a number of Indiana bats, 11 of which were sent to the rabies lab, from which we received them. All were adult female *Myotis sodalis*, affording us a late record for a maternity colony and the first in a more upland situation. Unfortunately, nearly all the trees in the area were cut by the next year and the bats were no longer to be seen.

POPULATION CHARACTERISTICS. Colony formation in Indiana begins in early May, reaches its maximum by mid-June, then slowly declines from mid-August through mid-September (Humphrey et al., 1977). In winter, however, the bats congregate in vast numbers in dense groups in a very few caves, although some hibernate in small clusters or alone. The largest reported number in an Indiana cave was 100,000 bats, in 1975, and the number hibernating in that cave now is about 80,000 bats each winter. In Indiana, bats hibernate from about mid-November to mid-April, in caves or mines with stable temperatures below 10°C (51°F), preferably at about 4–8°C.

Longevity was recorded for one banded bat at 20 years, and several of 13 and 14 years were found.

ENEMIES. Like most other bats, this species has few enemies, other than by chance encounters. Snakes and carnivorous birds and mammals undoubtedly capture them when opportunity arises. A housecat killed a number in Wyandotte Cave in Indiana one year.

PARASITES AND DISEASE. The most abundant ectoparasite of this species is the macronyssid mite *Macronyssus crosbyi*, but fleas and a myobiid mite have also been found. This bat and the gray bat are host to a peculiar mite, *Spinturnix globosus*, found only in the anus of the host. More peculiar, only females of this mite have been found. The mite is so host-specific that its presence can help identify the species of bat.

RELATION TO HUMANS. The Indiana bat was placed on the federal endangered species list on 11 March 1967 by the U.S. Fish and Wildlife Service. Before developmental projects can begin, the location of maternity colonies, hibernacula, and feeding areas of this species must be determined.

AREAS FOR FURTHER WORK. Much more information is needed on the summer behavior of males. How do the bats navigate back to a specific hibernaculum, a small cave opening that may be in deep woods? Are there differences in food habits with age, sex, and time of feeding (dusk vs. dawn)? Do first-year females breed?

## SUBSPECIES

None described.
Type locality: Wyandotte Cave, Crawford Co., Indiana.

### LITERATURE

Belwood, J. J. 1979. Feeding ecology of an Indiana bat community with emphasis on the endangered Indiana bat, *Myotis sodalis*. Unpubl. M.S. thesis, University of Florida, Gainesville. 103 pp.

Brack, V., Jr., and R. K. Laval, Jr. 1985. Food habits of the Indiana bat in Missouri. *J. Mammal.* 66: 308–315.

Brack, V., Jr., A. M. Wilkinson, and R. E. Mumford. 1984. Hibernacula of the endangered Indiana bat in Indiana. *Proc. Ind. Acad. Sci.* 93: 463–468.

Callahan, E. V., R. D. Drobney, and R. L. Clawson. 1997. Selection of summer roosting sites by Indiana bats (*Myotis sodalis*) in Missouri. *J. Mammal.* 78: 818–825.

Clawson, R. L. 1991. Report on the status of Priority 1 Indiana bat hibernacula, 1991. Unpubl. report, U.S. Fish and Wildlife Service, Minneapolis. 11 pp.

Clawson, R. L., R. K. Laval, M. L. Laval, and W. Caire. 1980. Clustering behavior of hibernating *Myotis sodalis* in Missouri. *J. Mammal.* 61: 235–253.

Cope, J. B., A. R. Richter, and R. S. Mills. 1973. A summer concentration of the Indiana bat, *Myotis sodalis*, in Wayne Co., Indiana. *Proc. Ind. Acad. Sci.* 83: 482–484.

Davis, W. H., and O. B. Reite. 1967. Responses of bats from temperate regions to changes in ambient temperature. *Biol. Bull.* 132: 320–328.

Gardner, J. E., J. D. Garner, and J. E. Hofmann. 1991. Summer roost selection and roosting behavior of *Myotis sodalis* (Indiana bat) in Illinois. Unpubl. report. Endangered Species Coordinator, Region 3, U.S. Fish and Wildlife Service, Minneapolis. 56 pp.

Garner, J., and J. E. Gardner. 1992. Determination of summer distribution and habitat utilization of the Indiana bat (*Myotis sodalis*) in Illinois. Unpubl. report, Illinois Natural History Survey, Champaign. 25 pp.

Hall, J. J. 1962. A life history and taxonomic study of the Indiana bat, *Myotis sodalis*. Sci. Publ., Reading Publ. Mus. and Art Gallery 12. 68 pp.

Humphrey, S. R., A. R. Richter, and J. B. Cope. 1977. Summer habitat and ecology of the endangered Indiana bat, *Myotis sodalis*. *J. Mammal.* 58: 334–346.

Kurta, A., J. Kath, E. L. Smith, R. Foster, M. W. Orick, and R. Ross. 1993a. A maternity roost of the endangered Indiana bat (*Myotis sodalis*) in an unshaded, hollow sycamore tree (*Platanus occidentalis*). *Amer. Midland Nat.* 130: 405–407.

Kurta, A., D. King, J. A. Teramino, J. M. Stribley, and K. F. Williams. 1993b. Summer roosts of the endangered Indiana bat (*Myotis sodalis*) on the northern edge of its range. *Amer. Midland Nat.* 129: 132–138.

Miller, G. S., Jr., and G. M. Allen. 1928. The American bats of the genera *Myotis* and *Pizonyx*. Bull. U.S. Natl. Mus. 144. 218 pp.

Thomson, C. E. 1982. *Myotis sodalis*. **Mammalian Species No. 163**. Amer. Soc. Mammal. 5 pp.

Patterson, A. P., and J. W. Hardin. 1969. Flight speeds of five species of vespertilionid bats. *J. Mammal.* 50: 152–153.

## Silver-Haired Bat
## *Lasionycteris noctivagans*
## (LeConte)                    Color plate 3

DESCRIPTION. The silver-haired bat can be distinguished at once from all other eastern bats by its color. The pelage, dark blackish brown or black, the ends of many of the hairs tipped with silver, is alike in the two sexes. This frosting is most pronounced along the middle of the back and is absent, or nearly so, on the face, crown, and throat. The fur extends on the upper surface of the interfemoral membrane for half its length. The short, rounded ear, nearly as broad as long, has a broad, bluntly rounded tragus. The flattened skull has a broad rostrum, the dorsal profile being practically straight, and there is a distinct concavity on each side of the rostrum. Bats of this genus, as in *Pipistrellus* and *Corynorhinus*, have two upper incisors on each side

*Silver-haired bat,* Lasionycteris noctivagans
*(Tony Brentlinger)*

and a *single reduced premolar immediately behind the canine. Myotis,* by contrast, has two (rarely one) reduced premolars, and the premolars in *Eptesicus* and *Nycticeius* are all full-sized (see p. 81).

MEASUREMENTS. Average measurements of 55 individuals from Indiana were: total length 99.7 (84–113), tail 38.8 (27–47), hind foot 8.2 (7–11), forearm 41.5 (39–44), wingspread 279–310 mm; and weight 10.5 (7.4–16.4) grams.
  Diploid number = 20.

TOOTH FORMULA

$$\frac{2}{3} \ \frac{1}{1} \ \frac{2}{3} \ \frac{3}{3} \ = \ 36$$

DISTRIBUTION. *Lasionycteris* is found only in North America, the single species occurring from the Atlantic to the Pacific, and from southern Canada (but to Alaska along the Pacific coast) south through most of the United States and barely into Mexico. In eastern United States this bat occurs from Maine and Wisconsin south to Mississippi, Alabama, and Georgia. It can best be characterized as a northern species, for

its summer range is essentially the north woods, and it is common in some northern regions. C. Hart Merriam, a century ago, stated that in the 1880s it was the most abundant bat of the Adirondacks. Although good data on its summer distribution are largely lacking, it appears to bear its young in Canada and across the northern states—Wisconsin, Michigan, New York, and New England, and south perhaps through the Appalachians. Silver-haired bats in the east pursue a well-developed migration to the south, where they hibernate. They spend the winter in the middle states from southern Illinois, Indiana, and coastal New Jersey south to Tennessee and South Carolina, Alabama, and northern and coastal Georgia. They do not occur in most of Illinois, Indiana, Ohio, Pennsylvania, Connecticut, or Rhode Island in either summer or winter, but are regular migrants through those states in spring and fall. Females apparently migrate farther north than males. The range of this species is mapped to show summer and winter range as well as areas where the species is known only during migration. A very few have been found hibernating in winter to the north of the range indicated.

HABITAT. Silver-haired bats inhabit wooded or semi-wooded areas, where they apparently live in holes in trees in the summer. Little is known of their hibernation, but at least some hibernate in cliff crevices, hollow trees, and caves and mines.

HABITS. This is a bat of the watercourses, flying about the trees and tall shrubs in coniferous or mixed forests bordering streams and lakes. It leaves its diurnal retreat early in the evening, and is often seen abroad before the sun has fully set. It is easily recognized by its slow, erratic flight. In fact, individuals have been brought down with a handful of alder switches as they repeatedly flew past on their hunting paths bordering a small northern bog pond.
  *Lasionycteris noctivagans* has long been regarded as a solitary, migratory, tree-roosting bat. It *is* clearly migratory, and it *is* often solitary, although cases of several occurring together are known, and it does form small maternity colo-

nies. Six individuals were captured at one time in a net operated by bird banders in New Jersey in the fall of 1963, indicating that they were flying (presumably migrating) together (Barbour and Davis 1969). These bats do not hang in foliage in the manner of red or hoary bats. Usually, one comes upon a single individual behind loose bark, under a shingle or shutter, in a rock crevice, or in a hollow tree. Some years this bat is rather common; at other times it may be quite scarce.

There are early, but questionable, reports of this species forming large maternity colonies, and more recent records of silver-haired bats, in Canada, indicate they form nursery colonies in hollows in trees. Novakowski (1956) found a nursery colony on 7 August in Saskatchewan, in a cavity in a balsam poplar about 5 meters above the ground. Included in the colony were three adults, three or four nonvolant young, and one pregnant female. The very late date given and the mixed reproductive stages described make one wonder about the details of this record, but the adults are preserved and their identity was verified by Parsons. Parsons et al. (1986) found a silver-haired bat maternity colony in a flicker hole about 5.4 meters above the ground in a partly hollow, living basswood on 26 June 1979 in Simcoe County, Ontario. The tree, 27 cm thick, was in an opening in a maple/birch/cedar wood. The bats—at least 15 adult females, one pregnant and eight of them with 12 young—were found when the tree was cut down. One female escaped with two young. Seven of the eight females were lactating, six each had two young, and one had one. Finally, among 11 roost trees found by Betts (1995) in northeastern Oregon were five maternity roost sites of this species.

*The summer and winter ranges of the silver-haired bat,* Lasionycteris noctivagans, *in the eastern United States*

The bats changed roost trees frequently. Of eight sites used by this species, one was under bark and seven were in woodpecker holes. Bats were observed exiting from five roost trees on eight nights, the number of individuals exiting varying from three to 16.

More data are needed, but it seems likely that the males remain in the wintering range throughout the year, and that mating takes place there when the females arrive in fall. The females migrate north to their summer range in April and May, and return to their winter range in September and October. Eleven males were collected in South Carolina on 7–11 June 1940 (Golley 1966), and all 16 individuals taken in that state have been males, seemingly confirming the notion that males remain in the winter range all year. Females, presumably, are in the winter range only in fall and winter. That males and females winter in the same area is indicated by the data of Layne (1958) and Pearson (1962), who between them found 21 silver-haired bats, nine males and 12 females, hibernating in silica mines in the Shawnee Forest of southern Illinois. That most males stay in the south in spring is indicated by the sex ratio of silver-haired bats taken in Indiana, where essentially all of the individuals are migrants; twenty-one of 25 taken in spring were females, whereas in fall, eight of 14 were females (Mumford and Whitaker, 1982). The males were presumably the young of the year. Much more striking is the fact that of 85 adult specimens killed by Merriam in Lewis County, New York, during the summer of 1883, there was but a single male.

In the northern parts of the winter range, the bats hibernate in caves, mines, hollow trees, crevices, buildings, and other protected places. They have been found hibernating in skyscrapers, churches, wharf-houses, and the hulls of ships in New York City, and in the silica mines of southwestern Illinois. Three individuals have been found hibernating in West Virginia caves, another beneath the loose bark of a tree in British Columbia. A number of silver-haired bats have been found wintering in Indiana, several in caves (many of these in Tunnel Cave in Jefferson County) and two in buildings. Tunnel Cave was checked every two weeks in the winter of 1990–91: no silver-haired bats were found un-til 29 December, when a male was discovered hibernating on the wall, and four females were sharing a crevice that had previously been checked four times. Others have been found hibernating in Wyandotte Cave. The available information suggests that in the south most silver-haired bats spend the winter in hibernation in cliff crevices and hollow trees, and only occasionally in caves or mines. Some in the south may be active at least part of the time, as evidenced by the five individuals that were mist-netted on 22 December 1965 in Arkansas (Baker and Ward 1967). Individuals have been found in hollow trees (perhaps the most common hibernating site) in North Carolina during the winter months, and there are records for Bermuda. In Tennessee, silver-haired bats have been found hibernating by woodcutters, and Merlin Tuttle has found them deep in the cracks of cliff faces and occasionally in cave entrances. Brack and Carter (1985) found one on 11 May in the burrow of a squirrel, probably *Spermophilus tridecemlineatus*, in a cemetery in Clinton County, Indiana.

During migration, the silver-haired bat commonly roosts in trees on a ridge along the shore of Lake Manitoba, near the University of Manitoba Field Station at Delta Marsh. A total of 177 silver-haired bats, most of them females, was found there in 36 different roosts. They were usually solitary (106 bats), but 30 were in pairs and 24 were three to a roost. Typical roosts were 0.9 to 3.5 meters high (3 to 11 feet) in narrow crevices in tree trunks, splits in trees, or narrow spaces between two trees.

FOOD AND FEEDING. This species feeds on a variety of foods, with Lepidoptera, Homoptera and Hemiptera (Cicadellidae and Corixidae), Coleoptera (Carabidae), Diptera, Isoptera, and others all reported. Being slow and highly maneuverable, *Lasionycteris* apparently detects and pursues prey over short distances (Barclay, 1985). It produces numerous feeding buzzes, about four to 12 per minute, and is commonly observed feeding on swarms of insects along streams or ponds or in small clearings. Barclay suggested that the species feeds opportunistically (see the discussion in the *Lasiurus cinereus* account).

REPRODUCTION AND DEVELOPMENT. Mating normally occurs prior to hibernation, but fertilization is delayed until spring. In silver-haired bats hibernating in southern Illinois silica mines, Layne (1958) found few sperm in males but viable sperm in uterine smears from females. Gestation is about 50 to 60 days, fertilization occurs in May and June, and the two (occasionally one) young are produced in late June or early July (Kunz, Mammalian Species, 1982). Kunz measured the birth weight of two young at 1.9 and 1.8 grams. The young remain clinging in their quarters while the parent forages, but grow rapidly from their mother's milk, and a little over a month later are strong enough to follow their parents on their nightly quest for food. They can easily be distinguished from the adults at this season by their relatively weak and hesitant flight; and, if one is captured, the pronounced silver tips on almost black hairs serve to distinguish it from the duller adults.

POPULATION CHARACTERISTICS. Little is known of population characteristics in this species. This bat is primarily solitary during hibernation and migration, but appears to form small maternity colonies in hollows in trees in summer.

ENEMIES. No information is available on predation on this species. That it normally bears two young suggests lower survival rates for the young than is the case in many other bat species. Perhaps squirrels find the young in tree holes.

PARASITES AND DISEASE. Some parasites of this species in the east include the sarcoptid mite *Notoedres lasionycteris*, essentially a mange mite (Boyd & Bernstein, 1950), which was found on this host in Pennsylvania in clusters "on the ears and in one case on one of the fingers on the underside of the wing. The clusters were composed of adults surrounded by their eggs. The mite appeared to burrow into the skin in a tick-like fashion." Nymphs and adults of the mite *Macronyssus macrodactylus* are the mites chiefly seen crawling about in the fur and on the wing membranes, although some myobiid mites, *Acanthophthirius* (probably new sp.), and cimicids (batbugs) occur. Streblid and nycteribiid flies have also been reported on this host, and trematodes, nematodes, and cestodes inhabit its intestines.

Rabies has been found in this species on several occasions, but the incidence is very low even in "suspect bats." Smith et al. (1995) of the Communicable Disease Center in Atlanta, Georgia, have recently been studying various rabies strains. First, as we long suspected, terrestrial and bat rabies are quite different. These we could term "street" or "carnivore" rabies and "bat" rabies. Among carnivores, there are separate skunk, fox, and raccoon strains, forming a related group; bat rabies includes, among others, two red bat strains, three big brown bat strains, a free-tail bat strain, and a silver-haired bat strain. These strains have most often been found in their proper host, but can be recognized in other hosts. There are eight recent cases of people having died from the silver-haired bat strain of rabies, but in none of these was there evidence of bite or close contact with bats; the first occasion to suspect rabies was when the symptoms appeared, which was too late. Later investigation did reveal some association with a bat in some of these cases, though the species was not known. Apart from the fact that in no case was there evidence of a bat bite or even close contact with bats, these situations are hard to understand, because the silver-haired bat is not one that humans often come into contact with. Much more work is needed on this conundrum, but might it be that the silver-haired bat strain was originally associated with a different mammal, such as the skunk or raccoon?

RELATION TO HUMANS. Like other insectivorous bats, this species helps maintain the balance of nature. In general, there seems to be little contact between this species and humans, but, as indicated above, the silver-haired bat rabies strain has recently been implicated in several human deaths, even though there was no evidence that the people afflicted had had any contact with bats.

AREAS FOR FURTHER WORK. For the most part, exceedingly little information is available on the habits and population dynamics of the silver-haired bat. Are the bats colonial or solitary during birthing? Are the maternity roosts usually in hollow trees? If so, how many bats are there in a maternity colony? A myobiid mite (*Acanthophthirius* sp.) that is found on these bats needs to be identified, and perhaps described, and much more needs to be learned about the occurrence and mode of transmission of the silver-haired strain of bat rabies.

## SUBSPECIES

None described.

Type locality: Eastern United States.

## LITERATURE

Baker, R. J., and C. M. Ward. 1967. Distribution of bats in southeastern Arkansas. *J. Mammal.* 48: 130–132.

Barbour, R. W., and W. H. Davis. 1969. *Bats of America*. Lexington: Univ. Press of Kentucky. 286 pp.

Barclay, R. M. R. 1985. Long- versus short-range foraging strategies of hoary (*Lasiurus cinereus*) and silver-haired (*Lasionycteris noctivagans*) bats and the consequences for prey selection. *Canadian J. Zool.* 63: 2507–2515.

Barclay, R. M. R., P. A. Faure, and D. R. Farr. 1988. Roosting behavior and roost selection by migrating silver-haired bats (*Lasionycteris noctivagans*). *J. Mammal.* 69: 821–825.

Betts, B. J. 1995. Roosting behavior of silver-haired bats (*Lasionycteris noctivagans*) and big brown bats (*Eptesicus fuscus*) in northeast Oregon. In: M. R. Barclay and R. M. Brigham, eds., *Bats and Forests Symposium*, pp. 55–61. October 19–21, 1995. Victoria, B.C.: Res. Br., B.C. Min. Forestry.

Boyd, E. M., and M. H. Bernstein. 1950. A new species of sarcoptic mite from a bat (Acarina, Sarcoptidae). *Proc. Entomol. Soc. Wash.* 52: 95–99.

Brack, V., Jr., and J. C. Carter. 1985. Use of an underground burrow by *Lasionycteris noctivagans*. *Bat Research News* 26: 28–29.

Golley, F. B. 1966. *South Carolina Mammals*. Charleston, S.C.: Charleston Museum. 181 pp.

Izor, R. J. 1979. Winter range of the silver-haired bat. *J. Mammal.* 60: 641–643.

Kunz, T. W. 1982. *Lasionycteris noctivagans*. **Mammalian Species No. 172**. Amer. Soc. Mammal. 5 pp.

Layne, J. N. 1958. Notes on mammals of southern Illinois. *Amer. Midland Nat.* 60: 219–254.

Mumford, R. E., and J. O. Whitaker, Jr. 1982. *Mammals of Indiana*. Bloomington: Indiana Univ. Press. 537 pp.

Novakowski, N. S. 1956. Additional records of bats in Saskatchewan. *Canadian Field-Nat.* 70: 142.

Parsons, H. I., D. A. Smith, and R. F. Whittam. 1986. Maternity colonies of silver-haired bats, *Lasionycteris noctivagans*, in Ontario and Saskatchewan. *J. Mammal.* 67: 598–600.

Pearson, E. W. 1962. Bats hibernating in silica mines in southern Illinois. *J. Mammal.* 43: 27–33.

Smith, J. S., L. A. Orciari, and P. A. Yager. 1995. Molecular epidemiology of rabies in the United States. *Seminars in Virology* 6: 387–400.

## Eastern Pipistrelle *Pipistrellus subflavus* (F. Cuvier)                            Color plate 3

DESCRIPTION. The name *Pipistrellus* is derived from an Italian word meaning "bat." This little bat is readily distinguished from all other east-

*Eastern pipistrelle*, Pipistrellus subflavus *(Charles L. Oberst)*

ern bats by its small size, its tricolored fur, and the pattern of its dentition. The dorsal hairs are dark at the base, then light almost to the tips, which are reddish brown. The fur is a light, uniform yellowish-brown below. Although color varies considerably, the general perception of the dorsum is of a reddish-brown tone. Northern individuals are darker, duller, and more yellow, and juveniles are grayish. The dorsal base of the interfemoral membrane is sparsely furred. The wing membranes are attached to the base of the toes. The thumb, about one-fifth the length of the forearm, is large for such a small bat. The ears are distinctly longer than broad, and they taper to a narrow, round tip. This bat has a total of 36 teeth, including five molariforms on each side of the upper jaw. The first molariform is reduced, creating an apparent space, containing only this small tooth, between the canine and second molariform. Bats of the genus *Myotis* have two reduced molariforms in this space; in only *Pipistrellus*, *Corynorhinus*, and *Lasionycteris* among eastern bats does the space contain one tooth (see p. 81). In other eastern bats, such as *Eptesicus*, the first molariform is full-sized, and no space is present.

MEASUREMENTS. Average measurements of seven specimens from Georgia were: total length 85.1 (81–89), tail 40 (36–45), hind foot 8.7 (8–10), ear 13–15, forearm 33 (32–34), wingspread 245 (208–258) mm; and weight 3.5–7 grams. In this species, the females are larger than the males, a departure apparently related to the needs of lactation and the relatively large size of the two embryos (Myers, 1978).

Diploid number = 30.

TOOTH FORMULA

$$\frac{2}{3} \quad \frac{1}{1} \quad \frac{2}{3} \quad \frac{3}{3} \ = \ 36$$

DISTRIBUTION. The pipistrelle occurs in most of the eastern United States, from northern New England south to central Florida and west to Wisconsin. Brack and Mumford (1984) found extensive correlation between the northern edge of the present range of the pipistrelle and the southern edge of the Wisconsinan glaciation in the Midwest, probably because of the lack of caves north of this line. Beyond the eastern U.S., the pipistrelle is occasional in southern Quebec, and occurs west to central Minnesota, Kansas, and Texas and south through eastern Mexico to the Yucatan peninsula.

subflavus

floridanus

*Distribution of the eastern pipistrelle, Pipistrellus subflavus, in the eastern United States*

HABITAT. Females form small maternity colonies in summer, but relatively few colonies have been found. Most are probably in hollow trees, but some are in buildings, and two are known from caves in Iowa (Humphrey et al., 1976). Little is known of the behavior of male pipistrelles in summer, but they are probably solitary, roosting in crevices, caves, mines, and other such places. Males and females both hibernate in caves, usually near their summer homes.

HABITS. These small bats are weak, erratic flyers, and can even be mistaken for large moths. They are early flyers, coming forth from a hollow tree, a building, or a cleft in a cliff early in the evening to course over the water and flit about shaded groves.

Pipistrelles are sociable little creatures and often remain together for several years in small maternity colonies, usually numbering not more than 30–35 adult females. A. A. Allen (1921) banded a cluster of four adult females at his Ithaca, New York, residence in 1916 and recaptured them in the same place three years later. This was the first use of banding for the study of bats in North America. With the invaluable assistance of a group of "cooperators" who observed the bats once during the day and once at night, from the bats' arrival in spring to their departure in the fall, we observed six maternity colonies of pipistrelles in Indiana over five years (Whitaker, in press). Because the bats were not banded, turnover could not be determined. The number of females remained relatively comparable from year to year, but ranged from two to 29 and averaged about 14. (A single colony in Massachusetts numbered 30 individuals when first observed.) The colonies we observed were mostly in small buildings (one in a garage, two in sheds, two on porches, and one in a pavilion), and we have located five other colonies in similar situations. In all of the six colonies actually studied, the bats had alternate roosts; the bats (adults or adults and young) would disappear for a time but would then reappear. In one of the colonies, the bats were not inside a structure at all, but remained on the outside wall of a house (on the front porch), in full daylight, protected only by the overhang of the roof, and there was a similar roost on the back porch.

Adults and young in most colonies changed roosts about two or three times per season.

Pipistrelles remain active late into October, but as food becomes scarce the bats, now very fat, retreat to some mine or cave, even in tiny caves or mines, often being found where no bats of other species are present. There they hang alone to pass the winter, males and females in the same caves. They may hibernate throughout larger caves, but usually in small numbers, and often in small side passages, where few other bats occur. They were found in all of the 13 caves having bats that we examined in the winter of 1974–75 in a study in the Shawnee National Forest in southern Illinois, and in eight of the 11 silica mines inhabited by bats. We know of one mine in west-central Indiana, however, where over 200 pipistrelles hibernated in the winter of 1987–88. Here the pipistrelles hang mostly in the warmer back rooms, and little brown bats occupy the cooler front rooms.

Even in Florida this species hibernates, though food supplies are available throughout the winter. McNab (1974) opined that hibernation has been maintained in this species in Florida largely because of the long period required for sperm storage. Its habit of hibernating singly and its small size have enabled it to hibernate successfully in the relatively warm caves of Florida when other species have been excluded. Layne (1993), however, found that pipistrelles also occur far south of the cave region in Florida. There they were flying at night during the winter, and it would appear that they were feeding. The bats were in nine concrete basement units under the Archbold Biological Station in Highlands County, Florida. The 16 bats (seven males, nine females) were present in every month but May from February 1972 to February 1973, but although 21 were seen in February, no more than four were seen in any other month between January and December. In a study between February 1992 and February 1993, one male was recorded 39 times, at least once in every month. Females, however, were present only in January, February, and October; Layne suspected that they may have had a permanent roost away from the basements. If he is correct, this suggests an alternate-roost strategy similar to that recently described in Indiana (Whitaker, in press).

Water often collects on hibernating pipistrelles until they become covered with fine droplets. Consequently, when the beam from a flashlight catches them, they so glisten as to appear white. From this fact, and because few were caught in traps at a mine entrance, we suspected that, unlike other cave bats, which often move about in their winter quarters, the pipistrelle would seem to move seldom from the site it has first chosen. Beth Vincent, however, put marks on the wall in a pipistrelle hibernaculum and found that they moved about much more than expected.

The first subadults reach the hibernating caves in early August, but peak numbers are not reached until late October or early November, at least in the northern part of their range. There may be significant mortality among young pipistrelles failing to store sufficient amounts of fat for their first hibernation. Hibernating males steadily lose about 39% of their weight from September to April, whereas females lose about 29% from September to March. These findings accord with the patterns of temperature decrease of the two sexes during hibernation, the females' temperature decreasing rapidly from November to January, then remaining uniformly low until April (Fitch, 1966), whereas in males the rapid decrease did not occur until the January-February period. In the laboratory, Davis and Reite (1967) found that this species rapidly increased heart rate in response to an increase of temperature from a range of 5 to 10°C up to 15°C (60°F), and, conversely, that the bats would wake when the ambient temperature fell below freezing. Because pipistrelles are so sedentary in their caves in winter (*Eptesicus* and *Myotis* wake from hibernation at intervals), because they so often collect water droplets, and because, in contrast with *Myotis* and *Eptesicus*, they seldom fly about or outside of the hibernacula, we wonder if their physiology might be quite different from that of *Eptesicus* and *Myotis*.

The bats emerge gradually from hibernation in April and early May, at which time the males and females move to their summer locations, usually not far distant from the hibernaculum. At most of the maternity roosts in buildings in Indiana, the first pipistrelles arrived between 13 and 29 April and reached their maximum numbers between 26 April and 9 June (Whitaker, in

press). The greatest distance recorded between summer and winter roosts was only 52.8 km (33 miles) (Griffin, 1940), and bats of this species tend to return year after year to the same summer and winter roosts. During the summer, segregation of the sexes is pronounced.

From August through October, bats of both sexes leave their summer quarters, the adults before the juveniles. The adults then begin to congregate at cave and mine entrances, along with other swarming bats. It is at this time when most copulation occurs, although spring copulations may occur as well. Some of the bats milling about at a cave entrance may hibernate there, but others move on to other hibernacula.

FOOD AND FEEDING. From a study of their droppings, Hamilton concluded that the chief food items of pipistrelles are tiny flies, beetles, and hymenopterous insects. Individuals collected in eastern Kentucky 15–20 minutes after they first appeared in the evening already had their stomachs greatly distended with small dipterous and coleopterous remains. In 23 individuals from Indiana, the primary foods identified were cicadellids (21.7% by volume), carabids (18.1%), unidentified flies (10.7%), unidentified beetles (7.8%), moths (7.3%), and delphacids (7.2%).

REPRODUCTION AND DEVELOPMENT. Pipistrelles ovulate in spring, probably in early May, and fertilization is effected by the sperms stored in the uterus since the previous fall, or perhaps by sperms from a spring mating. Gestation, as measured from implantation to birth, is at least 44 days (Wimsatt, 1945).

From late June to mid-July in northern latitudes, the females produce two young. The young at birth are quite large for such a small bat, a litter of two weighing about 1.9 grams, a third or more of the weight of the female. They can make loud clicking sounds by which the females may locate them (Fujita and Kunz, 1984). In the southern states the young are produced in late May through the first three weeks of June, and after a few days the young are left alone while the mother seeks food. When about three weeks old, the young begin flying and foraging with their mothers, and about a week later, the adult females leave.

POPULATION CHARACTERISTICS. Maternity colonies are small in this species, the maximum number in six colonies we studied being 29. Males are always solitary, and bats of both sexes are solitary in caves and mines in winter. Most hibernacula of the species contain few pipistrelles (less than 30), but one mine in Vermillion County, Indiana, harbors over 200, and a mine near Lewisburg, Ohio, surveyed in February 1996, contained 1400 eastern pipistrelles.

Like other bats, pipistrelles are long-lived. The greatest longevity known to date for this species was that of a male in Illinois recaptured 14.8 years after it was originally banded.

ENEMIES. Little is known of the natural enemies of this species. Most of the predation that might occur is presumably by chance. We suspect that the chief cause of mortality, as appears to be the case for many other species of bats, is from young falling from the maternity roost. There are two records of pipistrelles being attacked by hoary bats, but humans are probably the pipistrelles' most important enemies.

PARASITES AND DISEASE. Several species of trematodes and one protozoan, *Eimeria macyi*, have been found in eastern pipistrelles. Chiggers, *Euschoengastia pipistrelli*, appear to be the main ectoparasites of this species, but several other chigger species have been found, as well as the macronyssid mites *Macronyssus crosbyi* and *M. unidens* and spinturnicid and myobiid mites.

RELATION TO HUMANS. This is one of the species that often forms colonies in human structures, and because humans are so uninformed about bats, they often kill or eliminate them. For example, in five of the six cases of pipistrelle colonies we are observing, it was the "cooperators" who called *us*, seeking advice on how to rid themselves of the bats. The cooperators now find them totally fascinating and would not let anyone hurt them.

Pipistrelles are tiny bats, and the droppings are small. The bats pose absolutely no threat to anybody and leave relatively little mess. Unless they are causing some particular problem, and in view of how beneficial they are to us, it is difficult to see why anyone would not welcome them, rather than seeking ways to get rid of them.

AREAS FOR FURTHER WORK. The available data on colonies of this species are from buildings, but most pipistrelle colonies are presumably in hollow trees. Are they? If so, can alternate colonies be found, as were discovered in the roosts in buildings in Indiana? How many alternate colonies are there, and what determines their numbers? One could study the invertebrate fauna of the guano community in hollow trees occupied by pipistrelles. Do pipistrelles in Florida south of the cave region feed in winter? Do pipistrelles wake from hibernation about every other week, as other bats do? What is the cause of the water droplets so commonly found on pipistrelles during hibernation?

## SUBSPECIES

*Pipistrellus subflavus subflavus* (F. Cuvier)

As described above.

Type locality: Eastern United States, probably Georgia.

Other currently recognized eastern subspecies:

*P. subflavus floridanus* Davis

## LITERATURE

Allen, A. A. 1921. Banding bats. *J. Mammal.* 2: 53–57.

Brack, V., Jr., and R. E. Mumford. 1984. The distribution of *Pipistrellus subflavus* and the limit of the Wisconsinan glaciation: An interface. *Amer. Midland Nat.* 112: 397–401.

Davis, W. H., and O. B. Reite. 1967. Responses of bats from temperate regions to changes in ambient temperature. *Biol. Bull.* 132: 320–328.

Fitch, J. H. 1966. Weight loss and temperature response in three species of bats in Marshall County, Kansas. *Search* 6: 17–24.

Fujita, M. S., and T. H. Kunz. 1984. *Pipistrellus subflavus*. **Mammalian Species No. 228.** Amer. Soc. Mammal. 6 pp.

Griffin, D. R. 1940. Migrations of New England bats. *Bull. Mus. Comp. Zool., Harvard Univ.* 86: 217–246.

Humphrey, S. R., R. K. Laval, and R. L. Clawson. 1976. Nursery populations of *Pipistrellus subflavus* (Chiroptera, Vespertilionidae) in Missouri. *Trans. Ill. Acad. Sci.* 69: 367.

Layne, J. N. 1993. Status of the eastern pipistrelle *Pipistrellus subflavus* at its southern range limit in eastern United States. *Bat Research News* 33: 43–46.

McNab, B. L. 1974. The behavior of temperate cave bats in a subtropical environment. *Ecology* 55: 943–948.

Myers, P. 1978. Sexual dimorphism in size of vespertilionid bats. *Amer. Naturalist* 112: 701–711.

Whitaker, J. O., Jr. In press. Populations, young, and roost switching in six summer colonies of eastern pipistrelles. *J. Mammal.*

Wimsatt, W. A. 1945. Notes on breeding behavior, pregnancy and parturition in some vespertilionid bats of the eastern United States. *J. Mammal.* 26: 23–33.

## Big Brown Bat *Eptesicus fuscus* (Palisot de Beauvois)

DESCRIPTION. This bat is at once distinguished from all other eastern bats by its long, uniformly

*Big brown bat,* Eptesicus fuscus

sepia-brown fur and large size, the forearm averaging around 45 mm in length. The hairs are much darker at their bases than at the tips, and the fur of the ventral surface is paler than that of the dorsum. The short, black ears are furred at the base. On the wings and the interfemoral membranes, fur is lacking. There are two upper incisors on each side, and the tooth behind the canine is *not* reduced in size (see p. 81). This species and *Nycticeius humeralis* are quite similar in appearance, but *Eptesicus* is much larger.

MEASUREMENTS. Average measurements of 20 specimens from New York and Georgia were: total length 114.3 (106–127), tail 46 (42–52), hind foot 10.7 (10–11.5), ear 17–18, forearm 46.8 (44.7–48), wingspread 320 (325–350) mm; and weight 13–25 grams. Large females, even with embryos removed, may weigh up to 30 grams.

Diploid number = 50.

TOOTH FORMULA

$$\frac{2}{3} \ \frac{1}{1} \ \frac{1}{2} \ \frac{3}{3} \ = \ 32$$

DISTRIBUTION. The big brown bat occurs throughout most of the United States west to the Pacific, into the adjoining Canadian provinces, south through most of Mexico and Central America, and in most of the Caribbean area. In the east, it ranges from Maine and Wisconsin south to Florida and southernmost Louisiana. It becomes increasingly less common in the south and is lacking in southern Florida.

HABITAT. Most big brown bats now form maternity colonies in buildings or other structures, although a few use hollow trees, probably their ancestral summer roosting habitat. Most apparently winter in buildings, but some use caves or mines. Big brown bats feed in a variety of habitats, but often over cultivated fields.

HABITS. The big brown bat, easily recognized by its general brown color, large size, and strong, erratic flight, takes to the air as dusk descends. One by one, the bats drop into the air from their exit opening, often under a roof, and fly off into the night. Females live in maternity colonies of 20 to about 600 individuals in summer, most often in buildings; males are solitary, often roosting lower in the buildings where the females roost. Bats found in houses, especially in winter, are most often of this species. These bats are not deterred by the bustle and noise of the great cities, and individuals have frequently been seen flying above the crowded streets of New York City. *Eptesicus* is one of our most sedentary of bats; most recaptures of banded individuals have been within 50 km (30 miles) of the original capture.

The big brown bat is one of the last bats to disappear in the fall. Even in the northernmost parts of their range, these bats may occasionally be seen flying in the sun at midday in winter, and during mild spells, some may fly at night. Maternity colonies start to disperse in September, but the last individuals do not leave until November. Much fat, about one-fourth of the bat's body weight, is put on in preparation for hibernation. From November to late March, a few individuals are found in hibernation with *Myotis* and *Pipistrellus*, in the same caves and mines. *Eptesicus* usually hangs singly or in clusters of not more than two to four, often close to the hibernaculum's entrance, and usually in a cool, dry site. It is seldom found in large clusters, or in large numbers, in one cave or mine, though we did count 310 individuals of this species (up to 75 in one cluster) hibernating in Tunnel Cave (a 200-meter-long tunnel open at both ends) at Clifty Falls State Park at Madison, Indiana, on 14 February 1987, and between 100 and 200 continue to hibernate there annually. Wayne Davis (pers. comm.) reports two clusters of over 100 each in two mines in New York. We have also seen large clusters of this species in mines in Minnesota, and a recently discovered mine near Lewisburg, Ohio, sheltered 373 big brown bats.

Still, the modest numbers hibernating in caves and mines over much of the range of this species

*Distribution of the big brown bat,* Eptesicus fuscus, *in the eastern United States*

are not nearly adequate to account for the large numbers found in buildings in summer. That many of these bats hibernate in buildings was long suggested by the fact that single individuals are so often found in living quarters of buildings in winter, probably when they have been disturbed, or when environmental conditions in their roost have changed. Even exposed window sashes have been chosen for a place in which to pass the winter, and we have found them hibernating under piles of lumber or trash. In one church, large numbers hibernated horizontally in the insulation on the floor of the attic, each with a 20-25-mm vertical chimney to the surface. Indeed, hardly a week goes by in some years but that we get a call to come get a bat from a building on the Indiana State University campus or in the city of Terre Haute. These bats are invariably *Eptesicus*.

In the winters of 1987–88 and 1988–89, in Indiana, we visited 67 summer roost sites that appeared to be possible hibernacula as well (Whitaker and Gummer, 1992). Nearly all of those that were heated and well insulated, 32 altogether, housed hibernating bats numbering from one to 73, totals that are vastly reduced from summer numbers. (The second largest number in one of these hibernacula was just 32.) That same winter we also examined the attics in 28 homes where a bat (always *Eptesicus*) had been found. Hibernating big brown bats, numbering from one to seven, were found in 14 of the 28, hanging from rafters or jammed into tiny spaces. None of these buildings had served as a summer colony.

It appears, then, that the members of a summer colony spread out in winter, using many different buildings, one bat or only a few per building. They are not often found because they are solitary, they are usually in secluded spots, and they do not eat (at least in the north), thus produce no guano. We placed numbered tags under the bats in two of the larger winter congregations, and found that, on the average, the bats changed position once every two weeks, and that individuals often flew outside on warmer nights. We spread large sheets of paper under many of the bats, but found no guano deposition at all, indicating that no feeding was being done. Big brown bats will sometimes defecate when captured in winter, but the winter pellets we have

examined have all been of fine material constituting fecal plugs rather than coarser material indicating recent consumption of fresh food. Chrissy Sutter and George Bakken have accumulated information indicating that the bats probably do drink in winter.

*Eptesicus* hibernates at temperatures of about 0 to 18°C (32 to 58°F), and will rouse at temperatures below −6°C (22°F). The cave that harbored the cluster of 75 seen on 14 February 1987 is cold, and open at both ends. On 14 January 1994 (outside temperatures −6°F), we measured anal temperatures of seven big brown bats just inside this cave. Air temperatures close to the bats ranged from −1.4 to −8.8°C; anal temperatures of the bats ranged from 0.0 to 3.8°C. One big brown bat was found in winter on a hot steam pipe in a Cornell University building. The temperature there was 17°C (64°F). This bat had evidently been hibernating in the building, awoke, and temporarily roosted on the steam pipe, since, presumably, it could not have been hibernating at that temperature. There is a turnover of this species between hibernacula, even during the coldest months, and in Indiana we have caught them in mist nets or bat traps at cave entrances all through the winter.

Brigham (1987), examining 159 individuals taken in winter, 43 active ones from buildings and 116 inactive ones from mines, found a steady decrease in mass over the winter in the inactive bats, but no relation between weight and date in the active ones. Only six inactive individuals weighed less than 14.5 grams, and only two less than 14 grams. By contrast, only ten of the active bats weighed *more* than 14 grams. Brigham concluded that his data support the hypothesis that bats may become active at a critically low energy reserve, presumably to find food.

We suspect there is survival value in the solitary nature of both sexes of this species in winter and in these movements between hibernacula. Because big brown bats have so effectively adapted to human culture, especially to our buildings and other structures, they are probably much more abundant than ever before. The species can and will use hollow trees, but relies mainly on buildings for most of its maternity colonies and hibernacula. Buildings, however, are ephemeral—they burn down, or are torn down, and the heat may be turned off—but we think the solitary habit of *Eptesicus* in winter ensures that not too many bats will be without a hibernaculum, should a building disappear. Furthermore, their movements between buildings in winter may make big brown bats aware of alternate hibernacula, should one be needed in such an emergency.

FOOD AND FEEDING. Examination by Hamilton (1933) of 2200 fecal pellets of *Eptesicus* indicated the following food proportions: Coleoptera, 36.1%; Hymenoptera, 26.3%; Diptera, 13.2%; Plecoptera, 6.5%; Ephemeridae, 4.6%; Hemiptera, 3.4%; Trichoptera, 3.2%; Neuroptera, 3.2%; Mecoptera, 2.7%; and Orthoptera, 0.6%. Remarkably, no lepidopterous remains were found. Of beetles, scarabaeids occurred most frequently, followed by elaterids. The dipterans were represented chiefly by muscids. Examination of 184 stomachs of this species from Indiana gave similar results, the most important foods being Carabidae, 14.6%; Scarabaeidae, 12.4%; Chrysomelidae, 11.5%; Pentatomidae, 9.5%; and Formicidae, 8.5%. Many of the prey items eaten were fairly large, at least a centimeter long. Beetles amounted to 49.6% of the total volume in the stomachs; only 4.5% was of moths. Further data from 12 maternity colonies (Whitaker, 1995) from different areas in Indiana, one of them sampled throughout the active season, showed that about 80% of the insect food is of harmful insects; among them, spotted cucumber beetles (*Diabrotica*, the larva of which is one of the species of corn rootworms), scarab beetles, green stinkbugs, and leafhoppers were dominant.

Brigham (1990) compared the food of big brown bats and nighthawks. He found that the bats ate more beetles and flies than would be expected by chance, whereas the nighthawks fed more heavily on beetles and hymenopterans. The top food for both species was Trichoptera (caddisflies). At least 60% of the available prey items were midges, but midges were not preyed upon by either species, whereas caddisflies ranged from 3.6 to 13.3% in abundance.

In the laboratory, two postlactating females consumed 4.38 grams of food per day (Coutts et al., 1973). They would cull heavily sclerotized parts such as elytra and legs that exceeded certain sizes (in beetles, parts about 15 mm long); the larger the beetle, the greater the number of parts that were removed, and as increasing amounts of food were made available, increasing numbers of parts were discarded. The wings were removed from moths weighing between 0.1 and 0.8 gram, and the antennae were removed on those over 0.85 gram. In other cases, the heads and abdomens of larger moths were eaten, but abdomens containing eggs were not. The tips of the abdomens, which contain glands that produce an unpleasant smell, were not eaten when several were presented, but were eaten if less than seven were presented. As is true of the little brown bat, *Myotis lucifugus*, this species would not eat live arctiid moths, *Cycnia tenera*, which presumably taste bad and give ultrasonic warning calls.

Hamr and Bailey (1984) found that big brown bats could detect 1000-Hz sounds from insects, and that they used these low-frequency signals in prey discrimination. Buchler and Childs (1981) found that big brown bats could detect and orient on the low-frequency sounds of frogs or insects over distances of at least 600 meters (2000 feet). It was thought that these sounds could lead bats to concentrations of insects.

REPRODUCTION AND DEVELOPMENT. Big brown bats copulate primarily in the fall, but little information is available on the specifics of where or when this takes place. Mating also occurs in spring or even during the winter, and we have seen more matings in spring in buildings than in fall. During the winter, some individuals engage in a good deal of mating activity. This species incorporates delayed fertilization, but in view of the extent of winter activity pursued, one wonders about its function. Perhaps its main function is to help ensure fertilization by allowing matings over a protracted period. Tom Kunz believes its function is to allow fertilization to occur at a critical point in the annual cycle—very soon after the female's emergence from hibernation.

Females begin entering the maternity colonies about mid-March, gradually building to a peak adult population by early May. The females often group in the peak of a building, or behind beams or in a crack. The males hang separately, apart from the females, but often in the same building. The bats ovulate about the first week of April, depending on latitude, and the eggs are fertilized by the sperms that have been stored in the uterus.

The season of partus is from late May to mid-June in the north, earlier in the south, and gestation is about two months. Two young are the usual number in the east, although Francis Harper collected a Georgia specimen containing four embryos. Newborn young weigh 2.8 to 4 grams, with a forearm of about 18 mm. The newborn cling tightly to the mother's teats during the day, and lie sheltered under her wing membranes. When she flies, however, even the smallest young are left behind. (In the western United States a few young have been found on females that were taken in flight, probably after being disturbed.) The young grow rapidly, are weaned when about four weeks old, and are flying by early July. When two months old they are nearly as large as the parents.

The young are apparently recognized and sought out by their own mothers, probably by voice. The young emit a loud "cheep" call when separated from the mother, or when they fall from the roost. The mother will encourage or retrieve the young if they manage to climb up the wall. She will often leave a young if it cannot get off the floor onto a wall, although we know of one case where a young bat was retrieved from outside, on a lawn.

In New England, many of the nursery colonies break up soon after weaning, but in the Midwest they decline more gradually, the last individuals leaving in early November, or just prior to hibernation. On several occasions, however, we have known of bats forming colonies late in the season and in places not occupied by big brown bats at other times, after the young are volant and before hibernation. We have referred to these as postlactation colonies, and have found several in buildings and one in a cottonwood tree in a 650-ha (1600-acre) bottomlands lacking big brown bats in summer.

Kurta et al. (1990) calculated that the assimilated energy needed for lactating is twice that needed for maintaining pregnancy (105.1 vs. 48.9 kilojoules per day). About 2% of the total energy requirement went into fetal tissue and about 28% into milk production. Daily water flux in lactating bats likewise was twice that of pregnant bats (17.07 vs. 8.47 ml per day). The same authors calculated that more than 65% of the water ingested was obtained in food and that about 20–22% was obtained by drinking. Urination accounted for 72% of the water efflux during pregnancy and 56% during lactation (milk production accounted for 22% of the latter efflux). Keeler and Studier (1992) found that 34 june beetles (*Phyllophaga rugosa*) met the daily caloric intake and the yield intakes of water, magnesium, potassium, nitrogen, sodium, and iron, but not of calcium, for a pregnant big brown bat.

POPULATION CHARACTERISTICS. Big brown bats form maternity colonies numbering up to about 600 individuals, but colonies are more likely to contain 20 to 300 individuals. A small town may support a couple of colonies, but a larger city may house many colonies, one every few blocks. Still, much more information is needed on the relation of colonies to each other and to those of other species.

Cope et al. (1961) moved bats 20, 40, 100, and 250 miles from their home roosts. Most bats at the three shorter distances returned home in one to three nights, and most of those released at the greatest distance returned on the fourth and fifth nights. Banded *Eptesicus* have been known to live up to 20 years (Davis, 1986), but we suspect they are capable of living much longer.

ENEMIES. Bats have few enemies. Owls capture a few, and a pilot black snake living in the eaves of a two-story building decimated one colony. Mortality is highest during infancy, when the young often fall from the maternity colony, but otherwise is generally low, as it is in most bats.

PARASITES AND DISEASE. Bat bugs, *Cimex*, are common in nursery colonies. The most common external parasites are the macronyssid mites *Steatonyssus occidentalis*, which crawl around in the fur and on the wing membranes. The tick *Ornithonyssus kelleyi*, the myobiid mite *Acanthophthirius caudatus*, and the spinturnicid mite *Spinturnix bakeri* are also found, along with a few chiggers, the most abundant being *Euschoengastia hamiltoni*.

RELATION TO HUMANS. All North American bats are insectivorous, but the big brown bat of the Midwest is particularly beneficial, at least in the corn belt, for it feeds heavily on spotted cucumber beetles (*Diabrotica* sp.), a pest of vine plants in gardens. Moreover, the larvae of these beetles are one of the species of corn rootworms, a major agricultural pest. Thus the big brown bat is an active, ready-made mechanism of biological control, and farmers and gardeners should welcome them. This is, however, the bat that most often presents a nuisance in buildings.

AREAS FOR FURTHER WORK. Little information is available on where and when most of the copulations take place, or on how often big brown bats wake in winter, how long they stay awake, and how much energy they use in the waking period. How many times does an individual leave and return to its hibernaculum in winter, and how often does it change hibernacula? Big brown bats are capable of hibernating both at very low temperatures (near freezing) and very high temperatures (apparently up to 15°C, or 60°F). How are they able to tolerate such extremes, physiologically, and how do they even manage to hibernate at such high temperatures? To what extent do the young of the year disperse from a maternity colony, and how far? What is the function of the postlactation colonies? Perhaps to move the bats, especially the young, closer to a food supply?

## SUBSPECIES

*Eptesicus fuscus fuscus* (Beauvois)
 As described above.
 Type locality: Philadelphia, Pennsylvania.
 Other currently recognized eastern subspecies:
  *E. fuscus osceola* Rhoads

### LITERATURE

Beer, J. R., and A. G. Richards. 1956. Hibernation of the big brown bat. *J. Mammal.* 37: 31–47.
Brigham, R. M. 1987. The significance of winter activity by the big brown bat (*Eptesicus fuscus*): The influence of energy reserves. *Canadian J. Zool.* 65: 1240–1242.
———. 1990. Prey selection by big brown bats (*Eptesicus fuscus*) and common nighthawks (*Chordeiles minor*). *Amer. Midland Nat.* 124: 73–80.
Buchler, E. R., and S. B. Childs. 1981. Orientation to distant sounds by foraging big brown bats (*Eptesicus fuscus*). *Anim. Behav.* 29: 428–432.
Christian, J. J. 1956. The natural history of a summer aggregation of the big brown bat, *Eptesicus fuscus fuscus*. *Amer. Midland Nat.* 55: 66–95.
Cope, J. B., K. Koontz, and E. Churchwell. 1961. Notes on homing of two species of bats, *Myotis lucifugus* and *Eptesicus fuscus*. *Proc. Ind. Acad. Sci.* 70: 270–274.
Coutts, R. A., M. B. Fenton, and E. Glen. 1973. Food intake by captive *Myotis lucifugus* and *Eptesicus fuscus*. *J. Mammal.* 54: 985–990.
Davis, W. B. 1986. An *Eptesicus fuscus* lives 20 years. *Bat Research News* 27: 24.
Hamilton, W. J., Jr. 1933. The insect food of the big brown bat. *J. Mammal.* 14: 155–156.
Hamr, J., and E. D. Bailey. 1984. Detection and discrimination of insect flight sounds by big brown bats (*Eptesicus fuscus*). *Biologie Behavior Biologie Comportemente* 10: 105–121.
Keeler, J. O., and E. H. Studier. 1992. Nutrition in pregnant big brown bats (*Eptesicus fuscus*) feeding on June beetles. *J. Mammal.* 73: 426–430.
Kurta, A., and R. H. Baker. 1990. *Eptesicus fuscus*. **Mammalian Species No. 356.** Amer. Soc. Mammal. 10 pp.
Kurta, A., T. H. Kunz, and K. A. Nagy. 1990. Energetics and water flux of free-ranging big brown bats (*Eptesicus fuscus*) during pregnancy and lactation. *J. Mammal.* 71: 59–65.
Rysgaard, G. N. 1942. A study of the cave bats of Minnesota with especial reference to the large brown bat, *Eptesicus fuscus fuscus* (Beauvois). *Amer. Midland Nat.* 28: 245–267.
Whitaker, J. O., Jr. 1995. Food of the big brown bat *Eptesicus fuscus* from maternity colonies in Indiana and Illinois. *Amer. Midland Nat.* 134: 346–360.
Whitaker, J. O., Jr., and S. L. Gummer. 1992. Hibernation of the big brown bat, *Eptesicus fuscus*, in buildings. *J. Mammal.* 73: 312–316.

## Bats of the Genus *Lasiurus*

The bats of this genus are our most colorful. All are solitary tree bats. Their skulls are short and blunt in front, and there is a single upper incisor on each side. The first molariform tooth, tiny and peglike, is on the lingual, or tongue, side of the canine.

## KEY TO THE BATS OF THE GENUS *LASIURUS*

1. Pelage yellow-brown; posterior portion of interfemoral membrane sparsely furred . . . . . . . . . . . . . . . . . . . . . . . *L. intermedius*
1. Pelage not yellow-brown; interfemoral membrane densely furred throughout . . . . . . . . . 2
2. Pelage chestnut-colored . . . . . . . . . . . *L. seminolus*
2. Pelage *either* red *or* brown with white-tipped hair . . . . . . . . . . . . . . . . . . . . . . . . . . . . . . . . 3
3. Total length of adult 91–112 mm; pelage brick-red or rusty red, frosted with white . . . . . *L. borealis*
3. Total length of adult 134–140 mm; pelage brown, that of the dorsum strongly tipped with white, producing a hoary effect. . . . *L. cinereus*

## Eastern Red Bat
### *Lasiurus borealis* (Müller)    Color plate 4

DESCRIPTION. This is one of the most beautiful of all American bats; its conspicuous bright-reddish or rusty color at once distinguishes it from all other species. Its exquisitely soft, fluffy

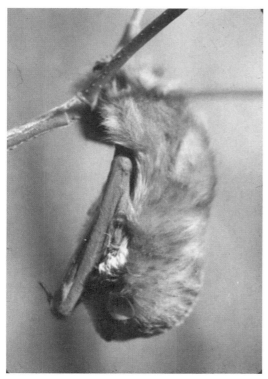

*Eastern red bat*, Lasiurus borealis, *male (Sherry L. Gummer)*

fur, the hair tips frosted with white on dorsum and breast, is in marked contrast to the more

coarse finish of the little brown bats (*Myotis*). The low, broad, rounded ear with its triangular tragus is naked on the inside, but the outer surface is densely furred on its basal two-thirds. The interfemoral membrane is thickly furred on its upper surface but only thinly furred on its proximal ventral surface. The fur also extends along the humerus to the wrist on the under-surface of the wing. The foot is small, about half the length of the calcar. This bat is one of a very few mammals in which the sexes are contrastingly colored. The coat of the females is a dull, buffy chestnut much frosted with white, that of the males a much brighter brick red (see the two color photos). On the front of the shoulder, of both sexes, is a buffy white patch or epaulet.

MEASUREMENTS. Average measurements of ten adults from New York, Pennsylvania, and Georgia were: total length 112.3 (95–126), tail 49 (45–62), hind foot 9.2 (8.5–10), ear 17–18, forearm 40 (37.5–42), wingspread 290–332 mm; and weight 9.5–16 grams.
  Diploid number = 28.

TOOTH FORMULA
$$\frac{1}{3}\ \frac{1}{1}\ \frac{2}{2}\ \frac{3}{3}\ =\ 32$$

DISTRIBUTION. The red bat occurs throughout the eastern United States, ranging from Canada to northern Florida and southernmost Louisiana in summer. It is common in the northern states in summer (less common in the far north), and migrates south in autumn to spend the winter from southern Illinois and southern Indiana south. In summer, the red and the big brown bat are the two most abundant bats in the Midwest. The red bat also occurs in Mexico and Central America to Panama, and in the western U.S. west to the Pacific, but not in the Rocky Mountain region.

HABITAT. This is a solitary, tree-roosting bat. By day, males and females hang among foliage; by night, they feed in and around trees, over watercourses, and often at lights. They migrate southward to hibernate in winter, but where they hibernate is not known. It may be in hollows in trees, in old squirrel nests, or in other protected places in woods where the temperature does not drop below freezing. Information on the winter whereabouts and behavior of this species is greatly needed.

HABITS. Long before darkness has fallen, the red bat is abroad on strong, narrow wings, pursuing its swift, erratic course. Red bats can often be easily identified as they swoop down for a drink from a pond or from someone's swimming pool. On still summer evenings these handsome bats may be seen at great heights, but they soon spiral down, at times flying but a meter or two above the ground as they search for insect prey. Elsewhere, on these late summer evenings, these bats will fly about the street lights of the city, attracted by the large numbers of insects, particularly moths, that are drawn to the lights. At times they will alight on the supporting poles to snatch up moths that have come to rest.

The roosting places of the red bat generally are thickly leafed above and to the sides, but clear below, where the bat launches into flight. Red bats usually roost 1 to 3 meters (3 to 10 feet) above the ground, partly concealed in a mass of leaves, but we have found them attached to cornstalks in full sunlight. Like many bats, they may become torpid at temperatures below about 20°C (69°F) during days as an energy-saving adaptation, and may remain torpid until the temperature returns to about 20°C (69°F). They also tolerate major temperature fluctuations without waking, which also conserves energy. If temperatures fall below freezing, their metabolism increases to keep their body temperature at a safe level. The shortness of the ears helps prevent heat loss, and the well-furred patagium

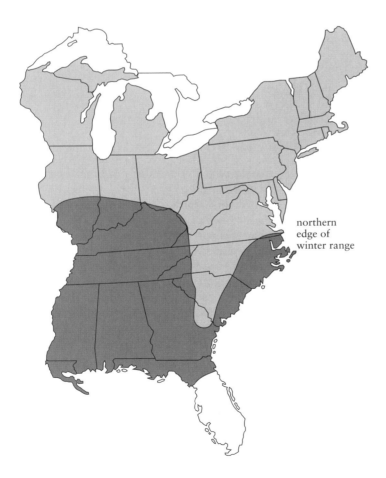

northern edge of winter range

*The summer and winter ranges of the eastern red bat,* Lasiurus borealis, *in the eastern United States*

wraps around the sleeping animal, forming a miniature blanket.

We have radio-tracked lone adult female red bats for a week at a time in late July in Indiana, in two consecutive summers. The area where we tracked, about 30 ha (72 acres) in extent, included several wooded areas, some open areas, and several small lakes. We were never able to find the radio-tagged bat itself, but could pinpoint its location to an area encompassing just three or four trees. The bat would roost in a different spot in one woodlot each day, returning to approximately the same spot only once during the week, and then not on consecutive nights. Presumably, red bats would return to a given spot when their babies had been left behind, but these data indicate that postlactation red bats may return to the same woods or general locality but not to the same specific spot.

During their migration, red bats often collide with large buildings, such as the convention center in Chicago, hit by 50 red bats, 48 of them in autumn (Timm, 1989). Timm postulated that the bats that hit the building were migrating through the area, that they concentrated along the shore of Lake Michigan owing to a funneling effect, and that they use visual cues to navigate along the shore during migration. Both bats and birds congregate in the fall at Cape May, New Jersey, to cross the mouth of Delaware Bay in their southern migration. In the early 1930s, many hawks were shot at this time, and the stomachs of sharp-shinned hawks examined by Hamilton contained red bats and bats of other species. Individuals have been observed several hundred kilometers at sea and on Bermuda, sometimes in flocks of 100 or more, but there are no data on the movements of individual bats, and few data from specimens in collections.

Analyses of dates and sex of bats in collections indicate that red bats become more abundant in the southern states from December to March, this area apparently constituting the species' main winter quarters, though red bats commonly winter at least as far north as Kentucky, Indiana, and Illinois. Late fall and winter records from West Virginia to Missouri are all of males. Early spring records in Illinois include

both sexes, but nearly all individuals in Indiana, Illinois, Iowa, Kansas, Louisiana, and Missouri during the breeding season are females, suggesting that these are nursery areas. Where the males are during the breeding season is not known. Apparently, males and females migrate at different times and have different winter and summer ranges. Most red bats leave the Midwest by October or November and return in March and April.

Bats, of course, usually fly at night, but they are occasionally seen in the daytime as well. Davis and Lidicker (1956) observed red bats emerge from a woods in Illinois in November, one at 1651 hours on 8 November, one at 1655 on 11 November. Davis reports counting 27 over roads in Mammoth Cave National Park, Kentucky, on warm afternoons in January 1957, and Russell E. Mumford has seen red bats flying on warm afternoons in southern Indiana. James B. Cope has seen them flying in Indiana every month but January, and Merlin Tuttle has seen them flying in winter in Tennessee. Mickey Weeks saw one apparently feeding near a water area at 1400 hours, 7 February 1987, and Whitaker saw a red bat, on two different occasions, flying along a lane in Clay County, Indiana, in the early afternoon in late February 1987, and another flying back and forth along a railroad track in Vermillion County, Indiana, on 30 January 1992. The first Clay County bat may have been frightened from its daytime roost; but the second was seen at the same location at dusk about a week later, and appeared to be foraging. The one in Vermillion County also appeared to be foraging, and Brock Fenton heard big brown bats emitting feeding buzzes while flying in winter in Canada. Some insects, such as midges and moths, do fly on warm winter days, but whether these bats feed during winter flight is unknown. Big brown, little brown, and northern bats thus fly about in winter seemingly foraging, but all our hard evidence indicates that they are not. Throughout the winter, red bats farther south, for example in the Great Dismal Swamp of Virginia and North Carolina, are active and feeding, primarily on flies and moths (Padgett and Rose, 1991). I would welcome fecal pellets, stomach contents, or, better yet, complete digestive tracts from red bats (and other species for that matter) found flying in winter in more northern areas.

Presumably, red bats enter torpor throughout the northern parts of their wintering range. They wake at 15°C (59°F), thus at much higher temperatures than do hibernating cave bats. This higher level of arousal would protect them from waking too frequently, and thus wasting energy, during the winter.

FOOD AND FEEDING. Examination of the stomachs of 128 bats of this species from Indiana revealed that moths formed 26.2% of the food taken, by volume. June bugs, planthoppers (Delphacidae), ants, leafhoppers, unidentified beetles, and ground beetles were the other more important foods; beetles, collectively, formed 28.1% of the volume in the sample. Red bats often fail to capture their prey on the first attempt. One was seen to make ten unsuccessful attempts to capture a glittering miller moth, *Estigmene acrea*, in the full glare of an electric street light.

Hickey and Fenton (1990) found that red bats concentrated their feeding around lights. The bats foraged for an average of 113.1 minutes per feeding, attacked an insect every 30 seconds, and were successful about 40% of the time. Acharya and Fenton (1992) found that longer feeding buzzes did not indicate larger prey, but the durations of the silent periods between feeding buzzes and the next echolocation call were significantly greater after successful attacks than after unsuccessful attacks.

REPRODUCTION AND DEVELOPMENT. Red bats copulate while in flight. During August, somewhat earlier than most bats, red bats mate. We have collected females in the first week of August that contained quantities of sperm in the uterus. Fertilization is delayed, and the three or four young—there is one case of five in a litter—are born about the middle of June, presumably while the female hangs alone in a tree. These are high numbers for bats, and the females possess four teats with which to nurse so great a quantity (most other bat species have two teats). Near-term embryos weigh about 0.5 gram and measure about as follows: total length 44, tail

15, hind foot 6 mm. Soon after birth the combined weight of the young exceeds that of the mother, but the young continue to nurse for some time. The young at this time hang by their feet but retain contact with the mother, grasping her with folded wings while her expanded membranes give them a measure of shelter. Their tiny but very sharp claws enable the young to cling easily to the mother's fur. By three to four weeks their eyes are open and they weigh about 4 to 5 grams. At four to five weeks they are large enough and strong enough to fly, although lactation continues for about 38 days (Kunz, 1971).

It has sometimes been thought that when the young of red bats are small, they accompany the parent on her flights, grasping the teat or loose skin of the breast with their tiny, recurved milk teeth, but this is not the case. The young are normally left behind. The recurving of the milk teeth may function to help the young remain attached to the female if she is blown about or frightened from her arboreal perch with the young attached—which would enable her to glide to the ground with the young, and then, when danger or the wind is past, climb back up a tree.

POPULATION CHARACTERISTICS. This is one of the more common bats in many of the areas where it occurs, as indicated by mist-netting, but to our knowledge no information is currently available on populations in this species. Though such information would be very valuable, it would probably be difficult to obtain.

ENEMIES. Greater predation than on many other species of bats would be indicated by the higher numbers of young, and blue jays appear to be a major predator (see Shump and Shump, 1982), but we suspect that babies falling from the roost may be the most important cause of mortality in this species. As mentioned above, migrating red bats can also fall prey to migrating hawks.

PARASITES AND DISEASE. The main ectoparasite of red bats is the macronyssid mite *Steatonyssus furmani*, and trematodes are common in the intestines. This species is relatively often rabid (about 4–5% of "suspect bats," which are those found dead or dying). Unlike other rabid animals, however, rabid bats pose no major threat. Rather, they suffer from "dumb rabies": they will bite to protect themselves if picked up, but are otherwise passive and do not attack.

RELATION TO HUMANS. Since they are solitary creatures and hang not in buildings but in trees, red bats seldom come into contact with humans and have little conflict with us. Contact typically occurs when someone finds one roosting on a cornstalk or among foliage, or comes upon a red bat on the ground with its young, the mother unable to take flight because of the weight of the young (a bat in these circumstances would presumably crawl up a tree).

AREAS FOR FURTHER WORK. Little is known about where and in what kind of roost red bats spend the winter, or whether red bats in northern areas feed in winter. The marked color difference between male and female in this species is correlated, I suspect, with some behavioral or perhaps geographical distinction peculiar to this species. An ecological study comparing males and females, with a view toward determining the function of this color difference, would be interesting. And, of course, the means by which red bats and other bats navigate during migration is in serious need of study.

## SUBSPECIES

*Lasiurus borealis borealis* Müller

As described above. The only subspecies in the eastern United States.

Type locality: New York.

### LITERATURE

Acharya, L., and M. B. Fenton. 1992. Echolocation behaviour of vespertilionid bats (*Lasiurus cinereus* and *Lasiurus borealis*) attacking airborne targets including arctiid moths. *Canadian J. Zool.* 70: 1292–1298.

Davis, W. H., and W. Z. Lidicker, Jr. 1956. Winter range of the red bat, *Lasiurus borealis*. *J. Mammal.* 37: 280–281.

Hickey, M. B. C., and M. B. Fenton. 1990. Foraging by red bats (*Lasiurus borealis*): Do intraspecific chases mean territoriality? *Canadian J. Zool.* 68: 2477–2482.

Kunz, T. H. 1971. Reproduction of some vespertilionid bats in central Iowa. *Amer. Midland Nat.* 86: 477–486.

Padgett, T. M., and R. K. Rose. 1991. Bats (Chiroptera: Vespertilionidae) of the Great Dismal Swamp of Virginia and North Carolina. *Brimleyana* 17: 17–25.

Shump, K. A., Jr., and A. U. Shump. 1982. *Lasiurus borealis*. **Mammalian Species No. 183.** Amer. Soc. Mammal. 6 pp.

Timm, R. M. 1989. Migration and molt patterns of red bats, *Lasiurus borealis* (Chiroptera: Vespertilionidae), in Illinois. *Bull. Chicago Acad. Sci.* 14: 1–7.

## Hoary Bat *Lasiurus cinereus* (Beauvois)

DESCRIPTION. Other than the rare mastiff bat, which occurs in the Miami, Florida area, the hoary bat is the largest of the eastern bats,

*Hoary bat,* Lasiurus cinereus

spanning a full 400 mm (16 inches) across the wings. Its yellowish-brown to dark mahogany-brown hair is frosted with silver over the entire

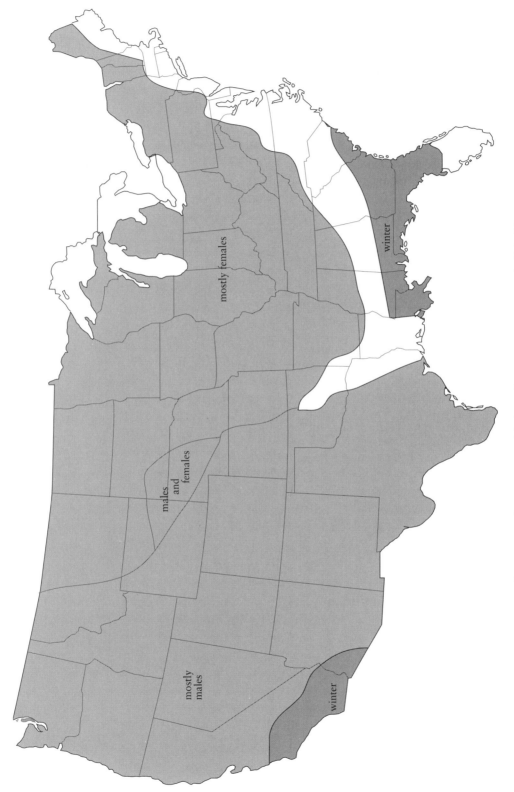

*The summer and winter ranges of the boary bat,* Lasiurus cinereus, *in the United States*

body, giving the animal a pronounced hoary appearance. The short, rounded ears have naked black rims. The throat and wing linings are buffy, and there are whitish wrist and shoulder patches. The top of the feet and the entire interfemoral membrane are well furred. The texture of the fur is unusually full and soft, and the furred patagium, when curled around the bat at rest, provides considerable insulation against the cold (Shump and Shump, Mammalian Species, 1982).

MEASUREMENTS. Average measurements of 41 adult females from Indiana were: total length 134.8 (102–152), tail 56.5 (49–65), hind foot 10.6 (6.0–13.5), forearm 54.9 (42–59), tragus 7.9 (5–11), wingspread 400 mm. Adults weigh from 18 to 38 grams, the females being the heavier.

Diploid number = 28.

TOOTH FORMULA

$$\frac{1}{3} \quad \frac{1}{1} \quad \frac{2}{2} \quad \frac{3}{3} \ = \ 32$$

DISTRIBUTION. The hoary bat is the most widespread of American bats, but has a rather complicated distribution. It occurs over much of temperate North America, extending north to southern British Columbia, the Districts of Mackenzie and Keewatin, and Labrador in summer and passing the winter well to the south. In South America this species occurs from Brazil to Argentina and Chile, and a subspecies of the hoary bat, *Lasiurus cinereus semotus*, is the only bat found in Hawaii. In the Gulf States the hoary bat is primarily a winter resident. Individuals that summer in North America winter in southern California, and in the Southeast (coastal South Carolina and northern Florida to Louisiana), and in Mexico and Guatemala (Watkins et al., 1972).

Hoary bats make a pronounced southerly migration in the fall, and indeed, a number of large migratory flocks have been reported. Findley and Jones (1964) summarized by means of maps much information on the distribution of hoary bats, one map for each month. We have used this and other information, such as that given by Zinn and Baker (1979), both in developing our own range map and in drawing the following tentative conclusions about distribution and migration in this species. As they are in the red bat, the sexes are largely separated during summer.

Females of this species are residents of the boreal region during the summer, but in the east they produce young at least as far south as Indiana and Pennsylvania, and there are records even for Louisiana. In summer, the females are found mostly in the area north of a broad arc extending from southern Alberta, eastern Wyoming, central Kansas, central Mississippi, western North Carolina, and northern Maine. During the period the females are on the maternity range there are very few females in western North America, nor are there hoary bats of either sex in the Southeast. At this time, hoary bats in the southwestern and northwestern United States are mostly males.

In August, migration toward the wintering range begins. It appears that most females move to the Southwest, where the males have spent the summer, rather than heading directly south across the Gulf of Mexico. They then probably move with the males back to the wintering grounds. Some males and females apparently move south along the Atlantic Coast through northern Florida and then perhaps across the Gulf to the wintering grounds.

It appears that the general wintering range of this species includes coastal Southern California and southwestern Arizona but is probably mostly south of the United States, apparently in Mexico and Guatemala, and a few individuals may spend the winter in a swath from South Carolina and Florida to Louisiana. There are also some scattered winter records to the north, which may indicate that a few individuals hibernate there. Mating probably takes place during fall migration or on the wintering grounds, or both.

HABITAT. Hoary bats are solitary and hang among the foliage, but very little is known concerning the particular habitats of this species. These bats often fly over woodland streams and ponds, but are also often seen feeding on moths around street lights.

HABITS. Again, the hoary bat is a solitary creature, although females have been observed hunting together, and five individuals have been seen within a short time over a small body of water. During the day, hoary bats generally hang among the foliage, but individuals have been found hanging on the sides of buildings, in a woodpecker hole, in caves, in a gray squirrel nest, and under a plank. Though this species is often said to be a late flyer, Caire et al. (1986) found, as is true of most other bats, much activity starting shortly after dusk, then several hours of reduced activity, followed by a period of minor activity before dawn.

Although the main wintering range of these bats is to the south, some apparently remain in the north. One was taken in winter from beneath a piece of driftwood on a Long Island beach. Hamilton observed one at Ithaca, New York, in early December. A hoary bat was seen flying about in a Pennsylvania forest in midday during a February thaw, and two have been taken in midwinter in Indiana. One of these was particularly interesting. It was taken on the side of a brick building at Terre Haute, on 31 January 1967, after a four-day warm spell. Maximum temperatures during the previous four days ranged from 14 to 20°C (58 to 67°F). The bat, a male in excellent condition, weighed 18.9 grams. The stomach, about a third full, contained grass, leaves, and shed snake skin; the small intestine was empty except for 25 trematodes; and the large intestine contained a mass of greenish vegetation, including grass leaves. We believe this bat had stopped eating insect food in the fall and had eaten vegetation prior to hibernation. It then voided the stomach and small intestine, leaving the vegetation in the large intestine as a fecal plug, and entered hibernation. But during the warm weather, the bat emerged and, with the return of cold weather, again fed upon grass leaves and, by chance, the snake skin.

Migration to the north occurs from March through April. Presumably, the majority of the males move northwest through Central America to their main summering range in the western United States, where only males occur in summer (Findley and Jones, 1964). Some of the males, however, apparently migrate eastward, presumably across the Gulf of Mexico, for Zinn

and Baker (1979) found both males and females of this species migrating through northern Florida in both spring and fall. These males probably account for the relatively few males occurring on the maternity range. The females apparently migrate directly north in spring over a broad area, for they occur in April throughout the southern United States, though they may initially head northwest with the males before heading north. That they do move more directly north, in contrast to the males, is indicated by the numerous female but not male records in the south-central states in April.

Hoary bats produce an audible chatter during flight. They have a rapid, direct flight, and can attain a rate of 21.3 kph (13.2 mph).

FOOD AND FEEDING. The hoary bat, because of its great size, can conquer large nocturnal insects, from which it will usually discard wings and head, allowing these to drop to the ground. The hoary bat is primarily a moth feeder, although it will also take other foods, and it has been recorded attacking pipistrelles. Ross (1967) found moths, numbering up to 25 per bat, in the digestive tracts of 136 of 139 hoary bats examined in New Mexico. There are strong differences in the food habits of bats, some being primarily moth feeders (this species and *Corynorhinus*), some feeding heavily on beetles (*Eptesicus fuscus* and *Nycticeius humeralis*), some on hemipterans (*Lasiurus borealis*), and some on smaller dipterans (*Myotis* and *Pipistrellus*). Though this differential resource utilization is incomplete, it does undoubtedly benefit the bats in reducing competition for food. Other foods taken by hoary bats include hemipterans such as stinkbugs and lygaeids, leaf and june beetles, and flies.

In Hawaii, where the hoary bat is the *only* bat, moth specialization would not be beneficial to it, and is not what is found (Whitaker and Tomich, 1983), although Belwood and Fullard (1984) found these bats feeding primarily on moths under lights in Hawaii.

The hoary bat uses a long-range foraging strategy (Barclay, 1985): detecting its prey, large prey, from a distance and pursuing it. Hoary bats fly fast and straight and are not particularly maneuverable. Barclay compared the food of *Lasiurus cinereus* with that of *Lasionyc-*

*teris noctivagans*, a slow, maneuverable, short-range feeder, and compared both with an insect sample gathered from the same place. Midges, Chironomidae, constituted the greatest biomass of insects in the available insect sample. Both bat species fed on a variety of foods, but *Lasionyc-teris* fed heavily on chironomids and other flies, and *Lasiurus cinereus* fed heavily on moths, beetles, and odonates. Even though they fed on radically different foods, Barclay (1985) concluded that both were feeding opportunistically, and that they did not partition their foods.

We suggest that these bats did indeed exhibit selectivity and did partition their food, since they fed on radically different proportions of items from the same prey base. As Barclay pointed out, much of this was because of their differential feeding strategies, but differential strategies—and differential flight capabilities—have evolved in part to allow bats to use different prey. Further, we do not believe most species feed either opportunistically *or* selectively as a general practice. This is too simplistic an approach to the question. We think bats select their food from among the available prey, and as Tom Kunz has pointed out, bats vary in the levels of selectivity they exhibit. It appears to us that opportunism is more important early in the season, at high latitudes, and in other situations in which the prey base is relatively low. Greater prey bases, conversely, allow greater selectivity.

Rolseth et al. (1994) has shown that the diets of adult and newly volant young hoary bats differ. Percent volumes of foods eaten by eight bats in their first week of flight in Manitoba consisted of about 40% midges (Chironomidae), 30% beetles (Coleoptera), 20% moths (Lepidoptera), and 4% Odonata. In their second week, seven bats ate these same items at rates of 2, 50, 24, and 9% by volume, already a different regimen. Adult foods, however, differed more markedly; adults fed on about 40% odonates, 30% moths, 20% beetles, and only 5% midges. We suspect that the swarms of midges allow the young bats to practice their echolocation skills, yet obtain meals much more easily—which is crucial in their first week—than feeding on other items would permit. During their second week they progress to catching beetles and moths, but are perhaps still not capable of capturing the odonates being eaten by the adults.

REPRODUCTION AND DEVELOPMENT. Hoary bats probably copulate during the fall, but, as in most vespertilionids, fertilization is delayed. Two young is the rule, although the female's four mammae will accommodate more. Birth usually occurs from mid-May through mid-June. At birth, the young weigh about 4.5 grams and have a forearm length of about 18–19 mm. Bogan (1972) and the author (Whitaker) have observed births of this species. After birth the female cradles the young in her wings, then grooms them until they are clean and dry. Fine, silvery-gray hair covers the backs of the newborn. The eyes open on day 12. Initially, the young cling to the female during the day, but remain among the foliage while she forages at night. The young grow very rapidly, attaining sufficient size and strength within a month to fend for themselves. Lactating females of this species were seen from 21 June to 22 July in Iowa, and the first volant young were seen on 22 July (Kunz, 1971). A female with two young attached was found on the ground in Denver. The combined weight of the two young exceeded 25% of the weight of the mother. A 24.8-gram female found in similar circumstances in Indiana had two young with a combined weight of 26.3 grams. This bat obviously could not have taken flight from the ground and would presumably have climbed back up a tree if she had not been found.

POPULATION CHARACTERISTICS. This species appears to be relatively uncommon over much of its vast range, and essentially nothing is known of its populations or home range. Nor have we information on the age attained by bats of this species.

ENEMIES. Almost nothing is known of the enemies of this species, although there are single records of kestrels and black snakes feeding on it. That it generally has two rather than three or four young suggests that it experiences lower mortality than does the red bat.

PARASITES AND DISEASE. The most abundant ectoparasite of this bat is the macronyssid mite *Chiroptonyssus americanus*. A myobiid mite, probably *Acanthophthirius lasiurus* but possibly an undescribed species, and other myobiid mites have been found. Several helminths have been reported in the intestines, but much more information is needed on the parasites of the hoary bat. The incidence of rabies is high (up to 25%) in this species in "suspect bats," those submitted to rabies laboratories for analysis. It would be very interesting to know the rate of rabies in hoary bats caught under other circumstances (by shooting, mist nets, or simply found in trees), but the high rate reported probably indicates simply that hoary bats are seldom found *unless* sick.

RELATION TO HUMANS. We seldom see this uncommon bat unless the bat is sick or we stumble upon its roosting spot by chance.

AREAS FOR FURTHER WORK. Nearly all aspects of the biology of this species need further work. The hypothesis on migration routes we propose here needs modification or verification, and more work on ectoparasites is needed. These bats make a very loud screech when handled. Is it simply a warning to a would-be predator, or does it have another function?

## SUBSPECIES

*Lasiurus cinereus cinereus* (Palisot de Beauvoir)

As described above. The only subspecies in the eastern United States.

Type locality: Philadelphia, Pennsylvania.

## LITERATURE

Barclay, R. M. R. 1985. Long- versus short-range foraging strategies of hoary (*Lasiurus cinereus*) and silver-haired (*Lasionycteris noctivagans*) bats and the consequences for prey selection. *Canadian J. Zool.* 63: 2570–2575.

Belwood, J. J., and J. H. Fullard. 1984. Echolocation and foraging behavior in the Hawaiian hoary bat, *Lasiurus cinereus semotus*. *Canadian J. Zool.* 62: 2113–2120.

Bogan, M. A. 1972. Observation on parturition and development in the hoary bat, *Lasiurus cinereus*. *J. Mammal.* 53: 611–614.

Caire, W., R. M. Hardisty, and K. E. Lacy. 1986. Ecological notes on *Lasiurus cinereus* (Chiroptera: Vespertilionidae) in Oklahoma. *Proc. Okla. Acad. Sci.* 66: 41–42.

Findley, J. S., and C. Jones. 1964. Seasonal distribution of the hoary bat. *J. Mammal.* 45: 461–470.

Kunz, T. H. 1971. Reproduction of some vespertilionid bats in central Iowa. *Amer. Midland Nat.* 86: 477–486.

Rolseth, S. L., C. E. Koehler, and R. M. R. Barclay. 1994. Differences in the diets of juvenile and adult hoary bats, *Lasiurus cinereus*. *J. Mammal.* 75: 394–398.

Ross, A. 1967. Ecological aspects of the food habits of insectivorous bats. *Proc. West. Found. Vert. Zool.* 1: 204–263.

Shump, K. A., and A. U. Shump. 1982. *Lasiurus cinereus*. **Mammalian Species No. 185.** Amer. Soc. Mammal. 5 pp.

Watkins, L. C., J. K. Jones, Jr., and H. H. Genoways. 1972. Bats of Jalisco, Mexico. Spec. Publ. Mus. Texas Tech Univ. 1. 44 pp.

Whitaker, J. O., Jr., and P. Q. Tomich. 1983. Food habits of the hoary bat, *Lasiurus cinereus*, from Hawaii. *J. Mammal.* 64: 151–152.

Zinn, T. L., and W. W. Baker. 1979. Seasonal migration of the hoary bat, *Lasiurus cinereus*, through Florida. *J. Mammal.* 60: 634–635.

## Northern Yellow Bat
### *Lasiurus intermedius*
### (H. Allen)                    Color plate 4

DESCRIPTION. This bat is somewhat similar in appearance to the red bat but is yellowish brown rather than red. The ear, of medium length, is more pointed than that of the red bat, and only sparsely haired on the inner surface, but furred more than halfway toward its tip on the outer surface. The tragus is broad at the base, tapering at the tip. The interfemoral membrane, naked below, is well haired above on only about the basal half. There is a sprinkling of fur on the underside of the volar membranes along the forearm to the wrist. The pelage is long and silky, and there are no white patches on the shoulders or wrists. There is no sexual dimorphism in color.

MEASUREMENTS. Measurements of 14 adults from Florida were: total length 126.8 (121–131.5), tail 54.2 (51–60), hind foot 9.8 (8–11), forearm 46.7 (46.7–50.0) mm (Hall & Jones, 1961). The wingspread is about 300–310 mm. There is little information on weights of this species. Four males from Louisiana ranged from 14 to 20 grams, and one pregnant female with a 15-mm embryo weighed 31.2 grams.

Diploid number = 26.

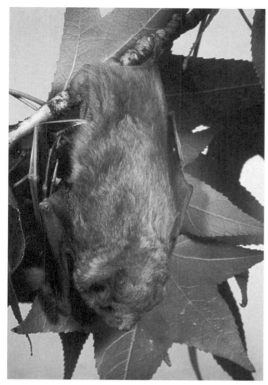

*Northern yellow bat,* Lasiurus intermedius
*(Roger W. Barbour)*

TOOTH FORMULA

$$\frac{1}{3} \quad \frac{1}{1} \quad \frac{2}{2} \quad \frac{3}{3} \quad = \quad 32$$

DISTRIBUTION. The yellow bat occurs in the southern parts of Louisiana, Mississippi, Alabama, and Georgia, nearly all of Florida, and north to southeastern South Carolina, and there are two accidental records north of this range. Beyond the eastern United States, it occurs across southern Louisiana and into east-central Texas.

HABITAT. This species is closely associated with Spanish moss, and, indeed, its range closely approximates that of Spanish moss.

HABITS. Little is known of the yellow bat's habits, but the available information has been summarized by Webster et al. (1980). Bats of this species, not common in collections, apparently do not resort to caves or buildings, as so many

other Chiroptera do. Most individuals collected have been shot, taken in mist nets, or captured by hand from trees. This species is a permanent resident throughout its range, and is often abundant where it occurs. In the northern extremities of its range, it does become torpid in cool temperatures.

FOOD AND FEEDING. The stomach of a yellow bat collected by H. B. Sherman (1939) at Gainesville, Florida, contained fragmentary insect remains that represented Homoptera, Zygoptera, Diptera (Anthomyiidae), Coleoptera (Dytiscidae and Scolytidae), and winged myrmicine ants. Yellow bats usually forage 5–10 meters (15–30 feet) above the ground in open or scrubby areas. Feeding aggregations are formed after the young begin to fly.

REPRODUCTION AND DEVELOPMENT. Little is known of reproduction in the yellow bat, although males appear to be reproductively active from August or September through mid-February. Bats of the genus *Lasiurus* are usually solitary, and this one, too, appears to be generally solitary, although maternity colonies have been found. Three or four young per litter are produced in late May or June. Newborn young weigh about 3 grams and their forearms are about 16 mm long. The young remain with their mother when she is disturbed from a daytime roost. Volant juveniles have been taken in June and July.

POPULATION CHARACTERISTICS. This bat is generally solitary, but on one occasion about 45 individuals were flushed from a day roost (Baker and Dickerman, 1956), and other groups have been reported. The sexes are apparently separated in winter.

ENEMIES. Nothing is known concerning the enemies of this species, but the fact that it bears three or four young per litter suggests that the mortality of the young, as effected by accidents or predators, must approach that of the red bat.

PARASITES AND DISEASE. The only parasite known to infest these bats is the macronyssid mite *Steatonyssus radovskyi,* which crawls around in the fur and on the membranes.

RELATION TO HUMANS. This species has little direct relationship to humans, since it roosts in vegetation, but like all insectivorous bats it helps to control insect populations and to maintain the balance of nature.

AREAS FOR FURTHER WORK. More information is needed on all phases of the biology of this species, but particularly on its food, parasites, and reproduction. Does this species generally form maternity colonies? Where are they, when do they form, how large are they, and when do the bats disperse? Or are the colonies occupied throughout the year? And in any event, where are the males?

## SUBSPECIES

The relationship between *Lasiurus intermedius floridanus*, the subspecies described for the east, and *L. intermedius intermedius* should be examined, but it appears that they form an intergrading series, and we see no reason to recognize them as separate.

*Lasiurus intermedius intermedius* (H. Allen)

As described above.

Type locality: Matamoros, Tamaulipas, Mexico.

Other currently recognized eastern subspecies:
    *L. intermedius floridanus* (Miller)

### LITERATURE

Baker, R. H., and R. W. Dickerman. 1956. Daytime roost of the yellow bat in Veracruz. *J. Mammal.* 37: 443.

Hall, E. R., and J. K. Jones, Jr. 1961. North American yellow bats, "*Dasypterus*," and a list of the named kinds of the genus *Lasiurus* Gray. *Univ. Kansas Publ. Mus. Nat. Hist.* 14: 73–98.

Sherman, H. B. 1939. Notes on the food of some Florida bats. *J. Mammal.* 20: 103–104.

*Distribution of the northern yellow bat,* Lasiurus intermedius, *in the eastern United States*

Webster, W. D., J. K. Jones, Jr., and R. J. Baker. 1980. *Lasiurus intermedius*. **Mammalian Species No. 132.** Amer. Soc. Mammal. 3 pp.

## Seminole Bat
### *Lasiurus seminolus* (Rhoads)    Color plate 4

DESCRIPTION. The seminole bat is similar to the eastern red bat, *Lasiurus borealis*, but much darker, the rufous shades of the more northerly species replaced by a rich mahogany brown, slightly frosted with grayish white.

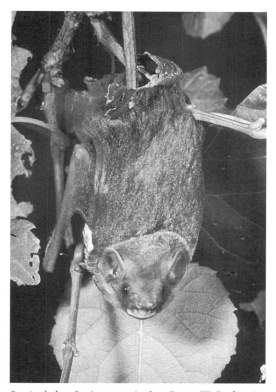

*Seminole bat,* Lasiurus seminolus *(Roger W. Barbour)*

MEASUREMENTS. Measurements of six adult specimens average: total length 111 (108–114), tail 48 (44–52), hind foot 8.5 (8–9), forearm 35–45 mm, and wingspread about 300 mm. Weights of ten adults from Georgia and Louisiana ranged from 8.6 to 13.8 grams.

Diploid number = 28.

TOOTH FORMULA

$$\frac{1}{3} \quad \frac{1}{1} \quad \frac{2}{2} \quad \frac{3}{3} \ = \ 32$$

DISTRIBUTION. The Seminole bat ranges across most of the Deep South, from Tennessee and North Carolina south to the Gulf Coast and most of Florida and west to eastern Texas. Two individuals have been taken in fall in Pennsylvania, one in Berks County and another in Lancaster County (Doutt et al., 1967), and another was taken at Ithaca, New York (Layne, 1955). Two were taken together in Posey County, Indiana, in 1994, and two were taken together after striking a high-rise in Milwaukee following a coastal hurricane.

HABITAT. Harper (1927) wrote of this species in the Okefenokee Swamp of southeastern Georgia, "In winter this appears to be the commonest bat of the swamp, but in summer it is outnumbered by Rafinesque's Bat. . . . The feeding grounds of this species appear to be very largely over watercourses, pine barrens, and cleared land, and to a lesser extent over prairies and hammocks. . . . In summer they likewise appear during the last half-hour before deep dusk. It seems to fly more directly than most of the other local species, and sometimes, at least, it travels comparatively slowly."

Through most of the year, this bat commonly roosts in long bunches of Spanish moss. The clumps chosen are at heights ranging from about 1 to 4.5 meters (3.5 to 15 feet) above the ground, and they are always above an area that is free of limbs, thus allowing the bat to drop free into flight. The trees occupied are usually at the edges of clearings.

HABITS. This is one of the most commonly seen bats in much of the South, but exceedingly little is known of its biology. It flies early in the evening but seldom at temperatures under 17°C (64°F). Apparently, the seminole bat is active throughout the winter, but it is more in evidence on warm evenings. It does appear to make limited northern and southern migratory movements.

FOOD AND FEEDING. The seminole bat may occasionally descend to the ground to feed. H. B. Sherman (1935), for example, collected a specimen at Gainesville, Florida, that had a flightless cricket in its jaws. Few data are available on the food of this species, but homopterans (Jassidae), dipterans (Dolichopodidae, Muscidae), and coleopterans (Scolytidae) were reported from one stomach, and T. L. Zinn (unpubl.) found seminoles to be eating 90% Odonata and 10% Coleoptera in July and 90% Coleoptera and 10% Hymenoptera in August (Wilkins, 1987). Shifts in consumption this dramatic occur often, as the prey base shifts. The presence of diurnal insects (Dolichopodidae, Odonata) in these stomachs suggests that the species often feeds before dark or gleans from vegetation after dark.

REPRODUCTION AND DEVELOPMENT. In Florida and southern Georgia, parturition occurs generally by the second week in June. Three or four young are the customary number (average 3.3), and they are supposedly capable of flight at no more than three weeks. Twenty-two pregnant females in one study had one young, two had two, nine had three, and ten had four.

POPULATION CHARACTERISTICS. The seminole bat is a solitary species, and essentially nothing is known of its population behavior.

ENEMIES. Like the red bat, this species bears three or four young, which suggests higher mortality through predation or from young dropping from the roost than is the case with most bats.

PARASITES AND DISEASES. We have no information on the parasites or diseases of this species.

RELATION TO HUMANS. As are all insectivorous bats, this species is undoubtedly highly beneficial in eating insects and thereby helping to maintain the balance of nature. Other than by

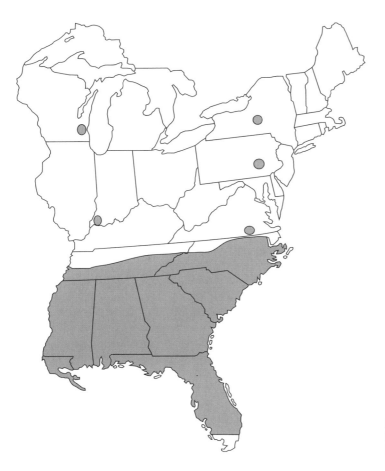

*Distribution of the seminole bat,* Lasiurus seminolus, *in the eastern United States*

chance, however, there is probably little contact between humans and this bat, since it is solitary and hangs inconspicuously in foliage.

AREAS FOR FURTHER WORK. Virtually all areas of the biology of this species are in need of study: reproduction, food, predators, parasites, populations, and winter behavior and movements.

## SUBSPECIES

None described.
Type locality: Tarpon Springs, Pinellas Co., Florida.

### LITERATURE

Doutt, J. K., C. A. Heppenstall, and J. E. Guilday. 1967. *Mammals of Pennsylvania*. Harrisburg: Pa. Game Comm. 288 pp.

Harper, F. 1927. The mammals of the Okefinokee Swamp region of Georgia. *Proc. Boston Soc. Nat. Hist.* 38: 191–396.

Layne, J. N. 1955. Seminole bat, *Lasiurus seminolus*, in central New York. *J. Mammal.* 36: 453.

Sherman, H. B. 1935. Food habits of the seminole bat. *J. Mammal.* 16: 224.

———. 1939. Notes on the food of some Florida bats. *J. Mammal.* 20: 103–104.

Wilkins, K. T. 1987. *Lasiurus seminolus*. **Mammalian Species No. 280.** Amer. Soc. Mammal. 5 pp.

## Evening Bat *Nycticeius humeralis* (Rafinesque)                    Color plate 5

DESCRIPTION. Evening bats closely resemble small big brown bats (*Eptesicus fuscus*), but the short forearm (about 36 mm, compared to the 45 mm of *Eptesicus*) and single upper incisors distinguish it from that species. *Nycticeius* can at once be distinguished from the several species of *Myotis*, which it somewhat resembles, by its short, rounded tragus, its short, sparse, dull-brown fur, the single upper incisor on each side, and the ample size of the first of the four molariform teeth behind the canine. In *Myotis*, there are two upper incisors per side, and the first two of the six molariform teeth are reduced in size, creating the appearance of a space between the canines and the large molariforms (see p. 81). The fur of *Nycticeius* is dull brown above, and the bases of these hairs are plumbeous. The ventral fur is paler than the dorsal. The young are considerably darker than the adults. The eve-

*Evening bat,* Nycticeius humeralis *(Roger W. Barbour)*

ning bat's fur is closely confined to the body, not extended onto the wing or tail membranes. The ears are small, thick, and leathery. The short, broad, low skull has a nearly straight dorsal profile. Bats of this species have an acrid odor, one strong enough to help in the identification of the live bat in the mist net, or of a colony in a building.

MEASUREMENTS. Average measurements of 30 adults from various parts of the species' range are: total length 92.7, tail 36.8, hind foot 7.1, ear 14–15, wingspread 260–280, forearm 35.6 mm; and weight 5–14 grams.
Diploid number = 46.

TOOTH FORMULA

$$\frac{1}{3} \quad \frac{1}{1} \quad \frac{1}{2} \quad \frac{3}{3} \; = \; 30$$

DISTRIBUTION. In summer, *Nycticeius humeralis* occurs sparingly north to Pennsylvania, southern Michigan, and Illinois, but it reaches its maximum abundance in the south, where it is found everywhere but in the Appalachians. It is becoming increasingly uncommon in the north, no maternity colonies being known today from either Illinois or Kentucky, and the species has been placed on the endangered species list in Indiana. Eleven maternity colonies were known in Indiana three decades ago, but all are now defunct; an additional one, discovered in a church in 1987, formed the basis of studies by Clem (1992, 1993), but it too is now defunct. In 1994, however, we discovered a colony in a silver maple tree in the Wabash bottomlands, in west-central Indiana. Outside of our range, evening bats occur west to northeastern Kansas, eastern Oklahoma, eastern Texas, and south into northeastern Mexico.

HABITAT. Evening bats almost never enter caves; a very few have been taken among bats swarming at cave entrances in late summer, and one was found roosting in a cave. Ancestrally, evening bats apparently roosted in hollow trees, and many still do, but this species is now often dependent on the structures of humans, and many nursery colonies have been found in buildings. One nursery was discovered in a hollow cypress in the Okefenokee Swamp, another in Spanish moss. Evening bats have also been found under loose bark. Matthew Crowder has found evening bats roosting under the bases left on palm trees when fronds are cut or broken off. We recently found a large colony of them using a pileated woodpecker hole about 12 meters (40 feet) up in a silver maple tree. The tree is in the Prairie Creek/Wabash River floodplain in a 650-ha (1600-acre) woodlot. There appear to be at least 350 bats using this tree, and this estimate is probably low. After the young become volant, the bats spread out to a number of alternate roost trees in the woods. In part because there are no buildings in the bottoms, which are often under a meter or two of water during flooding, we suspect that this population is behaving more like those of ancestral evening bats than are the colonies established in human structures. Bowles et al. (1996) also found evening bats often using alternate roost trees.

HABITS. Bain (1981), Bowles (1996), Clem (1992, 1993), and Watkins (1972) have given us much of our information on this species. As darkness falls, evening bats leave their roost in a hollow tree or building, falling one after another

humeralis

subtropicalis

*Distribution of the evening bat,* Nycticeius humeralis, *in the eastern United States*

into the air and flying off. Most of the bats in a church in Indiana left at dusk to feed for about two to three hours, then returned to the church for the remainder of the night (Clem, 1992). Mean foraging time per night was 78 minutes for pregnant females, 107 minutes for lactating females, and 127 minutes for postlactating females. The foraging was generally in open habitat, often over cornfields, within 2.7 km (1.7 miles) of the roost (Clem, 1993). These bats have a slow and steady flight—specimens have been secured simply by swishing a reed fishing pole in their path—and they will fly with other bats in the same area.

Nursery colonies have not generally been found in buildings also housing other species, except *Tadarida*, although Bain (1981) found *Nycticeius*, *Myotis austroriparius*, and *Tadarida brasiliensis* all roosting in the same building, *Nycticeius* and *M. austroriparius* together only in winter. In buildings, evening bats will spread out at higher temperatures, but pack together when it is cold. In Florida, they put on fat in winter, becoming torpid in cold weather and feeding during warm.

Bats inhabited a nursery roost in a building in Indiana from about the first of May to the last of October (Clem, 1992, 1993). Sometimes, however, some individuals did not return to the building, but took up alternate roosts in trees, remaining there from one to 12 nights. In contrast, the maternity tree in the woods in Indiana (discussed above) was inhabited by large numbers of bats only until the young became volant, the inhabitants then spreading out into numerous trees in the same woods. Some evening bats were present in the Florida maternity colonies in all months of the year but April, but the colonies declined through January and February, and single bats roosted there in February and early March. It is not known where the bats were from January to late April, but it appeared that a nearby alternate roost or roosts were being used, for females returned sporadically and a few solitary males were present. Judging from our experience in Indiana, we might suppose that the alternate roosts were in trees. The females returned to the colony in late April and early May, and a number of banded juvenile females born there the previous year returned to their natal colony. Roost temperatures in Missouri ranged up to 43°C (110°F); the bats moved about in the colony as temperatures rose and fell, thus placing themselves in optimum conditions, within a range of 23.8–35.5°C (75–96°F).

Adult males, seldom found in the northern part of the range, are more common in the south. Although the males are solitary, they appear sporadically in the nursery colonies at almost any time (in Missouri, however, none was found in the colony after 29 August). Young males desert the colony soon after taking to wing, but a few additional males arrived at the colony in October. It appears that males occasionally visit the colonies for mating in late fall or winter. They do not participate in the care of the young in any way.

Humphrey and Cope (1968) demonstrated that this species does migrate, by finding tagged individuals 176, 192, and 299 km south of where they had been tagged, and Watkins reported one 547 km (339 miles) south of where it had been originally tagged. Nonetheless, we have no idea where these bats hibernate. Evening bats in the north leave the summer roosts during September and early October. The deposition of fat in fall argues that these bats migrate, yet fat deposition occurs even in Florida. There, it appears that evening bats remain in the immediate vicinity, but their main winter roosts have not been found there either. Perhaps these bats are solitary in winter, at least in Florida, finding their own nook or cranny with proper conditions for hibernation, as *Eptesicus* does in the north.

FOOD AND FEEDING. Foods eaten by an Indiana colony of *Nycticeius* were monitored on a weekly basis throughout the season by guano analysis (Whitaker and Clem, 1992). The primary foods eaten were beetles, moths, and leafhoppers, comprising about 60, 20, and 7% of the total volume of food. The single food eaten in the greatest amount (14.2% by volume) was the spotted cucumber beetle, *Diabrotica undecimpunctata*. This beetle is a pest on vine plants, but less well known is the fact that its larva is the southern corn rootworm, a serious pest of corn. Carabid beetles (*Calathus* sp.), stinkbugs (Pentatomidae), and chinchbugs (Lygaeidae) were also important. We estimated that the 300 bats in this colony ate about 6.3 million insects per year.

REPRODUCTION AND DEVELOPMENT. In the south, the bats probably copulate in fall and winter, near the nursery colony but not within the colony itself. During August these bats appear unusually numerous, and at this time the two sexes are found together, probably for breeding purposes. We suspect that among bats in the northern part of the species' range, copulation occurs during migration to the south.

The two young (rarely one or three) are born synchronously in late May to mid-June, depending on latitude, and births have been recorded even into July. Females with embryos have been taken as far north as southern Michigan. The newborn, about 58% male, weigh about 2.5 grams, and the forearm is about 14 mm long at birth. The eyes open in about 12 to 30 hours, and short, grayish fur covers the babies within five days. Females nurse their own young in the two weeks following birth, then will nurse any young that approaches them, until weaning time. Just prior to leaving the roost, the females rub substances from their submandibular gland on the face of their young. Upon returning, they smell the faces of the young, presumably recognizing their own in this manner when the young fall to the floor. Young give a distress signal. Females fly to them, allow them to attach, then fly or crawl back to the roost with them. When foraging for food, nursing females leave their young in the recesses of the hollow tree or old building that serves as home. The young can fly at about three weeks. The colonies diminish greatly in July, owing presumably to dispersal, since the juvenile males tend to disappear. The juvenile females remain at the roost, foraging with their mothers but also continuing to nurse.

POPULATION CHARACTERISTICS. Much is yet to be learned of populations of this species. Females form maternity colonies in buildings or in trees. There are few adult males in the northern part of the range. Cope et al. (1961) reported a total of 460 bats in four colonies in buildings in southern Indiana, and 75 in one colony in adjacent Illinois. Bowles et al. (1996) state that these bats form maternity colonies of 25 to 950 individuals. Watkins and Shump (1981) recorded a maximum of 115 adult females in a colony in northern Missouri. High counts of evening bats at a church in Clay County, Indiana, in 1989 by P. D. Clem were 225 before the young were volant and 492 including volant young. In the Wabash bottoms of southern Indiana on 13 June 1995, an evening bat was radio-tracked to a silver maple tree and that night a minimum of 350 evening bats emerged from a pileated woodpecker hole about 12 meters (40 feet) up in the tree. The life span of *Nycticeius* is unknown.

ENEMIES. No information is available on the enemies of this species. We suspect falling from the roost is the greatest source of mortality. From the time evening bats began invading buildings in earnest, man has been the major enemy of the species. In nearly all of the 11 cases where colonies of evening bats are known to have disappeared in Indiana, the buildings that had housed them had been torn down or their exits closed.

PARASITES AND DISEASE. A macronyssid mite, *Steatonyssus ceratognathus*, is the most abundant parasite on the evening bat, but batbugs, *Cimex*, and a myobiid, *Acanthophthirius nycticeius*, also occur. Nematodes and cestodes have been found as internal parasites. Parasite populations were found to cycle in this species, peaking at the times when the newborn young were abundant.

RELATION TO HUMANS. Today, *Nycticeius* most often establishes its maternity roosts in buildings, which puts the species at risk of conflict with human concerns. Like the big brown bat, the evening bat feeds heavily on the spotted cucumber beetle, at least in Indiana, and is thus exceptionally beneficial, for the larva of this beetle is one of the corn rootworms, as a group the worst agricultural pests in the United States.

AREAS FOR FURTHER WORK. Where do the northern individuals of this species spend the winter? In trees along watercourses several hundred kilometers south of their summer range? And where do the males roost when the females are in the maternity roost? When and where does mating occur?

## SUBSPECIES

*Nycticeius humeralis humeralis* (Rafinesque)
As described above.
Type locality: Kentucky.
Other currently recognized eastern subspecies:
  *N. humeralis subtropicalis* Schwartz

### LITERATURE

Bain, J. R. 1981. Roosting ecology of three Florida bats: *Nycticeius humeralis, Myotis austroriparius* and *Tadarida brasiliensis*. Unpubl. M.S. thesis, University of Florida, Gainesville. 131 pp.

Bain, J. R., and S. R. Humphrey. 1986. Social organization and biased primary sex ratio of the evening bat, *Nycticeius humeralis*. *Fla. Scientist* 49: 22–32.

Bowles, J. B., D. Howell, J. W. Van Zee, and G. M. Wilson. 1996. Use of alternate roost trees by the evening bat, *Nycticeius humeralis*, in Iowa. In *Contributions in Mammalogy: A Memorial Volume*, pp. 217–224. Lubbock: Museum of Texas Tech University.

Clem, P. D. 1992. Seasonal population variation and emergence patterns in the evening bat, *Nycticeius humeralis*. *Proc. Ind. Acad. Sci.* 101: 33–43.

———. 1993. Foraging patterns and the use of temporary roosts in female evening bats, *Nycticeius humeralis*, at an Indiana maternity colony. *Proc. Ind. Acad. Sci.* 102: 201–206.

Cope, J. B., W. W. Baker, and J. Confer. 1961. Breeding colonies of four species of bats of Indiana. *Proc. Ind. Acad. Sci.* 70: 262–266.

Humphrey, S. R., and J. B. Cope. 1968. Records of migration of the evening bat, *Nycticeius humeralis*. *J. Mammal.* 49: 329.

Schwartz, A. 1951. A new race of bat (*Nycticeius humeralis*) from southern Florida. *J. Mammal.* 32: 233–234.

Watkins, L. C. 1972. *Nycticeius humeralis*. **Mammalian Species No. 23.** Amer. Soc. Mammal. 4 pp.

Watkins, L. C., and K. A. Shump. 1981. Behavior of the evening bat, *Nycticeius humeralis*, at a nursery roost. *Amer. Midland Nat.* 105: 258–268.

Whitaker, J. O., Jr., and P. D. Clem. 1992. Food of the evening bat, *Nycticeius humeralis*, from Indiana. *Amer. Midland Nat.* 127: 211–214.

## Bats of the Genus *Corynorhinus*

The big-eared bats of the eastern United States are plain brown but can immediately be recognized by their tremendous ears. On an animal less than 100 mm (4 inches) long, an ear about 35 mm (well over an inch) long is huge.

The New World big-eared bats have had a see-saw taxonomic history, shifting back and forth between *Plecotus* and *Corynorhinus*. For several years, following Handley (1959), they have been recognized as belonging in the genus *Plecotus*. Currently, however, we follow Tumlison and Douglas (1992), who evaluated the cladistic relationships of *Plecotus, Euderma, Idionycteris*, and *Corynorhinus* and concluded that the eastern U.S. big-eared bats should be assigned to the genus *Corynorhinus*, reserving the generic name *Plecotus* for the Old World big-eared bats.

### LITERATURE CITED

Handley, C. O., Jr. 1959. A revision of American bats of the genera *Euderma* and *Plecotus*. *Proc. U.S. Nat. Mus.* 110: 95–246.

Tumlison, R., and M. E. Douglas. 1992. Parsimony analysis and the phylogeny of the plecotine bats (Chiroptera: Vespertilionidae). *J. Mammal.* 73: 276–285.

### KEY TO THE BATS OF THE GENUS *CORYNORHINUS*

1. Tips of ventral hairs buff; accessory cusp on the first incisor lacking . . . . . . . . . . . *C. townsendii*
1. Tips of ventral hairs white; often an accessory cusp on the first incisor . . . . . . . . . . . *C. rafinesquii*

## Rafinesque's Big-Eared Bat
### *Corynorhinus rafinesquii* (Lesson)

DESCRIPTION. This species, about the size of the little brown bat, may at once be distinguished from all other eastern bats except *C. townsendii* by its tremendous ears, which are more than 30 mm long and joined at the base. A thick, wartlike enlargement between the eyes and the nostrils gives it the common name "lump-nose." *Corynorhinus rafinesquii* is distinguished from *C. townsendii* by its underparts, which are washed with white, and by having a cusp on the inner upper incisor.

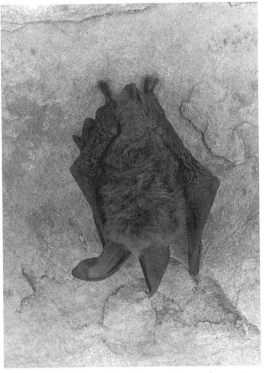

*Rafinesque's big-eared bat,* Corynorhinus rafinesquii, *its huge ears drooping below (Tony Brentlinger)*

MEASUREMENTS. Measurements of four adults from Tennessee and Georgia averaged: total length 99.5, tail 48, hind foot 40.2, ear 29–37, wingspread 265–301 mm; and weight 7–10 grams. The forearm is about 39 to 44 mm. Females average greater than males in weight.

Diploid number = 32.

TOOTH FORMULA

$$\frac{2}{3} \quad \frac{1}{1} \quad \frac{2}{3} \quad \frac{3}{3} = 36$$

DISTRIBUTION. Rafinesque's big-eared bat ranges widely over the southern states, from North Carolina and Kentucky south to the Gulf of Mexico and through most of Florida. It is still present in southeastern Illinois, but appears to have been extirpated from southern Indiana. The species ranges beyond the Mississippi River to southeastern Missouri, Arkansas, and Louisiana.

HABITAT. In choice of habitat, this species appears to differ most noticeably from eastern *C. townsendii* in establishing its summer colonies most often in hollow trees or buildings of wooded areas, rather than strictly in caves, and in Florida it occurs in areas that lack caves.

HABITS. Movement of bats within the colony is frequent, both winter and summer. In their summer roosts, the animals immediately become active if disturbed, moving their ears and their heads. When the bat is at rest, the long ears are coiled spiral-fashion about the neck, suggesting the horns of a ram.

The bats emerge after dark, presumably for a feeding bout followed by the use of a night roost, for they do not return to the day roost until just before dawn. Like other *Corynorhinus*, this is a versatile bat in flight, maneuverable but also capable of swift to nearly hovering flight.

In the northern parts of the species' range, hibernation is from about November to March, but these bats may be active longer in the south. *Corynorhinus rafinesquii* will hibernate in caves in the northern parts of its range, and in Kentucky there are some populations that live in caves year-round. In southern Illinois it sometimes hibernates in silica mines. Roosts are often shared with *Pipistrellus subflavus* in these mines, with *Myotis austroriparius* in the south, and very rarely with *Corynorhinus townsendii* in Kentucky caves. In Louisiana, *C. rafinesquii*, *P. subflavus*, and *M. austroriparius* may all share the same roost, although the species segregate themselves within the roost. There is no indication that this species often shares a maternity roost with *Eptesicus*, the big brown bat, the most abundant bat in buildings over much of its range, but it often shares hibernating caves with *Eptesicus*.

FOOD AND FEEDING. These bats emerge from their roost late, and their food, like that of other species of *Corynorhinus*, is mainly moths (Clark, 1991; Hurst and Lacki, 1997). Lepidoptera formed 90% or more of the volume of food in samples from four different roosts examined by Hurst and Lacki (1997). The moths involved were mainly noctuids and sphingids, especially *Catocala* sp. and *Deidamia inscripta*, as indicated by the wings discarded under roosts.

REPRODUCTION AND DEVELOPMENT. Copulation, in autumn and winter, is followed by delayed fertilization. A single young, weighing about 2.3 to 2.6 grams (Jones, 1977) is born in late May or early June. In about three weeks, the young have their permanent teeth and can fly.

POPULATION CHARACTERISTICS. Colonies number from a few to about 100 individuals, the colonies in the north larger on the average than those in the south. Longevity of at least ten years and one month was reported by Paradiso and Greenhall (1967), but we suspect individuals can live much longer than that.

ENEMIES. Because of its choice of roosting sites, this bat is highly susceptible to disturbance by humans and to predation by snakes, cats, raccoons, and opossums.

PARASITES AND DISEASE. We have no information on the parasites or diseases of this species.

RELATION TO HUMANS. This species helps keep insects, especially moths, under control. It often gets into buildings, but is usually not abundant enough to have much impact on the concerns of humans.

AREAS FOR FURTHER WORK. The habits of *Corynorhinus rafinesquii* are not well known, and would repay detailed study. This species is becoming quite rare and perhaps should be considered for threatened or endangered status. Study of its ecto- and endoparasites should be interesting, if only because nothing at all is currently known.

*Distribution of Rafinesque's big-eared bat,* Corynorhinus rafinesquii, *in the eastern United States*

## SUBSPECIES

*Corynorhinus rafinesquii rafinesquii* (Lesson)

As described above.

Type locality: Probably Le Conte Plantation, 5 mi [8 km] south of Riceboro, Liberty Co., Georgia.

Other currently recognized eastern subspecies:
*C. rafinesquii macrotis* LeConte

### LITERATURE

Clark, M. K. 1991. Foraging ecology of Rafinesque's big-eared bat, *Plecotus rafinesquii* in North Carolina. *Bat Research News* 32: 68.

Hurst, T. E., and M. J. Lacki. 1997. Food habits of Rafinesque's big-eared bat in southeastern Kentucky. *J. Mammal.* 78: 525–528.

Jones, C. 1977. *Plecotus rafinesquii.* **Mammalian Species No. 69.** Amer. Soc. Mammal. 4 pp.

Paradiso, J. L., and A. M. Greenhall. 1967. Longevity records for American bats. *Amer. Midland Nat.* 78: 251–252.

### Townsend's Big-Eared Bat
*Corynorhinus townsendii* (Cooper)

Today, *Corynorhinus townsendii virginianus* is recognized as an eastern subspecies of the western big-eared bat, but in the past there was much confusion between the two eastern species of *Corynorhinus.* Moreover, until recently both of these species were assigned to the genus *Plecotus* (for a discussion of that history, see the account for the genus *Corynorhinus*, above).

DESCRIPTION. This bat is at once distinguished from all other eastern species except Rafinesque's big-eared bat by its enormous ears. The

*Townsend's big-eared bat,* Corynorhinus townsendii *(Roger A Barbour)*

ears are about 35 mm long and, when laid back, reach to the middle of the body. Peculiar glandular masses rise high on the muzzle, well above the nostrils. The color above is clove-brown, shading imperceptibly into slaty gray at the base of the hairs. The bases of the inner margins of the ears are scantily furred, and the wing and tail membranes lack fur. This species can usually be separated from Rafinesque's big-eared bat by its buffy underparts, (in *Corynorhinus rafinesquii* the underparts are washed with white and the dorsal and ventral hairs are more sharply bicolored), and by the first incisor's having no accessory cusp (in *rafinesquii* there is usually an accessory cusp on the first incisor).

MEASUREMENTS. Average measurements of 11 adults from Pendleton County, West Virginia, were: total length 99.8 (96–110), tail 45.8 (42–52), hind foot 11.5 (11–12), forearm 44.4 (42–47), wingspread 291–319 mm; and weight 9–12 grams.

Diploid number = 32.

TOOTH FORMULA
$$\frac{2}{3} \quad \frac{1}{1} \quad \frac{2}{3} \quad \frac{3}{3} \;=\; 36$$

DISTRIBUTION. Eastern U.S. populations of this species, known as *Corynorhinus townsendii virginianus*, are restricted to caves in West Virginia and Virginia over 760 meters (2500 feet) altitude, except for one large colony (about 3700 individuals in 1993) in Kentucky.

HABITAT. In the east, this is a cave species, summer and winter. Specimens are usually met with in the twilight zone, close to the cave entrance, where they hang suspended from the walls or ceilings, their long ears spirally coiled and flattened against the neck. *Corynorhinus townsendii* does not move about much, although most individuals change caves seasonally. Barbour and Davis (1969) recorded movements of about 64 km (40 miles) in this species. Lacki et al. (1993) found that the Virginia big-eared bats use rock shelters (cracks and fissures) with large entrances and deep passages as feeding roosts, but otherwise the character of the rock shelters varied greatly.

HABITS. These peculiar bats excite much wonder in those who first make their acquaintance. Direct a beam of light on them in the caves where they live and they are immediately alert, the big ears upright and twisting alternately as if to catch the minutest sound. These are indeed among the wariest of bats, taking alarm at the least disturbance. They emerge late in the evening for a feeding bout, after which they probably repair to a night roost, and they probably pursue a predawn feeding bout before they return to the day roost. These bats are seldom taken in mist nets, perhaps because they have a very sensitive echolocation system. Many bats go into daily torpor, which serves to conserve energy, but this species does not.

There is no age or sex segregation during hibernation. Big-eared bats often hibernate in colder or well-ventilated parts of a cave, often near the cave entrances, and may lose up to half their weight during hibernation. If complex, the same caves may harbor both summer and winter populations in this species. There are several caves in eastern Kentucky (Barbour and Davis, 1974) where *C. townsendii* and *C. rafinesquii* have been found in the same cave at the same

*Townsend's big-eared bat in flight (J. Scott Altenbach)*

*Distribution of Townsend's big-eared bat,* Corynorhinus townsendii, *in the eastern United States*

time, but this is not known to occur elsewhere.

Although this bat flies at speeds of 2.9 to 5.5 meters per second (6.4 to 12.3 miles per hour) (Hayward and Davis, 1964), it is highly maneuverable and can fly at low speeds or even hover (Kunz and Martin, Mammalian Species, 1982). Presumably, the huge outer ears are of use in funneling sounds into the inner ear in connection with echolocation, but it has also been suggested that they may provide lift, since they are often directed forward when the bat is in flight. Bats of this species have exceptional ability to avoid obstacles, and to separate echolocation signals from background noise (Griffen et al., 1963). They are also able to emit echolocation pulses through the nose almost as well as through the mouth (Griffen, 1958).

FOOD AND FEEDING. These bats feed primarily on small lepidopterans, the basic food of bats of this genus. Moths formed 90% or more of the volume of food eaten by these bats in three caves in West Virginia (Sample and Whitmore, 1993), and 87.5% in 15 samples from West Virginia collected from 1983 to 1985 (Dalton et al., 1986). Minor foods were Coleoptera, Diptera, Hymenoptera, Homoptera, and Neuroptera. Sample and Whitmore (1993) found noctuid, geometrid, sphingid, notodontid, and arctiid wings in maternity caves of this species. The bats appear to use echolocation to capture individual moths in flight.

Burford and Lacki (1995) found that these bats spent much time over grassy fields, even though that habitat formed a relatively small part of their study, and moths, their principal food, were low in both species and numbers there. They suggested that moths are more easily captured in the uncluttered air above fields.

REPRODUCTION AND DEVELOPMENT. Pearson et al. (1952) studied reproduction in this species in the west. Mating is in the fall, but fertilization is delayed until spring, when ovulation, fertilization, and gestation take place, ovulation occurring about the time females leave the hibernacula. Gestation is about 56 to 100 days, depending on spring temperatures and varying degrees of torpor in the bats. Females return to the same maternity colonies year after year, but males are solitary at this time. The single young,

which develops in the right uterine horn, is born during late June, at 2.8 grams weighing about one-fourth the weight of its mother at birth. Its large ears cover the eyes its first few days, until the eyes open. The young produce "chirps" soon after birth and "squawks" a week later, and can fly at two and one-half to three weeks. The young probably make short forays out of the cave on their own over the next couple of weeks. By one month, the forearm is nearly as large as that of the adult, and by six weeks the young is weaned.

Lacki et al. (1994) monitored three maternity colonies and one bachelor colony in Kentucky. Two of the maternity roosts and the bachelor roost were in limestone caves; the third maternity colony was in a sandstone rock shelter. In maternity colonies in caves, some switching between roosts was observed. Females at the sandstone roost were pregnant on 10 May and lactating on 17 June, and the young were volant on 5 August. Numbers decreased in the bachelor colony in mid-August, coinciding with testis descent and presumably with the onset of mating.

POPULATION CHARACTERISTICS. In eastern populations, the bats usually hibernate singly or in small groups, although the groups occasionally number up to several hundred or more. Nursery colonies in the east are in caves, but the colonies are usually small, numbering not over 100 bats. At one time, there were several colonies of 100 to 300 bats in West Virginia, but the numbers have declined. A colony near Tazewell, Virginia, is quite large, and one of those in Kentucky numbers nearly 1000. These bats can live to at least 16 years of age (Paradiso and Greenhall, 1967).

ENEMIES. As is the case with other North American bats, this species has few important enemies.

PARASITES AND DISEASE. Bats of this species serve as host to large parasitic flies, *Trichobius corynorhini* (Streblidae), which are often obvious as they crawl about the bat, even during its hibernation. Occasionally, one can see one of them fly from one bat to another; the flight of these flies is slow, weak, and straight. Other ectoparasites are macronyssid mites, particularly *Macronyssus longisetosus*. Ticks, a chigger, and a sarcoptid mite have also been reported from this host. The internal parasites that have been identified are two nematodes, a cestode, and a trypanosome.

RELATION TO HUMANS. Because of its intolerance to disturbance, and its scattered eastern populations, continued efforts are necessary to protect this bat and the caves in which it lives. This eastern subspecies is now listed as federally endangered.

AREAS FOR FURTHER WORK. Relatively little is known of the life history of this species. The foods of the dusk and dawn feeding bouts could be compared. Further work on the parasites would be of interest. Trematodes are parasitic in the digestive tracts of many of our bats. Are they in this bat, primarily a moth feeder? Genetic comparison between eastern and western populations of this species and with *C. rafinesquii* would be interesting.

## SUBSPECIES

Eastern populations of this species are geographically separated from *C. townsendii townsendii*, which occurs in western North America, and therefore constitute a separate subspecies.

*Corynorhinus townsendii virginianus* Handley

As described above. This is the only subspecies that occurs in the eastern United States.

Type locality: Schoolhouse Cave, $4^2/_5$ mi [7 km] northeast of Riverton, Pendleton Co., West Virginia, for *C. townsendii virginianus*.

## LITERATURE

Barbour, R. W., and W. H. Davis. 1969. *Bats of America*. Lexington: Univ. Press of Kentucky. 286 pp.

———. 1974. *Mammals of Kentucky*. Lexington: Univ. Press of Kentucky. 322 pp.

Burford, L. S., and M. J. Lacki. 1995. Habitat use by *Corynorhinus townsendii virginianus* in the Daniel Boone National Forest. *Amer. Midland Nat.* 134: 340–345.

Dalton (Tipton), V. M., V. Brack, Jr., and P. M. McTeer. 1986. Food habits of the big-eared bat, *Plecotus townsendii virginianus*, in Virginia. *Virg. J. Sci.* 37: 248–253.

Griffen, D. R. 1958. *Listening in the Dark*. New Haven, Conn.: Yale Univ. Press. 413 pp.

Griffen, D. R., J. J. McCue, and A. D. Grinnell. 1963.

The resistance of bats to jamming. *J. Exp. Zool.* 152: 229–250.

Hayward, B., and R. Davis. 1964. Flight speeds in western bats. *J. Mammal.* 45: 236–242.

Kunz, T. H., and R. A. Martin. 1982. *Plecotus townsendii.* **Mammalian Species No. 175.** Amer. Soc. Mammal. 6 pp.

Lacki, M. J., M. D. Adam, and L. G. Shoemaker. 1993. Characteristics of feeding roosts of Virginia big-eared bats in Daniel Boone National Forest. *J. Wildlife Mgmt.* 57: 539–543.

———. 1994. Observations on seasonal cycle, population patterns and roost selection in summer colonies of *Plecotus townsendii virginianus* in Kentucky. *Amer. Midland Nat.* 131: 34–42.

Paradiso, J. L., and A. M. Greenhall. 1967. Longevity records for American bats. *Amer. Midland Nat.* 78: 251–252.

Pearson, O. P., M. R. Koford, and A. K. Pearson. 1952. Reproduction of the lump-nosed bat (*Corynorhinus rafinesquii*) in California. *J. Mammal.* 33: 273–320.

Rippy, C. L., and M. L. Harvey. 1965. Notes on *Plecotus townsendii virginianus* in Kentucky. *J. Mammal.* 46: 499.

Sample, B. E., and R. C. Whitmore. 1993. Food habits of the endangered Virginia big-eared bat in West Virginia. *J. Mammal.* 74: 428–435.

# FREE-TAILED BATS, Family Molossidae

As their name suggests, the tail of the free-tailed bats is partially free from the interfemoral membrane. These bats, with their long, narrow wings, are swift fliers. Their ears are thick and often meet on top of the head, but in our common free-tailed bat of the Southeast, *Tadarida brasiliensis*, they do not. Bats of the family Molossidae have long, stiff tactile hairs on the toes. Molossids, which are characteristic of the warmer parts of the world, include about 80 species in 12 genera. Three of these species, in three genera, occur in the eastern United States.

KEY TO THE GENERA AND SPECIES OF FREE-TAILED BATS OF THE FAMILY MOLOSSIDAE

1. Forearm more than 50 mm (57–66 mm long); ears joined at the midline; hairs bicolored (bats found in southern Florida) . . . . . . . . . . . . *Eumops glaucinus* (p. 152)
1. Forearm less than 50 mm (36–46 mm long); ears not joined at the midline; hairs not bicolored . . . . . . . . . . . . . . . . . . . . . . . . . . . 2

2. Lower incisors two or three; upper molariform teeth five; bats found over much of the
southeastern United States . . . . *Tadarida brasiliensis*
2. Lower incisor one; upper molariform
teeth four; bats found only in the Florida
Keys . . . . . . . . . . . . . *Molossus molossus* (p. 153)

### Brazilian Free-Tailed Bat, Mexican Free-tailed Bat *Tadarida brasiliensis* (I. Geoffroy St. Hilaire)    Color plate 5

DESCRIPTION. *Tadarida brasiliensis* is the only regularly occurring eastern bat with a free tail (the tail extending for some distance beyond the interfemoral membrane). It is a rather small bat with long, narrow wings. The fur, unusually short and velvety, is dark brown or dark gray, almost uniformly colored from base to tip, with a very short light-colored area at the base of the hairs. (Some individuals have scattered white hairs or patches of white.) The ears are short and wide, and their midlines are close together. Long hairs protrude from the toes. And there is only one upper incisor per side.

*Brazilian free-tailed bat,* Tadarida brasiliensis *(Roger W. Barbour)*

MEASUREMENTS. Average measurements of twenty adults from Florida, Alabama, and Louisiana were: total length 91.9 (88–98.6), tail 33.2 (26.8–37), hind foot 8.6 (7.4–9.2), ear 19–20, forearm 43.1 (41.5–45.5), wingspread 290–359 mm; and weight 8–14 grams.

Diploid number = 48.

TOOTH FORMULA

$$\frac{1}{2 \text{ or } 3} \ \frac{1}{1} \ \frac{2}{2} \ \frac{3}{3} \ = \ 30 \text{ or } 32$$

DISTRIBUTION. This *Tadarida* occurs in the South Atlantic states and Gulf Coast from Harnett County, North Carolina, through Georgia, Florida, Alabama, Mississippi, and Louisiana. It has suffered great decline, however, at least in Florida, and is nearly gone from north-central Florida (Bain, 1981). Conversely, it is the commonest bat in Louisiana, and has apparently moved north into North Carolina only in recent decades (Lee and Marsh, 1978). It has been taken in scattered northern localities, but is not regularly found there. This species occurs west to extreme southwestern Oregon, all of California, northern Baja California, and south into South America.

HABITAT. In the western United States, where this species is migratory, it forms huge colonies in caves. In the east, it uses buildings, never caves, and is usually thought to be nonmigratory. Lowery (1974), however, reported one large colony that disappeared in winter, and there are other, similar reports of large decreases during the winter. Free-tailed bats have also been found among the fronds of *Washingtonia*, a palm, and in hollow black mangrove trees.

HABITS. The free-tailed bat is exceedingly gregarious, often living in houses, stables, or business establishments by the thousands. Hundreds or even thousands leave their daytime retreat at dusk, flying considerable distances to a favorite feeding ground and not returning to their roosting places until dawn.

These are the swiftest of all North American bats, suggesting swifts in their mode of flight. They can fly at speeds of up to 65 to 95 km per hour (40 to 60 miles per hour) (Davis et al., 1962), and the flight is singularly erratic. Their homing abilities, too, are well developed: two of 12 individuals homed from 525 km (328 miles), the greatest of several distances from which Davis (1966) made releases. They take flight early in the evening, often in the afternoon, and some fly great distances to forage.

In the Southeast, *Tadarida* is often found in association with *Nycticeius humeralis*, less often with *Myotis austroriparius*. When together in one building, the three usually form separate clusters. One roost in Florida, in a barn, housed all three of these species (Bain, 1981). The evening bats were there primarily from mid-April through mid-January and bore their young there in late May. Southeastern myotis wintered there from November through March, then went to their maternity caves. The few free-tailed bats that used this barn were present from May through March. No bats of any species were present in early April.

Barbour and Davis (1969) stated that bats of

this species rarely use night roosts, and that they often appear to feed all night. Because freetail bats often spend much time traveling, they may miss the periods of greatest insect abundance and consequently have to spend more time hunting. Glass (1958) reported that they do use Alabaster Cave in Oklahoma as a night roost throughout the summer.

These bats exude a penetrating musky odor that can be detected at some distance from a site where a large colony is established. And when awake, they continually chatter.

FOOD AND FEEDING. Sherman (1937) found the chief insect-food items of this species, taken from the stomachs of eight individuals, to be winged ants, chalcids, dytiscid beetles, chironomid midges, and small lepidopterans. Ross (1961), however, found them to feed almost exclusively on moths. McCracken (1986) estimated that the 20 million free-tailed bats living

*Distribution of the Brazilian free-tailed bat,* Tadarida brasiliensis, *in the eastern United States*

in Bracken Cave, in Texas, eat more than 100 thousand kg (a quarter of a million pounds) of insects *nightly*. Whitaker et al. (1996) found that *Tadarida* in a Texas population fed largely on coleopterans and lygaeid bugs during evening feeding bouts, and mostly on moths during morning feeding bouts. Photographic studies by H. E. Edgerton and associates have shown that the tail membrane, although very short, may be extended and curled down in flight as an aid in catching insects.

REPRODUCTION AND DEVELOPMENT. This bat, unlike many others, does not store sperm in the uterus of the female for a considerable period prior to ovulation, but the females are pregnant when they return from their winter roosts to the maternity colonies. It may be that the females migrate to where the males are, spend the winter, then return after mating. H. B. Sherman (1937) has studied the breeding habits of this species in Florida. Although there are mature sperm in the testes throughout the winter, the males apparently have a short sexual season, from February to mid-April, the only time when spermatozoa are present in the epididymis, and are apparently incapable of breeding at other seasons. Mating occurs from mid-February to late March in various years, and ovulation occurs in late March. Gestation is about 77–84 days (Krutzsch, 1955). The single young (rarely two), nearly always produced in the right horn of the uterus, is born from late May to late June, the birth period varying from year to year. The full-term embryo measures about 25 mm crown-to-rump, has a forearm of about 18 mm, and weighs about 2.2 grams. Unlike those of vespertilionids, the young is not received in the interfemoral membrane at birth; the parent scratches the amnion to shreds, and, because the interfemoral membrane is so short and the wing membranes are not employed, the newborn young hangs by the cord until it can clamber to the breast. The placenta is not removed by the mother (it is, by many vespertilionids); rather, it remains attached for up to two days, then finally dries and falls. In the colony he studied, Sherman saw numerous young with placentas still attached.

The young of this species are not carried by their mothers, other than to move them to a different roosting site, and then usually because of disturbance at the original site. During the day, the adults and the young hang in separate roosting areas. The young cling together in huge masses, crawling about and continually squeaking, and the females come to feed them during the day. At this time the females have great amounts of milk. Using vocal and olfactory cues, most females find their own young even among very large numbers. Gelfand and McCracken (1986) showed that the young produce calls that are structurally distinct from one another. Nonetheless, the young will attempt to suckle any passing female, and in one study an estimated 17% of the females were nursing young that could not have been their own (McCracken, 1984; Gustin and McCracken, in press). The young bats nurse freely for about 30 minutes right after birth; and it may be that the females learn their odors at this time. It also appears that females mark young, perhaps not always their own, with odor from scent glands on their muzzles (Loughry and McCracken, 1991). The young apparently begin to fly at about five weeks, a good bit later than young vespertilionids do. The delay could be related to the greater development these bats need, since they are such fast, strong flyers. The females become sexually mature at about nine months.

Kunz and Robson (1995) used mark-recapture data to determine growth rates in *T. brasiliensis*. Forearm length and body mass in neonates averaged 18.5 mm and 3.2 grams. By 21 days, forearm length was about 35 mm, or 85% that of adults, and by 35 days the forearm was reaching adult length. By 21 days, body mass was approaching 80% of adult mass, and by the time the young were beginning to fly (at about 35 to 42 days) they had reached about 90% of adult weight, but then lost some body mass, owing to the increased exercise associated with flight.

POPULATION CHARACTERISTICS. *Tadarida* has occupied Carlsbad Caverns in New Mexico for centuries, and at one time the accumulated droppings covered an area a hundred feet or more in width, a quarter of a mile in length, and up to a hundred feet in depth. In the 1930s, there were about 8.7 million free-tailed bats in Carlsbad Caverns, but this number is now reduced to about a quarter of a million. About 20 million do still inhabit Bracken Cave, the world's largest bat colony, and about 6 million live under the Congress Avenue Bridge in Austin, Texas. In Florida in recent years, the free-tailed bat has undergone serious decline, to the extent that the species is uncommon there now. There are earlier estimates of 50,000 or more in single buildings in summer. Winter aggregations are much smaller: one building in Gainesville housed about 10,000 free-tailed bats in summer but only a few hundred were hibernating there in winter. It is not known where the remainder spend the winter, although individuals have been shot while in flight in South Carolina in January.

McCracken et al. (1994) found that neither summer nor winter populations of this species formed distinct genetic units. Rather, they showed a high degree of genetic variability, as would be expected in large populations. We have found no records taking the life span of these bats beyond five years. Like other bat species, however, they have few predators, and surely some individuals reach at least 15–20 years of age.

ENEMIES. Under favorable circumstances, great horned owls, barn owls, hawks, raccoons, opossums, skunks, and rat snakes feed on free-tailed bats.

PARASITES AND DISEASE. Parasites are abundant on these bats, the mite *Chiroptonyssus robustipes* (Macronyssidae) usually being the most common. Mites of the genus *Radfordia* and a flea, *Sternopsylla distincta*, have also been taken, in Florida. Rabies has been found in this species.

RELATION TO HUMANS. Bats of this species often come into contact with humans, since they often roost in houses and other structures. The Congress Avenue Bridge in Austin, Texas, which harbors millions of bats of this species, has become a major tourist attraction, through the efforts of Bat Conservation International, which is headquartered in Austin.

AREAS FOR FURTHER WORK. Much of our information on this species is from western populations, and more is needed on the eastern populations. What are its winter habits? Does it

sometimes occupy the same roosts all year? Does it migrate? Hibernate? Does it feed all winter? How much roost switching occurs in winter? In summer? What are the dates of occupancy of winter roosts? Summer roosts? Where do males spend the summer? The winter? We need long-term study of some of the southeastern colonies. Why has there been such a decline in these populations?

## SUBSPECIES

*Tadarida brasiliensis* was originally described from Brazil, but it occurs through Central America into the southern half of the United States. Although the nominate subspecies was described from Brazil, it occurs to the north through Panama, as well, and apparently intergrades through *T. brasiliensis intermedia* with *T. brasiliensis floridana*. We therefore consider the Brazilian free-tailed bat of the eastern United States to be *T. b. brasiliensis*.

*Tadarida brasiliensis brasiliensis* (I. Geoffroy)
As described above.
Type locality: Curityba, Parana, Brazil.
Other currently recognized eastern subspecies:
  *T. brasiliensis cyanocephala*

## LITERATURE

Bain, J. R. 1981. Roosting ecology of three Florida bats: *Nycticeius humeralis*, *Myotis austroriparius* and *Tadarida brasiliensis*. Unpubl. M.S. thesis, University of Florida, Gainesville. 131 pp.

Barbour, R. W., and W. H. Davis. 1969. *Bats of America*. Lexington: Univ. Press of Kentucky. 286 pp.

Davis, R. 1966. Homing performance and homing ability in bats. *Ecol. Monogr.* 36: 201–237.

Davis, R. B., C. F. Herreid II, and H. L. Short. 1962. Mexican free-tailed bats in Texas. *Ecol. Monogr.* 32: 311–346.

Gelfand, D. L., and G. F. McCracken. 1986. Individual variation in the isolation calls of Mexican free-tailed bat pups (*Tadarida brasiliensis mexicana*). *Anim. Behav.* 34: 1078–1086.

Glass, B. P. 1958. Returns of Mexican freetail bats banded in Oklahoma. *J. Mammal.* 39: 435–437.

Gustin, M. K., and G. F. McCracken. In press. Scent recognition between females and pups in the bat *Tadarida brasiliensis mexicana*. *Anim. Sci.*

Krutzsch, P. H. 1955. Observations on the Mexican free-tailed bat, *Tadarida mexicana*. *J. Mammal.* 36: 236–242.

Kunz, T. H., and S. K. Robson. 1995. Postnatal growth and development in the Mexican free-tailed bat (*Tadarida brasiliensis mexicana*): Birth size, growth rates, and age estimation. *J. Mammal.* 76: 769–783.

LaVal, R. K. 1973. Observations on the biology of *Tadarida brasiliensis cynocephala* in southeastern Louisiana. *Amer. Midland Nat.* 89: 112–120.

Lee, D. S., and C. Marsh. 1978. Range expansion of the Brazilian free-tail bat into North Carolina. *Amer. Midland Nat.* 100: 240–241.

Loughry, W. J., and G. F. McCracken. 1991. Factors influencing female-pup scent recognition in Mexican free-tailed bats. *J. Mammal.* 72: 624–626.

Lowery, G. H., Jr. 1974. *The Mammals of Louisiana and Its Adjacent Waters*. Baton Rouge: Louisiana State Univ. Press. 565 pp.

McCracken, G. F. 1984. Communal nursing in Mexican free-tailed bat maternity colonies. *Science* 223: 1090–1091.

———. 1986. Why are we losing our Mexican free-tailed bats? *Bats* 3: 1–4.

McCracken, G. F., M. K. McCracken, and A. T. Vawter. 1994. Genetic structure in migratory populations of the bat *Tadarida brasiliensis mexicana*. *J. Mammal.* 75: 500–514.

Ross, A. 1961. Notes on food habits of bats. *J. Mammal.* 42: 66–71.

Sherman, H. B. 1937. Breeding habits of the free-tailed bat. *J. Mammal.* 18: 176–187.

Whitaker, J. O., Jr., C. Neefus, and T. H. Kunz. 1996. Dietary variation in the Mexican free-tailed bat (*Tadarida brasiliensis mexicana*). *J. Mammal.* 77: 716–724.

## Wagner's Mastiff Bat
### *Eumops glaucinus* (Wagner)    Color plate 5

DESCRIPTION. The little-known free-tailed *Eumops* is somewhat like *Tadarida* in general appearance, but its much greater size and peculiar appearance easily distinguish it from the latter. *Eumops* is a dark-gray bat with long, narrow wings. Its forearm is 64 to 66 mm long and its wingspread is about 470 mm. The tail is free from the interfemoral membrane for about half its length. The fur is short and the basal half of the hairs is white. The wings are especially long and narrow, well adapted for rapid and prolonged flight. The ears are large, leathery, and rounded, joined at the midline, and projected forward.

MEASUREMENTS. A specimen from Havana, Cuba, preserved in alcohol in the Cornell Uni-

*Wagner's mastiff bat*, Eumops glaucinus
*(Bruce Hayward)*

versity Museum, has the following measurements: total length 130, tail 47, hind foot 11, forearm 59 mm. The forearm ranged from 58 to 69 mm in ten adults from Florida. The hind foot ranged from 11 to 15 mm in length, and the ear, in three individuals, ranged from 20 to 31 mm in length. Seven bats weighed from 30 to 44.5 grams, but a pregnant female taken later in Florida weighed 55.4 grams.

Diploid number = 38, 40.

TOOTH FORMULA

$$\frac{1}{2} \quad \frac{1}{1} \quad \frac{2}{2} \quad \frac{3}{3} \; = \; 30$$

DISTRIBUTION. The mastiff bat was first recorded from the United States at Miami, Florida, by Thomas Barbour (1936), who suggested that it may have come from Cuba via a fruit steamer. Flying distance over the Florida Straits from Cuba to the Florida Keys is less than 100 miles, no difficult achievement for this strong-flying bat. Barbour and Davis (1969), however, indicated that Florida individuals are much larger than those from Central America, and suggested that they might represent a separate subspecies. The species is usually uncommon, but might be as common in Florida as anywhere else. Charles English, a biology teacher at Miami High School, wrote Hamilton that five specimens of *Eumops* were collected in 1950 in the Miami area. A number of additional records have been noted in recent years, many of them from the Coral Gables area, from under the Cuban tile that is often used for roofing.

HABITS. The mastiff bat leaves its roost after dark and flies high. It has a loud, piercing call that can be heard over city noises once one learns to detect it. The young are born in June or July. These bats apparently do not hibernate.

AREAS FOR FURTHER STUDY. Almost nothing is known of the biology of this species. What is its present status? Where does it live and upon what does it feed? What is the genetic relationship of the Florida populations to other members of its species?

## SUBSPECIES

*Eumops glaucinus floridanus* (G. M. Allen)

As described above.

Type locality: Melbourne, Brevard Co., Florida, for *E. glaucinus floridanus*.

### LITERATURE

Barbour, R. W. 1936. *Eumops* in Florida. *J. Mammal.* 17: 414.

Barbour, R. W., and W. H. Davis. 1969. *Bats of America*. Lexington: Univ. Press of Kentucky. 286 pp.

Best, T. L., W. M. Kiser, and J. C. Rainey. 1997. *Eumops glaucinus*. **Mammalian Species No. 551.** Amer. Soc. Mammal. 6 pp.

## Little Mastiff Bat
### *Molossus molossus* (Pallas)

DESCRIPTION. This species is similar to the Brazilian free-tailed bat but has a single lower incisor per side, rather than two or three. It is

*Distribution of Wagner's mastiff bat,* Eumops glaucinus, *and the little mastiff bat,* Molossus molossus, *in the eastern United States*

variable in color: reddish brown, dark chestnut-brown, dark brown, rusty blackish, or black. There are also two color phases, one with a long, bicolored pelage, the other with short, velvety, unicolored fur. The bases of the ears are joined on the forehead.

MEASUREMENTS. Average measurements of 48 males are: total length 102, tail 36, hind foot 10, forearm 39 mm; and weight 15.4 grams. For 89 females they are: 100, 36, 10, 38 mm; and 13.3 grams (Eisenberg, 1989).

  Diploid number unknown.

TOOTH FORMULA

$$\frac{1}{1} \ \frac{1}{1} \ \frac{1}{2} \ \frac{3}{3} \ = \ 26$$

DISTRIBUTION. This species ranges through Central America, the Caribbean, and much of South America, and it has recently been found in the Florida Keys (Frank, 1997). Colonies have been found on Boca Chica, Stock Island, and at Marathon on Vaca Key, and one individual was taken from Key West on 28 November 1995 (see map p. 153). Individuals from each of these localities have been identified by Karl Koopman of the American Museum of Natural History, and specimens have been deposited in AMNH (269529–269532). These bats may have come from Cuba by normal dispersal, or they may have originated as a release from a bat tower on Sugarloaf Key by Richter C. Perky in 1929 (Layne, in press).

HABITAT. Bats of this species forage in dry, deciduous forest and moist, tropical evergreen forest. In drier areas, they frequently forage near ponds.

HABITS. At the beginning of the rainy season, females form nursery colonies in buildings, hollow trees, or caves. Individuals have also been known to roost in palm fronds. The three known colonies in the Florida Keys are all in the roof spaces of flat-roofed buildings. The Boca Chica colony is in the roof of a dormitory on the Key West Naval Air Station. The bats were resident there on 7 September 1994, when 268 were counted. The Stock Island colony is in the roof of an apartment building in a densely populated area. The bats were there on 14 February 1994, but not there on 15 March 1995. It was not possible to obtain an accurate count in 1994, although the bats were plainly visible leaving the roost at dusk. The Marathon colony is in the roof of a condominium in Key Colony Beach, adjacent to the ocean. About 80 bats were counted there on 8 September 1994. The three colonies have all been present for a long time, according to residents of the area. Temperatures have been known to reach 55°C (130°F) in the attic roosts of this species. These bats fly rapidly, in the manner of swifts. At least in a congener, *Molossus ater*, there are internal cheek pouches. These are filled to capacity with insects, whereupon the bat returns to the roosts to chew and swallow its prey.

FOOD AND FEEDING. Little mastiff bats feed on insects, perhaps chiefly moths, beetles, and flying ants.

REPRODUCTION AND DEVELOPMENT. Little is known of the reproduction of this species in Florida. *Molossus molossus* in Puerto Rico (Krutzsch and Crichton, 1985; treated as *M. fortis*) mated in February or March and gave birth in June and again in September. Each female produces one young, and lactation apparently persists for about six weeks, although Eisenberg (1989) stated that weaning occurs at about 65 days. When the females forage, they leave the young in a cluster. When they return, they identify their own young by their calls. Thirty-two bats of this species were caught in a church in Jalisco, Mexico, on 2 August; all but one were females, and 22 were pregnant (Watkins et al., 1972).

RELATION TO HUMANS. Too little is known of this species in Florida, but bats in buildings are often of concern to people.

AREAS FOR FURTHER WORK. A study of the biology of Florida populations of this species, contrasted with its habits elsewhere, would be of interest. Similarly, genetic comparison with this species elsewhere should afford us insight into the degree of isolation and evolution of this species in Florida. Almost nothing is known of this bat's population characteristics, enemies, parasites, or diseases, and more is needed on its food and reproduction.

## SUBSPECIES

*Molossus molossus molossus* (Pallas) occurs in the Lesser Antilles. Frank (1997) indicates that the *Molossus* from the Keys is *M. molossus tropidorhynchus*, the subspecies that occurs in Cuba.

*Molossus molossus tropidorhynchus Gray*
As described above.
Type locality for the subspecies: Cuba.

## LITERATURE

Eisenberg, J. F. 1989. *Mammals of the Neotropics. The Northern Neotropics.* Vol. 1: Panama, Colombia, Venezuela, Guyana, Suriname, French Guiana. Chicago: Univ. Chicago Press. 449 pp.

Frank, P. A. 1997. First record of *Molossus molossus tropidorhynchus* Gray (1839) from the United States. *J. Mammal.* 78: 103–105.

Krutzsch, P. H., and E. G. Crichton. 1985. Observations on the reproductive cycle of female *Molossus fortis* (Chiroptera: Molossidae) in Puerto Rico. *J. Zool.* 207: 137–150.

Layne, J. N. Nonindigenous mammals. 1997. In: D. Simberloff, T. Brown, and D. Schmitz, eds., *Strangers in Paradise: Impact and Management of Nonindigenous Species in Florida*, pp. 157–186. Covelo, Calif.: Island Press.

Watkins, L. C., J. K. Jones, Jr., and H. H. Genoways. 1972. Bats of Jalisco, Mexico. Spec. Publ. Mus. Texas Tech Univ. No. 1. 44 pp.

# 4. ORDER PRIMATES

## Apes, Monkeys, and Allies

PRIMATES INCLUDE HUMANITY and our relatives: the various monkeys, apes, baboons, and more primitive types, such as lemurs, lorises, and galagos. The order numbers 60 genera and 233 species found chiefly in the Old and New World tropics. Some of the major adaptations of primates have been toward increased brainpower, greater use of the eyes, greater awareness and manipulation of the environment, development and use of the hands, including the opposable thumb, and routine carriage in the upright position.

Humans will not be considered in this volume, but three other primates have become established in the eastern United States, all in Florida—the rhesus monkey, *Macaca mulatta*; the squirrel monkey, *Saimiri sciurus*; and the vervet monkey, *Cercopithecus aethiops*—of the three, the rhesus monkey has become sufficiently established to warrant consideration here.

### OLD WORLD MONKEYS,
### Family Cercopithecidae

This family comprises 19 genera and over 90 species. Old World monkeys have nonprehensile (nongrasping) tails, in contrast to the prehensile tails of the New World monkeys (Cebidae). The body is largely covered with hair, but the face is mostly bare. Old World monkeys have good vision and hearing and a good sense of smell, and they employ a broad repertoire of calls and facial expressions. They are mostly diurnal and are very much aware of their environment.

## Rhesus Monkey, Rhesus Macaque
*Macaca mulatta* Zimmerman

DESCRIPTION. The rhesus is a medium-sized monkey with strong limbs. The face is mostly bare except for the forehead. Rather long grayish-brown to rufous-yellow hair, a good bit lighter below, covers most of the body.

*Rhesus monkey,* Macaca mulatta *(Linda D. Wolfe)*

MEASUREMENTS. The head and body measure 40–55 cm (16–22 inches), and the tail is 17–25 cm (7–10 inches). Males are larger than females.

Diploid number = 42.

TOOTH FORMULA

$$\frac{2}{2} \quad \frac{1}{1} \quad \frac{2}{2} \quad \frac{3}{3} \quad = \quad 32 \quad \text{(the same as ours)}$$

DISTRIBUTION. The rhesus monkey is native to southern Asia, from Afghanistan and India to China and Vietnam. It was introduced near Silver Springs, Florida, in the late 1930s, probably as a tourist attraction. The monkeys were apparently released on an island in the Silver River. A jungle cruise ride originally began at the headwaters of the Silver River and ended at the island. The monkeys would be seen along the river and fed from the cruise boat. Until recently, when efforts were undertaken to remove the monkeys, there were two populations. One stayed near the island, and in time their descendants inhabited the Ocala National Forest. Other monkeys remained at the headwaters of the river, and their descendants were known as the Silver Springs monkeys. There are apparently two other free-living populations of this species in mainland Florida, one near Titusville and one near Dania. Efforts were initiated in

January 1996 to remove the entire population of rhesus monkeys from Silver Springs because of the presence of B virus, which is potentially dangerous to humans, and, as of this writing, most of them have been removed.

HABITAT. Most primates, including this one, live in tropical areas, but this species is also found in areas with freezing winter temperatures and snow. In Asia, rhesus monkeys live in mountains to 4,000 meters (13,000 feet), primarily in forests dominated by pines and firs, but also in regions supporting maples, horse chestnuts, and elms. In some areas in Asia, many live in towns. In Florida, these monkeys live in floodplain forest and mangrove swamp.

HABITS. In 1968 there were about 78 monkeys in the two Silver Springs populations. Serious investigation of these monkeys began in 1971, and

*Previous distribution of the rhesus monkey,* Macaca mulatta, *in the eastern United States*

in 1976 long-term studies were initiated on a single group of monkeys on the south side of the river (termed the Southside or S troop). Much information on the biology of these monkeys has been accumulated by William Maples, Michael Hutchins, Elizabeth Peters, and, most recently, Linda Wolfe, as summarized by Wolfe and Peters (1987). Their work compares the Southside population with native Asian populations (Lindberg, 1971; Roonwal and Mohnot, 1977).

Rhesus monkeys sleep in trees and spend much of the day on the ground, feeding on herbaceous plants. In warm weather they begin foraging before dawn, and rest at intervals through the day. These animals have a number of calls, including but not limited to an alarm bark, a guttural vocalization uttered in response to aggressive behavior, a scream when attacked, and a squawk when surprised.

FOOD AND FEEDING. The rhesus monkey is primarily a vegetarian but also gleans invertebrate prey. Clover, in particular, is an important part of the diet. The clover grows in patches where trees have been cleared. These patches may be quite rare, but the monkeys seek them out. They will feed on many other foods as they appear: young fir tips in early summer, strawberries, *Viburnum* berries, mushrooms, cicadas, jack-in-the-pulpit berries, and pine seeds. In winter, when it is more difficult for the monkeys to find good food sources, they will seek out such roots and tubers as they can find, but when necessary they will resort to evergreen oak leaves, which are hard to digest. Besides all these and the foods from feeding troughs along the cruise, the Florida monkeys feed on all types of plant parts: leaves, twigs, stems, bark, roots, fruit, buds, and seeds. The bud of the cabbage palm (*Sabal palmetto*) is one of the most commonly used items.

REPRODUCTION AND DEVELOPMENT. In the rhesus, there is a well-developed estrous cycle of about 28 days with vaginal discharge, although evidence is accumulating that this species is seasonally reproductive in parts of its native range. Gestation is 135 to 194 days, averaging 166. Females in the Himalayas produce at most one young every other year. Tropical individuals mature more quickly and bear young more frequently, the births falling as close as eight months apart. Reproductive rates are also related to the survivorship of previous young. In Florida, over a three-year period, 82% of the females had young, first giving birth at age four or five. Intervals between births averaged 14.3 months. The newborn, which weighs about 450 grams, clings to the belly of the female. Later, it may ride on the back *or* the belly. Sexual maturity is at about two and one-half to four years in females, later in males.

POPULATION CHARACTERISTICS. The social system of the Silver Springs monkeys was similar to that of native Old World populations. Rhesus monkeys live in troops of 11–70 animals, about half of them adults. The adult females are about two to four times as abundant as the adult males, because males disperse from the group and experience earlier average mortality. Females remain in the group in which they were born, though troops will sometimes divide. A matriarchal dominance hierarchy reigns in each troop, and the dominant female's daughters—who are also dominant to all other adult and juvenile females—achieve the number two position as they mature, at about five years of age, replacing their older sisters. Ultimately, the youngest daughter of the dominant female is the number two female, followed by her next youngest, and so forth. Closely related females form subgroups, grooming mutually and supporting each other in fights with other females. The males form their own dominance hierarchies, but these are much less stable than those of the females. Males usually disperse to other groups before reaching sexual maturity (at about seven years), gaining acceptance in the other groups either by being submissive or by challenging other males in the hierarchy.

Rhesus monkeys live perhaps 20 years in the Himalayas, up to 28 years in the tropics; the species capacity for population growth thus is much more constrained in the colder areas. Menopause occurs at about 25 years.

RELATION TO HUMANS. The rhesus monkey has been used extensively in biological and medical studies, over several decades. It was the species used in the first demonstration of the Rh factor in blood, and it was used in space flight. About 200,000 animals per year were exported to the United States for experimental purposes in the 1950s, but the rhesus population in India dropped from an estimated 20 million in the 1940s to just 180,000 by 1980. Populations there are beginning to recover as a result of bans on exportation instituted by India and on importation legislated by the United States.

AREAS FOR FURTHER WORK. From the time the Silver Springs monkeys were removed, and placed in captivity, further studies of this species in the wild have no longer been possible. Nonetheless, studies of genetic diversity in this small population, which has been isolated for about six decades, would be of interest, particu-

larly when pursued in comparison with the diversity of large Asian populations.

## SUBSPECIES

We are not aware of the origin or subspecies of the rhesus monkey populations in Florida.

## LITERATURE

Lindberg, D. G. 1971. The rhesus monkey in northern India: An ecological and behavioral study. *Primate Behav.* 2: 1–106.

Roonwal, M. L., and S. M. Mohnot. 1977. *Primates of South Asia.* Cambridge, Mass.: Harvard Univ. Press. 421 pp.

Wolfe, L. D., and E. H. Peters. 1987. History of the free-ranging rhesus monkeys (*Macaca mulatta*) of Silver Springs. *Fla. Scientist* 50: 234–245.

# 5. ORDER XENARTHRA

## *Armadillos and Allies*

THE XENARTHRA (formerly Edentata) are primitive mammals represented today by just four living families, all of them confined to the New World. The four, which differ greatly in habits and structure, are the armadillos (Dasypodidae, eight genera and 20 species), the sloths (Bradypodidae and Megalonchidae, one genus and one species each), and the anteaters (Myrmecophagidae, three genera and four species). The order had been recognized as Edentata for many years, but the name "Edentata," which means "lacking teeth," is a misnomer, since, of the four extant families, only the anteaters lack teeth. In fact, one of the xenarthrans, the giant armadillo, has as many as 100 teeth, probably more than any other mammal except some of the toothed whales. But where the teeth *are* present, they tend to be conical or peglike, rootless, and deficient in enamel. The name "Xenarthra" means "strange joint," a reference to the peculiar way in which the vertebrae connect: there are extra articulations, called "xenarthrales," between the lumbar vertebrae.

## ARMADILLOS, Family Dasypodidae

Armadillos are unique among living mammals in having an armor of ossified dermal plates covered by leathery epidermis. These plates form a shell with seven to eleven transverse, usually movable bands, the shell completely covering the dorsal surface of the animal. The forefeet, furnished with strong claws, are powerful digging tools. Though only one species (*Dasypus novemcinctus*) occurs in the United States, the order is currently represented by 29 species ranging widely through much of Central and South America (5 species of sloths, 4 of anteaters, and 20 of armadillos).

### Nine-Banded Armadillo *Dasypus novemcinctus* Linnaeus          Color plate 6

DESCRIPTION. This armadillo, an opossum-sized animal, is the only xenarthran occurring in the

*Nine-banded armadillo,* Dasypus novemcinctus *(Roger W. Barbour)*

United States, and it can be confused with no other species. It is best characterized by the shell-like, scaly skin, formed into eight to eleven (usually nine) transversely joined bands, that covers the back. Bony scutes cover the tail and the top of the head as well as the carapace. The simple, peglike teeth (usually eight above, eight below), the long, apparently segmented tail (it carries 12–15 rings of scutes), and the prominent claws likewise distinguish this peculiar animal. There are four claws on the forefeet, five on the hind. Soft, sparsely haired skin covers the belly and limbs. The prominent, erect ears are nearly half the length of the head. The eyes are small and weak, and the animal has a piglike snout. There are four mammary glands, two pectoral, two inguinal.

The generic name means "hairy-footed," and the specific name means "nine-banded."

MEASUREMENTS. McBee and Baker (1982) give the following measurements: total length 615–800, tail 245–370, hind foot 75–107 mm. Males are larger than females; males weigh 5.5 to 7.7 kg (12–17 lbs), females 3.6 to 6.0 kg (8–13 lbs) (Hall, 1955).

Diploid number = 64.

TOOTH FORMULA

$$\frac{7\ to\ 9}{7\ to\ 9}\quad (usually\ 8)\ =\ 14\ to\ 18$$

DISTRIBUTION. John J. Audubon and John Bachman first reported the armadillo in the United States from southern Texas, and it has been continually increasing its range since then. By 1925 it had entered Louisiana; by 1936 it occurred throughout Louisiana west of the Mississippi; and by 1943 it had moved east of the Mississippi River and now occupies western and southern Mississippi (Humphrey, 1974). It became established in Alabama by 1952, and is now widespread in the southern part of that state. The armadillo was introduced in Florida in the 1920s, and by 1952 could be found throughout much of the state. It also occurs in southern Georgia, western Tennessee, and South Carolina. West of the Mississippi, this species occurs in southeastern Kansas, much of Oklahoma and Texas, and south into South America.

HABITAT. The nine-banded armadillo is found in many habitats—such as brushy or waste lands, moist forests, pastures, and scrub—where the

*Distribution of the nine-banded armadillo,* Dasypus novemcinctus, *in the eastern United States*

soil permits easy digging and supports enough food for its needs.

HABITS. The armadillo is primarily crepuscular and nocturnal, usually becoming active near dusk, but during cold weather the animal is often active during the day. It forages by rooting here and there in the manner of a pig. While foraging, the armadillo will sometimes stand up on its hind legs, braced by the tail, and sniff the air.

E. W. Nelson, from his long acquaintance with this animal in Mexico, wrote:

Its sight and hearing are poor, and the armoured skin gives it a stiff-legged gait and immobile body. From these characteristics, combined with the small head hung on a short neck, it has in life an odd resemblance in both form and motion to a small pig; it jogs along in its trails or from one feeding place to another with the same little stiff, trotting gait and self-centered air. If alarmed it will break into a clumsy gallop, but moves so slowly that it may be overtaken by a man on foot. So poor is its eyesight that a person may approach openly within about thirty yards before being noticed. [One approached to within *three* yards of Bill Carver before it rose up, sniffed, and finally saw him.]

The armadillo is an accomplished digger, and each animal makes and maintains several prominent burrows, from which trails radiate in several directions through the scrubby thickets. In loose soil an armadillo can burrow out of sight in a few minutes. The nose and front feet dig into the soil, which is then pushed under the abdomen. The animal then balances tripodlike on the forefeet and tail, and swings the hind feet forward over the dirt. The back is then arched, and a sudden straightening of the body, coupled with a thrusting back and up with the hind limbs, throws the dirt behind. Burrows in Texas averaged 125 cm (about 4 feet) in length and about 50 cm in depth, although one was 151 cm deep. Half of the 26 burrows studied ended in an enlarged chamber housing a nest. Burrows are about 17 cm in diameter, and the enlarged nest chamber averages about 34 cm in diameter. In Florida, armadillos frequently take over burrows of the gopher tortoise, and, in turn, cotton-

tail rabbits, opossums, skunks, and many other animals use the burrows of the armadillos.

The nest, consisting of half a bushel or so of leaves or grass, is usually in a burrow but is sometimes in a small cave or crevice. When building a nest, the animal rakes plant material under its body with its forefeet, then grasps the material with its front legs—and backs to and into the burrow. The tail protrudes straight backward during this process, possibly serving a tactile function.

Although most authors state simply that armadillos nest in burrows, Layne and Waggener (1984) found over 100 above-ground armadillo nests in Florida, in situations where a high water table prevented underground nesting (Fig. 5.1b). Most were in prairie or pasture with saw palmettos, scattered shrubs, and cabbage palm/

*Surface nest of armadillo, Florida (James N. Layne)*

live oak hammocks; some were in slash pine woods with palmetto understory. Most of the nests were actually in saw palmetto clumps, but some were in the open. Each consisted of a shallow depression or form covered by much dry plant material, and resembled a miniature haystack. The form ranged from 15 to 30 cm deep, 20 to 30 cm wide, and 30 to 46 cm long. No obvious nest chamber was to be seen; rather, the interior was filled with fine vegetation. Most nests had one inconspicuous entrance, about

13–15 cm in diameter, at ground level. Nests varied in size from one habitat to another, those in open prairie being the largest (see the photo), ranging from about 40 to 60 cm high and up to 122 cm maximum diameter. Nests in saw palmetto thickets, by contrast, ranged from 25 to 36 cm high.

The clumsy gallop mentioned by Nelson is surprisingly rapid. If overtaken by a man or another enemy, the armadillo does not roll into a tight ball, as often claimed, although it *will* partially curl up, protecting the soft, vulnerable belly from attack. More often it will run rapidly away, traveling with considerable speed for such a clumsy-appearing beast. Its characteristic behavior when alarmed is to jump straight into the air and arch its back. This unexpected behavior is responsible for many highway deaths. When cornered in a burrow, too, the animal arches its back, which makes extracting it very difficult.

The armadillo swims in the manner of a dog. Occasionally, if the distance is short, it will walk across on the bottom—underwater. That its specific gravity exceeds 1 allows this behavior, but also means that the animal must ingest air by repeated gasping if it is to swim (or walk) any distance.

FOOD AND FEEDING. Some plant food (up to 10% or so of the diet) is eaten, but the food of the armadillo is primarily insects and other invertebrates, particularly beetles, ants, caterpillars, centipedes, millipedes, snails, and slugs. Vertebrates, particularly reptiles, may constitute up to 25% of the diet, especially in winter, but small birds or mammals and birds' eggs may be eaten whenever available. During wet periods, the animals will undertake local movements to higher, drier areas; during dry periods, they will move to streambeds and creekbeds, where digging for food is easier. The armadillo exposes insects with its sharp claws, then flicks them into its mouth with its long, sticky tongue. The scats of this beast are round mudballs, in the matrix of which are usually found numerous insect remains.

REPRODUCTION AND DEVELOPMENT. This interesting mammal almost always produces four young per litter, the four always of the same sex. The early embryo divides by fission to form twin embryos, and immediately these divide to give rise to two pairs of duplicate twins, or quadruplets. Thus the young are all derived from one fertilized egg and all inherit the same assortment of genes. Mating occurs in summer, but implantation is delayed into November, following which four months will elapse before the birth of the young. The young are born in an advanced condition; and although the armor is soft and pliable at birth, it soon hardens. One litter a year is the rule, and armadillos apparently remain paired for the season. Because of the shell, copulation requires that the female lie on her back.

POPULATION CHARACTERISTICS. Population-density estimates range broadly, from about 0.05 to 3 per ha (0.02 to 1.2 per acre). Averages for the home range were 20.3 ha (50 acres) for 13 animals in a Louisiana study site but only 3.45 ha (8.5 acres) for three animals at a Texas site, the latter monitored during a period of extreme drought and much home-range overlap. In Florida, the home ranges of eight animals ranged from 1.1 to 13.8 ha (3 to 35 acres). As one might guess from their large litter sizes, armadillos are short-lived. In the wild, few live more than two years.

ENEMIES. Although the dog can be an important armadillo predator, mortality on the highway probably accounts for more deaths than does predation. In spite of such persecution and unwitting destruction, armadillos seem to thrive, as the amazing extension of their range within recent decades so dramatically demonstrates.

PARASITES AND DISEASE. As one might expect, since so much of its outside is covered with hard plates, making for poor parasite habitat, the armadillo appears to be much less subject to ectoparasites than are many other mammals of comparable size. Ticks of the genus *Amblyomma* appear to be a principal assailant, and two species, *A. concolor* and *A. pseudoconcolor*, appear to be true armadillo parasites. A tiny hypopial mite, *Marsupialichus johnstoni*, can occur in large numbers around and in the ear (Pence, 1973). On the few armadillos we have examined, chiggers were also abundant, but fleas are rare. A number of internal parasites have been found, and the armadillo is a carrier of *Trypanosoma cruzi*, the causal agent of Chagas' disease.

RELATION TO HUMANS. Many armadillos are killed and their armored skins prepared as baskets for the tourist and curio trade. Armadillos are also sometimes used for food, roasted "in the shell." Natural cases of leprosy have been found in armadillos, and the species is an important laboratory animal in leprosy research.

AREAS FOR FURTHER WORK. Development of the armadillo from neonate through the juvenile stage has not been adequately described, and studies on geographic variation are in order. More information is needed on when and how tightly the animal curls up in a ball when disturbed.

## SUBSPECIES

The nine-banded armadillo occurs in South America, as well, but we do not know the relationship of the nominate subspecies in South America to *Dasypus novemcinctus* of the eastern United States, and thus have retained the current name for the eastern U.S. subspecies, *D. n. mexicanus*.

### *Dasypus novemcinctus mexicanus* Peters

As described above. The only subspecies in the eastern United States.

Type locality: Matamoros, Tamaulipas, Mexico, for the subspecies.

## LITERATURE

Breece, G. A., and J. L. Dusi. 1985. Food habits and home ranges of the common long-nosed armadillo *Dasypus novemcinctus* in Alabama. In: G. G. Montgomery, ed., *The Evolution and Ecology of Armadillos, Sloths and Vermilinguas*, pp. 419–427. Washington: Smithsonian Institution Press. 451 pp.

Clark, W. K. 1951. Ecological life history of the armadillo in the eastern plateau region. *Amer. Midland Nat.* 46: 337–358.

Fitch, H. S., P. Goodrum, and C. Newman. 1952. The armadillo in the southeastern U.S. *J. Mammal.* 33: 21–37.

Hall, E. R. 1955. *Handbook of Mammals of Kansas.* Misc. Publ. Mus. Nat. Hist. Univ. Kans. 7: 1–103.

Humphrey, S. R. 1974. Zoogeography of the nine-banded armadillo (*Dasypus novemcinctus*) in the United States. *BioScience* 24: 457–462.

Kalmbach, E. R. 1943. The armadillo: Its relation to agriculture and game. Austin: Texas Game, Fish and Oyster Comm. 60 pp.

Layne, J. N., and A. M. Waggener, Jr. 1984. Aboveground nests of the nine-banded armadillo in Florida. *Fla. Field Nat.* 12: 58–61.

McBee, K., and R. J. Baker. 1982. *Dasypus novemcinctus.* **Mammalian Species No. 162.** Amer. Soc. Mammal. 9 pp.

Pence, D. B. 1973. Notes on two species of hypopial nymphs of the genus *Marsupialichus* (Acarina: Glycyphagidae) from mammals in Louisiana. *J. Med. Entomol.* 10: 329–332.

Smith, L. L., and R. W. Doughty. 1984. *The Amazing Armadillo: Geography of a Folk Critter.* Austin: Univ. Texas Press. 134 pp.

Stangl, F. B., Jr., S. L. Beauchamp, and N. G. Konermann. 1995. Cranial and dental variation in the nine-banded armadillo from Texas and Oklahoma. *Texas J. Sci.* 47: 89–100.

Taber, F. W. 1945. Contributions on the life history and ecology of the nine-banded armadillo. *J. Mammal.* 26: 211–226.

Talmage, R. V., and G. D. Buchanan. 1954. The armadillo (*Dasypus novemcinctus*). A review of its natural history, ecology, anatomy and reproductive physiology. Rice Inst. Pamphlet, Monogr. Biol. 41. 135 pp.

Zimmerman, J. W. 1990. Burrow characteristics of the nine-banded armadillo, *Dasypus novemcinctus*. *Southwestern Nat.* 35: 226–227.

# 6. ORDER LAGOMORPHA

## Hares, Rabbits, and Allies

THE ORDER LAGOMORPHA embraces two families: the Leporidae, or rabbits (including cottontails) and hares (including jackrabbits); and the Ochotonidae, the much smaller pikas, or coneys. Lagomorphs are not a particularly diverse group, but do number about 13 genera and 80 species indigenous in most of the main land masses of the world except Antarctica, Madagascar, Australia, and New Zealand. The ochotonids, which live in rocky areas of Eurasia and our own West, include 26 species in two genera; the leporids, which are nearly worldwide in distribution, include 54 species in 11 genera.

Lagomorphs superficially resemble rodents, with which they have much in common. It was long thought that lagomorphs and rodents were unrelated, but it now appears that they do have common ancestry. Lagomorphs possess two pairs of upper incisors. The first pair is large and rodentlike, with a broad groove on the front surface. The second pair, emerging directly behind the first, is small, lacks the cutting edge, and is nearly circular in outline. A further feature of lagomorph dentition is that the lateral distance between the cheek teeth of the left and right sides of the lower jaw is considerably less than that between the two molar-tooth rows of the upper jaw. In consequence, only one molar row of the upper jaw and one of the lower jaw are capable of opposition at the same time, resulting in an ectalental, or sideways, chewing movement. Lagomorphs also have numerous fenestrae—small openings in the rostral area that serve to lighten the skull.

## HARES AND RABBITS, Family Leporidae

The terms "hare" and "rabbit" are much misused. Hares, technically, are members of the genus *Lepus*; rabbits, at least in eastern United States, constitute the genus *Sylvilagus*. Hares are generally larger and have longer ears and longer legs. Most species of hares, the snowshoe being one of the exceptions, live in more open habitat than rabbits and tend to outleap and outrun predators. Rabbits, by contrast, tend to run for cover when threatened. Hares do not make nests for their young; rather, the young are well developed (precocial) when born—fully furred and open-eyed. They are able to move about within hours after birth, but remain in the vicinity of their birth. Rabbits, for their part, are altricial, i.e. born in a relatively immature state, as are most mammals; at birth, they are pink and usually hairless, and their eyes are closed.

Some species, the European rabbit, *Oryctolagus cuniculus*, for example, make their own burrows, and some use the burrows of other mammals, especially those of woodchucks. But rabbits and hares alike often lie on the ground in a "form," which may be under cover or out in the open. The form is simply a shallow, temporarily cleared depression. When in the form they remain completely still, ears back, and are thus almost invisible. But if discovered, they burst forth, depending on their great speed and acceleration to outrun a predator. Lagomorphs are exceedingly prolific, their high reproductive rates offsetting the great numbers killed by predators, people, and the automobile. Ovulation is induced by copulation—which helps ensure that ovulation occurs at the optimum time for fertilization. The scrotal sac, entirely covered with hair, is visible only during the breeding season, when the testes are scrotal.

In the usual slow, more or less thorough digestion of food typical of the larger mammals, rabbits and hares form hard, brown fecal pellets. These are the familiar rabbit droppings seen in piles in the field. But in an alternative—faster and minimally digestive—process often practiced by rabbits and hares, soft, greenish pellets are formed. Most of the nutrients are removed from the hard pellets during the normal course of digestion, but the soft pellets still contain much nutritive material and large amounts of vitamin B. This alternative process, called *coprophagy,* or *reingestion,* allows the animals to feed on a large amount of food in a short period of time, and then return quickly to the safety of the form, thicket, or brushpile, where the soft pellets are eaten directly from the anus and digested more slowly, in safety.

Lagomorphs are generally silent except for foot thumps, alarm or aggressive signals, and the distress screams of captured animals. These animals appear to rely heavily on scent signals for communication.

Humans have introduced European rabbits, *Oryctolagus cuniculus,* into Australia and New Zealand, with dire results: with no predators to curb their spread, they multiplied beyond all expectations, and the Australian and New Zealand governments must now expend much revenue on rabbit control through the introduction of different strains of myxomatosis, an insect-transmitted viral disease of rabbits. Leporids often cause great damage to agriculture, especially in orchards, hay fields, or gardens. They also supply felt and hides to the hatter and furrier, and millions are killed for sport and food.

### KEY TO THE GENERA OF THE FAMILY LEPORIDAE

1. Hind foot usually more than 113 mm long; interparietals fused with parietals (hares) . . *Lepus* (p. 184)
1. Hind foot 113 mm long or less; interparietals distinct from parietals (rabbits). . . . . . . . . . . *Sylvilagus*

## Rabbits of the Genus *Sylvilagus*

The cottontails and other rabbits of the eastern United States—five species, three of them terrestrial and two semiaquatic—are all members of the genus *Sylvilagus.* (There may be just four; see the *S. obscurus* account.) Nine other species of the genus are distributed outside our confines.

Rabbits are sexually quiescent in midwinter, but as is the case with many other mammals, increasing day length stimulates the female's pituitary to secrete FSH (follicle stimulating hormone) into the blood, which in turn stimulates the follicles in the ovaries to grow and produce ova. The ova develop to a submature stage and the rabbit comes into heat, which is then maintained until copulation occurs. But there is no estrous cycle in rabbits; if copulation does not occur immediately, the rabbit can remain in "pre-estrus" for some time.

In rabbits (as in cats and some other species, collectively referred to as "induced ovulators"), copulation serves as the stimulant for the pituitary to secrete LH (luteinizing hormone), which in turn stimulates the maturation of the follicle and ovulation, followed by fertilization in the fallopian tube. The fertilized ova enter the uterus about day four and are implanted about day seven. Upon ovulation, as in other species, corpora lutea form in the old follicles. The corpora lutea secrete progesterone, which prevents additional ova from reaching maturation and begins to prepare the female for the production of young. Later, the placenta takes over progesterone production, but this source, too, diminishes in time, and fully mature follicles are present at the time of birth, permitting the female to breed again immediately following parturition. And she usually does, if a male is about, for she is also secreting pheromones at that time. These pheromones are probably formed by the maturing follicles.

Before the young are produced, the female digs a nesting depression. She then pulls out clumps of her belly fur to line the depression, thus creating a nest for them. Pulling out the belly fur also exposes her nipples, which facilitates nursing. The young live in the nest, which is capped with fur and vegetation, until old enough to fend for themselves. The mother visits the nest twice a day, at dawn and dusk, to nurse the young.

### KEY TO THE RABBITS OF THE GENUS *SYLVILAGUS*

In using this key, note that *Sylvilagus obscurus* and *S. transitionalis,* highly similar, are best distinguished by range and diploid number.

1. Hind foot more than 100 mm long; basilar
   length of skull greater than 63 mm . . . . *S. aquaticus*
1. Hind foot less than 100 mm long; basilar
   length of skull less than 63 mm . . . . . . . . . . . . . . 2
2. Underside of tail not white; postorbital process
   attached to skull along its full length . . . *S. palustris*
2. Underside of tail white; postorbital process free
   of skull, or attached only posteriorly . . . . . . . . . . 3
3. Nape rufous; often a white spot on forehead;
   supraorbital process present . . . . . . . . *S. floridanus*
3. Nape bearing a black spot; white spot on
   forehead nearly always lacking; supraorbital
   process lacking. . . . . . . . . . . . . . . . . . . . . . . . . . 4
4. Diploid number 52; found in New England
   west to the Hudson River and south to eastern
   Long Island . . . . . . . . . . . . . . . . . *S. transitionalis*
4. Diploid number 46; found in the Appalachians
   from west of the Hudson River south to
   Georgia and Alabama . . . . . . . . . . . . . *S. obscurus*

## Swamp Rabbit *Sylvilagus aquaticus* Bachman

DESCRIPTION. The swamp rabbit is the largest of the 14 species in its genus. Apart from its much larger size, it is distinguished from the cottontail by its short, sleek fur, slender, thin-haired

*Swamp rabbit,* Sylvilagus aquaticus
*(Karl H. Maslowski)*

tail, and dark coloration. Although it resembles the marsh rabbit, *Sylvilagus palustris*, its much greater size serves to distinguish it from this related species. (Still, the way in which the ranges of the two abut without overlapping tempts one to hypothesize that the two might belong to the same species.)

The top of the swamp rabbit's head is buffy brown, the back is buffy grayish brown to rusty brown, and the rump and the upper sides of the legs are rusty brown. The sides of the head and body are paler than the rest of the back. The upper sides of the feet and legs are cinnamon-rufous. The outsides of the ears are browner than the sides of the body. The lower neck is buffy gray, whereas the rest of the underparts, including the lower surface of the tail, are pure white. There is a black spot between the ears, but no white spot on the forehead, and there is a cinnamon-colored eye ring. Individuals from the narrow belt of swamps and marshes within the upper limits of tidewater along the Gulf Coast, from extreme southern Louisiana, Mississippi, and Alabama, are similar to other swamp rabbits in size, but much darker and more reddish; the upperparts are dark rusty or reddish brown strongly washed with black, becoming distinctly more rufous on the lower rump and the top of the tail. In summer the black wash is lacking, the reddish color fades, and the rabbit becomes pale brown, thus to some extent resembling a cottontail. (These Gulf Coast rabbits have been called *S. aquaticus littoralis*.)

MEASUREMENTS. Measurements of 18 individuals from Indiana were: total length 514 (462–545), tail 51 (40–60), hind foot 106 (100–113) mm; and weight 2.2 (1.8–2.7) kg (3.9–6 lbs). The ear averages about 70 (60–80) mm in length (Chapman and Feldhamer, Mammalian Species, 1981).

Diploid number = 38.

TOOTH FORMULA

$$\frac{2}{1} \quad \frac{0}{0} \quad \frac{3}{2} \quad \frac{3}{3} \ = \ 28$$

DISTRIBUTION. This rabbit occupies the southwestern portion of our area, from extreme southwestern Indiana, southern Illinois, and western Kentucky and Tennessee south to the

Gulf Coast and east through Alabama, northern Georgia, and extreme western South Carolina. West of our area it ranges to eastern Oklahoma and eastern Texas. This is a southern swamp species whose range limits extend north only as far as the southern swamp-forest community, and only to about the 24°C (12°F) isoline.

HABITAT. The swamp rabbit lives in the wet bottomlands, the river swamps, and the impenetrable jungles of cane, though it must have access to higher ground (ridges, knolls, or levees) for habitation during flood periods. Although plenty of bottomlands are still available in Indiana, this species has been nearly extirpated there because most of the adjacent higher areas have become farmland. Where swamp rabbits and eastern cottontails occur in the same area, they are generally separated by habitat, the cottontails not venturing into the swampy areas, where the swamp rabbits reign supreme.

*Swamp rabbit habitat*

HABITS. Swamp rabbits are accomplished swimmers. They will strike out across a sizable body of water when alarmed, or will visit the small islets that dot their watery home. When the rabbit is swimming, only its nose and ears are visible above water. Despite many assertions to the contrary, the available evidence suggests that

*Distribution of the swamp rabbit,* Sylvilagus aquaticus, *in the eastern United States*

this rabbit is a more accomplished swimmer than its smaller cousin, the marsh rabbit. In some parts of its range, the marsh rabbit ventures into the water only when pressed to the utmost, but the swamp rabbit swims for considerable distances, apparently as a regular means of getting about.

Like other rabbits, swamp rabbits use various tactics to confuse pursuers. Like cottontails, a swamp rabbit will walk along a log, then backtrack and jump off the log far to one side. It may then sit and watch its pursuer. When pursued, it will dive without hesitation. Swamp rabbits may also backtrack upstream, then enter the water and float downstream, and Hunt (1959) observed one, while being chased by a dog, swim under a bank, where it remained with only its eyes and nose above water.

Swamp rabbits commonly defecate on logs and stumps, often using the same log over and over, thus giving the hunter or biologist a clue that this species is about. The logs most commonly sprinkled with pellets are well-rotted and situated in relatively open places. They may vary in length from 60 cm (2 feet) on up, and may be as small as 5 cm (2 inches) in diameter. On a long log, there may be several groups of pellets. In Indiana, defecation on logs occurs mainly from about November through May. Zollner et al.

*Swamp rabbit pellets on log*

(1996) found that the swamp rabbits in their Arkansas study area defecated on logs throughout the year, though somewhat less often in summer. They found evidence supporting the "vigilance hypothesis," i.e. that rabbits favored logs from which they could keep watch for enemies, but

hypothesized further that the logs might serve other functions, such as marking territories. We think that defecation on logs is incidental to the rabbits' use of the logs as observation posts, and that this habit is practiced more often during the fall simply because vegetative growth tends to obscure the view. Swamp rabbit pellets average about 12.5 mm in diameter, whereas those of eastern cottontails average about 7.5 mm.

Swamp rabbits will hide in holes in the ground, in hollow trees or logs, in thickets of cane, honeysuckle, or elderberry, or in other such sheltered places. The great, splayed, slightly furred toes, with their sharp nails, support the swamp rabbit securely in the softest mud, where the marks of its characteristic gait, often a walk rather than a hop, indicate its presence.

Marsden and Holler (1964) studied the behavior of confined swamp rabbits. They found mutual toleration among females, but a dominance hierarchy among males. The hierarchy served to prevent fighting, and the top male accomplished most copulation. Swamp rabbits are territorial, and the males use "chinning" to mark territories with a distinctive pheromone. Chinning is the rubbing of the underside of the chin on branches, logs, stumps, and such.

FOOD AND FEEDING. The swamp rabbit feeds on a variety of herbs and succulent aquatic plants, and, of course, employs coprophagy. Its fondness for the stems of the ubiquitous cane (*Arundinaria*) is well known to southern hunters, who beat these tangles to put up the "cane-cutter." Terrel (1972) reported that other plants eaten in Indiana, in decreasing order of use, were crossvine (*Bignonia capreolata*), sedges, poison ivy, grasses, greenbrier, and tree seedlings. In Missouri a sedge, *Carex lupulina*, followed by blackberry, hazelnut, deciduous holly, and spicebush, were the plants most often eaten (Toll et al., 1960). These authors felt that items were eaten primarily in relation to their abundance.

REPRODUCTION AND DEVELOPMENT. Marsden and Holler (1964) reported mating behaviors similar to those of eastern cottontails: males chasing or threatening females, dashing about and jumping, often over the females, leading them in due course to copulation. Swamp rabbits are receptive shortly after giving birth, estrus lasting less than an hour (Sorensen et al., 1968). Crowded conditions brought on by flooding, or simply by high levels of population, lead to embryo resorption.

Two litters, but sometimes as many as five, at least in captivity, are usually produced in a year. The young number from one to six per litter, three being the most common, and first litters are smaller than second litters: in Alabama and Missouri, respectively, firsts averaged 2.8 and 2.7 young, seconds 3.2 and 4.1 young (Hill, 1967; Sorensen et al., 1968). In Louisiana, the young may be born in any month, births peaking from February through May, but the breeding season is progressively shorter to the north. In northern Alabama, breeding commences in early February or even late January, and the first litters are produced in mid-March. The gestation period is 35–40 days, 36 or 37 days the most common. Newborns, dark on the back, sides, and throat, but white below, average 53–62 grams, and their fur is about 5 mm long. The top of the head is tan and black. The eyes open at five to eight days, and the young leave the nest at 12 to 15 days. Early-spring young reach adult size by about ten months, late young not until the following year. The young can breed at 23 to 30 weeks of age, but seldom do breed until the year after their birth. The nest, as it is for many other rabbits, is a slight depression lined with fur; it may be in any protected place, but most of those found by Sorensen (1972) were under or against a fence, tree base, board, or similar support. Built before or on the night of parturition, the nest is about 4 to 7 cm deep, 15 cm wide, and 18 cm high, and its entrance is on the side. Active nests are lined with belly fur, but unused or "dummy" nests are not lined.

POPULATION CHARACTERISTICS. Home ranges of swamp rabbits have been estimated at 0.7 to 7.6 ha (1.2 to 19 acres) in different studies. Swamp rabbits live an estimated 1.8 years in Indiana (Terrel, 1972), but it would appear that they are capable of living much longer.

ENEMIES. This species is undoubtedly preyed upon by a host of predators—dogs and alligators have been reported—but little specific in-

formation is available. Flooding and hunting appear to be the major causes of swamp rabbit mortality, and habitat reduction for farming and other uses appears to be the major problem for this species.

PARASITES AND DISEASE. Swamp rabbits harbor cestodes, trematodes, nematodes, mites, ticks, and fleas.

RELATION TO HUMANS. A. H. Howell (1921) stated that where cultivated fields adjoin the swamps where they live, these rabbits often forage in corn or other crops and at times cause considerable damage. But because of the very nature of its habitat, this rabbit seldom causes problems for the farmer. For the hunter, however, the species has been a favorite. Its speed is more than a match for that of a dog, and few would be taken if it were not for the rabbit's unfailing habit of taking refuge in a hollow tree or other likely cavity after a short run. In the northern parts of its range, the swamp rabbit is now in need of protection because of habitat reduction.

AREAS FOR FURTHER WORK. This is one of the least studied species of *Sylvilagus*, and many of the available studies have been done in peripheral areas of its range. A major field study of the species in its optimum range, such as in Louisiana, should yield much more information about its life history. Does this species defecate on logs incidentally, while using them as observation posts, or does this behavior have other functions, such as territorial marking?

## SUBSPECIES

*Sylvilagus aquaticus aquaticus* Bachman
  As described above.
  Type locality: Western Alabama.
  Other currently recognized eastern subspecies:
    *S. aquaticus littoralis* Nelson

### LITERATURE

Chapman, J. A., and G. A. Feldhamer. 1981. *Sylvilagus aquaticus*. **Mammalian Species No. 151.** Amer. Soc. Mammal. 4 pp.

Hill, E. P. 1967. Notes on the life history of the swamp rabbit in Alabama. *Proc. Ann. Conf. Southeastern Assoc. Game and Fish Comm.* 25: 269–281.

Howell, A. H. 1921. A biological survey of Alabama. I. Physiography and life zones. II. The mammals. *North Amer. Fauna* 45: 88 pp.

Hunt, T. P. 1959. Breeding habits of the swamp rabbit with notes on its life history. *J. Mammal.* 40: 82–96.

Lowe, C. E. 1958. Ecology of the swamp rabbit in Georgia. *J. Mammal.* 39: 116–127.

Marsden, H. M., and N. R. Holler. 1964. Social behavior in confined populations of the cottontail and swamp rabbit. *Wildl. Monogr.* No. 13. 39 pp.

Sorensen, M. F. 1972. Parental behavior in swamp rabbits. *J. Mammal.* 53: 840–849.

Sorensen, M. F., J. P. Rogers, and T. S. Baskett. 1968. Reproduction and development in confined swamp rabbits. *J. Wildl. Mgmt.* 32: 520–531.

Terrel, T. L. 1972. The swamp rabbit (*Sylvilagus aquaticus*) in Indiana. *Amer. Midland Nat.* 82: 283–295.

Toll, J. E., T. S. Baskett, and C. H. Conaway. 1960. Home range, reproduction, and foods of the swamp rabbit in Missouri. *Amer. Midland Nat.* 63: 398–412.

Zollner, P. A., W. P. Smith, and L. A. Brennan. 1996. Characteristics and adaptive significance of latrines of swamp rabbits (*Sylvilagus aquaticus*). *J. Mammal.* 77: 1049–1058.

## Eastern Cottontail *Sylvilagus floridanus* (Allen)                     Color plate 6

DESCRIPTION. The eastern cottontail is the familiar "rabbit" of most of the eastern United States. The upper parts of the body are usually reddish brown with a cinnamon nape patch, and the underparts, including the fluffy underside of the tail, are white. In the coastal lowlands of peninsular Florida, the cottontail is small and dark, varying from dark grayish-buffy to a rusty, buffy brown. The nape and legs are a rich cinnamon-rufous. The ears are short, rounded, and darker than the back; on their outsides, they are dark grayish buffy, heavily bordered and washed with black, especially on the terminal half. The top of the head and back are dark buffy brown interspersed with reddish and dark-buffy hairs. The rump and sides of the body are dark buffy gray, washed with black. The top of the tail is dull rusty brown. The rusty color of the eastern cottontail is lost in the summer, however, replaced by grayish buffy brown. Animals

*Eastern cottontail,* Sylvilagus floridanus *(Roger W. Barbour)*

from extreme southern Florida are smaller and paler (grayer and less washed with black) than the northern Florida cottontails. Cottontails from the rest of the Southeast are larger and paler than those from Florida, with larger ears and a prominent gray rump patch. Animals from the north are also large, but their ears are shorter and the hind feet are longer.

Distinguishing *Sylvilagus floridanus* from the New England and Allegheny cottontails is most difficult. The eastern cottontail is lighter in color and often has a white spot on the forehead, whereas the New England and Allegheny cottontails rarely have a white spot on the forehead but often have a black spot between the ears. The eastern cottontail can be readily distinguished from the other two by examining the skull: in *S. transitionalis* and *S. obscurus*, the supraorbital process is short or missing and the postorbital process rarely touches the skull; in the eastern cottontail, the supraorbital process is present and the postorbital process touches the skull.

MEASUREMENTS. Average measurements of 20 Florida specimens were: total length 414 (355–485), tail 49 (37–70), hind foot 89 mm. Eleven individuals from extreme southern Florida averaged: total length 397 (370–424), tail 44 (32–51), hind foot 87 (80–95) mm. Average measurements of five North Carolina specimens were: total length 446, tail 65, hind foot 94 mm; and weight 1360–1430 grams (3–3.4 lbs). Average measurements of ten New York specimens were: total length 414, tail 56, hind foot 101 mm; and weight 1.2 kg (2.7–3.2 lbs). The ear in this species ranges from 49 to 68 mm in length.

Diploid number = 42.

TOOTH FORMULA
$$\frac{2}{1} \quad \frac{0}{0} \quad \frac{3}{2} \quad \frac{3}{3} \quad = \quad 28$$

DISTRIBUTION. The eastern cottontail has the widest distribution of any *Sylvilagus*, occurring west to southeastern Montana, central Colorado, and western Arizona, and south through Central America to northeastern South America. It is found throughout eastern United States except for northern New York and northern New England, and is moving into the southern Adirondacks. Prior to 1930, eastern cottontails occurred in New England only in northwestern Connecticut, but since then they have invaded all of Connecticut, Rhode Island, eastern Vermont, and southern New Hampshire (Litvaitis and Litvaitis, 1996).

HABITAT. Over its broad range, the cottontail occupies diverse habitats, from swampy woods and coastal dunes to upland thickets and farmlands, and is often found in residential areas of sizable cities. It seldom occurs in any numbers in heavy forest, but is quick to take advantage of new territory opened by lumbering. Cottontails are not abundant along the southern east coast of Florida but one does find them there in the pine woods. To the west, in the Everglades, they are replaced by *Sylvilagus palustris*.

HABITS. Cottontails are timid beasts, generally relying on their ability to blend into the back-

*Distribution of the eastern cottontail,* Sylvilagus floridanus, *in the eastern United States*

ground, but to escape their numerous enemies they will bolt suddenly and speed away. The white tail presumably functions as a "flash marking": the would-be predator goes to where the last white "tail flash" was seen, but in the meantime the rabbit has skulked away on a different course, into a hiding place. During the day, these rabbits sleep in a form, whether at the base of a suitable tree, in the scant shelter of a grass tussock, or in the more formidable cover of a blackberry thicket, ever ready to explode into flight if threatened by a fox, dog, man, or other enemy. At other times the rabbit will slink off to a place of cover. These rabbits are active chiefly at night, moving from their forms with the approach of dusk. During the colder winter months in the northern part of its range, they regularly utilize the burrow of a woodchuck, skunk, or other creature. A cottontail rarely, if ever, prepares its own burrow.

In their study of this species, Marsden and Holler (1964) reported dusting (rolling in dusty areas) and four types of grooming: grooming the face with the front paws (preceded by licking the paws), licking the body and legs, scratching with the hind legs, and biting and cleaning the feet.

Rabbits in a given area develop a peck order: one animal dominant over all, the number two animal dominant over the rest, and so forth. Dominant animals adopt an "alert posture" vis-à-vis subordinates and females, the rump raised and the ears erect. Submissive posture, by contrast, is a crouched position with the ears and tail down. Such behaviors—whether by cottontails or the many other animals that employ them— benefit the species, since they forestall actual fighting. Fights, which consist of biting and kicking, seldom occur, because of the elaborate dominance-submission patterns that develop.

Vocalizations in this species include distress cries, the high-pitched screams of injured or frightened animals; the squealing of males and females during copulation; and the grunting of females on the nest when the nest is approached too closely.

FOOD AND FEEDING. During the summer, cottontails eat a wide variety of green foods, chiefly grasses and the low, broad-leafed weeds.

They may become a nuisance in the garden, leveling rows of young cabbage and related plants, peas, beans, and early summer crops. Winter foods consist primarily of the buds and tender twigs of many types of small trees and bushes. Sumac bark is particularly favored. The canes of blackberry and other thorny stalks are neatly cut, and sapling sprouts are severed at the snow line. Cottontails make a clean diagonal cut when cropping twigs, whereas deer, lacking upper incisors, break them off, leaving a rough end.

Like many other lagomorphs, rabbits of this species practice coprophagy, or reingestion. Green food is swallowed rapidly, and the rabbit, having eaten its fill, returns to protective cover, where soft green pellets are defecated. These pellets, consisting of undigested vegetation, are then leisurely eaten, two or three pellets at a time, directly from the anus, and digested more thoroughly.

REPRODUCTION AND DEVELOPMENT. The cottontail is the most prolific species of the genus, some females breeding in the year of their birth. Cottontails are r-selected: they exhibit high reproductive rates and great mortality. K-selected species are sustained by an entirely different strategy: they have low numbers of young but a much greater proportion of the young enters the breeding population.

In early spring, even the casual observer can often see precopulatory behavior. When the male approaches, the female typically responds with a threat posture, facing the male (facing off). The male continues his advance, and the female then boxes, i.e. jabs with the front feet, or charges him. The male will then dash at the female, urinating in the process. If the female is receptive, jump sequences may follow the face-offs, the female jumping over the onrushing male, her leap followed by face-off once again. In due course, the female retreats, and the male follows and smells her hindquarters. Finally, after a brief chase, the female presents herself and copulation follows quickly. Dominant males copulate with most of the females.

Gestation in the cottontail ranges from 25 to 35 days, the mean 28 or 29 (Chapman et al., 1982). Breeding may commence in early January, but the first young are not commonly born until March. Three to seven litters of three to six young each (extremes are one to seven) are produced over a breeding season extending from February or March through September in the north, and even longer in the south (year-round in southern Texas (Bothma and Teer, 1977). Litter size, however, averages higher in the north. Conaway et al. (1963) found annual production in Missouri to be about 35 young per female; Pelton and Jenkins (1971) reported it as about 15 to 21 per female in Georgia.

The mother makes a warm nest by scraping out a shallow depression, or utilizing some natural cavity, then lining it with finely shredded leaves and grasses and a goodly amount of fur that she has removed from her belly and breast. This fur adds substance and warmth to the natal chamber, and its removal helps to expose her teats. The nest, which is carefully covered when the mother is away, may be almost any place, even in mowed lawns of residential areas. The nest cavity, usually slanting, averages about 180 mm deep and 126 mm wide (Chapman et al., 1982). At birth, the young are blind, essentially naked, and helpless. Total length is 90–110 mm, the hind foot is 21–28 mm long, and the weight is 35–45 grams. The eyes open on the fourth or fifth day, and the young can climb out of the nest at about two weeks of age. For about 16 days, the mother returns to the nest each dawn and dusk, opens the top, and lies over the babies to let them nurse. After she licks the young clean, she carefully closes the nest, then feeds and rests nearby. A gardener can weed and hoe within inches of the camouflaged nest without knowledge of its presence. Up to about half of the newborn breed during the year of their birth.

POPULATION CHARACTERISTICS. Cottontails are not territorial, though they seldom roam over an area greater than a few hectares in extent. Home range varies greatly with season, habitat quality, and population size, but one estimate puts it at about 2 ha (5 acres). The winter snow reveals the cottontails' trails, crisscrossing through a sumac patch or bit of swamp, the tracks often so numerous that one obtains a false notion of the cottontails' abundance. Usually, about 80 to 85% of cottontail populations are juveniles.

Populations can reach densities of 20 per ha (9 per acre), but most are much lower. In fall, in cottontail populations, there are animals with fixed home ranges and others without; the latter are the younger animals that have not bred. Assaulted by so many enemies, eastern cottontails are short-lived, only a quarter of the population, or less, surviving two years. Very few live for three or more years.

ENEMIES. Rabbits have many enemies. Scores of young are routed from their nest cavity by wandering bobcats, dogs, foxes, coyotes, skunks, and crows; and the growing young are preyed upon by hawks and owls, the larger snakes, and even red squirrels. The adults, too, fall prey to most of these enemies. Highway mortality is severe, for rabbits often run ahead of the automobile, confused by the headlights.

PARASITES AND DISEASE. Parasites are common in cottontails. Tapeworms are abundant, both as adults in the intestines and as large cysts in the liver. Because of these cysts, rabbits intended for the kitchen are often unnecessarily discarded by hunters, for many people believe the cysts to be indicative of tularemia. This disease is in fact indicated by numerous small white spots covering the liver, rather than a few large cysts. Tularemia, found in other species as well, is an important rabbit disease, always fatal to the rabbit. Most rabbits with tularemia will have died before the rabbit season begins, at least in the northern parts of the range. In Illinois, about 90% of the tularemia cases in humans are contracted from the flesh and blood of infected rabbits, or by eating improperly cooked rabbits. Ectoparasites consist of fleas, botflies, mites, chiggers, and ticks. Two flea species, *Cediopsylla simplex* and *Odontopsyllus multispinosus*, and one tick, *Haemaphysalis leporis-palustris*, are species primarily parasitizing rabbits.

RELATION TO HUMANS. The cottontail is the most important game animal of the eastern United States. Millions are shot each season, and the flesh is excellent; few meals compare with a well-prepared bowl of rabbit stew. Wearing rubber gloves while processing rabbits should help avoid tularemia, but the liver should be examined. A rabbit whose liver is finely covered with white dots should be discarded, but a liver ex-hibiting a few large, white objects need not lead one to discard the rabbit. The pelts are of little value, though they have long been used in trim-mings on children's garments.

AREAS FOR FURTHER WORK. Much could be learned, even in one's back yard, with the help of binoculars, from detailed observation of the morphological and behavioral development of this species. The natal nest and the interrelation-ships of the ectoparasite community of adult cottontails warrant study. Ectoparasite ecosys-tems are usually quite simple and lack their own predators, but rabbits often carry cheyletid mites, which are presumably predators. What do they prey upon and how do they fit into the ectoparasite community?

## SUBSPECIES

We see no reason to retain the several main-land subspecies that have been described, since there appears to be no evidence of primary isolating mechanisms; the populations simply grade into one another. Likewise, Litvaitis et al. (1997) found that mitochondrial DNA data did not support continued subspecific status for the various forms of *Sylvilagus floridanus* occurring in the northeastern United States. *Sylvilagus f. paulsoni* is partially isolated by the Everglades on the west and the Atlantic Ocean on the east, but it intergrades with *S. f. floridanus* in the north, in the Palm Beach area.

*Sylvilagus floridanus floridanus* (Allen)

As described above. Although eastern cotton-tails are variable, they form an intergrading se-ries throughout the eastern United States.

Type locality: Sebastian River, Brevard Co., Florida.

Other currently recognized eastern subspecies:
  *S. floridanus alacer* (Bangs)
  *S. floridanus ammophilus* Howell
  *S. floridanus mallurus* (Thomas)
  *S. floridanus mearnsi* (Allen)
  *S. floridanus paulsoni* (Schwartz)

*Sylvilagus floridanus hitchensi* Mearns

This subspecies occurs on Smith's Island, Fish-erman's Island, and Northampton Island, Vir-ginia. Since it is an island form, a primary iso-lating mechanism is in place. These rabbits are the size of *Sylvilagus floridanus* from the area of Raleigh, North Carolina. The color is described as being paler than on mainland cottontails, and "the bright colors" (black and rufous) "of the upper parts [are said to be] obsolete, giving a pale sandy fulvous shade to these parts." The backs of the hind legs are a slightly darker chest-nut than in the mainland form. The skull is "larger, heavier, broader interorbitally, with thickened rostrum and larger auditory bullae. All of the teeth are larger. Average measure-ments of six paratypes were: total length 420, tail 56.7, and hind foot 91 mm.

Type locality: Fisherman's Island, North-ampton Co., Virginia.

## LITERATURE

Bothma, J. du P., and J. G. Teer. 1977. Reproduction and productivity in south Texas cottontail rabbits. *Mammalia* 41: 253–281.

Casteel, D. A. 1966. Nest building, parturition, and copulation in the cottontail rabbit. *Amer. Midland Nat.* 75: 160–167.

Chapman, J. A., J. G. Hockman, and W. R. Edwards. 1982. Cottontails *Sylvilagus floridanus* and allies. In: J. A. Chapman and G. A. Feldhamer, eds., *Wild Mammals of North America*, pp. 83–123. Balti-more: Johns Hopkins Univ. Press.

Chapman, J. A., J. G. Hockman, and M. M. Ojeda C. 1980. *Sylvilagus floridanus*. **Mammalian Species No. 136.** Amer. Soc. Mammal. 8 pp.

Conaway, C. H., H. M. Wright, and K. C. Sadler. 1963. Annual production by a cottontail popula-tion. *J. Wildl. Mgmt.* 27: 171–175.

Kirkpatrick, C. M. 1956. Coprophagy in the cotton-tail. *J. Mammal.* 37: 300.

Litvaitis, M. K., and J. A. Litvaitis. 1996. Using mi-tochondrial DNA to inventory the distribution of remnant populations of New England cottontails. *Wildl. Soc. Bull.* 234: 725–730.

Litvaitis, M. K., J. A. Litvaitis, W.-J. Lee, and T. D. Kocher. 1997. Variation in the mitochondrial DNA of the *Sylvilagus* complex occupying the northeast-ern United States. *Canadian J. Zool.* 75: 595–605.

Marsden, H. M., and N. R. Holler. 1964. Social be-havior in confined populations of the cottontail and swamp rabbit. *Wildl. Monogr.* 13: 1–39.

Pelton, M. R., and J. H. Jenkins. 1971. Productivity of Georgia cottontails. *Proc. Ann. Conf. Southeastern Assoc. Game and Fish Comm.* 25: 261–268.

## Allegheny Cottontail *Sylvilagus obscurus* Chapman et al.

Until recently, the New England cottontail was thought to occur from southern Maine through the Appalachians to northern Georgia and Alabama. This presumption was called into question, however, when two chromosomal races were discovered, a northern one with $2N = 52$ and a southern race with $2N = 46$. The two races, recognized by Chapman et al. (1992) as separate species, are very similar, differing only in such characters as cranial shape, which can be delimited only by multivariate statistical procedures. Chapman et al. (1992) argued that "since there is no evidence of hybridization between the two karyotypes, it is probable that the chromosomal races represent two sibling species in what has traditionally been regarded as *S. transitionalis.*" We tentatively accepted the conclusion that two species should be recognized, although we did not completely agree with the taxonomic reasoning. That there are no hybrids is because the two are not sympatric, and, accordingly, we have no field test of what would happen if they occurred together. At the least, however, the two are separate subspecies of *S. transitionalis.*

Litvaitis et al. (1997) used mitochondrial DNA data to evaluate the recent separation of New England cottontails into two sister species, *S. transitionalis* of New England and *S. obscurus* of the southern Appalachians, and also compared those two species to eastern cottontails, *S. floridanus.* Sequence variation supported separation of *S. floridanus* from the New England cottontail group, and indicated that the two were not hybridizing. Their data, however, do not support the separation of *S. transitionalis* and *S. obscurus* into separate sister species, although these authors suggested that karyotypic and morphological differences between northern and southern populations should be considered during any efforts to restore declining populations of this species.

DESCRIPTION. There is usually a dark spot between the ears of the Allegheny cottontail, as there is in the New England cottontail, *Sylvilagus transitionalis*, but there are no diagnostic pelage characteristics to distinguish the two.

*Allegheny cottontail,* Sylvilagus obscurus *(Michael L. Kennedy)*

MEASUREMENTS. Measurements given for Pennsylvania are total length 382–425, tail 43–52; and weight 0.7–1.2 kg (1.5–2.6 lbs).
  Diploid number = 46.

TOOTH FORMULA

$$\frac{2}{1} \ \frac{0}{0} \ \frac{3}{2} \ \frac{3}{3} \ = \ 28$$

DISTRIBUTION. This species has a discontinuous distribution in the Appalachians from west of the Hudson River through New York, Pennsylvania, Maryland, West Virginia, Virginia, and Kentucky south to Tennessee, North Carolina, South Carolina, Georgia, and Alabama.

HABITAT. In contrast with the very closely related New England cottontail, the Allegheny cottontail is associated with dense cover of heaths, particularly *Vaccinium* and *Kalmia*, and with conifers at the higher elevations of the Appalachians. The type locality of this species, Dolly Sods, is a heath-covered Scenic Area in Grant County, West Virginia.

HABITS. The habits of this species are assumed to be generally similar to those of *S. transitionalis.*

FOOD AND FEEDING. No food-habits analysis has been undertaken for this species, but we assume that these rabbits feed heavily on green vegetation in summer and depend more on woody vegetation in winter.

REPRODUCTION AND DEVELOPMENT. Reproduction in this species is assumed to be similar to that of *S. transitionalis*. Tefft and Chapman (1983), during studies of captives from Maryland, gave average measurements of the hind foot and crown-rump length at birth, 4 days, 10 days, and 16 days as follows: 10.5, 73.8; 27.8, 81.4; 39.3, 105.8; and 49.7, 133.2 mm. The eyes began to open at about 2 days. At 16 days the young had excellent coordination and were entirely independent of the nest.

In Maryland and West Virginia, the breeding season is from March to September (Chapman et al., 1977). In West Virginia, about 18% of the juvenile females bred, whereas males were not potentially able to breed until the year after they were born. The average number of young per litter in Maryland was about 3.8.

ENEMIES. The traditional predators on cottontails, such as foxes, coyotes, and bobcats, are presumed to feed on the Allegheny cottontail as well.

PARASITES AND DISEASE. We have no information on the ectoparasites of this species, but suspect it harbors mites, fleas, and ticks.

RELATION TO HUMANS. Were it not that the Allegheny cottontail is rare, and is a candidate species for federal endangered listing, it would be, like other lagomorphs, a logical game species.

AREAS FOR FURTHER WORK. Practically no information is available on this species. Information on its food, parasites, and reproductive habits could be accumulated and compared with that of *S. transitionalis*, and much more information is needed on the relation between the two. Should they be considered as separate species? Or, as would be indicated at this reading, as separate subspecies?

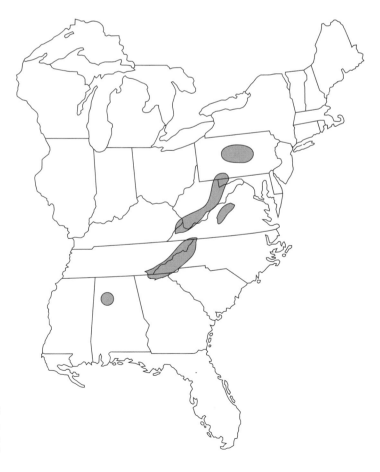

*Distribution of the*
*Allegheny cottontail,*
Sylvilagus obscurus,
*in the eastern United States*

SUBSPECIES

None described.

Type locality: Dolly Sods Scenic Area, Grant Co., West Virginia.

LITERATURE

Chapman, J. A., K. L. Cramer, N. J. Dippenoar, and T. L. Robinson. 1992. Systematics and biogeography of the New England Cottontail, *Sylvilagus transitionalis* (Bangs, 1895), with the description of a new species from the Appalachian Mountains. *Proc. Biol. Soc. Wash.* 105: 841–866.

Chapman, J. A., A. L. Harman, and D. E. Samuel. 1977. Reproductive and physiological cycles in the cottontail complex in western Maryland and nearby West Virginia. *Wildl. Monogr.* 56: 1–73.

Litvaitis, M. K., J. A. Litvaitis, W.-J. Lee, and T. D. Kocher. 1997. Variation in the mitochondrial DNA of the *Sylvilagus* complex occupying the northeastern United States. *Canadian J. Zool.* 75: 595–605.

Tefft, B. C., and J. A. Chapman. 1983. Growth and development of nestling New England cottontails, *Sylvilagus transitionalis. Acta Theriologica* 28, 20: 317–377.

## Marsh Rabbit *Sylvilagus palustris* (Bachman)                    Color plate 6

DESCRIPTION. The marsh rabbit is small and dark brown, with small, slender, dark-reddish-buffy feet. The tail, too, is small, but dingy (rarely white) on the underside. In no other *Sylvilagus* in the eastern United States is the underside of the tail not white. The ears are short and their leading edge is black. In general coloration, this rabbit is otherwise similar to the swamp rabbit, *S. aquaticus*, but it can be distinguished

*Marsh rabbit,* Sylvilagus palustris *(Joseph McDonald)*

by its smaller size and the dark underside of the tail. The upperparts are reddish brown; the nape is dark cinnamon-rufous; and the rump, the upper side of the tail, and the backs of the hind legs vary from chestnut-brown to dark rusty reddish. The middle of the abdomen is white, and the rest of the belly is buffy to light brown. Individuals from peninsular Florida, which have been called *S. palustris paludicola*, are smaller, darker, and more reddish brown than is typical *S. palustris*, and melanistic marsh rabbits are known from southern peninsular Florida (Layne, 1974).

MEASUREMENTS. Average measurements of seven adults from Florida and Georgia were: total length 441, tail 34.5, hind foot 92 mm; and weight 1.5 kg (3.5 lbs). Average measurements of eight adults from peninsular Florida were: total length 429, tail 42, hind foot 89 mm; and weight 1–1.06 kg (2.2–2.6 lbs).

Diploid number unknown.

TOOTH FORMULA
$$\frac{2}{1} \quad \frac{0}{0} \quad \frac{3}{2} \quad \frac{3}{3} \ = \ 28$$

DISTRIBUTION. The marsh rabbit occurs from Dismal Swamp, Virginia, south through southern Georgia and all of Florida (except for a gap between the upper and lower keys and another north of Miami) and west almost to Mobile Bay, Alabama.

HABITAT. The slender-footed little marsh rabbits are confined to wet areas, particularly where water is brackish. They inhabit the brakes, wet bottomlands, brackish marshes, and sea islands along the Atlantic Coast and the dense hammocks or the borders of freshwater lakes in Georgia and Florida. There is plentiful evidence of this rabbit in the sandy thickets lying back of the mangroves of South Florida beaches.

Fragmentation of habitats is thought to be a major environmental problem for these rabbits, since it may decrease the of usable habitat available to individuals and may adversely affect dispersal and genetic diversity. (The lower keys marsh rabbit, *Sylvilagus palustris hefneri*, is in a highly fragmented situation.) Forys and Humphrey (1996) found that radio-collared juveniles remained in their natal patch until sexual maturity. All subadults then dispersed, i.e., they made a one-way journey to another patch, but adult rabbits, having once established a new home range in the new patch, spent most of their lives in that one patch.

HABITS. Since marsh rabbit habitat includes extensive areas of lowland that periodically flood, these rabbits must be able swimmers. With their small, slender feet, they do not appear to be particularly modified for an aquatic life, but their hind limbs are less furred and their nails are somewhat longer than those of cottontails, and they will enter the water voluntarily and swim efficiently for considerable distances. Ivan Tomkins recorded an individual swimming strongly 640 meters (700 yards) from shore.

Marsh rabbits travel their own well-marked trails in the brakes and dense marsh vegetation. Although they can and do run like cottontails, they often "scurry" when running. They are likewise capable of stepping alternately with each foot in turn, much in the manner of a dog or a cat. Their slow gait when feeding is thus contrary to the hopping motions of other rabbits.

Marsh rabbits are nocturnal over much of their range, although variable tide levels may force them to move about to some extent during the day. During the day, they normally occupy a form, which they will leave only if approached very closely. The form consists simply of a spot bare of vegetation, about 22 by 30 cm in extent, in an area of thick vegetation. Hamilton noted that for several days one spring an immature Florida individual invariably returned each morning to the same resting quarters under a brush pile. Marsh rabbits are usually common throughout their range, and although they may

*Distribution of the marsh rabbit,* Sylvilagus palustris, *in the eastern United States*

be well hidden during the day, a strong light may reveal large numbers an hour or so after dusk.

Fecal pellets vary greatly in color. Thirty-four of them averaged 9 mm long and 8 mm wide (Blair, 1936). Marsh rabbits, like swamp rabbits, will deposit pellets on logs or stumps in hammock areas; those in marshes will deposit them along active runways.

Rabbits of this species, like many others, will thump the ground with the hind feet; frequently, they will squeal when flushed and making their escape; and one was heard to scream when wounded.

FOOD AND FEEDING. Observations by Blair (1936) showed centella (*Centella reparda*), greenbrier vines, and the pulp of tupelo to be among the natural foods of these rabbits, but in captivity and undoubtedly in the wild they eat a variety of plants, including aquatic emergents, such as cane, marsh grass, cattail, rush, and water hyacinths, the leaves and twigs of deciduous trees, marsh pennywort, the rhizomes of amaryllis, and the bulbs of several plants, including *Apios*. Marsh rabbits consumed about 29% of their body weight per day when fed centella in the laboratory. Like other rabbits, they practice reingestion (coprophagy).

REPRODUCTION AND DEVELOPMENT. Breeding occurs throughout the year, and gestation is 30 to 37 days. The two to four young (rarely five) are born in a warm, fur-lined nest of grass that occupies a rather sizable depression. The nests are about 36 cm (14 inches) in diameter, and about 50 cm (20 inches) high. Marsh rabbits, born with the pelage well developed but the eyes closed, remain in the nest for several days after they are weaned, and for a few days after they have first ventured out, they return to the shelter. A nest found by Hamilton under a cabbage palm in Lee County, Florida, was large enough to hold his foot. A mean of about six or seven litters is produced in a season; young and half-grown young have been found in October.

POPULATION CHARACTERISTICS. Little is known of populations, but the marsh rabbit is said to be quite abundant in good habitat. The greatest

populations of this species in Georgia are said to be along Ogeechee, Satilla, and St. Mary's rivers, and in swampy areas below the fall line. These rabbits probably live a maximum of three or four years in the wild.

ENEMIES. The main predators on this species appear to be the great horned owl and the northern harrier, or marsh hawk (Chapman and Willner, Mammalian Species, 1981), which must indicate that these rabbits are active a good bit during the day as well as at night. Other enemies are dogs and man, bobcats, foxes, and alligators. Water moccasins and diamondback rattlesnakes prey on the young.

PARASITES AND DISEASE. Marsh rabbits are known to harbor nematodes and cestodes in the intestines, but internal parasites were found in only one of 24 rabbits of this species examined. Blair (1936) found larval botflies (*Cuterebra* sp.) on every rabbit examined between 3 November and 20 December, but 15 rabbits examined later in December, through February, were not infested. All rabbits examined harbored ticks and/or fleas.

RELATION TO HUMANS. Marsh rabbits seldom exert economic pressure on our crops, but in the sugarcane fields of southern Florida, they are considered pests. They are widely hunted in the South, where the dried grasses are burned over to rout them into the open, where they can be clubbed or shot.

AREAS FOR FURTHER WORK. Detailed studies of the food and parasites of this species are needed.

## SUBSPECIES

*Sylvilagus palustris palustris* (Bachman)

As described above. Occurs over most of the range of the species.

Type locality: Eastern South Carolina.

Other currently recognized eastern subspecies:
    *S. palustris paludicola* Miller & Bangs

*Sylvilagus palustris hefneri* Lazell

Confined to the scattered islands in Florida's lower keys, this subspecies differs from rabbits of the mainland and upper keys in having a short molariform tooth row, high and convex frontonasal profile, broad cranium, and elongate dentary symphysis. The ventral pelage and the underside of the tail are both gray in this subspecies, whereas in *S. p. palustris* the tail and venter contrast in color, the venter hairs being nearly white-tipped.

Type locality: Lower Sugarloaf Key, Monroe Co., Florida.

## LITERATURE

Blair, W. F. 1936. The Florida Marsh Rabbit. *J. Mammal.* 17: 197–207.

Chapman, J. A., and G. A. Willner. 1981. *Sylvilagus palustris*. **Mammalian Species No. 153**. Amer. Soc. Mammal. 3 pp.

Forys, E. A., and S. R. Humphrey. 1996. Home range and movements of the Lower Keys marsh rabbit in a highly fragmented habitat. *J. Mammal.* 77: 1042–1048.

Holler, N. R., and C. H. Conaway. 1979. Reproduction of the Marsh Rabbit (*Sylvilagus palustris*) in South Florida. *J. Mammal.* 60: 769–777.

Layne, J. N. 1974. The land mammals of South Florida. In: P. J. Gleason, ed., *Environments of South Florida: Present and Past*, pp. 386–413. Miami, Fla.: Miami Geological Society, Memoir 2.

Lazell, J. D., Jr. 1984. A new marsh rabbit (*Sylvilagus palustris*) from Florida's Lower Keys. *J. Mammal.* 65: 26–35.

## New England Cottontail
### *Sylvilagus transitionalis* (Bangs)

Chapman et al. (1992) established southern populations previously considered to be *Sylvilagus transitionalis* as a separate species, the Allegheny cottontail, *S. obscurus* (see that account, above). Both species have disjunct ranges, indicating survival in portions of a larger original range. Morphologically, the two species are all but identical, differing only in such characters as cranial shape, allowing differentiation only by multivariate statistical procedures.

Litvaitis et al. (1997) used mitochondrial DNA to look for hybridization between eastern cottontails and New England cottontails in areas where New England cottontails were rare, and to evaluate the separation of New England cottontails into two sister species. *S. transitionalis* of New England, and *S. obscurus* of the south-

ern Appalachians. Sequence variation clearly supported separation of *S. floridanus* and the New England cottontail group, and indicated that the two were not hybridizing. However, these data did not support the separation of *S. transitionalis* and *S. obscurus* into separate sister species, although these authors stated that karyotypic and morphological differences between northern and southern populations should be considered during any efforts to restore declining populations of this species.

DESCRIPTION. The New England cottontail is a medium-sized cottontail with relatively short ears and a pinkish-buff coat heavily washed with black. There is usually a black spot on the forehead in both species, thus helping to distinguish both from the eastern cottontail, *S. floridanus*. Other pelage characters that help to distinguish New England and Allegheny cottontails from *S. floridanus* are their lack of the white blaze on the forehead and their shorter, black-rimmed ears. Skull characters also differ. The anterior supraorbital process of the skull is absent in *S. obscurus* and *S. transitionalis*, thus rendering the anterior notch obsolete or reducing it to a shallow concave depression. In *floridanus* the supraorbital is not only present, but broad and heavy. The postorbital process of *transitionalis* and *obscurus* usually tapers to a point and does not touch the skull, whereas in *floridanus* it is broad, nearly the same width throughout its length, and fused with the skull at its distal extremity.

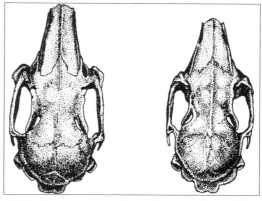

*Skulls of eastern cottontail,* Sylvilagus floridanus *(left), and New England cottontail,* Sylvilagus transitionalis *(right) (Tony Brentlinger)*

MEASUREMENTS. Measurements given by Chapman (Mammalian Species, 1975) for males and females, respectively, are: total length 405 (386–415), 411 (387–430); tail 43 (22–57), 47 (30–65); hind foot 93 (89–97), 93 (87–96) mm. The weight ranged from 756 to 965 grams (1.7–2.2 lbs) in males, and from 802 to 1038 grams (1.7–2.3 lbs) in females.

Diploid number = 52. This is the largest number for any *Sylvilagus* karyotyped to date (that for *S. floridanus* is only 42).

TOOTH FORMULA

$$\frac{2}{1} \quad \frac{0}{0} \quad \frac{3}{2} \quad \frac{3}{3} \ = \ 28$$

DISTRIBUTION. *Sylvilagus transitionalis* has a disjunct distributional pattern, probably indicating its survival in refugia representing portions of the original range. It occurs generally in much of New England north to southern Maine, west to the Hudson River in eastern New York, and south to eastern Long Island. Nine of 144 rabbits taken in New York in five counties east of the Hudson River during the 1994–95 hunting season were of this species, two from Putnam, one from Dutchess, and six from Columbia County. In Canada, this species barely reaches to southern Quebec.

Earlier, it was thought that the New England cottontail had been replacing the snowshoe hare as the northern coniferous forest was cut and the frontier of scrubby second growth took over. More recently, however, the species has been declining throughout the Northeast, owing perhaps to changing habitat and the introduction of other *Sylvilagus* species (Chapman and Morgan, 1973).

*Distribution of the New England cottontail,* Sylvilagus transitionalis, *in the eastern United States*

Since 1930, in fact, eastern cottontails have invaded much of New England. This has helped lead to a rapid decline in *S. transitionalis* in that area (Litvaitis and Litvaitis, 1996). Litvaitis and Litvaitis evaluated the use of mitochondrial DNA from tissue samples and from fecal pellets (tissue samples were recommended by the authors because they were hampered by the great amount of plant pigments in the pellets) to track declining populations of New England and eastern cottontails where they are sympatric in New England. New England cottontails are rapidly coming to occur only in southern New Hampshire and southwestern Maine, in three small areas in Massachusetts, and in one small area each in Connecticut, Rhode Island, and southeastern New York.

HABITAT. The New England cottontail inhabits open woods or their borders, or shrubby areas and thickets over more or less open areas.

HABITS. The behavior of this species is similar to that of *Sylvilagus floridanus* and *S. obscurus*. As dusk approaches, it leaves its retreat in a thicket and is particularly active during the few hours following sunset. Some behavioral differences between *transitionalis* and *floridanus* were noted by Olmstead (1970), principally that the former struggled more and squealed more frequently when held (*floridanus* usually froze and became docile). Olmstead thought this difference might have adaptive significance. Nugent (1968) found that *transitionalis* in pens venture into the open far less often than *floridanus* does.

There is one molt per year in this species; during late summer and fall.

FOOD AND FEEDING. During summer, the New England cottontail eats herbaceous plants, especially grasses and clover, often feeding well after sunrise. A variety of fruits and seeds, and various parts of many other plant species, are included. In winter, with the disappearance of herbaceous foods, feeding turns more heavily to woody species. Dalke and Sime (1941) believed the foods eaten by *S. floridanus* and *S. transitionalis* to be essentially the same, whereas Nottage (1972) believed *floridanus* to be better able to use a variety of foods than is *transitionalis*, but there is no reason for the two species to par-

tition their food resources, for in areas where the two are sympatric there is a superabundance of foods of the types eaten. Competition between these species, if any, would be for dens (woodchuck holes), for thickets, simply for space, or for some other essential in short supply. Reingestion (coprophagy) occurs (Eabry, 1968).

REPRODUCTION AND DEVELOPMENT. Increased day length has been demonstrated to induce the onset of reproduction in this species (Bissonnette and Csech, 1939). Precopulatory behavior, much like that in other rabbits, consists of chases by the males, the two sexes jumping over one another, face-offs, and one rabbit jumping straight into the air while the other dashes beneath it. Several litters are born, from late winter to late summer. Embryos in a pregnant female collected by Hamilton in late August probably would not have been born until mid-September. Gestation is believed to be about 28 days.

The nests of these rabbits are apparently like those of *S. floridanus*: simple depressions in the ground lined with fur and grass, capped by twigs and leaves (Dalke, 1942). Nests were in a variety of habitats: brush 43%, woods 25%, hayfields 16%, and other grasslands 16%. Three to eight young per litter are produced, the mean about 5.2, and lactation persists for about six days.

This rabbit generally shares the countryside with its larger relative, *S. floridanus*, and there is evidence that the two occasionally interbreed. Chapman and Morgan (1973) collected a hybrid female in western Maryland, and Dalke (1942) reported a hybrid litter, in his pens, between a male *S. floridanus* and a female *S. transitionalis*, but observed that fighting generally prevented crossbreeding. Fay and Chandler (1955) believed that the two interbreed in the wild. There are, in any case, genetic isolating mechanisms (52 chromosomes in this species vs. 42 in *S. floridanus*) that should tend to prevent interbreeding in the two.

POPULATION CHARACTERISTICS. Dalke (1937) found the home range of this species in the fall to be about 0.2 to 0.7 ha (0.5–2 acres), the range configuration more linear where individuals live along borders. In January and February, however, there were major movements of rabbits, apparently associated with the onset of reproduction; both sexes were found to move, up to 530 meters (1740 feet). Nugent (1968) found that males move farther than females.

ENEMIES. New England cottontails are probably preyed upon by the traditional predators of cottontails, such as foxes, coyotes, and bobcats.

PARASITES AND DISEASE. The parasites of these rabbits have not been well studied, but those identified are the parasites expected in rabbits: helminths, *Eimeria* (Coccidia), rabbit ticks, fleas, and botflies (*Cuterebra*).

RELATION TO HUMANS. Some hunters differentiate between the smaller *S. transitionalis* and the larger, longer-eared *S. floridanus*, calling the former the "wood rabbit" and the latter the "brush rabbit." *Sylvilagus transitionalis* will "hole up" when chased by dogs; *S. floridanus* is more apt to run. But because these animals are so similar morphologically and ecologically, and because they so often occur together, much confusion surrounds attempts to distinguish them. Conservation departments often refer to both simply as "cottontails."

AREAS FOR FURTHER WORK. Comparative ecological studies of this species, *S. obscurus*, and *S. floridanus* would be useful, and much more information is needed on their interbreeding, if any.

## SUBSPECIES

None described.

Type locality: Liberty Hill, New London Co., Connecticut.

## LITERATURE

Bissonnette, T. H., and A. G. Csech. 1939. Modified sexual photoperiodicity in cottontail rabbits. *Biol. Bull.* 77: 364–367.

Chapman, J. A. 1975. *Sylvilagus transitionalis*. **Mammalian Species No. 55.** Amer. Soc. Mammal. 4 pp.

Chapman, J. A., K. L. Cramer, N. J. Dippenaar, and T. J. Robinson. 1992. Systematics and biogeography of the New England Cottontail, *Sylvilagus transitionalis* (Bangs, 1895) with the description of a

new species from the Appalachian Mountains. *Proc. Biol. Soc. Wash.* 105: 841–866.

Chapman, J. A., J. G. Hockman, and W. R. Edwards. 1982. Cottontails *Sylvilagus floridanus* and allies. In: J. A. Chapman and G. A. Feldhamer, eds., *Wild Mammals of North America*, pp. 83–123. Baltimore: Johns Hopkins Univ. Press.

Chapman, J. A., and R. P. Morgan. 1973. Systematic status of the cottontail complex in western Maryland and nearby West Virginia. *Wildl. Monogr.* No. 36. 54 pp.

Dalke, P. D. 1937. A preliminary report of the New England cottontail studies. *Trans. Second North Amer. Wildlife Conf.*, pp. 542–548.

———. 1942. The cottontail rabbits in Connecticut: A report on the work of the Connecticut Wildlife Research Unit 1935–1938. Bull. Conn. State Geol. Nat. Hist. Survey No. 65. 97 pp.

Dalke, P. D., and P. R. Sime. 1941. Food habits of the eastern and New England cottontails. *J. Wildl. Mgmt.* 5: 216–228.

Eabry, H. S. 1968. An ecological study of *Sylvilagus transitionalis* and *S. floridanus* of northeastern Connecticut. Agric. Exp. Sta., Univ. Connecticut, Storrs. 27 pp.

Fay, F. H., and E. H. Chandler. 1955. The geographical and ecological distribution of cottontail rabbits in Massachusetts. *J. Mammal.* 36: 415–424.

Litvaitis, M. K., and J. A. Litvaitis. 1996. Using mitochondrial DNA to inventory the distribution of remnant populations of New England cottontails. *Wildl. Soc. Bull.* 234: 725–730.

Litvaitis, M. K., J. A. Litvaitis, W.-J. Lee, and T. D. Kocher, 1997. Variation in the Mitochondrial DNA of the *Sylvilagus* complex occupying the northeastern United States. *Canadian J. Zool.* 75: 595–605.

Nottage, E. J. 1972. Comparative feeding trials of *Sylvilagus floridanus* and *Sylvilagus transitionalis*. Agric. Exp. Sta., Univ. Connecticut, Storrs. 39 pp.

Nugent, R. F. 1968. Utilization of fall and winter habitat by the cottontail rabbits of northwestern Connecticut. Agric. Exp. Sta., Univ. Connecticut, Storrs. 34 pp.

Olmstead, D. L. 1970. Behavioral comparisons of two species of cottontails (*Sylvilagus floridanus* and *Sylvilagus transitionalis*). *Trans. Northeastern Sec. Wildlife Soc.* 27: 115–126.

## Hares and Jackrabbits of the Genus *Lepus*

Currently, there are four species of hares in the eastern United States. The snowshoe hare is native, the white-tailed jackrabbit was probably once native (its extant populations have probably resulted from reintroductions into Wisconsin), and the European hare and black-tailed jackrabbit are introduced exotics.

## KEY TO THE HARES AND JACKRABBITS OF THE GENUS *LEPUS*

1. Pelage brownish or grayish . . . . . . . . . . . . . . . . . 2
1. Pelage all white . . . . . . . . . . . . . . . . . . . . . . . . . 5
2. Tail black above and grayish below . . . . . . . . . . *L. americanus* (summer pelage)
2. Tail partly or wholly white. . . . . . . . . . . . . . . . 3
3. Tail all white (or exhibiting a faint dorsal line that does not extend onto rump). . . . . . . . . . . *L. townsendii* (summer pelage)
3. Tail black above. . . . . . . . . . . . . . . . . . . . . . . . 4
4. Hind foot white or whitish above; top of tail exhibiting a black stripe extending onto back . . . . . . . . . . . . . . . . . . . . *L. californicus*
4. Hind foot not white above; top of tail blackish. . . . . . . . . . . . . . . . . . . . . . . *L. europaeus*
5. Ear from notch less than 82 mm long; fur tricolored, the tips white, the median portion tawny, the bases gray to black . . . . . . . . . . . . *L. americanus* (winter pelage)
5. Ear from notch more than 82 mm long; white from base to tip, fur not tricolored . . . . . . . . . *L. townsendii* (winter pelage)

## Snowshoe Hare, Varying Hare
### *Lepus americanus* Erxleben

DESCRIPTION. The snowshoe hare, or varying hare, is a medium-sized hare with very large hind

*Snowshoe hare,* Lepus americanus, *winter (Roger A. Powell)*

legs admirably adapted for running and jumping. It has large ears, a short tail, and dense fur. The soles of the feet are well furred, particularly in winter. In summer, the upperparts are gray-brown to yellowish brown, slate-gray at the base, buffy in the middle, and brownish at the tips. The tail is black above, white below. The tips of the ears are bordered with black, summer and winter. The underside of the neck is variable, usually a buffy cinnamon, and the underparts are otherwise white. In winter, the tips of the ears are dusky and the rest of the pelage is white, though it consists of tricolored fur, the tips white, the median portion tawny, and the bases gray to black. Individuals from extreme eastern Maine have slightly longer ears and more cinnamon in the pelage; populations of the Allegheny Mountains area are the largest and most brightly colored; individuals from Wisconsin and western Upper Michigan are paler.

MEASUREMENTS. Measurements of snowshoe hares from Michigan (Baker, 1983) were: total length 380–505, tail 25–45, hind foot 120–150 mm; and weight 1.45–2.04 kg (3.5–4.5 lbs). The ears are 60 to 70 mm long.
Diploid number = 48.

TOOTH FORMULA
$$\frac{2}{1} \ \frac{0}{0} \ \frac{3}{2} \ \frac{3}{3} \ = \ 28$$

DISTRIBUTION. In the eastern United States, the snowshoe hare is found in northern Wisconsin, much of Michigan, and New England and New York southwest through most of the Alleghenies. It is now rare in the Great Smoky Mountains. This species is also found through most of Canada, south through most of Minnesota and North Dakota, and in the west to central California, southern Utah, and northern New Mexico.

HABITAT. The snowshoe hare is a forest species, never far from dense woods. It lives in brushy, semi-open tracts surrounded by evergreen forest, dense cedar swamps, or sparsely wooded hillsides that support much brush. These hares often occur in second-growth beech/birch/maple forest in West Virginia, and large numbers occur in young spruce stands. In the Ithaca, New York, region, they occupy areas where seedlings and saplings predominate; in the southern mountains, thickets of laurel and rhododendron are its home.

HABITS. The snowshoe hare appears to make no other home than its form, which it smooths out beneath a low coniferous branch, a tangled mass of brush, or an alder thicket. Occasionally, it utilizes a hollow log, the cavity beneath a rotting stump, or even a woodchuck hole. During the day, this large hare sits quietly in the form, ever alert to danger. If alarmed, it leaps away, covering almost 4 meters (a dozen feet) in a single bound and circling at prodigious speed through its broad home range. If not pursued, it soon comes to rest, the great ears raised and the twitching nose and big eyes alert for a new menace. The snowshoe hare can run up to 52 kph (31 mph), and will swim if necessary.

With the approach of the northern winter, the brown summer coat is shed and replaced by white. This phenomenon, a slow process, covers 70 to 90 days, beginning in October, and ends when all animals are white, generally in December. Not only is the white coat unquestionably of great aid in concealing the animal from its enemies, but its insulative qualities are about 27% better than those of the summer coat. There is also a seasonal weight change in snowshoe hares, from a low in the fall, then increasing about 200 grams to a peak in December (Cary and Keith, 1979). As one might suppose, there are two molts per year (Bittner and Rongstad, 1982); again, 70 to 90 days are required for the vernal reversion to brown, which begins in March and ends by May. Most are brown, with some white lingering, by April.

Their big, furry feet permit these hares to race with complete abandon across the snow, where other animals flounder. They usually run in well-marked trails, in both summer and winter, but especially in snow in winter. They will thump the hind feet, apparently as a means of communication, and a snowshoe hare handled by man or caught by a predator may utter a shrill cry. Clicking, doglike whines, a birdlike sound, and grunting noises have also been reported.

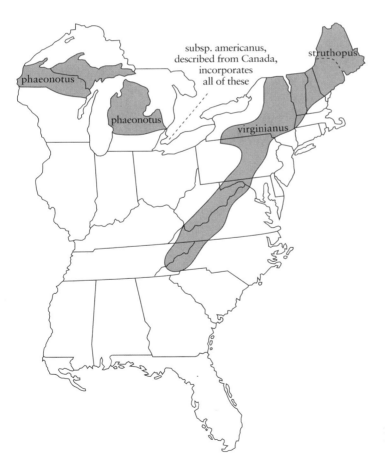

*Distribution of the snowshoe hare,* Lepus americanus, *in the eastern United States*

FOOD AND FEEDING. During the summer, grasses and other green plants are the primary foods of snowshoe hares. Many different plants may be eaten, but some of the favored ones are clovers, brome, bluegrass, vetches, asters, dandelions, strawberry plants, ferns, and horsetails. They may also eat the buds and young leaves of some woody plants, such as hazel, willow, aspen, alder, and birch. The twigs and buds of white and yellow birch, white cedar, sugar maple, quaking aspen, elm, jack pine, and red pine are some of the preferred winter foods, followed by white spruce, black spruce, hemlock, white pine, and beaked hazel (Bookhout, 1965b). Some of the foods eaten in quantity appear to be rather poor nutritionally (Walski and Hautz, 1977).

As successive snows add thickness to the winter blanket, the hares are forced to prune the higher branches, and at times may severely injure the bark and trunk by tearing the cambium with their strong, grooved incisors. Captive individuals in winter required about 300 grams of woody browse, about 3–4 mm in diameter, per day (Pease et al., 1979).

Coprophagy, or reingestion, occurs in this species, as in all lagomorphs. In coprophagy, some of the food passes through the digestive system twice. On its first passage, bacteria act on the food in the large caecum, reducing it to a more easily digestible form and concentrating it, particularly its vitamin B and protein content. The caecum, however, is past the portion of the digestive tract in which most resorption takes place. It is therefore necessary for the animal to reingest the resulting pellets, which are soft and green and mucous-covered, to realize the nutritional benefits of the process. These soft pellets are eaten directly from the anus. Another advantage is that the hares can eat quantities of food rapidly in the field, under threat of predation, then reingest it in the relative safety of their form.

REPRODUCTION AND DEVELOPMENT. Annually, prior to the mating season, the testes descend into the scrotum. Mating occurs from March or April through early August, its initiation dependent on latitude. Several males mate with one female after various precopulatory proceedings consisting typically of males and females ap-

proaching, sniffing, jumping into the air, and urinating on each other. One often races under its partner while the other leaps into the air, and the one overhead often urinates on the one below. Up to four litters are produced per year, the litters varying from one to seven young and the larger litters produced in the north (the average in Michigan was 6.5). First litters are the smallest. Meslow and Keith (1971) found increased numbers of young the year after greater amounts of snowfall, presumably because the deeper snow enabled the animals to stretch higher into the branches, thereby reaching younger and more nutritious branches. In the far north there are greater numbers of young per litter during the increasing stage of the snowshoe's population cycle, and just two during its declining phase. In Maine, all adult females have at least one litter, nearly 90% have at least two, and more than half have three or the maximum four litters per year. Most males become sexually inactive by July, but some are capable of mating through August. The last litters of the year are produced anywhere from July through September.

Unlike cottontails, the snowshoe hare gives birth to precocious young: they are covered with dense, fluffy fur at birth, and their eyes are open. The gestation period is about 37 (34–40) days, and no nest is prepared. The female is receptive again shortly after the birth of the young, and a few females produce litters during the summer of the year when they were born, but most do not until they are a year old. The newborn, which can walk and even hop feebly, weigh 65 to 80 grams. Until weaning they remain close to where they were born, and they will "freeze" at the approach of danger. Their weight doubles by about the ninth day, at which time they are eating green vegetation, and at eight weeks they have reached nearly 900 grams. By about 25 to 28 days, they are fully weaned and leave the nest area, though the last litter of the year may nurse for two months or even longer. The young hares spend their time in separate hiding places during the day, then regroup once a day when the female returns to nurse them for five to ten minutes. The female's form may be 200 to 300 meters (650 to 1000 feet) distant.

POPULATION CHARACTERISTICS. A characteristic of this species in the far north is its cycling of population levels—a marked fluctuation in abundance that peaks about every nine to ten years. Keith (1974) has suggested that the cycles are caused basically by an interaction between snowshoe hares and their food supply: the hares increase beyond the carrying capacity of the habitat, leading to a crash, which in turn leaves them far below the habitat's carrying capacity and able to increase once again. The lynx cycle parallels, but follows, that of the hare. In the eastern United States, where the winters are less severe, the snowshoe hare does not cycle. Home ranges ranged from 2.5 to 26 ha (6.3 to 64 acres) in Michigan, averaging about 9 ha (22 acres). Nursing females have smaller home ranges than males. Although individuals can live much longer, probably four or five years, most lagomorphs meet a violent end, and probably not more than 15% survive to breed during more than one season.

ENEMIES. The snowshoe hare is beset by many enemies. Bobcats, coyotes, dogs, and foxes succeed in capturing large numbers, and the fisher, lynx, goshawk, great horned owl, and other predators also prey on this species. Predators such as goshawks, great horned owls, snowy owls, and even lynx may move south during times when snowshoe hare populations are low.

PARASITES AND DISEASE. Ticks, especially *Haemophysalis leporis-palustris*, are abundant on these hares from April to October, and the hares harbor fleas and mites as well. Snowshoe hares also harbor many trematodes, cestodes, and nematodes (the practice of coprophagy may help concentrate these endoparasites). Tularemia (*Francisella tularensis*) and seven different viruses were found in snowshoe hares in Alberta and elsewhere. Shock disease due to low blood sugar has also been described, and can lead to death. There are two different syndromes of this disease. One consists of convulsions with sudden running movements of the legs, extension of the hind legs, and retraction of the head and neck, the eyes usually fixed. The other syndrome presents a lethargic state. The characters of the two syndromes can occur together.

RELATION TO HUMANS. The snowshoe hare is a favored game animal. Its spirited runs and the fact that it never holes up when pursued permit much sport. Moreover, its flesh is well flavored, and in earlier days in the far north the fleecy hide was stripped and sewn into warm robes. At times, snowshoe hares have caused damage in conifer plantations by nipping off terminal and lateral buds and girdling the bark of the trees.

AREAS FOR FURTHER WORK. A nutritional study of the snowshoe's food and of the soft and hard pellets would be of interest; more information is needed on the cycles of this species and the lynx; and a detailed study of the ectoparasites is in order.

## SUBSPECIES

*Lepus americanus americanus*, which also occurs to the north in Canada, intergrades broadly with the three subspecies currently recognized in the eastern United States. We therefore recognize all as *L. a. americanus*.

*Lepus americanus americanus* Erxleben
  As described above.
  Type locality: Fort Severn, Ontario.
  Other currently recognized eastern subspecies:
    *L. americanus phaeonotus* Allen
    *L. americanus virginianus* Harlan
    *L. americanus struthopus* Bangs

## LITERATURE

Baker, R. H. 1983. *Michigan Mammals*. East Lansing: Michigan State Univ. Press. 642 pp.

Bider, J. R. 1961. An ecological study of the snowshoe hare, *Lepus americanus. Canadian J. Zool.* 39: 81–103.

Bittner, S. L., and O. J. Rongstad. 1982. Snowshoe hare and allies *Lepus americanus* and allies. In: J. A. Chapman and G. A. Feldhamer, eds., *Wild Mammals of North America*, pp. 146–163. Baltimore: Johns Hopkins Univ. Press.

Bookhout, T. A. 1959. Reingestion by the snowshoe hare. *J. Mammal.* 40: 250.

———. 1964. Prenatal development of snowshoe hare. *J. Wildl. Mgmt.* 28: 338–345.

———. 1965a. Breeding biology of snowshoe hares in Michigan's Upper Peninsula. *J. Wildl. Mgmt.* 29: 296–303.

———. 1965b. Feeding coactions between snowshoe

hares and white-tailed deer in northern Michigan. *North Amer. Wildl. Nat. Resources Conf.* 30: 321–335.

————. 1971. Helminth parasites in snowshoe hares from northern Michigan. *J. Wildl. Diseases* 7: 246–248.

Cary, J. R., and L. B. Keith. 1979. Reproductive change in the 10-year cycle of snowshoe hares. *Canadian J. Zool.* 57: 375–390.

Grange, W. B. 1932. The pelages and color changes of the snowshoe hare, *Lepus americanus phaeonotus* Allen. *J. Mammal.* 13: 99–116.

Keith, L. B. 1974. Some features of population dynamics in mammals. *Proc. Int. Congr. Game Biol.* 11: 17–58.

Keith, L. B., and L. A. Windberg. 1978. A demographic analysis of the snowshoe hare cycle. Wildl. Monogr. No. 58. 70 pp.

Meslow, E. C., and L. B. Keith. 1971. A correlation of weather versus snowshoe hare population parameters. *J. Wildl. Mgmt.* 35: 1–15.

Pease, J. L., R. H. Vowles, and L. B. Keith. 1979. Interaction of snowshoe hares and woody vegetation. *J. Wildl. Mgmt.* 43: 43–60.

Walski, T. W., and W. W. Hautz. 1977. Nutritional evaluation of three winter browse species of snowshoe hares. *J. Wildl. Mgmt.* 41: 144–147.

## Black-Tailed Jackrabbit
### *Lepus californicus* Gray  Color plate 7

Because these hares range extensively across the West and occur in the East in only limited introduced population, most of the information presented here derives from accounts of western U.S. populations.

*Black-tailed jackrabbit,* Lepus californicus
*(Troy L. Best)*

DESCRIPTION. The black-tailed jackrabbit is a hare with very long ears and very large hind feet, its summer and winter pelage similarly colored. The back is buffish gray, interspersed with blackish. The ears are brownish, the last 20–30 mm usually black. The tail has a black stripe above, extending onto the rump, and on the tail the stripe is bordered by white. The soles of the feet are densely furred, and the upper lip is divided.

MEASUREMENTS. Ranges of measurements are: total length 465–630, tail 50–112, hind foot 112–145 mm; and weight about 1.8–3.6 kg (4–8 lbs).

Diploid number = 48.

TOOTH FORMULA

$$\frac{2}{1} \quad \frac{0}{0} \quad \frac{3}{2} \quad \frac{3}{3} \;=\; 28$$

DISTRIBUTION. The black-tailed jackrabbit occurs naturally in northern Mexico and the southwestern United States, north to southern Washington and Idaho, northern South Dakota, and east to western Missouri and northwestern Arkansas. It has been introduced in many eastern states, and apparently occurs now in Delaware and Maryland (on the Delmarva Peninsula), southern Florida and the Florida Keys, Massachusetts (Nantucket Island), Virginia (the Cobb Island area), and central New Jersey.

This species was introduced in the Miami region of Florida in the 1930s for the training of greyhounds. Many escaped and took up residence in the pastures and sand prairies west to the Everglades. At first, they became very abundant, but were then nearly exterminated by flooding. They persist, however, and are fairly common locally, especially around Miami International Airport.

These hares were also introduced on Nantucket Island, Massachusetts, from Kansas in 1925, solely for the purpose of sport, and hunted in the manner of English fox hunts. Additional rabbits were introduced on Nantucket in the 1940s.

HABITAT. In the West, this species is found in relatively barren areas, such as prairies, pastures, cultivated fields, and meadows, but also in areas of higher vegetation. On Nantucket it lives in the beach grass and other dune habitats, and in the open fields and adjacent cultivated areas, as well.

HABITS. Black-tailed jackrabbits are primarily nocturnal; they spend the day resting in their forms, but will sometimes lie on their sides in the morning sun. They scratch out the forms themselves, usually at the base of a plant that provides cover, and apparently never use burrows. A rabbit sitting in its form in the shade of a plant is a typical sight in the West. The animal may use a given form once, or during a short period, or over a long period. The young are born in a deeper form, one that is sometimes lined with fur from the female's breast. These hares often make trails through the vegetation.

The black-tailed jackrabbit is usually not gregarious, but aggregations sometimes occur. It is thought that these are due to exceptionally good food and cover conditions in local areas, rather than to any developed social-organizational qualities. Jackrabbits are acutely aware of their surroundings and are easily put on the alert, apparently trusting their ears and nose more than their eyes. At any indication of danger, they immediately raise their ears. While foraging, a jackrabbit will raise its head and survey the environment every 20 to 30 seconds.

Black-tailed jacks are excellent jumpers. They often move at great speed in hops 1.5 to 3 meters (5 to 10 feet) long, but can leap more than 6 meters (20 feet) at a jump, rising 0.6 to 1.7 meters (2 to 5.5 feet) off the ground. Every fourth or fifth jump is exceptionally high, seemingly giving the animal a better view of its surroundings. These hares are also swift runners, attaining speeds of 48 to 56 kph (30 to 35 mph) for short periods. They usually avoid water, but are good swimmers and will take to the water when frightened, occasionally swimming even when

*Distribution of the black-tailed jackrabbit,* Lepus californicus, *in the eastern United States*

*not* pressed. When they emerge, they shake in the manner of dogs.

Most rabbits are generally silent, but can squeal when in distress, and this species is no exception. Other calls are uttered when two are fighting, or to bring the young together.

FOOD AND FEEDING. The food of jackrabbits varies considerably with availability and locality. Principal foods are fresh and herbaceous plants (including crops) in summer, shrubs and dried herbaceous vegetation in winter. In a given area, many plant species are eaten, the feeding undertaken mainly in open areas near weed patches. Feeding is most common in the evening, but may take place at any time, day or night. A mature individual eats about 390 grams of food per day, of which perhaps 45% is assimilated (Johnson and Peek, 1984). At least in the West, this species has even been known to eat subterranean fungi (Maser et al., 1988). *Lepus californicus* is an important disperser of seeds, including those of the prickly pear, *Opuntia* spp. As many lagomorphs do, these jackrabbits eat and swallow their food rapidly, forming green "soft pellets." These pellets are then defecated and eaten in the relative safety of the form, a process called reingestion, or coprophagy. The soft pellets are gleaned directly from the anus, and the rabbit swallows them whole, thereby passing most food through the alimentary canal twice before producing the hard, fibrous fecal pellets seen in the field. Soft pellets from the mother are also eaten by her young— a vehicle, perhaps, by which microbiota are passed from mother to young. An average of 545 hard pellets are produced per day, each one flattened and about 13 mm in diameter. Hard pellets contain about 74% moisture, 14% protein; soft pellets are 80% moisture, 46% protein.

REPRODUCTION AND DEVELOPMENT. Black-tailed jackrabbits are promiscuous, and breeding may occur throughout the year in some localities. Precopulatory activity consists of complicated series of chases, jumps, leapfrogging, and fighting between male and female, the male frequently attempting to mount. Tufts of hairs are sometimes lost, owing perhaps to biting. Copulation, which usually follows a chase, lasts only a few seconds. Jackrabbits, like other lagomorphs, are induced ovulators—ovulation follows mating. (In the absence of fertilization, pseudopregnancy may occur.) Conception can occur immediately following parturition. Some sperm are present in males between five and seven months of age, but successful breedings probably begin at around eight months, when high numbers of sperm are available. Most females probably commence breeding in the year after their birth. Gestation is 41 to 47 days, and a female produces one to four litters per year, one to eight young per litter.

The young of the black-tail are precocious: they have teeth, they are fully furred, and their eyes are open. Nevertheless, they are born in a nest in a form, and the female covers the nest when she leaves. Measurements of the newborn in a litter from Arizona averaged: total length 140, tail 20, hind foot 34, and ear 27 mm; and weight 66 grams. The young do not exhibit well-coordinated hopping until about two to three days of age. The female comes to the nest to nurse them several times each night, and suckling may continue for 12 to 13 weeks, but is supplemented with solid food after ten days. The young are particularly active at night, but remain nearly motionless during the day. They tend to remain grouped at a particular resting site for about a week after nursing ceases.

POPULATION CHARACTERISTICS. These jackrabbits establish home ranges averaging about 10–20 ha (25–50 acres) and ranging from 2 to 140 ha (5 to 345 acres), with considerable overlap. The home ranges of females are larger than those of the males. For reasons not well understood, but probably related to quality of habitat, there are great fluctuations in the population levels of these jackrabbits. The great majority of individuals in the wild die in their first or second year, though they are capable of living four or five years.

ENEMIES. Black-tailed jacks, especially the young, are preyed upon by coyotes, foxes, hawks, owls, and snakes, but humans are probably their chief enemy.

PARASITES AND DISEASE. Jackrabbits have many ectoparasites (lice, fleas, ticks, and mites) and endoparasites (trematodes, cestodes, and nematodes). They also host botfly (*Cuterebra*) larvae. Diseases found in *Lepus californicus* in the West are tularemia, equine encephalitis, brucellosis, Q fever, and Rocky Mountain spotted fever. Ticks are the vectors for tularemia, and infected ticks have been found on *L. californicus*, at least in the West. Rabbits infected with tularemia die very quickly.

RELATION TO HUMANS. Black-tailed jackrabbits are still hunted on Nantucket.

AREAS FOR FURTHER WORK. Information is needed on the status of the introduced jackrabbit populations in the east. Differences in behavior, as related to differences in conditions between east and west, could be very instructive. Detailed studies of the ecto- and endoparasites of this species are also in order.

## SUBSPECIES

We presume the currently accepted name of the black-tailed jackrabbit on Nantucket to be *Lepus californicus melanotis* Mearns, since that is the subspecies from which it originated. But *L. californicus melanotis* appears to form an interbreeding series with *L. californicus californicus* of California through other western subspecies, and we therefore consider the population introduced into Nantucket to be *L. c. californicus*. The origin of the rabbits introduced into Florida is unknown.

*Lepus californicus californicus* Gray

As described above.

Type locality: "St. Antoine," California; probably on coastal slopes of mountains near Mission of San Antonio, Jolon, Monterey Co., California.

Other currently recognized eastern subspecies:
*L. californicus melanotis* Mearns

### LITERATURE

Best, T. L. 1996. *Lepus californicus*. **Mammalian Species No. 530.** Amer. Soc. Mammal. 10 pp.

Chapman, J. A., and J. L. Sandt. 1977. The black-tailed jackrabbit, *Lepus californicus*, in Maryland. *Chesapeake Sci.* 18: 318–319.

Clapp, R. B., J. S. Weske, and T. C. Clapp. 1976. Establishment of the black-tailed jackrabbit on the Virginia eastern shore. *J. Mammal.* 57: 180–181.

Dunn, J. P., J. A. Chapman, and R. E. Marsh. 1982. Jackrabbits *Lepus californicus* and allies. In: J. A. Chapman and G. A. Feldhamer, eds., *Wild Mammals of North America*, pp. 124–145. Baltimore: Johns Hopkins Univ. Press.

Harestad, A. S., and F. L. Bunnell. 1979. Home range and body weight—a reevaluation. *Ecology* 60: 389–402.

Haskell, H. S., and H. G. Reynolds. 1947. Growth, developmental food requirements and breeding activity of the California jackrabbit. *J. Mammal.* 28: 129–136.

Johnson, D. R., and J. M. Peek. 1984. The black-tailed jackrabbit in Idaho: Life history, population dynamics and control. Univ. Idaho College Agric., Coop. Extension Serv. Bull. 637. 16 pp.

Layne, J. N. 1965. Occurrence of black-tailed jackrabbits in Florida. *J. Mammal.* 46: 502.

Lechleitner, R. R. 1957. Reingestion in the black-tailed jackrabbit. *J. Mammal.* 38: 481–485.

———. 1958a. Certain aspects of behavior of the black-tailed jackrabbit. *Amer. Midland Nat.* 60: 145–155.

———. 1958b. Movements, density, and mortality in a black-tailed jackrabbit population. *J. Wildl. Mgmt.* 22: 371–384.

———. 1959a. Sex ratio, age classes and reproduction of the black-tailed jackrabbit. *J. Mammal.* 40: 63–81.

———. 1959b. Some parasites and infectious diseases in a black-tailed jackrabbit population in the Sacramento Valley, California. *Calif. Fish and Game* 45: 83–91.

Maser, C., Z. Maser, and R. Molina. 1988. Small-mammal mycophagy in rangelands of central and southeastern Oregon. *J. Range Mgmt.* 41: 309–312.

## European Hare *Lepus europaeus* Linnaeus

DESCRIPTION. Somewhat similar in appearance to our western (black-tailed) jackrabbits, this large hare may be recognized by its 12-cm (5-inch) ears and its thick mantle of somewhat kinky guard hairs, each with a black band and a buffy tip. Above, it is grizzled yellowish in summer and grayish brown in winter. The flanks, cheeks, and rump are grayish, and the neck and feet are buffy. The ears are brown with black tips. The underparts are mostly white. The rather long tail is blackish above, whitish below.

MEASUREMENTS. Measurements are: total length 600–750, tail 70–100, hind foot 150–170, ear

80–100 mm. The European hare weighs as much as 6.3 kg (14 lbs), but runs usually 2.7–5.4 kg (6–12 lbs).

Diploid number = 48.

TOOTH FORMULA

$$\frac{2}{1}\ \frac{0}{0}\ \frac{3}{2}\ \frac{3}{3}\ =\ 28$$

DISTRIBUTION. A native of Europe, this great hare was introduced into Dutchess County, New York, in 1893. Importations continued through 1911, the purpose being to provide a game species. A gradual buildup of the population resulted in rather widespread but spotty distribution in the Northeast. Nine individuals escaped from captivity near Brantford, Ontario, in 1912, and the animal is now established, if not particularly thriving, in Ontario. From there a few have moved into Michigan (Baker, 1983),

although there is no evidence that the species has become established there. The distribution and abundance of this species are not well understood, but it seems not to have done very well anywhere in North America.

HABITAT. The European hare is a creature of open fields, shunning the forest or heavy brushland.

HABITS. Its great hind legs allow the European hare to run like a dog, even occasionally standing on tiptoe. A speed of 55 kph (35 mph) has been recorded. Like other leporids, this hare is primarily nocturnal. It uses a form during the day, hollowed from vegetation or the ground, and during winter the animal may be completely covered by snow, bursting forth from its form in the manner of other leporids when approached too closely.

*Distribution of the European hare*, Lepus europaeus, *in the eastern United States*

FOOD AND FEEDING. Grass and herbs provide a summer diet, whereas the winter fare consists of twigs and buds and the bark of shrubs and small trees. The damage to orchards is often severe. In 1932, Hamilton inspected an apple orchard at Poughkeepsie, New York, where the hares had stripped the bark from the trunks of young fruit trees, leaving only shredded remains to indicate the destruction wrought by their nocturnal forays.

REPRODUCTION AND DEVELOPMENT. The two or three leverets (as first-year lagomorphs are called) are precocious at birth, covered with long, silky, grizzled fur, and it is well that they have this protective coat, for birth occurs in January or February. Females in northern areas probably produce two litters, chiefly from late winter through early summer. Gestation is about 30 to 40 days, following the typical leporid mating behavior of confronting, chasing, and jumping. Litters consist of one to seven young. The young are placed in different forms by the female, and she moves among them for nursing. The young probably do not breed in their first year.

POPULATION CHARACTERISTICS. This species may attain a population density of up to 15 hares or more per square km (25 per square mile), although 6 per square km is more typical.

ENEMIES. Coyotes, foxes, bobcats, and the larger hawks and owls are the major predators.

RELATION TO HUMANS. The European hare has been known to cause great damage in gardens and orchards in Ontario and New York. Though it may be an interesting addition to the fauna of our eastern states, the peril of an unwise introduction of this sort must also serve to remind us of past disastrous liberations. The European hare does provide fine sport for the hunter, for the hare can quickly outdistance the hounds. Bagging this swift animal is not easy, but the lucky hunter can be assured of a delicious meal.

AREAS FOR FURTHER WORK. Information is needed on the current occurrence, status, and abundance of this species in the eastern United States. Its interrelationships with other lagomorphs, in the areas where it occurs, should be studied. Its ectoparasites, too, are in need of study: how do they compare to those of native species? How do the isolated populations of this species compare genetically with its ancestral populations?

## SUBSPECIES

We know nothing of the subspecies from which our North American populations derive.

*Lepus europaeus* Linnaeus
  As described above.
  Type locality: Burgundy, France.

### LITERATURE

Baker, R. H. 1983. *Michigan Mammals*. East Lansing: Michigan State Univ. Press. 642 pp.

Dean, P. B., and A. de Vos. 1965. The spread and present status of the European hare, *Lepus europaeus hybridus* Desmarest, in North America. *Canadian Field-Nat.* 79: 38–48.

De Vos, A., and P. B. Dean. 1967. The distribution and the use of forms by European hares, *Lepus europaeus hybridus* (Desmarest 1822) in southern Ontario. *Saüg. Mitt.* 15 : 57–61.

Schneider, E. 1990. Hares and rabbits. In: S. B. Parker, ed., Grzimek's *Encyclopedia of Mammals* 4: 254–313. New York: McGraw-Hill.

## White-Tailed Jackrabbit
*Lepus townsendii* Bachman      Color plate 7

DESCRIPTION. The summer pelage of this large hare is pale buffy gray above. The tail is white both above and below, though there is sometimes a narrow, dusky stripe on the dorsal side that does not extend onto the body (the tail of the black-tailed jackrabbit is black above). In *Lepus townsendii*, the ears are buff or buffy gray on the anterior half of the outside, whitish on the posterior half, with a broad black patch extending to the tip. The venter is white or pale grayish.

This is the only jackrabbit that has two annual molts. Individuals are paler in winter than in summer, and those in the northern part of the range turn completely white in winter (most Wisconsin and apparently Illinois individuals

*White-tailed jackrabbit,* Lepus townsendii
*(Rod Planck)*

are pure white in winter). The white-tailed jack-rabbit and snowshoe hare (*L. americanus*) oc-cur in the same area in Wisconsin, and although their habitats differ, in winter pelage they can be confused. The pelage of *L. townsendii* in win-ter is wholly white, that of *L. americanus* tri-colored, the tips white, the median portion tawny, and the bases gray to black.

MEASUREMENTS. Measurements of Wisconsin individuals were: total length 575–650, tail 70–115, hind foot 148–175 mm; and weight 2.6–4.3 kg (5.8–9.5 lbs). The ear exceeds 90 mm in length.
  Diploid number = 48.

TOOTH FORMULA

$$\frac{2}{1} \ \frac{0}{0} \ \frac{3}{2} \ \frac{3}{3} \ = \ 28$$

DISTRIBUTION. In the eastern United States the white-tailed jackrabbit occurs (or occurred) in northwestern Illinois, and once occurred in most of Wisconsin, as well. It may once have been na-tive to Wisconsin, but was probably introduced there in 1908 (Jackson, 1961). It was quite com-mon in some areas of Wisconsin, particularly in Barron, Clark, Eau Claire, Marathon, Portage, Waushara, and Wood counties, but is now ex-tremely scarce and restricted to limited areas, mainly in the western part of the state. It is con-sidered to have extended its range from Wis-consin or Iowa into the sand-prairie area of

northwestern Illinois in the last 80 to 120 years, but may recently have been extirpated in Illinois. Beyond the Mississippi, the species occurs from southern Canada south to northeastern Cali-fornia, southern Utah, and extreme north-central New Mexico.

HABITAT. The white-tailed jackrabbit, a species of the prairie, also inhabits open areas such as plowed fields, stubble, pastures, grasslands, bar-rens, and burnt-over areas.

HABITS. Though the white-tailed jackrabbit is a very large hare, it is seldom seen. It is especially active at dusk and dawn, and can be active at any time during the night, but is seldom abroad during the day unless disturbed. When at rest, jackrabbits sit, often in a form, under a tussock or in a furrow, or simply on the open ground, with their ears folded back. The form is rather simple, consisting sometimes of only a slight de-pression, usually under protective cover, or it may be up to 60 cm long, 30 cm wide, and 15 cm deep, averaging probably 5 cm (2 inches) deep. When at rest in the form, the rabbit is nearly in-visible, its gray-buff color of summer blending into the soil, or the white of winter pelage blend-ing into the snow. Often it may be approached quite closely before it will suddenly spring up and bound away, 3–5 meters (12–16 feet) at a leap (up to a maximum to 7.5 meters, or 25 feet), and at speeds up to but seldom exceeding 58 kph (36 mph). When this jackrabbit is on the alert, it will move its great ears about in various di-rections, sometimes one backward and the other forward, as it listens to the sounds around it. This hare will also enter the water when cor-nered. It swims by paddling with the front feet and using the back feet in a leaping motion. Like other rabbits, it is usually silent, and is pro-tected chiefly by remaining motionless and blending into the environment. But like many other lagomorphs, it has a call: a series of three or four short notes in quick succession, which may be an alarm note. The young produce shrill squeals when distressed.

FOOD AND FEEDING. Summer food consists of various green vegetation, such as clover, grasses, alfalfa, dandelion, sedge, and the green shoots and leaves of many other species of wild and cultivated plants. In winter the rabbit browses on buds and twigs and on such dry vegetation as it may find, such as hay or straw, or the leavings from the previous year's harvest. Like most other rabbits and hares, jackrabbits exhibit coprophagy: they will take soft or green (undigested) pellets directly from the anus by squatting and placing the head between the hind legs.

REPRODUCTION AND DEVELOPMENT. The scrotal sac of jackrabbits is entirely haired and is visible only during the mating season, in mid-April or later, when the testes are scrotal. Apparently, both sexes commence breeding in their second year. Like those of other lagomorphs, mating encounters consist of dashes, jumps, and circling and chasing activities lasting for several minutes, and ending in a brief copulation. Small groups of males chase females during these proceedings. Gestation has been variously reported at 30, 36 to 43, and 42 days. There is no nest to receive the newborn young, which are precocious; the young may be simply dropped on the ground, or in a form used for resting by both sexes. The newborn, weighing about 90 grams, are well furred, their incisors protrude, and their eyes are open. They leave the form shortly after birth, usually within 24 hours, but stay together for a week or more after birth while nursing proceeds. They are soon active, doing some foraging for themselves when just two weeks of age. Weaning takes place at one month; the stomach of a four-week-old from Colorado contained both milk and plant material. At two months, the young are entirely independent. In Wisconsin, there may be two litters per year.

*Distribution of the white-tailed jackrabbit,* Lepus townsendii, *in the eastern United States*

POPULATION CHARACTERISTICS. This species is not colonial, and generally occurs in numbers too small to cause much harm. It is in fact one of the least social of hares, and tends to be solitary, although there may be a clustering of three or four individuals during the mating season, and there are reports of larger aggregations. In Iowa, this species generally occurred at densities of three to nine per square km (7.5 to 22.5 per square mile), with a high of 71 per square km (175 per square mile) (Kline, 1963). More information on the species' home range is needed, but it is larger than that of *L. californicus*, reported in one study to be about 90 ha (220 acres). Most individuals probably die in their first or second year.

ENEMIES. Predators on this species include coyotes, foxes, hawks, and probably many others.

PARASITES AND DISEASE. This species hosts lice, *Haemodipus setoni*, several fleas, probably ticks and mites, several tapeworms and nematodes, and botflies, *Cuterebra*. Like many other lagomorphs, it may contract tularemia.

RELATION TO HUMANS. This species is a fine game animal, both for the sport it provides and for its meat.

AREAS FOR FURTHER WORK. Does this species still occur in the eastern United States? If so, then the questions posed above for the European hare would be of interest here, as well.

## SUBSPECIES

*Lepus townsendii* Bachman
 As described above.
 Type locality: Near Wallula, Walla Walla Co., Washington.

## LITERATURE

Dunn, J. P., J. A. Chapman, and R. E. Marsh. 1982. Jackrabbits *Lepus californicus* and allies. In: J. A. Chapman and G. A. Feldhamer, eds., *Wild Mammals of North America*, pp. 124–145. Baltimore: Johns Hopkins Univ. Press.

Jackson, H. H. T. 1961. *The Mammals of Wisconsin*. Madison: Univ. of Wisconsin Press. 504 pp.

Kline, P. D. 1963. Notes on the biology of the jackrabbit in Iowa. *Proc. Iowa Acad. Sci.* 70: 196–204.

Lim, B. K. 1987. *Lepus townsendii*. **Mammalian Species No. 288.** Amer. Soc. Mammal. 6 pp.

# 7. ORDER RODENTIA

## Rodents, or Gnawing Mammals

RODENTS ARE FOUND the world over, far surpassing all other mammalian orders both in numbers of taxa (about 2021 species in 443 genera) and in actual numbers of individuals. In the eastern United States, there are 38 native species and five introduced species. Among them are terrestrial, fossorial, arboreal, and semiaquatic species, and even two gliders. As a group, they are best characterized by their large, chisel-like incisors, a single pair of them in each jaw, and the absence of canines. There is thus a wide space, the *diastema*, between the incisor teeth and the molariform or cheek teeth.

Some rodents, such as our western ground squirrels, the various introduced rats and mice, and the pocket gophers and field mice, often cause great loss to agriculture, and some are notorious disease carriers. Conversely, rodents are exceedingly important as prey species, the muskrat and beaver have been valuable fur bearers, squirrels have filled many a pot, and squirrels and chipmunks afford us much amiable entertainment.

Traditionally, North American rodents have been placed in three main suborders: the Sciuromorpha, or squirrel-like rodents; the Myomorpha, or mouse- and rat-like rodents; and the Hystricomorpha, or porcupines, capybaras, and allies. More recently, however, there has been considerable change in our thinking regarding the higher classification of rodents, and the tendency now is to recognize greater complexity among them, even as the three suborders have become two: the Hystricognathi and Sciurognathi.

The skull of the Hystricognathi incorporates a greatly enlarged infraorbital canal through which much of the masseter (jaw) muscle passes, but this muscle does not extend forward onto the rostrum (the preorbital part of the skull). The molariform teeth number four above and four below, and the postorbital process, prominent in squirrels, is absent in most hystricomorphs. Hystricomorphs also have long gestation periods and small numbers of young. Two families are represented in the United States, one by the native American porcupine (Erethizontidae), the other by the introduced nutria, or coypu (Myocastoridae).

The other suborder, the Sciurognathi, now subsumes several infraorders, three of which are represented in the eastern United States: the Sciuromorpha (squirrels and allies, family Sciuridae), the Myomorpha (three families: mice and rats, jumping mice, and pocket gophers), and the Castorimorpha (beavers, family Castoridae). The Sciuromorpha have a small infraorbital canal (not enclosing muscle tissue), a well-developed postorbital process, and four or five upper and lower molariform teeth. The Myomorpha have a small to large infraorbital canal through which part of the main jaw muscle passes before inserting on the side of the rostrum, and there is no postorbital process. The myomorph rodents of the eastern United States, as now classified, include the mice and rats proper (family Muridae), the jumping mice (Dipodidae), and the pocket gophers (Geomyidae). The murids have three molariform teeth above and below; the zapodines have a large, oval infraorbital foramen, three molariform teeth below, and three or four above; and the geomyids and castorids have a small infraorbital foramen and four molariforms above and below.

## SQUIRRELS AND WOODCHUCKS, Family Sciuridae

Squirrels are conspicuous residents in much of the world, except for Australia, southern South America, Malagasy (Madagascar), and many other islands. There are about 273 species of squirrels and their allies, 66 of them in North America north of Mexico, and 11 in the area covered by this book. Sciurids generally have large eyes and long, bushy tails. They often sit on their haunches and feed using their front feet. The thumb is reduced on the front foot, and there are five toes on the hind foot. Like our own, the cheek teeth are rooted in the jaws and have cusps. There are four molariform teeth in each half of the lower jaw and four or five in each half of the upper jaw. Squirrels are of various sizes, and they differ so substantially in habits and habitats as to be separated in both time and space, which reduces competition among them for food and habitat. Most sciurids are diurnal, the flying squirrels being a notable exception. Some are primarily arboreal (*Sciurus* and *Tamiasciurus*), some are burrowers (the ground squirrels, *Spermophilus*, and the woodchuck, *Marmota*), and some, such as the chipmunks (*Tamias*), are both. There is a general increase in tail bushiness with increased proportions of time spent in trees, probably to aid in balance and to help act as a parachute in case of a fall.

Squirrels have a great awareness of their environment. Their feeding strategy is one of moving about, sampling various items, and in the process locating the best of a variety of foods as they become available. Some species (chipmunks, ground squirrels, woodchucks) hibernate; the others are active all year. Whereas the chipmunks wake periodically and eat bits of the food they have stored, the other hibernating squirrels use stored fat for maintenance energy during hibernation. Most squirrels are primarily vegetarian, but some (ground and flying squirrels) are highly insectivorous, and some will take eggs, young birds, or other young vertebrates when the situation presents itself. Eastern squirrels range in size from the least chipmunk, averaging about 55 grams, to the woodchuck, which weighs up to 6 kg (13 lbs). The family name is taken from the generic name *Sciurus* (*sci* = shade; *urus* = tail), from the habit of tree squirrels of positioning the broad tail over the back like an umbrella when at rest.

3. Back lacking stripes or barring, usually of one
   color; tail proportionally longer and bushier
   (tree squirrels) ........................... 5
4. Dorsum with two or four pale stripes, but
   no spotting; infraorbital opening a foramen
   through a thin plate ................. *Tamias*
4. Dorsum with 13 alternating dark and light
   stripes and some spotting, *or* animal uniformly
   gray with an obscure spotting pattern; infraorbital opening a canal ..... *Spermophilus* (p. 214)
5. Animal large, more than 400 mm (15 inches)
   in total length; pelage orangish or gray
   above ...................... *Sciurus* (p. 222)
5. Animal smaller, less than 400 mm long;
   pelage reddish above ....... *Tamiasciurus* (p. 237)

## Chipmunks of the Genus *Tamias*

Originally, the chipmunks were placed in two
genera, the eastern chipmunks, *Tamias* (one species), and the western chipmunks, *Eutamias*
(several species, one of which occurs in our
area), but there is increasing evidence that the
two are best considered one genus (see Levenson et al., 1985). The name "chipmunk" is of
native American origin and probably relates to
their chipping call.

### Literature Cited

Levenson, H., R. S. Hoffman, C. F. Nadler, L. Deutsch,
and S. D. Freeman. 1985. Systematics of the Holarctic chipmunks. *J. Mammal.* 66: 219–242.

### Key to the Chipmunks of the Genus *Tamias*

1. Dorsum bearing four pale stripes; cheek
   teeth five in upper jaw, the first reduced
   in size......................... *T. minimus*
1. Dorsum bearing two pale stripes; cheek teeth
   four in upper jaw, none reduced in size .. *T. striatus*

## Least Chipmunk *Tamias minimus*
(Bachman)                          Color plate 7
DESCRIPTION. On the back of this small, long-
tailed chipmunk are five black stripes, the middle
one reaching from crown to base of tail, and four
pale stripes between the black ones, the outer-
most of these whitish. There is also a whitish
stripe above the eye, another below the eye; the
sides of the body are orange-brown or tawny;
the shoulders are often bright rufous; the belly
is grayish white; and the tail is pale brown, the

hairs near their tips marked with black. This
little chipmunk differs from *Tamias striatus* in

*Least chipmunk,* Tamias minimus *(Roger W. Barbour)*

its much smaller size, the narrower and closer
black stripes of the back, and the relatively
longer tail, which is usually held upright. The
first upper cheek tooth is reduced in this species, not in the eastern chipmunk.

MEASUREMENTS. Fifteen adults from northern
Wisconsin averaged: total length 202 (183–
223), tail 87 (81–95), hind foot 31 (28–33) mm;
and weight 40–70 grams.
Diploid number = 38.

TOOTH FORMULA

$$\frac{1}{1} \quad \frac{0}{0} \quad \frac{2}{1} \quad \frac{3}{3} \;=\; 22$$

DISTRIBUTION. In the eastern United States,
the least chipmunk occurs in north and south-
central Wisconsin and in the Upper Peninsula of
Michigan, but beyond, it ranges widely across
much of southern Canada and the western
United States.

HABITAT. The least chipmunk is widely distributed within its range, appearing to shun only
the thick evergreen forests, and even in such situations a few may occur. It is not as partial to
woodland as its larger cousin, *Tamias striatus*,
but may be found along the borders of the forest and the shorelines of lakes. Forbes (1966)
found this species most often in exposed, dry
habitats. It was often in clearings associated with
disturbed areas, such as rock piles, gravel pits,
and lumber yards, surrounded by raspberry

thickets, pines, and aspens. It also lives along rocky cliffs, open stands of jack pines, and river bluffs. Like the eastern chipmunk, *T. striatus*, it will occupy log and brush piles and stone walls. In hardwoods, the two species sometimes occur together, apparently in harmony.

HABITS. The least chipmunk is a fearless creature, visiting camp sites and work sites and making a fascinating nuisance of itself. It will sometimes feed from one's hand upon an hour's acquaintance. Like *Tamias striatus*, it is entirely diurnal.

*Tamias minimus* is an expert climber, often ascending trees or bushes to sun itself during the cool of the early morning, or it may construct a nest in a suitable stub or crotch, after the fashion of the true tree squirrels.

When disturbed, the least chipmunk is noisier and more active than the eastern chipmunk. Its most common call is a series of chip notes, but like its larger cousin it has a repertoire of calls. Reilly (1970) described a "qwip" often heard in late afternoon in spring and fall, a high-pitched "chit-chit" danger signal, and a lower "kek-kek" used as communication between individuals.

*Tamias minimus* is active from about April through much of October. It hibernates, and like the eastern chipmunk it wakes at intervals to eat from its cache, but the early snows and the ice-locked ponds may still find it about, weeks after its larger cousin has gone into winter dormancy. Even in northern Michigan and the Lake Superior region, its tracks may be seen on the winter snows, and mild spells during December and January may bring it out.

Least chipmunks may burrow into the ground or a bank, or they may use a nest in some protected place. The least chipmunk's burrow is built with the help of a "work entrance," which

*Distribution of the least chipmunk,* Tamias minimus, *in the eastern United States*

is later plugged; the burrow entrance later put to use is hidden, with no trace of dirt. Nests, which are of leaves, may be constructed in the burrow or in some safe retreat, such as among the roots of a tree, or perhaps in shredded bark among the evergreen foliage of a pine or spruce. Summer dens may be in hollow logs, stumps, rock or debris piles, or piles of brush. There are records of exposed leaf nests on branches, similar to those of fox squirrels, and the least chipmunk has been recorded rearing its young in an outside nest some distance above ground.

FOOD AND FEEDING. Food consists of a great variety of items, including seeds, nuts (especially hazelnuts), fruits, berries, grasses and green leaves, fungi, snails, insects, and quite probably small birds and mammals when opportunity arises. Great stores of food are cached from midsummer well into the fall, the busy creature filling its cheek pouches trip after trip. Banfield (1974) reported about 3700 blueberry seeds, 86 smartweed seeds, and 800 timothy seeds from the cheek pouches of just three individuals. A cache contained 487 acorns and 2734 cherry pits. Forbes (1966) most often found ants and other insects in stomachs.

REPRODUCTION AND DEVELOPMENT. Least chipmunks do not breed in the year of their birth. Mating behavior, initiated almost immediately upon emerging from hibernation, involves numerous chases and vocalizations between a female and several males. Litters, numbering two to seven young (usually five or six), are born from May through August, after a 31-day gestation period, but one litter per year is the norm (later litters are usually from females who have lost earlier litters). Newborn young weigh about 2–3 grams and are about 50 mm (2 inches) long. The eyes are open at 28 days, and the animal is fully furred by 40 days. The young leave the female at about two months, when they are two-thirds grown, and do not breed until their second year.

POPULATION CHARACTERISTICS. Least chipmunks occur at numbers up to about 36 per ha (15 per acre) in good habitat, but there are reports of up to 178 per ha (72 per acre). Home ranges are 0.2–1.7 ha (0.5–4.3 acres). Their lifespan is short, few individuals surviving to breed in a second year.

ENEMIES. There are few specific data, but the most likely predators are hawks, weasels, mink, foxes, and domestic dogs and cats.

PARASITES AND DISEASE. Fleas, ticks, mites, lice, and a nematode are known to parasitize this species.

RELATION TO HUMANS. Few mammals are so confiding as the least chipmunk, and its large numbers and the ease with which it can be observed give us reason to wonder why so little concerning its habits has been recorded.

AREAS FOR FURTHER WORK. Much work could be done on the reproductive and feeding behavior of these easily observed creatures and their relations with one another and with other species. Much more work could be done on its parasites, and its invertebrate nest fauna could be studied.

## SUBSPECIES

As in a number of other cases, the taxonomy of this species needs to be examined more closely, but we have no evidence of primary isolating mechanisms separating the subspecies described from the eastern United States, *Tamias minimus neglectus*, from other subspecies to the west. We therefore do not separate it from the nominate subspecies.

*Tamias minimus minimus* (Bachman)
  As described above.
  Type locality: Green River, near mouth of Big Sandy Creek, Sweetwater Co., Wyoming.
  Other current recognized eastern subspecies:
    *T. minimus neglectus* (J. A. Allen)

## LITERATURE

Baker, Rollin H. 1983. *Michigan Mammals*. East Lansing: Michigan State Univ. Press. 642 pp.
Banfield, A. W. F. 1974. *The Mammals of Canada*. Toronto: Univ. Toronto Press. 438 pp.

Criddle, S. 1943. The little northern chipmunk in southern Manitoba. *Canadian Field-Nat.* 57: 81–86.

Forbes, R. B. 1966. Studies of the biology of Minnesotan chipmunks. *Amer. Midland Nat.* 76: 290–308.

Reilly, R. E. 1970. Factors influencing habitat selection by the least chipmunk in upper Michigan. Unpubl. PhD. diss., Michigan State University. 108 pp.

Sheppard, D. H. 1969. A comparison of reproduction in two chipmunk species (*Eutamias*). *Canadian J. Zool.* 47: 603–608.

## Eastern Chipmunk *Tamias striatus* (Linnaeus) Color plate 7

DESCRIPTION. The eastern chipmunk is a small squirrel with prominent, rounded ears, a flattened, well-haired tail, and well-developed internal cheek pouches. Along its back are five

*Eastern chipmunk,* Tamias striatus *(Roger W. Barbour)*

black longitudinal stripes and two light ones. One of the black stripes is mid-dorsal; the others border the white or buffy stripes. The general color above is dark. The head is dark yellow-brown, with white facial stripes and clay-colored cheeks. The broader dorsal stripes are gray, the individual hairs barred with brown, and the black mid-dorsal stripe fades into the rump, which is rusty or brown. The sides of the body are rusty and the tail is blackish, peppered with gray above and rusty below. The feet are buffy and the belly is white, often suffused with buff. The darkest individuals occur in Kentucky and Tennessee and in the Carolina mountains. The smallest and palest individuals are found in the Northeast. Both albino and melanistic individuals have been seen. Snyder (Mammalian

Species, 1982) and Wishner (1982) summarized information on this species.

MEASUREMENTS. Eastern chipmunks from Indiana averaged: total length 242 (183–275), tail 86 (68–111), hind foot 34 (28–44) mm; and weight 111 (90–149) grams.

Diploid number = 38.

TOOTH FORMULA

$$\frac{1}{1} \quad \frac{0}{0} \quad \frac{1}{1} \quad \frac{3}{3} \ = \ 20$$

DISTRIBUTION. The eastern chipmunk occurs over most of the eastern United States from Wisconsin and Maine south to Louisiana, Alabama, northern Georgia, the panhandle of Florida, the western reaches of the Carolinas, and Virginia. The species varies in coloration considerably throughout its range, but individuals from any one locality usually show remarkably little variation. The eastern chipmunk occurs north into southern Canada and west essentially to the middle of the United States.

HABITAT. The half-cleared forest and the farm dooryard are equally attractive to the eastern chipmunk. Its favored habitat can perhaps best be characterized as the edges of oak/hickory or beech/maple forest, but it is at home in a variety of habitats. It frequents open deciduous woods, stone walls, half-rotted logs, and the thick underbrush that covers such places, but in contrast to such well-protected habitats, a number of these chipmunks at Terre Haute, Indiana, live on the mowed lawn of a cemetery in association with thirteen-lined ground squirrels.

HABITS. These chipmunks are small, solitary, diurnal squirrels that live primarily on the ground and store food. Burrow openings measuring about 40–60 mm (1.75–2.5 inches) in diameter are abundant along woodland banks, but because the dirt is carried off and scattered, there is no evidence of excavated earth. Unlike other hibernators, which burn stored fat for energy, the chipmunk eats bits of its stored food during frequent wakenings from hibernation.

Wherever chipmunks are at all abundant, their animated mellow "chuck" (a downward sweep from 3 to 1 kHz; Wishner, 1982) can be heard in fall in every woodlot, well into October in the northern part of their range. The call is likely to be taken up by several others, until the woods resound with their lively chatter. If a predator should approach one, it flees to its burrow or stone or brush pile with a startled whistle. Males whistle during mating chases, as well. Other important calls are a high "chip," a trill or series of closely spaced chips, and a low-pitched, repeated "cuk." The chip, a downward sweep from 10 to 3 kHz, may be uttered up to 130 times per minute, over as much as ten minutes (Wishner, 1982). The repetition rate of the calls apparently depends on the state of excitement of the animal. Calls are probably used as alarm signals and to indicate one's territory.

The chipmunk is an expert climber and often may be seen in small trees, or even climbing high up the sides of large trees. It shows a certain wariness when on slender limbs, however, and never exhibits the carefree, acrobatic behavior of the tree squirrels. Bowers (1995) found that distance to burrow was the most important factor governing where chipmunks spend their time—more important than such other ecological factors as microhabitat—probably because chipmunks need to be able to return to their burrow quickly and to defend their caches.

Chipmunks use two types of burrows, single-chambered hollows with one or two tunnels (see Allen, 1938) and extensive systems with many tunnels, chambers, and entrances. The single-chambered burrows may be only temporary retreats, or are perhaps produced by young animals to get them through their first year. Adult males, too, may live in simple burrows. The extensive burrow systems have up to five entrances, and one studied by Wishner had 30 entrances, although not more than about five were in use at any one time. Burrow systems may have up to 30 meters (100 feet) of tunnels,

*Distribution of the eastern chipmunk,* Tamias striatus, *in the eastern United States*

a nesting chamber up to about 60 by 40 by 25 cm (24 by 15 by 10 inches), and up to three storage chambers of about 25 by 40 by 15 cm (10 by 15 by 6 inches), as well as some smaller rooms and side pockets (Wishner, 1982). The burrows descend abruptly for several centimeters, then level off, extending beyond as far as 10 meters (30 feet), less than a meter below ground surface. Burrows are deeper in the north, about 60 to 74 cm (24 to 30 inches) in Wisconsin, and shallower in the south, 12 to 45 cm (5 to 18 inches) in Louisiana; and burrows are more abundant in areas with less ground cover (Thomas, 1974). Somewhere within the burrow, there is a large, bulky nest of leaves, where chipmunks not only sleep but bear their young. Fresh nests contain whole leaves (Thomas, 1974), but in nesting chambers there are often only parts of leaves or chewed leaves on the floor, owing perhaps partly to long use. (Sometimes, not all the stored food is eaten.)

There is a time in July and early August when chipmunks are relatively inactive, but in late summer and fall they become quite busy gathering stores of nuts and seeds for winter. In fall, they scamper up and down oaks gathering acorns, many of which can be heard falling to the ground. Nuts, acorns, and various kinds of seeds are carried to the storage chambers with great speed and stored in great quantity. Wishner (1982), for example, watched a chipmunk carry white oak acorns, six at a time, to its burrow. The round trip of about 60 meters (200 feet) required two minutes, and she carried three in one pouch, two in the other, and one in her mouth. At these rates, she was moving about 116 acorns per hour. Up to half a bushel of food may be stored in these storage chambers, but the amounts are usually much less. An extensive burrow system excavated by Thomas (1974) had two storage chambers; in one were 308 acorns and one hickory nut, the lot weighing 346 grams; in the other, 82 acorns and one hickory nut, totaling 227 grams.

Finally, a time approaches when the woods are silent, and the chipmunks are in various degrees of torpor in their underground retreats. But if December or January produces a mild spell, the snowy woods will display countless tracks of awakened animals. Actually, most animals will remain in the burrow for relatively long periods; only a few stay below for short, sporadic periods.

Since chipmunks wake periodically and eat, the question whether or not they are true hibernators had been in some doubt, but surgical implantation of temperature-sensitive radiotransmitters has now allowed biologists to confirm that they are. Respiration rates when active are greater than 60 breaths per minute, whereas in the torpid state they fall to less than 20. More significantly, body temperature ranges from 35 to 41°C (96 to 106°F) in the active state, 5 to 7°C (42 to 45°F) in the torpid state. Laboratory studies undertaken to determine what instigates hibernation have often been inconclusive, perhaps partly because the animals may not have been properly prepared for hibernation. We believe the proper initial questions are: what initiates preparation for hibernation, and what constitutes proper preparation? If we can answer these questions, then answering questions about hibernation itself should become easier. David E. Davis, in laboratory studies on woodchucks, found that food deprivation and temperature are influential in hibernation. At 6°C (44°F), woodchucks entered hibernation when deprived of food, whether fat or thin, but those being fed did not enter hibernation at that temperature. Moreover, woodchucks in the field might "deprive" themselves by remaining in the burrow. How much these data apply to chipmunks is debatable, since these were laboratory studies, on a different species. Since chipmunks wake to feed, it may be the presence of adequate food, rather than deprivation, that stimulates hibernation.

FOOD AND FEEDING. Over 60% of the volume of food from 59 chipmunks in Indiana was of mast (unidentified nut material). The rest, by volume, was chiefly various insects, 13%; fruits (*Rubus*), 8.3%; seeds, 6.4%; and vertebrates, 4.3%. Spores of the subterranean fungus *Endogone* were found, and other fungi are eaten. In spring, shadberry (*Amelanchier*) is often eaten, and in summer a chipmunk's face may be stained red from blackberries and raspberries. In a summer of high cicada emergence, chipmunks may feed heavily on them. In the fall the chipmunk busily stores food for winter, and its cheek pouches may be crammed with a dozen or more beechnuts or half a dozen acorns. Often one can hear chipmunks gnawing hickory nuts or acorns. Pyare et al. (1993) found that white oak acorns were selected over red, perhaps because they are smaller and contain less tannin. Chipmunks will drink water if it is available, but if not, they can apparently survive on dew, rainwater, and moisture from food.

REPRODUCTION AND DEVELOPMENT. By late February or March the testes have become scrotal and the females are in breeding condition. The animals are above ground on pleasant days and the males have found their prospective mates by exploring their territories and sometimes entering their burrows. At breeding time, males congregate on the territory of a female in heat. Males in this mode flick the tail up and down in the manner of an agitated gray squirrel, a behavior observed only when the male is ready to mate. Females not yet ready to mate are exceedingly antisocial and will chase and even attack a male. Mating itself is often preceded by chases, which can become quite frenzied if several males are present. Various vocalizations—growls, squeals, and chatters—are common during these chases. The female often eludes the males during the chase, and they will climb to high lookout perches to find her. The dominant male generally copulates with the female when not more than two or three other males are present; but when several males are present, the dominant one often spends so much time chasing other males away that he fails to mate. In the meantime, the female will have mated several times with one or more males, all within a matter of hours. Morphologically, females appear ready to breed for three to ten days, but they are actually receptive for only about 6.5 hours (Elliot, 1978).

Most spring matings occur between late February and early April. After a gestation of 31 to 32 days, the three to five young are born, each weighing in at 2.5 to 5 grams. The body at birth is 66 mm long, the tail 12 mm, and the hind foot 7.5 mm. At a week, the hair and stripes show. At one month, the young are 140 mm long, they weigh about 30 grams, and their eyes are open. At this point, they are fully weaned, look like small adults, and begin to venture from the nest.

Adult size and dentition are reached in three months.

Some females produce young in late July or August. Many of these mothers are probably the previous year's young that failed to breed in spring, but a number of chipmunks breed in both spring and summer, which is unusual in hibernators. Spring litters are usually more successful than fall, and there is no evidence of a second reproductive period in the north. Chipmunks do not breed in the year of their birth.

POPULATION CHARACTERISTICS. The basic chipmunk social unit is one adult per burrow system, other than when young share a system with a female. These chipmunks number up to about 38 per hectare, with great variation from year to year. The home range varies from about 100 square meters (1075 square feet) to a hectare (2.5 acres), and dispersing individuals travel up to about 875 meters (2870 feet) to set up camp. The home ranges are broadly overlapping, but chipmunks will defend small territories surrounding their burrows, and they will occupy their home ranges for long periods, perhaps for life. The average life span is over a year, and few live more than two or three years, but chipmunks are capable of living for several years, and there are records of up to 13 years under natural conditions (Wishner, 1982).

ENEMIES. Large snakes, hawks, foxes, bobcats, and house cats are all foes of the chipmunk, but the weasel is perhaps its most important enemy, its slim body enabling it to pursue a chipmunk into the innermost recesses of its burrow.

PARASITES AND DISEASE. Chipmunks harbor a variety of parasites, including protozoans, tapeworms, nematodes, trematodes, and spiny-headed worms among the internal parasites, as well as the large subcutaneous larvae of botflies, *Cuterebra emasculator*. External parasites include ticks, mites, chigger mites, fleas, and two host-specific lice, *Hoplopleura erratica* and *Enderleinellus tamiasis*. Many chipmunks are observed with damaged tails, either with the end gone completely or with the skin missing from the end. We think this damage is caused by large numbers of hypopial mites, *Aplodontopus sciuricola*, which live in the hair follicles of the tail; the skin of the chipmunk tail is naturally fragile, perhaps as an antipredator device, which makes it more vulnerable to the depredations of parasites.

RELATION TO HUMANS. Chipmunks occasionally dig holes in a yard or pilfer items from a garden. In the main, however, they are of little economic significance to humans. More to the point, their lively manner and interesting behavior add much to our enjoyment of the outdoors.

AREAS FOR FURTHER WORK. Behavior, the storage of food and the finding of the stored food, the composition of the nest fauna, and the dynamics of hibernation (preparation, causation, process, and arousal) all would provide good topics for further study. Close study of the epidermis of various acorns, nuts, cherry pits, etc., should allow us to separate the various nut materials we must now class indiscriminately as "mast" in food studies. Tail-follicle mites could be studied to see how they relate to damaged tails.

## SUBSPECIES

We are unaware of primary isolating mechanisms separating any of the subspecies described from the east, and thus recognize none of them.

*Tamias striatus striatus* (Linnaeus)

As described above.

Type locality: Upper Savannah River, South Carolina.

Other currently recognized eastern subspecies:

*T. striatus doorsiensis* C. A. Long
*T. striatus fisheri* A. H. Howell
*T. striatus griseus* Mearns
*T. striatus lysteri* (Richardson)
*T. striatus ohionensis* Bole & Moulthrop
*T. striatus peninsulae* Hooper
*T. striatus pipilans* Lowery
*T. striatus rufescens* Bole & Moulthrop

### LITERATURE

Allen, E. G. 1938. The habits and life history of the eastern chipmunk, *Tamias striatus lysteri*. *Bull. N.Y. State Mus.* 314: 1–122.

Bowers, M. A. 1995. Use of space and habitats by the eastern chipmunk, *Tamias striatus*. *J. Mammal.* 76: 12–21.

Elliot, L. 1978. Social behavior and foraging ecology of the eastern chipmunk (*Tamias striatus*) in the Adirondack Mountains. *Smithsonian Contr. Zool.* 265: 1–107.

Forbes, R. B. 1966. Studies of the biology of Minnesotan chipmunks. *Amer. Midland Nat.* 76: 290–308.

Levenson, H., R. S. Hoffman, C. F. Nadler, L. Deutsch, and S. D. Freeman. 1985. Systematics of the Holarctic chipmunks (*Tamias*). *J. Mammal.* 66: 219–242.

Pyare, S., J. A. Kent, D. I. Noxon, and M. T. Murphy. 1993. Acorn preference and habitat use in eastern chipmunks. *Amer. Midl. Nat.* 130: 173–183.

Snyder, D. P. 1982. *Tamias striatus*. **Mammalian Species No. 168.** Amer. Soc. Mammal. 8 pp.

Thomas, K. R. 1974. Burrow systems of the eastern chipmunk (*Tamias striatus pipilans* Lowery) in Louisiana. *J. Mammal.* 55: 454–459.

Tryon, C. A., and D. P. Snyder. 1973. Biology of the eastern chipmunk, *Tamias striatus*: life tables, age distributions, and trends in population numbers. *J. Mammal.* 54: 145–168.

Wishner, L. 1982. *Eastern Chipmunks: Secrets of Their Solitary Lives*. Washington: Smithsonian Institution Press. 144 pp.

Yahner, R. H. 1978. Burrow system and home range use by eastern chipmunks, *Tamias striatus*: Ecological and behavioral considerations. *J. Mammal.* 59: 324–329.

Yerger, R. W. 1955. Life history notes on the eastern chipmunk, *Tamias striatus lysteri* (Richardson), in central New York. *Amer. Midland Nat.* 53: 312–323.

## Woodchuck, Groundhog

*Marmota monax* (**Linnaeus**)     Color plate 8

DESCRIPTION. The woodchuck, our lone representative of a genus of circumpolar distribution, is the largest of the eastern squirrels. The origin of the name is not known, but it may have derived from a native American name for the animal, such as "wejack," "otchig," or "otcheck" (Lowery, 1974). The woodchuck may be any of various shades of brown, often grizzled, and has a relatively short but well-furred tail. The incisors are white, and the ears are short and rounded. The underparts are lighter, ochraceous buff to buffy white. The underfur is blackish brown at the base, tipped with grayish or buffy. The guard hairs are broadly tipped with buffy white. The lips, chin, and sides of the face are buffy, and the feet and legs are blackish brown

*Woodchuck,* Marmota monax *(Mark Romesser)*

to nearly black. The tail is colored as the legs, but the hairs on the tail are tipped with buffy white. In New York, two rather distinct color phases occur: one is light, the hairs of the dorsum broadly tipped with light buff; the other is dark, the long hairs tipped with chestnut-brown and the pectoral hairs more or less orangish. Melanism is common in this species, and albino specimens occur. The species is smallest in the north.

MEASUREMENTS. Average measurements of 64 males from Indiana were: total length 599 (475–673), tail 139 (117–172), hind foot 90 (77–100) mm; and weight 3.5 (2.2–5.3) kg (4.8–11.7 lbs). For 74 females they were 595 (440–700), 134 (107–182), 82 (75–95) mm; and 3.5 (2.0–5.9) kg (4.4–13 lbs). Five adults from Maine averaged: total length 505, tail 118, hind foot 75.5 mm. Measurements of eight individuals from Virginia averaged: total length 590, tail 142, hind foot 86 mm. Average measurements of 198 New York adults were: total length 555, tail 125, hind foot 76 mm; and

weight 2.7–5.4 kg (6–10 lbs), an occasional individual weighing up to 6.3 kg (14 lbs).

Diploid number = 38.

TOOTH FORMULA

$$\frac{1}{1} \quad \frac{0}{0} \quad \frac{2}{1} \quad \frac{3}{3} \; = \; 22$$

DISTRIBUTION. The woodchuck occurs in the eastern United States from Wisconsin and Maine south to northeastern Mississippi, central Alabama, northern Georgia, and northern North Carolina. Beyond its eastern U.S. range, the species occurs across southern Canada and into east-central Alaska, and in the United States west of the Mississippi to a line from eastern North Dakota to eastern Oklahoma.

HABITAT. The woodchuck inhabits areas with dry soil in rolling or flat country, but is especially abundant on stream banks or other raised areas. It often occurs along hedgerows or rights-of-way, or on dams or levees. It does not altogether shun its namesake habitat: the woodchuck, usually a solitary individual, may occasionally be found in rather dense stands of timber; it may even be abundant in the forested areas and wooded groves of the prairie states. Swihart (1991) found, in Connecticut, an increase in biomass of grass (orchard grass, *Dactylus glomerata*) and a decrease of biomass of forb (alfalfa, *Medicago sativa*) with decreasing distance from woodchuck burrows.

HABITS. When the country was first settled, the woodchuck was evidently scarce, but with the cutting of the forests, and the resultant appearance of meadows, open fields, and arable lands, its numbers increased greatly, until today the woodchuck is a familiar sight along many highways of the eastern United States. Woodchucks are both solitary and aggressive, in contrast with other species of *Marmota*, many of which are quite social.

Woodchucks are most active early in the morning and late in the afternoon, but they may be about at all hours, and if much hunted they sometimes feed at night. Feeding bouts last up to about two hours. Activity is erratic after emergence from hibernation, but later in the spring and in the summer, much sunning is done in the middle of the day, and the foraging is pursued in the morning and evening, especially as the days become warmer.

The woodchuck is an accomplished climber, and may ascend a sizable tree to survey its domain, or to take refuge when closely pursued by an enemy. It can also swim well. Again, woodchucks are more or less solitary, and usually only one adult occupies a burrow, but a male and female may occupy a burrow for a short time during the mating period, and several will live peaceably together in a small meadow. Much time is spent sleeping in the burrow. Woodchucks do exhibit an occasional nose-to-nose "greeting," mostly between young or between mother and young, but adults usually avoid each other, and

thus do not often get close enough for greetings. Raising of the tail appears to be a warning.

Woodchucks live in extensive burrow systems, the main entrance of which is often beneath a stone wall or tree stump. Summer dens are often in open areas with one to five entrances, and there are usually paths leading from the entrances to the foraging areas. There is usually a turnaround chamber below the main entrance, but otherwise there are all manner of variations in the size and number of entrances, rooms, and burrows. Some burrows, especially older ones, can be quite complex, and burrows are often plugged, concealing the entrance. A woodchuck burrow can be distinguished from those of other animals (foxes, skunks, badgers) by the mound of earth at the main entrance, which is always fresh, since the animal cleans out the burrow several times a week. A burrow sometimes de-

*Distribution of the woodchuck,* Marmota monax, *in the eastern United States*

scends to a depth of 1.5 meters (4.5 feet) and extends laterally up to 15 meters (50 feet). One or more of the tunnels terminate in a blind alley, where a nest of shredded leaves or grass about 38 cm (15 inches) in diameter is situated. The nest chamber is usually above the lowest point in the system, as modest protection against flooding. The nest cavity itself may be as much as 1.5 meters (4.5 feet) below the surface. There is normally at least one hidden plunge hole. A plunge hole, which goes straight down and acts as an escape hatch, is dug from inside in such a way that there is no telltale mound of earth to reveal it. The tunnel from the main entrance descends at an angle. Summer and winter dens differ, although in some cases the same den is used in summer and winter. Winter dens, which have only one entrance, are often in woods or brushy areas, and are often in a slope. Succeeding generations take over and enlarge established dens.

The woodchuck burrow can serve as home to many other species, but especially the cottontail rabbit, which depends on woodchuck dens in winter. Skunks, foxes, opossums, raccoons, mice, and many other animals also use woodchuck dens. The tracks of woodchucks are similar to those of raccoons, and a raccoon's residency in a burrow may thus be hard to detect, but raccoons have five toes on each foot, whereas woodchucks have five toes on the forepaws, four on the hind feet, and thus make alternating four- and five-toed prints.

The woodchuck spends much time standing upright, ever watchful, near the entrance to its burrow. If suddenly disturbed or startled, it will often give a sharp "whistle" (not actually a whistle, since it is produced with the vocal cords), followed by softer chuckling notes as it descends into the burrow entrance, from which it will then peek forth. Young have been seen to scurry to their burrow upon hearing this call made at the approach of a dog (Grizzell, 1955). These calls are given at about 2.7 to 4.8 kHz. The woodchuck may grind its teeth while chattering, and utter miscellaneous squeaks and barks when fighting. (The much more social western marmots have a whole series of calls.)

*Marmota monax* has three nipple-like glands inside the anus. When the animal is excited, they evert and disseminate a musky odor. The function is not known, but it may aid in identifying occupied (as opposed to unoccupied) burrows, or in bringing the sexes together.

Like other hibernators, woodchucks gain weight during the summer and lose weight during the winter. During late summer, woodchucks put on fat equaling about a third of their weight. It is not known exactly what stimulates them to put on fat, but photoperiod is probably involved. (Curiously, blood from a hibernating animal will trigger hibernation when transferred into an active animal.) As the first frosts blacken the fields, the woodchuck descends into a side passage of its burrow or perhaps a different burrow, often in the woods, even though the fall rains may produce abundant green food above. In Maryland, most woodchucks are hibernating by November 1, all by the second week in November. Animals attaining their full fat stores enter hibernation first. The woodchuck remains curled into an inanimate bundle through the long winter, drawing on the fat stored during the summer. Heart rate during this time is reduced from 100 beats per minute to 15, temperature from 35 to 8°C (96 to 47°F), thus conserving the energy the animal will need to survive the hibernating period. Early weaning affords the animal more time to store fat adequate for it to survive hibernation. Woodchucks lose about 20 to 37% of their body weight during hibernation (Lee and Funderberg, 1982), and animals not able to accumulate sufficient fat reserves may perish during the hibernation period.

Stored fat maintains the woodchuck not only through hibernation, but also during the period of food scarcity just after emergence, and it is

*Woodchuck burrow*

particularly important as an energy source for the female through pregnancy and lactation. Males emerge about a month ahead of females and then lose much weight; by the time the females emerge, the weight of the males has fallen to about the weight of the females. This is also a time of intense male-to-male competition, and the stress of this competition may contribute to the initial weight loss. The reason for the earlier emergence of the males is apparently to ensure themselves a place to live and a place in the dominance hierarchy. And indeed, in late February or early March, while snow yet covers the woods, woodchuck tracks may be seen between burrows, indicating a search for a mate.

Hibernation lasts just three or four months or even less in the southeastern portion of the range of the species, and at least as far north as central Indiana an occasional individual may sometimes remain active through the winter, feeding on the corn remaining on the ground after the harvest. Animals at higher latitudes and higher elevations thus hibernate longer; emergence dates are about one day later for each 16 km (10 miles) of latitude, given comparable altitudes. Emergence dates of *Marmota monax* in the south are less precise than those of the more northern populations, for those in the north are on a much more constricted seasonal schedule. Soon after emergence, the summer burrows are reopened. Often, however, the woodchuck may emerge from its den in late winter, but then resume its hibernation. In the northern parts of its range, spring emergence is in late February or early March.

The regularity of this habit has given rise to "Groundhog Day." Probably the most famous celebration each year occurs in Punxsutawney, Pennsylvania. On February 2, legend has it, the groundhog will emerge from its burrow; if it sees its shadow it will reenter hibernation, for six more weeks of winter are at hand. That this date is the approximate date of emergence is supported by the following: in Indiana, shortly after the "blizzard of 1978," with temperatures hovering near zero, a woodchuck emerged on 2 or 3 February, leaving a big mound of fresh dirt on top of the foot of snow on the ground. And in central Indiana, on 5 February 1971, five woodchuck dens were found to have been recently reopened. In eight years, woodchucks in Pennsylvania emerged between 29 January and 8 February.

Complexity of social structure in the various species of *Marmota* is inversely related to length of growing season (Lee and Funderberg, 1982). The Olympic marmot, *Marmota olympus*, resident in the Olympic Mountains of Washington, must survive a very short growing season (only 50 to 70 days). It is highly social, an adult male, two adult females, and some offspring from the previous two litters living together. *Marmota monax*, which enjoys the longest growing period (about 150 days in Pennsylvania), is solitary and aggressive. Other species fall between these extremes.

FOOD AND FEEDING. Food-habits analysis is very difficult on animals that feed on green vegetation, and no detailed stomach analyses have been performed on this species. The principal foods—as presumed from direct observation and limited stomach analyses—are grasses and other green plants, such as clover, alfalfa, plantain, and strawberry. Woodchucks will follow the rows of sprouting beans, peas, and other early vegetables; they will eat carrots, cabbage, celery, vine plants, and potato plants; and they will tear down corn. Some other recorded foods are the leaves, twigs, and fruit from apple trees, as well as blackberries, serviceberry, sedges, roses, sunflower, dandelions, vetch, and stonecrop. Unlike many other squirrels, the woodchuck seldom appears to eat flesh, although it has been known to eat poultry, insects, and snails.

Fecal pellets are deposited in a dry chamber in the burrow or buried in the dirt of the entrance mound, thus helping to avoid odor buildup. The young, too, bury their feces, a behavior not known in other sciurids.

REPRODUCTION AND DEVELOPMENT. The testes of the woodchucks are abdominal through much of the year. Some woodchucks (up to 25% of them) become reproductively active the year following their birth. Those that do breed in their second year do so later in the season than other animals. Essentially all fully adult females breed each year. Males emerge from hibernation before females, and sexually active individuals mate soon after emergence, usually in March and April. A captive pair showed interest in each other immediately upon arousal from hibernation. They chased and played together over a period of nine days. On the ninth day they boxed for a few seconds, the male then mounting the female and gripping the fur of her back with his teeth. Copulation occurred three times over the next hour or so, and they then lost interest in each other. Males and females may remain together for some time during the breeding season, but the male is driven from the female's den toward the end of gestation. It appears that a female mates with only one male during a season.

In April or early May, after a gestation of approximately 31 days, the blind, naked young, weighing about 26–27 grams, are born. They usually number four to six, but extremes of one to nine have been noted. The female remains in the burrow for about a week at the time she gives birth, and the young remain in the den until they are nearly a month old. Average measurements at one week are total length 120, tail 22, hind foot 16 mm; and weight 52 grams. The external ear pinnae are erect at birth, the back and the head are heavily pigmented, and the snout and forehead bear short, grayish fur (elsewhere, the young remain without fur). At two weeks, short fur covers the body, and the foreclaws are jet black. Measurements at this point are: total length 150, tail 35, hind foot 26 mm; and weight 80.5 grams. The eyes open between days 26 and 28, and at this time the entire life of the animals changes. The mother takes green food into the burrow, and the young begin to eat it. By five or six weeks of age, the young are weaned. Ferron and Ouellet (1991) present further information on the development of the young. Soon, they begin to move out of the nest, a few minutes at a time at first, and digging and burrowing behavior begins at about this same time. Young woodchucks, not being social animals, engage in little playing and fighting. Rather, they assume adult behavior rather quickly. By five weeks they have taken on the typical coloring of the adults, the upper incisors are just erupting, and the adult sounds, the whistle and the tooth grating, can be heard. Average measurements are now total length 260, tail 55, and hind foot 47 mm; and weight

247 grams. By early July they leave the parent to establish their own shallow burrows. There is only one litter per year.

POPULATION CHARACTERISTICS. Woodchucks are not territorial, except in the immediate vicinity of the burrow. Home-range size and shape are much influenced by the features and quality of the habitat, and there may be shifts from summer to winter dens. Woodchucks occur at densities of up to one per 4.3 ha (one per 11 acres), although in one case a density of one woodchuck per ha (2 acres) was estimated (de Vos and Gillespie, 1960). Snyder et al. (1961) captured 1700 woodchucks from an 810-ha (2000-acre) forest in two years in Pennsylvania. Adult male woodchucks can be rather sedentary "residents," but some individuals wander, rather than remaining in established home ranges. Resident male home ranges are about 10,000 square meters (108,000 square feet) and usually loosely encompass the ranges of one or two females. Wandering males generally avoid the local residents and seldom use dens. Home ranges of the females in spring are much smaller than those of males, typically about 2500 square meters (27,000 square feet), but later in the summer they expand, in due course becoming somewhat larger than those of the males. These greater home ranges probably reflect the greater needs of the mother and her young. Woodchucks disperse in the year of their birth, about two months after beginning above-ground activity, and yearling individuals have smaller home ranges than do adults. There is much variation in woodchuck populations, both between areas and between years, depending on habitat quality. One woodchuck lived ten years in captivity, but few individuals live more than five or six years in the field.

ENEMIES. Humans are the greatest enemy of the woodchuck. We hunt them and reduce or destroy their habitat, and the automobile takes its heavy toll, as it does with so many other wild species. Dogs also kill substantial numbers. The deadliest natural enemy of the woodchuck is the red fox; many young are taken to the den for the cubs. Coyotes, badgers, and red-tailed hawks also take some.

Flooding occasionally kills woodchucks. Fires, however, usually do not pose a major problem for them; they survive simply by remaining in their dens. They may have to travel some distance to find food at first, but their habitat, given additional nutrients by the burning, is often enhanced.

PARASITES AND DISEASE. Ninety-one woodchucks from Indiana harbored roundworms in the intestine and three species of chiggers (including *Euschoengastia marmotae*), three other species of mites (mainly *Androlaelaps fahrenholzi*), two species of ticks, one species of flea (*Oropsylla arctomys*), and one species of sucking lice (*Enderleinellus marmotae*) in the fur. Tularemia and sylvatic plague are occasionally carried by woodchucks.

RELATION TO HUMANS. Woodchucks at times do considerable damage to crops and gardens. The main crops damaged are hay or "mowed" plants, such as clover, alfalfa, and grass. A woodchuck or two can literally ruin a garden. Hidden burrows and the sprawling heaps of dirt and stones they push to the surface can injure unwary livestock and damage farm equipment, and can even endanger the equipment operator. Woodchuck hunting was once a popular sport. The hides are worthless, but the flesh, while coarse, is enjoyed by some.

AREAS FOR FURTHER WORK. A detailed study of the food of this species would be of value, since most extant data are from direct observation of woodchucks feeding and of the evidence of cuttings. A study of the invertebrates inhabiting the nests of woodchucks would also prove of interest.

## SUBSPECIES

We are not aware of primary isolating mechanisms separating any of the subspecies described for the eastern United States, and we therefore recognize none of them.

*Marmota monax monax* (Linnaeus)
  As described above.
  Type locality: Maryland.

Other currently recognized eastern subspecies:
  *M. monax canadensis* (Erxleben)
  *M. monax preblorum* A. H. Howell
  *M. monax rufescens* A. H. Howell

## LITERATURE

Barash, D. P. 1974. The evolution of marmot studies: A general theory. *Science* 185: 415–420.

———. 1989. *Marmots: Social Behavior and Ecology.* Stanford, Calif.: Stanford Univ. Press. 361 pp.

Bronson, F. H. 1962. Daily and season activity patterns in woodchucks. *J. Mammal.* 43: 425–427.

Davis, D. E. 1967. The role of environmental factors in hibernation of woodchucks (*Marmota monax*). *Ecology* 48: 683–689.

Davis, D. E., and J. Ludwig. 1981. Mechanism for decline in a woodchuck population. *J. Wildl. Mgmt.* 45: 658–668.

de Vos, A., and D. O. Gillespie. 1960. A study of woodchucks on an Ontario farm. *Canadian Field-Nat.* 74: 130–145.

Fall, M. W. 1971. Seasonal variations in the food consumption of woodchucks (*Marmota monax*). *J. Mammal.* 52: 370–375.

Ferron, J., and J.-P. Ouellett. 1991. Physical and behavioral postnatal development of woodchucks (*Marmota monax*). *Canadian J. Zool.* 69: 1040–1047.

Grizzell, R. A., Jr. 1955. A study of the southern woodchuck, *Marmota monax monax*. *Amer. Midland Nat.* 53: 257–293.

Hamilton, W. J., Jr. 1934. The life history of the rufescent woodchuck. *Ann. Carnegie Mus.* 23: 85–178.

Lee, D. S., and J. B. Funderburg. 1982. Marmots *Marmota monax* and allies. In: J. A. Chapman and G. A. Feldhamer, eds., *Wild Mammals of North America*, pp. 176–191. Baltimore: Johns Hopkins Univ. Press.

Lowery, G. H., Jr. 1974. *The Mammals of Louisiana and Its Adjacent Waters.* Baton Rouge: Louisiana State Univ. Press. 565 pp.

Schmeltz, L. L., and J. O. Whitaker, Jr. 1977. Use of woodchuck burrows by woodchucks and other mammals. *Trans. Ky. Acad. Sci.* 38: 79–82.

Snyder, R. L., and J. J. Christian. 1960. Reproductive cycle and litter size of the woodchuck. *Ecology* 41: 647–656.

Snyder, R. L., D. E. Davis, and J. J. Christian. 1961. Seasonal changes in the weights of woodchucks. *J. Mammal.* 42: 297–312.

Swihart, R. K. 1991. Influence of *Marmota monax* on vegetation in hayfields. *J. Mammal.* 72: 791–795.

Whitaker, J. O., Jr, and L. L. Schmeltz. 1973. External parasites of the woodchuck, *Marmota monax*, in Indiana. *Entomol. News* 84: 69–72.

## Ground Squirrels of the Genus
*Spermophilus*

There are many species of ground squirrels in the western United States, but only two in the east. One of these, the thirteen-lined ground squirrel, is the most wide-ranging of any of the ground squirrels. Ground squirrels are hibernators and are often colonial. The genus *Spermophilus* has, at times, been known as *Citellus*, but the name *Citellus* (Oken) is invalid (Wilson and Reeder, 1993).

### LITERATURE CITED

Wilson, D. E., and D. M. Reeder. 1993. *Mammal Species of the World: A Taxonomic and Geographic Reference.* Washington: Smithsonian Institution Press, in Association with Amer. Soc. Mammal. 1206 pp.

### KEY TO THE GROUND SQUIRRELS OF THE GENUS *SPERMOPHILUS*

1. Dorsum bearing a series of alternating brown and white longitudinal lines . . . . *S. tridecemlineatus*
1. Dorsum primarily gray, but with some flecking toward the posterior . . . . . . . . *S. franklinii*

## Franklin's Ground Squirrel
*Spermophilus franklinii* (Sabine)

DESCRIPTION. Superficially similar to the gray squirrel, Franklin's ground squirrel has a shorter

*Franklin's ground squirrel,* Spermophilus franklinii *(Roger W. Barbour)*

and less bushy tail, a tawny body, and shorter ears, and its behavior and habitat are quite different. It can be distinguished from the thirteen-lined ground squirrel by its lack of stripes and its larger size. The upperparts are brownish gray and blackish, the rump is often dull yellowish or olive, and the flanks are paler. The color pattern nonetheless suggests an animal distinctly barred or spotted, particularly on the hind quarters. The head is usually plain gray or grayish brown, and the tail is grayish, its margins tipped 214ull yellowish white, grayish white, or pinkish buff.

MEASUREMENTS. Measurements of ten Illinois and Wisconsin specimens averaged: total length 380 (351–401), tail 143 (133–156), hind foot 52 (49–55) mm. Weight in the spring is 350–450 grams; early in the fall, prior to hibernation, it is 500–700 grams.

Diploid number = 42.

TOOTH FORMULA

$$\frac{1}{1} \quad \frac{0}{0} \quad \frac{2}{1} \quad \frac{3}{3} = 22$$

DISTRIBUTION. East of the Mississippi this species is found in northwestern Indiana, central and northern Illinois, and north into central Wisconsin. Its range in Indiana has been greatly reduced in recent years. To the west, its range extends through about the eastern two-thirds of Kansas, Nebraska, South Dakota, and North Dakota, and in Canada to southern Manitoba, southern Saskatchewan, and east-central Alberta.

HABITAT. Franklin's ground squirrel inhabits open areas with some cover, more cover than is typical of *Spermophilus tridecemlineatus* habitats. It is seldom abundant, and in the east is now most often found along roads or railroad rights-of-way.

HABITS. Because of its large size, this ground squirrel should be a favorite object of study, but little is known of its habits. It is an accomplished climber, and is occasionally seen high up in a tree or bush, but it is less conspicuous than other ground squirrels and seldom assumes the upright posture. Moreover, it does not stop when its call is imitated, but heads for its burrow. The burrows of Franklin's ground squirrels are larger than those of the thirteen-lined ground squirrel, but are usually better concealed, much of the dirt being scattered away from the entrance so as to leave no more than a small mound. The burrow systems are extensive and are dug by the animals themselves. The entrances are no more than 75 mm (3 inches) in diameter, but the burrow may extend to a depth of 2.5 meters (8 feet). The construction of the burrows apparently differs from that of *S. tridecemlineatus* burrows, for we have been consistently unsuccessful in getting this species to emerge by filling its burrows with water, as is easily done with *S. tridecemlineatus*.

These squirrels, like most members of their genus, are most active on bright, sunny days. They are more vocal than others of their genus, producing a clear whistle as well as other bird-like twitters. These calls, uttered often while the animals are feeding or moving about, rather than when they are startled or on the alert, may serve as communication, since these animals live in heavier cover than do most other ground squirrels. Notwithstanding, Franklin's ground squirrels show much less evidence of social behavior than do other ground squirrels. One reflection of their stolidity is that they show little evidence of scent marking. The anal glands do give off a musky discharge, one that may play a role in the attraction of the sexes, or perhaps in marking home areas.

With the approach of cold weather, usually from late September to early November, depending on latitude, Franklin's ground squirrel, having acquired its winter fat, retreats to its underground chamber to spend half the year in deep hibernation. The young disappear later than the adults. These animals do not appear above ground until late March or early April,

*Distribution of Franklin's ground squirrel,* Spermophilus franklinii, *in the eastern United States*

the males preceding the females by a couple of weeks.

FOOD AND FEEDING. The food of this species consists of a great variety of plant and animal material, including much green plant matter. Grasses, clover, various mustards, cultivated plants, and numerous other species are eaten, the foods taken varying with season and locality. During the summer months, the thickets bordering the prairies provide a plentiful supply of berries, and on these the animals may subsist for weeks. Among animal foods, caterpillars, grasshoppers, crickets, beetles and their larvae, and ants are eaten. And like all its kinsmen, this squirrel often feeds on vertebrate flesh, at times taking young poultry or ducks, eggs, songbirds, toads, and frogs. It is also known to eat mice, the smaller thirteen-lined ground squirrel, and even small rabbits. Sowls (1948) described its method of feeding on duck eggs: the squirrel grasps the egg under its body, then with its hind legs pushes it forward into the incisors, thus making a small hole, which is then enlarged by further biting. Under controlled conditions Franklin's ground squirrel preyed heavily on duck eggs, whereas *S. tridecemlineatus* and *S. richardsoni* would not (Sargeant et al., 1987).

REPRODUCTION AND DEVELOPMENT. Mating, which involves much chasing of females by the males, occurs as soon as the females emerge from hibernation, about mid-April. As is usual in the members of this genus, a single litter is produced, generally by mid-May, after a gestation of 28 days. The young, numbering five to eleven and averaging about six to eight, are helpless at birth. They pass nearly a month in the den before appearing above ground. Hair appears at about 10 days and the eyes open at 20, by which time the young can whistle. Weaning is at about 40 days. The young remain with the parent for several more weeks, forming a loose-knit family, but finally disperse to seek their own territories as the summer advances. By hibernation time the young are nearly the size of the adults. These ground squirrels are peculiar in that they can appear in a given region, establish a community, but then, for no apparent reason, desert it, not to be seen again.

POPULATION CHARACTERISTICS. Franklin's ground squirrels form loose colonies, though these seldom number more than ten or twelve animals, and considerably fewer may occupy a hedgerow. Females occupy home ranges averaging about 135 meters (440 feet) in diameter. The animals occur at densities up to 20 per ha (8 per acre), although there is much annual fluctuation in numbers and there are reports of as many as 185 per ha (75 per acre). Dispersal is by juveniles, but, contrary to the practice of many other species of ground squirrels, both males and females disperse.

ENEMIES. The automobile is probably this squirrel's most important enemy, but predatory mammals, birds, and snakes levy a toll. The species is maintaining itself but is currently in trouble over much of the southern midwestern prairie. Its range has been diminishing in northern Indiana.

PARASITES AND DISEASE. Franklin's ground squirrels harbor lice, fleas, mites, protozoans, cestodes, and nematodes.

RELATION TO HUMANS. These squirrels sometimes produce holes in pastures, but generally are of little direct consequence to humans.

AREAS FOR FURTHER WORK. This species is worthy of much more study. Although its numbers are currently declining in many areas, valuable new data on its behavior, vocalizations, and interrelationships could doubtless be obtained in a study undertaken where it is still relatively common. Detailed study of its burrow and of its nest fauna, in comparison with those of the thirteen-lined ground squirrel, would also be instructive.

## SUBSPECIES

None described.
Type locality: Carlton House, Saskatchewan.

### LITERATURE

Bailey, V. 1893. The prairie ground squirrels or spermophiles of the Mississippi Valley. U.S. Dept. Agric., Div. Ornithol. and Mammal. Bull. 4. 39 pp.

Howell, A. H. 1936. Revision of the North American ground squirrels. U.S. Dept. Agric. *North Amer. Fauna* No. 56. 256 pp.

Nadler, C. F. 1966. Chromosomes of *Spermophilus franklinii* and taxonomy of the ground squirrel genus *Spermophilus*. *Syst. Zool.* 15: 199–206.

Sargeant, A. B., M. A. Sovada, and R. J. Greenwood. 1987. Responses of three prairie ground squirrel species, *Spermophilus franklinii, S. richardsonii,* and *S. tridecemlineatus*, to duck eggs. *Canadian Field Nat.* 101: 95–97.

Sowls, L. K. 1948. The Franklin ground squirrel, *Citellus franklinii* (Sabine) and its relationship to nesting ducks. *J. Mammal.* 29: 113–137.

## Thirteen-Lined Ground Squirrel
### *Spermophilus tridecemlineatus* (Mitchill)

The impropriety of common names is well-illustrated by this species. It is properly called the thirteen-lined ground squirrel, but in many areas of the Midwest it is called a "gopher," and the chipmunk is what is called a "ground squirrel" there. In the west, the "gopher" is the pocket gopher, and in Florida the "gopher" is the gopher tortoise. In many older books, *Spermophilus tridecemlineatus* is called the "thirteen-lined spermophile."

DESCRIPTION. This species is easily distinguished from any other mammal by the thirteen alternating light and dark stripes on the back. The

*Thirteen-lined ground squirrel,* Spermophilus tridecemlineatus

color above, basically dark brownish, is interrupted by seven long yellowish-white stripes,

really rows of spots. These stripes break up irregularly where they reach the top of the head. The face and underparts are tawny brown. The tail is mixed brown and white, the pattern of its coloration similar to that of the back: the central portion above is black, and the border is fringed with buffy-white hair tips.

MEASUREMENTS. Measurements of ten adults from Wisconsin averaged: total length 277 (250–310), tail 99.4 (83–110), hind foot 38.3 (35–41) mm. Weight, though variable, runs about 110 to 140 grams in June and twice that just prior to hibernation in late September. Males average slightly heavier than females.
Diploid number = 34.

TOOTH FORMULA

$$\frac{1}{1} \quad \frac{0}{0} \quad \frac{2}{1} \quad \frac{3}{3} \; = \; 22$$

DISTRIBUTION. In eastern United States, this species occurs throughout Wisconsin and south through the northern halves of Illinois and Indiana eastward to central Ohio. It was first observed in Lancaster, Ohio, in 1933, and appears to be extending its range into eastern and northeastern Ohio. To the west, it ranges to southeastern Alberta, much of Montana, Wyoming, Colorado, and New Mexico, east-central Utah, and northeastern Texas.

HABITAT. The thirteen-lined ground squirrel is partial to open areas with sparse vegetation, such as originally occurred in sandy short-grass prairie. This species appears to be much more abundant and more widely distributed than it was a century ago, for much shortgrass habitat suitable to its needs, such as mowed lawns, golf courses, cemeteries, and rights-of-way, has been developed by man.

HABITS. This squirrel is often conspicuous to the tourist driving from northwestern Ohio through northern Illinois as it scurries across the road, its short legs carrying it so rapidly that one fails to see the prominent dorsal markings. It can move at speeds up to 13 kph (8 mph). Like other ground-living squirrels, it is most active in the sun, although it will come out on cloudy days. If the weather is bad for several days, the animals will stay in their burrows and feed on stored foods.

The thirteen-lined ground squirrel appears to be quite sociable. Considerable numbers often occupy a relatively small area on a prairie knoll, in a cemetery, or on a golf course. Actually, however, it is one of the least social of the ground squirrels, and a squirrel will defend a small territory in the immediate vicinity of its main burrow. These ground squirrels rarely venture far from their burrows, standing up often to observe their surroundings. Occasionally, the tremulous whistle or trill, apparently a warning call, is heard; and if danger threatens, the ground squirrel disappears into a nearby burrow. This behavior, however, calls into question the value of the warning call. Presumably, some of the nearby animals are kin, and a warning call thus has selective value in preserving the caller's genes. The

trill is also used during breeding and agonistic behavior in this species (Schwagmeyer, 1980). It might at first seem unreasonable for the animal to be using the same call for both intraspecies use and antipredator use, but both are dangerous situations; both would favor alertness on the part of the squirrels, and much of the "social" calling is agonistic. There may be differences in the "urgency" of the calls, with respect to how closely a predator has approached and whether immediate action is needed. Moreover, nonrepetitive rather than repetitive calls seem better able to elicit the escape response, and calls may also elicit aid from neighbors against nonresident intrusion.

Ground squirrels also have a "greeting" behavior in which the noses and lips are brought together. Still other forms of communication are visual (the squirrels can see each other on the open ground in which they live), these prob-

*Distribution of the thirteen-lined ground squirrel,* Spermophilus tridecemlineatus, *in the eastern United States*

ably serving to indicate to others one's proprietorship of an area. Relatively little is known of the olfactory senses in communication, since they are difficult to study; but pheromones must be of great importance. Oral-labial glands are common in ground squirrels, and scent marking from these glands by "mouth" or "cheek" rubbing is also common, but occurs sparingly in this less-social ground squirrel. On the occasions when it is used, the squirrel approaches an object, sniffs it, then moves the head rapidly in a forward/sideways motion, pressing the sides of the mouth against the object. "Comfort marking"—rubbing the chin, throat, and belly against objects—is the major scent-related behavior in this species. The function of the anal glands (in the walls of the anal canal, eversible through the anus) is unclear.

The burrows of these ground squirrels vary in size, depending on the texture of the soil, the age of the individual, and the purpose of the burrow. There are three types of burrows: nesting burrows, escape burrows, and hibernating burrows, though the nesting and hibernation types may in some cases be one and the same. Adult squirrels may tunnel to a depth of 30 cm (a foot) or more, and the burrow may exceed 6.5 meters (20 feet) in length. In the course of things, a bulky nest of grasses is prepared in a side chamber. Young animals may make a shallow burrow not more than 2 meters (6 feet) long, with a single entrance. Escape burrows, scattered across the home range, are short. Squirrels remain inside the burrows at night, the burrows plugged for the night. Usually, there is only one squirrel per burrow.

Growth rates are slower in warmer or perhaps drier climates, the animals taking about two to three weeks longer to reach full weight in Kansas than in Michigan, but by late summer or fall, depending on locality, the squirrel—now resplendent in a new coat, rolling in fat, and as much as double its spring weight—is ready for hibernation. Decreasing day length apparently provides the cue for putting on fat and otherwise preparing for hibernation. (Young squirrels are later in building sufficient fat and may occasionally be seen into late November, and there are records of their activity even on warm days in winter.) In any event, this species belongs to that group that exhibits true hibernation, and these squirrels usually remain dormant until late March or early April, curled in a ball in the hibernating nest.

Like other hibernating animals, ground squirrels are known to wake periodically, but the reason for waking is not known. Energy during hibernation derives from the breakdown of fat (lipids). This breakdown produces much water and could lead to overhydration. It was once thought, in fact, that hibernators wake to empty the bladder, but it now appears that the only significant water loss by mammals during hibernation is through the skin, and that water balance is maintained by evaporation of the excess water produced by lipid breakdown. Hibernators awaken more frequently and stay awake longer, early and late in hibernation, than in mid-hibernation. Perhaps these awakenings are advantageous in late hibernation in helping the animal to determine its time of emergence. That time is probably in part determined by an endogenous cycle (an internal clock), but the specific stimuli for spring emergence are not known. The timing of entry into and exit from hibernation, and in turn the timing of reproduction, varies between populations and is related to length of growing season and to local conditions in any one year, including regional length and severity of winter. In Texas, adults begin entering hibernation in July, juveniles in August and September, but in Indiana, some individuals are still abroad through part of October. And in Texas, again, these ground squirrels exit from hibernation from early March through 5 April (McCarley, 1966). The early entrance into hibernation in Texas is apparently related to the dry weather there.

During hibernation, great changes occur. While active, these squirrels have a body temperature of 37°C (99°F), but in their profound winter torpor their temperature drops to 1–3°C above the temperature of the burrow. The heart-rate is reduced from a range of 200 to 350 beats per minute in active animals to not more than five beats per minute in the dormant individual. The respiration rate also falls, from 50 breaths per minute to perhaps four per minute. A hibernating individual uses about one one-hundredth as much energy and oxygen as an active one;

nonetheless, as much as 40–50% of the animal's weight is lost during hibernation.

FOOD AND FEEDING. These little mammals are omnivorous, devouring grains, seeds, succulent plants, berries, insects, and small mammals. A study of the stomachs of 125 thirteen-lined ground squirrels from Indiana indicated clover plants and caterpillars to be two of the most prevalent foods, followed by various kinds of grass and herb seeds, grasshoppers, beetles, and grubs. Only the internal organs are eaten from some of the larger insects. Birds and their eggs, lizards, and snakes are sometimes eaten. In one case, at least three young cottontail rabbits were taken from a nest over a period of days. Those who drive slowly will recognize these squirrels feeding on the crushed bodies of their less fortunate kin. They also store large quantities of seeds in their dens. Just when these are utilized is difficult to say, but they are most likely eaten early in the spring and during bad weather in summer.

REPRODUCTION AND DEVELOPMENT. Mating occurs soon after the animals have left their hibernating chambers in April or early May, the males emerging before the females. Males defend neither territories nor females; they simply search for receptive females, and numerous chases ensue. Copulations, in a population, occur over a period of about 12 days, although individual females are in estrus for short periods—one female was known to be in estrus at least six hours. Copulations are often above ground and may be conspicuous; as such, they can expose the animals thus preoccupied to greater danger of predation.

Females may mate with more than one male in years when enough males are available. There has been much discussion about the selective advantage of these multiple matings. The female's reproductive strategy is apparently to mate with any male that comes along during her receptive period. This should certainly help to ensure fertilization, and it probably contributes to increasing the population's genetic heterogeneity, although the largest males nonetheless attain the most matings. Conversely, we would see no obvious advantage in a female's mating only once, for the males play no role in the reproductive process beyond mating, no role in seeing to the needs of the female or her young.

Gestation is 27 to 28 days. The young are blind, naked, and helpless at birth and weigh about 6 to 7 grams. The lower incisors erupt at day 17, the uppers at day 19, the eyes open at 21–31 days, and the adult coloration appears by day 21–25. The six to 13 young (averaging about eight or nine) are not independent of the mother until about six weeks old. They then leave the natal chamber to dig their own burrows and forage for themselves, attaining adult weight by week 11, and in due course putting on a layer of fat in preparation for hibernation. In Texas, McCarley (1966) found that a few older females (five of 22) came into estrus again and produced a second litter, but apparently there is only one litter in the north.

POPULATION CHARACTERISTICS. These squirrels may occur in considerable numbers at times. Whitaker's family collected 147 individuals from an Indiana cemetery for hibernation studies in approximately 15 hours. Water from a hose was used to force them from their burrows. Population estimates of up to five ground squirrels per ha (2 per acre) in spring and 25 per ha (10 per acre) after the young emerge have been recorded. In Texas, home ranges averaged nearly 5 ha (12 acres) for males and less than 1.5 ha (3.7 acres) for females, the males expanding their ranges during the breeding season.

Females tend to remain near their birthplace; males disperse farther (Armitage, 1981). In one Texas study juvenile males dispersed from their place of birth an average of 267 meters (867 feet) and females 189 meters (620 feet); average male and female dispersal distances in a Wisconsin population were 80 and 53 meters (262 and 174 feet), respectively. In this species, dispersal may be either by adults, after breeding, or by the young of the year, but is male-biased in either case; juvenile and adult females both show a greater tendency to remain in the home area. Natal dispersal usually occurs in the first summer, at least a month after emergence from the natal burrow and a month before hibernation.

Despite heavy mortality among juveniles (80–90%), these animals live for several years; on one Texas site, 40% of marked individuals were still alive three years later.

ENEMIES. Many enemies help to hold down the numbers of these squirrels. Badgers, foxes, weasels, hawks, bull snakes, and other predators all take their share, and highway mortality is ever a threat. In late June 1940, Hamilton counted 107 dead squirrels on 18 km (11 miles) of Iowa highway and inadvertently ran over three in this stretch himself.

PARASITES AND DISEASE. Ectoparasites of this animal include ticks, mites, lice, and fleas. The endoparasites include protozoans, cestodes, nematodes, acanthocephalans, and spiny-headed worms. These squirrels are also regularly infested with botfly larvae, *Cuterebra*.

RELATION TO HUMANS. The thirteen-lined ground squirrel destroys substantial quantities of grasshoppers, grubs, and wireworms, but its detrimental effects cannot be overlooked. On the farm, it may dig up sprouting corn, sometimes necessitating a second planting, and heads of ripening wheat and oats may be leveled, though only a few kernels may have actually been eaten. Four or five squirrels to an acre (not a large number) will raise havoc in a ripening field of grain. Occasionally, these squirrels will enter a garden, where they may feed heavily on ripening tomatoes. The species has been controlled by means of gas, poisoned grains, traps, and shooting.

AREAS FOR FURTHER WORK. More work is needed on the stimuli for, and the process of, putting on fat for hibernation, as well as the stimuli for entering and emerging from hibernation. Much more information could be gained simply by watching these easily observed animals, recording their calls, and videotaping their actions in relation to each other and to squirrels of other species. Much remains to be learned concerning their glandular secretions. The development of behavior patterns in the young could be watched. Given the right circum-

stances and sufficient skill in the investigator, it might be possible to use one-way glass and red light to observe these ground squirrels in their nests, in much the way we observe ant farms.

## SUBSPECIES

*Spermophilus tridecemlineatus tridecemlineatus* (Mitchill)

As described above. The only subspecies in the eastern United States.

Type locality: Central Minnesota.

### LITERATURE

Armitage, K. B. 1981. Sociality as a life-history tactic of ground squirrels. *Oecologia* 48: 36–49.

Bridgewater, D. D. 1966. Laboratory breeding, early growth, development and behavior of *Citellus tridecemlineatus* (Rodentia). *Southwestern Nat.* 11: 325–337.

Fitzpatrick, F. L. 1925. The ecology and economic status of *Citellus tridecemlineatus*. Iowa State Univ. Studies Nat. Hist. 11. 40 pp.

Johnson, G. E. 1928. Hibernation of the thirteen-lined ground squirrel *Citellus tridecemlineatus* (Mitchill): I. A comparison of the normal and hibernating states. *J. Exp. Zool.* 50: 15–30.

Joy, J. E. 1984. Population differences in circannual cycles of thirteen-lined ground squirrels. In: J. O. Murie and G. I. Michener, *The Biology of Ground-Dwelling Squirrels*, pp. 125–141. Lincoln: Univ. Nebraska Press. 459 pp.

McCarley, H. 1966. Annual cycle, population dynamics, and adaptive behavior of *Citellus tridecemlineatus*. *J. Mammal.* 47: 294–316.

Michener, G. R. 1983. Kin identification, matriarchies, and the evolution of sociality in ground dwelling sciurids. *In*: J. F. Eisenberg and D. G. Kleiman, eds., *Advances in the Study of Mammalian Behavior*, pp. 528–572. Amer. Soc. Mammal., Spec. Publ. No. 7.

Schwagmeyer, P. L. 1980. Alarm calling behavior of thirteen-lined ground squirrel, *Spermophilus tridecemlineatus*. *Behav. Ecol. Sociobiol.* 7: 195–200.

Streubel, D. P., and J. P. Fitzgerald. 1978. *Spermophilus tridecemlineatus*. **Mammalian Species No. 103.** Amer. Soc. Mammal. 5 pp.

Wade, O. 1927. Breeding habits and early life of the thirteen-striped ground squirrel, *Citellus tridecemlineatus* (Mitchill). *J. Mammal.* 8: 269–276.

Whitaker, J. O., Jr. 1972. Food and external parasites of *Spermophilus tridecemlineatus* in Vigo County, Indiana. *J. Mammal.* 53: 644–648.

## Tree Squirrels of the Genus *Sciurus*

Two species of native squirrels of the genus *Sciurus* occur throughout most of the eastern United States, and the red-bellied squirrel, a native of Mexico, has been introduced on Elliot Key, Florida.

## Red-bellied Squirrel, Mexican Gray Squirrel *Sciurus aureogaster* Cuvier

DESCRIPTION. The red-bellied squirrel is related to the gray squirrel but is slightly larger and is distinguished by its bright reddish-chestnut belly and flanks. A large proportion (about half) of the individuals in Florida are completely melanistic.

MEASUREMENTS. Measurements are: total length 470–573, tail 235–276, and hind foot 63–70 mm. We have no information on the weight of the animals in this population.
Diploid number unknown.

TOOTH FORMULA

$$\frac{1}{1} \quad \frac{0}{0} \quad \frac{2}{1} \quad \frac{3}{3} \ = \ 22$$

DISTRIBUTION. This squirrel is not native in the eastern United States. It is native to much of Gulf coastal and southern Mexico and parts of Guatemala. Two pairs were liberated by a resident in 1938 on Elliot Key, Florida, about 20 miles (32 km) south of Miami, and the species is now well established there (see map on p. 224).

HABITAT. The red-bellied squirrel is now abundant in the dense jungle/hammock-type forest of Elliot Key.

HABITS. Brown and McGuire (1969) observed numerous leaf nests of the red-bellied squirrel in a variety of trees, but especially in Florida poisonwood and West Indies mahogany. Nests were rarely seen in gumbo limbo, even though this was the most abundant tree in the area. Where hollow trees were available, leaf nests were not seen.

FOOD AND FEEDING. Important foods are the fleshy yellow fruit of the mastic tree and the seeds of mahogany, coconut, sea grape, papaya, and thatch palm.

REPRODUCTION AND DEVELOPMENT. Litters of one or two young are produced at any time during the year. Both normal and melanistic phases may occur in the same litter.

POPULATION CHARACTERISTICS. The home range of females is about 0.9 ha (2.2 acre), that of males 2.3 ha (5.7 acres) (Brown and McGuire, 1975).

ENEMIES. There is little predation pressure on these animals, but competition for tree holes may limit the population.

AREAS FOR FURTHER WORK. As with any introduced species, an examination of the ecology of this species would be of interest, as it relates both to other species of mammals with which it occurs and to others of its own species in regions where it occurs naturally.

### SUBSPECIES

Two subspecies of this species—*Sciurus aureogaster aureogaster* and *S. a. nigrescens*—have been described for the native Mexican populations, but the origin of the squirrels on Elliot Key is not known. In any case, the two subspecies intergrade and thus do not fit our concept of subspecies.

*Sciurus aureogaster* Cuvier

Type locality: Altamira, Tamaulipas, Mexico.

LITERATURE

Brown, L. N. 1969. Exotic squirrel in Florida. *Fla. Wildl.* 23: 4–5.

Brown, L. N., and R. M. McGuire. 1969. Status of the red-bellied squirrel (*Sciurus aureogaster*) in the Florida Keys. *Amer. Midland Nat.* 82: 629–630.

———. 1975. Field ecology of the exotic Mexican red-bellied squirrel in Florida. *J. Mammal.* 56: 405–419.

# Eastern Gray Squirrel
## *Sciurus carolinensis* Gmelin

DESCRIPTION. This familiar, medium-sized tree squirrel has a long, bushy, somewhat flattened

*Eastern gray squirrel,* Sciurus carolinensis
*(Larry E. Lehman)*

tail. The upper parts of the body and top of the head are grayish to yellowish brown. The underparts are white, occasionally washed with yellowish brown. The ears, relatively short, but prominent, are rounded, and lack a tuft. The forefeet are gray above; the hind feet are light

brown above, the toes gray. The tail is brown at the base, its hairs blackish near their middle and broadly tipped with silvery gray. The winter pelage is dense and silvery, usually with a pronounced yellowish-brown dorsal band—this band, however, much paler than in summer. Adult gray squirrels molt twice per year: to the yellowish summer coat by late spring and to the more silvery-gray winter coat by late fall.

Northern gray squirrels are larger than those in southern populations, and those of the southern coastal plain are smaller and somewhat lighter and grayer than those elsewhere. Individuals from coastal Mississippi and Louisiana are darker than other southern gray squirrels; they are deep yellowish rusty with much black, lending a peppery appearance to the fur, and the underparts are smoky to dark buffy. Melanistic individuals are common, particularly in the northern part of the range; they are black above, the hairs near their tips frequently banded with brown, and they are pale brown below. Albinistic and erythristic (reddish) phases are less common. Olney, Illinois, is famous for its albinistic individuals. The eyes of albinistic individuals are sometimes pink, sometimes not. Some of the color variation in gray squirrels could be associated with thermoregulation, as suggested by Innes and Lavigne (1979).

The gray squirrel has five upper molariform teeth, the first reduced in size or "peglike." The fox squirrel, by contrast, has simply four large upper molariform teeth.

MEASUREMENTS. Average measurements of gray squirrels over their range are: total length 380–525, tail 150–250, hind foot 54–76, ear 25–33 mm; and weight 300–710 grams. Fourteen adults from central New York measured total length 487, tail 235, hind foot 68 mm; and weight 500–710 grams. Measurements of 179 individuals from Indiana were: total length 469 (404–530), tail 210 (177–285), hind foot 65 (50–76) mm; and weight 510 (403–610) grams. Average measurements of ten adults from north Florida and Georgia were: total length 439, tail 201, hind foot 61 mm; and weight 400–450 grams.

Diploid number = 40.

TOOTH FORMULA

$$\frac{1}{1} \quad \frac{0}{0} \quad \frac{2}{1} \quad \frac{3}{3} \quad = \quad 22$$

DISTRIBUTION. The gray squirrel occurs in suitable habitat essentially throughout the eastern United States. To the west, the species extends to southwestern Saskatchewan, most of North Dakota, and eastern Nebraska, Kansas, Oklahoma, and Texas.

HABITAT. The bottomlands of the rich Mississippi Valley and the oak/hickory forests of the Middle Atlantic states and the Southeast are home to this species, although it is found, in lesser numbers, much farther north. In Louisiana it is abundant in virtually every woodland. Higher densities occur where there is a diversity of nut trees (especially oak, hickory, beech, and walnut) providing food over a long season, and an abundance of den trees with cavities. In

much of the east where both gray and fox squirrels occur, the fox squirrel is found in the farmlands and the open woods, the gray squirrel in the deeper forest and riverbottom areas, but both thrive in many city parks and suburban areas. The greater the percentage of land that is wooded, the higher the percentage of gray squirrels, and the lower the percentage of fox squirrels.

HABITS. Gray squirrels are primarily arboreal. During warmer seasons, they are most active in the early morning hours and again in the late afternoon, when they forage for food. They also spend much time on the ground, especially in the fall, mainly to collect and bury nuts. They are active throughout the year, braving even extremely cold weather to dig in the snow for nuts buried the previous fall (see also "Food and Feeding," below). In colder weather, foraging is

*Distribution of the red-bellied squirrel,* Sciurus aureogaster, *and the Eastern gray squirrel,* Sciurus carolinensis, *in the eastern United States*

apt to occur during midday, the warmest period. Females are more active in spring and
summer, males in autumn and winter. Arboreal
activity peaks in summer and autumn and
greatly declines in winter, after the harvest is
gone from the trees.

Gray squirrels, like other tree squirrels, are
not social, and they are not particularly tolerant of one another or of other species. Male
gray squirrels are dominant over females, and
both are dominant over juveniles; residents are
very aggressive toward immigrants. Males regularly visit traditional marking points on trees,
where they gnaw the area and deposit scent
from urine and from oral-labial glands, and
males and females both mark areas with the
oral glands while moving about their home
sites. The two sexes come together only for
mating, when drawn by an abundance of food,
or, sometimes, in very cold weather in winter
dens. When feeding together at a concentrated
food source, they generally maintain a spacing
of 1.2 to 1.5 meters (4 to 4.5 feet). Pregnant or
nursing females will drive off other squirrels
from the den tree, by tooth chattering and by
lashing out with the forepaws.

Under high densities (seven or more squirrels
per ha, or three per acre), dominance hierarchies are established. Dominance, announced by
tooth chattering toward lower-ranking individuals, is determined by size, age, and experience.
Males and females establish their ranks in a
single mixed hierarchy, but males tend to be
higher-ranking than females. Under field conditions, the squirrels remain dispersed most of the
time, and the dominance hierarchy comes into
play when squirrels gather at mating time, at
food concentrations, or at den trees. Even at
feeders, gray squirrels have been noted to form
a social hierarchy, or "peck order," the males and
older animals the more likely to be dominant.

Gray squirrels often move slowly along the
ground, but can run at speeds of about 24 kph
(14 mph) with leaps up to 1.5 meters (4.5 feet).
They are exceedingly agile when moving in the
trees, and can make leaps of about 2 meters
(6 feet) between branches, or drop to branches
up to 5 meters (16 feet) below. The tail of the
gray squirrel is used primarily as a balancing organ for climbing about in trees, jumping from

limb to limb, and breaking falls. It may also be
coiled about the animal for added warmth, or
employed as a sunshade.

A characteristic rasping "whicker" or harsh
squall is given when the animal is disturbed, but
this species has several other calls, including
warning barks, chucks, and screams, buzzes
associated with mating chases, and "mews,"
"whistles," and "purrs" associated with group
interactions. Agonistic situations provoke tooth
chattering. Some of the calls are catlike, hence
the name "cat squirrel" sometimes given to this
animal. Various postures and tail movements
are associated with some of these calls. Neonates make lip-smacking noises and squeaks,
and older nestlings produce several calls.

Gray squirrels will hide from an enemy or simply sun themselves by lying on top of a branch,
with feet and tail hanging down. They may do
this anywhere from a couple of meters off the
ground to a place high in the trees, and a watchful observer can often spy them in this position.
A gray squirrel on a tree trunk will often move
quickly around the trunk, keeping all but its
face on the far side of an observer.

These squirrels use both tree cavities and leaf
nests. A large beech or oak, typically, is chosen
for the den tree, some natural cavity in the tree
housing the bulky nest. For optimum habitat,
there should be at least five to eight suitable cavities per ha (two or three per acre). A "suitable"
cavity is one at least 0.3 meter (12 inches) deep
with an opening at least 7.5 cm (3 inches) in diameter. An old woodpecker hole, or an opening
where a branch has broken off and rotted away,
will do. There are two types of leaf nests, better-
built ones for more permanent use and loosely
constructed ones that serve as rest sites. Both
are large; both are built of leaves, twigs, and
shredded plant material woven so firmly together as to be virtually waterproof. They are
usually built in the crotch of a tree, though they
may be in a grape vine or other tangle. These
nests are built of green leaves in summer, and
thus are quite well camouflaged at that time. In
the fall, when the nests have turned brown and
the leaves have fallen from the trees, the nests
are quite evident. Most often, a group of several
squirrels of the same or mixed sexes will occupy
a single nest in winter. This amicable behavior

may reflect the continuing cohesion of family groups. Koprowski and Koprowski (1987) reported a male and a female gray squirrel cooperating to build a nest; the male always gathered honey locust leaves, and the female always gathered hackberry leaves. Young individuals construct leaf nests when about 18 weeks old. In years when squirrels are abundant, their numerous nests are a familiar sight in the leafless winter woods. Leaf-nest counts can in fact be used to estimate relative numbers of squirrels, if done in the same way each year. Uhlig (1955) postulated that population sizes in West Virginia could be estimated by assuming 1.5 leaf nests per squirrel.

The irregular great squirrel emigrations or mass movements of early days, involving hundreds or thousands of squirrels, were a marvel to the pioneers, and many striking accounts of such movements are available. Gray squirrels in some numbers have emigrated westward from western Connecticut and neighboring New York, even crossing the Hudson River on bridges. The reason for these mass movements has probably been overpopulation and/or prolonged poor weather, resulting in reduced food supplies in the areas from which the squirrels came. These movements are much less common than in prior days, but such emigrations on a somewhat smaller scale have occurred more recently in New England and Kentucky. One in October 1968, when thousands of squirrels emigrated from areas in Tennessee, Georgia, and North Carolina was attributed to good mast production in 1967, which allowed for high winter survival and high levels of reproduction in 1968. A late spring frost then caused low mast production the following fall, resulting in overpopulation, food shortage, and mass emigration. In 1985, at least 90 squirrels drowned during a month-long emigration from a Lake Michigan island.

It is often thought that red squirrels drive away gray squirrels, or even that the smaller red squirrels emasculate the grays. Layne (1954), however, found no evidence of marked antagonism between the two species, although red squirrels did sometimes chase grays, or vice versa. Ackerman and Weigl (1970), in a laboratory situa-

tion, found no fighting between the two species. They also found that red squirrels would share nest boxes with each other; gray squirrels would not. Riege (1991) found that habitat specialization, not interspecific aggression, determined differences in distribution between red and gray squirrels.

FOOD AND FEEDING. The distribution of the gray squirrel coincides strikingly with that of oak and hickory forests. It is evident that the squirrel's mainstay during the colder part of the year is the mast of these trees—nuts and acorns, as well as maple samaras—that they have stored for later use. The gray squirrel also feeds on a multitude of other foods: buds, fruits and berries, and fungi are eaten; hawthorn fruits, apples, honey locust seeds, horse chestnuts, sycamore buds, and elm seeds may be important at times; magnolia fruits are important in the Everglades. Gray squirrels will eat the inner bark of maple or elm, or various animal materials, such as occasional insects or young birds. Calcium and other minerals are obtained by chewing on bones, including antlers and turtle shells. Packard (1956) indicated that they eat much soil. We wonder, however, had the soil been examined more closely, if it might have been found to contain subterranean fungi, such as *Endogone* or related forms (Endogonaceae). *Endogone* often looks like soil until examined at higher powers of a dissecting microscope.

Thompson and Thompson (1980) made a total of 7024 observations of gray squirrels feeding in Ontario. In every case the squirrel fed on a single kind of food during the observation, though a variety of foods was eaten during that spring. The most important foods were buried nuts and maple samaras that had survived the winter, but short-term foods such as the flowers of maple and oak were heavily used when available. Buried items decreased in importance as the season progressed. Silver maple samaras became totally dominant in summer when they ripened, forming two-thirds of the diet. In fall, hickory nuts, the first to mature, rapidly assumed dominance, and were followed by other available nuts as they matured. The most important fall food was sugar maple samaras, followed by horsechestnuts, acorns, and shagbark hickory nuts.

In the fall, as various nuts mature, there is a great increase of activity. Much time is spent gathering and storing these nuts for winter, but the squirrels continue to feed in areas of maximum abundance. Numerous nuts are cut from the trees, sometimes producing a veritable rain of nuts in the woods, especially when the squirrels cut white oak acorns. Gray squirrels are classic "scatter hoarders": nuts are carried in the jaws and most are stored by burying them individually (or sometimes in twos or threes) at least 2 cm (an inch) in the ground, but sometimes in quantities in cavities. Steele et al. (1996), in feeding experiments in Pennsylvania, found that gray squirrels cached significantly greater numbers than they ate of intact acorns of red and pin oak uninfested by weevils, but tended to eat the weevil-infested and shelled acorns. They ate significantly more of the white oak acorns, whether or not they were shelled or infested.

Thompson and Thompson (1980) showed that about 85% of the stored nuts are recovered, even under deep snow or after flooding. These authors observed 355 cases of caching behavior. This behavior was most prevalent in summer and fall, and the caches were mostly shallow. Many (28%) were visible at the surface, and a few were below 5 mm. The same authors also made 354 observations of food recovery between 15 October and May 3. Nuts that were experimentally cached by these authors were recovered at the same rate as naturally cached nuts, indicating that memory is not important in locating nuts, as has often been suggested. They concluded, through behavioral observations, that the squirrels located caches by olfactory cues, that the shallow burial aided in this process, and that squirrels could also find the caches of other squirrels.

REPRODUCTION AND DEVELOPMENT. Males and females both reach reproductive status in their second year at about 10 months of age, and two litters per year are generally produced. The main mating periods are in January and February and again in late May through early July.

Males use olfactory cues to locate females in estrus, and they will follow females in the five days before estrus. Mating behavior consists basically of chases, several males often in pursuit of a single female in estrus. A distinctive "buzzy" note accompanies mating chases. Gray squirrel females typically mate once, but on occasion several males will mate with one female. Again, there is a dominance hierarchy, and most matings are by the dominants. As in many vertebrates, especially rodents, copulatory plugs conclude matings. They are opaque white and waxy or rubbery, and their function is presumably to prevent copulation by other males. Nonetheless, female gray and fox squirrels often remove the plug within 30 seconds of copulation and discard it or eat it (Koprowski, 1992).

The female carries her young about 44 days, producing her litters about March and again in July or August. The young are born in a tree cavity or, especially those of the second litters, in the large leaf nests. Newborn gray squirrels weigh about 15 grams and are about 50–60 mm long. Hair appears, the ears open, and the lower incisors erupt by the 21st day; the eyes open at 25 days; and weaning begins at 50 days. The young stay with the female and may in fact nurse until the second litter arrives. The second litter often remains with the mother over the winter, although the young can fend for themselves at 80 days. From one to six young are produced in each litter, most often two to four, the larger numbers in better-quality habitat. There is one record of a litter of eight from North Carolina.

POPULATION CHARACTERISTICS. Gray squirrels were particularly abundant a century ago, and reports of a man killing a hundred individuals in a half-day hunt are not unusual. The frontiersman had to contend with the gray squirrel in raising his crops, and many a corn patch was torn up before the harvest. The squirrel hordes of Civil War days are gone, but the species still occurs in considerable numbers wherever suitable living conditions persist, attaining maximum densities of seven or more per ha (three per acre), sometimes up to 21 per ha (nine per acre) in urban parks.

Although squirrels are able to shift to other foods, such as buds, bark, roots, and fungi when available, mast failure has exceedingly serious consequences for both fox and gray squirrels, and two successive failures can substantially reduce a population. The massive gypsy moth depredations that denuded trees in southern Pennsylvania and elsewhere in the early 1980s practically wiped out squirrel populations in the hard-hit areas because there was virtually no mast production, and little cover to provide protection from predators. Gray squirrels were abundant in the woods at the Juniata College Biological Field Station, in Huntingdon County, Pennsylvania, in the summers of 1979–81, but when most of the forest was completely denuded, the squirrels nearly disappeared (Whitaker, unpubl.).

As with most mammal species, home-range size is influenced by habitat quality and the density of the animals. Gray squirrel home ranges usually average between 0.5 and 10 ha (1 and 25 acres), and those of males are larger than those of females (Flyger and Gates, 1982), but home ranges overlap extensively. Although some larger home ranges have been reported, those of gray squirrels are generally smaller than those of fox squirrels. Gray squirrels are much more active in fall than at other times, and during this time they may change home ranges frequently, to make the most of changing food availability. Gray squirrels may live six years, and there are records of individuals surviving 12 years in the field or 13 years in captivity, but the mortality rate is about 50% per year.

The ranges of gray and fox squirrels overlap extensively, and their foods are similar. Habitat, however, usually separates the two, the fox squirrels settling in the more open woods, the gray squirrels in the more dense woods. Where they occur together, female fox squirrels may displace gray squirrels in the breeding season, but gray squirrels are more efficient at finding food.

ENEMIES. Humans are a major enemy of the gray squirrel, through both hunting and the automobile. Red-tailed hawks are probably major predators, and the barred or great horned owl, moving on silent wings through the late afternoon, often surprises the unwary squirrel. Other birds of prey, bobcats, coyotes, foxes, diamondback rattlesnakes, and black rat snakes may also stalk the ground-foraging animal. There is heavy predation on nestlings by raccoons, snakes, and red squirrels. Gray squirrels do sometimes fall from trees, but are seldom killed by the fall.

PARASITES AND DISEASE. Mange is apparently the most important pathogen of gray squirrels, but tularemia and *Coxiella* have also been found. Gray squirrels are infested with numerous parasites, probably as a result of their tree-hole habitations. One species of flea, three of Anoplura, a subdermal botfly larva (*Cuterebra*), five species of mite, six species of chigger mites, and three species of ticks were found on 47 gray squirrels from Indiana. At least five species of protozoans, nine of tapeworms, and 18 of nematodes have been found as endoparasites. California encephalitis has been found in gray squirrels in the past, in Ohio and Wisconsin.

RELATION TO HUMANS. The gray squirrel is a favorite with the hunter. As many as 2.5 million per year are harvested in Mississippi, a 12.5-million-dollar impact in that state alone. It has been claimed that many Revolutionary era marksmen first gained their skill with the rifle during their early squirrel-hunting days. Besides the aesthetic and economic benefits we reap from squirrels, their caching behavior is of great importance in forest regeneration.

AREAS FOR FURTHER STUDY. A study of the invertebrate inhabitants of the leaf and cavity nests would be fascinating. How many of the forms are parasites, predators, or free-living forms, and what are the relations of the inhabitants to each other? Do the nest-inhabitant communities differ between leaf and cavity nests? Closer examination of the "soil" eaten by squirrels might show it to be mainly fungi. Much could be learned of the behavior of these animals simply by watching them with binoculars. What are their interactions with each other and with other species, and what is their time budget during the day?

## SUBSPECIES

Several subspecies have been described, but all apparently intergrade with the nominate, and we see no evidence of primary isolating mechanisms.

*Sciurus carolinensis carolinensis* Gmelin
As described above.
Type locality: Carolina.
Other currently recognized eastern subspecies:

*S. carolinensis extimus* Bangs
*S. carolinensis fuliginosus* Bachman
*S. carolinensis hypophaeus* Merriam
*S. carolinensis pennsylvanicus* Ord

### LITERATURE

Ackerman, R., and P. D. Weigl. 1970. Dominance relations of red and gray squirrels. *Ecology* 51: 332–334.

Barkalow, F. S., Jr., and M. Shorten. 1973. *The World of the Gray Squirrel*. Philadelphia: J. B. Lippincott. 160 pp.

Flyger, V., and J. E. Gates. 1982. Fox and gray squirrels, *Sciurus niger*, *S. carolinensis*, and allies. In: J. A. Chapman and G. A. Feldhamer, eds., *Wild Mammals of North America*, pp. 209–229. Baltimore: Johns Hopkins Univ. Press.

Habeck, J. R. 1960. Tree-caching behavior in the gray squirrel. *J. Mammal.* 41: 125–126.

Innes, S., and D. M. Lavigne. 1979. Comparative energetics of coat color polymorphism in the eastern gray squirrel *Sciurus carolinensis*. *Canadian J. Zool.* 57: 585–592.

Koprowski, J. L. 1992. Removal of copulatory plugs by female tree squirrels. *J. Mammal.* 73: 572–576.

———. 1994. *Sciurus carolinensis*. **Mammalian Species No. 480.** Amer. Soc. Mammal. 9 pp.

Koprowski, J. L., and M. M. Koprowski. 1987. Joint nest-building activity in the eastern gray squirrel, *Sciurus carolinensis*. *Canadian Field-Nat.* 101: 610–611.

Layne, J. N. 1954. The biology of the red squirrel, *Tamiasciurus hudsonicus loquax* (Bangs), in central New York. *Ecol. Monogr.* 24: 227–267.

Packard, R. L. 1956. The tree squirrels of Kansas: Ecology and economic importance. *Misc. Publ. Mus. Nat. Hist. Univ. Kansas* 11: 1–67.

Riege, D. A. 1991. Habitat specialization and social factors in distribution of red and gray squirrels. *J. Mammal.* 72: 152–162.

Steele, M. A., L. Z. Hadj-Chikh, and J. Hazeltine. 1996. Caching and feeding decisions by *Sciurus carolinensis*: Responses to weevil-infested acorns. *J. Mammal.* 77: 305–314.

Thompson, D. G., and P. S. Thompson. 1980. Food habits and caching behavior of the urban gray squirrels. *Canadian J. Zool.* 58: 701–710.

Uhlig, H. G. 1955. The gray squirrel: Its life history, ecology, and population characteristics in West Virginia. W. Va. Conserv. Comm., Final Report P-R Proj. 31–5. 175 pp.

## Fox Squirrel *Sciurus niger* Gmelin
Color plate 8

DESCRIPTION. The fox squirrel is the largest tree squirrel in the eastern United States and, for that

*Fox squirrel,* Sciurus niger *(Roger W. Barbour)*

matter, in the Western Hemisphere. There are five clawed toes on the hind foot, four clawed toes plus a rudimentary thumb on the forefoot. The fox squirrel lacks the gray squirrel's peglike first upper premolar, and is unique among mammals in accumulating uroporphyrin in teeth, bones, and soft tissue. This material produces pinkish bones and other tissues, in contrast to the white of the gray squirrel. The coloration it yields results from chromatophores (pigment granules) in the bone tissue. The color pattern is exceedingly variable; in fact, fox squirrels may be the most variably colored mammals in the United States. There are three basic color variants of fox squirrels, although intergradations between them are common: the *rufiventer* type of the Midwest, the *cinereus* type of the Northeast, and the *niger* type of the Southeast. Florida and Louisiana, moreover, have their own interesting variants. The various color phases range from black to buffy gray, but the top of the head in all is almost invariably black, and the nose and ears are often creamy white. There is a molt in late spring, but the summer and winter colorations are similar.

Midwestern or "rufiventer" fox squirrels are tawny brown grizzled with gray above, thus somewhat similar to the summer pelage of the northern gray squirrel. The ears are bright orange-brown, slightly tufted in winter. The cheeks, legs, and underparts are rusty or pale orange-brown. There is no light nose patch. The hairs of the tail are mixed black and tawny rufous. Individual coloration, however, is variable; some individuals are very dark, almost black, the hairs mixed with gray or tawny. The buff phase (which yields the name "rufiventer") is mixed black and tawny brown above. The underparts of the tail are much brighter, but the tail is bordered above and below with orange-yellow. The underparts and the feet are ochraceous orange. The top of the head is black, and the nose and ears are creamy white. Fox squirrels are larger in the north, smaller to the south.

The gray or "cinereus" type of the mid-Atlantic region is buffy gray or often steel-gray dorsally, the hair tips black. The feet and toes are cream to buff, and the top of the head is black. The nose and ears are white. The upper side of the tail is colored like the back, the long hairs black with creamy-white tips. The underparts are yellowish white, and the underside of the tail is ochraceous buff, particularly at its base.

The "niger" squirrels of the Southeast are very large (900–1200 grams) and are gray, agouti, or black dorsally except for the nose, lips, and ears, which are creamy white. The basic dark pattern is often modified by a wash of gold, tan, or reddish, mainly on the legs, sides, and tail. The gray or agouti squirrels, which can be quite dark, usually have a yellowish or off-white venter, whereas truly melanistic squirrels normally have a black belly. In North Carolina, about 75% of the squirrels are gray and 25% are completely or partially black (melanistic). Different color types often occur together within nest boxes and within litters.

Fox squirrels from southern Florida are similar to typical "niger," but are smaller and much darker, both above and below. The feet, however, are whiter, not tinged with buff. The nose, lips, and front of the face are white, and the ears are white, with a patch of cinnamon-buff at their base. The head and forelock are black, sprinkled with cinnamon, shading on the sides to an orange-cinnamon. The undersurface of the tail is a rich tawny. Harold H. Bailey states that the full-black pelage also occurs, and that these truly melanistic individuals occupy the pine- and cypress-timbered tracts and the mangrove swamps, from the region of Everglades City, Collier County, to the southern part of Dade County, Florida. Individuals from the Mississippi floodplain in Louisiana, Mississippi, and Alabama are smaller and of richer ferruginous coloration than is typical of *Sciurus niger*.

The reason for color variation in fox squirrels is not well understood, but the yellow coloration of the Midwestern squirrels blends in very well with the yellows of the hickories and oaks in fall, when the squirrels spend a great deal of time cutting nuts. Both the gray and black phases are difficult to see in the strong light-and-shadow environment of southern forests, much harder to see than a gray squirrel (Weigl et al., 1989). Color variation could also be associated with thermoregulation, as has been proposed for the gray squirrel, and it has been suggested that the black coloration in the south might be associated with periodic burning of the pine forests.

The species name, *niger*, means "black." The fox squirrel received this name because the original description was based on a black individual from the south. The species is called the "fox squirrel" because of its yellowish-red color, resembling that of the red fox. Much of the modern information concerning this species is based on midwestern squirrels, probably because they are more widespread and abundant.

MEASUREMENTS. Fox squirrels from Michigan measured: total length 500–570, tail 210–270, hind foot 62–80 mm. They weighed about 800 grams in autumn, the females somewhat larger. Measurements of 210 individuals from Indiana averaged: total length 534 (418–627), tail 244 (190–342), hind foot 71 (61–82) mm; and weight 787 (504–1207) grams. In North Carolina, fox squirrels are very large, weighing 900–1200 grams. Squirrels from the Florida

Parishes Area of Louisiana average total length 570 (530–620), tail 258 (178–295), and hind foot 66 (52–75) mm. Measurements of fox squirrels from southern Florida were: body length 281 (255–308), tail length 259 (237–276), hind foot 75 (71–80) mm. The biggest fox squirrels are supposed to be *Sciurus niger shermani*, from Florida, which have a hind foot averaging 85 mm and weigh from 900 to 1200 grams. This span of weights, however, is identical to that given by Peter Weigl for North Carolina (see above).

Diploid number = 40.

TOOTH FORMULA

$$\frac{1}{1} \quad \frac{0}{0} \quad \frac{1}{1} \quad \frac{3}{3} \quad = \quad 20$$

DISTRIBUTION. In the eastern United States, the fox squirrel occurs through much of the Southeast and Midwest, north through most of Wisconsin and Michigan. Fox squirrels in the coastal plain of the Southeast (of the "niger" type), which live in open pine or pine/oak habitats, have become increasingly scarce in recent years because of deforestation and the replacement of the pine/oak forest by pine monoculture, and those in the Northeast have been almost completely exterminated. Fox squirrels remain abundant only in mature pine/oak and open hardwood habitats. West of the Mississippi, the fox squirrel occurs through most of North Dakota, Kansas, Nebraska, Oklahoma, the eastern three-fourths of Texas, and into extreme northeastern Mexico.

HABITAT. The oak and hickory groves of the prairie states are the stronghold of the northern fox squirrel; in the Deep South, open forests of long-leaf pine and oak, or the open borders of cypress swamps and low thickets, are its favorite haunts. This big tree squirrel is seldom

*Distribution of the fox squirrel,* Sciurus niger, *in the eastern United States*

found in woods with a closed canopy, where the gray squirrel makes its home. It prefers the half-open or parklike oak or hickory stands, often surrounded by prairie and pasture land. In the Southeast, fox squirrels are often found on golf courses with open pine stands between the fairways. Fox squirrels are constantly establishing themselves in new locations by moving considerable distances along hedgerows and thickets, or across open ground. In the northern parts of their range, they are increasingly being replaced by the gray squirrel, as oak/hickory is replaced by beech/maple/hemlock. Riverbottom habitats may be suitable, provided there are adequate nut-producing trees. Tree cavities are important to this species, and the lack of cavities in the pine woods may be a factor in the decrease of fox squirrels in the Southeast.

HABITS. Fox squirrels are well known over much of the eastern United States, although they are becoming less common in the Southeast. They are most active in early morning and late afternoon in good weather, often more toward the middle of the day in winter or inclement weather. They can swim, using a dogpaddle stroke, and they can run at rates up to nearly 25 kph (15 mph). Most often, they feed while sitting and grasping the food in the forepaws. They are of course excellent climbers, and they are quite acrobatic, jumping between limbs and often hanging by the hindlimbs, leaving their front paws free to grasp food, but they rarely fall.

Fox squirrels are not particularly social, although they will feed in common areas and may den together in winter. The timing of denning in fall and winter appears to be tied to climatic conditions; warm, moist conditions and abundant food will slow their resort to the nests. Their lack of territoriality facilitates not only these types of behaviors but also the establishment of a "peck order" (see the account for the gray squirrel). Young squirrels are frequently seen chasing and wrestling with each other, on the ground and on tree trunks. Such rough-and-tumble behavior obviously helps them develop their skills of navigation and balance.

The fox squirrel spends much time on the ground, particularly late in the fall—probably much more time than the gray squirrel does. When disturbed, like the gray squirrel it will run for a tree, often climb up a meter or two, and brace itself against the trunk, head up and tail down, usually on the far side, all but unseen by the observer—but sometimes on the same side, and then it may even bark at the observer. Often one can tell that the squirrel is about to bark, because it starts stiffly waving its tail. Other times it will move on up the tree and enter a tree hole or leaf nest. Like the gray squirrel, the fox squirrel will also lie on top of a limb, legs and tail dangling. One can often approach quite closely to a squirrel in this position.

Two to four tree holes per ha (one or two per acre) are needed for suitable fox squirrel habitat. The openings should be no more than 12 cm (5 inches) in diameter and the cavities at least 35 cm (14 inches) deep. The opening must be such as to exclude rain and other mammals, such as raccoons. Many of the best cavities in the north are in beech and white oak trees, although soft maple and sycamore are also suitable. Cavities result from the natural falling of limbs, followed by central rot and perhaps additional work by woodpeckers and/or squirrels. Where cavities are inadequate, leaf nests assume greater importance, and leaf nests are heavily used when food is abundant and weather is mild. Leaf nests may be built in trees of many different species, and usually include leaves from the tree selected. Fox squirrels average about three to six active nests per squirrel, and additional nests may occasionally be visited. The nests are green when constructed, thus not conspicuous (yet not difficult to find when you look for them), but become very obvious after the leaves fall. Leaf nests may be up to 50 cm (20 inches) in diameter, and inside there is much shredded material. The entrance is on the side, and there is enough domed leaf material to keep the animals warm and dry. Tree holes appear to be preferred in winter, but fox squirrels will sometimes build leaf nests strong enough for winter use by incorporating twigs in their construction. Platforms, which squirrels simply lie on, are also built sometimes. One can develop relative estimates of squirrel density in a forest from the numbers of leaf nests observed. We once observed the completion of a nest in a scant half hour.

Activity patterns vary seasonally. In winter, squirrels are most active between 0800 and

1600 hours, whereas in summer there are two peaks of activity, one between 0600 and 1200 hours, the other between 1400 and 1800 hours. Activity is greatly reduced in July, the "disappearance" period, at least in the south. At this time, food supplies are often low, the days are hot, and squirrels reduce their activity, spending more time in leaf nests (instead of cavities), and more time in wetlands. Fox squirrels are increasingly active in damp weather, however, including light rain, for squirrels are better able to locate nuts and fungi when they are wet (Weigl et al., 1989), and wet weather may facilitate digging. In late summer and in fall, there is much more activity throughout the day, as the squirrels resume heavy foraging and begin to store food for winter.

Squirrels of this species produce several vocalizations, most of them lower and harsher than those of the gray squirrel. Most conspicuous are the repeated barking and the "que, que, que" calls.

The fox squirrel's closest associates are other squirrels, particularly the gray squirrel, red squirrel, chipmunk, and flying squirrels. The fox squirrel is most similar in size and habits to the gray squirrel, but these two are largely separated geographically or ecologically. When they occur together, the fox squirrel tends to occupy more savanna-like or parklike areas and the gray squirrel the deeper woods. The red squirrel is smaller, is more partial to conifers in areas where it occurs with the fox squirrel, and uses a much greater variety of den sites, such as hollow logs, burrows, rock piles, and manmade structures, as well as cavities and leaf nests. Flying squirrels, which are active at night, can use much smaller cavities than those used by fox or gray squirrels, and chipmunks, of course, are primarily ground dwellers. Thus the eastern squirrels have evolved to fill an area of rather different niches, and seldom compete seriously with one another. When they do compete, the smaller gray squirrel often outcompetes and replaces its larger cousin, the fox squirrel.

FOOD AND FEEDING. The distribution of fox squirrels is greatly influenced by habitat as that relates to food supplies. As indicated above, fall is (or should be) the time of plenty for the squirrels, time to store nuts for winter and early spring. The harvest season finds the fox squirrel busily engaged in burying acorns, hickory nuts, beechnuts, and other nuts in shallow (inch-deep) holes in the ground, from which they are recovered in time of need. Turkey oak is the oak most often important for food for fox squirrels in the pine forests of the Southeast. Many of the nuts not found by the squirrels produce new trees, and whole grasslands can be planted to nut trees by squirrels. Like gray squirrels, the fox squirrel caches most of its nuts in the ground individually, or sometimes in twos and threes, rather than in larger caches. Scatterhoarding nuts in low numbers per cache is advantageous to the squirrels, because it decreases pilfering by other nut feeders. An optimum cache distribution and density are reached when nut pilfering is balanced against the increased cost of transporting nuts for burial and against increased risk of attack by predators. These buried items are apparently the squirrel's mainstay during the fall, winter, and early spring, when the items are located apparently by the squirrel's simply visiting logical locations and using its sense of smell (Flyger and Gates, 1982). From about one-third up to nine-tenths of the stored nuts are recovered. Squirrels have sometimes dug up most of the walnuts that had been planted to start plantations.

Nuts are sometimes stored in tree cavities, and home ranges can sometimes overlap in such a way that nuts may be stored in the same tree by more than one squirrel. But fox squirrels do not subsist entirely on mast. Early spring is also a time of plenty, provided that the mast crop of the preceding fall was adequate. The ripening samaras of maples are often eaten; pine seeds and staminate cones, newly opening buds, and elm seeds are often important in spring; and various flowers, corms and bulbs, fungi, and insects are also available.

In many areas, early summer may be the hardest time for fox squirrels, especially in the pine forests. There, spring foods and the old mast supplies are gone, and available foods may be patchy. Squirrels often become much less active then, lose weight, and conserve energy by spending much time in their nests. The buds, flowers, and young fruits of tulip—cut from the trees in such numbers as to remind one of the fall nut harvest—are heavily eaten when available.

Catkins of willow and cottonwood, flowers of hackberry, beech, and elm, buds of elm and basswood, and mulberries and other berries and fruits are all known to serve as food, and birds' eggs and insects are occasionally eaten.

In late summer (August and September), conditions again improve for fox squirrels. In the Southeast, the ripening pine seeds provide an abundance of foods. The squirrels will sample various trees, then feed heavily on favored ones. But no caching occurs at this time. As the pine cones begin to open (late September) the squirrels will collect the seeds from the ground, but the fruits of holly, bay, grape, greenbrier, and persimmon are now available, along with insects. In the Midwest, the fox squirrel forages heavily on corn and soybeans left in the fields after harvest. Green pine cones are an important food of fox squirrels in typical pine-dominated habitats in the Southeast, as are osage orange fruits, and fox squirrels often strip bark from the twigs of sugar maple for sap. Calcium and other minerals are obtained by feeding on bones, antlers, and turtle shells. Salt is sought especially in spring and fall (Weeks and Kirkpatrick, 1978).

Fox squirrels will often feed on various types of fungi, especially truffles and subterranean clusters of spores of the family Endogonaceae, but many others as well. The squirrels make pits into the pine needles in search of the fungi, which are located by smell and provide food and nutrients, such as sodium and phosphorus. Many of the fungi are exclusively animal-dispersed, and their spores are relatively indestructible. They occur in huge numbers, and, once ingested, they remain in the digestive tract for some time, and are dispersed every time the animal defecates. The hypogeous fungi (*Endogone* and its relatives), which are mycorrhizal, form a mutualistic relationship with the roots of trees of various species, effectively increasing the absorptive surface of the roots. For its part, the fungus has a place to live plus a source of carbohydrate. Some of the fungi contain nitrogen-fixing bacteria, and thus produce nitrogen, some of which is available to the tree. Some of these fungi also produce auxins and cytokinins, which can influence plant growth. Thus, there is a complex relationship between the squirrels, the trees, and the fungi.

Animal foods, such as caterpillars, moths and butterflies, grasshoppers, scarabaeid beetles, ants, weevils (Curculionidae), birds and their eggs, and dead fish may be eaten in small amounts.

REPRODUCTION AND DEVELOPMENT. First-year females born in spring generally produce their first young the following spring; the fall young tend to produce their first young the following fall. Older squirrels are capable of producing two litters per year. In the male, the testes descend with about the same timing. Prenuptial chases, which are noisy and conspicuous, occur as early as late December, and first matings occur through January. The mating ritual includes various barks, purrs, and sucking notes, along with a variety of grooming, tail-flicking, and approach behaviors. It is usually the dominant males that successfully mate. As discussed above (for the gray squirrel), copulatory plugs are formed at mating, presumably to prevent copulation by other males, but females often remove these within 30 seconds of mating. A second peak of breeding occurs in May and June; like the gray squirrel, the fox squirrel can produce two litters per year in the north, just one in the south. Litter sizes are smaller in times of poor food supply, and smaller in the Southeast than in the West. Gestation is about 44 days.

The one to six (usually two to four) young are born primarily in late February and early March, and again in June and July (and infrequently into late August), although pregnant females have been taken in every month of the year. The young, born usually in tree-hole cavities but sometimes in leaf nests, are about 50 to 60 mm long, weigh 14 to 17 grams, and are pink and helpless. As with those of other tree squirrels, the young develop slowly. Hair appears on the dorsum at the end of a week, by which time the weight has doubled. The eyes open at the end of the fifth week. It is seven to eight weeks before the young leave the natal chamber, and about 12 or 13 weeks before they are weaned, first venture to the ground, and begin to fend for themselves. The young of spring litters may leave their mothers soon after weaning if a second litter is produced. Fall litters may remain longer with the mother, but all juveniles eventually disperse.

POPULATION CHARACTERISTICS. Fox squirrels occur at their greatest densities in April and May, and again when the young of the second litters are entering the population in September and October. It is at this latter season that active dispersal and movements of established adults are most likely to occur. This species has seldom launched major "migrations," however, and those that have been reported are not nearly so spectacular as those of the gray squirrel. Such movements probably result from good mast production the preceding year, which in turn results in a high squirrel population, at a time when mast production the current year is poor: too many squirrels, too little food. Populations vary in density up to about 1.0–3.5 squirrels per ha (0.4 to 1.4 per acre), although numbers can be much higher, up to 12 per ha (5 per acre) for short periods during good years. Weigl et al. (1989) found fox squirrels occurring at much lower densities in North Carolina, where they are in decline.

Home ranges in the West presumably average between 1 and 7 ha (3 and 17 acres), but Weigl et al. (1989) have recently found, in North Carolina pine forests, that the home ranges of 20 males averaged 26.6 ha (66 acres) and those of 20 females 17.2 (42 acres), but when using different methods of calculation the ranges of males averaged 43.7 ha (107 acres), those of females 25.0 ha (62 acres). Kantola and Humphrey (1990) calculated the average home-range size for males and females in Florida at 42.8 and 16.7 ha (106 and 41 acres), respectively, and those home ranges shifted during a food shortage. The much larger home ranges of the southeastern squirrels are related to the patchiness of their habitat; home-range size varies greatly with habitat quality and configuration and with density of squirrels. Using radio-tracking techniques, Adams (1976) found males in home ranges averaging 8 ha (20 acres), while those of females averaged half as large. Squirrels in one study in Ohio were traveling 1.2 km (0.7 mile) daily between woodlots. Home ranges break down during the mating seasons, and when the young leave their birthplaces.

Adult females apparently regulate population densities, but traditional scent-marking sites are regularly visited by males. Scent is deposited from the oral-labial glands. Females visit traditional scent sites but rarely scent. Both sexes do mark sites randomly as they travel in their home ranges. Duration of residence in an unhunted population in a given range was 4.7 months for juveniles, 13.5 months for subadults, and 25–27 months for yearlings and adults (Hansen et al., 1986).

In times of food abundance and food storage, fox squirrels are active most of the day in a small area. During scarcity in winter, the animals are forced to increase their home ranges to find adequate food. This is especially true of males, for females seem to outcompete them for home ranges. Much searching for hypogeous fungi occurs at this time. The large home ranges of the males may overlap those of several females, but males apparently avoid overlapping those of other males. During the period of summer scarcity, when fox squirrels reduce activity, they may move to the edges of swamps and bottomlands. Home ranges at any one time are thus only a part of the whole, their location and extent determined by local conditions and food availability.

Fox squirrels are large and mobile, and thus can respond to new food supplies as they become available. Bigger squirrels can more easily and more quickly move between food sources—which can often be far apart—and a particular advantage of large size in the Southeast may be the ability to tackle the very large cones of longleaf pine, which are up to 29 cm long and weigh up to 490 grams. The largest fox squirrels are found in northern Florida, and here there is a shorter period of food scarcity in spring. The longleaf pine cones become available in June, and food is abundant through September.

A large proportion of the population (at least one-third) turns over each year, as a result of mortality from hunting, the automobile, and natural predation, but tagging studies have indicated that individual squirrels can live for at least six years, and fox squirrels have lived up to 20 years in the laboratory.

Weather and its effects on local food supplies are of great importance to fox squirrels, for food failures such as those caused by heavy spring frost can destroy the flowers of oaks and hickories and lead to rapid decimation of the squirrel populations. At such times the squirrels expand their home ranges, seek out alternative food sources, and spend more time in tree cavities as an energy-saving measure. This level of inertia leads to low reproductive rates, high predation rates, and crashes in the squirrel population.

Fire has a positive influence on southeastern fox squirrel populations, for fire favors the pine forest by reducing hardwood competition and maintaining the widespread spacing of the trees. The gray squirrel begins to outcompete the fox squirrel when hardwoods move in and the canopy closes.

ENEMIES. Birds of prey, bobcats, raccoons, domestic dogs and cats, foxes, timber rattlesnakes, and rat snakes are some of the known predators, but predation is not a particularly significant cause of mortality in fox squirrels, other than on the young. People, through hunting, habitat destruction, and the use of automobiles, are their greatest enemies.

PARASITES AND DISEASE. Mange mites (*Notoedres*, *Sarcoptes*, and *Cnemidoptes*), which are common on fox squirrels, cause irritation and loss of hair, often severely enough to cause death. On 137 fox squirrels from Indiana (Whitaker et al., 1976) we found two species of fleas, three of sucking lice, the subdermal larvae of the botfly (*Cuterebra*), five species of mites, seven species of chigger mites, and three species of ticks. Species of all of the major groups of internal parasites (flukes, nematodes, cestodes, and protozoans) are harbored also.

RELATION TO HUMANS. Throughout its range, this species is a popular game animal. It is often hunted even in late summer, before other hunting seasons are open. One can simply sit quietly in the woods and wait for a fox squirrel to appear. Much more sporting is to listen for its call, for nuts being cut, or for the swish of branches as it moves through the trees, then test your skills against nature as you attempt to track the animal without alarming it. Man has played a major role in the distribution and abundance of the fox squirrel, especially in the Southeast, where cutting of the pristine long-leaf pine forest has reduced crucial fox squirrel habitat. Damage by fox squirrels tends to occur on a local scale, affecting, for example, corn crops, gardens, and fruit or nut trees. Their occasional gnawing of shingles or the wood around openings in buildings can be discouraged by applying mothballs or crystals to the damaged areas.

AREAS FOR FURTHER WORK. Further studies could be made of the leaf-nest and cavity-nest inhabitants, and of the "soil" eaten by fox squirrels, and much could be learned simply by observing them with binoculars. What are their interactions with each other and with other species, and what is their time budget? One interested in animal behavior could gain much from simple, quiet observation of this species, especially of its foraging and mating. The squirrel's techniques of gathering and feeding on the many foods it takes would be fascinating.

## SUBSPECIES

There is a great amount of color variation in this species, manifested both geographically and otherwise, and several subspecies have been described in consequence. We are not aware, however, of primary isolating mechanisms separating any of the subspecies of the eastern United States, although some of them—the Delmarva fox squirrel, *S. n. cinereus*, the mangrove fox squirrel, *S. n. avicennia*, and Sherman's fox squirrel, *S. n. shermani*—are considered to be threatened or endangered.

*Sciurus niger niger* Linnaeus 1758
   As described above.
   Type locality: Probably southern South Carolina.
   Other currently recognized eastern subspecies:
      *S. niger avicennia* Howell
      *S. niger bachmani* Lowery & Davis
      *S. niger cinereus* Linnaeus
      *S. niger rufiventer* Geoffroy St. Hilaire
      *S. niger shermani* Moore
      *S. niger subauratus* Bachman
      *S. niger vulpinus* Gmelin

### LITERATURE

Adams, C. E. 1976. Measurement and characteristics of fox squirrel, *Sciurus niger rufiventer*, home ranges. *Amer. Midland Nat.* 95: 211–215.

Allen, D. L. 1943. *Michigan Fox Squirrel Management*. Mich. Dept. Conserv., Game Div., Publ. 100. 404 pp.

Benson, B. N. 1980. Dominance relationships, mating behaviour and scent marking in fox squirrels (*Sciurus niger*). *Mammalia* 144: 143–160.

Dueser, R. D., and K. Terwilliger. 1987. Status of the Delmarva Fox Squirrel (*Sciurus niger cinereus*) in Virginia. *Virg. J. Sci.* 38: 380–388.

Flyger, V., and J. E. Gates. 1982. Fox and gray squirrels, *Sciurus niger, S. carolinensis*, and allies. In: J. A. Chapman and G. A. Feldhamer, eds. *Wild Mammals of North America*, pp. 209–229. Baltimore: Johns Hopkins Univ. Press.

Hansen, L. P., C. M. Nixon, and S. P. Havera. 1986. Recapture rates and length of residence in an unexploited fox squirrel population. *Amer. Midland Nat.* 115: 209–215.

Havera, S. P., and C. M. Nixon. 1979. Winter feeding of fox and gray squirrel populations. *J. Wildl. Mgmt.* 44: 41–55.

Havera, S. P., and K. E. Smith. 1979. A nutritional comparison of selected fox squirrel foods. *J. Wildl. Mgmt.* 43: 691–704.

Kantola, A. T., and S. R. Humphrey. 1990. Habitat use by Sherman's fox squirrel (*sciurus niger shermani*) in Florida. *J. Mammal.* 71: 411–419.

Koprowski, J. J. *Sciurus niger*. **Mammalian Species No. 479.** Amer. Soc. Mammal. 9 pp.

Layne, J. N., ed. 1974. Mammals. Vol. 1. In: *Rare and Endangered Biota of Florida*. Gainesville: Univ. Press of Florida. 52 pp.

Moore, J. C. 1957. The natural history of the fox squirrel, *Sciurus niger shermani*. Amer. Mus. Nat. Hist., Bull. 113. 71 pp.

Reichard, T. A. 1976. Spring food habits and feeding behavior of fox squirrels and red squirrels. *Amer. Midland Nat.* 92: 443–450.

Stapanian, M. A., and C. C. Smith. 1978. A model for seed scatterhoarding: Coevolution of fox squirrels and black walnuts. *Ecology* 59: 884–896.

Weeks, H. P., and C. M. Kirkpatrick. 1978. Salt preferences and sodium drive phenology in fox squirrels and woodchucks. *J. Mammal.* 59: 531–542.

Weigl, P. D., M. A. Steele, L. J. Sherman, J. C. Ha, and T. L. Sharpe. 1989. The ecology of the fox squirrel (*Sciurus niger*) in North Carolina: Implications for survival in the southeast. Tall Timbers Research Sta., Bull. No. 24. 93 p.

Whitaker, J. O., Jr., E. J. Spicka, and L. L. Schmeltz. 1976. Ectoparasites of squirrels of the genus *Sciurus* from Indiana. *Proc. Ind. Acad. Sci.* 85: 431–436.

Zelley, R. A. 1971. The sounds of the fox squirrel, *Sciurus niger rufiventer*. *J. Mammal.* 52: 597–604.

## Red Squirrel, Chickaree
### *Tamiasciurus hudsonicus*
**(Erxleben)**          Color plate 8

DESCRIPTION. The red squirrel can readily be recognized by its rufous color and small size,

*Red squirrel,* Tamiasciurus hudsonicus
*(Roger W. Barbour)*

about half that of the gray squirrel. In some areas it is referred to as the "chickaree," in northern Indiana it is the "piney squirrel," and in mountainous West Virginia it is the "fairy diddle."

There is a marked seasonal difference in color in this species. In winter, a broad rusty-red band extends along the entire dorsum, from between the ears nearly to the tail tip, the sides are olive-gray, with a sprinkling of black hairs, and there are prominent reddish or black tufts on the ears. In summer, a prominent black line separates the dorsal pattern from the white underparts, and the ear tufts are absent. The summer pelage is duller and more olive-colored than that of winter and lacks the bright rufous band. The ear tufts appear only in winter; and no other eastern squirrel possesses such tufts. The underparts, summer and winter, are grayish white, the hairs frequently marked with black, presenting a vermiculate appearance. The tail's upper surface is colored like the back, the outer hairs banded with black and tipped with yellowish rufous; its lower surface is yellowish gray, the tips blackish.

Red squirrels from Maine are smaller and darker, the underparts gray in winter, much vermiculated with dusky marks. The tail is dark, with much black, its outer fringe not conspicuously lighter than the median band. In the heavy spruce and fir forests of the higher southern Allegheny Mountains, red squirrels are distinctly darker on the head and sides, and the red of the dorsal area is deeper. The underparts are more grayish (less clear white) and more or less vermiculated with dusky. These characters show most strongly in winter pelage. There are two molts per year; the winter pelage is the brightest.

MEASUREMENTS. Average measurements of 28 adults from western New York were: total length 310, tail 120, hind foot 46 mm; and weight 140–220 grams. Average measurements of six adults from near Moosehead Lake, Maine, were: total length 290, tail 121, hind foot 45 mm. Average measurements of 32 adults from the Great Smoky Mountains were: total length 318, tail 132, hind foot 48 mm.
  Diploid number = 46.

TOOTH FORMULA

$$\frac{1}{1} \quad \frac{0}{0} \quad \frac{1 \text{ or } 2}{1} \quad \frac{3}{3} \; = \; 20 \text{ or } 22$$

DISTRIBUTION. The red squirrel occurs from Wisconsin, Michigan, and Maine south through northern Indiana and Ohio and through most of Virginia and the Appalachians to northern Georgia. Outside of our range, this species occurs through the southern two-thirds of Canada and into Alaska, and to the south through the Rocky Mountain area. On the west coast, it is replaced by the Douglas squirrel, *Tamiasciurus douglasii*.

HABITAT. Evergreen forest appears to be the original habitat of this species, but it now seems to exhibit utter disregard for a stereotyped habitat and occupies any area offering food and shelter. It may occur in a coniferous forest, a hardwood forest, or a mixed stand.

HABITS. The red squirrel is well known wherever it occurs, from the deep forests of northern Maine and Wisconsin to the mist-shrouded slopes of the Great Smoky Mountains. Its rolling chatter, nervous scampering, and mischievous

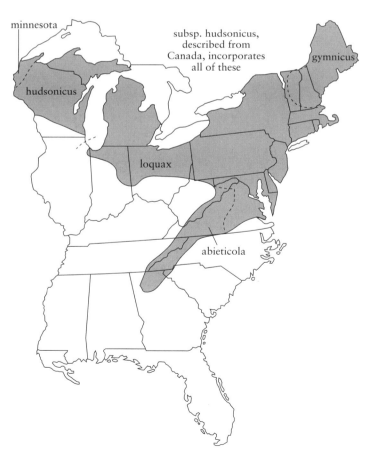

*Distribution of the red squirrel, or chickaree,* Tamiasciurus hudsonicus, *in the eastern United States*

ways have made it a favorite with naturalists, vacationers, and residents; as a consequence, it is one of our better-known mammals. Like most squirrels, it is diurnal, but it is particularly active at dawn and dusk.

Red squirrels spend a great deal of time on the ground, dashing from one tree to another or digging industriously for stored cones or buried maple seeds. When threatened, they will run up a tree, scamper from tree to tree over horizontal branches, remain on the far side of a tree trunk, or retreat to the safety of a leaf nest or a hollow in a tree, depending on circumstances.

Red squirrels may hole up for a few days in inclement weather, but otherwise are active all winter. In times of deep snow they are much less often in trees, but rather spend much time in burrows beneath the snow.

The red squirrel often constructs a nest of grass and bark in a deserted woodpecker chamber or a natural cavity in a hickory or oak, or it may be in a rock pile or a fallen tree. Sometimes it is a large structure of twigs and leaves in the branches of evergreens, built about 5 to 6 meters (16 to 20 feet) above ground. If a grape tangle is at hand, red squirrels may construct their nests of shredded grape bark. These they occupy throughout the year. Often the squirrel tunnels into the soil. Its piles of pine-cone remnants are everywhere in occupied coniferous forest.

Many people think that red squirrels, even though smaller, dominate gray squirrels and drive them out of their territories, and even that they castrate them. The latter story probably arose from someone's observing how often red squirrels chase gray squirrels, then linking that observation with the apparent lack of testes in gray squirrels, which are abdominal in the nonbreeding season. In a study of the interrelationships of these two species, Ackerman and Weigl (1970) attempted to determine the severity of the interaction between the two in captivity. Using a single cage with two nest boxes, a primary one with nesting material and a secondary, "unattractive" one, they introduced pairs of squirrels and found that red squirrels would nest together overnight, but that gray squirrels never did. Red and gray squirrels did nest in the same box on 18 nights, thus demonstrating remarkable tolerance for each other. The authors concluded that it is territorial be-

havior in the field that explains most of the red squirrel's observed intolerance.

Young squirrels spend much time learning, establishing territories, and engaging in early sexual behavior. When they wander into the territory of an adult they may be attacked, though a warning call will usually avert the attack.

FOOD AND FEEDING. James N. Layne (1954) found that acorns, hickory nuts, and beechnuts are among the year-round staple foods of this species, but other items, such as hemlock cones and tulip and sycamore seeds, which are more seasonal, are heavily utilized in some situations. The terminal buds of conifers and bark are important in winter. Various berries, the swelling buds of maple and elm, the fruits of sumac, the seeds of many conifers, many species of fungi, an occasional nestling or a clutch of eggs, various insects, and many other items are included in the red squirrel's fare. In the early fall the green cones of pine are cut and buried in the damp earth, for if they were allowed to dry, the seeds would quickly be wind-scattered and lost to the squirrel. Even the deadly amanita mushroom, *Amanita muscaria*, is eaten by red squirrels, apparently without harm. Red squirrels have been known to kill and partially devour young cottontails.

All tree squirrels are opportunistic and lavish in their feeding habits, sampling many items, discarding far more than they eat, and storing an excessive amount. This seeming waste is an adaptation to their needs, ensuring that the squirrel remains familiar with the potential foods in its environment. Weigl and Hanson (1980) demonstrated beautifully that young red

*Cones of white pine cut free and eaten by red squirrel*

squirrels can learn food-handling techniques from more experienced individuals (presumably their mothers, in most cases), techniques that require about half the expenditure of time and energy they needed on their own, proceeding through trial and error. This "edge" may be crucial to developing squirrels, in subsequent competition with other individuals.

It has long been known that red squirrels obtain sap from maple trees, and Heinrich (1992) presents much information on this behavior. Heinrich determined that the squirrels bite holes into the xylem of sugar maples, then harvest the sugar from these holes after the water has evaporated. The squirrels would make a quick bite, then move to the next site. The bites, in trunks or nearly vertical branches of saplings (4–15 cm in diameter at breast height), consisted of 2-mm-wide chisel-like grooves that pierced through the bark to the xylem. Fresh sap is only 2% sugar, but the squirrels revisited the maples after the sap had dried, and then licked it. At that time the sap is greater than 55% sugar. The squirrels would avidly return to these areas and lick the sugar, mainly in early morning, before the sap flow had begun. At one time Heinrich observed five squirrels in one maple grove all harvesting sap at the same time, though they were at least 20 meters (65 feet) apart and appeared to ignore each other. Where sugar maple trees occurred, no red maples were used, but at one site where there were no sugar maples, one red maple showed much evidence of use. The cuts were all healed by July. Heinrich observed the characteristic tooth marks at 23 sites in Maine and Vermont.

Some items are buried individually in the ground, but in contrast to other tree squirrels of North America, red squirrels store great numbers of items in large caches or "middens" for later use (Smith, 1970). Late summer and fall is the season when most of the caching is done. The caches may be in a hollow tree, in an underground den, or in a hollow at the base of a tree. Conifer cones are cut when green, then cached individually, or stored in middens either by burying them en masse or by piling them on the ground at the bases of trees or along logs. They are then often buried in a seepage or other wet area, which keeps them from opening; there they may remain fresh and viable even for a period of years. Other foods, such as acorns, hickory nuts, beechnuts, walnuts, butternuts, hawthorn, and sumac fruits, are also cached in this way. Fungi may be cut and placed in trees to dry, where they are available well into the winter, or they may then be cached. The many cached items may form the mainstay of the squirrels' diet through much of the late winter and early spring. Caches in hollow trees can be supplemented over years, and may even include additions from succeeding squirrels in a given territory. In years of mast failure, red squirrels are forced to feed on any other types of food they can find, and drastic declines in populations may occur. Smith (1968) presents information on energy budgets and caloric values of foods.

REPRODUCTION AND DEVELOPMENT. Through much of their range, red squirrels have only one litter per year, especially where winters are severe. In areas like New York, with less severe winters, the squirrels are less fiercely territorial and produce two litters per year. In New York, mating is in late winter and early spring (February and March) and again in June and July. The female defends her territory until she comes into heat, which she probably advertises by producing vaginal secretions. She is then receptive to males for just one day. At that time she permits nearby males to enter her territory, and she may mate with more than one of them. Appeasement calls given by the males at this time help them gain entry to the female's territory. At these times the males may be seen pursuing females, chasing and scrambling about the trees and over the ground with great celerity. Mating itself may occur on the ground or in a tree. In an interesting use of radiotelemetry, Helene Lair (1985) determined that free-living females were in estrus for one day, at which time several males would gather in their territories and engage in mating chases. A male dominance hierarchy is established at this time.

Gestation in the red squirrel is about 35 days. Most litters are produced in April and May and again in July and August, but Hamilton found nest young in late October in New York. The three to seven young (extremes are one to eight) are born pink and hairless. Increased numbers of young per litter occur in response to a good mast crop. The newborn are about 70 mm long and weigh about 7 grams. Hair is obvious by ten days, and the ears open at 18 days. When three and a half weeks old, the young have acquired the characteristic markings of the adult. At 28 days, they weigh 22 to 44 grams, and their lower incisors have erupted. The young may be moved between nests, the female carrying them by the nape of the neck. The eyes open at four to five weeks, and shortly thereafter the young make their first ventures from the nest. They are weaned at six to seven weeks of age, after which the female stays away from the nest. Chasing and mock fighting among litter mates are common, and the food-storing habit is manifested at this time. The female sometimes leaves the territory to the young, who then subdivide it. The young do not breed until their second year (at 10–12 months). It is not clear how many of the females produce two litters per year.

The reproductive system of the red squirrel is unique among tree squirrels in its morphology. The baculum is tiny, almost microscopic, whereas in a gray squirrel it is nearly an inch (2.5 cm) long. The vagina is coiled, a character unique to *Tamiasciurus*.

POPULATION CHARACTERISTICS. Fancy (1981) found that daily movements by females were shorter than those by males in prebreeding and breeding periods and during pregnancy, but that movements by females were longer than those by males during lactation and postweaning.

Red squirrels vary greatly in number, up to about 4.5 per ha (18 per acre) (Layne, 1954), but they may become much more abundant during short periods of plenty. In some seasons the woods appear full of them; at other times an entire summer may pass with only one or two being seen, and these few are strangely quiet. Individual red squirrels have home ranges of about 1.3 to 1.5 ha (3.2 to 3.7 acre), and both sexes defend a territory of about 0.2 to 1.2 ha (0.5 to 3 acres) in the area of the nest and the important feeding areas. Christopher C. Smith (1968) accumulated much information on the populations of this species. Territories, inversely proportional in size to the amount of available food, are fiercely defended against other red squirrels and other tree squirrels and birds. Red squirrels advertise their territories by their periodic trilling, and defend them by constant chat-

ter and tail jerking, threatening postures, and, sometimes, actual attack with the teeth and forepaws. Territories are contiguous, not overlapping; and they are defended by single squirrels, not by pairs. They are defended throughout the year in areas with cone mast, especially where winters are severe. They serve to spread the animals through the woods, as they do birds, thus minimizing conflict and perhaps regulating squirrel density.

Boundaries between territories are clear, and who holds rights to a favored cone-bearing tree on a boundary between two territories is never in any doubt. Territories are maintained by means of four territorial calls and an alarm call. One of these territorial calls is the extended trill so often heard in red squirrel country. The trill is modified into a loud, aggressive call upon the entrance of an intruder, and becomes a quiet, aggressive call when resident and intruder are in closer contact on territory. The fourth call, an appeasement call given by an intruder, results in inhibition of the aggressive behavior. This call is also given during the breeding season when a male enters the territory of a female for breeding. The alarm call is given in the presence of predators.

Occasionally, Smith (1968) observed a dispersing squirrel commandeering the territory of an established resident, forcing a change of ownership, but major conflicts, even death, can result from an attempted takeover. In hardwoods, however, where red squirrels may be abundant and where there is diverse food, they are often nonterritorial. Here they are also less vocal and less aggressive. The resource base in this case may have a marked effect on behavior.

There is much turnover within populations, owing to mortality and dispersal, but individual red squirrels live two or even three years, and in captivity they have been known to live for ten.

ENEMIES. The quickness of this little squirrel does not always save it from its enemies. The marten, the fisher, the bobcat, the larger hawks and owls, and other predators feed upon it, although Layne (1954) believed that predation was not particularly significant in red squirrel mortality. Red squirrel remains were, however, found in 10% of 1500 coyote scats from the Adirondacks.

PARASITES AND DISEASE. As do other tree squirrels, red squirrels harbor numerous fleas, lice, ticks, mites, and chiggers. A larvae of a botfly, *Cuterebra*, have also been found. The large numbers of parasites in tree squirrels probably arise from the inter- and intraspecific sharing of nest holes. Protozoans (three), trematodes, nematodes, and cestodes all occur as internal parasites of red squirrels. Tularemia, *Haplosporangium*, and some viruses have been reported.

RELATION TO HUMANS. This species, smaller than the other tree squirrels, is generally ignored by the hunter, but some people find it worthy both of hunting and of eating, and in former times it was eaten by both Indians and pioneers. It can be a nuisance in an attic or storage area, or in a plantation, where it may nip off the terminal buds of the crop plants. One of its habits, caching food in various locations, may help in reforestation, but another of its habits, stripping cones from the trees and concentrating them in one place, may hinder reforestation. Foresters needing pine seeds to plant sometimes find it economically feasible to hunt for red squirrel caches, rather than to cut the pine cones themselves.

AREAS FOR FURTHER WORK. The reason for the tiny baculum and coiled vagina in this species are unknown. Invertebrate faunas from ground and aerial nests could be compared, and both could be compared with the parasite fauna of the host.

## SUBSPECIES

We see no evidence of primary isolating mechanisms, and thus suggest that all eastern red squirrels are of one subspecies.

*Tamiasciurus hudsonicus hudsonicus*
(Erxleben)

As described above.

Type locality: Mouth of the Severn River, Ontario.

Other currently recognized eastern subspecies:

*T. hudsonicus abieticola* (Howell)
*T. hudsonicus gymnicus* (Bangs)
*T. hudsonicus loquax* (Bangs)
*T. hudsonicus minnesota* (Allen)

## LITERATURE

Ackerman, R., and P. D. Weigl. 1970. Dominance relations of red and gray squirrels. *Ecology* 51: 332–334.

Fancy, S. G. 1981. Daily movements of red squirrels, *Tamiasciurus hudsonicus*. *Canadian Field-Nat.* 95: 348–350.

Ferron, J., and J. Prescott. 1977. Gestation, litter size and number of litters of the red squirrel (*Tamiasciurus hudsonicus*) in Quebec. *Canadian Field-Nat.* 91: 83–84.

Flyger, V., and J. E. Gates. 1982. Pine squirrels *Tamiasciurus hudsonicus* and *T. douglasii*. In: J. A. Chapman and G. A. Feldhamer, eds., *Wild Mammals of North America*, pp. 230–238. Baltimore: Johns Hopkins Univ. Press.

Hamilton, W. J., Jr. 1939. Observations on the life history of the red squirrel in New York. *Amer. Midland Nat.* 22: 732–745.

Hatt, R. T. 1929. The red squirrel: Its life history and habits, with special reference to the Adirondacks of New York and the Harvard Forest. *Roosevelt Wild Life Annals* 2: 11–146.

Heinrich, B. 1992. Maple sugaring by red squirrels. *J. Mammal.* 73: 51–54.

Kilham, L. 1954. Territorial behavior of the red squirrel. *J. Mammal.* 35: 252–253.

———. 1958. Red squirrels feeding at sapsucker holes. *J. Mammal.* 39: 596–597.

Klugh, A. B. 1927. Ecology of the red squirrel. *J. Mammal.* 8: 1–32.

Lair, H. 1985. Length of gestation in the red squirrel, *Tamiasciurus hudsonicus*. *J. Mammal.* 66: 809–810.

Layne, J. N. 1954. The biology of the red squirrel, *Tamiasciurus hudsonicus loquax* (Bangs), in central New York. *Ecol. Monogr.* 24: 227–267.

Mayfield, H. 1948. Red squirrel nesting on the ground. *J. Mammal.* 29: 186.

Nadler, C. F., and D. A. Sutton. 1967. Chromosomes of some squirrels (Mammalia—Sciuridae) from the genera *Sciurus* and *Glaucomys*. *Experientia* 23: 249–251.

Reichard, T. A. 1976. Spring food habits and feeding behavior of fox squirrels and red squirrels. *Amer. Midland Nat.* 96: 443–450.

Rusch, D. A., and W. G. Reeder. 1978. Population ecology of Alberta red squirrels. *Ecology* 59: 400–420.

Smith, C. C. 1968. The adaptive nature of social organization in the genus of three [sic] squirrels *Tamiasciurus*. *Ecol. Monogr.* 38: 31–63.

———. 1970. The coevolution of pine squirrels (*Tamiasciurus*) and conifers. *Ecol. Monogr.* 40: 369–371.

———. 1978. Structure and function of vocalizations of tree squirrels (*Tamiasciurus*). *J. Mammal.* 59: 793–808.

———. 1981. The indivisible niche of *Tamiasciurus*: An example of nonpartitioning of resources. *Ecol. Monogr.* 51: 343–363.

Smith, M. C. 1968. Red squirrel responses to spruce cone failure in interior Alaska. *J. Wildl. Mgmt.* 32: 305–317.

Svihla, R. D. 1930. Development of young red squirrels. *J. Mammal.* 11: 79–80.

Weigl, P. D., and E. V. Hanson. 1980. Observational learning and the feeding behavior of the red squirrel *Tamiasciurus hudsonicus*: The ontogeny of optimization. *Ecology* 61: 213–218.

Yahner, R. H. 1980. Burrow system used by red squirrels. *Amer. Midland Nat.* 103: 409–411.

Yeager, L. E. 1937. Cone-piling by Michigan red squirrels. *J. Mammal.* 18: 191–194.

## Flying Squirrels of the Genus *Glaucomys*

Flying squirrels differ most notably from other squirrels in three ways: they are nocturnal, they can glide (not fly), and (especially the northern flying squirrel) they often feed on considerably more insect and fungal food than do the others. Flying squirrels are also characterized by their small size; their patagia, the prominent folds of skin that extend from the wrists to the ankles; and their broad, flattened, well-furred tail, the sides of which are nearly parallel. The fur is soft, dense, and silky, and the eyes are large, black, and lustrous.

The patagium, fully furred, is supported by slender cartilages extending from the wristbones; in conjunction with the soft, flat tail, it provides flying squirrels with the surface area necessary to carry out their long glides from tree to tree. When the legs are spread the patagium stretches, giving the squirrel a great amount of surface area in relation to its size and weight. Bachman credits the flying squirrel with a "sail" of 50 yards (46 meters), and we have witnessed at least one glide nearly that long. The squirrels routinely follow well-known routes in sailing from one tree to another. They can swerve to avoid obstacles by moving their legs to alter the configuration of the patagium; they can also spiral down rather than making a straight-line glide. Close observation of captive squirrels indicates that these creatures can turn virtually at right angles from their line of flight during a glide, and can elevate or depress the level of the glide by manipulating the patagium and tail.

The best way to see a flying squirrel in daylight hours is to pound or scratch on dead stubs, hollow limbs, or dead trees containing abandoned woodpecker holes. If a squirrel is present, it will often stick its head out, and it will emerge if one continues pounding. (We have found it much more difficult to get them to emerge from a cavity in a *living* tree by pounding.) Once the squirrel has emerged, it will generally glide to the base of a nearby tree. If pursuit is continued it will often try to elude the pursuer by sidling around to the far side of the tree, but if pushed will eventually run up the trunk to the uppermost parts of the tree, and sail through the air in a descending curve to the base of another. Just before terminating the glide, the squirrel deflects its course and pulls gently upward, alighting on all four feet, and then scrambles into the concealment of the foliage above.

The skeleton of flying squirrels is similar to that of other squirrels except for a styliform process connecting to the wrist, which supports the front part of the patagium during a glide. The patagium is not connected to the tail, but the patagia and the tail together give flying squirrels very efficient gliding ability similar to that of hang gliders.

Conserving dead snags and rotten logs, which provide nesting spots and refugia, is beneficial to flying squirrels and many other forest species.

There are two species of flying squirrels. Both occur in the eastern United States, and distinguishing one from the other is difficult. See Wells-Gosling (1985), which offers much more information on flying squirrels.

### Literature Cited

Wells-Gosling, N. 1985. *Flying Squirrels: Gliders in the Dark*. Washington: Smithsonian Institution Press. 128 pp.

Key to the Flying Squirrels
of the Genus *Glaucomys*

1. Hind foot of adult usually greater than 33 mm in length; belly hairs usually grayish at base; animal 250–370 mm in total length; skull usually more than 36 mm long; occurs in the North and along the Appalachian Mountains . . . . . . . . . . . . . . . . . . . . . . *G. sabrinus*

1. Hind foot of adult usually less than 33 mm
in length; belly hairs usually white to base;
animal 200–250 mm in total length; skull
less than 36 mm long; occurs over most of
eastern United States. . . . . . . . . . . . . . *G. volans*

## Northern Flying Squirrel
### *Glaucomys sabrinus* (Shaw)   Color plate 9
DESCRIPTION. A handsome species, the northern flying squirrel is larger and usually more

*Northern flying squirrel,* Glaucomys sabrinus
*(B. Moose Peterson)*

brownish than its cousin, *Glaucomys volans.*
Its dorsal coloration varies from light tan to
rusty brown. The belly hairs, basically white,
are gray at the base (but occasionally white
throughout). The pelage is much darker in summer than in winter.

MEASUREMENTS. Measurements of adult northern flying squirrels were: total length 276
(250–305), tail 126 (108–145), hind foot 36
(34–40) mm; and weight 70–140 grams.
Diploid number = 48.

TOOTH FORMULA

$$\frac{1}{1} \quad \frac{0}{0} \quad \frac{2}{1} \quad \frac{3}{3} \; = \; 22$$

DISTRIBUTION. In the eastern United States, the
northern flying squirrel occurs mostly in the
northern states, from Maine to central Pennsylvania and in northern and central Michigan and
Wisconsin, but also as two disjunct subspecies in
the southern Appalachians (see below). The species also ranges through most of southern Canada west into east-central Alaska, and in much
of northwestern United States to western Montana, northern Wyoming, and much of Utah.

HABITAT. Old-growth forest is the home of the
northern flying squirrel, for the large old trees
nicely accommodate its gliding locomotion and
its use of tree cavities for nesting. It inhabits the
dense spruce/fir forests and stands of yellow
birch and hemlock. In New York it often inhabits beech/birch/maple/hemlock stands, and in
the southern Appalachians it is found in northern hardwoods, especially near conifers. One
was taken above timberline at the summit of
Mt. Marcy in the Adirondacks, the highest
mountain in New York State (Gordon, 1961).
This squirrel's distribution is probably related to
that of its principal foods: various parts of certain conifers and hardwoods, certain lichens,
and subterranean fungi.

HABITS. At night, these soft-furred squirrels descend to the ground. Radio-tracking in summer
has shown activity peaks from dusk to midnight and in the one to three hours before dawn.
They spend considerable time foraging for food
in the forest-floor litter, and they also enter
many different nests or other refugia, apparently searching for food items. Even during the
severest weather, when the mercury tumbles
well below zero, at least to −31°C (−24°F),
northern flying squirrels are abroad. The southern flying squirrel occasionally enters torpor
(Wells-Gosling, 1985) in the coldest part of the
winter, but there is no evidence that this species
does. Rain, high wind, and fog do tend to reduce activity and also to impede gliding. When

abroad in adverse conditions, the animals appear to spend more time moving along branches than in gliding.

Northern flying squirrels commonly occupy tree cavities and old woodpecker holes in the cooler seasons, but in summer they often construct and use nests of shredded bark or leaves, well above ground in a crotch of a conifer. In winter they will use dense branches in the tops of fir and spruce trees as shelter (Weigl et al., 1992). Nests, whether in cavities or tree crotches, are lined with lichens, grasses or sedges, moss, or finely chewed bark. At least in the northern Rockies, northern flying squirrels make their nests almost entirely of arboreal lichens (Hayward and Rosentreter, 1995). They have also been observed entering holes in the ground, although the extent or purpose of this behavior is not known.

Northern flying squirrels are quite gregarious, and several are often found in the same nest, although their aggregations are not as great as those of *Glaucomys volans*. In the southern Appalachians, Weigl et al. (1992) found 33 aggregations of two to six northern flying squirrels, averaging 2.8, most often two adults. Apparently, the aggregations are often of family groups.

Using radio-tracking, Weigl et al. (1992) located 39 nests of *G. sabrinus coloratus*. Of these, 14 were in natural cavities, nine were in artificial nest boxes, and 16 were in outside nests. The natural cavities were woodpecker holes or decayed cavities, usually in yellow birch or beech trees. The outside nests, 20 to 25 cm (8 to 10 inches) in diameter and 15 to 20 cm (6 to 8 inches) deep, were all in red spruce trees, usually in dense branches near the top of the tree, from about 4.5 to 9 meters (15 to 30 feet) above ground. They were often on an old bird nest or on a pile of sticks. The outside of the nests was of spruce twigs, birchbark, and moss. Each had

*Distribution of the northern flying squirrel,* Glaucomys sabrinus, *in the eastern United States*

a single entrance about 4 cm (1.5 inches) in diameter. As in the nest boxes, the insides of the nests were lined with finely shredded birch bark. Both outside nests and cavities were commonly used in both summer and winter.

The two species of flying squirrels are marginally sympatric, and in the zone of overlap one species is common, the other rare. Except perhaps in Michigan's Upper Peninsula (Wells-Gosling, 1985), no areas are known where the two enjoy stable coexistence, for where their ranges overlap, they are often separated by habitat, in mosaic fashion. (It appears that *G. volans*, the southern flying squirrel, cannot long remain in an area lacking storable winter resources.) The two species do tolerate each other in captivity, even sharing nest boxes, but the smaller southern flying squirrel is more aggressive and sometimes displaces *G. sabrinus*, and there is no evidence of nest sharing in the wild. Weigl (1978) found that when given a choice experimentally, *G. volans* would choose deciduous vegetation, and *G. sabrinus* would choose either coniferous or hardwood vegetation. But when the two species were found together, *G. sabrinus* was always in the conifers.

*Glaucomys sabrinus* is less vocal than its southern counterpart, but it does have a low, soft chirp, and it produces a clucking sound when disturbed.

FOOD AND FEEDING. Unlike *Glaucomys volans*, this species is not heavily dependent on nuts and seeds, for the hickories and oaks are not major trees in most of the northern flying squirrel's range. Squirrels of this species feed heavily on fungi and lichens (Hall, 1991; Maser et al., 1985; McKeever, 1960; Weigl, 1978). Many of the fungi taken are tiny, subterranean hypogeous forms, truffles and their relatives, which are located by odor. Many of these fungi are available and eaten throughout the year, sometimes almost exclusively. The spores remain viable after passing through the digestive tract of a rodent (jumping mice, especially *Napaeozapus*, also feed heavily on these fungi). Maser and Maser (1988) have shown that northern flying squirrels in the Pacific Northwest are important in forest maintenance by dispersing nitrogen-fixing bacteria and fungal spores that

form mycorrhizal relationships with tree species. The mycorrhiza are mutualistic, gaining a home for themselves and helping the roots of trees to absorb nutrients and water and to exclude harmful fungi. Indians would not eat flying squirrels because they "ate dirt." We often tell our students to crank up the microscope to 30 or 40× or more during stomach-contents examination when they see "dirt," because "dirt" often turns out to be the spores of hypogeous fungi. At least in Virginia, lichens and northern flying squirrels were often found together.

Although fungi are heavily utilized, many other foods are eaten as well, and much more work is needed on the food of this species (Weigl et al., 1992). Staminate cones are used heavily in spring. Some other items recorded include fern sporangia, pollen, various seeds, buds, fruits, some epigeous (above-ground) fungi, insects, and other animal material. The squirrels will also lap sap from trees (Foster and Tate, 1966) and chew on bark, thus increasing sap flow, and they will sometimes feed on small vertebrates. At least in Alaska, northern flying squirrels will pilfer seeds from red squirrel storage middens, but unlike its southern cousin, *G. sabrinus* does not store food for winter.

REPRODUCTION AND DEVELOPMENT. The details of reproduction in this species are similar to those of the southern flying squirrel, but, in contrast, the northern flying squirrel produces only one litter per year. The breeding season commences in late March. Males are in reproductive condition most of the year, ten months or more, whereas although individual females were in heat as early as March, most are not until later. The two to four young (average three, extremes one to six) are brought forth in late May or June, some as late as September. Gestation is from 37 to 42 days. (A detailed description of the growth of the young is given in the account for the southern flying squirrel; events are roughly parallel, but proportionately more protracted in the northern species.) The newborn weigh 4 to 6 grams and are 70 mm long, and the patagium is already developed. The animals are well haired and crawl about by 18 days, the lateral hairs of the tail grow out in about three weeks, the lower incisors erupt by day 26, and the eyes open at 28–32 days. Juveniles are drab gray; adult coloration is attained at the first molt, which is completed at three to six months. The young first begin to venture from the nest and eat solid food at about 35 days, and are weaned at 55 to 60 days. The length of time that the young continue to remain with the female has not been determined, but some may stay with the female as a winter group.

The nest for the reception of the newborn is usually in some hollow stub, but may be in an outside nest high in a conifer. A large bird nest, capped with shredded bark and leaves, may also serve as a maternity shelter. An outside nest used to raise a litter is about 31 cm (12 inches) in diameter and has one or two entrances and an outer layer of twigs, bark, or roots. (Other outside nests housing individual squirrels are a good bit smaller.) As does the female southern flying squirrel, the mother moves the young by carrying them in her mouth, and the male plays no part in raising the young.

POPULATION CHARACTERISTICS. The presence of flying squirrels is not hard to determine, using either nest-box surveys or live traps. Nest boxes have the advantage that they can be erected and then checked perhaps two or three times per year, which allows one to keep tabs on the population easily. Old, inactive nests can be readily distinguished, for they will have caved in.

Home ranges usually range from 2 to 7 ha (5 to 19 acres), but telemetry data collected by Weigl (1978) indicates home ranges sometimes up to 35 ha (86 acres). Ten individuals tracked by Weigl had home ranges varying from 1.2 to 22.6 ha (the mean 8.9) (3 to 56 acres), those in winter averaging 11.6 ha (29 acres) and those in summer averaging 6.2 ha (15 acres). Food availability presumably is important in dictating both home-range size and mating behavior. Weigl found that northern flying squirrels would often travel great distances, sometimes more than 0.5 km (0.3 mile) in the first two hours of nocturnal activity, the two longest treks being 1164 and 1674 meters (3820 and 5490 feet; actual distance traveled, not linear distance from the nest). Densities in the north may reach ten animals per ha (four per acre).

Flying squirrels in captivity sometimes live 13 or 14 years, but in the wild most die much earlier, rarely living more than four or five years.

ENEMIES. Owls are the major predators on flying squirrels, and snakes often feed on them. House cats, bobcats, weasels, skunks, coyotes, foxes, and even sometimes hawks all get their share. The remains of one were even found in the stomach of a trout. Flying squirrels often are found drowned in open containers of liquid, such as sap buckets, cisterns, or stock-watering containers, and they can become entrapped in barbed wire. An encounter with a predator may result in the loss of part of the tail rather than the loss of the squirrel.

Introduced pests of the forest, particularly the balsam woolly adelgid (*Adelges piceae*, an aphid), are a relatively new threat to flying squirrels, through their damage to the trees. As with many introduced forms, the adelgid is relatively innocuous in its natural habitat in Europe, but in eastern North America it is a serious pest on the balsam and Fraser firs. It brings about the death of Fraser firs within two to seven years of infestation, and is radically reducing that species in the southern Appalachians. The effect on the northern flying squirrel there is unknown.

Concentrations of heavy metals (lead, copper, zinc, manganese) have been shown to be very high at high elevations in the southern Appalachians. On Mount Mitchell, North Carolina, for example, lead levels have been found to be up to ten times the levels in the surrounding lowlands, and at other localities they have been found to approach even those near highways. Heavy metal residues can be detrimental to small mammals, especially by causing lead poisoning.

PARASITES AND DISEASE. As is the case with its southern counterpart, ectoparasite diversity in *Glaucomys sabrinus* is high and includes several species of mites, fleas, and lice, some of them restricted to this host. Peter Weigl found that nematodes, *Strongyloides robustus*, would cause death in northern flying squirrels in captivity, though *G. volans* could tolerate them. Current work suggests that both low temperature and the ingestion of fir oil might limit *Strongyloides* populations in northern flying squirrels under natural conditions.

RELATION TO HUMANS. Because few ever see this animal, it would seem to have relatively little direct relationship to human concerns. Nonetheless, flying squirrels and several other small forest mammals play an important role in forest maintenance (see the discussion of food and feeding, above). *Glaucomys sabrinus* is an interesting visitor to bird feeders and often uses bird houses, and it makes an interesting pet, though it is not as easily tamed as the southern flying squirrel. It sometimes makes a nuisance of itself by living in an attic, and sometimes plays havoc with fur trappers by getting in their traps.

The two southern Appalachian populations of flying squirrels were not even known until 1936 and 1953, but the two subspecies there give us some rather unique opportunities for study with broad implications. They occur in what should be relatively unspoiled wilderness, yet introduced insect species (the balsam woolly adelgid and the gypsy moth) have invaded this area, and pollutants in the form of significant concentrations of heavy metals have been identified. The effects of these on forests or on flying squirrels can only be surmised at this point, but the occurrence of these pests and pollutants in these remote mountains should serve as still another strong warning that we should stop contaminating the world.

AREAS FOR FURTHER WORK. Work on communication among flying squirrels would be fascinating. Might they use echolocation at all? More information is needed on their food, and especially on how they find subterranean fungi. By odor? Finally, what is the relation between this species and the new factors to be dealt with—the gypsy moth and balsam woolly aphid, and the heavy metals that occur in quantity in the southern Appalachians.

## SUBSPECIES

Because northern populations broadly intergrade, there seems no reason to recognize *Glaucomys sabrinus sabrinus* and *G. s. macrotis* as separate subspecies, but there are two groups of populations isolated to the south, in the Appalachians, that do fill the subspecies criteria, and both are currently recognized as federally endangered. (The populations currently classed as *G. s. coloratus* in southwestern Virginia present special problems; they are under study, but appear to be intermediate in characters between *G. s. coloratus* and *G. s. fuscus*.) Fossil records indicate that the two southern subspecies once had much larger ranges, and they exist today as relict populations. A mix of conifers (especially red spruce and fir) and hardwoods appears essential to their survival, for they have not been found in the pure conifer forests of this area.

*Glaucomys sabrinus sabrinus* (Shaw)

As described above. Occurs over much of the range of the species in the eastern United States.

Type locality: Mouth of the Severn River, Ontario.

Other currently recognized eastern subspecies: *G. sabrinus macrotis*

*Glaucomys sabrinus coloratus* Handley

*Glaucomys sabrinus coloratus*, not described until 1953, is one of two relict southern Appalachian subspecies of northern flying squirrels. Both are endangered. This subspecies occurs as a disjunct population at high elevations (above 1230 meters, or 4035 feet) in the conifer/hardwood forests of the southern Appalachians along the North Carolina-Tennessee border and north into Virginia. It is similar to *G. s. fuscus* (see below) but is darker and somewhat larger (total length averages 286 mm). The undersurface is a pale yellow-orange to ochraceous-buff wash, with few or no white-tipped hairs. The cheeks are gray with a buffy wash. The 148 individuals of this subspecies measured by Peter Weigl averaged: total length 281 (191–315), tail 129 (102–160), hind foot 38 (34–50) mm. The weights of 121 animals from June to December averaged 108 (80–140) grams, whereas 80 taken from January to May averaged 112 (90–133) grams. About 150 northern individuals of this subspecies have been captured since it was federally listed as endangered in 1985. The southern Appalachian subspecies is found in red spruce/Fraser fir (*Abies fraseri* and *A. bal-*

*samea*) forests associated with beech, yellow birch, sugar or red maple, hemlock, and black cherry.

Type locality: Bald Knob, 5000 ft. [1525 meters], 3½ feet [1 meter] south of the Summit, Mt. Mitchell, Yancey Co., North Carolina.

### *Glaucomys sabrinus fuscus* Miller

This is the second relict subspecies of northern flying squirrel in the southern Appalachians. It occurs as a disjunct population at high elevations (above 1000 meters, or 3280 feet) in eastern West Virginia (Greenbrier, Pendleton, Pocahontas, Randolph, and Webster counties) and Virginia (Grayson, Montgomery, Smyth, and Highland counties), although those from Smyth and Grayson are more like those in North Carolina and are under further study. This subspecies, not described until 1936, averages about 20 mm shorter than *G. s. coloratus*. Size is as in typical *sabrinus*, but the color is darker. The tops of the fore and hind feet are fuscous. The cheeks are clear gray, not buffy gray as in typical *sabrinus*. The tail is darker and more extensively clouded on its terminal third than that of *sabrinus*. Five individuals averaged: total length 266 (256–274), tail 115 (108–127), hind foot 37 (35–39) mm. Prior to 1985, fewer than 30 specimens had been taken of this subspecies and *G. s. coloratus* combined, but since federal listing of this subspecies in 1985, intensive field work has led to the capture of at least 187 individuals of *G. s. fuscus* from West Virginia and 46 from Virginia.

Type locality: Mill Point, Cranberry River, 3450 feet [1050 meters], Pocahontas Co., West Virginia.

### LITERATURE

Foster, W. L., and J. Tate, Jr. 1966. The activities and coactions of animals at sapsucker trees. *Living Bird* 5: 87–113.

Gordon, D. C. 1961. Adirondack record of flying squirrel above timber line. *J. Mammal.* 43: 262.

Hall, D. S. 1991. Diet of the northern flying squirrel at Sagehen Creek, California. *J. Mammal.* 72: 615–617.

Hayward, G. D., and R. Rosentreter. 1995. Lichens as nesting material for northern flying squirrels in the northern Rocky Mountains. *J. Mammal.* 75: 663–673.

Maser, C., and Z. Maser. 1988. Interactions among squirrels, mycorrhizal fungi and coniferous forests in Oregon. *Great Basin Nat.* 48: 358–369.

Maser, C., Z. Maser, J. W. Witt, and G. Hunt. 1986. The northern flying squirrel: A mycophagist in southwestern Oregon. *Canadian J. Zool.* 64: 2086–2089.

Maser, Z., C. Maser, and J. M. Trappe. 1985. Food habits of the northern flying squirrel (*Glaucomys sabrinus*) in Oregon. *Canadian J. Zool.* 63: 1084–1088.

McKeever, S. 1960. Food of the northern flying squirrel in northeastern California. *J. Mammal.* 41: 270–271.

Muul, I. 1969. Mating behavior, gestation period, and development of *Glaucomys sabrinus*. *J. Mammal.* 50: 121.

Weigl, P. D. 1978. Resource overlap, interspecific interactions and the distribution of the flying squirrels, *Glaucomys volans* and *G. sabrinus*. *Amer. Midland Nat.* 100: 83–96.

Weigl, P. D., T. W. Knowles, and A. C. Boynton. 1992. The distribution and ecology of the northern flying squirrel, *Glaucomys sabrinus coloratus*, in the southern Appalachians. Unpubl. report, N.C. Wildlife Resources Comm., Morgantown. 120 pp.

Weigl, P. D., and D. W. Osgood. 1974. Study of the northern flying squirrel, *Glaucomys sabrinus*, by temperature telemetry. *Amer. Midland Nat.* 92: 482–486.

Wells-Gosling, N. 1985. *Flying Squirrels: Gliders in the Dark*. Washington: Smithsonian Institution Press. 128 pp.

Wells-Gosling, N., and L. R. Heaney. 1984. *Glaucomys sabrinus*. **Mammalian Spec. No. 229.** Amer. Soc. Mammal. 8 pp.

## Southern Flying Squirrel
### *Glaucomys volans*
### (Linnaeus)                    Color plate 9

DESCRIPTION. With their soft fur and their large, luminous black eyes, flying squirrels are beautiful animals. The southern flying squirrel, the smaller and more widespread of the two species, is somewhat grayer than the northern flying squirrel and its dorsal hairs are slaty gray at the base, steely gray to drab or pinkish cinnamon at the tips. The sides of the body are darker, and the tail is a uniform soft gray above, pinkish cinnamon below. The underparts are pure white or occasionally creamy white, the hairs white to the base (this character is best exhibited at the middle of the belly). The toes are white in winter. In the southern states, this species is a bit smaller and darker.

*Southern flying squirrel,* Glaucomys volans
*(Jerry Lee Gingerich)*

MEASUREMENTS. Measurements of 64 individuals from Indiana averaged: total length 228 (196–256), tail 100 (82–133), hind foot 31 (25–34) mm; and weight 63 (45–87) grams. Measurements of 66 individuals from Florida (courtesy of Jim Layne) were: total length 221 (192–244), tail 100 (71–112), hind foot 30 (27–34) mm; and weight 52 (38–75) grams.

Diploid number = 48.

TOOTH FORMULA

$$\frac{1}{1} \quad \frac{0}{0} \quad \frac{2}{1} \quad \frac{3}{3} \;=\; 22$$

DISTRIBUTION. Sollberger (1940, 1943) and Muul (1968, 1969, 1974) have given us much information on this species. The southern flying squirrel occurs throughout most of the eastern United States except for northwestern Wisconsin, parts of northern New England, and southwesternmost peninsular Florida. This species could as easily have been called the "eastern flying squirrel," since the main part of its range covers essentially the eastern half of the United

*Distribution of the southern flying squirrel,* Glaucomys volans, *in the eastern United States*

States. West of the Mississippi, it occurs only as far as western Minnesota, eastern Kansas, and eastern Texas, although there are isolated populations in Mexico and Central America.

HABITAT. The southern flying squirrel occurs in a variety of forest types, but its habitat can be generally characterized as deciduous and mixed woodland. It occurs from the oak, hickory, beech, aspen, and maple forests of the north to the moss-draped live oaks and gums of the Deep South. The northernmost limits of *G. volans* appear to be determined by the northern limits of mast-producing trees, mainly hickories and oaks. In the south it can be found in most wooded habitats of sizable extent.

HABITS. Because of its nocturnal habits, the southern flying squirrel largely escapes our notice. It often outnumbers the larger and more conspicuous tree squirrels, but often the only intimation of its presence is a luckless victim brought to the doorstep by a cat. We often think of this species as being confined mostly to trees, but it spends a great deal of time at night foraging on the ground or on logs, eating acorns in the manner of other squirrels. During summer, flying squirrels are more or less active all night. In cold weather, their activity may be restricted primarily to dusk and dawn, with an occasional third peak about midnight.

The flying squirrel is a sociable little beast. During cold periods several will gather together in a snug ball, to afford one another warmth. James B. Cope found 16 curled together in a wood duck nesting box on a cold February day at the Patuxent Research Refuge in Maryland, and there are many such records in the literature; up to 50 have been found in one nest. The best winter nest is a cavity in a tree that has rotted out but retains thick walls, which serve as insulation.

Illar Muul (1968) found that in very cold weather or in times of food scarcity southern flying squirrels would enter torpor, although not as deeply as in true hibernation. Their body temperatures dropped as low as 22°C (72°F), and even when lifted up they would remain inactive, sometimes taking up to 40 minutes to completely waken. Muul found an inverse rela-

tionship between temperature and number of squirrels in a nest, suggesting that the aggregations are indeed energy-saving adaptations.

Cavities in trees are the major nest sites, especially in the north, although the animals will readily use nest boxes set out for birds. Layne and Raymond (1994), in 841 occupied nest boxes in Florida, found 11% with litters, 81% with aggregations of two to 25 individuals, and just 9% with solitary individuals. Of the 676 with aggregations, 79% housed only adults, whereas the remainder had adults and sub-adults, rarely nestlings. Both males and females were represented in most aggregations. Communal nesting was most prominent in January, still common through spring, and lowest in September. Communal nesting in the north has thermoregulatory function, but these data would seem to indicate that it influences social organization as well.

Flying squirrels come to know and use every likely retreat in their home range, even sometimes underground. They thus have some nest or safe harbor to turn to at a moment's notice. An ideal den is an old woodpecker hole perhaps 2 to 6 meters (8 to 20 feet) from the ground. Entrance holes used by this species usually are about 4–5 cm (1.5–2 inches) in diameter. The nest is lined with finely shredded inner bark, though other plant materials are often used as well. In the Deep South, Spanish moss or palmetto fibers are used. The remains of food items are often abundant in nests. Besides the occupied nest there are usually several "secondary" nests, which are apparently used as sheltered feeding or defecating stations and may serve to divert the attention of predators from the main nest site. Some retreats are used exclusively for defecation, and some of these have been known over the years to develop humus half a meter deep. In the southern parts of their range, southern flying squirrels use outside leaf nests, and leaf nests are occasionally used in summer in the north. Leaf nests resemble those of fox and gray squirrels, but are much smaller, about 20 cm (8 inches) in diameter. Flying squirrels will also use abandoned fox or gray squirrel leaf nests, building their own nest on or in them.

The most often heard calls of flying squirrels are tiny "tssep" calls and chirps that remind one of the calls of night-flying birds. These calls, which often betray the presence of flying squirrels for one standing in a woodland at night, probably serve as a means of communication. It may be that the high-frequency sounds these squirrels produce during glides are used in echolocation, but, so far, direct evidence of this ability is lacking. In southern Indiana, an adult flying squirrel with her good-sized young glided into our mist net, which had been set for bats over a river. The adult escaped but the young became entangled. We removed the young and liberated it on a log. The female did not immediately find it, but moved about the area on logs and tree trunks, uttering a low "ruff" call that we picked up first on our bat detector. In due course, we were also able to hear it without the detector. The call appeared to be useful in uniting mother and young. Illar Muul (1968), who had earlier heard similar calls, indicated that they might be part ultrasonic.

FOOD AND FEEDING. The food of southern flying squirrels includes nuts and many types of seeds, but also an assortment of berries (especially juneberries, blackberries, and mulberries), fungi, bark, green buds, and other delicacies, and they eat quantities of insects, spiders, slugs, and other invertebrates. Hickory nuts, however, are undoubtedly the favored food of southern flying squirrels, followed by acorns, especially of the white oak. The range of hickory and oak trees corresponds closely with the range of the squirrels. Flying squirrels will pounce upon fluttering moths and eat large beetles, such as june beetles or various wood-boring forms; they will discard the hard parts, the larger moth wings, and other inedible parts. They will also occasionally take birds and their eggs. Hamilton has caught them in traps set for weasels and baited with a dead mouse. Flying squirrels will gnaw bark from maples and drink the sap that is exuded, and they also feed on the moths that come to the sap. In the south, pecans and the many berries of woody shrubs receive their attention. They also feed heavily on black-cherry pits. Hypogeous (underground) fungi are important, but not nearly so important as they are to the northern flying squirrel.

Flying squirrels will drink, but if water is not available, as is the case in the xeric long-leaf pine and turkey oak forests of Florida, the squirrels obtain their water from dew, food, and periodic rain. Sometimes, they derive moisture from fungi, which are about three-fourths water.

Decreasing day length stimulates this species to store great quantities of nuts, acorns, and seeds for winter use. Nuts are stored in their nests, in cracks or hollows in trees, in forks of tree limbs, or in the ground. Hickory nuts and acorns are buried throughout their home range, adding to the general store of nuts placed there by squirrels of several other species. Flying squirrels carry the nuts to the ground and bury them individually, using their front incisors to pound them into the soil. Alternatively, they will pound pieces of nut into a tree crotch, producing a sound that humans can hear from beyond 15 meters. Sometimes, flying squirrels will emerge even in daylight to store nuts. Illar Muul estimated that a flying squirrel can store perhaps 15,000 nuts in a season.

Nut shells the nuts of which have been eaten by flying squirrels are distinctively marked. The squirrel holds the nut in its forefeet and rasps it open at the end, where the husk is thinnest. It then uses its lower incisors to remove the meat. Therefore, a nut with a single, smooth-edged elliptical opening at one end is unmistakable evidence that a flying squirrel has been at work. Red squirrels leave a ragged edge, white-footed mice make two or three smooth-edged openings, and squirrels of the genus *Sciurus* chew the shell to fragments.

Flying squirrels have enlarged glands in their lips. These glands may be useful both in marking territories and in marking nuts already buried, so that the squirrel will not dig them up and rebury them.

REPRODUCTION AND DEVELOPMENT. In the northern states the breeding season for the southern flying squirrel commences in late February or early March, its onset triggered by increasing photoperiod. The testes of the males are abdominal from August to November, but are scrotal by mid-January, and female squirrels are receptive for one day. At that time, males gather about a female and vie for her attention. She will usually mate with the dominant male, but will then often solicit the attention of a subordinate male, the success of which could lead to greater genetic diversity.

Before the arrival of the young, the female goes off by herself and builds a nest in a cavity, where, after a gestation of 41 days, the two to seven young are born. They are blind, naked, and helpless, and weigh but 3 to 6 grams, but they already have their prominent lateral folds of skin, the patagia, and they are capable of uttering high-pitched distress squeaks. At one week, the skin of the head and back darkens as the tips of the dorsal hairs are formed in the follicles. The vibrissae are now less than 7 mm long. At two weeks, soft down covers the back, head, and chest, but the abdomen and chest remain naked; the toes are separated, the ear canals are open, and the vibrissae are about 10 mm long. The lower incisors have now erupted, and the young are able to right themselves. They weigh 10 to 15 grams and they are about 105 mm in overall length. At three weeks the young squirrel is well haired, and the lateral hairs of the tail appear, giving the animal a squirrel-like rather than ratlike appearance. Babies can now push themselves rapidly backward, and give a loud, rasping squeak. At four weeks, the babies are about 150 mm long and weigh about 25 grams, the vibrissae are about 24 mm long, the upper incisors are erupting, and the eyes are fully open. The young now resemble the parent. They are extremely active and will take bits of food, though they do not yet leave the nest. At five weeks they weigh about 30 grams and are about 175 mm long. By now they have the full juvenile (drab gray) color, and begin their first forays outside the nest. Weaning begins at about six weeks and is completed in a few more weeks.

Babies begin to glide on their own at about this time; they do not have to be taught—the behavior is instinctive—but the mother may coax them by calling from a nearby limb. By eight weeks they are gliding with celerity, and the female and young begin foraging together. The new young finally disperse, or else (after some foot stomping) they mix with, and are accepted into, the resident population. Molting of the gray juvenile pelage begins at about three months and is completed in a few weeks, the tail last. Compared to the adult tail, the juvenile tail is thin and wispy.

Females leave the young in the nest for short periods, so as to be free to forage. They will defend their young vigorously, and when potential danger looms they will move them to a different nest, one at a time. Each baby is carried in the mouth, and instinctively curls up when picked up by the scruff of the neck.

A second estrus occurs about late June, and a second peak of litters emerges in July or August. Young females usually have only one litter, but some of the older females may have two in one year (Wells-Gosling, 1985). Farther south (in Kentucky), breeding commences in January, and the first litter is produced in early March, the second litter during late August, but the time of production of young is highly variable.

POPULATION CHARACTERISTICS. Squirrels usually number two to eight per ha (one to three per acre), but up to 12 per ha (five per acre) have been reported. One observer claimed to have seen 100 in a small area in southeastern Pennsylvania, and Audubon and Bachman (1849–54) claimed to have seen at least 200 in and under large oak and beech trees near Philadelphia. Pregnant and lactating females defend a territory around the den tree against intruders of both sexes, thus establishing an exclusive area for mother and young. Males neither help care for the young nor defend territories. Average life span is probably about five years, potential life span about ten.

ENEMIES. Large mammalian predators and owls take a heavy toll of flying squirrels, but none can prove more relentless, particularly about suburban towns and villages, than the domestic cat. Almost every cat owner in rural districts has found the body or tail of a flying squirrel on the doorstep. Climbing snakes (particularly *Elaphe*) are also an occasional predator.

PARASITES AND DISEASE. This species suffers a diverse array of parasites, as is often the case with tree-hole-nesting mammals, probably be-

cause of increased opportunities for the intermixing of parasites, since various birds, mammals, and even insects use the cavities at different times. Audubon and Bachman reported a
purple martin house that contained about 20 flying squirrels, 20 bats, and six screech owls, all
at once! Southern flying squirrels harbor several kinds of fleas, mites, and lice; and some of
the fleas and the lice are host-specific. Recently,
*Rickettsia prowazekii*, the rickettsia responsible for epidemic typhus, was found in southern
flying squirrels in Virginia and other eastern
states. Also, several cases were found in humans
in Virginia, West Virginia, and North Carolina
between 1977 and 1980, apparently contracted
from flying squirrels, perhaps from their fleas
or lice.

RELATION TO HUMANS. Most people do not
even know these squirrels are around, even
though they are often as abundant as tree squirrels. We often encounter them by cutting down
a tree, or by finding them in a bird house in
winter. People often find them living in their attic or garage, or see them at a bird feeder. When
both flying squirrel species appear at a bird
feeder together, the smaller southern species is
the more pugnacious, and often chases away its
larger northern cousin (Wells-Gosling, 1985).

AREAS FOR FURTHER WORK. Much more information is needed on nocturnal behavior and on
calls. The latter should include testing for high-
frequency calls. The nest fauna of this species
could be studied with considerable profit, and
rickettsia-causing epidemic typhus in this species is in need of study.

## SUBSPECIES

We are unaware of any primary isolating mechanisms separating any of the described subspecies, and we therefore recognize none of them.

*Glaucomys volans volans* (Linnaeus)

As described above.

Type locality: Virginia.

Other currently recognized eastern subspecies:

    *G. volans querceti* (Bangs)

    *G. volans saturatus* Howell

## LITERATURE

Audubon, J. J., and J. Bachman. 1849–1854. *The
Quadrupeds of North America*, Vols. 1–3. Publ. by
J. J. Audubon.

Dolan, P. G., and D. C. Carter. 1977. *Glaucomys volans*. **Mammalian Species No. 78.** Amer. Soc. Mammal. 6 pp.

Jordan, J. S. 1956. Notes on a population of eastern
flying squirrels. *J. Mammal.* 37: 294–295.

Layne, J. N., and M. A. V. Raymond. 1994. Communal nesting of southern flying squirrels in Florida. *J. Mammal.* 75: 110–120.

Muul, I. 1968. Behavioral and physiological influences on the distribution of the flying squirrel, *Glaucomys volans*. Misc. Publ. Mus. Zool. Univ. Mich.
No. 134. 66 pp.

———. 1969. Photoperiod and reproduction in flying squirrels, *Glaucomys volans*. *J. Mammal.* 50:
542–549.

———. 1974. Geographic variation in the nesting
habits of *Glaucomys volans*. *J. Mammal.* 55: 840–
844.

Raymond, M. A. V., and J. N. Layne. 1988. Aspects
of reproduction in the southern flying squirrel in
Florida. *Acta Theriol.* 33: 505–518.

Sawyer, S. L., and R. L. Rose. 1985. Homing in and
ecology of the southern flying squirrel *Glaucomys
volans* in southeastern Virginia. *Amer. Midland Nat.*
113: 238–244.

Sollberger, D. E. 1940. Notes on the life history of
the small eastern flying squirrel. *J. Mammal.* 21:
282–293.

———. 1943. Notes on the breeding habits of the
eastern flying squirrel (*Glaucomys volans volans*).
*J. Mammal.* 24: 163–173.

Weigl, P. D. 1978. Resource overlap, interspecific interactions and the distribution of the flying squirrels, *Glaucomys volans* and *G. sabrinus*. *Amer.
Midland Nat.* 100: 83–96.

Wells-Gosling, N. 1985. *Flying Squirrels: Gliders in
the Dark*. Washington: Smithsonian Institution
Press. 128 pp.

## POCKET GOPHERS, Family Geomyidae

Pocket gophers are short-furred burrowing
rodents, characterized by prominent, fur-lined,
external cheek pouches, small eyes and ears,
prominent claws on the forefeet, and a short to
medium-length, nearly naked tail. They are confined to North and Central America and extreme
northern South America, ranging from Saskatchewan to Colombia. In the eastern United
States the Geomyidae are represented by two

species of the genus *Geomys*, one restricted in its distribution to the southeastern states (Alabama, Florida, and Georgia) and the other to parts of Indiana, Illinois, and Wisconsin.

These animals are admirably modified for a subterranean existence. The skull is massive and angular, and the incisors are large and somewhat protruding. Each upper incisor has two grooves on the anterior surface, a large one in the center and a smaller one toward the inner side. These grooves and the iron-oxide content of the outer enamel layer, which gives the incisors their orange pigment, render them stronger and harder cutting and digging tools.

### KEY TO THE POCKET GOPHERS OF THE GENUS *GEOMYS*

1. Nasal bones strongly constricted near middle (hourglass-shaped); found in Alabama, Florida, and Georgia. . . . . . . . . . . . . . . *G. pinetis*
1. Nasal bones not constricted near middle; found in Indiana, Illinois, and Wisconsin . . . . *G. bursarius*

## Plains Pocket Gopher
### *Geomys bursarius* (Shaw)

DESCRIPTION. The plains pocket gopher is a large gopher with a medium-length, scant-

*Plains pocket gopher,* Geomys bursarius
*(Tony Brentlinger)*

haired tail, the tip of which is nearly naked. The pelage is dark liver-brown, chestnut, or slate-gray above and below, somewhat paler on the belly, the coloration closely paralleling the soil color of the locality where it lives. The forefeet are white, and the hind feet are soiled white; the

hairs of the tail are brown on the basal half and white on the terminal half.

MEASUREMENTS. Males average 10–15% larger than females, some males measuring more than 300 mm in total length and weighing 500 grams. Average measurements of 48 males from Indiana were: total length 294 (252–328), tail 85 (67–105), hind foot 36 (35–38) mm; and weight 333 (230–451) grams. For 90 females they were: total length 286 (212–296), tail 74 (51–100), hind foot 32 (28–37) mm; and weight 231 (128–380) grams.

Diploid number = 70–72; fundamental number = 68–72.

TOOTH FORMULA

$$\frac{1}{1} \quad \frac{0}{0} \quad \frac{1}{1} \quad \frac{3}{3} \; = \; 20$$

DISTRIBUTION. This species occurs mostly in the center of the United States, reaching barely into south-central Manitoba and extending south through the northeastern two-thirds of Texas and west to eastern North Dakota, eastern Wyoming, Colorado, and New Mexico. East of the Mississippi, *Geomys bursarius* occurs in western Wisconsin, central Illinois, and northwestern Indiana.

HABITAT. Areas of brown sandy loam or prairie loam sparsely shaded by trees, and the open pastureland of agricultural areas, are home to these large pocket gophers. Intensive cultivation and new highways apparently disturb existing colonies and may limit potential range extensions of the species.

HABITS. Pocket gophers are solitary, living an antisocial existence in their underground chambers. Frequently, when two are placed together, they engage in savage combat, which can result in death.

Pocket gophers are apparently more active during the summer months, shuttling back and forth in the burrows with edibles for the storage chambers. Usually, they do not burrow much deeper than half a meter (a foot or two) at this season, but it is thought that when winter approaches they penetrate deeper into the soil, digging below the frost line and becoming less active. Melting snow often exposes the long, earthen cores of solidly packed loam that had been pushed into the snow when the burrow was being freed of dirt.

Conspicuous earth mounds are indeed the mark of gophers. Pushing up these mounds is the gopher's means of disposing of excess dirt as it extends and cleans its burrow system. The gopher digs with the front feet, then uses both front and back feet to push the dirt behind. Then it turns around and pushes the dirt along by using the front feet and head, bulldozer fashion. Often the mounds are in a line, with progressively fresher dirt indicating the newer burrows. Dirt is often taken out through a side passage, thence to the surface, and when that operation is complete, the side passage may be back-filled. As the animal moves backward in its burrow, the nearly naked tail serves as a tac-

tile organ. Although most of the digging is done by the forefeet, gophers do use the powerful incisors to cut away the dirt while burrowing. The upper lips, by being pinched together behind the incisors (the lips split just below the nose), keep the dirt from entering the mouth.

Jackson (1961) described a female's burrow he excavated. It consisted of one main tunnel 63 meters (206 feet) long with many short lateral branches, most of which did not reach the surface. The floor of the burrow was generally about 15 to 22 cm (6 to 9 inches) below the surface, but descended a meter (39 inches) in one place. The main burrow was about 7 cm (3 inches) wide and 11 cm (4.5 inches) high and was quite consistent in its dimensions throughout. Jackson estimated that the gopher had removed about 2 cubic meters (70 cubic feet) of soil in excavating this burrow. The single nest chamber was roughly in the center of the sys-

*Distribution of the plains pocket gopher,* Geomys bursarius, *in the eastern United States*

tem, its bottom 0.6 meter (2 feet) below the surface. The nest, 18 by 9 by 19 cm (7 by 3.5 by 7.5 inches), was of the abundant grasses in the area. Fecal material was all in plugged lateral passages. Two food stores were maintained, one in an enlargement at the end of a side tunnel and the other in a pocket at the side of the main tunnel.

In areas where pocket gophers are numerous, there may be sizable tracts that are quite barren of these animals. These have been termed *resting grounds*; they probably permit new growth of food plants, reconsolidation of soil, and perhaps disinfection and reduction of excreta, toward the day when the gophers return.

As it is for other members of the Geomyidae, water appears to be a formidable barrier to the dispersal of this pocket gopher, and rivers often mark the natural boundaries of its range or the ranges of its subspecies. Unlike most other small mammals, pocket gophers cannot swim, and make only ineffectual movements when tossed into the water.

FOOD AND FEEDING. The food of the plains pocket gopher is largely if not entirely vegetable. Most important are fleshy roots, bulbs, and tender green plants, many of which are probably cut off at the roots from below and pulled into the burrow. The roots of small shrubs and trees are not spared. Anderson (1990) found little relation between the location of tunnels and the natural distribution of the more palatable (or unpalatable) plants above ground, but some plants, perhaps, are reached from the mouth of a burrow. Quantities of food are stored in the underground chambers for use at times when growing plants are difficult to obtain.

The prominent external cheek pouches are used only to carry food to the storage chambers, and not to transport dirt, as is often erroneously believed. They are filled with incredible rapidity, the animal placing food in them with the forepaws, with "a sort of wiping motion" that forces the food into the open end of the pouch. To empty the pouches, the animal simply presses its forefeet against the sides of the head and brings them forward simultaneously; the contents of the pouches are thus extruded in a pile in front of the animal.

REPRODUCTION AND DEVELOPMENT. Pocket gophers are found in pairs only during mating, which occurs throughout the spring and summer but is most common from March through May. As many as two and sometimes three litters are produced per year, but the litter size is low for rodents, ranging from two to six but averaging only two to four young. Other than for mating, it is thought that the male leaves the female to pursue its solitary existence.

By raising two litters of these gophers in captivity, Sudman et al. (1986) have added greatly to our knowledge of the reproduction of the species. Gestation was at least 51 days. The young were naked at birth, and the eyes, ears, and cheek pouches were closed. Total length was 46 mm, and they weighed 5–5.5 grams. The upper incisors erupted at six days, the lower at nine days. Hair was evident by day ten, and the eyes opened on day 22 or 23. Digging and grooming behavior also commenced on day 22–23, and food was first noted in the cheek pouches on day 32. It was not clear when the cheek pouches opened, but the authors thought it was probably when the young were about four weeks old. By day 33, lactation had ceased. Fighting among the young was first noted on day 38, but they continued to live in the mother's burrow for some time despite their continued fighting, which was pursued to the point of drawing blood. Dispersal of the young from the female's burrow occurred at seven weeks, at a weight of 80 to 100 grams. Molting to adult pelage started at two months and was nearly complete by 4.5 months. Adult size was attained by day 100.

*Mounds of excavated soil from burrow of plains pocket gopher*

POPULATION CHARACTERISTICS. Population increases are not spectacular, as they often are in some of the smaller rodents, but even at their slow reproductive rate, the pocket gophers increase their numbers to levels where they can be serious agricultural pests, since they have few natural enemies. The maximum life span is about five years.

ENEMIES. The subterranean life of the pocket gopher largely precludes predation by mammals, snakes, or raptorial birds. They are most susceptible to predation when above ground. A gopher snake will occasionally poke its head through the mound and into the burrow, and thus lie in wait. It is normally a constrictor, but in the confined space of a gopher burrow it will make its kill by sliding alongside the gopher and pushing it against the wall of the burrow. Badgers and weasels would seem to be the only other regular enemies, although a house cat, owl, or other predator occasionally manages to capture one outside its burrow.

PARASITES AND DISEASE. The degree of their isolation from other species is reflected in the number of host-specific ectoparasites living on these creatures. In Indiana, all six of their major parasites are host-specific forms: a flea, *Dactylopsylla ignota*, a chewing louse, *Geomydoceus illinoensis*, and four species of mites, *Geomylichus floridanus*, *Androlaelaps geomys*, *Echinonyssus longichelae*, and *E. geomydis*. Biting lice, *Geomydoecus*, are common on pocket gophers, and are exceedingly host-specific. They have diverged as different species on different hosts, and only one species occurs on any one population of gophers (Timm, 1983). The lice are thus good indicators of taxonomic and biogeographic relationships of the gophers, and they support the current classification of gophers. *Geomydoecus geomydis*, for example, is found on both *Geomys bursarius bursarius* and *G. b. wisconsinensis*, and indeed, we question the validity of the subspecies *G. b. wisconsinensis*, since it is very similar genetically to *G. b. bursarius* (Hart, 1978). Both have a diploid number of 72 and a fundamental number of 72. Conversely, *Geomydoecus illinoensis* is restricted to a single subspecies, *Geomys bursarius illinoen-*

*sis*, the only subspecies (beyond the nominate) that we do recognize. This subspecies is separated from the nominate by primary isolating mechanisms, as indicated morphologically, genetically, and parasitologically.

RELATION TO HUMANS. Pocket gophers often become serious pests, particularly when they are attracted to the garden, vegetable patch, or alfalfa field, but they are not difficult to control. Specially designed gopher traps are very efficient in capturing these animals, as are small steel traps of any description when they are placed in an opened burrow and the hole is covered with cardboard and dirt to exclude light.

AREAS FOR FURTHER WORK. Radio-tracking could be used to great advantage with this subterranean species. One could use radio-tracking to determine when these animals are active (seasonally and daily), where they spend their time, where the nest is, how often (and how far) they move about within the burrows, and perhaps how much time is spent on the surface. It would also be interesting to study the invertebrate nest inhabitants, and to work out their own community relationships and their relationship to the *Geomys* parasite community.

## SUBSPECIES

*Geomys bursarius bursarius* (Shaw)

As described above. Occurs in western Wisconsin, and a number of other subspecies have been described west of the Mississippi River.

Type locality: Considered to be Elk River, Sherburne Co., Minnesota.

Other currently recognized eastern subspecies:
  *G. bursarius wisconsinensis* Jackson

*Geomys bursarius illinoensis*
Komarek & Spencer

*Geomys bursarius illinoensis* is separated from other subspecies of this species to the west by the Mississippi River. It differs from *G. b. bursarius* in being larger and having a longer rostrum and longer tail (33.9 to 44.3% of head and body, the mean 39.1%) (Heaney and Timm, 1983). It is also "distinctly slate-gray with no trace of brown or brownish on the back; hairs tinged with light brown or white on belly; nasals constricted medially, somewhat hour-glass shaped; superficial canals on palatine only extending to first molar, and from there more or less fused. Size large, measurements of 25 males: total length 265–322 mm, tail 88–98 mm, hind foot, 32–36 mm. Females: total length 253–273 mm, tail 69–73 mm, hind foot, 32–35 mm."

Type locality: 1 mile (1.6 km) south of Momence, Kankakee Co., Illinois.

## LITERATURE

Anderson, D. C. 1990. Search path of a fossorial herbivore, *Geomys bursarius*, foraging in structurally complex plant communities. *J. Mammal.* 71: 177–187.

Hart, E. B. 1978. Karyology and evolution of the plains pocket gopher, *Geomys bursarius*. Occ. Pap. Mus. Nat. Hist. Univ. Kans. No. 71. 20 pp.

Heaney, L. R., and R. M. Timm. 1983. Relationships of pocket gophers of the genus *Geomys* from the central and northern Great Plains. Misc. Publ. Mus. Nat. Hist. Univ. Kans. No. 74. 59 pp.

Jackson, H. H. T. 1961. *Mammals of Wisconsin.* Madison: Univ. Wisconsin Press. 504 pp.

Komarek, E. V., and D. A. Spencer. 1931. A new pocket gopher from Illinois and Indiana. *J. Mammal.* 12: 404–408.

Mohr, C. O., and W. P. Mohr. 1936. Abundance and digging rate of pocket gophers, *Geomys bursarius*. *Ecology* 17: 325–327.

Scheffer, T. H. 1931. Habits and economic status of the pocket gophers. U.S.D.A. Tech. Bull. 244. 26 p.

Sudman, P. D., J. C. Burns and J. R. Choate. 1986. Gestation and postnatal development of the plains pocket gopher. *Texas J. Sci.* 38: 91–94.

Timm, R. M. 1983. Fahrenholz's Rule and resource tracking: A study of host-parasite coevolution. pp. 225–265, In: M. H. Nitecki, ed., *Coevolution*. Chicago: Univ. Chicago Press.

Tuszynski, R. C., and J. O. Whitaker, Jr. 1972. External parasites of pocket gophers, *Geomys bursarius*, from Indiana. *Amer. Midl. Nat.* 87: 545–548.

Vaughan, T. A. 1962. Reproduction in the plains pocket gopher in Colorado. *J. Mammal.* 43: 1–13.

## Southeastern Pocket Gopher
### *Geomys pinetis* Rafinesque

DESCRIPTION. *Geomys pinetis*, smaller and paler than *G. bursarius*, is cinnamon-brown

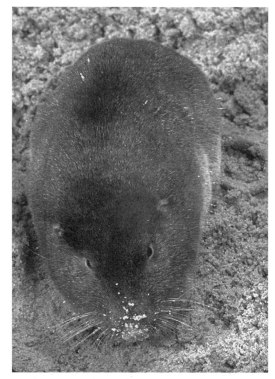

*Southeastern pocket gopher*, Geomys pinetis *(Roger W. Barbour)*

above, tinged with fulvous and buffy below; the feet and tail are pale buff to white.

MEASUREMENTS. Average measurements of 19 adults (ten males and nine females) from near Augusta, Georgia, are: total length 259, tail 86, hind foot 35 mm. The males are larger and heavier than the females. Four males from Georgia ranged from 145 to 208 grams, nine females 135 to 138 grams.

Diploid number = 42.

TOOTH FORMULA

$$\frac{1}{1} \quad \frac{0}{0} \quad \frac{1}{1} \quad \frac{3}{3} \;=\; 20$$

DISTRIBUTION. *Geomys pinetis* occurs only in the southeastern United States, from southern Georgia and Alabama to central Florida.

HABITAT. As one travels over the flat highways of coastal Georgia and much of Florida by car or train, irregular mounds of light sand, contrasting sharply with the burnt brush or brown earth of the pine woods, are seen by even the most casual observer. These are the mounds thrown from the tunnels of southeastern pocket gophers, or "salamanders," as they are known there (the name is probably a corruption of "sandy-mounder"). They are at times incredibly abundant, several hundred piles of pale sand dotting an acre (0.4 ha) of pasture or scrubby field. Wherever the soil is loose and friable and sufficiently high above the water table, *Geomys* sooner or later appears, to tunnel its way through the yielding earth in the longleaf pine country of our Southeast, though they are not restricted to this habitat.

Wilkins (1987) studied the habitat and distribution of *Geomys pinetis* in Florida. Prime habitat there consists of the rolling and well-drained sand hills characterized by longleaf pine (*Pinus palustris*) and turkey oak (*Quercus laevis*). The gophers are also found in the xeric hammocks commonly occurring amongst the sandhills. Dominant plants of the hammocks are live oak (*Q. virginiana*) and other hardwoods. The hammocks contain more organic material and a little more moisture than the sandhills. The species is less common in longleaf pine flatwoods and sand pine scrub habitats. There are two major rivers in Florida, the Apalachicola and the Suwannee, and both serve as barriers to range extension and gene flow in pocket gophers.

HABITS. Few mammals are so peculiarly modified for a special habitat as these. The strong, heavy, protruding incisors tear at roots or other obstacles as the long, heavy claws of the forefeet burrow through the ground. When a pile of dirt has accumulated in the burrow behind the gopher, the animal turns, and with head and

*Distribution of the southeastern pocket gopher,* Geomys pinetis, *in the eastern United States*

forefeet pushes the load, expelling it through a lateral passage to the surface. As the pile accumulates, a sizable mound is formed. Eventually, another lateral passageway is constructed and yet another pile formed, until the industry of a solitary individual gives the appearance of many at work. These piles often mark the course of the main subterranean passage, but when a number of piles have accumulated, it is difficult to follow the direction taken by the main tunnel. The tunnels are made at various depths, often only several centimeters below the soil but just as frequently a third of a meter to almost a full meter (1 to 3 feet) beneath the surface. The burrows are often of some size, more than large enough to accommodate their owner. The gopher can run backward with as much agility as forward, the tactile tail serving as an organ of touch when the gopher retreats. The burrows serve as home to about 80 species of arthropods, mostly insects, of which 14 appear to be obligate commensals.

FOOD AND FEEDING. The food of the southeastern pocket gopher consists chiefly of roots, fleshy rhizomes, and the green parts of the grasses, sedges, and forbs that can be reached from a tunnel opening. Probably few herbs are scorned. Considerable food is stored in the underground chambers—far more, it would seem, than the animal could possibly eat. It appears strange that such great quantities should be stored, for the gophers are active at all seasons, and thus, it would seem, need not be prepared for protracted periods when access to additional food is denied.

REPRODUCTION AND DEVELOPMENT. This species apparently breeds throughout the year, but mostly from January through August, with peaks of female reproductive activity in February and March and again in June through August. Litters range from one to three young, averaging 1.5, and individual females may give birth to two litters per year. Newborn are 50 mm long and weigh 5.8 grams. The young are weaned in one month.

ENEMIES. As indicated above (for *Geomys bursarius*), relatively few predators assault these pocket gophers. Gopher snakes and weasels are probably the most important.

PARASITES AND DISEASES. A nematode has been reported from the stomach of one of these gophers, and at least eight species of arthropods have been reported from its fur: a tick, four species of mites, two of biting lice, and a flea (Forrester, 1992).

RELATION TO HUMANS. In Georgia and Florida the pocket gopher is a pest of no mean consequence in agricultural regions. It is inordinately fond of sweet potatoes, destroying great quantities of them, and it attacks peanuts, sugar cane, and peas, as well.

AREAS FOR FURTHER WORK. A detailed study of the parasites of this species is in order, and the results could be compared profitably to those from studies of *Geomys bursarius*. A study of the nest associates would also be of interest. Specific information on the food of these rodents is needed, and much more could be learned concerning their burrows and burrowing. Why is so much food stored in the burrow? We have essentially no information on population characteristics. (See also the comparable questions under the account for *G. bursarius*.)

## SUBSPECIES

Pocket gophers are notoriously slow dispersers, partly because they are practically unable to swim. Thus even a small river can act as a primary isolating mechanism, but although they were earlier divided into several species and subspecies, the pocket gophers of the southeastern United States show little variation. Contrary to the views of earlier workers, Williams and Genoways (1980) concluded (and we concur) that all the southeastern pocket gophers belong to one species with two subspecies (including the nominate). The previously recognized *Geomys colonus* and *G. cumberlandius* are island forms, but series of specimens of those forms were not distinguishable from adjacent mainland populations, and so are accorded neither species nor subspecies status today.

*Geomys pinetis pinetis* Rafinesque

As described above. This is the form that we recognize as occurring in virtually the entire range of the species in the eastern United States. Type locality: Piney areas of Screven Co., Georgia.

*Geomys pinetis fontanelus* Sherman

This form, a relatively large, dark form known only from the type, is distinguished by having a "fontanel between the parietal and temporal bones." It is the only pocket gopher exhibiting this characteristic. The nasal bones are much compressed in their anterior third. This subspecies was described in 1940 (as a separate species), and the last individuals were taken in 1950. Recent efforts to find additional specimens have been unsuccessful. The subspecies occupies a very restricted range, and may have been obliterated by the expansion of Savannah, Georgia. Type locality: 7 miles [11 km] northwest of Savannah, Chatham Co., Georgia.

### LITERATURE

Brown, L. N. 1971. Breeding biology of the pocket gopher (*Geomys pinetis*) in Southern Florida. *Amer. Midland Nat.* 85: 45–53.

Forrester, D. J. 1992. *Parasites and Diseases of Wild Mammals in Florida.* Gainesville: Univ. Press of Florida. 459 pp.

Hickman, G. C., and L. N. Brown. 1973. Mound building behavior of the southeastern pocket gopher (*Geomys pinetis*). *J. Mammal.* 54: 786–790.

Pembleton, E. F., and S. L. Williams. 1978. *Geomys pinetis.* **Mammalian Species No. 86.** Amer. Soc. Mammal. 3 pp.

Wilkins, K. T. 1987. A zoogeographic analysis of variation in recent *Geomys pinetis* (Geomyidae) in Florida. *Bull. Fla. State Mus. Biol. Sci.* 30(1): 1–28.

Williams, S. L., and H. H. Genoways. 1980. Morphological variation in the southeastern pocket gopher, *Geomys pinetis* (Mammalia: Rodentia). *Ann. Carnegie Mus.* 49: 405–453.

## BEAVERS, Family Castoridae

Beavers are large, heavily built animals with a broad, scaly, spatulate (horizontally flattened) tail. They are the largest of North American rodents, some attaining a weight of 32 kg (70 lbs). The hind feet are prominently webbed. The three outer toes on the hind feet have typical claws; the two inner toes possess specialized claws that are used for grooming and combing the fur. The skull is massive and broad, and lacks a postorbital process.

Two species of beaver exist today: the New World beaver, *Castor canadensis*, and the Old World beaver, *C. fiber*. There had been a question whether the two were different or not, but they differ both in chromosome number (the diploid number is 40 in *Castor canadensis*, 48 in *C. fiber*) and in cranial morphology. We have also found recently that the New and Old World beavers differ almost completely in their ectoparasitic mite communities. They consist of entirely separate groups of species of host-specific chirodiscid mites of the genus *Schizocarpus*, with but one linking species in common, *S. mingaudi*. *Schizocarpus mingaudi*, then, would appear to have occurred alone on the progenitor beaver stocks that gave rise to *Castor canadensis* and *C. fiber*. These data support the recognition of two separate species of beavers.

## American Beaver
### *Castor canadensis* (Kuhl)

DESCRIPTION. The beaver is the largest North American rodent, and between its size and its large, scaly, paddle-like tail, it can be confused with no other North American mammal. The color is uniformly reddish brown to blackish brown. The guard hairs are about ten times the diameter of the dense, underlying underfur; they are longest on the back (50 mm) and are of one color, from tip to base. The longest underfur, about 25 mm long, is also found dorsally. The ears, short and rounded, are dark blackish brown. The hind legs are longer than the front legs, the hips thus higher than the shoulders when the animal is walking. The skull and teeth are massive, a necessity for cutting tough wood such as oak and maple. The upper incisors, a bright orange, are at least 5 mm wide and 20–25 mm long, and grow throughout the life of the animal. Some of the animal's adaptations for an aquatic existence are its closable nostrils and ears. Nictitating eye membranes and upper lips that close behind the incisors help keep water from the eyes and mouth just as they keep dirt out in burrowing animals.

*American beaver,* Castor canadensis
*(Larry E. Lehman)*

The reproductive organs are internal and open into a common anal cloaca with anal and castor glands. The castor glands, found in both male and female beavers, are often called musk glands or "castors." The anal and castor glands, both of them prominent, lie in a subcutaneous cavity at the base of the tail, the castors being anterior. There is no seasonal change in the size of these glands, and they are about the same size in the two sexes. In one beaver, the castor glands measured 87 by 57 mm (3.4 by 2.2 inches), the anal glands 76 by 25 mm (3.0 by 1 inches). The anal gland opens directly into the cloaca, and the castor opens into the urethra, which in turn opens into the cloaca. Secretions from these glands are used for scent-marking piles of mud and vegetative debris along the territorial boundaries of the colony. The castor glands give the beaver its peculiar odor and its generic name. See Svendsen (1978) for more details. There are four pectoral mammae.

MEASUREMENTS. Adult beavers measure: total length 900–1170, tail 300–440, hind foot 165–185 mm; and the tail is 110 to 180 mm wide. Adults (three years old or more) weigh from 13 to 32 kg (30 to 70 lbs), occasionally more. The record is 39 kg (86 lbs). A two-year-old beaver weighs about 13.5 kg, a six-year-old about 27 kg. Beavers are somewhat smaller in the south, and those in good habitat at midcontinent apparently attain the greatest size.
Diploid number = 40.

TOOTH FORMULA

$$\frac{1}{1} \quad \frac{0}{0} \quad \frac{1}{1} \quad \frac{3}{3} \; = \; 20$$

DISTRIBUTION. Although widely distributed throughout the eastern United States in former times, the beaver was nearly extirpated by 1900. Today, because of reintroduction and protection, it is becoming increasingly abundant, and it is found in regions where it had been absent for more than 80 years. It is now generally distributed in the eastern states, and reaches the Suwannee River in peninsular Florida. It is currently found throughout North America and barely into Central America.

HABITAT. The beaver again occupies much of forested North America wherever there are suitable rivers, streams, lakes, ponds, or even small seepages that can be dammed, even in suburban areas. It occurs at nearly all elevations where suitable water flows, although flatlands and valleys are preferred. Habitats with quaking aspen are particularly good beaver habitat, for aspen is their favored food tree.

HABITS. Often one's first indication that beavers are present is the sound of the slap of the tail on the water as a beaver dives. To the uninitiated, this slap often sounds as if someone had thrown a large, round rock into the water.
The engineering feats of the beaver, observed by many, are well known. The dams, the lodges, and the less-familiar canals are all remarkable

accomplishments. The haunts selected by the beaver for these construction projects are lakes and ponds or gently descending streams where their dams will create a pond deep enough for adequate food storage under ice—ice that will not freeze to the bottom. Food, in the form of edible branches, is cached under water, anchored in the mud at the bottom of the pond, near the entrance to the lodge or bank burrow. The beaver will use this cache in winter, but will continue to cut fresh logs when it can break through the ice. In the north, the food cache is critical in the life of a beaver, because it must stockpile food for up to six months.

Late summer and autumn is a busy season for beavers. It is then that they must build and repair the dams and lodges and accumulate the food piles that are essential for winter, when zero temperatures will lock them away from the shore and living trees. Usually, they carry on their activities at night, but at this season they work through much of the day if undisturbed.

To begin the construction of a dam, the beaver places thick branches with their butts facing upstream and their tips stuck in the mud. When a sufficient number are in place, spanning the stream from shore to shore, they are secured with mud, sod, and even sizable stones. More branches are then laid on top of these, and the process is repeated until water begins to back up and the desired pond depth is secured.

The lodge, constructed primarily of large branches or the trunks of saplings, is formed by building these materials up from the pond bottom, a small island, or a gently sloping bank. A roomy interior provides sleeping quarters, and a dry platform (but no nesting material) provides an area where the occupants may repair to feed on the bark of limbs dragged from their food pile (stripped limbs are common around an active beaver colony). There are two or three underwater entrances to the lodge.

*Distribution of the American beaver,* Castor canadensis, *in the eastern United States*

*Beaver dam*

At times beavers make no lodge, using instead a tunnel into a bank. In Indiana, such animals are known as "bank beavers." Beavers living along rivers routinely use bank burrows, and such homesites are otherwise more likely to be used about a natural pond or lake than on a pond created by a beaver dam. A pile of limbs may cover the entrance to the burrow, and a colony will sometimes construct both lodges *and* bank dens.

Canals, often of considerable length, are dug to facilitate the transport of branches from where they were cut back to the pond.

Fall is thus the primary tree-cutting season. One or two beavers will engage in cutting a tree. When the tree is felled (many are not completely cut through), the branches within reach, up to 12 cm (5 inches) or more in diameter, are cut off, reduced to lengths convenient for movement, depending on the size of the beaver and the diameter of the log, and transported to the food pile. Often the tree that has been felled catches in the branches of another, and leans far out of reach of the beavers; and of course every tree that is successfully cut through, of whatever size, is likely to retain many branches that the beaver cannot reach. If the bark is not eaten or the tree is not moved into the water within a week or two, the bark becomes dry and unpalatable and is not touched again by the beavers. Busher (1996) states that branches from woody vegetation can be eaten immediately, used in construction, stored in the food cache, or wasted. He set up a cafeteria-style experiment with piles of sticks marked with different-colored paints and showed that some species (e.g. witch hazel, *Hamamelis virginiana*) were more heavily cached, whereas red maple was usually consumed immediately, though these patterns changed with time.

The beaver is an excellent swimmer, and is able to remain under water for up to 15 minutes, though one or two minutes is more typical. The beaver has no unusual oxygen-storage capacity, however, that might allow it to remain under water for extended periods, but changes occur in heart rate and in circulation to the extremities, allowing it to conserve oxygen for longer dives. On land the beaver walks with an awkward waddle, but the forefeet have great dexterity, allowing the beaver to fold leaves and manipulate branches or small twigs with skill.

FOOD AND FEEDING. Beavers can be considered generalist feeders, feeding on a great variety of plants but choosing from among those available. From fall to spring the beaver feeds on bark, and, in the north, aspen is its staple. Entire stands of quaking aspen or "popple" may be removed—we have seen areas where aspens or willows have been leveled as if a mowing machine had gone through them—before serious inroads are made into stands of other trees, although maples, willows, alders, apple, birch, and many others are eaten with relish. Conifers are seldom eaten, but in Louisiana, loblolly pine is often taken. Sweetgum, silverbell, sweetbay, and ironwood are some of the other tree species heavily used in Louisiana. In the summer the aquatic succulents, pond lilies, bur reed, duckweed, pondweeds, algae, and the fleshy rootstocks of many other plants are eaten, and beavers will journey to neighboring fields to eat clover, alfalfa, and various herbaceous plants. Digestion is enhanced by extra digestive glands and a three-parted caecum (a side branch off the intestines) that harbors commensal microflora. Coprophagy, which allows greater digestive efficiency, also occurs. But the ability of the beaver to digest cellulose is no greater than that of other nonruminant mammals. To gain adequate nutrition, the beaver must ingest great amounts of fibrous woody material.

REPRODUCTION AND DEVELOPMENT. Beavers are monogamous. They mate between January and March in cold climates, in late November or December in the south. They first breed begin-

*Beaver cuttings along a road, the roadway almost awash from the effects of a dam*

ning about their third (second to fourth) year of life, depending on the quality of the habitat. There is one litter per year, and gestation averages about 105 to 107 days. The one to nine (usually three or four) young are born April through June, sometimes earlier. More young are produced in better environmental conditions. The young are remarkably well developed at birth, with well-furred bodies and open eyes. Newborn vary in color from brown or reddish brown to almost black and weigh about 0.5 kg (1 lb). By a year the young weigh 5 to 12 kg (11–26 lbs). They remain in the lodge for a month; at the end of that time they leave to swim and take solid food of the softer summer fare. Lactation can continue for at least 90 days, but beavers are usually weaned in two weeks.

POPULATION CHARACTERISTICS. Each beaver colony may consist of a pair of adults, their most recent set of young, and occasionally some of the yearlings or even older individuals. The number of beavers per colony is higher in better habitat, and the maximum number per colony is about 12, but a typical colony comprises five or six individuals. Colony densities reach maxima of about 1.9 colonies per km (4.2 per mile) of stream, but densities of 0.2 to 0.7 per km (0.4 to 1.5 per mile) are more typical. Beavers pursue several kinds of movements. Besides their normal movements within territories, and movements of the entire colony between ponds within their territory, yearlings may wander about, and adults that have lost their mates may make more miscellaneous movements. Just before the birth of another litter, the two-year-olds are driven

out, or leave the colony of their own accord, to establish a new residence, often several kilometers removed.

Beavers mark territories by placing mud and pieces of vegetation in piles near the colony's territorial borders. To these are added urine and the contents of the anal and castor glands. Dieter Müller-Schwarze and colleagues (Müller-Schwarze and Houlihan, 1991; Welsh and Müller-Schwarze, 1989) investigated the chemical and behavioral properties of beaver castoria and anal glands. Numerous chemicals have been identified in castoreum; 24 of them were used individually and collectively in creating artificial mudpiles both in free-ranging beaver territories and in uninhabited areas. Unoccupied (but suitable) sites thus artificially scented were colonized less often than the unscented control sites were, and thus appeared to be acting as repellents. At active sites, four compounds, two phenols and two ketones, elicited immediate responses. The most complete responses consisted of beavers sniffing the substances from the water, swimming toward the source, walking ashore and sniffing and pawing, and, finally, scent-marking the artificial mound themselves, using secretions from the anal and castor glands. Responses were strongest in the densest beaver population.

The life span of the beaver is 10 to 20 years.

ENEMIES. Its large size saves the beaver from many carnivores that would otherwise be its enemies. Humans, with their traps, are the worst enemies, and wolves and coyotes are the most important natural predators. The timber wolves' diet on Isle Royale, Michigan, included about 11% beaver. Coyotes are less important, but can occasionally kill a small beaver, especially when they encounter one away from water.

PARASITES AND DISEASE. The ectoparasites of beavers form an exceedingly interesting community, one made up entirely of host-specific forms. The community consists of two species of beetles plus a large group of tiny, tubular, hair-clasping mites, all in the genus *Schizocarpus*. One of the beetle species, *Platypsylla castoris*, is highly adapted to living on beavers and is widely known to trappers as "beaver flea." Until recently, it was thought that there was only one species of *Schizocarpus*, *S. min-*

*gaudi*, on Eurasian as well as North American beavers, but it is now known that *Schizocarpus*, found only on beavers, consists of a number of species—at least 15 on North American beavers and at least 33 others on *Castor fiber*, plus a single linking species, *S. mingaudi* (even the Eurasian and North American *S. mingaudi* may differ, though they are definitely closely related). It appears that when the beavers diverged they had a single mite of the *S. mingaudi* type, and that the subsequent speciation process ensued independently in Eurasia and North America (Fain et al., 1984). The North American *Schizocarpus* mites fall into four groups based on distinctions in the sucker plates of the males, the four groups all but restricted to certain parts of the beaver. Females are very similar between groups and at present impossible to identify within groups. This situation, nearly unique, is termed *multispeciation*.

Tularemia, a bacterial disease caused by *Pasteurella tularense*, has on occasion caused widespread mortality among beavers.

RELATION TO HUMANS. In the eighteenth and nineteenth centuries, the beaver was heavily trapped, leading to much exploration in the west and north, but also to near extirpation of the beaver by about 1900. Large pelts taken in 1942 brought $32, and by 1946 the price had risen to $65. By 1983, however, it had fallen to $35, and today a beaver brings roughly $10. Reintroduction and protection began in the 1920s and continued through the 1950s, until today, with low fur values, the beavers have so markedly increased their numbers as to become a pest species in many areas. They fell valuable trees and flood whole areas, and are considered detrimental by fishermen because the dams warm the water in trout streams.

But besides providing us with fur, beavers also create wetlands, control erosion, and aid many other species of wildlife. They also make excellent meat—as tasty as, and similar to, beef. Finally, the beaver can offer the instructor a memorable field trip. Standing by an active beaver pond, one can discuss the animal's role in American history, its life cycle, its effects on wildlands and other wildlife (whether for good or ill), and the construction and functions of the lodge and dam.

AREAS FOR FURTHER WORK. Comparative genetic work on American and Eurasian beavers, and on isolated populations of *Castor canadensis*, is needed. Much more work can be done on beaver mites, *Schizocarpus*. More species of mites will be found, and considerably more work is needed on the identification of their females and young individuals.

## SUBSPECIES

Because we see no evidence of primary isolating mechanisms separating any of the described subspecies, we recognize none of them.

*Castor canadensis canadensis* Kuhl
  As described above.
  Type locality: Hudson Bay.
  Other currently recognized eastern subspecies:
    *C. canadensis acadicus* V. Bailey & Doutt
    *C. canadensis carolinensis* Rhoads
    *C. canadensis michiganensis* V. Bailey

### LITERATURE

Busher, P. E. 1996. Food caching behavior of beavers (*Castor canadensis*): selection and use of woody species. *Amer. Midland Nat.* 135: 343–348.

Fain, A., J. O. Whitaker, Jr., and M. A. Smith. 1984. Fur mites of the genus *Schizocarpus* Trouessart, 1896

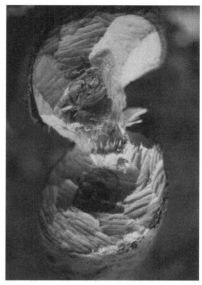

*Trunk of tree chewed through by beaver (Rita A. Veal)*

(Acari: Chirodiscidae) parasitic on the American Beaver *Castor canadensis* in Indiana, U.S.A. *Bull. Ann. Soc. Belge Entomol.* 120: 211–239.

Hill, E. P. 1982. Beaver *Castor canadensis*. In: J. A. Chapman and G. A. Feldhamer, eds., *Wild Mammals of North America*, pp. 256–281. Baltimore: Johns Hopkins Univ. Press.

Jenkins, S. H. 1975. Food selection by beavers: A multidimensional contingency table analysis. *Oecologia* 21: 157–173.

Jenkins, S. H., and P. E. Busher. 1979. *Castor canadensis*. **Mammalian Species No. 120.** Amer. Soc. Mammal. 8 pp.

Morgan, L. H. 1986. *The American Beaver*. Toronto: Dover. 330 pp.

Müller-Schwarze, D., and P. W. Houlihan. 1991. Pheromonal activity of single castoreum constituents in beaver, *Castor canadensis*. *J. Chem. Ecol.* 17: 715–734.

Novak, M. 1987. Beaver. In: M. Novak, J. A. Baker, M. E. Obbard, and B. Mallock, eds., *Wild Furbearer Management and Conservation in North America*, pp. 282–312. Toronto: Ontario Ministry Nat. Resources. 1,150 pp.

Rue, L. L., III. 1964. *The World of the Beaver*. Philadelphia: J. B. Lippincott. 155 pp.

Slough, B. G. 1978. Beaver food cache structure and utilization. *J. Wildl. Mgmt.* 42: 644–646.

Svendsen, G. E. 1978. Castor and anal glands of the beaver. *J. Mammal.* 59: 618–620.

Welsh, R. G., and D. Müller-Schwarze. 1989. Experimental habitat scenting inhibits colonization by beaver, *Castor canadensis*. *J. Chem. Ecol.* 15: 887–893.

## JUMPING MICE, Family Dipodidae

Representatives of this family are found in the northern portions of both the New World and Old World. They are characterized by a very large infraorbital foramen, which allows passage of muscles and nerves and, in one of the two North American genera, *Zapus*, by the presence of four upper cheek teeth. The incisors are compressed and very deeply grooved (Fig. 7.16b, below). In general, these animals are mouselike in form, but they are distinguished by an extraordinarily long tail and very long hind legs, which are adapted for leaping.

Jumping mice are found in forests, swamps, and meadows and are often common. They are profound hibernators. These mice were originally described in the family Dipodidae, then were placed in their own family, the Zapodidae, but recent work by Stein (1990) and Stenbrot

(1992) places them as the subfamily Zapodinae, back in the family Dipodidae.

### LITERATURE CITED

Stein, B. R. 1990. Limb myology and phylogenetic relationships in the superfamily Dipodoidea (birch mice, jumping mice, and jerboas). *Z. für Zool. Syst. und Evol.* 28: 299–314.

Stenbrot, G. I. 1992. [Cladistic approach to the analysis of phylogenetic relationships among dipodoid rodents (Rodentia, Dipodoidea)]. *Sbornik Trudov Zool. Muzeya* MGU 29: 176–201 [in Russian].

### KEY TO THE GENERA AND SPECIES OF THE FAMILY DIPODIDAE

1. Upper cheek teeth 4, the first small; tail tip not white . . . . . . . . . . . . . . *Zapus hudsonius*
1. Upper cheek teeth 3, tail tip white . . . . . . . . . . . . . . . . . *Napaeozapus insignis*

## Meadow Jumping Mouse *Zapus hudsonius* (Zimmermann)

DESCRIPTION. *Zapus* is basically mouselike in form, but has big feet, long hind legs, and a very long tail. The middle toe of the hind foot is the longest. The sides are yellowish, and the underparts and feet are white. Along the dorsum is a prominent, darker dorsal band interspersed with many black-tipped hairs, their bases slate-colored. The pelage is rather coarse. The tail, brownish above and white below, is sparsely haired and lacks the white tail tip of *Napaeozapus*. Anterior to the three enlarged molariform teeth, *Zapus* has a very small upper premolar.

*Meadow jumping mouse,* Zapus hudsonius
*(Dennis E. Clark)*

MEASUREMENTS. Thirty adults from New York averaged: total length 213 (207–222), tail 128 (119–136), and hind foot 31 (28–32) mm. May–June weights were 14–17 grams; September–October weights, 17–26 grams. The species is somewhat smaller in the southern parts of its range. Seven adults from Raleigh, North Carolina, averaged: total length 191, tail 115, hind foot 28 mm.

Diploid number = 72.

TOOTH FORMULA

$$\frac{1}{1} \quad \frac{0}{0} \quad \frac{1}{0} \quad \frac{3}{3} \;=\; 18$$

DISTRIBUTION. In the eastern United States the meadow jumping mouse occurs south to northern South Carolina, northern Georgia, and eastern Alabama. Elsewhere, it occurs across most of southern Canada, and in the U.S. West to southeastern Montana, eastern Wyoming, north-central Colorado, and northeastern Oklahoma.

HABITAT. Grassy fields or fields with mixed grasses and forbs, whether along ponds or streams or well removed from watercourses, are the home of the meadow jumping mouse. Small numbers may occupy grassy clearings in forested regions, and they often occur in early-successional-stage brushland. Where both *Zapus* and *Napaeozapus* occur, the meadow jumping mouse remains mostly in open areas, *Napaeozapus* mostly in the woods, but in areas where *Napaeozapus* is absent, the meadow jumping mouse often becomes abundant even in wooded areas, especially in thick, herbaceous vegetation. It is often particularly abundant in patches of touch-me-not (*Impatiens*), which often grows along streams or in wet places.

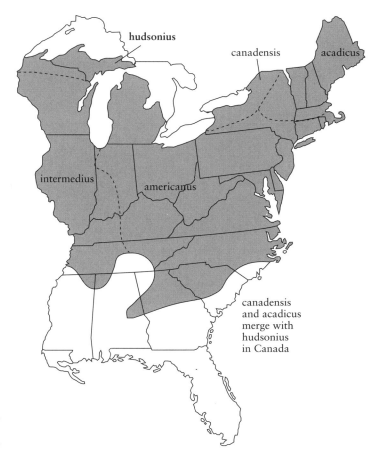

*Distribution of the meadow jumping mouse,* Zapus hudsonius, *in the eastern United States*

HABITS. As the mower clatters through the still June meadows, little balls of fur, propelled by incredibly long legs, occasionally burst from its path. For the most part, these little mice hide by day and feed during the night, but they are occasionally abroad during the day. They wander freely, seldom using runways, although in wet places they sometimes make ill-defined trails.

In prior years, this mouse was credited with making leaps of 3 meters or more (8 or 10 feet), the powerful hind limbs acting as the propulsive force while the long tail provides balance. In fact, meadow jumping mice normally skulk off among the vegetation or progress by a series of short jumps not exceeding 0.3 to 0.6 meter (a foot or two). On an open, paved parking lot we were unable to stimulate meadow jumping mice to jump farther than about a meter. The long leaps reported earlier were probably of the woodland jumping mice, not *Zapus*.

Jumping mice do not store food, but they acquire a substantial layer of fat (about 6 grams) for energy to sustain them during hibernation. At any one time, surprisingly few of the animals taken in traps in the fall have acquired their full fat complement (Whitaker, 1963). To put on this much fat, an individual needs about two weeks of heavy eating, which may occur at any time between 1 September and 20 October, but by 20 October essentially all animals have disappeared. The mouse then immediately enters hibernation, which explains why so few fat animals are taken. Hibernation, however, is not a period without risks, and only about a third of the meadow jumping mice present in fall survive to emerge in early spring. It appears that many of the individuals produced in late summer have had insufficient time to accumulate adequate fat and accordingly perish during the hibernating period. Muchlinski (1980) presented additional evidence supporting that scenario. He found that most adults and early-litter juveniles had disappeared by early September, that late-litter animals made up most of the fall population, but that early-litter juveniles had much higher survival rates than late-litter juveniles (3 of 11, or 27%, versus 4 of 50, or 11%).

The winter nest consists of a dry but often flimsy structure almost half a meter below the surface, often in a bank, mound, or other raised area. In this retreat, the mouse curls into a tight ball, its tail curled about the body, and in this rigid posture the dormant animal passes the winter, its temperature only a few degrees above freezing, its respiration slowed, and its heart rate reduced to a few beats each minute. This mouse apparently hibernates throughout its range, but the period of dormancy is somewhat shorter in the southern states. During the hibernating period the animal probably awakens on the average of once every two weeks. A mouse in hibernation in the laboratory for 19 days used only 86.6 calories per gram of weight, whereas exit from and reentry into hibernation, a period of only about five hours, required 93.6 calories per gram. An animal active for the whole 19-day period would have used at least 9,280 calories per gram, as compared to 180.2 calories per gram during the full hibernation bout (19 days asleep plus the single wake-up and reentry). Sometime in April, the time depending on latitude and altitude, the mouse emerges from hibernation, but on cold nights it is once again inactive.

FOOD AND FEEDING. When meadow jumping mice emerge from hibernation in spring, they take a variety of foods (Whitaker, 1963). Animal materials, especially beetles and cutworms, constitute about half the food, and various seeds about one-fifth of it. Few fungi are eaten. As the season progresses, more seeds, more fungi, and less animal materials are consumed, the seeds following one after another as they ripen. The seeds of various grasses, elm, touch-me-not (*Impatiens*), chickweed (*Cerastium*), sheep sorrel (*Rumex acetosella*), cinquefoil (*Potentilla*), and wood sorrel (*Oxalis*) are often important. The fungus *Endogone* and a few other tiny subterranean fungi are heavily utilized by this species, these forming 10–20% of the diet, especially in summer and fall. Jumping mice are particularly fond of berries and fruits that grow in their meadow habitat, such as blueberries, blackberries, and strawberries. Often one comes upon the little patches of 4-cm (inch-and-a-half) or longer cut grasses that demonstrate the industry of this mouse as it cuts away sections of the close-standing timothy or a few other grasses to bring the seed heads down within reach. After cutting the stalk off at as high a point as it can, it pulls the cut stalk to the ground, again cutting, and so on, until the head is reached. If one looks closely, the rachis and other parts of the seed head on the top of the pile can often be found. Other times the mouse will climb the stalk, cut off the head, and bring it to the ground to feed.

REPRODUCTION AND DEVELOPMENT. In the northeastern United States, there are three peaks of breeding in this species. Mating occurs soon after emergence from hibernation in spring, and the three to six young are born in May or June, after a gestation of about 18 days. Some individuals, most of them probably those not having borne a spring brood, produce a litter in July; and many of the mice mate again in late summer and produce a litter in August or even early September. Measurements of three newborn averaged total length 34, tail 9.2, and hind foot 4.7 mm. Average weight was 0.78 gram. Incisors erupt about the 13th day, the hair covering is complete by the 17th day, and the eyes open between the 22nd and 25th days (Quimby, 1951). And at that time the young mice begin to venture from the nest and eat solid foods, although they continue to take milk for another week or so. The well-constructed nest of grass and leaves is assembled in an underground chamber, underneath a log, or less often in a clump of shrubs or stout weeds a few centimeters above ground level. We have found the nests of young in open fields, the only cover being a weathered plank.

POPULATION CHARACTERISTICS. The home ranges of four females varied in size from 0.08 to 0.35 ha (0.19 to 0.87 acres), and those of five males varied from 0.06 to 0.4 ha (0.14 to 1.1 acres). At another site, the mean for nine males was 1.1 ha (2.7 acres), and for 18 females it was 0.6 ha (1.57 acres).

ENEMIES. The usual predators take their toll. Among the more important enemies are the raptors (particularly barn owls), foxes, skunks, weasels, and snakes.

PARASITES AND DISEASE. The most abundant ectoparasite of these mice is a tiny hypopial (nonfeeding transport-stage) mite, *Glycyphagus newyorkensis*, which can be found in large numbers on both *Zapus* and *Napaeozapus*. The widespread mite *Androlaelaps fahrenholzi* is the second most abundant mite on this host, and a few other mites, ticks, and fleas also occur.

RELATION TO HUMANS. Because *Zapus* is an innocuous little mouse that does not get into houses or other buildings, we are seldom aware of its presence. In general, its relation to humans has to be thought of as beneficial, since it eats large numbers of cutworms and other caterpillars, other insects, and numerous weed seeds.

AREAS FOR FURTHER WORK. Energy budgets, including calorific and nutrient intake, as compared with what is contained in the feces, could be worked out for these mice and for many other small mammal species. The physiological aspects of hibernation in these mice, their intraspecific social relationships, and the means by which they find subterranean fungi would be of interest.

## SUBSPECIES

There seems no logical reason to assign subspecies to this species in the eastern United States. Practically as much variation exists within individual populations as exists throughout the eastern range of the species. Moreover, there are no known primary isolating mechanisms separating major groups of populations.

*Zapus hudsonius hudsonius* (Zimmermann)
As described above.
Type locality: Hudson Bay, Canada; considered by Anderson to be Fort Severn, Ontario.
Other currently recognized eastern subspecies:
 *Z. hudsonius acadicus* (Dawson)
 *Z. hudsonius americanus* (Barton)
 *Z. hudsonius canadensis* (Davies)
 *Z. hudsonius intermedius* Krutzsch

### LITERATURE

Muchlinski, A. E. 1980. The effects of day length and temperature on the hibernating meadow jumping mouse (*Zapus hudsonius*). *Physiol. Zool.* 53: 410–418.

———. 1988. Population attributes related to the life history strategy of hibernating *Zapus hudsonius*. *J. Mammal.* 69: 860–865.

Quimby, D. C. 1951. The life history and ecology of the jumping mouse, *Zapus hudsonius*. *Ecol. Monogr.* 21: 61–95.

Whitaker, J. O., Jr. 1963. A study of the meadow jumping mouse, *Zapus hudsonius* (Zimmermann), in central New York. *Ecol. Monogr.* 33: 215–254.

———. 1972. *Zapus hudsonius*. **Mammalian Species No. 11.** Amer. Soc. Mammal. 7 pp.

## Woodland Jumping Mouse
### *Napaeozapus insignis*
### (Miller)                     Color plate 9

DESCRIPTION. The woodland jumping mouse is similar to *Zapus*, but differs in having a *white*

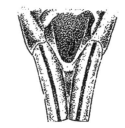

*Front of upper incisors of woodland jumping mouse, showing deep grooves (Thomas W. French)*

*Woodland jumping mouse*, Napaeozapus insignis *(Roger W. Barbour)*

TOOTH FORMULA

$$\frac{1}{1} \quad \frac{0}{0} \quad \frac{0}{0} \quad \frac{3}{3} = 16$$

DISTRIBUTION. In the eastern United States, this species occurs from Maine and eastern Ohio south through the Appalachians to northeastern Georgia, and in northern Michigan and northern Wisconsin. It is absent to the south except in the higher mountains. *Napaeozapus* also occurs in southeastern Canada and west to northern Minnesota and southeastern Manitoba.

tail tip, brighter reddish-yellow colors, and the absence of the small premolar in the upper jaw. The sides are yellowish or even reddish brown, sprinkled with black hairs; the darker dorsal band is dark brown interspersed with many more dark-tipped hairs. The underparts and the feet are pure white. The tail is bicolored, dark brown above and creamy white below, and the tail tip is all white. All jumping mice have prominently grooved incisors.

MEASUREMENTS. Measurements of 40 adults from New York averaged: total length 227 (210–249), tail 129.5 (126–152), hind foot 30.2 (28–34) mm. Weights of May–June specimens averaged 20 grams, and of September–October specimens just prior to hibernation, 25–28 grams. South through the Alleghenies, this mouse is smaller and considerably darker; measurements of eight adults from the Smoky Mountains averaged: total length 223 (185–233), tail 140 (120–148), hind foot 29.7 (29–30) mm.

Diploid number = 72.

HABITAT. The woodland jumping mouse is pretty much restricted to northern or cool moist woodlands, although where there is an intermixing of meadow and forest herbaceous vegetation in open glades at the edge of a forest or in other such ecotone situations, *Napaeozapus* and *Zapus* may both be found. The two are particularly apt to occur together where touch-me-not (*Impatiens*) occurs along a stream running from the woods into a field. *Napaeozapus* inhabits a variety of woodland types, from spruce/fir to mixed conifer/hardwood forests. It occurs in open, moist woods but is often taken near streams.

HABITS. Few small mammals can compare with the woodland jumping mouse in elegance of form or exquisiteness of color. This brightly marked little rodent is seldom seen, though it is at times fairly common. Between us we have trapped several hundred along tumbling brooks shaded by the tangled undergrowth and forest trees of central New York. This species is primarily nocturnal. It makes no discernible runways, but sometimes uses the burrows of other small mammals, or seeks the shelter of rotting logs or fallen trees, whose exposed roots provide sanctuary. Several observers have seen this mouse make a leap of from 3 to 4 meters (9 to 12 feet). We have seen one jump at least 8 feet, the powerful hind limbs acting as the propulsive force while the long tail provides balance. A nest is made of such material as is at hand; it is usually placed several centimeters below the surface, typically beneath a stump or slight eminence in the forest. Feed well this mouse must, for the first killing frosts signal the end of such bounty. Prodded by the shortening days of fall, the animals put on 7–8 grams of weight just prior to hibernation. The mouse passes the winter in a stiff ball, its life processes reduced to a minimum, but wakes from hibernation periodically, probably about every two weeks. Woodland jumping mice are the most profound of eastern hibernators, spending half the year in the dormant condition. These jumping mice may sometimes sleep in pairs, for the stomach of a November-caught skunk contained the remains of two of these mice.

FOOD AND FEEDING. The stomachs of 103 individuals of this species from New York contained tiny fungi of the genus *Endogone* and related genera, the fungi comprising about a third of the total food assayed. *Endogone* is poorly known and difficult to find even by sieving soil samples, yet *Napaeozapus* and many other small mammals feed on it in quantity, presumably locating it by olfaction. To the uninitiated, at low power of the dissecting microscope this fungus looks like dirt; one must increase the power to distinguish the individual spores. Seeds made up about a quarter of the food in the stomachs of the New York mice, lepidopterous larvae and various kinds of fruit each about 10%, and beetles 7.5%. Seeds of touch-me-not, easily identified by their brilliant turquoise color when found in the stomachs, are very important when ripe.

REPRODUCTION AND DEVELOPMENT. Gestation in the woodland jumping mouse appears to be about 29 days—quite long, considering that

*Endogone, a major fungal food of jumping mice and other small mammals, greatly enlarged (Mark O. Oster)*

gestation in its cousin, *Zapus hudsonius*, is only about 19 days. Three to six young are born in late June or early July, and some mice have a second litter in August. Layne and Hamilton (1954) described the development of the young in this species. The newborn are pink-skinned and hairless, and the four pairs of mammae are already visible, as light spots, in both sexes. The eye appears as a dark ring 1.5 mm in breadth. Standard measurements at birth are: total length 35.2, tail 11, and hind foot 5 mm; and weight 0.87 grams. By the tenth day the ear pinna has unfolded, but the external auditory meatus is still closed. Fine hairs appear by the 12th day, and the plantar tubercles (on the soles of the feet) have become black. By day 19, the claws are well formed and the lower incisors are protruding through the gums. By three weeks, the lower incisors protrude about 0.5 mm and the upper incisors are just appearing. The dorsal color pattern is developed by the 26th day, at which time the eyes open. The young are not weaned until a month old. By day 31 the mammae are no longer visible under the belly fur, the incisors are yellow, and the upper incisors are grooved; and by day 34 the young look like little adults.

POPULATION CHARACTERISTICS. Density estimates range up to 59 per ha (24 per acre). Home ranges of females range from 0.5 to 2.6 ha (1.2 to 6.4 acres), those of males from 0.5 to 3.6 ha (1.2 to 8 acres). Some individuals probably live to an age of three or four years, but it is unlikely that many live beyond two years.

ENEMIES. There are few reports of predators on this species, but most predators would certainly eat *Napaeozapus* if the opportunity were to arise. Known cases of predation are by skunks, weasels, mink, bobcat, screech owl, timber rattlesnake, and copperhead.

PARASITES AND DISEASES. The most abundant "parasite" of this species is the hypopus (transport) stage of the mite *Glycyphagus newyorkensis*. These mites are not really parasites, for they do not feed, but simply use the host for a ride. Few adults of any of the species have been seen, but the hypopi presumably drop off and transform to adults in the host's nest. Fain et al. (1985) have described the life cycle for this species, including the adult. A number of other mites and some fleas are also found on this host.

RELATION TO HUMANS. These mice are of little economic importance and are seldom found in the haunts of humans. Their usefulness probably lies in reducing the numbers of forest insects and furnishing a modest source of food for predatory birds and mammals.

AREAS FOR FURTHER STUDY. A third of the total food of this species may be subterranean fungi, especially *Endogone* and its relatives. How do the mice find it and what is its nutrient value? And where does this mouse hibernate? Much more information is needed on the life cycle of the hypopial mite *Glycyphagus newyorkensis*. (See also the questions asked in the *Zapus* account.)

## SUBSPECIES

Because there is no evidence of primary isolating mechanisms separating the subspecies described from the eastern United States, we recognize neither of them.

*Distribution of the woodland jumping mouse,* Napaeozapus insignis, *in the eastern United States*

Newborn masked shrew

Water shrew, *Sorex palustris*
(ROGER W. BARBOUR)

Northern short-tailed shrew, *Blarina brevicauda* (ROGER W. BARBOUR)

Three least shrews with earthworm (above), and young least shrews in nest, eight days old (below)
(JERRY LEE GINGERICH)

PLATE 1

Hairy-tailed mole,
*Parascalops breweri*
(ROGER W. BARBOUR)

Star-nosed mole,
*Condylura cristata*
(DWIGHT KUHN)

Jamaican fruit-eating bat,
*Artibeus jamaicensis*
(PHILIP A. FRANK)

Eastern small-footed myotis, *Myotis leibii*
(ROGER W. BARBOUR)

PLATE 2

Northern myotis, *Myotis septentrionalis*

Hibernating cluster of Indiana myotis in cave in southern Indiana

Silver-haired bat, *Lasionycteris noctivagans* (Tony Brentlinger)

Eastern pipistrelle, *Pipistrellus subflavus* (Charles L. Oberst)

PLATE 3

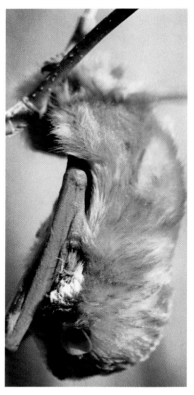

Eastern red bat, *Lasiurus borealis*, female
(ROGER W. BARBOUR)

Eastern red bat, *Lasiurus borealis*,
male (SHERRY L. GUMMER)

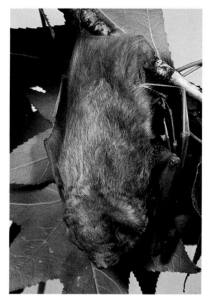

Seminole bat,
*Lasiurus seminolus*
(ROGER W. BARBOUR)

Northern yellow bat, *Lasiurus
intermedius* (ROGER W. BARBOUR)

PLATE 4

Evening bat,
*Nycticeius humeralis*
(ROGER W. BARBOUR)

Brazilian free-tailed bat, *Tadarida brasiliensis*
(ROGER W. BARBOUR)

Wagner's mastiff bat, *Eumops glaucinus*
(ROGER W. BARBOUR)

PLATE 5

Nine-banded armadillo, *Dasypus novemcinctus* (ROGER W. BARBOUR)

Eastern cottontail,
*Sylvilagus floridanus*
(ROGER W. BARBOUR)

Marsh rabbit, *Sylvilagus palustris*
(JOSEPH McDONALD)

PLATE 6

Black-tailed jackrabbit, *Lepus californicus*
(Troy L. Best)

White-tailed jackrabbit,
*Lepus townsendii*
(Rod Planck)

Least chipmunk, *Tamias minimus*
(Roger W. Barbour)

Eastern chipmunk, *Tamias striatus*
(Roger W. Barbour)

PLATE 7

Woodchuck, *Marmota monax*
(MARK ROMESSER)

Fox squirrel, *Sciurus niger* (ROGER W. BARBOUR)

Red squirrel, *Tamiasciurus hudsonicus*
(ROGER W. BARBOUR)

PLATE 8

Northern flying squirrel, *Glaucomys sabrinus* (B. Moose Peterson)

Southern flying squirrel, *Glaucomys volans* (Jerry Lee Gingerich)

Woodland jumping mouse, *Napaeozapus insignis* (Roger W. Barbour)

PLATE 9

Marsh rice rat, *Oryzomys palustris*
(ROGER W. BARBOUR)

Cotton mouse, *Peromyscus gossypinus* (ROGER W. BARBOUR)

Deer mouse, *Peromyscus maniculatus,* woodland form (ROGER W. BARBOUR)

PLATE 10

Golden mouse, *Ochrotomys nuttalli* (ROGER W. BARBOUR)

Southern red-backed vole,
*Clethrionomys gapperi*
(ROGER W. BARBOUR)

Rock vole, *Microtus chrotorrhinus*
(ROGER W. BARBOUR)

PLATE 11

Meadow vole, *Microtus pennsylvanicus* (ROGER W. BARBOUR)

Common muskrat, *Ondatra zibethicus* (ROGER W. BARBOUR)

PLATE 12

Lodge of common muskrat in winter

Black rat, or roof rat, *Rattus rattus* (Roger W. Barbour)

PLATE 13

Porcupine, *Erethizon dorsatum*

Nutria, or coypu, *Myocastor coypus* (ROGER W. BARBOUR)

PLATE 14

Coyote, *Canis latrans*
(Bill Brink)

Gray wolf, or timber wolf, *Canis lupus* (Roger W. Barbour)

PLATE 15

Red fox, *Vulpes vulpes* (Roger W. Barbour)

Gray fox, *Urocyon cinereoargenteus* (Roger W. Barbour)

PLATE 16

Black bear, *Ursus americanus* (ROGER W. BARBOUR)

Raccoon, *Procyon lotor*
(ROGER W. BARBOUR)

PLATE 17

Short-tailed weasel, *Mustela erminea* (ROGER A. POWELL)

Long-tailed weasel, *Mustela frenata* (ROGER W. BARBOUR)

PLATE 18

River otter, *Lutra canadensis* (Roger W. Barbour)

Spotted skunk, *Spilogale putorius* (Roger W. Barbour)

PLATE 19

Mountain lion, *Felis concolor*, known in Florida as the Florida panther (ROGER W. BARBOUR)

PLATE 20

Lynx, *Lynx canadensis* (Joe McDonald)

Bobcat, *Lynx rufus* (Joe McDonald)

PLATE 21

West Indian manatee, *Trichechus manatus,* cow and calf (Galen Rathbun, Sirenia Project, U.S. Department of the Interior)

Wild pig, or feral hog, *Sus scrofa* (James N. Layne)

PLATE 22

Fallow deer, *Cervus dama*
(Roger W. Barbour)

Wapiti, or elk, *Cervus elaphus* (Roger W. Barbour)

PLATE 23

Sika deer, *Cervus nippon*
(Ronald R. Keiper)

Sambar deer, *Cervus unicolor* (Phillip C. Roullard)

PLATE 24

*Napaeozapus insignis insignis* (Miller)

As described above.

Type locality: Restigouche River, New Brunswick.

Other currently recognized eastern subspecies:
  *N. insignis roanensis* (Preble)
  *N. insignis fructectans* Krutzsch

### LITERATURE

Brower, J. E., and T. J. Cade. 1966. Ecology and physiology of *Napaeozapus insignis* (Miller) and other woodland mice. *Ecology* 47: 46–63.

Fain, A., E. J. Spicka, G. S. Jones, and J. O. Whitaker, Jr. 1985. The life cycle of two astigmatic mites, *Glycyphagus* (*Zapodacarus*) *newyorkensis* (Fain, 1969) comb. nov. and *Glycyphagus* (*Zapodacarus*) *zapus* sp.n. Glycyphagidae. *Acarologia* 26: 155–169.

Layne, J. N., and W. J. Hamilton, Jr. 1954. The young of the woodland jumping mouse, *Napaeozapus insignis* (Miller). *Amer. Midland Nat.* 52: 242–247.

Whitaker, J. O., Jr., and W. E. Wrigley. 1972. **Mammalian Species No. 14.** Amer. Soc Mammal. 6 pp.

Wrigley, R. E. 1972. Systematics and biology of the woodland jumping mouse, *Napaeozapus insignis*. Ill. Biol. Monogr. No. 47. 117 pp.

## NEW WORLD RATS, MICE, AND ALLIES, Family Muridae

In the eastern United States, the myomorph rodents (rats and mice) are represented by two families, the jumping mice (Dipodidae, immediately above) and the rats and mice proper (Muridae). The Muridae, treated here, constitute the largest family of mammals, totaling about 281 genera and 1326 species distributed worldwide. Of these, 14 genera and 26 species are found in the eastern United States. The members of this vast family range in size from the tiny harvest mouse to the muskrat. Murids have no premolars, and only three molars on a side. The molars are topped by either flat crowns or tubercles. At one time, the Muridae included only the "Old World rats and mice," and the "New World rats and mice" were placed in their own family, the Cricetidae, which was divided into two subfamilies, the Cricetinae and the Microtinae. Today, however, because of a different understanding of their evolutionary

relationships, all the mice and rats of the region we treat here, except the jumping mice (now in Dipodidae), are placed in the Muridae, in three subfamilies: the Murinae (= old Muridae), the Sigmodontinae (= old Cricetinae), and the Arvicolinae (= old Microtinae).

The Murinae, or Old World rats and mice, include (in our area) the introduced house mouse (*Mus musculus*) and two introduced rats (*Rattus*). In the species included, the cheek teeth are rooted and their cusps, or tubercles, are arranged in three longitudinal rows.

The Sigmodontinae (previously Cricetinae) include the New World rats and mice. They typically have rooted, cusped molariform teeth, although *Neotoma* has flat-crowned molars with enamel loops and *Sigmodon* has transverse lophs (ridges) on the chewing surface. The cusps are in two longitudinal rows. The genera included are *Neotoma* (wood rats), *Sigmodon* (cotton rats), *Reithrodontomys* (harvest mice), *Peromyscus* (deer mouse, white-footed mouse, and others), *Podomys* (Florida mouse), *Ochrotomys* (golden mouse), and *Oryzomys* (rice rats).

The Arvicolinae (previously Microtinae), or microtine rodents, are the voles, including the muskrats. They have ever-growing, rootless molariform teeth with chewing surfaces formed into enamel loops and triangles rather than cusps. The genera in the eastern United States include *Synaptomys* (bog lemmings), *Ondatra* (common muskrat), *Clethrionomys* (red-backed mice), *Neofiber* (round-tailed muskrats), and *Microtus* (moles proper, or meadow mice).

### KEY TO THE SUBFAMILIES OF THE FAMILY MURIDAE

1. Tubercles, or cusps, of molar teeth in three longitudinal series . . . . . . . . . . . MURINAE (p. 370)
1. Tubercles, or cusps, of molar teeth in two longitudinal series, *or* flat-crowned . . . . . . . . . . . 2
2. Molar teeth usually topped with tubercles (with transverse lophs in *Sigmodon*, a prismatic pattern resembling rootless teeth in *Neotoma*); tail more than one-third of animal's total length . . . . . . . . . . SIGMODONTINAE
2. Molar teeth topped by complicated sets of loops and triangles; tail usually less than one-third of animal's total length. . ARVICOLINAE (p. 332)

*Upper molars of the Norway rat, with tubercles in three series (left), contrasted with those of the deer mouse, which have tubercles in two series (Thomas W. French)*

## NEW WORLD RATS AND MICE, Subfamily Sigmodontinae

This subfamily comprises a vast array (about 79 genera and 423 species) of small rodents, including the often familiar and abundant deer mice and white-footed mice, genus *Peromyscus*. Most are mouselike rodents with long vibrissae, pointed noses, long tails, and prominent eyes and ears. Among this large and variable group are species with diverse food habits. They are basically adapted to an herbivorous diet, although most are at least somewhat omnivorous. New World mice and rats have been given a bad name, but except for *Sigmodon* and sometimes some of the species of *Peromyscus*, few are major pests. We recognize 14 species of sigmodontines in the eastern United States, in seven genera: *Reithrodontomys*, three species; *Neotoma*, two; *Sigmodon*, one; *Oryzomys*, two; *Ochrotomys*, one; *Podomys*, one; and *Peromyscus*, four.

Key to the Genera
of the Subfamily Sigmodontinae

1. Front of incisors marked by a longitudinal groove; the smaller species much like a house mouse but with white underparts. . . . . . . . . . . *Reithrodontomys* (p. 282)
1. Front of incisors not grooved; the smaller species variable . . . . . . . . . . . . . . . . . . . . . . . . . 2
2. Animal large, over 200 mm in total length; tail variable . . . . . . . . . . . . . . . . . . . . . . . . . . . . . 3
2. Animal small, seldom exceeding 200 mm in total length; tail bicolored . . . . . . . . . . . . . . . . . . 5
3. Molars showing a prismatic pattern resembling that of rootless teeth; rostrum long and narrow; animals white below and very large, at least 310 mm long . . . . . . . . . . . . . . . *Neotoma* (p. 323)
3. Molars bearing cusps or lophs; rostrum not particularly long; animals variable below and much smaller . . . . . . . . . . . . . . . . . . . . . . . . . . . . . 4
4. Molars with transverse lophs; tail less than 40% of total length; fur blackish below, but with light tips, giving a grizzled appearance . . . . . . . . . . . . . . . . *Sigmodon* (p. 320)
4. Molars with cusps; tail about 50% of total length; fur more uniform in color, giving a far less grizzled appearance . . . . . . . . . . *Oryzomys*
5. Ears and body bright golden or ochraceous; posterior palatine foramina nearer to interpterygoid fossa than to anterior palatine foramina . . . . . . . . . . . . . . . . *Ochrotomys* (p. 317)
5. Ears dusky, contrasting slightly with body color; posterior palatine foramina midway between these openings . . . . . . . . . . . . . . . . . . . . . 6
6. Five plantar pads (on soles of feet) (p. 314) . . . . . . . . . . . . . . . . . . . . *Podomys* (p. 313)
6. Six plantar pads . . . . . . . . . . . *Peromyscus* (p. 289)

## Rice Rats of the Genus *Oryzomys*

Rice rats, *Oryzomys*, are long-tailed rats about the size of small Norway or black rats, and are often found in marshes. They have somewhat smaller ears than *Rattus* and are usually lighter underneath. They are similar also to cotton rats, which, however, have more grizzled fur. In separating the three, the most diagnostic character is in the teeth. The occlusal surface of *Oryzomys* molars has two rows of cusps, whereas that of *Rattus* has three; *Sigmodon* has transverse lophs (ridges).

Key to the Rice Rats
of the Genus *Oryzomys*

1. Digital bristles projecting beyond the ends of the median claws on hind feet . . . . *O. argentatus*
1. Digital bristles not projecting beyond the ends of these claws . . . . . . . . . . . . . . . *O. palustris*

## Silver Rice Rat
### *Oryzomys argentatus* Spitzer and Lazell

The silver rice rat was described as a new species by Numi Spitzer and James Lazell in 1978. Humphrey and Setzer (1989), however, found that the characteristics of *O. argentatus* fall within the overall variation of *O. palustris*, and thus did not give it even subspecific rank, but they did not compare it to adjacent mainland forms, nor did they use all of the characters outlined by Spitzer and Lazell. Because of the presence of a primary isolating mechanism and the evidence of differentiation given by Spitzer and Lazell, we have retained *O. argentatus* as a separate species.

DESCRIPTION. Spitzer and Lazell described this rat as being distinct from all other members of the subgenus *Oryzomys* in having the tufts of digital bristles not projecting beyond the ends of the median claws on the hind foot, large and widely open sphenopalatine vacuities, and a slender skull with long narrow nasal bones, their width contained in their length from 4.6 to 4.9 times. The pelage is brown dorsally, silver-gray laterally.

MEASUREMENTS. Measurements of two individuals were: total length 251 and 259; tail 121 and 132; and hind foot 32 and 32 mm.

Diploid number unknown.

TOOTH FORMULA

$$\frac{1}{1} \quad \frac{0}{0} \quad \frac{0}{0} \quad \frac{3}{3} \ = \ 16$$

*Silver rice rat,* Oryzomys argentatus *(Philip A. Frank)*

DISTRIBUTION. This rat was originally known from only two specimens from Cudjoe Key in the lower Florida Keys, but Numi Spitzer Goodyear has now found it on nine of the Lower Keys: Big Torch, Cudjoe, Johnston, Little Pine, Middle Torch, Raccoon, Saddlebunch, Summerland, and the Water Keys (see map under next species account), but it is relatively abundant only on Johnston Key. The silver rice rat has not been found on the Upper Keys, which are of a different geologic origin. They are of old coral reefs, whereas the Lower Keys probably once had a land connection with the peninsula.

HABITAT. The original two specimens of this species were collected along the edges of a small freshwater marsh bordered by white mangrove, with an understory of twig rush or sawgrass (*Cladium*) in the shallows. Where the water deepened to 15 cm (6 inches), the sawgrass was replaced by cattails. All of the individuals taken at later dates have been found in or adjacent to salt marshes.

Use of radio-tracking showed that the silver rice rat occupied three main zones, the first a low intertidal area of red, black, and white mangrove, much of it with little understory. This zone was used for foraging, for movement between foraging sites (saltwort swales), and for nest sites. The second zone was salt marsh flooded by spring or flood tides, supporting low grass (*Distichlis* and *Sporobolus*) and scattered shrubs and trees. Depressions here contain glasswort, saltwort, and black mangrove. Ten nests of shredded grass (*Distichlis* and *Sporobolus*) were found in mounds. Overstory in the third zone is of buttonwood or, in the wetter areas, buttonwood mixed with white mangrove, and the zone supports heavier growth of *Distichlis* and *Sporobolus* and more oxeye daisy than is found in the other zones. This area, which is seldom flooded, was used mainly for nesting, but also for foraging during flooding or very high tides.

This rat interacts little with *Sigmodon*, which occupies the higher areas on the Keys. It does overlap with the black rat, *Rattus rattus*, however, and competition from *Rattus* may have kept its populations low.

HABITS. The habits of this species are presumably much like those of *Oryzomys palustris*. Goodyear (1992) found eight nests of silver rice rats, all at least 10 cm (4 inches) below the ground and all constructed of balls of finely shredded grass (*Distichlis* or *Sporobolus*), though she had earlier found two nests 20 and 30 cm (8 and 12 inches) below the ground.

Goodyear used "dust-capsule tracking" to study the relationship of *Oryzomys* and *Rattus rattus* on five of the Lower Keys. The two occupied very similar habitat, although *Oryzomys* favored wetter areas more and *Rattus rattus* used higher areas more. The rice rats spent more time swimming and on the ground, but they also climbed. *Rattus* spent more time climbing, often jumped from place to place, and usually stayed out of the water.

FOOD AND FEEDING. Silver rice rats feed on the seed capsules of *Batis* in the depressions in the salt marsh. Remnants of items eaten by rice rats were *Rhizophora* propagules, snails (*Melampus*, *Cerithidea*), and crown conch (*Melongena corona*). In food-selection studies, the first choice of both *O. argentatus* and *Rattus* was *Ligia*, an isopod. Snails were eaten by *Oryzomys*, not often by *Rattus*. Propagules of *Rhizophora* and germinating *Avicenna* seedlings were eaten by both.

REPRODUCTION AND DEVELOPMENT. The reproductive characteristics of the silver rice rat are probably much like those of *Oryzomys palustris*.

POPULATION CHARACTERISTICS. Although this newly described species has been found on several islands, it is presumably quite rare. *Oryzomys* and the non-native *Rattus rattus* have probably coexisted on some or all of these islands for 500 years, and it would seem that they have long since adapted to each other. Goodyear (1992), however, is still of the opinion that the presence of *Rattus* on the Keys might pose a threat to *Oryzomys argentatus*, and the silver rice rat is currently listed as endangered.

ENEMIES. As indicated above, Goodyear (1992) believes the presence of *Rattus* may be detrimental to this species. Presumably, all the predators in the area would prey on the silver rice rat.

PARASITES AND DISEASE. The parasites of this species may be similar to those of *Oryzomys palustris*, but no information is available.

RELATION TO HUMANS. These animals have relatively little relationship with humans.

AREAS FOR FURTHER WORK. The habits of this species could be more thoroughly studied and compared to those of *O. palustris*, *Sigmodon*, and *Rattus*. Moreover, *O. argentatus* and *O. palustris* should be compared genetically, so that we might better understand their interrelationships.

## SUBSPECIES

None described.
Type locality: Cudjoe Key, Florida.

### LITERATURE

Goodyear, N. C. 1987. Distribution and habitat of the Silver Rice Rat, *Oryzomys argentatus*. *J. Mammal.* 68: 692–695.

———. 1991. Taxonomic status of the silver rice rat, *Oryzomys argentatus*. *J. Mammal.* 72: 723–730.

———. 1992. Spatial overlap and dietary selection of native rice rats and exotic black rats. *J. Mammal.* 73: 186–200.

Goodyear, N. C., and J. D. Lazell, Jr. 1986. Relationships of the silver rice rat *Oryzomys argentatus* (Rodentia: Muridae). *Postilla* 198: 1–7.

Humphrey, S. R., and H. W. Setzer. 1989. Geographic variation and taxonomic revision of rice rats (*Oryzomys palustris* and *O. argentatus*) of the United States. *J. Mammal.* 70: 557–570.

Spitzer, N. C., and J. D. Lazell, Jr. 1978. A new rice rat (genus *Oryzomys*) from Florida's lower Keys. *J. Mammal.* 59: 787–792.

## Marsh Rice Rat
### *Oryzomys palustris* (Harlan)  Color plate 10

DESCRIPTION. Superficially, the marsh rice rat is much like the Norway rat and the black rat, from which it can be distinguished by its two,

*Marsh rice rat*, Oryzomys palustris *(Roger W. Barbour)*

rather than three, rows of tubercles on the molars. It is gray or brown above, much paler below. The tail is long, slender, sparsely haired, and scaly. The body is grayish above, and the coat is mixed with black hairs and some brown hairs. The face is paler, either buffy or, in Georgia specimens, washed with yellowish-brown. The underparts are grayish white, the fur soft and rather woolly. The feet are white above, and the tail is dark brown or blackish above, slightly paler below, but not bicolored. Rice rats from Louisiana and western Mississippi are somewhat paler, and have a narrower skull, than those elsewhere. Individuals from peninsular Florida are larger and more tawny; they are a grizzled grayish brown to tawny olive, richest and darkest on the rump, and their underparts are white, sometimes suffused with buff.

MEASUREMENTS. Average measurements of 122 rice rats from Louisiana were: total length 237 (220–270), tail 117 (100–137), hind foot 28 (24–33) mm; and 26 individuals averaged 51.6 (40–75) grams. Ten adults from Florida averaged: total length 277, tail 143, hind foot 34 mm.

Diploid number = 56; fundamental number = 60.

TOOTH FORMULA

$$\frac{1}{1} \ \frac{0}{0} \ \frac{0}{0} \ \frac{3}{3} = 16$$

DISTRIBUTION. The marsh rice rat occurs from central New Jersey, southern Illinois, and southern Kentucky, excluding the Appalachians, south through Florida and west to Mississippi and Louisiana. To the west of the Mississippi it occurs to southeastern Kansas, eastern Oklahoma, and eastern Texas, and south to Panama.

HABITAT. The rice rat occupies a variety of habitats, from the salt marshes of the Atlantic and Gulf coasts to the clearings of wooded areas well into the slopes of the Appalachians. It is usually found where there is sufficient ground cover of grasses and sedges to afford it protection from its foes. Rice rats are amphibious by choice, exhibiting a preference for wet meadows and marshy areas.

HABITS. In the salt meadows, rice rats occasionally make extensive, well-defined runways, and they may tunnel into the banks for short distances. They will often build a nest of sedges and grasses in a low bush over water, far from land, even though occupying the shore. Nests may be placed under a mass of debris or woven into the rushes and aquatic emergents a foot or more (half a meter) above the high-water level. The nests are about 13 cm (5 inches) in diameter, and rice rats will sometimes take over an old marsh wren nest or a nest of *Neofiber* or *Ondatra*.

Rice rats are almost wholly nocturnal—an adaptation, perhaps, to avoid undue competition with the mostly diurnal *Sigmodon*, which often occupies the same habitat. Because they are abroad at night, rice rats are seldom seen, yet in certain parts of their range they may be the most abundant of all small mammals.

Rice rats are accomplished swimmers. When alarmed, they dive and swim below the surface for up to 10 meters (30 feet), then bob to the surface with water beading off their fur. Their presence is made evident by the mats of cut vegetation floating at irregular intervals in the tidal waters. Those who have kept them in the laboratory have remarked on their extraordinary cleanliness and extensive self-grooming. These efforts may help keep the fur water-repellent.

FOOD AND FEEDING. The name of this species reflects its habit of feeding on rice. During colonial times, the rice plantations suffered considerable loss at the hands of *Oryzomys*, which scratched up the rice when newly planted and before it had been flooded, ate it in its milky state, and gleaned the scattered grains right through the fall and winter. Its staple foods are in fact the seeds and succulent parts of available plants. It feeds on several grasses, including gama grass (*Tripsacum dactyloides*) and marsh grass (*Spartina glabra*). Much animal food, particularly of insects and small crabs, is also included in the diet. Such items were the dominant foods in summer and fall in the Georgia coastal salt marshes (Sharp, 1967). Rice rats are also known to feed on the eggs and young of the marsh wren, on adult birds, and on fishes, clams, and many other items.

REPRODUCTION AND DEVELOPMENT. The breeding habits of the rice rat are not fully known,

the best account being based on a Louisiana population. There, they breed from February to November. The one to six (usually three to five) young, born after a gestation period of about 25 days, are blind and naked at birth and weigh 3 to 4 grams. The pinna of the ear unfolds shortly after birth, but the ear opening remains closed until day eight. High-pitched calls are uttered on day one. The eyes open and solid food is taken on days eight to 11. Different studies put the age at weaning at 11 to 20 days. The weight of the developing young varies greatly, from 8 to 17 grams at 10 days, 18 to 27 grams at 20 days, and 40 to 60 grams at 60 days, which is about the time the young reach reproductive capability. In the Carolinas the young are born throughout the summer, but farther south there may be a lull in the hottest part of the summer. Specimens taken on Cape Charles,

*Distribution of the silver rice rat,* Oryzomys argentatus, *and the marsh rice rat,* Oryzomys palustris, *in the eastern United States*

Virginia, during early September were of all ages, from very small individuals to subadults. Several females contained three to five embryos.

POPULATION CHARACTERISTICS. Densities up to 50 per ha (20 per acre) have been reported, but usually they are not above ten. The average home range of males is about 0.37 ha (0.8 acre); and of females, about 0.23 ha (0.5 acre). Rice rats often occur with *Microtus pennsylvanicus* in the north and with *Sigmodon hispidus* in the south. The average life span in the wild is probably less than a year.

ENEMIES. Barn and barred owls, harriers and other raptors, mink, weasels, foxes, skunks, and other four-footed predators feed on these rats. Much of the rice rat habitat coincides with the range of the cottonmouth moccasin, and this big pit viper is said to eat many rice rats. Water snakes and alligators also take their toll.

PARASITES AND DISEASE. Ectoparasites include several species of mites, three species of lice, and one flea; endoparasites include several nematodes and trematodes, a pentastomid, and three protozoan species.

RELATION TO HUMANS. The rice rat is such a widespread species and often so abundant within its distributional limits that we would expect it to be much better known. That it is not is, perhaps, at least partly because it is usually of little consequence to humans.

AREAS FOR FURTHER WORK. More information is needed on reproduction in this species, and on most other aspects of its biology. *Oryzomys argentatus* and *O. palustris* should be compared genetically, behaviorally, and ecologically for better assessment of their interrelationships. Is there any place where the two are sympatric?

## SUBSPECIES

Humphrey and Setzer (1989) used a numerical taxonomic approach to compare the described taxa of rice rats morphologically. Three mainland forms of the rice rat have been described

from the eastern United States, *Oryzomys palustris palustris*, *O. p. natator*, and *O. p. coloratus*, as well as three island forms, *O. p. planirostris*, *O. p. sanibeli*, and *Oryzomys argentatus*. Humphrey and Setzer compared these taxa with rice rats throughout their ranges, rather than with the progenitor rice rats of the adjacent mainland, and found that they fell within the variation exhibited by a small part of those taxa. Unfortunately, they did not compare the three island forms with one another, nor did they compare them to the likely progenitors on the adjacent mainland, *sanibeli* and *planirostris* to *coloratus* and *natator* and *argentatus* to *coloratus*. Neither did they consider supplemental geographical or biological information.

On the basis of the presence of a primary isolating mechanism and the evidence of differentiation given by Spitzer and Lazell (1978), we have retained *planirostris* and *sanibeli* as subspecies of *O. palustris*, but not *natator* nor *coloratus*, for we have seen no evidence of their being separated by primary isolating mechanisms. We have also retained *O. argentatus* as a separate species (see the preceding account).

*Oryzomys palustris palustris* (Harlan)

As described above. Occurs throughout most of the range of the species in the eastern United States.

Type locality: "Fast Land," near Salem, Salem Co., New Jersey.

Other currently recognized eastern subspecies:
    *O. palustris coloratus* Bangs
    *O. palustris natator* Chapman
    *O. palustris texensis* Allen

*Oryzomys palustris planirostris* Hamilton

Known only from Pine Island and from one specimen referred to this subspecies from an area 3 km (2 miles) north of Fort Myers, Florida. Compared to the adjacent mainland form, these rice rats are small. Average measurements of 13 individuals were: total length 248, tail 120, hind foot 31.0 mm. In winter pelage, the upperparts are brownish gray; the top of the head and mid-dorsum are darker, with a slightly buffy suffusion on the sides and flanks, the buff color scarcely marked in some individuals; the underparts are dull white; the feet are white; and the tail is dark gray above, whitish below. The skull is small, and the supraorbital and temporal ridges are much less pronounced than in the peninsular Florida rice rats.

Type locality: Pine Island, Lee Co., Florida.

### *Oryzomys palustris sanibeli* Hamilton

Known only from the type locality, Sanibel Island, Florida, but probably occurs on Captiva Island as well. This subspecies is distinguished from the mainland forms by its much brighter dorsal pelage and markedly smaller size, as reflected in both body measurements and skull size. Average measurements of 11 adults are total length 257, tail 124, and hind foot 31 mm.

Type locality: Sanibel Island, Lee Co., Florida.

### LITERATURE

Humphrey, S. R., and H. W. Setzer. 1989. Geographic variation and taxonomic revision of rice rats (*Oryzomys palustris* and *O. argentatus*) of the United States. *J. Mammal.* 70: 557–570.

Negus, N. C., E. Gould, and R. K. Chipman. 1961. Ecology of the rice rat, *Oryzomys palustris* (Harlan), on Breton Island, Gulf of Mexico, with a critique of social stress theory. *Tulane Studies Zool.* 8: 93–123.

Sharp, H. F., Jr. 1967. Food ecology of the rice rat, *Oryzomys palustris* (Harlan), in a Georgia salt marsh. *J. Mammal.* 48: 557–563.

Spitzer, N. C., and J. D. Lazell, Jr. 1978. A new rice rat (genus *Oryzomys*) from Florida's lower Keys. *J. Mammal.* 59: 787–792.

Wolfe, J. L. 1982. *Oryzomys palustris.* **Mammalian Species No. 176.** Amer. Soc. Mammal. 5 pp.

### Harvest Mice of the Genus *Reithrodontomys*

The harvest mice include the smallest North American rodents. They are most similar to house mice or mice of the genus *Peromyscus*, but are immediately separated from both by their deeply grooved upper incisors. Harvest mice are known by few, other than biologists, and we assume they are called "harvest mice" because of their habit of harvesting seeds.

### KEY TO THE HARVEST MICE OF THE GENUS *REITHRODONTOMYS*

1. Tail more than 110% of body length; dentine of last lower molar in the form of an "S"; occurs *only* in Louisiana and Mississippi. . . . . . . . . . . . . . . . . . . . . . *R. fulvescens*
1. Tail less than 110% of body length; dentine of last lower molar in the form of a "C"; does not occur in *either* Louisiana or Mississippi. . . . . . . 2
2. First and second lower molars show a distinct labial shelf or ridge, often with distinct cusplets. . . . . . . . . . . . . . . . . . . . . . . . *R. humulis*
2. First and second lower molars show no such ridge. . . . . . . . . . . . . . . . . . . . . . . . *R. megalotis*

## Fulvous Harvest Mouse
### *Reithrodontomys fulvescens* (Allen)

DESCRIPTION. Mice of this species can be distinguished from the two other eastern harvest

*Fulvous harvest mouse,* Reithrodontomys fulvescens *(Roger W. Barbour)*

mice by their longer tail, which measures at least 80 mm in adults and exceeds 110% of the length of the body. The animal is golden brown with a darkish band down the dorsum. The sides of the face are a rich tawny or ochraceous orange. The underparts are grayish white, strongly washed with light pinkish cinnamon.

MEASUREMENTS. From Louisiana (Lowery, 1974), 133 individuals averaged: total length 158 (142–200), tail 88 (80–100), hind foot 19 (15–22) mm; and the weight of 49 individuals averaged 12.1 (8.5–17.8) grams.

Diploid number = 24.

TOOTH FORMULA

$$\frac{1}{1} \quad \frac{0}{0} \quad \frac{0}{0} \quad \frac{3}{3} \quad = \quad 16$$

DISTRIBUTION. In the eastern United States, the fulvous harvest mouse occurs only in southwestern Mississippi and in Louisiana. Beyond, it occurs from southwestern Missouri and most of Arkansas southwest through much of Texas, southeastern Arizona, and most of Central America.

HABITAT. This species is very common in Louisiana, where it inhabits old fields and thickets, coexisting with cotton rats and least shrews in dry areas, and with the rice rat in damp areas.

HABITS. Like other harvest mice, this species is nocturnal. Its nest is built several centimeters to a meter (several inches to 3 feet) above the ground, woven into clumps of grass or other plants. It consists of a compact mass of shredded grassy plant material about the size of a baseball. In the laboratory, nests contained one or two mice, and the entrances were plugged when the animals were inside. These mice evidently spend considerable time above ground; two-thirds of the captures by Cameron and Kincaid (1982) were made above ground.

FOOD AND FEEDING. The most important food of these mice in spring and summer was found to be invertebrates, whereas in fall and winter it was seeds. Considering the relative abundance of this species in Louisiana, it is surprising that more is not known of its biology.

REPRODUCTION AND DEVELOPMENT. Litters are usually of two to four young. In Texas, there are

*Distribution of the fulvous harvest mouse,* Reithrodontomys fulvescens, *in the eastern United States*

two peaks of breeding, one in March and one in July. Two newborn weighed just over a gram apiece. Dorsal hair appeared on the third or fourth day, and the eyes opened at about nine to 12 days. Weaning was at 13 to 16 days, when the young were about 3 to 3.5 grams.

POPULATION CHARACTERISTICS. In Texas, population peaks occur in summer and winter, the highs up to 11 animals per ha (4.5 per acre) in summer and up to 28 per ha (11.3 per acre) in winter. Fall and spring populations range up to 5.8 per ha (2.3 per acre). Home ranges are around 0.2 ha (0.5 acre). Individuals have a life expectancy of only 2.1 to 2.5 months, and a maximum life span of about 14–15 months.

ENEMIES. Barn owls and red-tailed hawks have been recorded as predators.

PARASITES AND DISEASE. Essentially nothing is known of the parasites and diseases of this species.

RELATION TO HUMANS. These tiny mice associate relatively little with humans.

AREAS FOR FURTHER WORK. Little is known of this species, and all phases of its biology deserve study.

## SUBSPECIES

Sixteen subspecies have been described, but it appears that they intergrade one into the other. However, we have listed only the subspecies that occurs in the eastern United States.

*Reithrodontomys fulvescens aurantius*
J. A. Allen

As described above. This is the subspecies that occurs in the eastern United States.

Type locality: Oposura, Sonora, Mexico, at 2000 feet [650 meters], for the species; Lafayette, Lafayette Parish, Louisiana, for the subspecies.

## LITERATURE

Cameron, G. N., and W. B. Kincaid. 1982. Species removal effects on movements of *Sigmodon hispidus*

and *Reithrodontomys fulvescens*. *Amer. Midland Nat.* 108: 60–67.

Goertz, J. W. 1962. Some biological notes on the plains harvest mouse. *Proc. Okla. Acad. Sci.* 43: 123–125.

Lowery, G. H., Jr. 1974. *The Mammals of Louisiana and Its Adjacent Waters.* Baton Rouge: Louisiana State Univ. Press. 565 pp.

Packard, R. L. 1968. An ecological study of the fulvous harvest mouse in eastern Texas. *Amer. Midland Nat.* 79: 68–88.

Spencer, S. R., and G. N. Cameron. 1982. *Reithrodontomys fulvescens.* **Mammalian Species No. 174.** Amer. Soc. Mammal. 7 pp.

## Eastern Harvest Mouse *Reithrodontomys humulis* (Audubon & Bachman)

DESCRIPTION. The harvest mice can be confused with house mice or with mice of the genus *Peromyscus*, but can be easily distinguished in the hand, since they are the only long-tailed sigmodontine rodents of the eastern United States *with grooved upper incisors*. The general color of the upperparts of the eastern harvest mouse is dark brown mixed with cinnamon, darkest

*Eastern harvest mouse,* Reithrodontomys humulis *(Roger W. Barbour)*

along the mid-dorsum. The underparts are ashy, tinged with cinnamon. The tail is fuscous above and paler below, but not sharply bicolored. The ears are fuscous or blackish and the feet are pale gray.

The eastern harvest mouse is probably more numerous than the numbers taken by collectors would suggest, but it seldom reaches the abundance of other small rodents. Very likely, inexperienced collectors have occasionally thrown away harvest mice, mistaking them for buff-colored house mice or *Peromyscus*. Any specimen of the latter with buffy underparts should be critically examined for grooved incisors, which will quickly establish its identity as *Reithrodontomys*.

MEASUREMENTS. Measurements of 12 individuals from Louisiana (Lowery, 1974) averaged: total length 120 (115–132), tail 56 (52–65), hind foot 16 (11–18) mm. This is one of the world's smallest rodents, the adults weighing only 6.5 to 12 grams.

Diploid number unknown.

TOOTH FORMULA

$$\frac{1}{1} \quad \frac{0}{0} \quad \frac{0}{0} \quad \frac{3}{3} \quad = \quad 16$$

DISTRIBUTION. The eastern harvest mouse occurs in the southeastern United States from Louisiana and southern Florida north to Kentucky, Ohio, West Virginia, and Maryland. West of the Mississippi, this species occurs in southern Louisiana west to southeastern Texas and as an isolated population in northwestern Arkansas.

HABITAT. Waste fields of matted grass and broom sedge, tangled patches of brier, roadside ditches, brackish meadows, wet bottomlands, and grassy flatwoods are the haunts of this dainty little creature. It shares its habitat with least shrews, meadow mice, and golden mice.

HABITS. Harvest mice construct small nests of shredded grass and plant fibers in the tangled herbage under a protecting fence, or at the base of a clump of grass or shrubs. Quite frequently, the nest is made in a small shrub several centimeters above the ground, or it may be woven into the matted aquatic uprights and rushes above wet ground. These nests, fitted with a single entrance, serve the mice throughout the

*Distribution of the eastern harvest mouse,* Reithrodontomys humulis, *in the eastern United States*

year, for they do not hibernate. These mice make no definite runways, but they frequently traverse the passageways of other mice.

FOOD AND FEEDING. Harvest mice feed on the multitude of small weed seeds that are everywhere abundant throughout the year. We assume they also feed heavily on lepidopterous larvae, as does the western harvest mouse. Limited storage is practiced; at the least, the mice garner small stores of grass seeds, such as those of brown sedge, crabgrass, and witch grass, and there is some evidence that the female may stock up her nest just before giving birth.

REPRODUCTION AND DEVELOPMENT. Breeding commences in March, and pregnant females have been taken in South Carolina as late as December, but in Florida, pregnancies may occur throughout the year. There is a lull in breeding in midsummer. A female from Florida produced eight litters in captivity in 11 months. The first litter was born on 31 March, and six of the litters followed at intervals of 28, 49, 31, 26, and 24 days, the last in January of the next year. Thus mating must often occur soon after birth. Gestation is about 21 or 22 days, and the young number from one to five (usually two or three).

The female from Florida normally weighed about 6.5 to 7 grams, but weighed 9.5 and 10.1 grams three and four days before birth of two of the litters. At birth, the young averaged 1.2 (0.8–1.6) grams. Growth was rapid in the first three weeks of age, the young gaining about a gram per week, then leveled off to a weekly gain of about 0.4 gram during the next four weeks, until adult measurements were attained at about seven weeks. The total length of newborn young ranged from 35 to 38 mm, the tail 10 to 11 mm, and the hind foot 5 to 6 mm. At three weeks, these measurements were about 90 to 105, 45 to 50, and 14 to 15 mm. The eyes and ears opened between days seven and ten, and by the end of the second week the animals looked like little harvest mice. The ferruginous color of the adults began to appear about the 17th day. The lower incisors were visible by the seventh day in all young, and all incisors were fully developed by the end of the third week.

For about the first three weeks, females protect the young and repeatedly pull them back into the nest out of danger. In the caged situation, the male showed some signs of defending the young, and on one occasion was observed to pull a young back into the nest, but other males in captivity during this time were excluded from the maternal nest and built separate nests. Weaning, and excursions of the young outside of the nest, took place between the second and fourth weeks. Two females caged with males did not become pregnant until their 11th and 20th weeks.

POPULATION CHARACTERISTICS. This species is usually quite uncommon. For example, in South Carolina at the Savannah River Ecology Laboratory, in 427 traplines (60 traps per line for three nights), the average capture of harvest mice was 0.11 per line (this calculates to only 47 animals for the whole project); for *Peromyscus polionotus*, by contrast, it was 3.14 per line. The greatest numbers of harvest mice were in broom sedge (Golley et al., 1965).

ENEMIES. We suspect that many or most of the carnivorous mammals and birds that hunt in meadows prey on these mice, and barn owls are known to be heavy predators.

PARASITES AND DISEASE. Little information is available on parasites and diseases of this species. Four species of mites have been reported, and the presence of a host-specific louse, *Hoplopleura reithrodontomydis*, on *Reithrodontomys megalotis*, suggests that *R. humulis* may harbor a louse.

RELATION TO HUMANS. Eastern harvest mice are seldom abundant enough in cultivated areas to cause harm, but even if they were, we suspect they would be highly beneficial on balance, because of the weed seeds and lepidopterous larvae they consume.

AREAS FOR FURTHER STUDY. Much more detailed information is needed on the habits, food, and parasites of this species. It would be interesting to compare its parasites to those of *R. megalotis*, and especially to determine if the host-specific louse *Hoplopleura reithrodontomydis* is present. Whitaker has many times heard (and recorded) a call from a captive western harvest mouse. It can be heard a room away and is suggestive of a diminutive blackpoll warbler call— a series of clicks, louder in the center, but trailing off at both ends. Can the call be heard in the field? Do the other harvest mice make similar calls? If so, it would be interesting to compare the calls via oscillograms. (See also the questions raised in the account for *R. megalotis*.)

## SUBSPECIES

One has been described, but it appears to intergrade broadly into the nominate, and we therefore do not recognize it.

*Reithrodontomys humulis humulis*
Audubon & Bachman

As described above.

Type locality: Charleston, Charleston Co., South Carolina.

Other currently recognized eastern subspecies:
*R. humulis virginianus* Howell

### LITERATURE

Golley, F. B., J. B. Gentry, L. D. Caldwell, and L. Davenport. 1965. Number and variety of small mammals at the AEC Savannah River Plant. *J. Mammal.* 46: 1–8.

Howell, A. H. 1914. Revision of the American harvest mice (genus *Reithrodontomys*). *North Amer. Fauna* No. 36. 97 pp.

Kaye, S. V. 1961. Laboratory life history of the eastern harvest mouse. *Amer. Midland Nat.* 66: 439–451.

Layne, J. N. 1959. Growth and development of the eastern harvest mouse, *Reithrodontomys humulis*. *Bull. Fla. State Mus. Biol. Sci.* 4: 61–82.

Lowery, G. H., Jr. 1974. *The Mammals of Louisiana and Its Adjacent Waters.* Baton Rouge: Louisiana State Univ. Press. 565 pp.

Stalling, D. T. 1997. *Reithrodontomys humulis*. **Mammalian Species No. 565.** Amer. Soc. Mammal. 6 pp.

## Western Harvest Mouse
### *Reithrodontomys megalotis* (Baird)

DESCRIPTION. Like other members of the genus, the western harvest mouse is recognized by its

*Western harvest mouse,* Reithrodontomys megalotis

long slender tail and grooved incisors. The middle of the back is brown, with numerous black-tipped hairs. The sides are buffy and the underparts are white; the tail is bicolored, dark brown above and white below. Molting occurs in spring and fall, the winter pelage being longer, more dense, and more buffy than the summer pelage.

MEASUREMENTS. Over 80 adults from Indiana averaged: total length 127 (114–146), tail 58 (50–69), hind foot 16 (15–18) mm; and weight 10.8 (9.1–21.9) grams.

Diploid number = 42.

TOOTH FORMULA

$$\frac{1}{1} \quad \frac{0}{0} \quad \frac{0}{0} \quad \frac{3}{3} \; = \; 16$$

DISTRIBUTION. East of the Mississippi this mouse was known through the 1950s only from LaCrosse and Racine, Wisconsin. The species was first taken in Illinois in 1953, in the extreme northwestern corner of the state (Hoffmeister and Warnock, 1955). There followed a series of reports indicating that the species was moving eastward across northern Illinois (Birkenholz, 1967; Jones and Mursaloglu, 1961; Stains and Turner, 1963), and it first moved into Indiana about 1969. By 1975, it was found in several northwestern Indiana counties. That the species was extending its range was clear, since some of the areas where the species now commonly occurs had earlier been extensively trapped. By 1995, it had moved 100 miles south into Vigo County, Indiana.

HABITAT. The western harvest mouse lives primarily in early-stage grassy or weedy fields. Fields of giant foxtail, *Setaria*, are often inhabited, but a huge Indiana population was in a Newton County rye field allowed to go fallow as wildlife habitat. This species occurs through much of the western United States and Central America.

HABITS. The western harvest mouse emerges at night to forage on weed seeds and lepidopteran larvae. Its nests, spherical and about 12.5 cm in diameter, are usually on the ground in bunches of grass or thickets, under shrubs, or under logs or other protected places, or they may be built in shrubs up to a meter above the ground. In Illinois, this species has been reported nesting in burrows, and we think it does so in Indiana, as well.

Except for the young, or when adults are courting, fighting, or injured, these mice are said not to vocalize often, but two that we have kept in captivity frequently vocalized; we taped their calls and induced them to call by playing the recording. The call suggested that of a blackpoll warbler: a series of notes, louder in the middle and trailing off at both ends.

FOOD AND FEEDING. A great variety of seeds and insects may be eaten by this species, depending to a considerable extent upon availability. The more important foods of western harvest mice in a rye field in Indiana were rye seeds (over half the diet), followed by moth larvae (about 22%). The most important items in other fields were moth larvae (31.1% of the volume of food) and grass seeds (29.2%), especially those of foxtail grass.

pectoralis

dychei

megalotis, a western subspecies, incorporates dychei and pectoralis

*Distribution of the western harvest mouse,* Reithrodontomys megalotis, *in the eastern United States*

REPRODUCTION AND DEVELOPMENT. Breeding occurs from March through October, and gestation is about 23 or 24 days. Litters run one to nine young (average between three and four). There may be a cessation of breeding during the dry part of the summer. Two individuals in captivity each gave birth to 14 litters, one of them producing 58 individuals in all. The newborn weigh 1 to 1.5 grams and are 7 to 8 mm long. The eyes and ears open at 11 to 12 days, and the young are weaned at 24 days.

POPULATION CHARACTERISTICS. There is essentially a complete turnover in each population of this mouse each year.

ENEMIES. Hawks, owls, snakes, canids, mustelids, and cats prey on these mice.

PARASITES AND DISEASE. Internal parasites of this species include protozoans, acanthocephalans, cestodes, and nematodes. Ectoparasites include fleas, several species of chiggers and other mites, and a host-specific louse, *Hoplopleura reithrodontomydis*.

RELATION TO HUMANS. This species probably has little direct relation to our concerns, but its feeding on weed seeds and lepidopterous larvae has to be considered beneficial.

AREAS FOR FURTHER WORK. No host-specific lice, *Hoplopleura reithrodontomydis*, were found in a relatively large sample of this species when it first invaded Indiana, but the lice later became quite common. Why were they not here originally, and are they generally present when this mouse invades? What is the function of the call of the western harvest mouse? How far will the species continue to disperse? What is its interrelationship with other species, such as wild populations of *Peromyscus* and *Mus*, in areas where harvest mice have not been found previously? The species' range is now separated by less than 240 km (150 miles) from that of the eastern harvest mouse, and it would be interesting to observe the relationship between these two should they become sympatric. Finally, little or nothing is known about social structure in harvest mouse populations.

## SUBSPECIES

Because the eastern form of the western harvest mouse intergrades through other forms of *R. megalotis*, we consider the eastern form to be of the nominate subspecies.

### *Reithrodontomys megalotis megalotis* (Baird)

Type locality: Between Janos, Chihuahua, Mexico, and San Luis Springs, Grant Co., New Mexico.

Other currently recognized eastern subspecies:
*R. megalotis dychei* Allen
*R. megalotis pectoralis* Hanson

LITERATURE

Birkenholz, D. E. 1967. The harvest mouse (*Reithrodontomys megalotis*) in central Illinois. *Trans. Ill. Acad. Sci.* 60: 49–53.

Ford, S. R. 1977. Range, distribution, and habitat of the western harvest mouse, *Reithrodontomys megalotis*, in Indiana. *Amer. Midland Nat.* 98: 422–432.

Hoffmeister, D. F., and J. E. Warnock. 1955. The harvest mouse (*Reithrodontomys megalotis*) in Illinois and its taxonomic status. *Trans. Ill. Acad. Sci.* 47: 161–164.

Jones, J. K., Jr., and B. Mursaloglu. 1961. Geographic variation in the harvest mouse, *Reithrodontomys megalotis*, on the central Great Plains and in adjacent regions. *Univ. Kansas Publ. Mus. Nat. Hist.* 14: 9–27.

Stains, H. J., and R. W. Turner. 1963. Harvest mice south of the Illinois River in Illinois. *J. Mammal.* 44: 274–275.

Verts, B. J. 1960. Ecological notes on *Reithrodontomys megalotis* in Illinois. Nat. Hist. Misc. Chicago Acad. Sci. No. 174. 7 pp.

Webster, W. D., and J. K. Jones, Jr. 1982. *Reithrodontomys megalotis*. **Mammalian Species No. 167.** Amer. Soc. Mammal. 5 pp.

Whitaker, J. O. Jr., and R. E. Mumford. Ecological studies of *Reithrodontomys megalotis* in Indiana. *J. Mammal.* 53: 850–860.

Whitaker, J. O., Jr., and G. R. Sly. 1970. First record of *Reithrodontomys megalotis* in Indiana. *J. Mammal.* 51: 381.

## The Mice of the Genus *Peromyscus*

In many habitats in the eastern United States, mice of the genus *Peromyscus* are the most abundant small mammals to be found. Usually, they can be recognized immediately by their large ears and eyes and their white underparts.

There are several particularly important works on the genus *Peromyscus*, each offering a wealth of information. The first is Osgood's (1909) "Revision of the genus *Peromyscus*," a monumental undertaking, considering how large and widespread the genus is. F. B. Sumner, L. R. Dice, and W. F. Blair were other early workers on *Peromyscus*; Dice's laboratory provided much information on hybridization, speciation, and genetics. John King (1968) edited "Biology of *Peromyscus*," a comparative approach to the genus with chapters by different authors on many facets of the life history of *Peromyscus*. Finally, a work edited by Kirkland and Layne (1989), "Advances in the Study of *Peromyscus*," presents summaries in five major areas where particularly exciting and innovative advances have been made. The five areas are systematics and evolution, adaptive physiology, reproduction and development, population biology, and social behavior. The last chapter contrasts *Peromyscus* with the genus *Apodemus*, its ecological counterpart in the Old World.

In this landmark work, Michael Carleton's summary of advances in systematics and evolution is based in large part on karyotypic and electrophoretic data. Advances have been made especially on Central American *Peromyscus* and on the relationships among the higher taxonomic categories. Carleton recognizes 53 species of *Peromyscus* in 13 species groups, including four species occurring in eastern United States: *P. maniculatus* and *P. polionotus* in the *maniculatus* group and *P. leucopus* and *P. gossypinus* in the *leucopus* group. There are six other very closely related groups, often listed as genera or subgenera, numbering an additional eight species. One of these, *Podomys*, is represented in the eastern United States by the Florida mouse, *Podomys floridanus*. Species of the *Peromyscus* assemblage range throughout North and Central America south to Honduras, and one of the closely related genera, *Icthomomys*, occurs in Panama.

Richard MacMillen and Theodore Garland, in the chapter on "Adaptive Physiology," show how the energy and water metabolism of mice of the genus *Peromyscus* establishes them as physiological generalists, thus helping to explain their ubiquitous nature and variable diet. These authors believe that selection has favored small size in the more stressful northerly regions, that torpor is more widespread in this genus than has generally been realized, and that this characteristic has allowed these mice to survive stressful periods.

John S. Millar, in his chapter on reproduction and development, generally supports Layne's earlier conclusions that the reproductive characteristics of *Peromyscus* are readily modified in response to environmental conditions. He shows that litter size is greatest and breeding season shortest in the northern areas. (For a discussion of birth in *Peromyscus* species, see the account for *P. polionotus*, below.)

Donald W. and Glennis A. Kaufman, in their chapter on population biology, found no relationship between niche width and heterozygosity. Allele frequencies vary across the range of a species, yet there is a high degree of genetic consistency within species, and island species are less variable than mainland species. Studies on distribution with regard to various environmental factors, and removal studies leading to increases of other species, have tended to support the reality of interspecific competition. Some species of *Peromyscus*, such as *P. leucopus*, store caches of food, especially in fall. What they cache is exceedingly various, thus helping them maintain a varied diet over time. Noncaching species, such as *P. maniculatus*, eat a less diverse array of foods, concentrating on high-energy foods. Resident animals, having to scavenge less because they are aware of their food sources, are more or less specialists, whereas immigrants are generalists, feeding on what they can find. Transient individuals are subject to greater predator risk because they are more intent on exploring, they do not know the area traversed as well, and they may be more active than are residents in their own home range. In vulnerability to predation, no sex differences have been found.

Jerry Wolff examined social behavior. Recent advances in our understanding of behavior in *Peromyscus* have come primarily through experimental manipulation and testing of hypotheses based on evolutionary theory but generated from descriptive and observational studies. The work has been done mostly on *Peromyscus leucopus* and *P. maniculatus*, and the conclusions thus apply primarily to those species. Home range can be quite well estimated by live-trapping, tracking, and radiotelemetry.

Wolff found that in both *P. maniculatus* and *P. leucopus*, female home ranges overlap male home ranges, but that the home ranges (territories) are mutually exclusive *within* sexes, and this appears to be the general pattern in *Peromyscus*. Territoriality and interspecific aggression become important only at high densities, ensuring males access to the females on their territories. Integrity of home ranges ensures the provision of food and living space for the young; and white-footed mice defend their territories to prevent infanticide by intruders. Mating systems in *Peromyscus* range from monogamy in *P. californicus* and *P. polionotus* to promiscuity in *P. maniculatus* and *P. leucopus*. Characteristic of monogamous species are the overlapping of home ranges of heterosexual pairs and the occurrence of family groups. The best evidence, however, emerges from electrophoretic evidence of mothers, pups, and possible fathers: in *P. polionotus*, successive litters had the same father; in *P. maniculatus*, about 20 to 40% of the litters were multiply sired. Juvenile males disperse in *P. leucopus*, but daughters remain in the home sites.

*Peromyscus leucopus* and *P. maniculatus* behaved territorially as one species, defending their territories against other animals of *either* species—which may constitute sort of an interdigitating mode of coexistence. Territorial defense was more intense at higher than at lower densities, and more intense with unknown animals than with neighbors—animals recognize neighbors, and neighbors are sometimes relatives, which might warrant the reduced aggression.

Wolff found that home ranges and territories are larger, and exhibit greater overlap, for males than for females, and that males spend more time on the periphery than do females. They also shift their home ranges to include those of females. Females use home ranges for nesting, rearing young, and feeding; males use them, in addition, to gain access to females. Competition for females is more intense at higher densities, but cuckoldry (a female breeding with several males) and multiple insemination nonetheless persist. At low densities, males may become vagrants in search of females. Territorial defense by females, which may protect their young against infanticide, is more intense when nursing young are still present. Intruding females, if finding the mother away, killed the pups in almost every case, which, especially in high densities, may help them to obtain territories. (Infanticide may be more common than was thought, but more information is needed.) Reproductive females are more aggressive than males, and overlap less in their territories, suggesting that they have a greater investment in territorial integrity than do the males. Territories are defined only during the breeding season, suggesting that their basis is the needs associated with reproduction, rather than other functions.

Dispersal in *Peromyscus* occurs throughout the year, but is especially common during the breeding season. Males disperse farther than females, and juveniles move about more than adults. None of 26 males, but seven of 23 females (29%) remained on their natal home ranges. The presence of a parent in *Peromyscus* suppresses sexual maturation in juveniles, a fact that may provide the key to dispersal and certainly helps to prevent inbreeding. Dispersal was greater at greater densities, but there appears to be little actual aggression between adults and juveniles, which suggests that the juveniles dispersed on their own, and were not forced out by adults. Juvenile males seldom remained on the natal home range, and then only if mothers and sisters were no longer there.

Resident adult males allow movement by juveniles, which facilitates recruitment, except at very high densities (over 25 mice per ha, or 10 per acre). At low densities, most juveniles attained maturation by fall; at high densities, they often did not. Thus at high densities, population regulation increases. Aggression is within sex, and aggression between females limits the numbers of females in a population.

Wolff's work, which has so nicely explored the social behavior of *Peromyscus leucopus* and *P. maniculatus*, can serve as a model for studies of other species of *Peromyscus* and, for that matter, other species of mammals.

## LITERATURE CITED

Carleton, M. D. 1989. Systematics. In: Kirkland and Layne, eds., 1989, pp. 7–141. (See below.)

Kaufman, D. W., and G. A. Kaufman. 1989. Population biology. In: Kirkland and Layne, eds., 1989, pp. 233–270. (See below.)

King, J. A., ed. 1968. Biology of *Peromyscus* (Rodentia). Spec. Publ. No. 2, Amer. Soc. Mammal. 593 pp.

Kirkland, G. L., Jr., and J. N. Layne, eds. 1989. *Advances in the Study of* Peromyscus *(Rodentia)*. Lubbock: Texas Tech. Univ. Press. 366 pp.

Macmillen, R. E., and T. Garland, Jr. 1989. Adaptive physiology. In: Kirkland and Layne, eds., 1989, pp. 143–168. (See above.)

Madison, D. M. 1977. Movements and habitat use among interacting *Peromyscus leucopus* as revealed by radiotelemetry. *Canadian Field-Nat.* 91: 273–381.

Millar, J. S. 1989. Reproduction and development. In: Kirkland and Layne, eds., 1989, pp. 169–232. (See above.)

Osgood, W. H. 1909. Revision of the mice of the American genus *Peromyscus*. *North Amer. Fauna* No. 28. 285 pp.

Wolff, J. O. 1989. Social behavior. In Kirkland and Layne, eds., 1989, pp. 271–291. (See above.)

Wolff, J. O., and B. Hurlbutt. 1982. Day refuges of *Peromyscus leucopus* and *Peromyscus maniculatus*. *J. Mammal.* 63: 666–668.

## KEY TO MICE OF THE GENUS *PEROMYSCUS*

The subspecies *P. maniculatus bairdii* is included because it behaves as a species where it occurs with other *P. maniculatus*; see text.

1. Animal small; hind feet usually 18 mm long or less .................................. 2
1. Animal larger; hind feet usually 19 mm long or more ................................. 3
2. Pelage very light; animals found in sandy areas of the Southeast ............. *P. polionotus*
2. Pelage dark grayish; animals found in open areas, including cultivated fields, of the north .................. *P. maniculatus bairdii*
3. Tail usually slightly more than half the animal's total length; color grayish, with an indistinct dorsal stripe or no stripe .......... *P. maniculatus* (excluding *bairdii*)
3. Tail usually slightly less than half the animal's total length; color brownish, usually with a well-developed dorsal stripe ............ 4
4. Hind foot usually more than 22 mm long; a southern species usually inhabiting lowlands ...................... *P. gossypinus*
4. Hind foot usually less than 22 mm long; a more widespread species............. *P. leucopus*

## Cotton Mouse
### *Peromyscus gossypinus*
### (LeConte)                    Color plate 10

DESCRIPTION. This medium-sized to large, dark-colored *Peromyscus* has a big hind foot (usually

*Cotton mouse,* Peromyscus gossypinus
*(Roger W. Barbour)*

greater than 22 mm long in adults, except in Florida). The tail, less than half the animal's total length, is blackish brown above and dull white below (but not sharply bicolored) and sparsely covered with short hairs. The dorsum is rufescent cinnamon, thickly interspersed with black hairs, creating a dark but poorly defined dorsal stripe. The nose, top of the face, and head are distinctly grayish, usually well delineated from the brown cheeks. The ears are grayish brown, and have no pale border. The underparts are dirty white and the feet are white. As in other species of *Peromyscus*, juveniles are gray.

Individuals from the general region of northern Georgia, Alabama, and Tennessee are larger and paler than typical *P. gossypinus*. They are less dusky on the sides, and their dorsal streak is less pronounced than that of the coastal form. The underparts are brighter, a creamy white.

Cotton mice from peninsular Florida are smaller and paler than typical *gossypinus*, and their underparts are often creamy or yellowish white. Finally, those from the southwest portion of the peninsula are small and brownish with a darker dorsum.

This species is very similar to *Peromyscus leucopus*, but heavier and considerably darker, the dorsal area broadly darkened. The distinctive characters of this mouse do not show well in the conventional museum skins, and the skull, except for its slightly larger size, differs only in minor respects from that of *P. leucopus*. In the flesh, however, these two are more easily distinguished. The underparts of *gossypinus* are much duller than those of *leucopus*, and the skull length in *gossypinus* generally exceeds 27 mm, whereas that of *leucopus* is less than 27 mm. Although occurring in the same localities as *leucopus* in the northern part of its range, and interbreeding with it in captivity, *gossypinus* in the field mates with its own kind, thus maintaining itself as a distinct species.

MEASUREMENTS. Average measurements of 30 adults from the mountains to the western lowlands of Tennessee were: total length 185 (160–205), tail 80.1 (63–97), hind foot 23.3 (20–26) mm; and weight 25–39 grams. Average measurements of 20 adults from Oak Lodge, east peninsula, Brevard County, Florida, were: total length 181, tail 71.8, hind foot 21.5 mm. Measurements of 15 males and females from Collier County, Florida, were: 166 (152–189), 71 (63–80), and 22 (21–23) mm. Cotton mice weigh 17 to 46 grams.

Diploid number = 48.

TOOTH FORMULA

$$\frac{1}{1} \; \frac{0}{0} \; \frac{0}{0} \; \frac{3}{3} \; = \; 16$$

DISTRIBUTION. In eastern United States, the cotton mouse occurs in the Southeast, from Louisiana and southern Florida north in the Mississippi Valley to southern Illinois and southern Kentucky, and through southern South Carolina to the eastern reaches of North Carolina and Virginia. West of the Mississippi, it occurs west to northeastern Oklahoma and eastern Texas.

HABITAT. The prime habitat of the cotton mouse is the bottomland hardwood forests and swamps of the Atlantic Coastal Plain, but this species occupies a variety of habitats, all the way to the open woodlands of the Great Smoky Mountain foothills at an elevation of 600 meters (2000 feet). It occurs in the dense underbrush in the lowest and wettest parts of overflowed lands. Remington Kellogg mentioned its occurrence on cliffs and rocky bluffs, especially in caves and crevices. Cotton mice burrow in the dry ridges bordering the Louisiana bayous, making their nests wherever high water will not invade their tunnels. Although its name suggests a habitat in cotton fields, the species is scarcely ever found in such places, unless the fields are along the borders of a timbered swamp. Major John LeConte, who described the species, mentioned its fondness for nesting under logs and the bark of decaying trees, making its home of cotton, and frequently using more than a pound of this material for the purpose. In Florida, these mice occur in flatwoods, scrub, sandhills, swamps, or inland hammocks, in the salt savannas, in piles of brush and rubbish about cleared fields, and in the shaded retreats provided by the saw palmetto thickets. They are seemingly ubiquitous, and they and *Sigmodon* are the commonest small mammals in Florida.

HABITS. This is the common dark-colored *Peromyscus* of the deep South. Like its white-footed relative to the north, the cotton mouse also inhabits the haunts of man, invading the house or camp for shelter and partaking of the crumbs and stores of its occupants. Francis Harper reports that a trapper of the Okefenokee Swamp whose provisions were being raided set a single trap and therewith captured 22 cotton mice during a single winter evening. Harper (1927) himself set a single trap and took five mice during the course of an evening.

Like *P. leucopus*, this species will climb, and nests are often located above ground. Individuals have been trapped nearly 5 meters (16 feet) up in trees, and several were found in a gray squirrel nest 6 meters (20 feet) above ground.

Other nests are in or under logs, stumps, or brush piles. They have even been found on moss on floating logs. This mouse is a good swimmer.

Frank and Layne (1992) used radio-tracking to locate 95 refugia of *Peromyscus gossypinus*. Of these, 67 were pocket gopher burrows, 23 were ground holes, and five were hollow tree cavities. The nests, of saw palmetto fibers (*Serenoa repens*), lichens, and cotton, were of platform or spherical form.

FOOD AND FEEDING. Little is known of the feeding habits of the cotton mouse, but there is no reason to suppose that its food differs much from that of other *Peromyscus*. Outram Bangs records their feeding largely on the seeds of sea oats along the Florida beaches.

REPRODUCTION AND DEVELOPMENT. The breeding season is long, and in Florida persists throughout the year, although breeding intensity there declines somewhat in summer, peaking in late fall and early winter. Gestation, generally about 23 days, was lengthened to 30 days in one nursing individual. Litters range from one to seven young, averaging about three or four. Most of the reproductive information we have is from Florida, but reproductively active individuals have been taken in Tennessee from August through October and in southern Alabama from February through December. One female from Alabama weighing only 10.1 grams contained three embryos. In eastern Tennessee, females with embryos have been collected in early March, and a Georgia specimen captured in late December carried one large embryo. The litter in these southern areas is apparently smaller than those of the northern forms, but the longer southern breeding season, which probably results in greater numbers of litters, enables these

*Distribution of the cotton mouse,* Peromyscus gossypinus, *in the eastern United States*

mice to maintain themselves in spite of heavy predation.

Measurements at birth are total length 47, tail 11, and hind foot 6.5 mm. The newborn weigh about 2.2 grams. By their fourth day, the ear pinnae unfold, and by day five the dorsum has acquired a covering of fine hair. The incisors erupt about the seventh day, the young are fully haired by day ten, and the eyes open between days 12 and 14. Weaning is between the third and fourth weeks, and molting to the adult pelage begins at five weeks.

POPULATION CHARACTERISTICS. Reported densities of this species have usually ranged from 0.25 to 7.2 per ha (0.10 to 2.9 per acre), although there is one report of 96.6 per ha (39 per acre) in low forestland along Reelfoot Lake, Tennessee. Population turnover is rapid, few individuals living more than five months in the field. Home ranges average 0.18 to 0.50 ha (0.4 to 1.2 acre), as they do for most small mammals, and those of the males are larger than those of the females. Home ranges tend to be smaller in more dense populations. This species appears to be polygamous.

ENEMIES. The enemies of the cotton mouse must include the barred owls, whose weird calls echo from every southern swamp, certain hawks, the abundant black racers and black and yellow rat snakes (A. H. Howell records finding a cotton mouse in the stomach of an Alabama rattlesnake), and of course all the mammalian predators, especially weasels, foxes, and skunks. These all serve to control the cotton mouse population.

PARASITES AND DISEASE. Pentastomid larvae, two trematodes, two cestodes, and two nematodes are the known internal parasites of this species, and eight mites, two chiggers, at least two ticks, and eight species of fleas are its known ectoparasites.

RELATION TO HUMANS. This species is the southern equivalent of the white-footed mouse, and like its northern counterparts it often inhabits houses and other buildings, pilfering what it can.

AREAS FOR FURTHER WORK. *Peromyscus leucopus* and *P. gossypinus* are so similar in structure and in habits that they would seem to be in rather direct competition where they are sympatric. A careful comparative life-history study of the two, both where they occur together and where they occur alone, should be interesting, and would perhaps reveal some differential behavior patterns. Work is also needed on the food, parasites, and social system of this species.

## SUBSPECIES

It appears that most of the described subspecies of *Peromyscus gossypinus* represent series of clinally occurring populations. Boone et al. (1993) studied several island and mainland populations of the cotton mouse, including populations from Cumberland Island, Georgia, and Anastasia Island, Florida, which had together been recognized as a separate subspecies, *P. g. anastasae*. They found that all populations were genetically and morphometrically variable, both within and among populations. Every population was statistically different from every other in at least one character, but none was unusually so. The island forms tended to be smaller than the mainland forms, but they did not cluster together, nor were they less variable than the mainland populations. The authors concluded that neither the Cumberland form nor the Anastasia Island form warranted recognition as a separate subspecies. The Key Largo population does warrant that status.

*Peromyscus gossypinus gossypinus* (LeConte)

As described above. Occurs throughout most of the range of the species in the eastern United States.

Type locality: Near Riceboro, Liberty Co., Georgia.

Other currently recognized eastern subspecies:
*P. gossypinus megacephalus* (Rhoads)
*P. gossypinus palmarius* Bangs
*P. gossypinus restrictus* A. H. Howell
*P. gossypinus telmaphilus* Schwartz

*Peromyscus gossypinus allapaticola* Schwartz

This is a large, reddish cotton mouse, larger than other cotton mice of the Florida peninsula.

Known only from Key Largo, Florida, it is more brightly colored and somewhat less overlaid with black on the mid-dorsal line, and has a distinctive grizzled appearance laterally. Standard measurements of 12 individuals from Key Largo averaged: total length 179 (170–189), tail 77 (72–87), hind foot 21 (21–23) mm.

Type locality: Key Largo, Monroe Co., Florida.

### LITERATURE

Batson, J. 1958. Studies of Rhoads' cotton mouse, *Peromyscus gossypinus megacephalus*, in Alabama. *J. Tenn. Acad. Sci.* 33: 123–132.

Boone, J. L., J. Laerm, and M. H. Smith. 1993. Taxonomic status of *Peromyscus gossypinus anastasae* (Anastasia Island Cotton Mouse). *J. Mammal.* 74: 363–375.

Frank, P. A., and J. N. Layne. 1992. Nests and daytime refugia of cotton mice (*Peromyscus gossypinus*) and golden mice (*Ochrotomys nuttalli*) in south-central Florida. *Amer. Midland Nat.* 127: 21–30.

Harper, F. 1927. The mammals of the Okefinokee Swamp region of Georgia. *Proc. Boston Soc. Nat. Hist.* 38: 191–196.

Pournelle, G. H. 1950. Reproduction and early postnatal development of the cotton mouse, *Peromyscus gossypinus gossypinus*. *J. Mammal.* 33: 1–20.

Wolfe, J. L., and A. V. Linzey. 1977. *Peromyscus gossypinus*. **Mammalian Species No. 70.** Amer. Soc. Mammal. 5 pp.

## White-Footed Mouse
### *Peromyscus leucopus* (Rafinesque)

DESCRIPTION. Mice of the genus *Peromyscus* are often difficult to distinguish. The tail of this medium-sized *Peromyscus* is usually slightly less

*White-footed mouse,* Peromyscus leucopus
*(Roger W. Barbour)*

than half the animal's total length, and less hairy than the tails of the *maniculatus* group; the tail's color is variable, and its penciled tuft is not prominent. In summer pelage the upperparts are grayish brown to dull orange-brown, and the mid-dorsum, interspersed with black-tipped hairs, is darker. The underparts are white, and although the bases of the belly hairs are bluish gray, they are usually effectively concealed by the white tips. The ears are grayish brown, pale white at the extreme margin. The preauricular tufts are of the same hue as the face (in *P. maniculatus* these tufts are often whitish). The tail is dark brown above and white below, though the line of demarcation between the two is usually not as sharply marked as it is in *maniculatus*. In winter, the pelage is grayer and the tail is more sharply bicolored. Immature mice are plumbeous gray above, and their belly and feet white.

In the northern and Appalachian forests, this species can easily be confused with the larger, long-tailed forest form of *P. maniculatus*, and both forms often occur together in the same forest. The best characters for distinguishing the two are tail length and skull differences. In *P. leucopus*, the tail is slightly *less* than half the total length, whereas in eastern woodland *maniculatus* it is slightly *more* than half the total length. The surest means of identification is skull comparison: *P. leucopus* has shorter nasal bones and a greater bulge of the maxillaries in front of the infraorbital foramen, and the anterior palatine slits are angulate in the middle rather than essentially parallel-sided. White-footed mice are paler than deer mice and are often of a pronounced orange-cinnamon shade on the back; they are also somewhat larger, and the tail is more thickly haired.

*Peromyscus maniculatus bairdii*, the prairie variant of the deer mouse, almost never enters the woods, but it can be confused with *P. leucopus*, which is often found in fields. *Peromyscus maniculatus bairdii* is a smaller, shorter-tailed, grayer form, with a hind foot usually measuring 18 mm or less (that of *P. leucopus* is usually 19 mm or more). The tail in *P. leucopus* is usually just less than half the total length of the animal, whereas in *bairdii* it is usually considerably less than half the total length. In the south, this species is easily confused with *P. gossypinus*, but the larger hind foot of that species (over 22 mm) is usually distinctive.

MEASUREMENTS. Nineteen adults from Tennessee averaged: total length 165 (152–181), tail 72 (59–83), hind foot 20 (19.5–22) mm; and weight 15–25 grams. Measurements of 30 adults from western New York were: total length 170 (157–189), tail 76 (60–92), hind foot 21 (18–23.3) mm; and weight 16–28 grams (Fig. 6.33).

Diploid number = 48.

TOOTH FORMULA

$$\frac{1}{1} \ \frac{0}{0} \ \frac{0}{0} \ \frac{3}{3} \ = \ 16$$

DISTRIBUTION. This species occurs throughout most of the eastern United States, from south-ern Maine south through Mississippi and Louisiana, the northern half of Alabama, Georgia, and the western two-thirds of South Carolina and Virginia. To the west it occurs to extreme southeastern Alberta, northeastern Wyoming, southeastern Colorado, and eastern Arizona, and south through much of eastern Central America.

HABITAT. The white-footed mouse is primarily a dweller of forest edges and brushy areas, frequenting woods and their borders, but it is also abundant in hedgerows and brushy areas. It less often ventures into open grassland and cultivated areas, except when hedgerows or woodlands are close by. It often takes up residence in houses; the first evidence of its presence may be a boot half filled with cherry pits or hickory nuts.

HABITS. The large black eyes, long, sensitive vibrissae, and big ears of this species are all stamps

*Distribution of the white-footed mouse,* Peromyscus leucopus, *in the eastern United States*

of a nocturnal existence, and it is rare to find these little mice abroad in daylight. White-footed mice are semi-arboreal; their home ranges often include patches of brush and trees. Because individuals become thoroughly familiar with their home ranges, they are quick to find hiding places when necessary. The tail is used both as a prop and as a balancing organ. Wherever this species occurs, it is likely to be one of the most abundant small mammals in the area.

As dusk descends, the white-footed mouse leaves its half-rotted stump or descends from a cavity in some venerable beech. In winter, or to produce its young, it may use an abandoned bird nest, perhaps capped with leaves or thistledown. Or again, the home may be the deserted nest of a squirrel high in the oak boughs, a ball of dead leaves beneath the forest floor, or a bird nest box, for this little mouse is adaptable and makes the most of its environment. Wolff and Hurlbutt (1982), using radiotelemetry, found eight nests in trees and 22 underground. Madison (1977), using the same technique, found ten summer nests in woodchuck dens and six in rockpiles, but in early autumn he found 13 nests in trees, either in hollow trees or in gray squirrel nests.

In summer, white-footed mice nest singly or, sometimes, in pairs or family groups. During the winter, most individuals remain active, even in the severest weather, but some individuals become torpid, exhibiting all the characteristics of a hibernating jumping mouse. In winter, too, they will often form aggregations in nests. Such communal nesting begins about mid-October, when the nests are often in trees. Later, in the grip of midwinter cold, the communal nests are more apt to be below ground. *Peromyscus leucopus* has even been recorded nesting with *P. maniculatus* on three occasions (see Wolff, 1989). Communal nesting, nesting below ground, and torpor are all energy-saving adaptations against midwinter cold in this species. These strategies can yield an energy savings of nearly 75%. (See the account for *Peromyscus maniculatus* for more on social behavior.)

FOOD AND FEEDING. Like many other rodents, white-footed mice are omnivorous, though their chief food appears to be the little nutlets, ber-

ries, and seeds that abound in the forest. Black-cherry seeds are a favorite food, though they must be removed from the pits. The seeds of jewelweed (*Impatiens*), known to many as touch-me-not, taste like walnuts and contain beautiful turquoise-blue endosperm. That the seeds are heavily feasted upon is evident from the turquoise-colored stomach contents of many individuals of this species in late summer. The small internal cheek pouches often are crammed with such tiny seeds, or various grass seeds, and these mice will store the seeds of raspberries, jewelweed, shadberries, and various species of viburnum, as well as wild-cherry pits. Several quarts of clover seed have been found in the galleries of a single mouse, and Hamilton once found nearly a peck of beechnuts that had been stored by a white-footed mouse in the cavity of a large beech almost 10 meters (30 feet) above the ground. As fall approaches, the mice harvest quantities of black-cherry pits, hickory nuts, basswood seeds, acorns, chestnuts, seeds of conifers, and other items.

Great quantities of insects are consumed during the summer months. Chief among these are caterpillars and ground beetles (Carabidae). These mice also eat centipedes, snails, an occasional small bird, and even other small mammals, including their own kind.

REPRODUCTION AND DEVELOPMENT. In early spring, white-footed mice seek mates. The breeding season lasts from spring (March through May) to fall (usually October or November, but as early as August in Wisconsin), the season varying with latitude (shorter in the north), and interrupted by a midsummer hiatus. About 23 days after mating, the tiny, naked young are born, in a warm nest of leaves and shredded bark. Gestation may be prolonged—by an average of five days but up to 14 days—if the female is still nursing a previous litter. The young average about four or five per litter (the extremes are two to eight), and weigh about 2 grams at birth. A lateral gradient in litter size finds larger litters being produced in the north. The young grow rapidly, the ear pinnae unfolding at about two days, the incisors erupting at about four to five days, and the eyes opening at about 11 to 13 days. When three weeks old the young are clothed in a handsome gray coat that contrasts sharply with their cottony white underparts. If the mother is disturbed when nursing her young, she flees the nest with the young clinging tenaciously to her teats, some often dropping off en route. She need not run far, for every hole and cranny in her intimate range has been explored previously, and down one of these she and her burden disappear.

Several litters are produced during the summer, and the young—which leave the nest between 16 and 25 days of age—are able to breed when they are but two months old, sometimes as early as 46 days. Small wonder that these mice sometimes attain vast populations. There is some indication that the females hold a territory during the reproductive season, defending it against other mice. Both sexes are involved in caring for the young, though females do so to a much greater extent than the males. Males are often found in the nest with their offspring after weaning (Schug et al., 1992), but the significance of this behavior is not known.

Apparently, *Peromyscus leucopus* is generally polygamous, but depending on conditions it may be monogamous, and in one case it even appeared to be polyandrous, one female living with several males (Wolff, 1985; Wolff, 1989). Promiscuity may serve as a protective mechanism for females and their young, in situations of potential infanticide, since males that have mated with a particular female will recognize her later and not kill her offspring.

POPULATION CHARACTERISTICS. Annual population turnover in this species is almost total. Home ranges are largest in the breeding season and smallest in the winter; overall, they average about 0.1 ha (0.2 acre). Densities usually range from about 2–23 per ha (1–10 per acre), but sometimes reach higher, up to at least 35 per ha (13 per acre). Males generally have larger home ranges than females. Aggressive behavior, when it does occur, is within the sexes, not between them.

Homing behavior is well developed. Hamilton marked individuals and released them fully a mile from their home territory and took many of them a few days later at the point of their initial capture. Individual recognition has also been demonstrated.

Dispersal is male-biased in *Peromyscus leucopus*. Juvenile males move out mainly during and just after the breeding season. The advantages accruing from dispersal are regulation of population density, prevention of habitat exploitation, the invasion of new territory, and, probably, the avoidance of inbreeding. The last of these functions may be more important to the species than are the density-related functions. Because the maturation of juveniles is suppressed when a parent is present, it is to the species' advantage for the young to disperse. For this reason, what drives the juveniles to disperse may be self-motivation, rather than eviction by their parents.

Few species of *Peromyscus* have been studied in detail, but Wolff (1989) outlined the social behavior of *P. leucopus* in the southern Appalachians in Virginia, suggesting that it is somewhat representative of the genus as a whole. Females reside in nonoverlapping home ranges maintained by mutual avoidance at low densities, by overt aggression at high densities. Males occupy home ranges overlapping those of one or more females, and mate with the included females. The male may share the nest with a female, but he is evicted at partus, perhaps as a protection against infanticide. Juvenile males and some juvenile females disperse voluntarily after weaning, and some juvenile females establish home sites in the general area of their birth. After fall breeding, some juvenile males disperse, but others remain and join the communal nests in winter. Communal nest sites can shift in winter, as can the membership of the associates in each nest, but at the onset of spring breeding, home ranges and territories are again established.

ENEMIES. The enemies of white-footed mice are legion, numbering every owl and hawk and many predatory mammals, chief among which are the weasel and red fox. Snakes also take their toll. The ubiquitous short-tailed shrew may overcome these mice in their tunnels upon occasion, but the shrew is hardly a match for a *Peromyscus* elsewhere.

PARASITES AND DISEASE. White-footed mice are parasitized by sucking lice, several species of mites, and fleas. This species is also the primary host for the larva of the tick that carries Lyme disease. Infestations of botfly larvae, *Cuterebra*, are very obvious as large brown protrusions in the anal area in late summer and fall. These larvae drop from the mouse and pupate in the ground in fall. Sometimes several of these larvae are found in one individual and utilize some of its body juices, but even then they seem to harm the host relatively little. Hantavirus can also occur in this species.

RELATION TO HUMANS. These pretty mice often invade our living quarters. They may pilfer food, leave their little black calling cards on a shelf, or cache a quart or two of cherry pits or wild bird-seed in a boot. One potentially serious threat from this and other species of *Peromyscus* in buildings is from hanta disease. One should not breathe air in confined spaces that has been contaminated by the nests, urine, or feces of *Peromyscus*. One can forestall their entering by finding and sealing off their entryway.

AREAS FOR FURTHER WORK. This species has been extensively studied, but even with all that we know, we have likely only scratched the surface. For example, social behavior, as described by Wolff (1989), could be examined and compared in animals from different latitudes, elevations, and habitats (including within and outside of buildings). Much more information on torpor could be gathered: how common is it, how long can it last, under what circumstances does it occur, and what instigates it? How does torpor relate to a supply (or lack) of stored winter food?

## SUBSPECIES

Because the mainland forms appear to form series of intergrading populations with no primary isolating mechanisms, we do not recognize subsp. *noveboracensis*.

### *Peromyscus leucopus leucopus* (Rafinesque)

As described above. Occurs throughout most of the range of the species in eastern United States.

Type locality: "Pine Barrens of Kentucky," restricted by Osgood to the mouth of the Ohio River.

Other currently recognized eastern subspecies:
   *P. leucopus noveboracensis* (Fischer)

### *Peromyscus leucopus ammodytes* Bangs

These mice are smaller than the typical *leucopus*, with a shorter tail; the color is very pale, above pale gray, below pure white to the base of the hairs. The tail is pale grayish above, white below. Average measurements of 24 adults of both sexes are: total length 162.5, tail 75.1, hind foot 20 mm.

This subspecies, restricted to Monomoy Island, Massachusetts, may be extinct. A rather permanent connection developed between the mainland and the island, allowing an influx of individuals from the mainland. This (temporary or permanent) breakdown of the primary isolating mechanism may have been sufficient to wipe out the subspecies as such, for a specimen collected in 1931 appeared to be of the typical mainland form, retaining only a slight remnant of *ammodytes* characters. This, then, may be a good example of the formation of a well-developed subspecies while a primary isolating mechanism is in effect, followed by a swamping out of the subspecies upon natural breakdown of the primary isolating mechanism. Knowledge of the current status of this form would be of interest.

Type locality: Monomoy Island, Barnstable Co., Massachusetts.

### *Peromyscus leucopus fusus* Bangs, 1905

Individuals of this subspecies are similar to those of typical *leucopus* but much larger; their color is not appreciably different from that of the mainland form. Average measurements of four adults were: total length 195.4, tail 90.4, hind foot 22.3 mm. Found on Nantucket Island and Martha's Vineyard, Massachusetts.

Type locality: West Tisbury, Martha's Vineyard, Dukes Co., Massachusetts.

### LITERATURE

Baker, R. J., L. W. Robbins, F. B. Stangl, Jr., and E. C. Birney. 1983. Chromosomal evidence for a major subdivision in *Peromyscus leucopus*. *J. Mammal.* 64: 356–359.

Batzli, G. O. 1977. Population dynamics of the white-footed mouse in floodplain and upland forests. *Amer. Midland Nat.* 97: 18–32.

Gaertner, R. A., J. S. Hart, and O. Z. Roy. 1973. Seasonal spontaneous torpor in the white-footed mouse, *Peromyscus leucopus. Comp. Biochem. Physiol.* 45A: 169–181.

Lackey, J. A., D. G. Huckaby, and B. G. Ormiston. 1985. *Peromyscus leucopus.* **Mammalian Species No. 247.** Amer. Soc. Mammal. 10 pp.

Madison, D. M. 1977. Movements and habitat use among interacting *Peromyscus leucopus* as revealed by radiotelemetry. *Canadian Field-Nat.* 91: 273–281.

Schug, M. D., S. H. Vesey, and E. M. Underwood. 1992. Paternal behavior in a natural population of white-footed mice (*Peromyscus leucopus*). *Amer. Midland Nat.* 127: 373–380.

Sutkus, R. D., and C. Jones. 1991. Observations on winter and spring reproduction in *Peromyscus leucopus* (Rodentia: Muridae) in southern Louisiana. *Texas J. Sci.* 43: 179–189.

Timm, R. M., and E. F. Cook. 1979. The effect of botfly larvae on reproduction in white-footed mice, *Peromyscus leucopus. Amer. Midland Nat.* 101: 211–217.

Wolff, J. O. 1985. The effects of food, density and interspecific interference on home range size in *Peromyscus leucopus* and *P. maniculatus. Canadian J. Zool.* 63: 2657–2662.

——— 1989. Social behavior. In: G. L. Kirkland, Jr., and J. N. Layne, eds. *Advances in the Study of Peromyscus (Rodentia)*, pp. 271–291. Lubbock: Texas Tech Univ. Press.

Wolff, J. O., and B. Hurlbutt. 1982. Day refuges of *Peromyscus leucopus* and *Peromyscus maniculatus. J. Mammal.* 63: 666–668.

## Deer Mouse
### *Peromyscus maniculatus* Wagner

*Peromyscus maniculatus*, one of the most abundant, widespread, and adaptable mammals in North America, poses a very interesting but difficult taxonomic problem in the eastern United States. Two morphological and behavioral types occur, one a large, long-tailed, big-eared woodland form, and the other a much smaller, short-tailed, small-eared field form. The two occur together geographically (but in different habitats) in large areas of Michigan, New York, and Pennsylvania, but presumably intergrade through a series of populations in Wisconsin and Michigan. Thus, the overlapping populations have well-developed secondary isolating mechanisms and are acting as true spe-

cies, whereas the Wisconsin populations are not even separated by primary isolating mechanisms. This situation, called *circular overlap*, defies logical taxonomic placement. If the two forms are deemed separate species, then one is in the position of accepting the fact of intergradation between two "species" in Wisconsin. But if they are called separate subspecies of one species, then one has two "subspecies" occurring together but not breeding. The latter choice, the more conservative of the two, is generally accepted today, and is followed here, but the two forms are given much more individual consideration here than are typical subspecies. There are other long- and short-tailed forms of *P. maniculatus*, and other instances of circular overlap of this species, in the western United States. The long-tailed individuals are generally the more arboreal of the two.

The two forms of *P. maniculatus* are treated here in the manner of separate species: a full text for each. "*P. m. maniculatus*" is in effect synonymous with "woodland deer mouse" (we do not recognize the three eastern "subspecies" that would effectively limit *P. m. maniculatus* to Canada). "*P. m. bairdii*" is in effect synonymous with "prairie deer mouse," which has *not* been partitioned into "subspecies," at least in eastern United States.

### *Peromyscus maniculatus maniculatus* (Wagner)
Woodland Deer Mouse                Color plate 10

DESCRIPTION. The long-tailed woodland form of this species shows much variation, some of

*Deer mouse,* Peromyscus maniculatus, *woodland form (Roger W. Barbour)*

which is discussed here. In southeastern Canada, it attains medium size for the species, the tail is shorter, less than half the animal's total length, and there is a prominent pencil of hairs at the tail's tip. On an adult in summer in Canada, the sides and lateral portion of the back are dark brown, the midstripe darker. The base of the whiskers and the orbital region are blackish, the ears are dusky, and the edges of the ears are paler. The underparts and feet are white. The tail is bicolored, dark brown to brownish black above, white below. Immature mice are steel gray above, the mid-dorsal stripe nearly black. To the south, in eastern and southern New York, western New England, northern Wisconsin, and Michigan's Upper Peninsula, deer mice of the woodlands are larger and their tails are longer. The color is brownish gray, the mid-dorsal stripe slightly darker than the rest. The feet are white and the tail is sharply bicolored, dark gray above and white below, with a prominent pencil at its tip. In central and northern Maine, this mouse is much grayer, the pelage of the adult suggesting that of an immature individual of a New York mouse. The dark dorsal stripe is faintly indicated or absent.

This mouse sometimes occupies the same woods as *Peromyscus leucopus*, and can be difficult to separate from that species, but it may be distinguished by its longer tail, the prominent pencil at the tail's tip, and its larger size, softer and grayer pelage, and larger ears. The color of *maniculatus*, however, is sometimes bright brown, approaching that of *P. leucopus*. The skull differs from that of *leucopus* in having longer nasal bones, a lesser bulge of the maxillaries in front of the infraorbital foramen, and parallel-sided palatine slits, which in *P. leucopus* tend to bow out in the middle.

MEASUREMENTS. Average measurements of 14 adults of both sexes from Canada were: total length 183, tail 87, hind foot 21 mm. Average measurements of 20 adult specimens from northern New York were: total length 191 (175–215), tail 93 (79–106), hind foot 21 (19–23) mm; and weight 16–29 grams. Eighteen adults from Lynch, Harlan County, Kentucky, taken at an elevation of 1220 meters (4000 feet), averaged: total length 178 (164–198), tail 89

(77–97), hind foot 20 (19–22) mm. Ten adults from Port Allegany, Pennsylvania, were somewhat smaller, averaging: total length 167, tail 84.1, hind foot 20.7 mm. Ten adults from the Mount Katahdin region of Maine averaged: total length 184 (171–195), tail 91 (81–100), hind foot 21 (20–23) mm; and weight 16–24 grams.

Diploid number = 48.

TOOTH FORMULA

$$\frac{1}{1} \quad \frac{0}{0} \quad \frac{0}{0} \quad \frac{3}{3} = 16$$

DISTRIBUTION. *Peromyscus maniculatus* is one of the most widespread of all North American mammal species, with greatly variable populations occurring from the Atlantic to the Pacific, from Labrador to Georgia and from Alaska to Mexico. The long-tailed woodland form of *Peromyscus maniculatus* occurs in Canada south into northern Wisconsin and northern Michigan, separately through New England and New York and throughout the Appalachians to northern Georgia. (See also the discussion and distribution of the prairie deer mouse under "Subspecies," below.)

HABITAT. These woodland deer mice occupy diverse habitats, even in the eastern United States. In northern Maine, *P. maniculatus* is at home in the dark spruce forests, whereas in New York it frequently chooses the hardwoods, which are also the resort of *Peromyscus leucopus*. In the cloud-blanketed slopes of the Great Smoky Mountains and the higher Alleghenies we may look for it in mixed woods or conifers.

HABITS. Like other members of the genus, deer mice are nocturnal, seldom being taken during daylight hours. Their lively nightly scampering and petty pilfering may drive the vacationer to distraction. They spend the daytime in permanent nests or temporary refugia.

The woodland forms of *P. maniculatus* climb with great agility and may take refuge in a squirrel nest or cavity many meters above the ground. When *P. leucopus* and woodland *P. maniculatus* occur together, *maniculatus* is much more apt to climb than is *leucopus*. Moreover, in the sympatric situation, *maniculatus* is associated with variable tree height and slash, *leucopus* with stumps and logs at ground level. Wolff and Hurlbutt (1982) found that 22 of 24 nest sites of *P. maniculatus* were in trees and only two were on the ground, in a situation where the two species occurred together. The figures were reversed for *P. leucopus*, 8 in the trees, 22 on the ground. Members of this species will huddle in communal nests in winter, thus gaining energy savings when not active.

Deer mice progress by a typical walking gait when moving slowly, such as when foraging. When moving rapidly, they leave two closely spaced pairs of tracks, quite unlike the trotting gait of shrews and woodland voles, and more like tiny rabbit tracks. The tail often leaves a conspicuous mark in the snow or sand.

FOOD AND FEEDING. Woodland deer mice feed largely upon the seeds and mast of the forest floor, or upon those that abound in the clearings, and for a long period during the summer, berries serve their needs. Numerous insects are eaten, and we have found in their stomachs the remains of brown and green caterpillars, centipedes, and even small birds and mice. Because they do not hibernate, they must cache a sizable store of nuts and seeds for the long winter months, and in summer their small internal cheek pouches may be found crammed with the seeds of blueberries, raspberries, and other items to be stored for those winter days, though these mice do not store to the extent that *P. leucopus* does.

REPRODUCTION AND DEVELOPMENT. Mice of this species are promiscuous. Breeding commences in early spring and lasts well into the fall, though there is a slight letup during the heat of the summer. The breeding season is from March to October or November in Michigan, from

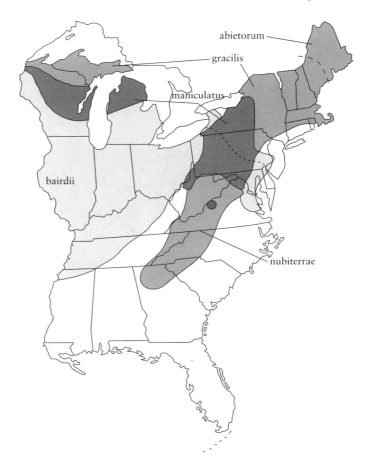

*Distribution of the deer mouse,*
Peromyscus maniculatus,
*in the eastern United States.*

April to August in Massachusetts, and from March to October in Virginia. Gestation averages about 23 to 24 days, about 27 if the mother is still lactating for the previous litter. From two to seven young (the average is about four to five) are born in a nest situated in a stump, beneath a log, or in a hollow stub. The young are blind, naked, and helpless at birth and weigh about 1.8 grams. The ear pinnae unfold at two to four days, the lower and upper incisors erupt at about seven and eight days, respectively, and the eyes open at 12–16 days. The young grow rapidly, are weaned before they are three weeks old, and are ready to commence family duties of their own in another three weeks. Litter size and length of breeding season vary geographically in this species, the larger litters and longer seasons in the more stressful northern areas.

POPULATION CHARACTERISTICS. This species, like many other small mammals, has periods of great abundance and periods of relative scarcity. It is difficult to determine the factors that produce these fluctuations, but habitat quality is presumably of prime importance. Wolff (1989) found the social behavior of *Peromyscus leucopus* and that of *P. maniculatus* to be similar, although males of *P. maniculatus* exhibited much more paternal behavior than did those of *P. leucopus*. Home ranges of *P. maniculatus* vary from about 240 to 3000 square meters (2500 to 32,000 square feet) of ground space, but one must consider the home range of this subspecies as three-dimensional, for the animals spend much time in trees. Home ranges tend to be smaller in good habitat with ample food, as well as in times of dense populations, although the relationship of home-range size to habitat, food sufficiency, and population density is not fully understood. Individuals of *P. maniculatus* clearly have their own territories, or at least mutually exclusive home ranges, but it is not clear whether these are maintained by aggressive behavior (i.e., they are true territories) or simply by mutual avoidance. It would seem likely that they are *established* by aggressive behavior, then *maintained* by mutual avoidance, perhaps with occasional readjustments. Above 24 mice per ha (10 per acre), the animals become much more defensive of their territories than do animals at

lower densities (Wolff et al., 1983; Wolff, 1985). Intensity of defense is also greater toward the center of the range than at its periphery, and bouts with strangers are more intense than are those with neighbors. At higher densities, core areas within home ranges appear to be established as territories. The home ranges and territories of males are larger than those of females and exhibit greater overlap. Males will also shift their boundaries to include more adult females.

The function of the range or territory for the male is basically to ensure him a place to feed and nest, but also to gain access to reproductive females. At low densities, in fact, males may abandon home ranges and seek females. It appears that the function of the home range for the female, however, is to ensure her a place to forage and nest during pregnancy and during the feeding and raising of her young. Providing a safe place to raise her young is particularly important, for invading females and males will attack the young. Lactating females will defend their territories against intruders of either sex, and infanticide may be more common than one would expect. At high population levels, intruding females may kill nest young in order to gain territory for themselves. Females are more aggressive than males in territorial defense, suggesting that they have more to gain from territorial defense than do males.

ENEMIES. Deer mice, because of their abundance and diversity of habitats, are eaten by a great array of predatory mammals, snakes, hawks, and owls, all of which seek to capture them at every opportunity.

PARASITES AND DISEASE. The first documented cases of hantaviruses in North America were diagnosed in May 1993, when several Native Americans died of a respiratory ailment on a reservation in Arizona. Since then, hantavirus has been found in many other western states. The first case east of the Mississippi was diagnosed when a man died in Indiana in January 1994, and cases have since been discovered in Florida and New York. Apparently hantavirus has been present nationwide for some time, but had gone unrecognized. It has been found in a number of other murid species besides *Peromyscus maniculatus*.

This species is parasitized by a number of species of fleas, ticks, mites, chiggers, and one of lice. Some of the more abundant are the flea *Orchopeas leucopus*, the louse *Hoplopleura hesperomydis*, and the mites *Androlaelaps fahrenholzi* and *Echinonyssus utahensis*.

RELATION TO HUMANS. In wooded areas, the long-tailed woodland subspecies of *P. maniculatus* often gets into buildings (the prairie deer mouse almost never does), but otherwise does not have much direct relation to humans, other than as a carrier of the recently discovered hantavirus. To avoid hanta, one should avoid breathing in enclosed areas anywhere mice of the genus *Peromyscus* have urinated, defecated, or nested.

AREAS FOR FURTHER WORK. These mice should be studied morphologically, ecologically, and genetically in the area where the long-tail and short-tail forms presumably intergrade. Much more work is needed on hantavirus. Specifically, how is it transmitted and under what circumstances?

## SUBSPECIES

Three woodland subspecies have been described from the eastern United States and Canada, but to our knowledge these are not separated by primary isolating mechanisms from the type, which occurs in Canada. We do recognize the prairie deer mouse, *Peromyscus maniculatus bairdii*, discussed separately below. Three subspecies of long-tailed woodland forms of *P. maniculatus* (*P. m. abietorum*, *P. m. gracilis*, and *P. m. nubiterrae*) occur in the eastern United States, but these intergrade with each other and with *P. m. maniculatus* to the north. We therefore consider them all as belonging to one subspecies, *P. m. maniculatus*.

*Peromyscus maniculatus maniculatus* Wagner
Woodland Deer Mouse

As described above. Ranges through northern Wisconsin and Michigan, across eastern Canada and south through northeastern United States and the Appalachians to northern Georgia, and includes, by our reckoning, the subspecies *abietorum*, *gracilis*, and *nubiterrae*, which we do not recognize.

Type locality: Moravian settlements, Labrador.
Other currently recognized eastern subspecies:
 *P. maniculatus abietorum* Bangs
 *P. maniculatus gracilis* (LeConte)
 *P. maniculatus nubiterrae* Rhoads

*Peromyscus maniculatus bairdii*
(Hay and Kennicott)
Prairie Deer Mouse

This is the small deer mouse of the open fields of much of the Midwest and parts of the east,

*Prairie deer mouse,* Peromyscus maniculatus bairdii
*(Tony Brentlinger)*

but it can easily be confused with the white-footed mouse, *P. leucopus*, which also is often found in fields, whereas the prairie deer mouse is almost never found in woods (although it may be found in dry savanna). For the reasons discussed above, we give this subspecies the treatment otherwise accorded to species.

DESCRIPTION. *Peromyscus m. bairdii* is smaller and grayer than *P. leucopus*, and its open-field habitat, shorter feet and tail, and smaller ears usually serve to distinguish it from that species. The tail is much less than half the total length of the animal, and the hind foot is seldom over 19 mm, whereas it generally exceeds 19 mm in *P. leucopus*. The upperparts, a brownish gray mixed with darker hairs, are brighter in winter, although considerable variation occurs even within a given locality. The underparts are white, though the basal gray of the underfur is often conspicuous. The ears are dark brown, the margins edged with white.

Woodland forms of *Peromyscus maniculatus* (*P. m. maniculatus*, described above) differ from *P. m. bairdii* much more than does *P. leucopus*. They are larger with bigger ears and bigger feet, and have a tail (in eastern United States forms) over half the animal's total length.

MEASUREMENTS. Average measurements of 388 individuals of *P. m. bairdii* from Indiana were: total length 136 (106–162), tail 52 (28–68), hind foot 16.7 (15–19) mm; and weight 16 (12.2–25.6) grams.

Diploid number = 48.

TOOTH FORMULA

$$\frac{1}{1} \quad \frac{0}{0} \quad \frac{0}{0} \quad \frac{3}{3} \quad = \quad 16$$

DISTRIBUTION. In the eastern United States, the short-tailed prairie form of the deer mouse occurs as far east as central New York (Tompkins County), southeastern Pennsylvania, Maryland, northern Virginia (there is also a recent record from Rockbridge County, Virginia), the panhandle of West Virginia (Avalon and Ohio counties), and west to at least western North Dakota and western Kansas, where it intergrades with additional described subspecies, and south through most of Kentucky and western Tennessee.

Ward (1965) suggested that some individuals previously identified as *P. polionotus* from Mississippi might actually be *P. maniculatus*, but the specimens need critical examination in conjunction with *P. maniculatus* from adjacent Tennessee and Arkansas (Wolfe, 1971). In recent years, with the cutting of the forest, the prairie form of this species has spread into new areas.

HABITAT. The prairie deer mouse shuns the woodland, inhabiting, instead, the open fields and sandy areas, but today reaches its greatest abundance in the corn, wheat, and soybean fields of the Midwest, not forsaking these fields even when the ground has been plowed, when it uses the soil itself as its only cover. It is one of very few mammals that shows an increase in abundance with a decrease in herbaceous cover. On the sandy beaches along the Great Lakes, where shelter is at a premium, it may seek no shelter at all, other than a partially burned plank or log from an old campfire.

HABITS. Prairie deer mice live in short burrows in the sandy soil or under piles of vegetation.

They will build a nest on the ground under an object or often in a short underground burrow. Nests are of grass or other plant material. In winter their tiny footprints are abundant on the snow in cultivated wheat fields, meandering from one burrow opening to another. We may also see the delicate tracery of their footprints on the sand dunes that border the Great Lakes.

FOOD AND FEEDING. The most important food of 444 prairie deer mice from Indiana, from a total of 51 categories of food, was lepidopterous larvae, which constituted about 15% of the total volume of food. Other important items were wheat seeds, soybeans, various other seeds, corn, and beetles, these foods ranging from 11.8 to 3.6% of the total volume, but a great variety of other foods, many of them various kinds of grass and forb seeds, had also been taken. Even when the ground has been plowed, prairie deer mice find plenty of food in the form of corn, soybeans, and grass seeds on or in the soil. Many of the seeds are stored in its burrows for winter use.

REPRODUCTION AND DEVELOPMENT. The young, usually two to four per litter, are born after a gestation of about 25 days. We have trapped pregnant individuals in Indiana in every month of the year; numbers of embryos ranged from two to eight and averaged 4.73, and the most common number was four. Three individuals contained both embryos and placental scars, indicating how rapidly one litter may follow another in this animal. *Peromyscus maniculatus* is generally polygamous, but Howard (1949) reported monogamy in this subspecies.

POPULATION CHARACTERISTICS. These little mice have well-developed homing behavior; individuals released 3 km (2 miles) from their point of capture have returned to the point of capture within a few days. The home range is usually about 0.2 to 1.0 ha (0.5 to 2.5 acres), the ranges of males larger than those of females. In summer, the ranges of a male, several females, and some juveniles may overlap. In winter, several individuals may huddle together in a burrow, thus conserving heat.

ENEMIES. One may surely suppose that nearly all of the predators abroad in the lands of these mice prey upon them when the opportunity arises.

PARASITES AND DISEASE. Endoparasites are cestodes, nematodes, and trematodes. Ectoparasites are fleas, one species of louse, at least nine species of mites, one chigger, and one tick.

RELATION TO HUMANS. The short-tailed prairie form of *Peromyscus maniculatus* is very common in the cultivated fields of the Midwest, and commonly gleans corn, wheat, and soybeans from them. These items, however, are mostly scavenged from the ground after harvest, and in our view these little mice cause little or no harm to the crops, but rather are exceedingly beneficial because so much of their food is of weed seeds and caterpillars. They rarely enter our buildings. This species is thought to be the prime carrier of hantavirus.

AREAS FOR FURTHER WORK. See above, in the account for the woodland deer mouse. One might also study the taxonomic relationship of this subspecies to *Peromyscus polionotus*.

Type locality: Bloomington, McLean Co., Illinois.

## LITERATURE

Blair, W. F. 1940. A study of prairie deer-mouse populations in southern Michigan. *Amer. Midland Nat.* 24 : 273–305.

Harris, V. T. 1952. An experimental study of habitat selection by prairie and forest races of the deer mouse, *Peromyscus maniculatus*. Univ. Mich. Lab. Vert. Biol. Contrib. No. 56. 53 pp.

Houtcooper, W. C. 1978. Food habits of rodents in a cultivated ecosystem. *J. Mammal.* 59 : 427–430.

Howard, W. E. 1949. Dispersal, amount of inbreeding, and longevity in a local population of prairie deer mice on the George Reserve, southern Michigan. Univ. Mich. Lab. Vert. Biol. Contrib. No. 43. 52 pp.

Kleiman, D. G. 1977. Monogamy in mammals. *Quart. Rev. Biol.* 52 : 39–69.

Martel, A. M., and A. L. Macauley. 1981. Food habits of deer mice (*Peromyscus maniculatus*) in northern Ontario. *Canadian Field-Nat.* 95 : 319–324.

Pitts, R. M., and G. L. Kirkland, Jr. 1987. A record of the prairie deer mouse (*Peromyscus maniculatus*

*bairdii*) from Rockbridge County, Virginia. *Proc. Pa. Acad. Sci.* 61: 205.

Ward, P. R. 1965. The mammals of Mississippi. *J. Miss. Acad. Sci.* 11: 309–330.

Whitaker, J. O., Jr. 1966. Food of *Mus musculus*, *Peromyscus maniculatus bairdii*, and *Peromyscus leucopus* in Vigo County, Indiana. *J. Mammal.* 47: 473–486.

Wolfe, J. L. 1971. Mississippi land mammals: Distribution, identification, ecological notes. Jackson: Miss. Mus. Nat. Sci. 44 pp.

Wolff, J. O. 1985. The effects of food, density and interspecific interference on home range size in *Peromyscus leucopus* and *P. maniculatus*. *Canadian J. Zool.* 63: 2657–2662.

———. 1989. Social behavior. In: G. L. Kirkland, Jr., and J. N. Layne, eds., *Advances in the Study of Peromyscus (Rodentia)*, pp. 271–291. Lubbock: Texas Tech Univr. Press.

———. 1991. Comparative paternal and infanticidal behavior of sympatric white-footed mice (*Peromyscus leucopus noveboracensis*) and deer mice (*P. maniculatus nubiterrae*). *Behav. Ecol.* 2: 38–45.

Wolff, J. O., M. H. Freeberg, and R. D. Dueser. 1983. Interspecific territoriality in two sympatric species of *Peromyscus* (Rodentia: Cricetidae). *Behav. Ecol. Sociobiol.* 12: 237–242.

Wolff, J. O., and B. Hurlbutt. 1982. Day refuges of *Peromyscus leucopus* and *Peromyscus maniculatus*. *J. Mammal.* 63: 666–668.

## Beach Mouse, Oldfield Mouse
*Peromyscus polionotus* Wagner

DESCRIPTION. In the dry, sandy fields and beaches of Georgia, Florida, and Alabama, a pale species of mouse has evolved. It is called

*Beach mouse, or oldfield mouse,* Peromyscus polionotus *(Roger W. Barbour)*

the "oldfield mouse" or "beach mouse," depending on the habitat it occupies, and it varies greatly throughout its range. In inland populations in the fields of cotton and corn, and in natural habitats such as the open scrub and sandhill associations in the Deep South, it is fawn-colored. In populations occurring along the coast on the white, sandy beaches, it is lightest, or even white. The darkest individuals are found above the fall line in south-central Tennessee, northern Alabama, northern Georgia, and northwestern South Carolina. Individuals from inland populations can be distinguished from other *Peromyscus* of the southern states by their smaller size, shorter tail, soft, brownish-fawn color, and pale underparts, the hairs of which are slate gray at the base except on the chin and throat, where they are white to the base. The upperparts are uniform brownish fawn, or brownish gray, slightly darker on the mid-dorsal line. The tail is bicolored, dusky above and white below. The hind foot is small, usually less than 19 mm long. Individuals from coastal Alabama and the western panhandle of Florida are a grayish-fawn color. The tail there is all white except for its basal third, the upper surface of which is dusky to pale grayish brown.

MEASUREMENTS. Measurements of twenty adults from Georgia, Florida, and Alabama averaged: total length 127 (122–138), tail 47 (40–51), hind foot 16.5 (15–18) mm. Weights vary from 8 to 19 grams, averaging about 14. Ten adults from St. Andrew's Point Peninsula and Cape San Blas, Bay and Gulf counties, Florida, are very pale and average total length 126, tail 49, hind foot 18 mm. Average measurements of eight adults from the southeast coast of Florida were: total length 136, tail 52, hind foot 18 mm. Ten adults from Anastasia Island averaged: total length 139, tail 54, hind foot 19 mm.

Diploid number = 48.

TOOTH FORMULA

$$\frac{1}{1} \quad \frac{0}{0} \quad \frac{0}{0} \quad \frac{3}{3} = 16$$

DISTRIBUTION. *Peromyscus polionotus* occurs only in the eastern United States. It ranges from central Alabama, south-central Tennessee, and western South Carolina south to the Gulf Coast

and through much of Florida. Three of the described subspecies, *P. p. trissyllepsis*, *P. p. allophrys*, and *P. p. decoloratus*, are considered by the state of Florida to be threatened or endangered, mainly because of beachfront development. Along with development, of course, has come the house cat, probably a major predator on this species. The house mouse, too, may depress *P. polionotus* by competing for its habitat.

HABITAT. These mice occur in sandy fields and beaches, but also venture into cotton and corn fields and occasionally occupy hedgerows or open timber tracts. In eastern Alabama, this species appears to favor sandy fields with abundant cactus but sparse growth of grasses.

HABITS. Beach mice are proficient burrowers. Their tunnels are marked by well-defined mounds of earth at their entrances. At times these mounds are surprisingly large, suggesting

*Burrow of beach mouse, Florida (James N. Layne)*

the work of a pocket gopher, but gopher tunnels do not normally have an entrance.

The beach mouse burrow normally slants down from the entrance to some greater or lesser depth, then levels off, and at the end of the burrow is a nest. Generally, a branch of the burrow extends directly above the nest to within a few centimeters (1 to 2 inches) of the surface. This extension may serve as an escape exit, should a marauding snake enter the burrow. Digging into the burrow entrance with a shovel will often cause the mouse to "explode" from the sand through the escape exit and go dashing off. The burrows are sometimes closed, sometimes open; but all occupied burrows appear to be quickly closed by the mice if heavy rains threaten to flood out the inhabitants. Many other species use the burrows of this mouse (Gentry and Smith, 1968), particularly house mice (*Mus musculus*), gopher frogs (*Rana areolata*), six-lined racerunners (*Cnemidophorus sexlineatus*), camel crickets (*Ceutophilus latibuli*), black widow spiders (*Latrodectus mactans*), Carolina wolf spiders (*Lycosa carolinensis*), and coach-whip snakes (*Masticophis flagellum*).

FOOD AND FEEDING. We know little about the food habits of this mouse, but available information indicates that it probably feeds on the seeds of grasses and forbs. Gentry and Smith (1968) found remnants of many types of food items in burrow entrances and nest cavities. Most were various types of seeds, but parts of

several insects were also found. Unfortunately, they gave no information on the relative abundance of the items, and stomach-contents analysis is sorely needed on this species. Howell has recorded the remains of blackberries in stomachs, and the oldfield mouse has been known to feed on wild pea (*Galactia*).

REPRODUCTION AND DEVELOPMENT. Mice of this species are monogamous. Reproduction can occur throughout the year in South Carolina, but in Florida it is most pronounced in fall. Gestation is 23 to 24 days, 25 to 31 if the mother is still lactating for her previous litter. The mean litter size is three to four. When birth is imminent, in this and other *Peromyscus* species, the female assumes a quadrupedal or bipedal crouching position, sometimes rising to a more erect position as each young is actually born, and one female *P. polionotus* was ob-

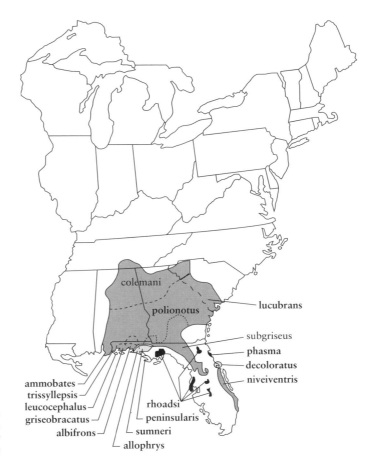

*Distribution of the beach mouse, or oldfield mouse,* Peromyscus polionotus, *in the eastern United States*

served to aid in the birth by gently pulling on the young with her front feet. The female may also facilitate the discharge of the placenta, again by pulling on it with the front feet. She then consumes it. The umbilical cord is broken by pulling or chewing at the time of birth, or as the placenta is eaten. Grooming and stretching may occur between deliveries. In one litter of *P. polionotus*, the young were washed after the last delivery. Birth usually occurs in the daytime in *Peromyscus*, an advantageous time for a nocturnal animal. Births may occur over a few minutes or even an hour or more in *Peromyscus*; they took 45 minutes in the *P. polionotus* litter observed, with intervals of 13 and 32 minutes between births. The newborn, ranging in this case from 1.1 to 2.2 grams, are pinkish. The pinnae elevate in three to five days, the lower incisors erupt in six to seven days, and the eyes open in ten to 16 days. Weaning occurs gradually between 20 and 25 days. First estrus in this species can occur at one month; first litters can then occur as early as about 53 days of age. As in all *Peromyscus*, juvenal pelage is some shade of gray. The post-juvenile molt occurs at about 30 to 45 days in most species, but at least some *P. polionotus* may be earlier. Young *P. polionotus* weigh about 4 grams at one week, 6 to 7 grams at three weeks and 8 to 10 grams at five weeks.

POPULATION CHARACTERISTICS. *Peromyscus polionotus* exhibits monogamous mating, as suggested by the home-range overlap of sexual pairs and the occurrence of family groups (Kleiman, 1977). Blair (1951) carried out extensive live trapping from November through January 1941–42 and in May and June 1942 on Santa Rosa Island, Florida. Total numbers of mice caught during various periods varied from 69 to 117 on a 26-ha (65-acre) grid. Estimated population densities ranged from 2.0 per ha (0.82 per acre) in early November to 3.5 per ha (1.40 per acre) in late December. Fourteen juvenile mice dispersed an average of 430 meters (1415 feet) before establishing residence. Only about 20% of the mice survived the four months that elapsed between the two trapping periods. Individual mice seemed to establish home ranges for life.

ENEMIES. Presumably, all of the avian and mammalian predators on small mammals feed on these mice when opportunity arises.

PARASITES AND DISEASE. In oldfield mice from Florida have been found six species of nematodes, one each of trematodes and acanthocephalans, and two of fleas.

RELATION TO HUMANS. Carlyle Carr informed Hamilton that *P. polionotus* in Florida may at times be a local nuisance to the planter, digging up melon seeds as soon as they are planted. Its repeated depredations necessitated three plantings of cantaloupes before a partial setting could be established.

AREAS FOR FURTHER WORK. Data are needed on the life history and ecology of this species in undisturbed natural inland habitats, since most information in hand has come from coastal-dunes populations or from disturbed habitats such as oldfields or cutover forests. The behavior and ecology of *Peromyscus polionotus* could be compared to those of *P. maniculatus bairdii*, for the two seem to share many traits. Information is also needed on the food and ectoparasites of this species, and much more is needed on its subspecies.

## SUBSPECIES

Several subspecies of *Peromyscus polionotus* have been described—more than for any other eastern mammal. Some intergrade insensibly one into the other, but others appear to be isolated geographically, and some show reduced fertility. South Carolina populations were studied by Albert Schwartz (1954), Gulf Coast populations by W. W. Bowen (1968). Bowen (1968) attempted to use essentially a biological-subspecies concept, although some intergradation is involved. He found reduced fertility between some adjacent populations and also a possible case of circular overlap. Since he did attempt to use a biological-subspecies concept, we have accepted most of his subspecies determinations here, but not *subgriseus*, since it intergrades broadly with *P. polionotus polionotus*. Bowen, in his extensive studies, used standardized color values for the various subspecies; mean reflectance values, average dominant wavelengths, and purity values. These values, given in Bowen's subspecies accounts, are not repeated here.

Much more work is needed on this variable and highly interesting group. We have attempted to apply our biological-subspecies concept, as usual, but to do so is particularly difficult in this case. We recognize 14 subspecies.

*Peromyscus polionotus polionotus* (Wagner)

As described above.

Occupies most of the range of the species: eastern Alabama, Georgia, western South Carolina, and much of western and northern Florida.

Type locality: Georgia.

Other currently recognized eastern subspecies (the former Suwannee Straits may have originally served as an isolating mechanism for these forms, but they apparently intergrade freely now):

  *P. polionotus colemani* Schwartz
  *P. polionotus subgriseus* Chapman

*Peromyscus polionotus albifrons* Osgood

This subspecies, which occurs in the Yellow-Shoal-Alaqua watershed of Walton Co., Florida, approaches typical *polionotus* in its yellow color, but is paler. The hair bases are very pale, grayish. Overall, these mice are very similar to *subgriseus* in overall size and ear size. This population is essentially semi-isolated, but some intergradation with *polionotus* to the north does occur. Head/body length 67–87, tail 42–58, hind foot 15–19 mm.

Type locality, as emended by Bowen (1968): About 4 miles [7 km] northeast of Whitfield (the dry, sandy area east of Alaqua Bay), Walton Co., Florida.

*Peromyscus polionotus allophrys* Bowen

Two mutually similar subspecies, *allophrys* and *sumneri*, were described from the west-central portion of the Florida panhandle, but the descriptions offered no indication of any primary isolating mechanism separating them. The two do, however, show reduced fertility when mated with individuals from adjacent populations to the north. Coloration in *allophrys* is variable, resembling that of *P. p. rhoadsi*, but often more yellow or orange. The tail and ears are longer than those of *rhoadsi*.

*Peromyscus polionotus allophrys* was described from the coastal dunes between Choctawhatchee and St. Andrew's Bays, Florida, whereas *sumneri* was described from the Merial Lake Area, where it occurs in the dry, sandy areas of the Choctawhatchee-Chipola watershed. Humphrey and Barbour (1981) indicated that *P. p. allophrys* has been extirpated from seven of its nine recorded localities, but that a remnant existed as one continuous population comprising about 158 individuals in 7.9 square km (3.1 square miles) of habitat near Topsail Hill. These workers also found a new population of 357 individuals in 9.4 square km (3.6 square miles) of habitat on Shell Island. The subspecies is listed as federally endangered.

Type locality: Coastal dunes near Morrison Lake, Walton Co., Florida.

*Peromyscus polionotus ammobates* Bowen

Individuals from the sandbar west of Perdido Inlet (Alabama Point), Baldwin Co., Alabama, are paler and grayer than *albifrons* and *griseobracatus* and have a longer hind foot. The venter is pure white. Measurements are: head/body 68–88, tail 42–60, hind foot 17–19 mm. This subspecies is found in Alabama, in the coastal dunes between Mobile Bay and Perdido Bay and also on Ono Island, at the mouth of Perdido Bay. The subspecies is listed as federally endangered.

Type locality: Sandbar west of Perdido Inlet, Baldwin Co., Alabama.

*Peromyscus polionotus decoloratus* Howell

We suggest that this subspecies might not really be distinct from *P. p. niveiventris*. This situation should be examined more closely, since *P. p. decoloratus* is considered as endangered by the State of Florida. Either way, however, it will be protected, since *P. p. niveiventris* is listed as federally threatened. Because *P. p. decoloratus* may already have been extirpated by beach development, the question may be moot.

Type locality: Ponce Park near Mosquito Inlet, Volusia Co., Fla.

*Peromyscus polionotus griseobracatus* Bowen

This subspecies is similar to *albifrons*, but more yellow-orange, with slightly longer hind feet and larger ears. In color, similar also to some *rhoadsi* populations (see below). Standard measurements are: head/body 66–84, tail 39–58, hind foot 16–18 mm. Known only from the coastline of Santa Rosa Sound, Florida, from Pensacola Bay to the northwestern shore of Choctawhatchee Bay.

Type locality: Twenty miles [32 km] west of Ft. Walton, Okaloosa Co. (= about 5 miles [8 km] west of Navarre, Santa Rosa Co.), Florida.

*Peromyscus polionotus leucocephalus* Howell

Similar to *P. p. phasma*, but the upperparts are drab instead of buff; the colored dorsal area is narrow, and the entire sides are white; the entire head and face are white, except the occiput and crown, which are light drab; these mice are slightly larger and more extensively white than *P. p. albifrons*. Restricted to its type locality.

Type locality: Santa Rosa Island, opposite Fort Walton, Santa Rosa Co., Florida.

*Peromyscus polionotus lucubrans* Schwartz

This subspecies is tentatively retained because it is isolated from adjacent Georgia populations by the Savannah River, and apparently from the northern South Carolina populations by the line demarcating the Piedmont (the fall line), but if populations are in fact continuous from northern through southern South Carolina, this subspecies should be synonymized. It resembles *P. polionotus* from Georgia and Alabama, but averages smaller in some of its measurements.

Type locality: 4.5 miles [7 km] east of the Savannah River on U.S. Highway 301, Allendale Co., South Carolina.

*Peromyscus polionotus niveiventris* (Chapman)

Along the sandy beaches of the southern half of eastern peninsular Florida, from Daytona Beach to Palm Beach, beach mice are slightly larger than typical *P. p. polionotus*, and the upper parts are paler; the dorsum is pale tawny gray to grayish white, the median dorsal area somewhat lighter; the color about the face and tail base is a clearer tawny; the underparts, including the feet and legs, the nose, and the lower half of the cheeks, are pure snowy white to the base; the tail is tawny gray above, white below. The palest individuals along the east coast of Florida occur in the region of Ponce Park, near Mosquito Inlet, and in Bulo (a region of Daytona Beach). In these individuals, the upperparts are pale pinkish buff; the pale-brown hairs on the back slightly darken it beyond the rest of the upperparts; the head is palest, but not actually white; the underparts and the sides of the head are pure white; the feet and tail are thinly clothed with whitish hairs; and the ears are brown on their outer surface. Average measurements of eight adults are: total length 136, tail 52, hind foot 18 mm.

Type locality: East peninsula, opposite Micco, Brevard Co., Florida.

*Peromyscus polionotus peninsularis* Howell

This form is similar to *P. p. leucocephalus*, but the back and ears are much darker and more brownish (the dorsal area, from crown to rump, is wood brown, and the ears hair is brown); the head, face, sides, underparts, feet, and tail are pure white. For ten adults from St. Andrew's Point Peninsula and Cape San Blas, Bay and Gulf counties, Florida, average measurements were: total length 126, tail 49, and hind foot 18 mm. This race, living on the ocean beaches connected with the mainland, and separated by only a few miles from the mainland *albifrons*, reflects the environment in its pale pelage. It occurs in Bay and Gulf counties, Florida, and is listed as endangered by the State of Florida.

Type locality: St. Andrew's Point Peninsula, Bay Co., Florida.

*Peromyscus polionotus phasma* (Bangs)

This subspecies occurs on Anastasia Island, along the northeast coast of Florida. The upperparts are pinkish buff with a grayish tinge in the middle of the nose; the nose, a spot above the eye, and the base of the ear are white; the underparts are pure white to the base of the hair; the feet and legs are pure white all around; the tail is completely white, with occasional faint traces of dusky on the upper side; and the ears are grayish white. This form differs from *P. p. niveiventris* in the conspicuous white spots on the nose, above the eye, and at the base of the ear. Measurements of ten adults average: total length 139, tail 54, hind foot 19 mm. The subspecies is listed as federally endangered.

Type locality: Point Romo, Anastasia Island, St. Johns Co., Florida.

### *Peromyscus polionotus rhoadsi* (Bangs)

This subspecies occurs as five separate groups of populations to the southwest and east of the range of *subgriseus* (a subspecies we do not recognize). It was found by Bowen to have low fertility rates in matings with *subgriseus*. Individuals are similar in size to typical *polionotus*, but differ in color; they are much yellower above; the hairs of the underparts are white to the base, and the tail is all of one color, either white or grayish white. The upperparts are a fawn color, shading on the cheek, the rump, and the lower sides toward orange-buff, and the dorsal midline has a few dark-tipped hairs but no pronounced dorsal stripe.

Type locality: the head of the Anclote River, Hillsborough Co., Florida.

### *Peromyscus polionotus sumneri* Bowen

This form, one of those recognized by Bowen (1968), appears to be a questionable subspecies, since it intergrades with both typical *polionotus* and *subgriseus* (a subspecies we do not recognize). It is darker and smaller than *allophrys*, and the hind foot is small. Measurements are: head/body 63–84, tail 40–57, hind foot 15–18 mm. These mice occur in the dry, sandy areas of the Choctawhatchee-Chipola watershed.

Type locality: Merial Lake, Bay Co., Florida.

### *Peromyscus polionotus trissyllepsis* Bowen

This subspecies is paler than *ammobates* and differs in pelage pattern from all other subspecies. It is similar to *albifrons* in color, but is much paler; the tail stripe is absent, the middorsal stripe indistinct; the venter is pure white, and to the west is lighter yet than that of *ammobates*. Humphrey and Barbour (1981) estimated the entire subspecies at 52 individuals in 10.4 square km of habitat at Gulf Island, and 26 in 2.6 square km at Gulf Beach State Park,

Alabama. This subspecies, listed as federally endangered, occurs in the coastal dunes between Perdido Bay and Pensacola Bay, Alabama and Florida.

Type locality: The sand bar east of Perdido Inlet (Florida Point), Baldwin Co., Alabama.

### LITERATURE

Blair, W. F. 1951. Population structure, social behavior and environmental relations in a natural population of the beach mouse (*Peromyscus polionotus leucocephalus*). Univ. Mich. Lab. Vert. Biol. Contrib. No. 34. 47 pp.

Bowen, W. W. 1968. Variation and evolution of Gulf Coast populations of beach mice, *Peromyscus polionotus*. Bull. Fla. State Mus. Biol. Sci. 12: 1–91.

Gentry, J. H., and M. H. Smith. 1968. Food habits and burrow associates of *Peromyscus polionotus*. J. Mammal. 49: 562–565.

Hayne, D. W. 1936. Burrowing habits of *Peromyscus polionotus*. J. Mammal. 17: 420–421.

Humphrey, S. R., and D. B. Barbour. 1982. Status and habitat of three subspecies of *Peromyscus polionotus* in Florida. J. Mammal. 62: 840–844.

Kleiman, D. G. 1977. Monogamy in mammals. Quart. Rev. Biol. 52: 39–69.

Schwartz, A. 1954. Oldfield mice, *Peromyscus polionotus*, of South Carolina. J. Mammal. 35: 562–565.

## Florida Mouse *Podomys floridanus* (Chapman)

DESCRIPTION. This large mouse looks like *Peromyscus* and was formerly placed as a mono-

*Florida mouse*, Podomys floridanus *(James N. Layne)*

typic subgenus in the genus *Peromyscus*. It can usually be distinguished from *Peromyscus gossypinus* and *P. polionotus*, which also occur in Florida, on the basis of its greater size and its color. It has big, nearly naked ears (16 mm long or more), a relatively short tail (about 80% of the body length), and a very large hind foot (24 mm long or more), and the *plantar tubercles number but five* instead of the usual six

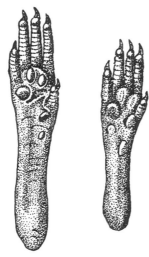

*Sole of the hind foot of* Podomys floridanus *(left) and that of* Peromyscus leucopus, *showing the five plantar tubercles of the former and the six of the latter (Thomas W. French)*

(a tiny sixth is occasionally present in *P. floridanus*). The fur (very soft and silky, as in *Peromyscus*) is brownish above, orangish on the cheeks, shoulders, and lower sides, and white below. Juveniles are gray, as are those of *Peromyscus*. Fresh specimens can be recognized at once by the number of plantar tubercles (on the soles of the feet) and the very large hind foot. Florida mice have a skunklike odor.

Smith et al. (1973) did an interesting study of biochemical polymorphism in this species in four sample areas. Electrophoretically demonstrable variation was found in one or more populations at 15 of 39 (38%) of the loci studied, and two and sometimes three alleles per locus were detected. These findings give some idea, at least, of the kind of genetic variation one may find between populations within a species. The amount of variation detected here was similar to that in such other rodents as *Peromyscus polionotus*, *Sigmodon*, and *Dipodomys*.

MEASUREMENTS. Average measurements of 30 adults (Jones and Layne, Mammalian Species, 1993) were: total length 195 (178–220), tail 88 (80–101), hind foot 26 (24–28), ear 19 (16–21.5) mm. These animals weigh about 25 to 49 grams.

Diploid number = 48.

TOOTH FORMULA

$$\frac{1}{1} \ \frac{0}{0} \ \frac{0}{0} \ \frac{3}{3} = 16$$

DISTRIBUTION. The Florida mouse is found chiefly in the central part of peninsular Florida, from coast to coast; there is also an isolated population in the panhandle, in Franklin County. *Podomys* is the only mammal genus endemic to Florida, and *P. floridanus* and *Oryzomys argentatus* are the only mammal species endemic to Florida.

HABITAT. This is the typical mouse of some of the driest Florida habitats; it is most common in the sand pine (*Pinus clausa*) scrub and in the high pinelands dominated by longleaf pine (*Pinus palustris*) and turkey oak (*Quercus laevis*). It is also found in the slash pine (*Pinus elliottii*)/turkey oak habitat of the southern ridge sandhills and in scrubby flatwoods and coastal scrub associations (Jones and Layne, Mammalian Species, 1993).

HABITS. The name "gopher mouse" has been applied to this species because it frequents the burrows of the gopher tortoise, *Gopherus polyphemus*. It shares the burrow with the tortoise, and makes small side passages and nest chambers in the sides of the burrow, sometimes building a pad on the floor of a chamber with oak leaves or wire grasses. These mice make small openings or chimneys to the outside through the roof of the burrow, and continue to use these chimneys after the main burrow entrance has collapsed. Radio-tracked Florida mice used only gopher tortoise burrows, and it did not matter whether the burrows were active or abandoned (Layne and Jackson, 1994). They used both the main entrances and the chimney entrances for access, but typically entered through side passages. The mice tracked used up to five different locations within burrows, and up to three different burrows within the tracking periods, which lasted up to 19 days. The cotton mouse, *Peromyscus gossypinus*, also makes extensive use of gopher tortoise burrows, but usually confines itself to the main burrows. *Podomys floridanus*, which uses burrows of pocket gophers, armadillos, and *Peromyscus polionotus*, as well as gopher tortoise burrows, does not dig as much as *Peromyscus*, probably because it relies so heavily on the burrows of other vertebrates. The species can and will climb, but is less arboreal than the cotton mouse.

FOOD AND FEEDING. Acorns, when available, are a mainstay in the diet of the Florida mouse, and this mouse will also eat seeds, nuts, insects, fungi, and other plant materials, but detailed food studies have not been conducted. Milstrey (1987) reported this species feeding on engorged ticks (*Ornithodorus turicata americanus*) that parasitize gopher frogs (*Rana areolata*) and gopher tortoises.

REPRODUCTION AND DEVELOPMENT. The number of young among eight litters conceived in the field but born in the laboratory varied from two to four, averaging 3.1. Embryos in 57 pregnant females varied from two to five, averaging 3.2. Gestation length has not been determined but is probably about 23 or 24 days. These mice breed throughout the year, but there is a major peak of breeding from July through December, a lesser peak in January and February, and cessation or near cessation in April and May. The newborn, which weigh 1.9 to 2.9 grams, measure about: total length 44,

*Distribution of the Florida mouse,* Podomys floridanus, *in the eastern United States*

tail 12, hind foot 8 mm. Weaning is at about three to four weeks. The young are half-grown by four weeks and have attained 80% of the adult weight by nine weeks, but are still slightly below adult weight at 15 weeks. The gray juvenile color pattern has developed by the end of the second week. The eyes open between the 12th and 20th days (average 16.5). The lower incisors are visible between days four and nine, the uppers between days seven and 11. By ten days of age, the young are active and fairly agile, and by the third week their behavior is essentially that of the adult. Weaning occurs at about three weeks of age, and the postjuvenile molt begins at about 36 to 42 days of age.

POPULATION CHARACTERISTICS. Populations of this species were greater (9.9 to 12.7 per 100 trap-nights) in scrub and scrubby flatlands than in high pinelands (2.5 per 100 trap-nights), and home ranges were smaller than in high pineland (16 meters versus 25 meters). One captive male lived seven years, four months.

ENEMIES. Predators on these mice are probably snakes, birds of prey, foxes, bobcats, and raccoons. This species shows relatively greater numbers of shortened tails than *Peromyscus gossypinus* does, apparently as a result of a modified integument that facilitates tail loss. This adaptation appears to foil the efforts of some predators.

PARASITES AND DISEASE. James N. Layne (1963) published a fine paper on the parasites of this species. In the research he reported, he had examined the parasites in relation to habitat and season. He and other authors have recorded seven species of mites (including three chiggers), five ticks, five fleas, and a louse among the ectoparasites, and the subdermal botfly larva, *Cuterebra*. The most common flea, *Polygenis floridanus*, is narrowly host-specific. Endoparasites known were three species of protozoans (found in fecal smears), one trematode, four cestodes, seven nematodes, and nymphal pentastomids (found in various internal organs).

RELATION TO HUMANS. This species probably has little or no direct effect on humans, other than maintaining its place in the ecosystem and its interest for the biologist. A major threat to the species is habitat loss from housing and agricultural development in the restricted habitats where it lives.

One of the greatest difficulties besetting the southern collector is the countless millions of ants occupying all the dry ridges. These insects riddle the stumps, tunnel the soil, and invade the very burrows of small mammals. They eat the bait from the pan as soon as a trap is set on the ground, and, if the collector is fortunate enough to take a specimen, it is often hopelessly mutilated before it can be removed. For this reason many mammalogists use live traps in the south, which offers the added advantage that a specimen can be released if not needed. This approach is excellent except for the needs of food-habits research, which suffers because food will usually have been digested by the time an animal is taken alive from a trap.

AREAS FOR FURTHER WORK. Study of the food habits and social system of this species would be of particular interest.

## SUBSPECIES

None described.
Type locality: Gainesville, Alachua Co., Florida.

## LITERATURE

Jones, C. A., and J. N. Layne. 1993. *Podomys floridanus*. **Mammalian Species No. 427.** Amer. Soc. Mammal. 5 pp.

Layne, J. N. 1963. A study of the parasites of the Florida mouse, *Peromyscus floridanus*, in relation to host and environmental factors. Tulane Studies Zool. No. 11. 27 pp.

———. 1966. Postnatal development and growth of *Peromyscus floridanus*. *Growth* 30: 23–45.

Layne, J. N., and R. J. Jackson. 1994. Burrow use by the Florida mouse (*Podomys floridanus*) in south-central Florida. *Amer. Midland Nat.* 131: 17–23.

Milstrey, E. G. 1987. Bionomics and ecology of *Ornithodorus* (*P.*) *turicata americanus* (Marx) (Ixodoidea: Argasidae) and other commensal invertebrates present in the burrows of the gopher tortoise, *Gopherus polyphemus* Daudin. Unpubl. Ph.D. diss., University of Florida, Gainesville. 260 pp.

Smith, M. H., R. K. Selander, and W. E. Johnson. 1973. Biochemical polymorphism and systematics in the genus *Peromyscus*. III. Variation in the Florida deer mouse (*Peromyscus floridanus*), a Pleistocene relict. *J. Mammal*. 54: 1–13.

## Golden Mouse *Ochrotomys nuttalli* (Harlan)                        Color plate 11

DESCRIPTION. The handsome little golden mouse is unique among eastern rodents in its rich, burnished, ochraceous to golden color. Florida individuals are a rich yellowish brown above, slightly paler on the sides, head, and ears. The feet and underparts are creamy white, the underparts often strongly suffused with ochraceous, particularly on the abdomen. The tail is slightly bicolored. The fur is exceptionally soft

*Golden mouse*, Ochrotomys nuttalli
*(Roger W. Barbour)*

and thick, and its golden color results from a lack of black guard hairs on the posterior dorsum. East-central Virginia individuals have darker underparts, and the ears are dusky, not tawny-ochraceous. In general appearance, adults are quite similar to reddish individuals of *Peromyscus leucopus*. Individuals from the western part of the species' range are rather small and pale. The young are somewhat duskier than the adults, but nonetheless golden, rather than the gray of the young *Peromyscus*.

MEASUREMENTS. Measurements of this species are: total length 176 (151–200), tail 85 (51–

97), hind foot 20 (16–21) mm; and weight 20–26 grams. In the southern parts of its range, *Ochrotomys* is smaller. Measurements of 28 adult golden mice from Florida averaged: total length 158 (135–178), tail 72 (60–85), hind foot 18 (13–19) mm.

Diploid number = 52.

TOOTH FORMULA

$$\frac{1}{1} \quad \frac{0}{0} \quad \frac{0}{0} \quad \frac{3}{3} \;=\; 16$$

DISTRIBUTION. The golden mouse occurs from southern Illinois and eastern Virginia south to Louisiana and central Florida. To the west it occurs through Arkansas and to eastern Texas.

HABITAT. Over their extensive range, golden mice are widely distributed in a variety of habitats. In the mountains of Virginia, Kentucky, and Tennessee, they occupy the pine and greenbrier thickets, the boulder-strewn slopes of dense hemlock forests, and the borders of broom sedge fields. In the southern swamps this beautiful little mouse is not uncommon, making its little nest in the strands of Spanish moss that drape the live oaks and bushes of these low-lying regions. In Alabama it occupies the canebrakes and swampy woodlands, or sometimes the dry, thickety flatwoods or among the wooded hills. In Florida it may be found in xeric upland oak/ pine habitats.

HABITS. The golden mouse is mainly nocturnal, with activity peaks near dawn and dusk. It is also largely arboreal, often climbing to a height of 10 meters (30 feet) or more, and running among the limbs with amazing celerity. The tail acts as a balance and even as a prehensile organ for clinging to branches when the footing becomes hazardous or when the animal is at rest. The animals will sometimes use the tail and hind feet to hang off of branches at nearly right angles. The feet are smaller than those of *Peromyscus* of comparable size, perhaps a scansorial (climbing) adaptation.

Golden mice usually build bulky globular nests of dead leaves, grass, and pine needles lined with finely shredded bark. Nests are usually said to be in greenbrier, honeysuckle, or grape vines, or, in Florida, in Spanish moss. The nests vary considerably in size, from that of a football to some scarcely larger than a baseball. The larger nests are occupied by several mice; occasionally, one finds as many as eight in a nest. These nests are usually reported at heights ranging from a few centimeters up to 10 meters (30 feet) above ground, but most are from 1.5 to 4.5 meters high. In Florida, however, Frank and Layne (1992), using radio-tracking, found 75 nests of this species under deep litter and only two above ground, both in shrubs. The nests, hollow spheres, were of saw palmetto fibers, Spanish moss, various twigs, leaves and grasses, and cotton. They were in small depressions in the ground under pine needles, oak leaves, and twigs. The litter cover at the nest sites averaged about 13 cm, whereas average litter depth in the area was less than 2 cm (the deep-litter nests apparently protect the animals from heat). Winter nests were larger than summer nests. Some of the nests, usually the smaller ones, are used mainly as feeding shelters, and seeds have sometimes been found in nests. The females often construct their breeding nests in impenetrable thickets of greenbrier, honeysuckle, or grape vines, or in Spanish moss, but nests are also often in conifers. When in trees they are often in forks. It has long been known that occasional nests are placed on the ground, in or under the mantle of a protecting log, stump, rock, or some other object, but the extent of ground nesting in this species may often have been underestimated, owing to the difficulty of finding the ground nests.

*Distribution of the golden mouse,* Ochrotomys nuttalli, *in the eastern United States*

FOOD AND FEEDING. A number of kinds of seeds have been found on the feeding platforms of this species, some of the more important of which are of sumac, wild cherry, dogwood, greenbrier, poison ivy, blackberry, and bedstraw, as well as acorns. Some caution must be used in interpreting this kind of information, however, since animals sometimes eat soft foods on the spot but carry off the less perishable items. These animals are in any case omnivorous. An analysis of golden mouse stomach contents from Tennessee revealed invertebrate remains in 47 to 57% of the stomachs examined. Like *Peromyscus*, golden mice have well-developed internal cheek pouches and they often stuff them with seeds for transportation.

REPRODUCTION AND DEVELOPMENT. Breeding extends from mid-March to early October in Kentucky and Tennessee, peaking in late spring and early autumn. In Florida, breeding occurs through at least eight months, perhaps peaking in early summer and autumn. In Louisiana, these mice may breed at any time during the year, although more young are produced in fall and early winter than at other times. Golden mice produce several litters per year, and females have been known to produce 17 litters in 18 months. The interval between litters generally ranges from 25 to 29 days, but can be as short as 25 days. Gestation is probably about 21 to 23 days, extended a bit if the female is still nursing her previous litter. In Tennessee, the number of young in 85 litters ranged from one to four, averaging about 2.7; there were 7 litters with one young, 30 with two, 33 with three, and 15 with four.

In captivity, males and females lived together in nests until the birth of the young. The males then left, and remained out of the nest. The young, blind and naked at birth, are about 51 (38–58) mm long, their tails average 15.3 (13–18) mm, their hind feet 7.2 (6–8) mm; and they weigh 2 to 3.5 grams. The young have dark-brown hair over the back and hips by the fifth or sixth day. The lower incisors erupt about the sixth day, the upper by days seven to eight, and the eyes open between days 11 to 15. Weaning occurs at days 17–21. Adult size is attained at the tenth week, after which growth is slow but sustained throughout life. Golden mice are better developed at birth than are many of their counterparts. They can cling to a finger at a 115° incline and they produce a loud, rasping squeak. By day one they can already take a few wobbly steps. The prehensile nature of the tail can be seen by the second day, and they can hang upside down by the fourth day. Climbing tendencies were evident by day ten.

POPULATION CHARACTERISTICS. The golden mouse is relatively rare in collections, but it is by no means a scarce creature. Those who are acquainted with its habitat have succeeded in taking large numbers in a short period. Home ranges of 0.05 to 0.6 ha (0.1 to 1.5 acre) have been recorded for this species, and population densities have run to nearly seven per ha (2.8 per acre) in Louisiana pinelands and nearly nine per ha (3.6 per acre) in Tennessee greenbrier thickets with an overstory of pine, maple, yellow poplar, and sumac. Under field conditions, golden mice, like many other small mammals, do not survive long, averaging perhaps six to seven months of life. In captivity, however, they fare much better. Donald Linzey (Linzey and Packard, Mammalian Species, 1977) kept five individuals as long as six years, and one lived eight years, five months, the longest life span recorded for a North American sigmodontine rodent.

ENEMIES. There appears to be little specific information on the predators on this species, but certainly many of the hawks, owls, snakes, and mammalian predators in its area would feed on it.

PARASITES AND DISEASE. The few parasites recorded from this species include mostly nematodes, internally, and mites, ticks, fleas, and the louse *Hoplopleura hesperomydis*, externally. The louse and mite species show much resemblance to those found on *Peromyscus*.

RELATION TO HUMANS. This is an interesting little animal, but probably has little direct relationship to humans.

AREAS FOR FURTHER WORK. Additional information is needed on the food, ectoparasites, and social system in these mice.

## SUBSPECIES

The described subspecies appear to intergrade one into another, and we therefore see no reason to distinguish them.

*Ochrotomys nuttalli nuttalli* (Harlan)

As described above.

Type locality: Norfolk, Norfolk Co., Virginia.

Other currently recognized eastern subspecies:

O. *nuttalli aureolus* Audubon & Bachman
O. *nuttalli floridanus* Packard
O. *nuttalli lisae* Packard

### LITERATURE

Frank, P. A., and J. N. Layne. 1992. Nests and daytime refugia of cotton mice (*Peromyscus gossypinus*) and golden mice (*Ochrotomys nuttalli*) in south-central Florida. *Amer. Midland Nat.* 127: 21–30.

Goodpaster, W. W., and D. F. Hoffmeister. 1954. Life history of the golden mouse, *Peromyscus nuttalli*, in Kentucky. *J. Mammal.* 35: 16–27.

Linzey, D. W. 1968. An ecological study of the golden mouse, *Ochrotomys nuttalli*, in the Great Smoky Mountains National Park. *Amer. Midland Nat.* 79: 320–345.

Linzey, D. W., and A. V. Linzey. 1967. Growth and development of the golden mouse, *Ochrotomys nuttalli nuttalli*. *J. Mammal.* 48: 445–458.

Linzey, D. W., and R. L. Packard. 1977. *Ochrotomys nuttalli.* **Mammalian Species No. 75.** Amer. Soc. Mammal. 6 pp.

McCarley, W. H. 1958. Ecology, behavior and population dynamics of *Peromyscus nuttalli* in eastern Texas. *Texas J. Sci.* 10: 147–171.

Packard, R. L. 1969. Taxonomic review of the golden mouse, *Ochrotomys nuttalli. Misc. Publ. Mus. Nat. Hist. Univ. Kansas* 51: 373–406.

## Hispid Cotton Rat
## *Sigmodon hispidus* Say and Ord

DESCRIPTION. The cotton rat, a large rodent of the open fields of the south, is brown above and only slightly paler below. It has a medium-long tail and a long, coarse, grizzled pelage, dusky above and paler below but not bicolored. The hairs are black on the tips, plumbeous at their bases. The ears are black, the feet vary from gray to dark brown, and the abdomen is pale gray or buffy. The tail is scaly and very scantily haired. Individuals from peninsular Florida are smaller, and the brown of the upperparts is much reduced and replaced by gray. The gray or yellowish gray, black-tipped hairs of these peninsular mice give a characteristic pepper-and-salt appearance, and the underparts are grayish white. Individuals of extreme southern Florida have a browner, less-gray dorsal pelage; the rump is cinnamon-rufous, and the tail is an almost uniformly dull black, slightly paler below.

MEASUREMENTS. Fifty individuals from Louisiana (Lowery, 1974) averaged: total length 267 (240–350), tail 106 (90–138), hind foot 31 (24–35) mm; and weight 80–120 grams. Twenty from Fort Myers, Florida, averaged: total length 258, tail 94, hind foot 28.5 mm.

Diploid number = 52.

TOOTH FORMULA

$$\frac{1}{1} \quad \frac{0}{0} \quad \frac{0}{0} \quad \frac{3}{3} = 16$$

DISTRIBUTION. The hispid cotton rat is a creature of the southern United States, from southwestern Kentucky and north-central North Carolina south through Louisiana and Florida, but is expanding its range northward in the east. It was first found in western Virginia in 1977, when six were taken in Lee County, and in southeastern Kentucky the same year, when seven were taken in Bell County (Davis and Barbour, 1979). Rose et al. (1990) recorded it for the first time in the Dismal Swamp in eastern Virginia. It occurs west to southern Arizona and south to Panama.

HABITAT. Every geographic region has its characteristic species, some more abundant than others, and often one species dominates the rest. In the waste fields and lush meadows of the North the meadow vole, *Microtus pennsylvanicus*, reigns, but in the grass-dominated fields of the South the cotton rat is king. It is generally more abundant on higher ground, but it can be found in the open sea-oats community on dunes;

and every field of broom sedge, every roadside ditch, even the open glades of the forest to elevations of 880 meters (1700 feet), has its quota. The canopy of grasses and weeds in typical cotton rat habitat covers a multitude of well-defined trails, and where the cover is thin these highways can be seen for some distance. These animals will sometimes ascend into bushes, to a height of almost 3 meters (10 feet).

HABITS. Though it is evident that cotton rat populations fluctuate from year to year, there is hardly a season in which these animals do not outnumber all other southern mammals. Though solitary animals, they are usually the most abundant species on the farmlands of the South. Occasionally, when an area has been burned over, many of these rats have emerged.

Cotton rats are active day and night, with peaks at dawn and dusk. They construct numerous long, shallow runways, and in them are chambers where they place their nests. The nests, which are built of grass, are small and spherical, with a small opening, or cup-shaped and open-topped. One can find them by following the numerous runways, or by looking in and under clumps of grass. Many other species of small mammals also use the cotton rat runways.

Wright and Pagels (1977) reported on the cotton rat's climbing activity, particularly in honeysuckle.

FOOD AND FEEDING. Grassy plants are the prime food, although cotton rats can do great damage in cultivated fields. The burrows are kept shorn of new growth, and little piles of cut sedges and various grasses appear at irregular intervals in the surface runways, as is the practice of meadow voles. These piles result when cotton rats cut the food plants into sections to get at the heads. At other times the rats feed mostly on the tender lower parts of grass stems, but cotton rats do not store food. Bachman wrote 140 years ago that this species is very destructive to quail, and Herbert Stoddard later confirmed this, finding that the cotton rat in Georgia destroys considerable numbers of eggs and chicks. The cotton rat also travels the ditches, feeding on crayfish and the little fiddler

*Hispid cotton rat,* Sigmodon hispidus
*(Roger W. Barbour)*

crabs, and its diet is occasionally supplemented with insects.

REPRODUCTION AND DEVELOPMENT. Few mammals are more prolific than the hispid cotton rat. Breeding commences in late winter and continues through October or November—perhaps at times, and in southern areas such as Louisiana, throughout the year. In late March, in southern Florida, these rats were not breeding. Females are in estrus every seven to nine days, and right after parturition, as well. Gestation is about 27 days. The young may number one to 15, but there are usually four to eight in a litter. Of six pregnant cotton rats collected in southern Arizona, the embryo number *averaged* 12. Spring litters are smaller than those of summer and fall. At birth, the young weigh 6.5 to 8 grams and are well developed. They are able to run about at that time, and have a fine coating of light-colored hair. The eyes open during the first day, and at the age of five or six days the young are weaned and begin to leave the nest and fend for themselves. At that time they weigh only 10 to 20 grams, and the species is thus one of the most precocious of all rodents. One female was pregnant at 38 days of age, another at 40. Following the birth of one litter, the parents may immediately produce another.

POPULATION CHARACTERISTICS. Population studies can be difficult in this species, because dominant animals are more likely to be trapped than subordinates (subordinates avoid traps scented by dominants), and because the exploratory behavior of subordinates is less adventuresome. Some maximum population densities in this species are 69 per ha (28 per acre) in Georgia and 25 per ha (10 per acre) in Florida. Adult home ranges range from 0.2 to 0.4 ha (0.1 to 0.2 acre), those of males larger, on average, than those of females, but the home ranges of established females are exclusive: they do not overlap those of other individuals. The average life span is probably less than six months, but one animal in captivity lived for 5 years and 2 months.

ENEMIES. Cotton rats are the mainstay of the predatory birds, mammals, and snakes of the southland. Even before it is fully dark, they are sought out by barred owls, gray foxes, raccoons, rattlesnakes, copperheads, and many other snakes.

PARASITES AND DISEASE. Cotton rats harbor a variety of parasites: endoparasites reported include six species of cestodes, seven of trematodes, and at least 14 of nematodes; ectoparasites include six species of fleas, two of lice, four of ticks, and nine of mites.

RELATION TO HUMANS. Bachman wrote of this species: "It is a resident rather of hedges, ditches, and deserted old fields, than of gardens or cultivated grounds; it occasions very little injury to the planter." Perhaps this was because of differences in farming in the early days, or perhaps the planter did not cultivate extensive truck crops for the northern markets in 1840. Today, in any case, the cotton rat is a pest of

hispidus

komareki

virginianus

hispidus incorporates all but exsputus and insulicola

littoralis

floridanus

insulicola

spadicipygus

exsputus

*Distribution of the hispid cotton rat, Sigmodon hispidus, in the eastern United States*

major importance to agriculture in many parts of the South, especially destructive of sugarcane, truck crops, and garden plants. It may cause 50% loss to sugarcane crops by cutting the stalks off close to the ground. The rats are particularly fond of sweet potatoes; a total of 513 were once killed in a 1-acre patch. (Bachman also reported—see "Food and Feeding," above—that these rats are very destructive to quail.)

AREAS FOR FURTHER WORK. This species replaces *Microtus* in the Deep South, and a detailed comparison of the ecology and behavior of the two would thus be of interest. Studies of the social structure, mating system, ectoparasites, and nest fauna of this species would all be instructive.

## SUBSPECIES

Most of the described subspecies appear to be clinally related, but we do recognize two island subspecies.

### *Sigmodon hispidus hispidus* Say and Ord

As described above. Occurs over most of the eastern range of the species.

Type locality: St. John's River, northeastern Florida.

Other currently recognized eastern subspecies:

    *S. hispidus floridanus* Howell
    *S. hispidus komareki* Gardner
    *S. hispidus littoralis* Chapman
    *S. hispidus spadicipygus* Bangs
    *S. hispidus virginianus* Gardner

### *Sigmodon hispidus exsputus* Allen
### Cape Sable Cotton Rat

This subspecies differs from animals in southern-peninsular Florida in having a proportionately longer tail. The dorsal surfaces of the head and body are pale ochraceous with slaty rather than blackish hair bases; the belly is clear white, and the hair bases are pale slaty gray. The type, an adult male, measures: total length 259, tail 117, hind foot 33.5 mm. These rats are known only from Big Pine Key.

Type locality: Big Pine Key, one of the southern Florida Keys, Monroe Co., Florida.

### *Sigmodon hispidus insulicola* Howell

The upper parts of these rats are paler and more grayish than are those of animals from the mainland, and the venter is lighter; the tail and hind foot are paler, and the animals and their skulls are smaller than is the case in mainland individuals. Standard measurements of six individuals are: total length 278, tail 114, and hind foot 31.7 mm.

Type locality: Captiva Island, Lee Co., Florida.

## LITERATURE

Cameron, G. N., and S. R. Spencer. 1981. *Sigmodon hispidus.* **Mammalian Species No. 158.** Amer. Soc. Mammal. 9 pp.

Davis, W. H., and R. W. Barbour. 1979. Distributional records of some Kentucky mammals. *Trans. Ky. Acad. Sci.* 40: 111.

Fleharty, E. D., J. R. Choate, and M. A. Mares. 1972. Fluctuations in population density of the hispid cotton rat: Factors influencing a "crash." *Bull. S. Calif. Acad. Sci.* 71: 132–138.

Kincaid, W. B., G. N. Cameron, and B. A. Carnes. 1983. Interactions of cotton rats with a patchy environment: Dietary responses and habitat selection. *Ecology* 66: 1769–1783.

Lowery, G. H., Jr. 1974. *The Mammals of Louisiana and Its Adjacent Waters.* Baton Rouge: Louisiana State Univ. Press. 565 pp.

Odum, E. P. 1955. An eleven-year history of a *Sigmodon* population. *J. Mammal.* 36: 368–378.

Randolph, J. C., G. N. Cameron, and J. A. Wrazen. 1991. Dietary choice of a generalist grassland herbivore, *Sigmodon hispidus. J. Mammal.* 72: 300–313.

Rose, R. K., R. K. Everton, J. F. Stankavich, and J. W. Walke. 1990. Small mammals in the Great Dismal Swamp of Virginia and North Carolina. *Brimleyana* 16: 87–101.

Wright, D. E., and J. F. Pagels. 1977. Climbing activity in the hispid cotton rat, *Sigmodon hispidus*, and the eastern meadow vole, *Microtus pennsylvanicus. Chesapeake Sci.* 18: 87–89.

Zimmerman, E. G. 1970. Karyology, systematics and chromosomal evaluation in the rodent genus, *Sigmodon.* Publ. Mus. Mich. State Univ., Biol. Ser. 4: 385–454.

## Woodrats of the Genus *Neotoma*

A woodrat, brown above and white below, looks much like an overgrown white-footed mouse. Norway and black rats of the genus *Rattus* are about the same size, but have dark rather than white underparts. Moreover, the tails of woodrats are furred and strongly bicolored, brown above and white below; *Rattus* tails are scaly rather than furred, and are not bicolored. The crowns of the molars in *Neotoma* are flat, the enamel thrown into prismatic folds; those of *Rattus* form three rows of cusps (p. 276). Woodrats have prominent vibrissae, the longest 90 mm; the longest vibrissae of *Rattus* are about 65 mm. There are four teats in *Neotoma*, located toward the rear of the abdomen; in *Rattus*, there are ten (these numbers of teats correspond with the low numbers of young produced by *Neotoma* and the high numbers produced by *Rattus*). Finally, along the midline of the abdomen in adult woodrats, there is a red-brown patch of discolored fur and exposed skin, up to 50–60 mm long and 5–7 mm wide, most prominent in males (Spencer, 1968).

Woodrats are nocturnal, but are occasionally abroad on dark days, and are seldom abroad on stormy nights. Bob Finley and others have used red light, which appears not to disturb them, to watch their nightly forays.

Among themselves, woodrats are aggressive creatures. They fight over their food or nest sites, and continually chase one another. Because of this intraspecific aggression, one seldom captures an adult that is not scarred; it may have torn ears or fresh skin wounds, and may even lack a piece of its tail. Foot-drumming is a common behavior in this species, especially during the reproductive period.

One of the characteristic behavioral traits of woodrats is to lug all sorts of rubbish to the den site. This booty may include bone scraps, leaves, bits of wood, tobacco tins, shotgun shells, glass, cast-off clothing, and the refuse from a camp site.

Many other animals use woodrat dens, including snakes, lizards, toads, insects, and a variety of small mammals, particularly white-footed mice and cottontails, and sometimes opossums.

Eastern woodrats were originally described as two separate species, a northern *Neotoma magister* and a southern *N. floridana*. These were later thought to constitute a single species, *N. floridana*. More recently still, John Hayes has concluded that the two are indeed distinct. Hayes and Harrison (1992) examined mito-

chondrial DNA in eastern woodrats, and Hayes and Richmond (1993) examined their clinal variation and morphology. This work indicated the presence of three major lineages of woodrats in the eastern United States, a northern (*magister*), a southern (*floridana*), and one now on the Keys (*smalli*), with relatively little variation within any of the three. Birney (1973) hypothesized that *Neotoma* may have been absent from the Northeast in Pleistocene times, and the data of Hayes and Harrison are consistent with that hypothesis, though they suggest that the three lineages were probably distinct during the Pleistocene, perhaps occupying separate refugia in the Southeast. Toward the end of the Wisconsinan glaciation, the Florida populations were apparently isolated from the rest of the range of the species by high waters across the northern part of the peninsula. It appears likely, however, that *N. magister* stocks separated from the other eastern stocks fairly early, probably before the Wisconsinan glaciation. On both genetic and morphological grounds, *N. magister* and *N. floridana* are best considered separate species.

Hayes found no evidence of hybridization between the two, "although [he] had some samples from near the species boundaries." The mountainous region along the North Carolina–Tennessee border would be worth exploring for hybrids. Elmer Birney attempted to force hybrid matings in the laboratory, but found that *N. magister* would usually attack and kill *N. floridana*.

### Literature Cited

Birney, E. C. 1973. Systematics of three species of woodrats (genus *Neotoma*) in central North America. *Misc. Publ. Mus. Nat. Hist. Univ. Kansas* 58: 1–173.

Hayes, J. P., and R. G. Harrison. 1992. Variation in mitochondrial DNA and the biogeographic history of woodrats (*Neotoma*) of the eastern United States. *Syst. Biol.* 41: 331–344.

Hayes, J. P., and M. E. Richmond. 1993. Clinal variation and morphology of woodrats (*Neotoma*) of the eastern United States. *J. Mammal.* 74: 204–216.

Spencer, D. L. 1968. Sympatry and hybridization of the eastern and southern plains wood rats. Unpubl. Ph.D. diss., Oklahoma State University, Stillwater. 85 pp.

## Eastern Woodrat
### *Neotoma floridana* (Ord)

This woodrat, *Neotoma floridana*, is closely related to and capable of hybridizing with the western woodrats *N. albigula* and *N. micropus*. *Neotoma micropus* and *N. floridana* occur together today, and *N. albigula* and *N. floridana* were sympatric in Texas around the turn of the century. The three do retain their mutual distinctions, however, with little or no introgression, and should remain classed as separate species.

DESCRIPTION. Woodrats look much like overgrown white-footed mice. The color above varies from pale cinnamon to brownish gray. The

*Eastern woodrat,* Neotoma floridana
*(Roger W. Barbour)*

sides are buffy brown, mixed with darker hairs, and are rather distinct in color from that of the middle of the back. The face and cheeks are buffy gray; the forehead is darker. The vibrissae are long. The underparts are creamy white, the dark basal part of the hairs showing prominently in the middle of the belly and on the flanks. The tail, dusky to brown above, slightly paler below, is fairly well haired and slightly bicolored in the south, definitely bicolored in the north.

MEASUREMENTS. Measurements of 24 adults from Georgia and Florida averaged: total length 393 (362–409), tail 181 (166–189), hind foot 38 (36–40) mm; and weight 200–275 grams. Diploid number = 52.

TOOTH FORMULA

$$\frac{1}{1} \quad \frac{0}{0} \quad \frac{0}{0} \quad \frac{3}{3} = 16$$

DISTRIBUTION. In the east-central United States, *Neotoma floridana* occurs in extreme southern Illinois, extreme western Kentucky, and Tennessee and Alabama south of the Tennessee River, and in the east from southwestern North Carolina, northwestern and southern Georgia, and southern South Carolina south through the Gulf states and all of northern and central Florida. There is also an isolated population in the upper Florida Keys. This species occurs west to eastern Colorado and eastern Texas.

HABITAT. The Allegheny woodrat, *Neotoma magister*, appears to be dependent on rocky habitat, or at least is currently restricted to that habitat, whereas *N. floridana*, much more of a habitat generalist, can subsist in rocky habitat when available, but is not dependent on it. In extreme southern Illinois, Florida woodrats live on the bluffs, just as *N. magister* does, but these conditions are not found in much of *floridana*'s range in the southeastern United States, and here the rats live a different life, on the flatlands. In much of Alabama, they appear to favor the osage orange hedges. In Georgia and Florida they are found on low, wet ground in hammocks and swamps, and in drier situations supporting, for example, sand scrub pine.

HABITS. In Alabama, woodrats build large nests in the branches of trees. In Georgia and Florida, they live in hollow trees or holes in the ground, or construct large houses, or lodges, of sticks, leaves, and rubbish along the banks of streams in dense stands of saw palmetto or, rarely, in trees. These houses are rather compactly constructed and sufficiently well knit to shed rain and provide protection from temperature extremes. The size and shape of the house vary with the situation, but a typical one is about 1.2 meters wide and a meter high and contains two or more nests, these opening to the outside by one or two entrances, although the exits may lead into the earth and extend a meter or so from the house before reappearing on the surface. The largest houses in the east are those of *Neotoma floridana smalli* on Key Largo, Florida. The house there is constructed primarily of sticks, often with the leaves still attached, but it generally contains many other items—paper, glass, dung, rocks, and especially bones. The inner nest material is prepared by the woodrat by shredding and fluffing it with its teeth; the rat then turns around and around in the nest, shaping the nest material with its head and forefeet. The house is used throughout the year, and perhaps throughout the life of the animal.

FOOD AND FEEDING. The diet of the woodrat, though varied, appears to consist almost entirely of vegetation. Included are many of the plants available in the habitat: fruits and berries, including dogwood, blackberries, mountain ash, wild cherries, and shadberries, the fruits and stalks of pokeweed and sassafras, fungi, ferns, rhododendron leaves, and parts of a host of other plants. These are often left in a green condition on the rocks, which may indicate a hay-making practice similar to that of the pika (a small relative of the rabbits, native to the Rockies). Different foods are used at different localities. Osage orange was the most important food at a Kansas study site; pecans were in Texas. A. H. Howell (1921) believed that woodrats feed in large measure on hickory nuts in Alabama, since he found a great accumulation of shells about the cliffs occupied by the rats.

*Distribution of the eastern woodrat,* Neotoma floridana, *in the eastern United States*

He likewise found pawpaw seeds about the dens. It appears that most foraging occurs close to the nest, within 20 meters (65 feet) or so. In summer, most feeding apparently occurs on the spot during foraging, since little material is brought back to the den at that time. Food storage commences in September or October, the food being placed in galleries at the top of the house.

REPRODUCTION AND DEVELOPMENT. In Florida and coastal Georgia, eastern woodrats breed irregularly throughout the year. In the north, the breeding season is from spring to fall. Gestation is from 32 to 38 days. Litters varied from one to seven young, most often two, with a mean of 3.2. There are two or three litters per year. At birth the incisors are already erupted and the vibrissae are prominent. Measurements of newborn were total length 87–96, tail 24–27, hind foot 13.5–14.8 mm; and weight 11.8–14.1 grams. The ears unfold in about nine days, and the eyes open in about 15 to 21 days. Weaning is at four weeks.

POPULATION CHARACTERISTICS. Assuming one rat per house, house counts have indicated up to 0.82 rat per ha (0.33 per acre), the density declining in years of extremely bad weather or low food production. Woodrats are basically solitary, one rat per house, and the houses are distributed through usable habitat in such a way as to lessen competition for food and living space.

ENEMIES. The spotted skunk, long-tailed weasel, pilot blacksnake, and timber rattler were the main predators recorded in one study, with the blacksnake and weasel being the most important. Fitch and Rainey (1956) include the great horned owl as a formidable predator.

PARASITES AND DISEASE. In some areas, botfly larvae (*Cuterebra*) are important parasites of *Neotoma floridana*. Interestingly, woodrats in the Florida Keys have fleas characteristic of gray squirrels rather than of woodrats (Layne, 1971). The fleas of woodrats from Illinois, *N. f. illinoensis*, are at least subspecifically distinct from those of other woodrats (Layne, 1958). The Florida Keys finding could reflect restraints on woodrat fleas, whereas the Illinois case probably reflects the isolation of this population of woodrats.

RELATION TO HUMANS. This species would generally seem to have little direct significance for us.

AREAS FOR FURTHER WORK. The ectoparasite community of this species could be studied and compared to that of *N. magister*, and the nest faunas of both these species could be studied and compared. What is the relation of *N. floridana* to the raccoon nematode, *Baylisascaris procyonis*, which appears to cause death in *N. magister*? Much more information is needed on reproduction in this species.

## SUBSPECIES

Other than for *Neotoma floridana smalli*, an island form, the various forms of this species appear to constitute series of intergrading populations.

### *Neotoma floridana floridana* (Ord)

As described above. A southeastern form that occurs from eastern Alabama and all but the southern third of Florida north through most of Georgia and southeastern South Carolina to extreme south-coastal North Carolina. This subspecies is confined on its western boundary by the Chattahoochee River. Eight adults from Wolf Lake, Illinois, averaged: total length 430 (390–475), tail 195 (187–205), and hind foot 38 (36–40) mm.

Type locality: St. Johns River, probably near Jacksonville, Duval Co., Florida.

Other currently recognized eastern subspecies:
  *N. floridana haematoreia* Howell
  *N. floridana illinoensis* Howell
  *N. floridana rubida* Bangs

### *Neotoma floridana smalli* Sherman

This insular form is known only from Key Largo, Florida, but was introduced to Lignum Vitae Key in 1970. The population thrived there for many years, but then underwent a precipitous decline, for unknown reasons. John Hayes was unable to capture any or find any evidence of their survival there in 1988, although numerous old houses were evident there at that time. It is "similar to *N. f. floridana* except the sphenopalatine vacuities are narrower and do not extend as far forward. They usually do not extend as far forward as the posterior edge of the bar which forms the posterior boundary of the optic foramen in *smalli*, and when they do, they overlap the bar not over half its extent. In *floridana* the anterior ends of the vacuities usually extend anterior to this bar or overlap it at least half its extent. The distance from the front of the incisor to the anterior end of the sphenotine vacuity is greater in adult specimens of *smalli* and usually less in *floridana* than the distance from the front of the incisor to the posterior edge of the third molar" (Sherman, 1955). Measurements from Key Largo are total length 290–420, hind foot 32–41 mm. Males are slightly larger than females.

Type locality: Key Largo, Monroe Co., Florida.

## LITERATURE

Birney, E. C. 1976. An assessment of relationships and effects of interbreeding among woodrats of the *Neotoma floridana* species group. *J. Mammal.* 57: 103–132.

Fitch, H. S., and D. G. Rainey. 1956. Ecological observations on the woodrat, *Neotoma floridana.* *Univ. Kansas Publ. Mus. Nat. Hist.* 8: 499–533.

Howell, A. H. 1921. A biological survey of Alabama: I, Physiography and life zones. II, The mammals. *North Amer. Fauna* No. 45. 88 pp.

Layne, J. N. 1958. Records of fleas (Siphonaptera) from Illinois mammals. Nat. Hist. Misc. Chicago Acad. Sci. No. 162. 8 pp.

———. 1971. Fleas (Siphonaptera) of Florida. *Fla. Entomol.* 54: 35–51.

Murphy, M. F. 1952. Ecology and helminths of the Osage wood rat, *Neotoma floridana osagensis,* including description of *Longistriata neotoma* n.sp. (Trichostrongylidae). *Amer. Midland Nat.* 48: 204–218.

Rainey, D. G. 1956. Eastern woodrat *Neotoma floridana*: Life history and ecology. *Univ. Kans. Publ. Mus. Nat. Hist.* 8: 535–646.

Sherman, H. B. 1955. Description of a new race of woodrat from Key Largo, Florida. *J. Mammal.* 36: 113–120.

Wiley, R. W. 1980. *Neotoma floridana.* **Mammalian Species No. 139.** Amer. Soc. Mammal. 7 pp. [Does not distinguish between *N. floridana* and *N. magister.*]

## Allegheny Woodrat *Neotoma magister* (Baird)

DESCRIPTION. *Neotoma magister* and *N. floridana* were originally described as separate spe-

*Allegheny woodrat,* Neotoma magister
*(Roger W. Barbour)*

cies, but later were considered conspecific (see discussion under "Woodrats of the Genus *Neotoma*," above). The two are nearly identical in appearance, but they can be distinguished on the basis of either genetic or morphological characteristics, and there is no evidence that the differences are due to clinal variability. Almost all individuals of the two species differ in two skull characters, the presence of a maxillovomerine notch in *Neotoma magister* and a strongly bifurcate anterior palatal spine in *N. floridana.* The notch does not occur in *N. floridana* and the bifurcation usually does not occur in *N. magister.*

MEASUREMENTS. Measurements of 30 individuals from Indiana averaged: 389.6 (348–431), tail 172.7 (141–191), hind foot 41.8 (37–46) mm; and weight 306.7 (193.6–383.5) grams. Measurements of ten adults from New York, Pennsylvania, and West Virginia averaged: total length 423 (405–441), tail 186 (170–200), hind foot 43.5 (40–46) mm; and weight 370–455 grams.

Diploid number = 52.

TOOTH FORMULA

$$\frac{1}{1} \quad \frac{0}{0} \quad \frac{0}{0} \quad \frac{3}{3} \quad = \quad 16$$

DISTRIBUTION. *Neotoma magister* occurs, or recently occurred, from southeastern New York southwest through much of Pennsylvania, extreme southern Ohio and Indiana, through western Maryland, all of West Virginia, most of Kentucky, and the western reaches of Virginia and North Carolina south through much of Tennessee, and into northern Alabama and northwesternmost Georgia. In the southern part of its range, it is separated from *N. floridana* by the Tennessee River. Poole (1940) lists localities from which Allegheny woodrats had earlier been recorded. The species has declined especially in the northern parts of its range. These woodrats were recently extirpated from New York (in 1987) and most of eastern Pennsylvania and New Jersey (one New Jersey site remains along the Hudson River).

HABITAT. Rocky cliffs, caves, and fissures or tumbled boulders on the sides of mountains are the preferred habitat of *Neotoma magister*. These rats earlier occurred further northward in Indiana and Ohio, but the range of this species has been reduced since Pleistocene times to include only selected rock bluffs along the Ohio and Mississippi rivers. Perhaps they disappeared due to long-term climatic changes, perhaps to the raccoon nematode, or perhaps to some other cause, yet unknown. There is still an old nest in a cave in Orange County, Indiana, but all recent records in Indiana are from Harrison and Crawford counties, and those in Ohio are from Adams County. Here the Allegheny woodrat is

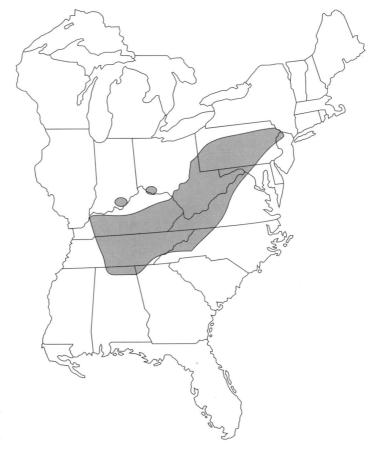

*Distribution of the Allegheny woodrat,* Neotoma magister, *in the eastern United States*

further restricted to areas with fissures, caves, or other rock shelters adequate to serve their needs. Stands of red cedar in the vicinity also appear highly beneficial to them, although not essential. In New York also, the species once occurred north of its recent range. Two caves near Albany, well north of the known historic range in New York, contained woodrat remains several thousand years old (D. Steadman, pers. comm.), but the species is currently extirpated in New York.

In the rock slides and extensive bare patches of the Appalachians, tumbled boulders form crevasses and extensive galleries, almost devoid of vegetation. Here the woodrats scurry by night, their presence made evident by their piles of droppings and by the trash that they lug to the dens and ledges. *Neotoma magister* is otherwise dependent on the rocky bluffs, caves, and other rocky habitats where they have managed to maintain a foothold since Pleistocene times. This species does sometimes nest in buildings.

The woodrat's presence may long go unsuspected in areas where they are not at all uncommon. The sense that they are absent is often due to their nocturnal habits and to the nature of the habitat they select, for the inhospitable cliffs invite few hikers. Where woodrats occur in and around cliffs, their presence is well demonstrated by the characteristic pellets on ledges and the piles of debris throughout the area. Here, woodrats run over the rocks with great agility, visiting the brush and open thickets in search of food; the foreign material in their nests suggests that they make extensive journeys into the bottomlands as well.

HABITS. The nest of the Allegheny woodrat is a bulky structure built in a fissure, behind rocks, or on a rock shelf or the level floor of a cave, well protected from the elements. It is open at the top, not unlike the nests of many birds. Nests in Indiana are often made of red cedar twigs and lined with shredded cedar bark, but any fine material may be used. Indeed, in Indiana we have often seen entire banks, above and below woodrat dens, strewn with cedar twigs. One nest, on a shelf more than 2 meters (7 feet) high, in an old building, was entirely of trash. It

covered the entire shelf, which was about 1.2 by 1.5 meters (4 by 5 feet). We have found these woodrats using shredded grape bark for nest-building in West Virginia caves.

Woodrats in Indiana characteristically build both middens and debris piles. The debris piles, consisting of sticks, bark, bones, feathers, paper, dung, and assorted trash, are commonly associated with den sites, apparently helping to protect the openings to fissures or other dens. Middens, which contain only potential food items, are quite characteristic of woodrat den areas. Formed in the fall, they serve as food caches, and are depleted by early spring. Midden materials line paths to the nest, or may be found on the ledges or fissures of the cliffs where woodrats live.

In New York, two of six piles examined by Ed McGowan (pers. comm.) could be described as debris pile/midden hybrids. Both piles contained food items (acorns, mushrooms, plant clippings) and debris (plastic trash, sticks, bones, etc.). McGowan also found raccoon feces in two food middens (gray birch leaves and fern clippings). Do the woodrats consider the feces food or not?

Kinsey (1976) found that dominant individuals in a captive population defended their nest sites, but that subordinates lived in communal aggregations and avoided the dominants. The number of dominant animals was limited to the number of available nest sites. Woodrats are normally intolerant of one another, their fighting consisting of jabs of the head and front feet when individuals cross paths. Woodrats seldom produce sounds, except for tooth chattering and foot thumping, the latter familiar to those who have kept them in captivity. There is some evidence that these rats socialize, for Francis Harper recounted the capture of three adult females at a group of three nests in the space of two days.

FOOD AND FEEDING. Poole (1940) listed 47 "materials found in and about nests" (probably partly food). These included five species of fungi (three mushrooms, two coral fungi), one lichen (*Parmelia* sp.), rock tripe (*Umbilicaria pustulata*), moss (*Dicranium*), five species of ferns, hemlock twigs, red cedar bark, and eight species of nuts and acorns. The remainder were other herbaceous and woody plant parts. He also reported the usual assortment of nonfood materials—nails, coins, bones, feathers, paper, shotgun shells, etc. From examination of a few stomachs, he definitely identified puffballs, hemlock (green twigs and seeds), black birch twigs and seed pods, chestnut (nuts), scrub oak (acorns), flowering dogwood (fruits), apple (fruits and seeds), black cherry (fruits and pits), mountain ash (fruits and seeds), and rhododendron (leaves, in winter). Newcombe (1930) gives similar data for woodrats taken in West Virginia.

Cudmore (1983) found that the most extensively used food items stored in the middens of the rock ledges in Indiana were foliage and sometimes samaras of tree of heaven (*Ailanthus altissima*), fruit of pokeberry (*Phytolacca americana*), foliage of red cedar (*Juniperus virginiana*), and leaves of Virginia creeper (*Parthenocissus quinquefolia*). The most important food items (by percent volume) in southern Indiana, as indicated by woodrat stomach contents, were tree of heaven, persimmon, Virginia creeper, acorns, Japanese honeysuckle, and red cedar. Some of the foods eaten by *N. magister* in Tennessee are honey locust, mint, acorns, and beechnuts; in Pennsylvania, mushrooms. Juterbock (1986) identified over 100 species of food items for *N. magister* in Ohio, from 1982 to 1986.

Animals kept in captivity by Poole (1940) commonly chewed on bones, which probably helps to keep their teeth sharp and provides a source of animal food. This behavior probably explains the abundance of bones in woodrat middens. Animals not given bones would chew on wood in their cages.

REPRODUCTION AND DEVELOPMENT. The breeding season for the Allegheny woodrat begins in early spring and continues until mid-fall, and three or even four broods may be produced, at least in a year with a good mast crop and a mild winter, and one female bred through the entire season in 1992 in New York (Al Hicks and Ed McGowan, pers. comm.). The litter usually numbers one to six, most often two. Gestation is 33 to 38 days, averaging about 35. As with other rodents, the young are born in an

*Nest of Allegheny woodrat (Russell E. Mumford)*

immature and quite helpless condition. The four curved upper and lower incisors, evident at birth, form an opening and are thus well adapted to grasping the teat. So firmly do the young grasp the teat that it is extremely difficult to remove them. The vibrissae, approximately 5 mm in length, are also prominent at this time. Standard measurements at birth are total length 87–96, tail 24–27, hind foot 13.5–14.8 mm; and weight 11.8–14.1 grams. The eyes open in the third week and another week passes before the young are fully weaned. At six to seven weeks, the young weigh about 120 grams. The first molt occurs at five to six weeks of age. It begins at the anterior venter and proceeds dorsally. This molt is followed immediately by a second. Young born early, may breed in the year of their birth, but most do not until their second year.

POPULATION CHARACTERISTICS. On the southern Indiana bluffs woodrats occur at rates up to about 70 animals per 1000 meters (3200 feet) of bluff.

ENEMIES. Woodrats have a number of potential enemies, but they do not seem to be particularly susceptible to predation. Although they share their country with the timber rattlesnake and the copperhead, Luther Hook, who examined many of these snakes in the woodrat country of New York and New Jersey, never found rat remains in their stomachs. Bobcats, foxes, weasels, and owls haunt the rocky cliffs and undoubtedly take some, but one of the most important predators is probably the great horned owl.

PARASITES AND DISEASE. Fleas, ticks, mites, and chiggers are all found on woodrats, and a few species, such as the flea *Orchopeas sexdentatus* and the mites *Echinonyssus neotoma* and *Myocoptes neotomae*, are very partial to woodrats, though not restricted to them. Nematodes and cestodes are found in the intestines, and the raccoon nematode, *Baylisascaris procyonis*, can be fatal to woodrats. Accidental ingestion of its tiny eggs, which are found in soil and in dung, is usually fatal. The adults found in the intestines are very large, 15 to 20 cm (6 to 8 inches) long and 1 cm (0.38 inch) thick (Kazacos, 1983). This nematode eliminated several released woodrats in New York (A. Hicks and E. McGowan, pers. comm.) and could be responsible for population declines in woodrats elsewhere in the Northeast, especially in areas where woodrats are collecting and storing raccoon feces.

RELATION TO HUMANS. This species would seem to have little direct significance to humans. We can say from personal experience, however, that its meat is excellent.

AREAS FOR FURTHER WORK. Much more information is needed on the relationship between this species and the raccoon nematode, *Baylisascaris procyonis*. This nematode appears to be limiting woodrats, at least in New York, but on the bluffs along the Ohio River in Indiana, woodrats appear to be holding their own. What is different? Habitat, distribution, or the abundance of the nematode? Why has this species declined at the northern edge of its range—in Pennsylvania, Ohio, and Indiana? In Indiana it is currently limited to rock bluffs along the Ohio River, whereas earlier, it occurred much farther north. Is this a response to climatic change? To the nematode?

## SUBSPECIES

None described.

Type locality: A cave near Carlisle, Cumberland Co., or near Harrisburg, Dauphin Co., Pennsylvania.

## LITERATURE

Birney, E. C. 1976. An assessment of relationships and effects interbreeding among woodrats of the *Neotoma floridana* species group. *J. Mammal.* 57: 103–132.

Cudmore, W. W. 1982. The distribution and ecology of the eastern woodrat, *Neotoma floridana*, in Indiana. Unpubl. Ph.D. diss., Indiana State University, Terre Haute. 148 pp.

Hayes, J. P., and R. G. Harrison. 1992. Variation in mitochondrial DNA and the biogeographic history of woodrats (*Neotoma*) of the eastern United States. *Syst. Biol.* 41: 331–344.

Hayes, J. P., and M. E. Richmond. 1993. Clinal variation and morphology of woodrats (*Neotoma*) of the eastern United States. *J. Mammal.* 74: 204–216.

Juterbock, J. E. 1986. A continuing study of eastern woodrats and green salamanders. Unpubl. report, Dept. Zoology, Ohio State University.

Kazacos, K. R. 1983. Raccoon roundworms (*Baylisascaris procyonis*): A cause of animal and human disease. Purdue Univ. Agric. Exp. Stat. Bull. 422. 25 pp.

Kinsey, K. P. 1976. Social behavior in confined populations of the Allegheny woodrat, *Neotoma floridana magister*. *Anim. Behav.* 24: 181–187.

Newcombe, C. L. 1930. An ecological study of the Allegheny cliff rat (*Neotoma pennsylvanica* Stone). *J. Mammal.* 11: 204–211.

Poole, E. L. 1940. A life history sketch of the Allegheny woodrat. *J. Mammal.* 21: 249–270.

Spencer, D. L. 1968. Sympatry and hybridization of the eastern and southern plains wood rats. Unpubl. Ph.D. diss. Oklahoma State University, Stillwater. 85 pp.

Wiley, R. W. 1980. *Neotoma floridana*. **Mammalian Species No. 139.** Amer. Soc. Mammal. 7 pp. [Does not distinguish between *N. magister* and *N. floridana*.]

## VOLES, MUSKRATS, AND LEMMINGS, Subfamily Arvicolinae

The arvicolines were long known as "microtines," but a different nomenclature was necessary to better reflect our current understanding of evolutionary relationships within the group. The arvicolines feed essentially on green vegetation, a food that wears teeth down very rapidly. They have evolved two major adaptations for dealing with the tough cellulose in this food: rootless teeth and flat, grinding occlusal surfaces on the molariform teeth. Rootless teeth generally continue to grow throughout the life of the animal (the teeth of older muskrats and red-backed voles develop roots), thus preventing early tooth loss; and the flat surfaces help in grinding the food.

There are nine species of arvicoline rodents in five genera in the eastern United States, 26 genera and 143 species worldwide.

## KEY TO THE GENERA
### OF THE SUBFAMILY ARVICOLINAE

1. Tail long, laterally flattened, animal more than 300 mm in total length (see also nutria, p. 389)............... *Ondatra* (p. 360)
1. Tail round or terete; animal less than 300 mm in total length ..........................2
2. Animal large (suggesting a small muskrat), usually more than 250 mm long; tail relatively long, at least one-third of total length .................... *Neofiber* (p. 356)
2. Animal smaller, usually less than 200 mm long; tail relatively short, less than one-third of total length ..........................3
3. A faint, shallow groove on outer anterior surface of incisors; tail very short, less than length of hind foot......... *Synaptomys* (p. 365)
3. Incisors lacking a groove; tail usually longer than length of hind foot....................4
4. Pelage generally reddish (sometimes grayish or blackish); posterior edge of palate forming a shelf, not connecting dorsally with skull proper at its posterior end........ *Clethrionomys*
4. Pelage brown; posterior edge of palate connecting dorsally with skull proper, thus not forming a shelf ....... *Microtus* (p. 339)

## Southern Red-Backed Vole
### *Clethrionomys gapperi*
(Vigors)            Color plate 11

DESCRIPTION. *Clethrionomys gapperi* is usually reddish-colored. It has small eyes, relatively prominent ears reaching above the fur, and a short tail. The pelage is characterized by a broad rusty or reddish dorsal band, grading into buffy on the sides, and pale gray underparts. The summer pelage is darker and more subdued. Immature animals exhibit a less prominent reddish dorsal stripe. A pronounced gray phase is occasionally found, the reddish dorsal stripe replaced by a brown or grayish-black pattern, causing the animal to resemble a meadow vole. Most of the gray animals are from north of the Gulf of St. Lawrence, but we took one in Wise

*Southern red-backed vole,* Clethrionomys gapperi *(Roger W. Barbour)*

County, Virginia, 5 km (3 miles) southeast of Big Stone Gap on 24 June 1967. (An unpublished work by Davis, Dalby, and Barnes at Clarion University indicates that gray is the dominant gene and red the recessive gene.) The posterior edge of the palate of *C. gapperi* forms a straight edge between the two sides of the maxillary bones, in contrast to the structure of the palate in other microtines.

Northern New England individuals differ from typical *gapperi* in their strongly ochraceous tints and almost entire lack of red. Individuals from the southern Appalachians are decidedly larger than their northern relatives. The broad, dull-chestnut dorsal stripe on these southern voles spreads out laterally, fading into the fulvous suffusion of the sides, which in turn encroaches on the white fur of the belly. The belly is usually strongly washed with ochraceous. The red-backed vole of mountainous southeastern Kentucky and southwestern Virginia is dark dorsally and a duller buff on the sides.

MEASUREMENTS. Average measurements of 20 adults from western New York and northern Pennsylvania (Allegheny County) were: total length 138.5 (123–155), tail 38 (34–44), hind foot 19 (17–20.5) mm; and weight 20–28 grams. Average measurements of 16 adults from Mount Washington, New Hampshire, were: total length 152, tail 40, hind foot 19.2 mm.

Twenty adults from the Great Smoky Mountains averaged: total length 146, tail 44.7, hind foot 20 mm. Eight adults from Black Mountain, near Lynch, Harlan County, Kentucky, averaged: total length 153, tail 38, hind foot 19.5 mm.

Diploid number = 56.

TOOTH FORMULA

$$\frac{1}{1} \quad \frac{0}{0} \quad \frac{0}{0} \quad \frac{3}{3} \quad = \quad 16$$

DISTRIBUTION. The red-backed vole occurs in the forested regions of eastern United States, from Maine and New York south through the Appalachians to northern Alabama, and also in northern Michigan and Wisconsin. Isolated populations are in New Jersey, eastern and western Pennsylvania, and Ohio. This species also occurs in the entire southern tier of provinces in Canada, and across the northern United States to the Pacific, farther south in the mountains.

HABITAT. The cool, shaded woods and moss-covered boulders are the haunts of the red-backed vole. The treeless alpine summit of bleak Mount Washington, where they are one of the most abundant mammals, the cold, damp sphagnum bogs of New Jersey, the spruce-covered, cloud-hidden summits of the towering Smoky Mountains, and the aspen meadows of northern Wisconsin all harbor these handsome little rodents. The red-backed vole seldom ventures from the forest, although it may be found in the grassy clearings of wooded regions, or on the treeless "balds" of the North Carolina mountains, and Gordon Kirkland (1990) reports that it commonly inhabits clearcut areas. In the southern part of its range it is mostly restricted to isolated bogs or mountaintops.

When introduced with *Peromyscus manicula-*

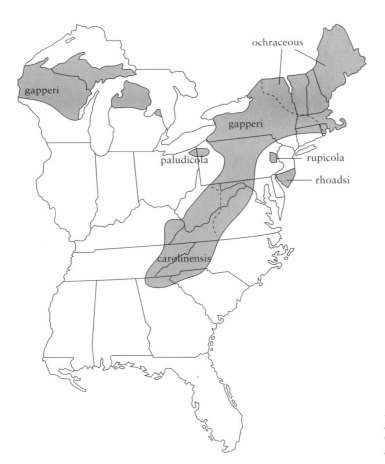

*Distribution of the southern red-backed vole,* Clethrionomys gapperi, *in the eastern United States*

*tus* on islands off the coast of Maine on which *Microtus pennsylvanicus* was resident, the red-backs displaced both *Peromyscus* and *Microtus* from the woods (Crowell and Pimm, 1976), and a complementary pattern with *Napaeozapus* has been noted in New Hampshire (Lovejoy, 1973).

HABITS. The red-backed vole makes little pretense of preparing elaborate tunnels like those of the meadow vole. It shares with other small woodland creatures the burrows made by moles and shrews, or wanders about under the shelter of fallen leaves. Unlike the deer mouse with its hopping gait, this species progresses by trotting. It is also an agile climber, scampering over the fallen logs or running up the windfalls to feed on the lichens and succulent edibles that carpet the rotting limbs. It may be active at any time, but tends to be nocturnal in warmer periods, more diurnal in winter. We have several times seen it about in broad daylight, scampering over the forest floor, its coat blending admirably with the forest carpet of dead beech leaves. Voles of this species will nest in various cavities, abandoned holes of other species, or nests of other small mammals, and one nest was located in a sphagnum hammock. The nests, globular in form and lined with various plant matter, range from 75 to 100 mm in diameter.

The red-backed vole is usually thought of as an inhabitant of the forest floor, but three were caught in traps for flying squirrels 2 to 3 meters (7 to 10 feet) above the ground (Muul and Carlson, 1963). *Clethrionomys gapperi* is known to have a "trilling song," and several individuals occasionally join in.

FOOD AND FEEDING. The red-back feeds on a variety of nuts, seeds, berries, green vegetation, succulent roots, and fungi. We have examined many stomachs but seldom found insect remains. Cut leaves of wild lily-of-the-valley (*Maianthemum*), bunchberry (*Cornus canadensis*), and other boreal plants here and there in the runs and among the rocks where this species abounds indicate its predilection for green vegetation. Fallen blueberries and the blackberries and raspberries that grow in the open woodland glades provide many meals. *Endogone*, other genera of related hypogeous fungi, and other fungi found in the soil are staple foods of

this species in late summer and fall. These fungi often make up about 20% of the diet of this species, even on clearcuts (Schloyer, 1977). Fisher (1968) found that *Endogone* and related genera comprised between 17.3 and 46.5% of the total food in different samples of red-backed voles in summer and fall in New York. In 1961–62, 25 of 76 voles contained 100% fungi.

Because this species is awake even during the most severe winter weather, when it cannot obtain adequate food, it must lay aside large stores of food during times of plenty. In November, Hamilton saw one of these mice busy cutting the petioles from the leaves of wintergreen and carrying them to an underground cache, and a friend once saw a dozen of these mice, in an afternoon, all busily searching for beechnuts, which they industriously carried to some storage place. Bark and roots are the main winter foods.

REPRODUCTION AND DEVELOPMENT. Breeding is from late winter or very early spring to late in the fall. Hamilton found large embryos in New York specimens taken in early December. The young, born after a gestation of 17–19 days, vary in number from two to eight, the litters larger at greater elevations and higher latitudes. The young mice grow rapidly and are capable of breeding at two to four months of age. Measurements of newborn at birth are crown-rump 30, total length 39, tail 6, hind foot 6 mm; and weight 1.7 to 2.3 grams. The young crawl at five days and 4.4 grams. The eyes open at 10 to 15 days. Weaning is usually completed by day 17. One litter follows another through the warmer months. The males apparently do not help care for the young, but nonetheless remain in the nest with the female and the litter, and leave when the young grow larger.

POPULATION CHARACTERISTICS. In the northern part of their range, red-backs are often the most numerous of all small mammals. In the White Mountains of New Hampshire and the Adirondacks of New York they are at times incredibly abundant, but there seems to be no well-marked population cycle in this species. Numbers range up to 65 per ha (26 per acre), declining gradually in winter. Home ranges vary from about 0.01 to 0.50 ha (0.02 to 1.2 acre), the ranges larger under snow. The autumn freeze, midwinter, and spring thaw all may be critical or stressful periods for this species.

ENEMIES. This animal is important in the diet of short-tailed weasels and hawks and certainly many other predators, and it is the major food of the American marten, *Martes americana.*

PARASITES AND DISEASE. Fleas, lice, ticks, and mites all parasitize this species, the mite *Listrophorus mexicanus* being exceedingly abundant. The mite *Glycyphagus hylandi* is restricted to this species and chipmunks. Protozoans, cestodes, and nematodes have been reported as internal parasites.

RELATION TO HUMANS. Occasionally, these mice prove a nuisance to plantings of ornamentals, and Merriam (1984) related how they girdle foot-thick trees to a height of a meter or more (3 or 4 feet) above the ground. The damage to deciduous trees may thus be great, but it is usually of a local nature. Merriam also remarked on the tender and well-flavored flesh of this mouse.

AREAS FOR FURTHER WORK. Information on social behavior and on the relationship of the male and female during the raising of the young would be interesting, and much more could be learned about food caches in this species. How does the red-back obtain underground fungi? Also valuable would be a comparative study of its ectoparasites and nest fauna.

## SUBSPECIES

*Clethrionomys gapperi* is a northern species, ranging across most of Canada and south into the United States. It is widespread in the northern part of its range, particularly in the mountains, but to the south it is restricted to disjunct populations in isolated bogs or mountaintops, where it may thus develop distinctive races.

### Clethrionomys gapperi gapperi (Vigors)

As described above. Occurs in virtually all of the eastern United States range of the species.
Type locality: Between Toronto and Lake Simcoe, Ontario.

Other currently recognized eastern subspecies:
*C. gapperi ochraceus* (Miller)
*C. gapperi carolinensis* (Merriam)
*C. gapperi maurus* Kellogg

### Clethrionomys gapperi paludicola Doutt

Similar to *C. gapperi gapperi*, but with a lighter back. This race is more golden, the sides are paler, and the belly is more washed with buffy. Distinguished from the lower Appalachian forms by the much lighter, more yellowish color of the back and sides; the belly and the underside of the tail are paler and more washed with buffy. Subspecies *paludicola* is known only from Pymatuning Swamp in extreme northwestern Pennsylvania, and at Conneaut Creek in extreme northeastern Ohio.
Type locality: Pymatuning Swamp, 1000 feet (300 meters), 4 miles (6 km) west of Linesville, Crawford Co., Pennsylvania.

### Clethrionomys gapperi rhoadsi Stone

In the cedar swamps and sphagnum bogs of southern New Jersey, where only diffused light penetrates, *C. gapperi* is much darker than typical *gapperi*, with a darker tail pencil. Unlike those of the typical form, the colors of the upper body reach down on the sides and are abruptly separated from the whitish underparts. The hind feet are dusky gray. *Clethrionomys gapperi rhoadsi* is slightly smaller than the type, ten adults from Ocean, Atlantic, Cape May, and Gloucester counties, averaging: total length 136 (121–150), tail 36.8 (33–40), hind foot 18.4 (18–20) mm; and weight 18–30 grams. This subspecies is apparently isolated in southern New Jersey, from the region of Lakehurst, northern Ocean Co., to the Delaware River and Cape May.
Type locality: Mays Landing, Atlantic Co., New Jersey, about halfway between Mays Landing Dam and Mare Run on Great Egg Harbor River.

### Clethrionomys gapperi rupicola Poole

This is another apparently isolated mountain population that has been separated long enough from other populations to have developed morphological distinctness. Individuals of *C. g. rupicola* are large, as large as or larger than redbacks from the southern Appalachians, and they are dull grayish. The subspecies is known only from Kittatinny Ridge of Berks and Schuylkill counties, Pennsylvania.

Type locality: Pinnacle, Berks Co., Pennsylvania.

### LITERATURE

Crowell, K. L., and S. L. Pimm. 1976. Competition and niche shifts of mice introduced onto small islands. *Oikos* 27: 251–258.

Davis, D. B. D., Jr., P. L. Dalby, and W. S. Barnes. The inheritance of coat color dimorphism in the red-backed vole (*Clethrionomys gapperi*). Unpubl. report, Clarion University, Clarion, Pa. 24 pp.

Fisher, R. L. 1968. An ecological study of the red-backed vole, *Clethrionomys gapperi gapperi* (Vigors) in central New York. Unpubl. Ph.D. diss., Cornell University. 79 pp.

Kirkland, G. L., Jr. 1990. Patterns of initial small mammal community change after clearcutting of temperate North American forests. *Oikos* 59: 319–320.

Lovejoy, D. A. 1973. Ecology of the woodland jumping mouse (*Napaeozapus insignis*) in New Hampshire. *Canadian Field-Nat.* 87: 145–149.

Merriam, C. H. 1884. The vertebrates of the Adirondack region: The Mammalia. *Transactions Linnaean Society of New York* 1: 1–214.

Merritt, J. F. 1981. *Clethrionomys gapperi.* **Mammalian Species No. 146.** Amer. Soc. Mammal. 9 pp.

Muul, I., and F. W. Carlson. 1963. Red-back vole in trees. *J. Mammal.* 44: 415–416.

Schloyer, C. R. 1977. Food habits of *Clethrionomys gapperi* on clearcuts in West Virginia. *J. Mammal.* 58: 677–678.

Watts, C. H. S. 1970. A field experiment on interspecific interactions in the red-backed vole, *Clethrionomys gapperi.* *J. Mammal.* 51: 341–347.

Wharton, C. H., and J. J. White. 1967. The red-backed vole, *Clethrionomys gapperi*, in north Georgia. *J. Mammal.* 48: 670–672.

## Voles of the Genus *Microtus*

There are four species of voles of the genus *Microtus* in the eastern United States (five, if one counts *M. breweri*, which we consider a subspecies of *M. pennsylvanicus*).

Voles of this genus are often the main small herbivores of open fields. They can invade habitats quickly and build toward large populations, then disappear as the habitat disappears. *Microtus* in fact is often only a temporary in-

habitant of an area, since many grasslands, except those constituting prairies, are simply the early successional stages in a progression toward woodlands. Meadow voles are seldom found in agricultural habitats other than in hayfield or meadow-type crops such as alfalfa, clover, timothy, and wheat. At times, exploding populations of voles have caused problems in these sorts of habitats. Their depredations can even lead to denudation. Vole outbreaks leading to major damage have generally occurred in the West. One of the worst was in Humboldt County, Nevada, from 1906 to 1908. Voles increased to about 25,000 per acre there and totally destroyed about 10,000 ha (25,000 acres) of alfalfa. And in one case in Illinois, they caused the loss of about 25% of a wheat crop.

Microtines have adapted to a high-fiber, low-nutrient diet. The enamel loops on their high-crowned molars provide hard surfaces for grinding. The caecum and large intestine are enlarged, those of the most herbivorous vole species being the longest of all. The functions of the enlarged caecum are the digestion of fiber and the production of protein and B-vitamins.

Little is known of nutrition in microtine diets (see Batzli, 1985), but it is clear that different microtine species eat and prefer different foods and have different nutrient requirements. Moreover, different plant compounds affect different microtines in different ways, and some compounds in plants are detrimental to microtines. As is true of all herbivores, voles derive little sodium from their diet, and they crave it. They conserve sodium by releasing minimal amounts of it in the urine and feces.

Voles of the genus *Microtus* exhibit a diverse array of mating systems, from extended family groups with monogamy as the predominant system (*Microtus pinetorum* and *M. ochrogaster*) to solitary males and mother/young units the females of which pursue either polygynous relationships (as in *M. montanus*) or promiscuous relationships (as in *M. pennsylvanicus*).

Reproduction in *Microtus* is controlled by an internal annual rhythm and several environmental stimuli: photoperiod, light intensity, temperature, nutrition, social cues, and certain chemical substances that occur in plants. It appears that there are pheromones in male urine that stimulate female reproduction: estrus is pheromonally induced, and ovulation is induced by either copulation or pheromones. Postpartum estrus also occurs in voles. The presence of a familiar male, with or without copulation, enhances the development of corpora lutea and early pregnancy, but the presence of a strange male can trigger the cessation of pregnancy, impair litter survival, and perhaps inhibit prolactin secretion. Certain chemical substances in plants, notably 6-methoxybenzoxazolinone (6-MBOA), lead to increased uterine and ovarian weights, increased testicular hypertrophy, and stimulated pregnancy rates. Other substances of plants (cinnamic acids and related vinyphenols) may bring on the cessation of reproductive activity. In many small rodents, gestation is lengthened somewhat if the female is still lactating for her prior litter; in New World *Microtus*, apparently it is not.

Although most species of mammals exhibit marked, sporadic changes in population size, some of the voles, the lynx, and the snowshoe hare are species that can be termed cyclic in this regard. That a population exhibits cyclic population behavior implies that there are major increases and decreases in population size, and that these changes are rather regular in both interval and amplitude. Lynx, hare, and lemming cycles were known much earlier, but Hamilton (1937) was the first to indicate that such cycles occur in *Microtus pennsylvanicus*. He observed that the cycles were associated not simply with good environmental conditions, but with changes in the reproductive success of the voles. During population increases, litter sizes and number of litters per season increased and the age of females at first breeding decreased; in the declining phase, these factors reversed. Populations as disparate as ten and 300 individuals per ha (4 and 120 per acre) are typical of population dearths and peaks in good habitat. Some argue that the population changes in *Microtus* species are not regular enough to be termed cycles, but they are prominent, and not at all like the more random changes one finds in populations of *Peromyscus* and other small mammals. We think "cycles" is an apt term in this case, but if one objects to its use here, then a new term is needed to distinguish the population behavior of *Microtus* from that of other species.

Many factors, such as habitat quality and levels of predation, affect population size at any given time, and many of these and other factors have been proposed as the causative agents of cycles (Taitt & Krebs, 1985). Basically, it seems to us, the declining phase of a cycle is a response to stress-induced changes in reproductive success. When populations are low in relation to the number of individuals the habitat can support, there is little stress and reproduction increases. But populations in voles can increase quite rapidly, quickly reaching levels the habitat cannot support. Overpopulation induces physiological stress, which in turn favors those factors that tend to inhibit reproduction. Cyclic population behavior could have evolved in voles as a strategy for taking advantage of good habitat rapidly when it is available and limiting populations in poor habitat. One test of this idea would be to see if voles always increase when in suitable and unexploited environment (whatever stage of cycle they may have been in at the outset of the test) or immediately decrease if large numbers of them are *introduced* into such an environment (again, without respect to cycle stage). After several years, normal cycling should ultimately become established if cycling is a normal strategy in these animals.

The fact that voles exhibit cyclic population behavior does not mean they vary between specific highs and lows (say, lows of ten per ha and highs of 100 per ha) and over exact spans of time (say, every three to four years). The picture is much more complicated than that (see Taitt and Krebs, 1985). Superimposed on a basic pattern of cyclic behavior in voles of the genus *Microtus* (some of them, anyway) are differences in habitat quality. These differences tend immediately to limit the population highs and lows through time. Moreover, habitat quality can change through time, and there are annual fluctuations (as well as cyclic changes) in *Microtus* populations. Populations increase greatly in the reproductive season; and because of the great predation pressure on voles, they decrease rapidly during the nonreproductive season. Consider further the phenomenal ability of these species to invade an area and increase their populations rapidly to take advantage of a newly produced, but likely short-lived, grassy field, be it natural or cultivated. Further, some populations, especially those in northern areas, exhibit more cyclic behavior than others.

Voles of the genus *Microtus* often exhibit exploratory behavior. They seek out new resources while running along edges of things, but they seldom jump, and they do not climb. All are apparently accomplished diggers, digging by simultaneous use of the rear paws and alternating use of the forepaws. *Microtus* is generally active day and night and uses well-established runway systems.

Several species of *Microtus* produce vocalizations, apparently defensive in nature, and neonates of at least some species, including *M. pennsylvanicus* and *M. ochrogaster*, produce ultrasonic calls (Colvin, 1973). Colvin believed that the calls elicit parental attention. The main agonistic display of the dominant animal consists of raising the body off the ground with the tail parallel to the ground behind and the ears held forward. One or both forefeet may be raised and teeth-gnashing may occur.

Mossing (1975) measured small-mammal activity with passage counters (small tubes placed in tunnel 7 cm by 5 cm). A small gate in the center of the tube is attached to a microswitch. When an animal passes through the tube the switch closes and the passage is recorded on an event recorder. More extensive use of these devices could be of great value to *Microtus* researchers.

In penned populations, the predatory effects of larger carnivores (feral cats, raccoons, foxes) resulted in more losses to a population of voles than did those of small carnivores (weasels) and raptors (Lin and Batzli, 1995), and snakes had low impact throughout the year. Raptor depredation peaked in autumn.

An excellent book on the genus *Microtus* is that edited by Robert H. Tamarin (1985).

## LITERATURE CITED

Batzli, G. O. 1985. Nutrition. In: R. H. Tamarin, ed., *The Biology of New World* Microtus, pp. 779–811. Amer. Soc. Mammal., Spec. Publ. No. 8.

Boonstra, R., B. S. Gilbert, and C. J. Krebs. 1993. Mating systems and sexual dimorphism in mass in microtines. *J. Mammal.* 74: 224–229.

Colvin, D. V. 1973. Analysis of acoustic structure and function in ultrasounds of neonatal *Microtus*. *Behav.* 44: 234–263.

Hamilton, W. J., Jr. 1937. The biology of microtine cycles. *J. Agric. Research* 54: 779–790.

Heske, E. J., and R. S. Ostfeld. 1990. Sexual dimorphism in size, relative size of testes and mating systems in North American voles. *J. Mammal.* 71: 510–519.

Lin, Y. K., and G. O. Batzli. 1995. Predation on voles: An experimental approach. *J. Mammal.* 76: 1003–1012.

Mossing, T. 1975. Measuring small mammal locomotory activity with passage counters. *Oikos* 26: 237–239.

Ostfeld, R. S., and E. J. Heske. 1993. Sexual dimorphism and mating systems in voles. *J. Mammal.* 74: 230–233.

Taitt, M. J., and C. J. Krebs. 1985. Population dynamics and cycles. In: R. H. Tamarin, ed., *Biology of New World* Microtus, pp. 567–620. Amer. Soc. Mammal., Spec. Publ. No. 8.

Tamarin, R. H., ed. 1985. *Biology of New World* Microtus. Amer. Soc. Mammal., Spec. Publ. No. 8. 893 pp.

## KEY TO THE VOLES OF THE GENUS *MICROTUS*

1. Tail about equal to hind foot in length; fur very fine and molelike (tending to lie either way); skull very similar to that of *M. ochrogaster*, the third upper molar showing only two triangles between anterior and posterior "loops" . . . . . . . . . . . . . . . . . . . . . *M. pinetorum*
1. Tail longer than hind foot; fur coarser; the third upper molar showing two, four, or six triangles between anterior and posterior "loops" . . . . . . . . . . . . . . . . . . . . . . . . . . . . . . 2
2. Nose yellowish; third upper molar showing six triangles. . . . . . . . . . . . . . . . . *M. chrotorrhinus*
2. Nose not yellowish; third upper molar showing two or four triangles . . . . . . . . . . . . . . . 3
3. Ventral fur silvery; tail usually much more than twice the length of hind foot; third upper molar showing four triangles . . . *M. pennsylvanicus*
3. Ventral fur usually buff-colored; tail usually about twice the length of hind foot; third upper molar showing two (three) triangles . . . . . . . . . . . . . . . . . . . . . *M. ochrogaster*

## Rock Vole *Microtus chrotorrhinus* (Miller)                    Color plate 11

DESCRIPTION. In general appearance, the rock vole is similar to the meadow vole, *Microtus pennsylvanicus*, but it can be distinguished by its orange or saffron nose. In body characters, too, it is similar to the meadow vole, but differs in having a larger ear and a smaller hind foot. In summer pelage the upperparts are grizzled

*Rock vole,* Microtus chrotorrhinus *(Roger W. Barbour)*

MEASUREMENTS. Average measurements of five adults from Mt. Washington, New Hampshire (the type locality), were: total length 168.5, tail 48, hind foot 19.5 mm; and weight 30–50 grams. Of five from Ulster County, New York, they were: 149 (133–172), 42 (39–48), 19.2 (19–20) mm; and weight 28.4 (21–39) grams. Diploid number = 60.

TOOTH FORMULA

$$\frac{1}{1} \quad \frac{0}{0} \quad \frac{0}{0} \quad \frac{3}{3} \quad = \quad 16$$

brown or bister, mixed with black. The facial region and to a lesser extent the area below the ears is orange-rufous or saffron, and the same color is faintly defined on the rump. The belly is silvery gray to plumbeous, the feet are silvery gray above, and the tail is sepia above, pale below.

DISTRIBUTION. The rock vole occurs from Labrador to southeastern Ontario and extreme northeastern Minnesota and south in the eastern United States to North Carolina and Tennessee. Its distribution is spotty, and it occurs only in the most suitable localities.

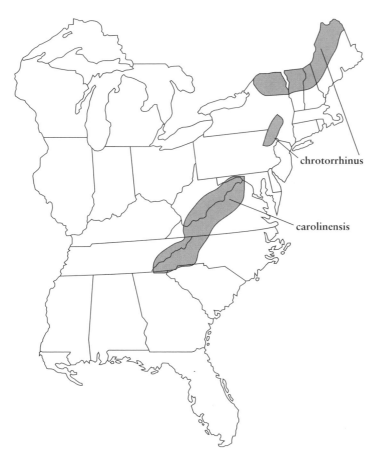

chrotorrhinus

carolinensis

*Distribution of the rock vole,* Microtus chrotorrhinus, *in the eastern United States*

HABITAT. Among the shaded retreats formed by the moss-covered boulders of northern mountains, or about the logs of the high, humid southern mountains, this little saffron-snouted mouse passes its days, seldom seen even by the professional mammalogist. Collectors have taken specimens in the rock slides of Mt. Washington, well above timberline. It is not uncommon in the Adirondack and Catskill mountains of New York, or in the cool forests of northeastern Pennsylvania, but other species usually greatly outnumber the rock vole, and it is uncommon in collections. Whitaker and Robert Fisher nonetheless found it to be abundant on Slide Mountain in the Catskills of New York, and took 25 individuals in two nights. Edwin and Roy Komarek (1938) took 37 specimens in the Great Smoky Mountains. Here, the mice were found even on the high grassy balds, among the rocky outcrops on the summit. These voles sometimes benefit from clearcutting.

HABITS. The habits of these microtines are poorly known. They live in shallow burrows and traverse runways that thread about rocks, and in some places they appear to be partial to a ferny habitat. They are active day or night, but perhaps are most active in the daytime. Fecal middens and piles of cut vegetation under rocks in a wooded or open talus slope are clear signs of the presence of this vole.

FOOD AND FEEDING. Whitaker and Robert L. Martin examined the stomachs of 47 individuals from New Hampshire, New York, Labrador, and Quebec, and found the most important food item to be bunchberry, *Cornus canadensis*, which made up nearly half the stomach contents, followed by unidentified green vegetation, lepidopterous larvae, and wavy-leaved thread moss, *Atrichum undulatum*. Rock voles will also feed on small rootstocks, green grasses, fresh shoots, and various berries. In Minnesota, they feed extensively on blueberry leaves and stems and bluebeard lily (*Clintonia*) plants. These voles presumably store food for later use.

REPRODUCTION AND DEVELOPMENT. The young are born from early spring well into the fall, the mean number of offspring per litter in differing localities running from 2.9 to 3.7.

POPULATION CHARACTERISTICS. Locally, living in small colonies, these mice may be quite abundant, but intensive trapping will soon take every member of a colony. They are absent from extensive areas that appear suitable for inhabitancy.

The thrill of trapping a rare mouse or shrew is graphically told by Morris M. Green (1930). He wrote:

Near Opperman's Pass, southwestern Wyoming County [Pennsylvania], in mid-October, 1927, my attention was drawn to a north-facing swale, filled with a tangle of ferns, moss-covered logs and boulders, shaded by yellow birches. The tinkling of an underground stream, beneath the boulders, could be plainly heard. A geologist might have said that this was a glacial moraine. There were many cozy little nooks between the boulders, for little forest folk, so I carefully placed a dozen mouse traps there. The next day there were a New York deer mouse, a short-tailed shrew, a red-backed mouse, in some of the traps. Peering down a cavity at one trap, there appeared to be a half-grown meadow mouse there. Drawing the trap out in the sunlight, my heart beat fast when I saw that the mouse had a saffron-colored nose with a brown body. Good luck had enabled me to record the first specimen of the rock vole from Pennsylvania.

PARASITES AND DISEASE. A number of parasites have been found on or in this species, including six species of chiggers, 17 of other mites, one tick, one botfly, nine species of fleas, three cestodes, and three nematodes. Timm (1985) details these data.

RELATION TO HUMANS. This species is little known even to professional mammalogists and therefore has little known relation to man.

AREAS FOR FURTHER WORK. Much more information is needed on virtually all phases of the biology of this species, its food, its mating and reproduction system, its distribution and abundance, and the factors limiting its distribution.

## SUBSPECIES

Two subspecies from the eastern United States have been described, one from the north and one from the southern Appalachians, and they appear to be separated geographically. Populations of this species are often separated by great gaps, and thus have great potential for divergent evolution and speciation.

### *Microtus chrotorrhinus chrotorrhinus* (Miller)

As described above. Occurs in northern New York and northern New England and (disjunctively) in southern New York and northeastern Pennsylvania.

Type locality: Mt. Washington, Coos Co., New Hampshire.

### *Microtus chrotorrhinus carolinensis* Komarek
### Southern Appalachian Rock Vole

Rock voles of the southern Appalachians are darker than, and differ from, the type in having a larger skull, a longer upper tooth row, and heavier zygomata. The upperparts are a dark, blackish bister; the sides are slightly blacker; the nose, to the eyes, is a deep orange-rufous; there is a small spot of rufous back of the ear, though this is not a constant feature; the underparts are dark plumbeous; above, the tail is colored like the back, and below, it is paler. Measurements of the skull, with those of typical *M. c. chrotorrhinus* following in parentheses, are: occipitonasal length, 26.5 (25.8) mm; greatest zygomatic breadth, 15.1 (14.3) mm; upper molar series, 7.1 (6.5) mm; weight, 26 (47) grams.

Type locality: Great Smoky Mts., North Carolina, about 5 miles [8 km] north of Smokemont, Swain Co., on a tributary of Bradley Fork, a small branch of the Oconalufty River, at 3200 feet [975 meters].

### LITERATURE

Green, M. M. 1930. A contribution to the mammalogy of the north mountain region of Pennsylvania. Ardmore, Pa., privately printed. 19 pp.

Kirkland, G. L., Jr. 1977. The rock vole, *Microtus chrotorrhinus* (Miller) (Mammalia: Rodentia) in West Virginia. *Ann. Carnegie Mus.* 46: 45–53.

Kirkland, G. L., Jr., and J. J. Jannett, Jr. 1982. *Microtus chrotorrhinus*. **Mammalian Species No. 180.** Amer. Soc. Mammal. 5 pp.

Komarek, E. V., and R. Komarek. 1938. Mammals of the Great Smoky Mountains. *Bull. Chicago Acad. Sci.* 5: 137–162.

Timm, R. M. 1985. Parasites. In: R. H. Tamarin, ed. *The Biology of the New World* Microtus, pp. 455–534. Amer. Soc. Mammal., Spec. Publ. No. 8.

Timm, R. M., L. R. Heaney, and D. D. Baird. 1977. Natural history of rock voles (*Microtus chrotorrhinus*) in Minnesota. *Canadian Field-Nat.* 91: 177–181.

## Prairie Vole *Microtus ochrogaster* (Wagner)

DESCRIPTION. The prairie vole is similar in appearance to the meadow vole, *Microtus pennsylvanicus*, from which it may usually be distinguished by its buffy belly (some individuals are

*Prairie vole,* Microtus ochrogaster

white-bellied) and shorter tail. Of further help are its having only five plantar tubercles and the grizzled appearance of the rather coarse dorsal pelage. The best means of identification, however, is to examine the crown of the third upper molar, which has but two triangles between the anterior and posterior loops. The ears are small and nearly hidden in the fur. The feet are pale buffy, and the tail is similarly colored, except for a narrow, slightly darker, dorsal stripe. Ohio individuals, which often have white underparts, have been described as *M. o. ohioensis*.

MEASUREMENTS. Measurements of ten adults from Illinois averaged: total length 148 (134–162), tail 31 (25–37), hind foot 19 (17–22) mm; and weight 25–55 grams.

Diploid number = 54.

TOOTH FORMULA

$$\frac{1}{1} \ \frac{0}{0} \ \frac{0}{0} \ \frac{3}{3} \ = \ 16$$

DISTRIBUTION. The prairie vole occurs from central Ohio and western West Virginia westward through southern Wisconsin, Illinois, Kentucky, and northwestern Tennessee. West of the Mississippi, it occurs west to southeastern Alberta, eastern Wyoming, eastern Colorado, and northern Oklahoma.

HABITAT. The prairie vole prefers drier, more sandy sites than its counterpart, the meadow vole, and it can subsist in situations offering much less ground cover. The meadow vole is often partial to grass/sedge habitats, the prairie vole to grass/sedge/forb habitats. The prairie vole has invaded much of Indiana and Illinois where farmland has replaced the forest.

In Clark County, Wisconsin, Schmidt (1931) found these mice abundant in sandy plains and on sandy slopes of sandstone mounds and in the woods of jackpine and jack oak, habitats that presented no heavy covering of grass. The mice were living in small colonies on large knolls formed by the uprooting of trees. The colonies, each of which numbered three or four adults and several young, were characterized by the great extent of their burrows. Most of the original prairie habitat of this species is now gone, and the species lives mostly in the remnants of dry, sparse grasslands resulting from farming operations. Orchards and areas along interstates and other highways often provide habitat for this species.

Under field conditions, *Microtus ochrogaster* and *M. pennsylvanicus* do not appear to compete. They avoid competition by partitioning the habitat, *M. ochrogaster* occupying drier, more sparse areas and *M. pennsylvanicus* occupying

*Distribution of the prairie vole,*
Microtus ochrogaster, *in the*
*eastern United States*

the more moist, heavily vegetated areas often of nearly pure grass. The two may occur together where the habitats blend or interdigitate.

HABITS. Prairie voles make their summer nests of shredded grasses in clumps of grass. The nests are about 125 mm (5 inches) wide by 80 mm (3 inches) deep. Prairie voles may be active at any time, but are most active at dawn and dusk.

These voles were said by Kennicott to build their winter nests in old anthills. But where they build them directly on the uncultivated prairie, they are characterized by little mounds of earth at the entrance. The burrows are reasonably shallow but are remarkable for their numerous, complicated chambers and side passages. The bulky nest of dried grasses is placed in one of these chambers, and has but a single, small opening on one side.

FOOD AND FEEDING. The food of the prairie vole is not unlike that of the eastern *M. pennsylvanicus*, in consisting almost entirely of finely ground vegetation; but in keeping with the greater numbers of plant species in its habitat, *M. ochrogaster* has a more varied diet. Earl G. Zimmerman (1965) found bluegrass, clover, lespedeza, old witchgrass (*Panicum*), fleabane, plantain, fescue, and black medic to be some of the more important foods at an Indiana locality.

These mice appear to store food for winter habitually, and several writers mention finding sizable quantities of tubers, roots, and small bulbs in their winter chambers.

REPRODUCTION AND DEVELOPMENT. In contrast to the reproductive system of the meadow vole, male and female prairie voles form monogamous pairs, sharing a nest and a home range, guarding each other, and seldom breeding with outsiders. The male takes the lead in attacking unfamiliar males and females, and the female will accept a strange male only if her mate is gone. Both male and female help in caring for the young, and the male may even build a second nest and care for some of the young there. Other paternal activities include nest and runway construction and food storage. The older young from one litter may help in the care of

the young of the next litter, thus allowing the mother time to be away from the nest for feeding or other activities.

The reduced number of teats (six) in this species argues for smaller litters than are produced by *M. pennsylvanicus*, and this is indeed the case. The number of embryos varies from one to eight, but most litters are of three or four young. Averages for different localities across the prairie vole's range varied from 3.2 to 5.1 young per litter. Pregnant females were found in every month, but fewer pregnancies were noted in December to January and in June to July. The breeding season usually runs from late March to October, but it can extend throughout the year under the right conditions, as when populations are rapidly increasing prior to peak densities and during particularly mild winters. Neonates, blind and hairless, weigh about 2.8 to 3.1 grams. They have brown fur at two days, the incisors erupt at one to two days, they crawl at four to five days, and the eyes open at five to ten days. They first eat solid food at ten to 14 days and they are weaned at about 12 to 19 days.

POPULATION CHARACTERISTICS. Although these mice are basically monogamous, they sometimes form communal-nesting social groups, mainly by the addition of philopatric offspring and nonrelated adults to male-female pairs (Getz et al., 1990; Getz et al., 1993). This behavior is more prevalent in winter, and although it occurs during the breeding season, as well, juvenile mortality then is usually high, and communal groups are thus usually small. Larger communal groups, equal in size to those forming in winter, formed in summer when predators were experimentally eliminated from the area where the population occurs (Getz et al., 1990). This finding led to the conclusion that formation of communal groups is the norm in this species, and that their number and size is related primarily to rates of juvenile survival (Getz et al., 1993). Mankin and Getz (1994) found that differences in burrow structure were not seasonal. Rather, they were related to the type of social group inhabiting the burrow: the burrows of communal groups were larger and more complex than those inhabited by pairs, and included larger nest chambers, more sections of burrow, and more entrances.

As does the meadow vole, this species exhibits a three- to four-year population cycle, though there is evidence that some populations do not cycle. Populations in Indiana and Illinois in good habitat reach levels of about 130 per ha (52 per acre) at the peaks and four per ha (1.6 per acre) at the lows. Emigration becomes prominent during the peaks of the cycle. Food availability does not appear to be a major cause of the cycles, for populations can decline even while food (and cover) are still abundant. The cyclic increase includes larger litters and an extension of the breeding period through the winter, although the greater litter size may be a function of the increased size of females that develops at this time. Aggressive behavior, especially by males, was more pronounced in peak populations. Reduced breeding parameters coincide with the down phase. Home ranges vary from 0.02–0.11 ha (0.05–0.27 acre), those of males being larger than those of females.

ENEMIES. Most of the avian and mammalian predators, such as red-tailed and rough-legged hawks, harriers (marsh hawks), short-eared owls, and least weasels, that hunt in the drier open-fields habitat of *Microtus ochrogaster* all have to be prime predators on this species. Kestrels also catch them occasionally. (That the least weasel, *Mustela nivalis*, is smaller than its cousin *Mustela erminea* is probably so precisely because *Microtus ochrogaster*, which is smaller than *M. pennsylvanicus*, is its chief prey, whereas *Mustela erminea* is a highly efficient predator on meadow voles.) Many of the snakes occurring in prairies must also feed heavily on *M. ochrogaster*.

PARASITES AND DISEASE. The prairie vole hosts nearly the full range of parasites one would expect on or in this species: 11 species of chiggers, 17 of other mites, four species of ticks, two of lice, 14 of fleas, eight of cestodes, and three of nematodes. For details, see Timm (1985).

RELATION TO HUMANS. Where they range into orchards, prairie voles often cause considerable loss among the young fruit trees by girdling

their bases. Fortunately, they are held in check by the numerous enemies.

AREAS FOR FURTHER WORK. More information is needed on the nests and burrows of these voles, and on their nest and burrow associates, as is the case for *M. pennsylvanicus*. The behavior associated with the formation of piles of cuttings in the runways could also be investigated. When are they made? How? Why?

## SUBSPECIES

There is no evidence of any primary isolating mechanisms separating *M. ochrogaster ohioensis* from *M. o. ochrogaster*, and we therefore do not recognize them as separate subspecies.

*Microtus ochrogaster ochrogaster* (Wagner)

As described above.

Type locality: Probably New Harmony, Posey Co., Indiana.

Other currently recognized eastern subspecies:

*M. ochrogaster ohionensis* Bole & Moulthrop

## LITERATURE

Abramsky, Z., and C. R. Tracy. 1979. Population biology of a "noncycling" population of prairie voles and a hypothesis on the role of migration in regulating microtine cycles. *Ecology* 60: 349–361.

Fitch, H. S. 1957. Aspects of reproduction and development in the prairie vole (*Microtus ochrogaster*). *Univ. Kansas Publ. Mus. Nat. Hist.* 19: 129–161.

Gaines, M. S., and R. K. Rose. 1976. Population dynamics of *Microtus ochrogaster* in eastern Kansas. *Ecology* 57: 1145–1161.

Getz, L. L., C. S. Carter, and L. Gavish. 1981. The mating system of the prairie vole, *Microtus ochrogaster*: Field and laboratory evidence for pair bonding. *Behav. Ecol. Sociobiol.* 8: 189–194.

Getz, L. L., B. J. Klatt, L. Verner, F. R. Cole, and R. L. Lindroth. 1987. Fourteen years of population fluctuations of *Microtus ochrogaster* and *M. pennsylvanicus* in east central Illinois. *Canadian J. Zool.* 65: 1317–1325.

Getz, L. L., B. McGuire, J. E. Hofmann, T. Pizzuto, and B. Frase. 1990. Social organization and mating system of the prairie vole *Microtus ochrogaster*. In: R. H. Tamarin, R. S. Ostfeld, S. R Pugh, and G. Bujalska, eds., *Social Systems and Population Cycles in Voles*, pp. 69–80. Basel, Switzerland: Birkhauser Verlag. 229 pp.

Getz, L. L., B. McGuire, T. Pizzuto, J. E. Hofmann, and B. Frase. 1993. Social organization of the prairie vole (*Microtus ochrogaster*). *J. Mammal.* 74: 44–58.

Harvey, H. J., and R. W. Barbour. 1965. Home range of *Microtus ochrogaster* as determined by modified minimum area method. *J. Mammal.* 46: 298–402.

Jameson, E. W., Jr. 1947. Natural history of the prairie vole (mammalian genus *Microtus*). *Univ. Kansas Publ. Mus. Nat. Hist.* 1: 125–151.

Keller, B. L., and C. J. Krebs. 1970. *Microtus* population biology: III. Reproductive changes in fluctuating populations of *Microtus ochrogaster* and *M. pennsylvanicus* in southern Indiana, 1965–1967. *Ecol. Monogr.* 40: 263–294.

Krebs, C. J., 1970. *Microtus* population biology: Behavioral changes associated with the population cycle in *Microtus ochrogaster* and *M. pennsylvanicus*. *Ecology* 51: 34–52.

———. 1977. Competition between *Microtus pennsylvanicus* and *Microtus ochrogaster*. *Amer. Midland Nat.* 97: 42–49.

Krebs, C. J., B. L. Keller, and R. H. Tamarin. 1969. *Microtus* population biology: Demographic changes in fluctuating populations of *Microtus ochrogaster* and *M. pennsylvanicus* in southern Indiana. *Ecology* 50: 587–607.

Mankin, P. C., and L. L. Getz. 1994. Burrow morphology as related to social organization of *Microtus ochrogaster*. *J. Mammal.* 75: 492–499.

Martin, E. P. 1956. A population study of the prairie vole (*Microtus ochrogaster*). *Univ. Kansas Publ. Mus. Nat. Hist.* 8: 361–416.

Rose, R. K., and M. S. Gaines. 1976. Levels of aggression in fluctuating populations of the prairie vole, *Microtus ochrogaster*, in eastern Kansas. *J. Mammal.* 57: 43–57.

———. 1978. The reproductive cycle of *Microtus ochrogaster* in eastern Kansas. *Ecol. Monogr.* 48: 21–42.

Schmidt, F. J. W. 1931. Mammals of western Clark County, Wisconsin. *J. Mammal.* 12: 99–117.

Thomas, J. A., and E. C. Birnie. 1979. Parental care and mating system of the prairie vole, *Microtus ochrogaster*. *Behav. Ecol. Sociobiol.* 5: 171–186.

Timm, R. M. 1985. Parasites. In: R. H. Tamarin, ed., *The Biology of the New World* Microtus, pp. 455–534. Amer. Soc. Mammal., Spec. Publ. No. 8.

Zimmerman, E. G. 1965. A comparison of food of two species of *Microtus*. *J. Mammal.* 46: 605–612.

## Meadow Vole, Field or Meadow Mouse *Microtus pennsylvanicus* (Ord)　　　Color plate 12

DESCRIPTION. This relatively large, robust vole has a long tail, one that is usually at least twice as long as the hind foot. The fur, dense and soft, is overlaid with a few coarser hairs. The short, rounded ears are prominent, but may be well hidden in the winter pelage. There are six tubercles on the soles of the hind feet (in *M. ochrogaster* there are but five). The last upper molar exhibits four intermediate triangles and a posterior loop (that of *M. ochrogaster* has two intermediate triangles and a posterior loop). The upperparts in summer pelage are a dull chestnut-brown, but a few individuals are bright chestnut. The dorsal pelage is interspersed with numerous black hairs. The belly is silvery, occasionally tinged with buff, as it is in *M. ochrogaster*. The feet and tail are dusky above, paler below, but the tail is not sharply bicolored. The winter pelage is darker, with more gray. Immature individuals are much darker, with black feet and tail. Individuals from the southern part of the range are larger and much darker. Those in a large series from Chincoteague, Virginia, are notably darker than specimens from New York and Michigan, being almost black on the rump.

MEASUREMENTS. Measurements of fifty adults from central New York averaged: total length 167 (149–196), tail 42 (32–57), hind foot 21 (19–23) mm; and weight 25.6 grams. Large adults may exceed 50 grams. Twelve adults from Chincoteague, Virginia, averaged: total length 171, tail 43.5, hind foot 23 mm.

Diploid number = 46.

TOOTH FORMULA

$$\frac{1}{1} \quad \frac{0}{0} \quad \frac{0}{0} \quad \frac{3}{3} = 16$$

DISTRIBUTION. The meadow vole (or field mouse, as it is often called) occurs from Maine to South Carolina and Georgia and westward through Michigan and Wisconsin, northern Illinois, and eastern Kentucky. This species has not definitely been recorded from Tennessee, though it probably occurs in some areas there. An isolated subspecies has recently been described from Florida (Woods et al., 1982). The meadow vole also occurs in much of Canada, south to northeastern Washington, northern Utah, northern New Mexico, and northern Missouri.

HABITAT. This adaptable creature is the most widespread species of *Microtus* in North America. Indeed, few rodents are so widespread or found in such a wide variety of habitats. This vole is best associated with moist fields of dense vegetation consisting chiefly of grasses and sedges. It occurs in low meadows and swampy pastures, in fields with a protecting cover of dead grass and herbs, and in the salt meadows of the coast. Bluegrass fields are especially favored. Less often, it is found in open glades in the woods, where the sun encourages the growth of rank vegetation and herbaceous annuals, and we caught one in a grassy patch at the summit of Mt. Marcy, the highest peak in New York State. It often does very well in grassy areas along the roadside and in orchards.

Klatt and Getz (1987) found that *Microtus pennsylvanicus* invaded areas along the interstate highway system in central Illinois that present thicker, heavier grassy vegetation, greater soil moisture, and fewer dandelions than the sites occupied by *M. ochrogaster*. This finding, which included even a replacement of *M. ochrogaster* by *M. pennsylvanicus*, was apparently related to the differential management of roadsides. These authors concluded that the meadow vole's need for thicker cover was associated with the production of above-ground nests, as contrasted with the prairie vole's below-ground nests. When with other vole species, such as *M. ochrogaster*, *M. pennsylvanicus* occupies the more moist portion of the habitat, but it will coexist in the same habitat with *Sigmodon hispidus*, *Zapus hudsonius*, *Synaptomys cooperi*, and *Oryzomys palustris*. Alicia Linzey found that the meadow vole outcompetes *S. cooperi*, forcing it into more marginal habitats.

HABITS. These voles spend much time above ground. In the meadows they make numerous trails, each about the width of a garden hose. These are kept bare and smooth by the sharp teeth of the voles, which soon level any green sprout that forces its way through the soil of the runway. At irregular intervals along the trails, one finds great masses of little brownish-green pellets, the communal toilets for these cleanly little beasts.

Meadow voles are active by day and night, but they often seem to favor the early-morning and

*Meadow vole,* Microtus pennsylvanicus
*(Roger W. Barbour)*

*Meadow vole cuttings*

late-afternoon hours. They are more active in the daytime in habitats with great amounts of cover, and at night during periods of high temperature. Meadow voles can swim but do not climb. They can orient themselves by the sun, evidently an unusual ability for a small rodent (Fluherty et al., 1976).

The nests of dried grasses are constructed either on the surface or at the ends of shallow burrows. The heat from the occupants melts away the snow during the winter months, forming a chimney that sometimes reveals the compact nest below. In swamps and other wet places the nest may be placed in the center of a grass tussock, well removed from the threat of high water.

FOOD AND FEEDING. It would almost be easier to list the vegetative foods that are *not* eaten by *Microtus* than to list those that it does consume. Grasses of all kinds and their maturing seeds, fleshy rootstocks, and the tender bark of even sizable trees are all relished. Even during the most severe winter weather, the tender bark of trees, the blanched shoots of grasses, and various seeds and rootstocks provide abundant food. As the spring thaws level the snowbanks, abundant evidence of the meadow vole's subnivean activity is revealed. In spring they will fell dwarf willows and eat the fruiting bodies. In the fields of closely growing timothy and grains, the stalks are so closely crowded that lopping them off at the base will not allow them to fall, and the voles must cut them into successive match-sized sections before the prized heads can be reached. This practice accounts for at least some of the little crisscross patches of cured grasses the puzzled farmer observes so frequently in his fields. In the salt meadows, various sedges and even the tiny littoral life are eagerly taken, but the meadow vole, unlike many of its kin, seldom appears to eat insects. It does store roots, tubers, leaves, and other parts of plants for winter sustenance.

The appetite of *Microtus pennsylvanicus* is prodigious, a vole often eating green food in excess of its weight in 24 hours. Though this seeming gluttony might suggest otherwise, it has an efficient digestive system, given the relative indigestibility of the cellulose and lignin in its food. Digestion is aided by the very large caecum, which extends from one end of the body cavity to the other. Since the caecum dumps its contents directly into the large intestine, vitamins are extracted by reingestion of feces. Cranford and Johnson (1989) found that meadow voles reingested about 12% of their feces when on a high-quality diet and about 15% when on a low-quality diet. Experimental prevention of coprophagy (by a snug plastic collar) caused significant weight loss.

*Distribution of the meadow vole,* Microtus pennsylvanicus, *in the eastern United States*

REPRODUCTION AND DEVELOPMENT. Among the many prolific mammals, the meadow vole is champion. One large litter follows another in rapid succession, until it seems that the countryside should boil over with these mice. A captive female observed by Vernon Bailey (1924) produced 17 litters in a single year, and one of her daughters from a first litter had produced 13 families of her own before she had reached her first birthday! Few other mammals can challenge such fecundity. Both male and female meadow voles are promiscuous, the males competing for females and mating indiscriminately. During the breeding season, the animals are arrayed as solitary males and mother/young units, and several groups of young may be produced. But at the end of the breeding season, as winter approaches, juveniles may remain with the females as extended-family groups, and one or two adult males may join these groups (Madison et al., 1984). But if a predator should find and destroy part of a group, the remainder may join other groups. Energy conservation appears to be the beneficiary of this behavior. These groups again disband at the onset of breeding in spring. Males often kill babies in nests they find, but not the babies of females with which they have mated, thus helping to favor their own genetic material. Mating with multiple males may therefore give the female some protection against male infanticide, and it should enhance genetic variability as well.

On average, the winter, spring, and fall litters of the meadow vole are smaller than those of summer. The gestation period is just 20–21 days, and the one to 11 young (with averages of 3.7 to 6.9 in different localities), although born in an immature state, are weaned when about 12 days old, and the females are ready to breed when they have attained the ripe old age of three weeks. The newborn young weigh from 1.6 to 3.0 grams. They have brown fur by the third day, vocal activity begins at day four, and the incisors erupt by the sixth or seventh day, the molars about day eight. The eyes and ears open, and the young begin to eat solid food, by day eight or nine. The young start crawling about day nine, and are weaned about the 11th to 14th day. Adult weight is attained in about 12 weeks. The breeding season is long, continuing from late March into November, and in some years meadow voles breed throughout the winter.

McShea and Madison (1986) found that in spring the females of the meadow vole were larger than the males, whereas in fall the males were larger, the pattern thus favoring females and reproduction in spring. Females may cull the smallest young, particularly under poor conditions or in large populations.

POPULATION CHARACTERISTICS. Meadow voles are often cyclic, their populations reaching highs rather regularly every three or four years, although in some populations cycling does not occur at all. Cycling has been studied in many geographic areas (Taitt and Krebs, 1985). In an area in Ontario, the highs averaged 410 per ha (166 per acre), the lows 120 per ha (49 per acre); and in Manitoba they averaged 90 and 10 per ha (36 and 4 per acre). Annual fluctuations (as opposed to cyclic fluctuations) ranged between 44 and 30 voles per ha (18 and 12 per acre) in the Manitoba population. Cyclic behavior is not as well developed in *Microtus pennsylvanicus* in Indiana as it is farther to the north. Long-term data there showed a pattern roughly intermediate between cyclic and annual fluctuations, and Charles Krebs referred to the pattern as a two-year cycle. Maxima were 180 voles per ha (73 per acre) and minima were four per ha (1.6 per acre). Hamilton (1937), who first described cycles in meadow voles, took them to be psychological and physiological responses to overpopulation (see the account for the genus *Microtus*, above). Although the causal factors of these cycles have received much attention in recent years, and remain in some dispute, all the reproductive measures (number of litters per year, young per litter, etc.) are high during the increasing phase of the cycle, and low during the decreasing phase.

Male home ranges are about three times larger than female home ranges and may overlap the ranges of several females and of other males as well. The home ranges of males are not well defined and may change often, and, unlike females, males are tolerant of one another. The sizes of home ranges of both males and females are inversely related to habitat quality and population density. Home ranges are 0.2 to 2 ha (0.1 to 0.8 acres), larger in summer, larger in marshes than in meadows, and smaller at high population densities. The home ranges overlap, but meadow voles will defend small areas ("territories") in the immediate vicinity of their nests. In summer the needs of the female and her young define her territory, an area she will defend against other females. Where overlap does occur, one of the females involved is usually dominant and much larger, and she is usually the only one of the two with young. Dale Madison suggested that these pairs are mother/daughter units, and that the mother's presence inhibits the daughter from reproducing. At cessation of breeding, females will tolerate other males in their nests.

Madison et al. (1984) studied 32 voles in an enclosure by radio-tracking. In October, these voles began forming nesting groups of two to five individuals, 69% of these groups being just two voles. The benefits of grouping were presumably heat conservation, from "huddling," and protection from predators. During snow cover, the voles often shifted their home ranges and nesting affiliations.

ENEMIES. Of all our small mammals, no other has such a long list of enemies. In the air above the woods and meadows, and even in the water, lurk many foes, always ready to snuff out a life in one savage rush of wings, feet, or fins. Weasels are one of the most important predators on meadow voles, and *Mustela erminea* is a particularly efficient near specialist on this and other species of *Microtus*. The house cat is another important predator. The short-tailed shrew is often said to be a predator, but we think this occurs only under exceptional circumstances, such as when *M. pennsylvanicus* levels are very high. Were it not for the widespread distribution and large numbers of this rodent, many predators would be hard-pressed to maintain themselves.

PARASITES AND DISEASE. As is the case with most burrowing rodents, this species hosts a full range and large numbers of both internal parasites (trematodes, cestodes, nematodes, and acanthocephalans) and external parasites (mites, ticks, chiggers, lice, fleas, and larval botflies). A tiny cigar-shaped mite, *Listrophorus mexicanus*, and the hypopial mite *Glycyphagus microti* are characteristic parasites of this species. For a detailed list of its parasites, see Timm (1985).

RELATION TO HUMANS. Meadow voles are of great economic significance. By girdling fruit trees and nursery stock they cause considerable monetary loss to the orchardist and horticulturist. Their constant pilfering of forage crops, though difficult to measure, is in the aggregate a great loss to the agriculturist. The best control in orchards is probably to clean-cultivate the entire orchard, i.e. eliminate vole habitat. Various chemical controls have been used, but for environmental reasons we generally recommend the avoidance of chemical controls. Voles do serve a useful function in providing predatory birds and mammals with an abundant source of food.

AREAS FOR FURTHER WORK. This and other species of *Microtus*, as well as meadow jumping mice and many lagomorphs, produce piles of cuttings in their runways. Some of these piles seem to result from the vole's reaching as high as it can reach, pulling the stalk down and cutting it off, then pulling it down again and cutting it again, until the head is reached. Might there be other reasons for this behavior? For example, might they be extracting material from the center of the stalk? A study of the microflora and microfauna of the parts of the gut might be of interest, and further information on nutrition intake should be of value.

## SUBSPECIES

We recognize five subspecies, including *M. pennsylvanicus pennsylvanicus*. Two of these (*M. p. breweri* and *M. p. provectus*) were originally described as separate species, but we see no reason to retain them as such. They seem, rather, to fit our concept of subspecies, although Tamarin and Kunz (Mammalian Species, 1974) recognized *M. pennsylvanicus breweri* as a full species. There are some morphological differences between *M. p. breweri* and mainland *M. p. pennsylvanicus*, and there is less genetic variation in the insular form than in the mainland form, as one would expect. The two have been crossbred in the laboratory, but further details are lacking.

Another subspecies, the Great Gull Island meadow vole, *Microtus pennsylvanicus nesophilus*, with dark yellowish bister on the upper parts, was described by Vernon Bailey in 1898. It was confined to Great Gull Island, at the entrance to Long Island Sound, New York, but the removal of suitable cover during construction shortly after the discovery of this subspecies undoubtedly led to its extermination. Its type locality was Great Gull Island, Long Island, Suffolk Co., New York.

### *Microtus pennsylvanicus pennsylvanicus* (Ord)

As described above. This is the form occurring in nearly all of the range of the species in eastern United States.

Type locality: Currituck, Currituck Co., North Carolina.

Other currently recognized eastern subspecies:

*M. pennsylvanicus nigrans* Rhoads

*M. pennsylvanicus nesophilus* [extirpated]

### *Microtus pennsylvanicus breweri* (Baird)
Beach Vole

The beach vole is a coarse, long-pelaged meadow vole somewhat larger than *M. pennsylvanicus*, with a palish gray coat; the upperparts are buffy gray with scattered black- and brown-tipped hairs, and the sides are rather paler; the belly is silvery, with a sulphur suffusion; the feet are gray or grayish white; the tail is dark brown above, dirty white below. Beach voles often have a white patch on the forehead or, sometimes, on the chin or throat. The young show the same coloration as the adult, rather than being much darker, as is the case in the field vole (the nominate subspecies). Fifteen individuals from Muskeget Island, off the coast of Massachusetts, averaged: total length 176.5 (153–191), tail 51 (45–60), hind foot 22.3 (22–23) mm. Beach voles live in areas supporting beach grass (*Ammophila*) and poison ivy (*Toxicodendron*). They breed from March through October and produce one to six (mean of 3.4) young. Unlike the field vole, they are not cyclic but maintain their populations at high levels. They also have a shorter breeding season and smaller litters (Tamarin, 1977). The subspecies is known only from Mukseget Island.

Type locality: Muskeget Island, off Nantucket, Massachusetts.

### *Microtus pennsylvanicus dukecampbelli* Woods, Post & Kilpatrick
Saltmarsh Vole

Individuals of this subspecies are dark black-brown, grading to dark gray on the belly. They are large, much larger than the nearest subspecies to the north; the ears are short; and the hind foot is long. Average measurements of five individuals are total length 186.1 (178–198), tail 48.8 (43–55), hind foot 23.4 (22–25) mm; and weight 61.2 (43–80) grams. This subspecies is apparently extremely rare, and known only from the type locality, where it inhabits saltmarsh flats of *Distichlis* and other low plants. Presumably, meadow voles moved south during the Pleistocene glacial advance, then managed to survive in isolation when the glaciers receded.

Type locality: Island Field Marsh in Waccasassa Bay, Levy Co., Florida.

### *Microtus pennsylvanicus provectus* Bangs
Block Island Meadow Vole

Similar in color to typical *pennsylvanicus* but larger; the skull is peculiar, its interparietal very wide and extending far forward between the parietals; the nasal bones are wide posteriorly and end squarely, thus neither rounded nor pointed behind as they are in *M. pennsylvanicus*. Measurements of 12 adults averaged: total length 185, tail 49, hind foot 22.4 mm. Restricted to Block Island, 32 km (20 miles) off the coast of Rhode Island.

Type locality: Block Island, Washington Co., Rhode Island.

### *Microtus pennsylvanicus shattucki* Howe

This large meadow vole was originally described by Howe (*Proc. Portland Soc. Nat. Hist.* 2: 201), considered invalid by Wyman (1922), and resurrected and redescribed by Youngman (1967). Color very dark gray brown. Total length and hind foot average 186.3 and 22.4 mm, respectively. This subspecies is known from Long Island, Tumble Down Dick Island,

and North Haven Island, all in Penobscot Bay, Maine.

Type locality: North Haven Island, Maine.

## LITERATURE

Bailey, V. 1924. Breeding, feeding and other life habits of meadow mice (*Microtus*). *J. Agric. Res.* 27: 523–535.

Boonstra, R., and F. H. Rodd. 1983. Regulation of breeding density in *Microtus pennsylvanicus*. *J. Anim. Ecol.* 52: 757–780.

Cranford, J. A., and E. O. Johnson. 1989. Effects of coprophagy and diet quality on two microtine rodents (*Microtus pennsylvanicus* and *Microtus pinetorum*). *J. Mammal.* 70: 494–502.

Fluherty, S. L., D. H. Taylor, and G. W. Barrett. 1976. Sun-compass orientation in the meadow vole, *Microtus pennsylvanicus*. *J. Mammal.* 57: 1–9.

Getz, L. L. 1960. A population study of the meadow vole, *Microtus pennsylvanicus*. *Amer. Midland Nat.* 64: 392–405.

Getz, L. L., D. F. Gudermuth, and S. M. Benson. 1992. Pattern of nest occupancy of the prairie vole *Microtus ochrogaster* in different habitats. *Amer. Midland Nat.* 128: 197–202.

Hamilton, W. J., Jr. 1937. The biology of microtine cycles. *J. Agric. Res.* 54: 779–790.

———. 1941. Reproduction of the field mouse (*Microtus pennsylvanicus*). Mem. Cornell Univ. Agric. Exp. Sta. No. 237. 23 pp.

Jones, E. 1990. Effects of forage availability on home range and population density of *Microtus pennsylvanicus*. *J. Mammal.* 71: 382–389.

Klatt, B. J., and L. L. Getz. 1987. Vegetation characteristics of *Microtus ochrogaster* and *M. pennsylvanicus* habitats in east central Illinois. *J. Mammal.* 68: 569–577.

Madison, D. M., R. W. Fitzgerald, and W. J. McShea. 1984. Dynamics of social nesting in overwintering meadow voles (*Microtus pennsylvanicus*): Possible consequences for population cycling. *Behav. Ecol. Sociobiol.* 15: 9–17.

McShea, W. J., and D. M. Madison. 1986. Sex ratio shifts within litters of meadow voles (*Microtus pennsylvanicus*). *Behav. Ecol. Sociobiol.* 18: 431–436.

Moyer, C. A., G. H. Adler, and R. H. Tamarin. 1988. Systematics of New England *Microtus*, with emphasis on *Microtus breweri*. *J. Mammal.* 69: 782–794.

Reich, L. M. 1981. *Microtus pennsylvanicus*. **Mammalian Species No. 159.** Amer. Soc. Mammal. 8 pp.

Taitt, M. J., and C. J. Krebs. 1985. Population dynamics and cycles. In: R. H. Tamarin, ed., *The Biology of the New World Microtus*, pp. 567–620. Amer. Soc. Mammal., Spec. Publ. No. 8.

Tamarin, R. H. 1977. Reproduction in the Island Beach vole, *Microtus breweri*, and the mainland meadow vole, *Microtus pennsylvanicus*, in southeastern Massachusetts. *J. Mammal.* 58: 536–548.

Tamarin, R. H., and T. H. Kunz. 1974. *Microtus breweri*. **Mammalian Species No. 45.** Amer. Soc. Mammal. 3 pp.

Timm, R. M. 1985. Parasites. In: R. H. Tamarin, ed., *The Biology of New World* Microtus, pp. 455–534. Amer. Soc. Mammal., Spec. Publ. No. 8.

Woods, C. A., W. Post, and C. W. Kilpatrick. 1982. *Microtus pennsylvanicus* (Rodentia: Muridae) in Florida: A Pleistocene relict in a coastal saltmarsh. *Bull. Fla. State Mus. Biol. Sci.* 28: 25–52.

Wyman, L. C. 1922. The validity of the Penobscot field mouse. *J. Mammal.* 3: 162–166.

Youngman, P. M. 1967. Insular populations of the meadow vole, *Microtus pennsylvanicus*, from northeastern North America, with descriptions of two new subspecies. *J. Mammal.* 48: 579–588.

## Woodland Vole, Pine Vole
## *Microtus pinetorum* (LeConte)

DESCRIPTION. *Microtus pinetorum* is a relatively small but robust vole with a very short

*Woodland vole, or pine vole,* Microtus pinetorum
*(Roger W. Barbour)*

tail (averaging 18–23 mm, or only slightly longer than the hind foot). It has soft, short, dense, somewhat molelike fur. The eyes and external ears are much reduced, and the latter are usually hidden in the fur. The woodland vole has five plantar tubercles (on the sole of the hind foot) and four mammae. The upperparts are bright brown or chestnut, the fur showing a distinct sheen, and the sides are somewhat lighter. The belly is dusky to silvery gray, the bases of the hairs plumbeous. The tail is brownish above, pale below, and the feet are pale gray. There is a biannual molt, the winter pelage darker than the light-chestnut summer pelage. The young are more drab. The skull of this species, flat and wide, is very similar to that of *M. ochrogaster*. The two can be distinguished from the skulls of other eastern microtines by the third molariform teeth, which show an anterior and a posterior loop and only two triangles between them. Woodland voles from Florida are decidedly smaller and paler.

MEASUREMENTS. Measurements of 15 adults from Ithaca, New York, averaged: total length 126, tail 19, hind foot 18 mm; and weight 25–35 grams. In the southeastern parts of the woodland vole's range (Alabama to North Carolina), a large series averaged: total length 114 (81–125), tail 18 (12–29), and hind foot 16 (13–19) mm. The average weight is about 24 grams.

Measurements of an adult female from Ocala, Florida, were: total length 94, tail 15, hind foot 14 mm.

Diploid number = 62.

TOOTH FORMULA

$$\frac{1}{1} \quad \frac{0}{0} \quad \frac{0}{0} \quad \frac{3}{3} \; = \; 16$$

DISTRIBUTION. The woodland vole occurs from southern Maine to Georgia and northern Florida, westward to southern Wisconsin and Louisiana. Beyond the Mississippi, it occurs to Iowa, eastern Kansas, eastern Oklahoma, and northeastern Texas.

HABITAT. The woodland vole has a wide range of habitats, from sea level in the south to the

schmidti

nemoralis

scalopsoides

carbonarius

auricularis

pinetorum

parvulus

*Distribution of the woodland vole, or pine vole,* Microtus pinetorum, *in the eastern United States*

spruce and birch forests of the higher northern mountains. Few small mammals are more adaptable to variation in habitat. It is most abundant in deciduous forest in moist, friable soils suitable for burrowing. There we poke our fingers into the ground to find its burrows. About coastal bays, they occur to the edge of tidewater; in the dry fields and truck gardens of the South, they occur in great numbers; and along with meadow voles, they are a pest of orchards in the Northeast. The name "pine vole" is a misnomer, for except in Florida the species is seldom found in stands of pines; "woodland vole" much better characterizes this species. In northern Florida this vole usually selects areas covered with dense trees and shrubs, mainly pine and scrub oak. No runways were found in openings lacking trees.

Rhodes and Richmond (1985) presented laboratory animals with choices between various conditions of soil texture, moisture, and temperature as they related to nest-site selection and burrowing. Woodland voles selected 19°C (67°F) in preference to 25, 30, or 35°C (78, 81, or 90°F); a loam/peat moss mixture over soils with gravel or stone; and medium rather than very moist or very dry conditions.

HABITS. This species is active day or night but spends most of its time in burrows. The burrows range from 30 to 35 mm (1.0 to 1.1 inch) in diameter. The globular nest, with its three or four openings, may be in the burrow. If under a log, the nest may be saucer-shaped. Nests, of dead grasses and leaves, are placed beneath a log or, more often, in a snug chamber several centimeters below the surface. One nest under an old board in Florida was of palmetto bark, lined with silky, fibrous material much like the inside of a milkweed pod. Around the nest were the hulls of about 200 pine seeds.

The short ears, sleek, molelike fur, and strong feet are all adaptations for a fossorial life, and *M. pinetorum* has need of them, for it seldom ventures any distance above ground, and then only to chase over the shallow surface runways into another burrow.

When digging in the forest floor or dry fields, the woodland vole threads its way just beneath the thick carpet of leaves, the carpet forming a thin but substantial ceiling for the burrow. It may on rare occasions tunnel to a depth of 30 cm (a foot) or more, but most of the tunnels do not exceed 7 to 10 cm (3 or 4 inches in depth. Burrowing involves a shoveling motion with the head to loosen the dirt, the incisors and forefeet assisting. The loosened dirt is pushed backward. After proceeding about 30 cm, the vole turns around and pushes the soil out of the tunnel with its head. Excess soil is deposited in piles under the leaf litter.

A mousetrap sunk crosswise of the burrow with its treadle at the tunnel's ground level will catch woodland voles as well as the shrews and other small mammals that use the maze of underground tunnels. A piece of bark or other cover placed over the opening to the burrow may enhance the catch. We have also caught many woodland voles in cans we had sunk for *Sorex hoyi* and *S. fumeus* in the unglaciated hill country of southern Indiana.

FOOD AND FEEDING. The food of the woodland vole is chiefly of vegetation, but its diet is more varied than those of the meadow and prairie voles. It feeds primarily on roots and stems, especially of grasses, in summer; fruits, seeds, and mast in fall; and bark and roots in winter and spring. A large variety of plant foods has been recorded: pokeberries, clover, beechnuts, *Crataegus*, wild onions, hickory nuts, morning glory rootstocks, dock, violets, various grasses, and *Ranunculus* leaves. The subterranean fungus *Endogone* has also been recorded, and insects are sometimes eaten.

REPRODUCTION AND DEVELOPMENT. In the north, the woodland vole's breeding season lasts from early March well into November, but occasionally the voles breed as early as January. In North Carolina, woodland voles may breed throughout the year. A vaginal plug that forms after copulation lasts about three days, but it is usually not visible externally. Implantation is about five to seven days after copulation, and gestation is from 20 to 24 days. Individual females produce one to four litters per year, and litters number one to five young (averaging 1.9 to 2.5 at different localities). Woodland voles do not exhibit cyclic population behavior.

Rather, they are K-selected; they have a low reproductive rate and tend to maintain a stable population size. Although their rate of increase is considerably less than that of meadow voles, they probably suffer fewer enemies, for their subterranean habits secure them in some measure from hawks and owls.

The young are blind and helpless at birth, but have a sprinkling of fuzzy hairs. They weigh 1.9 to 3.2 grams but grow rapidly, the ear pinnae unfolding at day eight and the eyes opening at days seven to nine. The ears open on day 11 or 12, and weaning is between days 17 and 21. Standard measurements are total length 46, tail 4, hind foot 6 mm, and weight 3.7 grams, at day three; 55, 5, and 8 mm, and weight 5.0 grams, at day seven; and 74, 9, and 12 mm, and weight 7.0 grams, at day 12. At three weeks, the young voles were 69 to 98 mm in total length and weighed 7.5 to 9.6 grams, and by week five they were 80–105 mm long and weighed 12.4–17.1 grams. Young females could conceive at 77 days, but most did not until about day 105. The woodland vole has four teats, half the number of the meadow vole. If the nursing female is frightened from the nest, the young cling tenaciously to her teats and can be dragged considerable distances without losing their grasp.

POPULATION CHARACTERISTICS. Using radio-telemetry, Fitzgerald and Madison (1983) found woodland voles arrayed in nonoverlapping family units averaging 4.2 voles per unit. A unit consisted most often of two adult males, one adult female, and one or two young. The voles studied were in orchards, and the animals were affected by the spacing of the trees. Territories there were about 3 by 15 meters (10 by 50 feet), and home ranges were about 40–45 square meters (430–485 square feet). Mating varied, depending on the family unit: the pattern apparently may be monogamous, polygynous, or even polyandrous, but monogamy is the predominant system in this species (Fitzgerald and Madison, 1983). Woodland voles may occur at densities up to 14.6 per ha (6 per acre).

ENEMIES. As indicated by its lower reproductive rate, and presumably because of its subterranean habits, this species is less subject to preda-

tion than many of the other voles are. Any of the mammal, bird, or snake predators in an area will undoubtedly prey on this species, given the opportunity.

PARASITES AND DISEASE. We have found this species, like most other burrowers, to be heavily populated by ectoparasites and other associated species. Examination of the fur of a fresh specimen will often reveal a large and varied community of tiny organisms. There are lice (one species has been found on microtine rodents), fleas (most commonly the same ones found on shrews), *Androlaelaps fahrenholzi* (a large laelapid mite found on many different hosts), some other laelapids most often parasitic on small microtines, chiggers, and several other small mites, including those of the genus *Pygmephorus*. There is thus an entire community here, practically unknown until recently. Small-mammal ectoparasite communities are almost never examined by mammalogists (or even by parasitologists).

The genus *Pygmephorus*, in particular, illustrates the advantages and thrills of examining the unknown. Only one species of *Pygmephorus* was previously known from North America. We have found 27 more species, several of them on woodland voles. Even today, very little is known about the ecology of these mites. The females, common on woodland voles and other burrowers, are phoretic (they use the host as a means of transportation) and hold to the hairs by enlarged foreclaws (see p. 19). For the species inhabiting the fur of mammals, both the males and the breeding patterns are totally unknown.

This species also hosts a wide range of endoparasites; see Timm (1985) for a detailed listing.

RELATION TO HUMANS. The woodland vole is a serious pest of the orchard and the truck farm. It girdles the roots of fruit trees, causing widespread damage in the fruit belts of eastern United States. Damage of this nature has been particularly severe in the Shenandoah Valley. We have seen uprooted apple trees wholly girdled, the smaller rootlets completely eaten or cut from the tree. On Long Island and elsewhere, severe damage to potatoes has been caused by this species.

*Round-tailed muskrat,*
Neofiber alleni
*(Jerry Lee Gingerich)*

AREAS FOR FURTHER WORK. Much additional work on this species is to be desired. Its ecological limiting factors, with a view to determining why it changes burrow systems periodically, would be especially interesting. More information on the food of this species is also needed. And this host and its nests would be an excellent starting point for studies on mites of the genus *Pygmephorus*.

## SUBSPECIES

Several subspecies occur in the eastern United States, but, except for one, they appear to intergrade. Thus, we suggest they not be recognized.

### *Microtus pinetorum pinetorum* (LeConte)

As described above. Occupies essentially the range of the species in the eastern United States.

Type locality: Pine forests of Georgia, probably on the LeConte Plantation, near Riceboro, Liberty Co., Ga.

Other currently recognized subspecies:
  *M. pinetorum auricularis* Bailey
  *M. pinetorum carbonarius* (Handley)
  *M. pinetorum nemoralis* Bailey
  *M. pinetorum parvulus* Howell
  *M. pinetorum scalopsoides* (Audubon and Bachman)

### *Microtus pinetorum schmidti* Jackson

Differs from any other described subspecies of *pinetorum* in its decidedly more grayish, less rufescent coloration in specimens of comparable age and season, and in its shorter (5.9 mm) average upper tooth row. Known only from the hardwood forests of Worden Township, Wisconsin, this subspecies appears to be separated geographically from the remainder of the species' range; thus we have provisionally recognized it. Standard measurements of 29 individuals are: total length 120 (102–132), tail 21 (18.5–25), and hind foot 17.7 (17.5–18) mm.

Type locality: Worden Township, Clark Co., Wisconsin.

## LITERATURE

Benton, A. H. 1955. Observations on the life history of the northern pine mouse. *J. Mammal.* 36: 52–62.

Fitzgerald, R. W., and D. M. Madison. 1983. Social organization of a free-ranging population of pine voles, *Microtus pinetorum. Behav. Ecol. Sociobiol.* 13: 183–187.

Goertz, J. W. 1971. An ecological study of *Microtus pinetorum* in Oklahoma. *Amer. Midland Nat.* 86: 1–12.

Hamilton, W. J., Jr. 1938. Life history notes on the northern pine mouse. *J. Mammal.* 19: 163–170.

Hiaason, B., R. Stehn, J. Bart, and M. Richmond. 1978. A bibliography of the genus *Pitymys* (Rodentia, Mammalia) and homonyms *Microtus pinetorum* and *Microtus subterraneus*. Cornell Univ. Agric. Exp. Sta., Nat. Resources Res. and Ext. Ser. No. 10, 43 pp.

Paul, J. R. 1970. Observations on the ecology, populations, and reproductive biology of the pine vole, *Microtus pinetorum*, North Carolina. Ill. State Mus. Rep. Invest. No. 20. 28 pp.

Rhodes, D. H., and M. E. Richmond. 1985. Influence of soil texture and temperature on nest-site selection and burrowing by the pine vole, *Microtus pineto-rum. Amer. Midland Nat.* 113: 102–108.

Smolen, M. J. 1981. *Microtus pinetorum.* **Mammalian Species No. 147.** Amer. Soc. Mammal. 7 pp.

Timm, R. M. 1985. Parasites. In: R. H. Tamarin, ed., *The Biology of the New World* Microtus, pp. 455–534. Amer. Soc. Mammal., Spec. Publ. No. 8.

## Round-Tailed Muskrat *Neofiber alleni* True

DESCRIPTION. In general appearance, *Neofiber alleni* suggests a small muskrat. The species has in fact been characterized as a living link between the meadow vole and the muskrat, an impression brought home by the sight of a very young round-tailed muskrat in the grass, looking very much like a meadow vole. The round-tailed muskrat has a dense, soft, lustrous, waterproof coat with very thick underfur and dark guard hairs. The small ears are almost hidden in the fur. Its scaly, round tail is almost devoid of hair, and its hind feet are slightly webbed. The upperparts are generally a dark, rich, uniform brown, and the underfur is gray at the base, buffy at the tips. Juveniles are lead-gray. The darkest individuals occur in southern peninsular Florida. The hind foot is much larger than the front. The skull is similar to that of *Ondatra*, but smaller (41 to 51 mm in condylobasal length).

MEASUREMENTS. Total length 285–381, tail 99–168, hind foot 40–50 mm. Males are slightly larger than females, 108 males averaging 279 (187–350) grams, 94 females averaging 262 (192–357) grams.

Diploid number = 52.

TOOTH FORMULA

$$\frac{1}{1} \quad \frac{0}{0} \quad \frac{0}{0} \quad \frac{3}{3} \ = \ 16$$

*Distribution of the round-tailed muskrat, Neofiber alleni, in the eastern United States*

DISTRIBUTION. *Neofiber* occurs disjunctively in southeastern Georgia, in most of peninsular Florida, and in the Florida panhandle.

HABITAT. The round-tailed muskrat replaces the common muskrat in the grassy marshes or prairies of Florida and extreme southeastern Georgia. In Florida, it is especially abundant in sandy areas with water 150 to 460 mm (6 to 15 inches) deep supporting stands of *Panicum hemitomon*, *Leersia hexandra*, and *Pontederia lanceolata*. Here, their houses, feeding platforms, and runways are quite prominent.

Among the salt savannas bordering the tributaries of the Indian River of Florida, *Neofiber* is abundant. Frank M. Chapman found it along the fringe of red and black mangrove in grass 60 cm to a meter (2 to 3 feet) tall and densely matted underfoot. In the great Okefenokee Swamp of southeastern Georgia, *Neofiber* is largely restricted to the so-called prairies—level, almost treeless bogs or marshes. For the most part these bogs are covered with water and aquatic plants, the plants rooted in the muck and peat that has accumulated to a depth of several feet above the sand bottom.

*Spherical house of round-tailed muskrat (James N. Layne)*

In some parts of Florida these rats tunnel in both cultivated and abandoned fields, in cane patches, and even in dooryards and gardens. A. H. Howell found the burrows ramifying through the friable peat in all directions, but none apparently extended to any great depth.

HABITS. Round-tailed muskrats make houses, and the houses usually include nests. Other

*Entrance to burrow of round-tailed muskrat, with sand mound (James N. Layne)*

times, nests are constructed at the bases of trees, inside stumps, or in other protected places. Dale E. Birkenholz (1963) made extensive studies of these rats in Florida. He found that the houses were spherical, 17.5–61 cm (7–24 inches) in diameter, and had an internal chamber about 10 cm (4 inches) in diameter. Plants used in construction are usually grasses, sedges, and the like, much finer than the cattails used by the common muskrat, *Ondatra zibethicus*. A house constructed for normal living had walls 50 to 75 mm (2 to 3 inches) thick, the floor as much as 50 mm above water level. The cavity was unlined and moist, and had two exit burrows on opposite sides. These houses are constructed by bending plants over the basal platform and, often, by bringing additional plants into the walls. Females about to give birth altered this type of house, making the walls much thicker, raising the floor, and lining the chamber with dry, fine-textured grasses. Sometimes, these rats build still more complex houses. In the freshwater ponds near Gainesville, Florida, they build large nests in button bush, *Cephalanthus*, or on the surface in water 0.3–0.6 meter (1–2 feet) deep. Nests are mainly of aquatic grasses, but other plants are also used. They are attached to emergent vegetation, often on a base of sunken plant material. The height of the house is increased as water level increases. There are usually two, sometimes three openings to the house beneath the surface of the water. Houses may be used for up to six months or, sometimes, from one year to the next, and each house is occupied by a single adult. Unused houses are often used by rice rats or cotton rats.

These muskrats also build feeding platforms, one to six of them, each about 100 by 150 mm (4 by 6 inches) in shallow water near their houses, where succulent grasses may be pulled within reach. The discarded plant material is added to the platforms, and the feeding station eventually attains considerable bulk. The platforms are often shared by other animals. Francis Harper describes the feeding platforms of Georgia animals as being slight, smooth-worn mounds of sphagnum, peat, herb stems, and the like, with two tunnels leading downward into the water on opposite sides. Here, the round-tailed muskrat brings seedpods of *Iris* and *Sagittaria*, and succulent root stocks.

*Neofiber* is much less aquatic than *Ondatra*, but it is an excellent swimmer and does take to the water readily, swimming and diving with ease. The tail is said to gyrate in a peculiar manner, but this apparently occurs only when the animal is turning. Sometimes, perhaps at times of low water, these animals live in burrows rather than houses. *Neofiber* is active primarily at night.

FOOD AND FEEDING. Birkenholz (1963) found from observation of the contents of 330 stomachs and from food remains at feeding sites in north-central Florida that this species has a rather restricted diet. Maidencane, *Panicum hemitomon*, was the principal food species in his study sites, but occasionally *Sagittaria lancifolia*, *Hydrotridia caroliniana*, and *Brasenia schreberi* were eaten. Birkenholz thought *Brasenia* might have been of considerable importance had it been more abundant. Elsewhere, *Nymphaea*, *Pontederia*, *Mariscus*, *Sporobolus*, *Panicum*, *Peltandra*, *Iris*, and other plants have been recorded. Crayfish remains are often found on feeding platforms, but have never been found in stomachs. They are likely left there by rice rats, which often use the platforms.

REPRODUCTION AND DEVELOPMENT. *Neofiber* breeds throughout the year; there are no well-marked breeding cycles, by reproduction increases in fall or when habitat conditions are good. Gestation is 26 to 29 days. The number of young per litter ranges from one to four, averaging 2.2, and four to six litters are produced per year. Placental scars remain visible for two to three months.

The newborn, blind and hairless, average 12 (10–15) grams in weight. Standard measurements at birth are total length 89–94, tail 20–22, and hind foot 12–13 mm. By days 14 to 18, the eyes are open and all teeth have erupted. The young are on adult food by three weeks, they resemble adults by 30 days, and they are sexually mature at 90 to 100 days. At that time they average about 275 grams.

POPULATION CHARACTERISTICS. Although populations can reach levels of up to 250–300 per ha (100–120 per acre), they fluctuate greatly, and population changes can occur rather rapidly. Most feeding takes place within an area 9 meters (30 feet) in diameter, but the animals travel over larger areas.

ENEMIES. Dogs, cats, water moccasins, harriers (marsh hawks), and barn owls are the more important predators on this species. Tom French found one in a barred owl pellet, and several other predators have been reported.

PARASITES AND DISEASE. Endoparasites include cestodes, a trematode, and two nematodes. The ectoparasite community of *Neofiber* shows superficial similarities to that of the common muskrat in having one laelapid mite, *Laelaps evansi* (*Ondatra* supports *L. multispinosa*) and three listrophorid mites, all recently described (*Listrophorus caudatus*, *L. laynei*, and *Prolistrophorus birkenholzi*; Fain et al., 1986). *Ondatra*, for its part, harbors six entirely different species of *Listrophorus*. These data suggest that *Ondatra* and *Neofiber* have long been separated.

RELATION TO HUMANS. Like that of *Ondatra*, the burrowing of this species may weaken dams or otherwise damage lakes and ponds. Round-tailed muskrats sometimes damage sugarcane crops, as well. Animals can be trapped with 110 Conibear traps set in their houses or on the feeding platforms or runways.

AREAS FOR FURTHER WORK. Information on the mating system of *Neofiber* is needed. The nest inhabitants of this species could be studied and compared to those of the common muskrat, and to the parasite populations of both hosts.

## SUBSPECIES

Five subspecies of *Neofiber alleni* have been described, but primary isolating mechanisms are lacking between three of them, thus allowing intergradation. Schwartz (1953) indicates that *N. a. exoristus* of the Okefenokee swamp and *N. a. apalachicolae* of the panhandle of Florida are separated geographically from *N. a. alleni*. We therefore recommend that three subspecies be recognized, as follows:

### *Neofiber alleni alleni* True

As described above. Occupies most of the range of the species.

Type locality: Georgiana, Brevard Co., Florida. Other currently recognized eastern subspecies:
    *N. alleni nigrescens* Howell
    *N. alleni struix* Schwartz

### *Neofiber alleni exoristus* Schwartz

This subspecies is known only from the sphagnous marshes and prairies of the Okefenokee Swamp, Georgia, but probably occurs in Baker Co., Florida, in the southern part of the swamp, as well. This is the smallest of the races of *Neofiber*, and it is paler than the races from peninsular Florida but darker than *N. a. apalachicolae* Schwartz.

Type locality: 12.1 miles [19 km] southeast of Waycross, Ware Co., Georgia.

### *Neofiber alleni apalachicolae* Schwartz

*Neofiber alleni apalachicolae* occurs in the eastern part of the panhandle of Florida, from Apalachicola, Franklin Co., east along the coast to St. Marks, Wakulla Co., and northeast to Jefferson and Madison counties. This subspecies is larger and darker than the neighboring conspecific races.

Type locality: Apalachicola, east side of Apalachicola River, Franklin Co., Florida.

### LITERATURE

Birkenholz, D. 1963. A study of the life history and ecology of the round-tailed muskrat (*Neofiber alleni* True) in north-central Florida. *Ecol. Monogr.* 33: 187–213.

———. *Neofiber alleni.* 1972. **Mammalian Species No. 15.** Amer. Soc. Mammal. 4 pp.

Fain, A., M. A. Smith, and J. O. Whitaker, Jr. 1986. The fur mites (Acari: Listrophoridae) of the round-tailed muskrat, *Neofiber alleni. Bull. Ann. Soc. Belge Entomol.* 122: 171–181.

Perry, H. R., Jr. 1982. Muskrats *Ondatra zibethicus* and *Neofiber alleni.* In: J. A. Chapman and G. A. Feldhamer, eds., *Wild Mammals of North America*, pp. 282–325. Baltimore: Johns Hopkins Univ. Press.

Schwartz, A. 1953. A systematic study of the water rat (*Neofiber alleni*). *Occ. Pap. Mus. Zool. Univ. Mich.* No. 547. 27 pp.

Wassmer, D. A., and J. L. Wolfe. 1983. New Florida localities for the round-tailed muskrat. *Northeast Gulf Sci.* 6: 197–199.

## Common Muskrat *Ondatra zibethicus* (Linnaeus)
Color plate 12

DESCRIPTION. The muskrat, the largest arvicoline, is a large, brown, robust aquatic rodent. It

*Common muskrat,* Ondatra zibethicus
*(Roger W. Barbour)*

has short legs and large hind feet, the toes of the latter partly webbed (the toes of the front feet are unwebbed). The tail is long, scaly, sparsely haired, and laterally compressed. The ears are small, almost hidden in the fur. The pelage is dense and waterproof, the underfur soft and overlaid by long guard hairs. The back and sides are usually rich brown, but may vary through tans, reddish, or black, the dorsum darker owing to the black-tipped guard hairs, which arise above the shorter underfur. The underparts are paler. In late winter the guard hairs, particularly along the sides of the body, are tipped with gold. Some albinos occur. Muskrats from extensive cattail marshes are usually larger and heavier than those from pasture streams.

MEASUREMENTS. Average measurements of 35 males from Indiana were: total length 537 (463–631), tail 231 (192–273), hind foot 78 (65–95) mm; and weight 724–1498 grams (1.6–3.3 lbs). For 23 females they were 516 (447–598), 222 (186–260), 78 (66–88) mm; and weight 1107 (618–1525) grams (1.4–3.4 lbs). Some maximum weights recorded were 1814 grams (4 lbs) in Maryland and 1959 grams (4.3 lbs) in North Carolina.

Diploid number = 54.

TOOTH FORMULA

$$\frac{1}{1} \quad \frac{0}{0} \quad \frac{0}{0} \quad \frac{3}{3} \; = \; 16$$

DISTRIBUTION. The muskrat is found from Maine, Michigan, and Wisconsin south to southern Louisiana, central Georgia, north-western South Carolina, and most of North Carolina. It also occurs in much of Canada and, except for some of the southern parts, most of the United States.

HABITAT. The muskrat is most abundant in marshes, where reasonably shallow water supports a varied assortment of cattails and other food plants. Streams and wooded swamps also provide a homesite, but in such places the rats are less abundant. The extensive marshes of Delaware, Maryland, and southern Louisiana are favorite resorts of these animals.

HABITS. The muskrat is seldom observed far from water. Its broad, webbed hind feet and flattened tail perform efficiently as oars and scull. When swimming, muskrats are propelled by the hind feet, the front feet held against the chin. The muskrat may remain submerged for

*Distribution of the common muskrat, Ondatra zibethicus, in the eastern United States*

up to 20 minutes (Errington, 1963). One was observed by F. R. Smith to submerge for 17 minutes, come up for three seconds, then submerge again for 10 more minutes. This level of endurance is made possible in part through a high tolerance for carbon dioxide. The muskrat can swim at rates up to 5 kph (3 mph), and it can swim backwards. The underfur traps air, providing both insulation and buoyancy; the trapped air averages more than 20% of the animal's dry volume.

The muskrat is so named because of the musky odor produced by the preputial glands, paired glands on the side of the penis, which enlarge during the mating season. These glands emit a yellowish, rather pleasant-smelling secretion into the urine through openings in the foreskin of the penis. The scented urine is then deposited on lodges, along travel routes, in defecation areas, and at other places throughout the home range of the lodge owner, as a means of advertisement. Females have similar, but less active glands. The musk oil contains a mixture of cyclopentadecanol and cycloheptadecanol with corresponding ketones. The musk probably helps bring the sexes together.

In marshes or swamps, the muskrat builds a house, or lodge, of cattails, sedges, or other dominant water plants of its habitat (a house in

*Lodge of common muskrat*

an Indiana pond contained much duckweed), on the thick mat of decayed vegetation that lies below water level. These lodges, usually constructed in water not more than 0.6 meter (2 feet) deep, are built up merely by the accumulation of vegetation. The lodge may be built in shallow water or actually amidst a clump of

willows or other shrubs. A snug, dry chamber, slightly above the water level, serves as a sleeping chamber, and from this chamber one or two plunge holes lead to the water. The lodges, which harbor from one to ten or more individuals, vary greatly in size and shape; usually they are dome-shaped structures, but houses in Maryland often have slanting or flat tops. Most lodge construction occurs in May and early June, and again in October. In winter, lodge temperatures are about 20°C (36°F) above outside temperatures (MacArthur and Aleksiuk, 1979).

Smaller feeding shelters (pushups), large enough to house only a single muskrat at a time, protrude only 30–40 cm (12–16 inches) above the water. Several runways enter these shelters from below. In a New York marsh, there were about two or three such feeding lodges per main lodge. Here, food is brought and eaten in comparative safety. In the South, simple and more flimsy feeding platforms, rather than the covered feeding lodges, are often used.

MacArthur (1992) observed muskrats under clear ice in a Manitoba marsh. Normal underwater swimming speed was about 0.81 meters (2.6 feet) per second, escape speeds 1.27 meters (4.2 feet) per second. Pushups there ranged from 1.7 to 147 meters (5.6 to 385 feet) from the nearest neighboring shelter. Because the muskrats could dive up to 96 seconds, they can reach even the most distant pushups without surfacing.

Where conditions are unsatisfactory for the construction of a house, the muskrat digs a tunnel into a bank below the water surface (thus the name "bank rats"). A bank den opening, 15 by 20 cm (6 by 8 inches), leads to an enlarged chamber well above high-water level, where a warm nest of grasses is constructed. A second entrance may open onto the top or side of the bank.

In the marshes of southern Louisiana, the lodges of pregnant muskrat females, or of females with newborn, can usually be recognized by the character of their outer surfaces, freshly worked with plastered muddy peat (O'Neil, 1949). Females copulate about ten days after giving birth, and a new nest is then constructed in the same house. This process is repeated until three or four nests have been built; these nests are then used over and over. The adults and young all work together on house maintenance, but as the young reach sexual maturity, they are forcibly evicted. Thus new colonies may be started. Usually, a house contains the two adults and two to four young, but a second house is sometimes connected to the first, forming a "double house," and 10 to 15 muskrats may live and work together there.

Especially in times of low water, the muskrats dredge channels through the underlying mud so that they can swim between areas of deeper water, or between their dens and feeding areas. They may dig an elaborate series of canals, 15 to 30 cm (6 to 12 inches) wide, piling the excess debris along the ditches. Ditches are dredged with the front feet, and the loosened material is removed with the hind feet.

Muskrats are at their most aggressive, and assert the greatest degree of territoriality, during the breeding season, when dominance hierarchies are established. Females are more aggressive than males. Sounds produced by muskrats are a squeak, a "high pitched n-n-n-n sound," and tooth chattering.

FOOD AND FEEDING. Muskrats are chiefly vegetarian. They eat the roots and stalks of cattails, three-square grass, and *Sagittaria*, and the leaves, stems, and fleshy roots of many other aquatics; they even invade fields to eat herbaceous plants or growing corn. The most important foods on the extensive Gulf Coast marshes are three-squares (*Scirpus*), needle grasses (*Juncus*), and paille-fin grasses (*Panicum* and *Spartina*). Large freshwater clams, fish, and crustacea usually form a minor share of the food. Muskrats sometimes store food in their houses. Like beavers, they can close their upper lips behind the incisors in order to cut materials underwater without taking in water.

REPRODUCTION AND DEVELOPMENT. The muskrat is prolific and polygamous. Females usually breed in their second summer, but a few individuals mate in the year of their birth. Copulation often or usually occurs in the winter, the animals partially submerged in water. Breeding occurs throughout the year in Louisiana, although the heaviest breeding is from November to April. In the northern states the first litter is born in late April or early May, after a gestation of 25–30 days, and postpartum estrus follows. The young are born blind but have a fine cover-

ing of hair. At two weeks, they can swim. The incisors erupt at six to eight days and the eyes open between 13 and 16 days. The young are weaned and shifting for themselves when about a month old; at this stage they look much like *Microtus*. At three and one-half months they are the size of small adults. Several litters are produced in a season. The young number from three to eight, averaging three or four in the Gulf states, whereas five or six is more usual in the north. Muskrats in poor-quality habitat tend to have fewer and smaller litters.

Because the clitoris lies anterior to the vaginal opening and resembles the penis, the male and female genitalia are superficially similar. The distance from the anus to the genitalia is greater in males, and the perineum is furred in males but naked near the urethra in females.

POPULATION CHARACTERISTICS. Muskrats spend about half of their time in a relatively small area, usually within 15 meters (50 feet) of their house or feeding lodge, though movements are greater on rainy days. Errington (1963) found that home ranges average about 61 meters (200 feet) in diameter. Muskrats are territorial, individuals seldom straying much beyond halfway to the next house. There are two or three (or up to about seven) houses per ha (2.8 per acre) in good feeding habitat. Carrying capacity for muskrats can run up to 64 per ha (26 per acre) in the best habitats. Home ranges are larger at smaller population densities.

Dispersal is by the yearlings, usually in spring. Those in small ponds are much more likely to disperse than those in large ponds, and those in streams seldom move to ponds or marshes. Overpopulation of muskrats leads to overgrazing and can ruin the habitat for several years to come. There is in fact some evidence that muskrat populations follow a ten-year cycling pattern. Although one individual lived four years, muskrats have a relatively short life span.

ENEMIES. The muskrat is plagued by many predators, including harriers (marsh hawks), the larger owls, foxes, and raccoons. The mink, however, is the most important enemy, for it enters the muskrats' houses and bank tunnels and feeds heavily on them. (Further illustrating the closeness of this relationship, we have often found highly host-specific muskrat parasites on mink.) Water moccasins capture some muskrats, and the larger turtles and even alligators occasionally prey on them.

A new problem for southern muskrats has been the introduction of the nutria from South America. The much larger nutria has habits similar to those of the muskrat, placing the two species in direct competition. Moreover, the marshes have deteriorated. The net result is that the nutria has now replaced the muskrat as the most important fur-bearing animal in Louisiana.

PARASITES AND DISEASE. Muskrats carry a number of parasites. From North America, 36 species of trematodes, 19 of nematodes, 13 of cestodes, and four of acanthocephalans have been reported, along with 19 genera of bacteria. Ticks, too, are often found, but mites, *Laelaps multispinosa*, and six species of *Listrophorus* (*L. americanus*, *L. dozieri*, *L. faini*, *L. kingstownensis*, *L. ondatrae*, and *L. validus*) are abundant on muskrats, several of them occurring together on one individual. The listrophorids each tend to occur on particular parts of the muskrat, but they overlap broadly. Diseases of muskrats are septicemia, coccidiosis, leukemia, gallstones, pasteurellosis, hepatitis, uremia, and pneumonia. Tularemia and Errington's disease, however, are the only diseases confronting muskrats as major problems. Tularemia, a bacterial disease, is caused by *Francisella tularense*. Errington's disease (or hemorrhagic disease) is highly infectious, and the causal agent is not known.

RELATION TO HUMANS. The muskrat is still the most important of our native furbearers. Formerly worth only a few cents, the pelts skyrocketed to four dollars during the boom following World War I, and from 1933 through the 1940s the price still averaged a dollar or more for prime pelts. Many trappers of Maryland's east shore, the coastal marshes of Louisiana, and even the extensive swamps of New York, Michigan, and Wisconsin supplemented their income from the muskrat. Carcasses were also sold for food in some numbers in the markets of Wilmington, Baltimore, and Washington. Average prices of

muskrat skins in Indiana were $.99, $1.46, $2.36, $1.89, $2.49, and $2.98 for the years 1970 through 1975, respectively. More than a million and a half pelts were harvested in the 1968–69 season in Louisiana, the pelts averaging $1.10 (Lowery, 1974). A million pelts taken during the 1987 season in New York averaged $5.00 per pelt. Indiana pelts in 1996 brought about $2.00.

Muskrats may cause significant damage, including leakage, in small ponds and lakes, and, as mentioned above, muskrats (and many other rodents) can contract tularemia, and tularemia can be passed to humans.

AREAS FOR FURTHER WORK. Because muskrat houses are built in water, a study of the nest parasites would be fascinating. One could compare the house associates to the parasite community of the host and also to the associates of the bank burrows of this species.

## SUBSPECIES

Populations from extreme southeastern Pennsylvania through eastern North Carolina were originally described as a separate subspecies, *O. z. macrodon*, one held to be larger than typical *zibethicus* and to have much brighter pelage, and less black, but there is no primary isolating mechanism separating this form, and we therefore do not recognize it.

### *Ondatra zibethicus zibethicus* (Linnaeus)

As described above. Occupies essentially the range of the species in the eastern United States.
Type locality: Lake Drummond, Dismal Swamp, Norfolk Co., Virginia.
Other currently recognized eastern subspecies:
    *O. zibethicus macrodon* (Merriam)

### *Ondatra zibethicus rivalicius* Bangs

The muskrat of the Louisiana coastal marshes, geographically separated from the northern muskrats, is slightly smaller than typical *zibethicus*; it colors are duller, lacking the reddish tints of the more northern forms. Average measurements of ten adults were: total length 547, tail 233, hind foot 78 mm; and weight 700–900 grams (1.5–2 lbs).

Type locality: Burbridge, Plaquemines Parish, Louisiana.

LITERATURE

Erickson, H. R. 1963. Reproduction, growth and movement of muskrats inhabiting small water areas in New York State. *New York Fish and Game J.* 10: 90–117.

Errington, P. L. 1963. *Muskrat Populations.* Ames: Iowa State Univ. Press. 665 pp.

Lowery, G. H. 1974. *The Mammals of Louisiana and Its Adjacent Waters.* Baton Rouge: Louisiana Wildlife and Fisheries Commission and Louisiana State Univ. Press. 565 pp.

MacArthur, R. A. 1978. Winter movements and home range of the muskrat. *Canadian Field-Nat.* 92: 345–349.

———. 1992. Foraging range and aerobic endurance of muskrats diving under ice. *J. Mammal.* 73: 565–569.

MacArthur, R. A., and Aleksiuk, M. 1979. Seasonal microenvironments of the muskrat (*Ondatra zibethicus*) in a northern marsh. *J. Mammal.* 60: 146–154.

O'Neil, T. 1949. *The Muskrat in the Louisiana Coastal Marshes.* New Orleans: Louisiana Dept. Wildlife & Fish. 152 pp.

Perry, H. R., Jr. 1982. Muskrats *Ondatra zibethicus* and *Neofiber alleni.* In: J. A. Chapman and G. A. Feldhamer, eds., *Wild Mammals of North America*, pp. 282–325. Baltimore: Johns Hopkins Univ. Press.

Willner, G. R., G. A. Feldhamer, E. E. Zucker, and J. A. Chapman. 1980. *Ondatra zibethicus.* **Mammalian Species No. 141.** Amer. Soc. Mammal. 8 pp.

## Bog Lemmings of the Genus *Synaptomys*

Bog lemmings, *Synaptomys*, can be recognized by their very short tails and lightly grooved incisors. They are rather difficult to capture, for they do not readily take bait. When they are caught in traps, the grip is often by the leg or across the hindquarters. Because so few are taken, they are not well known, although they do occur in a broad variety of habitats. The northern bog lemming, in particular, is very seldom taken.

KEY TO THE BOG LEMMINGS
OF THE GENUS *SYNAPTOMYS*

1. None of the hairs at the base of the ears appreciably brighter than the remainder of the pelage; lower molars showing triangles on outer sides; palate bearing a broad, blunt median projection . . . . . . . *S. cooperi*
1. A few hairs at the base of the ears distinctly rust-colored; lower molars not showing triangles on outer sides; palate bearing a sharp, pointed median projection . . . . . . *S. borealis*

## Northern Bog Lemming *Synaptomys borealis* (Richardson)

DESCRIPTION. *Synaptomys borealis* resembles *S. cooperi*, but the enamel pattern of the lower

*Northern bog lemming,* Synaptomys borealis
*(Dean E. Pearson)*

cheekteeth in the two species is quite different: there are no deep reentrant or closed triangles on the outer margins in *S. borealis*. Moreover, the incisors are not as heavy, they are paler, and their grooves are situated more medially; the incisors are also much more slender than those of *S. cooperi*, the maxillary incisors often having the outer corners unworn and in fact prolonged into sharp splinters of enamel. The color above is dull brown, often with an olive wash, brighter on the rump, anteriorly more grizzled; the tail is bicolored.

On some, but not all, individuals taken in Quebec (Peterson, 1966), the middle two claws were enlarged, suggestive of the condition in one of the true lemmings, *Dicrostonyx*. This condition has not been reported in *S. cooperi*.

MEASUREMENTS. Measurements are: total length 110–150, tail 19–27, hind foot 16–22 mm; and weight 18–36 grams.

Diploid number unknown.

Tooth formula

$$\frac{1}{1} \quad \frac{0}{0} \quad \frac{0}{0} \quad \frac{3}{3} \quad = \quad 16$$

DISTRIBUTION. In the eastern United States, this species is known from the type locality at Fabyans, at the base of Mt. Washington, Coos County, New Hampshire, and from Baxter State Park in northern Maine, and there is one specimen from Mt. Moosiyauke, Benton, Grafton County, New Hampshire (unpublished; specimen taken 11 October 1958, 1150 meters, or 3800 feet, elevation, Montshire Mus. #2748). To the west, this species occurs through much of Canada and into Alaska, south to northern Washington and Idaho and extreme northwestern Montana.

HABITAT. Peterson (1966) states that this species is perhaps the rarest in collections of any eastern Canadian rodent. Six individuals from Quebec were from a dry, partly wooded area, but like its southern counterpart it may occur in old sphagnum bogs or in dense woods. The subspecies that occurs in Maine and New Hampshire was named *sphagnicola* because the type specimen was from a thick mat of sphagnum. Specimens have been taken from a sphagnum-lined spring on Mt. Katahdin, Maine, and from spruce forest with a thick sphagnum floor near the base of Mt. Katahdin (both sites in Baxter State Park). Tom French has located the Fabyans site: it is a moist patch of woods (not a bog) with a solid floor of thick sphagnum, a situation similar to that at the base of Mt. Katahdin. In New Brunswick, French trapped both *S. cooperi* and *S. borealis* along the same mountain stream.

HABITS. Few individuals of this species have been taken, and little is known of its habits. Pre-

*Distribution of the northern bog lemming,* Synaptomys borealis, *in the eastern United States*

sumably, they are similar to those of the southern bog lemming.

ENEMIES. Tom French found several skulls in raven pellets in coastal Quebec (north of the Gulf of St. Lawrence).

RELATION TO HUMANS. This species is apparently too rare and isolated to have much effect on humans.

AREAS FOR FURTHER WORK. Almost nothing is known of this very rare species. All phases of its life history would merit study.

SUBSPECIES

*Synaptomys borealis sphagnicola* Preble

As described above. The species occurs over most of northern Canada, but this subspecies is disjunct from the nominate subspecies, occurring from the Gaspé Peninsula (Quebec) and New Brunswick south to northern Maine and central New Hampshire, thus embracing the entire eastern U.S. range of the species.

Type locality: Fabyans, Coos Co., New Hampshire, for *S. borealis sphagnicola.*

LITERATURE

Dutcher, B. H. 1903. Mammals of Mt. Katahdin, Maine. *Proc. Biol. Soc. Wash.* 16: 63–72.
Harper, F. 1961. Land and fresh-water mammals of the Ungava Peninsula. Misc. Publ. Mus. Nat. Hist. Univ. Kansas No. 27. 178 pp.
Peterson, R. L. 1966. *The Mammals of Eastern Canada.* Toronto: Oxford Univ. Press. 465 pp.
Preble, E. A. 1899. Description of a new lemming mouse from the White Mountains, New Hampshire. *Proc. Biol. Soc. Wash.* 13: 43–45.

## Southern Bog Lemming
*Synaptomys cooperi* Baird

DESCRIPTION. *Synaptomys cooperi* is a small, robust, short-legged vole with a large head and a very short tail, the tail scarcely longer than the hind foot and sometimes shorter. This lemming has broad, heavy upper incisors with a shallow groove on their outer anterior surface. The pelage is rather long and shaggy, the upperparts

*Southern bog lemming,* Synaptomys cooperi
*(Roger W. Barbour)*

*Front of upper incisors of* Synaptomys, *showing shallow grooves (Thomas W. French)*

mixed brown, gray, and black, with a hint of dark yellow, lending a grizzled appearance. The overall tone is brownish. The underparts are silvery gray, the bases of the hairs darker. The tail is brownish above, whitish below, but not sharply bicolored.

Paul F. Connor has provided much of what we know about the southern bog lemming.

MEASUREMENTS. Fifteen adults from eastern New York and Pointe au Baril, Ontario, averaged: total length 121 (114–130), tail 16 (13–18), hind foot 17.5 (17–18) mm; and weight 24–35 grams. Average measurements of nine adults from the Great Smoky Mountains were: total length 127.2 (120–136), tail 24 (20–27), hind foot 20.4 (19–21) mm; and weight 26–36 grams.

Diploid number = 50.

TOOTH FORMULA
$$\frac{1}{1} \ \frac{0}{0} \ \frac{0}{0} \ \frac{3}{3} \ = \ 16$$

DISTRIBUTION. Bog lemmings have an extensive range in boreal America, descending in the eastern mountains as far south as the Great Smokies. The southern bog lemming occurs in the eastern United States from Wisconsin and Maine south to southern Illinois, northeastern Tennessee, western North Carolina, and western Virginia. There is a disjunct population in the Dismal Swamp of North Carolina. It also occurs in southeastern Canada and in the U.S. West through Minnesota and to western Nebraska and western Kansas.

HABITAT. The southern bog lemming is exceedingly variable in the habitats it occupies. Dry hillsides with a growth of bluegrass, fields matted with a canopy of weeds, grassy areas with interspersed brush and small trees, and dense woods of hemlock and beech all may harbor these little mice, at least in some areas. Paul F. Connor (1959) believes a chief requirement of the species is that its habitat support green, succulent monocots, primarily sedges and grasses. In many localities along the East Coast, such as in the Pine Barrens of southern New Jersey, where Connor made extensive studies on this species, sphagnum bogs are apparently its chief habitat. There, among the patches of pine forest, bogs are the principal situations where sedges and grasses are abundant. *Synaptomys cooperi* has also been taken in bogs in Quebec, Ontario, Nova Scotia, Manitoba, Michigan, Minnesota, New Jersey, Maryland, and North Carolina, but we have seldom taken it in bogs in New York or Indiana. Rather, the species often occurs in woodland burrows in New York, New Hampshire, Connecticut, Ontario, and Michigan. Here, the animals tunnel just beneath the leaf

*Distribution of the southern bog lemming,* Synaptomys cooperi, *in the eastern United States*

mold, pushing beneath the black soil or running through the hidden tunnels of the hairy-tailed mole, where these little animals can be caught by sinking mousetraps crosswise into underground burrows in hardwood forests. In many other areas, however, such as Iowa, Indiana, Ohio, Pennsylvania, or Kentucky, we would set our traps in areas of thick grass, especially bluegrass, where runways are fashioned above ground, crisscrossing one another. The grass is cut and trimmed constantly to keep the highways smooth. These lemmings have also been taken in grassy areas in New York, Michigan, Minnesota, Virginia, and elsewhere. In southern Indiana we have taken them in dry fields of little bluestem or broom sedge (*Andropogon*), and Connor mentions this same grass in the New Jersey habitat.

Bog lemmings were traditionally the dominant small mammal in Kentucky woodland clearings, but *Microtus pennsylvanicus* has recently invaded and appears to be replacing the bog lemming in this habitat, possibly through competitive exclusion (Krupa and Haskins, 1996).

HABITS. Wherever they occur, southern bog lemmings are found in company with other small mammals—red-backed voles, deer mice, prairie voles, moles, and various shrews—and *Synaptomys cooperi* often shares the same burrows with them. Nests, constructed of dead grasses and leaves, are often well hidden beneath the surface at a depth of several inches, or less often built directly on the ground wherever there is sufficient cover to conceal them. Occasionally, the nests are lined with fur.

Southern bog lemmings are sociable little beasts and usually occur in colonies, the populations of which range from a few to several dozen. Even though a sizable area may be of consistent habitat, often only a rather small part of it will be occupied and the remainder will be devoid of these mice. Southern bog lemmings are mainly nocturnal, but are sometimes abroad during the day. A prominent sign of their presence is the little piles of grasses or sedges that are found in the burrows or along the runways. These cuttings, of matchstick length, are found in varying degrees of freshness.

The droppings of *Synaptomys*, which are scattered throughout the burrows or are massed at certain points of the runway, are characteristic. They are bright green, in contrast to those of *Microtus*, which are black or brown. The color difference could be indicative of differences in digestive physiology.

*Synaptomys cooperi* usually refuses all lures, but an unbaited trap carefully set across one of its runways will often prove successful in its capture. Like shrews and woodland voles, it is often taken in pitfalls. This mouse is relatively rare in collections, but it is by no means an uncommon animal, its colonial habits perhaps making it more restricted than other small species are.

FOOD AND FEEDING. The food of southern bog lemmings consists almost entirely of green plant material, although blueberries, blackberries, and other such foods may be eaten in season. Fungi and mosses are also often consumed. All the stomachs we examined contained a finely chewed mass of green vegetation, although seeds of raspberry, spores of the subterranean fungus *Endogone*, and mosses (in winter) were also found. Some of the grasses used are *Festuca*, *Poa*, *Panicum*, *Glyceria*, and *Andropogon*.

REPRODUCTION AND DEVELOPMENT. Litters of one to eight (most often three) are produced after a gestation of 23 to 26 days. The young can be produced in any month in some parts of the species' range, but in the eastern United States there is little winter breeding. One female produced six litters totaling 22 young in 26 weeks (Connor, 1959). The tails of newborns averaged 5.7 mm, the hind foot 7.9 mm, and the weight 3.9 grams. The young are furred by seven days and look like juvenile bog lemmings at two weeks. The eyes open at ten to 11 days. Weaning is completed by the end of the third week.

POPULATION CHARACTERISTICS. Local temporary concentrations of this species, up to 51 per ha (20.6 per acre), have been recorded, but four to 12 per ha (1.6 to 4 per acre) is probably closer to the usual number in good habitat. Home-range estimates range from 0.04 to 0.32 ha (0.2 to 0.13 per acre). An individual originally captured as an adult lived two years, five months, in captivity.

ENEMIES. Owls, hawks, predatory mammals, and snakes all prey upon this mouse. Its appearance in owl pellets is sometimes the best indication the species is present, since it is often hard to trap.

PARASITES AND DISEASE. A large number of ectoparasites have been found on this species, but *Androlaelaps fahrenholzi, Laelaps, Dermacarus hypudaei*, several chiggers, a louse, and several fleas are the most abundant.

RELATION TO HUMANS. We doubt whether most people have heard of a bog lemming, and its impact on us can be but little.

AREAS FOR FURTHER WORK. A genetic assessment of this species from the various localities and quite different habitats where it occurs might prove interesting: for example, from woodland burrows in New York, bogs in New Jersey, and grassy fields in Indiana. A study of its behavior, mating systems, and general ecology should also be productive.

## SUBSPECIES

Five subspecies, including the nominate, have been recognized in the eastern United States, but just two appear to be separated by primary isolating mechanisms.

*Synaptomys cooperi cooperi* Baird

As described above. Ranges through virtually all of the eastern U.S. range of the species, excepting only the region of the Dismal Swamp of Virginia and North Carolina (Map 7.39).
Type locality: Jackson, Carroll Co., New Hampshire.
Other currently recognized eastern subspecies:
  *S. cooperi gossi* (Coues)
  *S. cooperi kentucki* Barbour
  *S. cooperi stonei* Rhoads

*Synaptomys cooperi helaletes* Merriam

Best characterized by the large, heavy, broad skull and stubby rostrum. The zygomatic breadth is 17 mm or greater; the rostral breadth, 6.3 mm. In color, *S. c. helaletes* does not differ appreciably from *S. c. cooperi*. Average measurements of nine adults from Lake Drummond, Dismal Swamp, Virginia, were: total length 129, tail 21.4, hind foot 20 mm. So far as is known, this race occurs only in the vicinity of Dismal Swamp, in extreme southeastern Virginia and extreme northeastern North Carolina.
Type locality: Chapanoke, Perquimans Co., North Carolina.

## LITERATURE

Burt, W. H. 1928. Additional notes on the life history of the Goss lemming mouse. *J. Mammal.* 9: 212–216.

Connor, P. F. 1959. The bog lemming *Synaptomys cooperi* in southern New Jersey. Publ. Mus. Mich. State Univ., Biol. Ser. 1: 161–248.

Krupa, J. J., and K. E. Haskins. 1996. Invasion of the meadow vole (*Microtus pennsylvanicus*) in southeastern Kentucky and its possible impact on the southern bog lemming (*Synaptomys cooperi*). *Amer. Midland Nat.* 135: 14–22.

Linzey, A. V. 1983. *Synaptomys cooperi*. **Mammalian Species No. 210.** Amer. Soc. Mammal. 5 pp.

Linzey, A. V., and J. A. Cranford. 1984. Habitat selection in the southern bog lemming, *Synaptomys cooperi*, and the meadow vole, *Microtus pennsylvanicus*, in Virginia. *Canadian Field-Nat.* 98: 463–469.

Wetzel, R. M. 1955. Speciation and dispersal of the southern bog lemming, *Synaptomys cooperi* (Baird). *J. Mammal.* 36: 1–20.

## OLD WORLD RATS AND MICE, Subfamily Murinae

Two species of rats of the genus *Rattus*, and the house mouse, *Mus musculus*, have been introduced into the New World since colonization. These pests are now well established over most of the country. They are characterized by a long, naked tail, the typical mouse- or ratlike form, and, as in the other murids, their three molar teeth on each side of both jaws. The upper molars differ from those of all native rats and mice in having three longitudinal rows of tubercles, a character that can be observed even in well-worn teeth.

## KEY TO THE GENERA OF OLD WORLD RATS AND MICE, SUBFAMILY MURINAE

1. Total length less than 250 mm; tail less than 110 mm long; skull less than 25 mm long . . . . . . . . . . . . . . . . . . . . . . . . . *Mus* (p. 376)
1. Total length more than 250 mm; tail more than 110 mm long; skull more than 25 mm long . . . . . . . . . . . . . . . . . . . . . . . . . . . . . *Rattus*

## Old World Rats of the Genus *Rattus*

Old World rats have to be among the most hated mammals in the world. They have managed to move with man practically throughout the world, and to cause untold millions of dollars of damage annually. They also carry some of our deadliest diseases, such as bubonic or black plague, which has caused so many deaths throughout human history. Rats of the genus *Rattus* can be distinguished from all other eastern mammals by their size and long, naked tail, coupled with the character of their molariform teeth, each bearing three rows of cusps (p. 276).

## KEY TO THE OLD WORLD RATS OF THE GENUS *RATTUS*

1. Tail longer than head and body; hind foot less than 40 mm long; first upper molar showing distinct outer notches on first row of cusps; cranium dome-shaped . . . . . . . . . . . . . . . . . . . . . . . . . . . . *R. rattus*
1. Tail not longer than head and body; hind foot more than 40 mm long; first upper molar showing no such notches; cranium flattened . . . . . *R. norvegicus*

## Norway Rat, Brown Rat
### *Rattus norvegicus* (Linnaeus)

DESCRIPTION. The Norway rat, or brown rat is a coarse-furred rat with prominent, naked ears and a nearly naked, scaly tail, the tail not longer than the head and body combined. On the molars of the upper jaw are tubercles in three longitudinal rows, as in the house mouse. The general color above is brown, with scattered black hairs, darkest on the middle of the back; the underparts are pale gray or grayish brown. The Norway rat can be confused with the rice rat (*Oryzomys*), since the two sometimes occur in the same habitat, but the rice rat is smaller and has softer fur, lighter underparts and a much

*Norway rat, or brown rat*, Rattus norvegicus
*(Roger W. Barbour)*

more slender tail; it also lacks the characteristic roman nose of *Rattus*, and the tubercles of its molariform teeth are in two rows.

MEASUREMENTS. Measurements of 50 adults from New York and Washington, D.C., averaged: total length 399 (320–480), tail 187 (153–218), hind foot 41 (37–44) mm; and weight 300–540 grams.

Diploid number = 42.

TOOTH FORMULA

$$\frac{1}{1} \quad \frac{0}{0} \quad \frac{0}{0} \quad \frac{3}{3} \; = \; 16$$

DISTRIBUTION. The Norway rat is now nearly cosmopolitan wherever people live; it was not known in Europe until about 1553, and it was introduced into the United States about 1775, probably from Eurasia. Because it is now well established in every state in the Union, no map is given.

HABITAT. Rats occur wherever there is an abundance of food and shelter, from the subways and crowded tenements of the great metropolitan areas to the corn and grain fields of the farm country. They are often superabundant in the corncribs and grain elevators of the Midwest, and they are frequently seen in the salt marshes of the Atlantic Coast, where edible flotsam washes up on the beaches.

HABITS. Rats are largely nocturnal, leaving the shelter of their nests as dusk approaches. They are wary creatures, and although they often occur in incredible numbers on a farm, such great numbers are seldom suspected, for they are adept at hiding or scurrying away at the approach of humans. Their bulky nests are built in a burrow, in trash, in a crate, drawer, or woodpile, or in any of many other protected places. Their droppings, capsule-shaped and about 20 mm long, are often conspicuous in buildings. A good summary of information on rats was given by Jackson (1982).

FOOD AND FEEDING. The appetite of the rat is prodigious. It will eat a third of its weight in 24 hours, and often waste as much more. Few items are shunned. Its sharp teeth puncture the tin covers of jellies, and it consumes soap, candy, milk, meat, vegetables, poultry and eggs, and all grains; even cherries growing many feet from the ground are not exempt from its attacks. It will enter water to feed, and will eat some aquatic plants.

Some of the more important foods of 115 Norway rats from Indiana farms and granaries (Whitaker, 1977) were grain seeds, mostly wheat (39.7% of the total volume), corn (20.2%), flesh (6.3%), green vegetation (5.3%), mast (5.0%), clover flowers (3.9%), and garbage (3.2%). It has been estimated that rats eat perhaps 7000 tons of cultivated grains per year from Indiana's granaries and larger farms alone.

REPRODUCTION AND DEVELOPMENT. Much has been written on the reproductive potential of the rat, a great deal of which has been gross exaggeration. Rats are nonetheless among the most prolific of mammals. If food is abundant and shelter adequate, rats will breed throughout the year, though producing fewer litters in the winter. The gestation period varies from 21 to 23 days, but may be prolonged when a pregnant female is nursing her previous litter. The number of young in a litter varies considerably. We have counted from two to 14 embryos in rats, and there is one record of 22, but six to nine is the usual number. Six to eight litters per year are usually produced, but there is one record of 12. Blind, naked, and helpless at birth, the young grow rapidly, and the eyes

open in 14 to 17 days. They are weaned when three weeks old, and can be completely independent at about four weeks. The young rats commence to breed when just four months old, although there is a record of an eight-week-old female giving birth to 11 young, all of which were successfully raised.

POPULATION CHARACTERISTICS. Rats seldom overpopulate, evidently responding to built-in regulating mechanisms. Overpopulation leads to reduced birthrates, increased death rates, and emigration, although rats are not given to frequent movement. At high populations, or when food or habitat is limited, intraspecific tension and strife arise. Dominant animals (alpha males and pregnant or lactating females) will harass or kill subordinates, and cannibalism of newborn and subordinates may occur. Conversely, when conditions are right, Norway rats can multiply to the carrying capacity of the habitat very rapidly.

Home ranges are usually relatively small, and rats usually remain within about 45 meters (150 feet) of their nests, at least in cities. The larger, dominant males establish both territories and harems. Other males are forced to accept marginal areas, and may even be forced to leave. The life span of a rat may reach three years, although few probably live more than one year.

ENEMIES. The rat's many enemies, such as cats, dogs, snakes, hawks, owls, and weasels, all serve to lessen its numbers, but cannot begin to keep populations down when environmental conditions are propitious. We are of course the most important enemy of rats, by destroying their habitat and laying out traps and poison.

PARASITES AND DISEASE. External parasites of the Norway rat include fleas, lice, and mites; internal parasites include protozoans, trematodes, cestodes, nematodes, and acanthocephalans.

Black and Norway rats carry or cause many diseases, such as bubonic (black) plague, typhus, food poisoning, tularemia, trichinosis, and more. Rats played a prominent role in the spread of plague in the early fourteenth century, which killed about one-fourth of the inhabitants of Europe. Plague killed half the inhabitants of London in 1665, and, over a single 20-year period, about 9 million people in India. Murine typhus killed many people in the southern United States in the 1940s, and hantavirus has been found in this species in New York.

RELATION TO HUMANS. The rat is the greatest mammal pest of mankind. Its diseases have caused more human deaths than all the wars of history (see above). It harbors lice and fleas, dread disseminators of the plague, typhus, trichina, infectious jaundice, and many other but scarcely less serious diseases. These animals are usually a paramount factor in the spread of pandemics during war.

Rodents chewing on insulation or perhaps directly on matches can cause fires, power outages, or telephone interruptions, although the rat's role in this type of damage is not well documented. There are records of rats gnawing through a wide variety of building materials, including even cinder blocks and metal sheeting, and they often climb along horizontal wires, beams, or other structures, or up wires.

Man has waged war against *Rattus* for centuries, but the rats continue to be an unmitigated nuisance, causing an estimated 500 million to a billion dollars in damage each year in the United States alone. For what it is worth, the Norway rat appears to replace the black rat over much of its inland habitat, and the black rat appears to be more dangerous than the Norway rat as a disease carrier.

This species does have a few redeeming features, so far as we humans are concerned. First, it has given us the albino laboratory rat, widely used for medical and other research purposes. The medical discoveries emerging from research based on white laboratory rats (and mice) have probably saved as many human lives as the black plague killed. Much behavioral work (Calhoun, 1963) has been carried out in rats, as well, some of which has indicated the disastrous results befalling animals when they become overpopulated. They display bizarre behavior, then begin to starve and to kill each other, and in due course reproduction ceases and the population crashes. One wonders why the lessons learned from overpopulation in rats are not better learned and more closely applied to human societies.

AREAS FOR FURTHER WORK. If we could find a way to educate the citizenry and the political and religious leaders of the world about the effects of overpopulation in rats, and about the dark implications of these effects for humans, sufficiently that governments began taking concrete steps about our own overpopulation, we would be helping to solve the gravest problem facing humanity today.

## SUBSPECIES

The original range of this species was apparently southeastern Siberia and northern China, but it has been introduced worldwide. Apparently, only the nominate subspecies has been introduced into North America, but some authors consider the species to be monophyletic (undifferentiated into subspecies) in any case.

*Rattus norvegicus norvegicus* (Berkenhout)
As described above.
Type locality: England.

## LITERATURE

Barnett, S. A., R. G. Dickson, and W. H. Hooking. 1979. Genotype and environment in the social interactions of wild and domestic Norway rats. *Aggressive Behav.* 5: 105–119.

Bjornson, B. F., H. D. Pratt, and K. S. Littig. 1969. Control of domestic rats and mice. U.S. Publ. Health Serv. Publ. No. 563. 41 pp.

Calhoun, J. B. 1963. The ecology and sociology of the Norway rat. U.S. Publ. Health Serv. Publ. No. 1008. 288 pp.

Davis, D. E., J. Emlen, and A. W. Stokes. 1948. Studies on home range in the brown rat. *J. Mammal.* 29: 207–225.

Howard, W. E., and R. E. Marsh. 1976. The rat: Its biology and control. Univ. Calif. Coop. Ext. Serv. Leaflet 2869. 22 pp.

Jackson, W. B. 1982. Norway rat and allies. *Rattus norvegicus* and allies. In: J. A. Chapman and G. A. Feldhamer, eds., *Wild Mammals of North America*, pp. 1077–1088. Baltimore: Johns Hopkins Univ. Press.

Storer, T. I., and D. E. Davis. 1953. Studies on rat reproduction in San Francisco. *J. Mammal.* 34: 365–373.

Whitaker, J. O., Jr. 1977. Food and external parasites of the Norway rat, *Rattus norvegicus*, in Indiana. *Proc. Ind. Acad. Sci.* 86: 193–198.

## Black Rat, Roof Rat *Rattus rattus*
### (Linnaeus)                         Color plate 13

DESCRIPTION. The black rat, or roof rat, is similar in general form to the Norway rat, but it has a longer tail, one that is more than half the ani-

*Black rat, or roof rat,* Rattus rattus
*(Roger W. Barbour)*

mal's total length. It also has a shorter nose. The color is a darker grayish black above, light to sooty to very dark below. On Cedar Key, Florida, there are distinctly different brown and black color morphs.

MEASUREMENTS. Measurements of 12 adults from Alabama, Florida, Georgia, Massachusetts, New Hampshire, and Virginia averaged: total length 369 (327–430), tail 193 (160–220), hind foot 35.5 (33–39) mm. The weight of large males is about 200 (150–250) grams. Diploid number = 42.

TOOTH FORMULA

$$\frac{1}{1} \quad \frac{0}{0} \quad \frac{0}{0} \quad \frac{3}{3} \quad = \quad 16$$

DISTRIBUTION. *Rattus rattus* apparently arrived with the Spaniards in Central America in the 1500s and with the colonists at Jamestown in 1607. (The more aggressive Norway rat apparently arrived much later.) The black rat is generally distributed along the East Coast and through all of the Deep South, and is established in many southern inland cities, as well. Black rats are more abundant in the South, but they have been recorded from most of the states east of the Mississippi, and formerly were found in many cities along the Great Lakes. The black rat was once established in Springfield, Massachusetts, and elsewhere in southeastern New England, but except for occasional fresh immigrants, it has disappeared there and pretty much elsewhere in the North. The map attempts to show where black rats are currently established. They also occur in much of the western United States.

HABITAT. When black and Norway rats occur together in buildings, the black rat usually lives high in the buildings, the Norway rat below. Moreover, the Norway rat appears to outcompete the black rat, for when the former becomes established, the latter often disappears. Being a more adept climber, however, the black rat has managed to maintain itself in trees, in the roofs and upper stories of buildings, and to a great extent in ships. The roof rat lives chiefly about the roofs of dwellings and in smokehouses and outhouses, occurring less commonly in the open fields.

HABITS. The black rat may nest in a burrow under a building, but it is more likely to live in the walls. On small islands off the east coast of Cuba and in southern Florida, it nests in coconut palms. Its droppings, about 12 mm long, are spindle-shaped. Roof rats recognize one another by a muzzling behavior in which the dominant animal takes the muzzle of the subordinate in its mouth. Adults live in separate burrows, although advanced young may remain with the female for a time.

FOOD AND FEEDING. Rats will eat almost anything remotely edible, but feed heavily on grain or seeds if available. Roof rats feed heavily on nuts and fruits even while they are still on the trees. They often damage citrus fruits, macadamia nuts, coconuts, and cacao.

REPRODUCTION AND DEVELOPMENT. The black rat, or roof rat, is apparently somewhat less prolific than the Norway rat, producing fewer and smaller litters. Nevertheless, their natural rate of increase is sufficient to make them a pest of major importance, and their archenemy, humanity, is forever attempting to reduce their numbers. Breeding may occur at any time of year, but mostly in early spring or early summer, and there may also be a fall peak. Black rats first breed at two to three months, and produce four to six litters per year. Each female weans about 20 young per year. Gestation is 22 days. The young are blind and hairless and pink in color. At one week the ears have opened, and fine hair covers the body. At two weeks, the eyes have opened and the young animals begin to move from the nest. Soon they begin following the mother to nearby food sources. There is post-partum estrus, and if the female becomes pregnant again, the next litter will be born in about a month. The newly weaned young from the previous litter must then move on and fend for themselves. Rats are promiscuous, several males mating with each female in estrus.

POPULATION CHARACTERISTICS. The home range of the black rat has a radius of about 30–50 meters (90–150 feet). Contrary to popular belief, rats are relatively sedentary, moving mostly when they are overpopulated or lacking in habitat or food. Rats may move from fields into buildings in winter, and young rats disperse from their natal areas. Although captive rats may live several years, their wild counterparts usually do not live a year.

ENEMIES. Rats are of course preyed upon by any mammalian or avian predators and snakes

*Distribution of the black rat, or roof rat,* Rattus rattus, *in the eastern United States*

that can overcome them, but humans, with their traps and poisons, are surely the greatest enemy of this species.

PARASITES AND DISEASE. This species harbors a number of parasites: at least six protozoans, 11 cestodes, five nematodes, three lice, 11 fleas, and 31 mites and ticks. These rats or their parasites are capable of transmitting a number of diseases, particularly plague and typhus fever, to humans.

RELATION TO HUMANS. The black rat is a menace of major proportions in harboring the infectious agents of plague and typhus fever. Wherever it occurs, public health officers must be on the alert, so that these dread diseases will not take their toll of humans. Epidemic typhus fever of the Old World is transmitted to man by the rat-borne louse. New World endemic typhus fever, although milder, is nevertheless frequently fatal; it is transmitted from rats to man by the rat fleas *Xenopsylla cheopsis* and *Nosopsyllus fasciatus*. A severe localized epidemic of typhus occurred in August 1941 in Lavaca County, Texas; more than 100 cases were reported in a single week, and several of them resulted in death. During the late summer and fall of 1942, army duties took Hamilton to Texas, where he was assigned to work on the control of typhus; by mid-October, more than 900 cases of typhus fever had been reported in Texas, and the disease was also widespread in Georgia. Fortunately, with the spread of the aggressive Norway rat, the black rat appears to have declined in numbers.

Introduced exotics can have major ill effects on native species, as witness the rabbit in Australia and the mongoose in Hawaii. Black rats may compete with the endangered silver rice rat (*Oryzomys argentatus*), feed on rare *Liguus* snails, and damage palm trees in Key Biscayne National Park. They probably have a more significant impact on native plants and animals in the eastern United States than does the Norway rat, for they move more frequently into natural habitats, especially in the South, and feed heavily on fruit and nut crops.

AREAS FOR FURTHER STUDY. Much more information is needed on the behavioral and ecological interrelationships between this species and the Norway rat, by studying them in areas where each occurs alone, where they occur together, and, if opportunity permits, where one has invaded an area already occupied by the other. Work of this sort could be done using enclosures, as well.

## SUBSPECIES

At least three subspecies of *Rattus rattus*— *R. r. rattus*, *R. r. alexandrinus* (Desmarest), and *R. r. frugivorus* (Rafinesque)—have been introduced into North America, but we shall not attempt to delineate their (no doubt intermixed) North American ranges.

*Rattus rattus rattus* (Linnaeus)
  As described above.
  Type locality: Uppsala, Sweden.

### LITERATURE

Jackson, W. B. 1982. Norway rat and allies. *Rattus norvegicus* and allies. In: J. A. Chapman and G. A. Feldhamer, eds., *Wild Mammals of North America*, pp. 1077–1088. Baltimore: Johns Hopkins Univ. Press.

Schwarz, E., and H. H. Schwarz. 1965. A monograph of the *Rattus rattus* group. *An. Esc. Nac. Cienc. Biol. Mex.* 14: 79–178.

## House Mouse
## *Mus musculus* Linnaeus

DESCRIPTION. This species is native to Eurasia, but has spread with human culture throughout

*House mouse,* Mus musculus *(Roger W. Barbour)*

the world. It is sometimes confused with our native species, since it is often caught in natural habitats as well as in buildings. It is a long-tailed mouse with prominent ears and no line of demarcation between the dorsal and ventral colorations. It is grayish brown to brown, shading to lighter gray or brown on the belly, which is often buffy. The tail is scaly and nearly lacking in hairs. The house mouse's identity can be verified by observing the crowns of the molars in the upper jaw, the tubercles of which are arranged in three longitudinal rows. The odor of this species is so distinctive that one in a trap can frequently be recognized before it is even seen.

MEASUREMENTS. Measurements of 30 adults from central New York and Washington, D.C., averaged: total length 163 (148–205), tail 78 (69–85), hind foot 18 (16–20) mm; and weight 14–24 grams.
Diploid number = 40.

TOOTH FORMULA

$$\frac{1}{1} \frac{0}{0} \frac{0}{0} \frac{3}{3} = 16$$

DISTRIBUTION. This species was introduced from Europe probably about the time of the American Revolution, and is now widely distributed. Because it is found throughout the eastern United States, no map is given.

HABITAT. The house mouse is found wherever humanity is found, and in keeping with its common name it often makes its residence in houses and other buildings. Still, it should not be thought of as a species only or primarily of those habitats. It reaches its greatest abundance, in fact, in the fields of corn, wheat, sorghum, and (to a lesser extent) soybeans, at least of the Midwest, but only when good ground cover is present. Kaufman and Kaufman (1990) found few house mice in Kansas in either grasslands, woodland, or crop fields. The only situation in which many were taken there was in crop-field fencerows—where, we assume, there was good herbaceous ground cover. In the various crop

fields, the house mouse is nomadic: when the ground is plowed or the crop is harvested, the house mouse moves, perhaps to another field yet to be harvested, or to a grassy or weedy field. It is at this time, especially, that the house mouse enters buildings, but it almost never enters woods. It is—or at least was—the most abundant small mammal of Indiana, probably because of the state's preponderance of cultivated habitats. With the widespread introduction of herbicides onto farm fields, the house mouse's status there may have changed. It is often found in grassy fields and waste lands, and the inexperienced collector may fail to recognize it under such conditions. It colonizes the saw palmetto thickets of Florida's west coast, but often appears on dunes, in grassy fields, and in other habitats there. The house mouse may be confused with harvest mice, but the absence of grooves on the upper incisors in the house mouse will prevent mistaken identification. It may also be confused with mice of the genus *Peromyscus*, but *Peromyscus* has white underparts and only two longitudinal rows of tubercles on its molariform teeth (in *Mus*, there are three).

HABITS. The persistent gnawing in the walls, or the little black pellets in drawers and on counters and other surfaces, are often the first clue to the presence of this little beast. The droppings are elongate and tapered at the ends, and about 3 to 6 mm long. A single individual will not pilfer any great quantity of food, but the combined depredations of several dozen over a few months' time may be considerable.

House mice are mainly nocturnal. They can swim and climb, and they jump well. When outdoors, they excavate burrow systems in which they construct nests of grasses with soft lining. In buildings, their nests may be in debris, drawers, shoes, furniture, or other protected places.

House mice can sense salts, sugars, and other chemicals at low concentrations (a few parts per million). They use pheromones in recognizing each other, and various objects are marked as the mouse investigates them. A mutual chemical-stimulation system links the sexes, females in estrus stimulating males and male cues stimulating females, in a feedback loop. House mice use urine both as a range marker and to inhibit aggression between conspecifics.

House mice utter various squeaks and calls, and even songs. Ernest Thompson Seton (1909) wrote, "Out of the black darkness of a cupboard at midnight came a prolonged squeaking, trilling and churring, suggestive of a canary's song but of thinner and weaker quality. There could be no question that it was a 'singing mouse.' Many cases are on record." One night while checking traps in a weedy field at Willow Slough Fish and Game Area in Newton County, Indiana, we heard such a song over and over. We could not find the singer, but believe it was a house mouse.

The establishment of this species in vast numbers around the globe is probably due to its adaptability to life in buildings and on ships, but also to its ability to invade early successional situations, to multiply rapidly, and then to move on when the habitat changes. Similarly, house mice can take advantage of cultivated fields, increasing rapidly with the growing crop, but immediately dispersing when the habitat is obliterated at harvest time. Another factor favoring its success is its low water requirement; in this respect, it rivals some desert rodents. The only other species that inhabits Midwest cornfields in numbers is the prairie deer mouse. The latter remains on site all year by using soil rather than vegetation as its cover. House mice and prairie deer mice (and white-footed mice) appear to be mutually antagonistic.

FOOD AND FEEDING. In fields, house mice eat many different foods, the depredations governed, of course, by availability. Some of the most important foods of 458 house mice from Indiana were the seeds of foxtail grass, *Setaria*, lepidopterous larvae, corn, wheat seeds, other grass and weed seeds, and beetle larvae. In one field they fed heavily on the subterranean fungus *Endogone*.

In the home, they feed on various grains and cereals, candy, paste from the bindings of books, meat, and almost anything edible left out by the householder. We have even found them regularly chewing on soap. The damage they do is exacerbated by their droppings, which are often deposited on that which they have otherwise spared.

REPRODUCTION AND DEVELOPMENT. These mice, like their larger cousin, the Norway rat, are very prolific. It is not unusual for them to produce a litter of 10 or 11 young, though the usual number is but five to seven. The average number of embryos among 48 pregnant females from Vigo County, Indiana, was 6.02 (range of three to ten). Breeding continues without interruption from early spring until late fall, but is much curtailed or stopped altogether during the colder months (no pregnant females were taken in December or January in Indiana). After a gestation period of 19–21 days (somewhat longer if a pregnant female is nursing her prior litter), the blind, naked, and helpless young are born, at a weight of about 1 gram. Their eyes open in two weeks, and they are fully weaned in three weeks. When less than two months of age they are ready to assume their own family duties. Females become sexually mature at about 45 days and may have up to 14 litters (seldom over eight) in a year. One can fairly often find a female with two distinct sets of placental scars, and we caught one animal that had two sets of scars plus a set of embryos.

POPULATION CHARACTERISTICS. House mice fluctuate greatly in numbers between habitats, years, and land-use situations. They have been known to reach highs of 1235 per ha (500 per acre) in Louisiana, and 205,000 per ha (82,800 per acre) in 1926 and 1927 in Kern County, California. Two tons of house mice were killed in one granary at the California location. Overpopulation leads to high energy consumption and a cessation of population growth, through reductions of reproduction due to social and pheromonal influences. In the laboratory, increasing population density can even lead to cannibalism.

House mice in field situations have home ranges that average about 0.6 ha (1.5 acres). In one study, the home ranges of juvenile males, juvenile females, and adult females were found to be similar to one another in size, but those of adult males were larger (Mikesic and Drickamer, 1992). A house mouse that had wandered

290 meters (860 ft) from its homesite returned the next day.

Most house mice probably live less than a year under field conditions, perhaps slightly more in buildings. One individual in captivity lived five years, 11 months.

ENEMIES. Most mammalian and avian predators, as well as snakes, probably take house mice when available.

PARASITES AND DISEASE. The most abundant internal parasite in digestive tracts from house mice in Indiana was a nematode, *Heligmosomoides polygyrus*. Cestodes and two other nematodes were also found.

As is the case with most small terrestrial (nonburrowing) mammals, house mice are not heavily beset with ectoparasites. Two myobiids, *Myobia musculi* and *Radfordia affinis*, were the most common mites, but several other species were also found. Fleas are not abundant on this species, and the plague flea, *Xenopsyllus cheopis*, was not found in Indiana. Rickettsial pox can be transmitted by mites from infected mice, but it is not an important disease. A few cases are recorded each year, mostly in large city apartment houses in New York and New England. Most of the diseases attributed to murid rodents are carried by fleas from rats, not house mice.

RELATION TO HUMANS. The diseases borne by house mice, and their depredations on food and other articles of ours, are discussed above. In a cultivated field, however, they are generally beneficial, for they eat numerous weed seeds as well as cutworms and other larvae. What corn and other grain they eat—forgetting for the moment the harm they can bring to a granary—is mostly of waste on the ground after the harvest. But the greatest value of house mice, both albinos and other strains, is their widespread use in laboratories, where they make ideal subjects for biological, genetic, or medical research. Most of the laboratory strains are apparently derived from *Mus musculus domesticus* from Europe, but Schwarz and Schwarz (1943) indicated that the one called "*Mus bac-*

*trianus* Blyth" was derived from *M. m. wagneri* of central Asia.

AREAS FOR FURTHER STUDY. House mice were found to be the most abundant small mammal in the cultivated fields of Indiana in a study in the early 1960s, but they were found only in areas with good ground cover of grasses and other plants in addition to the crop plant. This study was conducted before the time of no-till farming and heavy use of herbicides. Now, many of the fields are clear other than for the crop. What effect has this had on the mice (and other small mammals) of the cropfields? Studies of the behavioral and ecological interrelationships between this species and various native rodents, where they occur together, are always of interest.

## SUBSPECIES

Native wild stocks of house mice in Eurasia are short-tailed (the tail shorter than the head and body) and have white underparts, with a line of demarcation between the upper and lower colorations. The derived forms have longer tails, grayer underparts, and little demarcation between the dorsal and ventral colorations.

Introduced house mice in the New World are considered feral forms derived from ancestors that have long been commensal with humans (Schwarz and Schwarz, 1943; Sage, 1981). In the United States, *Mus musculus domesticus* Rutty from Spain or Italy was introduced in the North, and *M. m. brevirostris* Waterhouse from England was introduced in the South. The difference between these two forms lies in the presence of a recessive dark-belly allele in *domesticus* mice, which yields bellies that contrast with the paler coloration of the *brevirostris* bellies. Since these two forms differ by a single gene (Sage, pers. comm.), and since they broadly intergrade, we find no reason to consider them separate subspecies. As Sage (1981) points out, "considerable divergent evolution has occurred" among house mice, the "systematic treatment [of them has departed significantly] from the earlier view of a single widespread polytypic species," and it must be understood that there are many different species hidden under the common name "house mouse." Further, Sage (1981) considers the form introduced into the New World to be *Mus domesticus* rather than *Mus musculus*, whereas Wilson and Reeder (1993) treat *Mus domesticus* as a synonym of *Mus musculus*. For more information, see Schwarz and Schwarz (1943), Sage (1981), and Wilson and Reeder (1993).

*Mus musculus musculus* Linnaeus

As described above.

Type locality: Upsala, Upsala Co., Sweden.

## LITERATURE

Breakey, D. R. 1963. The breeding season and age structure of feral house mouse populations near San Francisco Bay, California. *J. Mammal.* 44: 153–168.

Briese, L. A., and M. H. Smith. 1973. Competition between *Mus musculus* and *Peromyscus polionotus*. *J. Mammal.* 54: 968–969.

Bronson, F. H. 1979. The reproductive ecology of the house mouse. *Quart. Rev. Biol.* 54: 265–299.

Brown, R. Z. 1953. Social behavior, reproduction, and population changes in the house mouse (*Mus musculus* L.). *Ecol. Monogr.* 23: 217–240.

Clark, D. E. 1970. Parasites of *Mus musculus* taken from an inhabited building in Terre Haute, Vigo County, Indiana. *Proc. Ind. Acad. Sci.* 80: 495–500.

Crowcroft, P., and F. P. Rowe. 1963. Social organization and territorial behaviour in the wild house mouse (*Mus musculus* L.). *Proc. Zool. Soc. London* 140: 517–531.

DeLong, K. T. 1967. Population ecology of feral house mice. *Ecology* 48: 611–634.

Engels, W. L. 1948. White-bellied house mice on some North Carolina coastal islands. *J. Hered.* 39: 94–96.

Evans, F. C. 1949. A population study of house mice (*Mus musculus*) following a period of local abundance. *J. Mammal.* 30: 351–363.

Houtcooper, W. C. 1978. Food habits of rodents in a cultivated ecosystem. *J. Mammal.* 59: 427–430.

Jackson, W. B. 1982. Norway rat and allies. *Rattus norvegicus* and allies. In: J. A. Chapman and G. A. Feldhamer, eds., *Wild Mammals of North America*, pp. 1077–1088. Baltimore: Johns Hopkins Univ. Press.

Kaufman, D. W., and G. A. Kaufman. 1990. House mice (*Mus musculus*) in natural and disturbed habitats in Kansas. *J. Mammal.* 71: 428–432.

Lidicker, W. Z., Jr. 1966. Ecological observations on a feral house mouse population declining to extinction. *Ecol. Monogr.* 36: 27–50.

———. 1976. Social behaviour and density regulation in house mice living in large enclosures. *J. Anim. Ecol.* 45: 677–697.

Mikesic, D. G., and L. C. Drickamer. 1992. Factors affecting home-range size in house mice (*Mus musculus domesticus*) living in outdoor enclosures. *J. Mammal.* 73: 663–667.

Oakeshott, J. G. 1974. Social dominance, aggressiveness and mating success among male house mice (*Mus musculus*). *Oecologia* 15: 143–158.

Orr, R. T. 1944. Communal nests of the house mouse *Mus musculus* L. *Wasmann Collect.* 6: 35–37.

Pearson, O. P. 1963. History of two local outbreaks of feral house mice. *Ecology* 44: 540–549.

Petras, M. L. 1967a. Studies of natural populations of *Mus*. I. Biochemical polymorphisms and their bearing on breeding structure. *Evolution* 21: 259–274.

———. 1967b. Studies of natural populations of *Mus*. III. Coat color polymorphisms. *Canadian J. Genet. Cytol.* 9: 287–296.

Petras, M. L., J. D. Reimer, F. G. Biddle, J. E. Martin, and R. S. Linton. 1969. Studies of natural populations of *Mus*. V. A survey of nine loci for polymorphisms. *Canadian J. Genet. Cytol.* 11: 497–513.

Quadagno, D. M. 1967. Litter size and implantation sites in feral house mice. *J. Mammal.* 48: 677.

———. 1968. Home range size in feral house mice. *J. Mammal.* 49: 149–151.

Sage, R. D. 1981. Wild mice. In: H. L. Foster, J. D. Small, and J. G. Fox, eds., *The Mouse in Biomedical Research*, Vol. I, chap. 4, pp. 39–90. San Diego: Academic Press.

Schwarz, E., and H. K. Schwarz. 1943. The wild and commensal stocks of the house mouse, *Mus musculus* Linnaeus. *J. Mammal.* 24: 59–72.

Seton, E. T. 1909. *Life Histories of Northern Animals*, Vol. 1. New York: Charles Scribner's Sons. 673 pp.

Smith, W. W. 1954. Reproduction in the house mouse, *Mus musculus* L., in Mississippi. *J. Mammal.* 35: 509–515.

Whitaker, J. O., Jr. 1966. Food of *Mus musculus*, *Peromyscus maniculatus bairdi* and *Peromyscus leucopus* in Vigo County, Indiana. *J. Mammal.* 47: 473–486.

———. 1970. Parasites of feral house mice, *Mus musculus*, in Vigo County, Indiana. *Proc. Ind. Acad. Sci.* 79: 441–448.

Wilson, D. E., and D. M. Reeder. 1993. *Mammal Species of the World. A Taxonomic and Geographic Reference*, Second Edition. Washington: Smithsonian Institution Press in association with American Society of Mammalogists.

# PORCUPINES AND ALLIES,
## Family Erethizontidae

Porcupines and nutrias (Myocastoridae) are the two eastern U.S. representatives of the Hystricomorpha, the former native, the latter introduced. The suborder Hystricomorpha otherwise subsumes several families of South American rodents. In the hystricomorphs, much of the masseter muscle passes through the very large infraorbital foramen. Representatives of the Erethizontidae are found in both North and South America, but only one, the North American porcupine, *Erethizon dorsatum*, the lone species of the genus *Erethizon*, occurs in North America. Besides their spines, porcupines are characterized by their intricate, folded-and-rooted, flat-crowned cheek teeth. The stout skull of our porcupine, with its large infraorbital

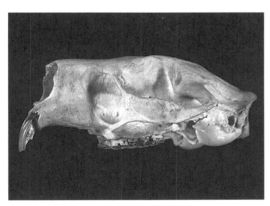

*The skull of the porcupine*

foramen and heavy incisors, is also characteristic of the family.

## Porcupine *Erethizon dorsatum*
## (Linnaeus)                    Color plate 14

Our knowledge of this remarkable animal has been greatly extended by the work of Uldis Roze (1989), who summarized his findings in *The North American Porcupine*, an excellent and very readable book. Roze and his wife came to know porcupines intimately by living among them for eight years on their 70 acres in the Catskill Mountains of New York. Much of this account is based on Roze's work, although some of his conclusions may not hold in the more

boreal habitat that makes up most of the porcupine's range.

DESCRIPTION. The porcupine is a heavy, thickset animal with a robust but relatively small

*Porcupine,* Erethizon dorsatum

head. The pelage comprises five different types of hair: the woolly underfur; the coarser guard hairs; the vibrissae, or whiskers; the stiff bristles on the undersurface of the tail, which are employed in climbing; and the quills, or spines. Quills, as many as 30,000 on a single animal, are stiff, highly modified guard hairs filled with a spongy matrix and bearing microscopic, backward-projecting barbs at the free ends. The quills, which are white or yellowish white with black tips, cover the body except for the venter, face, and ears. They vary in size, some reaching 110 mm in length and 2 mm in diameter, but all are slender and pointed. Because of their reversely barbed tips, the quills may work their way through the body of a would-be predator, all the way to its vital organs. The shorter spines of the neck, rump, and tail are stiffer than those of the flanks and back. The short, muscular tail is heavily armed above with quills, and the stiff bristles on its underside are useful for climbing. The soles of the animal's heavy feet are both naked and rugose (deeply wrinkled), another adaptation to a life in the trees. The pelage is brownish black above, although some of the longer hairs are tipped with white. In winter the pelage is longer and darker, often obscuring all but the longest spines. There are five clawed toes on the hind feet and four on the front. The incisors are heavily pigmented with yellow to orange enamel.

MEASUREMENTS. Measurements of adults from Minnesota were: total length 686 (612–740), tail 180 (160–223), hind foot 93 (75–110) mm. Adults weigh 2–7.6 kg (4.4–16.8 lbs).

Diploid number = 42.

TOOTH FORMULA

$$\frac{1}{1} \quad \frac{0}{0} \quad \frac{1}{1} \quad \frac{3}{3} \;=\; 20$$

DISTRIBUTION. In the northeastern United States the porcupine is found from northern New England through New York and much of Pennsylvania, and in northern Michigan and Wisconsin. It may still occur in the wilder parts of West Virginia, but probably never occurred as far south as the Great Smoky Mountains. Beyond the eastern United States, this species occurs throughout most of Canada and all of Alaska, and south through parts of California and Arizona, all of Nevada and New Mexico, and into western Texas and extreme northern Mexico.

HABITAT. The extensive northern stands of spruce, hemlock, birch, and deciduous and mixed forest are the home of the porcupine.

HABITS. The porcupine is a nocturnal herbivore, feeding almost entirely in trees. For the colder six months of the year, juveniles and females live in dens, and their movements are confined to small areas near them. Large males may spend a winter's day in trees, and may even remain aloft in one position for several days. Bitterly cold weather thus holds no terror for the porcupine, although its body temperature can drop several degrees on particularly brutal days. Its dense coat is sufficient guard against the severest winter storms, and sometimes only

original range south to here

*Distribution of the common porcupine,* Erethizon dorsatum, *in the eastern United States*

the protecting trunk of a large conifer guards it against the howling northern blizzard.

In winter, the porcupine feeds on bark, girdling the upper limbs. For the other six months, it ranges more widely and usually spends the day feeding on leaves and buds far out on the limbs, or simply resting in trees, except when moving on the ground between trees, or when occasionally retiring to its den. Bad weather will sometimes drive porcupines into holes in trees.

Like the skunk, the porcupine is a slow and deliberate animal, whether on the ground or in a tree. It can afford to be slow, for it has formidable, unique protective qualities, as any dog that has tangled with one knows. The porcupine does well, however, not to have to fight, and an elaborate system for warning predators has evolved along with this mode of life, one that involves sight, sound, and smell. The porcupine attempts to keep its posterior toward would-be adversaries (its face is unprotected), and on this aspect there are conspicuous markings of black and white. A black line that runs up the middle of the tail and expands along the lower back is outlined with white, and there is additional white on the head. The black-and-

*Porcupine ascending a tree, showing its black-and-white warning pattern (Uldis Roze)*

white pattern of the porcupine and the several skunk species is a standard visual warning to predators.

A second warning when attack is imminent consists of tooth-chattering, which lasts up to half a minute and can be repeated many times. A porcupine may even clack its teeth if it wants to come down a tree and a potential enemy is below.

When resorting to the third warning mode, under extreme stress, the porcupine produces a unique, pungent odor, one that can be very strong, depending on the size of the animal and the degree of its stress. In a confined area such as a porcupine den, the odor can cause the eyes to water and the nose to run. Roze believes the odor arises from a volatile fatty acid produced in an area of the skin above the base of the tail called the *rosette*. Naked skin is presented to the attacker when the quills in this area are erected.

When all else fails, the porcupine makes use of its spines, either defensively or offensively. Defensively, it erects the long quills of the nape and anterior back, forming a randomly projecting mass of needles. The quills are quickly embedded in the predator when it attacks the porcupine, their barbs holding them fast. An excess of quills in the mouth may even prevent feeding and cause the predator to starve. But the porcupine can also take the offensive, flicking its tail out rapidly and driving its quills into the victim. These shorter, slimmer tail quills are much more dangerous than the longer quills. They are sometimes driven so deeply into the flesh that they become internal projectiles, working their way through the body and even leading, in some instances, to permanent injury or death. Besides bearing barbs, which resist their extraction, they are covered with a grease that allows them to continue to move—always forward—in the flesh of the victim. The porcupine's defense is not always successful, of course (see the discussion of enemies, below). Unlike adults, baby porcupines lack the power to defend themselves; they hide and, to their benefit, they are all black.

Porcupines have an early spring molt in which the underfur, but not the quills or guard hairs, is molted all at once. At such times one can find masses of woolly hair in the area where the animals are active.

Porcupines must climb to reach their food. The long claws, one of their several adaptations for climbing, serve to grip crevices in the bark, working like the climbing hooks of telephone linemen. The claws are also used for grooming the quills and other hair, for pulling branches into reach, and for manipulating food. On the naked palms of the front and hind feet are tuberosities, footpads, and wrinkles, all of which increase friction when gripping surfaces. Porcupines can clasp a tree trunk too smooth and small for the use of claws, by the skin of the hind feet alone, leaving the forelimbs free to manipulate food. Finally, the stiff, backward-pointing bristles of the underside of the tail, directed against the bark in the manner of a woodpecker, keep the animal from sliding backward as it ascends, and the tail also becomes an exploratory organ, constantly lifted and lowered onto the tree trunk as the animal descends.

Porcupines of the Catskills den up for the winter around the first week of November, although some adult males spend the day in or under conifers. They do not build winter dens but, rather, use ready-made structures. They may return to the same winter dens every year, perhaps because dens are often in short supply. Porcupines change dens about every three weeks during the winter, but the reasons for the changes are not fully understood. Perhaps disturbance, perhaps a change in food supply. Although the porcupine is essentially a solitary animal, several may share a den in winter, especially if suitable dens are scarce. In northern New England a dozen or more may frequent a rock fissure or abandoned quarry during the cold winter days. Up to 100 animals were reported in an area of 1.6 to 2 ha (4 to 5 acres) with numerous ledges in Massachusetts, and six were found in one abandoned house in New Hampshire. (Den sharing appears to be unsettling to the individuals involved, at least in the Catskills, and members of the same sex are especially reluctant to share a den.)

About 70% of the dens in the Catskills were in fissures at least 3.5 meters (12 feet) deep in rock outcroppings, where drifting snow covers the entrance, leaving only a small opening. About 20% were in hollow trees, and the remainder were in hollow logs or outbuildings. There is no insulation or nesting material in the den, and the animal may even remove leaves that have blown in; the dens thus seem to offer little protection from cold, for the animals do not huddle and the entrances are open. There is little air flow, however, and the animals sleep in a sitting position with the front paws off the bare surface and the tail towards the entrance. At dusk, the animal leaves the den and heads for a tree normally within a hundred meters. It usually feeds on the inner bark of branches in the crown after first removing the dead outer bark, leaving a pattern of efficiently arranged scrapes on the branch.

Porcupines gain weight in summer and fall, and lose weight or tend to "starve in the winter," at least in the Catskills, where there are no evergreens, but they quickly gain weight when the maple buds burst forth in spring.

Since porcupines spend so much time in trees, much of it far out on limbs, it should perhaps not surprise us that they occasionally fall. Thirty-five percent of a sample of 45 museum skeletons examined by Roze showed healed fractures, and he found other evidence of falls, as well. Roze found also that the quills have antibiotic properties. He hypothesized that these properties protect the porcupines from infections when impaled by their own or each other's spines.

Many different vocalizations have been reported for the porcupine: moans, whines, grunts, coughs, squeaks, mews, chatters, shrieks, barks, wails, and others. Its hearing and sense of smell are excellent, but its sight is only fair.

FOOD AND FEEDING. Porcupines have few competitors for the niche in which they carve out their lives, for there are few other mammals that can climb that can also digest leaves and bark. These tissues are difficult to digest, since they contain cellulose, lignin, pectin, and other substances highly resistant to mammalian digestive enzymes, but they *can* be digested by enzymes secreted by certain bacteria found in the digestive tracts of many herbivores, including porcupines. Because these enzymes act slowly, the porcupine has evolved a long intestine, a large caecum, and protracted food-passage time. Indeed, the digestive system of a porcupine makes up about 25% of the animal's total weight. Much of the plant digestion takes place in the caecum, a vessel of high bacterial concentration.

The porcupine is one of few rodents that may be considered strict vegetarians. Most of its feeding occurs in the canopy, and the favored feeding trees can be recognized by their often cropped and stunted upper branches and bare bark. Unmistakable evidence of porcupine work are "the niptwigs" described by Roze. Niptwigs are terminal branches of trees that have been nipped off, leaving only short stubs or spurs

*Niptwigs dropped from tree by porcupine (Uldis Roze)*

where the leaves or buds have been cut off and eaten. Niptwigs often litter the ground under a favored tree. The parts eaten are those highest in nitrogen, which is essential for the development and maintenance of protein. Over time, a number of trees near a porcupine den may grow low and scrubby, owing to the constant pruning they endure.

Evidence of winter feeding is easy to spot, for porcupines feed heavily on the inner bark of trees, and their work is readily seen from a considerable distance. Bark from spruce, white

pine, elm, basswood, beech, and sugar maple are favored foods in winter, although the tree species selected vary between localities and even between individuals. Spruce trunks are often completely girdled of a strip several centimeters in breadth. Hemlocks are another favored winter food, but they are fed upon differently, since the bark is rich in ill-tasting tannins. Rather, the needles and small branches of the hemlocks are eaten, and some trees may be almost completely stripped of their smaller branches.

It is clear that porcupines exercise choice in their selection of foods from among those available in their environment. A porcupine usually limits its food to one or two tree species at any one feeding, and a favored tree may be visited many times. In the Catskills, each individual used at least two tree species, some of them three, over the winter; sugar maple is the favorite there. Red maple and white ash are almost never eaten. Changes in winter food are often related to changes in den site, but new dens are usually not far from the old ones.

In spring, porcupines feed on the buds of a variety of trees, such as sugar maple, basswood, and aspen. Roze found that sugar maple is eaten only in the bud stages, not later, for tannins build up in the young leaves, even more than in oaks, to a level intolerable to porcupines. (A function of tannins appears to be defense against insects, and apparently they taste bad to porcupines as well; red maple, which has high tannin levels even in the buds, goes untouched.) There is a progression of spring foods in the Catskills: first, sugar maple buds, then the leaves of young beech trees (not the canopy trees), and, in later spring, young ash leaves. In some areas porcupines graze on the ground in spring, on forbs such as grasses, violets, and dandelions, but in the Catskills there is a variety of good low-tannin arboreal spring food, and the only nontree food eaten there is raspberry leaves. (In the wilder agricultural lands, the porcupine may visit the corn patches and alfalfa fields.)

In early summer, in the Catskills study, beech and white ash were the mainstays in late summer, basswood. Other important foods were apples and the aspens (both bigtooth and quaking). Together, these three species were eaten during 90% of the feeding episodes. Yellow birch, shad, elm, and raspberry canes were fed upon less often. (The porcupines showed no preference among aspens, but aspens present a danger in having brittle branches.)

In late August, the favored summer trees become depleted, and mast (in this case acorns and beechnuts) becomes the next major food. In some years few acorns and beechnuts are produced, but in others there is a bumper crop. Porcupines are able to harvest a good percentage of these foods because they can forage on them before the ground-feeding species get to them. A porcupine might stay in a single large oak for several days, whereas a small tree in a poor year might be cleaned in minutes or hours. Acorns are a good energy source because of their fat content, but a poor nitrogen source; thus porcupines continue feeding on tree leaves through the mast season to obtain adequate protein. Because basswood, aspen, and apples were uncommon in the beech/maple/ash/oak forests of the Catskills, much of the summer food of porcupines is at the edge or outside of the forest.

Favored feeding trees are visited repeatedly. In the Catskills, certain basswood trees would be used, while others, even nearby ones, would be ignored. It turned out that the leaves of the favored trees had near-neutral pH, whereas those ignored were slightly acidic at a pH of 5.9 to 6.2. Perhaps these trees had a defense compound, since the pH itself is not low enough to be a problem. Excess acidity does reduce the efficiency of sodium conservation, and porcupines feeding on apples thus prefer the low-acid apples. Red delicious apples, which are preferred over many others, are the least acidic. (Favored apples had pH's of about 4, rejected ones about 3.) Small wonder, in any case, that porcupines feeding on apples showed increased craving for sodium. Feeding on tree leaves continued through the apple season, probably because apples are low in nitrogen.

The porcupine's fondness for salt is proverbial. Although a variety of food trees may be utilized in summer, all offer meager sodium, driving the porcupine to find salt, and thus bringing it into conflict with humans. Any article that has been handled by people, with their sweaty palms, is quickly chewed beyond repair. Today, the salt urge is now generally satisfied from road salt or from articles built with plywood. The salt urge is exhibited by all medium-sized and large herbivores; bison, for example, know where all the salt licks are to be found. Herbivores ingest huge amounts of potassium, but little sodium, and a major imbalance between the two will lead to apathy, declining muscular and circulatory function, and death. Herbivores have evolved several methods of sodium retention, and the moose, for example, has a "sodium reservoir," its rumen; sodium stored there can be used at any time of the year, as needed. Data are needed, but it may be that the caecum of the porcupine is such a reservoir. Salt use is heavy in spring, and a smaller peak follows in autumn. Salt is not sought during the winter, but there is a burst of salt feeding upon exit from the winter denning. Salt use is much heavier in females because of the loss of sodium in milk production; "salt chewing" occurs several times per year in females, typically only once in males.

How did porcupines find salt before roads were salted, cabins were built, and tools were used? There were early reports of porcupines feeding on yellow waterlilies (*Nuphar*), even swimming to get them (porcupines are good swimmers). It is also said that they follow the moose, feasting on the fleshy rhizomes that are torn from the mud by these great beasts. *Nuphar* was the best sodium source among all plants surveyed by Jordan et al. (1973): 9375 ppm, as opposed to 9 ppm in terrestrial vegetation. Arrowhead leaf and aquatic liverworts are other high-sodium foods, and fresh bone is another source of sodium (as well as calcium). Outer bark is a good source of sodium, but it is the inner bark that is the main food of porcupines in winter.

REPRODUCTION AND DEVELOPMENT. The porcupine's mating season is in fall, but actual mating is confined to an eight- to ten-hour heat period, when a membrane obstructing the vaginal orifice parts. While in heat, the female secretes a thick mucus; together with her urine, the mucus probably produces olfactory cues that attract males. Males do much wandering during this period, and they may fight over females. Courting is elaborate and incorporates much vocalization, but mating does not take place until the female is ready. Prior to mating, the male squirts high-pressure jets of urine all over the female, thoroughly wetting her. If nonetheless not ready, she will just walk away, but if ready, she will raise the hind quarters and curve her tail back. The mating act, though not unlike that of other mammals of comparable size, is very brief, and a copulation plug is formed. The female is then pregnant or lactating for the remaining 11 months of the year, her gestation lasting about seven months (205 to 217 days) and lactation about four months. One young is produced, although twins have been born to overweight females in zoos. The young, born April through June, are remarkable for their precocious condition at birth. The newborn is well clothed with fur and weighs about a pound (340 to 640 grams). During its birth, the young emerges headfirst in a sac, the amnion. The sac and the headfirst delivery protect the mother from quill damage. Following the birth, she eats the sac. The quills are soft at birth, but harden within an hour. The baby's eyes are already open and some teeth have erupted. The young weigh about 1 kg (2 lbs) at two weeks, 1.6 kg (3.5 lbs) at two months, and 1.8 kg (4 lbs) by about three months. Females first breed at about a year and a half.

POPULATION CHARACTERISTICS. In winter, the porcupine stays near its den, its home range averaging just 2.4 ha (6 acres) in both sexes, though it may be much greater in years of little snowfall. The female's nonwinter home range, by contrast, varies from 25 to 65 ha (62 to 160 acres), that of the male from 30 to 150 ha (75 to 370 acres). The female's home range usually includes a rock den, hollow log, or tree, or other suitable retreat. This is a small home range for an animal of this size, which accounts for the markedly local nature of porcupine distribution. Densities of 1.2 to 5.4 per square km (3 to 14 per square mile) have been reported in the east. The home ranges of females do not overlap, whereas those of males do, and the range of a male may overlap the ranges of several females. Large, dominant males have larger ranges than immature ones. The females return to the same ranges year after year, and use the same feeding trees; they will defend their ranges against other females. Males return to the same core areas, but the boundaries of their ranges, and their movements within them, may shift much more from year to year. Territorial boundaries may break down at scarce favored areas such as salt licks and apple trees. Unusual among mammals, only the juvenile females disperse, doing so during the fall mating season. Among adults, males are known to disperse, and although they do so at low frequency, they may actually be the dominant dispersing sex.

Few data are available on longevity, but both captives and wild animals have been known to live up to 18 years.

ENEMIES. The porcupine's formidable armor of quills provides substantial insurance against all potential enemies but humans, mountain lions, and fishers, although the red fox, the lynx, the bobcat, the wolverine, the wolf, the coyote, and the great horned owl have been known upon occasion to feed on the porcupine without suffering material harm. It is not known, however, whether these other predators killed the porcupines or simply fed on dead ones. The mountain lion will eat porcupine, and tolerates the ill effects, but in the eastern United States the mountain lion and the porcupine no longer inhabit the same areas.

The fisher is another matter, regularly and systematically hunting porcupines, and going out of its way to investigate their dens, although porcupines do not make up a major portion of its diet. Earl and Kramm (1982) found that porcupines were much less abundant where fishers occurred, at 0.4 per square km (1 per square mile), than when there were no porcupines (3.5 porcupines per square km, or 9 per square mile). The fisher makes its kill by avoiding the quills; it circles its quarry, parrying this way and that, and attacks the face. The attack may take 30 minutes and include repeated wounds before the porcupine is subdued. Often, the fisher is not successful and has to back away from the attack because the porcupine is too quick for it. But after a kill, the fisher rapidly devours the soft tissues of the head. Fishers were recently reintroduced into the Catskill Mountains of New York and have decimated the porcupine populations Roze has studied for so many years. Fishers introduced into the Ottawa National Forest of Michigan severely reduced the porcupine population there also. Sweitzer (1996) attached radiocollars to porcupines in Nevada and found higher rates of predation on them in open areas than in wooded areas. Predation there was by mountain lions and coyotes.

PARASITES AND DISEASE. Relatively few parasites have been reported from porcupines: one flea, two ticks, four species of mites (including a mange mite and two chiggers), a porcupine louse (*Trichodectes setosus*), five species of roundworms, and three species of tapeworms (at least two of them specifically porcupine tapeworms). Mange can be a major problem for porcupines.

RELATION TO HUMANS. Porcupines were important to Native Americans, who used the quills for quillwork. They would hold the quillwork together by split spruce root or sinew binding, or by sewing it with a bone awl. Quillwork was used for clothing, containers, ornaments, medicine bags, and many other items. Even today, many natives of the northern forests think the porcupine is an animal to be left alone, for it is a species that can be taken by someone lost in the woods and desperate. Indeed, we have found its flesh quite tender and palatable.

Today, unfortunately, the porcupine is often looked upon with disfavor, since it often conflicts with humans. It receives no protection at all in the United States; it may be hunted at any time, and, until relatively recently, bounties were paid on it. The two main focuses of conflict involve salt and timber. Porcupines today seek salt from roads where it has been used for ice control in winter, and from construction materials containing much salt, especially plywood. Porcupines have caused much damage to various kinds of wooden structures by chewing them for the salt, and they can disable a vehicle in a night by chewing on the tires, hoses, or electrical wiring on the undersides, where salt may have accumulated, or, for that matter, on

synthetic rubber, which contains sodium. Porcupines are often hated by foresters, since much of their feeding takes place in the treetops, where they girdle the limbs, in time yielding low and deformed trees. In the white pine stands of Minnesota, porcupines may kill more than 1% of the annual growth.

Notwithstanding these concerns, porcupines are a fascinating part of our natural heritage and should be preserved. Consideration should indeed be given to reintroducing them in areas where they have been extirpated.

AREAS FOR FURTHER WORK. More work on parasites, both internal and external, is in order, and we (Roze and Whitaker) are currently examining the fauna in the residue from dens of this species. Comparative-genetics work on isolated populations might also be of interest.

## SUBSPECIES

*Erethizon dorsatum dorsatum* Linnaeus

As described above. *Erethizon dorsatum dorsatum* is the subspecies described for the eastern United States; others, probably invalid by our criteria, have been described for the West.

Type locality: Eastern Canada.

## LITERATURE

Costello, D. F. 1966. *The World of the Porcupine.* Philadelphia: J. B. Lippincott. 157 pp.

Dodge, E. W. 1982. Porcupine. In: J. A. Chapman and G. A. Feldhamer, eds., *Wild Mammals of North America*, pp. 355–366. Baltimore: Johns Hopkins Univ. Press.

Earle, R. D., and K. R. Kramm. 1982. Correlation between fisher and porcupine abundance in upper Michigan. *Amer. Midland Nat.* 107: 244–249.

Jordan, P. A., D. B. Botkin, A. S. Dominski, H. S. Lowendorf, and G. E. Belovsky. 1973. Sodium as a critical nutrient of the moose of Isle Royale. *Proc. North Amer. Moose Conf. and Workshop* 9: 13–42.

Roze, U. 1989. *The North American Porcupine.* Washington: Smithsonian Institution Press. 261 pp.

Sweitzer, R. A. 1996. Predation or starvation: Consequences of foraging decisions by porcupines (*Erethizon dorsatum*). *J. Mammal.* 77: 1066–1068.

Taylor, W. P. 1935. Ecology and life history of the porcupine (*Erethizon epixanthum*) as related to the forests of Arizona and the southwestern United States. *Univ. Ariz. Bull.* 6. 177 pp.

Woods, C. A. 1973. *Erethizon dorsatum*. **Mammalian Species No. 29.** Amer. Soc. Mammal. 6 pp.

## NUTRIAS, Family Myocastoridae

A single species, the nutria, *Myocastor coypu*, constitutes the Myocastoridae. Nutrias, which occur from Brazil to Chile, have been widely introduced into Europe and North America. Though they were first introduced into North America in 1899 in California, it was in the late 1930s that substantial numbers of individuals were imported, for fur farms. Nutria fur farming proved unsuccessful because of low prices and competition with native furs, but in the course of events many nutria escaped or were released.

### Nutria, Coypu *Myocastor coypus*
### (Molina) Color plate 14

The nutria is a large, stout-bodied rodent with a long, scantily haired tail. Among native North

*Nutria, Myocastor coypus (Roger W. Barbour)*

American mammals, this species can be confused only with the muskrat, which is much smaller. The tail, somewhat less than half the total length, is terete (cylindrical in section), whereas that of the muskrat is laterally compressed. The head is large and squarish, and the nose and mouth are fringed with whitish fur. The skull is immediately distinguishable from that of the muskrat by the infraorbital foramen, which is approximately the size of the orbit. This is the case also in the porcupine, but the infraorbital opening of the muskrat is tiny. The enamel on the anterior faces of the incisors is

orange. The dense, soft underfur is overlaid with long, coarse guard hairs, coarsest on the back. Dorsal coloration is dark brown to yellowish brown. The vibrissae are pale, long, and stiff. The hallux and first three toes of the hind foot are prominently webbed; the fifth toe, free, is perhaps used in grooming. The teats are placed dorsolaterally in such a manner that the young can nurse while the mother is feeding in shallow water, or, more likely, so that she can lie on her belly on a nest and watch for predators as she nurses her young.

MEASUREMENTS. Eight Louisiana individuals measured by George Lowery (1974) averaged: total length 940 (837–1010), tail 344 (300–450), hind foot 131 (100–150) mm; and weight 4.5–11 kg (10–24 lbs). Average weight is about 26 kg (12 lbs).

Diploid number = 42.

TOOTH FORMULA

$$\frac{1}{1} \quad \frac{0}{0} \quad \frac{1}{1} \quad \frac{3}{3} \; = \; 20$$

DISTRIBUTION. Through accidental or purposeful releases, nutria have established themselves in wetland areas in many parts of the United States and Canada. Currently, New Jersey, Maryland, Delaware, Georgia, Florida, Alabama, Louisiana, and Mississippi among eastern states, have significant populations of these large rodents, but there are populations in the West also, at least in eastern Texas and Arkansas and some in the Northwest. The 1930s were considered the boom years for establishing nutria ranches, and with the advent of World War II, nutria farming virtually collapsed. Animals escaped, and ranchers released their stock; but it was promoters selling nutria as "weed cutters" who were responsible for transplanting them throughout the Southeast in the late 1940s. Although some of those populations have disappeared, nutria have adapted to a wide variety of conditions.

HABITAT. Nutrias are essentially animals of the freshwater or brackish marshes, and as such they compete for habitat with muskrats.

HABITS. Nutrias make their own burrows or utilize those of other mammals. Burrows are about 1.2 to 3 meters (4 to 10 feet) long, and are usually in banks that slope upward at 45 to 90%. They frequently occupy old muskrat houses or make surface nests in dense vegetation. Nutrias are not well adapted for cold conditions; bobbed tails and frostbitten ears and feet were found in nutria in Maryland during a year of severe freeze, and many froze to death at the Back Bay Refuge in Virginia in the severe winter of 1976–77. As can many other aquatic and burrowing mammals, the nutria can close its lips behind the incisors, thus allowing it to gnaw while underwater. Nutrias can remain underwater for up to ten minutes.

Nutrias are primarily nocturnal, becoming active just before sunset and returning to their nests a few hours before dawn. During most of that active period, they feed, groom, and swim.

They apparently become more diurnal in cold weather, and may huddle together on cold nights. They will sun themselves, and they often lie motionless in the water in the manner of muskrats.

Nutrias have well-developed auditory and tactile senses. They are gregarious, and except during mating, the females are dominant over the males.

Nutria feces are distinctive. They are oblong, about 5 cm (2 inches) long, and finely grooved longitudinally. Muskrat scats average less than 2 cm (perhaps an inch) long and are not grooved.

FOOD AND FEEDING. The nutria is entirely vegetarian, at least in North America, except for insects taken incidentally (in England and South America they sometimes eat crustaceans and freshwater mussels). The food otherwise consists of a wide assortment of vegetation, usually

*Distribution of the nutria,* Myocastor coypus, *in the eastern United States*

of an aquatic nature, but these creatures are adaptable and will eat bark, clover, and assorted roots, as well, and often feed on corn or other crops if the crops happen to be adjacent to the marshes. Like muskrats, they generally eat the more common aquatic plants of the habitats where they live, such as rushes (*Scirpus*), spike-rush (*Eleocharis*), pickerel weed (*Pontederia*), cattail (*Typha*), arrowhead (*Sagittaria*), smart-weed (*Polygonum*), and bur reed (*Sparganium*). Like the muskrat, nutrias often amass vegetation into feeding or resting platforms. After cutting food, they bring it to these areas, which range from small, flattened areas of plant material to large platforms up to a meter high. At other times they may eat the food while resting in shallow water or on logs. The nutria eats about a quarter of its own weight in food per night, in numerous small increments rather than larger meals. Coprophagy, or reingestion of feces, occurs as well.

REPRODUCTION AND DEVELOPMENT. In keeping with their tropical origin, the breeding of nutrias occupies the entire year. Females begin breeding in their first year, and embryos have been found in individuals six months old. Gestation lasts about 130 (127–132) days, and the three to seven young (up to 11 have been reported in Louisiana) are born in a well-furred condition with open eyes. Larger litters are produced in warmer climates and when food supplies are abundant. In good environmental conditions, females may have up to three litters totaling 15 young per year; yearly productivity in Maryland is about eight per year per female. Nutrias, weighing about 225 grams at birth, are precocial, and able to swim shortly after they dry off. Miscarriage is unusually high in this rodent, about a third of the litters being lost during pregnancy.

POPULATION CHARACTERISTICS. Nutrias generally remain in one area for life, moving about in home ranges. Various points in the home range are marked with secretions from an anal gland. Home ranges are estimated to run from 5 to 180 ha (12 to 445 acres), and density estimates range up to 25 animals per ha (10 per acre). Populations can be hit hard by severe cold

weather. These animals can live up to about six years, much longer in captivity, but few in the field live more than two years.

ENEMIES. The alligator is the chief predator on the nutria in the Southeast, but gar, cotton-mouths, and red-shouldered hawks are other predators in Louisiana. Nutria remains have also been found in bald eagle nests in Maryland and Louisiana.

PARASITES AND DISEASE. In Louisiana, 11 species of trematodes, 21 of cestodes, and 31 of nematodes were found in nutrias. One nematode, *Strongyloides myopotami*, which causes "creeping eruption" on the skin of humans, is referred to as "nutria itch" by Louisiana trappers. Biting lice, *Pitrufquenia coypus*, were found on the snout of one nutria from Louisiana, and ticks, *Dermacentor variabilis*, were abundant on nutria in Maryland. Other large aquatic rodents (beavers, muskrats, and round-tailed muskrats) all have large numbers of tiny listrophoroid mites (so small they are usually overlooked), involving exceedingly interesting complexes of species, with several species on each individual host. The nutria also harbors large numbers of tiny mites of this group, but all are of one species, *Myocastorobia myocastor* (family Atopomelidae), to judge from an examination of large numbers of mites from one nutria from Mississippi.

Leptospirosis, hemorrhagic septicemia, and paratyphoid have been found in nutria in Louisiana.

RELATION TO HUMANS. Nutrias are capable of doing damage to crops, to drainage systems, and to natural plant communities by selective feeding. In the coastal sugarcane and rice fields adjacent to Louisiana marshes, great loss is suffered, and the levees of commercial crawfish ponds in Louisiana must be checked regularly for leakage due to burrow construction by nutria.

On the credit side, the soft, fine underfur is valuable in the fur industry. In 1961, the average annual take of pelts was valued at over a million dollars. In more recent years, the sale of the pelts (used mostly in trim and lining) and of the meat (for pet food) has brought trappers several million dollars annually. The first nutrias appeared in the Louisiana market during the 1943–44 trapping season. Two years later, 8784 were taken, whereas in the 1976–77 season, Louisiana trappers took a record high of over 1.8 million nutria, yielding an income of over $14 million and making the nutria the foremost fur animal in the state. Since then we have seen the collapse of the fur industry, a collapse well illustrated by the fur harvests in Louisiana. Numbers taken and values of pelts have declined from the 1984–85 season to the 1990–91 season as follows (unpublished data, Louisiana Department of Wildlife and Fisheries): 1,214,600 ($4.25), 761,918 ($3.35), 986,014 ($3.53), 617,646 ($2.69), 273,222 ($1.72), 292,760 ($2.99), and 134,196 ($2.53). Inevitably, the decreasing harvest has resulted in a concomitant increase in nutria damage to marsh vegetation, levees, and agricultural crops.

AREAS FOR FURTHER STUDY. More nutria need to be examined for their small ectoparasitic mites. More detailed information comparing muskrat and nutria habitat, behavior, and food, gathered where the species occur alone and where they occur together, would be interesting. This information could be beneficial in developing means of management of both species.

## SUBSPECIES

Several subspecies have been imported (four have been described), but apparently *M. coypus bonariensis* from Argentina was the primary source of nutria in the United States.

*Myocastor coypus bonariensis*
Geoffroy St.-Hilaire

As described above.

Type locality: Rio Maipo, Santiago Province, Chile, for the species; Rio Parana, Paraguay, for *M. coypus bonariensis*.

## LITERATURE

Evans, J. 1970. About nutria and their control. Resource Publ. Fish Wildl. Serv., Bur. Sport Fish. Wildl., U.S. Dept. Int., No. 86. 65 pp.

Lowery, G. H., Jr. 1974. *The Mammals of Louisiana and Its Adjacent Waters*. Baton Rouge: Louisiana State Univ. Press. 565 pp.

Willner, G. R. 1982. Nutria, *Myocastor coypus*. In: J. A. Chapman and G. A. Feldhamer, eds., *Wild Mammals of North America*, pp. 1059–1076. Baltimore: Johns Hopkins Univ. Press.

Woods, C. A., L. Contreras, G. Willner-Chapman, and H. P. Whidden. 1992. **Mammalian Species No. 398.** Amer. Soc. Mammal. 8 pp.

# 8. ORDER CARNIVORA

## Carnivores, or Flesh Eaters

THE CARNIVORES ARE characterized by a dentition adapted for shearing and cutting flesh and organs. The incisors are small, but the canines are large and pointed, and project well beyond the other teeth. Most carnivores also possess a pair of specialized shearing teeth, one in the upper jaw, another in the lower jaw on each side, known as the *carnassial* teeth. Usually, there are five toes on each foot; these are invariably furnished with claws, the claws blunt in the dogs and bears but sharp and retractile in the cats.

Carnivores are native throughout the world, with the exception of Australia. (The dingo, which is actually a dog and is not native to Australia, was presumably brought to the continent long ago by human immigrants.) Today, there are 271 species of carnivores worldwide, in 129 genera and 11 families, including 34 species of pinnipeds (seals, walruses, and such) in 18 genera and three families.

As their name implies, carnivores are primarily flesh eaters, although many species, such as the bears, skunks, and foxes, eat large quantities of vegetation, as well. Carnivores are far less abundant than the rodents and lagomorphs, on which most are largely dependent for sustenance.

We like to think of animals as having homes, as people do. Often they do not. Other than for natal purposes, or for winter lodging (in those species that enter winter lethargy), few carnivores have nests that they use regularly. Rather, most use a nesting site once, or during a brief period when they are exploiting a particular food source, then move on.

Carnivores are usually larger than their prey—an obvious advantage in overcoming them—but large size has its disadvantages, especially in today's world, a world in which we have so disturbed the natural environments that suitable habitats occur in steadily smaller and more isolated patches. Habitat degradation, fragmentation, and elimination make both living and dispersing difficult. These effects adversely affect most animal species, but they have been particularly hard on carnivores, which, being generally larger than most other mammals, require relatively large patches of habitat if they are to find sufficient prey. Carnivores have other problems as well. They are often persecuted because they are perceived, rightly or wrongly, to be detrimental to the concerns of humans, in particular by killing our stock or game animals. They have long been hunted and trapped, and man has himself been the predator, the mortal enemy of many of them. But unlike other predators, man continues to hunt certain desired or unwanted species as long as they exist, even to extirpation or extinction. State agencies have thus been established or empowered to assess the status of wild species and, so that these species might maintain adequate population levels, set restrictions on our intrusions, lethal or otherwise.

Many carnivores of the eastern United States have been important to the fur trade, and for centuries trappers took great numbers of foxes, weasels, minks, skunks, otters, and raccoons. Recently, however, there has been a great decline in trapping, primarily because of pressures that have been brought to bear against the purchasing of furs. These pressures have come about mostly through the efforts of environmentalists and people concerned for the rights of animals. When growing awareness led to a reticence on the part of the public to buy items containing fur, the bottom fell out of the fur market, practically eliminating the monetary rewards of trapping. This change of attitude, which in the course of time has extended beyond the furbearers, is certainly warranted for some species, such as the timber wolf and the mountain lion, which are nearly extirpated in the East and need complete protection. Others, such as the black bear, bobcat, and river otter, need complete protection in some areas but not in others. Still others, such as the raccoon and such noncarnivores as the beaver and the white-tailed deer, have often exceeded the carrying capacity of the land and are in need of control over much of their range. Hunting and trapping are good ways to effect control, but each species must be assessed separately, on its own terms, by the responsible agencies, so that determinations can be made about how to treat it in each region. Obviously, the management of our animal resources is a complicated problem and a complex social issue. We cannot simply preserve the habitat and leave the animals alone. For example, since we have all but eliminated the traditional predators of deer, the mountain lion and the wolf, a cessation of deer hunting quickly leads to great overpopulation of deer. To prevent the destruction of habitat that ensues, destruction that affects many animal and plant species, deer need to be controlled. To the dismay of many, this is a task best effected by hunting or controlled shooting.

Six families, embracing 20 species of Carnivora, are represented in the eastern United States: the dogs (Canidae, five species), bears (Ursidae, one), raccoons (Procyonidae, one), weasels (Mustelidae, eight), skunks (Mephitidae, two), and cats (Felidae, three). The aquatic carnivores, constituting the old order Pinnipedia, are now included in the order Carnivora, but we have elected to confine ourselves here to the terrestrial and freshwater aquatic mammals. We omit, as well, the other great order of marine mammals, the cetaceans.

KEY TO THE FAMILIES OF THE ORDER CARNIVORA

1. Animal *either* very large with vestigial tail *or* doglike; molariform teeth six upper, seven lower . . . . . . . . . . . . . . . . . . . . . . . . 2
1. Animal not doglike and the tail well developed; molariform teeth not as above . . . . . . . 3

2. Animal doglike, its tail long and bushy; skull with long, narrow rostrum; upper tooth rows not parallel (dogs and allies) . . CANIDAE
2. Animal very large, its tail vestigial; skull with broad rostrum; upper tooth rows parallel (bears) . . . . . . . . . . . . . . URSIDAE (p. 422)
3. Animal with black facial mask and large, bushy, ringed tail; molariform teeth six upper and six lower (raccoons) . . . PROCYONIDAE (p. 427)
3. Face and tail not as above; molariform teeth not as above . . . . . . . . . . . . . . . . . . . . . . . . . . . . . 4
4. Form catlike; claws retractile and concealed in fur (when retracted); lower molariforms three; upper molariforms three or four (cats) . . . . . . . . . . . . . . . . . . . . . . FELIDAE (p. 478)
4. Form not catlike; claws not obviously retractile; lower molariforms more than three; upper molariforms four or five . . . . . . . . . . 5
5. Animals black and white; palate not extending appreciably beyond posterior edge of last upper molars; molariform teeth four (skunks) . . . . . . . . MEPHITIDAE (p. 469)
5. Animals basically brown (some are white in winter); palate extending appreciably beyond posterior edge of last upper molars; molariform teeth three to five (weasels, badgers, otters, and allies . . . . MUSTELIDAE (p. 433)

## DOGS AND ALLIES, Family Canidae

This family comprises about 41 species in 15 genera, of generally worldwide distribution. Of these, two species of foxes (in two separate genera) and four species of the genus *Canis* (the dog, the coyote, and two species of wolves) are found in the Eastern United States. Canids have 42 teeth (the ancestral placentals had 44), including well-developed canines, shearing carnassial teeth (the last upper premolar and first lower molar), and crushing surfaces on the teeth behind the carnassials. There are five toes on the forefeet, four on the hind; the claws are blunt and nonretractile.

KEY TO THE GENERA OF THE FAMILY CANIDAE

1. Tail vertebrae less than half as long as head and body; postorbital processes thickened, convex dorsally; basilar length of skull more than 147 mm (except in small dogs) . . . . . . . . *Canis*
1. Tail longer, its vertebrae more than half as long as head and body; postorbital processes thin, concave dorsally; basilar length of skull less than 147 mm (foxes) . . . . . . . . . . . . . . . . . . . . 2
2. Tail not white-tipped; sagittal crest U-shaped . . . . . . . . . . . . . . . . . . . *Urocyon* (p. 419)

Tail white-tipped; sagittal crest
V-shaped .................... *Vulpes* (p. 413)

## Dogs, Wolves, and Coyotes of the Genus *Canis*

There are eight species of *Canis* in the world, counting the domestic dog, and four of them occur in the eastern United States. The four are the red and gray wolves, the coyote, and the dog. Their interrelationships, however, are rather confused. All four can and sometimes do interbreed. Before the coming of the white man and the ensuing modification of the habitat, there was little interbreeding between these forms. Isolating mechanisms were in place and worked well. The gray wolf once occurred over much of the northern United States, but the question remains whether the gray wolf and the red wolf are really separate species. In earlier times, coyotes were not common or perhaps even present over much of the East, and may have been outcompeted by wolves, but upon the demise of the wolf in the East the coyote has greatly expanded its range and its numbers there. The red wolf has been reintroduced into the Alligator National Wildlife Refuge, in North Carolina, and of course the domestic dog has accompanied humans wherever they go.

KEY TO THE SPECIES OF THE GENUS *CANIS*

The domestic dog (*C. familiaris*) is often confused with the coyote (*C. latrans*), and, to complicate things further, the two hybridize (see the discussion in the coyote account). In the hybrids, the length of the molariform tooth row divided by the distance between the inside faces of the two anterior premolars ranges from 3.1 to 3.6.

1. Animal large, weighing far more than 30 kg; skull usually more than 250 mm long (found only in Upper Michigan, northern Wisconsin, and on Isle Royale) .................. *C. lupus*
1. Animal smaller, weighing not more than 30 kg; skull less than 250 mm long. ................ 2
2. Zygomatic breadth more than 105 mm; rostral breadth posterior to canines usually more than 32 mm (occurs here only where introduced; currently isolated in southeastern coastal localities). ......................... *C. rufus*
2. Zygomatic breadth less than 105 mm; rostral breadth posterior to canines usually less than 32 mm (found throughout the East). ........... 3
3. Rostrum long and thin; length of molariform tooth row divided by distance between the inside faces of

the two anterior premolars more than 3.6; individuals largely consistent in general form ........................... *C. latrans*
3. Rostrum relatively short; this ratio less than 3.0; individuals often vastly different in general form ........................ *C. familiaris*

## Domestic Dog, Feral Dog
*Canis familiaris* Linnaeus

DESCRIPTION. Most dogs cannot be confused with any native animal, and need not be described here, but some larger, shaggier, gray or gray-brown dogs with, for example, malemute or German shepherd blood can be confused with coyotes or wolves. Wolves are usually much larger than dogs and occur—in the eastern United States—only in certain areas bordering Lake Superior. And because wolves usually kill and eat dogs, free-living dogs do not last long in wolf country. People in Ely, Minnesota, for example, know that if their dogs run free they are likely not to come home. Coyotes, however, occur throughout the eastern United States, generally do not kill dogs, and even occasionally hybridize with them, producing *coydogs*. Many dogs carry their tails arched upward, whereas coyotes carry their tails straight, but slanted downward. The behaviors of dogs and wild coyotes differ sufficiently that one usually knows when one has seen a coyote. The snout of coyotes is long and thin compared to that of a dog, and the ratio of the length of the molariform tooth row to the distance between the inside faces of the first two molariform teeth is usually under 3.0 in dogs, 3.1 to 3.6 in hybrids, and greater than 3.6 in coyotes. (See also the accounts for the coyote, the gray wolf, and the red wolf.)

The domestic dog has apparently been domesticated from the gray wolf (*Canis lupus*), presumably from a small southern Eurasian subspecies, or perhaps from a Chinese wolf (see Olsen and Olsen, 1977; Clutton-Brock, 1995). The earliest documented records of fossils are from Idaho and Iraq, and date from 11,000 to 12,000 years ago. Today, there are more than 400 breeds of dogs (and innumerable mixtures). Clutton-Brock (1981) gives much information on the origins of dogs and other domestic animals.

MEASUREMENTS. These vary considerably with the breed, but total length varies from 36 to 145 cm (14.5 to 58 inches) and tail length from 13 to 51 cm (5.2 to 20.4 inches). Weight usually ranges from 1 to 79 kg (2 to 175 lbs), but the record weight is 155.6 kg (343 lbs), an Old English Mastiff.

Diploid number = 78.

TOOTH FORMULA

$$\frac{3}{3} \quad \frac{1}{1} \quad \frac{4}{4} \quad \frac{2}{3} \quad = \quad 42$$

DISTRIBUTION. This species is of course commonly kept as a house pet around the world, but it is frequently seen afield and often becomes feral in the eastern United States, as it does elsewhere. Some individuals evidently become feral by choice; many others, abandoned by their owners, are given little choice.

HABITAT. Most domestic dogs live in and around buildings, but feral individuals often use heavy vegetation or natural shelters, particularly in remote areas, if no dumps or abandoned human shelters are available.

HABITS. Domestic animals are not usually included in a book like this, but dogs do become feral, even in wilderness areas and urban situations. They often fill a predator niche, sometimes replacing natural predators, and they can have a serious impact on prey populations and livestock. Feral domestic dogs tend to be afraid of people, but they can become dangerous to both people and livestock when they form packs, which they often do. Feral animals generally seek shelter in and around buildings, under cars or stairways, or in any of various other protected areas, as available. They are most active morning and evening, avoiding the midday heat and perhaps people.

The tracks of dogs are usually not difficult to identify. They are usually round and almost cat-like, but they carry the imprint of the claws, especially the forefoot tracks. Wild canids have more elongate tracks, and their prints are usually in a straight line. Some well-bred working dogs single-track, but many dogs do not; rather, their prints alternate somewhat from side to side.

FOOD AND FEEDING. We know of no study of the food of feral domestic dogs, but they presumably eat a great variety of plant and animal items. In cities their food consists primarily of garbage, but in rural areas it is probably most similar to that of a fox or coyote. Some of the most important foods of rural dogs are likely to be mice, rabbits, other small vertebrates, larger animals found as carrion, the livestock of humans, and various fruits in season. They will also eat insects, vegetables, and most anything else that is remotely edible.

REPRODUCTION AND DEVELOPMENT. Females come into heat and can produce young twice a year, usually in late winter or early spring and in the fall. Heat lasts about 12 days. Domestic dogs produce about three to ten young after a 63-day gestation. Lactation usually lasts about six weeks, but may last up to about ten weeks, and the effects of stress can halt it abruptly.

POPULATION CHARACTERISTICS. Feral dogs may form packs and become fiercely territorial, but they will often forage in neutral or undefended zones. It has been estimated that half of the 80,000 to 100,000 dogs in Baltimore, Maryland, are free-ranging at least part of the time. This yields an average of about 230 per square km (595 per square mile). Density was estimated at about 150 per square km (388 per square mile) in Newark, New Jersey. Fully feral dogs may cover 0.5 to 8 km (0.3 to 5 miles) per day. Home ranges for free-ranging dogs have been calculated at 1.7 to 61 ha (4.2 to 150 acres), and up to 28,500 ha (70,000 acres) for feral packs. A pecking order is established in packs, and the leader of a pack may be of either sex. Feral dogs probably do not live long. See Beck (1971, 1973) for more information on feral dogs.

ENEMIES. People are the major enemies of feral dogs, but feral puppies probably fall prey to many larger carnivores.

PARASITES AND DISEASE. No study has been made on the parasites and diseases of feral dogs, but they would likely include those of pet dogs and wild canids, typically fleas, mange mites, ticks, heartworm, distemper, and rabies.

RELATION TO HUMANS. Feral dogs—most of them at one time pets—often prey on our livestock, though the blame for their attacks is likely to be placed on wild animals (we being predisposed to think well of dogs). Feral dogs in packs can also pose a distinct threat to humans, and they are often shot or poisoned. There are about a million dog attacks on people in the United States each year, and about 18 of these, mostly on children, result in death. The great fear that many of us show toward bats, by contrast, is simply ludicrous, given their nearly negligible threat, as compared to that of dogs (and automobiles).

AREAS FOR FURTHER WORK. Domestic dogs provide unparalleled opportunity for behavioral observation, given their tolerance of people. We believe, too, that major evolutionary insight could be gained from study of the evolution (including the genetics) of breeds of dogs, an evolution wherein human selection has been substituted for natural selection.

## SUBSPECIES

No subspecies have been described for the domestic dog, nor are they generally for domestic animals. This is probably so because dogs are not distributed in the patterns of naturally occurring species and subspecies. Naturally occurring species spread out over geographic areas, become separated in space (primary isolating mechanisms come into effect), and begin the process of speciation. Dogs, however, were developed; their evolution was controlled by humans. People long ago captured wild animals, probably from a wolf stock in this case, and then began selecting for different characteristics for different *strains* of dogs. The different strains, at least the pure ones, are presumably able to interbreed with one another, yet they are kept from interbreeding by humans. One therefore could say that the action of humans in keeping the dog strains distinct is akin to the natural formation of primary isolating mechanisms in natural selection. The pure strains could probably be considered as subspecies of a sort, related directly to the natural subspecies treated in this book. Rampant interbreeding, when the pure strains are allowed to mix, is then akin to the break-

down of primary isolating mechanisms, and results in various intergrades, or "mongrels."

One could proceed further with these thoughts. The process of speciation could be studied experimentally with dogs, cows, pigs, or other domestic animals having several distinct strains. One might develop hypotheses concerning evolution, then impose and manipulate artificial rather than natural selective pressures, in order to test the hypotheses. Charles Darwin used his studies of homing pigeons and other domestic stock as part of his evidence for, and his understanding of, the process of evolution.

*Canis familiaris* Linnaeus
  As described above.
  Type locality: Sweden.

## LITERATURE

Beck, A. M. 1971. The life and times of Shag, a feral dog in Baltimore. *Nat. Hist.* 80 (8): 58–65 (October).
———. 1973. *The Ecology of Stray Dogs: A Study of Free-Ranging Urban Animals.* Baltimore: York Press. 98 pp.
Clutton-Brock, J. 1981. *Domesticated Animals from Early Times.* Austin: Univ. Texas Press. 208 pp.
———. 1995. Chapter 1. Domestication and evolution; and Chapter 2. Origins of the dog: Domestication and early history. In: J. Serpell, ed. (see below), pp. 4–20.
Nowak, R. M. 1991. *Walker's Mammals of the World.* Fifth Edition. Baltimore: Johns Hopkins Univ. Press. 1629 pp.
Olsen, S. J., and J. W. Olsen. 1977. The Chinese wolf, ancestor of New World dogs. *Science* 197: 533–535.
Serpell, J., ed. 1995. *The Domestic Dog, Its Evolution, Behaviour and Interactions with People.* Cambridge, U.K.: Cambridge Univ. Press. 268 pp.
Wilcox, B., and C. Walkowicz. 1991. *The Atlas of Dog Breeds of the World.* Neptune City, N.J.: TFH Publications. 912 pp.
Wilson, D.E., and D. M. Reeder. 1993. *Mammal Species of the World.* Second Edition. Washington: Smithsonian Institution Press in association with American Society of Mammalogists. 1206 pp.

## Coyote *Canis latrans*
**Say**                                    Color plate 15

DESCRIPTION. The coyote is superficially similar to a small German shepherd, husky, or malemute, but it has longer fur and a shorter, bushier tail. The tail has an elongate black mark above,

*Coyote,* Canis latrans *(Bill Brink)*

MEASUREMENTS. Adult coyotes measure: total length 1075–1200, tail 300–390, hind foot 175–220 mm; and weight 9.1–22.7 kg (20–50 lbs). Exceptionally large individuals may weigh 25 kg (55 lbs). The females are smaller than the males.

Diploid number = 38. (See the account for the gray wolf.)

TOOTH FORMULA

$$\frac{3}{3} \ \frac{1}{1} \ \frac{4}{4} \ \frac{2}{3} \ = \ 42$$

toward the base, marking the site of a tail gland, and the tip is black. The tail is held straight and carried at a downward slant rather than upward or over the back. The overall color is exceedingly variable, varying from reddish through brown and yellowish to almost pure gray, the animals in drier habitats tending to be reddish. The base of the ears and nape are often yellowish or buff. The dorsal hairs are broadly tipped with black, and the abdomen and throat are pale. The legs are reddish with a blackish vertical line, the feet are light, and the face is gray above, more reddish on the snout.

Coyotes are often mistaken for timber wolves and are often called "brush wolves." In eastern United States, however, timber wolves are found only in those areas bordering Lake Superior, and can be distinguished immediately by their much larger size and much larger feet (and the coyote, again, carries its proportionately longer tail held low). Skulls are readily identified, but the pelts of some coyotes, wolves, and domestic dogs are indistinguishable. (See also the accounts for the dog, the gray wolf, and the red wolf.)

The track of a coyote paw measures about 70 mm long and 60 mm wide. Tracks of coyotes are very similar to those of dogs and foxes, but those of dogs can usually be distinguished, for they usually sidestep, whereas coyotes and foxes track in a straight line. The distance between the tracks of a coyote (the back feet fall into the tracks made by the front feet) is usually 10–15 cm (4–6 inches), that of foxes 7–10 cm (3–4 inches).

The name "coyote" derives from the Aztec Indian word *coyotl*. It should be pronounced "ky-o-tee" as in the Spanish, not "ky-ote."

DISTRIBUTION. The coyote has long been more or less common throughout the Midwest, but it has expanded its range, both naturally and through casual transplantations, and today we must include the whole eastern United States in its range. The great success of the coyote in the east in recent decades was apparently, at least in part, a filling of the void left by the decimation of wolves. In 1942, the coyote had not yet appeared in Louisiana, but 1500 individuals were taken in 1987 in Maine. Many of the eastern states have been populated by coyotes that have come as pets in the autos of tourists, only to escape later from their owners, or perhaps to be set free when they attained greater size. Others, particularly in the southern states, have been liberated by fox hunters who have had coyote pups shipped to them instead of young foxes, to which as pups they bear a striking resemblance. The coyote occurs to the west coast and from Alaska to Nicaragua.

HABITAT. Coyotes occupy a great range of habitats, ranging from open lands to forest, but they do not do well in dense forest. They do best in scrub country and open ranch lands, and in areas with a diversity of habitats, including brushy country, ravines, thickets, and small woodlots. Their dens are often in banks, mounds, or gullies, or under overhangs.

HABITS. In spite of the encroachments of civilization, the adaptable coyote manages to maintain its numbers, and appears to be increasing in many parts of its range. This is rather remarkable when we consider for how long this animal has been trapped, hunted, and poisoned.

Like most carnivores, coyotes do not have permanent homes, other than the maternal dens in which their young are raised. In the East, they spend the day well concealed in a dense thicket or woods, for they are most active in the hours near dawn and dusk, though it is not uncommon to see one abroad during the day. And of course they are often out at night, as anyone who has heard their vocalizing is well aware. In the West, coyotes are much more diurnal, since, like some other predators, they tend to be as diurnal as circumstances and the avoidance of people permit. Coyotes are active throughout the year, even on the coldest days, though they will remain in their dens during bad storms.

The basic social unit of coyotes is the mated pair, the bond sometimes sustained even for life, but some are solitary, and they may also occur in packs of three to seven individuals. Packs consist of the parents and young of different ages. There is a dominance hierarchy in the pack, the leader usually an older male. The boundaries of the territory are well marked with urine and feces, and nonmember coyotes are chased out. Postures and facial expressions convey all attitudes, from very submissive to very aggressive. Aggressive animals hold the head high with the neck arched, and the nape hairs are erect. The eyes narrow and the mouth opens, exposing the canine teeth. Submissive coyotes hold the head and body low, the tail between the legs, the ears back, and the tongue hanging out. Coyotes present dominant and submissive displays to one another, and whine when they greet each other. A submissive animal may lick the face of another, and may lie on its side, raise its leg, and urinate. A desire to play is indicated by raising the foreleg and making face-licking motions, and by tail-wagging with the front end of the body lowered.

An age-old symbol of the western plains is in fact the sharp, often protracted, yapping and

*Distribution of the coyote,* Canis latrans, *in the eastern United States*

thamnos

latrans

original range south to here

rustror

original range east to here

howling of the coyote in the evening, or on the still air at sunrise. Presumably the calling is intended to bring the group together. In the East, the bark is less often heard, but it has been greatly increasing in recent years. Until the mid-1980s, we had never heard coyotes howl in Indiana, but their call is commonplace today. The calls often start with the yapping of a single individual, then develop into a chorus as the others join in, and end in a mournful-sounding wail. A siren, the barking of a dog, or a clap of thunder often stimulates the chorus. Lone and group howls are often given when an individual or group is separated, and group yip-howls often ensue when the group is reunited.

Maternal dens may be excavated, or the coyote may use a remodeled woodchuck, fox, skunk, or badger hole for this purpose. The dens are often in brushy slopes, steep banks, or thickets, or they may be in hollow logs or rocky ledges. Dens are typically about 0.3 meter (1 foot) in diameter and up to 7.5 meters (24 feet) long, and they may have more than one entrance.

FOOD AND FEEDING. Coyotes eat a great variety of foods, including mice, rabbits, hares, ground squirrels, pocket gophers, woodchucks, wildfowl, snakes, insects, and many plant foods. Fruits and berries are eaten during the summer months, and carrion of larger animals such as deer is important in the winter. In 1500 coyote scats from the Adirondacks from throughout the year, mammals occurred in 78%, fruit 21%, insects 10%, and birds 3%, and amphibians, reptiles, and green grass were identified at yet lower percentages. The most important food was the snowshoe hare, occurring in 40% of the scats. Coyotes hunt singly, in pairs, or sometimes in larger groups, but little information is available on their hunting behavior. To locate prey, they depend on vision, hearing, and olfaction, in decreasing order of importance. Coyotes search for prey, orient to it, stalk it, and then either pounce, when the target is a mouse or other small prey, or rush, when the prey is the size of a ground squirrel or larger. Minta et al. (1992) reported an interesting opportunistic hunting association between coyotes and badgers, the badger digging into ground squirrel burrows and the coyote meanwhile guarding the burrow entrances. This pattern seemed to benefit both predators by increasing the vulnerability of the ground squirrels to predation (see the badger account for further discussion).

Although coyotes do not usually kill large game, Gese and Grothe (1995) observed nine attempts by coyotes in Yellowstone to hunt large prey cooperatively, and five of the attempts were successful. In deep snow, especially, and when the prey was in poor nutritional condition, two coyotes could kill a deer or even an elk. They kill a large animal by biting its throat and suffocating it.

The coyote is accused, often unjustly, of killing lambs, pigs, and poultry. This sort of depredation is much more often due to free-ranging dogs, but some individuals are undoubtedly responsible for the destruction of livestock.

Excess food is cached by burying it in the ground.

REPRODUCTION AND DEVELOPMENT. Premating behavior may begin two or three months before actual mating. Scent marking, for example, increases during this period, and the males become much more mobile, smelling the urine and feces of the female. Mating occurs in late winter, during the female's single period of heat. Male and female may howl in a duet before mating. Copulation ends in the typical "copulatory tie," the penis swelling and becoming locked into the female's vagina. The pair may remain locked together for 15 to 25 minutes. During this time they stand tail to tail, facing away from each other, the male having stepped over the female. Copulations may recur over several days. After a 58- to 63-day gestation, the five to ten pups (averaging six) are born, although litters of up to 19 are on record (Young and Jackson, 1951). At birth, the young are blind and helpless and weigh 250–275 grams (9–10 oz). Greater numbers of young are born in good rodent years than in poor.

Both parents and sometimes other individuals, usually siblings from an earlier year, assist in provisioning the young, all the while making circuitous trips to the den, presumably to avoid attracting attention to it. (One might ask why, if coyotes have no serious enemies, but humans are surely a serious enemy, and the behavior could in any case be a holdover from the days when larger predators, wolves and mountain lions, shared the land with the coyote.) The coyote pups' eyes open at about two weeks. The young first feed on solid food in the form of regurgitated items, and first begin emerging from the den at about three weeks. They are weaned at about six weeks. The family breaks up in the late summer or early fall, and the young hunt alone until late winter, when they are ready to pair and assume family duties themselves. They attain adult weight at about nine months of age, and then disperse, the males traveling farther than the females. Coyotes may keep the same mates for several years, but not necessarily for life.

POPULATION CHARACTERISTICS. The size of the home range of the coyote varies greatly with sex, season, habitat, and food availability. Home ranges of males in Arkansas averaged 21 to 42 square km (8.1 to 16.2 square miles), those of females 8 to 10 square km (3–3.9 square miles). Male home ranges overlapped; those of females did not. Movements during a single day are about 4.0 km (2.5 miles). Density is about 0.2–0.4 per square km (0.5–1.0 per square mile). Coyotes are less social than wolves, although they do sometimes form packs, the packs occupying territories of about 21 square km (8 square miles). Coyotes in packs defend their territories; those in pairs or alone do not (Bekoff and Wells, 1980).

Coyotes have lived in captivity for 18 years. The longevity record in the wild is 14.5 years, but few individuals, probably, live beyond six or eight years.

The experience of coyotes in the eastern United States points up an interesting aspect of population dynamics: changes in a biotic community can lead to unexpected rearrangements. For example, wolves often kill coyotes and may even exclude them (Berg and Chesness, 1978; Fuller and Keith, 1981; Carbyn, 1982) from local areas. Thus, the extirpation of wolves in the East may have afforded the coyote both increased abundance and an expansion of range, and the greater number of coyotes may be suppressing the red fox population (Sargent et al., 1987; Voigt and Earl, 1983; Dekker, 1990; Harrison

et al., 1989). In turn, because red foxes tend to limit long-tailed weasel populations, diminished red fox populations could lead to greater numbers of weasels. And because long-tailed weasels can exclude least weasels from areas with high populations of voles, via both scent marking and direct aggression, least weasel populations can also be affected.

Today, one hears much about "coydogs," or coyote-dog hybrids, in the Northeast. It is well established that dogs and coyotes mate and produce hybrids that exhibit characteristics of both species. Suspected crosses between coyotes and large dogs in New York have been examined and verified, but only a small percentage of more than 200 animals taken in the field in New York indicated a hybrid origin; most were either dogs or coyotes. Hybrids produce fewer offspring than do pure coyotes, and the timing of estrus is out of phase between the two, in effect yielding natural selection against hybrids. Coyotes come into heat in late winter, and male coyotes are capable of breeding only at that time. Female dogs come into heat twice a year, but not at any particular time, and male dogs are capable of breeding year-round. The result is that male coyotes are seldom able to impregnate a female dog in heat, whereas male dogs can impregnate a female coyote at any time. Most hybrids between dogs and coyotes thus result from male dog/female coyote crosses. This puts the female coyote at great disadvantage, for male coyotes help the female to raise the young; male dogs do not. Worse, estrus in coydogs comes especially early, producing young at a time unfavorable for survival. For these reasons, coydogs are uncommon and not apt to do well in relation to either dogs or coyotes. In short, coydogs are constantly selected against. Silver and Silver (1969) thought that the large coyotes of New England, the "New England canids," were the result of early introgression of dog and/or wolf genes.

ENEMIES. Man is the only serious enemy of the coyote. With dogs and gun, the coyote is hunted relentlessly, both in efforts (often misguided) to control predators and to match wits with this animal, perceived to be exceedingly cunning. Few dogs are swift enough to catch him, and in a serious scrap the coyote is the equal of any dog of comparable size, but there is no defense against the rifle.

PARASITES AND DISEASE. External parasites of the coyote include fleas, ticks, and lice, but usually not mites. Internal parasites are cestodes, nematodes, and acanthocephalans. Rabies, tularemia, and bubonic plague have all been found in coyotes.

RELATION TO HUMANS. Much of the hunting of coyotes in prior decades was for profit. The pelts were used in trimming ladies' garments and, to a lesser extent, for scarves. Many were dyed various shades of gray, brown, or black. Western skins from the Rocky Mountain areas at one time brought as much as $7.00 or more, but eastern hides of the best quality were traditionally worth only $2.00 to $3.00. From 1972 through 1977, eastern coyote pelts brought $9–$15, and in 1987 they brought $15–$25. Today, however, coyote pelts have little value.

For many years, state and local agencies offered bounties to encourage the killing of predators, but the bounty system was fraught with fraud and never accomplished much in the way of control. The predators were seldom in need of widespread control in any case. Individual predators known or suspected to be causing problems were usually dispatched locally, with or without bounty.

Coyotes, like foxes, are supposed to be shrewd animals, but the traits that lead us to think that certain animals are "shrewd" or "intelligent" are usually instinctive traits that have adapted the animal to its own environment. These traits usually have no real relation to shrewdness or intelligence.

Coyotes get blamed, usually unjustly, for all kinds of damage to our pets and to game and other wild animals that humans prize. As their numbers grow, they are increasingly thought by locals to be wreaking dire results on livestock and native species, especially rabbits and woodchucks. When the opportunity arises, they will kill livestock, and they obviously kill native species. Moreover, as discussed above, the addition of the coyote to our fauna has changed inter-relationships with other species, such as the red fox. These kinds of shifts in community structure are likely to produce yet other changes.

AREAS FOR FURTHER WORK. Studies of the inter-relationships of coyotes with animals of other species, both as competitive predators and as prey species themselves, should prove of interest, especially in comparisons of areas where coyotes have always existed with areas into which they have recently immigrated.

## SUBSPECIES

Most of the described subspecies of coyotes, including the three in the eastern United States, appear to intergrade imperceptibly.

*Canis latrans latrans* Say
 As described above.
 Other currently recognized eastern subspecies:
  *Canis latrans thamnos* Jackson
  *Canis latrans frustror* Woodhouse
 Type locality: Engineer Cantonment, about 19.2 km (11.5 miles) southeast of Blair, Washington Co., Nebraska.

### LITERATURE

Bekoff, M. 1977. *Canis latrans*. **Mammalian Species No. 79.** Amer. Soc. Mammal. 9 pp.

———, ed. 1978. *Coyotes: Biology, Behavior and Management.* New York: Academic Press. 384 pp.

———. 1982. Coyote, *Canis latrans.* In: J. A. Chapman and G. A. Feldhamer, eds., *Wild Mammals of North America*, pp. 447–459. Baltimore: Johns Hopkins Univ. Press.

Bekoff, M., and M. C. Wells. 1980. Social ecology and behavior of coyotes. *Sci. Amer.* 242: 130–148.

Berg, W. E., and R. A. Chesness. 1978. Ecology of coyotes in northern Minnesota. In: M. Bekoff, ed., *Coyotes: Biology, Behavior and Management*, pp. 229–247. New York: Academic Press.

Carbyn, L. N. 1982. Coyote population fluctuation and spatial distribution in relation to wolf territories in Riding Mountain National Park, Manitoba. *Canadian Field-Nat.* 96: 176–183.

Dekker, D. W. 1990. Population fluctuation and spatial relationships among wolves, coyotes and red foxes in Jasper National Park, Alberta. *Alberta Nat.* 20: 15–20.

Dobie, J. F. 1961. *The voice of the coyote*. Lincoln: Univ. Nebraska Press. 386 pp.

Fuller, T. K., and L. B. Keith. 1981. Non-overlapping range of coyotes and wolves in northeastern Alberta. *J. Wildl. Mgmt.* 62: 403–405.

Gese, E. M., and S. Grothe. 1995. Analysis of coyote predation on deer and elk during winter in Yellowstone National Park, Wyoming. *Amer. Midland Nat.* 133: 36–43.

Gier, H. T. 1968. *Coyotes in Kansas*. Revised. Agric. Exp. Sta., Kansas State Univ., Coll. Agric. App. Sci. 118 pp.

Harrison, D. J., J. A. Bissonette, and J. A. Sherburne. 1989. Spatial relationships between coyotes and red foxes in eastern Maine. *J. Wildl. Mgmt.* 53: 181–185.

Minta, S. C., K. A. Minta, and D. F. Lott. 1992. Hunting associations between badgers (*Taxidea taxus*) and coyotes (*Canis latrans*). *J. Mammal.* 73: 814–820.

Sargeant, A. B., S. H. Allen, and J. O. Hastings. 1987. Spatial relationships between sympatric coyotes and red foxes in North Dakota. *J. Wildl. Mgmt.* 51: 285–293.

Silver, H., and W. T. Silver. 1969. Growth and behavior of the coyote-like canid of northern New England with observations on canid hybrids. *Wildl. Monogr.* No. 17. 41 pp.

Voigt, D. R., and W. E. Berg. 1987. Coyote. In: M. Novak, J. A. Baker, M. E. Obbard, and B. Mallock, eds., *Wild Furbearer Management and Conservation in North America*, pp. 344–357. Toronto: Ontario Ministry Nat. Resources.

Voigt, D. R., and B. D. Earl. 1983. Avoidance of coyotes by red fox families. *J. Wildl. Mgmt.* 47: 852–857.

Young, S. P., and H. H. T. Jackson. 1951. *The Clever Coyote*. Philadelphia: Stackpole. 411 pp.

*Gray wolf, or timber wolf,* Canis lupus, *a very light colored individual (Roger W. Barbour)*

## Gray Wolf, Timber Wolf
### *Canis lupus* Linnaeus      Color plate 15

DESCRIPTION. A very large, broad-headed animal resembling a large domestic dog, *Canis lupus* is best characterized by its relatively larger feet, longer legs, narrower chest, and heavier muzzle. Much variation in color occurs, but the usual pattern is grayish, brownish gray, or brownish white, the middle of the back heavily marked with black. The underparts and legs are pale rufous brown to yellowish white. The pelage is heavier and shaggier in winter.

A wolf often runs with its tail carried high or horizontally, as a dog does, whereas a coyote carries the tail low. The wolf holds its tail straight, however; the dog, usually curved upward. The track patterns of wolves and large dogs also differ. Wolves and coyotes put their hind feet in the tracks of the front feet, thus walk or lope in a single line of tracks, whereas most dogs do not overlap their feet in this way, thus usually zigzag. Dog tracks are also rounder than those of coyotes. Wolf tracks are about 23 to 36 cm (9 to 13 inches) between tracks from tip of toe to tip of toe, coyote tracks about 15 to 20 cm (6 to 8 inches). Wolf tracks can normally be separated from those of a coyote by their greater size: the front feet, larger than the hind feet, are about 125 mm (5 inches) long and 39 mm (3.5 inches) wide; the hind feet are about 115 mm (4.5 inches) long by 80 mm (5.2 inches) wide. (See also the accounts for the dog, the coyote, and the red wolf.)

The domestic dog was probably first domesticated from the gray wolf about 12,000–15,000 years ago in southern Asia, or perhaps in China.

MEASUREMENTS. Adult males measure: total length about 1600 (1300–1800), tail 400, hind foot 250 mm. The shoulder height is about 70 to 80 cm. The nose pad of the adult wolf is broad, usually measuring more than 33 mm in width, and the skull is greater than 200 mm in length. Large adult males weigh from 20 to 80 kg (45 to 175 lbs), a few individuals approaching 70 kg (154 lbs, almost triple the weight of a large coyote), although this is exceptional. Females are usually noticeably smaller than males, their weight ranging from 18 to 55 kg (40 to 120 lbs).

Diploid number = 78. Wolves, coyotes, and dogs all have 39 pairs of chromosomes, and all are apparently interfertile.

TOOTH FORMULA

$$\frac{3}{3} \quad \frac{1}{1} \quad \frac{4}{4} \quad \frac{2}{3} \quad = \quad 42$$

DISTRIBUTION. A century ago, gray wolves roamed all through the forested east, south through Illinois, Tennessee, and northern Virginia. To the south, they were replaced by the red wolf. Originally, this species occurred throughout most of North America except for much of western California and most of the Southeast, where the red wolf was the resident canid. The gray wolf has been relentlessly persecuted, and today it is established in the United States in only five states. Just two of these, Michigan and Wisconsin, are in the east, and it is considered endangered in both these states. Wolves are still found throughout much of Canada and Alaska and parts of Montana, and a few apparently still occur in Wyoming, in Yellowstone National Park.

The timber wolf's last strongholds in the United States east of the Mississippi are Isle Royale (in Lake Superior) and the more extensive and more remote forested areas of northern Wisconsin and Michigan's Upper Peninsula. Wolves were last reported in Michigan's Lower Peninsula about 1910. In the Upper Peninsula, in 1955, the timber wolf population was estimated at about 100. Michigan repealed the bounty in 1960 and accorded the wolf legal protection in 1965, but by

Isle Royale

original range south to here.

*Distribution of the gray wolf, or timber wolf,* Canis lupus, *in the eastern United States*

then total populations were estimated at just 12 to 25, although there were sightings in at least nine counties in that year: Alger, Baraga, Chippewa, Delta, Gogebic, Iron, Luce, Ontonagon, and Schoolcraft. In 1973, the total population was estimated at six. Roger Powell photographed wolf tracks in Iron County, Michigan, that year. There are still sporadic reports, some of them of animals crossing over from Canada, but help for the native wolves of the Upper Peninsula was apparently too little and too late. (There was an experimental release in the 1970s, and the wolves found good habitat, but problems arose with humans.)

This leaves the only surviving viable population of wolves in Michigan on Isle Royale National Park, in northern Lake Superior. The species became established there in 1948 by crossing the ice from Canada, a distance of about 24 km (15 miles). Durwood Allen, L. David Mech, Rolf Peterson, and their associates have collected considerable information on this population, much of it by airplane and, recently, by radiotelemetry. The population normally numbers about 20 to 30 individuals, and in 1980 numbered as many as 50. It then declined dramatically, however, leaving only about seven or eight wolves there as of 1988, and 14 as of March 1990. The reasons for the decline are not known, but declining prey, disease, and decreased genetic heterozygosity have been proposed. It appears that the entire remaining population has derived from a single founder female (Wayne et al., 1991).

Wolves were considered to have been extirpated in Wisconsin by about 1960, but by 1981, wolves had returned (Mech and Nowak, 1981), and there was even evidence of breeding (Thiel and Welch, 1981). The estimated number of wolves in Wisconsin in 1986 was 15.

There are still frequent reports of gray wolves in various eastern states, but these animals usually prove to be coyotes or dogs.

HABITAT. Wolves range widely, across a great variety of open to wooded habitats.

HABITS. Gray wolves are exceedingly social animals. Their predilection for strong social bonds allows them to form packs, the packs numbering five to eight family members, sometimes more. Mech (1970) proposed that the basic component of the pack is the breeding pair, and a pack is realized when a lone male and a lone female breed. The pack of two then expands with the addition of the first litter, which remains with the parents for two years. After two years, however, the young have matured sexually, rivalries can develop, and some offspring may disperse to form new packs, although littermates sometimes mate and remain, thus increasing pack size. From then on, pack composition is reordered each year as the new crop of young matures. Moreover, two packs originating from the same family might meet and go on to hunt and breed together.

There are two strictly enforced hierarchies within the pack, a male order and a female order. The order is linear in each, and one male (the alpha male) is dominant over the entire pack, males and females alike. The beta male is second, and on down to the lowest-ranking male, though the dominant or alpha female may be dominant over some of the lower-ranking males. The alpha male and alpha female are usually the founding members of the pack. The dominance hierarchy affords the pack a strong measure of leadership and determines position in any competitive situation, the alpha male taking whatever he desires: food, bedding sites, and mates. (The hierarchy may be broken when a female has pups; she may then drive off a dominant male.) Leadership involves deciding, for the pack, when to rest, when and where to hunt, and when to feed. The leaders, clearly, are highly motivated individuals, but much can yet be learned of the mechanisms of leadership in wolf packs.

Although wolves usually occur in packs, three lone wolves, two of them females and one a male, are known to have successfully raised litters in Montana and British Columbia (Boyd and Jimenez, 1994). In the third case, a female had given birth in late April, but was killed in late May. The male then cared for the six young until he, too, was killed, in September. Thurber and Peterson (1993) found that lone wolves were greater in number, and average pack size was smaller, when wolf density was low, that territory size did not correspond with pack size, and that the kill interval varied inversely with the size of the pack. Lone wolves often teamed up with one or two other wolves for short periods, and pairs of wolves and even solitary wolves were able to kill adult moose.

The wolf's natal den is often in a hole in the ground, but it may be in a rock crevice, in a hollow log, under a stump, or in some other protected place. It is usually on high ground, near water. There may be several entrances, each about 0.3 to 0.6 meter (a foot or two) in diameter. The tunnel into the den extends about 1.3 to 4.5 meters (4.3 to 17 feet) into the ground. The same den may be used for years, but the young are sometimes shifted to a different den. Except for these natal dens, wolves do not regularly use shelters.

There are two main periods in the annual lives of wolves: the first, from April to late fall, finds them centering around the pups and the natal den (and, later, their rendezvous sites); The second period, which consumes the remaining months of the year, sees the wolves engaged in widespread wandering. During the summer, the wolves usually stay in or near the den in the daytime, for they do not tolerate the heat of the day well. Foraging begins near dusk, and the animals return to the den by morning. Wolves can move for long periods at a steady 8 kph (5 mph), but when necessary they can run at up to 70 kph (43 mph). They can detect odors at distances of up to 2.4 km (1.5 miles).

Wolves are territorial animals, and they mark their territories via urine posts, feces, and ground scratching. They are notorious for their howling, which may occur at any time of the day or year. The marking and the howling probably function in territory maintenance and in communication. Howls may initially be by one wolf, but after one or two howls by the one the whole pack may join in. A howling session begins with long, low howls and progresses to a series of shorter, higher ones. A howling bout averages about 85 seconds and may be followed by another. Individual howls last from half a second to about 11 seconds at a fundamental frequency of between 78 and 150 Hz. An important function of the howling, perhaps the most important, appears to be reassembling the pack, especially after a hunt, but other functions may be to advertise territories and to identify individuals. Other vocalizations of wolves are whimpering, which appears to be a greeting, growling, which is aggressive in nature, and barking, which serves as an alarm.

Assertions of dominance are bared teeth, with the mouth open; raised hackles (the hair on the neck and back); a wrinkled and swollen forehead, the ears erect and pointed forward; and the tail raised above the level of the back. Acknowledgments of subordination include a closed mouth, the teeth not visible; a smooth forehead; the eyes closed to slits; the ears flat against the head; and the tail held low, or between the legs. Free tail wagging is friendly; labored tail wagging is aggressive. Truly submissive postures are two. The first consists of lowering the hind quarters with the tail between the legs and pointing the muzzle toward the dominant, while thrusting the tongue forward rapidly. This stance is sometimes accompanied by whining and urinating. In the second posture, the wolf rolls onto its back, brings the paws in toward the body, and often urinates. Social interactions like these, which occur frequently, serve to limit fighting.

Subordinate animals can disperse, or perhaps move up in the dominance hierarchy. Dispersal is mostly in the fall, and dispersers often end up being shot by hunters, at least in Wisconsin. Packs will sometimes chase intruding wolves away; at other times they will accept one from one group but reject another from a different group.

FOOD AND FEEDING. The wolf's large size and its pack-forming proclivity, which allows cooperation in making kills, have adapted it well for feeding on large prey. During winter, the gray wolf subsists principally upon deer in Wisconsin and entirely on moose on Isle Royale. The animals most often killed are the young, the old, and the sick. The entire prey item is usually eaten at the time of the kill, but if not, the pack will return later to finish it. Other animals, such as crows, foxes, and weasels, may also feed on wolf kills. In spring and summer, snowshoe hares, ground squirrels, mice, birds, and some fruits and berries are eaten, but most effort is expended in hunting animals of beaver size or larger. In Wisconsin, the summer food of wolves is about 55% deer, 16% beaver, 10% snowshoe hare, and the rest a variety of other foods. Food is bolted down in chunks, with little chewing. Individuals eat up to 9 kg (20 lbs) of flesh per feeding, and have several feedings per day. On Isle Royale, Mech (1970) observed packs of about 15 wolves finish moose calves weighing 135 kg (300 lbs) in a day. He estimated that an adult wolf needs about 1.7 kg (3.7 lbs) of food per day to maintain itself, but if necessary, the pack can go without food for at least two weeks. When food *is* available, wolves gorge themselves.

Nearly all of the time they are awake, wolves are either hunting or eating, and on Isle Royale they will take up the hunt 35 minutes after feeding. Wolves find their prey by scent, by tracking, or by chance, the first being the most successful. In 42 of 51 hunts on Isle Royale, moose were first scented. The moose could usually be detected from 300 meters (950 feet), in one case from 3 km (2 miles). Tracking was the method used on nine of the 51 occasions, but only fresh tracks were followed. Once the prey is located it is stalked slowly at first, the pace then quickening as it is approached, but the wolves are often able to move to within 30 meters (100 feet) without being observed. When their presence is detected, the prey will stand its ground to fight or else bolt, the larger prey often managing to survive by driving the wolves off. Wolves are more apt to hesitate when the prey chooses not to run; but when the prey bolts, they rush to the attack. If they succeed in overtaking it, they bite at its rump, flanks, and shoulder. Most chases are very short, but a few stretch out to a kilometer or more, and occasional chases are much longer, even many kilometers. Feeding usually begins immediately following the kill, but when females are in the dens with pups, members of the pack will take food to the dens. Sometimes, a different female will stay with the pups while the mother joins the hunt. The net effect of wolf predation on the prey population appears to be generally beneficial, for it serves to cull ill or otherwise inferior animals, control the population, and stimulate the productivity of the herd. The current overpopulation of deer in many ar-

eas of the East, reflected in its distinct browse lines (removal of edible green material from ground level to as high as the deer can reach) and its habitat destruction, illustrates eminently the ill effects attendant upon predator removal.

REPRODUCTION AND DEVELOPMENT. Wolves mature in their second year, but most do not breed until their third. The female is in estrus for five to seven days. Mating is in late winter, the typical canid copulatory tie lasting up to 30 minutes. After a gestation of 63 days a litter averaging six pups (one to 11) is born. The newborn are dark gray to blackish and are blind and helpless. The mother remains with the young for much of their first two months, and the other pack members bring food for both young and mother. The growth of the young is much like that of domestic dog puppies. The eyes open during days 11–15. The young first emerge from the den at about three weeks of age, and are weaned by about week five. At about this time, they begin social activities. The pack then abandons the natal nest, and at about two months of age the young are moved to one of a series of "rendezvous sites" above ground. These sites consist of a series of trails and bedding areas near water where the pups apparently play, explore their environs, and learn to hunt. During this time, they develop their sociality, and the members of the litter begin following one another about, as a group. The young are weaned gradually from milk onto food regurgitated by the adults, and finally learn to capture their own food. These rendezvous sites are up to about 0.4 ha (1 acre) in extent, and several are used in a season, but as the summer progresses they are used less often, and in late summer the young commence to hunt with the parents. The adult dentition is in place by four to seven months, and the young attain their adult length (but not weight) at about ten months.

POPULATION CHARACTERISTICS. A maximum of about one wolf per 26 square km (10 square miles) is about the highest level at which wolf packs can maintain themselves, and density levels are usually lower. About 18 to 26 wolves are or were the norm on the 546 square km (210 square miles) of Isle Royale. In winter, when prey is scarcer and there are no ties to the natal den, home ranges are much larger than they were in summer.

Wolves spend much time traveling within their home range. Home ranges in Minnesota are about 130 km (80 miles) in diameter, and wolves may move up to 125 km (78 miles) in a day within the home range. Lone wolves range much farther, and they may be chased farther still by pack members whose range they intrude upon.

Wolves often disperse great distances, and may cross highways or pass through other developed areas. A 35-kg (77-lb) adult male was marked in St. Louis County, Minnesota, on 22 August 1979 and shot on 6 November 1982 in Pine County, Minnesota, 262 km (162 miles) away. A 10-kg (22-lb) male pup tagged on 25 August 1991, also in St. Louis County, was an adult weighing 38 kg (84 lbs) when it was recaptured on 12 June 1994 in Iron County, Michigan. A female captured in eastern Lake County weighed 13 kg (29 lbs) when it was tagged on 24 August 1993. In the winter of 1993–94 and through April 6, she belonged to a seven-member pack operating near the original capture area. She was seen alone on three occasions later in April, then was not seen again until she was killed by a motor vehicle on 30 August 1994 near Portage, Wisconsin, 555 km (344 miles) from the original point of capture.

Two wolf families may join to form a pack of 12 to 15 young. A pack observed in Ontario hunts over a large area, but returns to various points at quite regular intervals. The home range of a pack varies greatly, and is difficult to determine, but covers about 2000–3100 square km (770–1200 square miles). Wolves can live to 16 years, but few live more than ten under natural conditions.

ENEMIES. Humans (and their automobiles) are the only enemy of wolves. By hunting, trapping, and poisoning, humans have eliminated wolves from much of their vast original range.

PARASITES AND DISEASE. Several species of trematodes, cestodes, and nematodes and three species of acanthocephalans are the internal parasites of wolves. Lice, fleas, ticks, tongueworms, and a mange mite are the external parasites, and wolves are apparently bothered by mosquitos, deerflies, horseflies, blackflies, and stable flies. Rabies is the most important disease of wolves; it is not known if distemper occurs in wild populations.

RELATION TO HUMANS. Persistent hunting (often with the sanction of bounties), trapping, and poisoning hastened the gray wolf's extermination in Pennsylvania, New York, and New England well before the close of the nineteenth century. The eventual extirpation of the wolf over most of its original U.S. range was in large measure due to the settlement of the country, the consequent loss of adequate habitat, and our relentless harassment of the species. Fortunately, but almost too late, we are beginning to gain some measure of enlightenment about the plight of the many animal species we have decimated, the larger predators and so many others, and we have begun working to protect them.

There have long been cases of wolves killing people, as many as 300 over 500 years in Europe, for example, though many or most of these may have been instigated by rabies. But rabies or not, Europeans brought their fear of wolves to North America, and found the wolf to be in abundance here. The wolf of this continent is nonetheless very shy and retiring, and there are only three documented cases of attacks on humans in North America, none lethal. Peterson (1947) reported that a wolf pulled a man off a railroad "speeder" or velocipede (hand car) and attacked him for about 25 minutes. In the second case (Munthe and Hutchison, 1978), six wolves approached two people on Ellesmere Island, in Canada's far north, and one actually leapt at and glanced off one of the people. All six wolves then left. In the third encounter (Scott et al., 1985), three individuals were "treed" by three wolves.

There is no question that wolves have preyed on domestic stock, however, and from the earliest days of settlement that were at least *perceived* as a major problem for both sheep and cattle stockmen. The problem may have been exaggerated, however, for stockmen have a habit of too quickly blaming stock losses on predators, as when, for example, young stock succumb to illness or the elements. This response is especially likely if the dead carcass is later fed upon by predators. The spread of livestock in the Western Hemisphere, and the concomitant spread of rifles and hunters, was in fact the most critical factor in the demise of the wolf over most of its range. Where it still occurs, however, in Canada, the wolf has now reached a semblance of stability.

Wolf pelts were at one time used as scarves and trimmings, but this species is now granted full protection in the United States, excepting only Alaska.

AREAS FOR FURTHER WORK. Much information has been collected by Durwood Allen, Dave Mech, and Rolf Peterson on Isle Royale over many years, a period that has seen much change in the size of wolf populations there. Past and future data could be used to gain insight into these changes.

## SUBSPECIES

A number of intergrading subspecies invalid by our criteria have been described for Eurasia and North America; the one occurring in the eastern United States was the first of the North American subspecies to be described, in 1775. *Canis lupus lupus* occurs in the Old World.

*Canis lupus lycaon* Schreber

As described above. All native gray wolves of the eastern United States are of this subspecies. Type locality: Quebec, Quebec, for *Canis lupus lycaon*.

### LITERATURE

Boyd, D. K., and M. D. Jimenez. 1994. Successful rearing of young by wild wolves without mates. *J. Mammal.* 75: 14–17.

Harrington, F. H., and P. C. Paquet. 1982. *Wolves of the World: Perspectives of Behavior, Ecology and Conservation.* Park Ridge, N.J.: Noyes. 474 pp.

Mech, L. D. 1966. *The Wolves of Isle Royale.* Washington, D.C.: U.S. Natl. Park Service, Fauna Ser. 7. 210 pp.

———. 1970. *The Wolf: The Ecology and Behavior of an Endangered Species.* New York: Natural History Press. 384 pp.

———. 1974. *Canis lupus.* **Mammalian Species No. 37.** Amer. Soc. Mammal. 6 pp.

Mech, L. D., S. H. Fritts, and D. Wagner. 1995. Minnesota wolf dispersal to Wisconsin and Michigan. *Amer. Midland Nat.* 133: 368–370.

Mech, L. D., and R. M. Nowak. 1981. Return of the gray wolf to Wisconsin. *Amer. Midland Nat.* 105: 408–409.

Munthe, K., and J. H. Hutchison. 1978. A wolf-human encounter on Ellesmere Island, Canada. *J. Mammal.* 59: 876–878.

Murie, A. 1944. *The Wolves of Mount McKinley.* Washington, D.C.: U.S. Natl. Park Service, Fauna Ser. 5. 238 pp.

Peterson, Randolph L. 1947. A record of a timber wolf attacking a man. *J. Mammal.* 28: 294–295.

Peterson, Rolf. 1977. *Wolf Ecology and Prey Relationships on Isle Royale.* Washington, D.C.: U.S. Natl. Park Service, Fauna Ser. 11. 210 pp.

Scott, P. A., C. V. Bentley, and J. J. Warren. 1985. Aggressive behavior by wolves toward humans. *J. Mammal.* 66: 807–809.

Thiel, R. P., and R. J. Welch. 1981. Evidence of recent breeding activity in Wisconsin wolves. *Amer. Midland Nat.* 1006: 401–402.

Thurber, J. M., and R. O. Peterson. 1993. Effects of population density and pack size on the foraging ecology of gray wolves. *J. Mammal.* 74: 879–889.

Wayne, R. K., N. Lehman, D. Girman, P. J. P. Gogan, D. A. Gilbert, K. Hansen, R. O. Peterson, U. S. Seal, A. Eisenhawer, L. D. Mech, and R. J. Krumenaker. 1991. Conservation genetics of the endangered Isle Royale Gray Wolf. *Conserv. Biol.* 5: 41–51.

Young, S. P. 1944. *The Wolves of North America.* Washington, D.C.: American Wildlife Institute. 2 vols. 636 pp.

## Red Wolf *Canis rufus*
## Audubon and Bachman

In most modern works, the red wolf is listed as a full species, notwithstanding that its diploid number is shared with *C. latrans*, *C. lupus*, and *C. familiaris*. Evidence indicates that it has hybridized extensively with the coyote and perhaps also with the gray wolf, and some have suggested that it likely arose through hybridization between gray wolves and coyotes. It has also been suggested that massive hybridization helped lead to the demise of this species. The red wolf has often been thought to be conspecific with the gray wolf, or with the coyote, but it appears more likely that it was at one time a distinct species, then underwent extensive hybridization as its populations declined. Nowak (1979) presented the case for retaining the red wolf as a separate species.

DESCRIPTION. Named for its presumed overall rufescence (the term is misleading, for the color is primarily gray), the red wolf (Fig. 8.4) is simi-

*Red wolf,* Canis rufus *(Roger W. Barbour)*

lar to the gray wolf but smaller. Conversely, it is somewhat larger than a coyote, a typical specimen a bit closer to the gray wolf than to the coyote in length and weight. The face and saddle are liberally sprinkled with tawny or buffy hairs, but some animals' skins are indistinguishable from those of *C. lupus, C. latrans,* and even some breeds of domestic dogs. Melanism is common. Several authors have commented on the relatively long legs of this species, but this perception is probably a function of coat length, for the distinction is not apparent in winter.

MEASUREMENTS. Total length 1355–1650 mm (*C. latrans* is about 1050–1320 mm, *C. lupus* about 1370–2050 mm); weights of adults range from 20 to 36 kg (50 to 80 lbs), the females smaller than the males.

Diploid number = 78.

TOOTH FORMULA

$$\frac{3}{3} \quad \frac{1}{1} \quad \frac{4}{4} \quad \frac{2}{3} \quad = \quad 42$$

DISTRIBUTION. A southeastern species, formerly ranging north to southern Missouri, central Ohio, and southern New Jersey, and west to central Texas and Oklahoma, the red wolf was extirpated from most of its once vast range by the turn of the century. Today, red wolves

exist in the wild only through reintroduction and only in five small localities: the Alligator River National Wildlife Refuge, in Dare County, coastal North Carolina; Blount County, in southeastern Tennessee; Bull Island, in coastal South Carolina; Horn Island, on Mississippi's Gulf Coast; and on St. Vincent Island, on the coast of Florida's panhandle. The purpose of the introductions on the islands has been, first, to test the feasibility of reintroduction (Bull Island) and, then, to allow the wolves to reproduce in order to produce additional animals that can be trapped and introduced elsewhere.

Efforts are currently being made to introduce red wolves into Great Smoky Mountains National Park, in extreme western North Carolina and extreme eastern Tennessee (Blount County). A pair of wolves and their two pups were released near the Cades Cove area of the park in November 1991. Bull Island, too small for a permanent population, was used for the acclimation of the animals and as a site for a feasibility study.

By 1980, the red wolf was completely extirpated in the wild through destruction of habitat, persecution by humans, and apparently massive interbreeding with coyotes and domestic dogs while it was being increasingly forced into marginal habitats. In the early 1970s, however, the U.S. Fish and Wildlife Service began to obtain red wolves from Texas and Louisiana to initiate a breeding program, so as to stockpile animals for eventual release in favored sites. This program was essential, since the few remaining red wolves in the wild were hybridizing with coyotes, and genetic extinction was thus imminent. By 1985 there were 65 captive red wolves in six different zoos and parks, and as of 31 March 1992, there were 129 captive red wolves in 25 facilities. Wolves to be released are placed in acclimation pens on site. When the pens are opened, the wolves are allowed to leave at will. This is the first time a species considered extinct in the wild has been reintroduced, and it is hoped that the program will ensure biological survival (Parker, 1987).

The first attempts to establish a wild population were undertaken between 15 September and 1 October 1987, when several pairs were released in the Alligator River National Wildlife Refuge in Dare County, North Carolina.

This relatively isolated area of over 63,000 ha (155,600 acres) has proper cover and an abundance of prey species. A pair of replacement females was released in April 1988. As of November 1988, five of the first ten had survived. Two males had been killed by cars, one female had to be sacrificed after being badly hurt in a fight with another red wolf, and two females died from unknown causes. In 1988, two of the original four pairs of wolves produced litters. From 1988 through March 1992, 36 wolves have been introduced, of which six are still present. Of the rest, 21 died, seven were removed for management reasons, and the fate of two is unknown. At least two litters were produced in 1990, and at least three in 1991. Thus at least seven litters, totaling at least 20 wolves, have been produced in the wild at the refuge. In the spring of 1992, 19 wolves, including ten adults and yearlings and nine pups, were still alive in the wild in Dare County, North Carolina. It appears, then, that the release program at the Alligator River National Wildlife Refuge has been successful. The Cades Cove release, however, has not been nearly as successful, mostly because of the higher human density there.

Pairs of wolves, with and without pups, have also been released since 1988 on Bull Island, South Carolina; Horn Island, Mississippi; and St. Vincent Island, Florida. By now, three adult females and one female pup have been killed by alligators. (These islands serve as breeding areas, since they are too small to sustain permanent populations.) As of January 1992 there were 151 red wolves in existence, 26 in the wild, six on captive propagation islands, and the rest in captivity.

HABITAT. The original habitat of this species was apparently in densely vegetated areas of the

*Distribution of the red wolf, Canis rufus, in the eastern United States*

original range north to here

Southeast ranging from pine and hardwood forests to the coastal prairies and marshes.

HABITS. Red wolves are chiefly nocturnal, but become somewhat more diurnal in winter. They will sometimes bed down in a herd of cattle at night, but during the day they sleep in grassy or brushy areas. Mated pairs usually travel together or sometimes with an extra male, and packs of up to 11 animals sometimes form temporarily. Red wolves in the Alligator River Refuge are very social, forming packs that occupied particular territories. Their dens are in protected areas such as hollow logs, under stumps, in culverts, or in burrows or banks; the den openings are often behind a clump of briers or brush. The howl of a red wolf is between that of wolves and coyotes, but more like that of a coyote.

FOOD AND FEEDING. The primary food of the red wolf is the white-tailed deer, but wolves of this species regularly eat medium-sized mammals of several species, from lagomorphs to deer. Other, smaller prey are undoubtedly taken on occasion, and swamp and marsh rabbits may originally have been the primary prey of the red wolf. Scat analysis indicates that the most important food items of the species at the Alligator River Wildlife Refuge are deer, raccoon, and marsh rabbits, but corn and house mice are important also.

REPRODUCTION AND DEVELOPMENT. Copulations occur from late December and early January to late February and early March, but the animals do not mate until they are in their third year. Females with embryos have been taken from 18 February to 10 May, lactating females with young from 20 April to 6 June. Embryos range from two to ten (the average is 6.6). Gestation for one animal in a zoo in Texas was 60–62 days.

POPULATION CHARACTERISTICS. The home range of this species is smaller than that of the gray wolf, ranging from 15 to 100 square km (6 to 40 square miles). It averaged about 44 (19–70) square km, or 17 (7–27) square miles, for seven red wolves in Chambers County, Texas (Shaw, 1979). It was much larger in winter there

(average 40.9 square km) than in summer (8.5 square km). At the Alligator River Refuge, home ranges averaged about 100 square km (40 square miles) in wooded areas, and about 50 square km (19 square miles) in agricultural areas.

ENEMIES. Humans have been the paramount enemy of the red wolf. These wolves, like coyotes, can tolerate close association with humans, but in general seem less adaptable than coyotes, a factor that may have hastened their extermination. Perhaps the reason for the coyote's current success in the Southeast is that it is filling a niche previously occupied by the red wolf.

PARASITES AND DISEASE. Hookworms were prevalent in young red wolves in Texas, so seriously weakening them that they could not keep up with their parents, leading indirectly to mortality. The lives of adults, too, were shortened by hookworms and heartworms in Texas during the final years before extirpation.

RELATION TO HUMANS. As has been the case with so many species, especially the larger ones, humans have caused the extirpation of this species throughout its range. Ironically, it persists because of humans' efforts to capture the remaining individuals, raise them in captivity, and release them back into the environment.

AREAS FOR FURTHER WORK. The interrelations of this species with other predators and with prey species should provide fundamental knowledge about the dynamics of situations where a new species becomes part of a community.

## SUBSPECIES

Not all are in agreement that the red wolf is a species distinct from the gray wolf. Worldwide, *Canis lupus* includes morphological variants that differ more from North American gray wolves than does *C. rufus*, but fossil records indicate that the red wolf predates the gray wolf in North America by approximately 500,000 years (Nowak, 1979).

Originally, three subspecies were recognized: *C. r. floridanus*, *C. r. gregoryii*, and the Texas red wolf, *C. r. rufus*. The current breeding stock is of the *gregoryii* type. The other two subspecies are no longer extant, and we question, in any case, whether they met the subspecies criteria we have employed in this book. The dividing line between *gregoryii* and *floridanus*, at least, was entirely arbitrary.

*Canis rufus rufus* Audubon and Bachman
  As described above.
  Type locality: 15 miles (24 km) west of Austin, Texas.
  Other currently recognized eastern subspecies:
   *C. rufus floridanus* Miller
   *C. rufus gregoryii* Goldman

### LITERATURE

Nowak, R. M. 1972. The mysterious wolf of the south. *Nat. Hist.* 81: 51–53, 74–77.
———. 1979. North American Quaternary *Canis*. Univ. Kansas Mus. Nat. Hist. Monogr. No. 6. 154 pp.
Paradiso, J. L. 1965. Recent records of red wolves from the Gulf Coast of Texas. *Southwestern Nat.* 10: 318–319.
———. 1968. Canids recently collected in east Texas, with comments on the taxonomy of the red wolf. *Amer. Midland Nat.* 80: 529–534.
Paradiso, J. L., and Nowak, R. M. 1972. *Canis rufus*. **Mammalian Species No. 22.** Amer. Soc. Mammal. 4 pp.
Parker, W. 1987. Red wolves return to the wild. *Endangered Species Tech. Bull.* 12 (11–12). 4 pp.
Pimlott, D. H., and P. W. Joslin. 1968. The status and distribution of the red wolf. In: *Trans. 33rd North Amer. Wildl. and Nat. Resources Conf.*, pp. 373–389.
Shaw, J. H. 1979. Movements of the red wolf (*Canis rufus*). In: E. Klinghammer, ed., *The Behavior and Biology of Wolves, Proc. Symposium on Behavior and Ecology of Wolves*, pp. 501–524.
Wayne, R. K., and S. M. Jenks. 1991. Mitochondrial DNA analysis implying extensive hybridization of the endangered red wolf, *Canis rufus. Nature* 351: 565–568.

## Red Fox *Vulpes vulpes*
**(Linnaeus)**                    Color plate 16

  The native red fox of the United States was long recognized as a separate species, *Vulpes fulva*, but recent studies have indicated it to be of the same species as the Old World red fox, *V. vulpes*.

Some, indeed, have questioned whether the red fox was native in North America at all. Churcher (1959) believed it was native north of latitude 40, which runs roughly from northern California through Denver and Philadelphia. Red foxes have been introduced into the southern states for fox hunting, and some believe this was the origin of the North American red fox.

DESCRIPTION. The red fox is a reddish-colored canine, the size of a small dog, with pointed

*Red fox,* Vulpes vulpes *(Roger W. Barbour)*

nose, large, prominent ears, and a long, bushy tail. It is the only North American canid with a white-tipped tail. The upperparts are reddish yellow, mixed with black-tipped hairs. On the rump are reddish hairs mixed with white- and black-tipped hairs, giving a grizzled effect. The tail is reddish mixed with black-tipped hairs. The underparts, cheeks, and inner side of the ears are whitish, and the feet and the backs of the ears are black. Color varies with the season, the fur full and lustrous in winter, and faded, pale, and relatively short in summer. Various other color phases occur, the best known of these being the "silver fox," the melanistic coat of which is frosted with white, particularly about the head, shoulders, and rump. The pelt of the "cross fox" is mixed gray and yellow. These color phases may occur with normal red foxes in the same litter. The skull has prominent temporal ridges that unite to form a V-shaped sagittal crest. The upper incisors are lobed (in the gray fox, they are not).

MEASUREMENTS. Measurements of 195 male and 126 female red foxes from Indiana averaged: total length 1052 and 951 (890–1110), tail 376 and 356 (320–410), hind foot 160 and 150 (100–180) mm; and weight 4.9 and 4.0 (3.4–6.4) kg, or 7.5 to 14.1 lbs.

Diploid number = 34.

TOOTH FORMULA

$$\frac{3}{3} \quad \frac{1}{1} \quad \frac{4}{4} \quad \frac{2}{3} \quad = \quad 42$$

DISTRIBUTION. With the clearing of the forests, red foxes have increased in both abundance and range, and today they occur over most of eastern North America, except for southeastern Virginia and eastern North Carolina, though they are less common to the south. This species occurs throughout most of North America except for the far Southwest and the Rocky Mountain region.

HABITAT. Few animals occupy such a diverse range of habitats as the red fox. It is most common in rolling farmland mixed with sparsely wooded areas, marshes, and streams. It also occupies the forest edges and open areas in heavily forested regions and lives within the limits of the great metropolitan areas of Boston and New York, and probably others.

HABITS. The red fox is a rather small, solitary predator, and feeds mostly on small prey. It is primarily active when its prey is active, but especially near dawn and dusk. In summer, red foxes tend to be more active at night, but in winter, when they feed heavily on voles, they

*Distribution of the red fox,* Vulpes vulpes, *in the eastern United States*

become more diurnal, because voles are diurnal. Best known for its sagacity and cunning, the red fox continues to maintain itself in spite of constant persecution. Although it may live for years in quite thickly settled areas, the sight of a hunting fox should be recorded in the naturalist's notebook as a notable event. But if the observer be quiet and is not too distant, a bit of squeaking will draw the attention of the fox, and, if the wind is favorable, it may be drawn close to the observer. When Whitaker saw a fox hunting in a meadow in New York State, he fell to the ground and lay still. The fox then took a big circle and came up behind him to within 20 meters (60 feet) before making off.

Unlike those of most mammals, the red fox's ears are most sensitive to low sounds, at about 3.5 kHz, rather than to high-pitched squeaks. Most mammals have their most sensitive hearing at the range of their offspring's distress calls. The low-frequency noises detectable by the red fox are in the range of small mammals gnawing or rustling in leaf litter. It thus depends on its ears a great deal when hunting—listening for the movements or gnawing of their small prey.

These foxes can run at speeds up to 50 kph (32 mph). They are also good swimmers. Red foxes have a high-pitched bark, and also produce whines, screeches, and yaps. Other than the maternal den site, they do not have permanent homes, but they use urine to mark scent posts, as do other canids.

FOOD AND FEEDING. Red foxes feed on a variety of foods, plant and animal alike, taking advantage of what is available. Their chief food during the winter consists of mice, rabbits, such birds as they can secure, carrion, apples, and dried berries such as grapes. In spring and summer, rabbits, rodents and other small mammals, woodchucks, poultry, birds, snakes, turtles and their eggs, an occasional young fawn, and raspberries and blackberries provide a varied diet. In the fall, berries, particularly wild cherries and grapes, grasshoppers, and the ubiquitous mice are mainstays. Many of the birds eaten are ground nesters caught during nesting, when they are most vulnerable. David Henry has described the hunting behavior of red foxes.

By listening for the low-frequency noises of small mammals—their digging, gnawing, and rustling through the leaves—they can home in very close to the prey. Henry describes them sitting in 2 feet of snow, intently listening. They then dive into the snow and dig frantically, to unearth the prey they have heard. Red foxes often hunt along edges: just as the wildlife biologist knows that game is often more abundant at the interfaces between habitats, so does the fox come to learn that he is more apt to get a meal there. The cover is usually better there, and the plants more varied, thus increasing the chances of finding food—for predator and prey alike.

Red foxes, then, are very catlike in their hunting. Henry (1986) studied their hunting behavior by conditioning them. Because he would feed the foxes at the outset of a tracking session, they would come to accept him, and he would then be able to follow them. Canids generally capture prey by chasing it down after approaching it openly. Foxes, however, like felids, stalk their prey, then put on a quick burst of speed. They usually capture prey by biting it or pinning it to the ground with the forepaws. Almost all of the animals red foxes feed on are small ones; animals larger than rabbits are usually scavenged rather than killed. Henry observed foxes attempting to capture 34 different kinds of animal prey items—all small: 14 kinds of mammals (five species of voles and mice, three of shrews, three of squirrels including the woodchuck, snowshoe hare, pocket gopher, and muskrat), 13 kinds of birds (ten songbirds, two grouse, and mallard), and several categories of insects (crickets, grasshoppers, beetles, moths, and flies). Among 139 successful hunts observed by Henry, the foxes were successful in capturing insect prey 82% of the time (of all the prey, the insects were least able to escape), mammals 23% of the time, and birds only 2% of the time (only one of 71 attempts was successful).

The red fox hunts different prey groups differently. Insects are hunted rather casually—probably because they are so small and because they are so easily caught. Usually, the fox simply eats the insect. If he loses sight of it, he will poke his nose or stomp a forefoot into the area to relocate it, by making it move; alternatively, he may locate it by hearing its rustling sounds. To find rodents and shrews, a fox usually travels game trails. When it hears a mouse it stops, positions itself perpendicular to the trail, and stares intently at the area to locate the prey, using mostly its hearing but also olfactory efforts. It may crouch and stalk the prey, if necessary. When the prey is located, the fox lunges, arching through the air—usually up to 2 meters (6 feet) but up to as much as 5 meters (16 feet)—and attempts to pin the prey to the ground; it then bites it, but sometimes will carry it off and play with it, in the manner of a cat with a mouse. Birds and tree squirrels are stalked, the fox then attacking by a crouched, dashing run (they have little success with squirrels, just one of 43 hunts ending well). Rabbits and hares are also stalked. Typically, the fox crouches low to the ground and moves slowly forward, its eyes fixed on the prey, advancing as close as possible. The moment the prey bolts, the fox is in full gallop, straining to bite leg or rump, the prey suddenly and repeatedly changing direction in an attempt to distance itself from the fox. This sort of chase may cover considerable distances. Either the prey escapes into a dense thicket, or the fox gets a bite hold on it, pulls it to the ground, and pins it, and by a bite to the head or neck (the fenestrate rostrum of the rabbit may make an ideal place for the fox to bite) kills it.

Foxes will continue hunting when their stomachs are full, and will cache excess food in a very stereotyped way, each item in a different cache. A fox will hold the prey in its mouth while it digs a hole with the front feet, piling the dirt next to the hole. The prey item is put into the hole and pressed down. Dirt is then pushed over it and pressed down with the snout. Finally, leaves or other debris are raked over the cache. A fox can live on about 0.4 kg (1 lb) of food a day, and sometimes this total consists entirely of cached food. Henry (1986) believes a fox finds many of its caches by memory, aided by smell, but caches may be found and pilfered by other animals, too, especially by other foxes. Henry recorded one instance in which the same cache changed hands several times. To determine how valuable caching is in preserving the prey for a later meal, Henry set up a series of

caches himself, covering half (60) and leaving the other half in the bottom of the holes he had dug, uncovered. A week later, he returned. Sixty percent of the open caches had been pilfered, only 13% of the covered ones.

Foxes urine-marked up to 70 times per hour as they hunted for food, a few on obviously marked areas. Many of the marks, however, were seemingly at random or at least with no tree trunk, boulder, or whatever present. Henry concluded that the urine marks say to the fox, "No food here," in situations where there *had* been food or remnants of food but no usable material remained, the fox thus avoiding time wastage.

REPRODUCTION AND DEVELOPMENT. As winter begins to wane, in January or early February, foxes begin nocturnal barking. The mating season has started. The urine has now taken on a musky odor, and a skunky odor pervades the woods in the area where a pair of foxes have established their territory. The foxes have been living in solitary isolation, but they now seek one another out and spend much time traveling together. The female will locate and clean several dens on the territory, one of which will be chosen for her litter. The typical den is on a hillside in sandy loam or other soft soil, often in the forest but close to an open area, and usually there is water within a hundred meters (330 feet). There are usually several entrances to the den, the largest about 25 cm (10 inches) in diameter. The same den may be used for many years, and a daughter may even take it over upon her mother's death. One of the extra dens the female had cleaned can be used if the chosen den is disturbed.

In late March or early April, 51 days after mating, the mother gives birth to four to ten young, usually about five. The pups, a little over 100 grams each at birth, are similar to newborn coyotes or wolves, but most already show the white tail tip. During their first month, their coats are dark gray. The eyes open at about 10 to 12 days. The female remains in the den for a few days before and after the birth, and the male provides food for her during this period, a span of at least a couple of days in the south and up to ten days in the north. The female cuddles her body around the young during this time, apparently helping to keep them warm. By about two weeks they are well furred and she has resumed her normal activities, but she will return to the den to nurse and clean the cubs and play with them, and she eats their waste products. In their third week they begin to chew and suck meat. By three to four weeks they are fighting with each other and they have established a dominance hierarchy. The alpha animal (it may be a male or female, but is usually the largest) tends to get the food. Some may die as a result, but this behavior has survival value, since the number of young that survive will be proportional to the amount of food available. The outcome is that a few healthy individuals, rather than several in poor physical condition, survive the early weeks of their lives.

The pups come to the den entrance when they are about five weeks old, and by early May they are spending much time above ground; the dominance hierarchy is now well established and the fighting has greatly subsided. There is scarcely a more attractive sight to be seen than the youngsters disporting about the den entrance, rolling and tumbling in play, while the mother, ever alert, watches over them. The father, for his part, shares the burden of feeding the growing pups. When a parent brings food to the young, it calls and the young come out to get it. At first, they are still in their dark coats, but at around five weeks there is a molt to a sandy-colored coat, roughly matching the ground color of the soil in the area. This coat, still not the red coat of the adult, probably helps to protect them at this stage of their life, when they are spending much time outside. They do not attain the adult coat until late June. At about five weeks, too, the young begin the transition to adult life: they start eating solid food and weaning begins. The female will roll over on her stomach and repel attempts to suckle. Weaning is completed by eight weeks.

During this period the parents bring a great amount of food to the den and present it to the young, always in the same way. The parent arrives at the den with food in its jaws, chortles, and the young rush out. The food is given to the first pup that begs for it. The begging pup crouches low, beats its tail on the ground, and reaches up and smells, licks, and bites at the corners of the adult's mouth. Those pups that have not eaten recently often wait outside the burrow watching for the parent. This gives them the edge in the scramble for the next ration of food, but they must then defend the food from their fellow young. "Helper" foxes, usually daughters from a previous litter that have not yet left the territory, may also bring food to the young. The selective advantage to the helper may seem obscure, but she is genetically related to the offspring, and in helping the offspring she is thus helping to perpetuate her own genes. In poor years unbred females may serve as helpers, but in good years such unattached females may be bred by the male on the territory, and two litters can be produced, the male helping to raise both. This hypothesis, however, needs more exploration (Henry, 1986).

By mid-June the young, now called "kits," are two-thirds the size of the adults, and the parents are bringing them less food, but on their trips away from the den they begin to take one or more young along. Sometimes they bring the young back; sometimes they let them return on their own. During this time the kits explore near the den and eat such fruit, insects, and other prey as they happen upon. Each day, however, they tend to range farther from the den, and they soon find it is best to hunt their small prey alone, becoming "catlike canids" in the mold of their parents.

Kits and parents may continue to cross paths into late summer, but these meetings diminish, and in September, when the young males begin to mature, agonistic behavior increases, and the young begin to disperse, the males leaving first and going the farthest. Females leave later, and one or two may stay on territory if ample food is available, even up to several years (those that do will help with the litter but will not have pups of their own). Along with this pattern of development, red foxes have evolved monogamy, though it is not exclusively practiced. And along with a permanent pair bond has come great similarity between the sexes in red foxes.

The young remain in the den until they are about three and a half months old, when they begin to hunt for themselves. At that time, their catch is occasionally supplemented by the parents, as may be necessary, but by seven months they have learned to feed on their own. Now stress begins to develop between parents and young and the time to disperse is nearing. Soon, the young males do leave.

POPULATION CHARACTERISTICS. A midwestern red fox family unit occupies about 100 ha (250 acres), but territories can range from about 60 to 600 ha (150 to 1500 acres). Since these territories are small, they can be vigorously defended against other red foxes. Both sexes, but especially the males, do the defending. Because they take small prey, which is often rather abundant in small areas, red foxes can flourish in such areas, and they sometimes form stable, year-round, extended-family groups. A red fox normally lives about three to seven years.

ENEMIES. Young foxes are preyed upon by a variety of carnivores and raptors. Coyotes will kill adult red foxes, but otherwise they have few enemies other than people and their automobiles.

PARASITES AND DISEASE. Foxes sometimes contract rabies; in Illinois, for example, about ten foxes per year are diagnosed. Foxes may have furious, or aggressive, rabies, which for humans is the most dangerous form. Other times, rabid foxes may simply be visibly weak; we suspect this type may be bat rabies. Distemper is also a problem. Mange mites, which cause hair loss, are common on red foxes. Ear mites, ticks, one species of chewing louse, six species of fleas, and a number of internal parasites are also found, but as on other, larger predators, few mite species are present. The parasites present are often those of the prey species.

RELATION TO HUMANS. The red fox, an animal of the open, has done well in settled regions, and does especially well in broken country. Our opening of the land has benefited the red fox by providing more of this habitat, and this species, like the deer, probably occurs in greater numbers than ever before, in spite of continued persecution. Foxes do take some livestock, especially young chickens.

In the western world, fox hunting has long been considered great sport, whether on foot with the help of hounds, on horseback with a pack of hounds, or still-hunting when snow covers the fields. Although it is considered difficult, fox trapping was also once popular. An experienced trapper using a good clean set (one that could not be perceived) could sometimes catch a hundred foxes in a season. The value of fox pelts has varied greatly. Before World War II they were worth from $10 to $20 or more, but in the 1940s and 1950s they were of little value. In the 1970s long furs again became popular, and fox hunting was again on the rise. In the fall of 1976, for example, New York pelts brought $50, and 100,000 pelts were sold that year. Pelts still brought as much as $30 in 1987, but with increased emphasis on the conservation of predators, there is little call for fur today. The tremendous popularity of the silver fox (see "Description," above) once resulted in an extensive growth of the fur-farming industry, but today the number of foxes raised for their fur is negligible. Fox pelts have been used almost solely for trimming and scarves.

AREAS FOR FURTHER WORK. There are exceptions, but most of the large mammals have large ectoparasites—ticks, fleas, lice—but very few small mites. Why? The host certainly presents plenty of expanse and niches on which they could live.

## SUBSPECIES

Upon synonymy of the red fox of North America with the Old World *Vulpes vulpes*, the eastern U.S. subspecies became *V. v. fulva*. We suggest that *V. v. rubricosa*, which occurs in northern Maine, be combined with *fulva*, since we are aware of no evidence of a primary isolating mechanism separating the two. It may be, too, that non-native (European) subspecies have been introduced at times.

*Vulpes vulpes fulva* (Desmarest)

As described above. This is the subspecies that ranges across North America. Several subspecies have been described from western North America, but we suspect most are not valid.

Type locality: Virginia, for *Vulpes vulpes fulva*. Other currently recognized eastern subspecies: *V. vulpes rubricosa* Bangs

## LITERATURE

Ables, E. D. 1975. Ecology of the red fox in North America. In: M. W. Fox, ed., *The Wild Canids: Their Systematics, Behavioral Ecology, and Evolution*, pp. 216–236. New York: Van Nostrand Reinhold.

Churcher, C. S. 1959. The specific status of the New World red fox. *J. Mammal.* 40: 513–520.

Henry, J. D. 1986. *Red Fox, the Catlike Canine.* Washington: Smithsonian Institution Press. 174 pp. Henry offers insight that can come only from years of working intimately with a species. This book is highly recommended for anyone who really wants to know the red fox.

Larivière, S., and M. Pasitschniak-Arts. 1996. *Vulpes vulpes.* **Mammalian Species No. 537.** Amer. Soc. Mammal. 11 pp.

Pils, C. M., and M. A. Martin. 1978. Population dynamics, predator-prey relationships and management of the red fox in Wisconsin. Wisconsin Dept. Nat. Resources, Tech. Bull. 105. 56 pp.

Rue, L. L., III. 1969. *The World of the Red Fox.* Philadelphia: J. B. Lippincott. 204 pp.

Samuel, D. E., and B. B. Nelson. 1982. Foxes *Vulpes vulpes* and allies. In: J. A. Chapman and G. A. Feldhamer, eds., *Wild Mammals of North America*, pp. 475–490. Baltimore: Johns Hopkins Univ. Press.

Storm, G. L., R. D. Andrews, P. L. Phillips, R. A. Bishop, D. B. Siniff, and J. R. Tester. 1976. Morphology, reproduction, dispersal, and mortality of midwestern red fox populations. *Wildl. Monogr.* No. 49. 82 pp.

Voigt, D. R. 1987. Red fox. In: M. Novak, J. A. Baker, M. E. Obbard, and B. Mallock, eds., *Wild Furbearer Management and Conservation in North America*, pp. 378–392. Toronto: Ontario Ministry Nat. Resources.

## Gray Fox *Urocyon cinereoargenteus* (Schreber)                              Color plate 16

DESCRIPTION. Gray and red foxes are quite distinct, yet are often confused. The red fox is a reddish-colored canine with a white tail tip. The gray fox has reddish on the backs of the ears and around the neck, on the outsides of the legs, and on the sides of the belly, but otherwise is grizzled, or "salt-and-pepper" gray, with a black tail tip. The underparts are white. The sides of the nose and underjaw are blackish. On the upper side of the tail near its base is a con-

*Gray fox,* Urocyon cinereoargenteus
*(Roger W. Barbour)*

cealed mane of stiff black hairs, which can be felt by rubbing one's hand along the tail toward the body. The skull has prominent temporal ridges that join posteriorly to form a prominent lyrate or "U"-shaped configuration, as opposed to the V-shaped configuration on the skull of the red fox. The upper incisors are not lobed (in the red fox, they are). A notch near the bottom of the dentary bone produces four angles on the posterior portion of the lower jaw (in the red fox there are three such angles).

MEASUREMENTS. Average measurements of 112 gray foxes from Indiana were: total length 933 (805-1065), tail 334 (220–440), hind foot 135 (117–150) mm. Skull length is 124–130 mm. The weight ranges from 3.2 to 5.9 kg (7–13 lbs). Hamilton saw a 6.3-kg (14-lb) gray fox in New York, and J. E. Hill recorded an 8.6-kg (19-lb) specimen in Massachusetts. Gray foxes in the northern parts of the range are larger than those in the south, southern specimens seldom exceeding 4.5 kg (10 lbs). Two adults from central Florida averaged: total length 905, tail 285, and hind foot 125 mm.

Diploid number = 66.

TOOTH FORMULA

$$\frac{3}{3} \quad \frac{1}{1} \quad \frac{4}{4} \quad \frac{2}{3} \quad = \quad 42$$

DISTRIBUTION. The range of the gray fox includes all of the eastern United States, except for extreme northern Maine, and it is apparently not common in the Upper Peninsula of

Michigan. The gray fox has a more southerly distribution than the red. It occurs from about the Canadian border south through all of Central America and to northwestern South America, including all of the western United States except for a large area of the Northwest.

HABITAT. The gray fox does best in areas with diverse habitats, but in eastern North America it is typically associated with deciduous forest. It is also found in the swamps and the hammocks and pine woods of the southern states. The gray fox has recently moved into areas it had not previously occupied or from which it had been extirpated, such as New England and Michigan. It does not take as readily to the farmlands as the red fox does.

HABITS. Gray foxes are mainly crepuscular and nocturnal. They are adept climbers, often taking to trees when pursued. In climbing, the fox may leap cautiously from limb to limb, using its long, sharp, curved claws in the manner of a cat, or it may actually climb in a fashion not unlike that of a bear, by grasping the trunk with the forelegs and pushing upward with the hind feet. Gray foxes bark, a vocalization heard most often in February, during the breeding season.

Dens are used in the mating and reproductive season, seldom the rest of the year. A den may consist of a hollow tree or log, or a burrow in the ground, but these are seldom found in the open fields, as are those of the red fox. They may be on a brushy hillside, and are often the converted dens of other animals. Gray foxes and woodchucks have sometimes been found in the same dens. In contrast to its red cousin, a gray fox eluding the hounds usually takes to cover after a short chase, repairing to an underground retreat or climbing into the crotch of a suitable tree. Its diurnal resting sites are often above ground.

*Distribution of the gray fox,*
Urocyon cinereoargenteus,
*in the eastern United States*

Urine and scat deposition play a role in communication. Scats are often found on logs or rocks, or in bare areas. A musk gland, about 110 mm long, is associated with the mane on the top of the tail. Its secretion may be associated with individual recognition.

FOOD AND FEEDING. Gray foxes feed on a great variety of prey, their choices heavily influenced by availability, but their most important food is perhaps the cottontail rabbit. Smaller mammals, particularly mice and rats, form much of the prey, and shrews, birds, reptiles, insects and other invertebrates, fruit, nuts, corn, grasses, and carrion are also eaten. In the fall, grasshoppers and crickets may be particularly important.

REPRODUCTION AND DEVELOPMENT. Mating occurs January through April, its timing varying geographically, the earlier dates in the south. Some females breed at ten months, others not until their second year. The one to seven (usually three to five) young are born in March or April, depending on latitude. Data on the gestation period are meager, but it has been reported as 63 or 53 days. From the breeding season through late summer the foxes live in family units, each unit comprising a male, a female, and their young. (The gray fox may be monogamous, but this, too, has not been confirmed.) At birth, baby foxes average 86 grams, and their average weight progresses as follows: at 11 days, 129 grams; at 19, 169; at 23, 234; at 30, 249; at 51, 588; at 78, 1200; at three months, 1500 grams, at four, 2000; at six, 2300; and at eight months, adult size, 3700 grams (8.1 lbs). The young remain at the den their first month, and with the parents into early summer, and they stay with the mother until they are fully capable of maintaining themselves.

POPULATION CHARACTERISTICS. Home-range size varies with habitat type and quality, population size, and the configuration of natural features. Radiotelemetry has recorded ranges from about 85 ha (210 acres) to 3.2 square km (1.2 square miles). Home ranges overlap and are largest during the mating season, smallest for females when pups are in the den. Dispersal records for juveniles range up to 84 km (52 miles). Densities for this species are about one to two per square km (0.4 to 0.8 per square mile). Most gray foxes apparently die before the age of two, although captives have lived 14 or 15 years. Most mortality is from hunting, trapping, and roadkills.

ENEMIES. Humans are the most important enemy of the gray fox. We hunt them and trap them, and many fall to the automobile. Gray foxes are more easily lured and shot using predator calls that mimic the fear scream of a rabbit than are red foxes.

Other than ourselves, the adult gray fox has few enemies. Hamilton found the remains of one in the stomach of a large bobcat from Vermont, and coyotes may kill a few.

PARASITES AND DISEASE. Since a major food of this species is the cottontail rabbit, it is not surprising that its major flea is *Cediopsylla simplex*, a flea of the cottontail. Gray foxes are parasitized primarily by fleas, ticks, and lice, although two species of chiggers and a few species of mites have also been found. Among the internal parasites are at least five species of trematodes, eight of cestodes, 17 of nematodes, and two of acanthocephalans. Distemper and rabies are important diseases of foxes. Foxes may contract aggressive ("street") rabies or nonaggressive ("dumb") rabies; we suspect the nonaggressive type may be bat rabies.

RELATION TO HUMANS. The coarse gray fur of this species was widely used for collars and trimmings, but its quality does not match that of the red fox, and the trapper received less for it than for red fox hides. Gray fox pelts in Indiana brought an average of $10.48 and $19.51 in the 1974–75 and 1975–76 seasons, whereas red fox pelts averaged $19.09 and $34.26 those years. New York pelts had brought the trapper just $.75 in the 1930s, but in 1976 New York fur buyers paid $25.00 for pelts. In 1987, pelts brought the same price, $30, as red fox pelts did, but as of this writing, fox pelts, like other furs, are worth little.

AREAS FOR FURTHER WORK. Concerning ecology, much less is known of the gray fox than of the red fox. Much is yet to be learned of its hunting strategies and other behavior, and of its

*Black bear,* Ursus americanus
*(Roger W. Barbour)*

home life, home ranges, population size, and interrelations with other species.

## SUBSPECIES

Several subspecies have been described for the eastern United States, but we see no evidence of primary isolating mechanisms separating them. We consider all of them to be variants of the nominate subspecies.

*Urocyon cinereoargenteus cinereoargenteus (Schreber)*

As described above. This is the subspecies that ranges across eastern United States, from central New York to northern Mississippi, Alabama, and Georgia.

Type locality: Eastern North America.

Other currently recognized eastern subspecies:

    *U. cinereoargenteus borealis* Merriam

    *U. cinereoargenteus floridanus* Rhoads

    *U. cinereoargenteus ocythous* Bangs

## LITERATURE

Fritzell, E. K. 1987. Gray fox and island gray fox. In: M. Novak, J. A. Baker, M. E. Obbard, and B. Mallock, eds., *Wild Furbearer Management and Conservation in North America*, pp. 408–420. Toronto: Ontario Ministry Nat. Resources.

Fritzell, E. K., and K. J. Haroldson. 1982. *Urocyon cinereoargenteus.* **Mammalian Species No. 189.** Amer. Soc. Mammal. 8 pp.

Samuel, D. E., and B. B. Nelson. 1982. Foxes *Vulpes vulpes* and allies. In: J. A. Chapman and G. A. Feldhamer, eds., *Wild Mammals of North America*, pp. 475–490. Baltimore: Johns Hopkins Univ. Press.

## BEARS, Family Ursidae

This family numbers eight species in six genera. The grizzly bear and polar bear are two of the largest land mammals, each weighing up to 725 kg (1600 lbs), and the Alaskan brown bear can reach 780 kg (1720 lbs). Bears need little description. They are heavy-bodied, heavy-limbed animals with a vestigial tail. There are five toes on each foot, their claws nonretractile, and the posture is plantigrade (like us, bears walk on their heels). Bears have 42 teeth; the carnassials are flattened for crushing. They have small ears, heavy pelage, and a lumbering gait. The black bear, *Ursus americanus*, is the only species of bear to occur in the eastern United States in historic times.

### Black Bear *Ursus americanus* (Pallas)
                             Color plate 17

DESCRIPTION. The black bear is a large animal with rounded ears, coarse, dark fur, and essentially no tail. Individuals vary in color from cinnamon brown to black. The face and nose are tinged with tan; occasionally a white spot appears on the chest. The nose is long and tapering, the nose pad broad; the eyes are small and black. The feet, each with five clawed digits, are large and plantigrade. The teeth are bunodont (the cusps of the molariforms are blunt, like ours, an adaptation for an omnivorous diet). The first three premolars are rudimentary.

MEASUREMENTS. Total length of males 1370–1800 mm (54–70 inches), females 1200–1500

(47−59); tail 90−125 (3.5−5), 80−115 (3−4.5); hind foot 220−280 (8.7−11), 190−240 (7.5−9.5). Full-grown males weigh 113−227 kg (250−500 lb), females 50−204 (110−450), but exceptional individuals may weigh 270 kg (600 lbs) or more. The skull has a basilar length of 250 mm, a zygomatic breadth of 170−180 mm, and a prominent sagittal crest.

Diploid number = 74.

TOOTH FORMULA

$$\frac{3}{3} \ \frac{1}{1} \ \frac{4}{4} \ \frac{2}{3} \ = \ 42$$

DISTRIBUTION. The black bear formerly ranged over all the forested portions of North America and into central Mexico, but with encroaching civilization it has become increasingly scarce. It occurs throughout much of Canada and Alaska and has a spotty but widespread distribution in the West, occurring in Arkansas, Minnesota, and west of a line from central Montana to west Texas. In the east (Map 8.7), it is still present and sometimes abundant in parts of Maine, northern New Hampshire, most of Vermont, much of New York and Pennsylvania, northern Michigan and Wisconsin, the mountainous parts of West Virginia, Maryland, Virginia, Kentucky, North Carolina, Tennessee, and Alabama, and in the coastal swamps of North Carolina, including the Great Dismal Swamp. In the Deep South, the species can still be found in southern Alabama, the Florida panhandle, and Louisiana, and there is a major population in the Big Cypress region of southwestern peninsular Florida. Only remnant populations remain in western Massachusetts, South Carolina, Georgia, and northeastern Florida.

HABITAT. The black bear is today largely restricted to the wilder parts of the east—the

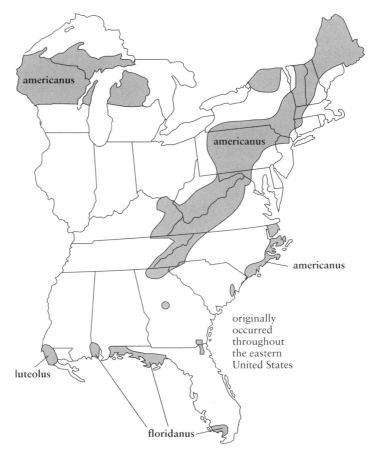

*Distribution of the black bear, Ursus americanus, in the eastern United States (Data courtesy of Michael Pelton)*

secluded northern forests and the almost impenetrable southern swamps. In the southern Appalachians, bears do best in oak/hickory or mixed mesophytic forest with an understory of blueberry, blackberry, raspberry, rhododendron, and mountain laurel. In the coastal areas of the Southeast, they live in wooded and swampy bottomlands where black gum and cypress are common in the wetter sites, vines and oaks in the drier sites. Holly, greenbrier, huckleberry, and evergreen woody species form the understory. Optimum bear habitat is relatively inaccessible terrain with thick understory and goodly supplies of mast. In Michigan, bears do best in areas with a series of wooded ridges alternating with swamps and marshes. Individuals frequently visit populated agricultural regions, but do not stay long.

HABITS. The black bear's presence is often easily detected, especially in fall. It leaves many signs—the very large tracks, trampled bushes, overturned logs and stumps, mud wallows, and gnawings and claw marks on trees. The claw marks result from climbing, or from the bear's behavior of rearing on its hind legs and digging its claws into a tree as high as possible. Such marks are especially prominent on beech, birch, and aspen trees. The function of this behavior is not understood, but the tree-marking behavior peaks during the midsummer breeding period. The marks could serve as territorial markers, but the spacing of males and females in this species is not well understood.

Black bears are active at dusk, and often even in daytime. Lindzey and Meslow (1977) reported them to be crepuscular in spring, diurnal in summer, and nocturnal in autumn, but there is little activity at temperatures below freezing, and activity usually slackens at temperatures above 25°C (78°F). Black bears, other than females with young, are solitary animals. They bed in shallow depressions in the forest floor, or in hollow trees—sometimes 20 meters (60 feet) up!

Bears have only adequate vision, but very sensitive noses and ears. Black bears are great travelers, sometimes covering many miles in a single night; they can move at speeds of more than 48 kph (30 mph); they can swim; and they are good climbers. Bears produce growls, bel-

lows, bawls, or, most commonly, "woof" calls. They pop their teeth in aggressive and fearful situations.

As cold weather approaches, bears feed heavily and become extremely fat, thus well equipped for winter. They may increase their weight by up to 100%: one black bear studied by Roger Powell increased from 50 to 100 kg (110 to 220 lbs). In the Upper Peninsula of Michigan, bears enter winter dens in October; in the South, later; even in Florida bears "hole up" during the coldest weather. The females seek some shallow cave, hollow tree or log, uprooted tree, or even the open floor of a sphagnum bog, sheltered only by overhanging conifer boughs. Erickson (1964) found 229 winter dens of bears in Michigan's Upper Peninsula. Of these, nearly half were in cavities under stumps and logs, 21% were in holes excavated in banks, and 11% were under brush piles. The rest were in a variety of situations—hollow standing trees, hollow logs, rock crevices, depressions, a beaver lodge, and beneath a deserted dwelling. In some areas, hollow trees may be critical, so as to avoid dogs. The males retire later to their winter quarters, but choose similar hibernacula.

There is a continuum of sorts between the deep sleep of raccoons, opossums, and gray squirrels and the true hibernation of ground squirrels and woodchucks, in which all bodily functions are greatly slowed. Bears are said not to truly hibernate, because although their bodily processes are slowed, they are not suppressed to the extent found in the deep hibernators. They also have their young during the period of dormancy. Black bears, however, if not true hibernators, are certainly close. Various terms—dormancy, ecological hibernation, and carnivoran lethargy, for example—have been used to indicate the black bear's various modifications to hibernation. They exhibit continuous dormancy for about seven months, without eating, drinking, defecating, or urinating. Their temperature does not fall to the extent it does in true hibernators, nor is respiration as greatly retarded. Body temperature decreases from a summertime 37–38°C (99–101°F) to 31–35°C (88–95°F), and the heart rate drops from about 40 to about eight to ten beats per minute. The black bear's elevated temperature is apparently an adaptation allowing her to care for her young during dormancy. Average loss of mass in one study was 260 grams per day; over the winter, that amounted to a drop of 23.1% from peak weight (Hellgren et al., 1990). Most hibernators wake periodically, but bears do not wake during winter unless disturbed. If they *are* disturbed, they will rouse readily. The ability of bears to recycle urea and to desist urinating, defecating, eating, or drinking during the entire denning period is unique. On emergence from dormancy, the bear faces a period of food scarcity and loses weight, still dependent in part on the fat stored in the preceding year.

A study in Maine found that food availability affected the date of denning. In one year, when beechnuts were scarce, most females denned in mid- to late October. The next year, when they were abundant, the bears foraged in hardwood forests more and did not den until November. Pregnant females tended to den earlier than those not pregnant. Emergence was in April, near the time of final snow melt.

FOOD AND FEEDING. Bears are omnivorous, selecting as wide a choice of food as any carnivore. They feed primarily on grasses and forbs in the spring, and on fruits and mast in summer and fall. They are inordinately fond of fruits, consuming great quantities of blueberries, blackberries, and shadberries or serviceberries (*Amelanchier* sp.), and their taste for honey is well-known. Mice, stranded fish, and other small animals are sometimes eaten, but only a small portion of the black bear diet is of animal material, and that mostly the larvae and pupae of colonial insects: ants, wasps, and bees. They also eat many beetles and their larvae. Most vertebrate material eaten consists of carrion. In fall, bears eat great quantities of acorns, hickory, and other nuts, grapes, and occasionally the leaves of hardwoods.

In Florida, the buds and fruits of the saw palmetto (*Serenoa repens*) and the berries and buds of cabbage palm (*Sabal palmetto*) are important foods. A large bear will climb to the top of a cabbage palm, wrap its arms around the top, and sway back and forth until the big bud loosens, then fall to the ground on its back, the tender cabbage secure in its paws.

REPRODUCTION AND DEVELOPMENT. Ovulation in black bears is induced by copulation. Mating is in mid-June to mid-July, but the blastocyst remains dormant in the uterus until late fall, when implantation occurs, followed by a normal development of about 70 days. The female gives birth to her one to five (normally two) cubs in her winter den in late January or early February, and reproductive success is lower following years with poor food. The cubs are remarkable for their diminutive size; the newborn offspring of a 90-kg (200-lb) adult scarcely exceeds 200 grams and is only about 180 mm (7.5 inches) long. (The minuteness of the cubs, in light of such a long gestation, is explained by the delayed implantation of the blastocyst.) Black hair appears dorsally at one week; the eyes open at about the 25th day. The ear pinnae unfold at about 46 days, when the cub weighs over 2.2 kg (5 lbs). The females emerge from their winter dens from late March through early May. The young may nurse until a year of age, remaining with their mother through summer, fall, and the following winter. But these cubs do not share their second denning with newborns, for bears ordinarily have young every other year, and females are not receptive in years when they are nursing. Females usually mature at three to five years of age, at a greater age in the north.

POPULATION CHARACTERISTICS. Black bear densities in Michigan have been calculated at one per 0.8 square km (0.03 square mile) to one per 32 square km (12 square miles). Black bears require an extensive area in which to live and roam, perhaps 20 square km (7.7 square miles), and males often cover perhaps twice the area used by females. In the Great Smokies, adult males used an average of 4.2 square km (1.6 square miles), females 3.8 square km (1.5 square miles). Black bears have returned to their home areas after being transported to localities up to 230 km (143 miles) distant. The minimum estimated home-range size, determined via radiotelemetry, of five bears in Louisiana averaged 5.5 square km (2.1 square miles) and ranged from 1.5 to 38 square km (0.6 to 14.7 square miles), the ranges of the males averaging about three to eight times greater than those of females. Three of the bears became inactive for periods of 74 to 124 days, and one gave birth during this period. Home-range size varies greatly, depending on habitat quality, the sex and age of the bear, the season, and population density, but home ranges overlap considerably, even in areas of high use; in one study, neighboring bears even used the same areas for the same activities at the same time (Horner and Powell, 1990).

Females and their offspring form social units that remain together for up to a year. In Minnesota, but not in North Carolina or Tennessee, the female defends a territory for the unit. Male territories are larger than those of females, and usually encompass those of two or more females. Young males are not allowed on anyone's territories. They presumably hunt for undefended habitat on which to settle.

ENEMIES. Other than humans and perhaps their dogs, black bears have few enemies.

PARASITES AND DISEASE. Black bear ectoparasites are a flea, six species of large mites, three ticks, and two mange mites. Internal parasites are protozoans, cestodes, trematodes, nematodes, and one acanthocephalan.

RELATION TO HUMANS. Bears have disappeared over much of their range because of the steady encroachment of humans. Nonetheless, they often live fairly close to settled land. The black bear's fur has little value, but its secretive habits and great size make it a favorite with hunters. Many hundreds are killed each year in the eastern United States, and the flesh is highly esteemed. Tate and Pelton (1980) described aggressive behavior toward humans in the Great Smokies, ranging from low moans, blow vocalizations with lip extensions, and lowered head to actual charge. Still, black bears usually retreat to the underbrush when humans approach; only 37 of 624 acts of aggression there ended in contact. Bears also take some livestock—hogs, calves, and poultry—and are considered a serious nuisance by beekeepers.

AREAS FOR FURTHER WORK. Genetic and morphological comparisons of the isolated bear populations in this slowly reproducing species would seem of interest. The data thus amassed could yield information on the effectiveness of the isolating mechanisms and on rates of evolution.

## SUBSPECIES

The black bear was once found throughout the eastern United States, but has been reduced there to occurrence in four general areas (the two northern forms are contiguous in Canada, and thus are retained as a single subspecies) and several remnant areas. Since primary isolating mechanisms now appear to be present, and since significant morphological variation can be demonstrated, we accept the three described subspecies (one of them the nominate), but given the great mobility of bears and their substantial populations in panhandle and southern Florida, the effectiveness of the isolating mechanisms might be questioned.

### *Ursus americanus americanus* (Pallas)

As described above. This is the black bear of the wilder regions of the northern and eastern portions of our area, including the Appalachians and coastal North Carolina. It is the smallest of the eastern subspecies. These bears occur through a series of integrading subspecies (thus not valid by our criteria) in Canada and the western United States.

Type locality: Eastern North America.

### *Ursus americanus luteolus* Griffith

A large black bear, differing from the northern subspecies by its greater size and different skull characters: the skull is long and flat, the frontoparietal region depressed; the profile of the top of the skull, including the crest, is nearly a straight line; the ratio of zygomatic breadth to basilar length of the skull is 2/3, whereas in *U. a. americanus* the same ratio is 3/4; and the last upper molar is particularly large, 17 mm in breadth and 30 mm in length. The distribution of *U. a. luteolus* has not been well defined. East of the Mississippi this bear occurs in Louisiana and probably along the Mississippi River and the Gulf in Mississippi. It occurs also into Arkansas, although bears from Canada and Minnesota have been restocked in that state. Until more specimens are available, the exact range cannot be determined.

Type locality: Louisiana.

### *Ursus americanus floridanus* Merriam

This is a large bear, a brownish black in captives from the Everglades, not so dark as *U. a. americanus*; the skull is very long, high, and narrow; the frontal region is remarkably elevated, highest immediately behind the postorbital processes; the brain case is very long and narrow (basilar length 280 mm); and the ratio of zygomatic breadth to basilar length is about 7/10.

Type locality: Key Biscayne, Dade Co., Florida.

### LITERATURE

Alt, G. L., G. T. Matula, F. W. Alt, and J. S. Lindzey. 1980. Dynamics of home range and movements of adult black bears in northeastern Pennsylvania. In: C. Martinka and K. L. McArthur, eds., *Bears— Their Biology and Management*, pp. 131–136. Bear Biol. Assoc. Conf. Ser., 3.

Eiler, J. H., W. G. Wathen, and M. R. Pelton. 1989. Reproduction in black bears in the southern Appalachian Mountains. *J. Wildl. Mgmt.* 53: 353–360.

Erickson, A. W. 1964. Breeding biology and ecology of the black bear in Michigan. Michigan State Univ., unpubl. Ph.D. diss. 274 pp.

Garshelis, D. L., and E. C. Hellgren. 1994. Variation in reproductive biology of male black bears. *J. Mammal.* 75: 175–188.

Garshelis, D. L., and M. R. Pelton. 1981. Movements of black bears in the Great Smoky Mountains National Park. *J. Wildl. Mgmt.* 45: 912–925.

Hellgren, E. C., and M. R. Vaughan. 1988. Seasonal food habits of black bears in Great Dismal Swamp, Virginia–North Carolina. *Proc. Ann. Conf. Southeast Assoc. Fish and Wildl. Agencies* 42: 295–305.

———. 1989a. Denning ecology of black bears in a southeastern wetland. *J. Wildl. Mgmt.* 53: 347–353.

———. 1989b. Demographic analysis of a black bear population in the Great Dismal Swamp. *J. Wildl. Mgmt.* 53: 969–977.

Hellgren, E. C., M. R. Vaughan, R. L. Kirkpatrick, and P. F. Scanlon. 1990. Serial changes in metabolic correlates of hibernation in female black bears. *J. Mammal.* 71: 291–300.

Horner, M. A., and R. A. Powell. 1990. Internal structure of home ranges of black bears and analyses of home range overlap. *J. Mammal.* 71: 402–410.

Landers, J. L., R. J. Hamilton, A. S. Johnson, and R. L. Marchinton. 1979. Foods and habitat of black bears in southeastern North Carolina. *J. Wildl. Mgmt.* 43: 143–153.

Lindzey, F. G., and E. C. Meslow. 1977. Home range and habitat use by black bears in southwestern Washington. *J. Wildl. Mgmt.* 41: 413–425.

Pelton, M. R. 1982. Black bear *Ursus americanus*. In: J. A. Chapman and G. A. Feldhamer, eds., *Wild Mammals of North America*, pp. 504–514. Baltimore: Johns Hopkins Univ. Press.

Poelker, R. J., and H. D. Hartwell. 1973. Black bear of Washington: Its biology, natural history and relationship to forest regeneration. Wash. State Game Dept., Biol. Bull. 14. 180 pp.

Rogers, L. L. 1987. Effects of food supply and kinship on social behavior, movements and population growth of black bears in northeastern Minnesota. Wildl. Monogr. No. 97. 72 pp.

Schooley, R. L., C. R. McLaughlin, G. J. Matula, Jr., and W. B. Krohn. 1994. Denning chronology of female black bears: Effects of food, weather and reproduction. *J. Mammal.* 75: 466–477.

Tate, J., and M. R. Pelton. 1980. Human-bear interactions in the Smoky Mountains: Focus on ursid aggression. 5th Int. Conf. Bear Research and Management. Madison, Wisconsin, Intern. Assn. Bear Res. Mgmt. 5: 312–321.

## RACCOONS, Family Procyonidae

There are about 17 species in seven genera in this remarkably diverse family. Except for the two species of pandas in Asia, which some think are not procyonids, all live in the New World. There are three species of this family in the United States—the coati, the ringtail, and the raccoon—but of these only the raccoon is found in the eastern United States.

The raccoon family evolved from the Canidae, the dogs. Most are medium-sized animals with long, ringed tails and pronounced facial markings, although the kinkajou, of Central and South America, is uniformly colored. The carnassial teeth of most carnivores are sharp, for shearing, but those of procyonids have evolved for crushing, as befits their omnivorous habits.

### Common Raccoon *Procyon lotor* (Linnaeus)                    Color plate 17

DESCRIPTION. The raccoon is a medium-sized mammal with a light-colored face broken by a prominent black facial mask from cheeks to eyes. It has a long, bushy, yellowish or grayish

*Raccoon,* Procyon lotor
*(Roger W. Barbour)*

tail with four to seven black rings, the rings not well defined below. Its pelage is long and thick. The muzzle is slender, the ears prominent and rather pointed. The feet are plantigrade and have five toes, each toe armed with a prominent claw, the claws useful for climbing. The toes are long and thin, even opposable to some degree, and they are extremely sensitive to touch. The soles of the feet are naked. These characters allow the raccoon a remarkable degree of dexterity in the manipulation of food and other items. The color of the raccoon varies, but the general tone is dull yellowish gray or grayish brown, darker on the back, and many of the hairs are black-tipped. There is a black streak on the forehead. The underparts are dull gray to yellowish gray, and the guard hairs are whitish or yellowish white. The feet are white. The skull is rounded, and the molars are broad and tuberculate. Individuals from Wisconsin and the Upper Peninsula of Michigan are the largest and darkest of the eastern raccoons, which become progressively smaller to the south. Individuals from Florida have a longer tail and proportionately longer legs; these animals stand much higher when on all fours. Florida raccoons vary in color between regions but often have a distinct, bright shoulder patch, ranging to deep orange-rufous in many individuals.

MEASUREMENTS. Measurements of 130 raccoons from Indiana averaged: total length 757 (550–853), tail 209 (146–254), hind foot 110 (85–124) mm. Adults commonly weigh 7–8 kg (15–18 lbs), very large individuals rarely to 14 kg (30 lbs). The record was a male of 28.3 kg (62 lbs). Measurements of ten adults from Florida and southeastern Georgia averaged: total length 812 (751–892), tail 262 (242–286), hind foot 122 (110–129) mm; and weight 5–7 kg (11–15 lbs). Raccoons of extreme southwestern Florida and the Keys seldom exceed 3.6 kg (8 lbs).

Diploid number = 38.

TOOTH FORMULA

$$\frac{3}{3} \quad \frac{1}{1} \quad \frac{4}{4} \quad \frac{2}{2} \quad = \quad 40$$

DISTRIBUTION. Raccoons are widely distributed across the eastern United States, from Maine to Wisconsin and south to the mangrove swamps of the Florida Keys and the vast bayou country of Louisiana. They also occur in southern Canada and across the continent to the West Coast, and except for a large area in the Southwest, through all of Central America.

HABITAT. The raccoon is found wherever suitable combinations of woods and wetlands provide acceptable food and den sites, from swamps and marshes (salt and freshwater) to mesic woods, cultivated areas, and urban situations. In contrast to most other carnivores, the raccoon is exceedingly successful today, having adapted well to humanity. Raccoons are often abundant in parks and in wooded portions of cities and towns, and often make pests of themselves in one way or another.

HABITS. The raccoon typically is a creature of the night, commencing to forage along the creeks and streams after sunset and remaining active to daylight, its activity peaking, however, before midnight. In the Midwest, the muddy banks and bottoms of small streams through wooded areas are often crowded with raccoon tracks in the low water of late summer and fall. The animals visit each pool in search of crayfish, frogs, fish, or other prey. Several times when we have been afield at night we have heard a rac-coon splashing through the water as it hunted by wading along the shore of a lake or stream. At dusk one can often see whole families of raccoons moving about in trees, and infrequently a family may even be surprised away from its den during the afternoon or early morning. Daytime activity has most often been recorded in coastal marshes at low tide, when the animals feed on mollusks and crustaceans, and on beaches, especially during dry seasons.

Other than the female with her young and some communal nesting during winter, the raccoon is basically a solitary animal, although it often appears in some numbers at campsites at night, and 30 were seen under street lights late one night at an intersection in California. It is an accomplished climber, its sharp claws enabling it to ascend a tree of any size with re-

*Distribution of the common raccoon, Procyon lotor, in the eastern United States*

markable celerity. It descends either headfirst or tailfirst; it is in fact one of a relatively few mammals that can descend headfirst, which it does by rotating the hind feet 180°. Raccoons are good swimmers, and though they usually walk, they can run for a considerable distance if necessary.

Raccoons use dens for a variety of purposes, for bearing the young, for winter sleep (they do not hibernate), and as temporary shelter. Hollow trees, when available, are usually favored over other dens and are most commonly used for winter sleep, but a raccoon may use a burrow or fissure or other protected situation, especially if hollow trees are scarce. A raccoon may change its winter den occasionally; one female was known to use three different dens in one winter. After mating, the female seeks out a natal den—a hollow tree, again, often being her first choice—but she may move the young to a surface den at about seven to nine weeks of age, which is about the time they start exploring outside the den. In summer, raccoons use a temporary daytime den consisting of almost any sort of shelter. It may be on the ground in a thicket, or in a salt marsh far from land. Raccoons may build a flat platform of grass or sedges for the purpose, or they may simply sleep on the upper surfaces of bare tree limbs, in old squirrel nests, or in clumps of Spanish moss during the day. Dens for whatever purpose are generally near water, and they vary greatly in the amount of use each receives, most summer dens being changed almost daily. Recent radio-tracking studies have shown that fissures in cliffs and abandoned woodchuck, fox, or skunk dens may provide suitable sites, and occasionally they are used even as maternal dens. In marshes, on rare occasions, muskrat houses have been used as dens, and in suburban areas, large drainage tiles, chimneys, and other manmade structures are used for sanctuary and for maternal dens. Communal denning is common, the members of the den usually being members of a family group. Rarely is more than one adult male present in these dens, but up to 23 raccoons have been reported in a single den.

In the northern parts of its range, in cold weather, the raccoon retires to some warm retreat, where it may stay for a month or more at a time, although snow cover may be more im-portant than temperature in the initiation of this process. Such dormancy or lethargy is not true hibernation, however, for the metabolism is not greatly lowered, whereas that of the woodchuck and other hibernators *is*. The raccoon is in fact easily roused, and if temperatures at night rise above freezing, it is up and about even in deep snow, and occasionally foraging, but little or no food is consumed during the winter in northern areas. Rather, the raccoon depends for energy on its stored fat, for it can store 30% or more of its body weight in fat. Northern animals may lose half of the fall weight during winter lethargy; in more moderate climates, raccoons may reduce activity but not become dormant.

Raccoons' hearing and sense of smell are excellent. They are colorblind, but their night vision is excellent, in keeping with their nocturnal habits. Young raccoons produce a variety of vocalizations, including a distress call described as a "winnowing" or a "quavering purr"; the female communicates with her young by a purr or a twitter. Otherwise, adult raccoons utter a variety of hisses, barks, growls, and snarls. The annual molt, which occurs in the spring and proceeds from the head rearward, takes about three months.

Scats are often deposited on logs or rocks, but they can easily be confused with those of other animals, especially those of foxes or opossums. The heaps of scats that are occasionally found indicate favored latrine areas, favored perhaps by more than one individual.

FOOD AND FEEDING. The raccoon is omnivorous, feeding on a great variety of plant and animal foods, and is highly opportunistic, making use of various food sources as available. In spring, animal food is most important, especially crayfish, followed by insects and other invertebrates, and although vertebrates are not particularly important at any time of year, they are generally eaten more in spring than at other times. What feeding is done in winter is most often on acorns and corn, but invertebrates continue to be important.

The five most abundant foods in the stomachs of 41 raccoons taken mostly in summer and fall in Indiana were corn (28.1% by volume), earthworms (11.6%), mast (9.9%), grain seeds, mostly wheat (4.8%), and grape (4.6%), and an additional 37 different foods were identified. This tally is presented simply as an example, since numerous different foods have been recorded for this species at different times and places. The raccoon is sometimes destructive to hole-nesting birds, including the wood duck. In midsummer, the raccoon will often take fruit and strip the ears of growing corn, and in late summer, like many other mammals, it feeds on the myriad crickets and grasshoppers. Apples and fall nuts, especially acorns, are favored fall foods. In season, raccoons feast heavily on black cherry, grapes, pawpaw, giant ragweed, blackberry, and pokeweed, as evidenced by the seeds in scats of raccoons. In suburban areas, raccoons often raid gardens and garbage cans, and carrion is readily consumed. In summer, sometimes, a family of coons will cut acorns in the manner of squirrels, then descend to the ground to consume them. They will also feed on small vertebrates, such as young turtles or muskrats, when these are readily available, and dig up the eggs of marine turtles in large numbers on some nesting beaches. Frogs are not eaten as often as one might expect, and salamanders are rarely eaten, but fish are often eaten when encountered in isolated pools. It is widely believed that the raccoon washes all of its food before eating—even its name, lotor, means "a washer"—but this practice is not washing, but is in fact the normal searching and kneading behavior of raccoons engaged in aquatic foraging.

REPRODUCTION AND DEVELOPMENT. Female raccoons commence breeding in their first or second year, most wild males not until their second year, mainly because they do not mature until late in their first year, after the females are already bred. One male probably mates with two or three females, and, although a pair bond is formed, a female will mate with more than one male at the peak of estrus. As is true of many carnivores, including canids and pinnipeds, the erectile tissue of the penis is reduced and its function supplanted by a penis bone, the baculum. In the raccoon, the baculum is long and curved, which helps the male maintain vaginal penetration. Mating, which occurs between January and March, immediately after emergence from

winter sleep, may last an hour or more in this species. The female retires to a maternal den, usually a hollow tree, a few days before birth, and scratches or chews off wood to create a crude nest. After a gestation period of about 63 days, the three to seven young (extremes are one to eight) are born, usually in April or May in the north (though a few births occur in late summer), probably throughout the year in the Deep South.

The newborns weigh about 60 to 75 grams and are well covered with fur. Though they soon acquire the markings of adults, their eyes do not open until they are nearly three weeks old. They are about 200 grams at seven days, about 450 grams at 19 days, and approaching 700 grams at 40 days. They may weigh up to 7 kg (15 lbs) in their first fall, and they attain their full weight in their second summer. The young are not able to stand upright until four to six weeks old, but they leave the den and begin running and climbing about by the end of the seventh week. As long as they remain in the den, they feed only on milk, but the mother may move them to a new den if disturbed. Beginning about the 8th to 12th week, the family forages together, and by about the 20th week the young are foraging more on their own. The young occasionally use a separate den, although the family remains together into the late fall or often well into winter, and usually dens together in cold weather. Some dispersal, especially in the south, is in autumn, but in the north the yearlings disperse in spring, when the new litter arrives.

POPULATION CHARACTERISTICS. There is great variation in the home ranges of raccoons, depending on season, sex, age, population, density, habitat quality, and other factors. Though they may reach 5000 ha (12,000 acres), most ranges are more like 40–100 ha (100–250 acres). As is often the case, males have larger home ranges than females. In the summer, raccoons generally use continually shifting portions of their home range, spending greater amounts of time near water and in the better-quality areas. Cornfields or fruit trees may encourage temporary forays outside of the normal range. In the city of Cincinnati, raccoons achieved a density of nearly 70 per square km (181 per square mile), but in rural areas densities of up to 20 per square km (52 per square mile) are typical. Males may be territorial at times, but females apparently are not. Raccoons often change nest sites, and dispersing juveniles have been known to move up to 264 km (165 miles). Raccoons appear to have little homing ability.

Captive raccoons may live up to 17 years, but in the wild most die before becoming independent. Very few, evidently, live to five years of age.

ENEMIES. Foxes, bobcats, coyotes, owls, and other predators undoubtedly kill many young raccoons, but for adult raccoons the automobile, disease, and accidents such as falling from trees are probably more important causes of death than are predators.

PARASITES AND DISEASE. Raccoons harbor a number of endo- and ectoparasites. They can also contract tularemia, but rabies and canine distemper are more important diseases of raccoons. Smith et al. (1995) have shown that bat rabies is molecularly different from carnivore or "street" rabies, and that there are different strains of both bat and carnivore rabies. One of these strains is raccoon rabies. In the Southeast, in the last decade, raccoons acquired a rabies epizootic, and for some years now it has been a major problem in the Northeast as well, probably originating from infected raccoons transported to Virginia and West Virginia. This strain, not found in raccoons in the Midwest, is essentially restricted to Alabama and 15 eastern states. All but 27 of the 5912 cases of raccoon rabies were from these states; rabid raccoons from elsewhere were usually infected with skunk or other strains.

A nematode found in raccoons, *Baylisascaris procyonis*, is dangerous to humans and other animals. Its tiny eggs, eliminated in the raccoon's dung, become more infective with time, and the resulting adult worms can be fatal to humans. Raccoons should not be encouraged to feed on porches, and raccoon dung should not be allowed to accumulate around living quarters or other places where people might become infected.

Major ectoparasites of the raccoon are a biting louse, *Trichodectes octomaculatus*, ticks *Ixodes texanus*, *I. cookei*, and *Dermacentor variabilis*,

and the cat flea, *Ctenocephalides felis*. The raccoon flea, *Chaetopsylla lotoris*, is less common. As is true with many larger carnivores, relatively few mites are carried.

RELATION TO HUMANS. In the fall, throughout much of the range of the raccoon, hunters and their dogs take to the woods for "coon" hunting. Aside from the excitement of pursuing the coon through swamps and beech ridges, and listening to their dogs, hunters for years were able to sell the pelts. Many raccoons were trapped, as well. Though coarse, the fur is thick and durable, and was widely used in the manufacture of short coats and trimmings. The average price of New York raccoons in 1976 was about $20, but, like other furs, the fur is worth little today.

Raccoons can be a pest in cities and towns, and in parks and camping areas. They will raid the garden or campground, get into garbage cans, and damage the roofing or siding of a building. More seriously, in the first half of the 1990s, rabies has become a major problem in raccoons in the eastern states. Raccoons are predators on wildfowl and other birds (Llewellyn and Webster, 1960), and they are one of the animals most frequently reported as nuisances (de Almeida, 1987).

AREAS FOR FURTHER WORK. It is now known that there are different rabies strains in different animal species, such as red bats (two strains), big brown bats (three strains), silver-haired bat, and free-tailed bat (Smith et al., 1995), and others in some of the various carnivores, including raccoons and skunks. Many questions arise concerning these various strains. How do they persist in the wild, since the infected hosts presumably die? Are they continually evolving? How do we explain two or more strains in one host species? Why is rabies a major problem in raccoons in the East but not in the Midwest?

## SUBSPECIES

Several subspecies have been described, but because we see no evidence of primary isolating mechanisms, we question most of them. The chain of keys bordering the southwest coast of Florida, however, known as the Ten Thousand Islands, and the great series of islands from

Biscayne Bay to Key West, the Florida Keys, have by virtue of their isolation and exposure given rise to several well-marked insular forms. In the nearly impenetrable mangrove swamps of the Keys, where freshwater streams are unknown, small raccoons exist (or at least existed) in great numbers. E. W. Nelson stated that single trappers took 800 in a season there when prices were high. We recognize three subspecies from these islands. Because the mainland raccoon populations grade one into the other, we recognize none of the subspecies that have been described for them.

### Procyon lotor lotor (Linnaeus)

As described above. Occurs across virtually all of the species' eastern U.S. range.

Type locality: Eastern United States.

Other currently recognized eastern subspecies:
*P. lotor elucus* Bangs
*P. lotor hirtus* Nelson & Goldman
*P. lotor litoreus* Nelson & Goldman
*P. lotor marinus* Nelson
*P. lotor maritimus* Dozier
*P. lotor megalodus* Lowery
*P. lotor solutus* Nelson & Goldman
*P. lotor varius* Nelson & Goldman

### Procyon lotor auspicatus Nelson

A very small raccoon, the smallest form from the Keys. *Procyon lotor auspicatus* is similar to specimens from the southern Florida mainland, but the upperparts are gray, the frontal area of the skull is much depressed, and the palatal shelf is short. Total length is 640–700 mm; and weight 2.3–2.7 kg (5 to 6 lbs). Restricted to Key Vaca and the immediately adjacent keys.

Type locality: Marathon, Key Vaca, Monroe Co., Florida.

### Procyon lotor incautus Nelson

The palest of the key raccoons, its black mask restricted, sometimes obsolescent, and the top and sides of the head whiter. The dirty-yellowish or dingy-whitish color of the worn pelage and the generally pale, faded tints reflect the brilliant light of the key environment. Weight of adults, about 3.6 kg (8 lbs). Found in the keys of the Big Pine Group, from Big Pine Key to Key West, Florida.

Type locality: Torch Key, Big Pine Key Group, Monroe Co., Florida.

### Procyon lotor inesperatus Nelson

Similar in weight and color to the mainland Florida raccoons, but the body and skull are smaller, the frontal area of the skull is much depressed, and the hind foot is relatively quite small (115 mm); *Procyon lotor inesperatus* occupies the group of keys beginning with Virginia and Biscayne keys on the north side of the entrance to Biscayne Bay and ranges south to the southern point of lower Matecumbe Key.

Type locality: Upper Matecumbe Key, Monroe Co., Florida.

### LITERATURE

Clark, W. R., J. J. Hasbrouck, J. M. Kenzler, and T. F. Glueck. 1989. Vital statistics and harvest of an Iowa raccoon population. *J. Wildl. Mgmt.* 53: 982–990.

De Almeida, M. H. 1987. Nuisance furbearer damage control in urban and suburban areas. In: M. Novak, J. A. Baker, M. E. Obbard, and B. Mallock, eds., *Wild Furbearer Management and Conservation in North America*, pp. 996-1006. Toronto: Ontario Ministry Nat. Resources.

Kaufmann, J. 1982. Raccoon and allies (*Procyon lotor* and allies). In: J. A. Chapman and G. A. Feldhamer, eds., *Wild Mammals of North America*, pp. 562–685. Baltimore: Johns Hopkins Univ. Press.

Llewellyn, L. M., and C. G. Webster. 1960. Raccoon predation on waterfowl. *North Amer. Wildl. and Nat. Resource Conf.* 25: 180–185.

Lotze, L., and S. Anderson. 1979. *Procyon lotor.* **Mammalian Species No. 119.** Amer. Soc. Mammal. 8 pp.

Rue, L. L., III. 1964. *The World of the Raccoon.* Philadelphia: J. B. Lippincott. 145 pp.

Sanderson, G. 1987. Raccoon. In: M. Novak, J. Baker, M. Obbard, and B. Malloch, eds., *Wild Furbearer Management and Conservation in North America*, chap. 38. Toronto: Ontario Ministry Nat. Resources.

Smith, J. S., L. A. Orciari, and P. A. Yager. 1995. Molecular epidemiology of rabies in the United States. *Seminars in Virology* 6: 387–400.

## WEASELS AND ALLIES, Family Mustelidae

There are 56 species of mustelids in 22 genera, inhabiting all major areas of the world except the Australian region. The skunks have traditionally been placed in this family, but recently they were removed and established as the skunk family, the Mephitidae (Dragoo and Honeycutt, 1997). The mustelids are quite variable, but most have short legs, long bodies, nonretractile claws, short heads, medium to long tails, and well-developed anal glands. The number of molariform teeth varies, but there is just one molar in the upper jaw, and only one or two in the lower jaw. Mustelids range in size from the least weasel, at about 40 grams, to the giant otter of South America, which can weigh up to 34 kg (75 lbs). This family includes some of the most efficient vertebrate hunters; some of the weasels can take prey several times bigger than themselves. Mustelids also include excellent climbers (*Martes*) and swimmers (*Lutra*).

The frontal sinuses of weasels and otters (and skunks also) are often infected by nematode worms of the genus *Skrjabingylus* Petrov, usually *S. nasicola* in weasels, *S. lutrae* in otters, and *S. chitwoodorum* in skunks. Advanced infection can cause deformities and lesions (skrjabingyliasis). The larval nematodes are found in slugs and snails. Carnivores become infected by eating the small mammals or other vertebrates that have preyed on these gastropods, or by eating the gastropods directly. Gamble and Riewe (1982) found damage in 100% of the adult individuals of *Mustela frenata* and *M. erminea* from Manitoba that he examined.

## LITERATURE CITED

Dragoo, J. W., and R. L. Honeycutt. 1997. Systematics of mustelid-like carnivores. *J. Mammal.* 78: 426–443.

Gamble, R. L., and R. R. Riewe. 1982. Infestation of the nematode *Skrjabingylus nasicola* Leukart 1842 in *Mustela frenata* (Lichtenstein) and *M. erminea* (L.) and some evidence of a paratenic host in the life cycle of this nematode. *Canadian J. Zool.* 60: 45–62.

## KEY TO THE GENERA
## OF THE FAMILY MUSTELIDAE

1. Feet broad and webbed; molariform teeth five above and below; skull flat and broad. . . . . . . . . . . . . . . . . . . . . . . *Lutra* (p. 465)
1. Feet neither broad nor webbed; tail long, thick, and with relatively short hair; molariform teeth not five above and five below; skull variable . . . . . . . . . . . . . . . . . . . . . . 2

2. Hind foot at least 75 mm long *and* top of head brown; molariform teeth five above and six below . . . . . . . . . . . . . . . . . . . . . . *Martes*
2. Hind foot less than 75 mm *or* top of head showing a white stripe; molariform teeth four above and five below . . . . . . . . . . . . . . . . . . 3
3. White stripe on head; hind foot more than 75 mm long; braincase triangular; skull more than 90 mm long; last molar triangular. . . . . . . . . . . . . . . . . . . *Taxidea* (p. 461)
3. No white stripe on head; hind foot less than 75 mm long; braincase elongate; skull less than 90 mm long; last molar dumbbell-shaped . . . . . . . . . . . . . . . . . . . . . . *Mustela* (p. 443)

## Martens and Fishers of the Genus *Martes*

The marten and fisher are fairly large, dark-colored, arboreal mustelids. Like many of the predators, they have greatly declined in numbers, but with the precipitous decline in the fur trade and the institution of management procedures, these two species are making a comeback.

### KEY TO THE MARTENS AND FISHERS
### OF THE GENUS *MARTES*

1. Orange on throat and chest; skull rounded behind; greatest length of skull less than 95 mm; total length of animal less than 700 mm; hind foot 70–90 mm long. . . *M. americana*
1. No orange on throat or chest; skull angular behind; greatest length of skull more than 95 mm; total length of animal more than 700 mm; hind foot more than 100 mm long . . . . . . . . . . . . . . . . . . . . . . *M. pennanti*

## Marten, Pine Marten
## *Martes americana* (Turton)

DESCRIPTION. An arboreal weasel with a long bushy tail, the marten is about the size of a small house cat or mink. It has soft, lustrous pelage, broad, rounded ears, a long, lithe body, and a noticeably bushy tail. Coloration in this species varies greatly, but ranges from yellowish brown to dark brown, richer and darker above. The throat and chest are conspicuously orange or ochraceous buff. The coat in summer is dark grayish brown or black, the throat patch is reddish yellow, and the pelage is thinner and coarser. The pelage is darker and thicker in winter. Martens of both sexes have prominent, elongated belly glands, which produce a characteristic oily marten odor, and paired anal scent glands. The claws are sharp and semi-retractile but not sheathed. Males are much larger than females. The marten differs from both the fisher and the mink in having the orange throat patch, and it is notably smaller than the fisher. The marten and fisher each have six upper and six lower molariform teeth; the mink has but five.

MEASUREMENTS. Males measure: total length 551–680, tail 150–205, hind foot 80–98 mm; and weight 0.7–1.3 kg (1.5–2.9 lbs). Females measure: total length 490–602, tail 135–182, hind foot 71–98 mm; and weight 0.6–0.78 kg (1.3–1.7 lbs). All males weighed by Roger Powell in Minnesota, however, weighed less than 1 kg (2.2 lbs), and adult males going into the breeding season in midsummer weighed about 0.75 kg (1.65 lbs).

Diploid number = 38.

TOOTH FORMULA

$$\frac{3}{3} \quad \frac{1}{1} \quad \frac{4}{4} \quad \frac{1}{2} \ = \ 38$$

DISTRIBUTION. In colonial times, the marten was distributed throughout the coniferous forests of the eastern United States, from Maine to Virginia and west to Wisconsin, but relentless trapping in conjunction with habitat reduction has extirpated it over most of this area. In the east today, it is found only in northern Wisconsin, the Upper Peninsula of Michigan and the northern part of the Lower Peninsula, and from northern Maine through northern New Hampshire, northern Vermont, and the Adirondack Mountains of New York, where it persists in some numbers.

HABITAT. The marten is an inhabitant of the cool northern spruce and balsam fir forests or mixed deciduous/coniferous forests, though it can adapt to other old-growth and mature forest types as well. The key is not the old-growth forest per se, but the complex physical structure of the forest floor. The dead trunks, branches,

*Marten,* Martes americana *(Tim W. Clark)*

and leaves that litter the floor form the habitat for rodents, particularly *Clethrionomys,* a major food of martens. This physical structure could be duplicated in managed forests to maintain their marten populations if we were willing to extend our efforts. The marten avoids early- and mid-successional forests, and usually avoids openings in the forest as well. It seldom ventures from these habitats, nor does it need to, for the red-backed vole and red squirrel, its chief prey, abound here.

HABITS. The marten is primarily solitary, but its habits are little known, owing in some measure to its relative scarcity and to the nature of the habitat it occupies. It retreats before the advance of civilization, yet is of an inquisitive and curious nature, falling easy prey to traps. It is often seen in trees, but most of its foraging time is spent on the ground, where it hunts red-backed voles and other edibles.

Natal dens may be in hollow trees, or in surface or below-ground sites. The marten's slender build enables it to use old woodpecker holes, where it prepares a nest of leaves or grass. It will spend the day in a daytime resting site, usually some rotten snag, hollow tree, rock den, or squirrel's nest, and will often remain in one of these sites during inclement weather. Martens are crepuscular and nocturnal, emerging at night to hunt, but they are often active during the day. They are active at all seasons, but more active in summer than in winter.

Martens cross and recross their own path when foraging, all the while investigating possible sources of prey, such as stumps, holes, and brush

*Marten aloft (Tim W. Clark)*

piles, and they will dig into the snow or actually forage under the snow in winter.

Their large feet afford martens a snowshoe effect in soft snow. They produce a typical mustelid "twin print," about 10 cm (4 inches) wide and up to 15 cm (6 inches) long in soft snow, but the tracks can be nearly impossible to distinguish from those of fishers. The distance between the twin prints ranges from 25 to 100 cm (10 to 40 inches). The normal walking stride of the male marten is about 22 cm (9 inches), of the female about 15 cm (6 inches). Of a fisher, these distances are about 32 cm (13 inches) for a male and about 22 cm (9 inches) for a female.

Martens drag their abdomens over branches and logs, using their belly glands for scent marking. Their vocalizations are various, but include huffs, pants, chuckles, growls, screams, whines, and "eeps."

FOOD AND FEEDING. Redback voles, *Clethrionomys*, which the marten captures by foraging around rotting logs, brush piles, and such, are its staple food everywhere, but other arvicolines are also heavily used when available. *Peromyscus*, though often available, is much less used, probably because it is much more difficult to capture. The marten uses a wide variety of foods, however, including birds, reptiles, amphibians, earthworms, and insects. It is also known to eat wild fruits, especially blueberries, when available. Martens eat many chipmunks and red squirrels, the latter especially in winter; most red squirrels are captured at night while they sleep. Flying squirrels and *Sorex* shrews are other common food items, and martens will also take snowshoe hares. To maintain themselves, martens need the equivalent of about three mice per day (80 kcal).

REPRODUCTION AND DEVELOPMENT. The mating season for martens is a three- to six-week period in late July or August. Courtship may last 15 days, and copulation, which occurs on the ground, may last up to 90 minutes, with two or three matings per day; the female may accept more than one male. During mating, the male holds the female by the nape with his teeth and may drag her around before actual copulation occurs. Shortly after the ova have been fertilized, development is arrested at the blastocyst stage for about six to eight months. The blastocysts, which are about 500–900 microns in diameter, remain free in the uterus. Thus, implantation of the embryo to the uterine wall is delayed, and embryonic development is not resumed until midwinter, when implantation is stimulated by increasing day length. The one to five young (the mean is about 2.85) are born from mid-March through mid-April, some 31 to 39 weeks after mating, but following an active gestation of only 22 days.

At birth the young are blind, helpless, and covered with fine yellowish hairs, and weigh about 30 grams. Sexual dimorphism in size becomes apparent by three weeks, and at one month the males weigh about 200 grams, the females about 175. The ears open at 24 days, the eyes at 5½ weeks. Adult weight is attained in three months, when the females weigh about 725 grams (1.6 lbs) and the males about 1135 grams (2.5 lbs). The weight of the young declines at six weeks, when they are weaned, and again at about three months, when they disperse. Males play no role in raising the young, but they do exclude other males from their home ranges, thus perhaps protecting available foods. The young travel with the female until dispersal. Breeding may occur the year after birth, or may be delayed an extra year.

POPULATION CHARACTERISTICS. The home ranges of martens extend about 10 to 20 km for males, 3 to 6 km for females, as indicated by radio-tracking techniques. Males defend territories against other males, but male home ranges encompass the ranges of one or more females. Before dispersal there may be 1.2 to 1.9 martens per square km (3 to 4.9 per square mile). Juveniles often disperse long distances. There is one record of a male dispersing 40 km (25 miles).

Martens are relatively long-lived. They can breed successfully until 15 years old, and there are several records of martens that age. One in the wild reached an age of 19 years.

ENEMIES. Although there are scattered reports of predation (coyote, fisher, fox, felids, eagles, and owls), the marten has few natural enemies. Its arboreal abilities and great agility help protect it from most terrestrial predators. We are or have been the most important enemy of the marten, through relentless trapping and steady reduction of habitat.

PARASITES AND DISEASE. Fleas, ticks (especially *Ixodes cookei*), and the mite *Listrophorus mustelae* are the main ectoparasites; nematodes, the main internal parasites.

RELATION TO HUMANS. Martens are easily trapped, even during periods of heavy snow. The fine quality of the pelt, and the high price it

original range south to here

*Distribution of the marten, or pine marten,* Martes americana, *in the eastern United States*

once commanded, sharply reduced marten populations. Lumbering operations likewise have dealt it a severe blow, for essentially all of its former habitat, the old-growth coniferous forest in the east, has now been destroyed. But with increased preservation of natural areas, martens have increased in the east, where some second-growth forests have come to resemble old-growth forests. Now there is even an open trapping season in Maine and New York. Beneficial management methods for this species are to preserve forests and to leave untouched the dead snags and hollow limbs (which the martens use as day resting spots) and the slash piles and downed logs (where *Clethrionomys* can thrive).

AREAS FOR FURTHER WORK. More work is needed on the ectoparasites of this species, and it would be interesting to learn more about the behavioral and ecological interrelations between martens and their principal prey species, the red-backed mouse and red squirrel.

## SUBSPECIES

Other subspecies have been described from western North America, but we are not sure that any should be recognized.

*Martes americana americana* (Turton)

As described above. The only subspecies that occurs in the eastern United States.

Type locality: Eastern North America.

### LITERATURE

Belan, I., P. N. Lehner, and T. Clark. 1978. Vocalizations of the American pine marten, *Martes americana*. *J. Mammal.* 59: 871–874.

Clark, T. W., E. Anderson, C. Douglas, and M. Strickland. 1987. *Martes americana*. **Mammalian Species No. 289.** Amer. Soc. Mammal. 8 pp.

Douglas, C. W., and M. A. Strickland. 1987. Marten. In: M. Novak, J. A. Baker, M. E. Obbard, and B. Malloch, eds., *Wild Furbearer Management and Conservation in North America*, pp. 510–529. Ontario Ministry Nat. Resources and Ontario Trappers Assoc.

Dragoo, J. W., and R. L. Honeycutt. 1997. Systematics of mustelid-like carnivores. *J. Mammal.* 78: 426–443.

Strickland, M. A., C. W. Douglas, M. Novak, and N. P. Hunziger. 1982. Marten, *Martes americana*.

In: J. A. Chapman and G. A. Feldhamer, eds., *Wild Mammals of North America*, pp. 599–612. Baltimore: Johns Hopkins Univ. Press.

## Fisher *Martes pennanti* (Erxleben)

DESCRIPTION. The fisher, sometimes called "pekan," is a large, dark-brown weasel-like an-

*Fisher*, Martes pennanti *(Roger A. Powell)*

imal about the size of a fox, but with shorter legs and less prominent ears. The face is somewhat pointed; the ears are broad and rounded. The neck, legs, and feet are stout, and the toes, five on each foot, bear strong, stout, semi-retractile claws, useful for climbing. The tail is tapering and bushy. The fur is dense, long, and soft, although that of the male is much coarser than that of the marten. The overall color is dark brown, and the face and shoulders are hoary; the underparts are nearly black, and there are a few white patches on the neck, throat, and genital area. The fisher is paler in late winter. There are both anal glands and glands on the pads of the hind feet. The hind feet can turn nearly 180°, allowing the fisher to descend trees headfirst. The fisher is plantigrade in gait (it walks on the soles of its feet).

MEASUREMENTS. Total lengths of adult male fishers range from 90 to 120 cm. The tail of a fisher averages about 360 mm; the hind foot, about 126 mm; and the weight, 3.6–5.5 kg (8 to 12 lbs). A large male from Maine weighed over 9 kg (20 lbs). Females are considerably smaller than the males, measuring 75 to 95 cm in length and weighing 2.0–2.5 kg (4.4–5.5 lbs).

 Diploid number = 38.

TOOTH FORMULA

$$\frac{3}{3} \ \frac{1}{1} \ \frac{4}{4} \ \frac{1}{2} \ = \ 38$$

DISTRIBUTION. Today, the fisher occurs primarily in the southern tier of Canadian provinces, dipping south into the northern United States and into northern California and northeastern Utah, but not into Nevada. The fisher originally occurred throughout the northern forest of the eastern United States and south through the Appalachians, but in the late 1800s and early 1900s it was extirpated over most of its eastern range by overtrapping and loss of habitat. The fisher is being reintroduced, however, and in the east today, it occurs in almost all of Maine, most of Vermont and New Hampshire, central Massachusetts, parts of the Connecticut River Valley in Connecticut, the Adirondack Mountains of New York, and northern Wisconsin and the Upper Peninsula of Michigan. Fishers have staged a dramatic comeback in New Hampshire, particularly in the southern part of the state; they are doing well in Vermont; and populations are now sufficiently large in New York and Maine to justify open trapping seasons. In Wisconsin, 559 fishers were trapped in 1917–18, but only 17, 5, and 3 the next three

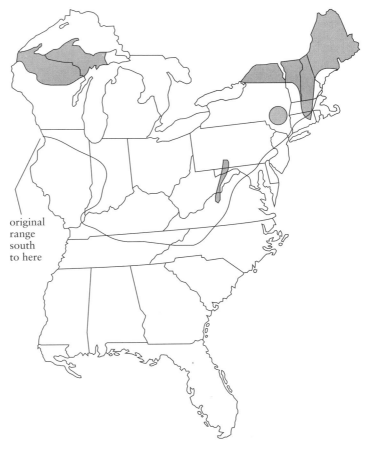

original
range
south
to here

*Distribution of the fisher,*
Martes pennanti, *in the
eastern United States*

*Fisher with snowshoe hare
(Roger A. Powell)*

years. Fisher season was closed in Wisconsin in 1921, but the species was believed to be extirpated there by 1932. The fisher disappeared from Michigan in the 1930s. But from 1956 to 1983, fishers were released in Nicolet National Forest in Wisconsin and Ottawa National Forest in Michigan's Upper Peninsula, and fisher populations have spread from those releases. A number were also released in the Catskill Mountains of New York in 1976, others were released in Massachusetts, and in the winter of 1969, 23 animals from New Hampshire were released in West Virginia, near the Virginia and Maryland state lines, apparently with some success.

HABITAT. The fisher is a dweller of continuous forest, a common resident of the coniferous and mixed conifer/hardwood forests of years past, and is now doing well in areas with extensive second-growth hardwood forest but, always, some conifers, as well. It is at home only where the wild country has not been invaded by humans. Fishers, however, are much more flexible in their habitat requirements than are martens, and have made a remarkable comeback. They are now relatively common and even trapped in areas where they had been extirpated.

HABITS. The fisher is a solitary denizen of dense forest. Of key importance is a closed canopy; fishers avidly avoid open areas. They are agile climbers, but the extent of their arboreal behavior has been much overstated. They are in fact mainly terrestrial except when they are in conifer forests or harassed. They may be active day or night.

Fishers run in typical weasel fashion, the forelimbs moving together and one slightly ahead of the other. The forepaws leave the ground just before the arrival of the hindpaws. This gait results in the characteristic weasel-type running track, "twin prints" one print slightly ahead of the other. Fishers will swim sizable lakes, and are often found in timbered northern bogs and swamps. They produce several vocalizations, including chuckles and hisses.

Fishers employ two types of dens, maternity dens and temporary dens used while the adult is moving about its home range. The temporary dens are selected from a variety of protected situations, but all the maternity dens discovered have been in hollow trees.

FOOD AND FEEDING. The name of this mustelid is a misnomer, for the fisher does not often prey on fish. Rather, it feeds extensively on snowshoe hares, porcupines, and other small and medium-sized mammals and birds. The prey of fishers is larger than that of martens, and fishers have a more diverse diet.

The fisher is an inveterate enemy of the porcupine in country where the latter occurs, but is not always immune to the sharp quills; an occasional fisher has been found decrepit and starving, its head and body riddled with quills. The fisher is one of the few mammals adapted for preying on porcupines, and thus has little competition for them when they are available. Few are actually killed by fishers, since the porcupine is not an easy kill, but they are important prey for the fisher because a single conquest provides so much food. The fisher kills porcupines only on the ground, by repeated attacks at the face, the only vulnerable area the porcupine presents. The fisher circles the porcupine waiting for its chance, the porcupine all the while rotating to keep its back to the fisher. The porcupine will also put its face against a tree or other object for protection, and the fisher may then climb the tree, come down headfirst, and thereby force the porcupine into the open. At length, when the porcupine has weakened from repeated facial wounds, the fisher makes the kill. The internal organs are eaten first, but the entire porcupine is carefully skinned and eaten. Porcupines are safe in trees or in hollow logs having a single entrance.

Other prey are much more commonly killed by fishers. The snowshoe hare is the most common prey item, but also eaten are carrion, grouse, rabbits, and squirrels of the genera *Tamiasciurus*, *Sciurus*, and *Glaucomys*. Carrion is mostly of larger mammals, such as deer and moose. Shrews are eaten much more often than one might expect, and some vegetation is consumed. Red squirrels are caught on the ground, usually in or near middens, probably never in trees. Energy expenditure during the nonreproductive period was estimated by Roger Powell at about 86 kcal per kg for a 2.4-kg female, to 94 kcal per kg for a 5.1-kg male. Food required by the fisher is estimated at about one snowshoe hare per week, a squirrel or two per week, or two to 22 mice per day, whereas a porcupine will feed a fisher for a month or so. When hunting for snowshoe hares, fishers frequently alter course, thus flushing hares from cover. When hunting porcupines they move long distances in one direction, directly toward known porcupine dens. Prey other than porcupines are generally killed by a bite to the back of the neck.

REPRODUCTION AND DEVELOPMENT. Female fishers first breed at one year of age and produce their first litters at two years of age. Almost nothing is known of courtship, but copulation is prolonged, lasting about an hour. Fishers are probably polygamous. The gestation period is a long one, lasting 327 to 358 days, including a 10- to 11-month period of delayed implantation. The blastocyst, an early embryo stage developed within about two weeks of mating, is a transparent sphere with an inner cellular mass measuring about 0.25 to 1.5 mm in diameter. Implantation of the blastocyst, stimulated by day length, can occur between January and April; post-implantation gestation is about 30 to 60 days, and birth occurs from early March to mid-April, most often in March. The timing of implantation and birth varies with latitude. The one to six young (average about two or three) are born in a nest in a cavity in a large hollow tree. About ten days after the young are born, the mother leaves the den to mate.

Newborn fishers are completely helpless and partially covered with light-gray hair, but they already exhibit the characteristic fisher shape. Hair covering, still gray, is complete at 18 days; the typical hair color emerges at about 10 to 12 weeks. The young weigh 40 grams at birth, about 800 grams by 96 days. They grasp with their claws at about 18 days, but are relatively helpless until about the sixth or seventh week. At about 53 days, the eyes open and the young start crawling. Climbing is initiated at about eight weeks. The young are weaned at 14 to 16 weeks, but they are not effective hunters until at least four months. The adult females begin to take meat to the young at about 62 days and the male apparently does not participate in rearing the young. The young learn to kill prey effectively by about 125 days, and they disperse in the fifth month.

POPULATION CHARACTERISTICS. Fisher densities in good habitat may be on the order of one fisher per 2.6 to 11.7 square km (1 to 4.5 square miles). Their home range varies from about 6 to 39 square km (2.3 to 15 square miles), and the home ranges of males are larger than those of females. Home ranges overlap substantially between sexes, but little between members of the same sex. Male fishers defend their territories against other males, and females defend against other females. Scent marking may be used to mark territories, but more information is needed on this aspect of fisher behavior.

The fisher is known to be a great traveler, holing up in suitable nesting dens—in hollow logs, under stumps or logs, in rock shelters, brush piles, holes, beaver lodges, or snow dens—as it moves about its home range. It comes to know the porcupine dens and hare habitat, but does not visit them on a regular basis. Fishers have been known to travel 45 km (28 miles) in two days and 90 km (56 miles) in three days. Males move about more than females, especially during the breeding season. Fishers have been known to live ten years in captivity; their longevity in the wild is not known, although there are records of up to seven years.

ENEMIES. Man is the fisher's only important enemy, for the prized pelt is highly sought by trappers. In 1976, prime New York pelts sold for $100; and in 1987, female pelts brought $150 and male pelts $175. The fisher is easily caught and is not infrequently taken in traps set for the coyote, fox, or marten. Recently, many states have given the fisher protection, and this respite should further its increase. Pollution is a problem of another sort: detectable levels of DDT, chlordane, dieldrin, Mirex, and PCB have been found in fishers from Ontario, apparently absorbed from aerial transmission of chemicals.

PARASITES AND DISEASE. Fishers harbor relatively few parasites, but two genera of cestodes, twelve of nematodes, two of trematodes, and one protozoan have been found. Ticks (*Ixodes cookei*) and fleas (*Oropsylla arctomys*) are known from fishers, and the mange mite (*Sarcoptes scabei*) causes mange in this species. Aleutian disease, leptospirosis, and sylvatic trichinosis are known to occur in fishers.

RELATION TO HUMANS. Fishers were nearly extirpated in the United States in the late nineteenth and early-twentieth centuries, owing to trapping and logging, for they are one of the easiest animals to trap and are greatly subject to habitat disturbance. In New York, trapping seasons were closed and farms were abandoned in some areas, and the fisher began to recover there. New York accordingly reopened a fisher season in 1949, Maine in 1950, New Hampshire and West Virginia in 1969, Massachusetts in 1972, Vermont in 1974, and Minnesota in 1977. New Hampshire reclosed in 1977 and New York limited its season that year. Porcupine populations had climbed as a result of the near-extirpation of the fisher, and damage complaints rose. In 1956, fishers began to be reintroduced into Wisconsin as a porcupine control, and Michigan followed suit starting in 1961. Both reintro-

ductions have been successful. Fishers have also been reintroduced into the Catskill Mountains of New York, and the fishers there have recently decimated the porcupine population that Uldis Roze (pers. comm.) had studied for so many years. Those interested in additional information on the fisher should read the excellent book by Roger Powell (1993).

AREAS FOR FURTHER WORK. A comprehensive study of the ectoparasites of this species is needed. The results could be compared to the faunas of the fisher's maternity and temporary dens to determine the origins of those faunas. Precopulatory behavior is little known in this species.

## SUBSPECIES

Other subspecies have been described from the western United States, but we are not sure that any should be recognized.

*Martes pennanti pennanti* (Erxleben)

As described above. The only subspecies occurring in the eastern United States.

Type locality: Eastern Canada.

## LITERATURE

Holmes, T., and R. A. Powell. 1994. Morphology, ecology and the evolution of sexual dimorphism in North American *Martes*. In: S. W. Buskirk, A. S. Harestad, M. G. Raphael, and R. A. Powell, eds., *Martens, Sables, and Fishers: Biology and Conservation*, pp. 72–84. Ithaca, N.Y.: Cornell University Press. 484 pp.

Powell, R. A. 1981. *Martes pennanti*. **Mammalian Species No. 156.** Amer. Soc. Mammal. 6 pp.

———. 1993. *The Fisher: Life History, Ecology and Behavior*. 2d ed. Minneapolis: Univ. Minnesota Press. 237 pp.

Strickland, M. A., and C. W. Douglas. 1987. Fisher. In: M. Novak, J. A. Baker, M. E. Obbard, and B. Malloch, eds., *Wild Furbearer Management and Conservation in North America*, pp. 530–546. Ontario Ministry of Nat. Resources and Ontario Trappers Assoc.

Strickland, M. A., C. W. Douglas, M. Novak, and N. P. Hunziger. 1982. Fisher, *Martes pennanti*. In: J. A. Chapman and G. A. Feldhamer, eds., *Wild Mammals of North America*, pp. 586–598. Baltimore: Johns Hopkins Univ. Press.

## Weasels and Mink of the Genus *Mustela*

In the eastern United States, the genus *Mustela* is represented by three species of weasels and the mink (the mink is larger than weasels and has a much bushier tail). These animals are characterized by their long, thin bodies and short legs, each leg with five digits. The claws are curved and nonretractile. The ears are short and rounded but more than ample in pinna area and ear-canal opening. All weasels are highly specialized for a carnivorous diet, as indicated by their sharply pointed milk teeth and adult teeth and the reduction of their cheek teeth. Only felids, among carnivores, have fewer cheek teeth. Highly carnivorous mammals like these need to ingest the body organs of their prey and the partly digested vegetation from prey digestive tracts, along with muscle tissue, in order to sustain a balanced diet. Associated with their body shape is a high ratio of body surface to mass and a high metabolic rate.

Northern weasels have thicker pelage and more hair on the soles of the feet than do those to the south. In winter, the pelt turns white on weasels in northern areas, not on those in southern areas. The molt is initiated by changes in day length, although the rate at which the changes occur can be affected by temperature. The fall molt begins on the venter and spreads upward, finally reaching the dorsum; the spring molt starts on the head and dorsum and spreads downward to the rest of the body.

In many mustelids, implantation is delayed. Mating, which occurs in summer, is followed quickly by fertilization and the development of the embryo. Development, however, temporarily ceases at the blastula stage, the sphere of cells that in due course implants and grows in the uterus. In weasels, the blastula remains free in the uterus for an extended period, usually through the winter, and implantation finally occurs at the moment when the brief ensuing gestation will bring the newborn young into the world at the optimum time for their survival.

One advantage of delayed implantation is that it conserves the energy necessary for mating during early spring, when energy is at a premium. But its greater advantage, perhaps, lies in allowing the female to become impregnated before attaining full size and before dispersal. In the early weeks of her pregnancy, then, her energy can be devoted to her own further growth and maturation, rather than to rapidly developing offspring.

Much of the reproductive strategy of weasels appears to be to ensure mating. That goal is important in all species, but it is particularly important in animals like weasels, which are solitary and relatively few in number. In contrast to larger predators, weasels are often preyed upon themselves, so are less likely to be around in their second year. Somewhat different reproductive strategies have evolved with different members of the genus *Mustela* in the eastern United States. The least weasel is smallest in size, thus likely to suffer the greatest predation rate. This disadvantage is compensated by a rapid growth rate and by having two litters in good years, without delayed implantation. Long- and short-tailed weasels, which are intermediate in size and also have many predators, have extended periods of delayed implantation. This strategy allows them to mate over a long period, yet ensures that implantation will occur at the optimum time. It also allows short-tailed weasels to become pregnant prior to dispersal, and long-tails to become pregnant in their first year. The mink is relatively large, and adult mink, at least, presumably suffer relatively little predation. Its reproductive strategy is similar to that of other, larger predators: female mink do not reach maturity until one year of age, and the species exhibits only a brief period of delayed implantation.

There is, again, a clear size difference between the various species of weasels. Apart from the mink, *Mustela frenata* is the largest, followed by *M. erminea* and *M. nivalis*, the smallest. There is also a clear size difference between the sexes; males are always larger than females. Just why these differences in the species and sexes occur has encouraged much conjecture. Hypotheses intended to explain the differences have been offered, yet there always seem to be examples and areas and situations that negate single-factor explanations. There may in fact be several factors affecting size, and these may not be the factors that were operative in earlier times and different areas. Those who have most thoroughly examined size relationships between species and between the sexes are Ralls and Harvey (1985) and Holmes (1987).

It would appear that differences in the size of weasel species are related to prey size, the larger species feeding on the larger prey. We think this is so in part because they have tended to partition the prey in areas where they are sympatric. The two smaller weasels occur together over much of their range, but *Mustela nivalis* occurs alone in the Southeast, and *M. erminea* occurs alone in the Southwest and Northeast. Further, *M. erminea* is larger toward the north, but the other two species do not show pronounced latitudinal variation. The size of voles also increases toward the north, but the ermine size increase is more closely tied to the latitudinal effect than is the vole size increase. *Mustela erminea* is much smaller in the southwestern part of its range, where *M. nivalis* is lacking. We think that the increased size of *M. erminea* to the north relates primarily to increased vole size, and that reduced ermine size in the Southwest relates to the absence of *M. nivalis*. We suggest, too, that the lack of northward increase in the size of *M. frenata* might be related to the prey available in its southern distribution: it presumably feeds heavily on *Sigmodon*, *Neotoma*, *Oryzomys*, and *Dipodomys* in the south, thus needs to be larger there, not in the north.

Thor Holmes found that the head, jaws, and teeth of weasels were less dimorphic than their bodies. Since these are the parts more important for feeding, one might infer that resource partitioning between the sexes is not influential, but body size itself may be the important factor, for weasels use their bodies in bringing down prey. Erlinge (1979) and Moors (1980) both proposed that the reason for marked sexual dimorphism in weasels is that it is more energy-efficient for females to be small, so that they may capture smaller food items, since they raise the young alone. It is better for males, they propose, to be large, so as to accumulate more females.

Male weasels do eat larger food than females, but we do not think that they are larger in order to take the larger food items. Rather, we think that the size disparity between the sexes in weasels relates to their reproductive strategies, and that the taking of different-sized food is secondary. The territories of the males encompass those of several contiguous females, and the bigger and stronger males can probably better defend a territory from other males. Weasels are small predators, thus more subject to predation than are larger predators, and they therefore have a shorter life span.

Weasels produce three vocalizations: trills, screeches, and squeals. The trills are often produced as the weasels investigate their surroundings, or during play, mating, or hunting. The screech, evidently a threat or defensive behavior, is a sudden sound given when the weasel is disturbed, and may be coupled with a lunge at an intruder. The squeal is a distress call.

Weasels, like skunks, have anal scent glands. They can discharge the odor when disturbed and it can be detected for some distance. Weasels that have been observed dragging the body along the ground may have been scent marking, but little is known of the function of these odors in weasels.

Roger Powell (1982) has discussed and experimentally studied the black tail tip of weasels (and the lack of it in *Mustela nivalis*). He suggested that the black tail tip of *M. frenata* and *M. erminea* directs the attack of a predator to the black, thus to the tail tip, thereby often sparing the weasel. The black tail tip, were it present in *Mustela nivalis*, would be too close to the body in this short-tailed form, and would thus have no protective effect. Powell used *M. frenata* and *M. nivalis* models to test these ideas experimentally. Predators significantly more often missed *M. frenata* models with black tail tips and *M. nivalis* models lacking the black tips than they did models lacking these characters.

Too often, and for too long, we have persecuted weasels. We should think of them as highly evolved, highly interesting animals that are necessary in the balance of nature. Like most predators, they are solitary, which has the advantage of spreading them out over the habitat, thus helping to maintain adequate prey for themselves and their offspring. Weasels do need to be near water, since they drink often, though relatively little at a time.

## Literature Cited

Erlinge, S. 1979. Adaptive significance of sexual dimorphism in weasels. *Oikos* 33: 233–245.
Holmes, T. 1987. Sexual dimorphism in North American weasels, with a phylogeny of the Mustelidae.

Unpubl. Ph.D. diss., University of Kansas, Lawrence. 694 pp.

Moors, P. J. 1980. Sexual dimorphism in the body size of mustelids (Carnivora): The roles of food habits and breeding systems. *Oikos* 34: 147–158.

Powell, R. A. 1982. Evolution of black-tipped tails in weasels: Predator confusion. *Amer. Naturalist* 119: 126–131.

Ralls, K., and P. H. Harvey. 1985. Geographic variation in size and sexual dimorphism of North American weasels. *Biol. J. Linnean Soc.* 25: 119–167.

## KEY TO THE WEASELS AND MINK OF THE GENUS MUSTELA

Because *Mustela frenata* and *M. erminea* vary greatly in size geographically, and because males in both species are much larger than females, they are difficult to key. The best single character is relative tail length.

1. Tail not black-tipped, or exhibiting only a few black hairs . . . . . . . . . . . . . . . . . . . . . . . . . . . . . 2
1. Tail clearly black-tipped. . . . . . . . . . . . . . . . . . . . 3
2. Animal small, less than 300 mm in total length; tail about 25 mm (1 inch) long; body light brown, the belly all white or cream; skull less than 40 mm long . . . . . . . . . . . . . . . . . . *M. nivalis*
2. Animal larger, more than 300 mm in total length; tail much more than 25 mm long; body dark brown, the belly with at most a few patches of white or cream; skull more than 40 mm long . . . . . . . . . . . . . . . . . . . . . . . *M. vison*
3. Tail usually more than one-half body length; postglenoid portion of skull (from point of articulation of lower jaw to posterior end of skull) less than 47% of distance from occipital condyles to tip of anterior incisor . . . . . . *M. frenata*
3. Tail usually less than one-half body length; postglenoid portion of skull more than 47% of this distance . . . . . . . . . . . . . . . . . . *M. erminea*

## Short-tailed Weasel *Mustela erminea* Linnaeus                          Color plate 18

Jones et al. (1992) use "ermine" as the common name for this species, in keeping with the epithet *erminea*. The term "ermine," however, best fits the white, or winter, stage of this species, and that of *Mustela frenata* as well. This difficulty has led some to use the term "stoat" for this species. "Stoat," however, best applies to the brown, or summer, phase of these two weasels. We have therefore opted for the term "short-tailed weasel" for this species.

DESCRIPTION. The short-tailed weasel is a small, slender, brown predator (white in winter) with

*Short-tailed weasel*, Mustela erminea *(Roger A. Powell)*

a black tail tip, scarcely larger than a chipmunk and built along much more slim lines. Its smaller size and shorter tail serve to distinguish it from the larger long-tailed weasel, *Mustela frenata*; moreover, its tail is about 40% of the head and body length, whereas in *M. frenata* the tail is usually more than 45% of the head and body length. (The least weasel, smaller yet, has an inch-long tail with no black tip.) The soft but rather thin fur of the short-tailed weasel is a uniform brown above in summer, slightly darker on the crown of the head. The underparts are whitish, often with a pronounced yellowish cast. Occasionally, there is a small brown spot or two on the throat or chest. There are two complete molts per year, the weasel retaining the black-tipped tail in winter but otherwise donning a pure-white coat. The ears are short and rounded, the eyes jet black. The soles of the feet, except for the toepads, are clad in hair in winter.

MEASUREMENTS. Average measurements of 31 adult males were total length 272 (251–295), tail 71 (65–80), hind foot 35 (32–38) mm. Of 15 adult females, they were: total length 236 (194–255), tail 55 (44–64), hind foot 29 (28–31) mm. Males from Michigan weighed 90 to 140 grams, females 45 to 75 grams.

Diploid number = 44.

TOOTH FORMULA

$$\frac{3}{3} \quad \frac{1}{1} \quad \frac{3}{3} \quad \frac{1}{2} \quad = \quad 34$$

DISTRIBUTION. This little weasel is a boreal species, most numerous in the coniferous forests of Canada and northern United States. It is a wide-ranging form, occurring from eastern Canada to Alaska, and south in the west to northern California, most of Utah, and north-central New Mexico. In the eastern United States the short-tailed weasel occurs throughout most of Wisconsin, Michigan, Pennsylvania, New York, and New England, but is uncommon in coastal regions.

HABITAT. This is an animal of the forest, partial to the deep conifer stands of the north. In the southern part of its range, it occupies a habitat similar to that of the larger long-tailed weasel, and is often found in brushy fields bordering cultivated areas. It seems to prefer the hedgerow or stone wall, where it can elude its many enemies and catch the small mammals and birds that are attracted to these coverts.

HABITS. Fagerstone (1987), King (1983, 1989), and Svendsen (1982) presented nice reviews of this species. Short-tailed weasels may be out day or night and are often fairly common, but they are seldom seen. They are active for short periods (10 to 45 minutes, but sometimes much longer), alternating with three- to five-hour rest periods throughout the day and night. The weasel is a curious animal, moving alertly through its territory investigating burrows, cracks, and such, and may often be attracted to an observer by squeaks.

All summer the weasel has a brown coat, but at the approach of winter a molt begins on the abdomen. Hairs on the lower flanks come in patchy white. The white hairs rapidly increase in number, and the white progresses up the sides and onto the back. The last brown to be seen is a stripe down the back, until, finally, the brown coat vanishes entirely, replaced by white—except for the black tail tip. This molt occupies

*Distribution of the short-haired weasel,* Mustela erminea, *in the eastern United States*

from three to five weeks, its duration varying with the individual. Some individuals taken in early November may show only incipient change; others, on that same date, may have almost completely lost their summer pelage. The timing of the change is governed basically by photoperiod. By early March a few brown hairs make their appearance, but the molt proceeds in reverse, beginning on the back and progressing downward over the sides, to the belly. In April, the weasel has again assumed its summer coat of brown.

This weasel seldom makes a den of its own; more often, it appropriates the chambers of a chipmunk, the cavity beneath some sizable stump, or a shallow excavation beneath a pile of boulders. And although its body shape is of value in catching prey, it does have its trade-off—it increases the cost of thermoregulation, since weasels cannot curl into a sphere, only into a disk, which means more exposed surface relative to mass. Weasels must then pile goodly amounts of insulation in their nests. The nest is a large, loose structure, usually composed of the fur and feathers of its prey. Several nests are included in the male's range, and he will use different nests at different times, depending on where he is.

Weasels, like skunks, have paired anal glands opening into the anus. The secretions of these glands are used in marking territories and for defense.

See the *Mustela frenata* account and the papers by Erlinge (1979), Holmes (1987), Moors (1980), and Ralls and Harvey (1985) for discussions of size differences in weasels, and Powell (1982) for a discussion of the black tail tip.

FOOD AND FEEDING. The short-tailed weasel feeds chiefly upon mice, chipmunks, shrews, and other small mammals, but it will also eat frogs, lizards, small snakes, small birds, and many kinds of insects, and has been known to feed quantities of earthworms to its young. Weasels can capture insects by tracking to their calls. But they do not always confine their hunting to such small prey, for they can and do capture small cottontails or other animals several times their own weight. The prey is killed by a bite to the neck. It is very dangerous, however, for weasels to attack prey larger than themselves, and they generally do so only when a particularly good opportunity arises, or in times of scarcity. Even then, they do it very cautiously, for a mistake can lead to their doom. Weasels first lick the blood from their vanquished prey, a practice that has perhaps given rise to the false notion that they suck blood. Weasels will kill all that is available and cache what is not eaten; and this weasel, in its white coat, spends much time burrowing under the snow for small rodents in winter.

REPRODUCTION AND DEVELOPMENT. Males and females of this species both reach about 85% of their adult weight by early fall, at about four months of age. As is the case in *Mustela frenata*, males do not mature and mate until they are into their second year, whereas females attain sexual maturity and mate in the year of their birth. Spontaneous ovulation begins in June and occurs monthly until the female is bred. During mating, the male grabs the female by the scruff of the neck and drags her about, the female passive all the while. Copulation, lasting two to 20 minutes, is often repeated.

Females come into estrus when their prior young are about six weeks old. At that time the adult female and her female offspring are bred by the male currently on territory. This male is probably not the newborn female's own father, for there is rapid turnover of males on territory. In some cases the newborn's eyes may not even be open at the time of mating. The fertilized eggs develop for about 14 days, then remain quiescent for nine to ten months in the uterus before implanting. Embryonic development resumes in the late winter, the resumption probably stimulated by increasing day length. Active gestation (implantation to birth) is about four weeks, and total gestation is about 280 days.

In the eastern United States, the four to nine young are usually born in mid-April. They are tiny creatures at birth, averaging 1.7 (1.5–2.0) grams, and are about 51 mm long and naked except for a covering of fine white hair. Standard measurements at a week are about 70, 10, and 7.5 mm and 5 grams; at two weeks they are 90, 13, and 10 mm and 10 grams. When the babies are about three weeks old (115, 16, and 12; and 169), a prominent mane appears on the neck; this mane persists for several weeks while the fur on the remainder of the body grows in. Milk teeth appear at about the third week, and size disparity between the sexes becomes evident at a month. The eyes do not open until the young weasel is five weeks old. At six weeks, females weigh about 37 grams, males about 55. The tails acquire their black tips at six to seven weeks. The young weasels first feed on solid food at weeks four to five, but continue to take milk until weeks 7 to 12. They will play outside the nest at weeks six to eight, and will begin to kill prey at 10 to 12 weeks, when their permanent dentition is complete. Adult size is reached by females in six months, by males in about a year. Young males at seven weeks weigh more than their mother.

POPULATION CHARACTERISTICS. The territories of males are larger and encompass those of several females, even though males and females live separate lives most of the year. A female will exclude other females, and will apparently avoid the male incorporating her territory. Territories of males range from 4 to 200 ha, usually 10 to 40 (10 to 495 acres, usually 25 to 100), and there is rather a rapid turnover of males occupying a given territory. Scent marks are used to mark territory, and they can be reinforced on each visit. Territories are larger with poorer food supplies. Density estimates run from one individual per 13 ha (32 acres) to one per 112 ha (278 acres), or one per 65 ha (160 acres) if only the area of good habitat is considered. One male short-tailed weasel moved 35 km (22 miles) in seven months.

ENEMIES. Owls, hawks, carnivorous mammals (including the house cat), and large snakes are this weasel's principal predators. Probably few individuals live beyond two years.

PARASITES AND DISEASE. The short-tailed weasel harbors a nasal nematode, *Skrjabingylus nasicola*, fleas, and tiny, highly specialized listrophorid mites, *Lynxacarus mustelae*. The nematode can cause gross deformation of the frontal region of the skull (Gamble and Riewe, 1982), although the direct effects to the host are not known.

RELATION TO HUMANS. Weasel pelts have never been very valuable, but when populations were large enough, the northern trapper might sometimes have found it worthwhile to lay out a line of traps for these handsome little animals. Weasels that are changing from brown to white are known in the fur trade as "graybacks" and were worth but a few cents. The weasel's greatest economic value lies in its role in rodent control.

AREAS FOR FURTHER WORK. A detailed study of this weasel's ectoparasites is needed. Radio-telemetry study of this species would also be fascinating. Such study could be used to locate various nests, and the invertebrate fauna of each could be compared to its ecological situation and the time the weasel uses it.

## SUBSPECIES

Two subspecies have been described, but the two intergrade broadly in southern Canada; thus no primary isolating mechanism can be shown to be present, and we do not recognize *M. erminea bangsii* as valid.

*Mustela erminea erminea* occurs in Eurasia. Several subspecies have been described from North America, most of which intergrade. The two earliest are *M. erminea cicognanii* and *M. erminea richardsonii*, both of which were described by Bonaparte in 1838, but *M. erminea cicognanii* has page precedence.

### *Mustela erminea cicognanii* Bonaparte

As described above. Occupies the entire eastern U.S. range of the species.

Type locality: Eastern United States, for *M. erminea cicognanii*.

Other currently recognized eastern subspecies:
   *M. erminea bangsi* Hall

### LITERATURE

Erlinge, S. 1979. Adaptive significance of sexual dimorphism in weasels. *Oikos* 33: 233–245.
Fagerstone, K. A. 1987. Black-footed ferret, long-tailed weasel, short-tailed weasel, and least weasel. In: M. Novak, J. A. Baker, M. E. Obbard, and B. Mallock, eds., *Wild Furbearer Management and Conservation in North America*, pp. 547–573. Toronto: Ontario Ministry Nat. Resources.

*Long-tailed weasel*, Mustela frenata
*(Roger W. Barbour)*

Gamble, R. L., and R. R. Riewe. 1982. Infestation of the nematode *Skrjabingylus nasicola* (Leukart 1842) in *Mustela frenata* (Lichtenstein) and *M. erminea* (L.) and some evidence of a paratenic host in the life cycle of this nematode. *Canadian J. Zool.* 60: 45–62.

Holmes, T. 1987. Sexual dimorphism in North American weasels, with a phylogeny of the Mustelidae. Unpubl. Ph.D. diss., University of Kansas, Lawrence. 694 pp.

Jones, J. K., Jr., R. S. Hoffman, D. W. Rice, C. Jones, R. J. Baker, and M. D. Engstrom. 1992. Revised checklist of North American mammals north of Mexico, 1991. Occ. Pap. Mus. Texas Tech University 146. 23 pp.

King, C. M. 1983. *Mustela erminea*. **Mammalian Species No. 195.** Amer. Soc. Mammal. 8 pp.

———. 1989. *The Natural History of Weasels and Stoats.* Ithaca, N.Y.: Cornell Univ. Press. 280 pp.

Moors, P. J. 1980. Sexual dimorphism in the body size of mustelids (Mammalia: Carnivora): The role of food habits and breeding systems. *Oikos* 34: 147–158.

Powell, R. A. 1982. Evolution of black-tipped tails in weasels: Predator confusion. *Amer. Naturalist* 119: 126–131.

Ralls, K., and P. H. Harvey. 1985. Geographic variation in size and sexual dimorphism of North American weasels. *Biol. J. Linnean Soc.* 25: 119–167.

Svendsen, G. E. 1982. Weasels. *Mustela* sp. In: J. A. Chapman and G. A. Feldhamer, eds., *Wild Mammals of North America*, pp. 613–628. Baltimore: Johns Hopkins Univ. Press.

## Long-Tailed Weasel *Mustela frenata* Lichtenstein
Color plate 18

DESCRIPTION. The long-tailed weasel is a long-bodied, short-legged carnivore; a few of the largest males approach the length of a small mink, but most individuals are much smaller. The head is short, the snout relatively blunt, and the ears rounded and set low. The tail is long (about 40 to 70% of the head and body length) and has a black tip that is quite noticeable in the live animal. The summer pelage is a rich brown above. The breast and belly sometimes have pale brown spots. The underparts, including the upper lips, are white to deep yellow. The fall molt ensues about November and takes three to four weeks. In the northern parts of its range, New York and upper New England to Wisconsin, nearly all the weasels become white, often stained with yellow on the hips, the tail tip alone remaining black. In Pennsylvania, considerably less than half of the individuals become white, and none do south of a line somewhere around the Pennsylvania/Maryland border. The vernal change to brown usually begins in March and takes six to ten weeks. In areas where the winter coat is not white, the color is a pale shade of brown, much lighter than that in summer.

MEASUREMENTS. Average measurements of twenty adult males from New York were: total length 405 (374–447), tail 135 (124–157), hind foot 44.5 (42–50) mm. Thirteen New York females averaged: total length 325 (306–362), tail 107.5 (95–117), hind foot 37 (35–41) mm. The weights of males range from 200–270 grams; those of females, 71–126 grams. The skulls of males measure 47–50 mm; those of females, 40–42 mm.

Diploid number = 42.

Tooth formula

$$\frac{3}{3} \quad \frac{1}{1} \quad \frac{3}{3} \quad \frac{1}{2} \quad = \quad 34$$

DISTRIBUTION. The long-tailed weasel is one of the most widespread carnivores of the Western Hemisphere. It is not found in southern Florida, but otherwise occurs throughout the eastern United States. It occurs in southeastern and south-central Canada, and in the entire western United States except for the states of Nevada, Utah, Arizona, and southern California; and it occurs south through all of Central America into South America.

HABITAT. This weasel is found in a variety of habitats, from dense hammocks and fringes of swamps, and from the thickets of low-growing shrubs along watercourses, to sparsely wooded second-growth forest. It even invades extensive marshes, wherever there is promise of abundant small vertebrates upon which to feed. It is a fearless little beast, hunting among the stone walls and through cut-over brush for its food.

HABITS. Long-tailed weasels are active throughout the year. They were once thought to be primarily nocturnal, but they are often out by day and they are generally active when hungry rather than on some daily schedule. Arvicoline rodents, one of their major prey groups, are mainly diurnal, but active especially near dawn and dusk. This weasel's insatiable curiosity leads it to prey but has often proved its undoing: if an

*Distribution of the long-tailed weasel,* Mustela frenata, *in the eastern United States*

observer remains quiet, it may actually run about the observer's feet.

Long-tailed weasels follow a zigzag pattern in the hunt, going from one rodent burrow to another. They run in typical weasel fashion, by a series of bounds with the back humped at each bound, the tail horizontal or raised at 45°. They will sometimes climb trees after prey, taking a vertical leap, then climbing upwards by 1-meter spirals.

A weasel will hole up in a shallow earthen burrow, underneath a large stump, or in the bank of a gully. At the end of a tunnel it will build a large nest in which to raise the young. The nest is often composed largely of the fur (and perhaps a few dried muzzles, tails, and feet) of its prey. Although weasels climb with agility, they never seem to make their dens in trees.

Long-tailed weasels produce the three typical weasel vocalizations—trills, screeches, and squeals—and Roger Powell has heard a fourth he describes as a "zeep." Powell heard this call during the weasels' courting behavior, and later a young male "zeeped" occasionally throughout one fall. Upon turning white, the weasel completely ceased making this call, but resumed it upon turning brown again in the spring. Powell thought this call was used at times of interest or nonaggressive excitement. Svendsen (1982) summarizes information on this species.

FOOD AND FEEDING. Weasels do not suck blood, as commonly thought, although they often lap blood from a wound. Stomach analyses show that these little carnivores eat flesh, bones, feathers, and fur. The weasel feeds on the head and thorax first, often caching food for later use. Weasels in search of food often cover several kilometers in a night, but these journeys may not encompass an area greater than 10 to 20 ha (25 to 50 acres). They will hunt in burrows or runways and will burrow under snow.

Weasels subdue mouse-size rodents by wrapping their body around them, thus pinning them, and biting the nape of the neck. Chipmunks and ground squirrels encountered above ground are caught and killed by a bite to the nape, the bite often severing the vertebral chord. Rabbits, too,

are attacked, but rabbits are a very dangerous choice of prey even for a large weasel, for they have the potential to kill the weasel. When other prey are available, then, weasels are less likely to attack rabbits, and most of the cottontails they take are likely young.

Although a large number of prey items have been recorded, and although the diet of weasels varies with the prey populations available, more than 96% of the food usually consists of small mammals, chiefly rodents. Meadow voles, because of their abundance, are a major food source. Long-tailed weasels successfully stalk and overcome cotton rats, wood rats, shrews, small birds, and snakes, and do not disdain insects or even earthworms. In 163 scats from New York, 34% of the prey were *Microtus* species, 17% were unidentified mice, another 17% *Sylvilagus*, 11% *Peromyscus*, 10% *Rattus*, and 6% *Blarina*, the rest consisting of *Sciurus*, *Tamias*, *Condylura*, and *Ondatra*. The food of this species overlaps considerably with that of other weasels, but because of its greater size, its prey averages larger.

REPRODUCTION AND DEVELOPMENT. Males reach adult body weight in three to four months, but do not mature sexually until about one year. The testes are inactive through the winter, begin activity at the time of spring molt, and reach a maximum volume in summer of about seven to eight times their inactive size. Males thus first mate at one year. Because females mature in three to four months, both the young of the year and older animals come into heat and mate in midsummer, June to August. Heat, indicated by a swollen vulva, lasts for three or four days from the time of the first mating, or several weeks if mating has not yet occurred. Unmated females come into heat again in 36 to 71 days, mated females not until the following summer.

When pregnancy is effected, development passes from the two-cell stage (at 70–85 hours) to the four-cell stage (at 81–99 hours), the eight-cell stage (at four to eight days), the morula (at 11 days), and the early blastula (at about 15 days). The blastula then remains quiescent in the upper uterus until spring, when it implants. Development of the embryo then proceeds, and the single litter of four to eight young is produced in April or May. Because the average total gestation is 279 days (range 205–314), there can be but a single litter per year.

The newborn of this species weigh about 3 grams, and their approximate standard measurements are total length 56, tail 13, and hind foot 7 mm. They have long, white hair and emit high-pitched vocalizations. At a week they weigh about 5 to 9 grams and are about 92 mm long. At week two sexual dimorphism begins to manifest itself, the females now about 89 mm long and 13.5 grams, the males 100 mm long and 17 grams. At two weeks the young can stand but not walk, but at three weeks (females 127 mm, 21 grams; males 150 mm, 27 grams) the carnassials and canines are erupting and the babies are crawling outside of the nest and feeding on meat. The dorsum is now gray, and the black tail tip is evident. At a month the female is about 196 mm long and weighs about 31 grams. Males are about 210 mm long and weigh about 39 grams. The upper incisors erupt and the babies, now trilling and squealing, are moving farther from the nest, even though they cannot see yet. At five weeks the eyes open, coloration is nearing that of adults, and the animals are weaned; at this point, they are eating about their own weight in food per day. At six weeks, females are about 215 mm long and weigh 62 grams; males are 240 mm, 81 grams. Only the female brings food to the growing young, which remain with her until midsummer, when they become independent. By seven weeks the young males are the size of the mother, at about 100 grams; the young females are about 73 grams.

POPULATION CHARACTERISTICS. In good habitat, long-tailed weasels reach a maximum density of about one weasel per 3 ha (7 acres). Although the sexes are separate for most of the year, the home ranges of males, about 10 to 24 ha (25 to 60 acres) are much larger and include those of more than one female, but home ranges tend not to overlap within sexes. Home range size and shape are affected by habitat factors, prey availability, and the proximity of other weasels, and home ranges are smaller in winter. Males may travel about 200 meters (655 feet) in their nightly forays, females about 100 meters (320 feet). The animals travel farther in open habitat than in dense vegetation.

ENEMIES. Weasels have many enemies, including foxes, coyotes, bobcats, hawks and owls, domestic dogs, house cats, and snakes.

PARASITES AND DISEASE. Fourteen species of fleas, two of biting lice (*Neotrichodectes minutus* and *N. mephitidis*), ten species of ticks, two species of chiggers, and 12 species of mites are known from *Mustela frenata*. Internal parasites include at least a trematode and two species of nematodes.

RELATION TO HUMANS. Weasels will visit the poultry yard, often with disastrous results, for they may kill far more than they can eat at a time. This makes sense, since the evolutionary development of weasel behavior has been toward killing when food is available, and we have created a situation in which prey is much more available than is normally the case in the wild. On the whole, as one of the predators helping to maintain the balance of nature, weasels are a distinct asset, for they often kill rats as well. Larger weasels were once profitable to the trapper, and many thousands of "ermine" pelts reached the fur markets each year. But weasel pelts, like other furs, are worth little today.

AREAS FOR FURTHER WORK. Telemetry studies of the spatial, temporal, and ecological relationships of this species, as compared to those of other members of the genus *Mustela*, might give us insight into questions of prey partitioning, the intersecting evolutionary patterns in this group, the different sizes of the sexes and species, the length of the tail, and the color of the tail tip.

## SUBSPECIES

Four subspecies have been described from the eastern United States, but all appear to intergrade one into the other and ultimately into the nominate subspecies, *M. frenata frenata*, which occurs in southern Texas and Mexico.

*Mustela frenata frenata* Lichtenstein
  As described above.
  Type locality: Ciudad Mexico.

*Least weasel,* Mustela nivalis,
*killing* Microtus ochrogaster
*(Roger A. Powell)*

Other currently recognized eastern subspecies:

*M. frenata arthuri* Hall

*M. frenata noveboracensis* [author?]

*M. frenata occisor* (Bangs)

*M. frenata olivacea* Howell

*M. frenata peninsulae* (Rhoads)

## LITERATURE

Fagerstone, K. A. 1987. Black-footed ferret, long-tailed weasel, short-tailed weasel, and least weasel. In: M. Novak, J. A. Baker, M. E. Obbard, and B. Mallock, eds., *Wild Furbearer Management and Conservation in North America*, pp. 547–573. Toronto: Ontario Ministry Nat. Resources.

Gamble, R. L., and R. R. Riewe. 1982. Infestation of the nematode *Skrjabingylus nasicola* (Leukart 1842) in *Mustela frenata* (Lichtenstein) and *M. erminea* (L.) and some evidence of a paratenic host in the life cycle of this nematode. *Canadian J. Zool.* 60: 45–62.

King, K. 1989. *The Natural History of Weasels and Stoats.* Ithaca, N.Y.: Cornell Univ. Press.

Powell, R. A. 1982. Evolution of black-tipped tails in weasels: Predator confusion. *Amer. Naturalist* 119: 126–131.

Sheffield, S. R., and H. H. Thomas. 1997. *Mustela frenata.* **Mammalian Species No. 570.** Amer. Soc. Mammal. 9 pp.

Svendsen, G. E. 1982. Weasels, *Mustela* sp. In: J. A. Chapman and G. A. Feldhamer, eds., *Wild Mammals of North America*, pp. 613–628. Baltimore: Johns Hopkins Univ. Press.

## Least Weasel *Mustela nivalis* Linnaeus

The North American form of the least weasel was originally described as a separate species, *Mustela rixosa*, but it is now recognized as being conspecific with the Eurasian "Maus-wiesel," *Mustela nivalis*, thus takes that name. Whether this is actually the case, however, is still in dispute.

DESCRIPTION. The least weasel is the smallest living carnivore, weighing but one ten-thousandth as much as the largest of our carnivores, the great Alaskan brown bear, which weighs up to 780 kg (1720 lbs). It is at once recognized by its diminutive size—total length 185 mm (7.3 inches)—and its *very short tail*, which scarcely exceeds 25 mm (1 inch) in length. The summer pelage of these little weasels is brown, except for the white underparts and toes. The tail tip contains a few black hairs, summer or winter, but the pronounced black tail tip so characteristic of other weasels is not a feature of the least weasel. Northern individuals become completely white in winter, but least weasels in most of their eastern U.S. range (from southern Michigan south) may remain brown throughout the year. Several white ones have been recorded from Pennsylvania, Ohio, Indiana, and elsewhere, but the majority acquire only a slightly paler brown coat with the approach of cold weather.

Individuals of this species might be confused with a female *Mustela erminea*, but the inch-long tail and small skull, totaling not more than 32 mm in length, are sufficient to distinguish it. The fur of this species fluoresces under ultraviolet light, producing a lavender color.

MEASUREMENTS. Average measurements of 34 males and 17 females from Indiana were: total length of males 185 (144–209), of females 173 (149–188); tail of males 31 (21–40), of females 28 (18–33); hind foot of males 21 (18–26), of females 19 (18–22) mm; and weight of males 45 (26–68) grams, of females 32 (21–52) grams. Diploid number = 42.

TOOTH FORMULA

$$\frac{3}{3} \quad \frac{1}{1} \quad \frac{3}{3} \quad \frac{1}{2} \; = \; 34$$

DISTRIBUTION. The least weasel occurs through much of Canada and south into east-central United States—from extreme western New York and western Pennsylvania southward into the mountains of North Carolina and Tennessee and westward through northeastern Kentucky, Ohio, northern Indiana and Illinois, and all of Michigan and Wisconsin. Two New York least weasels are known, both from Chautau-

qua County in extreme western New York. One was taken at French Creek in 1948 (Cooke, 1951), the second on 24 July 1981 in the basement of a home a mile west of Fredonia.

HABITAT. This tiny weasel is found in the deep forests of the high Alleghenies, but its primary habitat is the mixed grasslands, hedgerows, and pond edges of the midwestern agricultural lands where arvicoline rodents abound.

HABITS. The diminutive size of the least weasel is scarcely calculated to draw our attention, and we are seldom aware of its presence until one is trapped or otherwise turns up, often by chance—dead on the road, imprisoned in a freshly dug grave or fencepost hole, or in a swimming pool. It does not appear to be common in any part of its range. In Pennsylvania, where thousands of weasels have been trapped for

*Distribution of the least weasel,* Mustela nivalis, *in the eastern United States*

bounty, chiefly in the early years of this century, relatively few of these little weasels have been taken. For more on bounties, see the discussion in the account for the coyote; and see Hamilton (1946).

Least weasels are active any time of day or night, all year. They can dart about with amazing speed, up to 10 kph (6 mph), whether escaping an enemy or capturing prey, but they usually travel by a walk or slow gallop. When hunting, they move about their home range, investigating every hole and crack and frequently standing on their hind legs to check their surroundings for predator or prey. They often move about by bounds, and may even climb trees or bushes to examine the nests of birds or squirrels.

Nests of the least weasel, constructed of grasses lined with fur or feathers, have been found beneath corn shocks, in shallow burrows bordering streams, and in other sheltered places, including the nests and burrows of their prey species. One was found in Michigan in an abandoned beehive. As they are in the other weasels, the anal scent glands are well developed, and are used for marking territories and for defense.

Least weasels are rather vocal animals, uttering several chirps, squeals, squeaks, and hisses when threatened. The female also has a trill for calling the young. Least weasels hear high-frequency sounds, those in the range of their prey calls (Heffner and Heffner, 1985). Their "best" hearing is from 1 to 16 kHz, and at high frequencies as well, from 51 to 60.5 kHz.

FOOD AND FEEDING. Because of its petite size (body less than an inch, or 25 mm, in diameter), the least weasel can pursue its major prey within their own burrows. The least weasel is a specialist on small mammals, particularly arvicoline and sigmodontine rodents, but birds (including eggs and nestlings) and insects are also eaten. When prey are scarce, the males, being larger, readily shift to larger prey, but females generally continue to hunt in the small-mammal burrows. These animals consume about 40% of their own body weight per day, and thus must eat about nine or ten meals per day, each of a few grams (their stomach capacity is only about 10 grams, but food passes through the digestive tract in about 3.5 hours). Prey is captured by

grabbing it anywhere, the weasel wrapping its legs and long, thin body around it, in order to subdue it, prior to biting its neck and the base of the skull. The entire attack usually takes less than a minute. As do other weasels, the least weasel will kill many prey, whether it is hungry or not, storing excess food in side passages of its burrows, or in a cache near the kill site. Killing by weasels is innate, but hunting experience with the mother appears to make them efficient earlier.

REPRODUCTION AND DEVELOPMENT. The breeding habits of the least weasel differ from those of the larger weasels, which have prolonged gestation with delayed implantation and produce only one litter per year. Gary L. Heidt (1970) studied reproduction and development in *Mustela nivalis*. Ovulation is induced by copulation, and there are two or more litters per year, each of one to six young. Breeding can occur throughout the year, but is concentrated in spring and late summer. Young with unopened eyes have been discovered in midwinter, and lactating females and nest young have been found in Pennsylvania during October, January, and February.

The actual mating process in these weasels may last up to three hours and may be repeated a number of times over several days. Implantation is not delayed; the blastocysts implant in about 10 to 12 days. The young are born after a gestation of about 34 to 37 days, the newborn each weighing about 1–1.5 grams. Standard measurements at birth are total length 44, tail 5, and hind foot 3 mm. The first set of canines appears by day 11, and by 18 days the young are well furred and eating meat. By three weeks they have attained the adult pelage, and the carnassials and incisors erupt. The eyes open between 26 and 30 days, and at this time their permanent canines are in place and they have begun crawling about. The permanent dentition is in place by six weeks, and the young are weaned in six or seven weeks. They can kill prey by day 40, and in good years can attain adult length in eight weeks and adult weight in 12 to 15 weeks. Females are sexually mature at four months, males at eight months. Females, even from early litters, seldom produce litters the same year.

POPULATION CHARACTERISTICS. A population estimate in Michigan yielded one weasel per 1.2 ha (3 acres), but densities undoubtedly vary with the density of the prey species, especially the arvicoline rodents. Least weasels can perhaps reproduce rapidly to take advantage of high vole populations, but their numbers can also decline rapidly, because there is such great population turnover (most individuals die in their first year, though a few live up to three years). Males have much larger home ranges than females, ranging usually from 7 to 15 ha (17 to 37 acres); those of females are 1 to 4 ha (2 to 10 acres). Males and females remain apart except during the mating season. The home range of a male may include one or more females, but males exclude other males from their home ranges. There is some home-range overlap, but certain portions of the home range are the exclusive territories of their owners. Least weasels may have several dens or temporary shelters within their home range where they can rest or gain shelter from weather or predators.

ENEMIES. Hawks and owls are the most important predators of this species, but any larger predator, including the long-tailed weasel, may kill it. Predation on weasels can be heavy at times.

PARASITES AND DISEASE. Several roundworms are the least weasel's internal parasites; one is *Skrjabingylus nasicola*, which occurs in the frontal sinus of weasels and causes lesions in the skull. The most abundant ectoparasite of this species is the biting louse *Stachiella kingi*, but fleas and mites from its prey are often found on it. The second most abundant ectoparasite on this host in Indiana was *Myocoptes japonensis*, a mite of arvicolines. Ticks are also found.

RELATION TO HUMANS. Because of the small size and secretive habits of these weasels, humans are seldom aware of their presence.

AREAS FOR FURTHER WORK. This species is poorly known, and its populations are usually low. Studies of any aspect of its life history surely would yield valuable information, but radiotelemetry studies of its behavior in rela-

tion to other predators and to prey species would seem particularly valuable. Comparative studies of the invertebrate fauna of the nests, as it relates to the parasites of the weasel and of its prey species, would be interesting.

## SUBSPECIES

The North American least weasel was originally described as *Mustela rixosa*, but was later combined with *M. nivalis*, described earlier by Linnaeus from Eurasia. This merger left the name *M. nivalis rixosa* for the North American least weasel (see Reichstein, 1958: 169, for details). Other subspecies have been described from western North America, but they do not appear to be separated by primary isolating mechanisms.

*Mustela nivalis rixosa* Bangs

As described above. The only subspecies found in the eastern United States.

Type locality: Osler, Saskatchewan, for *M. nivalis rixosa*.

### LITERATURE

Cooke, A. H. 1951. The least weasel in New York. *J. Mammal.* 32: 225.

Erlinge, S. 1975. Feeding habits of the weasel *Mustela nivalis* in relation to prey abundance. *Oikos* 26: 378–384.

Fagerstone, K. A. 1987. Black-footed ferret, long-tailed weasel, short-tailed weasel, and least weasel. In: M. Novak, J. A. Baker, M. E. Obbard, and B. Mallock, eds., *Wild Furbearer Management and Conservation in North America*, pp. 547–573. Toronto: Ontario Ministry Nat. Resources.

Hamilton, W. J., Jr. 1946. The bounty system doesn't work. *Animal Kingdom* 49: 130–138.

Heffner, R. S., and H. E. Heffner. 1985. Hearing in mammals: The least weasel. *J. Mammal.* 66: 745–755.

Heidt, G. A. 1970. The least weasel *Mustela nivalis* Linnaeus. Developmental biology in comparison with other North American *Mustela*. *Publ. Mus. Mich. State Univ., Biol. Ser.* 4: 227–282.

———. 1972. Anatomical and behavioral aspects of killing and feeding by the least weasel, *Mustela nivalis* L. *Proc. Ark. Acad. Sci.* 26: 53–54.

King, C. M. 1989. *The Natural History of Weasels and Stoats.* London: Christopher Helm. 253 pp.

*Mink*, Mustela vison, *vaulting a log*
(Larry E. Lehman)

Reichstein, H. 1957. Schadelvariabilität europäischer Mauswiesel (*Mustela nivalis* L.) und Hermeline (*Mustela erminea* L.) in Beziehung zu Verbreitung und Geschlecht. *Zeitschrift für Saugetierkunde* 22: 151–182.

Sheffield, S. R., and C. M. King. 1994. *Mustela nivalis*. **Mammalian Species No. 454.** Amer. Soc. Mammal. 10 pp.

Svendsen, G. E. 1987. Weasels, *Mustela* sp. In: J. A. Chapman and G. A. Feldhamer, eds., *Wild Mammals of North America*, pp. 613–628. Baltimore: Johns Hopkins Univ. Press.

## Mink *Mustela vison* Schreber

DESCRIPTION. The mink is a dark, glossy brown, occasionally almost black animal with a white chin and variable white spots on the throat. The fur is soft and lustrous, overlaid with longer, glistening guard hairs. The richest color is attained in November; by midwinter the fur has commenced to fade. The tail, long and bushy and progressively darker posteriorly, constitutes about a third of the animal's total length. A weasel-like mammal, the mink has a long body, short legs, a long neck, and a comparatively short head tapering to a rather pointed snout. The ears are short and rounded. The toes of the hind feet are slightly webbed. The skull is small and lacks a sagittal crest. The anal glands are well developed. Males are about 10% longer than females.

MEASUREMENTS. Average measurements of eleven males from Quebec and the Adirondack Mountains, New York, were: total length 535 (491–590), tail 174.5 (158–194), hind foot 60 (57–66) mm. Five adult females averaged: total length 509 (481–597), tail 149 (144–155), hind foot 50 (47–54) mm. Males are generally 630–1000 grams (1.4–2.2 lbs), females somewhat lighter. Large males from the swamps of western New York weigh up to 1600 grams (3.5 lbs), although the usual weight is 700–900 grams (1.6–2 lbs). Measurements of ten adult males from the salt marshes of Florida and coastal Georgia averaged: total length 564 (526–615), tail 190 (179–203), hind foot 69 (61–72) mm. Ten adult males from Louisiana averaged: total length 563, tail 182.4, hind foot 70 mm. The mink attains greater size in inland marshes, possibly because of the better fare it can secure there.

Diploid number = 30.

TOOTH FORMULA

$$\frac{3}{3} \quad \frac{1}{1} \quad \frac{3}{3} \quad \frac{1}{2} \quad = \quad 34$$

DISTRIBUTION. The mink occurs throughout the eastern United States, wherever watercourses provide a sufficiency of food and shelter, except for a broad band from eastern North Carolina to southeastern Alabama and most of Florida Basically, mink occur throughout Canada and the United States except for the southwestern United States.

HABITAT. Diverse wetlands habitats, varying from the small streams of coniferous swamps to the tidal flats, are the home of the mink. Its greatest populations may be in cattail marshes, but it also occurs around small streams, rivers, lakes, bogs, swamps, and bottomland woods. The cypress/tupelo swamps of Louisiana are excellent mink habitats. During winter, when streams freeze over, the mink often resorts to the woods, occasionally occupying a rabbit burrow.

HABITS. The mink, an excellent swimmer, spends much time foraging along streams. It can swim underwater to a depth of over 5 meters (18 feet) or for a distance of 30 meters (100 yards). Although it is seldom seen, except by the trapper, it is not a rare animal. It is, however, a solitary animal, often out at night, but like other members of the genus, mink adapt their foraging time to hunger and availability of prey. The sexes associate only briefly, during mating.

The presence of den sites is very important for mink, and a male mink may have several dens in its home range. Sometimes they use one den repeatedly; at other times they den up wherever they happen to be. They often hole up under the large trees that line the banks of streams, the great tangle of roots protecting them from their few enemies. Mink also occupy the lodges or bank dens of muskrats, or natural cavities along the borders of rivers. Sometimes there are underwater entrances to their den sites. Like otters, mink will slide down muddy or snowy inclines on their bellies. The mink is a tireless wanderer, making extensive journeys, often over a broad range, and returning with marked regularity to the various parts of its range. Mink natal nests are 25 to 30 cm (10 to 12 inches) in diameter and lined with fur, feathers, or plant material.

Mink are provided with prominent anal glands that emit a powerful musky effluvium when the animal is excited or disturbed, the odor particularly pronounced during the mating season. This species, like the least weasel (and probably

*Distribution of the mink,*
Mustela vison, *in the*
*eastern United States*

other members of the genus *Mustela*), domestic dogs and cats, and raccoons, can hear high-frequency sounds in the range produced by their potential rodent prey (Powell and Zielinski, 1989).

FOOD AND FEEDING. The mink feeds on a variety of foods, both aquatic and terrestrial. It relies upon crayfish, fish, frogs, small mammals, birds, invertebrates, and snakes, taking such of these as it can secure. Mink often rely heavily on mammals in winter, on crayfish, fish, and frogs in summer, when the water is low, and especially when receding waters leave isolated pools, but relative importance varies greatly with habitat and availability. A mink captures mammals large enough to struggle by wrapping its body around them, and, in typical mustelid fashion, kills them by a bite to the nape of the neck. In extensive marshes where muskrats abound, male mink may feed heavily on these big rodents, though the muskrat is a dangerous and formidable foe. (Hamilton found a winter nest of a mink that consisted almost entirely of the fur of muskrats.) Female mink, being smaller, are more apt to take smaller mammals. Like weasels, mink will cache food for later use.

REPRODUCTION AND DEVELOPMENT. The testes begin to increase in size and activity in November, peaking in March. Ovulation is induced by mating in this species, and initial breeding is at ten months. Males search widely for females during the mating season, and mating behavior is accompanied by "chuckling" vocalization by both sexes. The male grasps the female by the nape during mating, but a fight may result if she is not receptive. Copulation may be prolonged, and mating periods may be interspersed with rest periods. Mating takes place from January through early April, but implantation is delayed from nine to 46 days.

In April or May, 40 to 75 days after mating, and 28 to 32 days after implantation, the one to ten young (average about four) are born. (Later in the season, the delay in implantation is more brief.) At birth the young weigh about 8 to 10 grams. Each is the size of a cigarette, covered with fine, almost white hairs that scarcely conceal the pink flesh. At two weeks, they have reddish-gray hair and the males are already larger than the females. The first teeth erupt about the beginning of the third week, and the eyes open at about three weeks. The young are weaned at five weeks, and the female alone thereafter brings food to the growing young. At seven or eight weeks, the young accompany the female on hunting journeys and can capture prey for themselves. The females reach adult weight by four months, the males by nine to 11 months. In summer, the entire family may sometimes be seen by day, hunting along the border of some quiet lake. The family disperses in early fall.

POPULATION CHARACTERISTICS. Male mink have larger home ranges than females, the females occupying 8 to 20 ha (20 to 50 acres), the males up to 760 ha (1900 acres). Females use their smaller ranges more intensively, and in winter both sexes have a much smaller locus of activity. Changes in home-range use are associated with differential food availability. Males encompass the home ranges of more than one female, but ranges do not overlap within sexes. Expressed in stream length, an adult male might occupy 2600 meters (8500 feet), female 1800 meters (5900 feet). Populations can reach levels up to about one animal per 12 ha (30 acres). Major movements of mink are during mating and at dispersal, most dispersers, however, moving less than 5 km (3 miles).

ENEMIES. Other than humans, the adult mink has few enemies, although great horned owls, bobcats, lynxes, foxes, and alligators are known to take them on occasion. People trap mink in large numbers, but more important, we have destroyed much of their prime habitat, and we continue to pollute vast reaches of it. It appears that the mink is highly susceptible to mercury and polychlorinated biphenyls (PCBs), both of them common in natural environments today, although PCBs are no longer produced in the United States. Mercury can kill mink, and PCBs can cause reproductive problems and, ultimately, death. Pesticides, which usually occur at low levels in the foods eaten by mink, are often a major threat to them.

PARASITES AND DISEASE. External parasites of mink are ticks, fleas, mites, and biting lice, but most parasites found on this host are acquired from their prey. A number of internal parasites, including at least 24 species of trematodes, three of cestodes, 19 of nematodes, and two of acanthocephalans, have also been reported. One of the nematodes is *Skrjabingylus*, which causes lesions in the nasal sinus area of several mustelids.

RELATION TO HUMANS. Trappers at one time took many thousands of mink each winter, for their durable and lustrous pelt commanded a high price. Trappers and hunters with trained dogs were largely responsible for the mink's decline over much of its range. A great number were taken in traps set for muskrats; in a good muskrat marsh, peak production of mink to the trapper was approximately 15 per 405 ha (1000 acres). From the 1930s to the 1960s, many mink were raised on fur farms, an enterprise that peaked in the 1960s at about 11 million pelts annually, in about 7200 mink ranches. In 1976, 40,000 wild northern mink pelts from New York averaged $15, and in 1987, good male pelts brought $35 and female pelts $18. But like other furs, those of mink are nearly worthless today.

AREAS FOR FURTHER WORK. Mink and other members of the genus *Mustela* have anal scent glands, as do the skunks. Comparative biochemical studies of these species and their glands might give clues to the evolutionary development of the group. Comparative behavioral studies of the several members of the genus *Mustela*, using experimentally planted scent markings, would be of value.

## SUBSPECIES

Mink occur, and apparently intergrade, throughout most of the eastern United States. The mink of Florida, however, occur in three disjunct populations (Humphrey and Setzer, 1989): *Mustela vison lutensis* along the Atlantic coastal plain of northeastern Florida, Georgia, and southern South Carolina; *M. v. halilimnetes* along the Gulf Coast, a form described as a new subspecies by Humphrey and Setzer; and *M. v. evergladensis*, which occurs in the saltmarshes (this name is somewhat a misnomer, since these mink are primarily associated with

the Big Cypress region rather than the true Everglades). If differentiation from nearly adjacent northern populations has indeed occurred, these three would meet our criteria for subspecies, and Humphrey and Setzer did demonstrate differentiation between the first two. They did not recognize the Everglades population, but in their description they ignored pelage characteristics, indicating that an insufficient number of skins was available to them for examination. Because they found its variation to be included in the variation of *M. vison mink* (a widespread form that we do not recognize as distinct from *M. v. vison*), they included it in that subspecies. *Mustela vison evergladensis*, however, includes only a small portion of the variation in *mink*.

Since this population is separated by a primary isolating mechanism, the next question is whether it has evolved from its ancestral population, but Humphrey and Setzer did not attempt to determine the ancestral population, which would appear to be *lutensis*, *halilimnetes*, or southeastern populations of *vison*. They showed *evergladensis* to be differentiated from *lutensis* and *halilimnetes*, but unfortunately did not compare it with the likeliest ancestral populations, the geographically closest populations of *M. v. vison*. In any event, since *evergladensis* is isolated, since it includes a relatively small amount of the variation found in the variable and widespread *vison*, and since it has an available name, we have chosen to retain it as perhaps a valid subspecies, pending further study.

We thus arrange the eastern U.S. subspecies of the mink as follows:

*Mustela vison vison* Schreber

As described above. The length of P1, lingual length of P4, and length of p4 average 4.30, 8.20, and 4.60 mm, respectively (Humphrey & Setzer, 1989).

Type locality: Eastern Canada (= Quebec).

Other currently recognized eastern subspecies:
    *M. vison letifera* Hollister
    *M. vison mink* (Peale & Beauvois)
    *M. vison vulvivaga* (Bangs)

*Mustela vison lutensis* (Bangs)

Humphrey and Setzer (1989) retained *M. v. lutensis* as a valid subspecies on grounds that it

*Badger*, Taxidea taxus
*(Charles A. Long)*

shows little morphological overlap with *M. v. mink*. Although it is not completely clear from their work, they imply that *lutensis* is geographically isolated and does not intergrade with *mink* (which we take to be embraced by *M. v. vison*). If *lutensis* is indeed isolated, then we would agree with this assessment and class it as a separate subspecies. The major characters used by Humphrey and Setzer are tooth size, especially the carnassial teeth, and the teeth of *lutensis* are in fact larger than those of *mink*, the length of M1, lingual length of P4, and length of p4 averaging 4.70, 8.95, and 4.95 mm, respectively, in *lutensis*.

Type locality: Salt marsh off Matanzas Inlet, St. Johns Co., Florida.

### Mustela vison evergladensis Hamilton

The characters of this subspecies are very similar to those of *M. v. mink*, though much less variable. Unfortunately, the values for *mink* and *evergladensis* are combined by Humphrey and Setzer (1989), but *mink* is smaller than both *lutensis* and *halilimnetes*.

Type locality: Tamiami Trail, 5 miles [8 km] southeast of Royal Palm Hammock, Collier Co., Florida.

### Mustela vison halilimnetes
Humphrey & Setzer

This subspecies occurs on the Gulf Coast of Florida, probably from Anclote (Pasco Co.) north to Ochlocknee Bay, Franklin Co. *Mustela v. halilimnetes* differs from *M. v. mink* in having "the first premolar more robust," a narrower interorbital, a narrower rostrum, and a

few other distinctions. External measurements of the type specimen were: total length 530, tail 134, hind foot 64 mm.

Type locality: West Yankeetown, Levy Co., Florida.

### LITERATURE

Enders, R. K. 1952. Reproduction in the mink (*Mustela vison*). *Proc. Amer. Philos. Soc.* 96: 691–755.

Errington, P. L. 1943. An analysis of mink predation upon muskrats in north-central United States. Iowa State Coll., Agric. Exp. Sta., Res. Bull. 320: pp. 797–924.

Humphrey, S., and H. W. Setzer. 1989. Geographic variation and taxonomic revision of mink (*Mustela vison*) in Florida. *J. Mammal.* 70: 241–251.

Linscombe, G., N. Kinler, and R. J. Aulerich. 1982. Mink *Mustela vison*. In: J. A. Chapman and G. A. Feldhamer, eds., *Wild Mammals of North America*, pp. 629–643. Baltimore: Johns Hopkins Univ. Press.

Powell, R. A., and W. J. Zielinski. 1989. Mink response to ultrasound in the range emitted by prey. *J. Mammal.* 70: 637–638.

### Badger *Taxidea taxus* (Schreber)

DESCRIPTION. The badger is a stout-bodied, short-tailed, short-legged member of the weasel family, easily recognized by its distinctive coloration, its broad body, and the large, heavy claws of the forefeet. The face is dark brown or black with white cheeks and a white stripe extending from behind the nose over the top of the head to the nape. The upperparts, including the tail, are clothed with long, shaggy hairs, these hairs white or yellowish white at the base, pale brown to black in the middle, and prominently tipped with white, giving the animal a distinctly grizzled appearance. The nose, crown, and neck are dark brown to blackish, and the hairs on the neck are tipped with white. The fur of the underparts is short and whitish. The legs are dark brown and the feet are black or brown. The middle claws of the forefeet are 25 mm (an inch) long or more.

MEASUREMENTS. Eleven males from Indiana averaged: total length 754 (605–843), tail 148 (115–250), hind foot 108 (93–121) mm. Eight females averaged: 689 (614–787), 124 (115–139), 102 (85–115) mm. Males are larger and heavier than females, the males in two populations averaging 8.4 and 8.7 kg (18 and 19 lbs), the females averaging 6.4 and 7.1 kg (13 and 15.5 lbs).

Diploid number = 32.

TOOTH FORMULA

$$\frac{3}{3} \quad \frac{1}{1} \quad \frac{3}{3} \quad \frac{1}{2} \quad = \quad 34$$

DISTRIBUTION. In the eastern United States, the badger ranges from northern and western Ohio westward through most of Indiana and Illinois and all of Michigan and Wisconsin. L. E. Hicks has indicated that badgers have always occurred in Wood, Henry, and Fulton counties in northwestern Ohio. Today, in Ohio, they are found principally in the sandy areas of the old postglacial lake beaches there. To the west, badgers occur from southeastern British Columbia and much of Alberta, Saskatchewan, and southern Manitoba south into central Mexico.

HABITAT. In the eastern part of their range, badgers frequent the open prairie country and flat,

*Distribution of the badger,*
Taxidea taxus, *in the*
*eastern United States*

rolling farmlands, shunning the woods and marshlands, and there is increasing evidence that these animals are extending their range. Their burgeoning numbers may be a side effect of lumbering operations, which encourage grassland, which in turn encourages the badger itself, as well as the rodent populations on which badgers are in large measure dependent.

HABITS. The badger is admirably adapted for a fossorial life. Its long, stout foreclaws, heavy forelegs, and squat, strong body enable it to dig with tireless energy and with amazing speed. Indeed, a badger can "dig itself in" in a matter of minutes. Dens are central to the existence of badgers. They are used for sleeping, the birth of the young, and food storage. Even when foraging, badgers operate from a den. Dens usually have a single entrance, around which is piled the excavated dirt. The entrance may be plugged during cold weather or when the badger is disturbed. Many old dens can be found in habitat occupied by badgers, and the badgers will reuse the old dens. An active badger uses a different den nearly every day, except when young are present. The natal burrow, its main tunnel branching and rejoining, and extending into dead-end lateral tunnels and pockets and chambers, is more complex than other burrows. The rejoining branch in the main tunnel presumably allows the badgers to pass one another. Some burrows noted were 2 meters (6.5 feet) deep and up to 11 meters (35 feet) long, others only 2 meters long and less than a meter deep. One female usually dug a new burrow each day in summer, commonly reused burrows for several days in autumn, and used a single den through much of the winter. There may be a nest of grass, though some workers report no nest.

The badger is basically solitary and largely nocturnal, but it may occasionally be seen in the early morning or, more often, in the late afternoon and early evening, just as dusk is approaching. It is usually a wary animal, and its presence may go unnoticed for many years in a region where it is relatively common. It is also a ferocious animal, and a fighter of great strength. It is more than a match for most dogs, for its loose skin affords little chance for a vital grip,

and its strong teeth are capable of inflicting deep wounds. It emits various grunts and growls, but its trademark, and the vocalization most likely to be heard by people, is its hiss. Badgers are solitary except during mating and when females are rearing young.

The badger may retire to its underground chamber for several days or perhaps a month or more during cold stretches in the winter, but it does not truly hibernate, and it may emerge during mild spells. It does enter torpor, however, an energy-conservation strategy critical for this species.

FOOD AND FEEDING. The badger is adapted for feeding on burrowing mammals, and most often eats its prey below ground. It feeds heavily on ground squirrels, and its depredations in a ground squirrel colony have all the appearance of an aerial blitzkrieg. In addition to ground squirrels, gophers, and other small rodents, they feed upon insects, ground-nesting birds, snails, reptiles, other small animal life, and sometimes carrion. They may even eat corn on occasion; the stomachs from four badgers taken in Iowa in the fall contained only corn. It has been estimated that an active 8-kg (17-lb) badger needs about two ground squirrels per day to meet its energy requirements.

Because potential prey often use old badger dens, badgers commonly forage simply by going from den to den. They probably sense the presence of prey in the dens from slight disturbance to the ground, or by smell around the entrance. Badgers may capture the inhabitants of a den by plugging all entrances but one (in cases where there are more than one), then digging the prey out. The behavior pattern may vary with the prey species and with the situation, but this method is often used to capture ground squirrels, a favored prey. In one case, badgers buried themselves near an open burrow entrance and waited for the ground squirrels to appear. Still another method used for the capture of pocket gophers and ground squirrels is to dig into the system at various points and close off parts, rather than digging up the entire burrow, thus reducing the amount of digging needed. Badgers often prey on hibernating mammals, as well.

Minta et al. (1992) found that badgers and coyotes occasionally form temporary hunting associations, as had much earlier been suggested. Such an association was observed in Wyoming, at Jackson Hole, where the Uinta ground squirrel, *Spermophilus armatus*, was the prey. The badger's excellent hearing and sense of smell helped it to pinpoint the location of the squirrel underground. It would then dig down and corner its prey, running back and forth to keep it from escaping, a tactic necessary because these dens often had multiple interconnecting passages. In due course, the badger would dig the squirrel out, but the coyote, meanwhile, may have helped keep the squirrel from escaping via the entrance. The coyote would remain at the various entrances and pounce on the emerging squirrels. Thus both above-ground and below-ground hunting were pursued, and both predators appeared to benefit. It appeared that the squirrels were much more at risk between the two predators than they would have been with either predator alone. The coyote certainly benefited from the badger's powerful assaults on the burrows, and the badger may have benefited from the coyote's superior ability to range out across the plains and find squirrels. How often this occurs is unknown, but it appears to have been a mutualistic relationship between two predators at the top of the food chain. The badger is not a particularly friendly animal, but the Mintas have even seen coyotes attempt to play with badgers—usually, and not surprisingly, eliciting aggressive behavior.

REPRODUCTION AND DEVELOPMENT. Badgers are promiscuous. Females typically become pregnant at one year, but occasionally as juveniles (at four to five months). Males, however, are not sexually mature until 14 months old, thus breed in their second summer. Badgers are in breeding condition from May to August, and mating peaks in late July and early August, but implantation is delayed until February. The young, numbering one to five (usually two or three, one record of seven), are born in late March or early April, furred but blind. They are apparently fed solid food while still in the den, and first emerge from the den at about four to five weeks. They remain in the den until they are fairly large; they are weaned in June; and they disperse at about 10 to 12 weeks.

POPULATION CHARACTERISTICS. Badgers often occur at densities of one badger (and its ten dens) per 2.6 square km (1 square mile), up to a maximum of two to six per square km (5 to 15 per square mile). The size of the home range varies considerably, but estimates vary from 237 to 1700 ha (585 to 4200 acres). In one case the "overall home range" was estimated at 850 ha (2100 acres), but varied from 725 ha (1800 acres) in summer to 53 ha (130 acres) in autumn and 2 ha (5 acres) in winter. Males extend their home ranges during the breeding season so as to encompass those of several females. The home ranges of females may overlap each other; those of males do not. A female remains near her young, but may often shift feeding areas by moving them. There are records of badgers living up to 15 years.

ENEMIES. Other than humans, the adult badger has few enemies.

PARASITES AND DISEASE. The internal parasites of badgers are nematodes, cestodes, and trematodes; their ectoparasites are biting lice, fleas, and ticks, but few mites.

RELATION TO HUMANS. The badger was once trapped for its coarse but handsome fur, which was used chiefly for trimmings and for "pointing" more valuable furs, principally fox. It was also used in the manufacture of shaving and paint brushes. Pelts brought $20 in 1986 and 1987. But like many of the other larger species of mammals, the badger has become increasingly uncommon in many areas in the east, and is now generally protected. Trappers and farmers are still killing many badgers, despite their importance in the destruction of rodents. Badgers can at times become problems by digging great holes and making mounds of earth while searching for food. These disruptions can damage crop fields and equipment.

AREAS FOR FURTHER WORK. A study of hunting strategies and other behaviors of badgers, via radiotelemetry and other methods, should

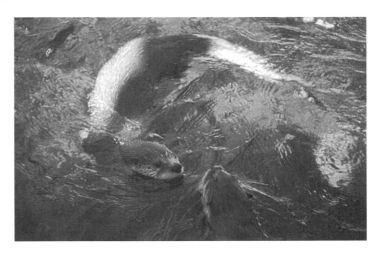

*River otter,* Lutra canadensis
*(Roger W. Barbour)*

prove of great interest. Coupled with a study of the energy budgets, such a study would be especially valuable. Another question of interest: How do badgers find hibernating prey?

## SUBSPECIES

Long (1972) recognized four subspecies of *Taxidea taxus* in North America, including two in the east, *T. taxus taxus* in Illinois and most of Indiana and *T. taxus jacksoni* in Wisconsin, Michigan, and northeastern Indiana. Because he showed that three of the subspecies—*taxus, jeffersoni,* and *berlandieri*—intergrade broadly, and because the original describer of *T. taxus jacksoni* (Schantz, 1945) indicated that *T. taxus taxus* and *T. taxus jacksoni* intergrade, we see no reason to recognize more than one eastern subspecies.

*Taxidea taxus taxus* Schreber

As described above.

Type locality: Probably southwest of Hudson Bay; restricted by Long (1972) to Carman, Manitoba.

Other currently recognized eastern subspecies:
*Taxidea taxus jacksoni* Schantz

### LITERATURE

Lindzey, F. G. 1982. Badger *Taxidea taxus.* In: J. A. Chapman and G. A. Feldhamer, eds., *Wild Mammals of North America,* pp. 653–663. Baltimore: Johns Hopkins Univ. Press.

Long, C. A. 1972. Taxonomic revision of the North American badger, *Taxidea taxus. J. Mammal.* 53: 725–759.

———. 1973. *Taxidea taxus.* **Mammalian Species No. 26.** Amer. Soc. Mammal. 4 pp.

Messick, J. P. 1987. North American badger. In: M. Novak, J. A. Baker, M. E. Obbard, and B. Mallock, eds., *Wild Furbearer Management and Conservation in North America,* pp. 586–597. Toronto: Ontario Ministry Nat. Resources.

Minta, S. C., K. A. Minta, and D. F. Lott. 1992. Hunting associations between badgers (*Taxidea taxus*) and coyotes (*Canis latrans*). *J. Mammal.* 73: 814–820.

Schantz, V. S. 1945. A new badger from Wisconsin. *J. Mammal.* 26: 431.

Wright, P. A. 1966. Observations on the reproductive cycle of the American badger (*Taxidea taxus*). *Symp. Zool. Soc. London* 15: 27–45.

———. 1969. The reproductive cycle of the male American badger, *Taxidea taxus. J. Reprod. Fert.* Suppl. 6: 435–445.

## River Otter *Lutra canadensis* (Schreber)                         Color plate 19

In his taxonomic and systematic revision of the genus *Lutra,* C. G. van Zyll de Jong (1972) concluded that the New World otters are generically distinct from *Lutra* of the Old World, and for the former he resurrected the name *Lontra* (Gray). I. I. Sokolov (1973), however, on the basis of a morphological analysis of recent and extinct forms of the subfamily Lutrinae, concluded that *canadensis* should be retained in the genus *Lutra,* and we agree with that determination.

DESCRIPTION. The otter is a large, aquatic member of the weasel family with a broad, flattened head, small eyes, small ears, long, stout neck, and a heavy, tapering tail constituting just over a third of the animal's total length. The otter's short legs and webbed toes, hairy soles, and thick, dense pelage are also characteristic. The color above is a rich glossy brown, occasionally nearly black. The underparts are much lighter, and the lips, cheeks, chin, and throat are a pale brown. The skull is flattened, the rostrum is short, and the auditory bullae are much flattened. Otters along the coast from New Jersey to South Carolina are paler in color than those to the north; those from the south are larger; and otters from Florida have a longer tail and less black.

MEASUREMENTS. Total length is 900–1300, tail 340–510, hind foot 110–135 mm. The male's weight is 5.4–9 kg (12 to 20 lbs), although one male from northwestern New Jersey weighed 10.7 kg (23.5 lbs).

Diploid number = 38.

TOOTH FORMULA

$$\frac{3}{3} \quad \frac{1}{1} \quad \frac{4}{3} \quad \frac{1}{2} \ = \ 36$$

DISTRIBUTION. The river otter originally occurred through nearly all of Canada and the United States except for some of the Southwest. This included all of eastern United States, but the species has been extirpated in much of its range. The last known record of the otter in Indiana, for example, was in 1942. More recently, however, the otter has been given protection, and it has been reintroduced into Ohio, Illinois, Indiana, and Pennsylvania, and in all these states it is making a comeback. Today, it occurs in the north in much of Wisconsin and Michigan and

*Distribution of the river otter,* Lutra canadensis, *in the eastern United States*

in most of New England and eastern New York. It also occurs through most of the south, northwest to western Kentucky, north to northern Georgia, and northeast through the Atlantic Seaboard to southern Maryland.

HABITAT. The otter needs areas with much water and much aquatic vegetation. It frequents the lakes and large rivers of the northern wilderness forests, the lonely bayous and cypress-lined rivers of the south, and it occurs in some numbers in the extensive marshes of the Gulf region. In recent years, it has increased in numbers, and it has actually become a nuisance in Massachusetts and in the Upper Peninsula of Michigan, where it invades the fish hatcheries and trout streams. The otter appears to favor fresh water in the north, but in the south it is found in brackish streams as well.

HABITS. The otter is a shy and retiring animal, nonetheless often occupying regions close to humans. Owing to its secretive habits it is seldom seen, even though its principal activity periods are from dawn to mid-morning and again in the evening. It is active throughout the winter.

The best-known and most obvious evidence of the presence of otters is their slides, although—at least in Wisconsin and the Upper Peninsula of Michigan—these are not obvious. In the north, slides are made on steep slopes coated with ice and snow; in the south, on clay banks. On these the otter slides to the pool or river below, its forelegs tucked under. The slides soon become slick, and several otters of a family may use the same slide. Other signs of otters are haul-outs (trails from water's edge, often scattered with droppings and crayfish parts), bedding sites (depressions on the ground edged with matted leaves or other vegetation), rolling sites (plants flattened along the bank in an area up to 2 square meters, or 20 square feet), scrapes (areas scraped completely clear of vegetation), and scent posts (usually recognized by the disturbance of the ground around them). The tracks of otters are distinctively wide, and often interspersed with the tracks are stretches where the belly drags, frequent short slides, and places where otters have been digging for turtle eggs, clams, or other items.

The otter is a strong and graceful swimmer, moving in an undulating course, or swimming with only its head above the surface. It can dive to about 18 meters (60 feet) and can swim at speeds up to 11 kph (7 mph) for 400 meters (a quarter-mile) without coming up for air. It can also tread water, projecting its long neck above the water to see. An otter need not travel far in summer, for foraging or hunting areas are usually readily available, but in cold winters it sometimes has to make long overland journeys to visit the infrequent pools—those that are kept free by cascading falls—to secure the fish that maintain it at this season. In spite of its short legs, the otter moves rapidly on land, and on the ice it expedites travel by sliding. In this mode, it moves by two to four loping bounds of 38 to 71 cm (15 to 28 inches), followed by a glide with the abdomen on the ground and the feet trailing behind. The glide may extend for about 1.5 to 4.5 meters (5 to 15 feet) in snow, or up to 7 meters (22 feet) on ice.

Dens are most often along a bank. A den may be a natural opening or another animal's burrow or lodge (beaver, muskrat, or woodchuck). It may be among tree roots, under a brush pile, in a hollow stump or log jam, or in some other protected place. The entrance to a den may be above or below the surface of the water. The main den may be used for several years. The nest itself may be of grasses, leaves, or aquatic vegetation, and otters will sometimes make a nestlike structure in the aquatic vegetation itself. Otters are extremely curious and appear to play with one another. They are able to manipulate items with their paws, and their tactile senses, especially those stimulated by the vibrissae, are well developed. When the vibrissae were experimentally removed from European otters, *Lutra lutra*, the animals took much longer to locate items in murky water. Vision is not acute, except under water, although otters can detect movement at great distances. An otter's hearing is good, and its sense of smell probably is as well, to judge from their extensive use of scent marking. Otters utter shrill chirps, growls, or hissing barks.

FOOD AND FEEDING. Fish are the main food of otters, but a great variety of other items constitute, collectively, an important part of the diet.

Crustaceans (primarily crayfish), other shellfish, frogs and toads, small mammals (especially voles), birds, and insects are some of the more important non-fish items. Small amounts of plant material, such as blueberries and rose hips, are occasionally eaten. Much has been written on the supposed destructiveness of otter to trout, and without question they successfully pursue and capture them. Hamilton saw rocks in "otter streams" literally plastered with the scales of these fish. Otters feed most heavily on the more abundant, slower-moving species, especially suckers, chubs, daces, darters, and catfish, and also such schooling species as bluegills and sunfish. Fast-moving and elusive species are taken at lower rates than would be dictated strictly by their abundance. Otters may capture fish by pursuit or by digging into the sand and lying in wait. Liers (1951), observing free-ranging captive otters, watched them stand on their heads in the pond and root out large frogs from their hibernacula in the mud, and dig out soft-shelled turtles from the sand. In a study of 141 Adirondack otters, Hamilton found that fish occurred in 70% of the stomachs, but only 5% of these were trout. Other foods taken were crayfish, frogs and tadpoles, and aquatic insects. Otters will sometimes forage on land, especially in winter. The otter is said to kill muskrats, but there is no direct evidence for this.

REPRODUCTION AND DEVELOPMENT. Otters mate shortly after the young are born, the females going almost immediately into a postpartum estrus lasting 42 to 46 days. Mating can occur at any point from December to May, but peaks in the north in March or April. The male presumably mates with one or more of the females whose home ranges fall within his. Females in heat may mark at scent stations and haul-outs. A 50% pregnancy rate in Alabama and Georgia indicates that females may breed only every other year there. Copulation, the female often caterwauling, usually takes place in the water but may be on land, and for a given female may recur several times over several days. Delayed implantation lengthens apparent gestation by 8 to 9.5 months, the blastocyst lying free in the uterus until implantation occurs—in about February in New York, earlier in the south.

The female establishes a natal den shortly before giving birth, and the young are usually born in March or April (range from November through May), but birth dates appear to show little relationship to latitude. The young, which normally number two to four, occasionally up to six, are fairly well developed at birth. They are fully furred, but their ears and eyes are closed, and they have no teeth. They weigh about 275 grams. The eyes open at 35 days, and at 40 days the young are active and playful. They forage with the mother at 10 to 11 weeks, soon after weaning, and disperse in the fall or winter of their first year, before production of the next litter. Otters reach sexual maturity at two years of age, although a few females mate at 15 months. Although *able* to mate sooner, many males are not successful in establishing territories and breeding until five to seven years of age.

POPULATION CHARACTERISTICS. Much of the available information on otters is on the closely related *Lutra lutra* in Sweden, rather than on the North American otter. Otters do not attain high densities, occurring at perhaps one otter per 3 or 4 km (2 to 2.5 miles) of waterway. Otters usually stay put after establishing themselves in suitable habitat, but dispersing individuals may move 120 km (75 miles) or more before establishing their own home ranges. Home ranges of males are large, perhaps 15 km (9 miles) wide, and include the much smaller ranges of one or more females. Both sexes maintain territories within the home ranges, and exclude others of the same sex. Some use the anal scent glands to mark territories; others mark territories by depositing scented feces (sprainting) and making scented dirt piles. Marking informs a transient that he is on claimed turf, thus helping to avoid conflict by allowing him passage without meeting the resident otter. The purpose of territories is apparently to secure feeding ranges, but territoriality is apparently relaxed at low densities.

ENEMIES. Humans have been the chief enemies of the adult otter, through both direct harvest and habitat destruction.

PARASITES AND DISEASE. Three species of ticks and a tiny listrophorid mite, *Lutracarus cana-*

*densis*, are found in the fur of otters. Internal parasites in the eastern states include six trematodes, one cestode, ten nematodes, and four acanthocephalans. One of the nematodes is *Skrjabingylus lutrae*, which causes lesions in the frontal sinuses area of the skull. Little is known of the diseases of otters.

RELATION TO HUMANS. This is the only otter species in the world that can be legally trapped. Its pelt is thick and lustrous and is the most durable of native American furs. Prime 1976 pelts brought $60, and 1987 prices ranged from $35 to $45. The pelts of both the river otter and the sea otter were the favorite furs of the Chinese mandarins and the Russian nobility, and many pelts were exported annually.

AREAS FOR FURTHER WORK. Much additional information is needed on the territorial relations and behavior of otters, and a detailed study of their ectoparasites would be in order.

## SUBSPECIES

Van Zyll de Jong (1972) recognized only two subspecies of otter in the eastern United States, and they are currently separated, but the discrimination of subspecies in this species will become increasingly difficult as reintroductions are made with stocks from various locations.

### *Lutra canadensis canadensis* (Schreber)

As described above. This subspecies, the smaller and darker of the two, occurs in the northeastern United States.

Type locality: Eastern Canada (= Quebec).

### *Lutra canadensis lataxina* F. Cuvier

This subspecies, somewhat larger and lighter-colored than *Lutra c. canadensis*, occurs in the southeastern United States.

Type locality: South Carolina.

### LITERATURE

Chanin, P. 1985. *The Natural History of Otters*. New York: Facts on File. 179 pp.

Liers, E. E. 1951. Notes on the river otter (*Lutra canadensis*). *J. Mammal.* 32: 1–9.

Melquist, W. E., and A. E. Dronkert. 1987. River ot-

ter. In: M. Novak, J. A. Baker, M. E. Obbard, and B. Mallock, eds., *Wild Furbearer Management and Conservation in North America*, pp. 626–641. Toronto: Ontario Ministry Nat. Resources.

Sokolov, I. I. 1973. Trends of evolution and the classification of the subfamily Lutrinae (Mustelidae, Fissipedia). *Bull. Moscow Priv. Biol.* 78(6): 45–52.

Toweill, D. E., and J. E. Tabor. 1982. River otter *Lutra canadensis*. In: J. A. Chapman and G. A. Feldhamer, eds., *Wild Mammals of North America*, pp. 688–703. Baltimore: Johns Hopkins Univ. Press.

van Zyll de Jong, C. G. 1972. A systematic review of the Nearctic and Neotropical river otters (genus *Lutra*, Mustelidae, Carnivora). Royal Ontario Mus., Life Sci. Contr. No. 80. 104 pp.

## SKUNKS, Family Mephitidae

The skunks have long been recognized in the family Mustelidae, subfamily Mephitinae, but Dragoo and Honeycutt (1997), using mitochondrial DNA sequencing data, have shown quite convincingly that the skunks should be placed in their own separate family, Mephitidae.

Skunks, familiar to us all, are characterized by their striking black-and-white color patterns, their slow, deliberate behavior, and their well-developed scent glands, which can spray foul-smelling scent with force and some accuracy. The behavior and color pattern together act as a warning, telling us and most predators to stay clear.

There are nine species in three genera in the family Mephitidae, all occurring in the New World. Two of the genera, each including one species, occur in the eastern United States.

As in weasels and otters, skunks are subject to heavy infestation by nematode worms of the genus *Skrjabingylus*, *S. chitwoodorum* being the species that afflicts skunks. Advanced cases cause deformities and lesions (skrjabingyliasis) in the frontal sinus area of the skull. Kirkland and Kirkland (1983) found *Skrjabingylus* damage in 50 to 100% of striped and spotted skunks in the United States, the percentage varying among regions.

### LITERATURE CITED

Dragoo, J. W., and R. L. Honeycutt. 1997. Systematics of mustelid-like carnivores. *J. Mammal.* 78: 426–443.

*Spotted skunk*, Spilogale putorius
*(Roger W. Barbour)*

Kirkland, G. L., Jr., and C. J. Kirkland. 1983. Patterns of variation in cranial damage in skunks (Mustelidae: Mephitinae) presumably caused by nematodes of the genus *Skrjabingylus* Petrov 1927 (Metastrongyloidea). *Canadian J. Zool.* 61: 2913–2920.

## KEY TO THE GENERA
## OF THE FAMILY MEPHITIDAE

1. Back showing four or more lines of broken stripes or spots; total length less than 500 mm; top of skull flat as seen in profile . . . . . . . . . . . . . . . . . . . . . . . . . *Spilogale*
1. Back typically showing continuous white stripes of varying length; total length more than 500 mm; top of skull angular as seen in profile . . . . . . . . . . . . . . . . . . *Mephitis* (p. 474)

## Spotted Skunk *Spilogale putorius*
## (Linnaeus)                      Color plate 19

As many as five separate species of spotted skunks have been described over time, and even today there is no strong consensus on the point. The spotted skunks of eastern United States are all of one species, and in our view none justify distinction as separate subspecies.

DESCRIPTION. A strikingly marked mephitid of moderate size, the spotted skunk is generally black in color, with four white stripes running along the dorsum, uninterrupted from the head to the middle of the back, and broken into patches on the hind quarters. There is a white patch on the forehead. The tail is long and broadly tipped with white on its terminal one-fourth or one-third. On spotted skunks from Louisiana, the amount of white is reduced; on those from Florida, it is increased.

MEASUREMENTS. Northern individuals of this species are larger than southern, and, as is true of all skunks, males are larger than females. Total length is 463–610 mm in males, 403–544 mm in females; tail length is 193–280 mm in males, 165–210 mm in females; and hind foot length is 43–59 mm in males, 39–47 mm in females. Weight is 444–999 grams (1–2.5 lbs) in males, 363–567 grams (0.8–1.25 lbs) in females.

Diploid number = 64.

TOOTH FORMULA

$$\frac{3}{3} \quad \frac{1}{1} \quad \frac{3}{3} \quad \frac{1}{2} \ = \ 34$$

DISTRIBUTION. In the east the spotted skunk ranges from extreme south-central Pennsylvania south through the Appalachians, west through central Tennessee and southeastern Mississippi to Louisiana and southeast through western South Carolina, northern and western Georgia, and most of Florida. There is an unverified sight record from southern Illinois, and the species has been found in Indiana cave deposits, but there is no evidence that it currently exists in either state. The spotted skunk occurs throughout most of the western United States and Central America.

HABITAT. The beautiful little spotted skunk is common in much of the south, inhabiting weedy cultivated fields and woodlots. It is common in the vicinity of farms and sometimes in the dense palmetto thickets of southern Florida, but seems to avoid heavy woods and wetlands.

HABITS. Skunks are best known for their odor and their color, and spotted skunks are remarkable for their handstands when under threat, a behavior unique among North American mammals. All of these characters—and their slow, deliberate behavior, for that matter—combine to form a protective strategy quite different from that of most other mammals. Most mammals avoid detection by blending into the background, on the strength of their color and behavior patterns. But there is something bad about skunks (and porcupines), and they advertise that fact. Both the black-and-white color and the slow, deliberate, and apparently uncon-

cerned behavior of the skunk announce "stay away" to most predators. Black-and-white is the color pattern most apt to be seen, day or night, and the strategy usually succeeds. Presumably, each would-be predator needs but one bad experience with a skunk to learn to stay away.

Spotted skunks are not belligerent, though they generally go wherever they please. They are docile creatures, so long as they are given a wide berth, but they are not easily intimidated, even by humans. Spotted skunks are well known for their handstands. If alarmed, they will often stomp their feet, raise their tail, stand on their front feet, and walk stiff-legged, all serving as warning that they may spray. They can spray while standing on the hands, which allows them to see and aim. Often they will run at an adversary, then abruptly stop and stand on their hands. Standing on the hands may also have the effect of making them look larger, thus more formidable to an adversary. The tail is usually

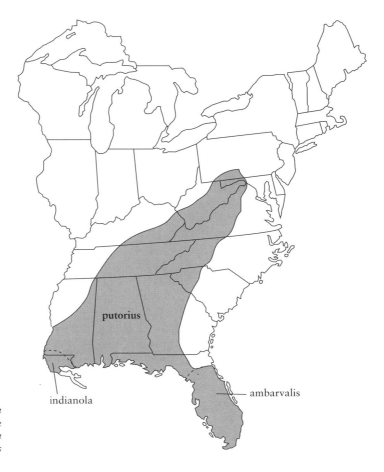

*Distribution of the eastern spotted skunk,* Spilogale putorius, *in the eastern United States*

*Scent glands of spotted skunk, everted
(Roger W. Barbour)*

held in an upright plume, always ready to be thrown over the back so that the rank effluvium may be discharged unimpeded from the anal glands. If the adversary persists, the skunk will spray, as a last resort. The stance when spraying is with both head and rump toward the adversary. The spray, which looks like skim milk with curds, is white to greenish yellow. The active component is mercaptan, a sulfide. Skunks can spray for several meters, with some accuracy, and can expel more than once before replenishing their spray. The odor can be nauseating and can cause momentary blindness.

The claws of skunks are used for digging, and those of the spotted skunk are useful for climbing, as well. Those of the forefeet of *Spilogale* are about 7 mm long, more than twice as long as those of the hindfeet.

Dens can be in any kind of protected area—crevices, buildings, foundations, hollow logs, often the burrows of other animals, such as woodchucks, armadillos, or even gopher tortoises—and occasionally a skunk will dig its own burrow. Skunks usually make nests of grass

or other suitable material. Dens are sometimes shared by two or more individuals at a time; at other times, dens are used alternately. But there is no sharing of the den when babies are present.

Scats, tracks, odor, and hair around burrows are the best indications of this skunk's presence. Scats, the best of these signs, are deposited anywhere along the skunks' runways, or on beams or braces, where skunks hole up in buildings. Each scat is about a centimeter in diameter and irregular in shape, and scat accumulation may reach a depth of 5 cm. Odor can also be a helpful sign; with a little experience one can distinguish the musk of spotted from that of striped skunks. Tracks are of several types. When the animal is hunting at a deliberate pace, the hind feet are placed in the tracks of the front, with a spacing of 13 or 14 cm (4 or 4.5 inches). A half-bounding gait leaves tracks in pairs, like those of weasels, the pairs roughly 23 to 36 cm (9 to 15 inches) apart. When the spotted skunk gallops, its tracks somewhat resemble those of the striped skunk.

The spotted skunk is almost entirely nocturnal, and seldom is abroad even on bright moonlit nights. Spotted skunks do not hibernate, but they may become inactive or even enter a winter sleep during bad weather. They are playful creatures, often romping with others of their kind like kittens.

FOOD AND FEEDING. *Spilogale*, like its larger cousin the striped skunk, is omnivorous, but it feeds heavily on many kinds of invertebrates, particularly crickets, grasshoppers, beetles, grubs, and earthworms. It is much quicker and more agile than the striped skunk, and will often catch small mammals, including many mice, baby rabbits, and others, especially during winter and spring. In summer and fall it eats fruit, corn, invertebrates, birds, and birds' eggs. The question arises, how does it catch birds. We assume this usually happens at night with the birds asleep or struggling to escape in the dark. In subduing birds and mice, it attacks the back first, then kills with a neck bite. It will root in peanut fields for the oily nuts, and feed on fallen persimmons and various fruits in season. Lizards, small snakes, and offal are not disdained.

Spotted skunks do not store food, but will exploit caches stored by weasels. They will also steal eggs and kill young chicks. They eat chicken eggs by biting into the side or end and lapping out the contents. An egg too large to be handled in this way will be straddled and kicked backwards with a hind foot. This process is repeated until the egg cracks against an object.

REPRODUCTION AND DEVELOPMENT. Mating is in late March and April, and the females produce two to four young (up to six) in early spring. The natal nest is in a woodchuck burrow, in a hollow log, under a foundation, or in some other protected place. Gestation is about 50–65 days in the eastern spotted skunk, and implantation is not delayed. This contrasts with the western spotted skunk (considered by most to be the same species), which incorporates delayed implantation into a total gestation of 210–230 days. Sometimes there is a second litter, following breeding in September, the young this time being produced in late October or early November. Second litters are more common in the south. The newborn are naked, but the growing hair visible beneath the skin surface already indicates how the color pattern will develop, and by 21 days the young resemble the adults in pattern. The eyes open at about a month, musk can be emitted at 46 days, weaning is at 54 days, and adult size is attained by 90 days. Males do not participate in the rearing of the young.

POPULATION CHARACTERISTICS. Little is known of the population biology of this species, but spotted skunks apparently do not occupy territories. They move from one area to another when not in the reproductive season, apparently denning wherever they happen to be, either alone or with others, depending on chance. When a female bears young, of course, there is a more permanent den. One density estimate, in Iowa, is 8.8 skunks per square km (14.2 per square mile). Alton Kinlaw found that there were at least 16 spotted skunks on a 5-km (3-mile) section of Canaveral National Seashore in Florida in 1982.

ENEMIES. Unless food is scarce and they are very hungry, few animals will tackle a skunk. Coyotes, great horned owls and perhaps barred owls, and a few other predators will occasion-ally kill one, but we suspect that even the owls and coyotes, hungry or not, are more likely to pass up a skunk and stick to their normal fare of smaller mammals. George Lowery states that dogs are the most important enemy of the spotted skunk in Louisiana. Humans, one way or another, have always been trouble for skunks.

PARASITES AND DISEASE. Ectoparasites include two biting lice, two fleas, and a tick. Endoparasites include a trematode, two cestodes, four nematodes, and an acanthocephalan. Among the nematodes, *Skrjabingylus* sp. infects the frontal sinuses of high percentages of these skunks, causing lesions to the frontal region of the skull. Rabies is the most important disease of skunks, but it occurs mostly in the striped skunk.

RELATION TO HUMANS. Humans are the chief enemies of skunks, formerly taking them for their pelts and, unfortunately, often killing them for no good reason. Many are killed on the highway. The pelts were at one time in demand, for they make up into beautiful jackets. The price paid the trapper was low, but in spite of this many thousands reached the market annually.

AREAS FOR FURTHER WORK. Much remains to be done. Radiotelemetry studies in an area where this species is common should provide much needed information on the behavior and ecology of these animals. A detailed study of their ectoparasites is also in order; surely they have mites, for example, but none has been found to date. More work is needed in the critical areas (Wyoming, Colorado, and northeastern New Mexico) where the ranges of the "eastern" and "western" reproductive forms of the spotted skunk approach each other, to determine whether the two types occur together or intergrade, if indeed they meet.

## SUBSPECIES

Two separate species of spotted skunks, *Spilogale ambarvalis* of Florida and *S. indianola* of Louisiana, were originally described from the east, in addition to *S. putorius*, but they were both later reduced to subspecies rank within *S. putorius* by Van Gelder (1959). Spotted skunks, genus *Spilogale*, occur throughout most

*Striped skunk,* Mephitis mephitis
*(Roger W. Barbour)*

of the United States, and most of Mexico and central America, and several subspecies have been described. Van Gelder (1959) revised the genus and considered *Spilogale* to include just two species, *S. putorius*, a variable species occurring throughout most of the range of the genus, and *S. pygmaea*, occurring along the Pacific Coast of Mexico. Ewer (1973), however, argued that *S. pygmaea* is also conspecific with *S. putorius*, and the way the ranges of the two abut suggests that that is the case.

Mead (1968), meanwhile, had found major physiological, cytological, and morphological differences between eastern and western spotted skunks, and suggested that they might constitute separate species, and Jones et al. (1992) accepted *S. putorius* and *S. gracilis* (a western entity) as separate, but both Hall (1981) and Wilson and Reeder (1993) consider eastern and western spotted skunks as conspecific. Any consideration of them as two separate species must confront the fact that their ranges abut over a great distance, a rather peculiar distribution pattern for distinct species. We agree, then, with Van Gelder (1959), Hall (1981), and Wilson and Reeder (1993) in considering all spotted skunks of the United States to be of one species, *S. putorius*. Moreover, the various eastern U.S. populations show no isolation of which we are aware, and we have not recognized any of them as separate subspecies.

*Spilogale putorius putorius* Linnaeus
  As described above.
  Type locality: South Carolina.

Other currently recognized eastern subspecies:
  *S. putorius ambarvalis* Bangs

## LITERATURE

Ewer, R. F. 1973. *The Carnivores*. Ithaca, N.Y.: Cornell Univ. Press. 494 pp.

Hall, E. R. 1981. *The Mammals of North America*. 2 vols. New York: John Wiley & Sons. 1181 pp.

Howard, W. E., and R. E. Marsh. 1982. Spotted and hog-nosed skunks *Spilogale putorius* and allies. In: J. A. Chapman and G. A. Feldhamer, eds., *Wild Mammals of North America*, pp. 664–673. Baltimore: Johns Hopkins Univ. Press.

Jones, J. K., Jr., R. S. Hoffmann, D. W. Rice, C. Jones, R. J. Baker, and M. D. Engstrom. 1992. Revised checklist of North American mammals north of Mexico, 1991. Occ. Pap. Mus. Texas Tech Univ. No. 146. 23 pp.

Mead, R. A. 1968. Reproduction in western forms of the spotted skunk (genus *Spilogale*). *J. Mammal.* 49: 373–390.

Van Gelder, R. G. 1959. A taxonomic revision of the spotted skunk (genus *Spilogale*). *Bull. Amer. Mus. Nat. Hist.* 117 (Art. 5): 229–392.

## Striped Skunk *Mephitis mephitis* (Schreber)

DESCRIPTION. So well known as to need little description, the striped skunk is a robust, medium-sized animal characterized by long black fur, a prominent, forked white dorsal stripe, and a long, bushy tail also bearing a white stripe. Both the pattern and the extent of white in the pattern are variable. The dorsal white stripes are usually broad, but may be narrow or all but absent, the white restricted to a dash on the nape. There is often a median white stripe between the eyes.

The claws of the forefeet, about twice the length of those of the hind feet, are well adapted for digging. The snout is pointed, and the ears are small and rounded. The dorsal profile of the skull is characteristically angulate, the top of it flat forward to the eye sockets, then sloping toward the nose. The auditory bullae are constricted and little inflated. The last upper molariform tooth is quadrangular and very large, and has an outer cutting ridge. The palate ends at about the posterior margin of the first upper molar. The anal glands are well developed.

The name "skunk" is of Algonquian origin.

MEASUREMENTS. Overall measurements for skunks from throughout their range are total length 575–800, tail 184–393, and hind foot 60–90 mm, but a sample of skunks from Illinois showed almost as much variation. Weights range from 1.2 to 5.3 kg (2.6 to 11.7 lbs).

Twenty-six individuals from Indiana averaged: total length 586 (447–635), tail 221 (159–290), hind foot 63 (48–71); and weight 1797 (907–2810) grams (1.6–5.1 lbs). Males are larger than females.

Diploid number = 50.

TOOTH FORMULA

$$\frac{3}{3} \ \frac{1}{1} \ \frac{3}{3} \ \frac{1}{2} \ = \ 34$$

DISTRIBUTION. The striped skunk occurs throughout the United States and southern Canada and south into northern Mexico. It is widely distributed over the eastern United States, from Maine and Wisconsin south to Florida and Louisiana, but is absent in southeasternmost Louisiana, eastern North Carolina, and extreme northeastern South Carolina.

*Distribution of the striped skunk*, Mephitis mephitis, *in the eastern United States*

HABITAT. Striped skunks are most abundant in agricultural areas, grassy fields, brushy areas, ravines, drainage ditches, hedgerows, and mixed-crop lands. They are often found around buildings.

HABITS. The skunk is of course well known, but not because of its handsome coat and gentle ways. Its chief claim to fame is its powerful effluvium, which is housed in the large anal glands. The skunk can project scent from one gland or both, through separate ducts from the glands to nipples that can be protruded from the anus. There is no question of the protective nature of these glands, which can shoot scent up to 5 meters (16 feet) when with the wind (more often, the spray reaches about 3 meters, or 8–10 feet). When startled or cornered, a skunk will generally face an intruder, arch and elevate the tail and erect the tail hairs, chatter its teeth and stomp the ground with the front feet, then shuffle backwards. If these threats are not sufficient, the skunk will face the intruder, twist the posterior quarters around, evert the anus to expose the scent-gland papillae, and quickly discharge the glands. A slight turning motion of the skunk's hindquarters ensures that the spray covers more territory. The glands are used only in times of great stress, for the warning of the uplifted tail is usually sufficient to intimidate all but the most insistent foe. The odor and the musk can cause nausea and temporary blindness. The active component of the musk is butyl mercaptan (chemically, it is trans-2-butene-1-thiol, 3-methyl-1-butanethiol, and trans-2-butenyl methyl disulfide). The striped skunk occasionally uses the handstand in its defensive posture, but that behavior is much more characteristic of spotted skunks. Verts (1967) saw the handstand only in young striped skunks.

Skunks are mainly nocturnal; one encountered in the daytime could be rabid or afflicted with distemper. They are abroad most of the night and return to their dens or resting sites before dawn. As fall approaches they put on much body fat, and in cold weather spend less time afield. During cold periods in winter, skunks may sleep for extended periods, the female and the young of the year usually the soundest sleepers. They do not hibernate, however, for their body temperature drops but a few degrees, from about 37° to 31°C (98 to 88°F). A warm spell, in fact, will tempt the skunk from its lair, its telltale tracks leaving an apparently aimless trail through the snow-covered fields and woods. In the southern part of their range, skunks remain active throughout the year.

Skunks can squeal, screech, grunt, growl, coo, twitter, and hiss, though they are usually silent. They can swim, but do so only when necessary. Skunks usually amble along at about 1.6 kph (1.0 mph), but they can gallop at speeds up to 16.5 kph (10 mph).

The burrow of a woodchuck, armadillo, fox, muskrat, or badger, or the sanctuary of an outbuilding or other protected place, serves as a retreat, but in areas where other burrowers are uncommon, the skunk may dig its own burrow. Burrows dug by the skunk itself are usually about 2 to 8 meters (6 to 25 feet) long, but may be longer, and they are about a meter (3 feet) deep. One to three chambers are included, each 30 to 38 cm (12 to 15 inches) in diameter, and the skunk makes a nest of dried grass in one of them. There may be up to five entrances to the burrow, all usually well hidden, each entrance about 20 cm (8 inches) in diameter. Natal and winter dens are below ground, but in other circumstances skunks often use above-ground retreats.

Skunks are not social animals, but they will gather in communal dens, especially in winter, when as many as 15 have been taken from a single large burrow. Communal dens usually consist of females, or females with one male, but the composition of the group in a den is continually changing. Males rarely form communal dens.

Other than during the reproductive period, the striped skunk is a rather docile creature. It usually goes about its business seemingly paying little heed to its surroundings, as it can afford to do, for its warning coloration is well known to both people and predators. During the reproductive season, however, a pregnant female will become aggressive, vocalizing and stomping her feet, fighting the male if he attempts to mount.

FOOD AND FEEDING. In spring and summer, skunks eat primarily invertebrates and small mammals; in fall and winter, plant material, particularly fruits, becomes important. But they will eat a great variety of the foods available to them, and they often make a nuisance of themselves about camps by raiding the garbage can. They dig grubs from lawns or golf courses, and they claw apart rotten logs and turn over rocks to find insects. Some of the more heavily eaten invertebrates are beetles and their larvae, grasshoppers and crickets, earthworms, lepidopterous larvae, spiders, snails, ants, bees and wasps, and crayfish. They eat quantities of may beetles and their grubs. Later, they haunt the wild raspberry and blackberry thickets, or blueberry bushes, filling themselves with the ripe fruit. Skunks raid beehives by scratching them to force the bees out. As fall approaches, wild cherries, ground cherry (*Physalis*), crickets, grasshoppers, and lepidopterous larvae become their mainstays, adding to the substantial layer of fat they have been acquiring since midsummer, fat they will use during the cold months (November to March). During that time female skunks may lose from 32 to 55% of their weight, males from 15 to 48%. Laying on fat, reducing aboveground activity, denning communally, and slightly reducing body temperature are all means by which skunks conserve energy in the winter months.

Skunks also take numerous vertebrates, especially *Microtus*, *Peromyscus*, and the eggs of ground-nesting birds. They must corner the mice under a tree stump or in a hollow log. They break birds' eggs by rolling them between their hind legs until they break upon a hard object. They catch insects and small vertebrates by pouncing on them with their front feet. We suspect that olfactory cues are most important in the hunt for vertebrates and invertebrates, followed by auditory and then visual cues. Caterpillars and toads are rolled on the ground before being eaten, the caterpillars apparently to scrape off hair or spines, the toads perhaps to rub away the secretion of the parotoid glands.

REPRODUCTION AND DEVELOPMENT. Skunks are polygamous. In northern climates, they become very active in mid-February, and the woods are covered with the tracks of wandering males searching mates. Mating occurs from mid-February to mid-April, but is concentrated in the third week of March. Loss of a litter or pseudopregnancy may lead to a later mating. Implan-

tation occurs about 19 days after mating, and gestation is usually 62 to 66 days. The four to eight young (extremes are two to ten) are born in May or early June. The newborn are blind, helpless, and hairless, but the striped pattern is already evident beneath the skin surface. They weigh 32–35 grams at birth, about 210 grams at four to six weeks. The eyes open at about 22 (17–35) days. Musk is present at birth and can be emitted on day eight. In June, following a six- to eight-week nursing period, mother and young begin to hunt together. A mother on the move, her young following in serpentine fashion, is a pleasant sight. Not long after these early hunts the young disperse.

POPULATION CHARACTERISTICS. In one study, home ranges averaged 234 and 284 ha (578 and 701 acres) for juvenile females and males, respectively, and 378 and 512 ha (934 and 1265 acres) for adult females and males. Skunks usually do not range more than 0.8 km (0.5 mile) from their dens to feed, and they often travel to the same feeding area by the same route for several nights, changing to a new den as new feeding areas become available or necessary.

Striped skunks live up to ten years in captivity, but in nature they survive less than a year on the average, and few live longer than five or six years.

ENEMIES. The mephitic odor of the skunk does not always deter predation, and the great horned owl rather often takes skunks. Bobcats, foxes, coyotes, and badgers have also been known to prey on them, but most predators probably take them only under great stress of hunger. People, with their traps and automobiles, are the main enemies of skunks.

PARASITES AND DISEASE. Striped skunks harbor several parasites: nematodes internally, fleas, lice, mites, and ticks externally. They carry a host-specific mallophagan, *Neotrichodectes mephitidis*, and a host-specific mite, *Echinonyssus staffordi*. Kirkland and Kirkland (1983) found cranial damage in skunks due to nematodes of the genus *Skrjabingylus*, varying from little or no damage to gross deformation of the frontal sinus region accompanied by perforation or erosion of the frontal bones. The frequency of this condition in striped skunks in the east ranged from 57 to 89%. Both the frequency and the severity of damage were greater in more moist areas and in older animals.

Skunks can contract a number of diseases, including distemper, histoplasmosis, tularemia, and Chagas' disease, but rabies is the most important. The striped skunk and the raccoon have now supplanted the dog as the species most often contracting rabies in the Midwest. Skunks contract either the well-known "furious rabies," in the throes of which the animal will attack anything moving, or "dumb rabies," which often leaves the animal completely docile. Dumb rabies is the variety carried in bats, and we suspect that a skunk with dumb rabies has eaten a rabid bat, whereas one with furious rabies has had an encounter with another rabid carnivore. These possibilities are currently under investigation, but strains of bat rabies have been found and identified in rabid carnivores.

Leptospirosis is another disease often common in skunks, ranging in occurrence from 13.6 to 60.1% in samples of skunks from Georgia, Illinois, Louisiana, and Pennsylvania. The disease is caused by a bacterium, *Leptospira* sp., and can be transmitted to humans through contact with infected water or mud. Symptoms are fever, muscular pain, and jaundice.

RELATION TO HUMANS. Skunks are not much liked by people, chiefly because of their odor, but also because they may learn to visit the poultry yard, and they may destroy numerous duck nests. All that aside, however, their destruction of insects such as cutworms, armyworms, crickets, grasshoppers, the larvae of scarab (grubs) and other beetles, and many other forms must do much to help keep these insects in check, and on balance they deserve our gratitude.

The thick fur of the skunk makes an attractive garment, and in an earlier day many thousands were trapped each year. The pelts varied greatly in value. A good New York skunk pelt brought $12 in 1928, but by 1976, New York pelts averaged only $2. Indiana pelts brought about $5 in 1995. Those mostly black brought the best price.

Thousands of skunks are destroyed on the roads every year. Hamilton once counted 27 dead skunks on a 34-mile stretch of paved road in New York during October. Insecticides are suspected of being toxic to skunks. Descented skunks have often been kept in captivity, and some compare them to cats as pets.

It is said that skunk odor can be removed from clothes by rinsing them in water with ammonia, and from the body by ammonia rinse, tomato juice, or a sponge saturated with turpentine.

AREAS FOR FURTHER WORK. Additional work is needed on communal denning; on the acquisition, strains, and transmission of dumb and furious rabies; and on populations and home ranges of skunks.

## SUBSPECIES

We are unaware of any primary isolating mechanisms separating the populations constituting the described subspecies, and we therefore do not recognize them as such.

*Mephitis mephitis mephitis* (Schreber)
As described above.
Type locality: Eastern Canada (= Quebec).
Other currently recognized eastern subspecies:
    *M. mephitis avia* Bangs
    *M. mephitis elongata* Bangs
    *M. mephitis hudsonica* Richardson
    *M. mephitis nigra* (Peale & Beauvois)

### LITERATURE

Bailey, T. N. 1971. Biology of striped skunks on a southwestern Lake Erie marsh. *Amer. Midland Nat.* 85: 196–207.

Godin, A. J. 1982. Striped and hooded skunks. In: J. A. Chapman and G. A. Feldhamer, eds., *Wild Mammals of North America*, pp. 674–687. Baltimore: Johns Hopkins Univ. Press.

Hamilton, W. J., Jr. 1963. Reproduction of the striped skunk in New York. *J. Mammal.* 44: 123–124.

Kirkland, G. L., Jr., and C. J. Kirkland. 1983. Patterns of variation in cranial damage in skunks (Mustelidae: Mephitinae) presumably caused by nematodes of the genus *Skrjabingylus* Petrov 1927 (Metastrongyloidea). *Canadian J. Zool.* 61: 2913–2920.

Mutch, G. R. P., and M. Aleksiuk. 1977. Ecological aspects of winter dormancy in the striped skunk (*Mephitis mephitis*). *Canadian J. Zool.* 55: 607–615.

Storm, G. L. 1972. Daytime retreats and movements of skunks on farmlands in Illinois. *J. Wildl. Mgmt.* 36: 31–45.

Verts, B. J. 1967. *The Biology of the Striped Skunk*. Urbana: Univ. Illinois Press. 218 pp.

Wade-Smith, J., and B. J. Verts. 1982. *Mephitis mephitis*. **Mammalian Species No. 173.** Amer. Soc. Mammal. 7 pp.

## CATS AND ALLIES, Family Felidae

Biologists generally agree that there are about 37 species of cats in the world, but just how many genera they constitute continues to provoke a good deal of controversy. Some authors place all cats in just two genera, *Acinonyx* (the cheetah) and *Felis* (everything else), while others recognize as many as a dozen or so genera. The house cat, most will agree, is a member of the genus *Felis*, and the three species of native cats of the eastern United States are also often included in that genus. The bobcat and lynx, however, are often included in their own genus, *Lynx*, and the mountain lion is often placed in the genus *Puma*. The controversy, of course, revolves around the question of relatedness: which cats are the most related to each other, and how close are those relations, evolutionarily speaking? Cats are a morphologically uniform group, as compared to most other mammalian families. We have used Jones et al. (1992) as our base list of species, and we have followed that source in using the genera *Felis* and *Lynx* for the cats present today in the eastern United States.

There are no cats in the Australian region, but otherwise cats are cosmopolitan. They are digitigrade (walk on their toes) and have five toes on the front feet, four on the hind, each toe bearing a retractable claw. Their skulls are very rounded. Cats, perhaps along with some of the smaller weasels, are the most carnivorous animals of the order Carnivora, feeding almost entirely on vertebrates. They are often at the top of the food chain, and most feline species have few enemies other than man. They use vision to locate prey, and they are one of the few groups of mammals that have color vision. They see about as well as we do in daylight, but their vision in low light is superior. All of the North American cats have the ability to purr, but not to roar. Their long, stiff, highly sensitive vibrissae are useful for sensing objects in the dark. Many felids are solitary, highly secretive tree dwellers and agile climbers that live in remote wooded areas, but this characterization certainly does not apply to the bob-

cat, panther, or house cat, and probably does not apply to the lynx. Many cats are near extinction because of man's relentless persecution, an assault pursued both from a primal fear of the big cats and from the lure of income from the sale of their skins.

The cats of the eastern United States are the two short-tailed species, the bobcat and the lynx, both of the genus *Lynx*, and the two long-tailed species, the mountain lion and the house cat, both here included in the genus *Felis*.

### LITERATURE CITED

Jones, J. K., Jr., R. S. Hoffmann, D. W. Rice, C. Jones, R. J. Baker, and M. D. Engstrom. 1992. Revised checklist of North American mammals north of Mexico, 1991. Occasional Papers Museum Texas Tech University 146: 1–23. (Earlier editions of this checklist are cited in the 1992 work.)

### KEY TO THE GENERA
### OF THE FAMILY FELIDAE

1. Tail long; upper molariform teeth
   (cheek teeth) four . . . . . . . . . . . . . . . . . . . . . . *Felis*
1. Tail short; upper molariform teeth
   three . . . . . . . . . . . . . . . . . . . . . . . . . *Lynx* (p. 488)

## Cats of the Genus *Felis*

As delimited here, there are only two species of the genus *Felis* in the eastern United States: the house cat, *Felis catus*, and the Florida panther, a subspecies of the mountain lion, *Felis concolor*.

### KEY TO THE CATS OF THE GENUS *FELIS*

1. Total length of animal much less than
   150 cm; skull about 8–10 cm long . . . . . . . *F. catus*
1. Total length of animal 150 cm or more;
   skull about 17–24 cm long . . . . . . . . . *F. concolor*

## Domestic Cat, House Cat
## *Felis catus* Linnaeus

The house cat was domesticated from the wild cat, *Felis silvestris*, which at one time was found extensively in deciduous woodland savanna and steppe of Africa and extreme southwestern Asia. Wild populations of *F. silvestris* have since de-

clined or been extirpated over much of the species' former range. Cats were found in towns in
Palestine at least 7000 years ago, but it was the
Egyptians, who took cats to be divine, who began serious domestication about 4000 years
ago. Clutton-Brock (1969) compared morphological data on contemporary cats to those from
cats interred in tombs in Jericho and found that
little change has occurred over the millennia.

DESCRIPTION. As cats go, the domestic cat is a
small one, about 75 cm in total length, almost
half of which is tail. There are more than 30
breeds, and the color and color patterns vary
greatly, since mixed breeds are probably more
common than pure breeds. The pupil of the eye
is a vertical slit in most house cats, round in
Persian cats. Lynxes and bobcats, both averaging much larger than house cats, have short
(bobbed) tails, and mountain lions are considerably larger than house cats.

MEASUREMENTS. The head and body together
average about 460 to 522 (300–800), the tail
about 300 (280–350) mm. Weight is 3 to 6 kg
(6.6 to 13 lbs). The largest known house cat
weighed 21.3 kg (46.95 lbs).
  Diploid number = 38.

TOOTH FORMULA
$$\frac{3}{3} \quad \frac{1}{1} \quad \frac{3}{2} \quad \frac{1}{1} \; = \; 30$$

DISTRIBUTION. This species is kept as a house
pet throughout much of the world. The domestic cat is usually not included in a book of this
sort, but individuals often escape and become
feral, thus have significant impact on natural
ecosystems and therefore are included.

HABITAT. The great majority of house cats live
in or around houses, barns or other buildings,
but completely feral cats presumably live in
or near grasslands or wastelands, raising their
young in some protected area such as a burrow,
thicket, rock pile, or hollow log. In the corn
belt, free-ranging cats spend most of their hunting time in linear edges containing cover, such
as roadsides or hedgerows; they spend relatively little time in corn or soybean fields. In
other areas, they spend time in grassy areas and

thickets, or wherever they can find small birds
or mammals (particularly *Microtus*) to hunt.

HABITS. Most free-ranging cats are pets living
in buildings, and as such are fed. Many, however, hunt, whether well fed or not, and compete with native predators for food. They appear to have a great impact on native wildlife in
suburban and agricultural areas, and they can
even be found deep in the forests in the mountains of North Carolina. They have been associated with extinctions of endemic prey species
on islands, and they have been implicated as
important predators in Wisconsin and Illinois.
We suspect that they have had an effect on the
decline of songbirds in the east. Males immi-
grating into an area must fight with the males
already there to determine their place in the
peck order, or they will be driven away.
  Haspel and Calhoon (1993) found that activity peaked at 0100 hours and again just before
dawn. Cats were more active at higher temperatures, less active during rain. House cats may
alternate between solitary and group behavior
for maximum efficiency in the obtaining of food
(Laundré, 1977).
  The footprints of the house cat are nearly round
and show no claw marks. The prints are usually
in a straight line, the smaller hind feet being
placed in the tracks of the larger front feet. The
tracks are about 22 or 23 cm (9 inches) apart,
and can easily be confused with those of foxes.

FOOD AND FEEDING. The stalking behavior of
domestic cats is frequently observed and familiar to most. Cats will remain on post for long
periods, wholly or partially hidden, then pounce
on prey as it appears. Mice, especially meadow
voles, are often the prey. Some of the more important foods found in 81 stomachs of house
cats (Latham, 1950; Mitchell and Beck, 1992)
were various mice and shrews (meadow and
woodland voles, white-footed mice, and short-
tailed shrews most often), birds, rabbits, insects,
squirrels, young rats, frogs, lizards, snakes, and
grass. House cats often deposit their various
prey on their owner's doorstep. The basis for
this behavior is not known, but it is probably instinctive, and more likely to occur where a kill
has been made in a situation where food is regularly supplied. Is it possible that it might be a

token presented to people perceived to be family members?

REPRODUCTION AND DEVELOPMENT. Ovulation in house cats is induced by copulation, and a female may produce two litters of one to eight young per year. Free-ranging house cats in Illinois produced an average of 1.6 litters per year, and an average of 4.4 kittens per litter, after a 62- to 65-day gestation. Births occurred throughout the year, most in March through August. The young weigh 85 to 110 grams at birth, and their eyes open at nine to 20 days. They are weaned at about eight weeks, and can fend for themselves by about four months of age. Male/female pair bonds can extend beyond the reproductive season, but a female may mate with more than one male in a season.

POPULATION CHARACTERISTICS. Feral males have larger home ranges than females. In Illinois (Warner, 1985), those of males averaged 228 ha (560 acres); those of females, 112 ha (275 acres). The home range of a male often incorporates the home ranges of more than one female. In Sweden, females live alone or in groups around buildings (Liberg, 1980), and their ranges (about 40–50 ha, or 110–125 acres) almost completely overlap, but between different female groups there is almost no overlap. Most females remained at one place throughout life, but a few moved, mostly to areas lacking other females. There were always six to eight males, with partially overlapping ranges, in the general area of the females. Young males remained at their birthplace until reaching the age of a year and a half to three years, then dispersed. Males urine-mark their territory.

Virginia Powell estimated the density of cats that hunt outside (at least sometimes) in the Powell neighborhood in Raleigh, North Carolina, at greater than 70 per square km (181 per square mile). Warner (1985) estimated the number of cats in an area of 5182 ha (12,800 acres) typical of the corn belt in Illinois at 326 (63 per square km, or 166 per square mile) in late summer. Estimates for Baltimore and Illinois (63 and 70 per square km, or 166 and 181 per square mile), were surprisingly similar. Haspel and Calhoon (1993) found cats to have been more than twice as abundant in a rundown apartment area as they were in a better-maintained residential area, in Brooklyn, New York, about 80 vs. 35 in two 16-ha (40-acre) plots. One house cat lived to be 34 years old, but few probably live beyond 10–14 years.

ENEMIES. Although cats often hold their own against dogs, dogs are presumably their traditional enemies, and a large dog will often chase, catch, and kill an adult cat by shaking it. Many other carnivores must prey on cats, especially the young, and numerous house cats are killed on the highway. In a study in Illinois, 26% were killed by vehicles, 17% by disease, 8% by humans, 7% by dogs, 5% by other cats, 4% by winter storms, 3% by machinery, 3% by farm chemicals, 2% by old age, and 1% by livestock; 27% either died of unknown causes or dispersed.

PARASITES AND DISEASE. House cats are parasitized by fleas, ear mites, mange, nematodes, and cestodes, and they can contract feline leukemia, rabies, and distemper. A sore may become infected with blowfly larvae.

RELATION TO HUMANS. We keep millions of house cats as pets or as mousers, and we tolerate their depredations on wildlife.

AREAS FOR FURTHER WORK. As we have with the domestic dog, we have substituted artificial for natural selection, and studies of the genetics and evolution of feral and domestic cats, especially in comparison with populations of wild *Felis silvestris* in Africa and Asia, could give valuable insight into the evolutionary process. Further studies of the impact of feral and domestic cats on wildlife populations are also in order. Comparison of the behavior of purely domestic, semi-feral, and completely feral house cats would be in order, as regards hunting and reproductive behavior, time budgets, social interactions, territories, shared feeding areas, and peck orders.

## SUBSPECIES

There are more than 30 different breeds of domestic cat, but no subspecies have been named. See the subspecies discussion for the domestic dog.

LITERATURE

Bradshaw, J. W. 1992. *The Behaviour of the Domestic Cat*. Wallingford, U.K.: CAB International.

Clutton-Brock, J. 1969. Carnivore remains from the excavations of the Jericho tell. In: P. J. Ucko and G. W. Dimbleby, eds., *Domestication and Exploitation of Plants and Animals*. London: Duckworth.

Haspel, C., and R. E. Calhoon. 1993. Activity patterns of free-ranging cats in Brooklyn, New York. *J. Mammal.* 74: 1–8.

Kitchner, A. 1991. *Natural History of the Wild Cats*. Ithaca, N.Y.: Cornell Univ. Press. 200 pp.

Latham, R. M. 1950. The food of predaceous animals in northeastern United States. Harrisburg: Pa. Game Comm. 69 pp.

Laundré, J. 1977. The daytime behaviour of domestic cats in a free-roaming population. *Anim. Behav.* 25: 990–998.

Liberg, O. 1984. Food habits and prey impact by feral and house-based domestic cats in a rural area in southern Sweden. *J. Mammal.* 65: 424–432.

———. 1980. Spacing patterns in a population of rural free roaming domestic cats. *Oikos* 35: 336–349.

Mitchell, J. C., and R. A. Beck. 1992. Free-ranging domestic cat predation on native vertebrates in rural and urban Virginia. *Virg. J. Sci.* 43: 197–207.

Pond, G. 1972. *The Complete Cat Encyclopedia*. New York: Crown. 384 pp.

Turner, D. C., and P. Bateson. 1988. *The Domestic Cat: The Biology of Its Behaviour*. Cambridge, U.K.: Cambridge Univ. Press.

Warner, R. E. 1985. Demography and movements of free-ranging domestic cats in rural Illinois. *J. Wildl. Mgmt.* 499: 340–346.

## Mountain Lion, Florida Panther, Puma, Cougar

*Felis concolor* Linnaeus          Color plate 20

DESCRIPTION. The mountain lion, also called panther (especially in Florida), painter, puma, cougar, or American lion, is a large, pale-brown, unspotted cat with a relatively small, rounded head and a long, dark-tipped tail. The ears are short and rounded, the limbs stout. The underparts, inner ear, lower cheeks, chin, and lips are white, and there is a dark spot at the base of the whiskers. There have been many reports of "black panthers" throughout the range of the species, but to date the only authentic case of a black panther is from Brazil. Young have black spots on a buffy fur until 18 months of age.

MEASUREMENTS. Total length of males is 2.2–2.3 meters (7.3–7.6 feet); of females, 2.0–

*Mountain lion or Florida panther,* Felis concolor *(Roger W. Barbour)*

2.1 meters (6.7–7 feet). Males generally weigh between 55 and 66 kg (121–145 lbs), females between 35 and 45 kg (77–99 lbs).

Diploid number = 38.

TOOTH FORMULA

$$\frac{3}{3} \quad \frac{1}{1} \quad \frac{3}{2} \quad \frac{1}{1} \; = \; 30$$

DISTRIBUTION. This species once occurred from parts of southern Canada south through nearly all of the United States and central America and into South America. It occurred throughout the eastern United States, but it disappeared over much of this range during the latter half of the last century. The last mountain lions in Pennsylvania were killed in 1871, in Virginia in 1882, and in West Virginia in 1887. The Adirondacks were the last stronghold of the mountain lion in the Northeast, the latest record from that wilderness being in 1903. The species apparently survived, at least for a time, in New Brunswick, and perhaps also in isolated pockets elsewhere, such as in southern Georgia and Alabama. Individuals moved from New Brunswick into Maine, where one was trapped at Little St. John Lake, Somerset County, in 1938 and was mounted (Wright, 1961). One was shot in Tuscaloosa County, Alabama, in 1956, and plaster casts of tracks and a reliable sight observation were made in Clarke County, Alabama, in 1961 and 1966, respectively.

The only known reproducing population of mountain lions in the eastern United States today is in southwest Florida, extending northward to the latitude of Lake Okechobee. The current documented range in Florida includes half or more each of Monroe, Dade, Collier, Henry, Glades, and Broward counties and part of Palm Beach County. There are also 12 confirmed records north of this area between 1983 and 1988, and some since.

Not long ago, the Florida population of the mountain lion (the "Florida panther") was estimated at no more than 30 individuals. As of May 1992, however, 24 Florida panthers were radio-collared, and the minimum number today has to be greater than 30. Perhaps about 50 panthers would be a more realistic estimate.

Persecution by hunters, disappearance of suitable habitat, and the fact that its main food, the white-tailed deer, was greatly reduced or extirpated over much of its range early in this century all contributed to the near elimination of this species in eastern United States. The Florida panther, a distinct subspecies of the more wide-ranging mountain lions of the west, is one of this nation's most critically endangered mammals. Until passage of the Endangered Species Act in 1973, it had no federal protection. A recovery team was appointed in 1976 to develop a recovery plan, and the plan was approved by

originally occurred throughout the eastern United States

*Distribution of the mountain lion, or puma,* Felis concolor, *in the eastern United States*

the U.S. Fish and Wildlife Service in 1981. Subsequently, a Florida Panther Interagency Committee (U.S. Fish and Wildlife Service, U.S. National Park Service, Florida Game and Fresh Water Fish Commission) was formed, and in 1987 this committee revised the recovery plan. One hopes that the research and management program developed by this committee can save this animal, and its plight does seem to be improving. Because the white-tailed deer is now abundant in many areas, the mountain lion could be reintroduced into various remote regions, although finding space sufficient for such populations to expand and receive local acceptance is a major problem.

Press accounts of these large cats in northeastern United States and in the southern Appalachians appear repeatedly, but most such stories lack authenticity. Throughout the eastern United States, mountain lion, bear, and wolf reports run rampant, even in places like Indiana, where none of these species has existed for many decades. Such reports make it difficult for us to rely on records not supported by good photographs, plaster casts, or actual specimens. See Tischendorf and Ropski (1996) for more information on cougars in the northeastern United States.

Still, deer populations have exploded, and many wilderness areas have been set aside in recent decades. Perhaps the mountain lion will once again roam some of these areas. W. C. Dilger observed the unmistakable snow tracks and tail markings of a mountain lion at a deer kill near Ithaca, New York, in January 1976, but we suspect that this and many of the other recent reports in the east may have been of escaped animals.

HABITAT. Original mountain lion habitat in the eastern United States was that of their principal prey, the white-tailed deer. It consisted of woods or, preferably, a mosaic (with plenty of edge) of wooded and open habitats, including some wetlands. But the only viable population of mountain lions still remaining in the eastern United States is in the ranchlands and wild, impenetrable swamps and hammocks of southwest Florida. Day beds and den sites are in areas with dense vegetation, especially saw palmetto

(Maehr et al., 1990b). Extensive radio-tracking indicates that Florida panthers spend more time in hardwood hammocks, mixed hardwood swamp, and cypress swamp than would be expected by chance, and less time in agricultural or barren land, or shrubby areas, than would be expected (Maehr and Cox, 1995).

The Florida panther requires extensive, biologically diverse habitat for its continued existence. Much of the more suitable land is privately owned, and cooperative agreements must thus be worked out between governmental agencies and the private landowners so that an effective long-range conservation strategy might be developed.

HABITS. This large, shy cat is rarely seen, and its occurrence is usually noted only by the spoor, although day beds—slight, ovoid depressions in the earth or dry leaves about 0.5 to 1 meter (1.5 to 3 feet) wide and 1 to 2 meters (3 to 6 feet) long—can also be found. Saw palmetto was the dominant plant at about two-thirds of the beds found by Maehr et al. (1990b). Mountain lions are solitary, the only groupings being that of a mother and her kittens and that during estrus, when a male may travel for a time with the female. This species, like many other carnivores, is both diurnal and nocturnal, hunting, basically, when it is hungry, although in Florida it currently hunts at night to avoid people. Its eyes are adapted for use day or night. The eye has enlarged pupils and lenses to gather more light at night, but the pupil contracts to the familiar "cat's eye" vertical slit during the day to protect the eye from excessive light. The mountain lion ranges widely, often covering several kilometers on a single, nightly hunting trip.

The ability of the lion to scream has been disputed by many, but it seems clear that these animals are capable of emitting unearthly wails. Charles B. Cory, an eminent naturalist who spent much time in Florida in the latter part of the nineteenth century, remarks that the "cry of the old panther somewhat resembles the screech of a parrot, but is much louder." Ned Hollister (1911) described the cry of the Louisiana panther as "a long-drawn-out, shrill trill, weird and startling. It commences low on the scale, gradually ascends, increasing in volume, and then lowers at the end." But during eight years of work on the mountain lion in Idaho, it was never heard by Seidensticker et al. (1973).

FOOD AND FEEDING. Deer seem to provide much of the food taken by the mountain lion over most of its vast North and South American range, but many other foods are eaten. Domestic livestock are occasionally taken, and there are records for raccoons, skunks, foxes, rabbits, armadillos, birds, turtles, turtles' and birds' eggs, alligators, snakes, and insects, as well. Mountain lions can drag carcasses several times their own weight. In times past, deer and porcupines were apparently the principal foods in the eastern United States. Maehr et al. (1990a) found, by examination of 270 scats, that wild hog (*Sus scrofa*) was the food most commonly eaten in Florida, with 42% frequency, followed by white-tailed deer, 28%; raccoon, 12%; and nine-banded armadillo, 8%.

Mountain lions search for prey by zigzagging back and forth across their home ranges, using cover as available and detecting prey visually. They capture large prey by working to about 15 meters (50 feet) from it, then rushing forward and lunging onto the prey, normally keeping the hind legs on the ground for support, control, and stability. The prey is killed by breaking its neck with a bite at the back of the neck, thus separating the vertebrae and breaking the spinal cord. The prey is often eaten under a bush or tree. When larger prey is killed, the liver, heart, and lungs are usually eaten first. The carnassial teeth are used to cut the meat into pieces, which are then swallowed whole. Portions not eaten are frequently covered with leaves, sticks, pine needles, and the like for later use, and this cache may be visited several times. In July 1940, Dwight Dyess was tracking a panther in the hammocks about 27 km (17 miles) east of Fort Myers, Florida, when he came upon the still-warm body of a half-eaten pig. It was a sow that had been pulled back into the palmettos; the body was covered with several branches. Dyess also found that the embryo from a doe killed by a panther had been removed and eaten.

Mountain lions prey especially on very young and old animals. That these are preferred may simply reflect the fact that they are easier prey, but choosing the young and the old may also be evolutionarily advantageous to the lion, because it emphasizes removing those that contribute the least to the reproduction of the prey population. Mountain lions will sometimes kill more prey than needed, but as weasels do, they appear to do so only in situations of excess prey, and those situations tend to arise only under conditions alien to those the predator has evolved to—the evolved behavior of killing and caching excess prey simply to guarantee the next meal has been driven to the extreme.

REPRODUCTION AND DEVELOPMENT. More than one male may accompany a female early in her estrus. These males may fight, but in the end the dominant male mates with the female. Copulation lasts less than a minute. First breeding is at age two and a half years, and individuals usually breed every other year, except under optimal conditions. Mountain lions may breed throughout the year in Florida, but most births are between April and September, after a gestation period of 82–98 days. The natal den is simple, with minimal nest material. One to three young (averaging about two) are produced in the east, but up to six have been recorded in a litter. Newborns, which are heavily spotted, weigh about 400 grams (14 oz).

The development of the kittens is not unlike that of the kittens of the domestic cat. The eyes and ears open between one and two weeks. Incisors appear at 10 to 20 days, canines at 20 to 30 days, and premolars at 30 to 50 days. Permanent incisors replace the milk teeth at five and a half months, canines at eight months. The kits are weaned at three months, but remain with their mother about one and a half to two years before dispersing. The mother and young communicate by licking, rubbing, and vocalizing, the young producing loud, chirping whistles. The spots disappear at 12–14 weeks, probably when the young begin to hunt with the mother. Weights of the young at 15 days average 1 kg (2.2 lbs); at weaning they weigh 3 to 4 kg (6 to 8 lbs). Sexual dimorphism, as manifested in weight, becomes apparent by the eighth month, and adult weights are attained at about two to four years. Females can remain reproductively active for at least 12 years, males for at least

20 years. The species breeds well in captivity, but many of the matings that have been arranged have been indiscriminate, undertaken without regard for subspecies or locality of origin.

POPULATION CHARACTERISTICS. Mountain lions maintain home ranges, but do not defend them. The home range consists of a "first-order home area," primarily a resting area, and a large hunting area. Home ranges are larger in summer and fall than in winter and spring, and may be mutually exclusive, for the most part, at least in the west. The home ranges of females with young are smaller, but increase to match the needs of the growing young. Home ranges averaged 519 (53–1183) square km, or 200 (20–456) square miles, for males, and 193 square km (74 square miles) for females. Dispersal distances averaged 58.7 km (36 miles) for subadult males (Maehr et al., 1991b). In one study, in Idaho, male home ranges showed little mutual overlap, but each overlapped more than one female range. Female home ranges overlapped, even completely in some cases. In another study, however, in Nevada, the home ranges of males overlapped, whereas those of females did not.

Males, and sometimes females, make scrapes (piles of dirt kicked up by the hind feet) in their home ranges. Scrapes, made primarily by resident males, transients, and females without kittens, measure 15 to 46 cm (6 to 18 inches) long, 15 to 30 cm (6 to 12 inches) wide, and 3 to 5 cm (1 to 2 inches) high. Scrapes are often in draws, on ridges, or on the downhill sides of trees, and they are more frequent when females are in heat. Scrapes apparently serve as boundary markers and thus as signals to other lions, and lions sometimes abruptly change direction at a scrape. Mountain lions will also scratch trees, as house cats do, though this is probably not territorial behavior, but, rather, simply a sharpening of the claws.

Forrester (1992) summarized information on the mortality of Florida panthers. Of 43 panthers documented by M. E. Roelke to have been injured or found dead from 1972 to 1990, 20 were hit by vehicles, seven were illegally killed, five died in fights with other panthers, one died of a heart defect, and five died of disease (rabies). Although highway collisions have been the most frequently documented cases of *known*

death among all panthers, radiotelemetry studies by Davis S. Maehr indicate that natural mortality, primarily intraspecific aggression, is the primary cause of death in the wild population. Annual mortality in the Florida panther averaged 17.2% from 1987 to 1990, a rate similar to that of other unhunted populations. Mortality in Florida was 46.9% by highway deaths, 28.1% by natural causes, 6.2% by illegal shooting, and 6.2% by research activities (Maehr et al., 1991a).

Recently, the literature has emphasized the possibility that problems in natural populations can have their basis in low genetic variability; and mountain lions, like cheetahs, do have low genetic variability. Both animals, however, are large, far-ranging, solitary predators whose greatest problem is probably finding mates. This sort of lifestyle tends to select for greater numbers of incestual matings than is the case in other species and in western populations of mountain lions, and this in turn leads to reduced genetic variability. Forrester (1992) found, in the Florida panthers, a number of anomalies—kinked tail, one testis descended rather than two, and close to 90% sterility. Forrester felt these anomalies to be due to inbreeding and decreased genetic diversity, but there are no data sufficient to support the contention that problems of the Florida mountain lion derive from these sources (Maehr and Caddick, 1995); indeed, the apparent inbreeding has not affected panther behavior or panther demographics. Florida panthers continue to reproduce at a rate that is more than capable of replacing lost residents; turnover among adults is infrequent; kitten survival is high (over 80% per year); and overall mortality in the population is low (less than 20% per year). This suggests that Florida panthers have adjusted well not only to a flat, sea-level, subtropical environment, but also to reduced outbreeding. Since 1987, births of kittens have exceeded deaths. The mean litter size in 25 litters is 1.92 (range one to four), and litters four to 12 months old still averaged 1.89 (range one to four). These values are in line with values that have been recorded in secure western populations. Moreover, several female Florida panthers have reproduced at 18 months of age, earlier than is generally thought to be the case for the species. It may be too early to conclude that the South Florida panther population is growing, but its present characteristics indicate that it certainly has the capacity to grow.

In spite of the lack of evidence that reduced genetic variability is debilitating the genetics of the Florida panther, the state of Florida released eight Texas cougars (*Felis concolor stanleyana*) into South Florida in 1995 with the intent of increasing genetic variability. This is a sad development, for it means that pure *F. concolor coryi* will no longer exist if the Texas cougars succeed in breeding. Worse, perhaps, the addition of new genetic material can itself cause problems (Maehr and Caddick, 1995). Such a drastic step should be taken only when the population's continued existence is clearly in jeopardy. A less drastic technique to accomplish the same goal, if one were felt to be necessary, would be to institute captive breeding and release programs, solely with captive Florida panthers.

ENEMIES. Humans are the only significant enemies of this large predator.

PARASITES AND DISEASE. *Toxoplasma gondii*, which causes toxoplasmosis, and several other protozoan parasites have been found in Florida panthers (Forrester, 1992). The felids are the definitive hosts of these parasites, but armadillos, raccoons, opossums, and roof, cotton, and rice rats all serve as intermediate hosts. Humans and other animals can become infected by eating infected meat or from feces. Toxoplasmosis is usually not serious in adult humans, but it can cause abnormalities such as mental retardation, convulsions, and spasticity in developing human embryos.

Fifteen species of helminths, two trematodes, three cestodes, and ten nematodes are known from Florida panthers (Forrester, 1992). Six species of ticks have been found, the most abundant of which are *Ixodes scapularis*, *Dermacentor variabilis*, and *Ixodes affinis*. One flea (*Ctenocephalides felis*) was found on one individual, and the mite *Lynxacarus morlani* and chigger-mite *Eutrombicula splendens* were both found on one individual. Five keds (dipteran larvae), *Liptoptena mazamae*, were found on two individuals.

Mountain lions have very few ectoparasites, but in the eastern United States they do harbor ticks and fleas. Tapeworms, flukes, and roundworms are the more common parasites of the digestive tract. Maehr et al. (1995) found notoedric mange in a Florida panther and its mother; the condition was successfully treated.

RELATION TO HUMANS. Earlier in this century, the mountain lion was bountied in Florida, but it was considered a game animal from 1950 to 1958. In 1958 it became fully protected by state law, and in 1967 was declared endangered by the U.S. Department of the Interior. These predators are certainly large enough to harm or even kill humans on occasion, and this can be a problem in some places in the west, where mountain lions are often in close proximity to humans. Mountain lions will also kill stock and pets when opportunity arises.

AREAS FOR FURTHER WORK. Radiotelemetry studies on the behavior and ecology of this species, currently under way in Florida, promise considerable return for our efforts, but thorough examinations for endo- and ectoparasites on individuals founds dead should also be done.

## SUBSPECIES

The subspecies designated as occurring in Florida is *Felis concolor coryi*, but whether it should be considered as separate from the northern *F. c. couguar* is questionable. Since it is now completely separated geographically from *F. c. couguar*, which occurs in western North America, we list it as a valid subspecies. *Felis concolor couguar* is now apparently extirpated in the eastern United States, but probably still occurs in southern Ontario and Quebec.

*Felis concolor coryi* Bangs

As described above.

Type locality: Wilderness back of Sebastian, Indian River Co., Florida.

This subspecies presumably has longer legs, but smaller feet, than *F. concolor couguar*. Typically, it has a rusty back and fulvous sides and is pale below. The nasal bones are remarkably broad and high-arched or expanded upward. Five males averaged 2,257 mm (89 inches); four females, 1,984 mm (78 inches). The tail and hind foot of the type specimen, an old adult male, were 760 and 280 mm, respectively, whereas corresponding measurements for an old adult female from the same locality were 670 and 271 mm. Florida mountain lions have a characteristic kink near the ends of their tails, gained presumably through genetic drift in a small population.

## LITERATURE

Currier, M. J. P. 1983. *Felis concolor.* **Mammalian Species No. 200.** Amer. Soc. Mammal. 7 pp.

Dixon, K. R. 1982. Mountain lion *Felis concolor.* In: J. A. Chapman and G. A. Feldhamer, eds., *Wild Mammals of North America*, pp. 711–727. Baltimore: Johns Hopkins Univ. Press.

Forrester, D. J. 1992. *Parasites and Diseases of Wild Mammals in Florida.* Gainesville: Univ. Press of Florida. 459 pp.

Hollister, N. The Louisiana puma. *Proc. Biol. Soc. Wash.* 24: 175–178.

Maehr, D. S., R. C. Belden, E. D. Land, and L. Wilkins. 1990a. Food habits of panthers in southwest Florida. *J. Wildl. Mgmt.* 54: 420–423.

Maehr, D. S., and G. C. Caddick. 1995. Demographic and genetic introgression in the Florida panther. *Conserv. Biol.* 9: 1295–1298.

Maehr, D. S., and J. A. Cox. 1995. Landscape features and panthers in Florida. *Conserv. Biol.* 9: 1008–1019.

Maehr, D. S., E. C. Greiner, J. E. Lanier, and D. Murphy. 1995. Notoedric mange in the Florida panther. *J. Wildl. Diseases* 31: 251–254.

Maehr, D. S., E. D. Land, and M. E. Roelke. 1991a. Mortality patterns of panthers in southwest Florida. *Proc. Ann. Conf. Southeast Assoc. Fish and Wildl. Agencies* 45: 201–207.

Maehr, D. S., E. D. Land, and J. C. Roof. 1991b. Florida panthers. *Natl. Geogr. Research and Explor.* 7: 414–431.

Maehr, D. S., E. D. Land, J. C. Roof, and J. W. McCown. 1990b. Day beds, natal dens and activity of Florida panthers. *Proc. Ann. Conf. Southeast Assoc. Fish and Wildl. Agencies* 44: 310–318.

Nowak, R. M. 1976. The cougar in the United States and Canada. Washington, D.C.: U.S. Fish and Wildl. Serv. and New York Zool. Soc. 190 pp.

Seidensticker, J., M. G. Hornocker, W. V. Wiles, and J. P. Messick. 1973. Mountain lion social organization in the Idaho primitive area. *Wildl. Monogr.* No. 35. 60 pp.

Tischendorf, J. W., and S. J. Ropski, eds. 1996. Proceedings of the Eastern Cougar Conference. 1994. American Ecological Research Institute. Fort Collins, Col.: 245 pp.

Wright, B. S. 1961. The latest specimen of the eastern puma. *J. Mammal.* 42: 278–279.

Young, S. P., and E. A. Goldman. 1946. *The Puma, Mysterious American Cat.* Washington: Amer. Wildl. Inst. 358 pp.

## Lynx and Bobcats of the Genus *Lynx*

The Canada lynx and the bobcat are the two short-tailed cats of the eastern United States. As is true of other genera of the cat family, members of the genus *Lynx* have often been considered to be properly assigned to the genus *Felis*.

### KEY TO THE LYNX AND BOBCATS OF THE GENUS *LYNX*

1. Tip of tail black on top and bottom; animal grayish brown; foramina at posterior inner corner of tympanic bulla one large, one small . . . . . . . . . . . . . . . . . . . . . *Lynx canadensis*
1. Tail white below, black above, the black grading into three or four bars distally; animal reddish brown with black spotting; foramina at posterior inner corner of tympanic bulla confluent, leaving a single opening . . . . . . . . . . . . . . . . . . . . . . . . . . . *L. rufus*

## Canada Lynx *Lynx canadensis* Kerr
Color plate 21

The Canada lynx is here considered a separate species, but it is often considered conspecific with the Old World lynx, *Lynx lynx*. As such, the North American lynx would become *Lynx lynx canadensis* Kerr.

DESCRIPTION. The Canada lynx is a short-tailed, medium-sized cat with large feet, prominent ear tufts, and a ruff of long, brown-tipped hairs on the sides of the head. The tail tip is wholly black. The hind legs are slightly longer than

*Canada lynx,* Lynx canadensis *(Roger W. Barbour)*

the forelegs, and longer than those of the bob-cat. The color is light gray sprinkled with pale brown, often producing a pinkish-buff hue, slightly lighter below. There are no prominent black or brown spots on the belly or flanks. The forefeet have five toes, the hind feet four.

The best way to distinguish the skull of the lynx from that of the bobcat is by examining the area just behind the inner corner of the tympanic bullae. There are two openings in this area in the lynx, but the two are confluent in the bobcat.

MEASUREMENTS. Measurements of males are: total length 780–1065, tail 75–138, hind foot 205–325 mm; and weight 6.7–17.2 kg (15–39 lbs). For the female, they are 765–965, 76–122, 180–250 mm; and 5.1–11.6 kg (11–25.5 lbs). The maximum weight of a North American lynx, one from Pennsylvania taken in the last century, is 19.9 kg (nearly 44 lbs).

Diploid number = 38.

TOOTH FORMULA

$$\frac{3}{3} \quad \frac{1}{1} \quad \frac{2}{2} \quad \frac{1}{1} \; = \; 28$$

DISTRIBUTION. The Canada lynx is found through much of Canada and south into the northern United States, primarily in the Rocky Mountain area. In the east, the lynx once ranged as far south as Indiana and Pennsylvania, but disappeared from Indiana about 1832 and apparently disappeared from Pennsylvania about the turn of the century, although one specimen was taken in Tioga County in 1921. It is difficult to define accurately the present range of the lynx, since few specimens are available, and because this species is often confused with the bobcat. It is not common anywhere in the eastern United States, and the dense coniferous forests of northern New England and extreme northeastern New York appear to be the remaining

original range
south to here

*Distribution of the lynx,*
Lynx canadensis, *in the*
*eastern United States*

home of the lynx in the northeastern states. Ten, nine, and five bounties were reportedly paid for lynx in New Hampshire in the periods 1951–55, 1956–60, and 1961–65, and the bounty was removed in 1965. A few individuals apparently still persist in the Upper Peninsula of Michigan, and there are relatively recent records for Iron, Washburn, Sauk, and Taylor counties, Wisconsin, and for Marquette County, Michigan, but the lynx is nearly gone from the Great Lakes states now. The lynx thus nearly disappeared from the eastern United States during the twentieth century; it still persists in Minnesota. In January 1989, a release of lynx in the Adirondack Mountains of New York began, but it is not yet clear whether this was successful.

HABITAT. The lynx lives in dense coniferous forest interspersed with rocky areas, bogs, swamps, or thickets, which serve as centers of activity and as resting areas. The regions it frequents are characterized by deep snow and extremely low winter temperatures.

HABITS. In the dense, snow-covered timber and swampy thickets, where only subdued light reaches the forest floor, the lynx hunts the snowshoe hare, which sustains it through much of the year. The large feet of the lynx, with their thick, furred pads, serve as snowshoes. The lynx is primarily nocturnal and solitary, associating with the opposite sex only at mating time. Like the house cat, it is a curious creature, investigating anything new in its environs. Lynx utter a number of purrs, hisses, mews, and growls, as well as shrieks and screams, the latter probably during the mating season.

The lynx has a single main den, but also maintains other resting sites in various parts of its home range. Dens may be in rock shelters or hollow trees, under stumps, or in brush. Bark, leaves, or other suitable plant parts are used as nest material.

Removed from its habitat of windfalls and logs, moss-covered boulders, and the uneven floor of the forest, the lynx is surprisingly slow. In open country it moves in a series of gallops, and is soon overtaken by a dog. But it is an adept climber and an able swimmer, and it has been known to cross sizable lakes.

FOOD AND FEEDING. Relatively few predators feed primarily on a single prey species, but these big cats subsist largely upon the snowshoe hare, which makes up about three-fourths of their diet. Ruffed grouse, mice, and squirrels are some of their main alternative foods when the snowshoe hare populations are low, or when these other animals become more abundant than hares. Skunks, beavers, foxes, or other larger prey may also be killed. White-tailed deer are sometimes eaten, but usually as carrion or young. An adult deer may be overcome occasionally, especially in deep snow, for the big feet of the lynx act as effective snowshoes, whereas the deer flounders helplessly until exhausted. Lynx will cache excess food near their dens for later use, but caching behavior is inconsistent. Diversification of food habits is more pronounced in summer. Grass is sometimes eaten, but it may be purgative rather than nutritional.

While hunting, the lynx apparently uses its eyes and ears more than its nose. It hunts by following established snowshoe hare trails and by concentrating its efforts in the hares' main areas of activity. Actual capture is effected by suddenly leaping at the prey from a position along a trail, in the manner of a house cat, using two or three long leaps totaling up to about 4.5 meters (14 feet).

REPRODUCTION AND DEVELOPMENT. As is true of the bobcat, much is yet to be learned about the mating behavior of the lynx. And as is true of the bobcat, several males may follow a female in heat, and there may be fighting between males. Caterwauling may precede mating. The female may produce loud yowls as part of the mating behavior, and this may be followed by a deep growl or muted purr from the male. The "scream" of the lynx has probably been exaggerated. Flehmen (smelling or tasting the urine of conspecifics) may help indicate a female in heat. Female lynx first become reproductively active at about 22 to 23 months, at least in times of low snowshoe hare populations, but some individuals may breed a year earlier if snowshoe hare populations are high. An alternate-year cycle is also possible. Males probably do not breed until their second year.

The lynx mates in February and March, and after a gestation of about 63–70 days the three or four young (extremes are one to six) are born, between late March and early June. Their eyes open when they are 12 to 17 days old. The kittens are streaked and spotted at birth and remain so colored for several months. At about 60 days, there is a molt to juvenile pelage and the young begin foraging with the mother. Weaning is by three months, canines appear at five to six months, and the adult pelage is complete at nine months. The play behavior exhibited by young lynx appears to be a precursor to adult behavior. The kittens stay with the mother until the beginning of the next mating season. As is the rule with wild cats, no more than a single litter is produced each year.

POPULATION CHARACTERISTICS. Adult lynx establish home ranges and then maintain them for several years. The largest and oldest animals usually have their home ranges in the best habitat, these ranging in size from 10 to 243 square km (4 to 93 square miles). The home ranges of the males are about twice the size of those of females. Males will tolerate females and their young in their home ranges, but when young are not present, their ranges rarely overlap those of females. Dispersing juveniles are faced with the task of finding unoccupied areas for themselves. Lynx often urinate on stumps or bushes, and scats are left unburied by adults (they are buried by the young). These behaviors suggest territorial marking or other communication, but much is yet to be learned of these behaviors in the lynx. Nightly movements within home ranges may average only 3 km (2 miles) or so. The distribution and abundance of snowshoe hares greatly influences the sizes and shapes of the home ranges, and also the densities of lynx.

The rates of survival of offspring are low in years of prey scarcity, mortality occurring, as in the bobcat, primarily after the young begin hunting for themselves. If food is plentiful they will be more apt to gain enough experience in capturing food to see them through the winter. If food is scarce, they may not be able to obtain enough food and/or enough experience to learn how to survive.

The snowshoe hare, the principal prey species of the lynx, shows a nine- to ten-year population cycle, particularly in the far north. The highs and lows are quite prominent, and in a situation where the chief predator of a species concentrates heavily upon that species, the reciprocal effects of the cycle are profound. Because low hare abundance leads to a reduction in juvenile lynx survival, the population cycle of the lynx follows that of the hare, lagging by about one year. The successive highs and lows are much more predictable than a basis of random fluctuations would yield. These highs and lows are quite apparent when one examines lynx fur-harvest data from the Hudson's Bay Company for the period 1850 to 1950. Numbers of lynx taken in this period of relatively stable economic history fluctuate greatly, but the highs occur about every nine to ten years. Density data for the lynx have had to be generated later, but density ranges from about one per 40 square km (16 square miles), during periods of low population, to one animal per 10 square km (4 square miles), in high years. Contrary to numerous indications in the literature, there are few cases of well-documented cyclic population fluctuation among mammals. Some of the voles of the genus *Microtus*, along with the lynx and snowshoe hare, are the best examples of the few mammals that have been clearly shown to be cyclic. *Microtus* exhibits a three- to four-year cycle.

In some areas where the lynx has been extirpated, the bobcat has moved in. These two species share many traits and thus are at least potentially in competition.

ENEMIES. As they are for most of the other larger predators, humans are the principal enemies of the lynx. Other than the northern trapper, the lynx has little to fear.

PARASITES AND DISEASE. Few parasite data are available, and a study of the parasites of this host is in order. Five species of fleas and several of tapeworms have been recorded.

RELATION TO HUMANS. Before the fur-market collapse, many lynx were taken for their dense,

*Bobcat,* Lynx rufus
*(Roger W. Barbour)*

lustrous pelts. The fur was used principally in scarves and coat trimmings. When the importation of spotted cat furs—cheetah, leopard, jaguar, and others—was first banned, both lynx and bobcats were suddenly much in demand, and the prices soared. Northeastern prime lynx pelts brought $400 in the mid-1980s, but today's attitudes toward fur have taken most of the pressure off this animal, and we can now concentrate on helping it to survive and perhaps thrive, at least in some areas.

AREAS FOR FURTHER WORK. A study of lynx and bobcats where the two occur together would be of great interest, and much more information is needed on the behavior, home range, and parasites of this interesting species.

## SUBSPECIES

Only the nominate subspecies occurs in mainland North America. *Lynx canadensis subsolanus* occurs in Newfoundland.

*Lynx canadensis canadensis* Kerr

As described above. The only subspecies occurring in the eastern United States.

Type locality: Eastern Canada (= Quebec).

## LITERATURE

McCord, C. M., and J. E. Cordoza. 1982. Bobcat and Lynx *Felis rufus* and *F. lynx*. In: J. A. Chapman and G. A. Feldhamer, eds., *Wild Mammals of North America*, pp. 728–766. Baltimore: Johns Hopkins Univ. Press.

Mech, L. D. 1980. Age, sex, reproduction, and spatial organization of lynxes colonizing northeastern Minnesota. *J. Mammal.* 61: 261–267.

Parker, G. R., J. W. Maxwell, L. D. Morton, and G. E. J. Smith. 1983. The ecology of the lynx (*Lynx canadensis*) on Cape Breton Island. *Canadian J. Zool.* 61: 770–786.

Saunders, J. K. 1963. Food habits of the lynx in Newfoundland. *J. Wildl. Mgmt.* 27: 384–390.

Tumlison, R. 1987. *Felis lynx.* **Mammalian Species No. 269.** Amer. Soc. Mammal. 8 pp.

## Bobcat *Lynx rufus* (Schreber)

Color plate 21

DESCRIPTION. The bobcat is one of the two medium-sized, short-tailed cats of the eastern United States. It can best be separated from the lynx by its reddish-brown, black-streaked coat, black-spotted underparts, short ear tufts (less than 3 cm, or just over an inch, and sometimes lacking), and the tail, which is white below and black above, the black grading into three or four poorly defined brownish-black bars distally. The lynx, by contrast, has unspotted brownish-gray fur and long ear tufts, and the tip of the tail is black both above and below. The fur of the bobcat is relatively short and sleek, contrasting sharply with that of the lynx. In winter the fur is longer and fuller, but the feet are never padded, as are the great "snowshoes" of the lynx. Southeastern bobcats are lightly built, with smaller feet. They are darker than northern bobcats and much more spotted, and they have black, wavy streaks down the back. Male bobcats are larger than females.

MEASUREMENTS. Forty-seven male bobcats from New Hampshire (Pollack, 1949) averaged: total length 865 (691–972), tail 155 (137–196), hind foot 177 (137–196) mm. Thirty-four female bobcats, also from New Hampshire, averaged: total length 805 (708–869), tail 145 (110–171), hind foot 165 (144–181) mm. Measurements of 37 males from North Carolina (measured by D. R. Progulske) were: total length 823 (610–940), tail 138 (113–178), and hind foot 159 (137–178) mm; and 51 females from North Carolina measured: total length 728 (610–864), tail 121 (90–152), and hind foot 145 (127–165) mm. Seventy-four Vermont specimens averaged 6.8 kg (15.3 lbs); seven weighed 13.6 kg (30 lbs) or more. The largest, an old male, was 16 kg (36 lbs). A New York winter-killed male weighed 18.9 kg (46.6 lb.) and was carrying 3.3 kg (7.3 lbs) of body fat. Lowery (1974) records a large specimen taken near Bains, Louisiana, that measured 112 cm (45 inches) from the tip of the nose to the tip of the tail and weighed 22 kg (45.3 lbs).

Diploid number = 38.

TOOTH FORMULA
$$\frac{3}{3} \quad \frac{1}{1} \quad \frac{2}{2} \quad \frac{1}{1} \; = \; 28$$

DISTRIBUTION. The bobcat originally ranged from southern Canada throughout the United States south to Oaxaca, Mexico, and still occurs in much of this range. It is no longer found in southern Minnesota, eastern South Dakota, Iowa, and most of Missouri. In the eastern states, it is widely distributed from Maine to Florida

*Distribution of the bobcat,*
Lynx rufus, *in the*
*eastern United States*

and westward to the Mississippi, and it often occupies wild areas close to large cities, but it is now absent from western New York and Pennsylvania and most of the Midwest, as well as from a large coastal swath from Massachusetts to Virginia. Hamilton, in the 1930s, found bobcat dens in the Ramapo Mountains less than 48 km (30 miles) from New York City. Bobcats can be present in low numbers in remote areas for extended periods without being detected. For example, they were long thought to have been extirpated in Indiana, even though there were persistent reports in several areas. In 1970, however, in a rugged area of Monroe County, one was shot by a hunter, and there have been 14 additional confirmed records between then and February 1997.

HABITAT. The bobcat is adaptable. It uses a wide variety of natural habitats, especially mixed habitats, and it is also able to change its way of life as civilization modifies the environment. It does not depend on the deep forest, as the lynx does, but rather makes its home in swamps, wooded areas, and mountainous regions. It often lives close to agricultural lands, so long as rocky ledges, swamps, or forested tracts are present. Its basic needs are for woodland—hardwood, coniferous, or mixed—and for resting and activity areas. Resting and activity areas most often center around rocky ledges and conifer swamps in the north, bogs and swamps or brier or palmetto thickets in the south. Here, its spotting helps it blend in with its normal background, the variegated pattern of thickets and rocks in which it hunts its principal prey, lagomorphs and rodents.

Even though it is heavily populated by people, Massachusetts harbors a good population of bobcats, because of its numerous rock ledges. Snow depth appears to limit the range of this species to the north, but the presence of the lynx might also be a factor.

HABITS. The bobcat is a solitary animal; the only association between the sexes, that during mating, is a brief one. This cat is basically crepuscular rather than strictly nocturnal, generally active from about three hours before sunset to midnight, and in the last hour before dawn to three hours after sunrise. Nightly movements

are on the order of 2 to 20 km (1.2 to 12 miles). The bobcat's vision and hearing are well developed. It is a good climber, and it has no aversion to water. The bobcat modifies its behavior in deep snow, bounding to get through, but often using roads, deer trails, logs, and other places where the snow cover is reduced.

Bobcats employ a natal den, often a cave or a rock shelter if one is in the area. They also have auxiliary or shelter dens around the less-visited reaches of their home range. Auxiliary dens may be in brushpiles, thickets, rock ledges, hollow logs, stumps, or the roots remaining from uprooted trees. The odor of these dens, and indeed of the cats themselves, is strong.

FOOD AND FEEDING. Bobcats, like many of the other larger predators, can tolerate extended periods when food is not available, then eat heavily when it is. When prey is scarce or hard to capture, a bobcat will often attempt to kill and cache a deer, which can supply its needs for longer periods. Such a circumstance often occurs when snow is deep and soft. Snow is less of a problem when it is crusted.

Bobcats feed by ambushing or stalking their prey, then pouncing. The preferred prey of the bobcat are mammals ranging from about 0.7 to 5.5 kg (1.5 to 12.5 lbs). Over most of the bobcat's range in the eastern United States, the cottontail rabbit is its main food, but it is replaced by the snowshoe hare in the north. Where both occur, as they do in New England, the two together form the principal fare of the bobcat. In the far north the lynx becomes the principal predator of the snowshoe hare, and in the Deep South the cotton rat sometimes replaces rabbits as the predominant food of the bobcat.

Although lagomorphs are often the mainstay, the overall diversity of foods in the diet of this species is great. The bobcat will take many other foods as the opportunities arise, and in response to changes in prey populations. Many species of squirrels (including woodchucks), mice and voles, opossums, moles and shrews, raccoons, foxes, house cats, and even skunks and porcupines have all been recorded as food, along with several species of birds, reptiles, insects, and snails. Deer, especially fawns, are often eaten. Bobcats and lynx are indeed capable of killing full-grown deer, though they seldom do except in winter in deep snow, or in times when their principal prey are in short supply. Many of the deer consumed are probably roadkills, or have been shot by hunters. Deer or other larger prey are cached and may be visited several times. Caches are covered with any material available, such as snow, leaves, or bark. There is often much hair from the prey mixed with the covering material. The mountain lion is of course a major predator on deer; bobcats and lynx usually are not. But as deer become more abundant, as is currently the case in Massachusetts, more and more are killed by bobcats.

Bobcats hunt animals of three different sizes, and employ a different hunting behavior for each. When feeding on small prey (mice and squirrels) where prey is abundant, they will lie, crouch, or stand motionless, waiting for the prey to approach, before pouncing. When hunting rabbits or hares, bobcats often crouch in a hunting bed or lookout, changing position in the lookout so as to scan the view in various directions. When prey is at hand, the bobcat may attack after a bit of stalking or by a sudden rush directly from the hunting bed. The rush is usually from within 10 meters (30 feet) of the prey. The bobcat hunts prey at rest, such as deer, by moving about more frequently. Bobcats are most apt to attack deer when they find them bedded down. After a great rush the bobcat will bite violently at the throat, the base of the skull, or the chest.

REPRODUCTION AND DEVELOPMENT. Most female bobcats breed in their second summer, but a few apparently breed as yearlings. Males do not breed until their second year. Sperm production begins in September or October, and males are generally fertile at least into the following summer. The mating season commences in February and March, at least in the north. Much is yet to be learned of the courtship and mating of bobcats, but a dominant male may mate several times with a female as the two run together, and may also undertake a series of chases, bumping behavior, and "ambushes." Other males may be in attendance, but they remain aloof during the matings (the female may in fact mate with other males later). When a female shows that she is receptive, the male apparently grasps her in the typical felid neck

grip. The one to six (usually two to four) young are born in spring or early summer, after a gestation period of about 62 days. Some births occur even into September, however, and it may be that two litters are occasionally produced. The young, well furred and spotted at birth, are about 255 mm long and weigh about 280 to 340 grams. By the ninth or tenth day, they open their eyes. They start exploring their surroundings at the end of the fourth week and are weaned when about two months old. By fall of their first year the young weigh about 4.5 kg (10 lbs) and are hunting by themselves, but they remain with the mother until nearly a year old.

POPULATION CHARACTERISTICS. Bobcats confine their activities to fairly well-defined territories, the territories varying in size depending on sex, season, and prey distribution and abundance. Resident animals spend much of their time in certain favored spots, such as around bluffs and ledges. Other residents are permitted to use these areas, but a dominance hierarchy may be established among the residents. Transients (usually young dispersing individuals) are generally excluded from these favored areas. Transients in these circumstances can either continue to disperse or remain near the residents, filling in if a resident dies. Home ranges of males in summer are about 0.9 square km (0.35 square miles); those of females are less than half that. Winter home ranges are much larger: in Maine they were calculated at about 100 square km (40 square miles); most other winter estimates run 25–50 square km (9.6–20 square miles). Home ranges of females are much smaller than those of males, and generally do not overlap those of other females, though two or more may be included in one male home range. The home ranges of males often overlap.

Bobcats mark home ranges by a complex system of scent marking involving urine, feces, scent from anal glands, scraping, and scratches in trees. They will scratch with their front claws as high as they can reach on dry, barkless, standing trees. At times they will cover their feces, at other times not, and they will sometimes prepare a scrape with the hind feet and deposit the feces in the scrape. Uncovered feces and scrapes are more often found around dens and in other areas most often frequented. Urine may be deposited in smaller or larger amounts, and may be covered or uncovered. Urine can be squirted across the anal glands as it is emitted.

There are no marked population cycles in this species, except perhaps in the far north. In Wisconsin, density was estimated at one animal per 13 square km (5 square miles), whereas in Alabama and Georgia it was about one per 0.9–1.3 square km (0.3–0.5 square miles). Overall annual survival averaged 0.624 among 15 bobcats that were tracked by radiotelemetry from 68 to 838 days (Fuller et al., 1995); the rate for females did not differ from that for males. Fewer bobcats survive to adulthood in years when prey populations are low. Most mortality probably occurs after the kittens are on their own, and while they are still learning to hunt. Many bobcats live six or eight years, but few live beyond ten.

ENEMIES. There are no major predators on adult bobcats; deaths of adults are from a variety of causes, including hunters, automobiles, starvation, accidents, and disease. Kittens may be killed by a variety of predators, including foxes, owls, and even adult male bobcats.

PARASITES AND DISEASE. Like many other predators, this species often harbors the larger parasites, mostly ticks and fleas, and often carries the parasites common on its prey, especially the fleas and ticks found on rabbits and squirrels. It does harbor one tiny mite, *Lynxacarus morlani*, found to date only on this host.

RELATION TO HUMANS. Bobcats, long hunted, trapped, and otherwise persecuted, are the only spotted cats in the world that can be trapped legally today. (The bobcat is listed in the CITES treaty with the provision that export of hides will be allowed only if the harvest has not been detrimental to the population.) Bobcats will usually tree after being run a short time by dogs, but they are more than a match for the average hound. Like many of the large cats, they seem to be more annoyed than frightened by the baying of a hound. In New Hampshire, bounties were paid on 1699, 1750, 1908, and 386 bobcats in the periods 1951–55, 1956–60, 1961–65, and 1966–70, respectively, but our efforts today are extended toward helping this animal. The species is doing very well through much of the south, where it is still extensively hunted, though hunters there now quite often tree the animal and then allow it to live, as a measure of protection.

An unprecedented rise in prices for long-haired raw furs in the 1970s and 1980s spurred interest in trapping bobcats. New York prime pelts, for example, brought $90 in 1976, but as is true of other furs, the pelts are worth little now.

AREAS FOR FURTHER WORK. Further radiotelemetry studies on this species should reveal much additional information about its behavior and ecology. Further study of its ectoparasites, including the mites of "hidden biotopes" (in follicles and skin pustules, in nasal and ear cavities, and behind the eyes) is also in order.

## SUBSPECIES

In the east there appear to be two groups of populations of bobcats, separated by Lake Superior, and these populations apparently do not meet in Canada, according to the maps in Hall and Kelson (1982) and Peterson (1966). One group is in the Upper Peninsula of Michigan and in Wisconsin. The other occurs over much of the eastern United States, excluding much of the Midwest. But although they do appear to be separated by a primary isolating mechanism, they are not well distinguished, and therefore we have not recognized them as separate subspecies.

*Lynx rufus rufus* (Schreber)

As described above. Found from Maine south to Louisiana and Florida.

Type locality: New York.

Other currently recognized eastern subspecies:

 *L. rufus gigas* Bangs
 *L. rufus floridanus* Rafinesque
 *L. rufus superiorensis* Peterson & Downing

## LITERATURE

Bailey, T. N. 1974. Social organization in a bobcat population. *J. Wildl. Mgmt.* 38: 435–446.

Fuller, T. K., S. L. Berendzen, T. A. Decker, and J. E. Cardoza. 1995. Survival and cause-specific mortality rates of adult bobcats (*Lynx rufus*). *Amer. Midland Nat.* 134: 404–408.

Hall, E. R., and K. R. Kelson. 1982. *The Mammals of North America.* New York: Ronald Press. 1083 pp.

Hamilton, W. J., Jr., and R. P. Hunter. 1939. Fall and winter food habits of Vermont bobcats. *J. Wildl. Mgmt.* 3: 99–103.

Larivière, S., and L. R. 1997. *Lynx rufus.* **Mammalian Species No. 563.** Amer. Soc. Mammal. 8 pp.

Lovallo, M. J., and E. M. Anderson. 1996. Bobcat (*Lynx rufus*) home range size and habitat use in northwest Wisconsin. *Amer. Midland Nat.* 135: 241–252.

Marston, M. A. 1942. Winter relations of bobcats to white-tailed deer in Maine. *J. Wildl. Mgmt.* 6: 328–337.

McCord, C. M., and J. E. Cardoza. 1982. Bobcat and lynx *Felis rufus* and *F. lynx.* In: J. A. Chapman and G. A. Feldhamer, eds., *Wild Mammals of North America*, pp. 728–766. Baltimore: Johns Hopkins Univ. Press.

Peterson, R. L. 1966. *The Mammals of Eastern Canada.* Toronto: Oxford Univ. Press. 465 pp.

Pollack, E. M. 1949. The ecology of the bobcat (*Lynx rufus rufus* Schreber) in the New England states. M.S. thesis, University of Massachusetts. 120 pp.

———. 1951. Food habits of the bobcat in the New England states. *J. Wildl. Mgmt.* 15: 209–213.

Rollings, C. T. 1945. Habits, foods and parasites of the bobcat in Minnesota. *J. Wildl. Mgmt.* 9: 131–145.

Van Wormer, J. 1963. *The World of the Bobcat.* Philadelphia: J. B. Lippincott. 128 pp.

Westfall, C. Z. 1956. Foods eaten by bobcats in Maine. *J. Wildl. Mgmt.* 20: 199–200.

Young, S. P. 1958. *The Bobcat of North America.* Harrisburg, Pa.: Stackpole. 193 pp.

# 9. ORDER SIRENIA

## *Manatee and Allies*

THE SIRENIANS INCLUDE the manatees, sea cows, and dugongs. These animals are vegetarian, wholly aquatic, and unlike any others. They likely have given rise to the traditional stories of mermaids and to the myths of the sirens in the ancient world.

There are two families of sirenians, the Trichechidae (manatees) and the Dugongidae. The Dugongidae include the dugong of North African and Asian waters, and the extinct Steller's sea cow, of the Bering Sea, which was exterminated by Europeans only 27 years after they first discovered it, in 1742. The survival of the remaining members of this order remains in question.

The extant sirenians are massive animals, often weighing over 500 kg (1100 lbs), and Steller's sea cow is estimated to have weighed three tons (2700 kg). There are no hind limbs and no dorsal fins on sirenians. The tail, horizontally flattened, propels the animal through the water; the paddlelike forelimbs exert control. Sirenians have a small mouth and a rounded snout; the nostrils are on the snout, their openings directed posteriorly. The molariform teeth are indeterminate in number and continuously replaced. The lips are prehensile.

## MANATEES, Family Trichechidae

Manatees have spatulate tails, and the upper lip is cleft in such a way that the two sides can move independently, a helpful feature when the animal is browsing on plants. The flippers are quite dexterous, and help some in locomotion on the bottom, but have limited use in food manipulation. The bones, especially the ribs, are heavy and dense, probably helping the animal to remain submerged.

There are three species of manatees, all in the genus *Trichechus*. One is an African species; the other two are found in the New World. The species that occurs in North America is *Trichechus manatus*, the West Indian Manatee. Isolation by the Straits of Florida has given rise to two subspecies, *T. m. manatus*, the Antillean manatee, and *T. m. latirostris*, the Florida manatee of the southeastern United States (Domning and Hayek, 1986). A workshop on manatees in 1992 produced a very useful summary of information on this species (O'Shea et al., 1995).

### LITERATURE CITED

Domning, D. P., and L. C. Hayek. 1986. Interspecific and intraspecific morphological variation in manatees (Sirenia: *Trichechus*). *Marine Mammal Sci.* 2: 87–144.

O'Shea, T. J., B. B. Ackerman, and H. F. Percival, eds. 1995. *Population Biology of the Florida Manatee*. Washington: U.S. Dept. Interior, Natl. Biol. Serv., Information and Technology Report I. 289 pp.

### West Indian Manatee
### *Trichechus manatus*
### Linnaeus                                    Color plate 22

DESCRIPTION. The manatee can be confused with no other mammal—other than, perhaps, a whale or dolphin. It is a huge, robust, aquatic mammal with a rounded body, a small head, no visible neck, and a thick, paddle-shaped tail. There are no paired posterior appendages; the front appendages, formed as flippers, each bear three or four vestigial nails. The snout is blunt, and the upper lip, cleft in the middle, overhangs the mouth. The lips are able to grasp. The nostrils are valvelike, and the eyes are small. The skin, about 2 to 3 cm (an inch or so) thick, is of-

*West Indian manatee,* Trichechus manatus, *cow and calf (Galen Rathbun, Sirenia Project, U.S. Department of the Interior)*

ten adorned with barnacles and algae, and the animal is gray to gray-brown to blackish. The skull, especially the lower jaw, is massive, but the nasal bones are vestigial. The incisors, concealed beneath a horny plate, are rudimentary, and are lost before maturity. The molariform teeth, five to seven of them present at any one time in each side of each jaw, are brachydont; the anterior ones wear down and fall out and are replaced from behind, a progression similar to that of elephants, although elephants have only three molariforms. The manatee has only six cervical vertebrae, rather than the normal seven. Fine hairs, 30 to 45 mm long, are found thinly over the body, but there are heavy bristles on the upper lip. The sexes are similar.

MEASUREMENTS. The total length of adults ranges from 250 to 450 cm (100 to 180 inches), and manatees weigh from 200 to more than 900 kg (440 to 2000 lbs), but adults generally range from 280 to 350 cm (111 to 140 inches) and weigh up to 500 kg (1100 lbs). The maximum recorded size was that of a 375-cm (150-inch) female weighing 1620 kg (3565 lbs).

Diploid number = 48.

TOOTH FORMULA

$$\frac{2}{2} \quad \frac{0}{0} \quad \frac{11}{11} \quad = \quad 52$$

DISTRIBUTION. The first record of the West Indian Manatee was made by Christopher Colum-

bus, who observed it along the shore of what is now the Dominican Republic. It occurs in coastal waters from the southeastern United States throughout the Caribbean region, and along the east coast of Central America and the northeast coast of South America. In the eastern United States it occurs along the Atlantic Coast from Beaufort, North Carolina, south and west to Louisiana and Mississippi, but it is found primarily in Florida. In recent decades, manatee numbers have diminished greatly in many parts of their range, but they are about equally abundant on the east and west coasts of Florida. Except for stragglers, essentially the entire U.S. population winters in Florida, moving back into neighboring states in summer. The total range today is similar to the historic range, but is fragmented by local extirpations (O'Shea and Ludlow, 1992).

Our manatees are widely dispersed in summer in rivers, canals, estuaries, lagoons, and bays south from the Suwannee River on the Gulf Coast and south from coastal Georgia on the Atlantic Coast. In winter, they move southward up to 200–300 km (125–180 miles) and congregate in warm-water areas, both natural and industrial. Major wintering areas are Crystal River, Homosassa River, Tampa Bay, Fort Myers, Port Everglades, Riviera Beach, near Titusville, and Blue Spring (O'Shea and Ludlow, 1992). The greatest numbers tend to be in the warmest waters, the manatees moving in and out of these waters as environmental temperatures change.

HABITAT. Manatees live in shallow coastal waters, lagoons, bays, and sluggish rivers along the coast, often in turbid water. They occur in salt water, but require access to fresh water, vascular aquatic plants for food, channels 1 to 2 meters (3 to 6 feet) deep, and warm-water areas for wintering (Hartman, 1979; O'Shea and Ludlow, 1992).

HABITS. Although manatees are normally solitary, they sometimes form groups. As many as 17 have been seen following a female in estrus, and such mating herds may persist for seven to 30 days. They also congregate in warm water in winter, often at power plants today, but also in proximity to natural springs. There are reports of manatees up the coast as far as Virginia, and they have been known to ascend rivers as far as 230 km (143 miles). Manatees appear to be primarily nomadic, but when they settle into a suitable locality, they may stay for extended periods.

Manatees can remain submerged up to 16 minutes, but they normally surface for air every three to five minutes. Often their presence can be determined by a series of upboilings in the water. They generally travel in channels at least one meter deep, preferably two or three. They usually travel at 3 to 7 kph (2 to 4 mph), but can swim at up to 25 kph (15.5 mph). Manatees are active day or night, feeding about one-fourth to one-third of the 24-hour period in one- to two-hour sessions, and they rest about six to ten hours. They may move as far as 12.5 km (7.75 miles) in 24 hours, and can travel during migrations at rates up to about 50 km (30 miles) per day. Manatees rest by lying motionless just under the surface or on the bottom, with their eyes closed. Hearing and vision are well devel-

*Distribution of the West Indian manatee,* Trichechus manatus, *in the eastern United States*

oped, but hearing seems to be their most important sense.

Manatees are usually quiet, but they can produce squeaks, chips, grunts, and groans audible to humans (Hartman, 1979). They are usually solitary, but they give each other nibbles, kisses, and embraces.

FOOD AND FEEDING. The food of manatees consists entirely of aquatic vegetation, although invertebrates are taken incidentally and may supply some protein. They feed on a great variety of aquatic plants, as well as sea grasses, bank grass, and overhanging mangrove (O'Shea and Ludlow, 1992). *Hydrilla* and other submerged aquatic vegetation are often staple foods in Florida. They have also been seen to eat dead fish. The animals graze just beneath the surface in shallow water, consuming about 45 kg (100 lbs) of food per day. Manatees may cease feeding for a week or so during cold spells in winter.

REPRODUCTION AND DEVELOPMENT. Males may become sexually active by their second or third year, spermatogenesis occurring in seasons other than winter. Most herd reproductive activity is observed in spring, when males gather about and follow a female, with much associated jostling and pushing as they attempt to get next to her, the female often attempting to escape. Courtship involves nuzzling and embracing, and mating is in shallow water. Manatees produce a single young (sometimes two) at any time of year (but seldom in winter) after a 12-month gestation. Rathbun et al. (1995) found that about 1.4% of the births were of twins. At birth, the young are about 120 to 150 cm (40 to 60 inches) long, weigh 28 to 36 kg (61 to 79 lbs), and are dark in color. Immediately following its birth the female takes the young to the surface to breathe, and it stays there for about 45 minutes. The calf then submerges and surfaces more frequently, staying down longer and longer each time, and after half a day it is surfacing and swimming on its own. After one to three months, the calf begins to take plant material on its own, but it continues nursing for one to two years, until it leaves its mother. The fact that calves of two different ages have been observed with a single female suggests that the young remain with the

female for more than one year. Sometimes the calf rides on its mother's back.

Females commence breeding activities at three or four years of age. The fact that about a third of the females are pregnant at any one time argues that an individual female is likely to give birth about every three years (the minimum birth interval is two years). Females can remain sexually active for at least 22 years; one female produced at least seven calves in 22 years and died giving birth at an estimated 29 years of age (O'Shea and Hartley, 1995).

POPULATION CHARACTERISTICS. The extent of the total U.S. manatee population is difficult to determine. One recent total manatee count was 1465, in the winter of 1991 (O'Shea and Ludlow, 1992), but at least 2639 were counted in Florida by aerial survey in the winter of 1996 (Florida Department of Environmental Protection). Though the later number might appear to demonstrate an increase, it could be reflecting better counting techniques; moreover, the manatees have become more visible in recent years because they tend to aggregate more in protected places. It is thus not clear what the total population trends are, currently, and since there are no reliable early estimates of manatee numbers, it is difficult to know how present populations compare with historical ones. We do know that winter populations at certain places have increased. Currently, the most reliable estimates can be made at Crystal River (Citrus County) and Blue Spring (Volusia County). None wintered at Crystal River in this century prior to the 1950s (Hartman, 1979), but about 45 were present in 1968, and over 300 winter there now. Eleven individuals were counted at Blue Spring in 1971, and more than 80 winter there now. Some other winter aggregation sites are at Homosassa River, Tampa Bay, Titusville, Indian River, Cape Canaveral, Vero Beach, Harbor Branch, Fort Pierce, Hobe Sound, Riviera Beach, Fort Lauderdale, and Port Everglades on the east coast, and at Fort Myers on the west coast. Generally, females are more sedentary than males in summer; the males, for their part, spend much of the summer traveling a circuit that encompasses the home ranges of several females. About 125 to 300 manatees are killed each year, about a third of the deaths attributable to human-related causes. An individual in captivity has lived more than 48 years.

ENEMIES. Humans are the only important enemies of manatees. In earlier times, manatees were killed extensively for their meat, oil, and skin, until they were in danger of extirpation in many areas. And although they are now completely protected in Florida, and are listed as endangered under the U.S. Endangered Species Act, they are still occasionally killed by poachers. Their gravest problems are encroachment and habitat alteration by residential and commercial development; environmental pollution; and the motorboat propeller. Habitat disappears, but sometimes new habitat opens up where channels are dredged or redirected. Herbicides containing copper are potentially harmful (O'Shea et al., 1984).

Since manatees graze just beneath the surface in shallow water, and since they are slow to react and slow-moving, boating accidents are their most serious problem. Many individuals show signs of past injury from boats, and the injuries are often fatal. The numbers killed by boats— 522 from 1974 through 1992, but 53 during 1991 alone—have increased considerably over the last few years (Ackerman et al., 1995), in part because boating of all sorts is becoming increasingly popular.

In Florida, manatees used to migrate upstream and spend the winter in the vicinity of warm springs, but today many remain in the heated outflow of powerplants. In these circumstances, the manatees are dependent on the heat from the outflow, and a winter shutdown of a powerplant can thus be fatal. Freezing weather is another major problem for manatees. One or two nights of freezing or near-freezing weather can cause pneumonia, which can lead to death. Manatees should be left alone in their warm winter quarters, so that they will not become alarmed and swim into the nearby colder water. They can be crushed in locks and flood-control structures, caught in fishing nets, poached, and poisoned by red tides (O'Shea et al., 1985). Florida Power and Light Company has aided in the conservation and study of these animals.

PARASITES AND DISEASE. Forrester (1992) summarized the information on the parasites of manatees. They include 48 species of bacteria, three of protozoa, four of trematodes, one of nematode, and one of cestode. Among ectoparasites, just two mites, both unidentified, have been found in skin sections.

RELATION TO HUMANS. This species is considered endangered in the United States, and is entirely protected, but manatees are sometimes wantonly killed, and motorboats pose a constant threat. The U.S. Department of the Interior, Florida Department of Natural Resources, private companies, and several nonprofit organizations have led efforts to encourage the public to avoid disturbing them, and to see that certain waterways are closed off. Although huge, manatees are completely harmless, and skin divers can swim among them safely.

AREAS FOR FURTHER WORK. Radiotelemetry studies and carcass salvage already under way will help us gain additional information on manatee biology. It would also be interesting to examine manatees for mites and other ectoparasites.

## SUBSPECIES

*Trichechus manatus manatus* occurs in the West Indies and northern South America. Since the Florida subspecies is completely separated geographically from *T. m. manatus*, we recognize it as valid.

*Trichechus manatus latirostris* (Harlan)
Florida Manatee

As described above.

Type locality: West Indies for the species; near the capes of eastern Florida for *T. manatus latirostris*.

## LITERATURE

Ackerman, B. B., S. D. Wright, R. K. Bonde, D. K. Odell, and D. J. Banowetz. 1995. Trends and patterns in mortality of manatees in Florida, 1974–

1992. In: T. J. O'Shea, B. B. Ackerman, and H. F. Percival, eds., *Population Biology of the Florida Manatee* (see below), pp. 223–258.

Forrester, D. J. 1992. *Parasites and Diseases of Wild Mammals in Florida.* Gainesville: Univ. Press of Florida. 459 pp.

Hartman, D. S. 1979. Ecology and behavior of the manatee (*Trichechus manatus*) in Florida. Amer. Soc. Mammal. Spec. Pub. No. 5. 153 pp.

Husar, S. L. 1978. *Trichechus manatus.* **Mammalian Species No. 93.** Amer. Soc. Mammal. 5 pp.

O'Shea, T. J., B. B. Ackerman, and H. F. Percival, eds. 1995. *Population Biology of the Florida Manatee.* Washington: U.S. Dept. Interior, Natl. Biol. Serv., Information and Technology Report I. 289 pp.

O'Shea, T. J., C. A. Beck, R. K. Bonde, H. I. Kochman, and D. K. Odell. 1985. An analysis of manatee mortality patterns in Florida, 1976–81. *J. Wildl. Mgmt.* 49: 1–11.

O'Shea, T. J., and W. C. Hartley. 1995. Reproduction and early age survival of manatees at Blue Spring, Upper St. John's River, Florida. In: T. J. O'Shea,

B. B. Ackerman, and H. F. Percival, eds., *Population Biology of the Florida Manatee* (see above), pp. 157–170.

O'Shea, T. J., and M. E. Ludlow. 1992. Florida Manatee *Trichechus manatus latirostris* Family Trichechidae Order Sirenia. In: S. R. Humphrey, ed., *Rare and Endangered Biota of Florida.* Vol. I. Mammals, pp. 190–200. Gainesville: Univ. Press of Florida. 392 pp.

O'Shea, T. J., J. F. Moore, and H. I. Kochman. 1984. Contaminant concentrations in manatees in Florida. *J. Wildl. Mgmt.* 48: 741–748.

Rathbun, G. B., J. P. Reid, R. K. Bonde, and J. A. Powell. 1995. Reproduction in free-ranging Florida manatees. In: T. J. O'Shea, B. B. Ackerman, and H. F. Percival, eds., *Population Biology of the Florida Manatee* (see above), pp. 135–156.

Reynolds, J. E., III, and J. R. Wilcox. 1986. Distribution and abundance of the West Indian manatee, *Trichechus manatus,* around selected Florida power plants following winter cold fronts: 1984–85. *Biol. Conserv.* 38: 103–113.

# 10. ORDER PERISSODACTYLA

## Horses and Other Odd-Toed Ungulates

PERISSODACTYLS ARE HOOFED mammals in which the axis of each limb passes through the middle or third toe, forming the enlarged hoof of the horse. Rhinoceroses and tapirs, with a similar axis, have three or four toes per foot. (See the Artiodactyl introduction for a more thorough explanation.) Perissodactyls, which include horses, rhinoceroses, and tapirs, digest fibrous plant material in the caecum and colon, where microorganisms aid digestion. But because digestive turnover is relatively rapid by contrast with that of artiodactyls, cellulose digestion is limited to about 45% efficiency. As a result, perissodactyls must consume large quantities of food.

Although perissodactyls were numerous and diverse in North America in earlier geological periods, no native representatives of the order remain today. Horses, however, have become established in several areas, particularly in the Southwest. In the eastern United States, wild horses have long been established on Assateague Island, a 37-mile-long island forming part of the barrier beach of Maryland and Virginia, and they occur on several smaller islands off the East Coast as well, in North Carolina and Georgia.

### HORSES AND ALLIES, Family Equidae

The family Equidae includes seven species with living representatives, all in the genus *Equus*—the horses, zebras, and asses. They are large animals the third toe of which has become a single large hoof. Native equines are now restricted to Africa and Asia. The domesticated horse, which occurred in wild form at least until recently in Mongolia and China, ranged as far west as Spain into the late eighteenth century. *Equus*

*asinus*, the wild ass, donkey, or burro, originated in Africa, but is now found only in domestication. Also included in the family are four species of zebras, the kulan or onager (*E. hemionus*) of four isolated areas in Asia, and the kiang (*E. kiang*), the largest wild ass, which is found on the Tibetan Plateau.

### Feral Horse *Equus caballus* Linnaeus

DESCRIPTION. The horse is too well known to need much description. It is the only established mammal in the eastern United States that has a single large hoof (actually the third toe) on each

*Assateague pony,* Equus caballus *(Ronald R. Keiper)*

foot. It is a very large animal with a long snout, a mane, and a long tail used as a switch to drive off flies. The free-ranging, unmanaged ponies of the Maryland section of Assateague Island have been extensively studied by R. R. Keiper, and most of the information here is from his excellent book (Keiper, 1985). It is assumed that the habitat relationships and behavior of the horses on the other east coast islands are similar to those on Assateague/Chincoteague.

The origin of the Assateague horses is not clear. Most likely, the early colonists kept horses there to escape taxes and fencing laws, bringing them to the mainland as needed. Other accounts claim that the ancestors of today's herd were the survivors from a Spanish galleon shipwrecked there in the late 1500s, or that they were put there by pirates. In any event, horses have been on Assateague for at least three centuries. (Part of Assateague Island is in Maryland and part is in Virginia.)

The Assateague ponies—a pony is simply an undersized horse—were privately owned for much of their existence, and the owners introduced and removed horses as they wished. But upon the establishment of the Assateague Island National Seashore in 1965, the privately owned ponies were removed and the ponies in the northern or Maryland extremity of the island came under the jurisdiction of Seashore personnel. (Fencing along the state line prevents mixing of the two herds.) The present herd on Maryland Assateague, the herd studied by Keiper (1985), originates from 21 original Assateague ponies donated to the Seashore at the time of the establishment of the Seashore. This herd has risen to about 150 animals, but apart from occasional birth-control measures executed to control the population, the herd is not manipulated.

The Virginia ponies are administered by the Chincoteague National Wildlife Refuge and owned by the Chincoteague, Virginia, Volunteer Fire Company, which is on Chincoteague Island, just west of the southern end of Assateague Island. This herd *is* managed to some degree. There are fences preventing access to the dunes; foals are sold at an annual auction to raise money for the fire department; and horses are added at suitable junctures.

The original Assateague horses were appar-

ently of a solid color, but many of those on the island today are piebald or pinto (brown and white), apparently as a result of interbreeding with Shetland ponies released in the early 1900s. The various brown-and-white patterns have facilitated research on the animals by allowing the recognition of individual animals, even at considerable distance.

MEASUREMENTS. Full-size horses elsewhere are over 14 "hands," 2 inches, or 58 inches (a hand is 4 inches) tall at the withers (the hump between the shoulder blades), thus about 145 cm in height. It is thought that the ancestral horses were full size, but animals of the Assateague population rarely exceed 13 hands, or 52 inches. The smaller size of the Assateague animals may indeed reflect poor diet; it is not genetically based, for animals that have been removed from the island as foals and given a high-protein diet grow to full size.

Diploid number = 64.

TOOTH FORMULA

$$\frac{3}{3} \quad \frac{1}{1} \quad \frac{3 \text{ or } 4}{3} \quad \frac{3}{3} \quad = \quad 40 \text{ or } 42$$

DISTRIBUTION. In the eastern United States, wild horses live on Shackleford Island, a small barrier island in the Cape Lookout National Seashore off North Carolina, on Cumberland Island off Georgia, and on Assateague. All of the world's extant horses either are domesticated or have descended from domestic stock. It is not known when or where horses were domesticated, but the domestic horse was common in China in 2000 B.C. The first domestications could have been in the Russian steppes around 3100 B.C., or perhaps in early postglacial times in central Europe.

HABITAT. The ponies spend most of their time grazing in the marshy grasslands of their low, offshore islands and resting in the higher and drier sandy areas.

HABITS. The Assateague ponies live in bands; some of the bands are called "harems." The Maryland ponies studied by Keiper (1985) currently distribute themselves in about 25 bands living from the north end of the island to the fence at the state line.

In general, the animals spend nearly 78% of

the daylight hours grazing and 19% resting; at night, about 54% grazing, 40% resting. Periods of grazing alternate with rest. All other activities occur without pattern, and consume an average of less than a minute per hour. Grazing, most pronounced in the early morning and late afternoon, increases in winter, probably because of the low nutritive value of the food at that time. When grazing, the animals are constantly moving. They move faster in summer (5 kph, or 3 mph) than in winter (0.2 kph, or 0.12 mph) because of the presence of flies, and because they make three rather than two trips to water on summer days. In winter they spend more time in small protected areas. Larger bands move slower than smaller ones.

The horses are usually standing while at rest; they stand on three legs, resting the fourth. They lock the legs, relax the muscles, hang their head, rotate their ears toward the outside, and close their eyes. They may sleep in this position for up to an hour and a half. Waking is usually accompanied by several yawns. Resting (and yawning) are contagious activities in horses. They may also rest by dropping heavily to the ground and tucking their legs under them (sternal recumbency) or by lying on their sides and extending their legs straight out (lateral recumbency). Recumbency would seem to be more restful, but it hinders breathing and circulation, and rising is difficult. In summer, adults seldom lie down during the day because of the heat and biting insects, but they may lie down at night or early in the morning. The horses rest less in winter, because greater amounts of the lower-quality food must be consumed.

Grooming occupies part of the horses' time. They self-groom by rubbing some part of the body against a tree or fencepost or other object, or they may roll over on their back and flex them-

*Distribution of the feral horse,*
Equus caballus, *in the eastern*
*United States*

*A band of ponies in the dunes*
*(Ronald R. Keiper)*

selves back and forth several times. Rolling, an-other contagious behavior, helps protect against biting insects and helps dry the fur. The horses may also bite at various areas with their teeth as a method of grooming. Mutual grooming, which finds two animals licking or biting each other, mostly at the withers but also at other areas, helps to establish and maintain social ties. Most mutual grooming is between close relatives or between animals of similar age and social rank, but it is often initiated by a subordinate to a dominant.

Mares urinate by spreading the legs and rais-ing the tail; males move quickly forward, then crouch, with the hind legs at about a 45° angle from the ground. These differential postures are obvious and can be used to determine sex at all ages. Males urinate more frequently, because they use urine to mark the defecation of others.

"Stud piles" of accumulated fecal matter are prominent features in the home ranges of some bands. They may be up to 2 meters long and more than half a meter deep, and are produced only by the stallion, the dominant horse in the band. Stallions also mark the urine and feces of their mares with their own urine.

The stallion, in fact, has exclusive rights to the mares in his harem, but he must continually tend the harem by keeping mares from leaving, by making other stallions keep their distance, and by driving out young males if they become a

threat. The stallion herds the mares by pressing his ears to his head, extending his neck, and dropping his head low to the ground, often swinging it from side to side. He will often bite their necks, flanks, or hindquarters if they move too slowly, not even ceasing when one slips or falls. The stallion must always be on the alert, for other stallions frequently attempt to start or increase their harems by raiding neighbors' har-ems. In confrontations between stallions, the two stand and stare at each other, some distance apart; each then defecates, smells the fecal pile, and again stares. The intruder may leave, but if not, the males move toward each other, necks arched and tails high. Their feet pound the ground in an exaggerated trot, called the "par-allel prance." Either may withdraw at this point, but if not, action escalates. They sniff each other and emit high-pitched screams, and a fight then ensues. They stand side by side, shouldering and biting each other. They may also kick with the forelegs, and sometimes one will rear and at-tempt to knock his opponent off balance. The two will rest or graze between "rounds," which resume when one of the opponents approaches the other. Fights often center around a fecal pile, the animals defecating on it and smelling it. During this ritualized defecating, neither will attack. Fights may last up to 45 minutes, but end only when one of the combatants leaves or is chased off.

Young males in the harem ward off attacks by the stallion by submissive behavior called "champing." The ears stand straight up, just the opposite of their disposition in aggressive behavior. These males then move toward the stallion and continue to champ, the two often almost nose to nose. This behavior is practiced by young submissive animals of both sexes, but older animals do not champ. Rather, they move away from the aggressor.

Both white-tailed and sika deer are present on Assateague, the latter far more abundant. All three species are herbivores, but food overlap among them is not great. Cowbirds often feed on the ground among grazing ponies, and red-winged blackbirds and starlings sit on the ponies and feed on the insects in their manes. Cattle egrets and horses maintain a mutualistic relationship: the egrets gain food and the horses are shorn of flies and parasites. The egrets walk about on the ground feeding on flies and other insects, many of them kicked up by the horses, or stand on the backs of the horses and snatch up flies and parasites. Cattle egrets, of African origin, migrated to South America by the late 1800s; they reached Florida by 1942 and Assateague by 1956.

FOOD AND FEEDING. All horses are primarily grazers, grinding their herbaceous plant food with highly specialized, ridged molariform teeth. The Assateague ponies graze on green plants in summer and become browsers on the tender parts of woody plants in winter. A little less than 80% of the Assateague Island ponies' diet is of grass, more than half of it saltmarsh cordgrass (*Spartina alterniflora*). Cordgrass is salty, fibrous, and abrasive, and it is abundant in the saltmarshes along the western shores of Assateague. The second most important grass in the diet is American beachgrass (*Ammophila breviligulata*), comprising 20% of the diet. Other plants eaten are American three-square rush (*Scirpus americanus*) and giant reed phragmites (*Phragmites* sp.) of the low-water areas, poison ivy (*Rhus toxicodendron*) and salt meadow hay (*Spartina patens* or *Diplachne maritima*) of the drier areas, greenbrier (*Smilax* sp.), and sandbur (*Cenchrus tribuloides*). They

will eat other items as available, such as sea lettuce (*Ulva lactuca*, a seaweed) in the low salt-marsh after storms; sea lettuce is more than 20% protein, thus much higher in protein than dead or dying grass (less than 9%). They will eat the seed heads of grass, the hips of beach rose, crabapples, and the underground tubers of grasses.

The ponies drink from the freshwater pools, but sometimes on hot days they will sip salt water for a few seconds. They usually go to the freshwater pools and drink three times a day in summer (before dawn, midday, and late afternoon or after dusk), but in winter they omit the midday drink. Movement to the water hole is an obvious activity. One member of the band starts, then all follow in single file until they near the water hole, when they break into a run. Drinking lasts one to three minutes. Because their food is so salty, the animals drink about twice as much water as domestic horses do.

REPRODUCTION AND DEVELOPMENT. Courtship is a protracted affair in this species, one pattern leading to the next. It begins with the male "tending" the estrous female by staying near her, often isolating her from the harem. He walks slowly, but sometimes rushes toward her with ears standing straight up, neck arched, and tail raised over the back. He sniffs, nibbles, nuzzles, and licks her. She may squeal and paw the air with a foreleg, and if near full estrus she will urinate. The male then paws the ground and sniffs the urine. He curls his upper lip, extends the neck, raises the head in a posture called *flehmen*, and inhales deeply, an effort that can be heard for some distance. If she remains receptive, mating will occur. The male may mate with several mares in one day, and several times per day per mare. Stallions can breed throughout the year, but most sexual activity is in the spring and early summer.

Gestation in Assateague ponies has not been ascertained, but is 330 to 340 days in domestic horses. Births occur in spring: about 13% in April, 52% in May, 22% in June, and 10% in July. An hour before giving birth to her single young, the mare usually separates from the band. The young are born forelegs first, usually

*Mare nursing foal
(Ronald R. Keiper)*

at night. They are at first unsteady, but are nursing within an hour. The female does not eat the placenta; rather, she moves the foal away from it as quickly as possible, presumably to avoid predators. The newborn are fully haired, and their eyes are open. Within a few hours of birth, they are running with their mothers or even swimming. And within three hours of birth, they return to the band, but a mare will keep the other horses away from her foal. The foals nurse about four to seven times per hour, the nursing bouts averaging 84 seconds. Later, the bouts decrease to about a minute, about one per hour. Mares do not nurse other foals, and will chase them off or even bite them, though the foals may champ to protect themselves. Mares that give birth to a new foal the next year wean their prior offspring just before or just after the birth of the new offspring; mares not having new offspring may continue to nurse for 20 months to two years. Foals practice coprophagy (ingestion of feces), perhaps obtaining necessary bacterial forms thereby. Foals initially spend most of their time nursing or resting, but increasingly greater amounts of time are spent in play with other foals of about the same age and in investigation of the environment. Play consists of chases, prancing, and biting one another.

First foaling is in the mare's third year, and 40 to 70% of the mares foal in any one year. Foaling rates were 27% for three-year-old mares, 41% for four-year-olds, 53% for five-year-olds, and 68% for females at least six years old. The rate is 80% in domestic horses and 74% on Virginia Assateague, because the foals are removed from their mothers at 6 to 12 weeks of age for sale at a yearly auction. Some females foal four or five years in a row before skipping a year. The northern herd is now being controlled by contraceptives, the southern herd through sale at the annual auction. The auction has kept the size of the population stable, at a ratio of about one male to 2.4 females.

POPULATION CHARACTERISTICS. The Assateague ponies form social groups known as "bands." The bands are family or harem groups usually containing a stallion, one to 16 adult mares, and their young up to three years of age. Some bands contain two to four mixed-sex or male-only young. Solitary animals, whether recent dispersals or older individuals, also occur. In 1974 the 45 ponies in the Maryland herd formed three harems averaging 14 mares each, and one male bachelor band. In 1984, there were ten harem bands, averaging just under nine per band, and three bachelor bands; and by 1988, herd size had increased to 19 harem bands with an average of 5.7 animals per band. The harem bands had become steadily smaller because of increased stallion pressure to establish harems. On the Virginia extremity of Assateague, however, there were fewer sexually mature stallions, thus fewer and larger harem bands. Social ties rather than the dominance of the stallion hold the harem bands together, and the bands remain together even if the stallion dies or disappears. A pecking order is established, thus reducing strife within the harem bands. The peck order is determined by age, temperament, and heredity; size and sex are of little importance, and the adult male is not necessarily the alpha animal.

Initially, of course, the peck order is established through aggressive behavior, which falls into five categories. The highest levels of aggressive behavior include (1) the threat to back-kick and (2) the actual back-kick. The threat consists of shifting the animal's posterior toward the second animal and waving the tail back and forth while backing toward it. The actual kick is directed backwards, both feet extended toward the opponent. The kick usually misses, but may catch the opponent in the chest or flanks. Lower-level aggressive behaviors are (3) displacement (the lowest level), wherein the aggressor simply occupies the space taken up by the opponent; (4) the threat to bite, with the ears against the head and the teeth sometimes bared; and (5) the actual bite. High-intensity aggression often includes high-pitched squeals.

The home range of the bands on Assateague ranges from 2.2 to 11.4 square km (0.85 to 4.4 square miles). Because the size of the home range is not related to band size, but rather to quality and amount of forage, bands in poor habitat are larger. Home range on Maryland Assateague averages 6.5 square km (2.5 square miles), whereas in Virginia, where habitats are considerably richer, it averages 1.7 square km (0.65 square miles).

Young males leave the harems between one and three years, some on their own, but most as they become increasingly harassed by their fathers. Most young males enter bachelor bands, occupying relatively small home-range areas, where they play-fight and otherwise mature until they are ready to establish their own harems. Other young males remain solitary. About one-fourth of the young females stay in their parental harems and are bred by their fathers, but most join new harems, at between one and three years. Some of the young join mixed-sex bands.

The lifespan of the Assateague ponies is about 20 years, as compared to about 30 for domestic horses. This disparity is at least partly due to malnutrition. As the ponies get older, the harsh diet wears their teeth down so badly that they are less able to grind their food adequately.

ENEMIES. The Assateague Island ponies have no important enemies other than flies and ticks, weather, and the actions of humans. One is occasionally hit by a car, and on Virginia Assateague, the Chincoteague Volunteer Fire department auctions off some of the ponies each year. Thirteen drowned in a winter storm in 1990.

PARASITES AND DISEASE. There are many ticks on the islands where our feral horses find their home, and these take blood meals from them, though they do not seem to bother the horses much. Mosquitos swarm around the animals also, but seldom seem to bother them except when they are inhaled; they are then blown out by the horses.

Biting flies are the most important enemy of the horses. They hurt, they can create open sores that can become infected, and they can transmit diseases such as equine infectious anemia and equine encephalitis. Outbreaks of these diseases have been recorded in both the Maryland and the Virginia populations, and in early 1990, two outbreaks of equine encephalitis each killed ten to 14 animals. Deerflies (*Chrysops*), three species of horseflies (*Tabanus*), and stable flies (*Stomoxys calcitrans*) are the important biting flies. Their effects are most serious in July and August. The horses often stamp their feet and bite in their efforts to shed them, and a band of horses will sometimes walk through thick brush to remove them. They may run to "refugia," open areas with higher wind, or enter the water, to get away from the flies. They may walk a kilometer (more than half a mile) into the bay, or go directly into the surf. Again, this is a contagious behavior: if one goes, the rest follow. They may remain in the surf up to 20 minutes, and then roll in the sand. The ponies seldom use woods as refugia, because of the deer flies there. Their most common defense is to seek an open area—mud flats, open sand, or parking lots—or a retreat under the cement bathhouses in Maryland State Park camping areas.

RELATION TO HUMANS. The northern (Maryland) ponies live on the Assateague Island National Seashore and are not managed, although contraceptives are administered by dart gun in order to maintain the population at about 150 animals. Over a million people visit the seashore annually, and the ponies are a major attraction. Some of the ponies are hit by cars, and ponies sometimes bite or kick visitors. Tents, coolers, and other items can also be damaged.

The southern (Virginia) ponies are owned by the Chincoteague Volunteer Fire Department and graze on the Chincoteague National Wildlife Refuge on southern Assateague Island. The southern herd likewise is maintained at about 150 animals. Each year there is a "swim," in which some of the animals on southern Assateague are herded into the water to swim the quarter of a mile to Chincoteague, where many of the foals and yearlings are sold at auction, thus helping to finance the fire department.

AREAS FOR FURTHER WORK. Comparative genetic studies of the Assateague, Chincoteague, Shackleford, and Cumberland Island horses should yield fascinating information on small-population evolution of a slowly reproducing species.

## SUBSPECIES

There are numerous breeds of horses, but no subspecies have been described. (See the subspecies discussion for the domestic dog.)

### *Equus caballus* Linnaeus

Type locality: Europe, perhaps Sweden.

## LITERATURE

Keiper, R. R. 1985. *The Assateague Ponies*. Centreville, Md.: Tidewater. 101 pp.

# 11. ORDER ARTIODACTYLA

## Pigs, Deer, and Other Even-Toed Ungulates

THE UNGULATES ARE the hoofed mammals. Evolution in ungulates has been toward large size, an herbivorous diet, and rapid locomotion. The functional toes have been reduced in number, usually to two, and the claws have transformed into thickened hoofs. The long bones of the front and hind feet, the metacarpals and metatarsals, and also, to some degree, some of the distal bones have elongated and elevated so that the ankle and wrist are above the ground and only the tips of the toes form the hooves or running surface. The two metatarsals and metacarpals have often fused into a "cannon bone." Effectively, the animal has an extra segment in its legs, and it walks or runs on the tips of its toes. Despite their size and speed, ungulates need to be alert for predators, and they have evolved excellent vision, smell, and hearing.

The herbivorous diet presents special evolutionary challenges. The cell walls of plants contain cellulose, which is indigestible to most mammals, and plant material is often low in protein. Protein is needed for the amino acids necessary for growth and the maintenance of tissues. The most abundant source of protein in plants is the seeds, but these are small, widely dispersed, and not always available. Ungulates and other herbivores exhibit great variety in the structure and function of their dentition and digestive tracts, because of variation in the way different species have solved the problem of feeding on plant material. This variation allows the various species to feed on different kinds of plant materials, and the molars of ungulates show various complicated patterns of grinding surfaces, each suited to a particular diet. The gut may be elongated, the caecum enlarged. This line of development reaches its extreme in the four-chambered stomach (rumen, reticulum, omasum, and abomasum) of the cows and other ruminants.

There are two groups, or orders, of ungulates, the odd-toed ungulates, Perissodactyla, and the even-toed ungulates, Artiodactyla. (In the eastern United States, the Perissodactyla are represented in the wild only by a few feral horses.) The Artiodactyla include about 220 species in 81 genera and ten families. They are worldwide in distribution, except for the Australian region. The Artiodactyla include three suborders: the Suina (pigs, peccaries, and hippopotamuses), the Ruminantia (deer, giraffes, cows, antelopes, and related forms), and the Tylopoda (llamas and camels). The Suina are rather primitive, relatively omnivorous artiodactyls with large tusks, bunodont teeth, and short, four-toed limbs. They do not feed on fibrous vegetation, but use mainly roots and fruits; their digestive system resembles that of other mammals. The Ruminantia and Tylopoda have broad, high-crowned, ridged molar teeth, adapted for grinding browse and grasses. The Ruminantia have a four-chambered stomach, the Tylopoda a three-chambered stomach. Both chew the cud. Microorganisms similar to those found in perissodactyls are present in the first three chambers of a ruminant, but food remains in the entire digestive tract much longer than it does in perissodactyls. Undigested food reenters the rumen to ferment. It will later be regurgitated as a cud, mixed with saliva, and chewed again. When reswallowed, the digested food will pass directly to the omasum, where digestion is completed.

Two families, the Suidae (pigs), with one introduced species, and the Cervidae (deer), with three native and three introduced species, are represented in the eastern United States.

KEY TO THE FAMILIES OF ARTIODACTYLA

1. Snout oval, elongate, mobile, and flat, the nostrils opening at the end; legs short; antlers lacking; dentition complete, the upper incisors present, the canines tusklike, the lower canines not incisiform . . . . . . . . . . . . . . . SUIDAE
1. Snout not as above; legs long; antlers in season in males; dentition reduced, the upper incisors lacking, the upper canines lacking or poorly developed, the lower canines incisiform . . . . . . . . . . . . . . . . CERVIDAE (p. 517)

*Wild pig, or feral hog,* Sus scrofa *(James N. Layne)*

## PIGS, Family Suidae

The pig family, the pigs and boars, includes 16 species in five genera, ten of the species in the genus *Sus*. Pigs are not ruminants; they have simple stomachs and do not chew the cud. There are three pairs of upper incisors, and the upper canines project laterally as tusks. The tusks, somewhat larger in boars than in sows, are rootless and therefore grow throughout the life of the animal, curving upward and outward. The cheek teeth are bunodont, as in humans, reflecting the omnivorous diet of these species. Suids are native to the Old World but have been domesticated, and also introduced into the wild, over much of the world. The European wild boar, though of the same species, differs from the domestic pig in having longer legs, a long, bristly hair tuft at the tip of the tail, and small, pointed, densely haired ears.

Domestication of the pig apparently occurred in China around 4900 B.C., but could have occurred even as early as 10,000 B.C. in Thailand (Lekagul and McNeely, 1977). Many breeds have been developed, especially in Europe.

### Feral Pig, Feral Hog
*Sus scrofa* Linnaeus          Color plate 22

The feral pig of the eastern United States is of the same species as the domestic pig and the European wild boar, a species that was originally widespread in the Old World. Pigs have probably survived in the wild in the southeastern United States for 400 years, since their escape from Hernando DeSoto in 1593, although there have been many other introductions since, and there is some evidence that pigs may have been present prior to the 1490s, to judge from an incisor found in Arkansas that was dated earlier than that (Quinn, 1970).

DESCRIPTION. The feral pig is smaller and rangier than the domestic pig. Wild pigs are also exceedingly variable in color. Most often, they are black and white, but they can be brown, brown and white, or all white. Wild pigs have sparse, bristly hair, more dense than the hair of domestic hogs, a truncate, naked snout, and short legs. Each foot has four toes: the middle two are flattened as functional hooves; the outer two (called "dewclaws") high on the leg, have small hooves and are accessory. The wild pig has small eyes, but fairly large, pointed ears. The nostrils face forward on the smooth disk of the movable snout.

MEASUREMENTS. Feral pigs measure: total length 900–1800 mm (35–70 inches), tail 300–400 mm (12–16 inches); and weight 50–200 kg (110–440 lbs). The females are generally smaller than the males. There is much variation in size, depending on how long a population has been established and on its density. An overpopulated coastal island in Georgia includes the smallest known individuals, averaging only 23 kg (50.5 lbs) and 96 cm (38 inches) total length, but the averages increased to 30 kg (66 lbs) and 101 cm (40 inches) when the herd was reduced in numbers.

Diploid number in European wild boars is 36; in domestic hogs, 38. One would expect the diploid number of feral pigs to be 38, as well, since they are descended from domestic pigs, but hogs from the Tellico Wildlife Management Area in Tennessee have 36, in line with their wild boar ancestry. The situation is further confused by interbreeding between individuals of domestic hog and wild boar origin.

Tooth formula

$$\frac{3}{3} \quad \frac{1}{1} \quad \frac{4}{4} \quad \frac{3}{3} \quad = \quad 44$$

DISTRIBUTION. Two forms of this species, the European boar and the wild pig, as well as many hybrids between the two, are present in the eastern United States. European boars, or at least animals that retain characteristics of European boars (some may be crosses between the European boar and the wild pig), are found in several states. In Tennessee they are found mostly in the Cherokee National Forest and Great Smoky Mountains National Park. An estimated 1500 individuals roam the National Forest and pri-

vate lands, and there are about 800 in the National Park. About 100–120 are killed annually on Forest Service and private lands. There are about 800 more in the six westernmost counties (especially Graham and Cherokee) of North Carolina, where about 100 are taken annually by licensed hunters. They have been reported from western Virginia, but no current populations are known to exist there (Mayer and Brisbin, 1991). In Kentucky, an estimated 300 are found in the Appalachians and on the Cumberland Plateau. Some were released in western West Virginia by the West Virginia Department of Natural Resources, and there is now a hunting season there.

The other form, the "feral hog," or "wild pig," is the escaped domesticated pig. Wild pigs are found in all of Florida and in coastal areas of extreme southern Virginia, North Carolina, South

*Distribution of the wild pig, or feral hog,* Sus scrofa, *in the eastern United States*

Carolina, Georgia, Alabama, Mississippi, and Louisiana. It is often difficult to determine whether free-ranging pigs in parts of Florida are wild or not, for wild ones are often difficult to observe, but in portions of the Everglades they are quite abundant and easy to observe.

HABITAT. The wild pig inhabits a variety of habitats, but especially bottomlands that include woods and water. It is limited in its distribution by both habitat and climate. It needs adequate cover in its habitat, both for protection from disturbance and to help reduce heat loss, and a moderate climate is important because rooting becomes more difficult with increased frost penetration. In Florida, the wild pig usually inhabits areas with a mixture of habitats, including relatively open areas for foraging and denser areas for resting. In the southern Appalachians, it frequents the higher elevations, where it lives in mixed wooded and open areas.

HABITS. Like its domestic cousin, the wild pig has a tough, cartilaginous snout and outward-turned canines, the whole assemblage well-adapted for rooting in the dirt or mud. The snout is supported by an accessory bone, the prenasal, situated under the tips of the nasal bones. Pigs live in bands of eight or less, most bands comprising not more than three adults. Large boars usually travel alone, except when with breeding groups. Bands of pigs are often almost nomadic within their home range, moving about as food becomes available, but their daily activity patterns are linked to thermoregulation, since they lack sweat glands and have so little hair. In summer, pigs are active at night, but especially active at dawn and dusk. Radio-tracked animals in South Carolina were mainly diurnal from October through May.

Pigs are swift runners. They also swim well and often wallow in mud, sometimes for hours. The tusks are fearsome offensive weapons; a cornered pig is well able to defend itself even against much larger animals. The tail serves as a fly switch. Wild pigs depend more on their noses and ears than on their eyes.

Wild pigs usually bed down in thickets, often on ridges but always in good cover. Sometimes they will construct shelters for shade, by cutting vegetation and spreading it on the ground. They then crawl under the grass and raise up with it on their back. This screen then catches in the standing grass, thereby forming a canopy. The pigs in the Smokies often rub trees with their bodies, leaving mud and bristles on the trees. These rubbing trees are usually located near trails and wallows. Wild boars also "tusk" trees, often pitch pines, and often these trees are their rubbing trees. Tusking leaves diagonal cuts through the bark.

FOOD AND FEEDING. Though wild pigs are omnivorous, they favor plant food, especially mast, but they will eat roots, tubers, shoots, leaves, fruits, and mushrooms. They root for food in mud and litter, and often feed on insect larvae, snails, earthworms, reptiles, birds, small mammals, and bird or reptile eggs, although, in one study in South Carolina, invertebrates and vertebrates each accounted for less than 3% of the diet, the most common invertebrates being scarabaeid grubs, centipedes, and earthworms. Wild pigs will also feed on carrion.

REPRODUCTION AND DEVELOPMENT. Boars gather as females come into heat, and several may gather around an estrous sow for about two days. When she becomes receptive, matings can take place day and night and as often as every ten minutes. All the while, there is a struggle for dominance that includes courtship displays and fighting. Wild pigs fight by circling, charging each other headfirst, and slashing at each other's shoulders, an area protected by fat and hair. The dominant boar copulates first, then usually lies down, allowing subordinates to mate. Gestation is about 112 to 115 days. Physiologically, litters can be produced at any time of year, but feral hogs in South Carolina had two peaks of farrowing, one in February and a smaller one in summer (Sweeney et al., 1979). In Tennessee, peaks occur in January/February and in May/June.

At farrowing time the female goes off by herself and greatly reduces her home range and activity. She makes a nest of vegetation, such as pine straw and broom sedge, in a shallow depression, usually in a shaded area on high ground. Litter size ranges from three to 12, averaging 7.4 in South Carolina (Sweeney et al.,

1979). One sow in South Carolina, after producing her young, would leave the piglets in the nest and forage from about 0900 to 1600 hours daily; by three weeks of age the young began following her, whereupon she soon left the farrowing area. Piglets in South Carolina remained together until their weight reached about 25 to 35 kg (55 to 82 lbs). Maturity is reached at about a year and a half, but the animals do not reach full growth until they are about five to six years of age. By 20–22 months, the milk teeth have been replaced.

POPULATION CHARACTERISTICS. The boars tend to be solitary, but there are bachelor herds and matriarchal herds, the latter formed of one or more sows with their young. Home ranges of 123 to 799 ha (304 to 1974 acres), averaging 396 ha (978 acres) in one study, and 203 ha (501 acres) in another, were reported from South Carolina, but the ranges of the sows averaged just 17 and 30 ha (42 and 74 acres) during the farrowing period. No territories are formed. The males establish a dominance hierarchy and move about in the female clan area. Wild pigs may live to 18 or 20 years.

ENEMIES. Human hunters are the most rapacious enemies of wild pigs. Predation on wild pigs is otherwise generally minimal, but alligators, mountain lions, and black bears have been known to kill adult feral hogs. In the Southeast, bobcats are important predators on the young.

PARASITES AND DISEASE. In the Southeast, old animals often show evidence of disease, including antibodies to vesicular stomatitis virus and eastern equine encephalomyelitis. Pseudorabies, hog cholera, and something resembling swine pox were suspected, but not demonstrated. Internal parasites found in wild pigs in the Southeast included lungworms (*Metastrongylus*), kidneyworms (*Stephanura*), and *Sarcosporidia* (but not trichina). The pig louse, *Haematopinus suis*, was abundant on pigs in the winter, and a few ticks were found in summer. Probably the most important bacterial disease of wild hogs is brucellosis, which has serious implications both for hunters and for domestic swine. It is caused by strains of *Brucella suis*, and it is found in about a third of the wild hogs

in Florida, but in certain areas the rates are higher still. Many wild hogs probably die from this disease (Forrester, 1992).

RELATION TO HUMANS. Rooting and compaction of the soil are problems that can arise from the presence of wild pigs. They may also feed on crops, and they compete for mast with other wildlife species (especially squirrels, deer, and turkeys). Damage to wildlife plantings can be a problem, and control programs often have to be implemented in natural areas. Wild pigs are currently causing considerable damage to vegetation, amphibians, and ground-nesting birds in the Great Smoky Mountains National Park, and even greater depredations in Hawaii.

Wild pigs are hunted under license in Georgia and South Carolina and some parts of Florida. From 1971 to 1976, sport hunting in Florida resulted in the killing of an average of 56,200 pigs per year (maximum 84,100). They are also hunted in many parts of their range where no license is required. In Alabama, Louisiana, and Mississippi, they are considered domestic livestock and not hunted.

AREAS FOR FURTHER WORK. How long and how often are feral pigs in estrus? More information on specific foods and feeding habits and additional data on ectoparasites would be desirable. The relationship between this introduced species and the various native species in its habitat would be of interest.

## SUBSPECIES

The feral hog, of domestic origin but living today in a wild state in the United States, is very closely related to the wild hog of Eurasia, and thus retains the same name.

*Sus scrofa scrofa* Linnaeus
  As described above.
  Type locality: Germany.

### LITERATURE

Bratton, S. P. 1974. The effect of the European wild boar (*Sus scrofa*) on the high-elevation vernal flora in Great Smoky Mountains National Park. *Bull. Torrey Bot. Club* 101: 198–206.

Forrester, D. J. 1992. *Parasites and Diseases of Wild Mammals in Florida.* Gainesville: Univ. Press of Florida. 459 pp.

Hanson, R. P., and L. Karstad. 1959. Feral swine in the Southeastern United States. *J. Wildl. Mgmt.* 23: 64–74.

Lacki, M. J., and R. A. Lancia. 1986. Effects of wild pigs on beech growth in Great Smoky Mountains National Park. *J. Wildl. Mgmt.* 50: 655–659.

Lekagul, B., and A. McNeely. 1977. *Mammals of Thailand.* Bangkok: Sahakarnbhat. 758 pp.

Mayer, J. J., and L. L. Brisbin, Jr. 1991. *Wild Pigs in the United States: Their History, Morphology and Current Status.* Athens: Univ. Georgia Press. 313 pp.

Quinn, J. H. 1970. Note on *Sus* in North America. *Soc. Vert. Paleontol. News Bull.* 88: 33.

Stegeman, L. C. 1938. The European wild boar in the Cherokee National Forest, Tennessee. *J. Mammal.* 19: 279–290.

Sweeney, J. M., and J. R. Sweeney. 1982. Feral hog, *Sus scrofa.* In: J. A. Chapman and G. A. Feldhamer, eds., *Wild Mammals of North America: Biology, Management and Economics,* pp. 1099–1113. Baltimore: Johns Hopkins Univ. Press.

Sweeney, J. M., J. R. Sweeney, and E. E. Provost. 1979. Reproductive biology of a feral hog population. *J. Wildl. Mgmt.* 43: 555–559.

Wood, G. W., and R. H. Barrett. 1979. Status of wild pigs in the United States. *Wildl. Soc. Bull.* 7: 237–246.

Wood, G. W., and R. E. Brenneman. 1980. Feral hog movements and habitat use in coastal South Carolina. *J. Wildl. Mgmt.* 44: 420–427.

# DEER, ELK, AND MOOSE,
Family Cervidae

In addition to their hooves, cervids retain remnants of the lateral digits, but they are best characterized by their antlers, those bony outgrowths arising from their frontal bones, and the absence of incisors in the upper jaw. The skull is tapering and the orbit is surrounded by a complete ring of bone. Cervids are generally grazers in summer, browsers in winter.

Antlers are deciduous, bony structures grown only by the cervids. They are the most rapid-growing bones of mammals. Each antler grows from a pedicel (or protrusion) of the frontal bone. Antlers begin to grow in the spring, and until they mature they are covered with "velvet," soft true skin liberally supplied with blood vessels and nerves, the blood vessels carrying

nutrients for antler growth. The antlers harden or ossify when they mature, about mating time, and the velvet then falls off or is rubbed off. The antlers are used in thrashing bushes and in fighting during the rut. After the mating season, decalcification takes place at the union between the base of the antler and the pedicel. The antlers then fall off, either under their own weight or by catching on brush. They are usually grown only by the males, but are present in both sexes in the caribou (called "reindeer" in Europe). Antlers evolved both as weapons and as display organs in relation to reproduction.

There are about 43 species in the family, and the family is distributed nearly worldwide except for the Australian region and Africa south of the Sahara. Only the white-tailed deer and the moose currently occur naturally in the eastern United States. One other, the wapiti, or elk, formerly wide-ranging in the east, has been reintroduced and currently thrives in Michigan and Pennsylvania, and there is even a small but persistent population of wapiti in central Florida. Three other species, the sambar, fallow, and sika deer, have been introduced in various locations.

## KEY TO THE GENERA
## OF THE FAMILY CERVIDAE

1. Huge animal (skull over 510 mm long); antlers palmate and animal unspotted; nose covered with hair all around nostrils; dewlap (bell) present (moose)...... *Alces* (p. 541)
1. Animal of more modest size (skull length well under 510 mm); *if* antlers palmate, *then* animal spotted; nose not covered with hair around nostrils; dewlap lacking.............. 2
2. Animals white-spotted at all ages; dorsum of tail black; dark stripe from nape to tail and around white rump patch; antlers palmate with brow tine (fallow deer)............. *Dama*
2. Adults not spotted except in *Cervus nippon*, on which most of dorsum of tail is white........ 3
3. Adults not spotted *and* weighing much less than 225 kg (500 lbs) (the common white-tailed deer of the eastern United States)................... *Odocoileus* (p. 531)
3. Adults white-spotted, the spots in seven or eight rows, *or* average weight greater than 225 kg (500 lbs); introduced exotics (sambar, sika deer) and wapiti, or elk ...... *Cervus* (p. 520)

## Fallow Deer
### *Dama dama* Linnaeus  Color plate 23

The fallow deer, a handsome animal native to Europe, Iraq, and Iran, is one of the world's most widely introduced ungulates. It has at times been placed in the genus *Cervus*, but *Dama* has now been validated as the generic name for this species by opinion 581, International Commission on Zoological Nomenclature (1960). The genus *Dama* contains only two species, *D. dama* and *D. mesopotamia*, the latter a closely related (if not synonymous) species of the Middle East.

DESCRIPTION. This deer is highly variable in color (white, cream, sandy, silver-gray, sooty, or black) but is spotted at all ages. The adult male has antlers in season and an "Adam's apple." The longer hind legs elevate the hind portions of the animal slightly. There is a black dorsal stripe from the nape of the neck to the tip of the tail and around the white rump patch. The spots, always white, are scattered chiefly on the back and flanks; there are fewer on the neck, and

none on the head or legs. Spots that occur on the lower parts of the sides and haunches fuse into a white line. In individuals three years old or older, the antlers are palmate. The beam of the antler is narrow, cylindrical, and about 50–70 cm (20–28 inches) long. It projects backward and laterally, and carries a well-developed, upswept brow tine. The bay tine is usually lacking, but a small tine projects laterally just below the palm. The palm, 7 to 20 cm (2.8 to 8 inches) wide, is inflected medially at the top, and has several posteriorly directed projections, the longest at the bottom. Upper canines are usually absent; the first lower incisors have large spatulate crowns; and the lower canines appear as incisors.

MEASUREMENTS. Weights of 20 adult males are 48–80 kg (105–176 lbs); for 15 females, 35–52 kg (77–114 lbs).

Diploid number = 68.

TOOTH FORMULA

$$\frac{0}{3} \; \frac{0}{1} \; \frac{3}{3} \; \frac{3}{3} \; = \; 32$$

DISTRIBUTION. In the eastern United States, fallow deer have been successfully introduced at several localities. There are an estimated 400 to 500 in Georgia, most of them on a privately owned island, Little St. Simons, but there are a few others on Jekyll Island, and they occasionally cross to St. Simons and Sea Islands. At Land Between the Lakes, in Kentucky, there are an estimated 600 individuals, and in central Alabama another 1000. There are also a very few, perhaps 10, along the eastern shore of Maryland in Talbot County. About 100 to 200 are taken by hunters annually in Kentucky and another hundred in Alabama, mostly in Wilcox and Dallas Counties. Some that had been introduced on Martha's Vineyard, Massachusetts, are no longer there.

HABITAT. Fallow deer seem to favor mixed older forest/grassland, but can maintain themselves in a variety of habitats.

HABITS. When undisturbed, fallow deer remain in herds all year, although adult males are usu-

*Fallow deer,* Dama dama *(Roger W. Barbour)*

ally solitary in summer. Bachelor herds may be formed in late summer. The largest herds occur just before rutting, in the fall, when the males join the herds. Groups are larger in open areas than in woods. When disturbed, females generally flee together; males flee individually.

By early autumn, adult males join the female groups and begin establishing territories. They paw the ground, creating "scrapes" into which they urinate, and they thrash vegetation with their antlers, in the fashion of white-tailed deer. The males also make low-pitched groans and grunts, they belch, and they spar with other males. Rutting reaches its peak in October, when females enter the rutting areas and the more dominant males chase off subordinates, which remain on the periphery of the herd. After the rut the females and younger animals form their own herds, usually of seven to 14 animals, sometimes more. The males may form bachelor groups.

Fallow deer have six vocalizations: a loud, explosive bark produced by females; "bleating" by pregnant females or mothers with fawns; "mewing," a submissive call given by any age or sex; "peeping" by fawns to contact their mothers or when in distress; "wailing" by fawns in intense distress; and groaning, a belchlike sound of adult rutting males. The groans are about a second in duration, but may be in a series with four to five seconds between groans.

A behavior pattern called "alerting" finds members of a disturbed herd assuming a rigid upright stance with the neck extended vertically. They may "stiff-walk," and the degree of tail elevation indicates degree of alarm.

FOOD AND FEEDING. The main foraging periods of fallow deer are at dusk and dawn; diet depends greatly upon availability, but from March through September, grasses, herbs, and tree leaves are preferred. Shrubs, including *Vacci-*

*Distribution of the fallow deer,* Dama dama, *in the eastern United States*

*nium*, *Rosa*, *Rubus*, and many others, become the staple in winter.

REPRODUCTION AND DEVELOPMENT. In North America the rutting season is the last half of October. Some females become pregnant when six to seven months old, although most do not conceive until about 16 months. Most produce one young, after a gestation of 33 to 35 weeks. Fawns are born from May through the summer, most in early June. The newborn is 55 cm (22 inches) in crown-rump length.

Pregnant females usually leave the herd and find a secluded place for the birth of the young. The female cleans the newborn by licking it. Soon she will leave the fawn alone for most of the day, returning only for nursing. Later, the fawns learn to recognize the mother's bleat. The fawn remains in the area of its birth for about a week, and is able to run with its mother at about one month of age. Nursing occurs about every four hours, until the young is four months old; weaning may continue until the spring after birth, when the young is about seven or eight months old. Males become fully mature and reach their greatest mass at about five to nine years of age, females at four to six years. Most males do not breed until they are four years old.

POPULATION CHARACTERISTICS. Home ranges, those of the larger males, vary greatly. Males occupy different home ranges depending on whether they are in bachelor herds or in rut. The two home ranges may or may not overlap. Defended territories are established only by males, only during rutting. Group size in summer in Kentucky averaged 3.6 in wooded areas, 5.2 in the open, but ranged up to 45 individuals, with mixed, male, and female herds averaging 9.2, 2.1, and 14.0 individuals per group, respectively.

ENEMIES. The enemies of this species today are humans and their automobiles, and coyotes and other predators, which prey especially on the young.

PARASITES AND DISEASE. Ectoparasites reported in North American fallow deer are lice (*Bovicola tibialis*), keds (*Lipoptena depressa* and *Neolipoptena ferrisi*), nasal bots (*Cephenemyia apicata*), and ticks (*Ixodes pacificus, I. scapularis, Amblyomma maculatum,* and *Dermacentor albipictus*). Numerous nematodes, six species of cestodes, and four species of trematodes have been reported as endoparasites. Evidence of avian tuberculosis, pseudotuberculosis, and brucellosis has been found in the United States.

RELATION TO HUMANS. This species is not native, and in none of the areas where these animals have been introduced are they protected. Rather, they are considered as deer and hunted for sport and food in regular season.

AREAS FOR FURTHER WORK. The particulars of the food of this species could be studied, and its parasites could be studied and compared to those of the native white-tailed deer where the two occur together.

## SUBSPECIES

*Dama dama* Linnaeus
  As described above.
  Type locality: Sweden.

## LITERATURE

Chapman, D. I., and N. G. Chapman. 1975. *Fallow Deer: Their History, Distribution and Biology.* Laverham, Suffolk: Terrence Dalton. 271 pp.

Chapman, N. G., and D. I. Chapman. 1980. The distribution of fallow deer: A worldwide review. *Mammal. Revue* 10: 61–138.

Feldhamer, G. A., K. C. Farrs-Renner, and M. Barker. 1988. *Dama dama.* **Mammalian Species No. 317.** Amer. Soc. Mammal. 8 pp.

International Commission on Zoological Nomenclature. 1960. Opinion 581. Determination of the generic name for the fallow deer of Europe and the Virginia deer of America (Class Mammalia). *Bull. Zool. Nomenclature* 17: 267–275.

## The Deer and Elk of the Genus *Cervus*

The genus *Cervus* numbers ten species worldwide. It includes our "elk," or wapiti, a native

*Wapiti, or elk,* Cervus elaphus
*(Roger W. Barbour)*

species considered to be conspecific with the red deer of Eurasia and Africa (which has been widely introduced elsewhere). The nine other species include two that have been introduced in eastern United States, the sika deer, *C. nippon,* and the sambar deer, *C. unicolor.*

KEY TO THE DEER AND ELK
OF THE GENUS *CERVUS*

1. Average weight less than 90 kg (200 lbs); skull less than 355 mm long; back showing white or yellowish spots in juveniles and adults . . . . . . . . . . . . . . . . . . . . . . *Cervus nippon*
1. Average weight greater than 225 kg (500 lbs); skull more than 355 mm long; back lacking light spots in juveniles and adults. . . . . . . . . . . . . 2
2. Nose, head, and neck dark brown, the back pale brown, a large yellowish patch on rump, the tail short and same color as rump patch; main tine of antler extending posteriorly from head, the antler bearing five tines . . . . . . *C. elaphus*
2. Animal uniformly brown above, the underparts a slightly lighter yellowish brown; main tine of antler projecting forward, the antler bearing a smaller, forked tine projecting posteriorly . . . . . . . . . . . . . . . . . . . . . *C. unicolor*

## Wapiti, Elk
### *Cervus elaphus* Linnaeus           Color plate 23

The wapiti, or elk, of the American continent is a large cervid originally described as *Cervus canadensis.* The current view is that the elk is conspecific with the red deer, *C. elaphus,* of Eu-

rasia. Since *C. elaphus* was the form of this entity described first, the wapiti is now known as *C. elaphus* as well. In Europe, unfortunately, the common name "elk" refers to *Alces alces,* which is called "moose" in North America. To avoid confusion with the European "elk," then, the preferred common name is "wapiti," although the name "North American elk" is often used. The name "wapiti," meaning "white deer" or, more specifically, "white rump," is of Algonquian origin.

DESCRIPTION. The wapiti is a very large, brown cervid with a large buff-colored rump patch. It is the second largest cervid in the world, second only to the moose. The antler can weigh over 13 kg (28 pounds). The fur is darker brown in winter, more tawny in summer. The head, throat, underparts, and legs are dark brown, in contrast to the lighter colors on the back and sides. In the adult male, or bull, the antlers consist of long main beams (to 1,500 mm, or 5 feet) that extend back from the head and carry five or more tines. A brow tine extends forward over the head, the second (bez) tine grows laterally over the ear, the third (trez) is about a third the length of the main beam and projects upward, the fourth is the largest, and the fifth projects somewhat posteriorly. The last point is the tip of the main beam. The antlers are shed in winter following the breeding season and soon begin regrowth. Under poor ecological conditions, the antlers are smaller and otherwise less developed. Unlike white-tailed deer, mule deer, and moose, the wapiti has an upper canine, or "elk tooth."

MEASUREMENTS. The wapiti stands about 1.7 meters (5 feet) at the shoulder. Head and body length averages 2400 mm (8 feet) in the male, or bull, and 2250 mm (7.5 feet) in the female, or cow. The tail is about 150 mm (6 inches) long. Bulls weigh 261–450 kg (580–1000 lbs), cows 225–293 kg (500–650 lbs).

Diploid number = 68.

TOOTH FORMULA

$$\frac{0}{3} \quad \frac{1}{1} \quad \frac{3}{3} \quad \frac{3}{3} \quad = \quad 34$$

DISTRIBUTION. Originally, the wapiti of North America ranged from southern Canada through most of the United States except for its southernmost reaches. In the eastern United States, the wapiti ranged from Wisconsin, New York, and west-central New England south to central Georgia and northwestern South Carolina. Wapiti were extirpated in the eastern United States by about the 1870s from overhunting and habitat destruction. The latest records were 1863 in Wisconsin, 1867 in Pennsylvania, 1875 in West Virginia, and 1877 in Michigan. Wapiti have been reintroduced, however, and there are now herds in Pennsylvania, Michigan, and Highlands County, Florida (Layne, 1993). It is hoped that wapiti are back in the east to stay.

There have been several attempts, both state and private, to return the wapiti to Michigan. The present herd apparently descends from seven Yellowstone Park wapiti that were liberated in Munda Township, Cheboygan County, in the north end of the Lower Peninsula, in

original
range
south
to here

*Distribution of the wapiti, or elk,* Cervus elaphus, *in the eastern United States.*

1918. This herd did well, and by 1958 the wapiti occurred in Montmorency, Otsego, and Presque Isle counties. By the 1960s, they also occurred in parts of Antrim, Charlevoix, and Emmet counties, these counties also in the Lower Peninsula, though they are no longer present in Antrim County. By 1979, they ranged over about 1500 square km (600 square miles) of Michigan. Populations were estimated at 200 in 1925, 300–400 in 1939, 900–1000 in 1958, and 2000–3000 in 1963–64. Herd size in Michigan in the winter of 1994–95 was estimated at 1140.

From 1913 through 1926, 177 wapiti were released in several counties in Pennsylvania, 145 of them from Yellowstone. Hunting was allowed from 1923 through 1931. During this time 98 individuals were legally harvested and 78 were killed illegally, or for damaging crops. The population was not regularly monitored but decreased to about 24 by the early 1970s. As of 1982, about 135 individuals resided in Cameron, Elk, and McKean Counties, in an area of about 200 square km (80 square miles). In 1992, the Pennsylvania herd numbered about 180 individuals, a number sufficient to cause appreciable crop damage. The current herd consists of about 250 animals, and 25 of these were captured and released in the Chequamegon National Forest, Bayfield County, Wisconsin, in 1994. There is currently discussion of elk releases in other states.

HABITAT. The natural habitat of wapiti is forested mountain terrain and plains. The Michigan elk now thrive in a mixed open and woodland environment. In summer they occupy areas of aspen/hardwood forest broken up by numerous openings. In winter they inhabit swampy areas with conifers, cutover areas, aspen/hardwoods, and upland conifer/hardwoods, again with openings. The openings are important; they can be relatively small in winter, larger in spring and fall.

HABITS. The wapiti shares its habitat primarily with the white-tailed deer, although it is more of a wilderness animal. It is more mobile in winter than the deer. Wapiti and deer could compete for habitat or food if either of these resources is in short supply.

Wapiti, especially females, are very gregarious, but both the degree of herding and the types of herds vary between seasons, sexes, and populations. Herd members are constantly alert. The detection of something unusual by a herd member may lead to barking. An adult stares at the source of alarm and struts stiffly to determine its cause. Response to the disturbance can range from none, to a coordinated attack by several wapiti (mobbing, as in defense against coyotes), to mass flight. Most of the time, males and females are in separate herds in their own discrete areas, the females and calves in large herds, the males in small herds. These herds break up during rutting in September, when males and females come together and the bulls compete to form harems. The harems tend to break up by mid-October, and the antlers are lost in late winter or early spring. After the mating season, the males commence to feed and rebuild their energy. Larger herds, containing both sexes and all ages, form at this time. These herds are led by a dominant female, the matriarch. Herds are largest in winter, and are especially large if winter range is limited. Smaller matriarchal nursery bands of females and young are formed in summer.

Antlers have apparently evolved as weapons for pushing, so as to obtain and maintain dominance and mates, but they are generally not used to inflict damage or pain intentionally. Sparring, which may serve to test dominance, is common among wapiti. It is ritualized and nonaggressive, though it sometimes escalates into an actual fight. Sparring consists of two bulls slowly putting their antlers together, then pushing and twisting. Aversion of the eyes by one or both bulls may temporarily end the sparring. One bull may wait with its head down during the break. Disengagement from sparring is also gradual, both bulls averting their eyes, and neither showing signs of submission. When real threat is needed, the wapiti stands on its hind legs and flails the forelegs, a spectacle that explains why an adult bull can dominate an antlered three-year-old male.

The wapiti is perhaps the most vocal of the eastern ungulates. The newborn produces a high "bleat or squeal," presumably to call to the mother. Females bark, grunt, or squeal, and males (and sometimes females) bugle during the rut. The male bugle usually begins as a roar, scales upward to a "high lucid, trimodal bugle." It tapers off as a grunt or series of coughing sounds.

FOOD AND FEEDING. As one would expect, wapiti eat enormous amounts of food. Adults eat 0.7 to 1.1 kg (1.5 to 2.5 lbs) per 45 kg (100 lbs) of body weight per day, depending on such factors as the type and quality of the food, the season, and the sex and behavior of the animals. Consumption rates of calves are higher, by weight.

Wapiti feed in early morning and late evening, taking food into the rumen, the first chamber in a four-chambered, ruminating stomach, where digestion begins. The rumen is both a storage organ and a culture chamber for bacteria (and some protozoa). Without these microorganisms, wapiti would not be able to digest cellulose. Much of the energy for the animal derives from the fermentation of cellulose, starch, etc., into volatile fatty acids, which are absorbed directly from the rumen. The reticulum returns large particles to the rumen for further processing; the omasum, which has many folds, presses water from the predigested food through muscular action; the abomasum is the true stomach. Later, when the animals are bedded down, material from the rumen is regurgitated as a "cud" and rechewed, before passing back into the rumen and through the remainder of the digestive tract. Rumination reduces the size of the food bits and damages their cell membranes, thus making the particles more digestible. Wapiti fecal pellets are similar to deer pellets but larger, about 35 mm (1.5 inches) long.

Large numbers of woody and herbaceous plants are eaten by wapiti, which are mainly grazers (feeding on herbaceous material) in spring and summer and browsers (feeding on woody stems) in winter, though they will feed on grasses, sedges, and forbs any time they are available. Bluegrass and brome are among the more important herbaceous plants eaten, and elk will eat mushrooms. Some of the woody species most often eaten by Michigan elk were white cedar, hemlock, staghorn sumac, and jack pine, but red maple, juneberry, basswood, cherry, striped maple, witch hazel, and aspen were also commonly eaten.

REPRODUCTION AND DEVELOPMENT. Male wapiti become progressively fatter in the pre-rut period, and this fat maintains them during rutting. Males reach maturity in three or four years, but those under four or five years of age are seldom able to form harems and are driven off by dominant bulls. These younger males manage to mate only when no adult bulls are present. Males about seven to ten years old are generally the most successful, and may gather up to 20 females; seldom, however, does any one bull father more than about four young in a given year. Elk have a polygynous mating system: the male's strategy is to maximize the number of females he breeds. He has two options for succeeding in this enterprise: he can search out females and stay with each until she is in estrus, or he can advertise his presence and attract females. The former is more successful in dense vegetation, the latter in more open areas.

By early fall, when the antlers of the adults have matured, courtship activities (the rut) are initiated by the bugling of the bulls. Bugling, like the call of the loon, is one of the beautiful wilderness sounds; the bigger the elk, the deeper and louder the call. A bull elk may dig a wallow, urinate in it, and roll in it, and he may return to the same wallow and rest in it for long periods. Thrashing of brush and urinating on it is an alternative type of advertisement. One way or another, cows and calf groups are attracted into harems. Once his harem is formed, the bull will follow or "herd" the females. Harem herding succeeds best in open country, where the male can follow and watch over the females, herding them along by blocking their exit when necessary. The actual mating activity, a spectacular affair, is in full swing between September 15 and October 10. Each female is receptive for only about 18 hours. The mature bulls defend their harems during the rutting, driving off other adult males to form their own groups, although some mature bulls may remain solitary. In Michigan, harem size varied from one to 21 cows. Yearlings can be bred if they are in good health;

in Michigan, about 23% of the yearlings, but about 90% of the adult females, were pregnant. At the end of rutting, about mid-October, the breeding bulls leave the herds.

In spring, just before giving birth, pregnant females leave the herds and disperse widely. Calves are born in May or June after a gestation of 249–262 days, usually one calf per female. The mother eats the placenta, urine, and feces of the young, then stays away from the young except when suckling, and will attack smaller predators or decoy larger ones away. At birth, the calf weighs about 10.4 to 20.4 kg, averaging 16.8 kg (37 lbs), the males about 2 kg heavier than the females. The newborn calf has fawn-colored, matted pelage with white spots. Even though the calf is large at birth, it is not very active, which enhances the likelihood of its remaining hidden. At four days of age, some lower incisors erupt and the calf can walk, in wobbly fashion. By seven days it can walk straight and run about, and at 15 days the mother and calf rejoin the herd. At that time the calf is left pretty much on its own; it must avoid conflicts with adults and is no longer protected by its mother. Nursing, however, continues until weaning is completed, in two months. Young elk will hide in protective situations until they are large enough to avoid predators. Besides the spots, their adaptations for hiding include a lack of scent and a capacity to remain still and silent. The juvenile spotting is lost with the molt to winter pelage in September.

POPULATION CHARACTERISTICS. Densities in Michigan vary up to about 1.5 to 1.9 elk per square km (four or five per square mile) in the best areas. Except for bulls in rut, there is relatively little individual movement, even seasonally.

Over their more extensive geographic range, some western elk migrate, some do not, depending on conditions. Most migration is elevational: up the mountains for the summer, down for the winter, presumably because of weather and food supply. High-elevation summer range is larger than the low-elevation winter range. Eastern elk, however, apparently do not migrate.

Wapiti have been known to live for at least 25 years in captivity, but animals seldom live nearly this long in the field. Females increasingly

outnumber males in the older age groups in the population. This disparity is related to rutting activities, when the males are injured, chased off, and more susceptible to predation.

ENEMIES. Few of the larger carnivores that feed on wapiti calves are present in the east today. Mountain lions and wolves would have been the main predators prior to their decimation or extirpation. Bears and coyotes probably capture some calves. Illegal hunting is the chief enemy; in Michigan, for example, 40 wapiti were known to have been shot in 1975 alone.

PARASITES AND DISEASE. Externally, wapiti harbor ticks of several species, scabies mites (*Psoroptes equi* var. *cervinae*), and two species of biting lice. They are also bothered by botflies (*Cephenemyia*) and several biting flies. Internally, they harbor tapeworms, flukes, nematodes, and protozoans. A meningeal worm, *Parelaphostrongylus tenuis*, normally of the white-tailed deer, can be highly pathogenic to wapiti.

Wapiti can contract several bacterial diseases. "Lumpy jaw," caused by *Actinomyces bovis*, is uncommon but produces bone lesions and, in chronic cases, grotesque growths on the jawbone. *Brucella abortus* causes brucellosis, a contagious disease that causes abortion and infertility. *Fusobacterium necrophorum* produces several diseases, including necrotic stomatitis, or foot rot, in elk and other animals. This bacterium is common both in the gastrointestinal tract and in the environment. It penetrates the host via wounds and can cause lesions on the jaws. It was said by Murie (1951) to be the most debilitating disease of elk in winter on the National Elk Refuge in Wyoming, primarily when the range is overpopulated.

RELATION TO HUMANS. The wapiti, always a popular game animal, was extirpated in the east by the 1850s. Even after reintroduction into Michigan and Pennsylvania, there were hunts in Michigan in 1964 and 1965, when 477 animals were harvested. There were then no more hunts until 1984, when 49 were harvested, and there have been hunts every year since. Harvests in the 1990s range from about 200 to 330 animals. The goal of the Michigan Department of Natural Resources is to maintain the winter herd at about 800 to 900 individuals. Because elk do better in areas away from people and vehicles, management efforts involve establishing large remote wilderness or prairie tracts.

AREAS FOR FURTHER WORK. Comparisons of food, habitat, and parasites with those of other species of deer, where they occur with elk, should prove useful in management and interesting in their own right.

## SUBSPECIES

Six subspecies of elk have been described for North America, but all intergrade one with the other, and we therefore do not recognize them. *Cervus elaphus canadensis* was the first of these to be described in North America, thus has precedence and is the name used here. The elk native to Michigan was of this subspecies. Individuals recognized as *C. e. nelsoni* have been reintroduced into several eastern localities from Yellowstone National Park, Wyoming.

*Cervus elaphus canadensis* Erxleben
  As described above.
  Type locality: Southern Sweden for the species; Quebec, Canada, for *E. elaphus canadensis*; Yellowstone National Park, Wyoming, for *C. elaphus nelsoni*.

## LITERATURE

Boyce, M. S., and L. D. Hayden-Wing, eds. 1979. *North American Elk: Ecology, Behavior and Management.* Laramie: Univ. Wyoming Press. 294 pp.
Boyd, R. J. 1978. American elk. In: J. L. Schmidt and D. L. Gilbert, eds., *Big Game of North America: Ecology and Management*, pp. 10–29. Harrisburg, Pa.: Stackpole.
Layne, J. N. 1993. History of an introduction of elk in Florida. *Fla. Field Nat.* 21: 77–80.
Murie, O. J. 1951. *The Elk of North America.* Harrisburg, Pa.: Stackpole. 376 pp.
Peek, J. N. 1982. Elk *Cervus elaphus.* In: J. A. Chapman and G. A. Feldhamer, eds., *Wild Mammals of North America*, pp. 851–861. Baltimore: Johns Hopkins Univ. Press.
Spiegel, L. E., C. H. Huntly, and G. R. Gerber. 1963. A study of the effects of elk browsing on woody plant succession in northern Michigan. *Jack-Pine Warbler* 41: 68–72.
Thomas, J. W., and D. E. Toweill. 1982. *Elk of North America: Ecology and Management.* Wildlife Management Institute. Harrisburg, Pa.: Stackpole. 698 pp.

## Sika Deer
*Cervus nippon* Temminck     Color plate 24

DESCRIPTION. Sika deer range through various hues of brown and exhibit numerous white spots in seven or eight rows. The spots are more con-

*Sika deer,* Cervus nippon *(Ronald R. Keiper)*

spicuous in summer than in winter. The center of the back is darker than the sides, forming a band from head to rump. A large white rump patch is evident throughout the year. The underparts are whitish or gray. The antlers, narrow and directed somewhat posteriorly with two to five points, are 300 to 660 mm (12 to 26 inches) high and 25 mm (an inch) in diameter at the base. They are shed in May and new ones begin growing immediately. They are in the velvet from May through August, by early September the velvet is lost. The upper canines protrude anteriorly from the maxilla, and the lower canines are incisiform. Sika deer are somewhat smaller than white-tailed deer. "Sika" means "deer" in Japanese.

MEASUREMENTS. Measurements of males from Maryland were: total length 1357 (1182–1510), tail 109 (76–130), hind foot 362 (340–378) mm. For females they were: total length 1254 (1029–1433), tail 97 (75–120), hind foot 340 (317–363) mm. Weights of males are 50–140 kg (110–310 lbs); of females, 40–60 kg (90–130 lbs).

Diploid number = 68. Other reported diploid numbers (64–67) probably reflect past hybridization with red deer.

TOOTH FORMULA

$$\frac{0}{3} \quad \frac{1}{1} \quad \frac{3}{3} \quad \frac{3}{3} \quad = \quad 34$$

DISTRIBUTION. The sika deer is native to Asia (Japan, Manchuria, Korea, and adjacent China) but has been widely introduced, several times in the United States. Feral populations persist in Texas and, in the eastern states, in Wisconsin, Maryland, and Virginia. Sika deer were released in Maryland on James Island in 1916 and on Assateague Island about 1930; today, they are present there and on Chincoteague Island, Virginia. By 1964 they were rarely encountered on the mainland, but in the last few years the Maryland populations have greatly increased, until sika deer occupy four counties on the eastern shore of Maryland: Dorchester, Wicomico, Somerset, and Worcester. Populations have increased so greatly that sika have displaced the white-tailed deer in some places. In the 1970s and 1980s the sika showed an increase of 25 to 65% in Maryland, while the white-tailed deer showed a corresponding decrease (Feldhamer and Armstrong, 1993).

HABITAT. In Maryland, sika deer are generally found around freshwater marshes. On Assateague Island, they frequent the loblolly pine forests and open marshes, but they are most often found in the myrtle, greenbrier, and poison ivy thickets at forest edge.

HABITS. Sika are primarily nocturnal, but they may be seen grazing during the day, singly or in small herds. On Assateague, they often graze while standing in water. They produce at least ten vocalizations. These utterances, most noticeable during the mating season, include soft whistles between females, "goatlike bleats" from doe to fawn, horse-like neighs from fawn to doe, and loud screams from males during the rut. Sika deer use a stiff gallop at lower speeds, making bounds up to 6 meters (18.5 feet) long. At higher speeds they move with a "stiff-legged, quadrupedal hopping," all four hooves up to 0.3 meter (a foot) off the ground at the same time. They can traverse obstacles up to 1.7 meters (5.2 feet) high in this gait. They are also good swimmers.

FOOD AND FEEDING. Sika deer feed during the night and occasionally at other times. They eat many different species of plants, primarily grasses and herbs in summer and woody plants in winter. In Maryland they eat wax myrtle, red maple, red gum, loblolly pine, largetooth aspen, pokeweed, and cordgrass (*Spartina*). Poison ivy (*Rhus radicans*), Japanese honeysuckle (*Lonicera japonica*), and greenbrier (*Smilax*) are also often important foods. The deer will feed on crops in spring and early summer, especially soybeans and corn.

REPRODUCTION AND DEVELOPMENT. Rutting season is from late September to December. Fierce fighting may ensue between rival bucks, and a successful male may mate with as many as 12 females. Males follow available females and attempt to drive them into their territories, where the mating occurs. The bucks, so intently engaged in herding, may not feed until late in the rutting. Females do feed, and may move about through adjacent territories.

Gestation is about 30 weeks, the young usually produced in May or June, sometimes as late as August. Females may be sexually mature as early as six months, but most probably breed first as yearlings. The newborn, usually one per female, weigh 4.5 to 7.0 kg (9.9 to 15.5 lbs) and average 570 mm (22 inches) in total length. By eight months they approach the weight of their mother.

POPULATION CHARACTERISTICS. These deer are not very gregarious; single animals are seen about as often as small herds. Adult males are usually solitary, but after the antlers are shed they can sometimes be found together. Females and young form groups of two or three during calving, perhaps including the young of the previous year. Larger groups may be formed at other times of the year. Adult males initiate territory formation in summer, digging holes up to 1.6 meters (5 feet) wide and 0.3 meter (1 foot) deep, with their forefeet and antlers. They frequently urinate in the holes. These holes, and the thrashed ground cover around them, indicate territorial boundaries. When three or more females group together on a territory, young males might also be present, vocalizing but not mating. Calving females face off and stomp the ground with their forefeet, apparently as a means of maintaining the isolation of female groups. The home ranges of a radio-collared male and female sika deer in Maryland were 182.5 ha (450 acres) and 127.8 ha (315 acres), respectively. Sika have lived up to 12 years in the wild, 25 in captivity.

ENEMIES. People and their automobiles are the chief enemies of this species.

PARASITES AND DISEASE. Ticks, *Amblyomma americanum* and *Dermacentor variabilis*, and the chigger *Eutrombicula splendens* have been reported from this species.

RELATION TO HUMANS. This species is an interesting addition to Assateague and Chincoteague and to the other areas where it occurs, but as is so often true of exotics, its invasion has side effects, often unwanted. This species has invaded the mainland in Maryland, and now appears to be replacing the native white-tailed

*Distribution of the sika deer,* Cervus nippon, *in the eastern United States*

deer. About 1460 animals per year are now harvested.

AREAS FOR FURTHER WORK. More work is needed on the ectoparasites of this species. Do they have lice of their own, or do they collect either of the mallophagan lice harbored by white-tailed deer? As with other introduced species, ecological comparison with native species, where they occur together and where they do not, should be of interest.

## SUBSPECIES

There is disagreement about the number of subspecies constituting this species, ranging from six to 14, but it is not clear which one occurs in the eastern United States.

*Cervus nippon* Linnaeus
Type locality: Japan, probably Kyushu.

## LITERATURE

Feldhamer, G. A. 1980. *Cervus nippon*. **Mammalian Species No. 128.** Amer. Soc. Mammal. 7 pp.
————. 1982. Sika deer. In: J. A. Chapman and G. A. Feldhamer, eds., *Wild Mammals of North America*, pp. 1114–1123. Baltimore: Johns Hopkins Univ. Press.
Feldhamer, G. A., and W. E. Armstrong. 1993. Interspecific competition between four exotic species and native artiodactyls in the United States. *Trans. 58th North Amer. Wildl. and Nat. Resources Conf.*, pp. 468–478.
Feldhamer, G. A., K. R. Dixon, and J. A. Chapman. 1982. Home range and movement of sika deer (*Cervus nippon*) in Maryland. *Sonderdr. Z. f. Saugetierk.* 47: 311–316.
Flyger, V., and N. W. Davis. 1964. Distribution of sika deer (*Cervus nippon*) in Maryland and Virginia in 1962. *Chesapeake Sci.* 5: 212–213.
Mullan, J. M., G. A. Feldhamer, and D. Morton. 1988. Reproductive characteristics of female sika deer in Maryland and Virginia. *J. Mammal.* 69: 388–389.

## Sambar Deer
### *Cervus unicolor* (Cuvier)          Color plate 24
DESCRIPTION. This large deer, about the size of a wapiti, is mostly a uniform brown in color with a shaggy mane on the throat. It is a lighter

*Sambar deer,* Cervus unicolor *(Phillip C. Roullard)*

yellowish brown under the chin, inside the limbs, between the buttocks, and under the tail. Males have three-tined antlers; a basal tine projects forward, and a second tine projects backward before forking. Rudimentary upper canine teeth are present in both sexes. The young are not spotted.

MEASUREMENTS. Total length is 1850–2150 mm (73–85 inches); weight is 160–340 kg (350–750 lbs). The males are larger than the females. Diploid number = 58.

TOOTH FORMULA

$$\frac{0}{3} \quad \frac{1}{1} \quad \frac{3}{3} \quad \frac{3}{3} \; = \; 34$$

DISTRIBUTION. This deer is native to India, Sri Lanka, the Malay Peninsula, Indonesia, and the Philippines. In the eastern United States it is established only at the St. Vincent National Wildlife Refuge, St. Vincent Island (Gulf County) on the Gulf Coast of Florida, where four deer were introduced in 1908. The 5003-ha (12,357-acre) island became a wildlife refuge in 1968. By 1940, the St. Vincent deer had increased to several hundred head, then were reduced to about 50 by illegal hunting by the mid-1950s. They are no longer hunted, and in the mid-1980s the population was around 200 (Flynn et al., 1990).

HABITAT. In its native land the sambar deer is found in open woodland. Its home here, St. Vincent Island, offers a varied habitat of wetlands, sloughs and marshes, dunes (scrub oak, live oak, and some hardwoods), and slash pine.

HABITS. Sambar deer are most often alone, but the most common social unit is the hind (cow) and her calf. Groups of four to seven individuals seen in summer included hinds, yearlings, and stags in velvet.

Antler rubs, scrapes, and wallows are often seen during the breeding season. Rubbed trees on St. Vincent were often rerubbed within and between breeding seasons. Scrapes, usually at the bases of small trees, were apparently used by different stags during the same breeding season. Active wallows, found only during the breeding season, were used only by large stags. These "signposts" were found from September through June, and males with hard antlers were found throughout this period.

Though there was much crepuscular activity, these deer were more nocturnal than diurnal. When disturbed, and usually just before they run for cover, these deer emit a high-pitched bark that serves as an alarm call. The bark is sometimes repeated several times, but was given by only one individual when a herd was disturbed. Hoof stamping by one front hoof was another common behavior of this species.

FOOD AND FEEDING. Foods consisted of a great many species of grasses, forbs, browse, and mast, but included many aquatic plants, whereas white-tails on the island fed almost entirely on terrestrial plants.

REPRODUCTION AND DEVELOPMENT. Breeding occurred over ten months, but rubbing and scraping activities were most intense from December through April, peaking in February, when 90% of the stags had polished antlers. A single fawn is produced after a gestation of about eight months. Young calves are difficult to observe, because the mothers keep them well concealed, but calves were seen from May

St. Vincent
Island

*Distribution of the sambar deer,* Cervus unicolor, *in the eastern United States* through February. The young stays with its mother for about a year. Females become sexually mature in their second year.

POPULATION CHARACTERISTICS. The median annual home-range size of the sambar deer is 312 ha (772 acres). Stags move about much more than females, except in the fall.

ENEMIES. Today, the sambar on St. Vincent are no longer hunted, and have virtually no enemies.

PARASITES AND DISEASE. Seven species of nematodes, one of trematodes, four of ticks, and one of mite have been found inhabiting sambar deer from St. Vincent Island.

RELATION TO HUMANS. Because their island has been declared a wildlife refuge, these deer can remain relatively undisturbed even while being observed by people.

AREAS FOR FURTHER WORK. Ecological and behavioral comparison with native deer should be both interesting and constructive.

### SUBSPECIES

*Cervus unicolor* Cuvier

Type locality: Sri Lanka.

### LITERATURE

Flynn, L. B., J. C. Lewis, E. M. Marchinton, R. L. Marchinton, and S. M. Shea. 1990. Ecology of sambar deer on St. Vincent National Wildlife Refuge, Florida. Tall Timbers Research Sta., Bull. 25. 107 pp.

Lever, C. 1985. *Naturalized Mammals of the World.* Essex, U.K.: Longman Group. 487 pp.

## White-Tailed Deer
### *Odocoileus virginianus* (Zimmermann)

Excellent summaries of information on this deer are presented by Halls (1984), Hesselton and Hesselton (1982), and Smith (Mammalian Species, 1991).

DESCRIPTION. The white-tailed deer differs from the mule deer (*O. hemionus*), the only other species in its genus, in the length of its ears, in its tail color, in the way it runs, and in its antlers. The mule deer is a resident of western North America. Its ears are larger, the tip of its tail is black

*White-tailed deer,* Odocoileus virginianus
*(Larry E. Lehman)*

rather than brown, and it runs with the left front and left hind legs moving together, then the right, rather than with the diagonally placed legs moving together as the white-tailed deer does.

The long, rather bushy tail of the white-tailed deer is brown above, white beneath. The seasonal color and general characteristics of the pelage vary markedly. The coat is bright tan to ruddy, darker along the mid-dorsum and paler on the face, throat, and chest. The nose is black, and the ears are large and prominent. A prominent nose band, the orbital region, the upper throat, the insides of the ears and legs, and the belly are pure white. Deer of this species tend to be darker-colored in humid forest areas and lighter in dry, open brush land. The skull is long and tapering. The young are spotted with white, and thus tend to blend into the background. The spots are lost by late summer, during the first molt to winter pelage.

Only male (buck) white-tailed deer carry antlers. The main beam of the antlers, directed forward, bears several unbranched tines. The main beam, less than 750 mm (30 inches) in length, carries no brow tine. Antler growth usually begins in April. The growing antlers are covered with "velvet," a soft, true skin containing an extensive matrix of blood vessels and nervous tissue. The blood vessels carry nutrients to the rapidly growing bone. When the full size of the antler is attained, usually about August or September, the bone hardens. The velvet then dries up and is sloughed off, some of it incidentally during routine activities, some by the buck's rubbing its antlers against small trees. These "rubs," often seen where white-tails are common, apparently serve in territorial marking. Antlers first grow in a buck's yearling year, that is, in the spring and summer when he is just over a year old. The first antlers are usually a pair of single spikes, but under optimum conditions each antler can carry up to five tines. Antler growth is rapid (no mammal bones grow faster), the full size being obtained in four months or less. Following the rutting season, and after the mature antlers have been carried for several months, a separation layer forms between the antlers and the skull. The antlers then become loose and fall off, or are knocked off by contact with branches or other obstructions. In the north the antlers are shed from late December to February, but in South Florida the bucks drop their antlers much earlier. Antlers are occasionally retained until spring.

It is commonly but incorrectly thought that the age of a buck can be determined by the number of its tines. Under good conditions, each new "rack" (set of antlers) will generally be greater in size and tine number, at least until old age. Nutritional factors, however, greatly influence tine number. On good range, bucks will develop an average of eight points as three-year-olds, but in overpopulated situations, and on poor range, they will have smaller antlers with fewer points and smaller beams. And where overpopulation is extreme, many bucks may never develop an eight-point rack. Females with excess testosterone may produce small antlers, but they can nonetheless produce and raise fawns.

A small but conspicuous metatarsal gland margined with white hairs is also characteristic of this species. It is about 2.5 cm (an inch) long and situated on the outer side of the hind leg, between the ankle and hoof. Some other glands in this species are the preorbital gland, at the inner corner of the eyes, which acts as a tear gland; the tarsal gland, on the inner sides of the hind legs at the hocks (the elongate ankles) which produce individual scents involved in rub-urination marking; and interdigital glands, between the toes, which scent the deer's trail. Odor is thus an important form of communication between members of the herd.

Wildlife biologists have worked out fairly accurate age-determination techniques for the white-tailed deer on the basis of tooth-eruption patterns and tooth wear. For details see Larson and Tabor (1980) or Dimmick and Pelton (1996).

MEASUREMENTS. Weights and measurements vary considerably, the largest animals occurring in northern areas and the smallest in southern areas. Measurements for adult male white-tails are: total length 1340–2062 mm (52–80 inches), tail 150–330 mm, and hind foot 362–521 mm. Height at the shoulder is 660–1143 mm. Weights of bucks usually range from 68.6 to 140.9 kg (150 to 310 lbs); and of does, 40.9 to 95.5 kg (90–210 lbs). Few bucks currently harvested, however, weigh much over 90 kg (200 lbs) whole weight. One buck taken near Trout Creek in Ontonagon County, Michigan, in 1919 weighed 161 kg (354 lbs) after being field-dressed. Deer from Louisiana and the Everglades are smaller than northern deer, and the key deer (from the Florida Keys) is the smallest, at a maximum weight of 36 kg (80 lbs).

White-tailed deer exhibit seasonal weight change. In bucks, weight loss begins during the rut, and weight gain begins in spring. Weight change may be 20 to 30% of total weight. In does and fawns, weight loss begins in January. For does, weight gain commences in summer after the fawns are weaned.

Diploid number = 70.

TOOTH FORMULA

$$\frac{0}{3} \quad \frac{0}{1} \quad \frac{3}{3} \quad \frac{3}{3} \ = \ 32$$

DISTRIBUTION. The white-tailed deer occurs throughout the eastern United States, and in greater numbers than before settlement. Once all but extirpated in the Northeast and Midwest, it is now common there. Its range in North America is from southern Canada south through most of the United States (except much of the Southwest) through Central America and into South America.

HABITAT. The white-tailed deer occurs in a variety of habitats, but thrives in early mixed successional stages, the more mixed the better. It is also found in open glades, swamps, and thickets on the coastal islands of the South Atlantic states, in the dense Florida hammocks, and even on the lower Florida Keys. The white-tail has responded very well to the cutting of the forest.

HABITS. White-tailed deer are active at all hours, but much less so during the day. They are most active at dawn and dusk, but they vary their activity patterns with local conditions. They often increase their activity prior to bad weather, and all but cease activity during bad weather. They usually spend the day bedded down in cover, often in woods, and move into open areas and begin feeding near dusk. They often continue to move about during the night, usually bedding down after dawn, but may also bed down for an hour or two in the middle of the night. Bedding situations are usually in cool areas in hot weather, sunny areas in cool weather, and more

protected areas in bad weather. Although these deer usually do not return to the same bedding area day after day, they do sometimes use the same spot repeatedly in winter yards, the areas where they congregate in winter. They may return to the same general area, a "core area," then pick a different spot, or they may bed down in an entirely different area on another day. At other times they may have one core area in the daytime, another at night.

White-tailed deer can run at speeds up to 58 kph (36 mph) and have been known to make vertical leaps of 2.6 meters (8 feet) and horizontal jumps of 9.1 meters (28 feet). They run at either a trot or a gallop and also walk. When galloping they generally take several long strides between each two high bounds. White-tails are good swimmers: they can swim from one small Florida Key to another, and they often enter large lakes to escape dogs or mosquitos or bit-

*Distribution of the white-tailed deer,* Odocoileus virginianus, *in the eastern United States*

ing flies. Owing to their hollow, air-filled hair shafts, deer are very buoyant; it is almost impossible for them to sink should they become exhausted while swimming.

White-tails are usually thought of as quiet animals, but 13 different vocalizations are recognized (Halls, 1984). Fawns make bleating and murmuring sounds, and the doe may grunt to call her fawn. Deer may bawl when in danger, and bucks make a short "ba" or bleat sound when trailing a doe during rut. The footstamp is a thumping noise used as an alarm, often in conjunction with the snort. The most commonly heard sounds are the snorts and footstamps given when deer are startled. The snort is a loud expulsion of air through the nostrils with the mouth closed. Snorts occur more often in family units than in buck groups. They are often given when danger is perceived but no direct threat is identified.

Three aggressive calls are known: low, guttural grunts of low intensity made by bucks or does at any time; snorts in higher-intensity situations, most often given by bucks in the sparring or breeding season (these two may be combined as grunt-snorts); and the grunt-snort plus a "wheezing inhalation through pinched nostrils" during the highest-intensity agonistic behavior. Males chasing females make a "drawn-out grunt that sounds like an unoiled hinge, or a branch swaying in the wind." The tail, or "flag," usually raised as an alarm, may otherwise serve as a means of communication between animals.

The white-tailed deer depends heavily on its senses of hearing, smell, and sight. Hearing determines the location and behavior of other animals, including predators and humans. Smell is used both to locate other animals and to identify food. Deer can detect differences in the palatability of food on the basis of smell, and bucks are attracted to does by smell. Having eyes on the sides of the head gives deer a wide field of vision, so wide that they are even able to see behind them when they are facing straight ahead. Deer have been considered color blind, but this has recently been called into question.

There are basically two types of social groupings: family groups, each consisting of a doe and her offspring, which remain together for nearly a year; and buck groups. Most doe groups

consist of just one mature doe and her young, but in more open country they may include more than one adult doe and more than one young. For short periods, this sort of grouping may contain two generations of the matriarch's offspring, but in early spring, about a month prior to giving birth, the doe normally will drive away her young from the preceding year. Bucks are more social than does, and buck-group membership constantly changes. Yearling males become solitary in spring or early summer, but then may form small male subgroups of about three to five individuals. Sometimes, yearling males and females forced out of the family groups may join buck groups for a short time, though they usually avoid the dominant bucks. The bachelor, or buck, group disbands shortly before the autumn rut. Feeding groups of males and females may also form, but these groups break up at the end of the feeding periods.

As is the case with many animal species, a dominance hierarchy forms within each white-tail social group. Dominance is determined mostly by size and age. Because bucks are larger than does, they are usually dominant to them in all age groups, though there is relatively little contact between adult bucks and does. Dominance, however, does not translate to group leadership. The doe is the leader in a single-family group, and there *is* no apparent leader in buck, multifamily, or mixed groups. Many of the interactions between individuals occur in dominant/subordinate situations. Once the dominant individual is established, fighting and energy waste are avoided by the subordinate animal's simply moving away as the dominant approaches. Subordinates also avoid eye contact with dominants, but a subordinate will sometimes be forced out of the herd entirely. Aggression is expressed by dominants in various ways. Low-level interactions are expressed by a direct stare coupled with lowered ears. Other, higher-level aggressive behaviors are head-up, head-down postures that indicate intentions to rear and strike, and to chase, respectively. The chase, which includes kicking or striking with the feet, is often used by the doe to drive off her yearlings before giving birth. Rearing, less commonly seen, involves flailing at the subordinate with the forelegs. Deer of equal rank may rear and flail at each other, but rarely for more than five seconds. The aggressive behaviors of bucks and does are basically similar, but bucks carrying mature antlers will use them in threats.

Grooming is a common social interaction in groups. Individuals often lick each other, in bouts lasting several seconds to several minutes. During grooming, individuals face in the same direction or away from each other, but never toward each other.

In winter, larger herds are often formed in areas of food abundance called "yards." Such herds may number up to 150 individuals; and again, leadership is matriarchal. Individuals may use the same yards for many years. Herding has its advantages: pathways are kept open by the passage of so many deer; and the herd is better protected from predation, although the major predators, the wolf and mountain lion, have all but vanished in the east. Food may become limited, however, and body fat too depleted, if deep snow keeps deer in yards too long. Under such circumstances, parasites and disease can increase, and many deer may perish from exhaustion and starvation; deer that lose more than 30% of their body weight die. Fawns are particularly vulnerable to starvation in winter.

FOOD AND FEEDING. The white-tailed deer seeks out and uses those food items best suited to its nutritional needs, using taste and smell to identify them, and natural selection has ensured that deer select from among the more nutritious foods. The four-chambered stomach allows deer to utilize plant foods not available to nonruminant species. The deer benefit not only from the nutrients occurring naturally in the foods, but also from the nutrients synthesized by microbial symbionts in the rumen, reticulum, and omasum. Symbiont nutrition may be particularly important in low-nutrient conditions.

Deer spend more time feeding than in any other activity. They often move to feeding areas along established deer trails, then spread out to feed. Deer are basically grazers, but they browse when herbaceous food is inadequate, especially in winter. Much of their summer food is grasses, forbs, and the new leaves of woody plants. They will feed on fruit or on such lily pads and pond plants as are easily obtained. They feed heavily on acorns, beechnuts, and other mast items as they become available. Acorns appear to be highly selected; deer will increase their home range to include acorn-producing areas in fall. Greenbrier, sassafras, maple and oak sprouts, honeysuckle, wild grape, and mushrooms are other foods often used. Corn, soybeans, and alfalfa can account for half their diet, in the right circumstances. In winter they feed on the buds and twigs of maples, birches, viburnums, blueberries, white cedar, and many other woody plants. Each deer consumes about 2.25 to 4 kg (5 to 9 lbs) of food per day. When deer become overpopulated, or forage is otherwise limited, they will often eat foods of little nutritional value, and may even die with full stomachs.

Deer often drink, but they can apparently go without free water for extended periods if rain, snow, dew, and succulent plants provide them with adequate alternatives.

REPRODUCTION AND DEVELOPMENT. The rut extends over several months and passes through several stages. As in other species, rutting activity is probably triggered by photoperiod. Rutting behavior, which begins with sparring among bucks, is stimulated by the annual increase of hormone levels, when antlers are fully grown and have lost their velvet. In the north, these changes occur in late summer and early fall. The timing of their inception varies considerably in the south. At the time of onset of the rut, bucks are in buck groups, and their sparring, a form of low-level aggression, seems to function to form the dominance hierarchy. One buck lowers his antlers and directs them toward another; the second often accepts the challenge, and the two may engage antlers. Sparring then consists of a shoving match, the younger, smaller buck usually being shoved backward and withdrawing. At other times the match may stop abruptly, with no apparent winner or loser. Sparring may last from a few seconds to several minutes. The larger bucks engage in the most serious sparring; the smaller bucks spar most often. The larger antlers of older deer tend to serve as visual signals of dominance. Sometimes, the antlers of two bucks become inextricably locked, and in time, after a desperate but futile battle, they perish from starvation.

Courtship begins about four to six weeks after the onset of sparring—around mid-October in the north. The buck groups break up at this time and the bucks, now solitary, begin to chase does. (About half of the northern does mate and conceive in their first year, whereas bucks do not mature reproductively until their second year.) Does become exceedingly active at night just before they come into heat, and bucks follow them continuously for five or six days, including the 24- to 36-hour period when a female comes into estrus and will allow mating. During chases, bucks put their noses to the ground and trot along about 50 meters (160 feet) behind the does, obviously following their scent. During these runs, the does do not allow the bucks to approach too closely. Early in courtship, males may chase females more than 200 meters (650 feet) before losing interest, but later a buck may chase a doe over 500 meters (1600 feet). A doe being pursued may pause to urinate; and her urine probably contains pheromones that signal her readiness to mate. The buck may sniff the urine, then often give a lip curl, or "flehmen," lasting for about five seconds, which consists of lowering the head and chin to a 45° angle and curling back the upper lip. During the chase, the privilege conferred by the male dominance hierarchy is clear. The largest buck follows the doe most closely, the smaller bucks, if any, following along behind. If a larger buck joins a chase already underway, the smaller bucks defer. Dominance is also exhibited in male encounters during the courtship period, but most such confrontations end with the subordinate backing off. Actual fights are rare, but consist of bucks charging at each other from a distance of a meter or two. They may circle before charging. Again, such an encounter consists of a shoving match that ends when one of the combatants chooses to retreat or is driven back.

A single buck may attempt to dominate up to about ten does—his "harem"—although larger doe groups may include more than one buck. The dominant buck then attempts to shield the does from other bucks, all the while courting the does. Antler threats usually serve to repel submissive subdominant bucks, but the presence of yearling and small bucks among the does is tolerated. Because the composition of the group constantly changes as both bucks and does move in and out, the term "harem" is really a misnomer. Young bucks may not have an opportunity to achieve dominance and breed until they are 3.5 to 4.5 years old. Dominant bucks may breed with several does during a single breeding season.

A buck and a doe in estrus may feed and bed down together, then mate several times over several hours. During the time the doe is in heat, the buck may remain with her wherever she goes and drive away other males.

Bucks produce two types of "signposts," each incorporating an olfactory component and a visual component. "Buck rubs" are portions of the stems of saplings or shrubs where a buck's rubbing, with its antlers and head, has removed the bark. Glands from the skin of the head deposit scent on these rubs. Rubs are most prominent just after the velvet is removed, but continue throughout the rut. The other signpost is called a "scrape": bucks travel a regular route during the rutting season, and along this route they thrash saplings with their antlers and scrape the adjacent ground bare with their hooves. A scrape thus consists of branches broken a meter or two above ground and a pawed depression directly below. Bucks revisit these scrapes regularly, and does are thought to visit them and to leave their own scent signs. The bucks then follow the doe trails near the scrapes. To assert his dominance, a buck may make a scrape in the presence of another buck. But even though they leave these signposts, bucks are not thought to be territorial.

Following the rut, the does separate from the bucks and return to their subherds until late spring (May or early June in Michigan), when they depart the subgroups to give birth, remaining apart for about two months. The young are born in late May or early June, after a mean gestation of about 200 (187–222) days. (In Florida and the Gulf states, mating takes place in summer, and the young are produced from January to March.) A young doe usually has a single fawn; twins are usual in a mature female, and occasionally triplets are produced. Food availability plays a major role in the number of offspring for a given birth. Birth occurs quickly, the doe either standing or lying. Labor took

28 minutes in one case and 24 minutes in another (Michael, 1964). Does immediately remove and eat the fetal membranes and afterbirth
of the fawns. This probably removes material
that would otherwise attract predators to the
birth site, and affords the doe some protein.
Does may return to the same site each year to
give birth.

At birth, the fawn is well-haired and spotted.
It weighs about 1.8 to 3.6 kg (4 to 8 lbs) and already has four lower incisors. Within an hour of
birth it stands on its own. The doe licks the newborn's body, and nursing begins in about 35 minutes. Fawns wag their tails during nursing and
the does lick the fawns' anal and genital areas
almost constantly. The fawn stays in a thicket
or other hiding place, blending so well with the
dappled shadows and standing so perfectly motionless that it is unlikely to be seen. Twin fawns
lie apart, apparently a protective behavior. By
the third or fourth day, fawns are able to travel
more. The mother makes a low grunt to call her
young, and she quickly responds to its bleat.
Nursing occurs one to three times per day, the
fawns then returning to their thicket to bed
down; nursing increases as the fawn grows.
Fawns sometimes attempt to nurse from the
wrong does, but are usually rejected.

Weaning is nearly complete by one month, but
sometimes lasts until ten weeks. Fawns apparently choose their own bedding sites, usually a
different one each day. The mother returns to
where the fawn was last seen, then searches for
it using olfactory cues (she also "mews" sometimes to call her young), and the fawn will often run 10 to 30 meters (30 to 100 feet) to meet
the doe. Fawns begin play behavior at two
weeks of age. At three weeks, they feed on grass
and rejoin the herd with the mother. Play bouts
increase with age, then decrease in autumn. By
about two months their activity periods have
come to equal that of the mother, and rumination is fully developed.

Fawns remain with the mother well into the
fall or winter, or longer. Some of the permanent
teeth erupt by nine to ten months of age, the
premolars not until 18 or 19 months. Female
fawns may stay with the mother up to two
years. Some breed at six to eight months, but
most not until their second year.

Fawn mortality is high when the mother is on
low-nutritive diets, and heavier fawns are produced when the female is in better nutritional
condition. Deer milk is richer in fat, protein,
and energy than cow's milk. If the quality of the
range is poor, the milk will still be of good quality, but the *amount* of milk the doe can produce
will be reduced. Where quality food is limited,
the doe may become stressed as the fawn continues to take milk.

POPULATION CHARACTERISTICS. Deer occupy
the same home range year after year. They are
not territorial, but will defend bedding sites.
Seasonal changes in home-range usage are related to food availability. Home ranges of individual deer vary from 16 ha (40 acres) in good
habitat to 135 ha (330 acres) in marginal habitat. Home ranges tend to be larger in open country, and smaller in woods or more heavily vegetated situations. Bucks usually have larger home
ranges than does or younger deer, and bucks
may extend their home ranges during the rut.
Winter home ranges are sometimes much larger,
up to 520 ha (1285 acres).

Daily movements of individuals vary greatly
(from 340 to 3000 meters, or 1090 to 9600 feet),
depending on age, sex, season, habitat, weather,
and the physical condition of the animal. Movements are reduced in winter, and movements by
malnourished individuals are much reduced.

Dispersing white-tailed deer at the Crab Orchard National Wildlife Refuge in Illinois were
mostly yearling males; 80% of yearling bucks
and 13% of the yearling does dispersed. Other
dispersers included 4% of the fawns, 7% of the
adult does, and 10% of the adult bucks (Hawkins et al., 1971). Nelson (1993) determined by
radio tracking that 28 of 44 (64%) male deer in
Minnesota dispersed between a year and a year
and a half in age, and seven of 35 (20%) females
did. Most dispersed less than 26 km (16 miles);
seven dispersed 32–38 km (20–24 miles),
whereas four dispersed 56, 67, 77, and 168 km
(35, 42, 48, and 104 miles), respectively. The
major causes of dispersal in this species are
thought to be social pressures, sexual competition, and foraging competition.

Deer do best in bottomland hardwoods, where
25 deer per square km (64 per square mile) may

be supported. Population density varies greatly, but 30 to 35 deer per square km (78 to 91 per square mile) in autumn is not unrealistic in good habitat. The nation is in fact experiencing a deer-population explosion. White-tails have even invaded Chicago's O'Hare airport, and the surrounding urban forests support deer numbers up to 38 per square km (100 per square mile), because the deer have no natural predators and are not hunted in areas of this sort. These large numbers have become both a hazard to the motorist and a problem for the agriculturist and forester. Elsewhere, various agricultural practices combined with a lack of predators have often led to overpopulations of deer.

Although it is nice to know the size of a herd, for management purposes it is much more important to know whether it is increasing, decreasing, or remaining stable, and how it relates to the carrying capacity of the range. Deer (and other animals) should be maintained near or below the carrying capacity of the range, so as to avoid damage both to the environment and to the health of the herd. Now that carrying capacity has been attained in most areas, annual mortality must equal annual recruitment if a healthy herd is to be maintained at or just below carrying capacity. Because annual recruitment is about 30 to 40% in a healthy herd, this percentage of deer should be removed from a population annually through hunting—the major factor in mortality in a deer herd today—and such other forces as roadkills and predation. Achieving this is difficult to do by taking only bucks, and it alters the age structure of the herd, as well. For these reasons, antlerless deer hunts have become essential to the maintenance of healthy deer herds.

An increasing hazard to deer today is a well-meaning but misguided populace that wants to halt deer hunting, for too many deer harm habitats both for the deer and for other species. Controlled hunting, then, leads to reduced numbers but healthier deer; outlawing hunting can lead to disaster. For example, in Brown County State Park in south-central Indiana in the late 1980s and early 1990s, deer became greatly overpopulated, to the detriment of themselves and most other plant and animal species within the park. For several years, nonetheless, the steadfast opposition of animal lovers stymied the obvious solution—to reduce the deer herd by harvest. Controlled harvest has now been introduced and in time the park should return to normal.

White-tailed deer can live up to 20 years, but few survive beyond four to five years in the wild.

ENEMIES. Deer meat is an important source of food for many predators, but much of the deer meat eaten by predators is carrion, and the effect of predation on the deer herd, although highly variable, is often negligible, except on fawns. Before its virtual extinction, the wolf and the mountain lion were probably the greatest enemies of the white-tailed deer. Nonetheless, most wolf/deer encounters probably ended in the escape of the deer, for deer usually respond to wolves by running rather than by standing their ground as moose do. Older deer tend to be killed in winter, fawns in summer. With the wolves all but extirpated, the most important predators on fawns in the east today are probably dogs, bobcats, and coyotes. Bobcats and probably coyotes manage to bring down even an occasional adult during winter, when the deer are hindered in their travels because of snow or limited food supply. Bobcats tend to hunt deer at night, often by stalking them, then attacking while they are bedded down. They will leap upon the deer's back, bite its neck, and puncture its windpipe. Dogs frequently chase deer, and today are probably the most important predators on fawns, and on deer of any age that have been weakened by winter. Still, dogs do not kill very many deer, and do not significantly affect populations of deer. Other than hunters, the major cause of mortality is the automobile: in 1987, for example, 34,000 deer were killed by automobiles in Indiana alone.

PARASITES AND DISEASE. The internal parasites of deer include liver flukes, lungworms, stomach worms and several other nematodes, tapeworm larvae, a flatworm, a whipworm, meningeal worms, and protozoans. Of these, only helminth worms cause significant health problems, but even these problems are usually associated with overpopulation of deer. A list of 35 helminths known from deer is given by Halls (1984, p. 180). The meningeal nematode has little effect on deer but may be fatal to wapiti and moose if not treated.

External parasites include the nose botfly (*Cephenemyia*), ticks, and two species of biting lice. Biting lice have an interesting and puzzling distribution on eastern mammals; they are found on carnivores and pocket gophers as well as deer. The deer tick, *Ixodes scapularis*, is the carrier of Lyme disease, first discovered in 1975 in Lyme, Connecticut. The disease, caused by a bacterium transmitted to humans by the bite of deer ticks, is often fatal to humans. Health officials throughout the Northeast are concerned with the spread of the disease, which has reached epidemic proportions on Long Island and north of New York City and is spreading northward.

Several diseases occur in deer. Epizootic hemorrhagic disease, which is caused by a virus, produces extensive hemorrhaging and is often fatal. It was first reported in 1955 in New Jersey, where about 700 deer died. Outbreaks have occurred in many other areas since, including, again, New Jersey, where about 1000 died in 1976. It is transmitted by arthropod vectors and usually occurs in late summer and early autumn. It is usually limited geographically, but there were outbreaks throughout the southeastern United States in 1971. An infected deer loses its fear of humans, fails to eat, grows weaker, salivates extensively, and finally becomes comatose.

Anthrax, a bacterial disease, has caused significant mortality in white-tailed deer. It is transmitted by animals that feed or drink in contaminated areas. Infected deer are listless, lose coordination, stagger, and become stiff-legged. There are often bloody discharges from nostrils and anus, and the animals usually die within two days. Humans are highly susceptible to this disease. A number of other diseases can infect deer, as well.

Deer often have skin tumors. They can occur on any part of the body, sometimes in great numbers. Because they are caused by a host-specific virus, they pose no threat to humans.

RELATION TO HUMANS. The white-tailed deer is the most important big-game animal in the United States. In the Northeast, great numbers of deer are killed annually. In Michigan, in 1975, 178,000 deer were taken from a herd numbering perhaps a million. In 1974, deer hunters in New York State killed 103,303 deer, a record harvest for the state; and in 1987, 204,715 were taken, again setting a record. Maine, New Hampshire, Vermont, Massachusetts, Pennsylvania, the Carolinas, and Louisiana are other states in which large numbers are killed. Some states where deer have been reintroduced after earlier extirpation, such as Indiana and Illinois, now have ample herds and good hunting. Illinois hunters, for example, harvested 142,233 deer in 1995.

AREAS FOR FURTHER WORK. Genetic comparison of the various subspecies and other isolated populations of white-tailed deer should give us a better understanding of interrelationships within the species. Birth control, in the form of chemosterilants, is a very active area of current research aimed at controlling deer populations in situations where it is not desirable to hunt them, such as in crops, yards, orchards, and parks, where deer can cause so much damage.

## SUBSPECIES

Deer were absent from much of the Midwest by the 1930s, but since then have often been transported around the country for restocking, causing considerable genetic mixing and taxonomic confusion in this species. Moreover, considerable intergradation occurs between most of the previously recognized subspecies, other than the island forms. Five island subspecies are recognized here. Four of them are quite similar to the mainland white-tailed deer, but the key deer, *Odocoileus virginianus clavium*, through long isolation, has evolved a unique set of characters. Whether it would remain distinct or would form a single interbreeding unit with mainland white-tailed deer if the two occurred together, thus whether or not it is a distinct species, is unclear. It has certainly evolved in that direction, and it is considered by Lazell (1989) to have reached species status.

*Odocoileus virginianus virginianus*
(Zimmermann)

As described above.

Type locality: Virginia.

Other currently recognized eastern subspecies:

*O. virginianus borealis* Miller

*O. virginianus mcilhennyi* F. W. Miller

*O. virginianus osceola* (Bangs)

*O. virginianus seminolus* Goldman & Kellogg

*Odocoileus virginianus clavium*
Barbour & Allen
Key Deer

The key deer is a remarkable animal. It is the smallest and palest of the eastern deer. The maximum shoulder height is only 76 cm (30 inches), and the animal appears stocky because of its short legs. Females weigh up to 28 kg (63 lbs), males up to 36 kg (80 lbs). The differences between the key deer and mainland deer, however, are based on much more than size alone. The skull is as broad as that of a mainland deer (greatest width of the skull across the orbits is 90 to 119 mm, the same as in mainland deer), but the molariform tooth row is shorter than in mainland deer, the maximum length (that of the type specimen) being 66.4 mm, whereas the *minimum* length for mainland deer is 68 mm. The nasal bones of key deer are broad, but short. The three measurements—width of skull, length of nasal bones, and length of molariform tooth row—separate all key deer from all Florida mainland deer (Lazell, 1989). Key deer also have proportionately longer tails, and although they are variable in color, they do not have the summer red and winter gray phases that characterize mainland deer.

Key deer have been isolated on the Keys for less than 10,000 years. They have had no predators other than man, but whereas other deer tend toward overpopulation, key deer seem to have adapted to their limited range by attaining a low reproductive potential. Breeding occurs in September and October, fawning in April and May, and there is usually only a single young, males outnumbering females at birth two to one. Males have home ranges of about 120 ha (300 acres), females around 52 ha (130 acres).

Some have considered key deer to be merely mainland white-tails, stunted because of poor conditions, but northern white-tails have been present on Lignum Vitae Key for generations and show no signs of stunting.

The key deer apparently once occupied the western half of the Keys from Key Vaca west. Its present range is in the western part of the Florida Keys, from the Johnson Keys north of Little Pine west beyond Lower Sugarloaf to some of the southern Saddlebunch Keys. The type locality (designated in 1922) is Big Pine Key. Key deer are found only on islands with year-round fresh water and extensive pine or hardwood woodland. At present, there are no deer on Johnston Key north of Sugarloaf. Most of the key deer occur in the National Key Deer Refuge, established in 1954 to protect them.

Key deer are in serious trouble, and are listed as federally endangered. Their population reached a low about 1950, then began to increase in response to protection from hunting and disturbance. As of 1978 (Layne, 1978) there were about 300–400 key deer, and at present there are about 250–300 (Humphrey, 1992). Dogs and traffic take their toll, but development is the biggest problem. The houses that are being built on the Keys are using up the land at a great rate. The fate of the key deer has been summarized by Carey (1987): despite the establishment of a federal refuge, "In one year 62 deer were killed by automobiles, a fifth of the fawns died in drainage ditches, dogs killed large numbers, and conflict with human population and reduction in habitat all pose a hazardous future for this tiny deer."

Low reproductive potential, coupled with rapid development of the land, will make it difficult for the key deer to recover and increase its populations unless more land is protected. Even today, major efforts should be made to begin buying as much of the land in the Keys as possible, so as to restore it to its natural state. Such a task might seem hopeless, but to many people transforming the area east of Chicago back to a natural condition as the Indiana Dunes Natural Lakeshore seemed similarly impossible. Such efforts should be made for the Florida Keys, with the goal of establishing a National Park.

Type locality: Big Pine Key, Monroe Co., Florida

## Odocoileus virginianus hiltonensis
### Goldman & Kellogg

Smaller than typical *O. v. virginianus*; the tarsal gland tufts are deeply colored, usually near burnt sienna, and the braincase is narrow and highly arched. Known only from Hilton Head Island.

Type locality: Hilton Head Island, Beaufort Co., South Carolina.

## Odocoileus virginianus nigribarbis
### Goldman & Kellogg

This subspecies is similar to the typical mainland form but much smaller; the antlers are more flattened; the pelage is shorter; the upperparts are a duller cinnamon in winter pelage; and the facial areas and ears are blacker, less grayish. The subspecies is found on Blackbeard and Sapelo islands, Georgia.

Type locality: Blackbeard Island, McIntosh Co., Georgia.

## Odocoileus virginianus taurinsulae
### Goldman & Kellogg

Similar to typical *virginianus* from Virginia, but smaller; the general color is somewhat darker; the upperparts are suffused with a darker cinnamon or cinnamon-buffy tone; the facial areas are distinctly darker, a dark brownish or blackish along the median line; and the skull is similar to that of *virginianus* but smaller, with a relatively shorter rostrum and broader nasal bones. Known only from Bull Island, South Carolina.

Type locality: Bull Island, Charleston Co., South Carolina.

## Odocoileus virginianus venatorius
### Goldman & Kellogg

Similar to the typical form, but smaller; the upperparts are paler buff, less cinnamon-buff or cinnamon than is usual in *virginianus* in winter pelage; and the skull is smaller than that of *virginianus*, the nasal bones more uniformly flattened and depressed anteriorly. Found only on Hunting Island, South Carolina.

Type locality: Hunting Island, Beaufort Co., South Carolina.

## LITERATURE

Carey, J. 1987. Trouble in Paradise. *Natl. Wildl.* 25: 42–45.

Dimmick, R. W., and M. R. Pelton. 1996. Criteria of sex and age. In: *Research and Management Techniques for Wildlife and Habitats*, 5th ed., pp. 169–214. Bethesda, Md.: The Wildlife Society. 740 pp.

Halls, L. K., ed. 1984. *White-Tailed Deer: Ecology and Management*. Harrisburg, Pa.: Stackpole. 870 pp.

Hawkins, R. E., W. D. Klimstra, and D. C. Autry. 1971. Dispersal of deer from Crab Orchard National Wildlife Refuge. *J. Wildl. Mgmt.* 35: 216–220.

Hesselton, W. T., and R. M. Hesselton. 1982. White-tailed deer. In: J. A. Chapman and G. A. Feldhamer, eds., *Wild Mammals of North America*, pp. 878–901. Baltimore: Johns Hopkins Univ. Press.

Humphrey, S. R. 1992. *Rare and Endangered Biota of Florida*. Vol. 1. Mammals. Gainesville: Univ. Press of Florida. 392 pp.

Larson, J. S., and R. D. Taber. 1980. Criteria of sex and age. In: S. D. Schemnitz, ed., *Wildlife Techniques Manual*, 4th ed., pp. 143–202. Washington: The Wildlife Society.

Layne, J. N. 1978. *Rare and Endangered Biota of Florida*. Vol. 1. Mammals. Gainesville: Univ. Press of Florida. 52 pp.

Lazell, J. D., Jr. 1989. *Wildlife of the Florida Keys: A Natural History*. Washington: Island Press. 253 pp.

McShea, W. J., and G. Schwede. 1993. Variable acorn crops: Responses of white-tailed deer and other mast consumers. *J. Mammal.* 74: 999–1006.

Michael, E. D. 1964. Birth of white-tailed deer fawns. *J. Wildl. Mgmt.* 28: 171–173.

Nelson, M. E. 1993. Natal dispersal and gene flow in white-tailed deer in northeastern Minnesota. *J. Mammal.* 74: 316–322.

Scanlon, J. J., and M. R. Vaughan. 1983. Social grouping of white-tailed deer in Shenandoah National Park, Virginia. *Proc. Ann. Conf. Southeast. Assoc. Fish and Game Wildl. Agencies* 37: 146–160.

Severinghaus, C. W. 1949. Tooth development and wear as criteria of age in the white-tailed deer. *J. Wildl. Mgmt.* 13: 195–216.

Smith, W. P. 1991. Odocoileus virginianus. **Mammalian Species No. 388.** Amer. Soc. Mammal. 13 pp.

Spielman, A., C. M. Clifford, J. Piesman, and M. D. Corwin. 1979. Human babesiosis on Nantucket Island, USA: Description of the vector *Ixodes (Ixodes) dammini* n.sp. (Acarina: Ixodidae). *J. Med. Entomol.* 15: 218–234.

Taylor, W. P., ed. 1956. *The Deer of North America*. Harrisburg, Pa.: Stackpole. 668 pp.

## Moose *Alces alces* (Linnaeus)

DESCRIPTION. The moose, known as "elk" in Europe, is the largest living member of the

*Moose,* Alces alces *(Bob Gress)*

deer family, and can be mistaken for no other animal. This massive creature, with its high, humped shoulders, broad, pendulous muzzle, long, coarse black hair, and whitish legs, is an impressive animal. The ears are large, and there is a prominent hairy dewlap, the "bell," on the throat. The bull has broad, palmate antlers. The pelage is reddish brown or brown to nearly black, not noticeably paler beneath; the lower parts of the legs are light brownish gray, giving one the impression of stockings. Two characteristics help distinguish the sexes when antlers are not present: whereas the bridge of the nose of adult females is noticeably lighter than the body color, that of males is usually the same color as the body; and whereas females have easily observed, fist-sized white vulva patches, males have no distinctive color marking around the tail.

MEASUREMENTS. Standard measurements of moose from Canada were: total length of males 2440–2900 mm (95–115 inches), of females 2000–2600 (80–100), tail (both sexes) 75–150 mm (3–6 inches), and hind foot (both sexes) 725–830 mm (29–33 inches). The greatest recorded antler spread is 204.8 cm (81 inches). Skull length in six individuals ranged from 538 to 686 mm (21 to 26 inches). Quinn and Aho (1989) obtained mean weights of 496 kg (1102 lbs) for mature adult males and 461 kg (1024 lbs) for mature adult females in Algonquin Park, Ontario. Two large bulls from Ver-

mont and New Hampshire weighed 425 kg (945 lbs) and 468 kg (1040 lbs) dressed weight and 617 kg (1370 lbs) and 679 kg (1508 lbs) live weight, the live weights calculated at 1.45 times dressed weight. Similar values for cows from Vermont and New Hampshire were 298 kg (662 lbs) and 383 kg (850 lbs) dressed weight and 432 kg (959 lbs) and 554 kg (1232 lbs) estimated live weight.

Diploid number = 70.

TOOTH FORMULA
$$\frac{0}{3} \quad \frac{0}{1} \quad \frac{3}{3} \quad \frac{3}{3} \quad = \quad 32$$

DISTRIBUTION. The moose occurs in most of southern and western Canada and Alaska, south into northern Minnesota, eastern North Dakota, and south through northern Idaho and western Montana to northeastern Utah, as well as in parts of New England, New York, and Michigan and much of northern Eurasia.

In the eastern United States, the moose formerly occurred over much of New England, the Adirondacks of New York, extreme northern Pennsylvania, and Wisconsin and northern Michigan (including Isle Royale). It was extirpated from Massachusetts in the early to mid-1800s (Vecellio et al., 1993). At least until very recently, the moose recorded in western Massachusetts since 1932 were probably escaped, semicaptive individuals from an estate in central Berkshire County. The moose is still common in northern Maine. There, it has increased from about 2000 head in the early 1900s to an estimated population of 25,000 and growing (Morris and Elowe, 1993). In New Hampshire, the moose reached a low of an estimated 13 animals by 1898, when moose hunting was outlawed in the state (Bontaites and Gustafson, 1993). Numbers then remained low for 80 years, mostly because of habitat reduction from clearing for agriculture. In the early 1900s, agriculture declined in New England, and habitat for moose again increased. Large area clearcutting, culling of the deer herds by severe winters, and continued legal protection led to excellent conditions for moose, and the species began to increase. The herd was estimated at 500 in 1977, 1600 in 1982, and as of this writing there are an estimated 5000 moose in New Hampshire. Moose were nearly extirpated from

Vermont by the 1850s, although a few remained in its northeastern extremity (Essex County). Complete protection was given in 1896, but the herd remained very low during the first half of this century. Increases began in the 1970s with improved habitat and fewer deer. Estimates of the size of the herd were 200 in 1980 to over 1500 and increasing in 1993 (Alexander, 1993). Moose are now hunted in both Vermont and New Hampshire. Moose were gone from New York by 1861, not to reappear until about 1980, when one was seen in Washington County. Moose now enter New York from Vermont and from Canada, but those from Canada probably originated in New England. Present populations are estimated at 80 to 100 individuals in Massachusetts and up to 50 in New York, mostly in the Adirondacks. They are now breeding and increasing in numbers in both states. A few wander into other ar-

*Distribution of the moose,*
Alces alces, *in the eastern*
*United States*

eas of New York, and a bull has wandered the Catskills and along the border of Pennsylvania the past two years. The moose is yet found in the Upper Peninsula of Michigan and occurs in some numbers on Isle Royale in Lake Superior.

HABITAT. The moose is a boreal-forest species, and its range corresponds closely with the limits of this forest. Moose frequent the coniferous forests, swamps, and aspen thickets that border the northern lakes and rivers, and willow/aspen areas form excellent moose habitat. The habitats (and in fact ranges) of moose and deer are largely separate. Moose are also far more tolerant of snow than deer are, and often winter on hilltops while deer concentrate in lowland conifers. Only at snow depths of roughly a meter do moose begin to rely on heavy conifer cover.

HABITS. The moose is a majestic beast, inspiring awe in anyone who has not previously seen it. In spite of its huge bulk and the tremendous palmate antlers of the bull, it is capable of trotting through heavy brush or the forest with amazing speed and stealth. It often haunts the waterways, particularly in the summer, both to seek relief from flies and to secure the tender roots and stems of a variety of aquatic plants, including water lilies. Moose may be active at any time, their activity often reaching several peaks within 24 hours.

As is the case for other cervids, the antlers begin to grow in spring, attain their full size by fall, and fall off or break off in winter at a line of weakness along their base, all within a year. The antlers are used for thrashing brush, in fighting for mates, and for rooting plants from the pond floor.

Moose are powerful swimmers, striking boldly across large lakes. Only an accomplished canoeist can overtake a moose in the water.

Moose are silent most of the year, but they emit several vocalizations. Males "croak" and "bark" during rut. Cows have a grunt that is useful in calling the young, and a "long, quavering moan" during the breeding season. Young calves "cry" under stress; their call may be heard from at least 3 km (1.8 miles) away. Both sexes have appeasement calls, and males under extreme stress utter "roar bellows." Ant-

lers produce nonvocal sounds during the thrashing or rubbing of brush, and during fights. These sounds often attract other males.

FOOD AND FEEDING. Like deer, moose are browsers during the lean months, but they will also feed on a variety of trees and shrubs during spring and summer. They strip the leaves from the last 0.3 to 0.5 meter (1 to 1.5 feet) of the branches by running the branch through their mouth. During the growing season, moose often repair to the shallow lakes, seeking the submerged rhizomes, petioles, and leaves of the spatter-dock (*Nymphaea*). We have watched a huge bull feeding in a pond on the slopes of Mount Katahdin, in northern Maine, during August. At times the bull would submerge and remain completely out of sight for many seconds. Then the huge head with its velvet-covered antlers would break the surface and the moose would chew its prize. Moose eat many different plant species. Some of the favored woody plants are willows, balsam fir, aspen, and birches. Moose consume about 20 kg (44 lbs) of food per day, more in summer than in winter. Dry weight consumed is about 5 kg (11 lbs) in winter, 10 to 12 kg (22 to 26.5 lbs) in summer.

The energy produced by fermentation during digestion in moose is about 30% *less* than needed in winter and up to more than 200% *more* than needed for maintenance in summer; thus moose lose weight in winter, and regain it in summer, because more food is eaten then than is required, and the excess is stored as tissue.

REPRODUCTION AND DEVELOPMENT. The mating season for moose commences in mid-September, peaking around the last week of September or the first week of October, then tapers off through the remainder of October. Females may breed as yearlings and can produce young until about age 18, but most young are produced in the fourth to twelfth years. During the mating season the bulls rush through the forest, ever alert for the grunting cows, or challenging rival bulls with their bellows. Males do not gather harems; rather, they vie for females, and there are "mock battles" preceding a major fight for a female during which the

*Moose, cow with calf (Bob Gress)*

males circle each other, then hit trees and shrubs. Either of the males can avoid a fight by withdrawing in the early stages, as is true for most cervids. Withdrawal is marked by "displacement feeding" with "jerky movements and exaggerated intensity, the eyes fixed on the opponent." The males then fight, or one may yield. Fights take the form of antler-pushing, back and forth; and if one bull falls, he may be hit with the antlers of the other. For a time, neither may gain the advantage, but either may withdraw at any time, and both remain in the area until one does withdraw.

The cow, for her part, remains passively by during all this uproar, until the one remaining male mates with her, over a one- to two-day period. The female is receptive for seven to 12 days. Bulls will mate with more than one cow, and 90% of the cows are usually mated, unless there is a very low bull-to-cow ratio. Following an eight-month gestation (240–246 days), the calves are born, in late May or early June. Twins are produced about 5 to 30% of the time, depending on habitat and the health of the herd. Triplets have also been seen. The newborn weighs 11 to 16 kg (24–35 lbs), and can stand up on its first day. The mother licks it all over at birth. The young are paler, more reddish brown, than the parents, but, unlike deer fawns, moose calves are not spotted. The young average over 1 kg (2.2 lbs) of weight gain per day over their first five months. They are weaned at six months,

but remain with the mother for a year. They are driven off just before the birth of the new young, although the yearlings may rejoin the parents after the young are born.

POPULATION CHARACTERISTICS. Moose are the least gregarious North American cervids, leading a solitary life except in fall, during breeding, and in winter, when the deep snows (over 60 cm, or 2 feet) limit movement. Moose have strong ties to home ranges and may use the same home ranges for years, though the size and shape of a range may vary through time (larger in summer, smallest in winter), thus availing the moose of the best habitat. The home ranges are relatively small, 2.2 to 16.9 square km (1.3 to 10.5 square miles). Moose do not gather in large numbers or yards, as deer and wapiti do. There is little socializing in winter; individuals appear to come together because of favorable habitat rather than for any social purposes. The greatest aggregations occur in late fall and early winter, immediately after the rut. Aggregations then decrease as winter progresses and snow depth increases. But because the moose are spread out, their combined efforts tend to pack the snow down over considerable areas. Within this "yard" the moose move easily, searching out the tender twigs of many kinds of trees.

ENEMIES. Wolves, when present, are the main predator on moose, and their depredations can cause declines in moose populations (see the account for the gray wolf). Wolves kill the highest number of calves or debilitated moose or moose in deep snow. Wolves often chase several moose before finding one they can kill. Adult moose in good condition are much less likely to be killed by wolves than are younger or debilitated ones. Black bears may prey on calves. Being shot by hunters, falling through ice, miring in marshes or bogs, falling into mines, becoming trapped in fires, inextricably locking antlers, and getting hit by vehicles are other hazards that kill some moose, and the domestic dog can also be a hazard.

PARASITES AND DISEASE. A nematode of the brain, *Parelaphostrongylus tenuis*, causes a neurological disease in moose. The white-tailed deer is the primary host. The nematode is harmless to the deer but when ingested by moose may cause incoordination, stiffness, circling associated with blindness, paralysis, and eventually death. In northern New England, deer are at the northern edge of their range, thus less abundant than farther south, and moose there are accordingly less subject to this parasite than they might be elsewhere. It had been felt that this worm could in fact prevent the moose from extending its range to the south, and could be the cause of the extensive wanderings of some moose far from their normal range. To the contrary, however, the moose *has* extended its range to the south. Murry Lankester (Thunder Bay, Ontario) suggests that moose can survive infection and develop an immune response if they are initially exposed to low numbers (one or two) of the worms, but initial dosages of many worms are often fatal.

Moose also harbor liver flukes (*Fascioloides magna*) and winter ticks (*Dermacentor albipictus*). Other parasites have been reported but are not known to be harmful.

RELATION TO HUMANS. Moose are hunted. Hunters call the bulls with crude birchbark horns, simulating the grunt of a cow. Often, a stick rattled in an alder thicket will attract them in September, for at this season they, too, rattle their antlers in the saplings to free them of the last vestiges of velvet. As one of the few true wilderness animals remaining in the eastern United States, the moose should be protected, and protecting the moose requires that we ensure that adequate amounts of good habitat be maintained. One of the more difficult problems of management is accurately censusing the herds. One needs to know the size of the herd and to determine how many moose the range can support, before arriving at a workable management plan. Then the herd can be protected, control measures can be instituted, and harvesting, if warranted, can be undertaken, the goal being to produce a sustained yield. For humans, collisions with cars are probably the most immediate problem the moose presents.

AREAS FOR FURTHER WORK. More study is needed on the interrelationships between moose and other large animals, particularly deer, since both species can greatly affect their habitats. Comparisons of food, habitat, and parasites where this species is sympatric with white-tailed deer (or other cervids) should prove interesting and useful in management. From a practical standpoint, we will need more information relevant to protecting both moose and people, especially as people become more numerous and still more widely distributed, and put more pressure on moose and moose habitat.

## SUBSPECIES

Moose are circumpolar in distribution, and all are now considered to be of the same species. Of seven currently recognized subspecies, three occur in the western United States, just one in the eastern United States.

*Alces alces americana* (Clinton)

As described above.

Type locality: Sweden for the species; "country north of Whitestown" (probably in the western Adirondack region, New York) for *A. alces americana*.

## LITERATURE

Alexander, C. E. 1993. The status and management of moose in Vermont. *Alces* 29: 187–195.

Bontaites, K. M., and K. Gustafson. 1993. The history and status of moose and moose management in New Hampshire. *Alces* 29: 163–167.

Coady, J. W. 1982. Moose *Alces alces*. In: J. A. Chapman and G. A. Feldhamer, eds., *Wild Mammals of North America*, pp. 902–922. Baltimore: Johns Hopkins Univ. Press.

Franzmann, A. 1978. Moose. In: J. Schmidt and D. Gilbert, eds., *Big Game of North America*, pp. 67–81. Harrisburg, Pa.: Stackpole.

———. 1981. *Alces alces*. **Mammalian Species No. 154.** Amer. Soc. Mammal. 7 pp.

Hicks, A. 1995. Past, present and future moose in New York. *Adirondack J. Env. Studies* 2: 26–31.

Morris, K., and K. Elowe. 1993. The status of moose and their management in Maine. *Alces* 29: 91–97.

Murie, A. 1934. The moose of Isle Royale. Misc. Publ. Mus. Zool. Univ. Mich. No. 25. 44 pp.

Peek, J. M. 1974a. On the nature of winter habitats of Shiras moose. *Nat. Canada* 101: 131–141.

———. 1974b. Dynamics of moose aggregations in Alaska, Minnesota, and Montana. *J. Mammal.* 55: 126–137.

Peterson, R. L. 1955. *North American Moose.* Toronto: Univ. Toronto Press. 280 pp.

Quinn, N. J. S., and R. W. Aho. 1989. Whole weights of moose from Algonquin Park, Ontario, Canada. *Alces* 25: 48–51.

Telfer, E. S. 1967a. Comparison of a deer yard and a moose yard in Nova Scotia. *Canadian J. Zool.* 45: 485–490.

———. 1967b. Comparison of moose and deer winter range in Nova Scotia. *J. Wildl. Mgmt.* 31: 418–425.

Vecellio, G. M., R. D. Deldinger, and J. E. Cardoza. 1993. Status and management of moose in Massachusetts. *Alces* 29: 1–7.

# APPENDIX

## Endangered, Threatened, and Extirpated Species

IN RECENT DECADES both the U.S. Fish and Wildlife Service and the state governments have been reexamining the various animal and plant species extant in the United States to see how each is doing and to identify those in need of help. Two main categories are included in these programs:

ENDANGERED. An endangered species is one that is in danger of extirpation or extinction throughout all or a significant part of its range.

THREATENED. A threatened species is one that is likely to become endangered in the foreseeable future.

Federally listed Endangered or Threatened species are automatically accorded at least that rating by the various states. A state may also list species that are endangered or threatened within that state, but not nationally. Federal listing requires the pertinent federal agencies to establish and maintain suitable programs of protection for both taxa and their habitats. Many or most of the "species" on the federal and state lists are actually subspecies. To ensure that distinct populations are accorded appropriate protection, the legal definition of species in the federal act includes full species, subspecies, and even particular populations, and the state criteria are similar.

The species listed as Endangered or Threatened by the states east of the Mississippi are listed in Table 1. Federally listed taxa are also indicated.

A number of other eastern U.S. taxa, most of them given as subspecies, are of concern and were being considered for federal listing in 1994. This entire category has been dropped. No such listing was included with the later lists of species considered as Endangered or Threatened (Endangered and Threatened Wildlife and Plants, USFWS, 31 October 1996). Even though this list no longer has any federal status, it still indicates taxa that we should be concerned about. The species that were under consideration for federal listing in 1994 (Federal Register, 59: No. 219, 15 November 1994) are the following:

INSECTIVORES

| | |
|---|---|
| *Blarina brevicauda aloga* | MA |
| *Blarina brevicauda compacta* | MA |
| *Blarina brevicauda shermani* [We have included this as *B. carolinensis shermani*.] | FL |
| *Scalopus aquaticus bassi* [We do not consider this to be distinct from *S. aquaticus aquaticus*.] | FL |
| *Sorex cinereus nigriculus* [We do not consider this to be distinct from *S. cinereus cinereus*.] | NJ |
| *Sorex palustris punctulatus* | MD, NC, PA, TN, VA, WV |

BATS

| | |
|---|---|
| *Eumops glaucinus floridanus* | FL |
| *Myotis austroriparius* | AL, FL, GA, IL, IN, KY, LA, MS, NC, SC, TN |
| *Myotis leibii* | CT, DE, GA, IL, IN, KY, MA, MD, ME, NC, NH, NJ, NY, OH, PA, RI, SC, TN, VA, VT, WV |
| *Corynorhinus rafinesquii* | AL, FL, GA, IL, IN, KY, LA, MS, NC, OH, SC, TN, VA, WV |

RABBITS AND HARES

| | |
|---|---|
| *Sylvilagus floridanus hitchensi* | VA |
| *Sylvilagus obscurus* | AL, GA, MD, NC, NY, PA, SC, TN, VA, WV |
| *Sylvilagus transitionalis* | CT, MA, ME, NH, NY, PA, RI, VT |

RODENTS

| | |
|---|---|
| *Geomys cumberlandius* [This is an island form but was synonymized with *G. pinetis* by Williams and Genoways (1980).] | GA |
| *Sciurus niger shermani* [We do not consider this to be distinct from *S. niger niger*.] | FL |
| *Neotoma floridana haematoreia* [We do not consider this to be distinct from *N. floridana floridana*.] | GA, NC, SC |

| | |
|---|---|
| *Neotoma magister* (= *N. floridana magister*) | AL, CT, GA, IN, KY, MD, NC, NJ, NY, OH, PA, TN, VA, WV |
| *Peromyscus polionotus leucocephalus* | FL |
| *Peromyscus polionotus peninsularis* | FL |
| *Peromyscus leucopus ammodytes* | MA |
| *Peromyscus leucopus easti* [We do not consider this to be distinct from *P. leucopus leucopus*.] | VA |
| *Peromyscus leucopus fusus* | MA |
| *Podomys floridanus* | FL |
| *Sigmodon hispidus insulicola* | FL |
| *Clethrionomys gapperi maurus* [We do not consider this to be distinct from *C. gapperi gapperi*.] | KY |
| *Microtus breweri* [We consider this to be a subspecies of *Microtus pennsylvanicus*.] | MA |
| *Microtus chrotorrhinus carolinensis* | NC, TN, VA, WV |
| *Microtus pennsylvanicus provectus* | RI |
| *Microtus pennsylvanicus shattucki* | ME |
| *Neofiber alleni* | FL, GA |
| *Synaptomys borealis sphagnicola* | ME, NH |

CARNIVORES

| | |
|---|---|
| *Felis concolor schorgeri* [Considered by us to be extirpated in the eastern U.S.] | IL, MN, WI |
| *Lynx canadensis* | ME, MI, NH, NY, VT, WI |
| *Mustela frenata peninsulae* [We do not consider this to be distinct from *M. frenata frenata*.] | FL |
| *Procyon lotor auspicatus* | FL |

| | |
|---|---|
| *Procyon lotor incautus* | FL |
| *Ursus americanus floridanus* | FL, GA |

ARTIODACTYLS

| | |
|---|---|
| *Odocoileus virginianus hiltonensis* | SC |
| *Odocoileus virginianus nigribarbis* | GA |
| *Odocoileus virginianus taurinsulae* | SC |
| *Odocoileus virginianus venatoria* | SC |

No species of mammal that occurred in the eastern United States in colonial times is extinct (gone everywhere, like the passenger pigeon and the Carolina paroquet), but three species of mammals present here then are now extirpated in the eastern United States: the bison, or buffalo, *Bison bison*; the wolverine, *Gulo gulo*; and the caribou, *Rangifer tarandus*.

The bison once occurred throughout much of the eastern United States, although apparently not in New England or on the Atlantic seaboard. Before the arrival of the Europeans, the bison probably numbered about 70 million, but by 1900 there were fewer than 1000 individuals on the whole continent. The bison was killed for food, hides, and sport, and to help subdue Native Americans, who were dependent on them. Today, there are some bison living wild in na-

tional parks, in bison ranges, and in private ranges in the west. All bison in the east today are in captivity. The last buffalo in Pennsylvania was killed in 1801, in Michigan shortly after the turn of the nineteenth century, in Ohio and Louisiana in 1803, in Virginia in 1825, in Indiana by 1830, and in Wisconsin in 1832.

The wolverine was originally present to the north in Canada and south in the eastern United States to southern Illinois, southern Indiana, and southern Pennsylvania. It was apparently always rare in New England, although there are a few records from New Hampshire and Vermont. It disappeared from Pennsylvania during the mid- to late nineteenth century, from Indiana by 1852, from Michigan apparently about 1860, and from Wisconsin about 1870.

The caribou originally occurred in much of Canada and south in the United States into northeastern Washington, northern Idaho, northern North Dakota, northern Minnesota, northern Wisconsin, Michigan, and Maine, and perhaps the Adirondacks of New York. In 1894 and 1895 caribou were fast disappearing but were still hunted in Maine, some 130 per year being shipped out. By 1900 the season was closed, and the last native caribou were recorded in Maine in 1905 and 1908 near Mt. Katahdin. The last one disappeared from Michigan (from Isle Royale) about 1915, and from Wisconsin perhaps 1910, although later records are not well documented.

Table 1. Endangered and Threatened mammals of the eastern United States as of 1996, excluding marine mammals.

| Species or subspecies | AL | CT | DE | FL | GA | IL | IN | KY | LA | ME | MD | MA | MI | MS | NC | NH | NJ | NY | OH | PA | RI | SC | TN | VT | VA | WV | WI |
|---|---|---|---|---|---|---|---|---|---|---|---|---|---|---|---|---|---|---|---|---|---|---|---|---|---|---|---|
| **INSECTIVORES** | | | | | | | | | | | | | | | | | | | | | | | | | | | |
| Cryptotis parva | | E | | | | | | | | | | | T | | | | | | | E | | | | | | | |
| Sorex dispar | | | | | | | | E | | | | | | | | | | | | | | | | | | E | |
| Sorex fumeus | | | | | | | | | | | T | | | | | | | | | | | | | | | | |
| Sorex longirostris fisheri* | F | | | | | | | | | | | | | | T | | | | | | | | | | T | | |
| Sorex palustris | | | | | | | | | | | | | | | | | | | | | | | | | | E | |
| Sorex palustris punctulatus | | | | | | | | | | | E | | | | | | E | | | T | | | | | | | |
| **BATS** | | | | | | | | | | | | | | | | | | | | | | | | | | | |
| Eumops glaucinus | | | | E | | | | | | | | | | | | | | | | | | | | | | | |
| Myotis austroriparius | | | | | E | | E | E | | | | | | | | | | | | | | | | | | | |
| Myotis grisescens | F | | | E | E | E | E | E | | | | | | E | E | | | | | | | | E | | E | E | |
| Myotis leibii | | | | | | | | E | | | | | | | | | | E | | T | | | | T | | | |
| Myotis sodalis | F | | | E | E | E | E | E | | | E | E | E | E | E | E | E | E | E | E | E | E | E | E | E | E | |
| Nycticeius humeralis | | | | | | | E | T | | | | | | | | | | | | | | | | | | | |
| Corynorhinus rafinesquii | | | | | R1 | E | | T | | | | | | | | | | | | | | | | | E | | |
| Corynorhinus townsendii virginianus | F | | | | | | | E | | | | | | | E | | | | | | | | | | E | E | |
| **LAGOMORPHS** | | | | | | | | | | | | | | | | | | | | | | | | | | | |
| Sylvilagus aquaticus | | | | | | | E | | | | | | | | | | | | | | | | | | | | |
| Sylvilagus obscurus | | | | | R1 | | | | | | | | | | | | | | | | | | | | | E | |
| Sylvilagus palustris hefneri | F | | | E | | | | | | | | | | | | | | | | | | | | | | | |

VA WV WI
SC TN VT
OH PA RI
NH NJ NY
MI MS NC
ME MD MA
IN KY LA
FL GA IL
AL CT DE

| Species or subspecies | F | AL CT DE | FL GA IL | IN KY LA | ME MD MA | MI MS NC | NH NJ NY | OH PA RI | SC TN VT | VA WV WI |
|---|---|---|---|---|---|---|---|---|---|---|
| **RODENTS** | | | | | | | | | | |
| *Geomys pinetis goffi** | F | | E | | | | | | | |
| *Glaucomys sabrinus coloratus* | F | | | | | E | | | E | |
| *Glaucomys sabrinus fuscus* | F | | | | | | | | | E E |
| *Microtus chrotorrhinus carolinesis* | | | | | E | | | | | |
| *Microtus ochrogaster* | | | | | | T | | | | |
| *Microtus pennsylvanicus dukecampbelli* | F | | E | | | | | | | |
| *Neotoma floridana* | | | E | | | | | | | |
| *Neotoma floridana floridana* | | | | | | T | | | | |
| *Neotoma floridana smalli* | F | | E | | | | | | | |
| *Neotoma magister* | | | | T | E | | E E T | E E T | | |
| *Ochrotomys nuttalli* | | | T | | | | | | | |
| *Oryzomys argentatus* | F | | E | | | | | | | |
| *Oryzomys palustris* | | | T | | | | | | | |
| *Peromyscus gossypinus allapaticola* | F | | E | | | | | | | |
| *Peromyscus gossypinus megacephalus** | | | | T | | | | | | |
| *Peromyscus gossypinus restrictus** | F | | E | | | | | | | |
| *Peromyscus polionotus allophrys* | F | | E | | | | | | | |
| *Peromyscus polionotus ammobates* | F | E | | | | | | | | |
| *Peromyscus polionotus decoloratus* | | | E | | | | | | | |

*(continues)*

Table 1 (*continued*)

| Species or subspecies | Federal | AL | CT | DE | FL | GA | IL | IN | KY | LA | ME | MD | MA | MI | MS | NC | NH | NJ | NY | OH | PA | RI | SC | TN | VT | VA | WV | WI |
|---|---|---|---|---|---|---|---|---|---|---|---|---|---|---|---|---|---|---|---|---|---|---|---|---|---|---|---|---|
| **RODENTS** (*continued*) | | | | | | | | | | | | | | | | | | | | | | | | | | | | |
| *Peromyscus polionotus niveiventris* | F | | | | T | | | | | | | | | | | | | | | | | | | | | | | |
| *Peromyscus polionotus peninsularis* | | | | | E | | | | | | | | | | | | | | | | | | | | | | | |
| *Peromyscus polionotus phasma* | F | | | | E | | | | | | | | | | | | | | | | | | | | | | | |
| *Peromyscus polionotus trissylepsis* | F | E | | | T | | | | | | | | | | | | | | | | | | | | | | | |
| *Sciurus niger avicennia*\* | F | | | | T | | | | | | | | | | | | | | | | | | | | | | | |
| *Sciurus niger cinereus*\* | F | | | E | | | | | | | | | E | | | | | | | | | E | | | | | E | | |
| *Spermophilus franklinii* | | | | | | | | T | | | | | | | | | | | | | | | | | | | | |
| *Synaptomys borealis* | | | | | | | | | | | T | | | | | | | | | | | | | | | | | |
| **CARNIVORES** | | | | | | | | | | | | | | | | | | | | | | | | | | | | |
| *Canis lupus* | | | | | | | | | | | E | | | E | | | | | | | E | | | | | | | E |
| *Canis rufus* | F | E | | | | | | | | E | | | | | | | | | | | | | | | E | | | | |
| *Felis concolor* | F | | | | E | | | E | | | E | | | | | | | | | | | | | | E | | | | |
| *Lutra canadensis* | | | | | | | | E | | | | | | | | | | | | | E | | | | | | | | |
| *Lynx canadensis* | | | | | | | | | | | | | | E | | | E | | | E | | | | | | E | | |
| *Lynx rufus* | | | | | | | T | E | | | | | | | | | | E | | E | T | | | | | | | |
| *Martes americana* | | | | | | | | | | | | | | T | | | T | | | | | | | | E | | | E |
| *Mustela vison evergladensis* | | | | | T | | | | | | | | | | | | | | | | | | | | | | | |
| *Taxidea taxus* | | | | | | | | T | | | | | | | | | | | | | | | | | | | | |
| *Ursus americanus floridanus* | | | | | T | | | | | | | | | | | | | | | | | | | | | | | |
| *Ursus americanus luteolus* | F | | | | | | | | | T | | | | | | | | | | | | | | | | | | |

| Species or subspecies | | AL CT DE | FL GA IL | IN KY LA | ME MD MA | MI MS NC | NH NJ NY | OH PA RI | SC TN VT | VA WV WI |
|---|---|---|---|---|---|---|---|---|---|---|
| **MANATEE** | | | | | | | | | | |
| *Trichechus manatus* | F | E | E  E | E | | E  E | | | E | E |
| **ARTIODACTYLS** | | | | | | | | | | |
| *Odocoileus virginianus clavium* | | | E | | | | | | | |

*Sciurus niger cinereus* has been reintroduced into Pennsylvania.

E = Endangered
F = Federally listed
T = Threatened

R1 = "Rare" forms in Georgia receive the same protection as Endangered or Threatened species.
Alabama, Kentucky, North Carolina, and West Virginia currently have no state lists, thus use the federal list.

*We do not consider these to be distinct subspecies. See the subspecies discussion in the species accounts.

# GLOSSARY

abomasum: The fourth or last part of the ruminant stomach, the part most similar to the true stomach of other mammals, and where the most absorption takes place. See *ruminant*.

acanthocephalan: A spiny-headed worm of the class Acanthocephala, an internal parasite found mostly in fish, birds, and other vertebrates, but sparingly in mammals.

acetabulum: Either of the two round openings of the pelvic girdle into which the head of a femur fits.

acre: An area of ground surface equal to 0.405 hectare.

acrocentric: Of a chromosome, having the centromere (attachment) positioned near the end during metaphase. Cf. *metacentric*.

aestivation: See *estivation*.

albinism: An unusual condition in which a genetically induced absence of pigmentation yields an albino, an animal with white hair and pink skin and eyes. Partial albinism results in a spotted animal, the pigmentation completely lacking in some areas; incomplete albinism results in an animal with reduced pigmentation throughout its body. Cf. *melanism, morph*.

albino: See *albinism*.

allantois: A saclike outgrowth of the embryonic gut of mammals, functioning in excretion, nutrition, and respiration. Cf. *amnion, chorion, placenta*.

allopatric: Occurring in different areas or in isolation, their ranges not overlapping, as for example two related or unrelated animal species. Cf. *sympatric*.

altricial: Of the young at birth, being blind, naked, immobile, and entirely dependent on parental care, as is the case with most mammals and many birds. Cf. *precocial*.

amnion: The fluid-filled sac enclosing the embryo in mammals. Cf. *allantois, chorion, placenta*.

anal gland: A gland associated with the anus of a mammal, particularly the odoriferous gland of a skunk (Mephitidae), or of weasels or other mustelids. Cf. *scent gland*.

analogous: Having correspondence in function between anatomical parts of different structure and origin, as for example the wings of bees and those of bats, or the horns of cows and those of rhinoceroses.

anestrous: Not exhibiting estrus.

annulation: A ring about the body, as on the earthworm.

anterior: At or toward the front. Cf. *posterior*.

anterodorsal: Toward the front of the upperparts.

anteroventral: Toward the front of the underparts.

anther: The pollen-containing structure at the end of the stamen of a seed-bearing plant.

antler: One of the paired, solid, annually shed bony growths arising from the frontal bone of an animal of the deer family, often incorrectly called a horn. Cf. *horn*.

aquatic: Growing or living in or frequenting water. Cf. *arboreal, subterranean, terrestrial*.

arboreal: Living in or frequenting trees. Cf. *aquatic, subterranean, terrestrial*.

arthropod: Any member of the vast invertebrate phylum Arthropoda, such as an insect, centipede, millipede, sowbug, spider, scorpion, or crustacean.

artiodactyl: Any of an order (Artiodactyla) of hoofed ungulate mammals (as for example the deer or pig) that have an even number of functional toes on each foot, the axis of each limb passing between the third and fourth toes. Cf. *perissodactyl*.

auditory bulla, tympanic bulla: The rounded, thinwalled, bony capsule enclosing the middle and inner ear of most mammals.

autosomal: Relating to a chromosome other than a sex chromosome. See *somatic cell*.

baby tooth: Any of the first set of teeth (milk teeth) of mammals, usually replaced by an adult (permanent) tooth at an early age. See *diphyodont*.

baculum (pl. bacula): A bone supporting the penis in many bats, rodents, carnivores, and some other mammals. Cf. *os clitoris*.

bay tine: An antler tine positioned beyond the brow tine.

bicornuate: Of the uterus, having two horns or extensions, the two showing much fusion at the base, but remaining evident, as in Insectivora, Carnivora, Sirenia, Perissodactyla, Artiodactyla, and some chiropterans and primates. Cf. *bipartite, duplex, simplex*.

bicuspid: A tooth, often or usually a molariform tooth, having two cusps.

binomial: The basic two-part unit of taxonomic classification, consisting of the generic (genus) name and the trivial name, or epithet, these together constituting the species or specific name, as for example *Procyon lotor*, the raccoon.

bipartite: Of the uterus, having two horns or extensions, the two showing a moderate amount of fusion, as in the cetaceans. Cf. *bicornuate, duplex, simplex*.

bipedal: Walking on two feet, as for example humans and birds. Cf. *quadrupedal*.

blastocyst: That early stage of a developing embryo of a placental mammal during which the embryo implants in the uterine wall.

blastula: An early embryonic stage of a mammal consisting essentially of a free-floating ball of cells, called a *blastocyst* in placental mammals.

brachyodont: Having low-crowned teeth, the teeth not as high as they are wide or long. Cf. *hypsodont*.

browse: To feed on twigs of trees or shrubs. Cf. *graze*.

brow tine: The tine closest to the base of an antler. Cf. *bay tine*.

buff: A dull, brownish-yellow color.

bulla (pl. bullae): See *auditory bulla*.

bunodont: Having teeth with low, rounded cusps, as in humans and pigs. Cf. *lophodont, myrmecophagous, selenodont, tuberculate*.

caecum (pl. caeca): See *cecum*.

calcar: The spurlike, cartilaginous projection on the ankle of a bat that helps to support the interfemoral membrane.

canal: An elongate opening through thickened bone, as opposed to a short opening through a thin plate. Cf. *foramen*.

canine: One of the lone, usually elongate, and more or less pointed teeth situated behind the incisors and in front of the molariform teeth of a mammal; the first tooth in the maxillary bone.

cannon bone: A single, elongate bone of the foot in perissodactyls and artiodactyls formed by fusion of the metacarpals. This bone actually forms the last segment of the leg, raising the ankle above the ground and effectively giving hoofed mammals an extra joint and leg segment, thus helping to account for their greater speed.

canopy: The uppermost spreading, branchy layer of a forest. Cf. *understory*.

carapace: A bony or chitinous case or shield covering the back or part of the back of an animal, as for example a turtle, crab, or armadillo.

carcass: The dead body of an animal. Cf. *carrion*.

carnassial: In many Carnivora, the last upper premolar or the first lower molar; the largest of the molariform teeth that are adapted for shearing rather than tearing or crushing.

carnivore: Any flesh-eating animal, especially a mammal belonging to the order Carnivora, presumably a meat-eater, but in many cases omnivorous.

carnivorous: Feeding on animal foods. Cf. *herbivorous, insectivorous, omnivorous*.

carrion: The dead or decaying flesh of an animal. Cf. *carcass*.

cartilage: A strong, translucent elastic tissue comprising most of the skeleton of embryonic and very young mammals and those of other higher vertebrates, mostly converted to bone in adult animals (but not in sharks and rays).

caterwaul: The wailing of mammals during breeding, especially that of cats.

caudal: Of, pertaining to, or near the tail or posterior part of the body.

cecum, caecum (pl. ceca, caeca): The blind sac or pouch behind which the large intestine of many mammals begins; the appendix of humans.

cellulose: A complex, relatively impervious, carbohydrate material forming the chief substance of plant cell walls. Mammals have evolved many adaptations of the teeth and digestive tract to help them break down cellulose.

centromere: The area of attachment of chromosomes during metaphase.

cervical: Of or pertaining to the neck.

cestode: A tapeworm, an internal parasite of the class Cestoda found in many mammals, usually consisting of a head, the scolex, followed by many body segments.

character, characteristic: Any of the various traits or features used to identify, distinguish, or classify organisms, most often, but not limited to, morphological or physical traits.

cheek teeth: The premolars and molars, taken together; the molariform teeth.

chigger: A larval mite of the acarine family Trombiculidae. Chiggers have three pairs of legs and piercing mouth parts; though small, they are often fairly obvious on hosts, often being highly colored (yellow, orange, red, or white), often solitary but some clustering in the ears or elsewhere on the body. Adult chiggers do not parasitize vertebrates but are the "red spider mites" often found crawling on the ground.

chitin: A horny substance secreted by the upper layers of the skin and forming the hard outer covering of insects, crustaceans, and various other arthropods.

chorion: The highly vascular membrane that envelops the entire embryo, including the allantois and amnion, and forming, in mammals, part of the placenta. Cf. *allantois, amnion, placenta*.

chromosome: One of the elongate chromatin-containing bodies of the cell nucleus, usually constant in number within a species. The chromosomes contain the individual's genetic material, its DNA. See *meiosis, mitosis, DNA*.

class: A taxonomic grouping, as for example Mammalia, that embraces one or more closely related orders.

classification: The systematic arrangement of entities, as for example organisms, into groups or categories corresponding to presumed lines of evolutionary development, according to specified criteria. Cf. *nomenclature, systematics, taxonomy.*

cline: A gradual gradation of characteristics from the individuals of one subspecies to those of another, usually geographic in disposition. Cf. *gradient, intergradation.*

cloaca (pl. cloacae): A chamber at the terminal part of the gut of many vertebrates into which the reproductive, digestive, and urinary systems (and often certain glands) empty and from which waste products (and newborn young) leave the body. Cf. *perineum.*

commensalism: A situation wherein individuals of two different (often markedly unrelated) species exist in close association, one benefiting from the association, the other not affected. Cf. *mutualism, obligate commensalism, parasitism, phoresis, symbiosis.*

common name: The non-Latinate, colloquial, everyday name for a species or other taxon, as for example "red fox." Because common names vary from region to region, nation to nation, language to language, and even within communities (note for example "mountain lion," "cougar," "puma," "panther," etc., all within English), they lack the rigor necessary for universal usage in scientific discourse. Cf. *scientific name, species name.*

condyle: An articular prominence of a bone, as for example the two occipital condyles where the skull articulates with the first cervical vertebra.

condylobasal length of skull: Of a vertebrate, the distance from the anterior end of the premaxillaries to the posterior end of the occipital condyle.

conifer: Any of various evergreen trees bearing true cones, as for example pines, firs. Cf. *deciduous.*

conspecific: Belonging to the same species, as for example individuals of two subspecies of a given species.

convergence: The evolutionary tendency of organisms that are not closely related to develop similar adaptations when subjected to similar environmental conditions and constraints.

coprophagy: The ingestion, by an animal, of its own undigested feces; also called *reingestion,* or *refection.* Rabbits, for example, feed rapidly on quantities of green vegetation, and the undigested material forms soft green pellets in the intestine. These are then defecated and fed upon in the safety of a burrow or thicket. Later, the typical brownish pellets, as often seen in the field, of digested material are defecated.

cranium: The braincase of a vertebrate, consisting of bone in mammals and most other cases.

crepuscular: Active during periods of twilight, whether dawn or dusk. Cf. *diurnal, nocturnal.*

cricetine: A mouse of the subfamily Cricetinae. (Eastern U.S. species previously assigned to the Cricetinae are now in the Sigmodontinae.)

crown-rump measurement: The distance from crown to rump of a developing embryo. Its virtue (and practical utility) is that it can be measured without removing the embryo from the reproductive tract.

cursorial: Adapted for running, as for example a wolf or hare or deer. Cf. *saltatorial, scansorial.*

cusp: A projection, or tubercle, on the biting surface of a mammalian molar tooth.

cyclic population behavior: Of a species, having populations normally and more or less regularly undulating in size, the highs and lows rather consistently attaining about the same levels through intervals of years (often three or four years per cycle in *Microtus,* nine or ten in northern populations of Canada lynx and snowshoe hares).

deciduous: Shed at a certain stage of growth (as the teeth of many vertebrates) or annually (as antlers in deer, or the leaves of many plants, typically in the fall). Cf. *evergreen.*

delayed fertilization: A condition wherein sperm remain viable in the uterus for an extended period before ovulation and then fertilization occur. In north-temperate bats, for example, copulation occurs usually in the fall, fertilization in the spring.

delayed implantation: A condition wherein, although fertilization occurs soon after mating and the embryo's development proceeds to the blastula stage, the blastocyst then remains free in the uterus for an extended period before implanting in the uterine wall. In some carnivores, mating occurs in summer, implantation the following spring.

dental formula: See *tooth formula.*

dermal plate: One of the external scutes of the armadillo.

deutonymph: An immature, nonfeeding "hypopus" of certain mites.

dewlap: A hanging fold of skin under the neck, such as of the moose.

diastema (pl. diastemata): A distinct space or gap between teeth, occurring as a normal character of various mammal species.

digitigrade: Walking on the toes, the heels not touching the ground, as for example cats and dogs. Cf. *plantigrade, unguligrade.*

diphyodont: Having normally two successive sets of teeth, deciduous (or baby) and permanent, as in humans and most other mammals.

diploid: Of the body cells of an individual organism, having the normal (2N) number of chromosomes, as opposed to the haploid number (N), the number in sex cells (sperms and eggs). Cf. *haploid, polyploid.*

disjunct: Of a population (or populations) of an organism, isolated geographically from the main range of its (their) species.

dispersal: Permanent movement of individuals or groups of a population, especially the young, to a new area, often from their birthplace to an area elsewhere. Cf. *emigration, immigration.*

displaced: Of an individual animal, being found in, or driven to, a new and unfamiliar location, as from a prior territory or home range.

distal: Farther, or farthest, from the main part of the body, as the tip of the tail. Cf. *proximal.*

diurnal: Active during daylight hours. Cf. *crepuscular, nocturnal.*

DNA: Deoxyribonucleic acid, the stuff of genetics; the basic material of chromosomes that transmits genetic information.

dormancy: A deep sleep, but not as deep as that in hibernation or estivation.

dorsal: On or pertaining to the back or dorsum. Cf. *ventral*.

dorsum: The upper surface of a body.

duplex: Of the uterus, having two horns or extensions, the two completely separate, as in rodents and lagomorphs. Cf. *bicornuate*, *bipartite*, *simplex*.

echolocation: A process by which an animal orients itself, or identifies the location, character, and perhaps movement of objects, by emitting high-frequency sounds and interpreting the reflected sound waves. Many bats and shrews navigate and locate prey by this method.

ectalental: Employing a sideways (rather than up and down) movement of the jaws. This mode of chewing, characteristic of rabbits, is reflected in them in the shorter lateral distance between the lower tooth rows than between the upper tooth rows.

ectodyte: Any organism found more or less regularly on the outside of an animal (on its hair or skin), as for example a parasite, a phoretic associate or other type of commensal, or an accidental guest, the nature of its relationship to the host unspecified. Replaces the cumbersome term "parasites and other associates." Cf. *ectoparasite*, *endodyte*, *endoparasite*.

ectoparasite: A parasite, such as a tick, occurring on the outside of the body of an animal, such as on the fur or skin, and by definition causing more or less protracted harm to its host. Cf. *ectodyte*, *endodyte*, *endoparasite*.

ectothermic: See *poikilothermic*.

effluvium: An offensive, invisible exhalation or smell, as for example that attending the musk of a skunk.

emarginate: Having a notched margin or tip, as for example the lower part of a bat's ear.

embryo: An animal in the early stages of growth and tissue differentiation, prior to assuming the essential form of its kind; often used synonymously with *fetus*, for example, "full-term embryo." Cf. *fetus*.

emigration: Leaving one's habitual home range or territory for a life or residence elsewhere. Cf. *dispersal*, *immigration*.

endangered: In danger of more or less imminent extinction with respect to its total, worldwide distribution, or, within a given region, of extirpation. Cf. *threatened*.

endemic: Restricted to a particular locality or region, as for example kangaroos to Australia.

endodyte: Any organism occurring naturally within the body of an animal, as for example a parasite or commensal, the nature of its relationship to the host unspecified. Cf. *ectodyte*, *ectoparasite*, *endoparasite*.

endoparasite: A parasite, such as a trematode, cestode, nematode, or acanthocephalan, occurring within the body of an animal, and by its nature causing more or less protracted harm to the host. Cf. *ectodyte*, *endodyte*, *ectoparasite*.

endothermic: See homeothermic.

environment: The total physical and biotic surroundings within the normal range of an organism. Cf. *habitat*, *niche*.

epipubic bone: One of a pair of bones, also called *marsupial bones*, extending forward from the anteroventral portion of the pelvic girdle in marsupials and monotremes, serving to support the pouch in which the female carries her young.

epithet: See *trivial name*.

epizootic: Said of a disease that affects many animals of one kind in one area or region at essentially the same time.

estivation: A dormancy similar to hibernation in being characterized by greatly slowed metabolic processes, but occurring in response to heat or drought during summer. Cf. *hibernation*, *torpidity*.

estrous, oestrous: Of or pertaining to estrus, or heat.

estrus, oestrus: See *heat*.

evergreen: Of a plant, such as a conifer, not shedding its leaves in an annual cycle. Cf. *deciduous*.

extinction: The complete and irrevocable disappearance of all individuals constituting a taxon throughout the worldwide range of that taxon. Cf. *extirpation*; see *endangered*, *threatened*.

extirpation: The extinction of a species within a particular geographic region, as for example North America or New England, but not from its total worldwide distribution. Cf. *extinction*.

fall line: The area or line where the uplands descend to the lowlands, often marked by waterfalls and rapids where rivers cross the fall line; specifically, the line of rapid descent east of the Appalachian Mountains, marking the change from the Piedmont Plateau to the Atlantic Coastal Plain.

fallopian tube: The small tube between the ovary and the oviduct in female animals, where fertilization often takes place.

family: A taxonomic grouping, as for example Felidae, that embraces one or more closely related genera, the genera in some cases assigned to two or more subfamilies. The names of animal families end in -idae, those of plant families in -aceae; for convenience, the members of animal families are often called by a modification of the family name, always ending in -id, thus "felid" for a member of the Felidae, or cat family. Cf. *subfamily*.

fecal: Consisting of (usually) waste material originating from the anus. Animals such as rabbits often produce undigested soft fecal pellets that are then reingested. See *coprophagy*.

feces: Animal excrement; scat. Cf. *spoor*.

femur: The upper bone of the hind leg of mammals and many other vertebrates; the thighbone.

fenestrate: Filled with a labyrinth of small openings, as, especially, the rostrum of a hare or rabbit.

feral: Wild; said of domestic animals (dogs, cats, pigs, horses) that have reverted to a wild state and are no longer dependent on humans.

fetus: An unborn or unhatched vertebrate, after attaining the basic structural plan of its kind. Cf. *embryo*.

fibula: The smaller and more slender of the two long bones in the lower part of the hind limb of most vertebrates. Cf. *tibia*.

flehmen: The smelling or tasting of the urine of conspecifics for purposes of identification, as often occurs in canids and felids. In many hoofed mammals, the act is characteristically accompanied by lip curling.

fluke: One of the two lobes of the flattened, tail-like appendage of cetaceans and sirenians; also, a trematode parasite.

follicle: One of the vesicles in the mammalian ovary wherein new ova develop, one ovum per vesicle; also, the subepidermal sheath that surrounds the lower part of a mammalian hair and provides nourishment to the hair.

forage: To search for food: for herbivores, typically by browsing or grazing or searching the ground for nuts; for bats, by searching the air for flying insects.

foramen (pl. foramina): A small opening or perforation through a thin plate, through which passes nervous tissue, blood vessels, or the like, as in the palate of many vertebrates. Cf. *canal, infraorbital foramen*.

foramen magnum: The large opening at the base of the skull in most vertebrates, into which the spinal cord passes.

forb: An herb, or nonwoody plant, other than grasses or grassy plants.

fossa: An anatomical pit or depression.

fossorial: Adapted for digging and burrowing and spending much time beneath the surface of the ground, as for example moles and pocket gophers. Cf. *aquatic, arboreal, subterranean, terrestrial*.

friable: Easily crumbled or pulverized, as soil.

frontal bone: The bone forming the front of the braincase of the mammalian skull, behind (or above) the nasal bones and maxillary bones.

gene: A bit of genetic material (DNA) controlling or influencing the rise of a particular characteristic in all or various individuals of a population.

gene flow: The movement of genetic material from one population of a species to another through interbreeding, or even from one species to another through hybridization.

gene pool: The collective genetic material within a closed or contiguous population, or an actually interbreeding unit.

genus: A taxonomic grouping, as for example *Felis*, that embraces one or more closely related species.

gestation, gestation period: The period of development of the embryo in the uterus from conception to birth, in some cases protracted by delayed implantation.

gradient: The span of change of one or more characters between one group or population of a species and another. Cf. *cline, intergradation*.

gravid: Pregnant.

graze: To feed on growing herbage or green plant material. Cf. *browse*.

gregarious: Living in groups, whether of fixed or variable membership, as for example many of the deer species.

grizzled: Streaked or flecked with gray and white.

guano: Bat or bird feces.

guard hairs: The long, usually coarser outer hairs that lie over the shorter underfur of most mammals.

habitat: The particular type of environmental circumstance, often highly specific in character, in which individuals or populations of a species of animal typically live, as for example forest, swamp, bog, or meadow. Cf. *environment, niche*.

hair: See *guard hair, molt, pelage, underfur*.

hallux: The first or preaxial digit of the hind limb of mammals and many other vertebrates; the "big toe."

haploid: Of the body cells of an individual organism, having half ($N$) of the normal number ($2N$) of chromosomes, thus the single set of chromosomes in a gamete (sex cell, whether sperm or egg). Haploid sets of chromosomes unite at fertilization to form the diploid or somatic number of the individual. Cf. *diploid, polyploid*.

harem: A group of females herded together, usually by one male, typically for purposes of mating.

heat: The typically annual period, from hours of duration in some species to weeks in others, during which a female mammal is sexually receptive to a male and reproductively fertile; estrus, or oestrus.

hectare: An area of ground surface (abbrev. ha) equal to 2.47 acres.

herb: A nonwoody seed-producing plant. Cf. *forb*.

herbaceous: Having the character of an herb.

herbivorous: Feeding on plant foods. Cf. *carnivorous, insectivorous, omnivorous*.

hertz: A unit of frequency equal to one cycle per second. Humans can hear up to about 20,000 hertz, or 2 kH. See *ultrasonic*.

heterodont: Having the teeth differentiated for various functions, as for example nipping, piercing, shearing, or grinding. Cf. *homodont*.

hibernaculum (pl. hibernacula): A shelter occupied in the winter by a hibernating animal.

hibernation: A period of winter inactivity, in many animals, in which normal metabolic processes and body temperature are greatly reduced. Cf. *estivation, torpidity, torpor*.

hispid: Rough, or covered with stiff hairs.

Holarctic: Of, relating to, or being the entire northern region of the lands (and seas) of the Old World and New World, south to but not including the tropics.

homeothermic, endothermic: Warm-blooded; having a body temperature that is internally regulated, thus remains relatively constant regardless of external temperatures. Cf. *poikilothermic*.

home range: The area, not defended, that an animal traverses on a day-to-day basis during its normal activities of food gathering, mating, and caring for its young. Cf. *territory*.

homing: The act of returning to familiar territory after wandering or having been displaced. See *philopatry*.

homodont: Having no differentiation of the teeth into incisors, canines, etc.; having all of the teeth essentially similar in both upper and lower jaws. Cf. *heterodont*.

hoof: The enlarged, hardened structure on the ends of one or more toes of the ungulate foot, each a greatly modified claw, on which the animals run.

horn: One of the usually paired, permanent projections arising from the head of a bovid, consisting of a bony core covered with keratin fiber substance; also, one of the two projections of the uterus in many mammal groups. Cf. *antler*; see also *bicornuate*.

humerus: The upper bone of the foreleg or arm of mammals and many other invertebrates.

hybrid: The offspring of a mating between individuals of two separate but related species, the offspring often infertile; a crossbreed.

hybridization: Mating between members of two separate but typically related species, the offspring often infertile, as for example a donkey.

hydric: Of a soil or habitat, characterized by an abundance of water; of an organism, requiring an abundance of moisture. Cf. *mesic, xeric*.

hypogeous: Growing underground; said of many fungi.

hypopus (pl. hypopi): A tiny, nonfeeding, immature deutonymph stage of certain mites that clings to fur or feathers, simply for transportation.

hypsodont: Having high-crowned teeth, the teeth higher than they are wide or long. Cf. *brachyodont*.

Ice Age: See *Pleistocene*.

immigration: Entering, and becoming established in, an area other than one's prior habitual home range or territory. Cf. *dispersal, emigration*.

implantation: The process by which the blastula or blastocyst stage of the developing mammal embryo imbeds in the lining of the uterus.

incisive foramen: One of a pair of openings in the anterior portion of the palate, just behind the incisor teeth, in many mammals.

incisor: One of the front teeth of most mammals, those ahead of (between) the canines, situated in the premaxillary bones of the upper jaw and in the anterior end of the mandible. The incisors are used by many animals for nipping, but by rodents and lagomorphs for the major cutting and shearing functions.

infraorbital foramen: An opening on the side of the rostrum, just anterior to the orbit, passing through the maxillary bone and into the orbit.

inguinal: Of or pertaining to the region of the groin.

innate: Inborn, as a particular behavior pattern or ability.

inner ear: An assemblage of three bones, the malleus, incus, and stapes, enclosed by the auditory bulla, constituting the essential organ of hearing and equilibrium in mammals.Cf. *middle ear, outer ear, pinna*.

insectivoran: A mammal of the order Insectivora.

insectivore: Any insect-eating animal, especially an insectivorous bat or anteaters. Mammals of the order Insectivora are not nearly as insectivorous as are many of the bats. Cf. *insectivoran*.

insectivorous: Feeding primarily on insects. Cf. *carnivorous, herbivorous, omnivorous*.

insular: Pertaining to, situated on, or living on an island.

interbreeding: Breeding between individuals of two different stocks or taxa. See *hybridization*.

interdigitated: Meeting or abutting along a highly irregular front, in the manner of the interlocked fingers of two hands, as for example adjacent habitats or populations.

interfemoral membrane: The membrane between the hind legs of a bat, usually enclosing the tail; also called *uropatagium*. Cf. *patagium*.

intergradation: A gradual change in characteristics, from population to population, in the interim range between two subspecies of a species. Cf. *cline, gradient*.

interparietal: A small bone, usually triangular, on the posterior part of the top of the skull in mammals.

interpterygoid: The opening in the skull above (not part of) the hard palate. See *palate*.

intertidal zone: The area along a shore between low and high tides, usually presenting distinct habitats and supporting a distinctive biome.

introduction: The intentional or negligent or accidental placing of individuals of a species from one region, e.g. Eurasia, in a region, e.g. North America, where that species had not previously existed, in sufficient numbers and in sufficiently suitable habitat that the species is at least potentially able to establish itself in the wild in the new region. Cf. *reintroduction*.

invertebrate: An animal without a spinal column: insects, spiders, millipedes, snails, worms, etc.

K-selected: With respect to a species or population, resulting from a reproductive strategy in which relatively few young are produced but those few are usually well cared for, such that many or most enter the breeding population. Cf. *r-selected*.

karyotype: The collective characteristics of the chromosomes of a cell, including chromosome number and the form and points of spindle attachment.

ked: The immature, wingless form of certain parasitic flies that give birth to living young (as opposed to eggs). The sheep ked is an example.

keel: A ridgelike projection on a bone or cartilage that provides an expanded surface for the attachment of muscles or skin, as for example the keel (ridge) on the sternum of a chicken or the calcar of some species of bats.

kilohertz: A unit of frequency equal to 1000 hertz.

labial: Of the lips; toward the lips from the teeth.

lactation: The production of milk by the mammary glands.

lagomorph: Any of an order (Lagomorpha) of gnawing mammals comprising the rabbits, hares, and pikas.

lambdoidal crest: The transverse ridge along the posteriodorsal portions of the occipital and parietal bones of the skull. Cf. *sagittal crest*.

larva (pl. larvae): A developmental form of many of the higher insects and many mites and ticks (in insects, a grub, maggot, or caterpillar) that is fundamentally unlike the adult in appearance and undergoes thorough reorganization at metamorphosis. The larvae of ticks and mites have only three pairs of legs, in contrast to the four pairs of adults. Cf. *naiad, nymph*.

leveret: A hare in its first year.

lingual: Of the tongue; lying near or next to the tongue; on the tongue side of the teeth. Cf. *labial*.

loph: A transverse ridge formed on the occlusal surface of a molar tooth.

lophodont: Of teeth, having transverse ridges. Cf. *bunodont, myrmecophagous, selenodont, tuberculate*.

luteinizing hormone (LH): The hormone that stimulates the maturation of the follicles and ovulation.

mamma (pl. mammae): See *mammary gland*.

mammary gland: One of the two or more milk-producing glands unique to mammals, developing in both sexes but rudimentary in males; the mammae.

mandible: The lower, movable jaw of a mammal or other vertebrate.

marsupial bones. See *epipubic bones*.

marsupium: The pouch of a marsupial, in which are provided mammae and shelter for the young.

masseter: One of the two jaw muscles that raise, thus close, the lower jaw.

mast: The accumulation, on the forest floor, of the fruit of various forest trees, such as acorns, beechnuts, and hickory nuts, often serving as food for animals.

maxilla (pl. maxillae): Either of the pair of bones in the upper jaw of vertebrates, closely fused to the skull, that bear the canines and molariform teeth. Cf. *premaxilla*.

maxillary: Of or pertaining to the maxilla; or, the maxilla.

meiosis: The cellular process that results in the number of chromosomes in gamete-producing cells being reduced to one-half, one of each pair of homologous chromosomes passing to each daughter cell. See *mitosis*.

melanism: The unusual darkening of coloration in some individuals of some animal species produced by a genetically induced excess of melanin (black) pigment in the skin and/or hair, as manifested, for example, in the black or melanistic morph of the gray squirrel. Cf. *albinism, morph*.

membrane: A thin, soft, pliable sheet of stretched skin, as for example on a bat or flying squirrel.

mesic: Of a soil or habitat, being of an intermediate condition of environmental moisture; of an organism, flourishing where there is neither an excess nor a paucity of water. Cf. *hydric, xeric*.

mesophyte: A plant that grows typically under medium conditions of moisture.

Mesozoic: The geologic era extending roughly from 200 to 65 million years ago, the Age of Dinosaurs, in which gymnosperms (conifers) were the dominant plants and toward the end of which the flowering plants and mammals made their appearance.

metabolic rate: The rate at which the chemical processes of the body occur, usually measured by the amount of oxygen consumed relative to an animal's mass.

metabolism: The sum of the chemical processes in an organism by which energy is provided for vital processes and activities.

metacarpal: One of the bones, often elongate and usually five, between the wrist bones (carpals) and the phalanges (finger digits) of the hand or front foot. Cf. *metatarsal*.

metacentric: Of a chromosome, having the centromere (attachment) positioned at the center during metaphase. Cf. *acrocentric*.

metaphase: The phase of mitosis and meiosis in which the chromosomes become arranged in the equatorial plane of the spindle.

metatarsal: One of the bones, often elongate and usually five, between the ankle bones (tarsals) and phalanges (toe digits) of the hind foot of a mammal. Cf. *metacarpal*.

microtine: A member of the old subfamily Microtinae (now the Arvicolinae).

midden: A refuse heap; specifically, a pile of guano, food, or other material, such as the piles of plant materials, bones, etc., deposited by woodrats; or, the stored cones or other foods of squirrels.

middle ear: A small cavity that is separated from the outer ear by the eardrum, and that transmits sound waves from the eardrum to the partition between the middle and inner ears, through a chain of tiny bones. Characteristic bones of mammals (the incus, malleus and stapes), from the temporal area of the skull of reptiles, occur here. Cf. *inner ear, outer ear, pinna*.

mid-dorsal: Situated at the middle of the dorsum.

migration: The two-way movement, usually seasonal, often of all or most individuals of an animal species, from one region to another for the purpose of feeding and/or breeding, and the return at a later date.

milk teeth: The first set of teeth of mammals, usually replaced by adult teeth at an early age.

mitosis: A process in the nucleus of a dividing cell that results in the formation of two new nuclei, each having the same number of chromosomes as the parent nucleus. See *meiosis*.

molar: Any of the hindmost teeth of the jaw in most mammals, typically robust and adapted for crushing, that are situated behind the premolars, not developmentally preceded by milk teeth. Cf. *premolar*.

molariform teeth: The premolars and molars, taken together; the cheek teeth.

molt: The periodic, typically annual or biannual, shedding and replacing of all or much of the hair by a mammal (or of skin or feathers or chitin in other animals). The presence of molting can be determined by examination of the fur from above, revealing the presence of short hairs pigmented to the base. The mature hairs of a "prime" or nonmolting pelt are usually light-colored at the bases (the pigmentation is above skin level), and the skin thus appears pinkish or whitish. Molt also shows on the underside of the skin where pigment deposition occurs as small dark dots in the new hairs as they are growing.

monestrous: Having a single estrous cycle (period of heat in the female) per year. Cf. *polyestrous*.

monogamous: Having a single mate for life, or at least for one breeding season. Cf. *polyandrous, polygamous, promiscuous.*

monotypic: Embracing a single subordinate taxon, as for example a genus consisting of single species.

morph: A form of an organism morphologically different from the typical form for the species, as for example the cross fox, or the black morph of the gray squirrel.

morphological: Of or pertaining to morphology.

morphology: The form and structure (anatomy) of an organism or any of its parts; the branch of biology that deals with the form and structure of animals or plants.

mutualism: A mutually beneficial, but not necessarily intimate, relationship between individuals of different animal or plant species, as for example the burying of acorns, by squirrels, for future consumption; the squirrel consumes many of the acorns, but many others later sprout and become trees, thus benefiting that species of oak. Cf. *commensalism, obligate commensalism, parasitism, phoresis, symbiosis.*

mycorrhiza (pl. mycorrhizae): The rootlike structures of a fungus that are in close association, perhaps in obligate mutualism, with the roots of a tree or other seed plant.

myrmecophagous: Of teeth, simple and peglike, lacking enamel, as in the armadillo. Cf. *bunodont, lophodont, selenodont, tuberculate.*

naiad: The immature aquatic stage of a mayfly, stonefly, dragonfly, or damselfly; the immature bears some features of the adult but undergoes major changes at metamorphosis. Cf. *larva, nymph.*

nasal bone: One of a pair of bones in the front of the mammal skull anterior to the frontal bones.

Negri bodies: Structures, found in the brains of rabid animals, that are diagnostic for rabies.

nematode: Any of a large number of roundworms of the class Nematoda; many are internal parasites of mammals.

niche: The typical role or "profession" of an organism within its normal habitat and environment; organisms can carve out niches for themselves in different ways in different habitats, or in different communities in similar habitats.

nictitating membrane: A thin, transparent membrane, present in most mammal species, often called a "third eyelid"; it is drawn over the surface of the eyeball from the inner angle of the eye to the outer angle, thus cleaning the eye.

nipping: Cutting free any of the various tender parts of a plant, typically by the incisors, for consumption.

nocturnal: Active during the night. Cf. *crepuscular, diurnal.*

nomenclature: The formal international system and procedure of assigning unique and universal New Latin names to taxa of organisms. Cf. *classification, systematics, taxonomy.*

nominate subspecies: The subspecies bearing the same name designation as the species, as for example *Sus scrofa scrofa*; the name thus given to the originally described population of a species when, in later years, some other population of that species is distinguished in some way, formally described, and accorded its own, new subspecific epithet. If in due course the newly described subspecies is formally deemed to be superfluous (synonymous), and no other subspecies has been described, the need for the nominate subspecies as a taxonomic entity becomes moot. See *subspecies.*

nose leaf: An upward projection from the nose of some bats, perhaps used in some way in echolocation.

notch (of an ear): The lowest indentation in the periphery of the ear. The length of the ear is measured from this notch to the farthest point on the periphery.

nymph: An immature individual of one of the more primitive orders of insects, as for example crickets or grasshoppers (Orthoptera), at any of several successive life stages each of which more or less closely resembles the adult; or, in mites and ticks, an immature individual having gained four pairs of legs, as in the adult, but not yet able to reproduce. Cf. *larva, naiad.*

obligate mutualism: The necessary and permanent relationship between two, often markedly unrelated, organisms, in which both benefit and without which neither would survive, such as that between cellulose-digesting bacteria and the ruminants whose alimentary tracts they inhabit, or that constituting a lichen, which is in fact a close linkage of an alga and a fungus. Cf. *commensalism, mutualism, parasitism, phoresis, symbiosis.*

occipital, occipital bone: The bone forming the back or base of the skull, containing the occipital condyles.

occipital condyle: One of the two protuberances on the back of the skull that articulate with the first cervical vertebra.

occlusal: Of or relating to the grinding surfaces of the teeth.

occlusion: The relationship between the opposing surfaces of the teeth of the two jaws when in contact.

ochraceous: Having a yellowish-red tint.

oestrous: See *estrous.*

oestrus: See *estrus.*

olfactory: Pertaining to the sense of smell.

omasum: The third of the four parts of the ruminant stomach, which presses water from the predigested food. See *ruminant.*

omnivorous: Feeding typically on both animal and vegetable foods. Cf. *carnivorous, herbivorous, insectivorous.*

orbit: Either of the two bony eye sockets of the skull.

order: A taxonomic grouping, as for example Carnivora, that embraces one or more closely related families.

os clitoris: A tiny bone or cartilage, the homologue of a baculum, often found in females of species, as for example seals and raccoons, the male of which possesses a baculum.

ossified: Formed of bone, as opposed to cartilage.

outer ear: The outer and visible portion of the ear that

collects and directs sound waves toward the eardrum; the pinna. Cf. *inner ear, middle ear, pinna.*

ovary: The typically paired essential female reproductive organ that produces eggs and in vertebrates female sex hormones.

oviduct: A tube that serves exclusively or especially for the passage of eggs from an ovary.

ovulation: The eruption, or release, of eggs, or ova, from the ovary, into the fallopian tubes of mammals.

ovum (pl. ova): Egg.

palate: The bony roof of the mouth in vertebrates. The palate has two pairs of openings into the skull, the anterior (incisive) and posterior palatine foramina. Cf. *interpterygoid.*

palatine: Of or pertaining to the palate.

palmate: Branched from a common point or area, as the fingers of a hand, or the principal veins of a maple leaf.

parasite: An organism that lives on or in, and at the expense of, but generally does not kill, its host. In most cases, a parasite is far smaller than its host and inhabits one or only a few hosts during its lifetime. See *ectoparasite, endoparasite*; cf. *ectodyte, endodyte.*

parasitism: A situation wherein two individual organisms, usually of markedly unrelated species and markedly different sizes, exist in intimate association, the one (on or within the other) benefiting from the association at the expense of the other. Cf. *commensalism, mutualism, obligate commensalism, phoresis, symbiosis.*

parietal: Either of the paired bones of the skull between the frontal bones and the occipital bones and forming the posterior portion of the braincase.

parturition, partus: The birth of offspring in most mammals; the process by which a fetus separates from the mother's uterine wall and leaves the mother's body.

patagium (pl. patagia): The membrane in flying squirrels and bats that typically stretches down the sides of the body between the forelimbs and hindlimbs and in bats usually includes the tail as well, forming the surface area necessary for gliding (flying squirrels) or flight (bats). Cf. *interfemoral membrane.*

pectoral girdle: In most vertebrates, the bony structure that supports the forelimbs.

pelage: The entire furred coat of a mammal, whether on the living animal or prior to skinning. Cf. *pelt.*

pelt: The entire furred coat of a mammal, after its removal from the animal. Cf. *pelage.*

pelvic girdle: In most vertebrates, the bony structure that supports the hind limbs and includes, on each side, a round opening, the acetabulum, into which the head of the femur fits.

perineum (pl. perinea): The area between the anus and the posterior extremity of the external genitalia of a vertebrate, especially in the female. Cf. *cloaca.*

perissodactyl: Any of an order (Perissodactyla) of nonruminant, hoofed ungulate mammals (as for example a horse, tapir, or rhinoceros) that usually have an odd number of toes on each foot, the axis of each limb passing through the middle toe. Cf. *artiodactyl.*

phalanx (pl. phalanges): One of the bones of a finger or toe of a vertebrate.

pheromone: A chemical substance produced by an animal that serves as a stimulation to other individuals of the same species for one or more behavioral responses, as for example mating.

philopatric: Characterized by, or exhibiting, philopatry.

philopatry: The tendency or drive of an individual animal to stay in, or return to, its home range.

phoresis, phoresy: A relationship between individuals of two species in which one uses the other simply for transportation purposes, the host neither benefited nor harmed, as for example the larvae of certain mites routinely found in the fur of certain mammals. Cf. *commensalism, mutualism, obligate commensalism, parasitism, symbiosis.*

phoretic: Of or pertaining to phoresis.

phylum: A taxonomic grouping, as for example Vertebrata, that embraces one or more closely related classes.

piedmont: A plain or plateau between a mountain range and a (lower) coastal plain, specifically the plain between the Appalachian Mountains and the Atlantic Coastal Plain. The Piedmont Plateau meets the Coastal Plain at the fall line, a zone of rapid descent.

pigmentation: Coloration in an organism produced by pigment granules, especially melanins (black or brown pigments), but also by anthocyanins (red pigments) or xanthins (yellow pigments).

pinna (pl. pinnae): Either of the external (fleshy) ears of a mammal, lacking in many aquatic and fossorial species; the outer ear.

placenta: The assemblage of vascular tissue, formed by the chorion and allantois of the embryo in placental mammals, that provides for the exchange of gases, nutrients, and waste materials between mother and embryo. The opossum (a marsupial mammal) has only a rudimentary placenta. Cf. *allantois, amnion, chorion.*

placental scar: One of the discolorations on the wall of the uterus marking former attachments of placentas.

plantar: Of or relating to the sole of the foot.

plantigrade: Walking on the soles of the feet, the heels touching the ground, as for example bears and humans. Cf. *digitigrade, unguligrade.*

Pleistocene: The Ice Age, or time of extensive glaciation, which lasted roughly from 1 million to 10,000 years ago.

plumbeous: Of a leaden-gray color.

poikilothermic, ectothermic: Cold-blooded; having a body temperature that varies with that of the environment. Cf. *homeothermic.*

polyandrous: Having more than one male mate per female. Cf. *monogamous, polygamous, promiscuous.*

polyestrous: Having more than one estrous cycle (period of heat) per year. Cf. *monestrous.*

polygamous: Having more than one female mate per male, the male thus having a harem. Cf. *monogamous, polyandrous, promiscuous.*

polyploid: Having for the chromosome number some

multiple of the haploid number (other than 2*N*, which is the diploid number), such as 3*N* (triploid) or 4*N* (tetraploid). Cf. *diploid.*

population: A group of interbreeding individuals of a single animal or plant species; a single reproductive unit or gene pool of a species, more or less isolated from other such units. Cf. *subspecies.*

posterior: At or toward the rear. Cf. *anterior.*

postorbital process: A process, or projection, of the frontal bone directly behind the orbit, or eye socket. Cf. *preorbital, suborbital, supraorbital.*

postpartum estrus, postpartum heat: The condition of a female wherein she becomes receptive to mating (and capable of conceiving) soon after giving birth.

precocial: Of the young at birth, being fully furred (or feathered), open-eyed, and able to move about immediately, as the young of snowshoe hares, deer, cows, horses, chickens, killdeer, and some other mammals and birds. Cf. *altricial.*

predator: An animal that lives, at least in part, by the killing and consuming of other animals, as is characteristic of many mammal species.

prehensile: Adapted for grasping by curling or wrapping, as for example the tail in the opossum and many New World monkeys.

premaxilla (pl. premaxillae): Either of a pair of bones (the anteriormost) of the upper jaw of vertebrates, between and in front of the maxillae, that bear the incisors. Cf. *maxilla.*

premolar: Any of the teeth of a mammal that are situated in front of the molars and behind the canines, developmentally preceded by milk (baby) teeth; in humans, the bicuspids.

preorbital: Anterior to the eye. Deer, for example, have preorbital glands just forward from the eyes.

preputial: Situated in the prepuce, or foreskin of the penis.

prey: Any animal seized or hunted by another for food, successfully or not.

primary isolating mechanism: Any factor (usually geographic) that separates the members of a species into two or more groups in such a way that interbreeding between the groups can no longer occur; the first of the two essential elements of speciation. Cf. *secondary isolating mechanism, speciation.*

promiscuous: Mating indiscriminately and perhaps often; said of an individual or a species. Cf. *monogamous, polyandrous, polygamous.*

proximal: Closer, or closest, to the main part of the body, as the base of the tail. Cf. *distal.*

pseudopregnancy: An anestrous state resembling pregnancy that occurs in various mammals usually after an infertile copulation.

pupa (pl. pupae): The dormant or inactive stage in the development of insects of species (for example butterflies) that undergo complete metamorphosis from larva to adult. During the pupal stage, the insect in most cases is enclosed within a protective covering such as an earthen cell, cocoon, or puparium (hardened outer skin).

quadrupedal: Having, and moving about on, four feet. Cf. *bipedal.*

quill: One of the many hardened, hollow, pointed, and barbed hairs of a porcupine or other species; a hardened spine.

r-selected: With respect to a species or population, resulting from a reproductive strategy in which numerous offspring are produced but relatively few survive to enter the breeding population. Cf. *K-selected.*

radiotelemetry: The use of radio transmitters and receivers to track the movements of, or to determine the den locations of, individual animals, the transmitter affixed in one way or another to the animal to be tracked.

radius: The anterior, thicker, and shorter of the two bones of the lower foreleg or the forearm of mammals and many other vertebrates. Cf. *ulna.*

reentrant angle: A fold or recess into the inner or outer side of a tooth, running typically from base to crown, such as are found in the teeth of arvicoline rodents.

refection: See *coprophagy.*

reingestion: See *coprophagy.*

reintroduction: The placing of individuals of a species in an area from which the species had previously been extirpated, in sufficient numbers and in sufficiently suitable habitat that the species is at least potentially capable of reestablishing itself in the wild in that area. Cf. *introduction.*

reticulum: The second of the four parts of the ruminant stomach, which returns large particles to the rumen for further processing. See *ruminant.*

retractile: Capable of being drawn back, or into sheaths, as a cat's claws.

riparian: Pertaining to the bank or shore of a river or other watercourse, or sometimes a lake or tidewater.

rostrum: The preorbital or snout part of the skull of a vertebrate.

rugose: Heavily wrinkled; roughened into ridges.

rumen: The first of the four parts of the ruminant stomach, a storage organ and a culture chamber for bacteria. See *ruminant.*

ruminant: One of the hoofed artiodactyls having a four-parted stomach (the stomach consisting of, in order, the rumen, the reticulum, the omasum, and the abomasum).

rut: The usually annual period of sexual excitement in the male deer and related mammals.

sagittal crest: A raised, median, anteroposterior ridge of bone on the cranium, or braincase, serving as an attachment area for muscles or skin. Cf. *lambdoidal crest.*

saltatorial: Adapted for jumping, as a jumping mouse or kangaroo. Cf. *cursorial, scansorial.*

samara: A dry, indehiscent, usually one-seeded, winged fruit, as for example of a maple, ash, or elm tree.

scansorial: Having the ability to climb by means of sharp, curved claws, as for example tree squirrels and porcupines. Cf. *cursorial, saltatorial.*

scapular: Pertaining to the region of the shoulder, or scapula.

scat: A unit of animal excrement, often diagnostic of species; feces. Cf. *spoor*.

scavenger: An organism that feeds habitually on refuse or carrion.

scent gland: Any of various glands, variously situated on the body of an animal, that produce a scent, or sometimes even an effluvium, the scent employed in different species for different (or unknown) purposes, but typically to mark territory, identify individuals, or attract the opposite sex. Cf. *anal gland*.

scientific name: The unique Latinate name, of universal application, of a species (or other taxon) of organisms, such as *Mus musculus*, for the common house mouse, or Chiroptera, for the order embracing bats. The classification of plants is similar to, but entirely separate from, that of animals; therefore the same name can denote a plant taxon and an animal taxon. See *species name*; cf. *common name*.

scolex: The head of a cestode, or tapeworm.

scute: An external bony or horny plate, as for example those on the dorsum of an armadillo. Also *dermal plate*.

secondary isolating mechanism: Any of various divergent adaptations of two or more populations or groups or populations of a species that prevent resumption of successful interbreeding between the groups, once a primary isolating mechanism (typically geographic in nature) has broken down and the groups are once again in contact. Secondary isolating mechanisms, the second of the two essential components of speciation, may take many forms, as for example genetic, ecological, behavioral, temporal, or mechanical (anatomical). Cf. *primary isolating mechanism*, *speciation*, *subspecies*.

selenodont: Having teeth in which the enamel of the occlusal surfaces takes the form of successive longitudinal crescents, as in deer. Cf. *bunodont*, *lophodont*, *myrmecophagous*, *tuberculate*.

seminal vesicle: The pouchlike or saclike structure, usually at the base of the penis in mammals, that stores seminal fluid (but not sperm) prior to ejaculation.

senescent: Showing characteristics of advanced age.

seral stage: One of the various stages in natural succession, as grassland or old-growth forest. See *succession*.

simplex: Of the uterus, having the horns completely fused into a single chamber, as in edentates, higher primates, and chiropterans. Cf. *bicornuate*, *bipartite*, *duplex*.

sirenian: Any of an order (Sirenia) of aquatic, herbivorous mammals including the manatee and dugong.

somatic cell: Any cell of the body other than the sex cells (sperm or egg).

spatulate: Flattened at the end like a spatula or spoon.

speciation: The evolutionary process whereby, over time, two or more species are produced where only one had existed previously, usually following the rise of primary and secondary isolating mechanisms. Primary isolating mechanisms (usually geographic) sep-

arate populations or groups of populations of a species, thus cutting off gene flow between them and allowing evolution (biological divergence) to proceed; secondary isolating mechanisms are those factors (genetic, ecological, morphological, ethological), that block resumed interbreeding if and when the primary isolating mechanisms break down. See *primary isolating mechanism*, *secondary isolating mechanism*, *species*.

species: A group of interbreeding or potentially interbreeding natural populations of organisms that are reproductively isolated from (generally genetically incapable of breeding with) all other organisms or groups of organisms; the basic unit of animal and plant life, and of taxonomy. See *speciation*, *subspecies*.

species name: The currently accepted binomial (two-word) name of a species, consisting of the generic and trivial names, as for example *Mus musculus*, or *M. musculus*. *Mus* is the generic name, *musculus* is the trivial name, or epithet. Development of the present system of rules of naming, the International Code of Zoological Nomenclature ("the code"), began in 1889, when the first Commission on Zoological Nomenclature met. The code established the tenth edition of Linnaeus' *Systema Naturae* (published in 1758) as the starting point of zoological nomenclature because Linnaeus was the first to apply binomial nomenclature consistently and systematically. The commission meets every five years to improve or modify the code as needed, and to rule on contested names. Cf. *common name*, *nominate subspecies*.

spoor: The track, trail, footprint, or droppings, of a wild animal; a manifestation, of whatever sort, of the more or less recent presence (and often identity) of an animal. Cf. *scat*.

stamen: The organ of a flower that produces the male gamete and consists of an anther (pollen-producing structure) and a supporting filament (stalk).

standard measurements: A set of measurements employed, by general agreement, in the description of an individual mammal or (as an average) of a species or population of a species, given as total length (TL), tail length (T), and hind foot length (HF), always presented in this order.

sternum (pl. sternums, sterna): The bone linking the ribs of a vertebrate along the length of the breast; the breastbone.

subfamily: One of two or more taxonomic groupings, as for example Arvicolinae, that embraces one or more closely related genera within a family. The names of animal subfamilies end in -inae, thus yielding "arvicoline" for a member of the Arvicolinae. Whereas the rules of taxonomy necessarily order all species into genera and families, the subfamily taxon (like the suborder or subgenus) is optional, typically employed in the classification of large families numbering many genera. Cf. *family*.

submaxillary gland: A small gland under the lower jaw of a mammal that supplies saliva to the mouth; in the shrew *Blarina*, the gland contains poison.

subnivean: Beneath a ground cover of snow.

subspecies: One of two or more populations, or groups of populations, of a species all deemed to be mutually distinct on some basis and given distinct names, as for example *Sorex hoyi hoyi*, deemed distinct from *S. h. winnemana*; as used here, and, as such, separated from other subspecific populations or groups of populations of that species by a primary isolating mechanism (for example a mountain range), thus lacking a clinal gradation to the other subspecies of its species (and perhaps embarked on a process of speciation) but nonetheless potentially capable of interbreeding with other subspecies of its species. (Historically, the problem of precisely defining the concepts *species* and *subspecies*, especially the latter, has been much in debate.) Cf. *nominate subspecies, population, primary isolating mechanism*; see *secondary isolating mechanism, speciation, species*.

subterranean: Living or occurring beneath the surface of the ground. Cf. *aquatic, arboreal, fossorial, terrestrial*.

succession: The gradual, and naturally occurring, replacement of one biotic (chiefly vegetational) community by another, such as occurs during the replacement of grassland by shrubland, and eventually by forest. See *seral*.

supraorbital process: A process, or projection, of the frontal bone above the orbit, or eye socket. Cf. *preorbital, postorbital, suborbital*.

suspect bats: Bats found on the ground, apparently sick, dead, or dying. The percentage of rabies in "suspect bats" (about 4% in Indiana, for example) is much higher than that in bats behaving normally, where the rate is far less than 1%.

swarming (of bats): The gathering of substantial numbers of individuals (of one or more bat species), in late summer and fall, in the air about cave entrances; the function of the behavior is not completely understood, but is probably related to mating. (See the account for *Myotis septentrionalis* for further discussion.)

symbiosis: The living together in a more or less intimate association or close union of two dissimilar organisms, whether with benefit or harm for either or both or not; often used in the meaning of mutualism or obligate commensalism. See *commensalism, mutualism, obligate commensalism, parasitism, phoresis*; see also *ectodyte, endodyte*.

sympatric: Occurring in the same range or area without loss of identity from interbreeding as for example two related or unrelated animal species. Cf. *allopatric*.

synonym: One of two or more scientific names deemed, at a given point in time and by a given authority, to be designating the same species or other taxon, one name recognized by that authority as the accepted name and the others relegated to synonymy. See *nomenclature, subspecies, synonymy*.

synonymy: A list of two or more scientific names all applying to the same species or other taxon, all once thought to be designating distinct taxa but having fallen into synonymy over time (displaced in usage and recognition) as the result of revisions of their subtending group by later specialists, or on the basis of new discoveries or other knowledge. See *synonym*.

systematics: In the broad sense, the science of classification and nomenclature of organisms. Cf. *classification, nomenclature, taxonomy*. Many consider systematics to be the theory and science of classification, of organisms, the placing of smaller groups within larger groups, hierarchically; and taxonomy to be the process of establishing the bounds of small or large groupings and according them names.

tactile: Having, or pertaining to, the sense of touch.

talus: A slope formed by rocky debris at the base of a cliff or mountain.

tawny: A brownish-yellow color.

taxon (pl. taxa): Any taxonomic unit, as for example one of the various subfamilies, genera, species, or subspecies within a family; more specifically, a group of organisms all members of which share characteristics such that all are deemed to be collectively distinct from all other organisms or groups of orgnisms. As such, a taxon is a representation of a natural unit, whether yet named or not. See *classification, nomenclature, synonymy, systematics, taxonomy*.

taxonomy: The formal and orderly classification of plants and animals into nested units (species within genera, genera within families, etc.) according to their presumed natural relationships and origins; systematics. Cf. *classification, nomenclature, systematics*.

terete: Circular in cross section.

terrestrial: Living primarily on the ground, as for example a wolf; or growing on the ground, as for example a daffodil. Cf. *aquatic, arboreal, fossorial, subterranean*.

territory: The portion of its home range that an individual animal routinely defends against members of the same or either sex of its own species, or, sometimes, different species. Cf. *home range*.

thermoregulation: The regulation of body temperature in warm-blooded vertebrates (mammals and birds). See *homeothermic*.

threatened: At risk of becoming endangered. Cf. *extirpation*.

tibia (pl. tibiae): The larger and more robust of the two bones in the hind limb of most vertebrates. Cf. *fibula*.

tine: One of the points on a cervid antler.

tooth formula, dental formula: The itemized distribution of the upper and lower incisors, canines, premolars, and molars of an adult mammal, expressed as, for example,

$$\frac{3}{3} \quad \frac{1}{1} \quad \frac{4}{4} \quad \frac{3}{3} \quad = \quad 44$$

where the "fractions" to the left represent numbers of teeth of each type (incisors first) in the upper and lower jaws of one side of the skull and the number at the right doubles the preceding total, thus counts *all* of the teeth in *both* sides of the skull.

torpidity: In mammals, a relatively short-term period of

winter inactivity during which the body temperature and rate of metabolism are somewhat reduced. Cf. *estivation, hibernation.*

torpor: A deep sleep.

track: The imprint of successive footprints in soil, snow, or other substrate.

tragus (pl. tragi): The often prominent, sometimes quite long lobe extending vertically from the base of the ear of a bat, the function of which is incompletely known but apparently relates to echolocation.

transponder: A tiny, passive (nonelectrical) unit barcoded with individual numbers, inserted under the skin of an animal, and read by a scanner similar to those employed in supermarkets, so as to identify that individual animal. As currently available, the barcode can be read only by a scanner situated immediately next to the animal, or by a scanner forming a loop around an exit/entrance opening.

trematode: A fluke, or internal parasite, of the invertebrate class Trematoda.

trichome: An epidermal, hairlike structure on a plant.

trivial name: The second element of a binomial (species) name, as for example *musculus*, of *Mus musculus*, the first element being the generic name. Also called *epithet*; see *subspecies.*

truncate: Terminating abruptly, as if the end were cut off.

tubercle: A small, rounded projection, such as is found on the crown of a tooth or on the sole of a foot.

tuberculate: Of teeth, a primitive low-crowned type with three cusps. Cf. *bunodont, lophodont, myrmecophagous, selenodont.*

tularemia: A bacterial disease, caused by *Pasteurella tularensis*, that can be contracted by humans principally through the bites of flies, fleas, ticks, or lice that infest rabbits, hares, and rodents.

tympanic: Pertaining to the ear, especially the middle ear.

tympanic bulla: See *auditory bulla.*

ulna: The posterior, thinner, and longer of the two bones of the lower foreleg or the forearm of mammals and many other vertebrates. Cf. *radius.*

ultrasonic: With respect to sound waves, above the range of human hearing, i.e. above about 20,000 Hz (20 kHz). See *hertz.*

underfur: The thick, soft fur lying beneath the longer and coarser guard hairs of most mammals.

understory: The layer of herbs, shrubs, and smaller trees beneath the forest canopy.

unguis: A nail, hoof, or claw of a mammal, usually at the end of a digit.

unguligrade: Walking in such a manner that only the unguis is in contact with the ground, as for example in deer and horses.

unicuspid: In shrews, one of the three to five small teeth between the anterior large two-cusped upper incisors and the large cheek teeth.

uropatagium (pl. uropatagia): See *interfemoral membrane.*

uterus: The internal organ of the female mammal that contains and nourishes the young during development previous to birth.

vacuity: An empty space.

vaginal plug: A plug formed of congealed seminal fluid that temporarily blocks the vagina, and during that time prevents further insemination. Such plugs are found in bats, arvicoline mice, squirrels, and various other mammals.

vascular: Of or relating to a channel or system of channels for the conveying of a body fluid, such as the blood of an animal or the sap of a plant.

velvet: The soft vascular skin that envelops and nourishes the developing antlers of deer and is shed prior to the rut.

venter: The underparts of the belly, or abdomen.

ventral: On or pertaining to the underside or belly (venter). Cf. *dorsal.*

vertebrate: An animal with a backbone, or spinal column; fish, amphibians, reptiles, birds, and mammals.

vesicle: A membranous and usually fluid-filled pouch or sac in a plant or animal. See *seminal vesicle.*

vestigial: Of the character of, or pertaining to, a vestige.

vestige: The evolutionary, often degenerate, remnant of an organ or structure that had been functional in ancestral organisms but is no longer in use, as for example the human appendix.

vibrissa (pl. vibrissae): One of the several stiff facial whiskers or hairs around the nose or mouth of certain mammals, as for example felines, evidently performing a tactile function.

viviparous: Of an animal species (including nearly all mammals and even some sharks), having the developing young become attached to, and receive oxygen and nourishment from, the reproductive tract of the female and, later, be born alive (not in eggs). See *placenta.*

volant: Flying; capable of flight, as for example when the developing young of a bat becomes able to fly.

xeric: Of a soil or habitat, characterized by minimal moisture; of an organism, requiring a very dry situation. Cf. *hydric, mesic.*

yearling: A one-year-old animal, i.e. one now in its second year.

zygomatic arch: The arch of bone forming the lower and outside edge of each orbit, or eye socket, of a vertebrate.

# GUIDE TO FURTHER READING

## Journals and Serials

American Midland
  Naturalist
Canadian Field-
  Naturalist
Canadian Journal
  of Zoology
Ecological Monographs

Ecology
Journal of Mammalogy
Journal of Wildlife
  Management
Mammalia
Oecologia
Oikos

## Additional General References

Allen, G. M. 1942. *Extinct and Vanishing Mammals of the Western Hemisphere, with the Marine Species of All the Oceans.* Amer. Commission Intl. Wildl. Prot. Spec. Publ. No. 11. New York Zool. Park. 620 pp.

Anderson, S., and J. K. Jones, Jr. 1984. *Orders and Families of Recent Mammals of the World.* New York: John Wiley and Sons. 686 pp.

Anthony, H. E. 1928. *Fieldbook of North American Mammals.* New York: Putnam. 674 pp.

Asdell, S. A. 1964. *Patterns of Mammalian Reproduction.* 2d ed. Ithaca, N.Y.: Comstock Publ. Assoc. of Cornell Univ. Press. 670 pp.

Boitani, L., and S. Bartoli. 1983. *Simon and Schuster's Guide to Mammals.* New York: Simon and Schuster. 511 pp.

Bookout, T. A., ed. 1996. *Research and Management Techniques for Wildlife and Habitats.* Bethesda, Md.: Wildlife Sciety. 740 pp.

Bourliere, F. 1954. *The Natural History of Mammals.* New York: Alfred A. Knopf. 363 pp.

Burt, W. H., and R. P. Grossenheider. 1976. *A Field Guide to the Mammals.* 3d ed. Boston: Houghton Mifflin. 289 pp.

Chapman, J. A., and G. A. Feldhamer, eds. 1982. *Wild Mammals of North America: Biology, Management, and Economics.* Baltimore: Johns Hopkins Univ. Press. 1147 pp.

Choate, J. R., J. K. Jones, Jr., and C. Jones. 1994. *Handbook of Mammals of the South-Central States.* Baton Rouge: Louisiana State Univ. Press. 304 pp.

Darlington, P. J., Jr. 1957. *Zoogeography: The Geographical Distribution of Animals.* New York: John Wiley & Sons. 675 pp.

Davis, J. W., and R. C. Anderson, eds. 1971. *Parasitic Diseases of Wild Mammals.* Ames: Iowa State Univ. Press. 364 pp.

DeBlase, A. F., and R. E. Martin. 1981. *A Manual of Mammalogy with Keys to Families of the World.* 2d ed. Dubuque, Iowa: Wm. C. Brown. 436 pp.

Doran, D. J. 1954–55. A catalogue of the Protozoa and helminths of North American rodents (in four parts). *Amer. Midland Nat.* 52: 118–128, 469–580; 53: 162–175, 446–454.

Eisenberg, J. F. 1981. *The Mammalian Radiations: An Analysis of Trends in Evolution, Adaptation, and Behavior.* Chicago: Univ. Chicago Press. 610 pp.

Eisenberg, J. F., and D. G. Kleiman, eds. 1983. *Advances in the Study of Mammalian Behavior.* Amer. Soc. Mammal. Spec. Publ. No. 7. 753 pp.

Eisentraut, M. 1956. *Der Winterschlaf mit seinen ökologischen und physiologischen Begleiterscheinungen.* Jena, Germany: VEB Gustav Fischer. 160 pp.

Errington, P. 1946. Predation and vertebrate populations. *Quart. Rev. Biol.* 21(2): 144–177; 21(3): 221–245.

Forrester, D. J. 1992. *Parasites and Diseases of Wild Mammals in Florida.* Gainesville: Univ. Press of Florida. 459 pp.

Glass, B. P. 1951. *A Key to the Skulls of North American Mammals.* Minneapolis: Burgess. 53 pp.

Greene, E. C. 1935. *Anatomy of the Rat.* Philadelphia: Trans. Amer. Philos. Soc. 27. 370 pp.

Grzimek, B., ed. 1989. *Grzimek's Encyclopedia of Mammals.* 5 volumes. New York: McGraw-Hill.

Gunderson, H. L. 1976. *Mammalogy.* New York: McGraw-Hill. 483 pp.

Halfpenny, J. 1986. *A Field Guide to Mammal Tracking in Western America.* Boulder, Colo.: Johnson Books. 111 pp.

Hall, E. R. 1981. *The Mammals of North America.* 2 vols. New York: Ronald Press. 1181 pp.

Hamilton, W. J., Jr. 1939. *American Mammals.* New York: McGraw-Hill. 434 pp.

Hazard, E. B. 1982. *The Mammals of Minnesota.* Minneapolis: Univ. Minnesota Press. 280 pp.

Headstrom, R. 1971. *Identifying Animal Tracks of Mammals, Birds and Other Animals of the Eastern United States.* New York: Dover. 141 pp.

Howell, A. B. 1926. *Anatomy of the Wood Rat.* Baltimore: Williams & Wilkins. 225 pp.

Jameson, E. W., Jr. 1949. Some factors influencing the local distribution and abundance of woodland small mammals in central New York. *J. Mammal.* 30: 221–235.

Jones, J. K., Jr., D. M. Armstrong, R. S. Hoffmann, and C. Jones. 1983. *Mammals of the Northern Great Plains.* Lincoln: Univ. Nebraska Press. 379 pp.

Jones, J. K., Jr., and E. C. Birney. 1988. *Handbook of Mammals of the North-Central States.* Minneapolis: Univ. Minnesota Press. 347 pp.

Jones, J. K., Jr., R. S. Hoffmann, D. W. Rice, C. Jones, R. J. Baker, and M. D. Engstrom. 1992. Revised checklist of North American mammals north of Mexico, 1991. Occ. Papers Mus. Texas Tech Univ. No. 146. 23 pp. [Earlier editions of this checklist are cited in the 1992 work.]

Kayser, C. 1961. *The Physiology of Natural Hibernation.* Oxford: Pergamon. 325 pp.

Lawlor, T. E. 1976. *Handbook to the Orders and Families of Living Mammals.* Eureka, Calif.: Mad River Press. 244 pp.

Lyman, C. P., and A. R. Dawe. 1960. *Mammalian Hibernation.* Bull. Mus. Comp. Zool. 124, Harvard Univ. 549 pp.

Lyman, C. P., J. S. Willis, A. Malan, and L. C. H. Wang. 1982. *Hibernation and Torpor in Mammals and Birds.* New York: Academic Press. 317 pp.

Macdonald, D., ed. 1984. *The Encyclopedia of Mammals.* New York: Facts on File. 895 pp.

Marler, P., and W. J. Hamilton III. 1966. *Mechanisms of Animal Behavior.* New York: John Wiley and Sons. 771 pp.

Martin, A. C., H. S. Zim, and A. L. Nelson. 1951. *American Wildlife and Plants: A Guide to Wildlife Food Habits.* New York: Dover. 500 pp.

Merritt, J. F. 1984. *Winter Ecology of Small Mammals.* Spec. Publ. Carnegie Mus. Nat. Hist. No. 10. 380 pp.

Miller, D. 1981. A guide to animal tracks of eastern North America. Berkeley, Calif.: Nature Study Guild. 61 pp.

Miller, G. S., Jr., and R. Kellogg. 1955. *List of North American Recent Mammals.* U.S. Natl. Mus. Bull. 205. 954 pp.

Miller, M. E. 1952. *Guide to the Dissection of the Dog.* 3d ed. Ann Arbor, Mich.: Edwards Bros. 369 pp.

Morris, D. 1964. *The Mammals: A Guide to the Living Species.* New York: Harper and Row. 448 pp.

Murie, O. J. 1954. *A Field Guide to Animal Tracks.* Boston: Houghton-Mifflin. 375 pp.

Nelson, E. W. 1930. *Wild Animals of North America.* Washington: National Geographic Society. 254 pp.

Nowak, R. M. 1991. *Walker's Mammals of the World.* 5th ed., 2 vols. Baltimore: Johns Hopkins Univ. Press. 1629 pp.

Peterson, R. 1966. *The Mammals of Eastern Canada.* Toronto: Oxford Univ. Press. 465 pp.

Schwartz, C. W., and E. R. Schwartz. 1981. *The Wild Mammals of Missouri.* 2d ed. Columbia: Univ. Missouri Press and Missouri Dept. Conservation. 356 pp.

Sealander, J. A., and G. D. Heidt. 1990. *Arkansas Mammals: Their Natural History, Classification, and Distribution.* Fayetteville: Univ. Arkansas Press. 308 pp.

Seton, E. T. 1929. *Lives of Game Animals.* 4 vols. Garden City, N.Y.: Doubleday, Doran.

Simpson, G. G. 1945. *The Principles of Classification and a Classification of Mammals.* Bull. Amer. Mus. Nat. Hist., New York, 85. 350 pp.

Smith, R. P. 1982. *Animal Tracks and Signs of North America.* Harrisburg, Pa.: Stackpole. 271 pp.

Stokes, D., and L. Stokes. 1986. *A Guide to Animal Tracking and Behavior.* Boston and Toronto: Little, Brown. 418 pp.

Van Gelder, R. G. 1969. *Biology of Mammals.* New York: Charles Scribner's Sons. 197 pp.

———. 1982. *Mammals of the National Parks.* Baltimore: Johns Hopkins Univ. Press. 310 pp.

Van Zyll de Jong, C. G. 1983. *Handbook of Canadian Mammals.* Vol. 1: Marsupials and insectivores. Ottawa: National Mus. Canada. 210 pp.

———. 1985. *Handbook of Canadian Mammals.* Vol. 2: Bats. Ottawa: National Mus. Canada. 212 pp.

Vaughn, T. A. 1986. *Mammalogy.* 3d ed. Philadelphia: Saunders. 576 pp.

Walker, E. P., ed. 1968. *Mammals of the World.* 3 vols. Baltimore: Johns Hopkins Univ. Press.

Whitaker, J. O., Jr. 1968. *Keys to the Vertebrates of the Eastern United States, Excluding Birds.* Minneapolis: Burgess. 256 pp.

———. 1996. *National Audubon Society Field Guide to North American Mammals.* New York: Alfred A. Knopf. 937 pp.

Wilson, D. E., and D. M. Reeder. 1993. *Mammal Species of the World: A Taxonomic and Geographic Reference.* Washington: Smithsonian Institution Press, in assoc. with American Society of Mammalogists. 1206 pp.

## State Mammal Publications

### ALABAMA

Howell, A. H. 1921. A biological survey of Alabama. I. Physiography and Life Zones. II. The Mammals. Washington: *North Amer. Fauna* 45. 88 pp.

### CONNECTICUT (see also New England)

Goodwin, G. G. 1935. *The Mammals of Connecticut.* Conn. State Geol. and Nat. Hist. Surv. Bull. 53. 221 pp.

## DELAWARE

Ernst, C. H. 1975. Skull key to the adult land mammals of Delaware, Maryland, and Virginia. *Chesapeake Sci.* 16: 198–204.

## DISTRICT OF COLUMBIA

Bailey, V. 1923. The mammals of the District of Columbia. *Proc. Biol. Soc. Wash.* 36: 103–138.

## FLORIDA

Brown, L. 1996. *The Mammals of Florida*. Miami, Fla.: Windward Publ. 224 pp.

Forrester, D. J. 1992. *Parasites and Diseases of Wild Mammals in Florida*. Gainesville: Univ. Press of Florida. 459 pp.

Humphrey, S. R., ed. 1992. *Rare and Endangered Biota of Florida*. Volume I. Mammals. Gainesville: Univ. Press of Florida. 392 pp.

Lazell, J. D., Jr. 1989. *Wildlife of the Florida Keys: A Natural History*. Washington: Island Press. 253 pp.

Stephenson, H. M. 1976. *Vertebrates of Florida: Identification and Distribution*. A Florida State University Book. Gainesville: Univ. Presses of Florida. 607 pp.

Layne, J. N. 1974. The land mammals of South Florida. *Mem. Miami Geol. Soc.* 2: 386–413.

Bangs, O. 1898. The land mammals of peninsular Florida and the coast region of Georgia. *Proc. Boston Soc. Nat. Hist.* 28: 157–235.

## GEORGIA

Neuhauser, H. N., and N. E. Baker. 1974. Annotated list of mammals of the coastal islands of Georgia. In: A. S. Johnson et al., eds., *An Ecological Survey of the Coastal Region of Georgia*, pp. 197–209. U.S. Natl. Park Serv. Sci. Monogr. No. 3. 233 pp.

Golley, F. B. 1962. *Mammals of Georgia*. Athens: Univ. Georgia Press. 218 pp.

Harper, F. 1927. The mammals of Okefenokee Swamp region of Georgia. *Proc. Boston Soc. Nat. Hist.* 38: 191–396.

## GREAT LAKES REGION

Kurta, A. 1995. *Mammals of the Great Lakes Region*. Rev. ed. Ann Arbor: Univ. Michigan Press. 376 pp.

Burt, W. H. 1954. *Mammals of the Great Lakes Region*. Ann Arbor: Univ. Michigan Press. 246 pp.

## ILLINOIS (see also Great Lakes Region)

Hoffmeister, D. F. 1989. *Mammals of Illinois*. Urbana: Univ. Illinois Press. 348 pp.

Layne, J. N. 1958. Notes on mammals of southern Illinois. *Amer. Midland Nat.* 60: 219–254.

Hoffmeister, D. F., and C. O. Mohr. 1957. *Fieldbook of Illinois Mammals*. Manual 4. Urbana: Nat. Hist. Survey Div. 233 pp.

Necker, W. L., and D. M. Hatfield. 1941. Mammals of Illinois. *Bull. Chicago Acad. Sci.* 6: 17–60.

Cory, C. B. 1912. *The Mammals of Illinois and Wisconsin*. Chicago: Field Mus. Nat. Hist. Publ. 153, Zool. Ser. Vol. XI. 505 pp.

Kennicott, R. 1851. *The Quadrupeds of Illinois*. Exec. Doc. 32, 35th Congr., House Repr. 1856: 52–110; 1857: 72–107.

## INDIANA (see also Great Lakes Region)

Mumford, R. E., and J. O. Whitaker, Jr. 1982. *Mammals of Indiana*. Bloomington: Indiana Univ. Press. 537 pp.

Mumford, R. E. 1969. *Distribution of Mammals of Indiana*. Ind. Acad. Sci., Monogr. No. 1. 114 pp.

Brooks, D. M. 1959. *Fur Animals of Indiana*. P-R Bull. 4. Indianapolis: Indiana Dept. Conservation. 195 pp.

Lyon, M. W., Jr. 1936. Mammals of Indiana. *Amer. Midl. and Nat.* 17: 1–384.

Hahn, W. L. 1909. The mammals of Indiana: A descriptive catalogue of the mammals occurring in Indiana in recent times. 33rd Annual Report, Ind. Dept. Geology and Nat. Resources, pp. 417–654, 659–663.

## KENTUCKY

Barbour, R. W., and W. H. Davis. 1974. *Mammals of Kentucky*. Lexington: Univ. Press of Kentucky. 322 pp.

## LOUISIANA

Lowery, G. H., Jr. 1974. *The Mammals of Louisiana and Its Adjacent Waters*. Baton Rouge: Louisiana State Univ. Press. 565 pp.

Arthur, S. 1928. *The Fur Animals of Louisiana*. Louisiana Dept. of Conservation, Bull. 18 (revised). 444 pp.

## MAINE (see also New England)

Norton, A. H. 1930. The mammals of Portland, Maine, and vicinity. Proc. Portland Soc. Nat. Hist. No. 4. 151 pp.

Durcher, B. H. 1903. Mammals of Mount Katahdin, Maine. *Proc. Biol. Soc. Wash.* 16: 63–71.

## MARYLAND

Webster, W. D., J. F. Parnell, and W. C. Biggs, Jr. 1985. *Mammals of the Carolinas, Virginia and Maryland*. Chapel Hill: Univ. North Carolina Press. 255 pp.

Ernst, C. H. 1975. Skull key to the adult land mammals of Delaware, Maryland, and Virginia. *Chesapeake Sci.* 16: 198–204.

Paradiso, J. L. 1969. Mammals of Maryland. Washington: *North Amer. Fauna* 66. 193 pp.

## MASSACHUSETTS (see also New England)

Cardoza, J. E. 1985. List of the mammals of Massachusetts (3rd ed.). Westborough, Mass.: Massachusetts Div. Fisheries and Wildlife. 10 pp.

Allen, J. A. 1869. Mammalia of Massachusetts. *Bull. Mus. Comp. Zool. at Harvard College* No. 8. Vol. 1: 143–252.

## MICHIGAN (see also Great Lakes Region)

Baker, R. H. 1983. *Michigan Mammals*. East Lansing: Michigan State Univ. Press. 612 pp.

Burt, W. H. 1954. *The Mammals of Michigan*. Ann Arbor: Univ. Michigan Press. 288 pp.

## MISSISSIPPI

Jones, C., and C. H. Carter. 1989. Annotated checklist of the recent mammals of Mississippi. Occ. Papers Mus. Texas Tech Univ. No. 128. 9 pp.

Kennedy, M. L., K. N. Randolph, and T. L. Best. 1974. A review of Mississippi mammals. Stud. Nat. Sci., Eastern New Mexico Univ. No. 2. 36 pp.

Wolfe, J. L. 1971. Mississippi land mammals: Distribution, identification, ecological notes. Jackson: Miss. Mus. Nat. Sci. 44 pp.

Ward, R. P. 1965. The mammals of Mississippi. *J. Miss. Acad. Sci.* 11: 309–330.

## NEW ENGLAND

Godin, A. J. 1977. *Wild Mammals of New England*. Baltimore: Johns Hopkins Univ. Press. 304 pp.

Allen, G. M. 1904. Check list of the mammals of New England. Fauna of New England. Occ. Papers Boston Soc. Nat. Hist. No. 7(3). 35 pp.

## NEW HAMPSHIRE (see also New England)

Carpenter, R. G., II, and H. R. Siegler. 1945. List of New Hampshire mammals and their distribution. New Hampshire Fish and Game Dept. 13 pp.

## NEW JERSEY

Van Gelder, R. G. 1984. The mammals of the State of New Jersey: A preliminary annotated list. New Jersey Audubon Soc. Occ. Pap. No. 143. 20 pp.

Shoemaker, L. M. 1963. Mammals of New Jersey. New Jersey State Mus., Bull. 8. 20 pp.

Stone, W. 1907. The mammals of New Jersey. New Jersey State Mus. Report, 33–110.

Rhoads, S. N. 1903. *The Mammals of Pennsylvania and New Jersey*. Philadelphia: privately printed. 266 pp.

## NEW YORK (see also Great Lakes Region)

Connor, P. F. 1971. The mammals of Long Island, New York. New York State Mus. and Sci. Serv. Bull. 416. 78 pp.

———. 1966. The mammals of the Tug Hill Plateau, New York. N.Y. State Mus. and Sci. Serv. Bull. 406. 82 pp.

———. 1960. The mammals of Otsego and Schoharie counties, New York. N.Y. State Mus. and Sci. Serv. Bull. 382. 84 pp.

Harper, F. 1929. Notes on mammals of the Adirondacks. N.Y. State Mus. Handbook No. 8, pp. 51–118.

Miller, G. S., Jr. 1899. Preliminary list of New York mammals. Bull. N.Y. State Mus. 6: 271–390.

Merriam, C. H. 1884. The vertebrates of the Adirondack region: The Mammalia. Trans. Linnean Soc. New York No. 1. 214 pp.

Dekay, J. E. 1842. Zoology of New York. Pt. 1. Mammalia. Albany: White & Visscher. 146 pp.

## NORTH CAROLINA

Linzey, D. W. 1995. Mammals of the Great Smoky Mountains National Park: 1995 update. *J. Elisha Mitchell Sci. Soc.* 111: 1–81.

Webster, W. D., J. F. Parnell, and W. C. Biggs, Jr. 1985. *Mammals of the Carolinas, Virginia and Maryland*. Chapel Hill: Univ. North Carolina Press. 255 pp.

Lee, D. S., J. F. Funderburg, Jr., and M. K. Clark. 1982. A distributional survey of North Carolina mammals. Occ. Pap. N.C. Biol. Surv. 1982–10. 70 pp.

Linzey, A. V., and D. W. Linzey. 1971. *Mammals of Great Smoky Mountains National Park*. Knoxville: Univ. Tennessee Press. 114 pp.

Komarek, E. V., and R. Komarek. 1938. Mammals of the Great Smoky Mountains. *Bull. Chicago Acad. Sci.* 5: 137–162.

## OHIO (see also Great Lakes Region)

Gottschang, J. L. 1981. *A Guide to the Mammals of Ohio*. Columbus: Ohio State Univ. Press. 176 pp.

Bole, B. P., Jr., and P. N. Moulthrop. 1942. The Ohio recent mammal collection in the Cleveland Museum of Natural History. *Sci. Publs. Cleveland Mus. Nat. Hist.* 5: 83–181.

## PENNSYLVANIA (see also Great Lakes Region)

Merritt, J. F. 1987. *Guide to the Mammals of Pennsylvania*. Pittsburgh: Univ. Pittsburgh Press. 408 pp.

Genoways, H. H., and F. J. Brenner, eds. 1985. *Species of Special Concern in Pennsylvania*. Pittsburgh: Carnegie Mus. Nat. Hist. 430 pp.

Williams, S. H. 1980. The mammalian fauna of Pennsylvania. *Ann. Carnegie Mus.* 19: 225–234.

Doutt, J. K., C. A. Heppenstall, and J. E. Guilday. 1977. *Mammals of Pennsylvania*. 4th ed. Harrisburg: Pa. Game Comm. 288 pp.

Grimm, W. C., and R. Whitebread. 1952. Mammal survey of northeastern Pennsylvania. Harrisburg: Pa. Game Comm. 82 pp.

Roberts, H. A., and R. C. Early. 1952. Mammal survey of southeastern Pennsylvania. Harrisburg: Pa. Game Comm. 70 pp.

Gifford, C. L., and R. Whitebread. 1951. Mammal survey of south-central Pennsylvania. Harrisburg: Pa. Game Comm. 75 pp.

Roslund, H. R. 1951. Mammal survey of north-central Pennsylvania. Harrisburg: Pa. Game Comm. 55 pp.

Grimm, W. C., and H. A. Roberts. 1950. Mammal survey of southwestern Pennsylvania. Harrisburg: Pa. Game Comm. 99 pp.

Richmond, N. D., and H. R. Roslund. 1949. Mammal survey of northwestern Pennsylvania. Harrisburg: Pa. Game Comm. 67 pp.

Rhoads, S. N. 1903. *The Mammals of Pennsylvania and New Jersey*. Philadelphia: Privately publ. 266 pp.

RHODE ISLAND (see also New England)

Cronan, J. M., and A. Brooks. 1968. The mammals of Rhode Island. Rhode Island Dept. Nat. Resources, Wildl. Pamphlet No. 6. 133 pp.

SOUTH CAROLINA

Webster, W. D., J. F. Parnell, and W. C. Biggs, Jr. 1985. *Mammals of the Carolinas, Virginia and Maryland.* Chapel Hill: Univ. North Carolina Press. 255 pp.

Golley, F. B. 1966. *South Carolina Mammals.* Charleston, S.C.: Contrib. Charleston Mus. 181 pp.

TENNESSEE

Linzey, D. W. 1995. Mammals of the Great Smoky Mountains National Park: 1995 update. *J. Elisha Mitchell Sci. Soc.* 111: 1–81.

Kennedy, M. L. 1991. Annotated checklist of the mammals of western Tennessee. *J. Tenn. Acad. Sci.* 66: 183–185.

Linzey, A. V., and D. W. Linzey. 1971. *Mammals of Great Smoky Mountains National Park.* Knoxville: Univ. Tennessee Press. 114 pp.

Kellogg, R. 1939. Annotated list of Tennessee mammals. *Proc. U.S. Natl. Mus.* 86: 245–303.

Komarek, E. V., and R. Komarek. 1938. Mammals of the Great Smoky Mountains. *Bull. Chicago Acad. Sci.* 5: 137–162.

VERMONT (see also New England)

Osgood, F. L., Jr. 1938. The mammals of Vermont. *J. Mammal.* 19: 435–441.

Kirk, G. L. 1916. The mammals of Vermont. Vermont Bot. and Bird Clubs, Joint Bull. 2: 28–34.

VIRGINIA

Linzey, D. W. In press. *Mammals of Virginia.* Saltville, Va.: McDonald and Woodward.

Handley, C. O., Jr. 1991. Mammals. In: K. Terwilliger, coord., *Virginia's Endangered Species*, pp. 539–616. Blacksburg, Va.: McDonald and Woodward.

Webster, W. D., J. F. Parnell, and W. C. Biggs, Jr. 1985. *Mammals of the Carolinas, Virginia and Maryland.* Chapel Hill: Univ. North Carolina Press. 255 pp.

Handley, C. O., Jr. 1979. Mammals of the Dismal Swamp: A historical account. In: P. W. Kirk, ed., *The Great Dismal Swamp*, pp. 297–357. Charlottesville: Univ. Press of Va. 428 pp.

Ernst, C. H. 1975. Skull key to the adult land mammals of Delaware, Maryland, and Virginia. *Chesapeake Sci.* 16: 198–204.

Handley, C. O., Jr., and C. P. Patton. 1947. *Wild Mammals of Virginia.* Richmond: Va. Comm. Game and Inland Fisheries. 220 pp.

Bailey, J. W. 1946. *The Mammals of Virginia: An Account of the Furred Animals of Land and Sea Known to Exist in This Commonwealth with a List of Fossil Mammals from Virginia.* Richmond, Va.: Williams. 416 pp.

WEST VIRGINIA

McKeever, S., and W. G. Frum. 1951. A survey of West Virginia mammals. Pittman-Robertson Proj. 22–R, Conserv. Comm. W. Va. 126 pp. [mimeo]

Brooks, F. E. 1911. The mammals of West Virginia. W. Va. Bd. Agric. Report No. 20: 9–30.

WISCONSIN (see also Great Lakes Region)

Long, C. A. In preparation. *Mammals of Wisconsin.*

Jackson, H. H. T. 1961. *Mammals of Wisconsin.* Madison: Univ. Wisconsin Press. 504 pp.

Cory, C. B. 1912. *The Mammals of Illinois and Wisconsin.* Chicago: Field Mus. Nat. Hist. Publ. 153, Zool. Ser. Vol. XI. 505 pp.

## References Treating Major Mammal Groups

### Didelphimorphia

Gardner, A. L. 1973. The systematics of the genus *Didelphis* (Marsupialia: Didelphidae) in North and Middle America. Mus. Texas Tech Univ., Spec. Publ. No. 4. 81 pp.

Hartman, C. G. 1962. *Possums.* Austin: Univ. Texas Press. 174 pp.

Hunsaker, D., II. 1977. Ecology of New World marsupials. In: D. Hunsaker II, ed., *The Biology of Marsupials*, pp. 95–156. New York: Academic Press. 537 pp.

### Insectivora

Choate, J. R. 1970. Systematics and zoogeography of middle American shrews of the genus *Cryptotis*. *Univ. Kansas Publ. Mus. Nat. Hist.* 19: 195–317.

Crowcroft, Peter. 1957. *The Life of the Shrew.* London: Max Reinhardt. 166 pp.

Cudmore, W. W., and J. O. Whitaker, Jr. 1984. The distribution of the smoky shrew, *Sorex fumeus*, and the pygmy shrew, *Microsorex hoyi*, in Indiana, with notes on the distribution of other shrews. *Proc. Ind. Acad. Sci.* 93: 469–474.

Diersing, V. E. 1980. Systematics and evolution of the pygmy shrews (subgenus *Microsorex*) of North America. *J. Mammal.* 61: 76–101.

Genoways, H. H., and J. R. Choate. 1972. A multivariate analysis of systematic relationships among populations of the short-tailed shrew (genus *Blarina*) in Nebraska. *Syst. Zool.* 21: 106–116.

Gorman, M. L., and R. D. Stone. 1990. The natural history of moles. Ithaca, N.Y.: Comstock Publ. Assoc. of Cornell Univ. Press. 138 pp.

Gould, E., N. C. Negus, and A. Novick. 1964. Evidence for echolocation in shrews. *J. Exp. Zool.* 156: 19–38.

Hamilton, W. J., Jr. 1930. The food of the Soricidae. *J. Mammal.* 11: 26–39.

Jackson, H. H. T. 1915. A review of the American moles. Washington: *North Amer. Fauna* 38. 100 pp.

Jones, C. A., J. A. Choate, and H. H. Genoways. 1984. Phylogeny and palaeobiogeography of short-tailed shrews (genus *Blarina*). In: H. H. Genoways and M. R. Dawson, eds., *Contributions in Quarterly Vertebrate Paleontology: A Volume in Memorial to John Guilday*, pp. 56–148. Spec. Publ. Carnegie Mus. Nat. Hist., Pittsburgh.

Merriam, C. H., and G. S. Miller, Jr. 1895. Merriam: Revision of the shrews of the American genera *Blarina* and *Notiosorex*. Miller: The long-tailed shrews of the eastern United States. Merriam: Synopsis of the American shrews of the genus *Sorex*. Washington: *North Amer. Fauna* 10. 124 pp.

Merritt, J. F., G. L. Kirkland, Jr., and R. K. Rose. 1994. Advances in the biology of shrews. Carnegie Mus. Nat. Hist., Spec. Publ. 18. 458 pp.

Miller, G. S., Jr. 1895. The long-tailed shrews of the eastern United States. Washington: *North Amer. Fauna* 10: 35–56.

Tate, C. M., J. F. Pagels, and C. O. Handley, Jr. 1980. Distribution and systematic relationship of two kinds of short-tailed shrews (Soricidae: *Blarina*) in south-central Virginia. *Proc. Biol. Soc. Wash.* 93: 50–60.

Whitaker, J. O., Jr., and R. E. Mumford. 1972. Food and ectoparasites of Indiana shrews. *J. Mammal.* 53: 329–335.

## Chiroptera

Allen, G. M. 1939. *Bats*. Cambridge, Mass.: Harvard Univ. Press. 368 pp.

Altringham, J. D. 1996. *Bats: Biology and Behavior*. New York: Oxford Univ. Press. 262 pp.

Baker, R. J., and J. L. Patton. 1967. Karyotypes and karyotype variation of North American vespertilionid bats. *J. Mammal.* 48: 270–286.

Barbour, R. W., and W. H. Davis. 1969. *Bats of America*. Lexington: Univ. Kentucky Press. 286 pp.

Barclay, R. M. R., and R. M. Brigham, eds. 1996. Bats and forests symposium, October 19–21, 1995. Victoria, B.C.: Res. Br., B.C. Ministry Forests, Working Paper 23/1996.

Bickham, J. W. 1979. Chromosomal variation and evolutionary relationships of vespertilionid bats. *J. Mammal.* 60: 350–363.

Davis, R. 1966. Homing performance and homing ability in bats. *Ecol. Monogr.* 36: 201–237.

Davis, W. H., and O. B. Reite. 1967. Responses of bats from temperate regions to changes in ambient temperature. *Biol. Bull.* 132: 320–328.

Fenton, M. B. 1983. *Just Bats*. Toronto: Univ. Toronto Press. 165 pp.

———. 1992. *Bats*. New York: Facts on File. 207 pp.

Fenton, M. B., and G. P. Bell. 1979. Echolocation and feeding behavior in four species of *Myotis* (Chiroptera). *Canadian J. Zool.* 57: 1271–1277.

Fenton, M. B., P. Racey, and J. M. V. Rayner, eds. 1987. *Recent Advances in the Study of Bats*. Cambridge, U.K.: Cambridge Univ. Press. 470 pp.

Griffin, D. R. 1940. Migrations of New England bats. *Bull. Mus. Comp. Zool.* 86(6): 217–246.

———. 1958. *Listening in the Dark*. New Haven, Conn.: Yale Univ. Press. 413 pp.

Hall, E. R., and W. W. Dalquest. 1950. A synopsis of the American bats of the genus *Pipistrellus*. *Univ. Kansas Publ. Mus. Nat. Hist.* 1: 591–602.

Hall, E. R., and J. K. Jones, Jr. 1961. North American yellow bats, "*Dasypterus*," and a list of the named kinds of the genus *Lasiurus* Gray. *Univ. Kansas Publ. Mus. Nat. Hist.* 14: 73–98.

Handley, C. O., Jr. 1959. A revision of American bats of the genera *Euderma* and *Plecotus*. *Proc. U.S. Natl. Mus.* 110: 95–246.

Harvey, M. J. 1986. Arkansas bats: A valuable resource. Little Rock: Arkansas Game and Fish Comm. 48 pp.

Hill, J. E., and J. D. Smith. 1984. *Bats: A Natural History*. Austin: Univ. Texas Press. 243 pp.

Humphrey, S. R. 1975. Nursery roosts and community diversity of Nearctic bats. *J. Mammal.* 56: 312–346.

Kunz, T. H. 1971. Reproduction of some vespertilionid bats in central Iowa. *Amer. Midland Nat.* 86: 477–486.

———. 1973. Resource utilization: Temporal and spatial components of bat activity in central Iowa. *J. Mammal.* 54: 14–32.

Kunz, T. H., ed. 1982. *Ecology of Bats*. New York: Plenum Press. 425 pp.

———. 1987. *Ecological and Behavioral Methods for the Study of Bats*. Washington: Smithsonian Institution Press. 533 pp.

Lewis, S. E. 1995. Roost fidelity of bats: A review. *J. Mammal.* 76: 481–496.

McNab, B. K. 1974. The behavior of temperate cave bats in a subtropical environment. *Ecology* 55: 943–958.

Miller, G. S., Jr. 1897. Revision of the North American bats of the family Vespertilionidae. Washington: *North Amer. Fauna* 13. 135 pp.

———. 1907. *The Families and Genera of Bats*. U.S. Natl. Mus. Bull. 57. 282 pp.

Mohr, C. E. 1933. Pennsylvania bats of the genus *Myotis*. *Proc. Pa. Acad. Sci.* 7: 39–43.

Myers, P. 1978. Sexual dimorphism in size of vespertilionid bats. *Amer. Midland Nat.* 112: 701–711.

Nagorsen, D. W., and R. M. Brigham. 1993. Bats of British Columbia. Roy. Brit. Columbia Mus. Handbook. Vol. 1. The Mammals of British Columbia. 165 pp.

Patterson, A. P., and J. W. Hardin. 1969. Flight speeds of five species of vespertilionid bats. *J. Mammal.* 50: 152–153.

Ransome, R. 1990. *The Natural History of Hibernating Bats*. London: Christopher Helm. 235 pp.

Ross, A. 1961. Notes on the food habits of bats. *J. Mammal.* 42: 66–71.

———. 1967. Ecological aspects of the food habits of insectivorous bats. *Proc. West. Found. Vert. Zool.* 1: 205–263.

Schmidly, D. J. 1991. *The Bats of Texas*. College Station: Texas A & M Univ. Press. 185 pp.

Slaughter, B. H., and D. W. Walton, eds. 1970. *About Bats: A Chiropteran Symposium.* Dallas: Southern Methodist Univ. Press. 339 pp.

Thomas, D. W. 1995. The physiological ecology of hibernation in vespertilionid bats. In: P. A. Racey and S. M. Swift, eds., *Ecology, Evolution and Behaviour of Bats,* pp. 223–244. Symposia Zool. Soc. London. No. 67. 421 pp.

Thomas, D. W., G. P. Bell, and M. B. Fenton. 1987. Variation in echolocation call frequencies recorded from North American vespertilionid bats: A cautionary note. *J. Mammal.* 68: 842–847.

Tuttle, M. D. 1974. An improved trap for bats. *J. Mammal.* 55: 475–477.

———. 1988. *America's Neighborhood Bats.* Austin: Univ. Texas Press. 96 pp.

Whitaker, J. O., Jr. 1972. Food habits of bats from Indiana. *Canadian J. Zool.* 50: 877–883.

———. 1973. External parasites of bats in Indiana. *J. Parasitol.* 59: 1148–1150.

Wimsatt, W. A., ed. 1970 and 1977. *Biology of Bats.* New York: Academic Press. Vol. 1, 406 pp. Vol. 2, 477 pp. Vol. 3 (1977), 651 pp.

## Primates

Clutton-Brock, T. H., ed. 1977. *Primate Ecology: Studies of Feeding and Ranging Behaviour in Lemurs, Monkeys and Apes.* London: Academic Press. 631 pp.

Michael, R. P., and J. H. Crook, eds. 1973. *Comparative Ecology and Behaviour of Primates.* London: Academic Press. 847 pp.

## Xenarthra

Montgomery, G. G. 1985. *The Evolution and Ecology of Armadillos, Sloths and Vermilinguas.* Washington: Smithsonian Institution Press. 451 pp.

## Lagomorpha

Corbet, G. B. 1983. A review of classification in the family Leporidae. *Acta Zool. Fennica* 174: 11–15.

Diersing, V. E. 1984. Lagomorphs. In: S. Anderson and J. K. Jones, eds., *Orders and Families of Recent Mammals of the World,* pp. 241–254. New York: Wiley, and Amer. Soc. Mammal.

Lord, R. D. 1963. The cottontail rabbit in Illinois. Illinois Dept. Conservation Tech. Bull. No. 3. 94 pp.

Nelson, E. W. 1909. The rabbits of North America. Washington: *North Amer. Fauna* No. 29. 314 pp.

## Rodentia: Squirrels and Marmots

Flyger, V., and J. E. Gates. 1982. Fox and gray squirrels, *Sciurus niger, S. carolinensis* and their allies. In: J. A. Chapman and G. A. Feldhamer, eds., *Wild Mammals of North America,* pp. 209–229. Baltimore: Johns Hopkins Univ. Press.

Howell, A. H. 1915. Revision of the American marmots. Washington: *North Amer. Fauna* 37. 80 pp.

———. 1918. Revision of the American flying squirrels. Washington: *North Amer. Fauna* 44. 64 pp.

———. 1938. Revision of the North American ground squirrels. Washington: *North Amer. Fauna* 56. 256 pp.

Lee, D. S., and J. B. Funderburg. 1982. Marmots. In: J. A. Chapman and G. A. Feldhamer, eds., *Wild Mammals of North America,* pp. 176–191. Baltimore: Johns Hopkins Univ. Press.

Lowery, G. H., Jr., and W. B. Davis. 1942. A revision of the fox squirrels of the Lower Mississippi Valley and Texas. *Occ. Papers Mus. Zool., Louisiana State Univ.,* No. 9: 153–172.

MacClintock, D. 1970. *Squirrels of North America.* New York: Van Nostrand Reinhold. 184 pp.

Packard, R. L. 1956. The tree squirrels of Kansas: Ecology and economic importance. Univ. Kansas Mus. Nat. Hist. and State Biol. Survey, Kansas Misc. Publ. No. 11. 67 pp.

Weigl, P. D. 1978. Resource overlap, interspecific interactions and the distribution of the flying squirrels, *Glaucomys volans* and *G. sabrinus. Amer. Midland Nat.* 100: 83–96.

Wells-Gosling, N. 1985. Flying Squirrels: Gliders in the Dark. Washington: Smithsonian Institution Press. 128 pp.

## Rodentia: Mice and Rats

Anderson, P. K. 1989. Dispersal in rodents: A resident fitness hypothesis. Amer. Soc. Mammal. Spec. Publ. No. 9. 141 pp.

Bailey, V. 1900. Revision of the American voles of the genus *Microtus.* Washington: *North Amer. Fauna* 17. 88 pp.

Burt, W. H. 1940. Territorial behavior and populations of some small mammals in southern Michigan. *Misc. Publ. Mus. Zool. Univ. Mich.* No. 45: 7–58.

Davis, D. E. 1953. The characteristics of rat populations. *Quart. Rev. Biol.* 28: 373–401.

Elton, C. 1942. *Voles, Mice and Lemmings.* New York: Oxford Univ. Press. 496 pp.

Goldman, E. A. 1910. Revision of the wood rats of the genus *Neotoma.* Washington: *North Amer. Fauna* 31. 124 pp.

———. 1918. The rice rats of North America (genus *Oryzomys*). Washington: *North Amer. Fauna* 43. 100 pp.

Hamilton, W. J., Jr. 1937. The biology of microtine cycles. *J. Agric. Res.* 54: 779–790.

———. 1941. The food of small forest mammals in eastern United States. *J. Mammal.* 22: 250–263.

Hollister, N. 1911. A systematic synopsis of the muskrats. Washington: *North Amer. Fauna* 32. 47 pp.

Howell, A. B. 1927. Revision of the American lemming mice (genus *Synaptomys*). Washington: *North Amer. Fauna* 50. 97 pp.

Howell, A. H. 1914. Revision of the American harvest mice (genus *Reithrodontomys*). Washington: *North Amer. Fauna* 36. 97 pp.

Johnson, M. L., and S. Johnson. 1982. Voles. In: J. A. Chapman and G. A. Feldhamer, eds., *Wild Mammals of North America*, pp. 326–354. Baltimore: Johns Hopkins Univ. Press.

King, J. A., ed. 1968. *Biology of* Peromyscus *(Rodentia)*. Amer. Soc. Mammal. Spec. Publ. No. 2. 593 pp.

Kirkland, G. L., Jr., and J. N. Layne. 1989. *Advances in the Study of* Peromyscus *(Rodentia)*. Lubbock: Texas Tech Univ. Press. 366 pp.

Krebs, C. J., B. L. Keller, and R. H. Tamarin. 1969. *Microtus* population biology: Demographic changes in fluctuating populations of *M. ochrogaster* and *M. pennsylvanicus* in southern Indiana. *Ecology* 50: 587–607.

Krebs, C. J., and J. H. Myers. 1974. Population cycles in small mammals. In: A. MacFadyen, ed., *Advances in Ecological Research*, pp. 267–399. New York: Academic Press.

Miller, G. S., Jr. 1896. The genera and subgenera of voles and lemmings. Washington: *North Amer. Fauna* 12. 84 pp.

Osgood, W. H. 1909. Revision of the mice of the American genus *Peromyscus*. Washington: *North Amer. Fauna* 28. 285 pp.

Preble, E. A. 1899. Revision of the jumping mice of the genus *Zapus*. Washington: *North Amer. Fauna* 15. 42 pp.

Schwartz, A., and E. P. Odum. 1957. The woodrats of the eastern United States. *J. Mammal.* 38: 197–206.

Tamarin, R. H., ed. 1985. *Biology of New World* Microtus. Amer. Soc. Mammal. Spec. Publ. No. 8. 893 pp.

Wolfe, J. O. 1985. Comparative population ecology of *Peromyscus leucopus* and *Peromyscus maniculatus*. *Canadian J. Zool.* 63: 1548–1555.

Wolfe, J. O., and D. S. Durr. 1986. Winter nesting behavior of *Peromyscus leucopus* and *Peromyscus maniculatus*. *J. Mammal.* 67: 409–412.

### Rodentia: Pocket Gophers

Merriam, C. H. 1895. Monographic revision of the pocket gophers, Family Geomyidae (exclusive of the species of *Thomomys*). Washington: *North Amer. Fauna* 8. 258 pp.

### Carnivora

Bekoff, M., ed. 1977. *Coyotes: Biology, Behavior and Management*. New York: Academic Press. 384 pp.

Carbyn, L. N., S. H. Fritz, and D. R. Seip, eds. 1995. *Ecology and Conservation of Wolves in a Changing World*. Edmonton: Canadian Circumpolar Institute, Univ. Alberta. 620 pp.

Cook, D. B., and W. J. Hamilton, Jr. 1957. The forest, the fisher and the porcupine. *J. Forestry* 55: 719–722.

Coues, E. 1877. *Fur-Bearing Animals: A Monograph of the North American Mustelidae*. Dept. Interior, U.S. Geol. Survey of the Territories, Misc. Publ. No. 8. 348 pp.

Crabb, W. D. 1948. The ecology and management of the prairie spotted skunk in Iowa. *Ecol. Monogr.* 18: 201–232.

Dearborn, N. 1932. Foods of some predatory fur-bearing animals of Michigan. Univ. Mich. School of Forestry and Conserv. Bull. No. 1. 52 pp.

Gittleman, J. L., ed. 1989. *Carnivore Behavior, Ecology, and Evolution*. Vol. 1. Ithaca, N.Y.: Cornell Univ. Press. 620 pp.

———. 1996. *Carnivore Behavior, Ecology, and Evolution*. Vol. 2. Ithaca, N.Y.: Cornell Univ. Press. 644 pp.

Goldman, E. A., and H. H. T. Jackson. 1950. Raccoons of North and Middle America. Washington: *North Amer. Fauna* 50. 153 pp.

Hall, E. R. 1951. *American Weasels*. Univ. Kansas Publ. Mus. Nat. Hist. No. 4. 466 pp.

Hamilton, W. J., Jr. 1933. The weasels of New York: Their natural history and economic status. *Amer. Midland Nat.* 14: 289–373.

Hollister, N. 1913. A synopsis of the American minks. *Proc. U.S. Natl. Mus.* 44: 471–480.

Howell, A. H. 1901. Revision of the skunks of the genus *Chincha (Mephitis)*. Washington: *North Amer. Fauna* 20. 62 pp.

———. 1906. Revision of the skunks of the genus *Spilogale*. Washington: *North Amer. Fauna* 25. 55 pp.

Johnson, A. S. 1970. Biology of the raccoon (*Procyon lotor varius* Nelson and Goldman) in Alabama. Auburn Univ. Agric. Exp. Sta. 148 pp.

Latham, R. M. 1950. The food of predaceous animals of northeastern United States. Harrisburg: Pa. Game Commission. 69 pp.

Mengel, R. M. 1971. A study of dog-coyote hybrids and implications concerning hybridization in *Canis*. *J. Mammal.* 52: 316–336.

Van Gelder, R. G. 1959. A taxonomic revision of the spotted skunks (genus *Spilogale*). *Bull. Amer. Mus. Nat. Hist.* 117: 229–392.

### Sirenia

O'Shea, T. J., B. B. Ackerman, and H. F. Percival, eds. 1995. *Population Biology of the Florida Manatee*. Washington: U.S. Dept. Interior, Natl. Biol. Service, Inf. and Technol. Report 1. 289 pp.

Reeves, R. R., B. S. Stewart, and S. Leatherwood. 1992. *The Sierra Club Handbook of Seals and Sirenians*. San Francisco: Sierra Club Books. 359 pp.

### Perissodactyla

Keiper, R. R. 1985. *The Assateague Ponies*. Centreville, Md.: Tidewater Publishers. 101 pp.

### Artiodactyla

Halls, L. K. 1984. *White-Tailed Deer Ecology and Management*. A Wildlife Management Institute Book. Harrisburg, Pa.: Stackpole. 870 pp.

Mayer, J. J., and L. L. Brisbin, Jr. 1991. *Wild Pigs in the United States: Their History, Morphology and Current Status*. Athens: Univ. Georgia Press. 313 pp.

Putnam, R. 1989. *The Natural History of Deer*. Ithaca, N.Y.: Comstock Publ. Assoc. of Cornell Univ. Press. 224 pp.

Schmidt, J. L., and D. L. Gilbert. 1978. *Big Game of North America*. Harrisburg, Pa.: Stackpole. 494 pp.

Thomas, J. W., and D. E. Toweill. 1982. *Elk of North America: Ecology and Management*. Harrisburg, Pa.: Stackpole: and Wildlife Management Institute. 698 pp.

Taylor, W. P. 1956. *The Deer of North America: The White-Tailed, Mule and Black-Tailed Deer, Genus* Odocoileus, *Their History and Management*. Harrisburg, Pa.: Stackpole; and Wildlife Management Institute. 668 pp.

# INDEX